Theory
in
Anthropology

Theory in Anthropology

A SOURCEBOOK

EDITED BY ROBERT A. MANNERS AND DAVID KAPLAN

BRANDEIS UNIVERSITY

ALDINE PUBLISHING COMPANY / *Chicago*

First published 1968 by
ALDINE Publishing Company
529 South Wabash Avenue
Chicago, Illinois 60605

Library of Congress Catalog Card Number 67-17606
Designed by David Miller
Printed in the United States of America

Second Printing 1969

CONTENTS

v

PART VIII: STRUCTURALISM AND FORMAL ANALYSIS — 473

INTRODUCTION:
THE PLAN OF THE BOOK

READERS in the social sciences and their various divisions and subdivisions have proliferated so rapidly in the past few years that it is now very difficult to assemble a collection which does not come out looking like a reader of readers, or what someone has referred to as a non-book, out of non-books by non-authors. Consequently, any new collection of old writings must justify itself. Our reasons for compiling the present sourcebook were twofold. First, since a collection of this kind had not been done before, we were not really embarking on a "reader of readers." But, more important, our experience with courses in anthropological theory persuaded us of the need for making accessible in a single volume a sample of those important pieces which are presently scattered in numerous publications, some of which are difficult for the student to obtain.

Our second reason had to do with certain convictions we hold about the aims and methods of anthropology. Kluckhohn's 1939 assertion that "the very word 'theory' has a pejorative connotation for most American anthropologists," and his conclusion: "To suggest that something is 'theoretical' is to suggest that it is slightly indecent," impress us as no longer appropriate, because anthropologists nowadays do a great deal of talking about theory ("The Place of Theory in Anthropological Studies," *Philosophy of Science,* VI: 333). However, it seemed to us that there was considerable confusion about theory—how it might be defined, how it was developed, how it was applied, and how one went about confirming or disconfirming it. To us, therefore, the more exciting reason for undertaking this book was that it offered an opportunity to examine and evaluate these intellectual concerns of anthropology.

There are, of course, many different ways to organize a book which deals with these concerns, and organization as well as content will obviously reflect the biases and the interests of the compilers. This book is no exception. We have, however, made a strong effort to keep our own biases and particular views on theory from dominating the final product. As a matter of fact, it was precisely because our own views on

theory seemed often to differ from those of many anthropologists that we felt impelled to write the introductory essay which follows.

As the process of selection progressed we were often torn between the anthropologists' broader view of theory, on the one hand, and our own somewhat more restricted view of theory, on the other. Now, looking at the end result, we find we have in effect straddled these two views of theory. And we believe that this seeming vacillation imparts to the book a balance within our biases.

We should also like to make it clear that we were far less interested in putting together a reader in the *history* of anthropological theory than we were in assembling a collection that would reflect the *current* theoretical interests of anthropology. This will explain the absence from our Table of Contents of the names of many distinguished anthropologists of the past, such as Tylor, Boas, Malinowski, and Kroeber. In some cases their theoretical ideas have either been superseded by or incorporated into the writings of contemporary anthropologists and have been improved in the process. In other cases their work, whatever other merit it may have, seems to have left little or no impress on current anthropological theory.

The reader will note that while we have thus omitted from our collection a number of outstanding figures in the history of anthropology, we have included a number of essays by writers outside the discipline—writers who in our view have illuminated problems that are of direct concern to anthropological method and theory. We found that on a variety of theoretical issues writers in other fields had either said it better than it had been said before or, in some instances, were saying things that had not been said before—at least not by anthropologists.

A few words about the organization of the book are in order here. The first of the eight sections into which the volume is divided is entitled "Overview." We have included in this segment a number of essays meant in a general way to convey something of the scope of anthropology and to introduce some of its basic concepts.

Each of the five pieces in this section addresses itself to a somewhat different issue: The Gluckman essay emphasizes the "scientific" aspect or dimension of anthropology, while Evans-Pritchard is concerned with the more "humanistic" side of the discipline. Eggan's contribution attempts to reconcile the traditional British and American approaches to the subject at the same time that it stresses the significance to anthropological inquiry of the method of "controlled comparison." David Kaplan's essay is addressed to the vexed issue of the autonomy of sociocultural phenomena and the general question of reductionism in the sciences. White's critique of Kroeber and Kluckhohn is concerned with the problem of defining culture. A central point of his argument is that confusion often flows from the failure to distinguish nominal from real definitions.

While most American anthropologists continue to view culture as their key concept, a great deal of criticism has been leveled at this emphasis on the grounds that the term is too broad, too all-inclusive, to be used as an analytic tool. It has often been agreed that a term less broad, such as social structure, proves in practice to be more useful for the analysis and understanding of sociocultural systems. In this latter view, culture is often seen as epiphenomenal—as the product of social relationships. In our view, however, there are at least two important respects in which the culture concept has heuristic advantages over more restricted concepts like social structure. First, human social life is preeminently shaped by culture, and even if one is prepared to attribute "proto-culture" to species other than man, certainly the impact of culture on human social life is incomparably greater than it is on the social life of all other animal species. Such concepts as social system, structure, or society used by themselves tend to obscure this important difference.

Second, most anthropologists, whether they are guided in their work by the culture concept or by such concepts as social structure, do in fact deal with the interrelationship among the various institutional orders of the systems they study, that is, ideology, politics, technology, kinship, etc. Indeed, much of the controversy about theory in anthropology has centered on the issue of the degree to which one or another of these institutional orders exhibits what Har-

sanyi has called "autonomy" (see his essay in Part II). According to Harsanyi, while the various institutional orders are interrelated, that order which shows a higher degree of autonomous development will tend to exert the greater causal influence on the system as a whole. Some term or concept seems to be required which refers to the larger system of which these various institutional orders are a part.

In a review of Murdock's *Social Structure in Southeast Asia,* Marshall Sahlins remarks on this *"larger system* of which social relations are but one component." He then goes on to say:

. . . the "concrete reality" after all includes as coordinate and influential elements such things as tools, techniques, tenure arrangements and the like. They are *in* the system. They enter into functional relations with social structure; in these relations they, and not social elements alone, may be forces of constraint. It is a system of things, social relations, and ideas, a complex mechanism by which people exist and persist. It is organized not merely to order relations, but to sustain human existence. An understanding of the design of such mechanisms, then, would probably have to consider still wider nets of relation, would consider the influential context, natural and superorganic, in which societies are enclaved. Our vision is magnified several powers. Most important, it is extended to that complex mechanism—including the set of social relations—the name of which in American anthropology is "culture." ("Remarks on Social Structure in Southeast Asia," *Journal of the Polynesian Society* [1963], 72:49. Emphases in original.)

In Part II, "Explanation in Social Science," only two of the six selections are by anthropologists. The remaining pieces are by philosophers, with one by an economist. This unbalance may strike one as strange, since anthropologists are ostensibly engaged in formulating explanations of a wide range of cultural phenomena. However, we—along with many of our colleagues—have been struck by the great frequency with which so-called explanation fails either to explain or to conform to the most elementary logical canons of what Karl Popper has called "satisfactory" explanation. For these reasons we felt very strongly that a section on explanation should be included in the book.

Because most anthropologists apparently have not considered explanation as a problem in itself, they have rarely dealt with it as a philosophical issue nor have they, with one or two notable exceptions, treated it as an issue of relevance to proper explanation in their own work. A search of the anthropological literature, therefore, turned up very little about the real problems of explanation. Thus we have had to rely heavily upon philosophers who have dealt with this issue. It is our hope that the inclusion of this section may stimulate anthropologists to be more self-conscious about the materials they advance by way of "explanation" in their own writings.

Part III contains seven articles on "Methodology." Since anthropologists have been concerned with problems of method, especially as these arise in connection with field work, there is a relative abundance of essays from which to select in this category. We found, however, that many of these were directed at some specialized aspect of anthropology, such as kinship analysis. Since it was our aim in this reader to stress the broader issues in anthropology, we have tried in our present sample to present a group of papers that make certain general methodological points and are not limited to a narrow range of substantive problems. While some of these essays appear to fall in the latter category, such as Goodenough's essay on "Residence Rules," in our view they utilize limited substantive materials to illuminate a wider methodological issue.

Originally we had intended to entitle this book *Method and Theory in Cultural Anthropology*. But as the work progressed we realized that it was theory rather than method that was our greater concern, and we re-titled the book as it now stands. Of course, method considered as theories about the conduct of research bears close relationship to theory itself, and we felt strongly, therefore, that the book must include a section on method. But while methodology may assist in theory formation, it cannot by itself generate theories. A number of scholars have remarked that an overconcern with methodology is often a substitute for coping theoretically with empirical problems. S. Andreski has put it this way:

Methodology is prophylactic in its essence. In the same way as hygiene can help us to avoid some contagions but is powerless to insure health, methodology can warn us of pitfalls but will not help us conceive new ideas. The so-called methods of induction are in reality methods of verification: they tell us how to test hypotheses but not how to arrive at them. Indeed, the latter process is just as much a mystery as it was in the days of Socrates: all that is known is that, in order to conceive fruitful original ideas, one must have talent, must immerse oneself in the available knowledge and think very hard (*The Uses of Comparative Sociology*, Berkeley, 1965, p. 34).

Part IV includes a number of essays under the traditional rubrics of structure and function, evolution, and history, since these are the theoretical banners under which anthropologists have frequently grouped themselves in order to carry on their intramural polemics. While these approaches can, of course, be separated analytically, in actual practice anthropologists tend to employ them in varying combinations—often using all three approaches at the same time. As Linton Freeman notes in the paper that introduces this section of the book, the conflict waged under these banners is more apparent than real: "when we look to their hypotheses their conflict disappears—they become congruent—a single theory of socio-cultural form and process."

Furthermore, within these traditional theoretical frames anthropologists have taken more specific theoretical positions with regard to the cultural mechanisms of stability and change. Here we are referring once again to the issue raised above—the relative weight to be assigned to the different subsystems of culture. Thus, in Parts V, VI, and VII, we have included essays that deal with such mechanisms and approaches as ecology, culture-and-personality, and ideology. Again, as in the case of functionalism, history, and evolution, it should be pointed out that these divisions are not mutually exclusive and that anthropologists have in practice often utilized two or more of these approaches in combination. But at the same time each position reflects, in some measure, the theoretical bias of the particular anthropologist.

Finally, and because no book on contemporary theory would be complete without a section on the new ethnography and structuralism, we have included in Part VIII eight pieces that attempt to convey something of the method and the theoretical foundations as well as the limitations of these recent developments. While some of the techniques and methods used by the "new ethnographers" come out of recent work in such fields as linguistics, symbolic logic, and cybernetics, from a theoretical point of view these ethnographers have, in effect, raised once more the ancient issue of the insider's versus the outsider's view of a culture; or, to use Goldstein's phrasing of the issue (see his essay in Part II) "phenomenological versus naturalistic approaches" to the sociocultural.

It has been a common practice among editors compiling readers and sourcebooks of this kind to preface each of the book's sections with some introductory remarks. These generally take one of two or three forms: either a few brief summary paragraphs, which do little more than list the title and main point of each essay in the section, or lengthier editorial prefaces, which may go into much greater detail or present a historical and bibliographical survey of the subject matter.

We ourselves originally planned to prepare the shorter type of preface to each section, having rejected the alternative of lengthy editorial statements for two reasons. First, eight such essays would have added significantly to the total length of the book and have raised already high publication costs to a prohibitive level. Second, such lengthy introductions seemed, somehow, to imply that our selecting might not have been adequate and that the essays did not cover the ground we wished to cover. But we believe this is not the case; the selections speak for themselves and do not require any lengthy exegeses.

After preparing the full series of shorter introductions, we realized they were superfluous and, therefore, we dropped them also. We have tried to compensate for the absence of lengthy introductory essays with this preface, the following introductory essay, and the selected bibliography appended to the book.

With two exceptions, the texts of all the essays are reprinted here without abridgement. The two exceptions are Anthony Wallace's "Psychic Unity of Human Groups," excerpted from the first chapter of his book, *Culture and Personality;* and Kingsley Davis and Judith Blake's "On Norms and Values," the first half of a longer article entitled "Norms, Values, and Sanctions." We think that both selections, in addition to having something important to say, can stand alone. To conserve space we have also, in almost all cases, deleted bibliographies and footnotes that do not make a substantive point or advance the argument of the text. Here again there are two exceptions: Bert Kaplan's "Personality and Social Structure" and William Sturtevant's "Studies in Ethnoscience." Although the bibliographies of both of these survey articles are lengthy, we have left them in because they seemed to us to be an integral part of the essays.

Finally, a word about a number of articles that were clearly significant enough to merit inclusion in a collection of this kind but do not appear here. In most of these cases, we decided in favor of omission because the article had been reprinted elsewhere or because it was so long that its inclusion might have required the sacrifice of two or three other pieces of comparable value. In those few cases where we have included unusually long articles or essays already reproduced in other collections, we did so because we were unable to find an adequate discussion covering substantially the same ground.

We wish here to acknowledge our special debt to the authors of all the pieces included in the volume. We should like also to express our appreciation to Carroll McLure Pastner and Carol Bigham for typing assistance, and especially to Elinor Abbot, who served as editorial assistant through the long and tedious process of the book's preparation. Finally, to Alexander J. Morin of Aldine Publishing Company we want to offer a special word of gratitude for his assistance, encouragement, and especially for his gentle impatience with a pair of editors who (repeatedly) threatened publication deadlines and announcements.

R. A. M.
D. K.

Theory
in
Anthropology

NOTES ON THEORY AND NON-THEORY
IN ANTHROPOLOGY

IN the Introduction we have dealt with some of the principles that guided us in the selection of the materials that go to make up this volume. The resulting collection thus reflects, at least implicitly and in part, our common point of view about the nature and meaning of theory in anthropology. We would like now to enlarge these views and to make them more explicit, not only because they have been responsible for determining the kind of book this is, but because we have not found anywhere in our reading a set of statements which lay out in fairly concise fashion what we take to be the character and role of theory in anthropology. On the contrary, the search has tended to confirm our view that anthropologists use the term theory in a great variety of ways—almost whimsically—sometimes as a synonym for a concept, or a synonym for an inductive generalization or for a model (often itself a term used in a number of different ways), sometimes merely to lend tone or dignity to the obvious.

In what follows, therefore, we want to offer a few tentative observations on the nature and role of theory in anthropological research and inquiry. While we do not expect our comments to move anthropologists any closer to consensus with reference to the vexed question of the nature and role of anthropological theory, we hope we may be able to clarify somewhat the source of our dissatisfaction. At the same time we would like to highlight some of the disciplinary circumstances which have contributed to the present confusion associated with ideas about theory in anthropology.

Since we believe that part of the reason for the paucity of "authentic" anthropological theory as well as for some of the uncertainties about the use and meaning of the term itself comes, ironically enough, from the discipline's emphasis on field work, we begin this part of our discussion with the relationship between field work and anthropological theory.

Looking back over the last one hundred years one notes a rather striking change in the role of field work in anthropological inquiry. From an almost incidental feature of the discipline, it has come to occupy a position of central significance. Field work is now not only the "device" used by anthropologists to provide the discipline with its empirical materials, but it has become much more than this, a kind of touchstone of adequacy, a *rite de passage* prerequisite to membership in the profession. Almost twenty years ago Max Gluckman commented astringently on the extent to which field work had come to dominate anthropology:

The romantic device "field work" became a slogan: everybody rushed to primitive areas, and later to more civilized ones. On the other hand, everyone who had been to a primitive field was able to contribute something, instead of being regarded as, generally, fit only to be an informant. Once "the jargon" was learnt, he could rank as a professional. Worst of all, the "field work" cry carried a sneer at those who had not done it: better a missionary who'd seen an African than a Lévy-Bruhl who had not; better an African himself, than a Frazer (1949, p. 27).

But while Gluckman deplored the mystique that had grown up around field work, he did not in any sense suggest that the practice should be abandoned. What in fact he called for was a shift of emphasis, a move toward more creative speculation, using field work as a means rather than the end toward which it often appeared to be moving. Thus he continued:

I am the last to decry field work. . . . But when I reflect on the broad generalizations that have emerged in the history of our science, I find that the most stimulating have come on the whole from armchair students, who saw no tribe though they studied European society: Van Gennep's analysis of *rites de passage,* Lévy-Bruhl's of pre-logical collective representations, Durkheim's of division of labor, Hubert and Mauss' of sacrifice and offering, and the many works of Tylor, Frazer, Marett, Engels, Freud, Pareto. When I consider the type of data with which they worked, I can only wish that they might be here again to use the data provided by modern field-research in even more fruitful hypotheses. This is not to deny that some modern field workers have produced as stimulating hypotheses: but, if we are to learn from our history, I hope that some of them will forsake the savage for the study (*ibid.,* pp. 27–28).

In short, we agree with Gluckman that field

work has demonstrated its worth as a data-gathering and data-testing device. But there is another, and complementary, consequence of anthropology's concern with field work which Gluckman does not emphasize but which, in our opinion, may have operated to inhibit the discipline's growth as a science. A sizable body of field research has been undertaken not with a self-conscious interest in contributing to generalization and theory formation, but rather with the intention of documenting the differences, the great variety in the patterns of human behavior. While it is true, as we suggest below, that such documentation may provide others with the materials out of which theory can be constructed, the results have tended in these instances to the creation of books and articles closer in plan and execution to natural history—see below—or to literature and art than to what we would characterize as science. In their concern for what is unique their authors have, implicitly or explicitly, deflected attention from the recurrent or the repetitive patterns of cultural behavior and social institutions to the particularities of the societies they have studied.

It thus seems fairly clear that field work, and the way in which it has been carried on, has yielded mixed emphases in anthropology. In part the aim has been to develop theoretical concepts and propositions, and field work has been seen as an adjunct to this endeavor. And in part field work has been approached as a kind of natural history or as a way of presenting a unique or special "slice of life." Thus, a number of anthropologists, like Evans-Pritchard (1950), Redfield (1953), and Benedict (1947), have, in their own work and in their comments on the work of others, drawn attention to the strong literary and humanistic flavor of much anthropological writing. It is this latter aspect of the subject that John Bennett seems clearly to have in mind when he says:

The Trobriand Islanders have found their way into countless literary and scientific documents, in person and in disguise, as testimony of the human condition. What relationship these mythic Trobriand natives bear to the living creatures observed by Malinowski, or indeed, to the people of the contemporary archipelago, no one knows. . . . Malinowski in a sense created a culture or a people in the course of many volumes of reportage. They continue to be recreated by the reader and by those who mine the volumes for exemplary materials. The Trobriands—small, insignificant pocket of humanity, doomed to eternal obscurity and anonymity until Bronislaw Malinowski happened to find them, now

elevated to a major intellectual myth of the western world—are a people no scholar will ever forget, no librarian ever ignore. From time to time it will be necessary to review current interpretations of Trobriand culture and the causes it has been made to serve, by rereading Malinowski's volumes. I have little doubt that the Trobrianders painted in recent commentaries are not identical with Malinowski's originals. . . .

Wherever we find a major ethnological compilation on a particular people, there we shall also find the makings of myth and legend: the conversion of that people into a special Personage or Culture which lives in the "ethnographic present" and which becomes a type case of the human reality of variation and the inexhaustible novelty of man's behavior and relations with Nature (1964, pp. 76–77).

Others, too, notably Kroeber and Wolf, have commented on the several faces of anthropology —the literary, artistic, aesthetic, humanistic, or natural history side, on the one hand, and the more abstract, generalizing, social scientific side, on the other. Kroeber observes:

The older anthropology saw some broad problems and made generalizations—Tylor alone woud establish that. But it contained also a strong sensory, aesthetic, and experimental interest. It liked artifacts and it established museums; it was interested in the land and scenes in which people functioned; it liked to experience—at first vicariously and then in the flesh—how these people looked and behaved and what they had to say. It was part natural history in character, part humanities; but the humanities-like ingredient was non-normative, comparative, and broad-ranging instead of intensely particularistic, and therefore somewhat more prone than most humanists were to generalize, though its generalizations mostly remained fairly humble, step-by-step, "low-level" (1955, p. 307).

Kroeber then went on to contrast this approach with the more formal "social science" orientation which seems now to occupy the attention of an increasing number of anthropologists. He concluded by observing:

With two intellectual ancestries and motivations now represented among anthropologists, we are de facto having two streams of thought flowing. This is perhaps the major development in anthropological thought of the past generation, and it seems to me by now incontrovertible (p. 308).

Wolf also deals with the strong literary emphasis in much anthropological writing:

Hence, the anthropologist will always pay tribute to true skill in observing detail and eliciting meaning. There is a sense in which, in the private ranking systems of American anthropologists, the first-class recorder of ethnographic detail ranks more highly than the most gifted theorist. Just as the historian will always take delight in reconstructions that evoke *wie es eigentlich gewesen,* so the anthropologist will always relish expert descriptions of Hanunoo betel chewing, of the use of indigenous weights and measures in a Haitian market, of children as errand runners in a Mexican Indian community.

In this emphasis on the particular—indeed, on the characteristics of the individual case as an ultimate touchstone against which theory must be tested—anthropology resembles literature. For literature, too, focuses on the particular as *ultima ratio.* Good literature is not written by constructing frames of universal applicability; these frames must first be filled with the vibrancy of particular life, *in order* to become universally meaningful. So anthropology, too, seeks this vibrancy of particular life. Nevertheless, it differs basically from literature, and this not only because its heroes are collective heroes, as in *Solomon Island Society, We the Tikopia,* and *The People of Alor.* Literature likewise can portray collective heroes, even if it must do so through the portrayal of individualized men, as—for instance—in André Malraux's *Man's Fate* or *Man's Hope* or Lawrence Durrell's *Alexandria Quartet.* The writer, however, creates his work of art; the anthropologist, to the contrary, describes and analyzes a phenomenon he has done nothing to create. The work of art with which the anthropologist is concerned exists when he comes to it—it is the culture wrought by Siuai or Tikopia or the people of Atimelang—all he can do is capture the phenomenon with fidelity and insight (1964, pp. 89–90).

In a particularly lucid passage, Robert Brown emphasizes this distinction between the natural history approach which has characterized much of anthropological field work and a more broadly theoretical approach:

The natural historian of human society resembles the social scientist in that, unlike the historian, he has no particular concern with actions of the past as distinct from those of the present. Neither has he any concern with problems of dating or questions of tracing social developments. On the other hand, the natural historian of human society resembles the ordinary historian in that both try to establish "true statements about particular events, processes and situations." The social observer is satisfied if he can show that a particular custom exists to a specified degree in a given society or that a particular cause operates. He leaves it to the social scientist or to the historian to explain either why the custom and the cause are present at all or why they are present in the specified degree. Thus it is not correct to say that natural historians are not interested in causal explanations. They are; what does not interest them are *general* explanations, ones which account for all cases of a certain type, rather than merely this case or that case (1963, p. 35).

We are not, of course, suggesting that field work—whether "slice of life," natural history, or any other kind—needs to be defended, deplored, or abandoned. For it is only through field work that anthropologists have been able to compile at first hand a rich corpus of data on a broad variety of cultural arrangements and adaptations. It is obvious that such a corpus could not have been put together by any other means. Not only has the richness and the diversity of ethnographic materials provided a basis for meaningful comparison, but it has documented, as well, the striking malleability of "human nature."

In point of fact, to both the lay public and the intellectual community at large it has been the literary-humanistic kind of anthropology which has most effectively and dramatically demonstrated this malleability. Susan Sontag, for example, in an interesting essay, "The Anthropologist as Hero," finds Lévi-Strauss' *Tristes Tropiques* great art and, therefore, great anthropology.

The profoundly intelligent sympathy which informs *Tristes Tropiques* makes all other memoirs about life among preliterate peoples seem ill-at-ease, defensive, provincial. . . .

Anthropology has always struggled with an intense, fascinated repulsion towards its subject. The horror of the primitive (naively expressed by Frazer and Lévy-Bruhl) is never far from the anthropologist's consciousness. Lévi-Strauss marks the furthest reach of the conquering of the aversion. The anthropologist in the manner of Lévi-Strauss is a new breed altogether. He is not, like recent generations of American anthropologists, simply a modest data-collecting "observer." Nor does he have any axe—Christian, rationalist, Freudian, or otherwise—to grind. Essentially he is engaged in saving his own soul by a curious and ambitious act of intellectual catharsis.

The anthropologist—and herein lies his essential difference, according to Lévi-Strauss, from the sociologist—is an *eye-witness.* "It is sheer illusion that anthropology can be taught purely theoretically." (One wonders why a Max Weber writing about ancient Judaism or Confucian China is permissible, if a Frazer describing scapegoat rituals among the Tagbanua tribe in the Philippines is not.) Why? Because anthropology, for Lévi-Strauss, is an intensely personal kind of intellectual discipline, like psychoanalysis. A spell in the field is the exact equivalent of the training analysis undergone by candidate psychoanalysts. The purpose of field work, Lévi-Strauss writes, is to "create that psychological revolution which marks the decisive turning point in the training of the anthropologist." And no written tests, but only the judgement of "experienced members of the profession" who have undergone the same psychological ordeal, can determine "if and when" a candidate anthropologist "has, as a result of field work, accomplished that inner revolution that will really make him into a new man."

But then Miss Sontag seems to deplore Lévi-Strauss' retreat from these high esthetic peaks into abstract scientism:

However, it must be emphasized that this literary-sounding conception of the anthropologist's calling —the twice-born spiritual adventure, pledged to a systematic *déracinement*—is complemented in most of Lévi-Strauss' writings by an insistence on the most unliterary techniques of analysis and research. His important essay on myth in *Structural Anthropology* outlines a technique for analyzing and recording the elements of myths so that these can be processed by a computer. . . . But his nearest affinity is to the more avant-garde methodologies of economics, neurology, linguistics, and game theory. For Lévi-Strauss, there is no doubt that anthropology must be a science, rather than a humanistic study. . . .
   Linguists—as well as economists and game theorists—have shown the anthropologist "a way to get out of the confusion resulting from too much acquaintance and familiarity with concrete data."
   Thus the man who submits himself to the exotic to confirm his own inner alienation as an urban intellectual ends by aiming to vanquish his subject by translating it into a purely formal code. The ambivalence toward the exotic, the primitive, is not overcome at all, but only given a complex restatement (1966, pp. 72, 75–77).

We would like once more to make it clear that we are not, of course, opposed to the kind of personal-humanistic approach that Miss Sontag finds so appealing in certain aspects of Lévi-Strauss' work. But we believe that this emphasis is unlikely to generate theoretical propositions in anthropology. As a matter of fact, its results, if not its purpose, seem to us to point in the opposite direction.
   Thus, along with the positive contributions of the emphasis on field work seem to have come certain negative consequences for the development of anthropological theory. There has been a strong tendency for the individual anthropologist to immerse himself so completely in the intricacies and unique features of the people he studied that it became difficult for him to discuss the culture except in terms of its uniqueness or special flavor. Indeed, as we have noted earlier, many anthropologists have seen this portrayal of the unique as the main mission and contribution of the discipline.
   Many others who were willing to work toward more general formulations found themselves so intimidated by the sheer weight of ethnographic

detail that they retreated in dismay from an essential task of theory formation, namely, abstraction. Thus, ironically, anthropology's empirical riches have tended often to act as a deterrent rather than a stimulus to theory formation.
   On the one hand, the extreme particularists, pluralists, humanists, or radical relativists have insisted on the uniqueness of each culture—either by referring to its genius, flavor, configuration, style, pattern, and so forth, or by emphasizing the self-evident, "that no two cultures are exactly alike." Because they were right, in the sense that no two anything are exactly alike, their opposition to generalizations, speculations about cross-cultural regularities, or cause-and-effect statements applied comparatively carried enough weight to discourage free theory formation in anthropology. It always turned out that "my people don't do it that way." And because the speaker had done extensive field work among "his people" and therefore had a firsthand familiarity with their lifeways, his observation could not be easily dismissed. Too often it was assumed that the validity of a general proposition about cultural patterning, structure, or process depended upon identity of details. Thus, many twentieth-century anthropologists overreacted to the errors and excesses of the grand theorists and speculators of the nineteenth century when careful field work revealed some of the glaring errors in the data and the assumptions with which the nineteenth-century thinkers had operated. When old theories were "destroyed by new facts," many field workers began to distrust all generalizations in the realm of culture.
   There were always, of course, a number of professionals who continued to insist that generalization was not only possible but potentially more fruitful than it had been when imagination filled the gaps left by inadequate, erroneous, or even non-existent data. In one form or another, these anthropologists—who might prefer to be called "generalizing" or "scientific," to distinguish them from the particularist or extreme relativist anthropologists—insisted that it was the discipline's special grace, or even its mission, to formulate theories or general propositions about culturally patterned human behavior. They pointed out what theoreticians in the "hard sciences"—and many others in the softer sciences as well—had known for a long time: one can only generalize about *types* of situations or events, and, in doing so, one inevitably performs

a process of abstraction and violates the individuality of the event or phenomenon. Not only have anthropologists tended to demand realism of ethnographic accounts (witness the recent concern with "getting at native categories") but they have also demanded realism of their theories. This insistence, in our view, has been a major deterrent to theory formation in anthropology. For the role of theory is to *explain* reality and not to mirror or reproduce it.

Of course, comments about the issue of particularizing as opposed to generalizing have been made often in the past. We have gone over the ground again briefly as a way of leading into what is the central concern of this essay—the relationship of theory to generalizations and facts, and the special problems of theory formation in anthropology.

THE NATURE OF THEORETICAL KNOWLEDGE

Few anthropologists would dispute the assertion that ultimately the main goal of anthropology is the development of a body of reliable knowledge about sociocultural phenomena—how these come into being, how they are maintained or altered over time, and how they interrelate. Yet there continue to be sharp differences of opinion as to how we can best achieve such knowledge and even as to the form its presentation ought to take. Most anthropologists in their more philosophic moments and when they come to reflect upon what it is they do, have tended to espouse a form of narrow empiricism. Thus, they have favored the notion that one simply observes the objective world, collects the relevant facts about this world, and then by a process of induction synthesizes a theory that somehow fits and accounts for the facts. Not only has this view led anthropologists to dichotomize "factual knowledge" and "theoretical knowledge" more sharply than is warranted, but it has also led them to embrace the former as the more solid, basic, and reliable knowledge of the two. In one of the few comprehensive and systematic attempts to explore the theoretical foundations of anthropology, Nadel expressed this viewpoint quite explicitly:

Facts are safer than theory and more solid than explanation, as observation is safer and more solid than thinking about observation (1951, p. 24).

Nor is Nadel here offering a purely idiosyncratic or minority view. We are fairly certain that many if not most anthropologists would find nothing objectionable in his position. As a matter of fact, the above quotation came to our attention because it appears on the flyleaf of a recent ethnographic monograph (Reina, 1966). It is curious that while anthropologists often endorse this point of view in their "theoretical" pronouncements, in their empirical research the realities of field work force them to abandon what is, essentially, an artificial distinction. In short, as Nadel himself recognizes in the very paragraph from which the above quote was excerpted: "When we, as scientists, speak of 'only facts' we mean a product of omission, selection, and inference" (Nadel, 1951, p. 24).

It is a commonplace that observation is always selective and requires some interest, some point of view, or some theoretical framework if it is to be meaningful. Not only do we *not* want to observe and describe everything, but it is not clear just what describing everything could possibly mean. Thus, what we choose to call "observed" or "ethnographic" facts is very much dependent upon the conceptual or theoretical framework within which the observations are carried on. If nothing else, every ethnographer comes to his observations armed with the conceptual apparatus of the anthropological intellectual tradition. What is more, no anthropologist in his role as ethnographer has been content simply to relate discrete and disconnected facts about the culture he is describing. Every ethnographer—including, of course, the humanist–literary–natural history–"slice-of-life" kind—makes some attempt to tell us how the facts hang together, how they interrelate causally, and what makes the particular society in question what it is.

Yet to assert, for example, that a particular event, *x*, occurred because of certain other events, *y* and *z*, presupposes, more broadly, that events of type *x* are linked to events of type *y* and *z* in certain determinate ways. It implies, in other words, some degree of generalization or theoretical interpretation which in most ethnographies tends to remain implicit. Without some such background of theoretical information we have no warrant for crediting what an ethnographer chooses to call *facts* as being significant nor for accepting his representation of how these facts "hang together."

There is no need to belabor these points. The view that any field of systematic inquiry begins with raw observation and the collection of hard facts from which it proceeds by some process of induction to formulate theories, has long since been shown by philosophers of science to be mistaken on both logical and psychological grounds. We could cite a long list of authorities to support this contention, but we shall not. Instead, we have selected a statement by Gunnar Myrdal, first because he is a social scientist rather than a philosopher, and second because he has expressed so clearly the position we have tried to present here:

Theory is necessary not only to organize the findings of research so that they make sense but more basically, to determine what questions are to be asked. Scientific knowledge never emerges by itself, so to speak, from empirical research in the raw, but only as solutions to problems raised; and such solutions presume a logically co-ordinated system of problems stated. Theory, therefore, must always be *a priori* to the empirical observations of the facts. Facts come to mean something only as ascertained and organized in the frame of a theory. Indeed, facts have no existence as part of scientific knowledge outside such a frame. Questions must be asked before answers can be obtained and, in order to make sense, the questions must be part of a logically co-ordinated attempt to understand social reality as a whole. *A non-theoretical approach is, in strict logic, unthinkable* (1957, p. 164, emphasis added).

Thus far, we have been talking of the relationship between fact and theory, and we now want to say something more directly about what it is that makes a theory a theory. The following remarks lay no claim to being either definitive or especially original, but in view of the vagueness with which the term theory has been used by many anthropologists, some attempt at clarification does seem to us to be worthwhile.

As noted earlier, anthropologists have used the term in a variety of ways. Sometimes they apply a concept to a phenomenon or process and call it a theory; sometimes certain kinds of conceptual distinctions are said to be theories; and in other cases, models or conceptual schema are referred to as theories. For example, with reference to the particular issue of models (which have become so fashionable in recent social science literature) there seems to be a strong tendency to equate models with theories. Yet a number of philosophers of science have pointed to the strictly analogic character of models and labored to define the distinction between models and theories. (See, for example,

Brodbeck, 1959; Rapoport, 1959; and Braithwaite, 1953.)

The political scientist, Eugene J. Meehan, has spelled out the importance of this distinction in the following passage:

A theory should be differentiated clearly from a model. A model is not an explanatory instrument, in the sense that theory explains generalizations. Modles are an aid to understanding, and they may contribute indirectly to explanation, but they do not have a part in the process. A model, very generally, is an analogy, an isomorphic construction that is similar in some, but not all, respects to the theory or phenomenon for which it is a model. To use a model is to use an analogy, and it is subject to all of the limits imposed on analogous reasoning. In no case is the model causally related to the theory or object, and in all cases the model is a simplification, a partial isomorph.

Models are very useful tools, of course, and a model of a complex theory or phenomenon can facilitate comprehension and discussion enormously. What are called "postulational" models, formal structures in which the postulates are "educated guesses," can aid the exploration of observable phenomena and relationships. Max Weber's "Ideal types," which are essentially models and not theories, do this very well, as do many of the models used in economics. . . .

The uses of models in engineering, medicine, biology, science, and elsewhere are so obvious and manifold that they hardly need further elaboration here. But the results obtained from the study of models are not knowledge, and strictly speaking a model is not an explanatory tool. Models can perform some of the functions of theories, properly employed. But the very properties that make models useful also make their use dangerous.

It is very easy to confuse model and theory, to assume that a property of a model is a property of a theory or object. It is also easy to forget that models are always partial and incomplete, that some variables have been eliminated, that some relationships have been dropped, that structure has been simplified. No amount of study of formal models can produce knowledge unless the axioms of the model are linked to observables by rules; in that case, the model becomes a theory. Finally, as [Abraham] Kaplan rightly points out, extensive reliance upon models can lead to overemphasis on rigor and precision, hence to unrealistic and unattainable criteria of inquiry. In the world of observable facts, rigor must always be sacrificed to human capacity and precision is limited by the tools of inquiry. Rigor may be bread and butter to the logician but it can be an extremely expensive luxury for the field worker in social science (1965, pp. 49–150).

While some, and perhaps all, of the operations of model building, definition, conceptualization, classification and so forth may be helpful and even necessary to theory formation, they do not constitute theories *per se*. Thus, there is, in our view, a useful distinction to be made between what might be called "theoretical work" (Homans, 1964) or "quasi-theories" (Meehan, 1965), on the one hand, and theories properly so-called, on the other. In this view, theories are generalizations or, more commonly, sets of interrelated generalizations, that explain facts, general statements and even other theories. To put it another way, theories are generalizations, but generalizations of a particular kind, namely, those which relate classes or types of phenomena to one another in certain determinate ways. It follows, then, that theories are not simply inductive or empirical generalizations of the sort that are related to observational data in a direct and immediate way. Theories, if they are any good, should tell us *why* certain empirical generalizations or regularities of nature obtain. Thus, all theories are framed to answer a "why" question.

Theories, it seems to us, have three distinguishing characteristics. First, theories are never subject to confirmation or disconfirmation by simple and direct observation, unlike factual statements or empirical generalizations. The major reason for this has been neatly summarized by Meehan:

Theories are abstract and symbolic constructions, and not descriptions of data or inductive generalizations from observations. Theories relate general statements by appealing to underlying similarities, not to observable properties. Theories supply a wider framework in which generalizations appear as special cases of broader principles. The link between theory and generalization is conceptual and not empirical. Some of the non-logical terms in a theory will refer to observables, but others will refer to nothing that is directly observable. These "theoretical terms" are extremely important, for they give a theory its generalizing power and provide the linkage between theory and generalization (1965, p. 131).

In anthropology, we find such theoretical terms as "role," "status," "integration," "segmentary lineage system," "values," and "class," which must in some sense be "operationalized" or linked to observed phenomena before judgment can be passed on the explanatory fruitfulness of the theories in which they appear. In short, it is the consequences of the theory—arrived at deductively or in some other fashion—which are subject to observational test, rather than the theory directly.

Second, since theories are not simply abbreviated summaries of factual data, they must go beyond what has already been observed. (This, incidentally, is why the formulation of theories always involves an imaginative leap and is never arrived at by a simple process of induction from the empirical data.) In other words, fruitful theories must account for more than the facts and generalizations they were designed to explain. They must explain not merely the facts which may have suggested them in the first place, but other facts besides. What is more, they should direct our attention to new facts and observations. A theory which only accounts for the data which suggested it, is always in danger of collapsing into a tautology, of becoming nothing more than a verbal or *ad hoc* explanation. (For example, why do sleeping pills put people to sleep? Because of their dormative powers.)

Finally, and most important, theories not only bring together and systematically relate discrete and disconnected observed phenomena, but they also in some sense explain these phenomena. Anthropologists often speak in terms of theories making phenomena "intelligible" or in terms of theories promoting "understanding." But "intelligibility" and "understanding" are essentially subjective processes—what may be intelligible to one anthropologist may not be intelligible to another, depending upon a host of personal, psychological factors. There are, however, certain non-subjective, logical criteria for evaluating the explanatory adequacy of a theory, so that in deciding among theories we are not wholly dependent upon an appeal to authority or upon considerations such as which theory "satisfies" us the most. Of course, as Philipp Frank (1961) has argued, even in the physical sciences one can never completely eliminate subjective judgments from the acceptance or non-acceptance of a theory. However, theoretical maturity in a science is at least in part measured by the degree to which it has reduced the subjective or the purely personal factor in the evaluation or acceptance of its theories. On this score, anthropology—and social science in general—is relatively immature. But there are, as well, other characteristics of the discipline which help to account for its failure to build up a body of theory about which there is general consensus. We refer here to the way in which anthropological theories have often been formulated.

Much of what purports to be theory in anthropology tends to be circular, tautological, *ad hoc* in nature, or phrased in such a way as to be perfectly compatible with any possible contingent event in the empirical world; we can think of nothing which would count as evidence against it. Such theories can be rejected on purely logical grounds. To give an illustration, Beattie has noted that:

> . . . explanations of particular social institutions by reference to the maintenance of the "functional unity" of whole societies tend to be either tautologies or unilluminating, or just plain wrong. For example, if we explain the institution of communal feasting on certain occasions by saying that such commensality conduces to the maintenance of social cohesion, and if (as is very likely) part of what we mean by social cohesion is just such joint activities as eating together, our explanation amounts to little more than saying that when people are together they are together, or at best that the more they are together now, the more likely it is that they will be so in the future (1964, pp. 58–59).

The philosophic and scientific literature dealing with explanation is voluminous and often controversial. There is no point in trying here to review the various stands taken by those engaged in the controversy (for a sample, see the General Bibliography at the end of this volume). However—and in brief—we take the position that factual statements or empirical generalizations are explained when it is shown that they can be subsumed under a set of theoretical statements, either by being derived from such statements in formal deductive fashion, or when the connection between the theoretical statements and the generalizations and facts is a probabalistic one. While one finds both types of explanation in the physical sciences, it is rare that one encounters formal deductive explanatory systems in the social sciences. This raises once more the ancient issue of the difference between the physical and social sciences to which we turn now.

SPECIAL PROBLEMS OF THEORY FORMATION IN ANTHROPOLOGY

Most of what we have had to say in the preceding paragraphs about the nature of theory has come not from anthropologists but rather from the writings of philosophers of science and philosophically minded scientists. Such discussions of theory, however, have had the natural sciences, especially physics, in mind. Thus, when philosophers of science speak of theory, they invariably mean by theory a set of general statements hierarchically and deductively interrelated. Deductive theory is considered to be the "ideal" form, and the advantages of this kind of theory are, first, that all general statements in such theory tend toward universality, and all relationships are deductive; hence powerful mathematical techniques can be employed. This enables the deductive consequences of a given set of axioms or postulates to be fully explored, thus facilitating the discovery of significant gaps and pointing the way toward the exploration of new problem areas. What is more, formal deductive relations are usually more easily grasped than the kind of irregular relationships that depend upon long familiarity with and a profound knowledge of the subject matter. This is certainly one of the major reasons why relatively young scientists can often make significant contributions in the physical sciences, but why this is uncommon in the social sciences.

In a recent article on "Contemporary Theory in Sociology," George Homans (1964) adopts a rather strict view of theory. Following the English philosopher of science, Braithwaite, Homans defines theory as a deductive explanatory system containing one or more hypotheses of universal scope. It is not surprising, therefore, that he concludes by taking a very dim view of theory in sociology. As a matter of fact, he finds very little sociological theory worthy of the name. And we are certain that if we were to measure anthropology against this view, we too would be hard pressed to find very much theory. First of all while generalizations in the physical sciences as well as in anthropology are probabilistic in form, the conditions of the former promote greater statistical reliability, and therefore such generalizations can often be considered universal hypotheses for all practical purposes. For as Braithwaite has noted, it is "safer for the philosopher or the scientist or the social scientist to make statistical hypotheses as being the normalcy and to regard universal hypotheses as being extreme cases of statistical hypotheses when the proportions in question are 100 or 0%" (1953, p. 116). This would make universal hypotheses, theories, or laws in any of the sciences—but especially in the social sciences—rare and tricky propositions, to say the least. Further, social science "theories," rather than taking a strictly formal-deductive shape, are more often than not what Abraham Kaplan has called "concatenated theories" (and what Quentin Gibson has referred to as "factor theories"). That is, rather than relating general statements in a deductive and hierarchical fashion, these statements are related by their relevance to a particular question or phenomenon. This type of theory leaves an uncomfortably large area for personal judgment and subjective evaluation on the part of the individual investigator.

Why is there this difference in the kinds of theories which may be formulated by anthropology and the social sciences on the one hand, and certain of the physical sciences on the other? Why has anthropology not produced the elegant formal-deductive theories that philosophers so admire? Is it simply a matter of the immaturity of anthropology as a science, or is there some inherent intractability in the kind of data studied by anthropologists? We believe that there are some special problems anthropologists face in formulating theories as well as in gaining consensus for them, and that these problems do not stem either from the immaturity of the discipline or altogether from the inherent nature of its data.

Three or four such problems seem to us to be especially noteworthy. First, there is the matter of complexity. Now complexity is not simply an ontological attribute of the external world but, to a large extent, is relative to the knowledge we have about the world. In other words, empirical phenomena are what they are. It is the kinds of questions we ask of reality and the kinds of conceptual pictures that we build up of this reality that are more or less complex. Anthropologists, because of the questions that they have traditionally asked, are faced by complex systems which contain the interaction between many more and different types of variables than are usually handled by the physicist. This point has been made in somewhat different ways by both May Brodbeck and Anatol Rapoport:

The physicist may know all the principles involved yet be quite at a loss to predict, say, how many leaves will blow off a tree in the next storm. The poignant difference is, of course, that in social matters we desperately want explanation in detail, while in physical changes we are frequently indifferent. Laws in social science, if we had them, would contain many more variables than those of physics. Yet we berate the social scienties for not being able to do what even the model sciences cannot do (Brodbeck, 1954, pp. 146–147).

Now physics is a science in which from the very beginning a few fundamental measureable quantities were singled out for study. In mechanics, for example, these quantities are length, time, and mass.

Their unambiguous "measurability" was intuitively self-evident and, until the advent of modern positivist critique, there was no question that these quantities were objectively real. This framework of thought sufficed and was constantly reinforced by the success of celestial and terrestrial mechanics in describing and predicting events with remarkable accuracy.

When mathematical physics was extended to other classes of events, involving heat, electricity, and magnetism, it became necessary to isolate other measurables, such as temperature, electric charge, and magnetic field. But the list of these physical quantities is still small, and physics, by definition, deals with those events which can be described entirely in terms of these few fundamental quantities and their combinations.

Now the social scientist has no such list. In fairness to the social scientist, it must be admitted that he does try to invent one. The trouble is that whereas a Newton could begin with intuitively evident quantities (length as measured by sticks, time as measured by clocks, forces as felt in the muscles), the social scientist cannot make such a beginning. The stuff from which human relations and social structure are made is not evident intuitively. It must somehow be distilled or abstracted from innumerable "events," and the selection of these events depends to a great extent on one's experiences, cultural background and biases.

Nevertheless, the social scientist does try to select the fundamental entities of his field of interest. This process of selection, however, is so laborious and involved that it often constitutes the bulk of the social scientist's efforts, and so he hardly ever gets around to stating "postulates." He must first relate his terms to referents. These referents cannot be simply exhibited; they must themselves be abstracted from a rich variety of events, generalizations, and relations. By the time a number of these referents have been so abstracted and christened, one already has a bulky "system" before the work of seeking out "laws" has ever begun. Such "system," particularly in sociology, is sometimes taken to be "theories" (Rapoport, 1959, pp. 350–351).

A second difficulty faced by anthropologists in their efforts to formulate theories is that the systems they deal with are open systems. It is true, of course, that in nature there are no closed systems. Physical scientists, however, perhaps because of the kinds of variables they are concerned with and perhaps because of their ability to control such variables in the experimental situation, seem to have had more success than the social scientists in stating the conditions of closure of the systems they investigate. Anthropologists, on the other hand, have had great difficulty bounding their systems, both on the ground (for example, village, tribe, nation) and in the kinds of explanations they offer (for example, "levels" and the problem of reductionism). We have sometimes tried to get around this problem by introducing the "other things being equal" clause, but unless one can state specifically just what other things have to remain equal this rider may act primarily as a means of masking our ignorance. It should, however, be pointed out in this context that the so-called comparative method, which all anthropologists employ explicitly or implicitly, does give us some measure of limited control over the variables with which we deal.

A further difference is that the kinds of systems investigated by the hard sciences are featured not only by a relative stability, but the internal processes of these systems tend to be repetitive. Thus, under properly controlled conditions the Brownian effect or movement may be investigated at any time and place and will exhibit the same characteristic features. Things are not so easy for social science, where the Industrial Revolution really takes place only once, or where, as Evans-Pritchard observes in his discussion of false analogies from the biological sciences, "A society, however defined, in no way resembles a horse, and, mercifully, horses remain horses—or at least they have done so in historic times—and do not turn into elephants or pigs, whereas a society may change from one type to another, sometimes with great suddenness and violence" (1962, p. 55).

The upshot of all this is that while we often can state many of the necessary conditions for the occurrence of an event, we rarely can state the necessary *and* sufficient conditions. Our explanations, in short, are highly probabilistic and open-ended.

Finally, theories in anthropology (indeed, in all of the social sciences) also function as ideologies, and the reaction to them is often in terms of their ideological rather than their scientific implications. It is, of course, true as many historians of science have pointed out, that the acceptance of various theories in the physical sciences has often hinged upon ideological, esthetic, and other extra-scientific factors. But we do not believe that such extra-scientific factors intrude themselves so prominently in the physical sciences as they do in anthropology and the other social sciences. What is more, theories in the physical sciences do not function in this dual context as commonly as do theories in anthropology. The theory of relativity or the Copernican theory are not ideologies in the same way that theories about the nature of culture (for example, functionalism or evolutionism) are. Thus it is not surprising that where

physical theories have impinged most directly on man they have produced the greatest ideological reaction and ferment. The discovery of the Brownian movement raised no ideological eyebrows. The Copernican theory did.

CONCLUSION

Social scientists are generally embarrassed and apologetic about the paucity of their theoretical achievements as compared with those of the physical scientists. For while the latter have developed a respectable body of well-confirmed laws and theories, many social scientists would question whether their combined disciplines have produced any laws or theories deserving those designations.

In the preceding section we have tried to point up some of the distinctions between the physical and social sciences that might help to account for these differences in the volume and significance of their respective theoretical achievements. (It was not our intention, however, to suggest that such differences in any way constitute a logical or ontological gap between the two fields of inquiry.) Paradoxically enough, greater theoretical demands are made on the social sciences than are made on the physical sciences—as the quote by Brodbeck in the previous section implies. Thus, one looks to the social sciences for answers to the many social problems that afflict us, and one wants detailed answers so that something may be done to correct them. Every man is a social scientist of sorts. The physicist, by contrast, has not had to cope to the same degree with a body of folk or common-sense physical theory. And this has left him much freer to select his own problems in terms of the internal logic and development of his discipline. For example, celestial mechanics, one of the first great theoretical formulations in the physical sciences, concerns itself with only four variables: mass, position, velocity, and time. It asks nothing about such features as color, shape, inhabitants, mineral composition, or atmospheric conditions of the planets. Yet it is with complex questions parallel to these (in the sociocultural realm) that social science often attempts to deal.

Anthropology, like all other fields of systematic inquiry, seeks to generate public, reliable knowledge about its subject matter. As noted earlier in this chapter, anthropology's outstanding achievement thus far has been the production of a rich and varied literature, depicting in often vivid fashion the lifeways of an enormous range of human societies, both past and present. But this literature is largely natural history, not theoretical science. Theory is knowledge organized so that facts are subsumed under general principles. Not only is theoretical knowledge therefore more easily comprehended and transmitted than knowledge organized in any other form, it also has a potentiality for growth and development that the mere accumulation of facts does not have. Indeed, one could question whether accumulated facts by themselves ought to be termed knowledge at all.

Because it takes all cultures at all times and places as its subject matter, anthropology has always been the most comparative of the social sciences. But the failure to exploit more fully the potentialities of comparison as well as the failure to cast knowledge in theoretical forms has made for a great deal of wasteful reduplication. Scattered through the anthropological literature are a number of hunches, insights, hypotheses, and generalizations, some tentative and limited, some of broader scope and more generally accepted. But they tend to remain scattered, inchoate, and unrelated to one another, so that they often get lost or forgotten; and the tendency has been for each generation of anthropologists to start out fresh without any very clear sense of what is known about an area of research. (We are tempted here to paraphrase Santayana: Those who have no memory of the history of anthropology are doomed to repeat it.) Among the consequences of this failure is that theory-building in cultural anthropology comes to resemble slash-and-burn agriculture as Anthony Wallace has recently noted: "After cultivating a field for a while, the natives move on to a new one and let the bush take over; then they return, slash and burn and raise crops in the old field again" (1966, p. 1254).

This "slash-and-burn" character of anthropological theory-building also stems from the failure of anthropologists to be more self-conscious about the logical properties of theories and about what it means to assert that a theory "explains" a set of phenomena. A more explicit awareness of such issues would, if nothing else, greatly reduce the output of what often passes for explanation in anthropology. Here, we believe, anthropologists may learn a great deal from philosophers of science, provided that their learning is somewhat tempered by the knowledge they have of their own discipline. After all, it is the anthropologist who knows the significant empirical problems of his discipline, and not the logician or the philosopher.

But there is always the danger that anthropologists can become so over-awed by the impressive technical arsenal of the mathematicians, logicians, and philosophers that, in an attempt to achieve greater methological rigor and to do what philosophers and mathematical logicians say they ought to be doing, they may unnecessarily constrict the discipline rather than liberate it. We are all for greater logical and methodological sophistication. But if we permit methodology to suggest the problems we deal with rather than allowing problems to determine the methodology, we clearly run the risk of becoming more precise about a continually narrowing range of cultural issues or phenomena.

REFERENCES

BEATTIE, JOHN.
　1964　*Other cultures.* New York: Free Press.
BENNETT, JOHN W.
　1964　Myth, theory, and value in cultural anthropology: questions and comments. In Earl W. Count and Gordon T. Bowles (Eds.), *Fact and theory in social science.* Syracuse: Syracuse University Press.
BRAITHWAITE, RICHARD B.
　1953　*Scientific explanation.* Cambridge, England: Cambridge University Press.
BRODBECK, MAY.
　1954　On the philosophy of the social sciences. *Philosophy of Science,* 21: 140–156.
　1959　Models, meaning and theories. In L. Gross (Ed.), *Symposium on sociological theory.* New York: Harper and Row.

BROWN, ROBERT.
  1963 *Explanation in social science.* Chicago: Aldine Publishing Company.

EVANS-PRITCHARD, E. E.
  1962 Anthropology and history. In E. E. Evans-Pritchard, *Essays in social anthropology.* London: Faber and Faber.

FRANK, PHILIPP G.
  1961 The variety of reasons for the acceptance of scientific theories. In P. G. Frank (Ed.), *The validation of scientific theories.* New York: Collier Books.

GIBSON, QUENTIN.
  1960 *The logic of social inquiry.* New York: Humanities Press.

GLUCKMAN, MAX.
  1949 *An analysis of the sociological theories of Bronislaw Malinowski,* Rhodes-Livingstone Papers No. 16. London: Oxford University Press.

HOMANS, GEORGE C.
  1964 Contemporary theory in sociology. In Robert E. L. Faris (Ed.), *Handbook of modern sociology.* Chicago: Rand McNally.

KAPLAN, ABRAHAM.
  1964 *The conduct of inquiry: methodology for behavioral science.* San Francisco: Chandler.

KROEBER, ALFRED L.
  1955 History of anthropological thought. In William J. Thomas, Jr. (Ed.), *Yearbook of anthropology.* New York: Wenner-Gren Foundation for Anthropological Research.

MEEHAN, EUGENE J.
  1965 *The theory and method of political analysis.* Homewood, Ill.: Dorsey Press.

MYRDAL, GUNNAR.
  1957 *Rich lands and poor.* New York: Harper and Row.

NADEL, S. F.
  1951 *The foundations of social anthropology.* Glencoe, Ill.: Free Press.

RAPOPORT, ANATOL.
  1959 Uses and limitations of mathematical models in social science. In L. Gross (Ed.), *Symposium on sociological theory.* New York: Harper and Row.

REINA, RUBEN E.
  1966 *Law of the saints: a Pokomam pueblo and its community culture.* Indianapolis: Bobbs-Merrill.

SONTAG, SUSAN.
  1966 The anthropologist as hero. In Susan Sontag, *Against interpretation.* New York: Dell.

WALLACE, ANTHONY F. C.
  1966 Review of *The revolution in anthropology* by I. C. Jarvie. *American Anthropologist,* 68: 1254–1255.

WOLF, ERIC R.
  1964 *Anthropology.* Englewood Cliffs, N.J.: Prentice-Hall.

PART I

Overview

ON THE CONCEPT OF CULTURE

LESLIE A. WHITE

Culture: A Critical Review of Concepts and Definitions, by Kroeber and Kluckhohn, is presented as "a critical review of definitions and a general discussion of culture theory" (p. 157). Its purpose is threefold: "First, . . . to make available in one place for purposes of reference a collection of definitions by anthropologists, sociologists, psychologists, philosophers and others. . . . Second, . . . [to document] the gradual emergence and refinement of a concept . . . [the authors] believe to be of great . . . significance. Third, . . . to assist other investigators in reaching agreement and greater precision in definition by pointing out and commenting upon agreements and disagreements in the definitions thus far propounded" (p. 4).

The work is divided into four parts. Part I deals with the "General History of the Word Culture" (30 pp.). Part II, "Definitions" (38 pp.), offers 164 definitions of culture—"close to three hundred 'definitions'" are included in the monograph as a whole (p. 149). Part III, "Some Statements about Culture" (58 pp.), presents more extensive quotations from numerous authors in which the "nature of culture," the relationship between culture and language, culture and society, individuals, etc., are treated. In Part IV, "Summary and Conclusions," (46 pp.), the authors review the history of the concept of culture, survey critically the numerous and varied conceptions now extant, and offer their own conception of culture. There are two appendices by Alfred G. Meyer: (a) on the concept of culture in Germany and Russia, and (b) on the use of the term "culture" in the Soviet Union.

Kroeber, Kluckhohn, and their five research assistants have gone through a great mass of literature, tracing the history of the use of

the term culture and collecting innumerable definitions of, allusions to, and statements about culture. Their history of the use of the term will no doubt impress some readers as somewhat tedious and pedantic. And few readers will require "close to three hundred definitions" of culture to make them realize that great diversity of usage prevails. But these tasks needed doing, and the authors have done them so thoroughly that no one else need do them again.

"The most significant accomplishment of anthropology in the first half of the twentieth century," Kroeber has said, "has been the extension and clarification of the concept of culture." I am not at all prepared to accept this statement. It is true that the concept of culture has been exended to fields other than anthropology; but that it has become "clarified" in the process is something that I doubt very much, and I do not believe that the monograph under review will substantiate this claim. On the contrary, I believe that confusion has increased as conceptions of culture have been multiplied and diversified.

Thirty years ago most anthropologists—in the United States at least—knew what they meant by culture. And most of them meant, I believe, what Tylor meant in 1871 when he formulated his "classic" definition. It was this conception that Lowie, for example, subscribed to in the first paragraph of *Primitive Society.* But who knows what Mr. *X* means by culture today? Culture is "learned behavior"; it is not behavior at all but an "abstraction from behavior"; it is "intangible," a "logical construct"; it is a "psychic defense system," a "precipitate of social interaction," a "stream of ideas"; it "consists of *n* different social signals that are correlated with *m* social responses," etc. One anthropologist at least has gone so far as to question the "reality" of culture. It is difficult to discern much "clarification" of conception during the past twenty-five years. On the contrary, many, no doubt, will sympathize with Radcliffe-Brown who has felt that "the word culture has undergone a number of degradations

Reprinted from "Review of *Culture: A Critical Review of Concepts and Definitions* by A. L. Kroeber and C. Kluckhohn," *American Anthropologist,* 56 (1954): 461–486, by permission of the American Anthropological Association and the author. Leslie A. White is Professor of Anthropology, University of Michigan.

which have rendered it unfortunate as a scientific term."

The problem of "clarifying the concept of culture," which I take to be the chief purpose of this monograph, is, it seems to me, primarily a philosophical and semantic problem. And I finished the treatise with the feeling that the authors have not been overly successful in their attempts to reach an adequate or satisfactory solution to it. They run head on into such ontological problems as the nature of culture, its reality, its abstract or concrete character, and so on, without quite knowing how to handle them— or at least without showing the reader how to handle them. And they become involved, if not entangled, in semantic difficulties which they appear at times not to recognize, or at least to appreciate fully.

We may distinguish two quite distinct kinds of problems: (1) What is the chemical composition of the atmosphere of the sun? Is it determinable? What is the velocity of light? Is it determinable? (2) To what class of phenomena do we wish to apply the term *bug,* or *gentleman*? In the first we are concerned with sensory exploration of the external world: Does the sun's atmosphere contain hydrogen or doesn't it? Does light travel 186 or 187 thousand miles per second? In the second kind of problem we merely have to decide how we shall use words. Are spiders to be included in the category—labeled with the word—bug or not? If a man does such and such do we wish to call him—include him in the category—gentleman?

Is culture a thing, or class of things, in the external world whose nature we have to determine as we would ascertain the chemical composition of the sun or the velocity of light? Or is culture a word the use of which we have arbitrarily to determine—like deciding whether to include spiders or butterflies in the category *bug*?

Some anthropologists seem to feel that a conception of culture must depend upon our ability to ascertain the properties, or nature, of things in the external world. Thus, D. G. Haring asks "Is *Culture* Definable?" (emphasis added) and comes to the conclusion, as I interpret him, that it is not—just as one might conclude that the chemical composition of the sun is not determinable.

Kroeber and Kluckhohn do not make it clear which kind of problem one is faced with in regard to conceptions of culture. They appear to feel, however, that it is the "chemical com-

position of the sun" kind, for they say that one of the purposes of their study is "to assist other investigators [*sic*] in reaching . . . greater precision in definition . . ." (p. 4), and they tell us what culture "basically" *is* (p. 155). Investigators are indeed needed to ascertain the chemical composition of the sun. But we do not need to resort to any investigation whatever to decide whether we wish to include spiders in the category *bug* or not. Bug-ness is not a thing in, or an attribute of, the external world whose nature we have to discover through investigation, like the chemical composition of the sun's atmosphere. Neither, we suggest, is *culture. Culture,* like *bug, is a word* that we may use to label a class of phenomena—things and events —in the external world. We may apply this label as we please; its use is determined by ourselves, not by the external world. "It cannot be too clearly understood," says Whitehead, "that in science, technical terms are *names arbitrarily assigned,* like Christian names to children. There can be no question of the names being right or wrong. They may [however] be judicious or injudicious . . ." (emphasis added).

As for "precision of definitions," definitions are not more or less precise—like measurements of the velocity of light. A definition of *bug* that includes spiders is neither more nor less precise than one that does not. Needless to say, a "definition" that does not mark boundaries, set limits, in short, which does not define, is not a definition. "Culture is learned behavior" is precise enough; behavior patterns are acquired by learning or they are not; those that are so acquired may arbitrarily be labeled *culture.* The same can be said of "culture is a psychic defense system," or "a stream of ideas."

To be sure, a definition may be precise without being useful or fruitful in scientific interpretation. "A *doko* is any man between the ages of 23 and 37, who has red hair, wears number 10 shoes, and has one glass eye," is precise enough as a definition, but it has no apparent value. Neither does, or can, a definition tell us *all* we want to know about the thing defined, just as no witness can ever tell "the truth, *the whole truth, etc.";* "culture is learned behavior" is the beginning of one intellectual process as it is the end of another. Definitions are conceptual tools, man-made and fashioned for certain purposes, to do certain things—in science to render experience intelligible. A conception of culture must be more than precise; it must be fruitful; its value is proportional to its contribution to understanding. Until anthropologists distinguish clearly between two quite different kinds of problems—determining the chemical composition of the sun, and determining the use of the word *bug*—in short, until they distinguish sharply between *things and events* in the external world, and *verbal concepts* with which these phenomena are represented, they will continue to grope and flounder, trying to discover what culture "basically is," striving for "greater precision of definition."

Professors Kroeber and Kluckhohn appear to be definitely committed to the view that "culture is an abstraction": ". . . culture is inevitably an abstraction" (p. 61); it is "basically a form or pattern . . . an abstraction . . ." (p. 155). They do not tell us explicitly and precisely what they mean by abstraction; we are left to figure that out for ourselves. They seem to use the term in two different senses: (1) a form or pattern, and (2) a statistical concept of average or mean. They emphasize repeatedly the point that culture is not behavior, but something abstracted from behavior (pp. 114, 155–56, 189, etc.). Behavior, they say, "seems . . . to be that within whose mass culture exists and from which it is conceptually extricated or abstracted" (p. 156). Concrete behavior is the subject matter of psychology, according to their view, whereas forms or patterns, abstracted from behavior, are culture and are therefore the subject-matter of cultural anthropology (p. 155). Anthropologists have tended to be "concrete rather than theoretical minded about culture" (p. 156). And Kroeber and Kluckhohn feel that "the greatest advance in contemporary anthropology is probably the increasing recognition that there is something more to culture than artifacts, linguistic texts, and lists of atomized traits" (p. 62). In short, to proceed from conceiving of culture as a class of objective observable things and events in the external world to regarding it as an intangible abstraction is a significant achievement.

A man casts a ballot: is this behavior or culture? Kroeber and Kluckhohn would say that dropping the ballot in the box is behavior, not culture; culture would be something intangible, a form or pattern, "extricated or abstracted from" this act. Is a Chinese porcelain vase an article of merchandise, an *objet d'art,* or a scientific specimen? It all depends. A vase is a vase. It becomes a commodity when it is placed in one kind of context, an *objet d'art* when placed in another. Similarly, casting a ballot— dropping a piece of paper in a box—is an act,

an event. It "is" what it is. When we interpret this act in terms of the ideas, sentiments and habits of an individual we may call it *behavior* and call the kind of interpretation *psychological.* When we explain it in the context of the extra-somatic tradition of things and events dependent upon symboling we may call it *culture,* and the explanation *culturological.* The thing, the event, is the same in either case; we merely refer it to different contexts for purposes of explanation. The matter need not be one of concrete versus abstract at all, but merely different contexts to which the event is referred for purposes of explanation. And there need be no antithesis between concrete and theoretical; a physicist may be as theoretical as you wish in his interpretation of concrete particles. Conrtariwise, it does not follow that one is more advanced theoretically because he defines his subject matter as "abstraction."

"Even a culture trait is an abstraction . . . [it] is an 'ideal type' because no two pots are identical nor are two marriage ceremonies ever held in precisely the same way" (p. 169). Are we then to cease calling pots, axes, songs, rituals, etc., culture traits because no two items in a class are exactly alike? Could we not say that a culture trait is any thing or event—objective and observable, like a pot or a marriage ceremony—that is dependent upon symboling? Could we not say that pot is a culture trait, and that *pot* is the name of a class of objects and also of any member of that class? This, of course, is being "concrete minded," which is just what Kroeber and Kluckhohn want to get away from.

"Culture is not behavior but something abstracted from behavior." Similarly, a pot, or pots, are not culture; it is the "ideal type" of pots that is culture. An "ideal type" is a statistical conception in the mind of the anthropologist. We now face this question squarely: are we to use the term culture to label objective things and events in the external world, or conceptions in the anthropologist's mind? Kroeber and Kluckhohn, it seems to me, are definitely committed to the latter course. I feel also that they are not fully aware of the consequences to which their "culture is an abstraction" definition commits them.

No two foxes are exactly alike—just as no two pots are. But we do not wish to say that *fox* is an abstraction, an "ideal type" to which all the little concrete bushy-tailed creatures correspond in varying degrees. Fox is the name of a class of objects and also of each member of this class. "Ideal type" is actually a way of designating this class, in terms of an average or mean about which the individual members cluster. The situation in which the cultural anthropologist finds himself is exactly like that confronting the mammalogist, the physicist or any other scientist. We have objective, observable things and events in the external world (i.e., outside our own individual minds) on the one hand, and conceptions in our minds with which we represent these things and events and with which we try to render them comprehensible, on the other. The cultural anthropologist can use the term culture to label a class of things and events in the external world—as Tylor did and as generations of anthropologists have done until recently—or he can use the term to label conceptions in his own mind—which we suspect he does not fully recognize as such because he calls them "ideal types" or "abstractions" whose place of residence is not so obvious. So can the mammalogist use the term fox to label a statistical conception in his own mind rather than a quadruped with a bushy tail. But if the anthropologist is to use the term culture to label conceptions in the mind, is not Cornelius Osgood to be complimented for having made this conception explicit: "Culture consists of all ideas concerning human beings which have been communicated to one's mind . . ." (p. 66)?

Despite Kroeber and Kluckhohn's feeling that "the greatest advance in contemporary anthropological theory" is the shift from "concrete-mindedness" to traffic in abstractions, I venture to predict that anthropology will again revert to defining culture in terms of concrete, objective, observable things and events in the external world. I make this prediction with some confidence because it is the procedure in every other science—in all of the more mature sciences, at least—and we believe that cultural anthropology will mature some day. Fox is the name of a class of objects; electron is the name of a thing in the external world—it traverses an observable path in a cloud chamber. A "gene" or a "magnetic field" may not be directly observable, but the referents of these terms are unequivocally things or events in the external world. It goes without saying that mammalogists and physicists have *conceptions* of foxes and electrons in their minds. But they do not readily confuse foxes and electrons with conceptions of the same. The time will come again when cultural anthropologists will once more distinguish a particular class of objective phenomena in the external world as their subject matter, just as every other scientist does, and they will label their subject matter *culture,* just as other scientists label their subject matter atoms, mammals, parasites, etc.

Kroeber and Kluckhohn attach great importance to *values.* But what are values? The authors make a very considerable attempt to explain them to us, but with rather little success. "They are the products of men, of men having bodies . . ."; they are "intangible," and "empathy" is required to "perceive" [*sic*] them; but they receive objective expression and "can be viewed as observable, describable and comparable phenomena of nature" (pp. 156, 172–73). Values are imponderable and unmeasurable (p. 174), but they are definitely "part of nature, not outside it" (p. 172)—as if science could deal with, or mankind experience, anything outside of nature. "Values are primarily social and cultural [what are they secondarily?]: social in scope, parts of culture in substance [*sic;* culture is an abstraction, it must be remembered] and form" (p. 172). Values have their "locus or place of residence" in "individual persons and nowhere else" (p. 172). They are "the structural essence" of culture (p. 172). Thus, *a value is the structural essence of an abstraction.* Kroeber and Kluckhohn need not be surprised if some readers do not always comprehend them and follow them at all points. Finally, values "provide the only basis for the fully intelligible comprehension of culture" (p. 173). If only we had a basis for a "fully intelligible comprehension" of values!

Is *value* the name of something that people or culture *do?* Or, does it designate *how* something is organized or done? Or is value the name of a way that some anthropologists feel-and-think about culture? *Value* is a word employed in ordinary and in philosophic discourse. It has some connotations, rather vague and indefinite, and it is also soaked with feeling. Kroeber and Kluckhohn take this term and then try to determine what, in the external world, corresponds with it. Would it not be better to begin with observation of things and events as we find them in the external world and then to determine what word-concepts are needed to represent them? The latter course, if followed scientifically, *could,* of course, lead to use of the term value. But we doubt very much that it would. *Value* has been so identified through usage with the subjective and the imponderable that we doubt if it can—or will—ever be usable as a scientific term.

Values are intimately related to "cultural relativism." Cultures are comparable, the authors tell us, but comparison on an objective basis is limited and of little significance, apparently (p. 176). Cultures derive their meaning and significance from their value systems. Cultures are therefore imponderable as their values are imponderable. Each culture is to be measured by its own yardstick; a yardstick that would measure all cultures—such as the amount of energy harnessed and put to work per capita per year, or the amount of food, measured in calories, produced per unit of human energy—they call "absolute," and they will have no truck with absolutes. They defend their theory of cultural relativism against its critics and opponents—whom they do not identify—with a warmth and vigor that suggests a feeling on their part that it needs defending. They anticipate "some attempts to escape from relativism" (p. 175). But cultural relativism is an "inescapable fact" that has been "completely established" (pp. 175–76, 178). And, we are told peremptorily, "there must be no attempt to explain it away or to deprecate its importance because it is inconvenient, hard to take, hard to live with" (p. 178). And that, it would seem, is that.

There are many other points in this monograph that invite and need discussion, but our review has already grown long. We might merely mention a few of them, however.

"It is perfectly true . . . that culture 'conditions' individuals but is also 'conditioned' by them" (p. 110); "personality shapes and changes culture but is in turn shaped by culture" (p. 114). This proposition, which seems so obviously valid—or reasonable—to many anthropologists is one that this reviewer would challenge; it is confusing or misleading, to say the least.

We find the old dichotomy "history and science," which obscures the evolutionary process by identifying it with history (p. 161): "If a natural classification implicitly contains an evolutionary development—that is, a history . . ." (p. 175)—as if *evolution* and *history* were synonyms. But we have gone over this ground before.

We were disturbed, in reading this monograph, by what appears to us to be ambiguities, inconsistencies and uncertainties. Culture is usually an abstraction; but it is also "an abstract

description . . ." (p. 182), and sometimes it seems to be something observable in the external world. It "must never be forgotten . . . that only persons and not cultures interact . . ." (p. 186). Yet, "at the cultural level of abstraction it is perfectly proper to speak of . . . the mutual influencing of cultures . . ." (p. 186). Can we formulate—they say "discover" (p. 167)—laws of culture or not? They appear to say, "Yes, we can—we have—discovered and used 'statistical laws,' but 'we do not anticipate the discovery of cultural laws that will conform to the type of those of classical mechanics,'" (p. 167; see also, pp. 182, 188–89). Many of their statements are so qualified as to make it difficult to know what they are driving at.

Culture is an important monograph—important because (1) it deals with the most significant concept in cultural anthropology, and (2) because it will undoubtedly exert considerable influence, not only among anthropologists, but upon others as well. Since Tylor's day—and chiefly within the last twenty-five years—conceptions of culture have multiplied and become so diverse as to present a picture of confusion, not to say chaos. The authors have tried to bring some order into the situation. We believe that they have expressed a prominent—perhaps the dominant—trend in conceptions of culture during the past twenty-five years, and they have done it effectively and well. This trend is away from the conception of culture as objective, observable things and events in the external world and toward the conception of culture as intangible abstractions. We deplore this trend because we believe that it is a veering away from a point of view, a theoretical standpoint, that has become well established and has proved itself to be fruitful in the tradition that is science: the subject matter of any science is a class of objectively observable things and events, not abstractions. This shift in conceptions of culture will, therefore, only make the achievement of a science of culture more difficult. The magnitude of research that has gone into this monograph, the earnest consideration of the theoretical problems involved, the confident tone in which the authors' conclusions—or at least their point of view—is expressed, and, finally, the prestige of the authors, which is very great indeed, will all tend to impress many readers and to lend substantial support to the "abstraction" conception of culture, thus delaying and making more difficult a return to the scientific tradition of a direct and immediate concern with objective things and events: Culture as the name of a class of things and events in the external world; the *conception* of culture a conception (why use the ambiguous term abstraction?) in the mind of the culturologist. Let us not mistake the one for the other.

If today we find ourselves confused with regard to culture and conceptions of culture, perhaps it is not to be wondered at. The science of culture is very young, and its most appropriate name, *culturology,* even younger. Culture may be the subject matter of cultural anthropology. But what is culture? "It is a well-founded historical generalization," says Whitehead, "that the last thing to be discovered in any science is what the science is really about."

2

THE SUPERORGANIC: SCIENCE OR METAPHYSICS?

DAVID KAPLAN

I

ALMOST a century ago, E. B. Tylor in the opening chapter of his classic work *Primitive Culture,* argued for the creation of a naturalistic and autonomous science of culture. During the intervening years a number of other writers—more or less echoing Tylor's plea—have attempted to set forth the case for the superorganic view of culture (e.g., Durkheim, Kroeber, Murdock, Lowie, White); which in turn has provoked a variety of rebuttals from the opposing camp (e.g., Sapir, Goldenweiser, Spiro, Bidney, among others). Indeed, few theoretical issues in anthropology have been perennially debated with quite the fervor that has been generated by this one.

By now the whole topic has received such a thorough working over that it would appear there is scarcely anything left to be said on the matter. In reviewing some of the literature of this logomachy, however, I have been struck by how large a portion of it has been couched in metaphysical terms: theoretical discussions dealing with the concept of culture have usually ended up as discussions about the ontological status of culture. A great deal of effort and

From *American Anthropologist,* 67 (1965): 958–976 © by permission of the American Anthropological Association and the author. David Kaplan is Associate Professor of Anthropology at Brandeis University.

philosophic ingenuity has gone into the exploration of such questions as: Is culture real or just an abstraction from reality? If real, then what is the nature of its reality and where does this reality have its locus? If an abstraction, then how can we speak of it as influencing the behavior of individuals? and so forth.

While all of these may be important questions in certain realms of philosophic discourse, as practicing anthropologists we need not await the resolution of ontological issues before getting down to the scientific business of the discipline, which I take to be to provide the best explanations we can of how cultural systems have come to be as they are and how they work. We can, in other words, separate methodological and epistemological questions from ontological ones. In fact, if it were not possible to make such a logical separation, and indeed if such a distinction had not been made long ago, the various scientific disciplines would still be branches of metaphysical philosophy. As Goldstein has aptly pointed out:

The term "electron" is frequently found in physical theory and it too has given rise to ontological questions. What is an electron? What is its status in the world? The realistic view holds that it is a tiny bit of something, so small that the human eye cannot detect its presence, which makes itself known by its manifested effects. Phenomenalists say that it is senseless to talk of such bits, and that all one can possibly mean by the term "electron" are the so-called effects or manifestations. Whichever view one favors, the actual theoretical science is in no way affected, nor is it difficult for advocates of these metascientific interpretations to collaborate in specifically scientific work. And the objects of concern to other sciences are also amenable to both realistic and phenomenalistic interpretations without affecting the actual work of these sciences.

The following discussion is an attempt to re-examine the superorganic conception of culture in the light of the logic of scientific methodology. Put more specifically, the central problem of this paper is whether from the viewpoint of the logic of scientific explanation it makes any sense to speak of explaining "culture in terms of culture"; or whether, as we have so often been told, cultural phenomena must, in the final analysis, be explained in psychological terms. The crux of this issue, as I see it, hinges not upon a determination of the ontological structure of the world, but rather upon a formulation of those conditions under which one science is reducible to some other one, i.e., the logical and empirical requirements which must be satisfied if the laws and other theoretical statements of one discipline can be said to be explained by the theoretical statements of a second discipline. There are, of course, a number of different theoretical perspectives which have as their focus the relationship between cultural and psychological phenomena, and not all of them are reductive in their implications. One might, for instance, be interested in exploring the psychological concomitants of cultural events in an attempt to supplement culturological explanations with some statements about the character of such psychological processes; or one might wish to investigate the congruence or lack of congruence between certain types of personality systems and certain kinds of cultural systems. But since these theoretical concerns, as I understand them, would not entail a denial of the logical possibility of explaining cultural phenomena in terms of themselves, I will not be concerned with them here.

Perhaps it ought to be emphasized at the outset that this paper lays no claim to settling this issue once and for all. Its purpose is essentially a more modest one, namely, to shift the dialogue from the spongy ground of metaphysics to the arena of scientific methodology—where the whole question properly belongs.

Probably the best place to begin is with a few brief remarks about the concept of culture itself. I think it is fair to say that most anthro-

pologists, at least in the United States, look upon culture as their master concept. Yet if one were to judge from the recent exhaustive review of the concept by Kroeber and Kluckhohn, it would appear that anthropologists are sharply at odds about the nature of their subject-matter, as well as where to set the logical limits of its boundaries. On the face of it, this is a curious state of affairs for a discipline to find itself in— somewhat like a group of mammalogists at loggerheads over what a mammal is. I think, however, that if we put aside what anthropologists assert to be the essential nature of culture when they don their philosophic caps, and instead look at how they actually work with the concept in the context of their empirical research, we will find a greater degree of agreement than the bewildering array of definitions contained in the Kroeber-Kluckhohn compendium might suggest. After all, despite their diverse metascientific conceptions of culture, most of the time anthropologists do manage to communicate with each other about the kinds of things they are doing. When we undertake a piece of research, whether it be in the field or the library, we do not first spend time in deciding what and where culture is—as though culture were some object to be located out there in the external world: we allow our theoretical interests to dictate the kinds of phenomena and conceptual "entities" with which we will be concerned. As a matter of fact, a cursory glance through a sample of ethnographic monographs will reveal that anthropologists concern themselves with roughly the same kinds of conceptual "entities": modes of subsistence, kinship systems, political institutions, magical and religious rituals, and so on.

I would suggest that the basis for this common universe of discourse—beneath all the ostensible definitional diversity—is that anthropologists engaged in empirical research, however they may philosophically define the concept, tend to view culture as a class of phenomena, conceptualized for the purpose of serving their methodological and scientific needs. And while it is one's theoretical concerns which ultimately determine the kinds of things and events which go to make up the class of phenomena termed culture, it may be useful at this point to summarize briefly some of the major pragmatic considerations which seem to have entered into what might be called the anthropologist's "pre-philosophic" conception of culture.

To begin with, things and events are identified

as a cultural phenomena principally by their traditional aspect. Or to put it in somewhat different terms, cultures are built up out of patterned and interrelated traditions—traditions in technology, social organization,[1] and ideology. When physical anthropologists, for example, are confronted with the task of deciding whether certain fossil forms did or did not have culture, they base their judgments upon the presence or absence of *tool traditions.*

Among the important features of the varying traditions which make up culture, two stand out as being especially noteworthy: first, they are transmitted across time and space by non-biological mechanisms; and second, they do not appear to be explainable by an appeal to either genetic or panhuman psychic traits. That is, while the psychobiological characteristics of the hominids would seem to be relevant to an explanation of the emergence of cultural traditions from their infrahuman background as well as the early development of these traditions, there does not appear to have been any significant change in the neural structure of the human species since the Upper Pleistocene, perhaps as much as 50,000 years ago. Since that time, therefore, the psychological characteristics of the human species would not be relevant to an explanation of either the specific content or the variations in time and space of these traditions—or so the present evidence would strongly indicate.[2] The burden of proof would be on those who contend otherwise. Such panhuman psychobiological characteristics, however, might be relevant to explaining why certain *general* features turn up in all cultural traditions, e.g., Wissler's "universal culture pattern."

Now, it can legitimately be argued that in some infrahuman species one does find non-genetically transmitted traditions of a rudimentary sort. But a distinctive attribute of human cultural traditions is that they are cumulative over time in a way that the incipient traditions found associated with infrahuman species are not. This is undoubtedly related to the fact that man has come to be wholly dependent upon these cultural traditions for his biological survival as a species, a fact not true of any other animal species. Some writers stressing the existence of such inchoate traditions (sometimes called protoculture) exhibited by infrahuman species, view the behavioral differences between man and the rest of the animal kindom as constituting a difference in degree. Others have stressed the cumulative nature of human cultural

traditions and view the difference as being one of kind. All writers, however, seem to agree that the behavioral differences between man and his infrahuman relatives are sizable and significant. Finally, there appears to be widespread agreement among anthropologists that the building up and cumulative nature of cultural traditions is made possible by man's ability to create and use symbols, which takes its most prominent form in human language. Some scholars would question whether the ability to symbolize is unique to man, but all would agree, I think, with Fried that "only man, on this planet, engages in massive, systematic and continuous symboling."

II

Most of the critiques which have been levelled at the superorganic conception of culture can be grouped within two broad categories. The first—and probably the one that anthropologists have found most convincing—would reject the possibility of explaining cultural phenomena wholly in terms of themselves on the grounds that such phenomena have no independent ontological existence, but in "reality" are always found intimately associated with psychological phenomena. In other words, because culture cannot exist without its human carriers, and because in "reality" man and culture are inseparably linked, this position would maintain that to separate culture conceptually from man does violence to the nature of this "reality."

The second type of critique is of a different sort and stems from a moralistic stance. This position would reject the attempt to explain cultural phenomena in terms of themselves on the grounds that this view entails a kind of determinism which reduces man to a mere cipher caught up by impersonal cultural forces over which he has no control. Each of these arguments will now be taken up in turn.

We are indebted to David Bidney for one of the most explicit and thoroughgoing expositions of what can be called the ontological critique of the superorganic position. In his *Theoretical Anthropology* he writes:

The interdependence of the levels of natural phenomena implies that no level is in fact completely intelligible apart from reference to the levels below it. Physical and chemical phenomena are most closely related, but biological and biochemical processes now seem to be inseparably connected also.

Similarly, it is to be expected that with the development of psychosomatic medicine we shall learn more about the interdependence of psychological, cultural and biological phenomena.

At each level we may begin with the postulation of certain data which cannot be deduced from the lower levels. As a methodological device, or fiction, it may be pragmatically useful to study the phenomena of a given science "as if" they were independent of other levels. This is particularly easy for physicists, chemists, and biologists, who deal with disparate objects which may be segregated for special treatment. The problem becomes more difficult in the case of psychologists who wish to study psychological phenomena to the exclusion of biological processes, since the two sets of data obviously pertain to the same object. Similarly, sociologists and anthropologists, who are interested in social behavior and its products, cannot investigate their data except by reference to actual human organisms. That is, psychological, sociological, and cultural phenomena do not exist independently, and hence may not be said to constitute distinct ontological levels or be conceived through themselves alone. Methodologically, it is possible to abstract the latter phenomena and to treat them temporarily "as if" they were independent of the organisms upon which they depend.

It might appear from the above excerpt that Bidney's aim is to distinguish a methodological version of superorganicism from an ontological one, in order to reject the latter in favor of the former. If this were indeed the case, then we would have no difference of opinion and there the matter would end. That this is not his intention, however, is evident from the fact that nowhere in his work does he discuss how such a methodological superorganicism might be used as a procedure in the scientific study of cultural phenomena. The reasons for this, I think, are abundantly clear. In Bidney's view, the scientific disciplines are primarily distinguishable not on logical grounds, i.e., by their methodogical procedures or theoretical structures, but rather by their different ontological assumptions and commitments. If Bidney thought otherwise, he would be obliged to give serious consideration to the logical and scientific implications of methodological superorganicism. But this would commit him to entertaining the possibility of a naturalistic, autonomous science of culture, and Bidney will have none of that. An examination of the reasons for his rejection of such a science of culture would carry us too far afield. Suffice it to note that Bidney is not so much interested in what anthropology *is,* but in what it *ought* to be; and his vision of what it ought to be stems from his own very personal appraisal of anthropology in particular and the human condition

in general. Bidney is not especially concerned with the kinds of empirical questions that are of interest to most anthropologists. What interests him most are a broad range of humanistic and metaphysical questions having to do with such matters as—human freedom, the nature of cultural reality, and how man freely creates his cultural environment as a means of fulfilling his basic needs and desires. It is this humanistic concern which leads him to seek a metascientific or ontological theory of culture, and it is this search which impels him to develop his critique of the superorganic conception of culture—indeed one might well construe this to be the major purpose of his book:

Those who insist so repetitiously upon the autonomy of culture, namely, the superorganicists, mean to assert an ontological principle as well as an epistemic fact. The ontological issue is whether cultural phenomena constitute a closed system and are independent of psychological processes, that is, superpsychic, or whether in the last analysis they cannot be understood or said to exist, either wholly or in part, independently of the mind of man. . . . Our thesis is that neither psychology nor history is a sufficient cause or condition of culture, because the latter is an inherently complex phenomenon comprising both psychological and historically acquired experience of nature. Concrete, actual experience is psychocultural and involves a creative synthesis of psychological activity and cultural achievement in relation to a given environment.

The crux of Bidney's argument seems to be as follows: that each of the sciences strives to isolate for special consideration its own particular segment of reality; but the interdependence of the levels of reality makes for certain difficulties in this endeavor. Some scientific disciplines, such as physics, chemistry and biology find it methodologically easy to accomplish because they deal with "disparate objects which may be segregated for special treatment." In the case of the cultural sciences, however, it is clearly impossible. Since there is no separate segment of reality (ontological level) which corresponds to cultural phenomena, we cannot speak of explaining these phenomena in terms of themselves, but must always include as an integral part of our explanations, statements about psychological phenomena as well.

Now one can readily agree that in "reality" all cultural phenomena are intimately linked with psychological phenomena; but is it not also the case that psychological phenomena are at the same time intimately associated with physiological phenomena and these in turn with physiochemical and subatomic phenomena. Yet it is not claimed (at least not by Bidney) that to explain cultural or psychological phenomena we must show how they are related to the biochemical and sub-cellular physical processes going on within human organisms—although some writers might contend that this is the ultimate goal of science.

Bidney, it should be pointed out in all fairness, explicitly asserts that his psychocultural approach does not seek to reduce cultural phenomena to the psychological level—as a matter of fact, he labels any such attempt the "naturalistic fallacy." I must confess, however, to being somewhat uncertain as to the meaning which Bidney attaches to the terms "reduction" and "psychocultural." In support of his psychocultural approach, for example, he contends: "An adequate theory of culture must explain the origin of culture and its intrinsic relations to the psychobiological nature of man. To insist upon the self-sufficiency and autonomy of culture, as if culture were a closed system requiring only historical explanations in terms of other cultural phenomena, is not to explain culture, but to leave its origin a mystery or an accident of time."

Bidney is so acutely attuned to the detection of logical fallacies, it is surprising that he should be guilty in the above passage of the genetic fallacy. The psychobiological nature of man, to be sure, *is* revelant to explaining the origins of culture (who ever denied this). But to account for the initial origins of culture is quite a different matter from providing an explanation of its present-day diversity of content and form.

Basic to Bidney's view of culture is his notion of "human nature." He maintains that "culture is a direct necessary expression of human nature" and furthermore that this "human nature, like culture, evolves or unfolds in time." He then goes on to add: ". . . while the innate biological potentialities of man remain more or less constant the actual, effective psychophysical powers and capabilities are subject to development in time. . . . The point I wish to make does not raise the problem of racial differences, but only the possibility of the cultural perfectibility of human nature as an acquired, historical achievement which varies with different cultures."

But how are we to determine empirically what these "psychophysical powers and capabilities" are, which seem to unfold independently of man's innate biological potentialities, and which give rise to cultural variations in time and space? Bidney does not tell us, except to say that they vary with the state of human culture. Ultimately what we are left with is a mode of explanation that goes something like this: Cheyenne culture differs from Arunta culture because they are expressions of different human natures. And how do we know that Cheyenne and Arunta human natures are different? Obviously, because their cultures are different. The sterility of this kind of verbal explanation is, I think, apparent and scarcely needs further comment.

As for Bidney's disavowal of reductionism, his remarks about the connection between chemical and physical phenomena and the development of psychosomatic medicine casting light on the interdependence between cultural, psychological and biological phenomena, indicate not only a readiness to deal with several (and perhaps even all) levels simultaneously, but also a conviction that phenomena at the "higher" levels *can* be explained by those at the "lower" levels. If we are to deal with a number of different levels at once, however, what is required are empirical laws which permit us to connect logically the phenomena (or more accurately the concepts and statements which describe and explain these phenomena) of the several levels. The success of a field such as biochemistry, for example, stems from the fact that as a result of empirical developments in biology and chemistry, such laws and hypotheses have been formulated, making it possible logically to derive statements about certain biological phenomena from statements about certain chemical phenomena. We will return to this issue shortly, when considering reductionism more fully.

III

What appears to be involved in Bidney's position, and, indeed, in the whole ontological critique of the superorganic, is an erroneous view of the rationale for the division of labor between the various scientific disciplines, as well as the basis for making logical distinctions between them. Bidney sees the world in terms of a series of emergent levels of reality. Moreover, he writes about these levels of reality as though the "nature" of things and the interrelationships between those natures were somehow given to us to be read off by direct inspection. But the world does not present itself to us neatly packaged into cultural events, psychological events, bio-logical events or physiochemical events; nor does it present itself to us in terms of "levels of reality" or "natural phenomena." It comes to us as a stream of concrete events which are "just what they are." Out of the countless properties associated with any given event, the ones that are selected out for special concern will depend upon one's theoretical interests and scientific purposes. Since language is by its very nature abstractive—and all knowledge about the world if it is not to remain private must be stated in propositional form—we can never exhaust the total "concreteness" of an event. Nor is it the purpose of any theoretical science to faithfully reproduce "reality," either in whole or in part. We are, in effect, constantly engaged in a proc-ess of theoretical selecting-out, and it is for this reason that the notion of "pure" description is a chimera. To put it in a slightly different way, while there may be one "reality," there are many different kinds of questions which one can ad-dress to that reality and in consequence many different ways of conceptualizing it. And since this reality is never grasped directly, but only through our conceptualizations of it, the nature of reality turns out to be as varied as there are different theoretical formulations of it. We can-not somehow get behind our concepts to a non-conceptualized "real" world. The point of all this is that the *logical* independence of a science is not based upon having its own separate "chunk of reality" with which to deal—for this is not true of any science. Rather, it is based upon the fact that it has a set of distinct ques-tions or problems which are its special concern, and that in seeking answers to these probelms it has developed a body of distinct terms and con-cepts (which determine its subject-matter), as well as laws and theories (which organize and explain its subject-matter).

Now, I would submit that cultural anthro-pology has a set of *cultural* questions which it has traditionally sought to answer (e.g., the re-lationship between types of residence, types of descent and types of kinship terminology; the relationship between changing modes of sub-sistence and complexity of social organization; the relationship between centralized political sys-tems and such features as trade or the construc-tion and maintenance of large-scale public works or ecological differentiation—to name but a few that come readily to mind). I am aware that in addition to the kinds of questions mentioned above, anthropologists have, especially within recent decades, been interested in asking ques-tions about all sorts of things, e.g., national character, socialization, basic personality struc-ture, values, themes, etc. I am not so much con-cerned here, however, with the special interests of particular anthropologists, as I am in logical distinctions between different theoretical struc-tures and the modes of questioning from which they issue. If an anthropologist wishes to ask psychological questions, then he is obliged to operate within the conceptual and theoretical framework of psychology. But this does not mean that anthropology as a discipline is *about* psychology, it merely signifies that some anthro-pologists are interested in psychological ques-tions. It is the failure to fully appreciate the fact that different kinds of questioning logically necessitate the use of different concepts and theoretical schemes which has sometimes made culture-personality research so vulnerable to criticism. For example, in an excellent survey of recent work in this field, Bert Kaplan [See pp. 318–42. EDS.] has made the point that all-too-frequently anthropologists have inferred person-ality configurations wholly or in large part from cultural data, rather than dealing with person-ality in more autonomous, i.e., psychological, terms. Since they then want to relate personality back to culture, their methodological procedure becomes circular and a great deal of their theo-retical statements tautological.

Some of the questions traditionally posed by cultural anthropologists have also been asked by some of the other cultural sciences such as sociology; some are unique to anthropology. The science of psychology, on the other hand, has focused on problems relating to the intraorgan-ismic psychic processes of individuals, usually in relation to a specific environmental setting. Anthropologists, in contrast, have not been so much concerned with the inner processes of in-dividuals *qua* individuals, as they have in *tradi-tional ways* or *patterns* of behaving. Moreover, in seeking answers to its questions about these traditional patterns of behaving, anthropology has developed a body of concepts (e.g., segmen-tary lineage, virilocal residence, cross-cousin marriage, ramage, redistribution, irrigation state, etc.)—as well as theoretical statements relating these concepts to each other—which appear no-where in the conceptual framework of psy-chology. This, at least in part, is the logical rationale for the methodological assertion that cultural phenomena can be explained in terms of themselves.

To many anthropologists, who view culture as merely an "abstraction" or a "logical construct," the notion that cultural phenomena can be said to explain or cause anything (no less themselves) would seem to be patent nonsense. Thus, Wallace quotes with an approving nod the well-known remark by Radcliffe-Brown that, "To say of culture patterns that they act upon an individual . . . is as absurd as to hold a quadratic equation capable of committing a murder." Woodger has graphically characterized the type of philosophy expressed in the above quote as "finger and thumb" metaphysics—the view that a "thing is real or exists only if it can in principle be picked up between the finger and thumb." But its metaphysics to one side, Radcliffe-Brown's comment is also highly misleading because it tends to confuse the purely formal or logical structure of a science with the empirical implications or relevance of that structure. From a strictly formal point of view, all conceptual entities in science are in some sense "abstractions" or "logical constructs"—since science is a form of sociolinguistic behavior, what else could they conceivably be? But those who espouse a logical-construct view of culture are claiming much more than this: they mean to assert that while culture patterns are constructed (or abstracted) out of a welter of observations, they are not in themselves directly observable— the implication being that this makes them somehow less real and causally significant than, say, persons or sticks and stones.

First, we ought to be reminded that scientific concepts, while they may be suggested by empirical data, are not abstracted from such data by a simple process of induction. They are, rather, the products of an informed and creative imagination, or as it has so often been put "free inventions of the human intellect." What is more, few conceptual entities in science are directly observable, or can be said to be physically real in the sense in which sticks and stones are real. (It is not inappropriate to note here that *names,* in addition to sticks and stones, *can* hurt me). This does not mean, however, that such entities have no empirical referents, although their logical relationship to observational data is rarely a simple and direct one; nor does it mean that such entities may not form part of the logical structure of causal explanations. As was noted earlier in the quote by Goldstein, whether different investigators take a realistic, phenomenalistic, or perhaps no view at all toward the ontological status of conceptual en-

tities, the empirical work of the science is in no way importantly affected since, whatever one's metaphysical position, the *observational* data to be explained are the same. From the standpoint of the development of a science, the explanatory power of conceptual entities is of far greater importance than are questions about their ontological status. Mayo makes this quite clear: "If theoretical concepts are only to be explained by referring to the particular theory in which they have a place, and if the only justification for accepting a particular theory as established is that it enables us to explain known facts and successfully predict new ones, then it follows that we can gain nothing by either attaching or withholding the epithet 'real.'" And Toulmin writes in a similar vein: "Evidently, then, it is a mistake to put questions about the reality or existence of theoretical entities too much in the centre of the picture. In accepting a theory scientists need not, to begin with, answer these questions either way . . ."

Within recent decades the whole problem of the ontological status of theoretical entities has come in for a great deal of discussion in the physical sciences because of certain conceptual difficulties arising out of developments in subatomic physics. But anthropologists do not deal in sub-microscopic phenomena; they are concerned with what, by contrast, are macroscopic events. And as far as the conceptual entities formulated by anthropologists to explain these events are concerned, there are two crucial questions that ought to be asked of them: Do they have empirical referents which can be specified with any degree of precision? And do they have explanatory power, i.e., where would we be in organizing and interpreting our data without them? In this sense at least, culture patterns such as, for example, "castes," "markets," "lineages" are just as real and may be causally significant in scientific explanations as "atoms," "genes," and "gravitational fields"—or for that matter, "drives," "habit strengths" and "cognitive maps."

Thus far in the discussion we have been skirting the problem of reduction in the sciences, and it is time that we faced it more directly. The term "reduction" turns up frequently in social science literature, usually appended to the phrase "the fallacy of," as though reductionism were some sort of illicit logical practice. Actually, the reduction of one science, either wholly or in part, to some other one may, under certain conditions, represent a significant advance of scientific knowledge.

One science is said to be reducible to another science (or one part of a science to another part) when all the terms and concepts of the one science are logically "connected" to those of the other (either by the terms of the one being explicitly defined in terms of the scientific vocabulary of the other, or more commonly through suitable empirical hypotheses) in such a way so as to make it possible for all the theoretical statements of the one science to be derived logically from the theoretical statements of the other. Thus, to reduce one science to another does not somehow decrease the diversity of the natural world or make a certain range of phenomena illusory, as some writers believe; it merely implies that the theoretical structure of one science can, either entirely or in part, be subsumed under or explained by, the theoretical structure of a second.

To cite one of the classic cases of a successful reduction in science, physicists are agreed that the laws of thermodynamics which contain such concepts as heat, temperature, and entropy are reducible to the laws of mechanics which contain no references to these concepts at all. Making this reduction possible are certain empirical hypotheses which logically connect the concepts of the two sciences, e.g., temperature is posited as being proportional to the mean kinetic energy of gas molecules As a result, physicists are enabled to introduce as premises in their explanations hypotheses (kinetic theory of matter) which omit all references to such concepts as heat, temperature, etc., and which substitute in their place only concepts referring to the things that are part of the subject-matter of mechanics, such as the motion of molecules. In consequence, all the statements in thermodynamics can be logically derived—and without these statements losing in the process any of the theoretical content that they have in thermodynamics—from statements in mechanics.

The same formal requirements would hold in the case of reducing the science of culture to psychology. Concepts such as "lineage," "caste," "polygyny," "levirate" would have to be logically connected to such terms as "drive," "sublimation," "ego processes," "aggression" and "conditioned reflex," so as to provide a basis for specifying in *psychological* terms the conditions which give rise to the occurrence of different cultural phenomena. Clearly, we are a long way from any such reduction. Take the concept of "lineage," for example. A lineage, to be sure, is a particular grouping of individuals interacting

in certain ways. But the lineage also has an organizational structure which persists through time irrespective of the particular individuals who may be members of the lineage at any given moment; and it is precisely these organizational features of the lineage in which anthropologists have been most interested. In other words, the kinds of questions we want to ask of lineage organization are not the same questions we wish to ask about psychological make-up of the individuals who may be members of the lineage at any given moment in time. Nor is it possible, and this is really the crux of the argument, to derive logically statements about the organizational features of the lineage from statements about the psychological characteristics of its members. Any attempt to explain lineage organization in terms of the behaving of its individual members would require that we conceive of these individuals not in psychological terms, but in terms of the statuses they occupy and the roles they perform. And since the concepts of status and roles would be meaningless except if interpreted as part of the organizational structure of the lineage, we would, in effect, be assuming a knowledge of the very phenomena we were trying to explain. The point here is that the lineage concept, while its scientific usefulness may be validated by observing individuals interacting in certain social situations, is not simply an abstraction from these observations. Rather, it is "invented" precisely for the purpose of making sense out of that observed behavior. Maurice Mandelbaum, who has similarly argued for the irreducibility of societal concepts, has put it this way: "In order that we may claim to know as inclusive and long-enduring an entity as the Catholic church we must be in a position to single out for consideration the activities of those individuals who, by reason of their status, were important in the history of that institution; but to know what it means to have a particular status in an institution involves us in knowing the institution and is not reducible, without circularity, to how an individual influences the actions of other individuals."

Finally, this part of the discussion would hardly be complete if it were not noted that anthropologists *have* explained lineage organization in cultural terms, e.g., by economic arrangements, inheritance of strategic resources, etc.

The main drift of the argument up to this point has been to show that given the present stage of development of both sciences, the science of culture is not fully and without loss of theoretical meaning reducible to the science of psychology. But what of the future? Has not the general trend in science been toward greater reductionism? And is it not likely therefore that eventually the science of culture will be reduced to psychology (or indeed that psychology will be reduced to physiology and so on)? This is clearly an empirical question which relates to the future state of the sciences being considered, and therefore is not answerable on logical grounds alone. Culturology may at some future date be reduced to psychology, it may not—we can only wait and see. In either case, the outcome will depend upon the direction taken by the empirical development of both disciplines. In this connection, it is important to emphasize that the reducibility or irreducibility of a science is not an inherent characteristic of it; the possibility and scientific significance of reduction is always relative to the given state of development of the sciences concerned. If future theoretical developments should make it possible for the science of culture, or portions of it, to be reduced to psychology—and from the vantage point of this moment in time such developments seem very remote indeed—then psychology will have become a very different science from what it now is.

Turning from the future to the present state of the sciences of culture and psychology, it is difficult to imagine what would be gained scientifically if one were reduced to the other at the current time, assuming that such a reduction was now logically feasible. One can scarcely speak in any meaningful way of reducing culturology to psychology until there is a science of culture to be reduced, and a science of psychology for it to be reduced to. As Nagel has noted, if reduction is to represent a genuine advance of scientific knowledge and not merely an arid formal exercise, the sciences concerned must be at appropriately mature levels of development. It need hardly be pointed out that the sciences being considered here are a long way from achieving such levels of theoretical sophistication. And if we can further judge from the history of science, scientific knowledge has never been significantly advanced by the simple addition of the terms and theories of one science to another. What I am suggesting here is this: that given the present undeveloped state of both the sciences of culture and psychology, the cause of the advancement of the

two disciplines in particular, and scientific knowledge in general, can best be served by each continuing to further develop and refine its own conceptual and theoretical structures.

From everything that has been said it should be apparent that it is not sufficient merely to assert, as Spiro has done, that ". . . personality variables are as important for the maintenance of social systems as for their change. Without the use of personality concepts, attempts fully to explain the operation of these [cultural] systems, either in terms of efficient causes or in terms of functional consequences, are seldom convincing." One must demonstrate how personality variables are to be logically connected to cultural variables through empirical hypotheses so as to yield explanations of how cultural systems undergo change as well as how they operate. This Spiro has not done. As a matter of fact, in the essay from which the above quote was excerpted, it is evident that Spiro is not concerned with explaining why different cultures are the way they are and how they have come to be that way, but with the very different question of how individuals are motivated to assume the social roles necessary to keep the cultural system going. In other words, his entire analysis assumes an on-going cultural system, and then provides an explanation of how it perpetuates itself; it does not explain the cultural system itself (why this set of roles rather than some others?).

This matter of keeping the questions being posed sorted out, as this paper has tried to show, is an important one. Anthropology has often been characterized by a great deal of futile and unproductive controversy because some writers have accused others of not adequately answering questions that they did not ask in the first place. White and Kroeber, for example, have sought to explain cultural innovations by the antecedent cultural matrix out of which they arise (I am not so much concerned with the substantive content of the explanations offered by these writers, as with their methodological approach). The question White and Kroeber are concerned with is why it is that certain innovations are made in certain cultures and not others, and why in certain historic periods and not others. In short, theirs is essentially a question about *rates* or *patterns* of innovation. They are not asking why in a particular culture at a particular time, individual A makes an innovation rather than individual B. This is patently a biographical question which cannot be answered by their methodological approach. Thus, Copeland's recent remarks that White's thesis fails to explain why Ghandi, Churchill, Hitler and Mussolini and not some other persons did what they did, misconstrues White's intention.

Nor will the Kroeber-White approach tell us anything about the psychological processes involved in making an innovation. Barnett in his book on innovation views the innovative process as being essentially a mental one, involving the recombination of two or more "mental configurations." A major limitation of this perspective, as Wallace sees it, is that it fails to ". . . state the conditions under which a particular innovation will occur; i.e., to predict which of several possible recombinations will be made, by whom, and when." Wallace has his own view of the innovative process, based upon what he calls the "principle of maximal organization," which asserts ". . . that an organism acts in such a way as to maximize under existing conditions, and to the extent of its capacity, the amount of organization in the dynamic system represented in its mazeway; that is to say, it works to increase both the complexity and the orderliness of its experience."

Wallace adds that if a particular innovative recombination is to occur, the necessary "prototypical and stimulus configurations" must be present. He then sums up his position by saying that ". . . in itself innovation is an 'instinctive' propensity of the human organism activated under the merest provocation of desire for richer or more orderly experience."

Now, one can conceptualize innovation in any way that one's theoretical interests demand, but if I understand them correctly, I do not see how either Barnett's or Wallace's conceptualization of the innovative process will help us very much in answering questions about varying *rates* of innovation in time and space.

IV

The ontological objection to the superorganic view of culture has been discussed at considerable length because it is clearly the most frequently expressed criticism of that position. The second type of critique can be dealt with more briefly.

As mentioned earlier, one gets the impression from reading many of the strictures directed at the superorganic view of culture that often the objection is not a logical or scientific one but rather a moralistic one; that is, the objection is to the alleged deterministic implications of the position. Opler, for instance, has recently fired a verbal fusilade at those deterministic "culturologists" who would strip anthropology of its "warmth and purpose, its concern with humanity." Why the attempt to explain cultural phenomena in terms of other cultural phenomena should indicate a lack of concern with humanity, or turn men into mechanical robots, is not readily apparent. One would think that, on the contrary, only to the extent man is able to develop a body of reliable knowledge about how cultural systems work, will his efforts to exert some measure of control over his cultural environment meet with any degree of success. I suspect one of the major reasons some writers find the superorganic position so repugnant is they tend to see it as entailing the view that, regardless of what man does, cultural forces will grind away inexorably to their fated end. But this is to misinterpret wholly the character of causal explanation in science and to confuse it with some brand of metaphysical fatalism. Causal explanations do not somehow shape and constrain events in the phenomenal world; they merely enable us to understand and predict them. The laws of gravitation do not cause apples to fall from trees, nor can we object to meteorology for making it rain so often.

This is not the place to undertake a full-scale review of the logic of scientific explanation and its relationship to the issue of determinism versus indeterminism, but a few brief remarks are warranted.

Whether or not a universal determinism can be attributed to the world in the sense that for every event there is a unique set of conditions without whose presence the event would not have occurred, and that given these conditions the event in question will always occur, is a doctrine which cannot be proved or disproved on either *a priori* grounds or by citing empirical evidence. It is an *assumption* that we make about the world which says, in effect, that all events have determinate causes and that we ought to look for them. Such assumption would seem to be a precondition of our very ability to understand and effectively cope with the world in which we live, for the opposite assumption calls up a kind of Kafkaesque world in which events occur with maddening whimsicality, without apparent rhyme or reason. As a heuristic principle, determinism is basic to doing science, since the goal of the scientific enterprise is explanation, and the ideal of scientific explanation is to be able to state the necessary and sufficient conditions for the occurrence of an event. It is of course true that many events cannot now be explained in strictly causal terms (some may never be so explained), and that much of our knowledge about the world is of a statistical or probabilistic nature. But to say this is to say something about the present state of our theoretical knowledge of the world, and not to describe its ontological structure. For to argue from the epistemic fact that our theories do not at the present time permit us to explain causally the occurrence of a specific event to the conclusion that "this event has no cause," is to advance a metaphysical proposition which can never be verified. And it may, of course, with future theoretical developments, be falsified.[3]

The superorganic position, therefore, is neither more nor less deterministic than any other scientific procedure. It merely asserts that from a methodological standpoint, cultural events can be explained in terms of other cultural events, and that the motives, drives and psychological dispositions of individuals are not relevant to answering certain cultural questions. If an investigator comes back with the counter-assertion that such psychological phenomena are relevant, then he must demonstrate logically and empirically in what way they are. But the introduction of individuals and their psychological characteristics as explanatory factors would not make his explanations any the less deterministic than they would be if these phenomena were excluded. The science of psychology, in short, is no less deterministic than the science of culture.

CONCLUSIONS

The development of a naturalistic and autonomous science of culture for which Tylor argued so cogently rests squarely upon the possibility of explaining cultural phenomena in terms of themselves. For if this cannot be done, then there can be no autonomous science of culture, and the study of cultural phenomena becomes a branch of whichever scientific discipline can provide explanations for them. This paper has attempted to demonstrate that there are no *logical* or *scientific* reasons why culture cannot

be explained in terms of culture, and that in answering certain kinds of questions it makes perfectly good methodological sense to do so. This position, as I have tried to show, does not commit us to any metaphysical view of the constitution of the world—although it is true that often proponents of superorganicism have phrased their arguments in terms (e.g., "levels of reality" or "reality *sui generis*") which might lead one to believe that this is the case.[4] It does not, in other words, compel one (as Bidney contends) to conceive of culture as some sort of metaphysically closed system. Obviously, cultural phenomena do in "reality" interact with all kinds of noncultural phenomena. But our attempts to explain cultural phenomena are something else again, and it is here that we strive to achieve logical closure. The ultimate ideal of any science is the formulation of a comprehensive and systematic theoretical structure, i.e., a set of highly interconnected, hierarchically ordered and "logically closed" theoretical propositions. Few sciences have ever even approached this kind of theoretical maturity, and there are good reasons for thinking that a science of culture may never do so. But certainly we ought not to abandon the quest, since much can be learned from just trying.

The main burden of this paper has been a logical one. It has been maintained that there is indeed a set of strictly cultural questions and problems which have never been the concern of the science of psychology, and that these have formed the traditional core of the anthropological enterprise. Moreover, in seeking answers to these problems, anthropology has formulated concepts, theoretical entities, laws (or if one prefers, generalizations) and theories which do not form any part of the theoretical apparatus of psychology and cannot be reduced to it. This is the logical basis for treating culture as an autonomous sphere of phenomena, explainable in terms of itself. It is wholly beside the point to maintain that anthropologists cannot proceed in this way or that they ought not proceed in this way, for the brute fact of the matter is that in their empirical research this is precisely the way they do most often proceed. In this regard, it is a curious fact that when cultural phenomena are explained in terms of themselves in the context of anthropological empirical work, few eyebrows are raised. It is only when anthropologists get philosophical and start to talk about what they are doing that all the trouble begins.

NOTES

1. Throughout this paper I have assumed, as I think most American cultural anthropologists do, that "human society" is a sub-system or part of culture. If one wanted to, therefore, the terms "socio-cultural" or "social" could be substituted for the term "cultural," and I do not think the basic argument of the paper would have to be altered.

2. Wallace has recently written: "The observations of ethologists, the recent discoveries in biological psychiatry, and the increasing attention to physiological process in the new physical anthropology have conspired to make highly questionable the assumption that biological factors in behavior are for all practical purposes constants. Biological determinants of behavior—working *via* disease, nutrition, exposure to sunlight, etc., as well as *via* constitutional factors—are now to be regarded as significant variables for both the group and the individual." I am somewhat puzzled as to what biological determinants of "group" behavior Wallace is referring to here, especially since later in the same essay he says: "With regard to biological determinants of behavior, I do not mean only constitutional, hereditary factors—which can be regarded as constants at least for a major part of a given population (a few deviants excepted). . . ." And while such factors as disease, nutrition and exposure to sunlight certainly do have important biological consequences, the varying importance of these factors in different societies would clearly seem to be a function of cultural determinants and not biological ones. Simply because biological factors are involved in an event it does not follow that the expanation of the event need be biological. Finally, on a somewhat different but related theme, Wallace

has written in another place: "Little evidence is available to suggest any substantial inter-racial differences in cognitive capacity."

3. Recent developments in microphysics, or more precisely philosophic interpretations of these developments, have cast doubt on the heuristic value of the doctrine of determinism. It is proclaimed that causality has been dethroned and indeterminism once again reinstated in Nature. Physicists seem to be sharply divided on this issue. But from the vast literature on the subject one thing is clear, namely, that the dispute is about the theoretical interpretation of the data and not the data themselves. What the dissenters from the orthodox interpretation, such as Einstein, de Broglie, and Schrödinger, seem to object to, are the ontological conclusions which have been drawn from what they regard as conceptual and theoretical difficulties in formulating strictly causal laws at the quantum-mechanical level. Moreover, as a number of writers have pointed out, the theoretical foundations of microphysics are not as acausal as they have often been made out to be. In any case, these developments are not very relevant to the phenomena dealt with by anthropologists, since they are macro-events and physicists agree that the interpretation of macro-events are just as deterministic as they ever were.

4. It is interesting to note that one of the staunchest adherents of the superorganicist position, Leslie A. White, in one of his more recent statements, defines culture as a "class of things and events, dependent upon symboling, considered in an extrasomatic context," which I take to be a methodological assertion and not a definition at all in the sense in which White intends it to be.

3

THE DIFFICULTIES, ACHIEVEMENTS, AND LIMITATIONS OF SOCIAL ANTHROPOLOGY

MAX GLUCKMAN

THE primary work of the Rhodes-Livingstone Institute is sociological research, and that work is about to expand under a grant from the Colonial Development Fund. I consider therefore that in this first issue of our journal addressed to the citizens of British Central Africa,

From *Journal of the Rhodes-Livingstone Institute*, 1 (1944): 22–43. Copyright © 1944 by the Rhodes-Livingstone Institute. Reprinted by permission of the author and the publisher. Max Gluckman is professor of Social Anthropology. Manchester University.

I may well explain what social anthropology is, what are its difficulties, limitations and achievements, and what its researches contribute to an understanding of human problems.

Social anthropology is that branch of sociology which concerns itself with the so-called primitive peoples. This division of the science into branches dealing with civilised and primitive peoples is largely historical, not logical, particularly since the "primitive" African today is part of modern industrial civilisation—he works in its mines and factories and he consumes their products. Therefore I shall speak of "sociology" rather than of "social anthropology," but I shall draw my examples from studies of primitive tribes, as they were and as they are. In doing so, I shall tend to choose examples from work done in this region, as being of more interest to my readers. This is my excuse for an apparent overemphasis on the work of my immediate colleagues and myself.

The status of sociology largely depends on how far it can claim to be scientific in its procedure and the results it obtains. The control which we have obtained over nature and our lives is based in the advances of physicists, chemists, etc., in studying nature scientifically, and a problem of immediate practical importance is how far the social sciences can be developed to enable us to understand and control the social organisation in which we live.

Science is essentially a method of studying nature. The scientist begins by making observations of fact, which are the impressions that nature makes on his senses, and he may assist these with machinery. Each of these impressions is called an event—a sound, a colour, a smell, these are all events. He describes and classifies these events, and with the aid of controlled experiments formulates a law to describe universal uniformities in these events, of the general type: given A, then B is always found; and conversely, given B, then A is always found. For example, the old rhyme

"Red at night is the shepherd's delight,
 Red in the morning is the shepherd's warning,"

states that rain and red morning skies go together, as do red evening skies and good weather. A number of these laws are brought together into a theory which includes them all, and enables the scientist to predict other events and relations between them, which must again be tested by observation and experiment.

In the unending flow of impressions (of events) which enter our senses, some are permanent and persist, like the country that a particular people live in; others are very transient, like spoken words, though words may be given more durable existence by being carved on stone or written on paper. However, permanent or transient, everything that we observe is nature, the field of study of all the sciences.

Now science does not describe the whole of any particular event which occurs in nature. First, it isolates certain aspects of events, and abstracts what we may call type-events for study. We shall see later that these type-events very rarely coincide exactly with anything that actually occurs in nature. The scientist to work, must simplify, and to simplify he must distort. Thus, for the law of gravity the colour and smell of bodies is irrelevant and does not appear in the formulation of the law. Newton is supposed to have formulated the law by comparing an apple's falling with the moon's not falling. Though this story is not true, the law covers these events; but it does not consider the red of the apple and the white of the moon, or the edibleness of the apple and the inedibleness of the moon—even if the old nursery belief is right and the green cheese of the moon is edible. The law of gravity was concerned with bodies in space, and the apple was such a body; but the law did not describe exactly what an apple was.

Second, science classifies these type-events: as the moon not falling and the apple falling are both examples of the movement of bodies in space. Newton was not interested in the exact history of each falling apple, but in all bodies that moved in space. Similarly, the sociologist does not describe the history of the relationship of an African chief with every member of his tribe, but the relation between "the chief" and "the subjects."

Third, as we have seen, science tries to establish uniformities between these type-events, which occur always. E.g. the law that if a body be immersed in a fluid, it will lose weight equal to the weight of fluid it displaces, relates together a body, its immersion in fluid, its weight before and after immersion, and the weight of fluid it displaces. Science does not say this of any particular body or fluid—it says this of all bodies and all fluids brought together in the above way. That is, science does not study any particular event, for in nature each event tends to be unique, and events are often not repeated exactly, except under laboratory conditions or in industrial processes.

I must elaborate this last point, for it leads to the fundamental difficulty which confronts the sociologist. Science does not describe exactly raw nature, any particular events which we observe in nature, and often cannot predict their future course. Scientific laws are said by some to be abstract conceptions of the human mind— fictions, Vaihinger calls them. By this they mean that a scientific law practically never occurs in uncontrolled nature, for a single scientific law never operates alone on natural events. But scientific laws do explain natural events.

The point I want to make appears in the firing of a rifle. Each of the laws of ballistics will not by itself explain the path a fired bullet will take, but all the laws dealing with the velocity of projectiles, of certain charges of powder, through muzzles of a certain kind of rifling, and so on, are needed to give the muzzle velocity of a bullet. The further path of the bullet will be affected by laws describing the effect of the resistance of air on bullets of certain shapes and weights; and the actual course of the bullet will be determined by events affected by laws of other sciences, physics and meteorology, which explain particular conditions of wind, temperature, etc. in the atmosphere in the bullet's path. The history of physical science has an example which makes the point even more clearly: Galileo's formulation of the law of falling bodies, that in a vacuum bodies fall at the same speed, irrespective of their weights and shapes. Galileo is said to have "proved" this before the members of the University of Pisa as they marched by the Leaning Tower; from the top of the tower he dropped lead and a bundle of feathers and these reached the ground at approximately the same time. Approximately only, for their course was affected by resistance of the air. For at that time there was no such thing as a vacuum: both the event "a vacuum" and the more complex relation of two events "falling bodies in a vacuum" were then purely abstract conceptions in Galileo's mind. But he had formulated a scientific law, though it had never yet appeared in nature; it was a tendency, operating with many other tendencies, on all falling bodies in the atmosphere. Its first actual appearance, alone and unaffected by other tendencies, was many years later when the development of laboratory apparatus made it possible to create vacuums artificially. For essentially the laboratory is a place where two or more types of events can be isolated from other factors, to determine their interrelationship. Thus the vacuum eliminates air resistance and wind effects, and the relation between masses and shapes of falling bodies and the rate of speed of their fall can be determined accurately.

I ask the reader to bear with me while I make another introductory point, in order to pave the way for the first main subject of this essay, the difficulties of social anthropology. Implicit in the above examples, is the fact that the way in which nature behaves is affected not only by the many scientific laws of different types at work, but also by the actual history of each event occcurring in nature. Let us refer again to the firing of a rifle bullet. The ballistician may know all the laws affecting the muzzle velocity of the bullet and its passage through the air, and also all the laws affecting the condition of the atmosphere in the bullet's path, but he cannot say more than that the bullet will drop to the ground within a certain area. For he cannot measure all the events that will actually affect the bullet's trajectory: the charge of cordite in a particular bullet may vary slightly in strength or age, the heating of the barrel from shot to shot, as well as wear in its rifling and smoking, may alter the velocity of the bullet. Finally, it is extremely difficult to measure all the atmospheric conditions that may affect the air in the immediate path of the bullet, so as to cause slight winds and currents, under the operation of other scientific laws. Nevertheless, the ballistician can predict the trajectory within close limits, and the marksman, firing with a rifle and bullets designed on the basis of the laws of ballistics, allows for varying conditions to shoot accurately.

II

With this general introduction, I consider how these fundamental concepts, methods, and limitations, of science in general, apply to sociology, the would-be science of society. For many years sociologists, in terms of an older scientific philosophy which held that science is the analysis of substances, searched to define the substance they were studying. They formulated this as society, as the group-mind, as culture, as social institutions, which they broke up in analysis. This involved them in major logical difficulties into which I need not go here—they were accused of personifying society, of importing purposive arguments, and so on. I must say here at once that this does not discredit their work which has been of the highest value, and our recent advances have been made on the basis they laid. Nevertheless, Radcliffe-Brown's definition of the field of sociology, as the relations between events in a social system, eliminates many difficulties. These events are acts of human behaviour, and material events like the sun and land and tools where these are parts of acts of human behaviour. Human beings live in communities and we assume that their actions form a system with an ordered pattern —a fundamental assumption of all sciences— and it is the analysis of this pattern that is sociology. Psychology also studies acts of human behaviour, but, as Radcliffe-Brown puts it, psychology studies these acts in their relations within mental systems: i.e. each act of behaviour is studied in relation to other acts by the same person. Sociology studies the same acts in their relations in the pattern of community behaviour. The same act (event) may be studied by different sciences in different sets of relationships. For example, eating is the subject of physiological, psychological, and sociological, analysis. The physiologist studies eating in relation to blood circulation, digestion, defoecation; the psychologist is interested in its relations to a man's repressed complexes, his sublimations, etc.; while the sociologist analyses its relations with the community's methods of production and distribution, its social groupings and relationships, its taboos and religious values. Thus to understand the simple action of eating in its entirety, it might be necessary to call in the laws of the above three sciences, and also those of biochemistry, chemistry, and yet other sciences. They are all necessary to give us complete understanding of the whole event of eating. Again, if a man accuses his wife of bewitching their child, the psychologist may relate this to the man's ambivalent attitude to his mother, for whom his wife is a surrogate while his child is a surrogate for himself; the sociologist, while interested in that relation as defined by the psychologist, also must interpret the accusation within the total system of witchcraft-divination-magic of the tribe. However, it is clear from this example that psychology and sociology are closely related sciences, and that their principles will have to be subsumed within psychosociology as those of chemistry and biology are in biochemistry.

The reader of a psychological or sociological analysis must therefore remember that it never can claim to explain the whole of a real situation—the events, the acts of behaviour—which it has studied. For these are affected by a large number of psychological and sociological laws, and also by physiological, biological, and ecological laws, and ultimately by chemical and physical laws. Moreover, if the actual events which are studied by the physical sciences (such as the path of the bullet) are affected by a large number of other events which cannot be exactly measured (the conditions in the atmosphere), even more is this true of the acts of human beings which sociology studies. Imagine the long history, both of a community and of an individual, and all the manifold and varied influences which may cause a man to act at a certain moment in this way, and not in that, and you will see how difficult the task of the social sciences is. For example, we know that many of our tribes suffer from malnutrition and disease. Nutritional and medical research would examine the conditions in each tribe's life which are related to the health of its members. The ecologist, agriculturalist, veterinarian, and piscatologist, might study the tribe's use of its environment. The sociologist would study the effects on food production, distribution and consumption, of the form of social groupings including class differences, the economic organisation, type of land tenure, labour incentives, religious and magical beliefs, indigenous physiological concepts, ideas about disease, reaction to modern medicine, sex customs, the effects on the above of modern conditions such as labour migration, etc. He would require the assistance of physiologist and psychologist to study the formation of dietetic habits, etc., in children. It would be necessary to calculate the effect of these health conditions on the reproduction rate of the tribe and this is the task of the demographer. Should he find the population is declining, the cause(s) might lie in any one or more of the factors involved. All might be at work in every tribe, but only some might reach such an intensity as to affect the reproduction rate: the intensities of each might vary from tribe to tribe. "Poor health" is such a complex phenomenon that a large number of scientific correlations of different type, as well as a study of the detailed and varying history of each tribe, would be required to understand it fully, and therefore tackle it.

III

The major difficulty of sociology therefore is that the "falling bodies in a vacuum" which Galileo imagined, is far more difficult to imagine in the study of human behaviour. When better apparatus was made, Galileo's vacuum could in fact be created, and his law shown in the controlled experiment relating different weights of bodies with the rate of their fall. The physicist and the chemist can isolate, under laboratory conditions, any two types of events and test and measure their interdependence. Workers in the biological sciences can do this to a lesser extent. The psychologist and sociologist can hardly do it at all. We cannot control a man's life, cutting him off from all stimuli except one, save when we are testing very simple reactions. The failure to evolve a system of intelligence testing, which eliminates the effects of the conditions of upbringing, is proof of this. It is even more difficult to isolate a community, as in a test-tube or crucible, away from all factors except one, and study the effect of that one factor. On the physical plane, it is as if the ballistician had to measure the laws of projectiles on actual bullets fired, under constantly varying conditions in rifle barrels, cordite charges, bullet shapes and weights, atmospheric conditions. The psychologist and sociologist have to work on the acts of behaviour they observe: and these we have seen are produced by many laws in each of many sciences—ranging from sociology to physics on the scale of life—, and by a long history of preceding events, ranging from rain and drought to disease, to individual temperaments, to social factors such as forms of economic organisation. We are caught in the web of reality. You can experiment with inorganic matter; an experiment with social facts creates groups, relationships, and interests, from which it is difficult to return.

This is one of the chief reasons why exact scientists often say that history and sociology cannot be sciences, that they will remain arts, descriptions of particular events and not of the inevitable and universal relations between types of events. Thus a physicist, Campbell, says: "The view to which I incline is that history cannot be usefully grouped with the characteristic sciences. . . . The main concern of history is not with laws, but with particular events.

The decision concerning economics is more difficult. A civilised community is part of 'nature' and there is no reason for thinking that such a community may not be subject to laws in the scientific sense. But I have very grave doubts whether any economic 'laws' hitherto enunciated are laws in [the scientific] sense." This is the opinion of a sympathetic physicist, who came to this opinion after considering the difficulties which beset the social scientist, and developments in the exact and social sciences since he wrote in 1921 may have led him to change his opinion. Nevertheless, it expresses an attitude I have found among exact scientists.

One point that many of them make against sociology, is that it is qualitative, and not quantitative, and I shall deal with this here, for it arises from the fundamental difficulty described above. We cannot measure emotion, apply the yardstick to *esprit-de-corps*, evalute numerically a father-son relationship. In many fields this is a great weakness in sociology and psychology, inherent in our material, though in others, as I shall show later, it has been overcome. For many facts are now measured by social scientists, and valuable results have been obtained thus. However, many social relations are not yet susceptible of measurement. It does not follow that because an event cannot be measured that it cannot be understood scientifically, as I hope to show. Even before the making of barometers, etc., "red at night is the shepherd's delight" may have stated a universal relationship between the colour of the sky and the weather. Unfortunately, because of this criticism some sociologists have either restricted their work to measurable things, which is stupid since they thus often exclude consideration of major problems and concentrate on minor problems; and even more foolish ones have measured whatever they could, for measuring's sake. Thus one sociologist counted all the yams in all the gardens of the tribe he was studying, and with a stop-watch timed a woman digging, her periods of work and of rest. (Fortunately, the rest of his work was good). The absurdity of this attitude is well shown in the following quotation from an article on the circumcision ceremony of the Cokwe (Jok) tribe in Angola. "The two boys for whom the ceremony was to be performed were brothers about twelve and fourteen years of age respectively. Both were about 5'5" in height. Their weight was about 120 lbs. each. They showed good muscular development and were apparently in good health. Their skins were smooth and glossy and rather deep bronze than black in colour. They were mesocephalic. Their hair was scanty and woolly, eyes black, cheekbones slightly prominent, noses platyrrhine, lips thick and chins short." The investigators might have added size of calves, length of fingers, colour of finger-nails, and so on, for these have as much to do with an analysis of the circumcision ceremony as has the width of the nose. Nowhere do the authors refer again to this meticulous, and very factual, description of the events making up the boys, nor do they relate to anything else. Though this particularly blatant example of mensuration gone mad is not from the work of professional sociologists, it typifies a tendency that is found among them.

IV

To sum up, let us return to the point that science does not study particular events. The physicist quoted above considered that "it is here that science is distinguished from history; history studies particular events but science does not. . . . Science studies certain relations between particular events"—I would prefer to say, between type-events. However, I must stress here that science must be anchored to nature, and that the scientist continually returns to nature to test whether the relations he states to exist between type-events, do in fact occur in nature, and that the theories and hypotheses he creates from these relations do in fact explain nature.

The above comment on history applies equally to sociology, for history is that branch of sociology which studies recorded past social systems. It is true that this criticism is justified by certain so-called historical and sociological studies, which do describe only a succession of events in the life of communities. They do not state relations between social facts which are logically correct, they associate social facts on the grounds that they are actions of the same people. Thus one sociologist, in an admirable book, analyses the organisation of production, etc., but he begins his account by telling us that the farmer puts his clothing, food, and water-gourds under a shady tree, while his small sons, who may accompany him to the fields, play by themselves nearby. He tells how each seed is planted. This adds as little to our understanding of the economic process as the clothes under

the shady tree and the playing boys do to the next season's crop. Their presence might be relevant to a study of education. A scientific relation must be of the type: given A, always B. The above statement describes what happens in a particular series of real events, but it does not establish a scientific relation between the three distinct events. Here is a second example from my own experience. In my *Economy of the Central Barotse Plain* I tried to establish that there was a relation of high interdependence between the mode of production of the people and their social organisation, such that their mode of production explained certain salient facts about their social organisation, and why it has one form and not another. In the course of this argument I mentioned that goods were exchanged in various ways, one of which was by barter. One of my colleagues criticised me because I did not describe the actual bargaining which took place in this barter. But the actual process of barter had nothing to do with the relation I was discussing (interdependence of mode of production and social organisation), and the only reason for asking that it be described, was that it occurred—that is, it had a connection in nature with what I was considering, though it had no logical relation to my analysis. I might as well have been asked to count the barbs on the fish-spears, and the size of mesh of the nets, used by the people in fishing—and there would be no end to any sociological book.

I cite these examples to show that certain sociologists have not yet appreciated that there is this fundamental difficulty in sociology: that we are striving to establish scientific relations. and not to describe precisely what we have observed, or explain the whole of what we have observed. To establish general relations is the only road by which sociology can make advances, and not remain generalised descriptions of particular societies repeated on yet other societies. Our difficulty is to break loose from the web of nature and postulate universal relations, and this requires special methods to get over the fundamental difficulty that we cannot isolate type-events and see if the presence of one implies the presence or absence of the other.

V

We have now considered the difficulties that sociology has to overcome if it is to be a science, like the other sciences. They will continue to emerge in the succeeding analysis. How far then has sociology been able to adapt standardised scientific techniques to its material, and what has it achieved?

Sociology has practically to eschew all experiment, and work on deductions made from descriptions of societies, which it tests over a number of descriptions which record certain significant similarities, variations, and differences. I shall let this method emerge from my examples, and not expand it here.

I begin with one of the doyens of our science, Sir James Frazer. Latterly, parts of his great comparative work on the relations of science, magic and religion, have been criticised, but most of it remains to stimulate further research. Notable is his analysis of the basic principles of magical thought in *The Golden Bough*. "If we analyse the principles of thought on which magic is based, they will probably be found to resolve themselves into two: first, that like produces like, or that an effect resembles its cause and, second, that things which have once been in contact with each other continue to act on each other at a distance after the physical contact has been severed. The former principle may be called the Law of Similarity, the latter the Law of Contact or Contagion. From the first of these, namely the Law of Similarity, the magician infers that he can produce any effect he desires merely by imitating it; from the second he infers that whatever he does to a material object will affect equally the person with whom the object was once in contact, whether it formed part of his body or not." Subsequent researches have on the whole confirmed Frazer's hypothesis. Nearly every magical rite, spell, or medicine, recorded has one or other of these characteristics. I cite only single examples of each. Ila warriors eat of the skilfully hiding quails to become undetectable—that is the law of similarity. Zulu believe that a man can be made ill by having his footprints stabbed with a quill containing certain medicines—this the law of contagion. However, in Africa especially, many magical substances are used which do not seem to have this symbolism, but as far as we know are considered to have an inherent magical power. Nevertheless, Frazer's generalisations are scientific laws, of the type: All events *A* will have characteristics *b* or *c*. These laws of magical thought express a relation between acts of behaviour to achieve a purpose, and associations of ideas.

They are probably true of a large number of magical acts which have not been observed by scientists, in the past, at this moment, and in the future; and if I write a book on Lozi magic, I need merely refer to Frazer's laws to sum up my material. Of course, Frazer goes far beyond this simple statement: he illustrates, elaborates, and analyses the laws in great detail, and they have been developed by his successors.

The psychologist Freud showed that the beliefs of the neurotic in our civilised society are very similar to these fundamental magical beliefs of primitive man; that is, he found that the laws applied in another field. For magical beliefs are not abnormal, they are normal in certain societies. While Frazer and other English students began their study of these beliefs from individual psychology, Lévy-Bruhl asserted that magic could not be thus derived. The believer in magic believes in it because he is born into a community which has magical beliefs. The pattern of magical thought is external to the individual and imposed on him. There is no doubt that this is true, but I do not want to go into its full analysis by Lévy-Bruhl. I cite him here because his emphasis shows that similar relations can be shown in the thought-patterns of certain kinds of societies, external to the individual, and in the thought-patterns of abnormal persons in non-magical societies, as demonstrated by Freud. That is, Freud and Lévy-Bruhl show that Frazer's relation of association of ideas with power to act on other things (which is part of magical power), applies in two entirely different fields, and we have an example of the way in which scientific knowledge expands. The implications of this have not yet been worked out: it is the sort of point that will be treated by psychosociology.

I omit reference to many valuable studies of magic, and come to a work in which they all flowered: Evans-Pritchard's study of *Witchcraft Magic and Oracles among the Azande* of the Sudan. I cannot here analyse it in detail and part of its argument is considered elsewhere in this journal, in my article on *The Logic of African Science and Witchcraft*. In brief, starting like Lévy-Bruhl from the fact that magical (mystical) ideas are social, Evans-Pritchard analyses the whole system of behaviour and beliefs involved in witchcraft, magic, and divination. He describes witchcraft as a philosophy of causation and a philosophy of morals; he shows how it is related to a particular social organisation, so that its relations in other social organisations can be predicted; we learn that every part of the system buttresses every other part, and that it works so that in fact the results it pretends to achieve do in fact occur in reality. Evans-Pritchard's work illuminated not only the study of magic and witchaft among primitive peoples, but also, I was told by an historian, witchcraft in the history of Europe. That is, it established relations between types of events, not specific events: and that is scientific.

But there is another, possibly more important, aspect of his analysis. If we regard magic-witchcraft as a system of beliefs based on invalid premises, i.e. on descriptions of nature which are not scientifically true, Evans-Pritchard's principles can be applied to all similar systems of thought. In taking the example of Nazism, I obviously do not do more than describe one aspect of it; I abstract, to simplify, and therefore distort. I do not even consider Nazism's main origins. Nazi ideology argues that most of Germany's troubles are due to the Jews, who have an inherently evil nature and power (like witches). All Jews are bloated capitalists who sweat the German worker, and at the same time all Jews are bloody-minded communists who threaten the German capitalists. Within this Nazi system of thought, the cause of all misfortune is known in advance: "it is the Jews." Here is the similarity to witchcraft beliefs, for in Africa the cause of all misfortune is known in advance: "it is a witch." I have space here to apply only a couple of the relations formulated by Evans-Pritchard for a witchcraft ideology to the Nazi ideology. For example, he states that all events which appear to contradict the system of belief, in fact strengthen it, for they are explained in terms of the system. Thus even scepticism is formulated in terms of the system. African magicians who themselves use sleight-of-hand to deceive their clients, do not therefore believe that the magic system is false. They believe that there are magicians who do know the magic which makes it unnecessary to deceive, and if they themselves could get that magic they would not have to cheat. We all know the phrase "the decent Jew," even Nazis have used it. The existence of this phrase implies that even if all Jews were decent, this would not affect the social belief that they are all evil, for the existence of each decent Jew, known to each German, does not disprove that all the Jews he does not know are evil. As Evans-Pritchard puts it of witchcraft beliefs, each individual's experi-ence of the system is limited, and only the man with a full knowledge of what is happening throughout the society, can see that its premises are false. In another field I used this principle to explain that since Zulu think all farmers are bad employers, even if most of the farmers are good employers the Zulu belief may persist. The behaviour of a good farmer will not change his own employees' ideas about other farmers, or the opinions about himself held by other farmers' employees, who do not know him. Thus these apparently academic principles have practical value for an understanding of labour problems. Further, he shows that if an effect promised by a magical act does not occur, this is explained by breach of a magical taboo, lack of skill of the magician, or stronger counter-magic; i.e. in explaining the failure, people have to do so in the only system of thought they know, and therefore the system is strengthened. I am afraid that this will apply to the Nazis, and that the defeats they are now suffering will be interpreted by their fanatical members as being due to the Jews, inside Germany and among the United Nations. Defeat will strengthen their hatred of the Jews, not persuade them that the Germans are not herrenvolk destined to conquer the world. Therefore, as defeat comes nearer, the Germans will more and more blame it on and persecute the Jews. Of course, this applies to the dyed-in-the-blood Nazi, but fortunately Nazism is not a closed system of thought. Many Germans grew up before it was established, and both social forces and ideas from outside operate on them: just as economic forces are shaking the Africans' beliefs in witchcraft. I have given another example of how a similar principle acts in Nazism, in my article on *The Logic of African Science and Witchcraft*, where I discuss how the Nazis published a book of anti-Hitler cartoons from the world's newspapers, to "prove" to the Germans that all other countries were dominated by Jews who hated the god, Hitler. Even accusing the Jews of being at once all capitalists and all communists is explained by Evans-Pritchard's interpretation of witchcraft, where he shows that it may be believed that a man died because he was killed by a witch and because he was killed by vengeance magic for being a witch.

Evans-Pritchard in an article related to his book, analysed the difference between magic-witchcraft and ancestral-cult beliefs. One of the main points he makes is that the ancestral-cult operates within the boundaries of a kinship-group, magic can operate across them. This relation is true of all African ancestral-cults; the spirits of the ancestors are believed to have power to affect the lives of their own descendants. Even the chief's ancestors on the whole affect only their own descendants, though exceptionally among the Lozi, for determinable reasons, they can affect commoners' health and economic success. In general, however, the royal spirits influence commoners only by providing or withholding tribal well-being. This relation, postulated by Evans-Pritchard of the Sudan Azande, can be applied to the study of changing Zulu life. When I worked in Zululand, I found that the practices of the ancestral-cult were less and less used, but witchcraft-magic beliefs were burgeoning. In seeking an explanation, I adopted a general principle that all social changes have to be expressed in terms of customs and ideas available to the members of the changing community. Then I permuted the concepts:

(a) *new and old conflicts,* and (b) *new and old customs,* to yield the following arguments.

(1) *If new conflicts can be expressed in terms of old customs these will tend to persist.* Thus, Zulu can explain their ill-luck or success in the struggle to work for Whites by saying that they were bewitched, or had powerful magic, for this relates their fortunes to their competing with people who are not their relatives, in work outside the tribal milieu. But the ancestral-cult, since it operates in the kinship group only, cannot as adequately cover the struggle for wage-work for Whites.

(2) *If old conflicts which persist can be expressed in old customs these will tend to persist.* Conflicts within the kinship groups which are still important in Zululand, have been increasing. These conflicts have always been expressed in witchcraft charges, rather than through the ancestral-cult which is dependent on kinship hierarchies.

I need not refer here to the permutations which cover the adoption of new customs, for these do not affect the present argument. There are also other reasons why the witchcraft-magic system persists, but here I am only concerned with those that arise from the relations formulated of kinship groupings on the one hand with magic-witchcraft, and on the other hand with the ancestral-cult. It is immediately obvious that the former, and not the latter, can be extended to the whole range of relationships with non-kinsmen which mark the new White-Black society of Africa. Thus Evans-Pritchard's "laws"

can be applied to interpret new relations in new situations; and in turn these new relations cover other sets of facts. E.g. the conflict between separatist and White-church sects can be expressed in witchcraft-magic-divination beliefs, not in ancestral-cult beliefs, for the dissident sects consist of non-related people and therefore their priests can use the former, but not the latter, set of beliefs. Thus from establishing one or two relations, we begin to establish whole sets of relations which cover new ranges of events, and this is the procedure of science.

Now I can revert to some of our major difficulties. First, the principles I have enunciated above operate on magic and on ancestral-cult beliefs, but at the same time there are many other events and social laws acting on these. That is to say, if my analysis is correct, we have got two reasons ("laws") tending to maintain the magic-witchcraft system as against the ancestral-cult system. But this does not mean that in fact the former will survive. For many other forces, notably our economic motives, are attacking it at the root. Because it is impossible to isolate magic together with work for Whites in one test tube, and the ancestral-cult with work for Whites in another, we cannot prove experimentally that the above postulated interactions are valid. The constellations of events are complicated and the explanations given must take the form: these factors tend to maintain magic, but not the ancestral-cult; those factors tend to cause magic to die out. The general probability of its surviving is so-and-so.

What then is the proof of the above formulations, if there is no experimental proof? Obviously they are explanations after the event, deduced from generalised description. However, the relations described by Evans-Pritchard are observable relations, and assuming for the moment that my principles relating conflicts and customs are true, the deductions from them and from his relations are logical. The test of my conflict-customs principles must then be how far they cover other ranges of fact. Let us apply them to another descriptive generalisation. Take the following analysis of political principles: in strongly organised African states "the regional devolution of powers and privileges, necessary on account of difficulties of communication and transport and of other cultural deficiencies, imposes severe restrictions on a king's authority. The balance between central authority and regional autonomy is a very important element of the political structure. If a king abuses his power, subordinate chiefs are likely to secede or to lead a revolt against him." That is, subordinate political authorities, who are often heads of local groups, as well as being bureaucrats under the central authority, are also checks on it. This relation is established by a large number of independent studies. What happens to it under modern conditions, if we apply to it the two principles I formulated above?

(1) *If new conflicts can be expressed in terms of old customs these will tend to persist.* The modern political balance in Africa is dominated by the antithesis of European administrator and chief, and the checks of subordinates under the old system operate on the chief to prevent his becoming too far a bureaucrat of the modern government. Thus the local councillors get a new basis for their authority.

(2) *If old conflicts which persist can be expressed in old customs these will tend to persist.* The conflicts between the central authority and the local units under it persist into modern political organisation; therefore the relationships between the chief and his subordinates also persist. Thus these principles get logical support from their application to other facts.

VI

Many primitive peoples have what is known as the classificatory system of kinship nomenclature. In this, whole groups of related people are called by one term—so that a man has many mothers, fathers, brothers, sisters, etc. with whom his physical kinship connections are often very distant in time. Sociologists have postulated various hypotheses to explain this system of nomenclature. One is that it is a survival from a time when all societies had group marriage, so that a man did not know his father, and any woman was potentially his mother before he was born, and all their children were in fact his brothers and sisters. Morgan, Engels, and later Rivers, were all exponents of this theory.

Logically the hypothesis does explain the system, but it has certain weaknesses. (a) It requires a series of subsidiary hypotheses, first, to explain why the terms of relationship survived even after group marriage became obsolete, and second, to explain how it came to vary over a number of tribes where the details of the nomenclature vary. (b) It is a theory of historical origin, and does not explain relations that can

be observed, so that once we have deduced from a particular system of nomenclature a type of marriage we cannot observe, we are at the end of our study. (c) It is an hypothesis which cannot be tested on the facts, since it relates the system to types of marriage which have passed away and can no longer be observed. But here there are sound points in it, which are subsumed in the hypothesis of Radcliffe-Brown given below, where I shall refer to it again.

A second hypothesis, that of Malinowski, in one part amounted to saying that the system provided social insurance, by providing everyone with a number of substitute kinsmen. Malinowski also emphasised that the individual fathers and mothers etc. of children were clearly distinguished from what we call the classificatory ones. This hypothesis too is subsumed in Radcliffe-Brown's hypothesis. Malinowski's hypothesis suffers from being teleological, i.e. explaining the existence of the extended kinship relationships by the purpose they serve.

Radcliffe-Brown's hypothesis may be summed up briefly as: siblings (i.e. brothers and sisters) tend to be socially identical. This does not mean that they do not differ in individual temperament, and the hypothesis allows for differences of sex and age, but it states that siblings tend to be in identical relationships to other people. Then: all siblings of the same mother and father call each other brother and sister (as among us), but in addition all children of all these siblings call the males among them "father," and similarly the children of the women call them all "mother." The system then extends on this principle. In its simplest form, all members of the higher generation are father and mother, of one higher are grandparent, and below are child and grandchild (found in Hawaii). But the same principles can be used to explain more complicated systems. For example, many South African Bantu call the mother's brother "my male mother," and the father's sister "my female father": these can be explained by Radcliffe-Brown's principle of the equivalence of siblings, but not by the group marriage theory, since whom did your female father marry in her role as a male, and how did your male mother bear in his role as a woman? Under Radcliffe-Brown's hypothesis, the combination is simply explained. A woman is socially identical with her brother: therefore you call your paternal aunt "father" for she is assimilated to your father; and the designation "female" allows for her sex. Similarly, your mother's brother is "male mother," though he is sometimes called "mother." A District Commissioner asked by the Army to find out if it was true that an African soldier had overstayed his leave to attend the funeral of his "mother," as he said, found in fact that it was the mother's brother who had died. He therefore replied: "Ask him if his mother was a man or a woman. If he says his mother was a man he is telling the truth; if he says a woman, he is lying."

I cannot go into all the ramifications of the system which can thus be interpreted, but note a few points. First, obviously the hypothesis embraces Malinowski's hypothesis of the "substitution" of one person for another for social insurance. Second, the group marriage hypothesis is used to explain such facts as that a Lozi man may call his sister's daughter "my wife," jokingly, while she is small. It is deduced that in the past they could marry and that the nomenclature survived when the marriage became obsolete. Radcliffe-Brown has explained this kind of fact equally well in terms of his own principle of equivalence of siblings, together with a general analysis of what he calls "joking and avoidance relationships." Finally, his theory embraces that part of the group marriage hypothesis which explains how, when a person marries, whole sets of his or her spouse's relatives become siblings-in-law and parents-in-law. It also explains the levirate and sororate (under which a widow or widower marries a sibling of the deceased spouse) as well as group marriage does, and also does justice to the fact that future children of this second marriage still rank as children of the deceased spouse.

The hypothesis is further validated since it can be applied to other types of kinship system, such as our own, where we class many people as uncles and aunts, and in addition it explains more by interpreting other ranges of fact. Thus Schapera has used it to explain the reaction to twins: for here the principle is carried to its extreme form. Two siblings are identical in age, and perhaps in sex, and since these distinguishing characteristics are absent, two people, absolutely identical socially, have to be fitted into the system. Sometimes, they are eliminated; in other societies they are inducted into the system with special ritual.

Concluding this evaluation, we may note that this hypothesis not only explains most facts, but it is also the simplest and it is invariably found in science that the simplest hypotheses are the best. In addition, as it refers to relations between present events, it is susceptible of observational study.

I take one last example on this point. "It should be remembered that in these [African] states there is only one theory of government. In the event of rebellion, the aim, and the result, only is to change the personnel of office and never to abolish it or to substitute for it some other form of government. When subordinate chiefs, who are often kinsmen of the king, rebel against him they do so in defence of the values violated by his malpractices. They have an interest greater than any other section of the people in maintaining the kingship. The ideal constitutional pattern remains the valid norm, in spite of breaches of its rules." This principle, true for all African states, can be observed in Oriental and European history. Let us look at some of its implications. In setting out some of these, I know that I am jumping some logical steps, and including fresh data, but I merely want to show how a coherent set of relations between political acts of behaviour, in *rebellions,* to change officers as contrasted with *revolutions* to change the political system, can be reached. However, we must first note that these relations seem to be true only of societies with non-expanding techno-economies. In this type of society, where it is based on kingship, then:

(1) There can be rebellions to change the personnel of rulers, not revolutions to alter the political system.

(2) Therefore the rulers fear rivals in their own class, not revolutionaries from other classes.

(3) Since the king is considered bad for not observing the values of kingship, the rebellion is waged in defence of the kingship—i.e. people have an interest in the values of kingship and fight in defence of it.

(4) Since the rebellion is to put someone, who it is hoped will observe these values, in the king's place with the same powers, a rebellion in fact (paradoxically) supports the kingship.

(5) Where the leader of the rebellion is a member of the royal family, the rebellion confirms his family's title to the kingship though it attacks his kinsman king.

(6) Every rebellion therefore is a fight in defence of royalty and kingship: the hostility of commoners against aristocrats is thus subli-

mated to maintain the power of the aristocrats, some of whom lead the commoners' rebellions.

We have here a set of relations between social events, which is logically consistent. The full implications of the relations are not analysed, nor are the complicated constituent events. Nevertheless, I think I can claim that in establishing these principles sociology has established its claim to be a science. For these relations are true of all societies of the defined type. Moreover, they can be applied to societies of a different type, those with expanding techno-economies; and it will be found that even in these, in which social change occurs by what I have defined as revolutions as against rebellions, the rebellion-tendency, with all its implications, is present. That is, the hypothesis can be tested on a new range of facts.

I make four more points.

(a) These principles are logically consistent with one another, given a set of premises on the facts. This is a characteristic of every body of scientific knowledge.

(b) They can be corrected with other sets of principles. Thus if we refer back to the principle of local autonomy vs. central authority, which is an observable fact I used in an example above, this can be fitted in with the principles we are considering here to give a greater body of logically consistent relations. This too is an important method of scientific advance.

(c) Logical deductions can be made from these relations to give others, another method of scientific advance. For example, we can deduce that if all members of the royal family tend to want to become king, then they intrigue against their ruling kinsman without threatening the kingship they wish to achieve.

(d) Finally, logical deductions from these relations can be tested against observable facts. Thus: it is a fact that though the Zulu welcomed the assassination of the tyrannous Shaka, yet nevertheless they appeal to his spirit to assist them and believe it to be a source of strength for them. This is related to the fact that the movement against him disposed of him personally, but did not affect his kingly office; therefore, in the national ancestral-cult, he figures benevolently though he was killed with his people's approval.

Here are two other examples briefly given. Most primitive societies have only primary goods: simple food, houses, furnishings, etc. with few luxuries. The chief cannot build himself a palace out of a grass hut or consume all the meat and milk from his herds. There is a limit to every individual's consumption of these goods. Therefore in these societies the range in standards of living, from chiefs to the poor, is very small. It follows logically that a man who has many goods, since he cannot exchange them for luxuries, or invest them to make profits, must either destroy them, let them rot, or give them away to others. Various primitive societies have all these solutions: their effect is the same. Where plenty is distributed to others, these are strongly attached to the giver; where plenty is destroyed or exposed, groups compete in rivalry against each other in this waste, so again the same basic principle appears in establishing social relationships. This fundamental economic situation can be correlated with the set of relations described for "rebellions" above. Moreover, its basic principle produces different correlated institutions in societies which have luxuries. An economist has argued from it that since no man can consume more than a certain amount of primary goods, the solution for the over-investment in industries to produce other industries, which characterised the pre-war world, is to make more and more factories to produce luxuries. I cite this as an example of logical deduction, not necessarily of sound politics, for other deductions can be made. Thus Marx argued from the basic principle that the rich man, unable to use his wealth, must invest more and more in heavy industry, which thus outpaces industry producing consumers' goods; but he suggested very different solutions from the one above.

The same principle is probably basic to the explanation which sociologists have given of bride-wealth (the giving of cattle for brides), which they have correlated with extended kingship systems, circulation of women and wealth, legitimacy, and so on.

VIII

I have given a few from many examples of how sociology has formulated relations between specific types of events which are scientific relations, and not pure descriptions of particular events. I now pass to aspects of sociological work which deal with problems of greater scale, and which, though not giving full understanding, contribute precise knowledge.

The sociologist can give a meticulous and

accurate description of facts in a given social field, so as to indicate the actual events in that field, even if he cannot show the necessary relations between them. He can indicate generally a connection between two or more very complicated constellations of events. Important examples, near to us, are Schapera's study of *Native Land Tenure in the Bechuanaland Protectorate* and Richards' of *Land Labour and Diet in Northern Rhodesia* (among the Bemba). Both these books, covering every aspect of their work, show the interacting effect of many different elements by which the people "make their living." Incidentally, they state many relations of the type formulated above. One important part of the descriptions, is that they do enable us to generalise broadly about fields not yet studied. Thus from Schapera's work and others, we can predict that in every Bantu society the so-called communal ownership of land will be found to consist in "clusters" of rights, of different types and priority, of various people to any piece of land, or rights to graze or fish in particular places. Similarly, on the basis of what has been observed of migrant labour throughout Africa, in England in the industrial revolution, in Tsarist Russia, in Mexico, we can say: wherever one finds migrant labour, one will find certain other concomitant conditions. This is a scientific statement. It is made with one proviso: "other things being equal," and this brings me back to the point which I stress again and again as our major difficulty.

The complicated constellations of events which we study are produced by a large number of laws studied by several sciences and by an immensely complicated history of actual events of many types. Therefore, in making the comparisons suggested above, and in predicting what will happen in any social field, the sociologist necessarily has to say "other things being equal." But it is sometimes forgotten by critics of the claim of sociology to be a science that in fact the predictions of all sciences contain, by implication, this phrase. Astronomers are able to predict the movements of the heavenly bodies almost exactly, for they know the major laws, and can measure exactly the events, which affect these movements. The meteorologist predicts less accurately, largely at present because the world lacks sufficient meteorological stations, particularly at the Poles. But even the physicist predicts in the formula "other things being equal," save under laboratory and industrial conditions where he knows all the events and

the laws operating in a given set of circumstances. This, we have seen, is a condition which the sociologist cannot establish. I may say that the effects of the migration of men from our Eastern Province, which has not been systematically studied, will probably be similar to the effects of the labour flow from Bechuanaland, Zululand, Barotseland, etc., but there might be factors in the Eastern Province which would alter the situation. More than that, even if one studied the Eastern Province, and on the basis of that and comparative studies, said that so-and-so will happen, other factors might come in to upset the prediction; as the popularising of a Native craft, which for instance has enriched the Pueblos of New Mexico. Nevertheless—and this is the important point—the statement that certain social events are related to the institution of migrant labour from and back to rural areas would remain a definite scientific relation. That is, it is always true that migrant labour is characterised by inefficiency in both industries and country; and even if there were a special campaign of education to increase skills in both areas which did in fact increase them, the inefficiency would remain in the sense that the same education campaign on stabilised workers in town and country would have produced even more skill.

Sociologists and psychologists are themselves often to blame for not properly appreciating the implications of this point. For example, Freud's theory of the unconscious mind has advanced psychological science enormously. It has been generally, and usually unintelligently, criticised because it relates most of human behaviour to the sexual and death instincts. And there is this much in the criticism, at least— that I do not think that all Freud's followers realised fully that in relating human behaviour to the sexual instinct he was not excluding other factors, and they have defended his emphasis on sex as factually, instead of logically, correct. Nevertheless, obviously in the actual human organism sex, like every impulse, must interpenetrate every reaction. When a physicist says, under the law of gravity, that bodies at sea-level in a vacuum fall to earth at the speed of 32.8 feet per second, he knows that air resistance, presence of mountains, types of rocks below, all in fact affect falling bodies in nature so that they do not fall at that speed. But he excludes these factors in formulating this law. He would not attempt to justify his law by saying that it explains all the facts about actually falling bodies in nature. Similarly, when human behaviour is obviously affected by a variety of external stimuli, and probably by a variety of internal impulses, it is absurd for a psycho-analyst to attempt in a few formulae to cover them all. But he is justified in asserting that one factor among the many involved is related to such-and-such other factors in such-and-such ways. To take a simple example: a child refuses to eat, and the parents wish to know why. A dietician must establish that the food offered is good, and a physiologist that there is nothing wrong with the child's stomach, before the psycho-analyst comes in to relate the child's refusal to eat to its mental complexes. Events in the field of each of these sciences, and laws of each of these sciences, affect the actual events studied, and none can claim in advance to give a complete interpretation by itself.

I take another example from my own work. After working in the Barotse Plain on the Upper Zambezi, I wrote a paper to establish certain relations between the Lozi tribe's use of its environment in its productive system and the forms of its social organisation. I have been criticised for neglecting other factors, and the criticism is perhaps justified from people who do not appreciate the methods of science, in so far as I failed openly to state that I was not arguing that the whole social organisation was produced by the relation of the people to their environment, and that I admitted that many other factors, which I was excluding for the time being, also operated. Thus, obviously, when I ascribe the form of the Lozi family and kinship system to their mode of production, I do not wish to imply that the family is not also related to sex, rearing of children, etc. What I wished to establish was a certain relation between two sets of events, themselves intra-related in complicated patterns, and I was justified in excluding all events and relations which were irrelevant to the relation I was studying. The same is true of a similar work by Evans-Pritchard, which inspired mine, on the Nuer of the Sudan. I did not myself appreciate as fully as I might have, that the analysis of these relations as they operated in the past was also an analysis of the relations of the modern system. For the relations I formulated still operate, though other things are no longer equal. The induction of Loziland into the modern world system complicates the actual events in Loziland, but nevertheless the indigenous mode of production is still related to the present social organisation,

though migrant labour, money, purchase of luxuries, and so on, have altered the real events in which these relations appear. However, I did suggest this at the beginning when I said that the procedure of analysing the past economy "at any rate enables us to understand these principles as they operate in the modern system."

IX

Here is an example from a work in which the sociologist appreciated that his explanation was incomplete, which also leads to one method of measurement in sociology. Durkheim made a study of suicide in which he began from the statistical fact that in all civilised communities, and most primitive tribes, there were suicides. That is, suicide in society is related to social forces which push a number of individuals to kill themselves. He defined three types of suicide and showed how they vary in number with social conditions. I do not propose to present his analysis here, but emphasise that he was not concerned with the mentality of the various people who killed themselves or did not kill themselves, i.e. with the psychological motives which are to be studied by psychology, but with the external pressure of social forces on a determinable number of people to commit suicide. To understand why a particular man killed himself, one would have to know sociological and psychological laws, and also the history of the society and of that individual. Here is a fruitful measurement of social facts: it states that a certain number of people of a certain type, but which specific people cannot be predicted in advance, will kill themselves under certain social conditions. This is a calculation of a statistical probability, found in the exact sciences. E.g. "Out of a large number of radium atoms, one in every two thousand ejects an α particle in the course of a year. The atoms are alike both in intrinsic properties and in external environment, and there is presumably no reason why one should die rather than another." Again, a physicist may state that a certain number of electrons revolving about an atom's neutron will jump out of their orbits, but he cannot say which particular electrons will do so.

I recently applied a similar computation to data on the entry of Lozi into political life, in three chief's councils. These councils consist of permanent titles to most of which people succeed by election. I found that successions to kinsmen in a particular title constituted 24%, 25%, and 26%, of the cases I had recorded in each council, and there was similar consistence over a number of other categories which I formulated. I could not say that such-and-such a person is likely or unlikely to become a member of a council, but I calculated the chances that various types of people would have to succeed to titles. Thus it is probable that the succession to over 25% of the present title-holders will be from close relatives (since the tendency is increasing), though it is more difficult to say to which particular titles this would happen. The same applies to the other categories I investigated: a chief's attendant has a chance to succeed to about 9% of the titles. These principles have practical importance: most of the sons of the higher councillors are better educated than the mass of the people, so it is likely that the councils will increasingly consist of educated men.

X

We have examined the difficulties which confront the sociologist, described the limitations of his work, and considered some of his achievements. What, then, does he contribute to our understanding and control of our present problems? This is a whole subject in itself, so I can only refer to it briefly, and I assume that it is agreed that knowledge, as accurate as possible, is necessary for proper planning. Clearly a sociological analysis describes only one of the many sets of relations which actually determine that human beings shall behave thus, and not otherwise. For a full understanding of a specific human problem it is necessary that sociological analysis should be supplemented by psychological, physiological, ecological, etc., analyses. On the other hand, sociology has demonstrated that it can establish scientific relations between acts of human behaviour correlated in a social system, which are different from the relations established by other sciences. Therefore ecological, physiological, psychological, etc., analyses must be supplemented by a sociological analysis, if we are to understand fully the situation with which we are dealing, and the probable results of any projected line of action. I comment on this general statement briefly.

The sociologist can describe accurately and comprehensively a certain range of social facts, and the practical value of this is that it enables people acting in that field to do so with a full knowledge of the facts and some idea of the broad connections between them. The sociologist can make large scale predictions for a given field, within certain limits and possibilties, as to future developments and the probable effect of certain policies. On the basis of these studies, predictions can also be made about other areas of social activity where the same general situation occurs. The sociologist, by comparative analysis, may know more about an area he has not visited than do the people who work there. What is ultimately most important, is that sociologists are increasingly formulating relations which are not true of any particular events, but of certain types of events. That is, sociology is becoming a science. The development of this set of relations, by further observation and by the ordinary processes of scientific logic, is beginning. As more and more relations are formulated, they can be applied in advance to social fields in which most of the facts are known. A fuller elaboration of this subject must await a second essay on applied sociology.

NOTES

1. Professor A. R. Radcliffe-Brown of Oxford has clarified my ideas on this subject in stimulating lectures and discussions, and as he has not recently published on this theme I gratefully acknowledge my debt to him. Drs. E. E. Evans-Pritchard and M. Fortes have in a long friendship contributed directly to my formulation, as did Mrs. A. W. Hoernlé, my first teacher in social anthropology. I thank Dr. J. M. Winterbottom for most pertinent criticisms of the first draft of this essay.

4

SOCIAL ANTHROPOLOGY:
PAST AND PRESENT

E. E. EVANS-PRITCHARD

Mr. Rector, Fellows and Scholars, I have been greatly honoured by your invitation to deliver this lecture in commemoration of Rector Marett, a great teacher of social anthropology and my friend and counsellor for over twenty years. I am touched also, Mr. Rector, at delivering it in this familiar hall.

I have chosen to discuss a few very broad questions—questions of method. The considerable advances made in social anthropology during the last thirty years and the creation of new departments in several universities would seem to require some reflection on what the subject is, and which direction it is taking, or ought to take, for anthropology has now ceased to be an amateur pursuit and has become a profession. There is a division of opinion on these matters among anthropologists themselves, broadly between those who regard the subject as a natural science and those who, like myself, regard it as one of the humanities, and this division, which reflects quite different sentiments and values, is apparent whenever there arises a discussion about the methods and aims of the discipline. It is perhaps at its sharpest when the relations between anthrolopoly and history are being discussed, and since consideration of this difficult question brings out the issues most clearly, I shall devote a large part of my lecture to it. To perceive how these issues have come about it is necessary to cast our eyes back over the period of the genesis and early development of the subject.

EIGHTEENTH-CENTURY ORIGINS

A subject of scholarship can hardly be said to have autonomy before it is taught in the uni-

From E. E. Evans-Pritchard, *Essays in Social Anthropology* (New York: The Free Press, 1962). © 1962 by E. E. Evans-Pritchard. Reprinted with permission of The Macmillan Co. E. E. Evans-Pritchard is Professor of Social Anthropology, Oxford University. This essay was originally presented as the Marett Lecture in 1950.

verstities. In that sense social anthropology is a very new subject. In another sense it may be said to have begun with the earliest speculations of mankind, for everywhere and at all times men have propounded theories about the nature of human society. In this sense there is no definite point at which social anthropology can be said to have begun. Nevertheless, there is a point beyond which it is hardly profitable to trace back its development. This nascent period of our subject was the middle and late eighteenth century. It is a child of the Enlightenment and bears throughout its history and today many of the characteristic features of its ancestry.

In France its lineage runs from Montesquieu and such writers as D'Alembert, Condorcet, Turgot, and in general the Encyclopaedists, to Saint Simon, who was the first to propose clearly a science of society, and to his one-time disciple Comte, who named the science sociology. This stream of French philosophical rationalism was later, through the writings of Durkheim and his students and Lévy-Bruhl, who were in the direct line of Saint-Simonian tradition, to colour English anthropology strongly.

Our forebears were the Scottish moral philosophers, whose writings were typical of the eighteenth century: David Hume, Adam Smith, Thomas Reid, Frances Hutcheson, Dugald Stewart, Adam Ferguson, Lord Kames and Lord Monboddo. These writers took their inspiration from Bacon, Newton and Locke, though they were also much influenced by Descartes. They insisted that the study of societies, which they regarded as natural systems or organisms, must be empirical, and that by the use of the inductive method it would be possible to explain them in terms of general principles or laws in the same way as physical phenomena had been explained by the physicists. It must also be normative. Natural law is derived from a study of human nature, which is in all societies and at all times the same. These writers also believed in limitless progress and in laws of progress. Man, being everywhere alike, must advance along certain lines through set stages of development, and these stages can be hypothetically reconstructed by what Dugald Stewart called conjectural history, and what later became known as the comparative method. Here we have all the ingredients of anthropological theory in the nineteenth century and even at the present day.

The writers I have mentioned, both in France and England, were of course in the sense of their time philosophers and so regarded themselves. In spite of all their talk about empiricism they relied more on introspection and *a priori* reasoning than an observation of actual societies. For the most part they used facts to illustrate or corroborate theories reached by speculation. It was not till the middle of the nineteenth century that systematic studies of social institutions were conducted with some attempt at scientific rigour. In the decade between 1861 and 1871 there appeared books which we regard as our early classics: Maine's *Ancient Law* (1861), Bachofen's *Das Mutterrecht* (1861), Fustel de Coulanges' *La Cité antique* (1864), McLennan's *Primitive Marriage* (1865), Tylor's *Researches into the Early History of Mankind* (1865), and Morgan's *The Systems of Consanguinity* (1871). Not all these books were concerned primarily with primitive societies, though those that were least concerned with them, like *Ancient Law,* were dealing with comparable institutions at early periods in the development of historical societies. It was McLennan and Tylor in this country, and Morgan in America, who first treated primitive societies as a subject which might in itself engage the attention of serious scholars.

NINETEENTH-CENTURY ANTHROPOLOGY

The authors of this decade, like those of the generation before them, were anxious to rid the study of social institutions of mere speculation. They, also, thought that they could do this by being strictly empirical and by rigorous use of the comparative historical method. Using this method they, and those who followed them, wrote many large volumes purporting to show the origin and development of social institutions: the development of monogamous marriage from promiscuity, of property from communism, of contract from status, of industry from nomadism, of positive science from theology, of mono-

theism from animism. Sometimes, especially when treating religion, explanations were sought in terms of psychological origins as well as in terms of historical origins.

These Victorian anthropologists were men of outstanding ability, wide learning and obvious integrity. If they overemphasized resemblances in custom and belief and paid insufficient attention to diversities, they were investigating a real and not an imaginary problem when they attempted to account for remarkable similarities in societies widely separated in space and time; and much of permanent value has come out of their researches. Nevertheless, it is difficult to read their theoretical constructions today without irritation, and at times we feel embarrassed at what seems complacency. We see now that though their use of the comparative method allowed them to separate the general from the particular, and so to classify social phenomena, the explanations of these phenomena which they put forward amounted to little more than hypothetical scales of progress, at one end of which were placed forms of institutions or beliefs as they were in nineteenth-century Europe and America, while at the other end were placed their antitheses. An order of stages was then worked out to show what logically might have been the history of development from one end of the scale to the other. All that remained to be done was to hunt through ethnological literature for examples to illustrate each of these stages. It is evident that such reconstructions not only imply moral judgments but must always be conjectural; and that in any case an institution is not to be understood, far less explained, in terms of its origins, whether these are conceived of as beginnings, causes or merely, in a logical sense, its simplest forms. For all their insistence on empiricism in the study of social institutions the nineteenth-century anthropologists were hardly less dialectical, speculative and dogmatic than the moral philosophers of the preceding century, though they at least felt that they had to support their constructions with a wealth of factual evidence, a need scarcely felt by the moral philosophers, so that a very great amount of original literary research was undertaken and vast repositories of ethnological detail were stocked and systematically arranged, as, to mention the largest of these storehouses, in *The Golden Bough.*

It is not surprising that the anthropologists of the last century wrote what they regarded as history, for all contemporaneous learning was radically historical, and at a time when history in England was still a literary art. The genetic approach, which had borne impressive fruits in philology, was, as Lord Acton has emphasized, apparent in law, economics, science, theology and philosophy. There was everywhere a passionate endeavour to discover the origins of everything—the origin of species, the origin of religion, the origin of law and so on—an endeavour always to explain the nearer by the farther which, in reference to history proper, Marc Bloch calls '*la hantise des origines.*'

In any case, I do not think that the real cause of confusion was, as is generally supposed, that the nineteenth-century anthropologists believed in progress and sought a method by which they might reconstruct how it had come about, for they were well aware that their schemata were hypotheses which could not be finally or fully verified. The cause of confusion in most of their writings is rather to be looked for in the assumption they had inherited from the Enlightenment that societies are natural systems or organisms which have a necessary course of development that can be reduced to general principles or laws. Logical consistencies were in consequence presented as real and necessary connexions and typological classifications as both historical and inevitable courses of development. It will readily be seen how a combination of the notion of scientific law and that of progress leads in anthropology, as in the philosophy of history, to procrustean stages, the presumed inevitability of which gives them a normative character.

THE TWENTIETH CENTURY

The reaction against the attempt to explain social institutions in terms of parallel, seen ideally as unilinear, development came at the end of the century; and though this so-called evolutionary anthropology was recast and represented in the writings of Westermarck and Hobhouse it had finally lost its appeal. It had in any case ceased to stimulate research, because once the stages of human development had been marked out further investigation on these lines offered nothing more exciting than attachment of labels written by dead hands. Some anthropologists, and in varying degrees, now turned for inspiration to psychology, which at the time seemed to provide satisfactory solutions of many of their problems without re-

course to hypothetical history. This has proved to be, then and since, an attempt to build a house on shifting sands. If I say no more in this lecture about the relation between psychology and anthropology it is not because I do not consider it important, but because it would require more time than I can spare, and also more knowledge of psychology than I possess, to treat adequately.

Apart from the criticism of evolutionary theory implied in the ignoring of it by those, including Rector Marett, who sought psychological explanations of customs and beliefs, it was attacked from two directions, the diffusionist and the functionalist. Diffusionist criticism was based on the very obvious fact that culture is often borrowed and does not emerge by spontaneous growth due to certain common social potentialities and common human nature. To suppose otherwise and to discuss social change without reference to events is to lapse into Cartesian scholasticism. This approach had, unfortunately, little lasting influence in England, partly, no doubt, on account of its uncritical use by Elliot Smith, Perry and Rivers. The other form of attack, the functionalist, has been far more influential, as it has been far more radical. It condemned equally evolutionary anthropology and diffusionist anthropology, not merely on the grounds that their historical reconstructions were unverifiable, but also, and simply, because both were historical approaches, for in the view of writers of this persuasion the history of a society is irrelevant to a study of it as a natural system.

The same kind of development was taking place at the same time in other fields of learning. There were functional biology, functional psychology, functional law, functional economics and so forth. The point of view was the more readily accepted by many social anthropologists because anthropologists generally study societies the history of which cannot be known. Their ready acceptance was also partly due to the influence from across the Channel of the philosophical rationalism of Durkheim and his school. This influence has had, on the whole, not only a profound but a beneficial effect on English anthropology. It injected a tradition which was concerned with broad general questions into the more piecemeal empirical English tradition, exemplified by the way in which theoretical writers like Tylor and Frazer used their material and by both the many first-hand accounts of primitive peoples written by travellers, missionaries and administrators and the early social surveys in this country. On the other hand, if students are not firmly anchored by a heavy weight of ethnographic fact, they are easily led by it into airy discussions about words, into arid classifications, and into either pretentiousness or total scepticism.

THE FUNCTIONAL THEORY

The functional or organismic theory of society which reigns in social anthropology in England today is not new. We have seen that it was held in their several ways by the early and mid-Victorian anthropologists and by the moral philosophers before them, and it has, of course, a very much longer pedigree in political philosophy. In its modern and more mechanistic form it was set forth at great length by Durkheim and, with special reference to social evolution, by Herbert Spencer. In yet more recent times it has been most clearly and consistently stated by Professor Radcliffe-Brown. Human societies are natural systems in which all the parts are interdependent, each serving in a complex of necessary relations to maintain the whole. The aim of social anthropology is to reduce all social life to laws or general statements about the nature of society which allow prediction. What is new in this restatement of the theory is the insistence that a society can be understood satisfactorily without reference to its past. Almost without exception the eighteenth-century moral philosophers presented their conception of social systems and sociological laws in the form of history in the grand style—a natural history of human societies; and, as we have seen, the enduring passion of their Victorian successors was seeking for origins from which every institution has developed through the working of laws of progress. The modern version of a naturalistic study of society, even if lip-service is sometimes paid to the possibility of a scientific study of social change, claims that for an understanding of the functioning of a society there is no need for the student of it to know anything about its history, any more than there is need for a physiologist to know the history of an organism to understand it. Both are natural systems and can be described in terms of natural law without recourse to history.

The functional orientation, by its insistence on the inter-relatedness of things, has been largely responsible for the comprehensive and detailed professional field studies of modern anthropology, such as were entirely unknown to the anthropologists of the nineteenth-century, who were content to let laymen collect the facts on which they based their theories. It is also largely due to it that the anthropologist of today sees more clearly than his predecessors that an understandnig of human behaviour can only be reached by viewing it in its full social setting. All social anthropologists now accept that the entire activities of primitive societies must be systematically studied in the field, and all have the same holistic approach when they come to set down and interpret their observations.

But a theory may have heuristic value without being sound, and there are many objections to the functional theory. It is no more than an assumption that human societies are systems of the kind they are alleged to be. Indeed in the case of Malinowski the functional theory, in spite of the wide claims he made for it, was little more than a literary device. The theory assumes, moreover, that in the given circumstances no part of social life can be other than what it is and that every custom has social value, thus adding to a naive determinism a crude teleology and pragmatism. It is easy to define the aim of social anthropology to be the establishment of sociological laws, but nothing even remotely resembling a law of the natural sciences has yet been adduced. What general statements have been made are for the most part speculative, and are in any case too general to be of value. Often they are little more than guesses on a common-sense or *post factum* level, and they sometimes degenerate into mere tautologies or even platitudes. Also, it is difficult to reconcile the assertion that a society has come to be what it is by a succession of unique events with the claim that what it is can be comprehensively stated in terms of natural law. In its extreme form functional determinism leads to absolute relativism and makes nonsense not only of the theory itself but of all thought.

If for these and other reasons I cannot accept, without many qualifications, the functional theory dominant in English anthropology today, I do not assert, as you will see, that societies are unintelligible or that they are not in some sense systems. What I am objecting to is what appears to me to be still the same doctrinaire philosophy of the Enlightenment and of the stage-making anthropologists of the nineteenth century, with only the concept of evolution substituted for that of progress. Its constructions are still posited dialectally and imposed on the facts. I attribute this to anthropologists always having tried to model themselves on the natural sciences instead of on the historical sciences, and it is to this important issue that I now turn. I must apologize to historians if, in considering it, what I say may seem obvious to them. My observations would be hotly disputed by most of my anthropological colleagues in England.

ANTHROPOLOGY AND HISTORY

In discussing the relations between history and social anthropology it is necessary, if the discussion is to be profitable, to perceive that several quite different questions are being asked. The first is whether a knowledge of how a particular social system has come to be what it is helps one to understand its present constitution. We must here distinguish between history in two different senses, though in a literate society it is not so easy to maintain the distinction as when speaking of non-literate societies. In the first sense history is part of the conscious tradition of a people and is operative in their social life. It is the collective representation of events as distinct from events themselves. This is what the social anthropologist calls myth. The functionalist anthropologists regard history in this sense, usually a mixture of fact and fancy, as highly relevant to a study of the culture of which it forms part.

On the other hand they have totally rejected the reconstruction from circumstantial evidences of the history of primitive peoples for whose past documents and monuments are totally, or almost totally, lacking. A case can be made out for this rejection, though not in my opinion so strong a case as is usually supposed, for all history is of necessity a reconstruction, the degree of probability attending a particular reconstruction depending on the evidence available. The fact that nineteenth-century anthropologists were uncritical in their reconstructions ought not to lead to the conclusion that all effort expended in this direction is waste of time.

But with the bath water of presumptive history the functionalists have also thrown out the baby of valid history. They say, Malinowski the most vociferously, that even when the history of a society is recorded it is irrelevant to a

functional study of it. I find this point of view unacceptable. The claim that one can understand the functioning of institutions at a certain point of time without knowing how they have come to be what they are, or what they were later to become, as well as a person who, in addition to having studied their constitution at that point of time, has also studied their past and future is to me an absurdity. Moreover, so it seems to me, neglect of the history of institutions prevents the functionalist anthropologist not only from studying diachronic problems but also from testing the very functional constructions to which he attaches most importance, for it is precisely history which provides him with an experimental situation.

The problem here raised is becoming a pressing one because anthropologists are now studying communities which, if still fairly simple in structure, are enclosed in, and form part of, great historical societies, such as Irish and Indian rural communities, Bedouin Arab tribes, or ethnic minorities in America and other parts of the world. They can no longer ignore history, making a virtue out of necessity, but must explicitly reject it or admit its relevance. As anthropologists turn their attention more to complex civilized communities the issue will become more acute, and the direction of the theoretical development in the subject will largely depend on its outcome.

A second question is of a different kind. We ask now, not whether in studying a particular society its history forms an integral part of the study, but whether in making comparative sociological studies, for example of political or religious institutions, we ought to include in them societies as presented to us by historians. In spite of their claim that social anthropology aims at being a natural history of human societies, that is, of all human societies, functionalist anthropologists, at any rate in England, have, in their general distaste for historical method, almost completely ignored historical writings. They have thereby denied themselves access in their comparative studies to the valuable material provided by historical societies structurally comparable to many of the contemporaneous barbarous societies which they regard as being within their province.

A third, and to me the most important, question is a methodological one: whether social anthropology, for all its present disregard of history, is not itself a kind of historiography. To answer this question we have first to observe what the anthropologist does. He goes to live for some months or years among a primitive people. He lives among them as intimately as he can, and he learns to speak their language, to think in their concepts and to feel in their values. He then lives the experiences over again critically and interpretatively in the conceptual categories and values of his own culture and in terms of the general body of knowledge of his discipline. In other words, he translates from one culture into another.

At this level social anthropology remains a literary and impressionistic art. But even in a single ethnographic study the anthropologist seeks to do more than understand the thought and values of a primitive people and translate them into his own culture. He seeks also to discover the structural order of the society, the patterns which, once established, enable him to see it as a whole, as a set of interrelated abstractions. Then the society is not only culturally intelligible, as it is, at the level of consciousness and action, for one of its members or for the foreigner who has learnt its mores and participates in its life, but also becomes sociologically intelligible.

The historian, or at any rate the social historian, and perhaps the economic historian in particular, will, I think, know what I mean by sociologically intelligible. After all, English society in the eleventh century was understood by Vinogradoff in quite a different way from the way it would have been understood by a Norman or Anglo-Saxon or by a foreigner who had learnt the native languages and was living the life of the natives. Similarly, the social anthropologist discovers in a native society what no native can explain to him and what no layman, however conversant with the culture, can perceive—its basic structure. This structure cannot be seen. It is a set of abstractions, each of which, though derived, it is true, from analysis of observed behavior, is fundamentally an imaginative construct of the anthropologist himself. By relating these abstractions to one another logically so that they present a pattern he can see the society in its essentials and as a single whole.

What I am trying to say can perhaps be best illustrated by the example of language. A native understands his own language and it can be learnt by a stranger. But certainly neither the native himself nor the stranger can tell you what are its phonological and grammatical systems. These can only be discovered by a trained linguist. By analysis he can reduce the complexity of a language to certain abstractions and show how these abstractions can be interrelated in a logical system or pattern. This is what the social anthropologist also tries to do. He tries to disclose the structural patterns of a society. Having isolated these patterns in one society he compares them with patterns in other societies. The study of each new society enlarges his knowledge of the range of basic social structures and enables him better to construct a typology of forms, and to determine their essential features and the reasons for their variations.

I have tried to show that the work of the social anthropologist is in three main phases or, otherwise expressed, at three levels of abstraction. First he seeks to understand the significant overt features of a culture and to translate them into terms of his own culture. This is precisely what the historian does. There is no fundamental difference here in aim or method between the two disciplines, and both are equally selective in their use of material. The similarity between them has been obscured by the fact that the social anthropologist makes a direct study of social life while the historian makes an indirect study of it through documents and other surviving evidences. This is a technical, not a methodological, difference. The historicity of anthropology has also been obscured by its pre-occupation with primitive societies which lack recorded history. But this again is not a methodological difference. I agree with Professor Kroeber that the fundamental characteristic of the historical method is not chronological relation of events but descriptive integration of them; and this characteristic historiography shares with social anthropology. What social anthropologists have in fact chiefly been doing is to write cross-sections of history, integrative descriptive accounts of primitive peoples at a moment of time which are in other respects like the accounts written by historians about peoples over a period of time, for the historian does not just record sequences of events but seeks to establish connexions between them. Nor does the anthropologist's determination to view every institution as a functioning part of a whole society make a methodological difference. Any good modern historian aims—if I may be allowed to judge the matter—at the same kind of synthesis.

In my view, therefore, the fact that the anthropologist's problems are generally synchronic while the historian's problems are generally diachronic is a difference of emphasis in the rather peculiar conditions prevailing and not a real divergence of interest. When the historian fixes his attention exclusively on a particular culture at a particular and limited period of history he writes what we would call an ethnographic monograph (Burckhardt's *Culture of the Renaissance* is a striking example). When, on the other hand, a social anthropologist writes about a society developing in time he writes a history book, different, it is true, from the ordinary narrative and political history but in all essentials the same as social history. In the absence of another, I must cite my own book *The Sanusi of Cyrenaica* as an example.

In the second phase of his work the social anthropologist goes a step farther and seeks by analysis to disclose the latent underlying form of a society or culture. In doing so, he goes farther than the more timorous and conservative historians, but many historians do the same. I am not thinking of philosophers of history like Vico, Hegel, Marx, Spengler and Toynbee, not of those who can be exclusively particularized as social historians or writers of the *Kulturgeschichte* school like Max Weber, Tawney, and Sombart or Adam Smith, Savigny and Buckle, but of historians in the stricter and more orthodox sense like Fustel de Coulanges, Vinogradoff, Pirenne, Maitland, or Professor Powicke. It is perhaps worth noting that those historical writings which we anthropologists regard as examples of sociological method generally deal with early periods of history, where the societies described are more like primitive societies than the complex societies of later periods of history, and where the historical documents are not too vast to be grasped and assimilated by a single mind; so that the total culture can be studied as a whole and contained in a single mind, as primitive cultures can be studied and contained. When we read the works of these historians we feel that we and they are studying the same things in the same way and are reaching out for the same kind of understanding of them.

In the third phase of his work the anthropologist compares the social structures his analysis has revealed in a wide range of societies. When a historian attempts a similar study in his own field he is dubbed a philosopher, but it is not, I think, true to say, as it is often said, that history is a study of the particular and social anthropology of the general. In some historical writers comparison and classification are quite explicit; always they are implicit, for history cannot be written except against a standard of some kind, by comparison with the culture of a different time or people, if only with the writer's own.

I conclude therefore, following Professor Kroeber, that while there are, of course, many differences between social anthropology and historiography they are differences of technique, of emphasis and of perspective, and not differences of method and aim. I believe also that a clearer understanding that this is so will lead to a closer connexion between historical and anthropological studies than is at present provided by their meeting points in ethnology and prehistoric archaeology, and that this will be greatly to the benefit of both disciplines. Historians can supply social anthropolgists with invaluable material, sifted and vouched for by critical techniques of testing and interpretation. Social anthropologists can provide the historian of the future with some of his best records, based on careful and detailed observations, and they can shed on history, by their discovery of latent structural forms, the light of universals. The value of each discipline to the other will, I believe, be recognized when anthropologists begin to devote themselves more to historical scholarship and show how knowledge of anthropology often illuminates historical problems.

SOCIAL ANTHROPOLOGY AS ONE OF THE HUMANITIES

The thesis I have put before you, that social anthropology is a kind of historiography, and therefore ultimately of philosophy or art, implies that it studies societies as moral systems and not as natural systems, that it is interested in design rather than in process, and that it therefore seeks patterns and not scientific laws, and interprets rather than explains. These are conceptual, and not merely verbal, differences. The concepts of natural system and natural law, modelled on the constructs of the natural sciences, have dominated anthropology from its beginnings, and as we look back over the course of its growth I think we can see that they have been responsible for a false scholasticism which has led to one rigid and ambitious formulation after another. Regarded as a special kind of historiography, that is as one of the humanities, social anthropology is released from these essentially philosophical dogmas and given the opportunity, though it may seem paradoxical to say so, to be really empirical and, in the true sense of the word, scientific. This, I presume, is what Maitland had in mind when he said that 'by and by anthropology will have the choice between becoming history or nothing.'

I have found, both in England and America, that students are often perturbed at these implications. There is no need for them to be, for it does not follow from regarding social anthropology as a special kind of historiography rather than as a special kind of natural science that its researches and theory are any the less systematic. When therefore I am asked how I think that social anthropology should proceed in the future I reply that it must proceed along much the same lines as do social history or the history of institutions, as distinct from purely narrative and political history. For example, the social historian seeking to understand feudal institutions would first study them in one country of Europe and get to know all he can about them there. He would then study them in other European societies to discover which features were common to European civilization at that time and which were local variations, and he would try to see each particular form as a variation of a general pattern and to account for the variations. He would not seek for laws but for significant patterns.

What more do wo do, can we do or should we want to do in social anthropology than this? We study witchcraft or a kinship system in a particular primitive society. If we want to know more about these social phenomena we can study them in a second society, and then in a third society, and so on, each study reaching, as our knowledge increases and new problems emerge, a deeper level of investigation and teaching us the essential characteristics of the thing we are inquiring into, so that particular studies are given a new meaning and perspective. This will always happen if one necessary condition is observed: that the conclusions of each study are clearly formulated in such a way that they not only test the conclusions reached by earlier studies but advance new hypotheses which can be broken down into fieldwork problems.

However, the uneasiness I have noted is not, I think, on this score, because it must be evident to any student who has given thought to the matter that those who have most strongly urged

that social anthropology should model itself on the natural sciences have done neither better research than those who take the opposite view nor a different kind of research. It is rather due to the feeling that any discipline that does not aim at formulating laws and hence predicting and planning is not worth the labour of a lifetime. This normative element in anthropology is, as we have seen, like the concepts of natural law and progress from which it derives, part of its philosophical heritage. In recent times the natural-science approach has constantly stressed the application of its findings to affairs, the emphasis in England being on colonial problems and in America on political and industrial problems. Its more cautious advocates have held that there can only be applied anthropology when the science is much more advanced than it is today, but the less cautious have made far-reaching claims for the immediate application of anthropological knowledge in social planning; though, whether more or less cautious, both have justified anthropology by appeal to utility. Needless to say, I do not share their enthusiasm and regard the attitude that gives rise to it as naive. A full discussion of it would take too long, but I cannot resist the observation that, as the history of anthropology shows, positivism leads very easily to a misguided ethics, anaemic scientific humanism or—Saint Simon and Comte are cases in point—*ersatz* religion.

I conclude by summarizing very briefly the argument I have tried to develop in this lecture and by stating what I believe is likely to be the direction taken by social anthropology in the future. Social anthropologists, dominated consciously or unconsciously, from the beginnings of their subject, by positivist philosophy, have aimed, explicitly or implicitly, and for the most part still aim—for this is what it comes to—at proving that man is an automaton and at discovering the sociological laws in terms of which his actions, ideas and beliefs can be explained and in the light of which they can be planned and controlled. This approach implies that human societies are natural systems which can be reduced to variables. Anthropologists have therefore taken one or other of the natural sciences as their model and have turned their backs on history, which sees men in a different way and eschews, in the light of experience, rigid formulations of any kind.

There is, however, an older tradition than that of the Enlightenment with a different approach to the study of human societies, in which they are seen as systems only because social life must have a pattern of some kind, inasmuch as man, being a reasonable creature, has to live in a world in which his relations with those around him are ordered and intelligible. Naturally I think that those who see things in this way have a clearer understanding of social reality than the others, but whether this is so or not they are increasing in number, and this is likely to continue because the vast majority of students of anthropology today have been trained in one or other of the humanities and not, as was the case thirty years ago, in one or other of the natural sciences. This being so, I expect that in the future there will be a turning towards humanistic disciplines, especially towards history, and particularly towards social history or the history of institutions, of cultures and of ideas. In this change of orientation social anthropology will retain its individuality because it has its own special problems, techniques and traditions, Though it is likely to continue for some time to devote its attention chiefly to primitive societies, I believe that during this second half of the century it will give far more attention than in the past to more complex cultures and especially to the civilizations of the Far and Near East and become, in a very general sense, the counterpart to Oriental Studies, in so far as these are conceived of as primarily linguistic and literary—that is to say, it will take as its province the cultures and societies, past as well as present, of the non-European peoples of the world.

5

SOCIAL ANTHROPOLOGY
AND THE METHOD OF CONTROLLED COMPARISON

FRED EGGAN

I

THE contemporary student of anthropology is in a difficult position in attempting to achieve a sound orientation in our rapidly changing and developing discipline. Nowhere is this more true than in the general field of cultural anthropology, where there is an apparent schism between those who call themselves ethnologists and the newer group of social anthropologists. Ethnology, which has had its major development in the United States, has been concerned primarily with culture history and culture process; social anthropology, on the other hand, is primarily a product of British anthropology and has emphasized social structure and function as its major concepts. These differences

From *American Anthropologist*, 56 (1954): 743–760. Reprinted by permission of the American Anthropological Association and the author. Fred Eggan is Professor of Anthropology, University of Chicago.

in emphasis and interest have led to considerable misunderstanding on both sides. As one who has had a foot in both camps for some two decades I may perhaps be permitted some observations on this situation, along with some suggestions as to a common meeting-ground.

Since World War II rapid changes have taken place in all branches of anthropology. Genetics and the experimental method, plus a host of new fossil finds from Africa, are revolutionizing physical anthropology; archeology, with the aid of radiocarbon dating and other new techniques, is beginning to achieve a worldwide chronology and is turning to cultural anthropology for further insight into cultural development; linguistics, with structural methods well established, is returning anew to historical problems and re-examining the relations of language and culture. But ethnology, one of whose tasks it is to synthesize and interpret the conclusions reached by its sister disciplines, is lagging behind.

It is not clear how long anthropology can

remain partly a biological science, partly a humanity, and partly a social science. As we shift from the descriptive, data-gathering phases of anthropology to analysis, interpretation and theory, it is inevitable that realignments will come about. My predecessors in the presidency during the postwar period have sketched some of these new developments and realignments as they have seen them. It is highly probable that the forces for fusion will prevail over the tendencies to fission in the near future, so far as the United States is concerned; in England the forces are more nearly balanced, and the outcome is more uncertain. In the long run we may or may not follow the patterns set by other disciplines.

Turning to the field of cultural anthropology, one of the important developments of the last few years has been the series of articles and books defining, denouncing, or defending "social anthropology." Murdock, in the most outspoken attack, notes that: "For a decade or more, anthropologists in other countries have privately expressed an increasingly ambivalent attitude toward recent trends in British anthropology—a curious blend of respect and dissatisfaction." His analysis of the strengths and weaknesses of British social anthropology, as revealed in current productions, and his diagnosis of the social anthropologists as primarily "sociologists" have led to replies and counterreplies.

At the International Symposium on Anthropology sponsored by the Wenner-Gren Foundation a special session was devoted to "Cultural/Social Anthropology," in which various scholars presented the usages current in their respective countries. Tax's summary of the consensus is to the effect that we ought to "use the words 'cultural' and 'social' anthropology interchange-ably and forget about the question of terminology"; but Kroeber in his "Concluding Review" returns to the problem of society and culture and finds distinctions. If these distinctions were merely a question of factional dispute or of alternate terms for similar activities, we could agree, with Lowie, on some neutral term such as "ethnography"—or allow time to make the decision in terms of relative popularity.

But the distinctions being made are not merely a matter of British and American rivalry or of terminology, and it is essential that we realize that there is a problem and that it is an important one. After accepting contemporary British social anthropologists as "true enthnographers" interested in the realities of culture,

Lowie goes on to unequivocally reject Fortes' contention that "social structure is not an aspect of culture but the entire culture of a given people handled in a special frame of theory." However, many British social anthropologists would go even further than Fortes! In general they make a clear distinction between the concepts of *society* and *culture* and think of social anthropology as concerned primarily with the former. Murdock's startling conclusion that the Britishers are sociologists was anticipated by Radcliffe-Brown and recently reaffirmed by Evans-Pritchard: "I must emphasize that, theoretically at any rate, social anthropology is the study of all human societies. . . . Social anthropology can therefore be regarded as a branch of sociological studies, that branch which chiefly devotes itself to primitive societies." In contrast, the current Americanist opinion subsumes social structure as one aspect of culture, following Tylor, or separates the two but gives primacy to the concept of culture.

Before we read our British brethren out of the anthropological party, however, it might be wise to see whether we may not have taken too narrow a view of cultural anthropology. Lowie, who, along with many American anthropologists, takes his cultural text from Tylor, defines the aim of ethnography as "the *complete* description of all cultural phenomena everywhere and at all periods" (italics Lowie's). It may be both possible and useful to view the "capabilities and habits acquired by man *as a member of society*" under the heading of social structure, despite the fact that Lowie finds it inconceivable. We might wait for the remainder of Fortes' materials on the Tallensi before rendering a verdict. And if we look more closely at Tylor's famous definition it seems clear that anthropology should be concerned with *both* society and culture, as they are interrelated and reflected in human behavior. We need a complete description and interpretation of both social and cultural phenomena, not to mention those concerned with the individual, if we are going to think in global terms. I would agree with Hallowell that society, culture, and personality may "be conceptually differentiated for specialized types of analysis and study. On the other hand, it is being more clearly recognized than heretofore that society, culture and personality cannot be postulated as completely independent variables." We can wait until we know more about each of these concepts before we rank them as superior and inferior.

More important, we cannot afford to ignore the contributions of the British social anthropologists to both theory and description. In the last thirty years they have been developing a new approach to the study of man in society, which is currently producing significant results. It is no accident that many of the best monographs of the postwar period have come out of the small group of British social anthropologists. Reviewing *African Systems of Kinship and Marriage,* Murdock states that "the ethnographic contributions to the volume reveal without exception a very high level of professional competence in field research and in the analysis of social structural data, equalled only by the work of the very best men in other countries." What some of these contributions are has been recently pointed out by Firth, Evans-Pritchard, and Fortes, among others. While Fortes recognizes that they lack the wide and adventurous sweep of American anthropology, "the loss in diversity is amply balanced by the gains we have derived from concentration on a limited set of problems." Most American anthropologists are inclined to attribute the relative excellence of these contributions to good field techniques or perhaps to superior literary abilities, considering the British theoretical approach as rather barren and lifeless. But this seems to me to be a mistake. The structural point of view makes possible a superior organization and interpretation of the cultural data, and good monographs may well be related to this point of view. If we are to meet this competition (particularly in view of Firth's account of their new directions) we need to do more than label our British colleagues as "comparative sociologists" or invoke the magical figures of Tylor and Franz Boas.

If I may venture a prescription based on my own experience, we need to adopt the structural-functional approach of British social anthropology and integrate it with our traditional American interest in culture process and history. For the weaknesses of British social anthropology are in precisely those aspects where we are strong, and if we can develop a way of relating the two approaches we can perhaps save ethnology from the destiny to which Kroeber has assigned it—"to a premature fate or a senescent death as one may see it." I feel encouraged in this attempt because I have a genuine interest in both culture and social structure and because Murdock believes I have succeeded "in fusing functional analysis with an interest in history and an awareness of process in a highly productive creative synthesis."

In contrast to most of my contemporaries I arrived at this synthesis without too many conflicts. My early anthropological education was in the Boas tradition as interpreted by Cole, Sapir, and Spier—with additions from Redfield. But before the mold had hardened too far I came under the influence also of Radcliffe-Brown. The early thirties was a period of intense excitement among graduate students at Chicago, enhanced by debates between Linton and Radcliffe-Brown and heated arguments about functionalism. Redfield's account gives something of the flavor of this period, as well as a brief characterization of Radcliffe-Brown's contributions to anthropology. And Linton's *Study of Man* shows definite evidence of the impact of the structural and functional points of view on his thinking: culture and society are clearly differentiated, though they are mutually dependent, and concepts such as social system, status and role, integration and function are intermixed with the more usual cultural categories. But *The Study of Man,* while widely admired, was little imitated by Linton's colleagues—though it has had important effects on social science as a whole and on some of his students.

Once we were in the field, however, some of us discovered that the alternatives about which we had been arguing were in reality complementary. We found that the structural approach gave a new dimension to the flat perspectives of American ethnography and allowed us to ask new kinds of questions. Functionalism gave us meaningful answers to some questions and enabled us again to see cultures as wholes. But we also maintained an interest in cultural regions and a concern for culture process and cultural development. The resulting data were utilized for a variety of purposes. Some students prepared "descriptive integrations" which approximated to that complex reality which is history. Others were attracted to the formulation of general propositions as to society or culture. I, myself, began by working in limited areas on problems of kinship and social structure, untilizing comparison as a major technique and attempting to see changes over time. When Radcliffe-Brown went to Oxford in 1937 we put together some of these studies under the ambitious title, *Social Anthropology of North American Tribes.*

The distinction between society and culture,

far from complicating the procedures of analysis and comparison, has actually facilitated them. Generalization requires repeatable units which can be identified, and social structures, which tend to have a limited number of forms, readily lend themselves to classification and comparison. Cultural data, on the other hand, tend to fall into patterns of varying types which are more easily traced through time and space. Social structures and cultural patterns may vary independently of one another, but both have their locus in the behavior of individuals in social groups. Depending on our problems one or the other may be central in our analysis, and we may utilize one or another of the basic methods of investigation—history or science. I would agree with Kroeber that these latter need differentiation, "precisely because we shall presumably penetrate further in the end by two approaches than by one," but I see no reason why we should not use the two approaches together when possible.

The crucial problem with regard to generalization, whether broad or limited, is the method of comparison which is used. In the United States, for reasons which I will mention later on, the comparative method has long been in disrepute and was supplanted by what Boas called the "historical method." In England, on the other hand, the comparative method has had a more continuous utilization. Nadel discusses the techniques and limitations of the comparative method and the nature of the results which may be obtained from its application. As Radcliffe-Brown has stated: "It is only by the use of the comparative method that we can arrive at general explanations. The alternative is to confine ourselves to particularistic explanations similar to those of the historian. The two kinds of explanation are both legitimate and do not conflict; but both are needed for the understanding of societies and their institutions."

The particular adaptation of the comparative method to social anthropology which Radcliffe-Brown has made is well illustrated in The Huxley Memorial Lecture for 1951, where he begins with exogamous moiety divisions in Australia and shows that the Australian phenomena are instances of certain widespread general tendencies in human societies. For him the task of social anthropology is to "formulate and validate statements about the conditions of existence of social systems . . . and the regularities that are observable in social change."

This systematic comparison of a world-wide variety of instances, while an ultimate objective of social anthropology, is rather difficult to carry out in terms of our present limited knowledge of social systems. We can make some general observations about institutions such as the family; and the war between the sexes in aboriginal Australia has some interesting parallels with the world of Thurber. But I am not sure, to give one example, that the "Yin-Yang philosophy of ancient China is the systematic elaboration of the principle that can be used to define the social structure of moieties in Australian tribes," through Radcliffe-Brown's analysis and wide experience give it a certain plausibility.

My own preference is for the utilization of the comparative method on a smaller scale and with as much control over the frame of comparison as it is possible to secure. It has seemed natural to utilize regions of relatively homogeneous culture or to work within social or cultural types, and to further control the ecology and the historical factors so far as it is possible to do so. Radcliffe-Brown has done this with great skill in *The Social Organization of Australian Tribes* (1931). After comparing the Australian moiety structures and finding their common denominators, I would prefer to make a comparison with the results of a similar study of moiety structures and associated practices of the Indians of Southern California, who approximate rather closely the Australian sociocultural situation. The results of this comparison could then be matched against comparable studies of Northwest Coast and other similar moiety systems, and the similarities and differences systematically examined by the method of concomitant variation. I think we would end up, perhaps, with Radcliffe-Brown's relationship of "opposition," or the unity of opposites, but we would have much more, as well, in the form of a clearer understanding of each type or subtype and of the nature of the mechanisms by which they are maintained or changed. While I share Radcliffe-Brown's vision of an ultimate science of society, I think that we first have to cultivate more intensively what Merton has called the middle range of theory. I suggest the method of controlled comparison as a convenient instrument for its exploration, utilizing covariation and correlation, and avoiding too great a degree of abstraction.

Before examining the ramifications and possible results of such exploration it may be useful to glance at selected aspects of the history of anthropology to see how certain of the present differences between American and British anthropologists have come about. We are somewhere in the middle of one of Kroeber's "configurations of culture growth," and it is important to see which patterns are still viable and which are close to exhaustion.

II

The early developments in American cultural anthropology have been delineated by Lowie and parallel in many respects those which were occurring in England. In addition to Morgan, Bandelier, Cushing, J. O. Dorsey, Alice Fletcher, and others were among the pioneers whose work is today largely forgotten in the the United States. For with the advent of Franz Boas a major break was made with the past, resulting not so much from his program for cultural anthropology as in its selective implementation. Boas in "The Limitations of the Comparative Method" (1896) outlined a program which included two major tasks. The first task involved detailed studies of individual tribes in their cultural and regional context as a means to the reconstruction of the histories of tribal cultures and regions. A second task concerned the comparisons of these tribal histories, with the ultimate objective of formulating general laws of cultural growth, which were psychological in character. This second task, which Boas thought of as the more important of the two, was never to be fully implemented by his students.

Boas formulated this program in connection with a destructive criticism of the comparative method as then practiced in England and America. After stating as a principle of method that uniformity of processes was essential for comparability, he goes on to say: "If anthropology desires to establish the laws governing the growth of culture it must not confine itself to comparing the results of growth alone, but whenever such is feasible, it must compare the processes of growth, and these can be discovered by means of studies of the cultures of small geographical areas." He then compares this "historical method" with the "comparative method," which he states has been remarkably barren of results, and predicts that it will not become fruitful until we make our comparisons "on the broader and sounder basis which I

ventured to outline." The requirement that only those phenomena can be compared which are derived psychologically or historically from common causes, valuable as it may have been at that time, has had the effect of predisposing most of Boas' students against the comparative method—except in linguistics where genetic relationships could be assumed—and hence against any generalizations which require comparison. And the processes which Boas sought in a study of art and mythology on the Northwest Coast proved more difficult to isolate than was anticipated. Kroeber notes that though Boas was "able to show a multiplicity of processes in culture, he was not able—it was impossible in his day and perhaps is still—to formulate these into a systematic theory."

In the "Formative Period" of American ethnology, from 1900 to 1915, these were minor considerations. There were the vanishing Indian cultures to study, and it was natural for the students of Boas to concentrate on the first portion of his program. They wrote theses, for the most part, on specific problems, or to test various theories which had been advanced to explain art, or myth, or ritual, generally with negative results. This clearing of the intellectual air was essential, but it also led to excesses, as in Goldenweiser's famous study of totemism. It also resulted in the ignoring of earlier anthropologists and even contemporaries. Alice Fletcher's *The Hako: A Pawnee Ceremony* excellently describes and interprets a ritual but was never used as a model.

The major attention of the early Boas students was devoted to the task of ordering their growing data on the American Indian in tribal and regional context. During this and the following periods many important monographs and studies were published, which formed a solid base for future work. The climax of this fact-gathering revolution was reached with the culture-area concept as crystallized by Wissler, and in the studies by Boas on the art, mythology, and social organization of the Northwest Coast.

The period which followed, from 1915 to 1930, was a "Florescent Period" in American ethnology. The culture area provided a framework for the analysis and interpretation of the cultural data in terms of history and process. Sapir opened the period with his famous *Time Perspective*, which began: "Cultural anthropology is more and more rapidly getting to realize itself as a strictly historical science. Its data cannot be understood, either in themselves or in their relation to one another, except as the end-points of specific sequences of events reaching back into the remote past." Wissler, Lowie, Kroeber, Spier, Benedict, and many others provided a notable series of regional studies utilizing distributional analyses of cultural traits for chronological inferences—and for the study of culture process. Wissler developed the "law of diffusion" and then turned his attention to the dynamic factors underlying the culture area itself. In *The Relation of Nature to Man in Aboriginal America* he thought that he had found them in the relationship of the culture center to the underlying ecology. The great museums dominated this period, and American anthropology shared in the general prosperity and optimism which followed the first World War.

One result of these distributional studies was that chronology tended to become an end in itself, and some ethnologists became so preoccupied with seeking time sequences that they did not pay much attention to culture as such. The analysis of culture into traits or elements and their subsequent treatment often violated principles of historical method by robbing them of their context. The normal procedure of historians of basing their analysis on chronology was here reversed—the chronology resulted from the analytic study. The generalizations as to process which were formulated were used as short-cuts to further historical research.

Another important result of these studies was the conception of culture which gradually developed. Culture came to be viewed as a mere aggregation of traits brought together by the accidents of diffusion. Here is Benedict's conclusion to her doctoral dissertation: "It is, so far as we can see, an ultimate fact of human nature that man builds up his culture out of disparate elements, combining and recombining them; and until we have abandoned the superstition that the result is an organism functionally interrelated, we shall be unable to see our cultural life objectively, or to control its manifestations."

The revolt against this mechanical and atomistic conception of culture came both from without and from within. Dixon criticized both Wissler's procedures and his conceptions of the processes of culture growth, as well as his formulation of the dynamics of the culture area. Spier renounced historical reconstruction as misleading and unnecessary for understanding the nature of the processes of culture growth, advocating in its place a consideration of the actual conditions under which cultural growth takes place. Benedict was soon engaged in the study of cultural patterns and configurations, and her *Patterns of Culture* represents a complete reversal of her earlier position—here superstition has become reality.

During this period there was little interest in social structure as such, even though Kroeber, Lowie, and Parsons all studied Pueblo life at first hand. The shadows of Morgan, McLennan, Spencer, and Maine still loomed over them, and sociological interpretations were generally rejected in favor of psychological or linguistic ones. Lowie, however, began to develop a moderate functional position and sociological orientation with regard to social organization, perhaps best exemplified in his article on "Relationship Terms."

The "Expansionist Period" which followed, 1930–1940, was a time of troubles and of transition for American ethnology. The old gods were no longer omniscient—and there was an invasion of foreign gods from overseas. The depression brought the great museums to their knees and temporarily ended their activities in ethnological research; the center of gravity shifted more and more to the universities, as the social sciences grappled with the new social problems. This was a period of considerable expansion for cultural anthropology, much of it in terms of joint departments with sociology. Archeology also experienced a remarkble expansion during the decade, partly as a byproduct of its ability to utilize large quantities of WPA labor. The chronological framework that resulted, based on stratigraphy and other techniques, further emphasized the inadequacy of the reconstructions made from distributional analyses alone.

In the meantime *Argonauts* and *The Andaman Islanders* had been published but had made relatively little impression on American scholars. Malinowski's field methods were admired, and his functional conception of culture struck some responsive chords; as for Radcliffe-Brown, his "ethnological appendix" was utilized but his interpretations of Adamanese customs and beliefs were largely ignored. Soon afterwards, however, Malinowski began developing social anthropology in England on the basis of the functional method and new techniques of field research. Brief visits by Malinowski to the United States, including a summer session at the University of California, plus the work of his early students in Oceania and Africa, led to a considerable increase in his influence, but during the 1930's he was largely preoccupied with developing a program of research for Africa.

In 1931 Radcliffe-Brown, who had been first in South Africa and then in Australia, brought to this country "a method for the study of society, well defined and different enough from what prevailed here to require American anthropologists to reconsider the whole matter of method, to scrutinize their objectives, and to attend to new problems and new ways of looking at problems. He stirred us up and accelerated intellectual variation among us."

As a result of these and other forces American ethnologists began to shift their interests in a variety of directions. Kroeber re-examined the relationship between cultural and natural areas in a more productive way and formulated the concept of culture climax to replace Wissler's culture center. He also explored the problem of culture elements more thoroughly, in the course of which he organized the Culture Element Survey; at the other end of the cultural spectrum he wrote *Configurations of Culture Growth*. Herskovits, who had earlier applied the culture-area concept to Africa, developed a dynamic approach to the study of culture which has had important results. Redfield, in the meantime, was beginning the series of studies which resulted in *The Folk Culture of Yucatan*—a new and important approach to the study of social and cultural change.

During this period, also, Steward was beginning his ecological studies of Great Basin tribes, Warner was applying social anthropological concepts and methods to the study of modern American communities, and Sapir was shifting his interests in the direction of psychiatry. Linton, with his perception of new and important trends, had put them together with the old, but his interests also shifted in the direction of personality and culture. Acculturation became a respectable subject with the Redfield, Linton, and Herskovits' "Memorandum on the Study of Acculturation," and applied anthropology secured a foothold in the Indian Service and in a few other government agencies.

These developments, which gave variety and color to American ethnology, also tended to leave a vacuum in the center of the field. We will never know for sure what might have developed out of this interesting decade if World War II had not come along.

The "Contemporary Period"—the decade since the war—is difficult to characterize. In part there has been a continuation of prewar trends, in part a carry-over of wartime interests, and in part an interest in new problems resulting from the war and its aftermath. There is a growing interest in complex cultures or civilizations, such as China, Japan, India, and Africa, both at the village level and at the level of national culture and national character, and new methods and techniques are in process for their study and comparison.

One postwar development of particular interest in connection with this paper has been the gradual but definite acceptance in many quarters in this country of social anthropology as a separable but related discipline. Of even greater potential significance, perhaps, is the growing alliance between social phychology, sociology, and social anthropology as the core groups of the so-called "behavioral sciences," a relationship also reflected in the Institute of Human Relations at Yale and in the Department of Social Relations at Harvard, as well as elsewhere.

Perhaps most important of all the postwar developments for the future of anthropology has been the very great increase in the interchange of both students and faculty between English and American institutions, including field stations in Africa. The Fulbright program, the Area Research Fellowships of the Social Science Research Council, the International Symposium on Anthropology of the Wenner-Gren Foundation, and the activities of the Carnegie, Rockefeller, and Ford Foundations have all contributed to this increased exchange. I am convinced that such face-to-face contacts in seminar and field represent the most effective way for amalgamation of techniques and ideas to take place. The testimony of students back from London or Africa is to the general effect that our training is superior in ethnography and in problems of culture history but is inferior in social anthropology: kinship, social structure, political organization, law, and so on. There are exceptions, of course, but we would like the exceptions to be the rule.

III

For the details of the complementary developments in England we are indebted to Evans-Pritchard's account in *Social Anthropology* and to Fortes' inaugural lecture entitled *Social Anthropology at Cambridge Since 1900*. There are differences in emphasis between the Oxford and Cambridge versions, but in general the developments are clear.

In England cultural anthropology got off to a fine start through the efforts of Tylor, Maine, McLennan and other pioneers of the 1860's and 1870's, but their attempts to construct universal stages of development ultimately fell afoul of the facts. The nineteenth-century anthropologists in England were "armchair" anthropologists; it wasn't until Haddon, a zoologist by training, organized the famous Torres Straits expedition of 1898–1900 and converted an assorted group of psychologists and other scientists into ethnologists that field work began. But from this group came the leaders of early twentieth-century British anthropology: Haddon, Rivers, and Seligman. According to Evans-Pritchard, "This expedition marked a turning point in the history of social anthropology in Great Britain. From this time two important and inter-connected developments began to take place: anthropology became more and more a whole-time professional study, and some field experience came to be regarded as an essential part of the training of its students."

During the next decade a gradual separation of ethnology and social anthropology took place, culminating, according to Radcliffe-Brown, in an agreement to use "ethnography" for descriptive accounts of nonliterate peoples, "ethnology" for historical reconstructions, and "social anthropology" for the comparative study of the institutions of primitive societies. The institutional division of labor also took a different organization which has led to different views as to how anthropology should be constituted.

Sir James Frazer dominated social anthropology in the early decades of this century, and the conceptions of evolution and progress held sway long after they had given way in American anthropology. But Fortes notes that, while anthropologists had a magnificent field of inquiry, the subject had no intrinsic unity: "At the stage of development it had reached in 1920, anthropology, both in this country and elsewhere, was a bundle-subject, its data gathered, so to speak, from the same forest but otherwise heterogeneous and tied together only by the evolutionary theory."

Ethnology flourished for a period under Haddon, Rivers, and Seligman, but with the advent of Malinowski and Radcliffe-Brown "social anthropology has emerged as the basic discipline concerned with custom and social organization in the simpler societies." From their predecessors the latter received their tradition of field research and the principle of the intensive study of limited areas—a principle that Malinowski carried to its logical conclusion.

Beginning in 1924 Malinowski began to train a small but brilliant group of social anthropologists from all parts of the Commonwealth in the field techniques and functional theory that he had developed from his Trobriand experience, but his approach proved inadequate for the complex problems encountered in Africa. This deficiency was remedied in part by the advent of Radcliffe-Brown, who returned to the newly organized Institute of Social Anthropology at Oxford in 1937 and proceeded to give British social anthropology its major current directions. Evans-Pritchard discusses this period with the authority of a participant, and I refer you to his *Social Anthropology* for the details —and for a summary of what a social anthropologist does.

The postwar developments in England have been largely a continuation of prewar developments together with a considerable expansion stimulated by government support of both social anthropological and applied research. Unlike the situation in the United States there is no large established group of sociologists in England, and social anthropology has in part filled the gap. Major theoretical differences as to the nature of social anthropology as a science or as a humanity are developing, but these differences are subordinate to a large area of agreement as to basic problems, methods, and points of view. Just as the American ethnologist of the 1920's had a common language and a common set of problems, so do the British social anthropologists today.

One important key to the understanding of British social anthropology resides in their conception of social structure. The contributions in this field with regard to Africa have been summarized by Fortes in "The Structure of Unilineal Descent Groups." Here he points out that the guiding ideas in the analysis of African lineage organization have come mainly from Radcliffe-Brown's formulation of the structural principles found in all kinship systems, and goes on to state that he is not alone "in regarding them as among the most important generalizations as yet reached in the study of social structure." For Fortes the social structure is the foundation of the whole social life of any continuing society.

Not only have the British social anthropologists produced an outstanding series of monographs in recent years but they have organized their training programs in the universities and institutes to insure that the flow will continue. In the early stages of training there is a more concentrated program in social anthropology in the major British universities, though the knowledge demanded of other fields is less, and linguistics is generally conspicuous by its absence. Only the top students are given grants for field research. As Evans-Pritchard sketches the ideal situation, the student usually spends at least two years in his first field study, including learning to speak the language of the group under observation. Another five years is allotted to publishing the results, or longer if he has teaching duties. A study of a second society is desirable, to avoid the dangers of thinking in terms of a single society, but this can usually be carried out in a shorter period.

Granted that this is the ideal procedure, it still offers a standard against which to compare our American practices. My impression is that our very best graduate students are approximating this standard, but our Ph.D. programs in general require considerably less in terms of field research and specific preparation. We tend to think of the doctorate as an earlier stage in the development of a scholar and not a capstone to an established career.

This proposed program, however, has important implications for social anthropology itself. If each anthropologist follows the Malinowskian tradition of specializing in one, or two, or three societies and spends his lifetime in writing about them, what happens to comparative studies? Evans-Pritchard recognizes this problem: "It is a matter of plain experience that it [the comparative study] is a formidable task which cannot be undertaken by a man who is under the obligation to publish the results of the two or three field studies he has made, since this will take him the rest of his life to complete if he has heavy teaching and administrative duties as well."

In place of the comparative method he proposes the "experimental method," in which preliminary conclusions are formulated and then tested by the same or other social anthropologists on different societies, thus gradually developing broader and more adequate hypotheses. The old comparative method, he says, has been largely abandoned because it seldom gave answers to the questions asked.

This concentration on intensive studies of one or two selected societies has its own limitations. The hypotheses advanced on such a basis can often be modified in terms of studies easily available for comparison. Thus Schneider points out that some of Evans-Pritchard's generalizations about the Nuer could well have been tested against the Zulu data. The degree to which comparison may sharpen hypotheses is well illustrated by Nadel's study of "Witchcraft in Four African Societies." There is further reason for this lack of interest in comparative studies on the part of Evans-Pritchard in that he thinks of social anthropology as "belonging to the humanities rather than to the natural sciences" and conceives of his task as essentially a historical one of "descriptive integration." His colleagues are currently disagreeing with him.

Schapera has recently reviewed a number of studies utilizing some variation of the comparative method and finds most of them deficient in one respect or another. The comparative approach he advocates involves making an intensive study of a given region and carefully comparing the forms taken among the people of the area by the particular social phenomena which are under scrutiny, so as to classify them into types. These types can then be compared with those of neighboring regions. "Social anthropology would benefit considerably, and have more right to claim that its methods are adequate, if in the near future far more attention were devoted to intensive regional comparisons."

One difficulty in the way of any systematic and intensive comparison of African data is being remedied by the Ethnographic Survey under the direction of Daryll Forde. The absence of any interest in linguistics is a major criticism of a group who advocate learning a language to carry out researches in social structure but who ignore the structure in the languages which they learn. Lévi-Strauss has pointed out some of the problems in these two fields, and it is difficult to see why they are neglected.

Ultimately the British anthropologists will discover that time perspective is also important and will encourage archeology and historical research. The potentialities of Greenberg's recent genetic classification of African languages, and the subgrouping of Bantu languages through shared correspondences and lexico-statistical techniques, are just beginning to be appreciated. And for those who demand documents there are the Arab records and historical collections such as the Portuguese records for Delagoa Bay. That the same tribes speaking the same languages are still in this region after four hundred years suggests that there is considerable historical material which needs to be utilized. For our best insights into the nature of society and culture come from seeing social structures and culture patterns over time. Here is where we can distinguish the accidental from the general, evaluate more clearly the factors and forces operating in a given situation, and describe the processes involved in general terms. Not to take advantage of the possibilities of studying social and cultural change under such relatively controlled conditions is to do only half the job that needs to be done.

IV

These brief and inadequate surveys indicate that cultural anthropology has had quite a different development in the United States and England and suggest some of the reasons for these differences. They also suggest that the differences may be growing less. In the United States ethnology began with a rejection of Morgan and his interest in the development of social systems, and an acceptance of Tylor and his conception of culture. Tylor's views by-and-large still prevail, though since the 1920's there have been many alternative definitions of culture as anthropologists attempted to get a more *rounded* view of their subject. In England, as Kroeber and Kluckhohn have pointed out, there has been more resistance to the term "culture"; on the other hand, Morgan is hailed as an important forerunner, particularly for his researches on kinship. Prophets are seldom honored in their own country.

Both Kroeber and Redfield have recently reviewed the role of anthropology in relation to the social sciences and to the humanities and have emphasized the virtues of a varied attack on the problems that face us all. With Redfield, I believe we should continue to encourage variety among anthropologists. But I am here particularly concerned with cultural anthropology, and I am disturbed by Kroeber's attitude toward ethnology: "Now how about ethnology?" he writes in his Concluding Re-

view of *Anthropology Today,* "I am about ready to abandon this baby to the wolves." He goes on to detail some of the reasons why ethnology appears to be vanishing: the decrease in primitives, the failure to make classifications and comparisons, and the tendencies to leap directly into large-scale speculations. His solution is to merge ethnology with culture history and, when that is soundly established, to extricate the processes at work and "generalize the story of culture into its causal factors." This is a return to the original Boas program.

My own suggested solution is an alternate one. While there are few "primitives" in our own backyard, there are the new frontiers of Africa, India, Southeast Asia, Indonesia, and Melanesia to exploit. Here is still a complete range in terms of cultural complexity and degree of culture contact. Africa alone is a much more challenging "laboratory" in many respects than is the American Indian. And for those who like their cultures untouched there is interior New Guinea.

The failure to make adequate classifications and comparisons can in part be remedied by borrowing the methods and techniques of the social anthropologists or by going in the directions pioneered by Murdock. Social structure gives us a preliminary basis for classification in the middle range while universals are sought for. Steward's "sociocultural types" are another step in the directions we want to go.

The tendency to leap directly into large-scale speculations is growing less and will be further controlled as we gradually build a foundation of well-supported hypotheses. Speculations are like mutations in some respects—most of them are worthless but every now and then one advances our development tremendously. We need to keep them for this reason, if for no other.

If we can salvage cultural anthropology in the United States, I do not worry too much about the "anthropological bundle" falling apart in the near future. As a result of the closer co-operation among the subdisciplines of anthropology in this country new bridges are continually being built between them, and joint problems, and even new subfields, are constantly being generated. So long as our interaction remains more intensive than our relations with other disciplines, anthropology will hold together.

One thing we can do is to return to the basic problems American ethnologists were tackling in the 1920's and 1930's, with new methods and points of view and a greater range of concepts. I have elsewhere discussed the potential contributions that such a combined approach could achieve, and for the Western Pueblos I have tried to give a specific example. But in terms of present possibilities, not one single region in North America has had adequate treatment. Nor are the possibilities of field research in North America exhausted. The Cheyenne, for example, are still performing the Sun Dance pretty much as it was in Dorsey's day. But despite all the studies of the Sun Dance we still do not have an adequate account giving us the meaning and significance of the rituals for the participants and for the tribe. One such account would enable us to revalue the whole literature of the Sun Dance.

The Plains area is now ripe for a new integration which should be more satisfying than the older ones. In addition to Wissler's and Kroeber's formulations, we now have an outline of cultural development firmly anchored in stratigraphy and radiocarbon dates, and a considerable amount of documentary history as well as a series of monographs on special topics. By centering our attention on social structure, we can see the interrelations of subsistence and ecology, on the one hand, and political and ritual activities, on the other. For those interested in process we can ask: Why did tribal groups coming into the Plains from surrounding regions, with radically different social structures, tend to develop a similar type? The answer is not simply diffusion. Once this new formulation of the Plains is made, new problems will arise which will require a more complex apparatus to solve.

Another type of comparative study which has great potentialities is represented by the investigation of the Southern Athabascan-speaking peoples in the Plains and the Southwest. Here the same or similar groups have differentiated in terms of ecology, contacts, and internal development. Preliminary studies by Kluckhohn, Opler, Hoijer, Goodwin, and others suggest the possibilities of a detailed comparative attack on the problems of cultural development in this relatively controlled situation. Bellah's recent study of Southern Athabascan kinship systems, utilizing Parsons' structural-functional categories, shows some of the possibilities in this region.

In the Southwest I have attempted to work within a single structural type in a highly integrated subcultural area and to utilize the archeological and historical records, which are here reasonably complete, to delimit and interpret the variations which are found. Clyde Kluckhohn looks at the Southwest from a broader standpoint and with a different but related problem: "One of the main rewards of intensive study of a culture area such as the Southwest is that such study eventually frees investigators to raise genuinely scientific questions—problems of process. Once the influence of various cultures upon others in the same area and the effects of a common environment (and its variant forms) have been reasonably well ascertained, one can then operate to a first approximation under an 'all other things being equal' hypothesis and intensively examine the question: Why are these cultures and these modal personality types still different—in spite of similar environmental stimuli and pressures and access over long periods to the influence of generalized area culture or cultures? We are ready now, I believe, for such studies—but no one is yet attempting them seriously."

The Ramah Project, directed by Kluckhohn, has been planned so as to furnish a continuous record of a series of Navaho from childhood to maturity and of the changes in their culture as well. This project is in its second decade, and a variety of participants have produced an impressive group of papers. So far Kluckhohn's major monograph has concerned *Navaho Witchcraft,* which he has interpreted in both psychological and structural terms and which breaks much new ground. A newer project in the same region involves the comparison of the value systems of five groups: Navaho, Zuni, Mormon, Spanish-American, and Texan, but the results are not yet available.

Comparative studies can also be done on a very small scale. The few thousand Hopi are divided into nearly a dozen villages, each of which differs in significant ways from its neighbors in terms of origins, conservatism, contacts, independence, degree of acculturation, and specific sociocultural patterns. And on First Mesa the Hano or Hopi Tewa, who came from the Rio Grande around A.D. 1700, still maintain their linguistic and cultural independence despite biological assimilation and minority status—and apparently differ significantly in personality traits as well. Dozier's preliminary account of this interesting situation suggests how valuable this comparison may eventually be.

How much can be learned about the processes of social and cultural change by comparative field research in a controlled situation is illustrated by Alex Spoehr's researches in the Southeast. Here some preliminary investigations by the writer had led to tentative conclusions as to the nature of changes in kinship systems of the Creek, Choctaw, Chickasaw, and other tribes of the region after they were removed to reservations in Oklahoma. Spoehr not only demonstrated these changes in detail but has analyzed the historical factors responsible and isolated the resulting process.

Here Redfield's comparative study of four Yucatecan communities in terms of progressive changes in their organization, individualization, and secularization as one moves from the tribal hinterland through village and town to the city of Merida should also be mentioned. The significance of its contributions to comparative method has been largely overlooked in the controversies over the nature of the "folk society" and the usefulness of ideal types.

We can also begin to study particular social types wherever they occur. Murdock's *Social Structure* demonstrates that similar social structures and kinship systems are frequently found in various parts of the world. We can compare matrilineal social systems, or Omaha kinship systems, in different regions of the world without restricting ourselves to the specific requirements originally laid down by Boas. Thus Audrey Richards' comparison of matrilineal organizations in Central Africa will gain in significance when set against the Northwest Coast data. When variant forms of matrilineal or patrilineal social systems are compared from the standpoint of structure and function, we will have a clearer idea of the essential features of such systems and the reasons for special variants. The results for matrilineal systems promise to give quite a different picture than Lowie originally drew of the "Matrilineal Complex," and they will help us to see more clearly the structural significance of cultural patterns such as avunculocal residence and cross-cousin marriage.

These and other studies will enable us ultimately to present a comprehensive account of the various types of social structure to be found in the regions of the world and to see the na-

ture of their correlates and the factors involved in social and cultural change. It is clear that new methods and techniques will need to be developed for the evaluation of change over time; quantitative data will be essential to establish rates of change which may even be expressed in statistical terms.

I have suggested that there may be some virtues in combining the sound anthropological concepts of structure and function with the ethnological concepts of process and history. If we can do this in a satisfactory manner we can save the "ethnological baby" from the fate to which Kroeber has consigned it—what we call the infant when it has matured is a relatively minor matter. In suggesting some of the ways in which comparative studies can be made more useful I have avoided questions of definition and ultimate objectives. This is only one of the many ways in which our science can advance, and we have the personnel and range of interests to cultivate them all.

After this paper was substantially completed the volume of papers in honor of Wilson D. Wallis entitled *Method and Perspective in Anthropology* became available. Much of what Herskovits says with regard to "Some Problems of Method in Ethnography" is relevant to points made above, particularly his emphasis on the historical approach and the comparative study of documented change as well as on the importance of repeated analyses of the same phenomena. And Ackerknecht's scholarly survey of "The Comparative Method in Anthropology" emphasizes the importance of the comparative method for cultural anthropology: "One of the great advantages of the comparative method will be that in a field where the controlled experiment is impossible it provides at least some kind of control." He sees signs of a renaissance: "In whatever form the comparative method may reappear, it will express the growing desire and need in cultural anthropology to find regularities and common denominators behind the apparent diversity and uniqueness of cultural phenomena."

Kroeber, in commenting on the papers in this volume, subscribes "whole-heartedly to Ackerknecht's position. My one criticism is that he doesn't go far enough. He sees the comparative method as something that must and will be revived. I would say that it has never gone out; it has only changed its tactic." He goes on to point out that all science ultimately seeks knowledge of process, but that this must be preceded by "description of the properties of the form and substance of the phenomena, their ordering or classification upon analysis of their structure, and the tracing of their changes or events." These are the essential points that I have tried to make with reference to cultural anthropology.

On both sides of the Atlantic there is an increasing willingness to listen to one another and a growing conviction that the varied approaches are complementary rather than competitive. We can agree, I think, with Radcliffe-Brown: "It will be only in an integrated and organized study in which historical studies and sociological studies are combined that we shall be able to reach a real understanding of the development of human society, and this we do not yet have." It seems to me that it is high time we made a start—and indeed it is well under way.

In time we may be able to simplify and further order our conceptual schemes in terms of direct observations on human behavior. Sapir, in perhaps a moment of insight, once defined culture "as a systematic series of illusions enjoyed by people." But culture, like the "ether" of the nineteenth-century physicists, plays an essential role today and will do so for a considerable time to come. The distant future is more difficult to predict—I think it was Whitehead who remarked that the last thing to be discovered in any science is what the science is really about!

PART II Explanation in Social Science

6

ON EXPLANATION

JOHN HOSPERS

WE are sometimes presented with a statement describing some observed fact, and when we ask "Why?" we are presented with another statement which is said to constitute an "explanation" of the first. What is the relation between these two statements? What is it that constitutes the second statement an "explanation" of the first? By virtue of what does it "explain"? Though everyone is constantly uttering statements which are supposed in one way or another to explain, few persons are at all clear about what it is that makes such statements explanations.

It is sometimes assumed that when we set out to explain anything we are always trying to answer the question "Why?" But it should be evident at once that this is not the case. We offer many statements as explanations although they do not answer the question "Why?"; they sometimes explain how, or when, or who, or whither; and often when we are asked to explain some statement we merely make it clearer to the listener by stating it in other words. As the word is commonly used, any kind of clarification is likely to be called an explanation; and a statement can be clarified in many different ways.

Thus explanation covers a good deal more ground than merely answering the question "Why?"; and it might be worth while to disentangle various senses of the word "explain," showing what different kinds of questions are answered by statements which are commonly called explanations. In this paper, however, I shall be concerned only with the sense of "explain" which tries to answer the question "Why?" It may develop that to answer "Why?" also involves, or is involved in, answering the question "How?" but my present object is

simply to inquire into the "Why?" I shall, moreover, restrict the field of inquiry to empirical concepts, neglecting explanations in mathematics and logic, where we would generally be said to ask for reasons rather than for explanations (although both these words are very loosely used, and overlap a good deal). My remarks will be designed not so much to add any new contribution to this issue as to analyze and correlate statements which have already been made about it. And considering the uncritical meekness with which people have accepted claims that "science has explained the universe," or, on the other hand, that "science doesn't really explain anything," the analysis of explanation has received little enough attention.

There have been a number of statements, some overlapping and others contradictory, of what the "true nature" of explanation is. (1) Perhaps the most obvious, and certainly the oldest, is that of "explanation in terms of purpose." We have explained why an event occurred when we have stated its purpose. "Why did you walk through the snow for ten miles when you could have taken the bus?" "I wanted to win a bet." "Why does that dog scratch at the door?" "He's cold and he wants to get in." In these cases, when such answers are given, we feel quite satisfied that our question has been answered and that the phenomenon in question has been explained; and it has been explained with reference to a purpose which some sentient being(s) had in attaining a certain end. This is the most primitive conception of explanation. People like to feel that there is a purposive explanation for everything: if not in terms of human purposes, then of divine ones, or mysterious forces and powers. The impulse to explain everything in terms of purpose doubtless springs in part from an attempt to extend what holds true of some events in the human realm to all events whatever: we know what conscious motivation is like from our own experience of it, hence we "feel at home" with this kind of explanation.

But if all explanation must be in terms of

From *Journal of Philosophy*, 58 (1946): 337–356. Copyright © 1946 The Journal of Philosophy. Reprinted by permission of the publisher and the author. A revised version of this essay appears in Anthony Flew (Ed.), *Essays in Conceptual Analysis* (New York: St. Martins Press, 1956). John Hospers is Professor of Philosophy, California State College, Los Angeles.

purpose, then physical science can never be said to give explanations. Surely, however animistically the nature of explanation was once conceived, this is not its meaning now. To have recourse to the whims of malignant demons to explain why the watch misbehaves is surely to desert explanation altogether. Many reasons could be adduced for this, but it is enough here to state that what we want is something that will tell us why this event happened rather than that one; and, outside contexts in which human (and perhaps also animal) agencies are operative, this can not be done by appealing simply to "purpose." (An account of the nature of purposive explanations, what renders them explanations, and their place among other explanations, will appear later in this paper.)

Another account of the nature of explanation is that (2) an event is explained when it has been shown to be an instance of some kind or class of events which is already familiar to us. For example, when a person's behavior seems strange to us, we are satisfied when it is "explained" to us as being really impelled by the same sort of motives and desires—love, greed, etc.—as occur in us, and are therefore familiar to us. "Why is he introducing the man he hates to the woman he loves?" "Because he wants them to fall in love with each other" would not generally be accepted as an explanation, for this very reason. When we observe that a balloon ascends rather than descends, unlike most objects, and it is made clear to us that air has weight and that the gas inside the balloon weighs less than an equal volume of air would weigh, we are satisfied; the phenomenon has been "explained" to us by "reducing" it to something already familiar to us in everyday experience, such as a dense object sinking in water while a hollow one floats. The event is no longer unusual, strange, or unique; it has been shown to illustrate a principle we were already acquainted with and accepted. When we want to know why gases diffuse when released into a chamber from which the air has been pumped out, the explanation offered by the kinetic theory of gases is satisfactory to us because it asserts that molecules behave *like* particles with which we are already acquainted in our everyday experience. Norman Campbell notes:

Only those who have practised experimental physics, know anything by actual experience about the laws of gases; they are not things which force themselves on our attention in common life, and

even those who are most familiar with them never think of them out of working hours. On the other hand, the behavior of moving solid bodies is familiar to every one; every one knows roughly what will happen when such bodies collide with each other or with a solid wall, though they may not know the exact dynamical laws involved in such reactions. In all our common life we are continually encountering moving bodies, and noticing their reactions; indeed, if the reader thinks about it, he will realize that whenever we do anything which affects the external world, or whenever we are passively affected by it, a moving body is somehow involved in the transaction. Movement is just the most familiar thing in the world; it is through motion that everything and anything happens. And so by tracing a relation between the unfamiliar changes which gases undergo when their temperature or volume is altered, and the extremely familiar changes which accompany the motions and mutual reactions of solid bodies, we are rendering the former more intelligible; we are explaining them.

Professor Bridgman holds that all explanation is of this kind: "I believe that examination will show that the essence of an explanation consists in reducing a situation to elements with which we are so familiar that we accept them as a matter of course, so that our curiosity rests."

One might object to this that the term "familiar" is a rather subjective one. What is familiar and every-day to us may be strange and unfamiliar to the savage; what may be familiar to you may even be unfamiliar to me. Hence some statements will be explanations for some persons and not for others. Explanation will then be a relative matter—relative to the person to whom the explaining is done. Professor Bridgman is quite willing to accept this consequence: "An explanation is not an absolute sort of thing, but what is satisfactory for one man will not be for another." But there is a more serious objection: we ask for explanations not merely of phenomena that are strange and unusual. We ask for explanations of the simplest and most familiar phenomena in the world. We can ask not only why balloons rise, but why heavier-than-air objects fall. We can ask why trees grow, why our memories fail as we get old, why January is colder than July. And the principles in terms of which the scientist claims to explain these things are principles which most of us have never heard of before. Surely the fact that light blinds you as you emerge from the darkness but not after you have been in the light for a few minutes, and the fact that you can see better in darkness when you have been in it for a while, is more familiar than its explanation in terms of the contraction and expansion of the pupil of the eye. And surely the formation of rust on iron is more familiar than the chemical combination of iron with oxygen, of which most observers of iron rust have never heard.[1]

It is sometimes asserted that (3) an event is explained when it has been classed as an instance of some general law (the degree of familiarity of this law being irrevelant). A seemingly isolated phenomenon is shown to be an instance of a general law, and thus is explained. "Why are there more suicides (in proportion to the population) in New York City than in Mudville Flats?" "There are always more suicides in large cities." But surely this is no explanation. It is true that we have learned something—in this case, that the size of the city is relevant to the frequency of suicide, rather than, say, its longitude. Moreover, by showing that the phenomenon in question is not unique, that it is only one of many occurrences in a class, or subsumed under some law, we have taken away from most questioners the curiosity which prompted them to ask for an explanation in the first place; people most frequently (though not always, as we have seen) ask for explanations of what is bizarre or strange, and when an event has been shown not to be so ("It's just like a lot of other things") they are no longer so curious. But to have removed the impulse to ask the question is surely not to have answered it. And if people were asked whether a statement such as the one above really explained the phenomenon in question, they would very probably answer "No"; they would still know nothing about the phenomenon except that it belongs to a class of similar phenomena.

I do not believe that laws can ever be explained by inclusion in more general laws; and I hold that, even if it were possible so to explain them, the explanation would not be that which science, developing the tendencies of common sense, demands. . . . To say that all gases expand when heated is not to explain why hydrogen expands when heated; it merely leads us to ask immediately why all gases expand. An explanation which leads immediately to another question of the same kind is no explanation at all (Campbell).

Let us compare the two answers given to each of the following questions:

(1) Why do the water-pipes in my basement burst in winter?

(*a*) It always happens under certain specific conditions (cold weather, a certain pressure on the pipes, etc.).

(*b*) The pipes are filled with water, which expands when it freezes, bursting the pipes.

(2) Why are there more suicides in New York City than in Mudville Flats?

(*a*) Suicides are always more prevalent in large cities.

(*b*) In large cities, conditions leading to discouragement and despair are more prevalent: loneliness, mass unemployment, poverty. . . . When people are in such situations, they more often commit suicide.

(3) Why do animals in the Arctic so often have white fur?

(*a*) Many animals exhibit protective coloration.

(*b*) Those that don't have protective coloration are more easily seen against their snowy background by animals which prey on them, with the result that they are more likely to be killed by them; the white ones live to perpetuate the species and their young, in turn, have a better chance for survival; thus, the white ones multiply in increasing numbers, while the others are gradually obliterated.

We have, in the first of the two cases in each example, a simple general statement ("explanation by generalization," which I have just described); in the second, a principle or set of principles in terms of which the phenomenon can be understood. In each case we have shown the phenomenon to be an instance of a general law which is accepted as true. (These laws are not necessarily more familiar—so long as they are accepted as true, that is sufficient. In more cases than not, they are both more familiar and more general than the phenomena to be explained. But their familiarity has nothing to do with the validity of the explanation. "If they aren't familiar they should be.") How, then, does the second kind differ from the first? In that it does not simply repeat the statement in general form. Instead of saying with regard to the broken water-pipes, "This regularly happens when it is cold, etc.," we give another general law, "Water expands when it freezes," which, when we combine it with other statements, of whose truth in this case we are already aware (e.g., that when things expand they may break whatever stands in the way of their expansion), yields us a satisfying explanation of why the pipes burst. We have not simply made a statement which generalizes on the instance adduced: we have, at last, shown *why* the phenomenon occurred. Or again: it is true (as well as familiar) that animals beget other animals like them, that animals that prey on others often kill them and keep them from propagating their species, that animals are most likely to catch the animals they can most easily see, etc. These things being true, it is understandable that so many animals in a white environment are white. In this example, many such general principles are involved; but be they many or few, every explanation involves them and is made on the basis of them.

Before discussing this view of explanation further I want to mention a closely related one: namely, the notion that (4) we are said to explain the concurrence of two phenomena (the reason for whose concurrence we do not understand) when we indicate intermediate factors which provide a connection between them. For example, we may explain the high correlation between the presence of cats in a certain region and the abundance of clover there, by showing that the cats catch the mice which would otherwise eat the bees (and other insects) that are required to pollinate the clover.

It will be seen that this—"explanation by intermediary agencies"—is really a special case of explanation in terms of general principles, just discussed. The links are fitted into the chain by general principles: in this case, that cats eat mice, that bees pollinate clover, etc. Illustrations of the other type could equally well be made to fall under this one: we could say, for example, that we are trying to explain the correlation between sub-freezing temperature and the bursting of the water-pipes, and the principle of the expansion of water on freezing supplies us with the required connection; it is the intermediate link in the chain, so to speak, just as the predatory habits of cats and mice and the fact that bees pollinate clover are general principles constituting the intermediate links in the other chain. A large proportion of explanations are of this type: they break down gross phenomena into components which are, or are instances of, general principles which serve to explain the concurrence of these phenomena.

It is sometimes said that (5) an event is explained by reference to its *cause*. Now I do not propose here to attempt an analysis of just what the causal relation is—the volumes devoted to this subject constitute a large fraction of the entire literature of philosophy—except to say that the word "cause" is used so vaguely, and often ambiguously as well, that to say that an event is explained in terms of its cause is to substitute for a term that requires analysis one that requires analysis still more. So loosely is this weasel-word used that I feel safe in saying that every explanation is in *some* sense or other a causal explanation.

For example: When someone asks, "Why did that book fall to the floor?" he may receive such diverse answers as "Somebody accidentally dropped it" and "On account of the law of gravitation." Both of these answers may be claimed to state the *cause* of the book's falling —and yet they are manifestly answers of quite a different order. The first answer would be more likely to satisfy the average inquirer than the second. What he wants to know is the particular circumstance in this case—did someone drop it in anger, did the cat playing on the table dislodge it, etc. But he may, on the other hand, know the circumstances of the book's falling— may have seen it fall—and then when he asks why it fell he is not asking for the same sort of thing at all. He is asking for some general principle, a law, not a particular event in time. (Perhaps the timeless principle enunciated in the law of gravitation will not satisfy him, on grounds that it merely classifies the event, just as "All gases expand when heated" did not satisfy the person who asked "Why does hydrogen expand when heated?" In this case he is asking for a general principle, but not one that merely generalizes on the present instance. Sometimes no other answer is possible, however —"explanation by generalization," if this can be called explanation at all, is all that can be offered; but this will be discussed below under the heading of "brute fact.") Without doing too much violence to Aristotle, we might call the first answer adduced the efficient cause of the event and the second, the general principle, the formal cause. In contemporary philosophical terminology the second would be unlikely to be called a cause at all.

Generally when we ask for the cause of an event we mean the efficient cause—though I shall not here try to describe an efficient cause (whether it is a necessary condition of the event, or a set of them, or a sufficient condition, or both, etc.) other than to say that it is a particular prior event or set of events. When we ask, "Why is the water in the lake frozen?" the answer we want is not "Because water freezes at 32° F." (a general law) but rather "Because the temperature dropped to below 32° F. during the night" (a particular prior event). In a case such as this we *presuppose* acquaintance with the general law that water freezes at 32° F. but want to know the efficient cause in this instance, just as in the case of the book we presuppose that objects do fall under certain circumstances and want to know the particular circumstances of the fall on this occasion.

To connect this now with the discussion of explanation: When the phenomenon requiring explanation is not a particular event but a general statement (law in its widest sense) referring to a class of events (Why do water-pipes burst in winter? etc.), then no particular event is needed by way of explanation—only general principles are involved. But when the phenomenon requiring explanation is a particular event, then the complete explanation consists not only of the general principle(s) but also of the particular antecedent(s) in this case. Thus, again: "Why did the water in the lake freeze?" "Water freezes at 32° F. (under standard conditions)" (general principle) *plus* "The temperature dropped to zero last night" (antecedent event), which together constitute an explanation of the phenomenon to be explained. But if we ask in general, "Why do lakes freeze in winter?" we are answered with the non-temporal principle that water freezes whenever the temperature reaches a certain low, which it generally does in winter in northern climates.

It should be evident here that explanation in terms of purpose is just one species of explanation in terms of general principles—or, in the case of a particular event, general principles plus particular antecedent events. If there is a satisfactory explanation, there is some general principle involved: "Why did you go to New York last night?" "There was an opera I wanted to see." Seeing the opera was the person's *purpose* in going; but there are general principles presupposed here, such as "People, in general, do what they want to do, unless prevented by some other force"—and it is only by virtue of such accepted general principles that wanting to do a thing is considered in any way an explanation of doing it. For example, in this instance it is presupposed that the act in question is something we *can* do if we want to; with many others this is not the case. "Why did the Allies win the war?" "Because they wanted to" would not be a sufficient explanation; after all both sides wanted to; wanting to and having the physical power to are *both* requisite, and all the wanting to in

the world will not alone explain its happening, any more than the desire of a paralytic to walk is sufficient to enable him to do so.

In connection with explanations of particular events, it should be pointed out here that the analysis just given applies to all "genetic" explanations. On the tidal hypothesis, for example, the fact that the largest planets in the solar system are in the middle is explained by the fact that when the passing star approached the sun, the tides raised on the sun were the largest at the star's point of closest approach; this tidal material, ejected from the sun by the star's gravitational attraction, condensed into the planets, leaving the largest in the middle where the amount of ejected material was the greatest. Many principles are involved here: the law of gravitation, Newton's laws of motion, etc. Some, indeed, such as the principle of moment of momentum, can not be rendered consistent with certain consequences of the hypothesis and thus serve to cast doubt upon the whole hypothesis. But *if* this is what happened several billion years ago and if our formulation of the laws involved is correct, then surely the present state of affairs (the position of the larger planets, and many other things) is explained, exactly as in the case of the lake freezing.

I shall now touch on a number of points which I hope will clarify certain points in the above account, and which I consider more important than the analysis of explanation itself.

(1) The laws alleged must be true ones, else there is no true explanation. If, in the cats-clover sequence, we had been told that cats eat *books* and that the books in turn eat the bees, we would never have accepted the explanation, inasmuch as these statements are false. *If* true, they would provide a connecting link, but since we are quite sure that cats do not eat books and that books do not eat bees, we would reject any alleged explanation depending on such proffered laws. As it is, we may not believe that mice eat bees; and if they do not, the whole explanation breaks down and we must cast about for another one. A chain is no stronger than its weakest link.

Sometimes explanations are offered in terms of intra-molecular states and other unobservable entities, where we can not observe directly even a single instance of the truth of the general statement. But again the principle is the same: *if* the statements about intra-molecular states are true, they do indeed provide the explanations we are after; and if the truth of the statement is something that can not be determined for certain, then whether this explanation is true or not can not be determined either. (I do not want to become involved here in the question of whether the only *meaning* of saying that a statement, e.g., about atoms, is true is that certain phenomena—"pointer-readings"—are observable. This would be too lengthy a digression.)

The "simplicity" of explanations has been much emphasized, often at the expense of their truth. All other things being equal, I suppose, the simplest explanation is most likely to be accepted (not psychologically the simplest, i.e., the easiest to understand, but the one involving the fewest principles). But many accepted explanations are far less simple than rejected ones. The simplest explanation of the cats-clover correlation, I suppose, would be that certain effluvia released into the atmosphere in the exhalation of the cats' breath served to pollinate automatically all the clover in the region. A true explanation is very often very complicated, and many alleged explanations turn out to be gross oversimplifications which overlook the actual complexity of events. Simple explanations could, I daresay, be devised for any occurrence whatever, in terms of principles which are dubious or false, like the one just mentioned. The explanation of many things remains unknown simply because of the complexities involved. This is true in submicroscopic phenomena as well: the atom can not be constructed on any such simple model as was accepted a century ago; if it is to explain the observed phenomena, it must be made bewilderingly complex, and there is much question of whether any model will suffice at all.

(2) Sometimes the explanatory principles are theories, and sometimes laws. (I have used the term "general principle" to cover both.) The relation between these two must be indicated.[2] It is usual in discussions of this kind to state that individual events are explained by laws, and that laws are explained by theories. But this is a misleading statement, to say the least. I may ask for the explanation of some individual event, such as the appearance of the aurora borealis on a certain night, and be answered with statements about electrical storms on the sun (sunspots) and streams of electrons flowing from the sun toward the earth's magnetic poles —most of which certainly comes under the head of theory, since it is not directly observable.

Of course it might be objected that this is actually an explanation of why the aurora borealis occurs at any given time, and not why it appears tonight, and that thus we would still be explaining the individual event (its appearance tonight) in terms of laws (aurora occurs under certain observable conditions, e.g., involving sunspots), and the laws (specifying the conditions under which the aurora occurs) in terms of theories (about streams of electrons, etc.). But might it not be the case that there was no discoverable regularity in such an occurrence (if not in the aurora example, then in others), and hence no law under which the instance could be subsumed, and we would have to invoke theory to explain the individual event, no law being discoverable? Moreover, we have seen in the first part of this paper that when individual events are explained by laws they are not explained by laws alone but by laws *plus* antecedent events (to explain the state of the solar system at some future moment we must know not only the laws describing the behavior of bodies but also the state of the solar system at the present, or some past time). Nor is it always true that laws are explained in terms of theories. Both the explanation and the phenomenon to be explained may be laws, of which instances are directly observable. The explanation of the cats-clover correlation can be entirely in terms of other laws (not mere "explanation by generalization" such as "Cats are generally more plentiful when there's clover about" but rather statements about the predatory habits of cats and mice, etc.) and never once invoke theory; that is to say, the general principles in terms of which a law can be explained may very well be other laws, into which theory does not enter at all.

Nevertheless there is a substantial difference between laws and theories as explanations. To use an example I have used often before in this paper, we may perfectly well explain the bursting of the water-pipes on the principle of the expansion of water on freezing—a law of nature. Lest the phenomenon to be explained be taken for an individual event, we may put it in a general way: not "Why did they burst just now?" but "Why do they always do so under certain specifiable conditions (when it's cold etc.)?" The explanation would be in terms of the expansion of water on freezing, a physical law referring again to something perfectly observable, with no theories involved. But suppose one goes on to ask, "Why does water expand when it freezes?" Here the explanation is not in terms of any general law of which we can directly observe instances ("Most liquids do" would not be an explanation, but simply a generalization, as we have seen, even if it were true, which it isn't). The explanation generally offered, and the only *kind* of explanation I can think of, is in terms of the crystalline structure of the water molecule. This is theory; the structure of the water molecule has not been observed; but *if* we suppose it to have such a structure, we can see how water *would* expand on freezing.

(3) Perhaps the most important matter yet discussed in this paper is the extent to which explanation can be carried, and when it must stop.

To take again the case of the pipes bursting: we can explain this in terms of the expansion of water on freezing; and when we are asked in turn why this happens, then on the ordinary macroscopic level we can say nothing—"it just is that way"—although, as I have just indicated, attempts have been made to explain this in terms of the structure of the water molecule. (Whether this is actually a true explanation, and what precisely is meant by saying that it is true, I am not concerned with here. Assuming that the explanation is satisfactory, we can go on.) This only suggests the next question: "Why is the molecule constructed in this way?" Perhaps some explanation might be suggested in terms of intra-molecular or intra-atomic forces; but when an explanation of these is demanded, it seems that we can only say, "That's just the way it is, that's all." Here, it appears, explanation comes to an end; we have reached the level of "brute fact." "This is the way things are, this is how the world is constituted, and that's all we can say about it." Most persons would probably say this before such a level of analysis had been reached; they would say it is just a brute fact that water starts to expand again below 39° F.[3]

There are many phenomena which were formerly considered "brute fact" which are no longer considered so. Why does this element have this color, this melting-point, these spectral lines? Why does it combine with this substance and not with that? etc. For many of these phenomena, of which formerly it was said "These are just (brute-fact) properties of this substance," explanations are now offered in terms chiefly of atomic structure and activity. But are not these explanations (assuming that they are satisfactory) brute fact? or if not, then the explanations of these? Must we not sooner or later come to a standstill in our process of explaining?[4]

At any given stage of scientific investigation, surely, there is a level of brute fact, in which the phenomena can not be explained in terms of anything more ultimate though they themselves may afford an explanation of other phenomena on a "higher" level. As has just been said, a level that was once thought to be ultimate may turn out not to be so—like layers of varnish that keep peeling off, revealing others below. But how can we be sure, at any given point, that we have come to the end, reached *the* ultimate brute fact and not just what is thought at any particular time to be so? The answer is, of course, that we never can be sure. If ever we *have* arrived, no further explanation is possible; but that we have arrrived is never certain.

It is sometimes said that people who keep asking Why? Why? even with regard to what we now consider brute fact, are asking meaningless questions. It might be observed, however, that if such questions had not been asked in the past, we would not have reached such "deep" levels of explanation as we now have; and the progress of science depends in large measure on the fruitfulness of explanatory hypotheses. Moreover, I suggest that the question has meaning when we have some definite conception of a more ultimate structure in terms of which the structure now considered brute fact can be explained, even if such a conception be highly tenuous and hypothetical, e.g., if we know what kind of structure *would* explain the behavior of the electrons, etc., just as the present electron-proton hypothesis explains the failure of certain elements to combine with others. Explanation is always in terms of something else, and there can be no explanation (to request one is to make a demand logically impossible of fulfillment) if there is nothing even hypothecated in terms of which to make it. But once such a hypothesis has been conceived, our answers in terms of it will make sense even though they may not be true and even though it may seem unlikely that we shall ever know whether they are.

There are many realms in which explanation, at the present stage of inquiry, comes to an end long before the molecular or sub-molecular level is reached. This is particularly true in cases dealing with biological behavior. And perhaps biological phenomena—some of them at any rate—are inherently incapable of explanation in this way; does not the controversy between vitalism and mechanism (in at least one of the many meanings of those much-abused terms) involve precisely this issue?

Nor do I want to leave the impression that all explanation must be in terms of the more minute. This is not even true in physics. As Bridgman says, speaking of the "elements" in terms of which an event or law is explained,

There is no implication that the "element" is either a smaller or a larger scale thing than the phenomenon being explained; thus we may explain the properties of a gas in terms of its constituent molecules, or perhaps some day we shall become so familiar with the idea of a non-Euclidean space that we shall *explain* (instead of describe) the gravitational attraction of a stone by the earth in terms of a space-time curvature imposed by all the rest of the matter in the universe.

The terms which we apply in trying to explain phenomena make it seem as if explanations are being given, while actually in many cases the terms are simply names for the phenomena themselves, or the class into which they fall, and nothing more. When someone asks, "Why do stones fall?" and the "explanation" is given, "All heavier-than-air objects tend to fall," it is clear at once that one is simply generalizing on an individual case—"explanation by generalization" which we have already seen to be unsatisfactory. But it is not so clear to most people that the answer "Because of the law of universal gravitation" is of exactly the same kind as the first one. The classification has been extended —the behavior of the stone is now of a kind in which all objects in the universe partake, not merely terrestrial ones—but neither statement does more than classify the present phenomenon. It has been classified but not explained. Appeals to gravitation are just ways of saying that all bodies behave in a certain ways of saying that all bodies behave in a certain manner, and this mode of behavior is entitled "gravitational attraction." We are not explaining the fall of bodies as we did the bursting of the pipes or the comparative abundance of white animals in arctic regions.

To make this quite clear let us compare it with another instance.

All plants, so far as is known, I believe, *start* upwards as regards their stems, however these may begin soon afterwards in some cases to creep. And they all equally start downwards as regards their roots, whatever direction these may subsequently

take. When we enquire as to the cause of this tendency, . . . the scientific man does not attempt here to interpose a technical term like "gravitation"; in fact, owing to the novelty of the enquiry he is not provided with such a term as yet. Had the particular question been raised a couple of centuries ago, the difficulty would probably have been smoothed away by the introduction of a well-selected expression, on the analogy of "plastic form" or "vital force." But this resource is not available, and consequently to the semi-scientific, who are greatly influenced by the appropriate introduction of a term, it often seems in such a case as if some admission were being made as to the inferior position which we occupy (John Venn).

To have given a name, however impressive it may be, is not to have given an explanation.

There seems to be one kind of case in which the brute-fact level is reached at once and bids fair to remain so: I mean the correlation of certain mental states with certain physical states. We can often explain physical phenomena in terms of other physical phenomena, as has been done constantly in this essay; but what can we do in the case of mental phenomena except note that certain of them seem to be uniquely correlated with certain physical states? *Why* do I have a certain color-sensation, which I call red, when light-waves of a certain frequency strike the retina of my eyes, and another and indescribably different sensation, which I call yellow, when rays of another frequency strike the retina? That this frequency is correlated with this unique experience, and that one with that experience, seems to be sheer brute fact, which no amount of information about physics and physiology alone could have enabled us to predict. Or, again, is it not just an ultimate brute fact that this peculiar and unique taste-sensation occurs when salt is in contact with my palate, and another when the substance is cinnamon?

But is not the salty taste of a certain food explained when we discover that one of its chief ingredients is salt? Yes, indirectly: I mean that *if* one grants the brute fact that this substance is correlated with this kind of sensation, then the occurrence of the salty taste in this dish is explained by the presence of salt in it; but that this taste is correlated with the presence of this substance, is still brute fact. (When we are ill the dish may not taste salty; but this shows only that the presence of salt is not the whole physical state; many other things enter into the picture as well; but the *whole* complex—or, some would say, the brain-event which is the end-product of a whole series of states in the brain, nerves, sense-organs, and external world—is what is, as a matter of brute fact, correlated with this particular sensation.) If we know that a physical state x is correlated with mental state x', the production or removal of that mental state can be explained indirectly in terms of the production or removal of the physical state x by means of agencies (in this case chemical) a, b, etc. Thus it is the physical state in each case that is explained, and the brute-fact character of the mind-matter correlation remains.

One further point should be made before leaving this subject. There are many cases in which the question "Why?" is asked and no answer is forthcoming. It may be that there is an explanation but we do not yet know what it is: for example, we do not as yet know why potassium thiocyanate relieves certain types of migraine, although we shall probably come to know this in the future. If, on the other hand, we are at the brute-fact level, then by definition we can no longer meaningfully ask for further explanations. Of course, as we have seen, we can not be sure at any given stage whether this level has been reached (with the possible exception, just noted, of the correlation of mental states with physical ones); it might be described as the theoretical limit of our investigations; and physical science can always keep on speculating and investigating the possibility of further explanations. But there are other cases in which the question "Why?" is asked, and the inquirer has no notion what he is really asking for. The child asks, "Why is Mummy sick?" and on being given a lengthy physical description of germs attacking certain blood-corpuscles which are necessary to the maintenance of health because they perform certain essential functions in the body, etc., the child, even if he understands the physical explanation, may still ask, "But *why* is she sick?" What is the child asking for? Perhaps he is asking for an explanation in terms of purpose (and might then be satisfied with "God willed it so" or even "Some evil spirit wanted to torture her") just as he receives an answer in terms of purpose to questions such as "Why did Daddy go to Chicago?" (I daresay that most of the first explanations a child receives are in terms of purpose, and he may assume that all others will be in those same terms.) It is notorious that uneducated persons as well as children demand explanations in such terms when none is in order. But on the other hand the child may have no idea what he is asking and may simply feel a general dissatisfaction which he voices by repeating the question "Why?" So too may the man in the street and the philosopher when they ask (respectively) "Why is life like that?" and "Why are there sense-data?"—little realizing that they have removed the very possibility of an answer by the very nature of the question —or group of words in the form of a question.

In such cases the word "why" simply becomes an "expectation-formula"; having received answers to questions beginning with "why" when these questions were meaningful and explanations could be given, they continue to use the word "why" even when they do not know what it means in this case, and really do not know what they are asking for. One need not be surprised that no answer is forthcoming to such questions. We are all too prone to terminate an exasperating series of questions beginning with "why" with a remark such as "That's just something we don't know," as if it were like the cases where something definite is being asked but we do not yet happen to know the principles which explain the phenomena we are asking about. If something in the case is not known, there must be something in the case which we could fail to know. If we are to ask a meaningful question, we must know what it is that we are asking for; only then can we recognize an answer as being one when we do find it. And if no statement, even if true, would satisfy as an answer, what does the question itself mean?

(4) Closely related to this is the contention that science actually explains nothing, but only describes. "Science doesn't tell us *why* things happen," the complaint runs, "it only tells us *how* things happen." Now I confess that the exact intention of the user of the question beginning with "why" is often not very clear—as we have just seen. In the way in which the term is commonly used, science *does* explain; once again, the bursting of the pipes, the formation of ice at the top of ponds rather than at the bottom, and many other phenomena, are explained by reference to the principle of the expansion of water on freezing. The phenomenon is now understandable to us, we see why it occurs as it does, and we say it has been explained. (If someone says we have *not* explained why the pipes burst, then what does he mean by "why"? What sort of thing is it that he is asking? What *would* answer his question? Let him state in other terms what it is that he wants to know.)

"But is not explanation after all merely description?" I have no objection to saying that when we explain something we actually describe, but this does not preclude the fact that we *are* explaining. When the question is asked why pressing the button turns on the light, we explain the phenomenon by describing just what (we believe) goes on—currents, closed and open circuits, conduction of electricity, dynamos in the power plant, etc. But have we not in so doing explained the phenomenon? We have explained *by* describing, if you will—by stating the principles which describe these states-of-affairs; but certainly we have explained. To deny this would be like saying that because an object is red it can not also be colored.

(5) In any given case the explanation that will satisfy us depends on our intent in asking the question. We may be interested in only one aspect of a phenomenon, and yet, roughly speaking, say that we have found "the explanation" whereas others, looking for something else, but asking the same question, may find "the explanation" to be quite different. Each of them is looking for some item in the total explanatory scheme, which in the case of human affairs is often bewilderingly complex. Why did the man steal the money out of that safe? "He picked the lock," says the detective; "He knew that the Madame was out," says the maid; "We needed the money," states his wife; "Look at his background," says the sociologist, "and you'll discover why." These explanations do not exclude each other, but rather complete and supplement each other. In these cases we should speak not of *the* true explanation, but of *a* true explanation; or, more precisely still, a part or aspect of the complete explanation.

In this connection it is in point once again to allude to explanation in terms of purpose. What can be explained in terms of purpose can also be explained—in a different dimension, so to speak—on other levels. Whether the explanation satisfies depends on what the inquirer was asking for. "Why did he go downtown?" "Well, in response to impulses from certain centers in his brain, some muscles in his arms and legs started moving and. . . ." "No, that's not what I mean. I mean, why did he go? what purpose did he have in view?" "Oh—he wanted to buy a new suit." Contrast this with the following: "Why did he die?" "Well, a bullet entered his lung, puncturing some blood vessels, and the blood filled his lung so that he couldn't breathe any more, and. . . ." "No, that's not what I

mean. I mean *why* did he die?" But here we can give no answer in terms of conscious purpose. (We could answer in terms of purpose in *another* sense, e.g., what purpose did it serve? How was the world benefited by his death?) The inquirer here is assuming that just as the conscious purpose of some individual resulted in that individual's going downtown, so also the conscious will of some superhuman individual, presumably God, resulted in the death by shooting of the person in the second example. But unless we introduce *ad hoc* such an agency into the scene, the question in the second case is not in order (of the philosophical difficulties entailed by such an introduction I shall here say nothing), but merely derives its appearance of reasonableness from an analogy with cases like the former. Explanation in terms of purpose works only where there *is* a conscious agent purposing to do this or that; purposive explanations are out of order in cases where inanimate objects (and all others incapable of sensation and volition) alone enter into the picture, i.e., where there is nobody to have the purpose.

(6) Scientific explanation has been viewed with fear or abhorrence in some circles because it was believed that explaining meant "explaining away." The precise meaning of this latter term I have never been able to discover. Surely explanation deprives us of no facts we had before. To "explain color" in terms of light-waves is not, of course (as should have been obvious), to take away the fact of color-sensations. "Thinking is nothing but the occurrence of certain neural impulses" should be changed into *"When* thinking takes place (and it is just as incontrovertible a fact as the neurons are), there are neural impulses." To "explain away" someone's politically reactionary tendencies by saying "He's old, and people get over-conservative when they get old" does not for a moment impugn whatever truth the person's opinions may have. The same reasoning could undermine his opponent's assertions: "You needn't pay any attention to that young upstart, they're all hot communists when they're young." Reference to biography may explain why a person held a certain belief at a certain time, but the truth or falsity of the belief is utterly unaffected by this and is tested on different grounds entirely. The idea that reference to a person's mental or physical condition could "explain away" the truth of any belief is one of the most flagrant blunders of the materialistically-inclined laity of our day.

In this paper I have tried (1) to analyze the nature of explanation, particularly in the natural sciences, and (2) to clarify several related questions, such as the ultimacy of explanations, laws and theories as explanations, and the relation of explanation to description. There are many other related topics, such as that of *ad hoc* explanations and the predictive value of explanations, which would require far too lengthy a treatment for a single essay, and which, moreover, are much more usual problems for discussion in current philosophy, having been amply discussed in a number of textbooks and articles in periodicals.

NOTES

1. We must beware, however, of a misuse of this argument. The freezing of the water-pipes in my basement in winter may be more familiar to me than the principle that water expands when it freezes, but once we have learned that water does expand when it freezes (unfamiliar though that fact may have been), the principle employed as explanation is indeed more familiar than the phenomenon we wanted explained: namely, that when things expand they "have to go some place" and in doing so can be expected to break whatever they are enclosed in. This is surely one of the most familiar facts of experience. Thus in one sense, at least, the explanation is really more familiar than the thing explained—the general phenomenon (things bursting other things when pressure is exerted) is more familiar, but not the fact that this class of phenomena (the expansion of water on freezing) is an instance of it. It is probable that many explanations are actually in terms of something more familiar although at first they may not seem to be so. On the other hand, many do not seem to be so in any sense. And, I am tempted to ask, what does it matter? Does the familiarity of a principle to some person or group really affect its value as an explanation? Many phenomena which are more familiar than others are not explanations of them; and many which are less familiar, are.

2. I am using the word "theory" as Campbell uses it, to denote statements involving unobservables, such as atoms and electrons. Generalizations involving only observables, such as that all crows are black and that bees pollinate clover and that ice mets at 32° F., are laws and not theories, even if some generalizations of this kind may be doubtful or even false—in this case they are false laws or dubious or alleged laws. It would be confusing to apply to these not-definitely-accepted laws the name "theories," and so confuse them with statements incapable of direct observation. Thus the statement that the hydrogen atom has one electron is a theory, but the statement that hydrogen burns is a law.

3. There is a rather elementary but widely pervasive confusion on this point. It is said that unless an explanation has been given all the way down to the level of brute fact, no explanation has really been given for the phenomenon at all; e.g., unless we know why water expands on freezing, why the water-molecule has a crystalline structure, etc., we do not really know why our pipes burst. But surely this is not the case. Whether we know why water expands on freezing or not, we do know that it does so, and that it is because of its doing so that the pipes burst in cold weather. When we have asked why the pipes burst, the principle of expansion of water does give an explanation. When we ask why water expands on freezing, we are asking *another* question. The first *has* been answered, whether we can answer the second or not.

4. I am tempted to remark here that there has been much unjust criticism of the Humian doctrine of causation because the process of analysis is not carried far enough. Thus, in cases of death by arsenic poisoning, he would be no more content than would a physician to say that there was simply a constant conjunction and no connection (between arsenic and death); he would analyze it down further, to the action of this substance on the stomach, etc. To deny this is to reduce Hume's view of causation to an absurdity. But ultimately, having performed such a detailed analysis, do we not come to a series of brute-fact "constant conjunctions"? (One might say: Yes, if you like, there are connections, but those connections consist of a lot of constant conjunctions.) This, however, is too large a topic for me to explore any further here.

7

THE "NATURAL SCIENCE IDEAL" IN THE

SOCIAL SCIENCES

LEWIS WHITE BECK

THE ORIGIN OF THE "NATURAL SCIENCE IDEAL"

IMAGINE a man who builds a house like the Joneses, at considerable inconvenience to himself because actually he needs something quite different. As soon as he gets the foundations laid, the Joneses begin tearing down parts of their house, adding new wings, and overhauling its foundations. Our poor social climber has committed himself; he has to continue to build according to his plans whether he likes them or not. To comfort himself, he says he has the kind of house the Joneses have and ignores the fact that they are doing a big job of renovating.

This little fable of keeping up with the Joneses fits the relations existing until a short time ago between the social and the natural sciences. The climbers, the social scientists, have tried to imitate the Joneses, the natural scientists. Now the social sciences have an immense house much of which is not very useful; it lacks many of the modern conveniences; but it seems to be scientific, just the same, and that often seems to be enough. But the social scientist might be far happier in his house, or he might be more successful in renovating it to meet modern needs, if he gave up pursuing the past glory of the great edifice of nineteenth-century physics.

When splitting off from philosophy in order to become scientific, the social studies took a bad moment to imitate the natural sciences. They did so just before the natural sciences themselves began to undergo major changes. The result is that many social scientists pride themselves on being natural scientists or regret that they cannot be, whereas the science they emulate or would like to emulate became obsolescent fifty years ago.

From *Scientific Monthly* 68 (1949): 386–394. Copyright © 1949 American Association for the Advancement of Science. Reprinted by permission of the publisher and the author. Lewis W. Beck is Professor of Philosophy, University of Rochester.

In imitating the natural sciences, the social sciences attempted to follow both the methods and the metaphysics of the former. The social studies tried to attend only to observable and measurable entities and to connect these by simple causal or functional laws. If the social scientists thought that they were like the natural scientists in studying "reality," they became mechanists or materialists. If they feared equating their verified hypotheses with "reality," as many natural scientists did, they became positivists. In either case they took over ready-made philosophies of the nature of scientific objects. But there was no unanimity on the philosophical foundations current among the natural scientists, and the "unity of the natural sciences," by virtue of which they might have served as an unequivocal model, was an illusion even before the death of Comte.

The social sciences, therefore, neither emerged from, nor could they later merge into, a homogeneous body of natural science doctrine. The natural science ideal, which many social scientists wished to pursue but which was vehemently rejected by others, was much more ambiguous than it appeared to be in the work of Comte and Spencer. By the time of Dilthey, with his emphasis on the function of sympathetic imagination in social studies, the opposition of the natural and the social sciences was predicated upon an almost complete misunderstanding of the methodological foundations and metaphysical implications of the natural sciences. It would have been much more to the point to have compared the status of the new social sciences with that reached by physics in the time of Galileo than to compare these nascent sciences with a physics already showing signs of passing through the change of life. The contrasts between explanation and description, between nomothetic and ideographic procedures, and between the ideals of a *beschreibende* and a *verstehende* psychology were not so much contrasts between the natural science ideal and the ideals perhaps more germane to the social studies, as they were signs of problems which every science, whether it be natural or social, must face in the early stages of its development.

It is consequently beside the point to contrast the natural and the social sciences in the language used in the early part of this century. Neither the natural nor the social sciences were homogeneous bodies of doctrine in simple conflict with each other. No clear-cut decision could have been intelligently made between the alternative of following or rejecting the natural science ideal. There were analogous conflicts within both bodies of knowledge between opposing strategies. In each case these conflicts have been resolved in analogous ways during the present century. There is now a continuity of method and philosophy in the two branches of science that could not have been dreamed of even by the most naturalistic of social scientists of the time of Spencer, because this continuity is a consequence of a *rapprochment* in which both sciences have actively participated. We shall see this in detail throughout this essay; at the moment let it suffice to mention the vocabularies of the two. It would not be possible, upon looking into the index of a scientific book, to tell whether it was a book on natural or social science if it contained only the following entries: constitution, dimension, experiment, field, migration, population, prediction, probability, space, statistics, vector. And the list of common terms is growing year by year.

It would be going too far to say that there is no difference between the two groups of sciences, but we should not overemphasize their differences, as was frequently done early in the century, or underestimate them, as has been fashionable since then. It is sound scientific procedure to substitute differences of degree for differences in kind whenever apparent differences in kind can be interpreted as consequences of variation of some common factor. The common variable that I believe will account for both the unmistakable differences and the current *rapprochements* between the natural and the social sciences is "complexity of subject matter." It is my belief that the major differences between them are due to the greater complexity of the subject matter of the social sciences, and that differences of method and interpretation of results are due primarily to awareness of this difference.

If this is correct, we should be able to test it empirically, by seeing whether the social sciences, when they deal with simple subject matters, are able to approach the natural science methods, and whether the natural sciences, when they deal with complex subject matters, appropriate social science methods. Let us, then, turn to an examination of their respective subject matters in order to answer the question: Will differences in complexity account for differences in their observational, experimental, and conceptual techniques?

SUBJECT MATTER OF NATURAL AND SOCIAL SCIENCES

When we think of the social sciences as only the "poor relations" of the natural sciences, we forget that an insight into the order of society was prior to that into nature. Every primitive people sees nature by an analogy with its social organization. Science began when laws, like those given by governments and tribunals, were projected into nature.

The great Greek philosophers approached nature with the anticipation that it would conform to simple principles, some aspects of their society providing them a model for the interpretation of nature. Anaximander (*ca.* 550 B.C.), in an epoch-making analogy, held that changes in nature are regulated by *justice,* anticipating the function later ascribed to *laws.* Henceforth nature was to be seen as a cosmos.

But in searching for regularity and simplicity and lawfulness, the philosophers and early scientists found that they had to work with abstractions from observations and not with complex observations themselves. From the time of Galileo, at the latest, we feel that the "right abstractions" were made, because he chose to report those aspects of his observations which could be related to each other by simple mathematical laws.

Since Galileo, the subject matter of the natural sciences has been relatively simple and repetitive series of simple events. Such series are repetitive because they can be isolated from many other events and understood without reference to them. The natural sciences deal with isolated systems, because the variables they choose to observe are controllable by means of varying other chosen variables. Solely for this reason are simple experiments possible. Only a small number of variables have to be known for us to give functional laws relating one to another.

Certainly every event in nature is related to an untold number of others, perhaps even to everything else in nature. But by abstraction and material isolation, we are able to reduce the effects of most of the others to negligible quantities, and to attend only to the functional relations of certain chosen events. In the natural sciences, lack of repetitiveness in a series of events, as this occurs when an experiment "turns out wrong," is always taken as evidence that the systems were not isolated, and we thereupon carry through a process of successive approximations toward complete isolation.

Nature not only has serial orders which can be studied in relative isolation; the things of nature also come in "vertical" arrangements, or wholes with contemporaneous parts. Field concepts, rather than merely serial concepts, apply to this aspect of nature. But because we can isolate systems, we can determine the boundaries of these fields, and eliminate the factors which would make our study of a given whole unmanageably complex. By moving the "isolation partitions," we can determine experimentally the effects of parts on wholes and wholes on parts, even though we never deal with an entity which is not a part of some whole.

The subject matter of the social sciences, on the other hand, consists of highly complex constellations of complex events in systems that are only poorly isolated. Instead of indistinguishable atoms, as the chemist considers his subject matter, the social scientist must deal with societies of individuals of almost infinite internal complexity and variability. No one has yet made the fortunate discovery comparable to that of Galileo in physics: though we know that science cannot deal with an unlimited number of variables, no social scientist has yet shown us precisely which ones to choose to interrelate and which ones may be safely neglected.

When we try to isolate systems in the social sciences, we therefore do not know what to include in them and what to try to eliminate. We cannot move our partition boundaries at will, because the contexts within which we find human beings are not variable to such an extent that we can try out many different wholes for a single part. We cannot isolate a child from all social environments to see where the partition between eliminable and noneliminable environmental factors should be drawn. Until we do so, however, we have no generally acceptable rule by which we can decide what

factors to include in our descriptions of the relevant environment or social field. We have parts always within wholes; and, though the social sciences have advanced on the basis of this recognition, which has often in the past not been given sufficient weight, it is hard to specify the relevant part-whole relation because it *always* obtains.

Let us not overlook the fact that these differences are differences of degree, and that as the social sciences approach the stage where they may be able to decide which few variables may be most profitably observed, the natural sciences are undergoing developments of techniques for taking more and more variables into account. It is now recognized that the high regularities of the physical sciences are only statistically simple; as the physical scientist gets closer to the individual object, as it were, the complexities that had been neglected before reappear. Instead of attending only to serial collocations of simple events, the physicist is now finding it necessary, in spite of all his efforts, to deal with field concepts and probabilities as ineluctable parts of his conceptual system. We should not forget that "statistics" is originally a concept and technique of social science, and its use in physical science signifies an often overlooked appropriation of social science methodology.

OBSERVATIONAL TECHNIQUE IN NATURAL AND SOCIAL SCIENCES

Observation in the natural sciences differs widely from that of everyday life. Most observations in natural science are instrumental results, usually observations of pointer readings. The major part of natural science work is not the taking of observations, but deciding what to observe and constructing instruments to make the observation. The observations of the natural scientist, therefore, are never the raw data or brute facts of common sense; they come to him already conceptually transformed and instrumentally abstracted from irrelevancies. They are what Loewenberg has aptly called "postanalytical data." In getting these postanalytical data, the scientific instrument reduces the subjective contribution of the observer almost to zero and "narrows the field of vision" to a specific observable event uniquely correlated with some unobservable we are interested in measuring.

Until about a century ago, observations in the social sciences hardly differed at all from those of everyday life. The student of social phenomena observed the phenomena of society as a physician would observe a patient if he had no thermometer or laboratory reports. The data of the social studies were "preanalytical." Where the contribution from the object ended and that from the observer began, no one could tell. Because there was no standardized instrument to narrow the field of vision to specific and relevant phenomena, the facts of social science might vary from common-sense observations to the narrow observations of a man with an *idée fixe*. The facts of the social studies were about as objective as journalistic observation, and no science could be based on such unstable and disputable facts.

As the social studies became scientific, they did so in part by the use of instruments. Usually these were not "brass instruments," but conceptual devices that served comparable purposes—reducing the subjective contribution to observations, and abstracting the desired observable from irrelevant data normally given along with it. But these conceptual devices served the same purpose as physical instruments: they gave an indisputable postanalytical datum which seemed to be uniquely correlated with some vague preanalytic observation or with some wholly unobservable entity in which the scientist was interested.

Consider an intelligence test, perhaps the most nearly perfect of all social science instruments. For a quality not directly observable but the object of many common-sense judgments, the test substitutes a postanalytical datum, a ratio between two observed quantities, namely, age and a set of marks on a paper. The set of marks and this ratio are obtained by standardized and conventional procedures. "Intelligence" is not only measured by this instrument; it is operationally defined by the methods used to measure it. Until the test is devised, "intelligence" is not a part of scientific vocabulary at all.

Even with this instrument, the results still differ widely in scientific standing from those obtained with, say, a galvanometer. The galvanometer substitutes a postanalytical datum, a number, for a preanalytical datum, the shock we all feel when we hold a wire under some conditions. The galvanometer standardizes the conditions, eliminates subjective differences between observers, disregards irrelevancies such

as the "appearance" of the circuit, and gives us a "hard" and indisputable datum. With a galvanometer, we can forget all about the original shock we felt. But with an intelligence test, we still think that it is measuring something that we already knew about, and if its results conflict too widely with those of our common sense, we decide the instrument must be changed. The social scientist does not trust his instruments as much as the natural scientist trusts his. The social scientist rightly reserves some insight against the reduction that his instrument would effect. However much the instruments of social science localize and control the subjective contribution to observations, the design, choice, and evaluation of instruments still depend upon the same kind of insight that social philosophers have always possessed or claimed; otherwise the results of instrumental observation may be very neat and elegant, but they have no noticeable relevance to the prescientific problems which led to the development of these, rather than other, instruments.

Hence the social scientist, equipped with the finest batteries of tests, is still in the position of the legendary people who wished to weigh a pig very accurately. They planed the board to which the pig was to be tied until it was of identical thickness, measured in "milli-micro-mulahs," throughout its length; they used as counterweights stones whose sphericity had been established within limits of one "milli-micro-mullah"; they carefully balanced the pig and board against the stones—then they asked the first stranger who came along to estimate the weight of the stones.

Because the operational definitions of the objects of natural science are applied to terms of no great emotional significance, and are definitions of which there are no counterparts in everyday language, we tend to forget that the way in which the natural scientist has obtained them is logically not unlike that of the social scientist or the legendary pig-weighers. The natural scientist's objects themselves do not determine what aspects shall be observed. The instruments he uses are extensions or projections of the questions he asks. With other questions, there would be other instruments and other data. The choice of his instruments is not ultimately determined by the object, but by the kind of answers he wants. In this respect, he is exactly like the social scientist.

But here, again, the natural scientist knows better what he is looking for. As he is interested in correlating his data in simple functional laws, he is interested only in an instrument whose reading will be a variable in an equation by which he can predict what the reading on another instrument will be. He uses only those types of instruments which will give him such results; even further, he uses only those *specific* instruments which will give him those results, and sends the others to the shop. The social scientist, however, is lucky if he possesses even a single instrument for getting data. Outside a few fields, such as that of factor analysis in psychometrics, he must correlate his instrumental results with his vague common-sense preanalytical observations; he therefore has little or no check on the accuracy of his instruments. In consequence, although the introduction of instruments into the armory of social sciences has given intersubjectively valid data which the social scientist did not formerly have, it has not permitted him to state categorically what is the conceptual significance of his results. He must still "estimate the weight of the stones."

Hence observation in both the natural and the social sciences necessarily involves a subjective element of choice of observable variables. But, whereas in the natural sciences this choice is constantly modifiable by reference to other chosen observations, in the social sciences the choice is usually corrigible only by reference to the "enlightened common sense" of the observer, which tells one social scientist (but unfortunately often him alone) what weight is to be attached to the results, which observations are worth getting, and which ones are not. We can see the reason for this in the differences in complexity of the sciences: the instrumental "sieving" of the facts of nature is very precise and fine-grained, whereas the facts of society are large-grained and recalcitrant to narrow abstractive procedures, whether instrumental or conceptual.

EXPERIMENTAL TECHNIQUES IN THE NATURAL AND SOCIAL SCIENCES

Often the contrast between the natural and the social sciences is as succinctly drawn as that between experimental and observational sciences. But there are nonexperimental natural sciences, and there are experiments in the social sciences. This contrast, therefore, is not perfect; but it throws light on another conse-

quence of the different complexity of the two kinds of science.

The natural sciences, as we have said, can establish physically isolated systems in which only a small number of variables play a significant role; therefore, an experimental determination of their correlation is possible. The social sciences cannot physically or temporally isolate their subjects. Though experiments may be performed under conditions of imperfect isolation, neither in physics nor in sociology would we know how much of the object we were experimenting with. The physicist can meet this objection by moving his partition boundaries; the sociologist cannot. An experiment on children puts the boundary, let us say, at 9:00 A.M. in a classroom; but the previous history of the child, the home conditions, the hereditary conditions, and so on are uncontrolled variables from which the subjects of the experiment are by no means isolated. The social scientist, therefore, has to perform the same experiment over and over again with the idea that the uncontrolled variables will be randomly distributed in the series and thus cancel each other out. Hence in the experiments of social science there is a large inductive element lacking in the interpretation of good experiments in the natural sciences.

In recent years the social scientists, especially Lewin, have developed techniques for deriving results from only one or a very small number of experimental situations. This is possible when there are a large number of variables within the "field," so that some interconnection between them can be found and little or no recourse has to be made to relatively unknown variables outside the field. Work of this kind, in which the conceptual apparatus is adequate to the complexity of the subject matter, is one of the most encouraging signs of a further affiliation between the natural and the social science techniques. In contrast, when the external trappings of a natural science experiment are imitated, so that only a few highly abstract data are obtained, the lack of isolation of the variables being measured really prevents the experiment from being comparable to those of the natural sciences.

There is another difference between the experiments of the two branches of science which is dependent upon differences in their complexity. Isolation from the operator is difficult to achieve in the social sciences; the adventitious circumstances of the experimental setup, the isolation partitions themselves, function as significant causal variables. From the experimental results we can extrapolate to "normal situations" only with a wide margin of error, since these variables may be very important in the experiment and wholly absent in the situation we wish to make predictions about.

In experiments in natural sciences, the experimental situation is comparable to the normal, or at least the effects of the experimental situation can usually be estimated and conceptually eliminated. Certainly putting a new meter into a functioning circuit affects the circuit as a whole, but this effect can be measured in other experiments on the meter itself and we can eliminate the interference.

As the physical sciences come to deal more and more with the "individual physical object" —e.g., a single particle—it is found that the experimental conditions may play a more disturbing role which cannot be eliminated. The Heisenberg principle of uncertainty is illustrative of this comparatively unusual situation in the natural sciences, but one very common in the social. The study of individual members of a population of electrons may suffer from many of the same disabilities as the study of human individuals in society. As physics turns its attention to the complexities of the individual case, and sociology finds itself able to deal with large numbers of cases, their operational conditions and results become more nearly comparable.

Each science begins with "middle-sized" facts, those which are within range of convenient observation. The middle-sized facts of physics have a specious simplicity because individual differences have been statistically canceled out; if physics, like the human sciences, had begun with the individual case, it is likely that it would have made no more rapid progress than sociology. The middle-sized fact of sociology is the small community, and this is more complex and variable than the individual particle in physics. As sociology approaches statistically evened-out states of affairs, it may approach the simplicity of classical physics, which dealt only with its evened-out, middle-sized facts.

THEORETICAL STRUCTURE OF THE NATURAL AND SOCIAL SCIENCES

The differences between the theoretical structures of the natural and the social sciences are even more obviously contingent upon differences of complexity in their subject matter. We shall see this in two respects: the parsimony of the two systems, and the modes of explanation in the two systems.

First, a word about the theoretical structure of any science. In scientific research there are three types of hypotheses functioning. First, there is the *substantive* hypothesis, the hypothesis being tested. Second, there is an *operational* hypothesis, stating that if such and such things are done, such and such observable results should be attained, provided the substantive hypothesis is true. The operational hypothesis is always formulated as a basis for experiment or observation, and it is chosen in the light of the substantive hypothesis we wish to test. Finally, there are *collateral* hypotheses, which are not being tested at the moment, but which provide the route by which the mind moves from the substantive to the choice of the operational hypothesis.

To illustrate these hypotheses, let us take an exceedingly simple example. We have the substantive hypothesis "Salt is soluble in water." We test it by performing an experiment based on an operational hypothesis: "If I put the crystals from this bottle into water, they will disappear." How do we move from the former to the latter hypothesis, by which it is to be tested? We do so by means of certain collateral hypotheses, viz., "These crystals are salt," "This liquid is water."

A given hypothesis is not inherently substantive while another is always collateral. We may subject any one of them to test. In our previous example, for instance, we could test the hypothesis "These crystals are salt," using the other hypothesis, "Salt is soluble in water," as collateral.

When an observational result differs from the prediction from a set of hypotheses, it is always possible to choose whether we shall consider (*a*) the operational hypothesis to have failed (experimental error); (*b*) the substantive hypothesis, the one we intended to test, to be wrong; or (*c*) some collateral hypothesis, by virtue of which we choose this experiment, to be in error (systematic error).

If we decide on the first alternative, we are in effect "testing a fact by a theory." This is sometimes necessary in even the best-organized sciences in order to avoid renegade instances and to give credit to the obvious fact that not all observations are equally trustworthy. But science becomes dogmatic if this procedure is always followed, because then there can be no occasion to modify a theory once adopted. We have already seen the difficulty of eliminating experimental error in the social sciences, and consequently in them frequent recourse is had to this expedient; if the result is not as predicted, we can always say that there were disturbing and uncontrolled factors, or the observer was inaccurate, or the like.

Assuming that the experiment has been done well, we then have a choice as to which of the other hypotheses is to be modified or rejected. In the natural sciences this choice can be made by performing still other experiments involving different collateral hypotheses (in our example, we could use crystals from another bottle), or by undertaking other experiments in which the collateral hypothesis is tested without reference to the hypothesis in which we were originally interested. (In our example, we could undertake a chemical analysis of the crystals in the bottle to see if they are sodium chloride.) The result of this multiplicity of approach is that in the natural sciences there need be no untestable hypotheses, and every well-performed experiment is crucial for *some* hypothesis in the body of the science.

Because of the complexity of each hypothesis in the social sciences, testing seriatim is rarely possible. For instance, we wish to determine the existence or nonexistence of racial differences in intelligence. We give a test to a group of children of different races. Their marks differ significantly. Does that prove the hypothesis that there are significant differences? Not unless we assume the collateral hypothesis, namely, that the test is independent of cultural differences. Can we test that experimentally? Only by devising a test in which the different cultural groups make approximately the same marks. But usually we cannot independently control the racial and cultural components; therefore, we do not know which hypothesis—a hypothesis about our particular intelligence test, or a hypothesis about the intelligence of different races —must be rejected.

Because some assumptions are untested in our experiment, there will be disagreement about them. The result is that we have "schools" of psychology and sociology (e.g., "racial theories" and "cultural theories") that are distinguished by disagreement about collateral hypotheses which function as "presuppositions." Crucial experiments which might resolve controversies be-

tween schools are thus almost unknown in the social sciences. The route by which we move from a substantive hypothesis to an observation or experiment is so circuitous, and involves so many assumptions, that experiments can usually be cited equally well by both sides in a controversy.

The hypotheses of the natural sciences are so simple that they can be tested seriatim; those of the social sciences are so complex and interpenetrating that we have to take them in families. Nevertheless, here again the difference is one of degree, and recent science is narrowing the distance between the two theoretical structures. The natural scientist now realizes that no hypothesis can be tested without assuming others, and ultimately a circle in testing is completed. There now exist in physics several alternative families of hypotheses in which the circle has been completed. All the observations of one are translatable into results of the other, though the two sets are not logically equivalent, and future observations *may* lead to decision between them. At present, the choice must be made in terms of their relative parsimony. Yet the estimation of the degree of parsimony involves aesthetic, procedural, and subjective considerations of elegance, ease of inference, and the like. The philosophy of science during this century has largely emphasized subjective elements in even the most objective sciences, and we find a prominent physicist speaking of science as "nature refracted through human nature." If the subject matter of physics were as complex as that of the social sciences, this human refractivity and selectivity would be more obvious than it is. If the subject matter of physics permitted the same variety of abstractions to be parsimoniously organized, it is likely that the conceptual structure of the natural sciences might appear as arbitrary as that of sociology or political science.

Finally, we come to the general strategy of explanation in the two branches of science. I do not refer to the age-old problem of mechanical *vs.* teleological explanation, for this metaphysical controversy appears in both types of science. I refer rather to the logic of explanation. In the natural sciences, the chief mode of explanation is description of the more pervasive and abstract features of the situation, whereby prima-facie different states of affairs are described in the same terms. For instance, a freely falling body and the moon are special cases falling under Newton's laws. Explanation in the natural sciences is therefore analytic or reductive, through discovery of common and simple conditions of diverse effects whose prima-facie description would involve a very large vocabulary. Hence a phenomenon in chemistry is explained when it is described in the simpler terms of physics; the motions of the planets and of bodies rolling down an inclined plane are explained when a common set of variables is discovered in the description of each phenomenon.

Certainly this relation between explanation and description is met with also in the social sciences. We would, for instance, describe war and migration in quite diverse terms; but we might explain them in terms of a condition not obvious in either but underlying both, e.g., "population pressure." We shall, in the following section, deal with the limits of this type of explanation as one of the unsolved problems in the logic of the social sciences. Still, it must be admitted that at least at present the common mode of explanation in the social sciences is not reductive and analytic, but synthetic. That is, we predict some event in terms of psychology alone; but for more complex events we have to add to the psychological causes sufficient factors to get to the effect we actually find. Thus we say that we must attend not only to the psychological conditions, but draw in also the sociological, the economic, and the like. What would be called explanation in the natural sciences is all too often seen as "oversimplification" in the social sciences.

The extent to which reductive techniques should be universally employed, especially in psychology in its relation to physiology, is one of the crucial problems in the philosophy of social science. Just as physiological description is translated into physiological explanation, it is often held that the logically simpler is everywhere the explanation of the more complex, and psychology must be "reduced" to physiology. If this is the case, then of course there is no autonomous social science; it is simply a division of labor to be tolerated only until the natural sciences are able to effect a reduction. Such reducibility, if it exists, strengthens the thesis that the difference between the two branches of science lies in their differing complexity. The argument of the reductionist is that in the future the natural sciences will become better able to deal with states of affairs of high complexity, and the social sciences will have succeeded in conceptually diminishing the complexity of societal facts, so that the transition can be made. At present it cannot be done, perhaps because of the great disparity in degrees of complexity. Whether it can and should be done is one of the unsolved problems to which we now turn.

SOME UNRESOLVED QUESTIONS OF SOCIAL SCIENCE STRATEGY

There are two problems we have lightly touched on, but which deserve more than passing notice even in a brief discussion. The first is strictly metaphyiscal: Are there any indigenous and irreducible categories of societal nature (e.g., culture, personality) that will successfully resist all attempts at reduction? Is the *only* difference between societal and natural reality a difference in complexity?

I have called this question metaphysical rather than scientific, for, whatever answer we give to it, the effect on scientific procedure will be the same. Different answers to this question will affect only the philosophical evaluation of the findings and procedures of the social sciences. Admitting irreducible categories would not in the least exempt the social scientist from reducing all that he can in order to increase the likelihood that the remaining ones *are* irreducible and not simply nonreduced. He would still do everything in his power to diminish the scope and importance of the not-yet-reduced concepts. Following the principle of parsimony, he would and should try to account for as much as possible by means of reductive explanation.

Analogous questions are met with in the natural sciences. The world of nature is not prima facie homogeneous, but has manifold discontinuities, levels of organization, and emergent properties. Acceptance of these with "natural piety" would have arrested the development of science. Yet the natural scientist does not have to explain them away in order to be scientific; he has only to attempt to explain them by showing the conditions under which they occur. Inasmuch as the necessary, but not the sufficient, conditions of life have been found in chemical studies, there still remains a task for the biologist—the description of his own phenomena, and the interrelation of them under unreduced biological categories. There can thus be purely biological explanation if he is successful in elaborating a general system of biological categories.

Similarly, in the social sciences it may be argued that, though it is important to know the natural conditions of societal phenomena, the social sciences have an indigenous subject matter, their own categories for its elaboration (e.g., "meaning" or "value"), and their own techniques for dealing with them (e.g., "understanding"). Much can be said for this point of view so long as it is not allowed to arrest the reductive procedures by which societal phenomena can be related to those of non-human nature. We have to deal here with two basic principles of method.

In the logic of science there is a principle as important as that of parsimony: it is that of sufficient reason. The former directs us to look for simplest causes, the latter cautions us not to simplify so far that the explanation is inadequate to the facts to be explained. Opposition to the hegemony of reductionism, insisting on the autonomy of social science categories, emphasizes the importance of the maxim that the adduced reasons shall be sufficient, rather than that they shall be parsimonious. Parsimony is not itself a simple criterion of a good methodology; we cannot simply count the factors of explanation and say that the theory containing the smallest number is the best. The ideal of parsimony cannot be expressed without the proviso that the conditions for which it is a norm shall themselves be adequate. But if simplicity is difficult to define adequately, how far from simple it is to define adequacy!

Whether an explanatory system is adequate depends in the final analysis on what we want of an explanation. No one holds a brief for an "autonomous chemistry" and for the "indigenous and irreducible facts of chemistry" and thus fights physicalistic reduction. But for practical, even if not for metaphysical, reasons, a comparable reduction of social science concepts to those of natural science may be quite legitimately resisted. Even if we overlook the possibility of metaphysical discontinuities between nature and man, the social sciences, if they are to be of use either practically or for the sake of an insight into social problems, are inextricably tied to enlightened common sense with its terminology. Operational simplification of sociological terms may be oversimplification in the sense that the problems as solved in the reduced vocabulary of natural science are not practically or intuitively equivalent or germane to the problems that originally led to the undertaking of the study. It may be that we ask for the bread of social insight and are given stones of natural science. It may be that an explanation of societal events in natural terms will have to be translated back into original language before anyone will admit that the explanation is adequate to the problem at hand.

Translations of this kind seem trivial and inadequate to the understanding of the initial problem. At the present stage of social sciences, then, it is quite defensible to hold that the explanatory concepts shall be germane to the motivating problem and not simply statements of correlations between societal and nonsocietal phenomena. This being the case, the tasks of the social sciences are the determination of adequate germane categories, such as culture, meaning, function, and value; their rigorous definition within the context of social science phenomena; their theoretical elaboration into parsimonious explanatory systems; and the establishment of rigorous procedural rules for their empirical application. For these tasks, the history of the more highly developed sciences may provide useful cues, but no more.

The second problem, though closely related to the former one, is logically independent of any answer we give to that question. Assuming that reduction will be practiced as far as possible, we still have to decide the proper procedures with respect to the concepts and hypotheses which have not yet been reduced. It is a question of the strategy of theorizing in the social sciences themselves. To be more specific: The social scientists now debate the question as to whether the chief desideratum is a general overarching theory or a series of particularistic hypotheses of relatively low degrees of generality.

The history of the natural sciences provides a valuable guide to the answer to this strategic problem. The physicists kept their hypotheses as close to observations as possible; their theories were integrations of hypotheses, not highly abstract summaries of concrete facts all on the same level. Galileo and Kepler had to do their theoretical as well as observational work before there could be Newton's. But, we may be told, the social scientists now have almost as many hypotheses as facts; more unkindly, they may be said to be long on hypotheses and short on facts.

The mind of man, however, is not so prodigal of imaginative hypotheses that it can generate an infinite variety of them. Hypotheses show an inner kinship of common parentage in a given milieu and in the inventiveness of the social scientists—the demonstration of this being one of the great accomplishments of the sociology of knowledge. Hypotheses are increasing in number, but the variety of their types may be diminishing. General theory is not to be built by addition of hypotheses, except indirectly; it arises from their analysis and reduction.

Hence it may be expected that when a plethora of facts is elaborated in hypotheses of low generality, the broad outlines of an overarching theory may be subtly adumbrated. But in view of the complexity of subject matter, the looseness of theoretical structure, and the uncontrolled character of many of the observations of society, it is too soon to expect—indeed, it is too soon to be impatient for—a Newton of the social sciences.

8

EXPLANATION AND COMPARATIVE DYNAMICS IN SOCIAL SCIENCE

JOHN C. HARSANYI

INTRODUCTION

AMONG social scientists there is now an increasing interest in fundamental theory, in *explaining* social facts rather than merely *describing* them. At present the only social sciences possessing a well-developed systematic theory are economics and demography. But there is a clear trend towards greater emphasis on theoretical analysis in social and cultural anthropology, sociology, social psychology, social and cultural history, political science, legal theory, etc. There is also a growing realization of the fact that society is a causal mechanism so closely inter-connected as to require analysis to a large extent in terms of one basic theory common to all social sciences rather than merely in terms of independent theories particular to the various disciplines. The interest of social scientists in recent years has tended to center upon problems which by their very nature require study by a cooperative effort of specialists in different social sciences, such as the problems

From *Behavioral Science*, 5 (1960):136–145. Copyright © 1960 by Behavioral Science. Reprinted by permission of the publisher and the author. John C. Harsanyi is Professor of Business Administration and Economics, University of California, Berkeley.

of cultural change, economic development, the relation between culture and personality structure, comparative politics, etc.; and experience with interdisciplinary research projects in such fields has made even clearer to what an extent our understanding of social phenomena is restricted by the lack of an integrated explanatory theory of society.

When a social scientist (e.g., a historian) tries to explain the behavior of a given individual, he will use the social institutions and cultural patterns of the relevant society as explanatory principles without necessarily attempting to explain these institutions and cultural patterns themselves. But at a deeper level of analysis the main task of the social sciences is precisely to explain the institutions and cultural patterns of each society. The purpose of this paper is to propose certain heuristic criteria for explanatory hypotheses and general theory construction at that level of analysis. Of course, heuristic considerations can never save us the trouble of actually setting up specific explanatory hypotheses and testing them against the social facts of the present and the past. But they may help us to devise fruitful hypotheses and to avoid blind alleys if we can make it clearer to ourselves what sort of theory we are after and what kinds of explanations we are looking for.

STATIC AND DYNAMIC MODELS

The most "natural" explanation for a social fact is in terms of some other social variables belonging to the *same* time period. For instance, the most obvious way of explaining the nature of English literature in the Victorian age is to refer to certain characteristics of English society in that period. But a little reflection will show that this type of explanation cannot be pressed very far. For, English literature of the Victorian age evidently carried forward (or reacted against) the English literary traditions of earlier ages and was also subject to literary influences from abroad. Hence, what contemporaneous English social conditions can explain about Victorian-age English literature are not so much the prevailing *literary patterns* themselves as are rather the *deviations* that occurred from the literary patterns of the previous period (as well as from the foreign models used). That is, what contemporaneous social conditions directly explain are not the relevant social *variables* themselves but are only their *time trends* (time derivatives), i.e. the directions and rates of their change.

Following the terminology used by economists, we shall speak of *static explanation* when a social variable is explained exclusively in terms of variables belonging to the *same time period;* and we shall speak of *dynamic explanation* when at least some of the explanatory variables used belong to an *earlier period* than the variables to be explained. More generally, we shall speak of dynamic explanation also if what we directly try to explain, and/or what we offer as explanation, involve not only the *values* of certain social variables at a given time, but also their *time trends* (time derivatives), i.e. the directions and rates of their change.

Social scientists making use of a static explanation often do not sufficiently realize how restrictive the assumptions are to which they are committed by adopting this type of explanation. A static explanation implies a static model of the social system. That is, it implies the assumption that all social variables relevant to the problem on hand always adjust to one another (and to the variables defining the natural environment) without any considerable time lag. More particularly, if the value of a certain variable Y is to be explained in terms of the

contemporaneous values of some other variables $X_1, \ldots, X_n$, then the following assumptions have to be satisfied:

1. At any moment the values of $X_1, \ldots, X_n$ must determine an equilibrium value for Y.
2. Should Y be removed from this equilibrium value by any disturbing force, it must return again without any significant delay [1] to this equilibrium value when the disturbing force ceases to operate.
3. Should there be any change in the values of $X_1, \ldots, X_n$, then Y must move to its new equilibrium value (determined by the new values of the X's) also without any significant delay.

Clearly, these are very strong assumptions, in particular 2 and 3. No doubt, there are within the social system subsystems to which static models are applicable at least as crude first approximations. For instance, the analysis of economic and political institutions in terms of static models and in terms of the concepts of economic or political equilibrium (balance of power) does have its usefulness. But the social system as a whole can hardly be regarded as a static mechanism. If nothing else, at least the evident inertia of cultural traditions and of social institutions must prevent any immediate all-over adjustment to changing conditions as would be required by a static model.

Therefore, in general we have to use dynamic models, which allow for slow, delayed or staggering adjustment, and which include the social conditions of earlier periods (and/or the time trends due to the changes going on in society) among their explanatory variables. This means that normally the explanation of a given cultural pattern or social institution will have to refer to the cultural patterns and social institutions of the previous period; and the conditions of the present will explain no more than the cultural and institutional *differences* between the present period and the previous one.

Very often when empirical observation fails to discover any consistent relationships between two important groups of social variables, we can quite confidently expect to find meaningful relationships between *changes* in these two groups of variables. For instance, the examples of the United States, Great Britain and the Soviet Union show that there is no uniform connection between the productive technology of a society and its economic and political institutional framework, as in each of these societies basically the same productive technology is associated with very different economic and political institutions. In contrast, between *changes* in technology and the consequent changes in economic and political institutions (as well as the other way round) there do appear to exist well-defined recognizable relationships. For example, we already know a good deal about what economic and political changes tend to follow the adoption of Western technology by a non-Western country (and how the nature of these changes depends on the economic, political and cultural conditions of the country prior to Westernization). Similarly, we also have a good idea of the social and cultural changes that regularly tend to follow technological innovations in Western countries.

The point is that dynamic laws represent the general case of causal laws while static laws form a very special case, found only in causal systems of special descriptions.[2] Therefore society must be subject to dynamic laws if it is subject to causal laws [3] at all, but there is no reason to expect that it will be subject to static laws, except for certain special fields.

Greater care in distinguishing between static and dynamic models would no doubt enhance the theoretical value of certain analytical tools now commonly used by social scientists. For example, social institutions and cultural patterns are now often explained in terms of the *functional adjustment* hypothesis. It is argued that every society must display a certain minimum degree of functional efficiency, i.e. correspondence between social needs and social institutions —at least as much as is needed for the very survival of the society. This leads to the inference that all social institutions tend to serve some real social needs and that all important social needs tend to be catered for by some social institutions: the task of empirical research is simply to find out which social institutions are connected with which social needs and vice versa.

Another, closely related, analytical tool is the hypothesis of *cultural consistency*. It is assumed that the value-attitudes, beliefs and activity patterns of each society form a well-integrated self-consistent system. Once certain basic value-attitudes of the society are given, the other elements of the culture can be explained to a large extent in terms of this consistency requirement.

Both the functional adjustment and the cultural consistency hypotheses certainly contain a good deal of truth: there are strong forces that tend to adjust social institutions to social needs or alternatively to eliminate societies with extreme institutional maladjustments; and there are also strong forces that tend to iron out inconsistencies among the cultural patterns of a given society. But it is sufficiently clear that all these forces are often quite slow in operation (and often have to work in the face of strong counteracting forces which try to preserve maladjusted institutions or inconsistent cultural patterns) so that the requirements of a static model are not met. Consequently there is no presumption whatever to the effect that the institutions and cultural patterns of any given society will be found to be particularly well adjusted or particularly consistent. Undue insistence on such hypotheses can only lead to existing functional maladjustments or cultural inconsistencies being explained away. A satisfactory model of functional adjustment and cultural integration cannot be static but rather has to include specific assumptions, at least in a rough qualitative sense, about the *speeds* at which the relevant adjustment and integration processes operate in different parts of the social system (as well as about the strength of the counteracting forces they have to overcome).

EXPLANATION AS A PROBLEM OF COMPARATIVE DYNAMICS

If society were a static mechanism the task of social science would be to explain differences and similarities between different societies or different parts of the same society in terms of certain basic social variables of the same period. That is, the fundamental problem would be a problem of *comparative statics*. As, however, society is a dynamic system the fundamental problem becomes a problem of *comparative dynamics*. The problem is to explain similarities and differences in the development over time of different societies or of different parts of the same society, in terms of the *initial conditions* (i.e. the conditions prevailing at some arbitrary point of time chosen as the starting point of our investigation) and in terms of the subsequent *external influences* (boundary conditions) affecting their development. On reflection it turns out that the explanation of *any* social fact is always a problem of comparative dynamics even if at first it is not stated in this form. For example, explaining the existence of industrial capitalism is the same thing as explaining why the Western society of the 18th century did produce a capitalistic industrial revolution while other societies, even those at comparable levels of economic and cultural development, did not have independent capitalistic industrial revolutions of their own. It was one of Max Weber's greatest contributions to social science to point out the reducibility of every question about explanation to a question in comparative dynamics.

Indeed, if an explanation proposed for a social fact does not explain why this fact appears or appeared in some societies or social groups but not in others—i.e., if it does not supply an explanation in a comparative dynamic sense—then we cannot accept it as full explanation of this social fact at all (though we may very well accept it as an important step towards a future explanation). For instance, even if the scapegoat theory of racial prejudice should be correct as far as it goes it cannot be regarded as full explanation of racial prejudice so long as it cannot explain why racial prejudice emerged in some societies or social groups but not in others, or why it is increasing in some social environments but is decreasing in others.

The fact that the social system is a dynamic system means that all problems in social science have an essential historical dimension and that in effect the main task of social science is to *explain historical development*. So it is most unfortunate that it has become customary for social scientists with a sense for theoretical analysis to neglect history and for social scientists with historical scholarship to keep themselves innocent of theoretical analysis.

Of course, in many cases the reluctance of historians to offer explanations (except on rather superficial levels) for the course of social development is simply a matter of there being no worthwhile analytical theory they could have drawn upon. For instance, so long as we have no theory to speak of on the dynamics of political institutions, we cannot blame historians if they fail to offer a satisfactory explanation for the fact that democracy works reasonably well in some countries but could never take firm roots in some other countries at comparable levels of cultural development. Even in economic history, progress in explaining the patterns of historical development was up to quite recently greatly hindered by the fact that available economic theory did not provide a satisfac-

tory theory of economic growth. Only in the last few years have both economic theorists and economic historians shown a more active interest in explaining the differences in the rate and direction of economic development among various societies at different periods, and in setting up dynamic models consistent both with sound economic theory and with the established results of historical research.

As the main purpose of a comparative dynamic theory of society would be to explain the course of historical development, our present interest in comparative dynamics to some extent represents a return to problems that used to occupy the evolutionary theorists of the 19th and early 20th centuries—in contrast to the anti-theoretical, or at best static, approach fashionable in the more recent past (roughly in the inter-war period).[4] But of course there are also fundamental differences. Evolutionists were looking for a law determining a uniform sequence of evolutionary stages for all societies. Comparative dynamics, on the contrary, is based on the idea that different societies often show very different patterns of development, and its main objective is to explain these differences in development in terms of differences in the initial conditions and the external influences.

Instead of assuming a law directly determining the course of social development (as a uniform sequence of evolutionary stages), a dynamic theory of society will have to explain social development in terms of the basic causal laws governing the interaction among the various social and environmental variables. It will have to set up analytical models based on specific—and, if possible, quantitative—assumptions concerning the causal influence that each major social and environmental variable has on the other variables, and concerning the causal mechanisms which transmit this influence. And of course ultimately all these causal laws will have to be explained in terms of interaction among the social groups—and, more fundamentally, among the individuals—who make up the social system.

EXOGENOUS VARIABLES AS EXPLANATORY VARIABLES

Among explanatory variables, special logical status belongs to variables *exogenous* to the social system, i.e., to the variables describing the natural environment of the society, and the biological properties of the population, in their aspects independent of human intervention. For, if a social scientist suggests an explanation for a social fact in terms of other social facts (i.e., in terms of variables endogenous to the social system), his explanation will be incomplete so long as he cannot offer explanation for these latter social facts themselves. But if he puts forward explanation for a social fact in terms of variables genuinely exogenous to the social system his analytical task will be completed, as it will not be his business as a social scientist to find an explanation for these exogenous variables themselves. In this sense the exogenous variables represent the only vehicles of "ultimate" explanation in social science.

For instance, if the differences between Western European and Indian economic development could be fully explained in terms of differences in the natural resources (as they in fact cannot), no further explanation would be required. But if we try to explain these economic differences, say, in terms of the religious differences (as between Christianity and Hinduism), this explanation will be incomplete so long as we cannot explain these religious differences themselves. Indeed, any explanation of the economic differences in terms of religion will carry full conviction only if there is some evidence that the religious differences themselves in turn can be explained by factors *independent* of the economic differences we have started from in the first place.

To be sure, experience shows that we very often cannot follow all causal chains back to the basic exogenous variables. In effect, if we want to restrict our analysis to a period shorter than the whole history of the human race, we have to admit as explanatory variables initial conditions which are already social variables; and if we want to limit our attention to a social system smaller than mankind as a whole, we have to admit as explanatory variables influences coming from other societies. But even apart from the natural limitation of the scope of our analysis in time and in space, the failure of all theories of environmental determinism (and the even more complete failure of theories of racial determinism) shows that our explanation of social development can hardly ever be so complete that we would avoid admitting "historical accidents," i.e., events that we can subsume only under statistical laws. This means that the connection between the known exogenous variables and the detailed course of social development has to be visualized in terms of stochastic (probabilistic) rather than deterministic models.

Of course, the concept of historical accidents must be handled with great care to make sure that its use will satisfy the requirements of probability theory. For instance, suppose that a given society did not make a certain invention in a given period even though there would have been a strong social need for it and even though all basic technological principles required were known. Then, as inventions are no doubt to some extent matters of luck, we may legitimately regard this failure to make the invention in question as a mere historical accident, if the period involved was reasonably short. But if the invention failed to occur over a long period the assumption that this was due to mere chance will have a very low probability, and a specific explanation, e.g., in terms of negative social attitudes towards invention, will be required.

But, even though explanation in terms of exogenous variables is not always possible, whenever it is possible it has a very special theoretical interest; and one of the basic tasks for a causal theory of the social system will be to discover the causal (deterministic or statistical) laws according to which the natural environment and the other exogenous variables influence the social variables, and to identify the causal mechanisms which transmit this influence. Not only the exogenous variables themselves have a privileged position as explanatory variables but so do all endogenous social variables which bear the direct impact of major exogenous variables and play a principal role in transmitting the latter's influence to the rest of the social system.

One of the reasons why explanation of social phenomena in terms of *economic* forces is often so fruitful lies in the fact that the economic system is one of the main channels through which the natural environment (in particular, the presence or absence of natural resources and of natural routes of communication) acts upon the social system. To be sure, the economic system is not the only causal channel through which the environment exerts its influence. For instance, geographical conditions have an important effect on the sizes and boundaries of political units; climate influences patterns of recreation and social intercourse, etc. In trying to explain differences in the development of different societies, of course, all these influences of the natural conditions have to be taken into account.

STABLE ENDOGENOUS VARIABLES (SOCIAL INSTITUTIONS AND CULTURAL TRADITIONS) AS EXPLANATORY VARIABLES

Social institutions and cultural traditions have an important role as explanatory variables fundamentally because of their *stability*.

Though only the exogenous variables are fully independent of the other variables, any stable endogenous variable also represents a relatively *independent source of causal influence* in that (so long as it maintains its stability) its value is independent of changes in the other variables.

The task of a dynamic theory of society is to explain social development in terms of the initial conditions associated with some arbitrary "initial" period (and in terms of the subsequent external influences). Hence special theoretical interest attaches to those causal channels which transmit the influence of the initial conditions to later periods. These causal channels are represented primarily by the stable variables of the social system. A given initial condition tends to have a persistent influence on later development either if it itself represents a relatively stable social variable (a stable social institution or cultural tradition) or if it has a lasting effect on another variable with a high degree of stability (e.g., the social conditions, themselves possibly of short duration, which give rise to a lasting institution or cultural tradition). In effect, the influence of *any* initial condition can always be represented in principle by a constant parameter in the equations describing the behavior of the system over time—though this constant parameter may not always correspond to a directly observable constant variable of the system.

To be sure, the effect of a stable social variable on social development, even if persistent, need not be large. In particular, variables connected with some causally isolated part of the social system may exhibit great stability—maybe precisely as a result of their isolation from influences coming from other parts of the system—and may still have very little influence

on the rest of the system. For example, the social structure of an isolated rural community may remain practically constant for centuries without this fact having any important effect on society at large. But any social or cultural variable that tends *both* to show a high degree of stability *and* to remain in close interaction with other important variables can hardly fail to be a variable with a significant long-run influence. Even if the influence of such a stable variable should remain small in the short run, its long-run influence will tend to be considerable as it will represent the cumulative effect of a force persistently pressing in the same direction over a long period.

In view of the great causal importance of such relatively stable social institutions and cultural traditions, it is of particular interest to explain the behavior of these institutions and traditions themselves—both their stability over time and the changes, if any, they display.

There are, of course, certain familiar stabilizing mechanisms which help to preserve all institutions and cultural traditions once they exist—such as education by teaching and example, social pressure for conformity, fear of the new and unfamiliar. But social scientists from Marx to the modern functionalists agree that an institution or cultural pattern cannot persist for long unless it satisfies some specific *interests* or psychological *needs* on the part of society as a whole or on the part of particular social groups. This means that the *stability* of all other social variables greatly depends on those *fundamental structural variables* which determine the common interests and psychological needs of the society as well as its division into the major social groups, and the separate interests and psychological needs of these groups themselves. These fundamental structural variables include the natural environment of the society and its way of utilization; the society's position among, and relation to, other societies; the prevailing basic value attitudes and the basic personality structure of the members of the society; the social structure and its major subdivisions according to class, status, occupation, residential area, ethnic origin, religion, etc., as well as the basic economic, political and social relations among these groups. These fundamental structural variables, or rather changes in them, also play an important role in explaining *changes* in other social institutions and cultural patterns (if the relevant time lags are allowed for). Hence the differences between two societies in these fundamental structural variables must go a long way towards explaining the differences in their other social variables.

ACCUMULATIVE VARIABLES

If we apply the method of comparative analysis, not to two different societies, but rather to two different periods of the same society, obviously we cannot explain the observed differences in terms of completely stable social variables, which did not change from one period to the other. Rather, we have to rely on variables which did significantly change from one period to another but which at the same time remained approximately constant within each (short) period under comparison —that is, on variables which tend to change at a very slow rate but so that this adds up to large changes in the long run. Such variables may be called *accumulative* (or decumulative) *variables*. Examples are: population, the stock of capital, the stock of natural resources (the latter is a "decumulative" variable subject to depletion), the "stock" of technological knowledge, the sizes of slowly growing social organizations, etc. Obviously accumulative variables of this sort represent very important causal links in explaining the fundamental long-run changes that occur in a society in the course of social development. In the short run they can be regarded as constant, and therefore as independent variables, while in the long run they are themselves subject to the moulding influence of other social variables.

These latter, i.e., the social and cultural conditions that decide the rate and direction of change in each of these accumulative variables, are of course another most important class of explanatory variables. For instance, it would be a major advance in economic theory if we would decide which are the main economic and social variables that determine the rate of increase in capital and in technological knowledge.

We have argued above that one reason for the fruitfulness of an economic analysis of social institutions lies in the fact that the economic system is one of the main causal channels through which the natural environment acts upon the social system. We can now add an additional reason: the economic system (if defined so as to include productive technol-ogy as one of its variables) contains at least three of the major accumulative variables, viz., capital, natural resources and productive technology. Therefore a good deal of the differences between the social conditions of two different periods can be explained in terms of economic differences. But of course a full explanation will have to bring in cumulative variables which are not "economic" in nature, e.g., population, the "stock" of pure scientific knowledge, military technology, communication and organization methods, etc.

INTERACTION BETWEEN DIFFERENT SUBSYSTEMS OF THE SOCIAL SYSTEM

Perhaps the most interesting methodological problem facing a social scientist is what working hypothesis to adopt about the likely direction of the causal influence between certain major groups of social variables (i.e., between different subsystems of the social system). Should we, with Max Weber, assign causal priority to the religious-ethical variables and explain the emergence of Capitalism in terms of Protestant ethics, or conversely should we, with Karl Marx, assign causal priority to the economic variables and explain Protestantism itself in terms of the economic conditions of late-medieval towns? Should we explain economic development in terms of political factors and regard Capitalism the by-product of the fiscal policies of national governments, or should we adopt the opposite explanation and make the national governments themselves the agents of Capitalistic economic interests?

Sometimes attempts have been made to dismiss all problems of this kind with the pronouncement that in society all causal relations are two-way affairs and that no social variable has causal priority over any other. But this is not, in my view, a fruitful approach. Maybe most causal relations run in both directions but no doubt one direction is often much more important than the other, and if so this fact will be very interesting information to us. In particular, so long as we have to work with very rough and often non-quantitative models, the only way of gaining insight into the causal structure of the social system is to find out the principal directions of causal influence among the major social and environmental variables.

In effect, hypotheses as to causal priority

96   EXPLANATION IN SOCIAL SCIENCE

can always be translated into comparative dynamic hypotheses concerning the causal importance of the revelant social variables as initial conditions. For instance, Max Weber's theory is essentially a hypothesis on what difference it would have made to later economic development in Western Europe if Protestantism had not figured among the initial conditions of the relevant period. Likewise, the Marxian theory on the causes of the Reformation is a hypothesis about what difference it would have made to Western European religious development if the economic conditions of late-medieval towns had been different. Of course, without the possibility of experimental testing (and we cannot set up a society similar to Western European society of the relevant period, except for the absence of Protestantism, and then observe what will happen), hypotheses of this sort can be supported only by indirect evidence. As in other nonexperimental sciences, the analysis of historical facts may be a partial substitute for experimentation. For example, Max Weber was able to test his thesis up to a point by comparing the economic development of the Western European society with that of other societies with different religions but otherwise more or less similar social institutions. But of course observation is never a full substitute for experimentation. The societies Max Weber used for comparison inevitably differed from Western European society in many other respects besides religion, e.g., in certain economic and political characteristics, and this involved the possibility of alternative interpretations for the historical facts.

However, this type of historical evidence may be supplemented by study of the causal mechanisms operative in social development and by investigation of the dynamic behavior of the relevant social variables.

What does it mean to ascribe causal priority to one subsystem of the social system over another? It essentially means to assume that, while the main aspects of the first subsystem's development can be explained in terms of internal factors, i.e., in terms of interaction among its own variables, the second sybsystem's development has to be explained in essential respects in terms of influences coming from the first subsystem. Obviously all parts of the social system and all parts of culture show some measure of relatively autonomous development and on the other hand none of them can claim full autonomy. But the various subsystems seem to exhibit conspicuous differences as to the degree of autonomy they possess. Philosophy, art, religion, law, etc., may for a while apparently follow their own internal logic in their development, but soon this development takes an unexpected turn, old ideas are abandoned for no apparent good reason and new ideas emerge which in no way represent a further development of the old. If an attempt is made to explain these developments in terms of their internal logic alone they remain profound mysteries. But if we bring in external factors, such as social, political and economic changes, things become at once meaningful and understandable. The economic system and even more so the larger system including, besides the economic variables, also technology, political organization and the size and composition of the population) shows a much higher degree of autonomy. If someone wants to explain Capitalism as a product of Protestant ethics he has to find an explanation for the emergence of Protestant ethics itself—presumably in terms of the autonomous evolution of Christian theology. But Max Weber himself admits that Protestant ethics is by no means a logically necessary implication of Protestant theology; indeed he thinks that fatalistic ethics would have been logically more consistent with the doctrine of predestination. So the explanation of Protestant ethics in terms of autonomous theological developments fails at the very first step, and extra-theological social factors have to be invoked to explain why the early Puritans adopted the ethical attitudes so highly favorable to the development of Capitalism. On the other hand, if we try to explain Protestantism as a result of the social conditions prevailing in late-medieval towns, we have no fundamental difficulty in explaining how these social conditions themselves emerged as a result of economic, technological and political developments.

Over relatively short periods, of course, practically any subsystem of the social system may show largely autonomous developments, which may then have important effects on other parts of the social system. The point is only that in many subsystems such spells of relatively autonomous developments tend to be soon interrupted by outside influences. Indeed, as Kroeber has pointed out, many fields of culture simply do not possess the ability to display continual development in one particular direction indefinitely: if no outside influence intervenes they will soon exhaust their internal developmental possibilities and simply stop or exhibit endless repetition of the same patterns.

CONCLUSION

To sum up, we have tried to show that the fundamental problem of social science is to explain social facts in terms of a *comparative dynamic theory* of social development.

We have argued that among explanatory variables special theoretical importance attaches to those which are relatively independent of the other variables of the social system, and which are therefore in a position to exert relatively *independent causal influence* on the other variables.

On the basis of this criterion we have discussed six groups of important explanatory variables, viz., (1) exogenous variables; (2) endogenous variables that mediate the influence of major exogenous variables; (3) endogenous variables with a high degree of stability (i.e. stable institutions and cultural traditions); (4) basic structural variables, which determine the values, interests and psychological needs of the members of the society and in that way largely determine the stability of other social variables; (5) accumulative variables, connected with the basic changes of society in the long run; (6) the variables that determine the rate of growth of the accumulative variables.

We have used the same criterion of relative causal independence also for judging the likely direction of causal influence between different subsystems of the social system. We have argued that a subsystem is more likely to have causal priority over other subsystems the more it is intrinsically capable of persistent autonomous long-run movements of its own, and the more it is able to preserve these movements against disturbing influences coming from other parts of the social system.

NOTES

1. For, the equilibrium value of Y can be used to explain the actual value of Y only if Y is most of the time actually at or near its equilibrium value.

2. Any system subject to static laws is always also subject to dynamic laws but not vice versa. This is so because any static law can always be expressed in the form of a dynamic law, e.g. by adding a vacuous conditional clause involving a variable of the previous period, etc.

3. This is true irrespective of whether these causal laws are deterministic or merely statistical.

4. Economic theory in many ways followed a course different from that of most other social sciences in that it felt the influence of extreme evolutionist doctrines much less, and later largely avoided the anti-theoretical current that swept over sociology and anthropology. But it likewise went through a period of purely static theorizing and of neglect for development problems.

9

THE PHENOMENOLOGICAL AND NATURALISTIC APPROACHES TO THE SOCIAL

LEON J. GOLDSTEIN

I

IN an interesting essay not long ago, Maurice Natanson contrasted two approaches to the

From *Methodos,* 14 (1961): 225–238. Copyright © 1961 *Methodos.* Reprinted by permission of the publisher and the author. Leon J. Goldstein is Professor of Philosophy, State University of New York, Binghamton.

study of sociocultural phenomena and concluded that one of them, the naturalistic, is entirely wanting and not adequate to dealing with such phenomena, and that the other, the phenomenological, is, on the contrary, entirely suited to the task. It seems to me, however, that he has said too much, and in the course of what follows I want to show that far from opposing one another, these two approaches are complementary and both of them necessary if we are to have a full account of the phenomena in question. Each does a different job, and there is no reason why we cannot have both.

The terms "phenomenological" and "naturalistic" suggest schools or procedures within philosophy, and I think it best if I make some preliminary remarks as to how I intend the distinction between them in this paper. It is not my intention when speaking of the phenomenological approach to speak of the application to the social of the methods of Edmund Husserl and his followers. I do not know whether the approach I mean to deal with is or is not phenomenological in that sense, but for what it is worth the reader may be informed that Alfred Schutz seems to think that it is, Hans Neisser that it is not, and Natanson himself takes both views, depending on whether he intends phenomenology in a broad or a narrow sense. For the purpose of the distinction that I want to make, "the phenomenological approach" will mean one that is primarily oriented toward description, not theory formation, and in which the vantage point of subjectivity, in a way to be made clear, is of first importance.

By the naturalistic approach I shall mean any concern with the social not from the standpoint of subjectivity. Naturalistic social science seeks to explain how sociocultural phenomena come to be as they are, how they develop and change. For reasons which have been sufficiently discussed by well-known methodologists and will simply be assumed here, such explanation presupposes reference to general laws. But I do not think that one can say that it is the utilization of general propositions that distinguishes the naturalistic from the phenomenological approach, for a descriptive or phenomenological account of the social world can always be formulated so as to contain general propositions. Our account might say that things are such in our social world that if anyone having specificable social characteristics were to find himself in a given situation he would act in a determinate way. Most anyone in the given society may be expected to *understand* the action, thus the element of subjectivity is seen to be entirely compatible with generality. (This is not to say that people ordinarily bother

to set out the common characteristics of their social life in the form of general propositions, and it is not unreasonable to think that many, even most, people of a given community could not do so if asked. Nevertheless, people generally know what to expect of their fellow participants in the social and cultural life of their community; they seem to "know" implicitly what the ethnographer or sociologist sets forth explicitly).

I have still to make clear, even in a preliminary sort of way, what I mean by the naturalistic approach to the social. In a paper written some twenty years ago but only recently discovered and posthumously published, Schutz opposes to the subjectivism of his favored phenomenological approach what he calls objectivism. "Objectivism" does not refer to just one specific alternative to phenomenology in social science, but seems to be used as a general name for all social research which does not take as its task the attempt to understand some social world from the standpoints of those who live in that world. At the extreme position of the objectivist spectrum, Schutz finds behaviorism, but, unlike the view he seems to hold in a later paper, he recognizes that there are alternative objectivist possibilities. "There is rather a basic attitude conceivable—and, in fact, several of the most successful social scientists have adopted it—which accepts naively the social world with all the alter egos and institutions in it as a meaningful universe, *meaningful namely for the observer* whose only scientific task consists in describing and explaining his and his co-observers' experiences of it" (italics added). Whether or not it is fair to speak here of naive acceptance, I do agree with Schutz that we can, and do, have social science the purpose of which is to make intelligible to the observer the social phenomena he elects to study. This is a social science which takes as its point of departure not the living experiences of the members of a society, but, rather, the questions that the investigator thinks are worth answering.[1] It is this kind of social science that I intend by the term "naturalistic social science," and I think that it is this kind of social science that Natanson finds wanting.

It seems, then, that naturalistic social science is one kind of nonsubjective social science subsumed by Schutz under the rubric "objective." We have seen that in addition to this he recognizes and rejects an approach he calls "behavioristic." I must confess that I am not able to make any sense of the idea that there can be such a thing as behavioristic social science, though I can appreciate the polemical value it may have for a subjectivist who wishes to make his opponents seem to be defending an impossible position. Behaviorism, if it can be carried off at all, seems to be an orientation in the study of individual behavior or psychology and purports to describe such behavior using only terms which refer to overt or public movements and the like. Since meanings of some sort and in some sense are necessary—as we shall see in the sequel—for human action to be understood as social, there cannot possibly be a behavioristic approach to the study of sociocultural phenomena.

Perhaps advocates of the view that only the phenomenological approach is ultimately tenable think behaviorism is the extreme alternative to their position because it is obviously the extreme alternative to views they hold in psychology. There, too, subjectivists have inclined to think that *the* purpose of psychological investigation is to present an account of the mental life from the standpoint of the subject himself. One need not, of course, deny that this is a possible subject for study, but I do think it a mistake to conclude therefrom that no other approach in psychology is possible. I should imagine that if those who follow behavioristic procedures emerge with conclusions which do not violate the accepted canons of scientific procedure, if, that is, their results are confirmable by others and their predictions realized, anyone would admit that their discipline is a scientific one. What I am saying is rather like Rollo May's suggestion that what both Kierkegaard and Freud have to say about anxiety is useful and admissible even though they seem to be pursuing different lines of investigation. "What powerfully struck me then was that Kierkegaard was writing about *exactly what my fellow patients and I were going through.* Freud was not; he was writing on a different level, giving formulations of the psychic mechanisms by which anxiety came about." Kierkegaard's approach was to offer a subjectively oriented account of anxiety, and the acceptability of his work depends upon the extent to which it results in descriptions of anxiety that actually accord with the experience of those who experience it. That Freud's results do not accord with such experiences does not invalidate them, for they are judged by different criteria entirely, namely those of scientific method. In

just this way we may distinguish between those criteria with reference to which we are to judge the work of behaviorism and those relevant to assessing psychological descriptions from the standpoint of subjectivity. For those who prefer only the latter to rule out the possibility of the former on the ground that psychology *must* characterize the mental life as it is experienced is simply dogmatism. It seems, however, that this view of psychology came to be accepted by behaviorists, who then proceeded to deny that there was a subjective standpoint at all. And this is clearly incredible. One may suggest that the source of both dogmatism and incredibility is the treatment, by denizens of both camps, of the methodological prescriptions of their respective procedures as if they were more fundamentally metaphysical, and on that basis proscribing entirely what failed to be in accord with them.

To return to our present purpose, I think it is not difficult to see that the same sort of distinction I have been making for psychology can be made for social science. And so we may come to recognize that far from confronting each other as incompatible ways of studying the same phenomena of experience, the phenomenological and the naturalistic approaches to the social are simply different undertakings for the purpose of acquiring different kinds of knowledge. I do not wish to suggest that they are so disparate that there is no point of contact between them; rather, on the contrary, I hope that one of the conclusions which will emerge from the discussion to follow is that the two approaches are complementary and, in fact, mutually require one another.

Schutz himself may be pointing in the direction of our distinction when he says the following: "The fathers of behaviorism had no other purpose than that of describing and explaining real human acts within a real human world. But the fallacy of this theory consists in the substitution of a fictional world for social reality by promulgating methodological principles as appropriate for the social sciences which, though proved true in other fields, prove a failure in the realm of intersubjectivity." Implicit in this statement is recognition of the fact that the behaviorists could do whatever job behaviorism is capable of doing within that area of investigation suited to their methods, but that it was a mistake to extend them beyond their proper limits. The notion that they substituted "a fictional world for social reality," is just Schutz's

way of saying that they treated their methodological principles as metaphysical ones, thus
imposing unwarranted restrictions upon the
possibility of theoretical developments.

Schutz then goes on to recognize that it is
possible to do useful social scientific work
which does not treat the social world from the
standpoint of subjectivity. In his own words:
"Doubtless *on a certain level* real scientific work
may be performed and has been performed
without entering into the problems of subjectivity. We can go far ahead in the study of
social phenomena, like social institutions of all
kinds, social relations, and even social groups,
without leaving the basic frame of reference,
which can be formulated as follows: What does
all this mean for us, the scientific observer?"
But this, he adds, "does not alter the fact that
this type of social science does not deal directly
and immediately with the social life-world, common to us all, but with skilfully and expediently
chosen idealizations and formulizations of the
social world which are not repugnant to its
facts" (italics added). Schutz's view is that no
matter how well it does its work, naturalistic
social science is defective and inferior precisely
because it fails to deal directly with the common social world as it presents itself to those
who experience it. He also holds that it is
always possible to go back to the subjective
standpoint and that we must go back to it if our
interest is at all in the social. He holds that
even naturalistic social science rests upon the
phenomenological standpoint. I think that in
what follows it will emerge that there is a sense
in which this is justified. Yet I think, too, that
there are problems confronting social science
which can only be resolved along naturalistic
lines. Our problem, then, is not to arrange the
approaches to the study of sociocultural phenomena in an hierarchial order and so conclude
that the phenomenological approach is or is
not higher than the naturalistic, but, rather, to
sketch the purposes and domains of each and
to pay some attention to their possible points of
contact.

II

Professor de Laguna is entirely correct in
her claim that what the phenomenologists call
the *"Lebenswelt,"* the social world the description of which Schutz and Natanson both take
to be preeminently the task of social science,

and what anthropologists describe as the cultural
world are, in the end, two ways of referring to
the same data of experience. The main point
of those who defend the phenomenological
standpoint is that human action is informed
by meanings, and that it is purposive in a way
that only meaningful behavior can be. This
means that to observe an action as if it were
simply a physical event in a physically causal
nexus would not enable the observer to apprehend the action as social, as something which
cannot be reduced to the non-social. As long
as we confine our attention to investigations of
the social world which the investigator shares
with the people he studies, it is easy to take
the meanings which are involved for granted,
and by concentrating attention upon the behavior of individuals to ignore the fact that we
have to do with more than individual behavior
in a behavioristic sense.

If I prick my finger, or cut it or bruise it, I
am very likely to put it into my mouth. My
companions may express concern, but they certainly find nothing odd in my response to the
accident, as they might, say, if a man of my
age were to be seen sucking his thumb. Likely,
they think that putting the hurt finger in my
mouth has some beneficial effect, and likely,
too, they would expect that most sensible people
share their belief. Of course, the subject never
comes up for discussion and these beliefs are
rarely explicitly elicited, yet I suppose that most
readers will agree that what I have just said
obtains for most of the people they know. But
once an anthropologist was riding somewhere
in the western part of the United States in the
company of an American Indian, and, catching his finger in some appurtenance of his
saddle, he hurriedly put the finger into his
mouth only to find himself an object of amuse-
ment to his companion. To the Indian, the
sudden act of the anthropologist was odd, even
silly, and apparently made no sense as a sequel
to the accident. Presumably for him, the
"theory" which underlay the anthropologist's
action had no standing at all: it was not an element of his own culture and he simply never
heard of it. Instances of this kind can be multiplied indefinitely, and we shall be satisfied
simply to add a few words of Raymond Firth,
who observes that "if the anthropologist is
traveling in the Plateau of Northern Nigeria
. . . he may meet men from the Bi Rom and
other pagan tribes living there. They will probably shake their clenched fists in the air as he

approaches. According to his fears or his politics, he may interpret this as a symbol of anger or of solidarity among fellow-workers. In time, he will find it is merely the normal greeting." Firth calls this "contextualization," and means that in time the anthropologist comes to understand the sense of the behavior as he comes to appreciate its context.

The experiences of anthropologists when they first try to get their bearings in a new community entirely different from their own amply evidence the fact that the behavior of people when observed but not understood within the context of the way of life it exemplifies is entirely unintelligible. I do not say that this understanding is of the motives of the particular agent whose behavior is observed, though, of course, there are times when these motives are quite central to any effort to make sense of his behavior. These are times when he, behaving as the rational agent he sometimes is, does what he does in order to effect some end in view, and unless we are cognizant of the end we are neither able to make sense of what he does nor to assess the adequacy of his action. But much of human action is not purposive in this way yet, nevertheless, cannot be made intelligible without the kind of understanding that is simply not to be had if one limits one's apprehension of it to accord with the prescriptions of behaviorism. What must be understood to make sense of such action is the mode of social existence which makes this sort of behavior the thing to expect or the thing to do. To think that the kind of understanding called for is of "subjective states of mind" (Nagel) is simply to miss the point, for it seems to suggest that its advocates treat all social action as if it were the purposive behavior of rational agents. And this is surely not the case.

My last remarks may seem to have a peculiar effect upon our notion of social inquiry from the standpoint of subjectivity for they seem to suggest that such inquiry is not concerned with the idiosyncratic standpoint of the individual, though this is the only standpoint which is actually that of a subject. It may well be that those—or many of those—who have defended some version of the phenomenological standpoint in social science would find any attempt to limit the centrality of the idiosyncratic standpoint unacceptable. We have seen, for example, that Schutz objects to those who would place emphasis upon the standpoint of the observer rather than that of the participant

in social action, and since the participant is always a particular individual one might think that this requires that only the discovery of the individual's particular purpose in doing what he does will suffice to make it intelligible. The difficulty with such a view, however, is that there is no reason for thinking that every —perhaps even most—human action is done with an end in view, and this would seem to result in that much such action could not be made intelligible as social-meaningful rather than biological-behavioral. Actually, we do not have to impose such a narrow interpretation upon Schutz, for it seems clear enough that writers such as he and Natanson take the regularities of social life to be part of the *Lebenswelt* that phenomenological social science is called upon to describe, and these are not subjective in the idiosyncratic sense. The standpoint, then, that this approach is supposed to make explicit is that which the actor may be thought to acquire in the course of his enculturation and which comes to inform his life and actions, even though he need not be explicitly aware of it as one standpoint among others. The behavior of the subject becomes intelligible to the observer when the observer has come to understand the presuppositions of social action in the subject's community. If the observer is an enculturated member of the same community and not a scientific observer then the understanding is un-selfconscious and not explicit. If he is not, then his understanding is likely the outcome of the kind of painstaking effort we have come to expect from ethnographers. For the first, the activity in question makes sense and is natural. For the second, it is intelligible in light of what he has come to know about the culture of the actor.

In sum, the purpose of the phenomenological approach to the study of social behavior is to make explicit what is implicit in the social action of the members of a given community. In a sense, Schutz is right in seeing this as the exploration of the social from the standpoint of the subject or the actor in that the whole point of the investigation is to reveal just what precisely it is that makes the actor's action intelligible. Yet the ordinary—naive—actor acts in ways he takes to be "natural" and not the consequence of adherence to a standpoint. That it is the consequence of such adherence is precisely the point of view of the observer. In view of the way that writers like Schutz make so much of their claim that the standpoint of the subject is the only *real* standpoint for the study of social phenomena, this may seem somewhat paradoxical.

III

I think that from what we have already said, it is possible to argue that between the phenomenological and the naturalistic conception of the social there is really no fundamental difference. Such an argument would be based upon the facts that the phenomenological social scientist does not concern himself with the merely idiosyncratic and the naturalistic social scientist does not adopt the standpoint of behavioristic psychology. For both of them social inquiry has to do with socially meaningful action, action the entire point of which depends upon the presence of shared meanings or values.

But even if the idea of the social implicit in the work of both phenomenological and naturalistic social science is identical, it is still the case that some social research is not phenomenological. Not all social inquiry is directed toward determining the character of the system of shared meanings in terms of which the action of the members of a given society is seen to make sense. In seeking such intelligibility one assumes that some system of ideas or what have you exists and that one must only discover what it is in order to discover the standpoint of the acting subject. To think that this approach exhausts the possibilities of work in the social sciences, however, is simply to think that we cannot ask of any such system of ideas —or any system of institutional arrangements which are reflected in the system of ideas— how it came to be as it is. But here we find ourselves trying *to account for the development* of a particular social world, and this is not the same as trying to constitute that social world in order to understand the activities of those whose world it is. Only the latter is pointed at the recovering of the standpoint of subjectivity as this is intended by Schutz and Natanson. The kind of inquiry I am now concerned about, however, is, to speak metaphorically, outside of the given standpoint and seeks to account for it. Consequently, it is is clearly not social science of the sort that the phenomenological philosophers insist is the only proper way to achieve the most desirable kind of social knowledge.

Any historical account which is not an attempt to reconstitute a social world which once was but is no more, but is, rather, an attempt to trace the development of institutions, must, perforce, fail to satisfy the requirement of the phenomenological approach. While at each stage in the development recounted one may hope to reconstruct the standpoint which renders intelligible the actions of the men and women whose standpoint it is, it is clear enough that the sweep of the development as presented cannot possibly be from the subjective standpoint of any of the actors in question but must be entirely from that of the observer or historian. The development as reconstructed is introduced for the purpose of making sense of what the observer finds before him, namely, the sundry documents, artifacts and such which constitute his historical evidence. Presumably, the historian purports to be characterizing the standpoint of the people and leading actors with whom he is concerned, but that in no way alters our point that his characterization is made from the standpoint of himself confronting the evidence which lies before him. Given the nature of historical research, this is the only standpoint which is possible to him. (It may be noted, by the way, that one may always take ethnography, presumably the model of phenomenological social science, as being entirely like history in the respect just noted. Instead of dealing with documents and artifacts, the ethnographer is faced with the task of making intelligible his observations or his field notes. We have tended to think of the ethnographer as *reconstructing* the subjective standpoint of the people whose actions he observes, but we can just as easily think of him as *postulating* that standpoint in order to explain what he observes. This latter way of putting the matter would be part of an attempt to characterize the standpoint of the ethnographer himself, part of a methodological account of ethnography.)

Just as historians may be interested in the development of events, institutions, and the like in the course of time, so too sociologists and anthropologists. It will serve no purpose of this paper to deal in any detail with the kind of investigation that such scholars call "diachronic," and it will suffice to call passing attention to the fact that the development characterized cannot possibly be in accord with the subjective standpoint of given actors. It may be agreed that each stage of the development is a reconstruction of a subjective standpoint, but what is done in such investigations is not to confront subjects engaged in action in order to discover the standpoint which renders their action intelligible—something which can only be done at the very most with contemporary actors who must always be at the end of the sequence of development—but rather to assume or postulate past stages or standpoints in order to render present practice or presently existing evidence intelligible.

In addition to such investigations, there is also the interest of at least some social scientists in the formulation of general laws, and it is easily seen that such formulation can hardly be the reconstruction of a subjective standpoint. It was noted above that the phenomenological approach to the social involves the discovery of the expected regularities characteristic of the social world being reconstructed. It might be thought that the formulation of these regularities represents a contribution to theoretical social science—hence that such theory is phenomenological—but this would be mistaken. Though from the standpoint of the acting individual we have to do with a recurrent phenomenon, from the standpoint of describing a given social world we have to do with a single fact: this is a social world in which when such-and-such is the case then some determinate sequel may be anticipated. But there are other social worlds in which it is not the case, and so our formulation is not a general or theoretical statement about social worlds. This recurrence may be said to form part of the constant background for the action of those who participate in the given social world, but the discovery of its presence there is hardly a theoretical matter. On the contrary, it is the task of theory, together with history, to explain how the given feature of the social world has come to be as it is. Our explanation refers to antecedent conditions, i.e., must make use of history, but in order to render intelligible or to justify the claim that the present feature emerged out of the antecedent condition one must have recourse to some system of theoretical social science. Whatever one wants to say about such laws, they surely cannot be reconstructed subjective standpoints, since their purpose here is to help us understand the transition from one such standpoint to another. And, indeed, even if we were not explicitly aware of their purpose here, enough is known about the logic of scientific theory and

the general character of scientific propositions to see that it simply would make nonsense to think of theoretical social science as being the reconstruction of a subjective standpoint. Such propositions are intended to state that the elements of systems characterized in determinate ways bear certain specified or specifiable relationships to one another. To rule these out of social science on the ground that they do not conform to the ideal of a phenomenological social science would be most arbitrary indeed. I find it difficult to believe that writers such as Schutz and Natanson actually intend that this be done.

IV

We have seen that there are at least two kinds of approach to the study of the social and that to suggest that only the so-called phenomenological approach is true to the reality of its subject-matter is somewhat arbitrary. Indeed, if one were required to choose between the two approaches, we shall see that it is the phenomenological approach which would have to be rejected in favor of the naturalistic. But there is really no reason for not adopting a position of methodological tolerance and keeping what may be derived from both of these procedures.

If one agrees with the phenomenologist that inquiry must proceed from the standpoint of the subject, I do not see how one may gainsay the fact that the ultimate subject of any investigation is the investigator himself. No account of what the investigator does, or, more generally, no attempt to characterize the methodology of the sort of investigation it is, can fail to conclude that what is produced is produced from the investigator's own standpoint. The ethnographer purports to reconstruct a standpoint which is supposed to make the action of the people he observes subjectively meaningful, i.e., meaningful from their own point of view. But this cannot be established beyond peradventure, and it is always possible that the reconstruction corresponds to nothing in the feelings and experiences of the observed behavers and is only introduced by the observer because it makes the best sense of what he has observed. I am not saying that this must be the case and that the observer is never able to come to understand the standpoint of the community in which his investigation is being carried out. But I am saying that it is always possible to wonder if the reconstructed standpoint is the standpoint of the behavers, and that a strict account of its genesis and its function in the work of the social scientist makes it clear that its formulation in the way that the investigator formulates it has its origin in his need to understand what he observes. Hence, if we are required to choose between the phenomenological and naturalistic standpoints, it would seem that the latter must win out. But this notwithstanding, it also appears that the results of the two approaches point to each other and may even be thought to require one another. No one wants to assert that the social world in which we now find ourselves always was, and so we must recognize that any account of our social world or *Lebenswelt* is an account of something which is but the latest stage of a series which cannot be constituted in the same way that this latest stage itself can. And this is only another way of saying that what is constructed by the phenomenological approach to the study of the social cannot be said to stand by itself in the sense that it had no antecedents but simply came into the world fullblown the way it is. It clearly presupposes what can only be known through the naturalistic approach.

On the other hand, one may wonder how much sense the study of the social, from any standpoint you please, would make to us if we were not acquainted, even pre-reflectively, with the idea of a social world which comes to us from participating in one. Merely being social creatures ourselves does not enable us to understand the behavior of others who do not share our social life, but it is only because we are social beings that we can come to know that to understand that behavior we are required to understand the point of view that underlies it. That the data or evidence which is the starting point for naturalistic social or historical studies are recognized by us to be the starting point for such enterprises, and not merely objects in space and time, is precisely because we experience the world as social beings. And that way of experiencing the world which we take for granted is just what the phenomenological sociologist wants to make explicit, just as the ethnographer wants to do for contemporaries who do not share our *Lebenswelt*. We have seen that any such effort may be challenged and that we can never be absolutely certain that a reconstruction of this kind actually accords with the subjective standpoint of the people being studied. But this only shows that the phenomenological standpoint cannot be made entirely independent of the naturalistic, not that the attempt to understand human behavior from the standpoint of subjectivity must be abandoned.

NOTES

1. For an instance of complete refusal to see any point of view other than that of the participants in the social world being studied as worthy of consideration, see G. Dalton, "A Note of Clarification on Economic Surplus," *American Anthropologist,* 1960, LXII, 483–90. Dalton considers that a question raised from any other standpoint is an imposition of the "values" of the investigator upon the people being studied (p. 487), and reserves the honorific adjective "empirical" solely for the standpoint of the subjects (p. 489).

10

CAUSES, FUNCTIONS, AND CROSS-COUSIN MARRIAGE: AN ESSAY IN ANTHROPOLOGICAL EXPLANATION

MELFORD E. SPIRO

ALTHOUGH addressed to the problem of unilateral cross-cousin marriage, this paper is primarily concerned with the methodological issues involved in the explanation of this, or of any structural type, and more particularly with the relative merits of functional and causal explanations. Cross-cousin marriage provides a useful vehicle for the examination of these different explanatory modes because the recent controversy [1] concerning differential cross-cousin marriage raises most of the important issues entailed in anthropological explanation in general, and in causal versus functional explanations in particular.

What, then, do these rival theories of cross-cousin marriage say? In the first place, we must distinguish between their respective explanations for observed phenomena, and the extrapolation of these explanations to account for past phenomena. That is, Needham as well as Homans and Schneider attempt to account for the *origin* of differential unilateral cross-cousin marriage on the basis of their explanation for its current practice. This is an invalid procedure. Both, moreover, offer the same explanation for the prescriptive *rule* of cross-cousin marriage as they offer for the practice of cross-cousin marriage. This, too, is an invalid procedure. In this section, however, we shall evaluate their explanations for the *practice* of unilateral cross-cousin marriage, from which both deduce their explanations for both the origin of and the rule prescribing its practice.

The Homans-Schneider causal hypothesis can be simply stated: a man marries his matrilateral (or patrilateral) cross-cousin because he is

From *Journal of the Royal Anthropological Institute*, 96 (1965): 30–43. Copyright © 1965 by the Journal of the Royal Anthropological Institute. Reprinted by permission of the publisher and the author. Melford E. Spiro is Professor of Anthropology, University of Chicago.

'fond' of her. Assuming that Ego wishes to marry *somebody,* his fondness for his matrilateral cross-cousin renders this form of marriage 'sentimentally appropriate'. Homans and Schneider then attempt to account for this 'sentiment' in each generation of Egos. Fondness for MoBrDa, they argue, stems from the system of unilineal jural authority found in unilineal societies. In societies in which jural authority is patripotestal, the child develops warm and close ties with his nurturant mother and, by generalization, with those relatives with whom she is identified, including MoBrDa. (In some societies these positive 'sentiments' toward the class of MoBrDa are reinforced by interaction with a specific MoBrDa.) This positive sentiment felt for MoBrDa provides a motivational basis for marriage with her. (At the same time, the negative sentiments toward father and his kin, evoked by patripotestal jural authority, are generalized to include FaSiDa, rendering marriage with her 'sentimentally inappropriate'.)

In short, although Homans and Schneider attempt to provide a motivational explanation for the *practice* of this form of marriage, they do not derive the motivation from some universal characteristic of the human mind, or from some *assumed* characteristic of the members of this society, but rather from early learning experience in the context of a certain type of institutional structure, that is, patrilineal authority and matrilineal nurturance. Moreover, they are careful to point out that jural authority is a necessary, but not a sufficient, condition for its practice. It follows that the type of jural authority can be deduced from the type of unilateral cross-cousin marriage, but that the latter cannot be deduced from the former.

This type of explanation—whether or not the particular theory is true—seems to be exemplary. Needham, however, takes issue with the formal aspects of this explanation on the grounds that it is causal, 'psychological', and non-contextual. Since the last objection is tangential to his argument, we shall address our comments to the former two only.

Needham's first objection to the Homans-Schneider explanation is that it is 'fundamentally not sociological at all, but psychological, and inapt to the solution of a sociological problem'. Agreeing with Durkheim, he maintains that ' "the psychological factor is too general to predetermine the course of social phenomena. Since it does not imply one social form rather than another, it cannot explain any" '. Since this quotation presumably reflects Needham's understanding of 'psychological explanation' the fallacy inherent in his criticism of Homans and Schneider is obvious. The 'psychological factor' which they employ is not 'general', nor is it used to explain 'directly' a social phenomenon. Their procedure is, in fact, the reverse of what Needham interprets it to be. The antecedent condition, by which they attempt to explain matrilateral cross-cousin marriage, is not a general 'psychological' factor, but a specific jural institution. From this jural institution, they deduce a specific sentiment which, they argue, is the intervening variable between jural authority, as the independent variable, and matrilateral cross-cousin marriage, the dependent variable. Thus, Needham's characterization of the Homans-Schneider hypothesis is not only a caricature, it is false.

Needham's second objection to the Homans-Schneider explanation is that it is causal, and causal explanations, for him, are as inappropriate as non-contextual methods. This objection can be dealt with adequately only after an analysis of the strategy of causal analysis. Before proceeding to this analysis, in the next section, we must first examine Needham's functional explanation for unilateral cross-cousin marriage. His hypothesis is difficult to state because the argument in which it is contained is confusing and contradictory. Embedded, however, in his contradictory argument, there seems to be the following thesis: Although both types of unilateral cross-cousin marriage are found in unilineal societies, the matrilateral type is to be found most frequently (perhaps always) in those societies in which residence and descent rules are parallel ('harmonic regimes'). This is to be explained by the high degree of social solidarity, resulting from the generalized exchange inherent in this type of cross-cousin marriage, and by the 'instability and confusion' inherent in the patrilateral type.

It would seem, then, that the issue is joined. The Homans-Schneider hypothesis seemingly is causal and 'psychological'; the Needham hypothesis seemingly is functional and sociological. These types of explanations will first be examined in terms of their logical properties, following which the specific theories will be evaluated. Are they what they claim to be? Are they supported by the data?

CAUSAL EXPLANATION

Causal theories attempt to explain a variable, y, by reference to some antecedent condition, x, which, allegedly, produces y. In causal explanations, then, the *explanandum* (the variable to be explained) is some consequent condition, and the *explanans* (the variable which provides the explanation), is some antecedent condition. In any causal explanation, the relationship between antecedent and consequent conditions must satisfy one, and only one, of three mutually exclusive logical paradigms, depending upon whether the antecedent, x, is stipulated as a necessary, a sufficient, or a necessary *and* sufficient condition for y. Since each type of antecedent condition yields a distinctive set of logically permissible predictions and/or deductions, and since both antagonists in the present controversy exhibit some confusion about these different types of causes, we must examine these paradigms. Thus if we let x stand for an antecedent condition, and y for a consequent condition; and if we let $>$ stand for a logically permissible prediction from the term on its left to the one on its right, and np stand for a non-permissible prediction; and if we let $*$ stand for the absence of a condition, we then can explicate the meaning of the three paradigms below (Table I):

TABLE I. *Logical Paradigms for Causal Explanations*

Necessary	Sufficient	Necessary and Sufficient
$x\ np\ y$	$x>y$	$x>y$
$*x>*y$	$*x\ np\ *y$	$*x>*y$
$y>x$	$y\ np\ x$	$y>x$
$*y\ np\ *x$	$*y>*x$	$*y>*x$

Theories which stipulate an antecedent condition, x, as a necessary but not sufficient condition for a subsequent condition, y, must comply with the following model in their predictions and deductions. The absence of x

entails the absence of *y*, and the presence of *y* entails the presence of *x*. However, if *x* is present, the presence of *y* is not entailed, and if *y* is absent, the absence of *x* is not entailed. In other words, the first paradigm tells us that *x* is a necessary, but not sufficient cause of *y*, if, and only if, *x* is a condition without which *y* would not have occurred. It does not tell us that *x* is a condition in whose presence *y* always occurs.

If *x* is stipulated as a sufficient, but not as a necessary condition for *y* the paradigm reveals that the presence of *x* entails the presence of *y* and the absence of *y* entails the absence of *x*. However, the absence of *x* does not entail the absence of *y*, and the presence of *y* does not entail the presence of *x*. In other words, *x* is a sufficient, but not necessary cause of *y* if, and only if, *x* is a condition in whose presence *y* always occurs. It is not a condition without which *y* would not have occurred.

The paradigm for theories which stipulate *x* as a necessary and sufficient condition for *y* is uniformly symmetrical: the presence of either condition entails the presence of the other, and the absence of either entails the absence of the other. That is, *x* is a necessary and sufficient cause of *y* if, and only if, *x* is a condition without which *y* would not have occurred, and moreover, whenever *x* is present *y* occurs. This is 'causation' in the classical sense, in which *x* is not merely a determinant of *y;* it determines *y*.

Although necessary and sufficient causes are almost never discovered in the social sciences, it is nevertheless important to describe this type because frequently causal explanations of types 1 and 2 are 'refuted' by showing that they do not satisfy the paradigm for type 3: and this, in effect, is the basis for Needham's empirical objection to the Homans-Schneider hypothesis. Since there may be very few, if any, instances of patrilateral cross-cousin marriage, and since in their own sample there are many instances in which patripotestal jural authority is not accompanied by matrilateral cross-cousin marriage, their hypothesis, according to Needham, is disconfirmed. Although this argument, stated in many different ways, is repeated throughout the book (pp. 34, 57, 63, 68, 69, 70, 101–2, 111), it is fallacious. In the Homans-Schneider theory, jural authority is stipulated as a necessary, but not as a sufficient condition for differential cross-cousin marriage. Hence, in testing their hypotheses, the prediction, as the paradigm

for necessary conditions indicates, is from marriage to jural authority—'given patrilateral cross-cousin marriage, then . . .'—rather than the reverse.

In short, having demonstrated that in the absence of patripotestal jural authority, matrilateral cross-cousin marriage is absent—and this Homans and Schneider have done even by Needham's data—they have demonstrated that patripotestal jural authority is a cause or a determinant—to be distinguished from 'it is *the* cause', or 'it *determines*'—of matrilateral cross-cousin marriage. This part of their hypothesis is confirmed. If it is then the case that there are no empirical instances of patrilateral cross-cousin marriage, this part of their hypothesis is not disconfirmed; it is not an empirical hypothesis. (Patrilateral cross-cousin marriage is then a null-class.)

Although a causal hypothesis is criticized invalidly when criticism is directed to implications which are not entailed by the argument, deductions from the hypothesis are invalid if they make claims which are not entailed by it; and Homans and Schneider invalidly convert their causal explanation for the practice of this marriage custom into an explanation of its origin. This can be seen by examining the following statement, embodying the Homans-Schneider theory:

The practice of matrilateral cross-cousin marriage, *Cm*, in societies with unilineal descent systems, can be explained in terms of patripotestal jural authority, *Fp*, which is a necessary, but not sufficient, antecedent of *Cm*.

Since the cause, *Jp*, is stipulated as necessary, but not sufficient, it can be deduced from, or probabilistically predicted on the basis of, the practice of *Cm*. Let us assume that the hypothesis is tested against a representative sample of unilineal societies, and that it is confirmed at a certain probability level, *p*. On the basis of this finding can it then be further concluded that *Jp* can explain the origin of *Cm*, which is what the Homans-Schneider argument claims? Obviously not. For since an origin theory implies that *Jp is chronologically* antecedent to *Cm*, the hypothesis must be capable of test in the form 'if *Jp* then *Cm*'. But the latter hypothesis stipulates *Jp* as a necessary and sufficient condition; and, on their own data, this hypothesis is conclusively disconfirmed. There is, of course, another difficulty inherent in the deduction of past events from the explanation for current practices. Since there is no available evidence for testing the hypothesis, to argue that the evidence from present practice is also evidence for past origin is to commit the obvious fallacy of assuming that which is still to be proven.

FUNCTIONAL EXPLANATION

Unlike causal explanations which attempt to account for some structural unit, y, by reference to an antecedent condition, x, functional explanations attempt to account for y by reference to some consequent condition z—in which z constitutes the contribution of y to the maintenance of some system (social, biological, etc.) taken collectively, or of its several members taken individually. Thus, if x is a cause of y, the satisfaction of z is a function of y. In both causal and functional explanations y is the *explanandum;* but in the causal case an antecedent condition, x, is the *explanans,* while in the functional case, a consequent condition, z, is the *explanans.* Functional explanation, then, takes the form, if y then z, in which y (a structural unit) is a sufficient condition for the satisfaction of z—the satisfaction of z is the function of y—and z is a functional requirement of some system.

It is obvious from the formal statement, first, that 'function' may refer not only to those contributions which a structural unit makes to the maintenance of a social system or a social group, but also to the contribution which it makes to the maintenance and persistence of the several members of the group taken individually. The former are termed 'social functions', the latter 'individual functions'. (Unless otherwise specified, 'function' will refer to social functions exclusively.)

Second, whatever doubt there may be concerning the *empirical* status of any or all of the functions imputed by functional theory to those structural units by which functional requirements are satisfied, there can be no doubt about their *logical* status. Functions are necessary, but not sufficient, conditions for the maintenance of a social system. (If each were necessary *and* sufficient, any one of them would be sufficient to insure the maintenance of the system.) Hence, a complete inventory of social functions comprises 'a set of conditions that are individually necessary and jointly sufficient'.

Although functions are necessary, but not

sufficient, the structural units by which they are achieved—i.e., the institutions which satisfy the functional requirements—are, by contrast, sufficient, but not necessary. Because of the great diversity in man's social and cultural systems, different structural units may, in cross-cultural perspective, achieve the same function—they are functionally equivalent structures—and the same structural unit may achieve different functions. Indeed, it is rare that a given structural unit is even a sufficient condition for the satisfaction of a functional requirement, for often, in the same society, a number of such units jointly serve this function. Hence within societies it is a set of units, rather than any member of the set, which jointly constitute the sufficient condition for the satisfaction of a functional requirement. It would be somewhat rash to conclude that in any society social solidarity is achieved by means of one structural unit (although it should be possible, in principle, to rank the relative contribution of each member of the set).

If structural units are sufficient, but not necessary, for the satisfaction of functional requirements, no amount of knowledge concerning a functional requirement will, by itself, permit us to predict which structural unit, among a range of functionally equivalent structural alternatives, will in fact satisfy the requirement. And from the fact that some custom in a given society can be shown to satisfy this requirement in that society, it cannot be deduced that the functional requirement was a necessary, let alone a sufficient, condition for its origin. The fallacy in these procedures can be shown by examining the following statement which embodies Needham's functional theory:

I. The custom of matrilateral cross-cousin marriage, Cm, in 'harmonic' societies can be explained in terms of social solidarity, So.

This statement exhibits the ambiguity that characterizes most functional explanations. First, 'custom' may refer either to the origin or to the practice of a form of marriage; second, 'because of social solidarity' may refer either to a consequent, (function) or an antecedent, (functional requirement) condition of this type of marriage. In short, this statement contains at least two meanings which are expressed in statements $1a$ and $1b$ below, and it is not difficult to show that many functional explanations, including Needham's explanation for cross-cousin marriage, commit the fallacy of transforming statement 1*a* (which is valid) into 1*b* (which is not valid).

> 1*a*. Matrilateral cross-cousin marriage, *Cm* satisfies the functional requirement of social solidarity, *So*, and the satisfaction of *So* is the function of *Cm*.

Notice that in this statement *Cm* is the *explanandum* and the 'satisfaction of *So*' is the *explanans*. The *explanandum,* as in any functional explanation, is an antecedent condition which is explained by a consequent condition. Notice too, that this functional statement can be readily transformed into a causal statement by a simple transformation of *explanans* and *explanandum.* That is, instead of explaining a custom in terms of its functional consequences (a functional explanation in which the function is the *explanans*), the functional consequence can be explained in terms of the custom by which it is produced (a causal explanation in which the function is the *explanandum*). Hence, the functional expression in statement 1*a*, '*So* is the function of *Cm*' can be converted into the causal statement, '*Cm* produces *So*'. (The logical requirements for testing these statements is, of course, different.) In short, many functional explanations, but not all functional theories, are essentially causal. Let us now examine the invalid transformation of 1*a* into 1*b*.

> 1*b*. Matrilateral cross-cousin marriage, *Cm,* exists because it is caused by the functional requirement of social solidarity, *So*.

As in statement 1*a*, *Cm* is the *explanandum,* but in this case it is imputed as the consequent, rather than the antecedent, condition. Moreover, *So* in this statement differs from *So* in statement 1*a* in one crucial respect. In 1*a*, *So* refers to the function of social solidarity; in 1*b* it refers rather to the *functional requirement* of social solidarity. Whereas in 1*a*, a particular structural unit is said to satisfy the functional requirement, in 1*b* it is an unsatisfied functional requirement which is said to produce the structural unit.

This, in essence, is Needham's hypothesis. It should be noticed, in the first place, that despite his objection to causal explanation, this is a causal, not a functional, explanation. It seems to be functional because of the expression 'functional requirement'. But this should not

obscure the fact that the functional requirement, *So,* is imputed (invalidly) as the cause of the marriage type, *Cm.*

The imputation of causal efficacy to *So* is invalid for obvious reasons. Even if it were demonstrated that *So* is the function of *Cm*, and only of *Cm*, (statement 1*a*) the latter can only be a sufficient, never a necessary cause of *So*. Hence to deduce the existence of *Cm* from *So* is invalidly to convert a sufficient, into a necessary, condition. The fallacy is egregiously compounded (statement 1*b*) when the function, social solidarity, is confused with the functional requirement of social solidarity, and the latter is then deduced as the cause of the former.

Although functional explanation does not permit us to deduce the origin of *Cm* from *So*, it does permit us to explain the persistence of *Cm* in terms of *So*, *So* being necessary, but not sufficient for its persistence. Thus, if in a certain type of social system, 'harmonic' societies for example, *Cm* alone can produce *So*, then for the social group with this type of system, but not for some other social group, *Cm* is necessary, and not only sufficient, for *So*. Hence, if *So* is a functional requirement, the absence of *So* would, by definition, entail changes in the social system; and since *Cm* is one of its units, it follows that the absence of *So* would effect *Cm*, either directly or indirectly, as well.

In short, the persistence of a custom can be explained, but only in part, in terms of the functional requirements of a social group which it satisfies, and the following statements at least can be supported by numerous ethnographic and historical examples. If the net balance of functional consequences (as Merton terms it) resulting from the performance of any custom or set of customs is disfunctional with respect to, for example, the functional requirement of social solidarity, the interpersonal strains attendant upon this condition of *anomie* would either lead to the disintegration of the social group, physically, socially, or culturally, or it would lead to the acceptance of innovations in that custom or set of customs such that social solidarity is achieved.

In this example, the explanatory strategy of functional theory with respect to unintended social functions is viewed as analogous to the explanatory strategy of natural selection theory in biology. Natural selection theory is, of course, a functional theory: the survival of a biological character is explained in terms of a functional consequence, adaptation. Although new traits are adaptive with reference to particular environments, they do not occur in response to environmental stimuli, but are produced by genetic mutation. Now, just as mutations occur at random, regardless of their adaptive functions for the species, we may assume similarly that social and cultural innovations occur at random within a group. (It is obvious, of course, that social, like biological innovations, are products of individual members of the group.) But just as in biology, new structural items which satisfy functional requirements of a species survive; so, too, social and cultural items which satisfy the functional requirements of a social group tend to survive.

Of course, this analogical model cannot be pressed too far, and it has one important and obvious flaw. Although the source of biological innovation (genetic mutation) is not purposive, the source of social innovation (human cognition) does exhibit, at least on occasion, purposive behavior. Hence, to the charge that functional explanations are teleological (and therefore non-scientific!) the functional theorist can only agree that his explanations are, at times, teleological; but that given the nature of man, they nevertheless remain scientific. Thus if certain social functions are intended—and it cannot be denied that some, at least, are—then it can plausibly be argued that some institutions were instituted with the intention of satisfying certain functional requirements. One must hasten to add, however, that those social functions that have been of greatest interest to functional theorists—social solidarity, social integration, etc.—are obviously unintended consequences of the institutions that are explained; and to offer teleological explanations, as is all too frequently done, for these functions, is to commit the obvious fallacy of converting a consequent into a antecedent condition, as we have already noted.

If the argument thus far is valid, Homans and Schneider are not justified in claiming that if their causal explanation is confirmed, Lévi-Strauss's functional explanation is neither 'right' nor 'wrong', but rather 'unnecessary' (p. 59). If his—and Needham's—theory is a final cause theory, it is not only unnecessary, it is wrong. If it is not a final cause theory, and if its predicted functional consequences can be empirically demonstrated, Lévi-Strauss's and Needham's theory (taken as an explanation for the persistence, rather than for the origin, of this custom) is both 'right' and 'necessary'. Necessary, but not sufficient. For it is not the custom, but its practice, which satisfies a functional requirement; and the practice of the custom is always 'caused' by a psychological (motivational) variable, sometimes, but not always, of the type stipulated in the theory of Homans and Schneider. Indeed, in converting the functional consequence of a custom into a causal functional requirement (statement 1b above) functional theorists implicitly recognize the crucial importance of motivation for functional analysis. And, indeed, there would be no fallacy in this procedure if—but only if—the functional consequence were stipulated as intended by the actors. In this case, the social function is internalized as a personal need which, in turn, instigates the practice of the custom.

But notice that in the process of making these transformations at least three consequences follow, all entailing important changes in classical functional theory. First, a functional theory is embodied in a causal explanation; second, the causal variable becomes a psychological and, specifically, a motivational variable; third, a new type of function is introduced into functionalist theory—functions for the several members of a social group taken individually (individual functions). It is obvious, however, that the intention of satisfying the functional requirement of social solidarity is not the motivational basis for the practice of matrilateral cross-cousin marriage, and the cause of its practice, therefore, must be sought in some other motivational variable (of which the type suggested by Homans and Schneider is one among other possibilities). In short, to explain the imputed functions of customs, functional theory requires causal explanations of the 'psychological' type employed by Homans and Schneider.

But just as functional theory must incorporate causal and psychological variables in order to explain the social *functions* (and hence the persistence) of a custom, causal theory must incorporate functional, and indeed teleological, variables in order to explain the *practice* of the custom. Thus, if some need, N^1, common to the members of a social group G^1, is postulated as an antecedent condition for the practice of a marriage custom, *Cm*, it is obvious that it is not N^1 but rather the *intention* or *expectation* of satisfying N^1 that causes its practice; and *Cm* persists because it does in fact, satisfy N^1. Here, then, a causal explanation embodies a functional theory: Cm is explained by reference to an anticipated consequent condition, the satisfaction of N^1. It is the (personal) function of the custom which accounts for its practice.

In the discussion this far, we have ignored the important distinction between a *rule* of marriage and its *practice*, a distinction which Needham, but not Homans and Schneider, is careful to make. The implications of this distinction are very important for a more considered evaluation of the two types of explanation being examined here.

WHAT IS MEANT BY A 'RULE' OF UNILATERAL CROSS-COUSIN MARRIAGE?

Both the leading theorists, at least implicitly, agree that a rule can take one of four forms: it can prescribe, stipulate a preference for, permit, or proscribe some activity. Now when these four types of rules are combined with two types of unilateral cross-cousin marriage, there are six empirically possible combinations of these four rules and two marriage customs. From Table 2 the following observations may be made: When one of the forms of unilateral cross-cousin marriage is proscribed by a marriage rule, the other form may be combined with it in one of three regulations: it may be prescribed, preferred, or permitted. (The fourth combination, in which both are proscribed, does not concern us here because we are concerned with a rule of cross-cousin marriage, and the latter combination precludes cross-cousin marriage.)

Thus, (*a*) if patrilateral cross-cousin marriage is proscribed, the only *rule* that would ensure the practice of cross-cousin marriage is a rule of *prescriptive* matrilateral marriage. For clearly, if *permission* to marry the matrilateral cousin is deduced from the proscription of the patrilateral, permission to marry all other females (except for those governed by incest taboos) may also be deduced; and if marriage with MoBrDa is designated as a *permissive rule* of matrilateral marriage, then, by the same token, the society may be said to have many other permissive rules of marriage as well. In the latter case, however, matrilateral marriage does not occupy a privileged position, and it would be misleading to characterize this society as having a rule of matrilateral marriage. Moreover, the expected probability of the ocurrence of matrilateral marriage, as deduced from the proscription of the patrilateral form, is no higher than that of any other non-patrilateral form of marriage. In short, even if it were the case that a patrilateral system is as 'difficult' and 'confusing' as Needham (p. 113) claims; that it is 'less effective' than matrilateral systems 'as a solidary arrangement' (p. 115); that societies which practice it are 'always in a precarious position', because this system does 'not produce an organic type of solidarity' (p. 117); even if all this were true it would still be irrelevant for an explanation of the practice of patrilateral cross-cousin marriage; there are other forms of marriage which could have been adopted by harmonic societies. Indeed, the vast majority did adopt one of these other forms.

(*b*) If patrilateral cross-cousin marriage is proscribed, it is equally misleading to speak of a *rule* of preferential matrilateral marriage. A cultural *rule* can be proscriptive or prescriptive; but 'preferential' is a characteristic of a human motivational system, not a cultural normative system. Although preferential matrilateral marriage is a motivational, rather than a jural (cultural) concept, it obviously leads to behavioral predictions of a high order of probability. From the statement, 'people prefer to marry matrilateral cross-cousins', it may be deduced, since there is no jural impediment to such marriages, that the incidence of such marriages is much higher than other forms of permitted marriage. Hence, although we cannot characterize this society as having a rule of

TABLE 2. *Combination of Rules of Matrilateral and Patrilateral Cross-Cousin Marriage*

Matrilateral Cross-Cousin Marriage:	Patrilateral Cross-Cousin Marriage:
Prescribed	Proscribed
Preferred	Proscribed
Permitted	Proscribed
Proscribed	Permitted
Proscribed	Preferred
Proscribed	Prescribed

matrilateral marriage, it is certainly characterized by the uniform practice of matrilateral marriage choice which, however, must be explained by some antecedent condition other than a rule.

In short, if patrilateral marriage is proscribed, the only cross-cousin marriage *rule* that can properly be said to characterize this society is a rule governing the *non*-practice of patrilateral marriage (or the practice of patrilateral marriage avoidance), rather than one governing the practice of matrilateral marriage. Consequently, no hypothesis concerning a rule of matrilateral marriage can be tested by a sample which includes cases of prescriptive, as well as of preferential and permissive matrilateral marriage. This, as Needham (pp. 8–11) correctly observes, is a major criticism of the Homans-Schneider study if it purports to be a study of rules of cross-cousin marriage. If the hypothesis is addressed to rules the only data that constitute evidence for testing the hypothesis are data concerning *prescriptive* rules.

Returning to Table 2, it is apparent that, unlike a proscriptive rule, which can be combined with three regulations concerning the other form, a prescriptive rule concerning one form of cross-cousin marriage can be combined with only one regulation concerning the other form. (1) If matrilateral cross-cousin marriage, for example, is prescribed, patrilateral marriage is necessarily proscribed, whether there is or is not an explicitly stated proscriptive rule. For the prescription of the one automatically eliminates the other from the class of either permitted or preferred (let alone prescribed) marriage partners.

But notice, (2) the prescription of marriage with matrilateral cross-cousins necessarily entails the proscription of marriage with *all* other classes of females, including, but not especially referring to, patrilateral cross-cousins. In short, the proscription of patrilateral cousins, as a deduction from the prescriptive rule of matrilateral cousin marriage, is to be included in the more general class of proscribed marriages. If this be so, a functionalist hypothesis can address itself either to the functional advantages of this prescriptive rule, or to the functional disadvantages of the marriage types implicitly proscribed by this rule. Thus, if Needham argues that the function of the prescriptive rule of matrilateral marriage consists in precluding the disfunctional consequences of patrilateral marriage, then, unless the patrilateral

cousin is explicitly proscribed, it must be demonstrated that the other proscribed marriages have equally disfunctional consequences. But if Needham were then to argue that it is an explicitly stated proscriptive rule (rather than an implicit rule deduced from the prescription of matrilateral marriage) that is stipulated by his hypothesis, unless the rule proscribing patrilateral marriage is accompanied by an explicit prescriptive rule of matrilateral marriage, the society cannot properly be designated as having a *rule* of matrilateral marriage, however frequently its practice may occur. But since Needham insists that he is concerned with rules of marriage, his hypothesis would have to be addressed to a proscriptive patrilateral, rather than to a prescriptive matrilateral, rule.

WHAT IS MEANT BY THE 'PRACTICE' OF UNILATERAL CROSS-COUSIN MARRIAGE?

When it is said that a people *practices* cross-cousin marriage or, for that matter, any other custom, such a statement unless otherwise specified is ambiguous. In some cases, 'custom' refers to some socially-learnt behaviour pattern which, without reference to prescriptive norms or rules, is widely, if not uniformly, performed by the members of a social group. In this sense of 'custom', driving a car in the United States or attending professional athletic matches, are both customs, whose occurrence is based on personal choice, and not on rules. 'Custom' may, on the other hand, refer to some socially-learnt behaviour pattern, widely performed by the members of a social group, whose performance must be understood with reference to some norm or rule. If the norm is prescriptive, the custom reflects the norm; if the norm is proscriptive with respect to one member of a class of behaviour patterns, and permissive with respect to the other members of the class, the ensuing practice is related to the norm without reflecting it. In the prescriptive case, we may say that the practice is isomorphic with a rule; in the proscriptive case it is not isomorphic with a rule. Needham recognizes this distinction, but he does not recognize some of the difficult implications for his hypothesis which stem from this distinction. Homans and Schneider seem to pass over this distinction much too rapidly. We shall examine each type with special reference to the 'practice' of cross-cousin marriage.

(1) The practice is isomorphic with a rule: If matrilateral cross-cousin marriage is prescribed, the 'practice' of matrilateral marriage means compliance with a prescriptive marriage rule, and whatever may be the explanation for the practice, lack of compliance will normally be expected to evoke some punitive sanction, whether of a psychological (superego pain) or social (social sanctions) character. (It may, therefore, be presumed that it is the potential presence of a punitive sanction, implicit or explicit which, psychologically, serves to distinguish a practice which is isomorphic with a rule, from a practice which is not.)

(2) The practice is not isomorphic with a rule: If, for example, patrilateral cross-cousin marriage is proscribed, and matrilateral marriage is permitted (but not prescribed), no punitive sanction will influence the actual practice of matrilateral marriage, and there is no reason to believe (merely from our knowledge of the rules) that it will occur more frequently than the other permitted forms of marriage. In this case, if matrilateral marriage does not occur, or if it occurs with less frequency than the other permitted forms, this society has neither the rule nor the practice of matrilateral marriage. On the other hand, if it occurs as frequently as the other permitted forms of marriage (and, especially, if its incidence is greater than any other form), we can certainly refer to a 'practice' of matrilateral marriage in that society. In this case, however, the practice of matrilateral marriage reflects personal preference rather than cultural norms.

THE EXPLANATION FOR RULES AND PRACTICES

Although there is some ambiguity in what the conflicting theories in the cross-cousin marriage controversy purport to explain, it would seem that they are both addressed to the origin and persistence of a prescriptive rule for one or the other form of unilateral cross-cousin marriage. Homans and Schneider seem to be arguing that the origin and persistence of a prescriptive rule can be explained in the identical manner in which the practice of a non-prescriptive custom is explained. Although their explanation for the latter is logically valid, its extrapolation to the former two is, as we have seen, not valid. Needham seems to be arguing, on the other side, that the origin and practice of (i.e. compliance with) a prescriptive rule can be explained in the identical manner in which its persistence is explained. As in the Homans-Schneider case, the explanation for the latter is valid, but its extrapolation to the former is not.

For Homans and Schneider, the origin and persistence of a proscriptive rule of marriage is to be explained in terms of patri- or matripotestal jural authority as an antecedent condition which renders 'sentimentally inappropriate' desire for marriage with females in the jural line. For them, it appears to be obvious that the origin of a rule which proscribes a class of marriage partners is chronologically subsequent to the absence of sentimental ties with this class of potential partners. This assumption seems obvious neither to Needham nor to me. To explain the *practice* of marriage with the non-proscribed cousin, Homans and Schneider postulate a pro-marital sentiment with respect to females in the non-jural line. Since the marriage practice is merely permitted, the explanation for its practice is appropriately sought in some motivational tendency of the actors, whose origin, in turn, is sought not in some universal need, but in the institutional arrangements of the society. The origin of a prescriptive marriage rule is then explained as a cultural codification of this motivational tendency. This, however, is not only counterintuitive, but is refuted by their own data. Most of the cases in their sample of unilateral cross-cousin marriages are cases in which the practice of this custom represents a personal preference of the actors rather than compliance with a rule. If it is the case that the practice of a custom based on preference is chronologically prior to the prescription of that practice, it surely follows that the non-prescriptive customs in their sample should have long ago been prescribed. Hence, their own data exemplify a contrary thesis: that where the practice of any permitted custom is instigated in the first instance by the motivational tendencies of the actors, there is no theoretical basis for the expectation that it will become prescribed, if it is practiced by a relatively homogeneous society. The contrary expectation is more probable: that prescriptive rules arise when marriage with a prescribed class of marriage partners has no motivational basis (*i.e.* when the actors are psychologically indifferent to the members of a class of prescribed mates, or when their personal preferences would have led them to mate with a class of females other than those prescribed).

Since Homans and Schneider do not distinguish between practice as compliance with a prescriptive rule, and practice as an expression of preference, their explanation for the latter is applied to the former as well. This explanation is entirely appropriate, although its import is different from the one that they would maintain: when the practice of a marriage custom means compliance with a prescriptive rule, their theory becomes a theory of social control, or of cultural conformity, rather than one of origin. Thus, given the prescriptive rule of matrilateral cross-cousin marriage, their theory can explain the practice of this marriage custom without the necessity of invoking psychological, social, or supernatural sanctions: the jural authority of the paternal line, combined with nurturant behaviour of the maternal line, creates a differential perception of mother and father, such that the child is motivated to marry MoBrDa. Thus, the institutions of jural authority and of prescriptive marriage are, as they claim, interrelated. The sentiments created by the former lead to marital choices that are consistent with the latter. When such a situation obtains, there is no conflict between the needs of the actors and the demands of the norms. (And, moreover, there is no emotional conflict within the individual.)

Let us now turn to Needham. Consistent with general functional theory, Needham argues, in effect, that a rule persists if the practice which stems from it has consequences which satisfy a functional requirement of that society, or, to put it less strongly, that it would not persist if the practice which stems from it has consequences which are disfunctional for society. From this, however, it does not follow as Needham believes it does that present social functions, even if intended—and in this case, this is a highly dubious assumption—are the basis for the origin of the rules. For example, the prescription may have been imposed on a group by force to support the interests of a ruling class; or by the charisma of a shaman or religious zealot for entirely irrational reasons. (The objection applies, *a fortiori*, to unintended functions.)

But the fallacy is compounded when Needham purports to explain the practice of a prescriptive custom (that is, compliance with a prescriptive rule) in the same manner in which

he explains its persistence. That is, for Needham, compliance with the rule of prescriptive matrilateral cross-cousin marriage is explained by its social functions. Now if this means anything it can only mean that in these societies the personal decision to marry MoBrDa (and this marriage *must* be based on a decision, since the rule cannot *force* a man to marry his MoBrDa) is based on the intention (conscious or unconscious) of satisfying the functional requirement of social solidarity. This assumption is not only counter-intuitive, but it is not borne out by the meagre data available. In the majority of societies that practice MoBrDa marriage, this type of marriage occurs in the absence of a prescriptive rule. Would it then be argued that *their* choice also is motivated by the intention of promoting solidarity? If so, this argument encounters a difficulty similar to that encountered in the Homans-Schneider argument: if the members of a social group are already motivated to achieve a desirable social end by practicing some custom, there is no reason for the custom to become prescribed. Needham might argue, of course, that once the rule exists compliance with the prescription is indeed motivated by the intention of serving its function. But apart from other difficulties inherent in this argument, it commits a logical fallacy, indeed, the obverse fallacy of the one committed by Homans and Schneider. It is just as fallacious to deduce the motivational basis for compliance with a rule from the social functions of compliance, as it is to deduce the origin of a prescriptive custom from the motivation for the practice of a non-prescriptive custom.

SUMMARY

To summarize this discussion, if distinctions are made (as they must be made) between rules and compliance with rules; between the origin of, and the persistence of, behaviour and rules; and between statistically normative and culturally normative customs, the following statements are either logical requirements for any theory, or are reasonable assumptions for the formulation of a theory. (1) If the theory is intended to explain the origin of a rule, then, (*a*) if the 'rule' is permissive, no explanation is required because this is really not a rule. (*b*) If the rule is prescriptive, its origin cannot be explained in terms of individual desires nor in terms of intended social functions because the rule, in either case, would then be redundant. It is reasonable, rather, to assume that the prescription is one to which the members of a group are either indifferent, or to which they are opposed; and its origin is to be sought in an individual or group of individuals who, either for their selfish interests or for the interests of the group (as they perceived it), imposed the rule upon the larger group. In the absence of data, however, the theory remains speculative, and no amount of data concerning the basis for present compliance with the rule allows us to convert an explanation for compliance into an explanation for origin. (*c*) The same logic applies to proscriptive rules.

(2) If the theory is intended to explain the practice of a custom, there are again three possibilities. (*a*) If the custom is permitted, rather than prescribed, the explanation may be based on a desire to satisfy either the personal needs of the actors, or some functional requirement of society—the latter, however, if (and only if) the social function is intended (but then the social function is a personal need, and the theory is motivational). (*b*) If the practice complies with a prescriptive rule, and if the motivational tendencies of the members of society are inconsistent with this rule, it can only be explained

in terms of motivational anxiety based on internalized (superego) or extrinsic (natural or supernatural) punitive social sanctions. If, on the other hand, the motivational system of the members of a group is consistent with the prescriptive rule, its practice may be explained by a desire to satisfy personal needs (as the model of Homans and Schneider suggests), or by a desire to satisfy social functions, the latter if (and only if) these functions are intended (but then the social function is a personal need, and the theory is motivational). (*c*) The same logic applies to the practice of proscriptive rules.

(3) If the theory is intended to explain the persistence of a custom based on a rule, which means, in effect, the persistence of behaviour which complies with the rule, or of the persistence of a custom not based on a rule, explanation can be in terms of (*a*) motivational tendencies of the kind stipulated by Homans and Schneider, (*b*) motivational tendencies based on the various kinds of anxiety discussed above, (*c*) unintended social functions.

NOTES

1. George C. Homans and David M. Schneider, *Marriage, Authority and Final Causes.* Glencoe, Ill.: Free Press, 1955.

Rodney Needham, *Structure and Sentiment.* Chicago: University of Chicago Press, 1962.

11

UNDERSTANDING AND EXPLANATION IN SOCIAL ANTHROPOLOGY

JOHN H. M. BEATTIE

ANY REASONED INQUIRY seeks to understand its subject-matter, and the kind of understanding appropriate in any particular case will depend both upon the interests of the inquirer and upon

From *British Journal of Sociology,* 10 (1959: 45–59. Copyright © 1959 by Routledge and Kegan Paul Ltd. Reprinted by permission of the publisher

the kind of material he is investigating. Social anthropologists have not always been agreed as to exactly what their sub-matter is or as to the nature of their interest in it. It may therefore be useful to see, first of all, what it is that present-

and the author. John H. M. Beattie is Lecturer in Anthropology, Oxford University.

day social anthropologists really study and, secondly, to consider how they attempt to make sense of what they study, that is, to understand it. One way of understanding things is to explain them, so I shall undertake a brief review of some of the types of explanation used in, and appropriate to, social anthropology.[1] What follows does not purport to be an original contribution to the methodology of the social sciences; its aim is the very limited one of making more explicit certain methods of analysis already commonly used.

First of all, how do present-day social anthropologists conceive their own subject? Here are a few fairly characteristic answers. For Radcliffe-Brown social anthropology was 'that branch of sociology which deals with "primitive" or pre-literate societies', 'sociology' being defined as 'the study of social systems', and a 'social system' as consisting of 'individual human beings interacting with one another within certain continuing associations'. (The same author had earlier defined social anthropology as 'the investigation of the nature of human society by the systematic comparison of societies of diverse kinds'.) According to Evans-Pritchard social anthropology studies

social behaviour, generally in institutionalized forms, such as the family, kinship systems, political organization, legal procedures, religious cults, and the like, and the relations between such institutions; and it studies them either in contemporaneous societies or in historical societies for which there is adequate information of the kind to make such studies feasible.

For Nadel 'the primary object of social anthropology is to understand primitive peoples, the cultures they have created, and the social systems in which they live and act'. As a final example, Piddington states simply that 'social anthropologists study the cultures of contemporary primitive communities'.

Even these few definitions exhibit very varying degrees of what social anthropology is about. Three of them restrict the social anthropologist's field to 'primitive' or pre-literate peoples; the other (Evans-Pritchard's) explicitly disavows any such limitation. Radcliffe-Brown affirms that social anthropologists study societies or social systems, entities which, he implies, are comparable as totalities. Evans-Pritchard speaks of social behaviour and social institutions rather than of social systems. Nadel, though apparently regarding social systems as legitimate objects of

study, differs from the other two in admitting culture as a proper theme for social anthropology. And Piddington would have social anthropology concern itself altogether with the latter topic.

We shall do better to consider what social anthropologists actually do. First, what do they not do? To begin with, they do not confine themselves to 'primitive' or pre-literate peoples, though it is true that their discipline grew up in the context of the investigation of simpler societies: studies usually regarded as anthropological have been and are being made in European, American and Asian communities which are in no sense primitive. Secondly, and here there lies a more fundamental misunderstanding, social anthropologists do not study or compare 'whole' societies, if 'society' be taken (as it is usually is) to stand for some kind of empirical totality; such a thing would be impossible.[2] What they do, or at least one of the things that they do, is to abstract from the social behaviour which they observe certain enduring or institutionalized aspects or qualities which seem to go together and make sense, in terms of some particular interest of the observer. Thus particular social institutions, such as a kinship relation, a marriage rule, a jural, ritual or economic complex, are identified and defined, and it is these, not whole societies, which may be and are compared. So the subject-matter of social anthropology, or at least of a very important part of it, is more accurately characterized as institutionalized social relations and the systems into which these may be ordered, than as 'society' or 'societies', considered as totalities somehow given as empirical entities to the observer.

But we must be more explicit. What are these social relations? Briefly, when social anthropologists speak of social relations they have in mind the ways in which people behave when other people are objects of that behaviour. At this preliminary level there are always two basic facts to be ascertained about any social relationship; what it is about, and whom it is between. This distinction is often expressed in the familiar distinction between status and role. Already it is becoming apparent that something more than just observed behaviour is implied in the notion of a social relationship; for a status is something that is inferred, not observed, and it exists only in so far as it is recognized and acknowledged, that is to say, in somebody's mind. Essential, therefore, to the notion of a social relationship are the kinds of expectations which the parties to it entertain about one another's (and their own) behaviour. It is, of course, this 'reciprocity of expectations' (in Parsons' phrase) that makes ordered social interaction possible. It follows that social relations cannot be intelligibly conceived or described apart from the expectations, intentions and ideas which they express or imply; certainly no social anthropologist has ever attempted so to describe them. Behaviour can have no social significance apart from what it means to somebody, and unless such 'meanings' are taken into account nothing remotely resembling sociological understanding is possible.

Social anthropologists, then, study both what people do and what they think about what they do. If data of the latter kind be regarded as cultural, then evidently they do and must have regard to some part, at least, of the cultures of the peoples they study.[3] Now the thoughts that people have about what they do are of (at least) two kinds; first, their notions about what they actually do, and, second, their beliefs about what they ought to do, their ethical norms or values. So it may be said that social anthropologists in fact concern themselves with three different kinds or levels of data; (i) 'what actually happens',[4] (ii) what people think happens, and (iii) what they think ought to happen, their legal and moral values. Modern anthropological monographs almost always give some account of all of these three different kinds of data, though sometimes one rather than another is emphasized, and they are not always clearly distinguished.

There may be some degree of coincidence between two or even all three of these things, but they differ in important ways. And kinds of explanation appropriate to one may be less so to the others. Thus (to take an obvious example) 'what actually happens' is often susceptible of quantitative treatment in a way in which —or at least to an extent to which—data of the other two kinds, beliefs and values, are not. A statement like 'in a sample of a thousand marriages bride-wealth was paid in seventy-five per cent of the cases' may be both true and informative. It is at this factual level that statistical treatment is most appropriate; it is less feasible to make quantitative statements of this kind about, say, sorcery beliefs or ideals of filial piety. Moreover, it should be noticed that even a statistical assertion demands, if it is to mean anything, a qualitative statement of what its terms signify; the statement quoted above is

only sociologically informative when it is known what 'marriage' and 'bride-wealth' mean in the social and cultural context being investigated.

Social anthropologists, then, study the different kinds of institutionalized social relationships which they abstract from the observed behaviour of the peoples they study, and they are also concerned with the beliefs and values which are intrinsic to these relationships. It is in terms of the systematic interrelating of these relationships that they define and analyse social institutions, as, for example, such an institution as kingship implies a complex of (*inter alia*) ruler-subject relations, which as it were 'hang together' both in the social field itself and (in terms of his conceptual interests) in the anthropologist's theoretical interpretation of it. But his interest in beliefs and values does not end with their implications for systems of social relations. Many, perhaps most, social anthropologists are interested in such ideal configurations and 'meanings', not only in so far as they are directly relevant to such systems, but also as constituting systems in their own right. Thus social anthropologists have written about primitive religions and cosmologies, and their concern with these themes has not been restricted to their social significance. Forde writes, in his Introduction to *African Worlds* (a collection of essays by social anthropologists), that 'each study seeks to portray and interpret the dominant beliefs and attitudes of one people concerning the place of Man *in Nature* (my italics) and in Society'. The essays are studies of beliefs and attitudes, not of social relations. Of course it is true that most of the contributors are interested in social relations, and take note of the implications for them of the ideas they are investigating, where such implications can be shown. But they do not abandon their enquiries where they cannot. Again, in his *Nuer Religion* Evans-Pritchard defines his inquiry as 'a study of what they [the Nuer] consider to be the nature of the Spirit and of man's relation to it'. His book is about religious ideas and practices, not about social relations, and this is so notwithstanding that the author has constantly in mind the social contexts of the beliefs and rites he is describing. It is plain, then, that although the central concern of social anthropologists has been with social relations, many of them are also interested in systems of beliefs and values even where these have no direct relevance to social relations. They are sociologists, but they are also something more.

II

I turn now to my central question: how do social anthropologists go about explaining the different kinds of data they deal with? It will be said that their first task is descriptive, for description must precede analysis. But although the distinction between descriptive and analytic studies is indispensable it can be misleading, especially in social science. It is not one between studies which imply abstraction and those which do not. It is rather one between levels and kinds of abstraction, for even the most matter-of-fact descriptions are shot through with abstractions, usually unanalysed 'common sense' ones. This must be so, because all description must use general terms, and general terms are the names of classes, that is, of abstractions, and not the names of things. So description does more than merely describe; it is also in some degree explanatory.

Any account of unfamiliar data, social or otherwise, must begin at this everyday level. To start with, the appropriateness of any particular framework of explanation must be a hit-or-miss affair, subject to continuing revision and reformulation. We must now ask what are the kinds of explanation which are applied, and appropriate, to the material which social anthropologists study. For there are different types of explanation, and they are sometimes confused with one another. But what every kind of explanation has in common, what in fact makes it an explanation, is that it relates what is to be explained to something else, or to some order of things or events, so that it no longer appears to hang in the air, as it were, detached and isolated. Explanation 'adds meaning to "just so" existence', as Nadel puts it. What is unintelligible considered in and by itself becomes meaningful as soon as it is seen as a part or as an exemplification of a wider system or process; that is, as soon as it is placed in an appropriate context.

Now it is an over-simplification to suppose that explanation is simply a process of subsuming the particular under the general, and to leave it at that. For things can be related to other things, and so explained, in a number of different ways. Of these four at least play an important, if rarely explicit, part in social anthropology. These are (i) explanation in terms of antecedent events, or efficient causes; (ii)

explanations in terms of mediating factors; (iii) explanation in terms of ends, or purposes, teleological explanation, and (iv) explanation in terms of general laws or principles. It will be worth while to consider separately each of these types.[5]

Explanation in terms of antecedent events is what we commonly call historical explanation. A certain existing state of affairs is supposed to be better understood if it can be shown to have followed from some pre-existing state of affairs, in accordance with certain principles of efficient causation already familiar from other contexts.[6] Thus if it is found that certain social institutions are as they are because of certain historical happenings, the anthropologist takes (or should take) notice of these happenings, provided that there is evidence for them. But there is another and no less important sense in which history is significant for social anthropology, and this is in its aspect not as a record of past events but rather as a body of contemporary ideas about these past events; 'incapsulated history', in Collingwood's phrase. These ideas may be potent forces in current social attitudes and relations. We should note, however, that explanation in terms of these ideas is not, strictly speaking, historical explanation at all, but rather explanation in terms of the interconnectedness of things, the second of the kinds of explanation distinguished above.

This mode of explanation consists simply in the demonstration of connections between things which at first sight appear to be quite separate. If the entities connected are on the 'what actually happens' level, these connections will in the last resort be found to be of a causal kind, different events being seen to be linked in a common causal nexus with other events. Thus Durkheim explained the statistical incidence of suicide among persons in certain categories by establishing causal connections with other social factors, such as marital status and church membership. And social anthropologists have added to our understanding of the widespread institution of marriage payment by showing how it is linked with other social institutions such as the system of statuses or the maintenance of inter-group relations. Anthropological literature affords innumerable examples of this kind of explanation. If the entities brought together are mental events, such as the ideas or 'collective representations' current in a society, then the connections may be in terms of mutual consistency or inconsistency, moral and intellectual compatibility, and so on, as well as in terms of their implications for social behaviour.

The pointing out of necessary but not always obvious interdependences between things is an integral part of the functionalist approach, as this has been variously understood in social anthropology. But it is not the whole of this approach. For functionalism always implies two quite different kinds of explanation. The second, to which I now turn, involves reference to an end or purpose, which is seen to be achieved by the causal interdependences which have been discovered.

The term 'teleological explanation' may itself mean at least two different things. Strictly speaking, it consists in showing that it is a quality of what is being explained to bring about a certain consequence. But not just any consequence; to say, for example, that it is a quality of fire to burn is not to offer a teleological explanation of fire (though certainly it adds to our comprehension of what fire is). For an explanation in terms of consequence to be teleological it is necessary that the consequence should be some sort of meaningful complex, such that when the causal implications for that complex of what is to be explained have been pointed out, it is possible to say of the latter 'so *that* is the point of it'. Thus the circulation of the blood is teleologically explained in terms of its re-oxygenation and so the maintenance of the life of the organism. What is implied in teleological explanation, then, is not simply reference from a cause to an effect, the simple converse of historical explanation which refers an effect to a cause; what is essential to it is the notion that what is explained has causal implications for some kind of complex, comprehended as a working system, and having some kind of value, such as utility or efficiency, attached to it. What is being explained is teleologically understood when it is shown how it contributes to the maintenance or working of that system.

But just as in explanation by reference to antecedent events the mind cannot rest content with mere correlation in space and time, but demands efficient causation, so in the case of teleological explanation efficient causation is as it were reversed, and the factor to be explained is understood to be as it is *because* it achieves the consequences it does achieve. This provides the second meaning of teleological explanation. The end is thought of as somehow foreseen (by somebody or something), and the thing to

be explained is understood when it is seen to be adapted (by somebody or something) to that end.

Now it is plain that this latter kind of explanation is appropriate to much social data. It often enables us to understand the conscious behaviour of human individuals, who do act teleologically (in this sense), at least some of the time.[7] It may even, it seems, help us to understand the behaviour of physical organisms, as the expansions and contractions of the amoeba are understood when they are seen as means to the acquisition of food. But clearly we do not mean quite the same thing in this latter case as we do when we say, for example, that a man is slaughtering a goat with the object of providing a feast. For we can say nothing about the amoeba's intentions, or even know that it has any. Nor can we (as empirical investigators) regard the amoeba's behaviour as due to somebody else's intentions, which provide that amoebae (or a sufficient number of them) will generally do what conduces to their survival.

But we are already on the edge of a confusion, for we are really asking two different questions at once. Not content with observing that a certain kind of event contributes to the working of a certain kind of (already comprehended) system, we are now asking (in terms, it should be noted, of efficient causation) how it comes about that this is so. We are turning, in fact, from teleological explanation to explanation by reference to some antecedent event, for instance somebody's previous act of intelligence or will. So we have two questions here, to one of which a teleological answer is sufficient, and to the other of which it is not. The first question is: how are we to understand the form of a certain phenomenon (whether this be the behaviour of an amoeba or a marriage regulation)? And the strictly teleological answer is: by seeing that that particular form conduces to the production or maintenance of a particular systematic complex; the maintenance of life through the ingestion of food, for example, or the integration of distinct social groups. Once this is seen the particular form which has been puzzling us is, so far, understood. The second, and quite different, question is: how did it come about that the form of what is to be explained is so conveniently adapted to the consequences by which we explain it? This is clearly a question of another sort: it is an aetiological one and not a teleological one at all, for it does not look forward to an end, but backward to a beginning. And like all historical questions, the usefulness of asking it depends on the likelihood of finding an answer to it.

Now in social anthropology the teleological approach which looks for the social ends served by institutions is a useful one, but that which attempts to provide a historical explanation of existing institutions in terms of somebody's purposes or intentions is much more rarely so. This is so, of course, because social anthropology has, as I have noted, tended on the whole to concentrate on the analysis of social institutions rather than on the study of the human individuals who have these institutions. And these two different approaches are very easily confused. In a social context, the presence of a certain institution and the fact that it contributes to certain socially significant ends may be due historically to any of a number of quite different kinds of factors: perhaps to the conscious intention of past or present members of the society, perhaps to its diffusion from elsewhere, perhaps to some kind of social 'natural selection', most likely to a combination of some or all of these factors. Where the answers to historical questions of this kind are ascertainable they are, as we have said, of considerable interest to social anthropologists. But where they are not, understanding in a different if more restricted dimension may be provided by teleological explanation in the narrower sense specified above.

Functional explanation, as it is usually understood, always implies two, sometimes all three, of the kinds of explanation I have so far discussed. It implies, first of all, the second kind of explanation which I distinguished, that in terms of mediating factors. For an essential part of the functional approach is the investigation of the causal links between different institutions. But it also implies the quite different notion (the strictly teleological one) that it is enlightening to regard institutions not simply from the point of view of their effects on some other institution or institutions considered in themselves, but rather in respect of their implications for some kind of enduring and socially significant system, the efficient maintenance of which depends upon (*inter alia*) the institution or institutions being examined. Here the accent is not simply on the causal links between institutions, but rather on the part one institution plays in a systematic and already apprehended complex of inter-locking institutions; on what may in a sense be said to be a part-whole rela-

tionship. Thus, for example, the institution of vassalage is explained functionally—and teleologically—when it is shown that it contributes to the maintenance of the particular complex of inter-personal relations which is usually called feudalism. And, thirdly, functional explanation may imply (though it need not) that it is because they bring about certain ends that the institutions studied have the form they do; it may, that is, attempt explanation on the level of effective causality. The ends which are thought of as being brought about may be, and have been, very differently conceived: sometimes they are thought of in terms of particular complexes of institutions localized in the society being studied; sometimes they are conceived as grandiose sociological ends like social equilibrium, integration, or the perpetuation of the social structure; sometimes they are taken to be non-social ends, like biological survival. Evidently the kinds of ends to which a particular institution is seen as conducing will depend to a very large extent on the kinds of interests held by the analyst.

I cannot here undertake a comprehensive analysis of the functional model as it has been developed and used in social anthropology; I simply indicate the parts played in it by the kinds of explanation I have considered. It may be said, however, that since the functional approach derives most of its weight from the analogy with organisms, which are usefully regarded as wholes composed of causally interacting parts or members, this approach is more illuminating where social institutions are being dealt with on the level of systems of social interaction rather than on the level of normative or ideal systems. Such systems may and indeed commonly do have a social dimension, but, as we have seen, it has proved enlightening to examine their interrelations in cultural as well as in social terms. It has, further, often been pointed out that the organic analogy can provide no model for the understanding of social change.

The fourth type of explanation which I distinguished is that which refers to general laws or principles. I might reasonably have put this kind of explanation first instead of last, for very often this reference is classificatory rather than explanatory, and in a sense all other kinds of explanation imply it. As a rule all that this kind of explanation does is to assert that the datum to be explained falls into a particular class or category, and so either possesses the characters by which that class is defined (in which case the 'explanation' is tautologous), or else possesses some character or characters with which members of that class have been found invariably to be associated (in which case the association itself demands explanation in some other terms). When, however, there already exists some understanding of the category to which the datum to be explained is referred, then the process of subsuming the particular under the general (as, for example, Mauss referred the institutions known as the *kula* and the *potlatch* to the general class of prestations) certainly adds to our understanding, and so may be called explanatory. But it would not be so unless we already understood the general class of phenomena to which reference is made; that is, unless it were already explicable in other terms. Thus the process of classification really consists in bringing the datum to be explained within the range of some already existing explanation. Of course a great deal depends on what is meant by such very ambiguous terms as 'law' and 'principle', but in any case what is explanatory is not the generality of the law invoked, nor any kind of regularity in the data which it expresses, but rather the explanatory synthesis which (perhaps implicitly) it entails. I have been concerned to suggest that the types of explanatory synthesis which we have discussed are among those most used—and most useful—in social anthropology.

III

So far we have been concerned with the ways in which social anthropologists go about understanding particular institutions. But social anthropologists, like others, have sometimes sought to provide understanding not simply of particular institutions, but of societies—or cultures—regarded as wholes, or even of the abstraction 'society' itself. I now consider briefly whether such approaches can be said to be explanatory and, if so, in what way.

I consider first those characterizations which are intended to illumine 'society' as such; which are, that is, supposed to be valid for all human societies everywhere, and to add to our understanding of what society is. The functional model which, as we have seen, combines two or more different kinds of explanatory synthesis, provides one such approach. Functionalism,

when it is conceived not (as it may most usefully be) as a useful technique for investigating and explaining particular social institutions, but rather as a key to the understanding of society itself, has assumed two main forms. First there is that associated with Malinowski, which holds that society is best understood as an assemblage of contrivances for satisfying the biological and psychological needs of the human organisms which compose it. Few if any social anthropologists nowadays use this approach: though indeed such needs must be met if societies are to survive, it is not instructive to analyse social institutions solely in terms of them. Their satisfaction is a condition of the maintenance of life at all, not only of social life, so they can hardly throw any distinctive light on the latter.

The second type of 'total' functionalism, taken over by Radcliffe-Brown from Durkheim, asserts that the function of any social institution is the correspondence between it and some general need (or 'necessary condition of existence', to use the term adopted by Radcliffe-Brown) of society. The ultimate value for any society may be said to be its continued existence, and this, so the argument goes, can be achieved only through the maintenance of social solidarity between its members. Cohesion, or social solidarity, is accordingly the end to which social institutions are to be conceived as contributing more or less effectively. Thus for Radcliffe-Brown social function is the contribution made to the functioning of the 'total social system', and functional unity is achieved when 'all parts of the social system work together with a sufficient degree of harmony or internal consistency; i.e. without producing persistent conflicts which can neither be resolved nor regulated'.

I am not concerned here to analyse this approach; in the present context I wish only to point out that it implies the notion that a total social system is some kind of empirical entity to which definite properties can be ascribed. It is, however, now becoming increasingly plain both that this 'holistic' view of society is of less analytic value than used to be supposed, and that in any case society or 'the social system' is not something given in experience, but is rather an intellectual construct or model. The use of a model of this kind is not to be justified by identifying it with something else that is 'really there'; its validity rests simply on its usefulness in helping to order and make sense of data under investigation. Society is not a 'thing'; it is rather a way of ordering experience, a working (and in certain contexts indispensable) hypothesis: if we impute to it some kind of substantial reality we saddle ourselves with an entity more embarrassing than useful. When this is realized, the needs or necessary conditions of a society no longer appear to be analogous to the needs of a physical organism; they appear rather as the logical implications of the particular theoretical model which we have constructed. Thus, for example, the American sociologist Levy uses a logical, rather than a teleological, frame of reference; he elaborates a number of 'functional requisites of any society', thus in effect saying (though he says a good deal more than this) how he conceives it to be most useful to employ the term 'society'.

I am not suggesting that attempts to characterize the concept 'society' are mistaken or useless; what I am saying is that such exercises, important though they may be for theoretical sociology, have little or nothing to do with the analysis of the kinds of data which are given in field investigation, which is the main business of social anthropologists. It is no part of their task to say what 'society' is; their work is cut out for them in explaining the data given to them in fieldwork. But although the concept is of limited usefulness for social anthropologists in its substantive form, the empirical entity to which it sometimes refers being better designated (after Emmet) 'social aggregate', it is none the less an indispensable part of the social anthropologist's analytic equipment (as it is of his title) in its adjectival form. So a minimal connotation must be ascribed to it, at least in a relational, if not in a substantive, sense. It is plain, I think, that what the term 'social' essentially implies is the idea of bringing together, associating, human beings, and it is simply this relational aspect of human life that we indicate by the terms 'social' and 'society'. 'Society' is simply the context in which the social anthropologist carries out his inquiries; as has been said, analysis of the concept itself need form no part of the anthropologist's task, which is simply the understanding of social and cultural institutions.

Anthropologists, then, do not, or at least need not, study 'Society'. But they can and do study specific societies, or 'social aggregates', which is a very different thing. What it usually means is that they study the social institutions in terms of which some at least of the members of a particular social aggregate are inter-related. The people so associated usually share a common territory, and they may—or may not—think of themselves in unitary terms. In this context what terms like 'society' or 'culture' do is broadly to delimit a particular field of ethnographical or sociological inquiry. My final question, then, must be: is any understanding of particular societies or cultures possible, over and above our understanding of the several institutions which characterize them?

The answer to this question depends, of course, on the way in which it is formulated; but in a certain sense it can, I believe, be answered in the affirmative. It may even, perhaps, be claimed that this kind of understanding is something which the social anthropologist is peculiarly qualified to provide. For it is to be achieved, if it is achieved at all, by coming to understand the dominant beliefs and values of the people being studied, and the social anthropologist, who lives in the society he studies and as far as possible as a member of it, may with luck achieve, or approximate to, this kind of understanding. When the major values of the people being studied have been apprehended in this way it may fairly be claimed that the society or culture has been 'understood', for only then can the investigator represent to himself—and perhaps to others—what it would be like to be a member of that society. Of course this kind of interpretation is extremely hazardous and a particular anthropologist may be mistaken; another anthropologist might conceivably select some other values in terms of which to interpret the same culture, for the student's predilections will affect what he sees and emphasizes. But the last word must be with the people whose society and culture are being studied; no doubt Evans-Pritchard's *Nuer* and Fortune's *Sorcerers of Dobu* (to choose but two examples) would have been very different books if they had been written by other anthropologists, but even if they had been they could hardly have failed to stress the pervasiveness of notions of descent, and the ubiquity of sorcery beliefs, respectively, as they do now. Social anthropology is not wholly hallucinatory. And, as I have noted, the key to this kind of understanding is not to be found simply by watching what people do (which is in any case unintelligible apart from what they think), but through the understanding of their language and familiarity with its idioms and the values it embodies. By these means an anthropologist may be able to give an account of the people he studies which conveys something of how they conceive their own social life, and which may thus possess unity and vitality as a work of art no less than as a scientific record.[8]

I conclude this very summary survey by recapitulating its main points. I discussed, first of all, the kinds of things that social anthropologists study, and I concluded that they study both systems of social relations and systems of beliefs and values. I then considered the types of explanatory synthesis appropriate to these kinds of material, and suggested that four types of explanation could usefully be distinguished for practical purposes. The parts played by these in contemporary anthropological theory were then briefly considered. I then asked how far social anthropologists could usefully address themselves to questions about the nature of society in general, and suggested that such inquiries often tend to become merely definitional, and that in any case the methods of social anthropology are not particularly appropriate to them. I concluded, finally, that the characterization of particular societies or cultures in terms of the prevalent value-orientations institutionalized in them is a proper activity of social anthropologists, though one to be engaged in with due caution.

NOTES

1. Explanation is not, of course, the only means to understanding, at least where the behaviour of human beings is concerned; understanding may also be achieved through imaginative identification with the character described. But social anthropologists, unlike poets and novelists, seek to convey understanding mainly (though not only) by explaining.

2. In the course of a critical discussion of the dangers of the 'holistic' approach in the social sciences, Popper points out that, 'If we wish to study a thing, we are bound to select certain aspects of it. It is not possible for us to observe or to describe a whole piece of the world, or a whole piece of nature . . . since all description is necessarily selective.'

3. Not, most social anthropologists would agree, to the whole of any culture. In most of its usages the term 'culture' is far too broad usefully to designate a specific field for systematic study. There is no need in the present context to elaborate the familiar society-culture distinction. It may be said, however, that as the terms are generally used by anthropologists the difference lies rather in the interest of the observer than in what is observed: where the interest is 'social' the emphasis is on social relationships; where it is 'cultural' it is on configurations of beliefs and values. But the reality which is given to the observer is one, not two.

4. It may be acknowledged at once that 'what actually happens' is a construct of the analyst, built up by abstraction and inference from what people do and say. The important point here is that it is the anthropologist's construct, not necessarily that of the people studied. It approximates to Lévi-Strauss's 'statistical model', as distinct from his 'mechanical model', which is the social system as its members conceive it. We cannot here examine the ontological status of sociological 'facts'. Here what is important to note is that whatever the level of abstraction involved 'what actually happens' is only one of the social anthropologist's concerns.

5. I do not here inquire into the epistemological status of these several types of explanation, nor into the question whether any of them can be reduced to any other, or all to a common type (in a certain sense they certainly can). For practical purposes they can be distinguished, and they can be shown to imply different kinds of interests in the data being examined.

6. Plainly 'historical' explanation implies reference to general principles (the fourth type of explanation distinguished above). None the less it is not explanation in terms of these general principles, but in terms of past events. The principles involved are usually psychological ones of the unanalysed, 'common-sense' kind.

7. Social anthropologists, as I have noted, tend to be more concerned with social institutions than with the behaviour of particular human individuals. But where they are concerned with the latter, of course the purposes of those individuals must be apprehended if their behaviour is to be 'understood'. Nadel, in particular, was concerned to stress the pervasiveness of purpose: thus 'behaviour is sociologically relevant only if it is aim-controlled or enters into aim-controlled action patterns'; and 'there must be, somewhere in the task pattern, consciousness, and somewhere in its activation, purpose. Without these two factors there can be no social understanding; more precisely, there can be no material susceptible of such understanding'.

8. This process of 'translation' from one culture into another has been recognized as one of the most important parts—if not the most important part—of the social anthropologist's task. Cf., for example, Evans-Pritchard, *Social Anthropology: The Broadcast Lectures* (London: Cohen and West, 1951), p. 61; also (for a non-anthropological view), Berlin, *Historical Inevitability* (London: Oxford University Press, 1954), p. 61: 'the modes of thought of the ancients or of any cultures remote from our own are comprehensible to us only in the degree to which we share some, at any rate, of their basic categories'.

PART III Methodology

12

LEVELS OF SOCIOCULTURAL INTEGRATION:
AN OPERATIONAL CONCEPT

JULIAN H. STEWARD

I

MANY ANTHROPOLOGISTS who began their careers in research on tribal societies now find themselves involved in the analysis of such complicated contemporary sociocultural systems as China, Russia, India, or the United States. It is not surprising that they bring to these newer tasks methodological tools that were devised primarily for the study of tribal society. Valuable as these tools are for many purposes, they are not adequate to deal with all the phenomena encountered either in the study of modern nations or in the analysis of the acculturation of native populations under the influence of these nations. There is some tendency to meet the difficulty by borrowing concepts and methods from the other social sciences which have had long experience in dealing with contemporary societies. Where this leads to new interdisciplinary approaches it represents healthy scientific development, but often it appears that anthropologists are ready to abandon the unique methods of their own science to imitate the other social sciences. It should be possible to revise basic anthropological concepts and methods to meet the needs of the new and enlarged subject matter.

The greatest need is an adequate conceptualization of the phenomena of sociocultural systems above the tribal level. Because anthropology is distinctive in its primary concern with culture—a concept which perhaps represents its greatest contribution to the social sciences—it seems to be widely held that a general definition of culture is sufficient to dictate problem and method in the study of *any* culture. There would probably be no great disagreement with the bare statement that culture consists of learned modes

From *Southwestern Journal of Anthropology*, 7 (1951): 370–390. Copyright © 1951 by the Department of Anthropology, University of New Mexico. Reprinted by permission of the publisher and the author. Julian H. Steward is Research Professor of Anthropology, University of Illinois.

of behavior that are socially transmitted from one generation to the next and from one society or individual to another. To have operational utility, however, this definition would have to be modified in the case of each particular kind of culture. Our present working definition of culture was devised largely for the study of tribal societies, and it does not at all meet certain needs in the analysis of the more complicated contemporary cultures.

The concept of tribal culture is based on three fundamental aspects of the behavior of members of tribal societies. First, it is a construct that represents the ideal, norm, average, or expectable behavior of all members of a fairly small, simple, independent, self-contained, and homogeneous society. It is a norm derived from the somewhat varied or deviant modes of individual behavior. It represents essential uniformities, which are shared by all persons, despite some special modes of behavior associated with sex, age, occupation, and other roles; for there are definite and fairly narrow limits to deviant behavior in most tribal cultural activities. Tribal society is not divisible into genuine subcultural groups which have a quasi-independent existence and distinctive way of life. The concept of tribal culture emphasizes shared behavior.

Second, tribal culture is usually said to have a pattern or configuration. Pattern has a considerable variety of meanings, but it seems generally intended to express some underlying consistency and unity, some overall integration. Pattern should perhaps connote structuring; but it is difficult to express structure concretely except in terms of some special component of culture, such as social organization. Benedict met this difficulty by conceiving pattern as synonymous with basic attitudes, life view, or value system shared by all tribal members and thereby giving uniformity to behavior. It is a natural step from this definition of pattern to the concept of cultural personality; for attitudes are an expression of a personality type which has been produced by cultural uniformities. Emphasis is again upon shared characteristics, although the auxiliary concept of status and role personality is introduced to explain certain special deviants.

Third, the concept of tribal culture is essentially relativistic. The culture of any particular tradition—the norm and the pattern manifest in the tradition—is seen in contrast to cultures of other traditions. It is viewed as unique. The tendency to emphasize the persistence of patterns—and usually also of content—within a tradition plays down the qualitative differences between developmental levels or stages.

Conceptualization of tribal culture in terms of its normative, patterned, and relativistic aspects has been a useful tool for analysis and comparison, especially when contrasts are sought. But as a tool for dealing with culture change it has found little utility, even on the primitive level. Archaeology has continued to deal primarily with element lists, and even ethnology has relied extensively upon element distributions in attempting to reconstruct cultural history. It is significant that the more functional and genuinely holistic ethnological approaches have either stressed the normative and persistent quality of primitive cultures—and in many cases been forthrightly antihistorical or unhistorical—or, if dealing with a culture that has been greatly altered under the influence of modern nations, have paid primary attention to the disruption, imbalance, and internal conflicts of the culture. In cases where the native culture has been substantially changed but has not broken down, the concept of pattern is usually abandoned and acculturation is treated in terms of categories of elements, that is, subpatterns, such as religion, economics, social organization, and the like.

In the analysis of cultural change and acculturation of more complicated sociocultural systems, there are phenomena which cannot be handled by the normative and relativistic concept of culture. The culture of a modern nation is not simply a behavioral norm, which may be ascertained by the observation of all or of a significant sample of individuals. Different groups of individuals are substantially dissimilar in many respects. Moreover, certain aspects of a modern culture can best be studied quite apart from individual behavior. The structure and function of a system of money, banking, and credit, for example, represents supra-individual aspects of culture. To say that in the final analysis a banking system, like all culture, exists in the minds of men is not to say that its

operation can best be ascertained by using the ethnographic method to study the behavior of bankers. The system not only has complicated rules, regulations, and principles of its own, but it cannot be understood without reference to world trade, industrial development, marketing, legal systems, and many other factors. The national aspects of banking can be ascertained from economists who have made them their specialty. It would certainly be approaching the problem in the most difficult way to use the ethnographic method.

Not only is the normative concept of culture inapplicable to certain aspects of modern culture, but the tribal meaning of pattern is a clumsy tool for dealing with contemporary society. A contemporary society is not integrated through uniformities of individual behavior. It is an extremely heterogeneous entity, whose total "pattern" consists of intricately interrelated parts of different kinds. When tribal acculturation under the influence of a modern nation is being examined, therefore, it is impossible to think of the replacement of the tribal pattern by the national pattern. No individuals or groups of individuals carry an entire national pattern. They participate only in very special portions of the entire culture. The "assimilation" of any ethnic minority, therefore, can only mean that certain aspects of the national culture affect the minority culture so as to integrate the latter as a specialized dependent part of the whole. The loss of native features does not mean that a national pattern has finally been adopted. Just what has been adopted will depend upon the individual case.

We need, therefore, to examine some of the different characteristics or aspects of modern cultures that must be taken into account in analytic and historical studies. In order to adapt methodology to the different kinds of cultures, we need a comparative cultural morphology; just as a biologist needs to distinguish the kinds of life forms he deals with.

In an effort to delineate some of the significant components of contemporary sociocultural systems and thereby to indicate the features which are susceptible to analysis by the ethnographic method, I have previously suggested that these systems can be viewed in terms of levels of sociocultural integration. According to this concept a total national culture is divisible into two general kinds of features: first, those that function and must be studied on a national level; second, those that pertain to sociocultural segments or subgroups of the population. The former include the supra-personal and more or less structured—and often formally institutionalized—features, such as governmental forms and legal systems, economic institutions, religious organizations, educational systems, law enforcement and military organizations, and others. These have aspects which are national, sometimes international, in scope and which must be understood apart from the behavior of the individuals connected with them.

The sociocultural segments are subcultural groups of individuals whose behavior lends itself to the methods of direct observation used by anthropology. There are several kinds of subcultural groups in modern states and nations. First there are vertical or localized groups, which may represent differentiation that has occurred during national development—for example, subcultures arising from local specialization in production—or else ethnic minorities, which survive from a pre-national period or which as immigrants brought a distinctive culture into the nation. Second, there are horizontal groups, such as castes, classes, occupational divisions, and other segments, which hold a status position in an hierarchical arrangement and usually crosscut localities to some extent. These, too, may represent segments which either have been differentiated during national development or have been incorporated from the outside.

The distinction between national institutions and sociocultural segments suggests that the ethnographic method is applicable only to the latter. Much recent anthropology, however, has dealt with "nations," "national culture," and "national characteristics." "National" cannot have the same meaning as "tribal," for many aspects of modern cultures do not represent shared behavior which lends itself to the direct observation of individuals. "National culture" has in fact several special meanings apart from the totality of culture, and it is necessary to distinguish these.

First, "national culture" may signify "cultural products" or national achievements in the fields of science, literature, philosophy, religion, and the like, which presuppose a national level of sociocultural integration. In some societies, these may be limited largely to the upper classes. Second, "national culture" may be understood to mean governmental, economic, religious, and other institutions which function on a national scale. Although all members of the society will be affected by these institutions, the effect may be quite different among the various sociocultural segments.

Third, "national culture" may mean the common denominator of behavior that is shared by all members of the nation and that can be ascertained by direct observation of the individual. The method of study presumably requires a technique for sampling large populations, although some use has been made of indirect evidence, such as "cultural content analysis" of novels, motion pictures, and the like. It is not my purpose at present to review the methods for ascertaining the common denominator of national characteristics. I would stress, however, that current research seems to be more concerned with the problem of how to ascertain these characteristics than with the question of what they signify. Once the characteristics have been determined, they are evidently considered, especially by the more psychoanalytically-minded social scientists, as evidence of a basic personality which constitutes the mainspring of all national behavior. If, however, one were to regard the national common denominator as a composite of behavior traits of different orders it would be easier to recognize that some traits do change fairly readily, that national character is not perhaps the tightly integrated entity it is sometimes represented to be.

An analysis of national characteristics from the point of view of levels of sociocultural integration suggests that the common denominator may consist of the following components. First, there are behavior traits which result from practices of child rearing, that is, which are acquired by the individual as a member of the family. In a large, heterogeneous society it seems unlikely that families of all sociocultural subgroups will be essentially similar; but the question is a purely empirical one. Second, there is common behavior to the extent that all members of a society are subject to the same national institutions. All individuals obey the same laws, and they may share in some measure national religious, military, social and other institutions. Third, there may be a common denominator that derives from the influence of mass means of communication. These three kinds of traits are not wholly comparable and they may change somewhat independently of one another. International relations, we know, have changed recently at a dizzy rate, and national attitudes toward other nations have changed correspondingly. This does not mean that attitudes toward internal political ideologies have undergone similar transformation. Nevertheless, the latter may change significantly under the pressure of economic factors and the influence of mass communications, while commensurate alteration of family types and ideals does not occur. This view is not in conflict with a functional interpretation. It merely stresses the importance of recognizing the heterogeneity of a modern society and of regarding even the common denominator of shared behavior as a composite, as wheels within wheels, some turning faster than others and each geared to some different aspect of national culture.

The distinctions between the different aspects of national culture clearly imply that a great many different methods must be used to study any national culture in its totality. The problem of how to study a national culture does not ordinarily arise in most of the other social sciences. Except anthropology and sociology, the other disciplines usually deal with a special category of data representing an aspect of culture which functions on a national level. This cannot mean, however, that these categories represent the only significant components of a national culture as is the case of tribal culture. Each category has manifestations on the national level and on the level of the subcultural groups. Religion, for example, may have a state or even international organization and a formal doctrine, but it also has a great variety of local meanings and manifestations. The utility of distinguishing levels of sociocultural integration as well as categories of phenomena can be strikingly illustrated in studies of culture change and acculturation.

In the growth continuum of any culture, there is a succession of organizational types which are not only increasingly complex but which represent new emergent forms. The concept is fairly similar to that of organizational levels in biology. In culture, simple forms, such as those represented by the family or band, do not wholly disappear when a more complex stage of development is reached, nor do they merely survive fossil-like, as the concepts of folkways and mores formerly assumed. They gradually become specialized, dependent parts of new kinds of total configurations. The many-faceted national culture previously delineated represents a very high development level.

The application of the concept of developmental levels, or emergent evolution, to cultural phenomena is not new. The idea that

"advanced" cultures are differently integrated than "simple" cultures is implicit in most studies. But its methodological utility has been pretty much ignored, partly, I suspect, because it suggests the now widely discredited schemes of cultural evolution. The concept of levels of integration does not presuppose any evolutionary sequence. In biology, the concept that higher levels of life have different organizing principles than lower ones is in no way concerned with the evolution of particular life forms, such as birds, mammals, or reptiles. Similarly, the same concept applied to culture is not concerned with the developmental sequences of particular cultural types. The cultural evolution of Morgan, Tylor, and others is a developmental taxonomy based on concrete characteristics of cultures. The concept of levels of sociocultural integration, on the other hand, is simply a methodological tool for dealing with culture of different degrees of complexity. It is not a conclusion about evolution.

Another obstacle to the use of the concept of levels of sociocultural integration is the very strong hold of the concept of relativity. So long as the differences between cultural traditions are regarded as the only important qualitative differences, that is, so long as each culture area is seen primarily in terms of a fixed pattern which endures throughout its history, developmental stages will be thought of in terms only of quantitative differences, as matters of mere complexity. The concept of levels of sociocultural integration provides a new frame of reference and a new meaning to pattern; and it facilitates cross-cultural comparison.

II

Few efforts have been made to specify significant levels of sociocultural integration. The historical approach has been divided between a relativistic emphasis upon the continuity of the traditional pattern and postulation of particular evolutionary stages. Where the approach has been less committed to one of these extreme positions, it has usually dealt only with special aspects of culture, suggesting developmental stages in such features as religion or political organization.

An outstanding contribution which bears directly upon the problem of integrational levels, even though it approaches it somewhat tangentially, is Redfield's concept of the folk society and the folk culture. The characteristics which Redfield ascribes to such a society and culture and which are attributable to a large number of tribal societies and cultures, are descriptive of an organizational type rather than of a particular cultural type. That is, they are intended to characterize societies at a certain level of sociocultural integration in wholly different cultural traditions. Further comparative analysis will no doubt require redefinition of the concept, but for the present purposes we can assume that most of the diagnostic features are significant. Folk societies are small, isolated, close-knit, homogeneous, patterned around kinship relations, oriented toward implicit goals and values, and pervaded by general supernaturalism.

Redfield did not attempt to conceptualize supra-folk levels of sociocultural integration, but in his studies of Yucatan he uses the urban society as a contrasting type. Subjected to urbanization, the folk society is secularized, individualized, and disorganized. Urbanization, however, is but one of the processes through which a folk society may be integrated into a larger sociocultural system; for cities are but specialized parts of such systems. Some folk societies are incorporated into states and nations as regionally specialized subcultures which do not undergo urbanization at all and which are readapted rather than transformed. Even when the folk society is transformed, the individual is not only secularized, individualized, and disorganized but he adopts scientific or naturalistic explanations in place of supernatural ones, he participates in occupational, class, ethnic, or other sociocultural segments of the city, and in general he is reintegrated in a new kind of system.

Redfield's concept of the folk society and the folk culture are based largely on his studies of the Maya Indians of Yucatan. Historically, the Maya villages were once parts of city states and federations, sometimes called "empires," and they became relatively independent after the Spaniards destroyed the state or national superstructure. The evident stability of their society and culture through the upheavals of the Spanish Conquest and later events suggests a fairly high degree of integration. Whether the nature of this integration is essentially similar to that of tribal societies and to what is broadly called "folk societies" in other cultural traditions is a question to be answered by comparative, cross-cultural analysis. It is significant that the term "tribal society" remains an exceedingly ill-

defined catch-all. Once a typology of integrational levels is established empirically, it will be possible to examine the reintegration of simpler societies into larger sociocultural systems and to make generalizations about process which go beyond what Redfield derived from the process of urbanization.

It is certain that further discriminations will require recognition of integrational levels that are lower than the folk level. The biological or nuclear family represents a level that is lower in a structural sense, and in some cases it appears to have been historically antecedent to higher forms. Among the aboriginal Western Shoshoni, practically all features of the relatively simple culture were integrated and functioned on a family level. The family was the reproductive, economic, educational, political, and religious unit. It reared its children in comparative isolation, obtained its own food, and cared for its members at birth, sickness, death, and other crises. It made its own decisions on virtually all matters. Family dependence upon outsiders was rare and fairly unpatterned. The family sometimes called a shaman to treat the sick, cooperated with other families in communal hunts and dances, and visited relatives and friends when the opportunity permitted. But it could and did exist during most of the year without these extra-familial relations. Extra-familial dependency represented only a slight tendency toward a higher level of organization; patterns of multi-family unity had not become fixed.

The nuclear family, despite its many varieties, is basic in every modern society, and it seems safe to suppose that it has always been basic. In many cases, it was probably antecedent to the extended family, band, community, and other multi-family forms. In any event, there are probably several levels of sociocultural integration between the family and the folk society which should be distinguished. And above the folk society there are many significantly different levels of integration. For the purpose of the present exposition, however, it is sufficient to discuss only three levels—the nuclear family, the folk society, and the state These are qualitatively distinctive organizational systems, which represent successive stages in any developmental continuum and constitute special kinds of cultural components within higher sociocultural systems.

Folk societies or multi-family sociocultural systems develop when activities requiring a supra-family organization appear. Productive processes may become patterned around collective hunting, fishing, herding, or farming. Property rights requiring interfamilial understandings are established. Unity achieved in economic behavior may be reinforced through group ceremonialism, through patterned forms of extended kinship and friendship, and through recreational activities. Society acquires a structure appropriate to the particular kinds of interfamilial relations that develop in the cultural tradition, and patterns of social control and leadership emerge.

One of the most common forms of multifamily integration is an extended kin group of some kind. Not all peoples, however, have a supra-family organization based on extended kinship. The nuclear family may be integrated directly into a larger, multi-kin structure.

What may be called roughly a state level of integration is marked by the appearance of new patterns that bring several multi-family aggregates, or folk societies, into functional dependence upon one another within a still larger system. Communities or other sociocultural segments of a folk type may participate in state projects, such as the construction of irrigation works, roads, religious edifices, and so on; they may produce special foods or manufactured objects for exchange with other communities and for state purposes; they may join other communities in offensive and defensive warfare; they may accept state rules, regulations, and standards concerning property, credit, commerce, and other matters of mutual concern. They frequently accept a state religion. The systems of controls arising from economic, military, and religious needs creates a political hierarchy and a social system of classes and statuses. Qualitatively new institutions appear on the state, or national, level: governmental structure and control of those aspects of life which are of state concern; social stratification; and national cultural achievements. All of these have national aspects that are distinguishable from their varied folk manifestations.

There are many kinds of state sociocultural systems, each having characteristics determined by factors which are peculiar to the area and to the cultural tradition. But all states can be said to represent a broad level of sociocultural organization which is more than the sum-total of the families and communities of which it consists.

There is nothing new in the idea that each

stage of sociocultural development entails new forms of cooperation and interaction, and that societies may be arranged in general developmental series, such as family, village, and state, gemeinschaft and gesellschaft, and others. The point we wish to stress is that the concept of levels may be used as an analytic tool in the study of changes within any particular sociocultural system, for each system consists of parts which developed at different stages and through different processes and which, though functionally specialized in their dependency upon the whole, continue to integrate certain portions of the culture. The problem of acculturation may be rephrased so that the phenomena can be handled not merely in terms of categories of elements and total patterns but also of functional levels. This is necessary in any acculturational situation involving a modern state or nation, for the different categories of cultural features—religion, economics, government, and the like—cut across the nation, community, class, and family levels, and function differently at each. National religions, for example, involve a formal organization and dogma, but their community or class manifestations may be quite varied, while a considerable amount of supernaturalism is particular to the individual or family.

III

Three brief examples will suffice to illustrate the utility of the concept of sociocultural levels in acculturational studies. These are offered to show how the concept could be used as a research tool and not to present definitive, substantive results, for the detailed research has not yet been done. Western Shoshoni acculturation exemplifies the influence of a modern nation upon a family level of sociocultural integration. Changes in the Inca Empire under the Spanish Conquest illustrate how the culture of a native state may be more radically affected at the national level than at lower levels. Postconquest changes in the Circum-Caribbean culture show loss of state functions and deculturation to a folk level.

1

The distinctive features of Western Shoshoni acculturation are best understood if contrasted to the acculturation of other Indians who had a tribal culture.

American Indians are potentially subject to influences from both the national and folk levels of United States culture. National influences consist of trade relations, such as the selling of furs, farm produce, and craft objects, and the purchase of manufactured goods. They include governmental services, such as schools, hospitals, work projects, grants of money and goods, and farm extension aid. They also include laws, establishment of reservations, and other restrictive measures. In some cases there was armed intervention in tribal affairs. National influences likewise have been introduced through special groups, such as churches. All of these influences are mediated through agents of one kind or another. But the contacts with the agents of the national institutions are rarely so continuous and powerful that the personal behavior patterns of the individual agents are adopted to any appreciable degree by the Indians.

In many cases, however, the Indians come into daily contact with White settlers—miners, farmers, and ranchers—which presents the opportunity for acculturation of each group toward the folk culture of the other. In early times, the White trappers were often strongly acculturated toward the Indian way of life. Later, the White farmers introduced rural American patterns which began to influence the Indians.

The reaction of the Indians to these national and folk patterns depended upon their own native level of cultural development. Most Indians had some kind of tribal organization, some fairly cohesive in-group, which made it difficult for an individual to detach himself from the tribe and enter the context of the neighboring rural White culture. The reservation is a result as well as a cause of tribal cohesion. It is only the extremely acculturated individuals who have been able to break from tribal life and, race prejudice permitting, behave like rural Whites.

But native patterns do not necessarily remain intact because individual Indians do not participate in White society. All tribes have been brought into a relationship of dependency upon American national culture through economic, governmental, and often religious institutions. In most cases, this influence of the institutions of the larger sociocultural system has been sufficient to destroy the native tribal pattern, often to destroy it with traumatic effects. It has been

the most serious weakness of the New Deal policy for the Indians to suppose that an uncontaminated native core of attitudes and values could be preserved while the tribe became increasingly dependent upon national institutions. One of the most tragic cases of present cultural conflict is the Navaho. Their very dependence upon livestock as cash produce for a national market puts them into competition with each other and threatens to destroy the native culture. The situation is aggravated by the limited grazing resources.

The Western Shoshoni were spared the more crucial difficulties experienced by Indians who had a fairly tightly-woven fabric of community culture. When White miners and ranchers entered their country a century ago, individual families readily attached themselves to white communities. Their hunting and gathering resources partly destroyed, they worked for wages sufficiently to maintain their very low standard of living. Later, they were given reservations, but these consisted of little more than small residence sites. A few who obtained arable land undertook farming in a small way, very like their White neighbors. Most Western Shoshoni, however, were only loosely tied to any locality or group, for there were no community bonds beyond kinship and friendship. Persons commonly wandered from place to place, covering distances of several hundred miles if they could manage transportation.

On the whole, Western Shoshoni acculturation has come about more through association with Whites than through governmental services. The influence of schools, health services, work projects, and other Federal benefits has been sporadic. Facilities have been poor, and the Indians have been too mobile. Association with rural Whites has not been very sustained, but it has been sufficient to acculturate the Shoshoni toward the rural American culture, especially where economic needs have forced them into the role of nomadic wage laborers. But it has not wiped out all Indian practices. Acculturation has consisted primarily of modification of those patterns necessary to adjust to the rural White culture. It has brought wage labor, White styles of dress, housing, transportation, food, and other material items, use of English and some literacy, and considerable adaptability in dealing with Whites, though race prejudice has prevented full participation in White social relations. The Shoshoni retain, however, many practices and beliefs pertaining to kinship relations, child rearing, shamanism, supernatural powers and magic, and recreation, especially gambling games.

Many other American Indian tribes retain features of this kind after other portions of their native culture have been lost. These features, however, are those that functioned on a family level and may survive apart from tribal patterns. The difference between the Western Shoshoni and most other tribes is that the former did not have to experience the break-up of tribal institutions. The individual families were quite free to adjust to changed circumstances in the most expedient way without facing conflict. Perhaps this is why they are generally quite amiable toward the Whites, exhibiting no deep-seated hostility.

2

At the time of the Spanish Conquest, the Inca of the South American Andes had a fairly elaborate empire. The Conquest produced radical changes in the national institutions, but the lower levels of the native sociocultural system were affected far less.

The native Inca empire was controlled through highly centralized political, military, economic, and religious institutions. These had developed in the course of empire growth, national or imperial institutions being imposed upon the local states just as local state institutions had evidently been imposed upon the earlier communities. The Inca institutions affected the states and communities to the extent that it was necessary to make the empire function, but this did not mean that everything at the lower levels had to be changed. Much was left alone. The imperial political structure consisted of a hierarchy of positions, the more important being held by members of the royal family while the lesser were left to native rulers. Community affairs that did not conflict with the state were evidently handled much as in pre-Inca times. Economic production was reorganized in order to channel a portion of goods and services to the ruling bureaucracy and to the Inca Sun Temple, but production for community and household purposes seems to have been little affected. The kinds and quantities of goods consumed in the home and village were not greatly changed, except perhaps through the introduction of methods of quantity production. The Inca Sun God was forced upon all communities as the supreme deity, but local

gods, cults, and rites and household fetishes, shrines, and beliefs were not disturbed.

Under the Conquest, Spanish national institutions replaced those of the Inca, but the lower levels of native culture were not so drastically altered. Spaniards took over the key positions in the political hierarchy and Spanish law was imposed to the extent necessary to maintain the Spanish institutions. But many native rulers were retained in lower positions and a large portion of village activities went on as in native times. Spanish economic patterns introduced a system of cash produce, money, credit, and commerce, but this was designed at first primarily to drain off wealth, especially gold, for the Spanish Crown and the upper classes. Instead of contributing goods and services to the Inca ruling classes, people were drafted into the mines to produce gold for export and were forced to pay tribute in various forms to their conquerors. Once these obligations were discharged, however, village and family affairs seem to have been carried on in traditional ways.

Spanish religion likewise affected the Inca culture differently at different levels. The Catholic Church, which in feudal Spain had sanctioned and implemented state policies, completely replaced the Inca Sun cult, for it could not tolerate a rival national religion. All Peruvians became nominal Catholics, accepting the Christian god and saints and contributing to Church support, but they did not abandon local shrines, ancestor worship, household gods, shamanism, and other lower level forms of religion. And the Catholic fathers were content to class these community and family practices as mere "paganism," which was innocuous provided it did not threaten the state religion.

Modern, republican Peru is very different from sixteenth century colonial Peru, but a great deal of native community and family culture has survived in the areas least touched by commercialism. Over the centuries, however, national economic patterns have struck deeply at the heart of community culture. The production of cash crops, both by independent small farmers and by plantation wage laborers, has linked the people to the national society. Wage labor in pottery, textile, and other factories, service in the army, work on roads and other government projects, and other cash-oriented occupations, together with loss of lands, is destroying the basis of the native communities and converting the mass of the Indians into a national laboring class. The local sociocultural segments are being replaced by horizontal or class subcultural groups. This trend is occurring in all parts of the world as native populations are drawn into the orbit of an industrial world through specialized production of cash commodities.

3

Among certain of the Circum-Caribbean tribes, the Spanish Conquest destroyed native state institutions without effectively substituting Hispanic national patterns. These tribes were consequently deculturated to a community level of sociocultural organization.

This deculturative process may be illustrated by the Cuna-Cueva Indians of the Isthmus of Panama. Archaeological evidence and historical documents show that at the time of the Conquest this tribe had a rather elaborate state organization. There was a ruling class, consisting of chiefs and nobles, whose status is evidenced by rich burials. These rulers were interred with several wives or retainers and a wealth of luxury goods, including gold objects, carved stone, pearls, precious stones, and ceramics. The priests were among the upper classes, and they presided over a cult which depended in part upon human sacrifice. As prisoners of war became sacrificial victims, warriors could achieve some upward mobility of status through taking captives. The common people were the farmers and the producers of the luxury goods. At the bottom of the scale were some kind of slaves, apparently female captives and perhaps males who were not sacrificed.

The Spanish Conquest struck the Cuna with sufficient force to wipe out the national or state institutions. Military expeditions eliminated the upper classes and confiscated their wealth. Human sacrifice and the state religion based on it were suppressed. But Spanish rule and the Catholic Church were not very effectively substituted for the native institutions, for the people moved into regions where the Spaniards did not care to follow. Left comparatively unmolested and yet unable to maintain state functions, the Cuna resumed life on a community basis. The content and organization of the Cuna community is strikingly like that of the Tropical Forest tribes, and it must be assumed that this type of culture was always part of the more elaborate Circum-Caribbean state

type of culture. Today, the Cuna farm for home consumption and make their own fairly simple household goods and utensils. The luxury objects were no longer made after the upper classes for which they were intended were wiped out. The manufactures now include pole-and-thatched houses, dugout canoes, basketry, simple pottery, and bark cloth. The village is the largest political unit, and it is controlled by a headman assisted by one or more shamans. These shamans do not have the priestly functions of the native Cuna, for loss of state religion has left little more than a simple village religion which centers around girls' puberty ceremonies and death rites.

IV

In the three cases we have briefly described, much of the significance of the acculturation would have been lost if we had attempted to view changes in the native society solely in terms of some total cultural pattern or configuration. Whether the substantive conclusions suggested are correct or not, it is clear that cultural and social interaction takes place on different levels. We selected the national community, and family levels for illustration, but there are no doubt other levels which will have greater significance for certain problems.

The concept of levels of sociocultural integration is a conclusion about culture change only in the sense that there do appear to be phenomena which cannot be explained by any other frame of reference. Any aspect of culture—economic, social, political, or religious—has different meanings when viewed in terms of its national functions and of its special manifestations in different subcultures. Stated differently, the individual's participation in culture is of a somewhat different order at the family, community, and national levels. As a member of the family, he is concerned with the most basic human needs—procreation, subsistence, child rearing, sickness, and death. Even where community or state institutions intervene to assist the family, these functions still remain the primary reason for the existence of the family. Because they are directly concerned with biological survival, they are charged with emotions—emotions involving sex, hunger, fear of sickness and death, and social anxieties. In the development of the individual, they are among the earliest learned and the most deeply ingrained. This presumably is why behavior which functions on a family level is the most difficult to change in a changing culture.

The individual, of course, reacts as a total person to his function as a member of the family, community, and nation. Nevertheless, community functions may develop without completely altering the family. New patterns of cooperation and social interaction lift certain responsibilities from the family and make it a specialized dependency of a larger sociocultural unit. But they by no means supercede all of its functions.

State functions, too, may be mediated to the individual through the community or they may reach him directly. But he does not surrender his role in the family and community by virtue of becoming a member of a nation. His relationship to the nation is specialized according to the subculture of his local group or class.

The inference of these observations for studies of national characteristics and national character is clear. Personal behavior is not something that can be understood simply by studying random samples of the total national population. The several aspects, or levels, of national culture we have previously defined— national institutions, national cultural achievements, subcultural patterns, family patterns, behavior in situations involving different subcultural groups, and the common denominator —should be distinguished and the role of each appraised. The significance of each of these aspects will depend upon the particular culture, and for this reason proper conceptualization of the culture studied is essential.

These comments on the usefulness of the concept of levels of sociocultural organization to studies of national characteristics and national character are offered because such studies have wide current interest. The concept, however, will have value to another problem or objective of anthropology which will surely become of major importance in the future. The search for cross-culturally valid laws or regularities has suffered as much for want of adequate methodological tools as for lack of interest. So long as developmental stages within any cultural tradition are regarded primarily as quantitative differences and the traditions are assumed to be qualitatively unique, formulation of cross-culturally significant regularities is foredoomed. If, however, stages are recognized as qualitatively distinctive, the way is clear to establish developmental typologies that are valid for more than one tradition. Even if this typology were based solely on general forms of the kind we have discussed, it would facilitate the analysis of the processes of change from one form to another. Distinction of levels of internal organization within sociocultural systems would also facilitate the discovery of regularities. Instead of dealing witih total configurations, which are made virtually unique by definition, it would be possible to isolate special components, which, having been analyzed in their relation to the whole, could safely be compared with similar components in other cultural traditions.

13

ZUÑI:

SOME OBSERVATIONS AND QUERIES

LI AN-CHE

MY interest in the study of Zuñi was twofold: to get a cultural perspective by acquainting myself with a different culture, and to learn

From *American Anthropologist*, 39 (1937): 62–76. Reprinted by permission of the publisher.

the field technique of American anthropology. In other words, I would rather take the study of Zuñi as an illustration of larger issues involved than as a limited piece of ethnography. Thus in the present paper if I raise many questions, my effort is to be taken as trying to seek light and not as trying to make criticisms. In fact, my choosing Zuñi particularly was because of its rich literature by outstanding authorities.

I arrived at Zuñi, in western New Mexico, on June 15, 1935, and except two weeks' excursions, I spent all the time in a native family at Zuñi until September 16th when I left for the east. My role was more of a participant observer than of an active inquirer, except for some census-taking, after I was taken in by the community quite as a matter of course. I explained myself as one from China who was anxious to learn the wisdom of other peoples in order to teach my own people better. I repeatedly told them that I was not interested in getting secrets of any sort, and that they could tell me anything they cared, but that, should I happen to ask something which they would not like to tell, I would appreciate their telling me so. About the end of my stay, they seemed to be not very conscious of me, especially the family in which I lived, which assumed joking relationship with me and would not break their conversation on my entering their living room. Once in a while they would volunteer some information, and a few days before I left they were ready to discuss group activities at large, either public or esoteric. I participated in the family planting of feathers in the field before the rain dances, of which I observed six, being all that took place that summer.

The present paper is concerned only with some aspects of interpretation of Zuñi life. Due to lack of space, factual information and the problem of adaptation are reserved for other occasions.

When going over earlier publications on Zuñi, one cannot help having all sorts of curiosity and bewilderment, yet field experience with enough reflection inevitably corrects both second-hand impressions and immediate irrelevant comparisons. True perspective and objectivity can be gained by distinguishing between judgments based on isolated cultural traits and those based on contextual relations, between absolute schemata of one's own culture and relative significance of another cultural pattern, between the selective nature of old mechanisms and the penetrating power of an intrusive system.

RELIGION

The prevailing impression among ethnologists in America is that Zuñi religion is a purely formalistic thing without much bearing on personal feelings. Perhaps Benedict and Bunzel are responsible for this. In her book on the *Patterns of Culture,* Dr Benedict spoke of "the acts and motivations of the individual" in Zuñi religion as "singularly without personal reference." As her intention was to establish clear-cut types of culture by contrasting Zuñi life with that of the Kwakiutl and that in Dobu, it is understandable that the pictures are probably over-simplified. But once the pictures are so painted with all the process of elimination and selection, they tend to appear as independent entities, as complete in themselves, and thus very misleading.

Dr Bunzel's presentation on the other hand, in spite of strong emphasis on the formalistic side, is more balanced because of its intensive concentration on Zuñi alone. Yet one's discerning power in reading between the lines is easily confused once her characterization has taken hold of the mind, particularly when the emphasis is reinforced by Dr Benedict. A few quotations from Dr Bunzel's report will serve as concrete examples. In one place she says:

In Zuñi, as all the pueblos, religion spreads wide. It pervades all activities, and its very pervasiveness and the rich and harmonious forms in which it is externalized compensate the student of religion for the lack of intensity of that feeling. For although the Zuñi may be called one of the most thoroughly religious peoples of the world, in all the enormous mass of rituals there is no single bit of religious feeling equal in intensity and exaltation to the usual vision quest of the North American Indian.

Elsewhere Zuñi prayer is said to be

not a spontaneous outpouring of the heart. It is rather the repetition of a fixed formula. . . . Practically all the techniques employed by primitive or civilized man to influence the supernatural are known at Zuñi—fetishism, imitative magic, incantation, and formulae figure largely in ritual while the more personal approaches of prayer (which in Zuñi, however, is largely formulistic), purification, abstinence, and sacrifice are also conspicuous. The weighting is on the side of the mechanistic techniques which are highly developed.

One naturally has this question in mind: Why should "the spontaneous outpouring of the heart" be antithetical to "the repetition of a fixed formula?" In consideration of the social content of an individual mind, one's aspirations need not necessarily be in conflict with the cultural framework in which one finds oneself, and indeed the most developed forms of self-sacrifice are the result of an intensified super-ego. If one's interest is in the contrast between a self-possessed mental attitude and that of a vision quest, it is legitimate to make the contrast. But one form of mental process needs no greater amount of personal feeling than the other, so far as religion is concerned. Both excited and contemplative types of religion may be following respective cultural patterns to the same degree, and both may be as personal below the surface of social conformity. Upon entering a different culture, one is likely to forget all the intricacies of one's own cultural forms. Should an American student of ethnology be asked whether the Holy Rollers or a church group, with its methodically conducted ceremony, have a greater degree of personal feelings in their religion, he is more apt to make a refined judgment. And the analogy of the Christian church serves to show that the participants in a well conducted service, following stereotyped prayers and songs, may differ immensely in their levels of participation. One may respond to the outside collective behavior with all individual fantasies quite irrelevant to the service. Another may be identifying himself so well with the surrounding fellowship that collective behavior is an embodiment of his personality as a whole for the time being. No doubt some of the Holy Rollers, as some of those who indulge in vision quest, are entirely mechanical in their yelling and frenetic manifestations. After all, there is a tremendous difference between the official appearance and the inner reality.

After all the emphasis on the fixed nature of individual prayer, in form and content, Dr Bunzel herself has given some hint to the contrary. For she speaks of its being "individually varied in degree of elaboration" and quotes her informants as saying: "Some men who are smart talk a long time, but some are just like babies." And on the same page she goes on to mention the occasions "on which men display their skill in handling the poetic medium." She also speaks of "the compulsive force" of Zuñi dance.

According to the testimony of Mrs Stevenson, all the prayers "are repeated in low and impressive tones." The mode of behavior characterized by low and impressive tones is always observed by any student of Zuñi culture, and is easily forgotten as characteristic of personal feelings when one jumps to contrasting Zuñi with something else, as if personal feelings were strangely absent among these Pueblos. In speaking of a myth to persuade the Corn Maidens to go to the people, she had some more symbolic statement to make: "All spoke with their hearts; hearts spoke to hearts, and lips did not move." If the symbolic significance is to have hearts speak to hearts without outward manifestations, is it not just the opposite of mechanical prayers? Personally I was very much impressed with the deeply religious atmosphere in the truest sense of personal communion when I intruded unwittingly one early morning on an old man in all solitude in the open field, praying to the rising sun. I retreated instinctively even before I realized that I was in the "Holy of Holies." Such a living picture was much more impressive than that reproduced by Stevenson in Figure 1, facing page 15 of her above-mentioned work. Having been made aware of this event, I had more occasions to watch such scenes from afar.

Having established the place of personal elements in Zuñi religion, let us pay some attention to another aspect of the problem of religion. In consideration of the all-powerful religious activities at Zuñi, one often wonders how the people find time and interest for the activities in the domain of the profane world. Here again, the exclusive preoccupation of almost all the students of Zuñi culture in the esoteric and the abstract has left some impressions of its lack of balance. But a moment's reflection will show that, whatever the impression, a society cannot function forever if actually unbalanced. Moreover, what seems strange to an outsider, may not be strange at all in the inner mechanism of the culture itself because of its well rounded checks. One trait transplanted in another culture without its previous background and context will be strange indeed. Thus all the unbalanced picture of a treacherous Dobuan or of a vision-seeking Plains Indian will lose its significance in its proper context. American college games might be taken by an outsider to mean that American students must have no time for studies. The plain fact in Zuñi seems to indicate that the esoteric interest is simply an aid to the ordinary struggle for existence. Its activities are not only meant to cope with the unknown, but also to orient the activities of the profane world. For instance, the religious dramatic dances are not only so much prayer for rain or snow, which is the most desirable thing for arid Zuñiland, but they serve both as calendar and as harmonizing force for the community. That other groups, the fraternities, are largely curing societies is too obvious to need comment. Most significant of all is this fact, that although theoretically all the male members are supposed to belong to the dancing groups, they participate only in turn; the service of those who do participate is called on at regular intervals, because dances come regularly; and apart from those who are performing the sacred duties, the people in general do not attend as bystanders all the time on such occasions. As a rule they attend their farming or other business in spite of the dances taking place in the community. It is toward evening or on days that they are free from such duties that a large audience surrounds the performers. Even the high priests take care of their own farms. But whenever the dances are crowded with large audiences, both the latter and the dancers seem to cooperate unconsciously to produce a harmonious atmosphere. In other words, the audience is also performing the sacred duty as well. Such a phenomenon does not seem to have drawn much attention from the students of Zuñi, but it is worth while to point it out, particularly because such performances take place in the open air, attended by all sorts of people, without any effort on anybody's part to give directions to the audience. In view of the regular noise in any indoor gathering, be it a church assembly or a dinner party, it is remarkable to find responsive quietness prevailing on the plazas of Zuñi in the public dances. Dr Bunzel, in speaking of the pleasurable activity of group dancing, has this happy remark: "Joy is pleasing to the gods and sadness a sin against them."

The participants in dramatic dances are affiliated in six groups, with headquarters in six kivas corresponding to the six directions. Although the whole male population is supposed to belong to these groups, not every man is active. The active membership of these groups is given in Table 1.[1]

In native consciousness there are six categories of dances out of the great mass of those performed by any one of these groups which are considered basic to genuine sacred drama.

TABLE 1. MEMBERSHIP IN KIVA GROUPS

Name of group*	Kiva number	Cardinal point and color	Number of kiva tenders (olah' amosi)	Membership
he'ikwe	1	north, yellow	4	45
tcupa'kwe	2	south, red	3	48
'ohekwe	3	east, white	5	40
muhekwe	4	west, blue	3	36
'upsanakwe	5	above, many colored	2	42
hekiapakwe	6	below, black	4	50

* Following Bunzel's orthography

These are tcakwena (with drum), towa tcakwena (without drum), wotemla (mixed dance with drum), towa wotemla (mixed dance without drum), muluktak'a, and hemiciikwe.

Apart from these basic forms, there are imitations of the dances of other tribes, which in turn are classified into masked and unmasked dances, the latter being just for fun. Of the former kind there are the Cow, Mountain Sheep, and Butterfly dances of the Hopi, the Kumance and Apache dances composed at Zuñi, and the Nahahico dance borrowed from Laguna. These are more or less serious, comparable to their own dances. The imitations without masks, which are just for fun, include the Hopi Butterfly dance, a Navaho Squaw dance, a made-up Kumance dance, and a made-up Sa'techiwe Squaw dance. I observed one of the made-up dances, meant to make

TABLE 2. MEMBERSHIP IN FRATERNITIES

Names*	Membership
ne'wekwe (Galaxy fraternity)	42
shi'wannakwe (including three orders: Mystery medicine, Jugglery, and Fire)	41
hä'lo'kwe (Ant fraternity)	41
ma'ᵗke ᵗsan'nakwe (Little Fire Fraternity)	50
ma'ᵗke 'hlan'nakwe (Great Fire fraternity)	20
pe'shä'silo'kwe (Cimex fraternity)	29
ᵗsän'iakiakwe (Hunter's fraternity)	45
ᵗhle'wekwe (Wood fraternity)	25
chi'kialikwe (Rattlesnake fraternity)	27
ᵗko'shi'kwe (Cactus fraternity)	(extinct ten years ago)
shu'maakwe (from the spiral shell)	18
u'huhukwe (Eagle-down fraternity)	38

* Following Stevenson's orthography

fun of the Navaho. Boys and girls were dressed like Navaho men and women, sang Navaho songs, and the artificial mustaches were exceptionally ludicrous.

Besides the six groups of katcina dancers associated with the kivas, there are twelve active medicinal fraternities, some of whom also participate in the above dances. They are shown in Table 2.

LEADERSHIP

After this digression for some factual information, we find another one-sided statement on returning to the problem of interpretation of Zuñi life. Avoidance of leadership in social life is a corollary of the lack of personal feelings in religion. If one is not interested in vision quest and if "Man is not lord of the universe," so that "The forests and fields have not been given him to spoil. He is equal in the world with the rabbit and the deer and the young corn plant" (Bunzel)—if all this is true, what is more natural than the supposition that leadership among men is not desired. But here is just a case in which the premise is correct enough while the conclusion does not necessarily follow.

Dr Benedict reports that a Zuñi is afraid of becoming "a leader of his people" lest he should "likely be persecuted for sorcery," and that he would be only "interested in a game that a number can play with even chances," for "an outstanding runner spoils the game." The basic fallacy seems to lie in the tendency to reason with the logical implications of one's own culture. In the competitive Western world where one is brought up to assume that the world is made for his exploitation and where, if one does not push ahead, one is surely pushed behind, it is certainly logical that lack of personal acquisitiveness implies the denial of leadership. But in another society where a mutual give-and-take is more harmoniously assumed among all the beings of the world, one might be as humble as may be and yet exercise high power of discrimination among differences and values. Thus leadership is naturally assumed by those who are recognized by their associates, as well as followed by others who do not see in the act of following any degree of humiliation. The problem is not the contrast between leadership and its denial, but the valuation of the ways and means of

achieving it. In any face-to-face community it is safe to assume that no individual with common sense will try to make himself ridiculous by seeking what is obviously beyond his reach, and that even the most eager and legitimate aspirants to high position will make the ordinary official declination of an offer. Modern societies have asylums to take care of the insane, but a primitive community would have to charge the mentally dangerous with sorcery in order to follow the policy of "safety first" for the communal welfare.

That there are so many public functionaries with well-guarded prerogatives in Zuñi is a proof of the existence of social ambitions. Dr Bunzel reports a case in which an old priest refused to give information as to the order of events in a rarely performed ceremony, although he was persuaded to reveal a particular prayer for a consideration. "In Zuñi a 'poor man' is one who has no special knowledge or position in the ceremonial system. A 'valuable' man has knowledge and prestige."

A healthy amount of ambition is in existence in any living society. Only the means of acquiring prestige and realizing ambitions are different, being culturally conditioned. Once agree to play the game, it must be played according to the rules of the game. The rules are different in different societies but their existence is universal. With reference to Zuñi in particular, not only do ordinary forms of struggle for individual supremacy exist, but violent forms also occur once in a while. When Dr Hodge was excavating the ruins near Zuñi, a Protestant Zuñi got the information from him that a sacred object valued by the people was but a small figure of St. Francis, inherited from the early Franciscan padres, and he used this information to discredit his Catholic opponents to his own advantage. Previous to this the priests of Zuñi valued the object as indigenous, and with this discovery a strife of immense magnitude took place between the Catholic and the Protestant elements. Backed by the victorious party, the particular Protestant assumed the governorship of the reservation. More recently a high priest put himself above the other priests who were much more respected, and his means were pure politics which would have been beneath contempt in earlier days. His underhand campaign was linked with that of a new governorship whose incumbent was to be his right-hand man. Both were successful, and the general public was sharply divided between the advocates of the old order and those of the new politicians.

DISCIPLINE

Another case of oversimplified interpretation of Zuñi is in connection with child behavior. The universal idea of the students of the area is that the child is not chastised at all and behaves well automatically. This sounds strange to those who have had much experience with children in any other culture, but it is more or less accepted by all on the authority of universal agreement. Here is a typical passage from Mrs Stevenson, which is by no means an isolated example. One can read almost the same remark in any writings on Southwestern ethnography whenever such a topic is commented on.

The Zuñi child is rarely disobedient, and the writer has known but one parent to strike a child or to use harsh words with it. The children play through the livelong day without a quarrel. The youngest children never disturb or touch anything belonging to others. In years of experience with the Zuñis and other Indians the writer has never lost an article through them, either of food or otherwise.

Because of the universal acceptance of this sort of judgment, those who are sympathetic with the Indians tend to idealize Indian life in this particular, and those who are hostile, especially the White traders, say that the Indians have no discipline from the time they are babies so that even the grown-ups are just spoiled children. Here again, what seems unjustified is not so much the observation as an interpretation based on an incomplete recognition of the factors involved. The observers are easily led astray by their own background in supplying the missing logic with their own.

The working mechanism seems to be something like this in Zuñi. First, the responsibility of supervision does not fall too heavily upon any one individual. All the members of the family besides the parents cooperate to see that the child behaves well. In fact, any member of the community who happens to pass by will say something to correct some misbehavior of a child. Confronted with this united front of the adults, so to speak, the child does not have much chance in trying to play one against the other. And if he is not unduly constrained, why should he make it unpleasant both for himself and for others? It is often observed that a very obstreperous child is easily hushed by a slight sound of any adult, in fact, by any facial expression which is seen by the child. It would be a wonder indeed that such things happened were there not sufficient conditioning beforehand. Second, in spite of all signs of parental love, the children are allowed a much greater independence in the free world of their own. The parents do not fondle them beyond the necessary physical care. To get bodily enjoyment by caressing the baby as a plaything and calling this love is not the pattern in Zuñi. Early in life the baby is put in a cradle for most of the time. He is often nursed in the cradle. As soon as he can play by himself, he joins the other little fellows and is out of sight of the threshold of the family. He comes back for food or for attention whenever he feels the need for it. He enjoys the world of his associates most of the time, and when he is near his parents he does not feel the need to show off to please them or to demand too much from them. They are taken for granted as the source of his wellbeing. Third, chastisement does occur once in a while, as acknowledged by Mrs Stevenson. But it is done deliberately and effectively, There is no fussing around on the part of the mother, nor is there endless talk among the adults so that the child is encouraged to be mischievous by giving him so much publicity and attention. It is with the introduction of a new educational philosophy into Zuñi that some of the parents are beginning to feel uncertain of their children. Formerly the children had one well-recognized authority, but lately they are made to understand that missionaries and school teachers are trying their best to discredit their parents. And the new educational philosophy referred to is the fear on the part of the educators of the Fear lest it be instilled in the tender minds of children. The teachers are afraid that the children be made afraid. In other words, the family is losing control of the child, and the school is not adequate yet to handle the situation. This is no place to deal with this fundamental problem with any degree of fairness, but the point is that here is a problem due to transition.

To instill in the child all the education for daily life in a sense more pervasive than formal school education, there is the religious system of the people as a fourth factor. As early as the child is able to recognize anything he is subject to the impressive dramatic dances coming regularly the year round. To him, of course, the performance is undertaken by supernaturals. The unmistakable moral derived from all these is that they will be angry over any misbehavior. When he is initiated into one of the dancing societies, there is more formal lecturing on the moral philosophy of life, and he is whipped as a sign of purification. And above all, there are special functionaries among the supernatural beings, whose duty it is to punish the misbehaving. Apart from those who are purely religious guardians, each kiva has an atocle, either man or woman, to take over the unpleasant job of frightening any notorious child on any necessary occasion. Sometimes it is done in connection with occasions of dance ceremony. I happened to see one of the katcina gods in full regalia go to a family in late evening after the public service was over. He had long hair covering his face and a large sword in his hand. A child, supported by two elderly women, presumably his mother and maternal grandmother, stood before this frightful figure, who made a long speech and all sorts of gestures with his hand. Finally he seemed to be satisfied with the intent look of the child and the assurances of the women behind him, and got himself out after receiving the blessing of the family in terms of prayer, prayer meal, and material gifts. The child must have been notorious somehow; and that impressive scene, I believe, must be a lasting memory. Again, it must be pointed out that the present interest is not in the wisdom of such a procedure, but in the actual mechanism used to mold the child's behavior. It seemed a sound policy, though, to have the child supported by the helping hands of two elderly women, while he himself was standing on his own feet.

MAN AND WIFE

The next point of my interest in the interpretation of Zuñi life is stimulated by Dr Kroeber. In speaking of woman's title to the house, he has the following remark:

When a building is pulled down, it is the men who do all the heavy work. When it is re-erected, or an entirely new house built outside the old town, the men quarry and lay the stone, cut and lay the roof logs, and carpenter the doors and windows; the woman's part is auxiliary throughout, except for the light labor of plastering, in which she holds sway. Yet when a man has built such a house, and he and his wife quarrel and separate, even though for no other reason than her flagrant infidelity, he walks out and leaves the edifice to her and his successor without the least thought of being deprived of anything that is his. Men have shown me the houses that they have put up for a wife who subsequently installed another man as her husband, and have pointed out the glass windows, which they had purchased from the storekeeper with their own earnings, still in place; but the information was given casually, and without implication of injustice being involved.

From the standpoint of Western culture, this is extraordinary indeed. And Kroeber goes on to say that "the Zuñi does not have an inkling of having been chivalrous in such an abandonment" and that "his conduct is as much a matter of course as resigning oneself to anything inevitable, like a cloudburst washing out one's cornfield." But a more intimate knowledge proves that there is no reason whatsoever for "an inkling of having been chivalrous in such an abandonment." The truth is this. A man has no worries about a house. If he is married, he lives with his wife. If divorced, he either goes back to his parents (his mother's house) as before his marriage, or to his sister's home in case of the lack of the former, or he is married into another woman's family and lives with them. A widower without any near relatives, such as parents, sisters, or daughters, is taken care of by any maternal relative. And further, there is the question of responsibility, over and above that of a property claim. Bunzel has this apt statement: "With his departure obligations cease, and his successor fathers his children." From this angle, he has nothing to lose, but everything to gain. However, he is not unduly favored by his culture requirements. If he leaves behind all his children to be fathered by his successor, he is likely to be supplied with other men's children to be fathered by him when he joins a new wife. Individual cases may be fortunate or otherwise, but in the mill of the community mechanism no one set of people can afford to be so obviously favored or disfavored, if the community is to persist.

Although there is no intention of presenting factual information in this paper, it may be of some interest to note that, of 1,420 case records of the Zuñi (the total population is 2,036) divided among 219 households, there are 14 houses owned by men, all the rest being owned by women. Men own houses when they have absolutely no other relatives to live with, when their wives come from other tribes than Zuñi, or when they want to follow the White pattern of establishing families of their own, not to be bothered by the wives' relatives. Of the same number of case records, it is found that there are 22 cases of patrilocal residence and 7 cases of clan endogamy. Although inter-clan marriage is the rule, these cases of marry-ing within a clan do not seem to draw much attention from the public, when they have de-cided to "marry anyway."

In order to view the family situation in a more complete context, let us examine sex relations more closely. Both Cushing and Mrs Stevenson give detailed account of the ways in which marriage was arranged. But "to marry Zuñi-fashion" today is synonymous with any physical cohabitation without public sanction. Although marriage certificates issued by state or reservation officials do exist, they represent cultural distinction rather than sanction of marriage as such. Marriages of this sort are not many. Fetching water from the well or cisterns is, as of old, a good opportunity of arranging for a liaison. The difference lies only in the fact that water vessels of pottery were once on the heads of the maidens and now water buckets are in their hands. Young men scatter around, either singly or by twos and threes, either behind street corners or against fences, with large sombreros to shade them-selves when they do not want to be recognized. Such a scene begins in the early evening and lasts until everything is perfectly dark. Then they go back home for supper. After that the unmarried ones make night calls according to arrangements made earlier in the evening. This accounts for a late supper as a rule. One minds one's own business, so far as the boy is con-cerned. His favor is determined by the girl, whose ex-lovers may be quite friendly to one another. But during the evening manoeuvres between the sexes in general the maidens are not simply interested in love-making, but each girl is equally interested in spying on the af-fairs of her lover. No one hastens in the eve-ning, but walks leisurely and with a great air of casualness. A visitor cannot be aware of this until with sufficient time it inevitably dawns on him that open-air evenings at Zuñi are magically charged, that everybody seems to be sneaking around in a sneaking atmos-phere, with occasional inquisitive eyes cast upon the stranger who is not in harmony with the general setting.

Night calls are made by men with or with-out intention of marriage. One Zuñi youth, who has been a widower for some time, says that had he sufficient money he could arrange to sleep with any young woman whose hus-band happened to be away or who was not married. "This is not boasting," he says, and seems to corroborate the impression of White residents in general. The parents of the girl give informal consent by not objecting to the youth's presence. Scandals arise only when the parents are not in favor of him. They may set to work in favor of one man at the expense of another. The parents of the youth do not care where their son finds living quarters, until they are informed that a relationship of some per-manency is established. Lest some substitute should take his place during his absence, a husband will try to stay home as much as pos-sible. Sheepherding requires camp life, but as it is not yet the fashion to take one's wife to the camp, one would try to remain away from the sheep. A boy as a rule is found to attend them. A group of sheep with a burro (which is displaced by the horse for any other pur-pose and is not seen in the pueblos), herded by a young boy or boys in cooperation, and visited once in a while by the owner to take back one or two sheep for food, is the usual arrangement.

Infidelity seems to be one of the major causes of the rapid dissolution of marriage at Zuñi, and certainly is the major cause of all the petty troubles among the young people— troubles which exhaust their interests beyond the immediate horizon of rivalries. These diffi-culties are not between the girl's lovers as such, but appear as competitive efforts of each sex to outwit the other and as friction indirectly produced among men who are otherwise re-lated. The local government can settle any trouble of daily life except that connected with sex relations, to which it refuses to give a hear-ing. Thus below the calm surface of Zuñi life, most of the individuals have some marital trouble or other, and it is a rule rather than an exception to find that each has more than one matrimonial history. Two cases of divorce came to my immediate knowledge. They oc-curred in one family; one man returning to it after he had left his wife in another household, and another leaving his wife left behind while he found temporary lodging with his maternal relatives. The first was angry with his wife because she was jealous of his "alleged" intimacy with an unmarried girl. The one who walked out was accused of spending money on somebody else, while he himself was dissatisfied with the "meanness" of the family, which depended on his money for securing credit from a White store to get daily supplies. I mention these two cases, because they illustrate the general situation—particularly the latter case.

In this connection, it is curious to note that characteristics of a joint household based on the kinship principle stand out very strikingly. This in spite of the fact that "the Zuñis do not have large families" (Stevenson), the average size of a Zuñi household being still about seven and one half persons as found by Dr Kroeber. (Yet an unusually large household of over twenty members is not at all conspicuous in the minds of the Zuñi.) What we find as an attitude typical of the wives of brothers in a Chinese family is surprisingly comparable to that of the husbands of sisters in a Zuñi family. I cannot resist the temptation of making a comparison, in spite of my conscious effort to keep away from any irrelevant associations. While Chinese wives are married into the husbands' family, or rather the husbands' parents' family, the Zuñi husbands are married into their wives' parents' family. It is true, as Dr Kroeber has pointed out, that the Zuñi "are not woman-ruled people" and that "the position of woman is not materially different from that which she occupies in nations of non-matriarchal institutions," but to a Chinese the role of Zuñi women seems much more important. It is not correct to say that woman rules man in Zuñi, but what is true and important is the fact that woman is not ruled by man at all. To have an abstract statement of this sort does not mean anything, but the realization of the carefree atmosphere surrounding Zuñi womanhood carries significance. She is the naturally protected person in her own home. It is the husband who must make the necessary adjustment. And this makes all the difference in the world. She and her unmarried brothers and her sisters, either married or unmarried, have only themselves to care about as far as external behavior is concerned, while her husband has to be considerate and calculating. If the others are slow in coming to the table, for instance, he must not show signs of eagerness and impatience. In case he has something in mind to do and his father-in-law has something else to let him do, he will inevitably conceal his own intentions and comply with the desire of his father-in-law. If he is not quite satisfied with his wife's sister's husband, he has to be tactful and not too frank. All these circumstances do not imply that the other people need be malicious. A one-sided adjustment is enough to make his situation not as comfortable as that of others. Thus he is quite comparable to a Chinese woman who is married into the man's family. She may be well treated, yet the very fact of *being treated* is the core of her difficulties. She cannot take anything for granted, however well she is treated. It is she who makes the adjustment to her husband, her parents-in-law, her husband's sisters and brothers, and his brother's wife. We are likely to believe in China that the petty troubles among the wives of the brothers are the result of definitely womanish qualities. It is a revelation to find the husbands of Zuñi sisters in similar difficulties, and what is more, such difficulties are due to similar adjustments irrespective of sex. An American woman may find it strange that co-wives could manage to live together at all, and it is equally strange for a Chinese to see the friendly relations between the ex-husbands of a particular Zuñi woman. America seems to lie in between in making emotional judgments; but a Chinese must actually see the matrilineal community at Zuñi in order to realize with any degree of vividness that a woman can be the carrier of a clan, which would become extinct were there no longer women members. So long as community life is a kind of symbiosis and is human, individuals must observe the rules of the game, once the rules are set.

NOTES

1. The population (1935) is 2,036, with 880 females and 1,156 males; of the latter, 768 are more than fourteen years old.

14

A CHINESE PHASE
IN SOCIAL ANTHROPOLOGY [1]

MAURICE FREEDMAN

SOME twenty-six years ago Malinowski was visited by Professor Wu Wen-tsao of Yenching University. He learned from him, as he tells us, 'that independently and spontaneously there had been organized in China a sociological attack on real problems of culture and applied anthropology, an attack which embodies all my dreams and desiderata'. These words were written in 1938 in the Preface to Fei Hsiao-tung's *Peasant Life in China,* a book which Malinowski thought would be counted 'as a landmark in the development of anthropological fieldwork and theory'. One reason for Malinowski's confidence in Fei's work was that it pushed the frontiers of anthropology outwards from savagery to civilization. And Malinowski went on to quote a forecast he had made on another occasion: ' "The anthropology of the future will be . . . as interested in the Hindu as in the Tasmanian, in the Chinese peasants as in the Australian aborigines, in the West Indian negro as in the Melanesian Trobriander, in the detribalized African of Haarlem [sic] as in the Pygmy of Perak".'

We are now in the midst of the future of which Malinowski wrote. If we ignore the reference to the Trobrianders (who generously provide opportunities to present-day anthropologists for fruitful non-field work), some of us might well say that the prophecy erred only in suggesting that we are *equally* interested in savagery and civilization. The bold ones among us might not be shy to confess that Hindus and Chinese seem rather more interesting than Australian aborigines. This is the point from which I start. Since the thirties a number of Chinese, British, and American anthropologists—let us call them 'social', most of them will not object —have tried to study Chinese society. What can we learn from their efforts to go beyond

the older boundaries of their subject? I shall suggest some answers to this question which should enable us, like the eponym of my lecture in his time, to guess at the near future of social anthropology.

The young Fei Hsiao-tung was one of several Chinese eager to study their own society by methods developed for investigating primitive social life. Francis L. K. Hsu, who followed Fei's example in taking his Ph.D. here at the School, belonged to this group, as did Lin Yueh-hwa, who will be known to you as the author of *The Golden Wing.* After the war the next generation was represented in England by T'ien Ju-k'ang. The presence of determined Chinese scholars in Britain and the United States, as well as the potent attraction of a civilization which since the eighteenth century has had a special place in western thinking, excited some of our number to interest themselves in China. Radcliffe-Brown taught at Yenching University in 1935, Dr. Fortune at Lingnan University in 1937–39. Professor Firth began to learn Mandarin, but, unfortunately for Chinese studies, decided to go no further than the Malayan coast of the China Sea. It is said that Dr. Leach, during his earlier incarnation as a businessman in China, first began to dabble in the anthropology which he has since been acrobatically rethinking. By the time the war had been over a couple of years a good deal of anthropological energy was ready to be released in Chinese studies. In China Fei and his associates wanted to continue the field work which they had bravely pursued during the war. W. H. Newell from Oxford, G. W. Skinner from Cornell, and M. H. Fried from Columbia established themselves in China, while Isabel Crook, having studied here at the School returned to China, where, as Isabel Brown, she had earlier been at work. In 1948 Redfield went to teach at Fei's own university, Tsinghua. But the potentialities of this talent could not be realized. Fei first butted his head against the political wall under the Kuomintang

From *British Journal of Sociology,* 14 (1963): 1–19. Copyright © 1963 by Routledge and Kegan Paul, Ltd. Reprinted by permission of the publisher and the author. Maurice Freedman is Professor of Anthropology, London School of Economics.

and then, as far as anthropology is concerned, succumbed to the alternating blandishments and severities of the Communists. The coming of the People's Republic generally put an end to field studies by Western scholars; happily Professor Fried managed to complete a study of a county seat in Anhwei Province in good time; and Mrs. Crook, working under Communist auspices, produced some material on land reform. For the period up to about 1950 there is little else to show. The outlook was unpromising. But since that time an encouraging lesson has been built into the history of our subject by the very handicap from which Chinese specialists thought they were suffering. The act which slammed the gates of China in the face of field anthropologists, cutting them off from the land for which they had studiously prepared themselves, turned them to other tasks which began by seeming to be inferior substitutes and are proving, as I shall contend, to be more and not less central to the social anthropology of the sixties.

Three kinds of field study of Chinese social organization began to be undertaken. From both Britain and the United States a handful of people went off to study communities of Overseas Chinese, especially in South-east Asia. A few British and American anthropologists carried out field investigations in the New Territories of Hong Kong. Finally, a small group of Americans, for the most part connected with Cornell University, turned their attention to Taiwan. This activity has been increasingly shaped by interests for which there are few precedents in the studies of China made by anthropologists before the coming of the Communists. Let me return to what Malinowski wrote in his Preface to Fei's book. He argued that Wu Wen-tsao and his pupils were on the right lines in striving to understand China by the study of 'present reality'. The anthropological approach was an indispensable supplement to historical research. There is nothing to quarrel with in that statement; it is a version of a common and defensible view of the contribution of anthropology to history. But the argument then proceeds to discuss how 'present reality' was to be studied. The 'methodological foundations of the modern Chinese School of Sociology' were sound, Malinowski wrote, as we could see from Fei's study of peasants. 'By becoming acquainted with the life of a small village, we study, under a microscope as it were, the epitome of China at large'. Mali-

nowski then offers us a glimpse into Fei's future work which would include, sooner or later, 'a wider synthesis of his own works and that of his colleagues, giving us a comprehensive picture of the cultural, religious and political systems of China'. Now it is true that Fei did in fact later produce some general essays on the nature of his own society, but he never came near realizing the programme expressed for him by his teacher. Nor could he have come near doing so as long as he was under the sway of the anthropological ideas of the thirties. His expertise was too narrowly confined to villages. Of course, he was also interested in factories and other non-rural things, but his studies of them did not widen his competence to the extent envisaged by his British teacher.

The idea Malinowski was putting forward was part of the accepted dogma of the day— and it is by no means entirely extinct a quarter of a century later. A few years before Malinowski was introducing his Chinese pupil to Western readers, Radcliffe-Brown was speaking in China on the transfer to complex societies of anthropological methods of investigation. In China, he told his audiences, the most suitable unit of study was the village, both because most Chinese lived in villages and because it was possible for one or two field workers to make a fairly detailed study in a year or so. According to Lin Yueh-hwa, who sat at his feet in China, Radcliffe-Brown said that the best way to begin the study of Chinese social structure was to select a very small 'social area', examine it meticulously, compare it with other specimens studied in the same manner, and then proceed to draw generalizations. It would seem that from this patient induction from studies of small social areas would emerge a picture of the social system of China. Of all the biases to which the anthropological approach has been subject this seems to me the most grievous. It is the anthropological fallacy par excellence. And it must strike us as a particularly ironical one if we remember that it springs directly from a preoccupation with totalities. When we study primitive societies we must take them in their entirety, but as soon as we turn to complex societies we find our instruments so adapted to the investigation of the small in scale that we must carve out from the unmanageable whole little social areas which, if I may make a pastiche of Malinowski and Radcliffe-Brown, are epitomes of convenient size.[2]

The anthropologists working on Chinese

themes since about 1950 have wanted to catch some of the things which a miniaturizing method of this sort must let slip. Had China not gone Communist they might still today have been piling up samples of local communities; the ethnographic map of China would have had many more flags in it, but the anthropologists would probably have been no nearer that understanding of Chinese society of which Malinowski wrote than they were ten years ago. New experiences in the study of Chinese society outside mainland China have taught new lessons. Consider first the case of the anthropologists who have tried to study Overseas Chinese. There are few villages, at least in the traditional sense, to tempt them, while the towns for the most part lack that convenience of size which would allow a simple transfer of traditional technique. Social relationships among Overseas Chinese do not round themselves off neatly in suitable localities, and it is at once apparent that to delimit a 'community' and confine one's attention to it would miss the very characteristic of the society which makes it interesting: its scale and its scatter. Trying to study the Overseas Chinese a man must find his anthropological prejudices corroded away. He must be mobile. He must learn to contain his impatience when he cannot see all his subjects acting out their many roles. He must be content with fragmentary direct observation. He must adjust his vision so that he may see behaviour and ideas within the framework not only of the immediate locality but also of the society from which the migrants have come, of the largest territorial settlement within which they find themselves, and of the non-Chinese society in which they are embedded. All this imposes its own wearying discipline, but that it can be rewarding by bringing anthropological, linguistic, and historical talents to bear on interesting problems I can illustrate by referring you to Professor Skinner's splendid work on the Chinese in Thailand. Not the least important aspect of that work is its use of sociological techniques to lay bare the essential ties between individuals and corporations which constitute the channels of control and command in a heterogeneous, highly differentiated, and dispersed segment of Thailand society.

The case of those who have studied and those who are yet to study in Hong Kong is rather different. In the New Territories of that Colony, as Miss Barbara Ward and Miss Jean Pratt have shown us by demonstration, Chinese villages can be studied by conventional anthropological methods to conventional anthropological benefit. The work they have pioneered is, I hope, the beginning of a long series of studies in the New Territories of problems of Chinese rural organization, especially since, by one of the practical jokes of history, a British Crown Colony has become the last refuge of a Chinese imperial administrative system. But to be in Hong Kong is also to have vividly before one's eyes a complex urban society reaching out, through two cities and many towns, into the life of the countryside. It offers a temptation, which surely cannot be resisted much longer, to remedy many of the lacunae in our understanding of urbanism in China.

The moral to be drawn from the experience of the anthropologists who have been at work in Taiwan is of yet another kind. Taiwan is China—that at least is not in dispute—but the anthropologists are able to seize on the benefit accruing from one important respect in which it is different from the rest of the country. It was for half a century a Japanese colonial possession, with the result that a remarkable descriptive and statistical documentation is here stored up which can hardly be matched elsewhere in China. This material is capable of answering questions independently of particular field studies and of providing information about the modern past of areas chosen for field work.

One might say of all this work that it has carried Chinese specialists along a road also traveled in the fifties by other anthropologists: towards a wider conception of the anthropological vocation. But I think that the people concerned with Chinese matters have been made especially sensitive to the challenge implied in the names of 'history' and 'sociology'.

Social anthropologists in Britain have swung round to commend historical studies when formerly they merely did them. (I think this summarizes a significant part of Professor Schapera's recent Presidential Address to the Royal Anthropological Institute.) At any rate, the case for the obvious has now been authoritatively made, and we have all a general licence to sit in archives (or at least in libraries) and interview the dead. Good. But if we are to be fruitful in our historical researches we must talk to historians. What will the conversation be like? Listen to an eminent historian of China invoking the social scientists in an argument with another eminent historian of China. Professor Mary Wright of Yale is rebuking Professor Fairbank of Harvard for telling the sinologues that they have been naughty historians for having been seduced into social science. The historians, Professor Wright says, need to understand the social sciences more not less, but however far they succeed in this understanding,

they cannot themselves become social scientists of China, and not only because they haven't time. The historian's business, ideally, is to study all the varied and interrelated facets of some particular process of change in time. The social scientist's business, I take it, is to study similar facets abstracted from many varied phenomena, related not in origin but in type. Each approach can learn from the other, but the aims are quite different. Any one who supposes he is doing both understands neither. If the social sciences are to make their full contribution to our comprehension of the Chinese (or any other) historical record, social scientists must themselves do research in the primary sources.

The argument goes on: the historian must persuade 'men of real skill in political science, economics, law, sociology and anthropology to apply these skills to the Chinese sources and tell us what they find'. But there are few signs that the Chinese records are attracting the social scientists. The data are abundant and 'the language can be learned'. Are the social scientists going to abandon to the historians the 'whole vast ranges of documented experiences to which [they] once laid formal claim'? And Professor Wright concludes with this provocation:

So far as I can ascertain . . . these questions have not attracted [the social scientists'] . . . attention. We must, therefore, now ask them whether the Chinese (or other non-Western) historical record is of professional interest to them. If so, do they intend to encourage their students to exploit it? If not, will they tell us why, so that we may understand more clearly what their professional interests are?

I am not 'they' and cannot speak for them, but I shall try to give what I think is a reasonable anthropologist's reply, at least in the context of scholarship in this country. One may make many nice and valid distinctions between the respective aims of history and anthropology. In many cases the two disciplines require each other because they have a common interest in establishing and interpreting a body of facts relating to the past. Co-operation between them would, to take a simple example, prevent the historian making silly remarks about Chinese

kinship in his ignorance of the properties of kinship systems, and the anthropologist perpetrating anachronisms for lack of an understanding of the changes in Chinese kinship over time. In my opinion, the problem raised by Professor Wright is much more practical than she seems to realize. She says the language can be learned. So it can, but who will teach it and how fast? The response to the Hayter report [3] should have convinced us that many of the orientalists are unhappy about accommodating the man whose interests are not engrossed by the civilization they teach. The young anthropologist with a technical literature to master which would have astonished even so recent a figure as Malinowski, and facing a mental discipline that makes great demands on him, cannot afford the time assumed by the traditional Chinese language training. On this score it is the sinologues who must make concessions if they are eager to have non-historians working on the records. But there is a practical difficulty which the anthropologists on their side could remove. Our profession is structured to produce field workers, for if we are not field workers are we anything? If the answer is no, then I think we are making poor use of our human resources and taking an excessively narrow view of our subject. Why should every young anthropologist have to be blooded in the field? Why should the field trip be the essential mark of the acceptable scholar? There are excellent grounds for saying that the tradition of field work is the core of the profession, but it does not follow that absolutely everyone must be given a ticket to far places. An obsession which created a magnificent esprit de corps among a small band of worthies of the older generation is now degenerating in a much expanded profession into a snobbery which threatens to cut us off from a kind of scholarship which would benefit us as much as the historians for whom Professor Wright has spoken.[4]

I have tried to present what I consider a reasonable anthropologist's answer to Professor Wright's challenge. But not all anthropologists are reasonable; yet their views are influential. There appear to be some who think that their subject is fundamentally about primitive society, or at least about the kinds of things that are best studied in primitive society. In the course of a general essay on, say, marriage, or feud, or ancestor worship, one may legitimately draw in scraps of information on civilized societies, but one must not stray too far from home ground. (Incidentally, how Frazerian this kind of comparative method sometimes looks is not clear to those who practice it.) Despite all the false rumours that the primitive world is shrinking to nothingness (circulated chiefly, I suspect, by jealous sociologists), the men who are for little anthropology were, are, and are likely to remain princes of the profession, however much they have belied Malinowski's prediction and however much of a nuisance they are to big anthropology.

On the other hand, there are some among us who, while they acknowledge the importance of venturing beyond the limits of the primitive, nevertheless are worried by the consequences of having too many institutional contacts with people like historians. They are in our ranks the analogues of the traditional orientalists who consider the Hayter report a subversive document. Both kinds of men can be goaded by the mention of area studies. What are such studies, they say, but an insipid dilution of several kinds of knowledge in the interests of current affairs, intelligence work, or, worst of all, imitating the Americans? The anthropological purist considers the historian a sort of temptress who will lure his young men away from the puritanical pleasures of disciplined enquiry and theory-building. To such an objection the reply is, in fact, very simple. If we set our pupils at the feet of the historians (or the geographers or the political scientists) in order to deepen their understanding of a particular part of the world, and they forget what we have taught them, then we have either taught them badly or they were no good anyway. If they fail to put our old questions to their new knowledge and cannot see in what their new teachers say ways of extending anthropology, then again the failure is in our subject or in those supposed to be carrying it on.

I turn to sociology. Like their fellows working in other complex situations, anthropologists studying the Overseas Chinese have found that the field work tradition of their subject does not equip them fully for their enquiries. In circumstances for which sociologists have devised techniques of investigation the anthropologist at best takes them over, and at worst, in ignorance of their existence, laboriously and inefficiently invents them all over again. No anthropologist who has faced the difficulties of large-scale inquiries is likely to look down his nose at the sociologist's techniques for surveying and counting. On this I need say nothing further, because

it seems to me that there is no intellectual question at stake. Either one uses appropriate sociological techniques or one does not.

The important question is whether we can learn ideas from the sociologists to help us in our efforts to study complex societies. We can, because their subject is constitutionally adapted to big issues and large phenomena. They, unlike us, have never made a virtue of narrowness. Of course, in reality many sociologists are as narrow as many anthropologists, and if sociologists can, in their casual way, sting anthropologists by asking them 'Are you still talking about kinship?', the insult is repayable by the question whether they have got beyond thinking about social stratification. And if there are anthropologists who live, breathe, and talk Africa, there are sociologists similarly confined to Western Europe. There are failures of imagination all around. But as a discipline sociology knows about things which are essential to anthropologists striking out into the study of civilization. We must go to the sociologists whenever we have problems to tackle in, say, ideologies, population growth, urbanism, industrialization, education, communications, or social mobility. We must not imagine that because we are studying China and they are not (as is the case in Britain), we can dispense with their concepts and their experience.

It must seem strange to anyone unfamiliar with academic relations if, having spoken of the need for my profession to learn from sociology, I go on to say that most social anthropologists in this country appear to think of themselves as sociologists. (Some of them, I understand, are duly recognized by the sociologists, others not.) They are tempted to justify their continued existence as a separate profession, or a distinct branch of the larger profession, by appealing to that special interest in the small-scale which I earlier argued to have hampered the development of anthropological studies of China. We learnt, when we were being brought up on savages—and Malinowski, of course, showed us brilliantly how it could be done—to examine small communities, subject them to minute observation, tease out the threads linking individual to individual, activity to activity, and idea to idea. As new and larger fields of enquiry open up we must look around for what, in terms of scale, are the equivalents of primitive societies. In 1938 Professor Firth sent a paper to the Chinese journal *The Sociological World* which appeared in a special issue dedicated, charm-ingly, to 'The London School of Anthropology'. In that paper Firth used the term micro-sociology to describe the special contribution to be made by anthropologists to the study of Chinese society. Six years later, speaking at a forum in London on possible post-war developments in anthropology, Professor Firth inserted the term into the British record. 'Much of the anthropologist's work', he said, 'has lain hitherto in what may be called micro-sociology—the study of small groups or of small units in larger groups; of how relationships operate on a small scale, in personal terms . . . I think that the most valuable contribution of the social anthropologist may well still lie in this micro-sociological field'. He returned to the theme again in 1951 when he argued the many advantages of confining observation to a small unit.

Now these advantages are indeed impressive, and the fruits of micro-sociology bear witness to its virtues. In one of the most interesting discussions I have read of the relations between history and the social sciences Professor H. Stuart Hughes, referring to the aim of 'the more imaginative historians of today . . . to grasp in a coherent pattern the economic, social and psychological manifestations of a given society', argues that it is primarily from the anthropologists that they can learn how to go about their tasks. And he goes on, citing Bloch's work and Wylie's study of a French village, to say that on-the-spot study of a small community seems to him 'the best possible training ground for the historian whose mind is orientated toward social and psychological synthesis'.

I remain suspicious of some of the implications of these statements. Professor Firth says that although our technique is micro-sociological, our theory is macro-sociological. We use 'the microcosm to illumine the macrocosm, the particular to illustrate the general'. But how do we, in fact, jump from microcosm to macrocosm? Professor Firth warns anthropologists that they should be careful to show the representativeness of the small sample they select for study, but he does not seem in this statement to face the question of whether, be the sample as perfect as may be, it is anything more than a sample of like small units instead of a microcosm of a total society.[5]

There can be no quarrel with an argument which says that anthropologists are so good at first-hand observation of small units that they should do it whenever they have the chance. And it is undoubtedly true that, as a result of their habituation to the small-scale, anthropologists are especially skilled in certain kinds of institutional analysis, above all in the field of kinship. What needs to be disputed is the view that anthropologists should be chained by their virtues and made nervous of trying to do bigger things. Fei Hsiao-tung did his micro-sociology very well, and our knowledge of Chinese society would be vastly poorer if his books were expunged from the record. But he thought his understanding of his villages, coupled with his radical-mandarin insight into his society, gave him privileged access to the social secrets of China. In my opinion he erred in his judgment because he lacked enough historical knowledge of China and a full understanding of its broader institutional framework. And I think that Fei's mistake illustrates a risk inherent in the anthropological preoccupation with the small in scale: the risk of speaking generally of a society with the confidence bred of an intimate acquaintance with local communities in it.

The big question of the anthropologist's contribution to the study of complex societies was taken up last year in an international parish magazine called *Current Anthropology*. Professor Eisenstadt, the Israeli sociologist, who has for many years now taken a sympathetic interest in the doings of anthropologists, set out his estimate and appraisal of the contribution and was then given the 'treatment' for which Professor Tax's journal is noted. The arguments and criticisms of which the 'treatment' was composed show some of the intellectual and emotional barriers which need to be crossed before anthropologists really feel at home in the study of complex society. There is a suggestion that we have been studying it all along, for, after all, was not Nadel's Nupe society complex, and what does complex mean anyway? As for the difficulty that anthropologists turning their attention to complex society cannot cope with the total society, well, that is a false problem, because a total society cannot be studied, whether we call it complex or primitive. There is some resistance to the implication that anthropologists may have a special role to play in the study of the complex. There is support for the view that the frontiers between anthropology and certain other social sciences must be removed. And so on.

I stand by my earlier statements. There is a valid sense in which, however imperfectly they may in fact do it, anthropologists are able realistically to aim at observing and analysing a total society when that society is small and relatively undifferentiated. And the statement remains true even when, as in the case of the Kachin and the Tallensi, the authors of the books describing them have only the vaguest notions of where the boundaries of the societies lie. The point is that Dr. Leach and Professor Fortes are able to convince us that there would be little to gain in our understanding of what they have discussed by our looking beyond the limits they themselves have imposed.

I am not sure that I myself know what a complex society is, or, more accurately, where along a continuum from most to least simple a complex society can be said to fall; but I think I know when I am in the presence of a civilization. In a civilization an ethnographer cannot do what ethnographers have done elsewhere; total society is beyond his individual grasp. And yet, if he is to be informative when he pronounces on his findings, he must have had access to material bearing on the total society and be able to bring his own work into relation with it. It is in this limited sense that anthropologists working on China must aim at the total society. Of course, the more competently they equip themselves in history and sociology, the larger the circuit they will be able to cover, although it is not necessary to assume that their activities as straightforward field ethnographers of the old type are of no use in the grand enterprise.

But today mainland China is closed to field work. As a result, the thoughts of anthropologists sometimes turn to historical problems, and, casting about for ways to compensate for the loss of field work opportunities, they consider the possibilities of reconstructing aspects of Chinese society from data collected in interviews with émigrés, by means of analogies drawn from Hong Kong and Overseas Chinese settlements, and by interpreting present-day official Chinese writings; and they often resort to torturing the existing information on nineteenth and twentieth century China to make it yield up answers to important questions. But in this very odd position they are automatically exempt, so far as the mainland is concerned, from conducting campaigns to endear themselves to the political controllers of the society and from adapting their activities to the wishes of its intellectual élite.

Elsewhere in Asia, where study on the spot is relatively free, the problem of accommodating scholarship to national interests already

exists and may, I suggest, grow sterner. A price may have to be paid for the privilege of being a disinterested scholar, and paid in the coin of applied anthropology, so that the currency corrupts the purchase. In countries in which their leaders are struggling to assert national independence, cultural and political, and crying out for economic development, knowledge can easily come to be defined as that which is immediately useful. Some anthropological knowledge is immediately useful, and there is a case for giving advice in the post-colonial world just as there was in the days when Malinowski was enthusiastic about culture change and applied anthropology.[6] But there is a nasty booby trap in the new situation. In the classical colonial setting, when the anthropologists, as it was very natural for them to do, presented to their sponsors the circumstances and views of the underdogs, they were more or less liked and more or less believed. They were not, however, generally looked upon as subversive. The anthropologist nowadays may, by threatening the myths of determined élites, get himself seen as a national danger. He may, for example, demonstrate that peasants conduct their affairs in contravention of principles laid down for them in an ideological heaven; the peasants are individualists when the élite says they are collectivists. The exclusion of such an anthropologist is perhaps imminent, and he too ought to be thinking of doing historical research—although that also is not without its myth-breaking dangers.

But there is more to it than that. There can be no new generation of anthropologists in China, at least as we understand the name. In other countries of Asia we hope for a great expansion in our numbers, and we look around eagerly for Asian students to come to us to be prepared and in their turn to set up centers of anthropological learning. And indeed in one or two places—outstandingly in India—there are signs that our hopes are not in vain. But I suggest that there are reasons for moderating our optimism. New civil bureaucracies are great soakers up of talent; little prestige, let alone income, is left for the unpractical scholar. In the press for political and economic development there is scant tolerance of fundamental scholarship in the social sciences. These in their theoretical aspects are easily damned as postponable luxuries and persecuted by 'priorities'. If I am right in this dark assessment, our own responsibilities become greater. We have to further the study of oriental civilizations among us, not simply because it is a matter of national security that we have people equipped in Asian languages and cultures, but because our own title to civilization must be kept alive by our capacity to view the world impartially.

I have spoken of developments in anthropological studies of China in the last decade or so as having marked a step forward from the traditional social anthropology. This is, of course, a very small phase in a much larger one in which our subject tries to cope with new circumstances and fresh ideas. The Indianists have done much better than their colleagues on the Chinese side; their field is open.[7] The Africanists for their part have not been slow to take the hint from the growth of towns, industry, trade unions, electoral systems, new states, and the Africans' awareness of their past. The anthropological study of Asia, let alone that of China, can show nothing so grand as the panorama displayed by the International African Institute. But before the Chinese phase is dead—for who can say how long it will survive the attraction of talent to more accessible fields?—an interesting section will have been added to the annals of what Radcliffe-Brown liked to call comparative sociology.

The only study which Radcliffe-Brown himself attempted directly to sponsor during his stay in China was an investigation in the Yellow River region of 'paired intermarrying clans'. He was interested in the subject because he thought it was still possible to study in action a marriage system which, many centuries before, had been associated with the development of a philosophy of complementary opposites epitomized in the concepts of yin and yang. Speaking in 1951 Radcliffe-Brown thought it might still not be too late for such a study to be done (it had been prevented in the thirties by the Japanese attack); it would enable us, he said, 'to evaluate more exactly the historical reconstruction of Marcel Granet'. He was surely too optimistic to speak like this in 1951, but his recommendation still has a point in it for us. The historians, so they tell me, now know better than Granet; the anthropologists have moved on from Radcliffe-Brown in the study of marriage systems. It is possible to pose, in the light of theory as it now stands, many problems in Chinese marriage, affinity, and kinship which could be examined in the Chinese records for a great span of time, shifts in the proscription of marriage, in the scale of the marriage network, in the duties of affines, in the depth of lineage organization,

and in the arrangements of the ancestor cult being brought into relation with one another and with changes in political and economic circumstances. As for the present, Hong Kong and Taiwan remain open.

My first example of what can be done is typically anthropological in the sense that it calls upon the traditional stock of interests and ideas. Take, then, towns and cities. The historians can tell us a little about them—I recommend to you Jacques Gernet's recent study of Hangchow in the second half of the thirteenth century. The anthropologists have in the last few years been looking at social organization in cities such as Bangkok and Singapore where great numbers of Chinese have come together. I have already referred to Professor Fried's study of a county seat in central China. Again, we have opportunities in Taiwan and Hong Kong. At least as far as the big cities are concerned, we begin to see some regularities. We notice that agnatic principles create solidarity between 'clansmen' as well as 'kinsmen'; that men adapt themselves to the city through loyalties built around the villages and regions from which they come; that political and economic order in the city is to a great extent a function of interlocking voluntary associations of a bewildering variety.

Consider too migration. Several of the anthropologists now working on Chinese themes are interested in the Hakka, a people identified in the first place by the dialect of Chinese they speak and widely dispersed in China. Much has been written on them and a recent, as yet unpublished, historical study by a young American anthropologist, Mr. Myron Cohen, has raised the interesting question of how different kinds of Chinese maintained their several identities, competed and came into conflict with one another, and moved on to new places. Those who have studied Overseas Chinese have for long been asking about the reasons why particular villages in south-eastern China specialized in sending their members abroad, and the consequences of the emigration for village economy and organization. Partial answers to these questions may be supplied by historical material, and a field study would certainly take us a long way to understanding, for example, the viability of village institutions in the absence of large numbers of men and the economic aspect of self-perpetuating migration such that, once well launched, the movement must continue, perhaps increase, because of the adaptation to external income. Now it happens that at this moment we have in Hong Kong and on our own door-step the two ends of a classical Chinese village migration; for the owners of and waiters in the Chinese restaurants which have sprung up around us in this country are apparently recent emigrants from a few villages in the Hong Kong New Territories, villages which are themselves challenged by immigrants to Hong Kong who rent rice fields and turn them into intensively cultivated vegetable gardens.

A number of important works have been appearing in recent years on social mobility in China, a topic which, because of the nature of the imperial examination systems and recruit-ment to the bureaucracy, lends itself to detailed historical treatment. An anthropological critique needs to be inserted into the discussion, not merely to help clarify, under sociological guid-ance, the technical apparatus for treating class and status, but also to work out the modes of life and structures of relationship which were transformed as individuals ceased to be peasants to become merchants, came first to be recog-nized as belonging to the gentry, or moved into higher officialdom.

The accumulation of wealth is an aspect of social mobility, but it needs to be taken with a different question, which has a history of its own in the social sciences: why did capitalist enterprise in China prove abortive? Students of Hong Kong and the Overseas Chinese know something of the way in which Chinese com-merce and industry can thrive outside the frame-work of the Chinese state, and, with a friendly push from the economists, might succeed in describing how Chinese entrepreneurs manage their affairs (the account would certainly not be dull) and in throwing light on the factors which have favored and retarded Chinese economic innovation.

I shall take the themes of law and social control to illustrate in an especially acute form how the study of Chinese society challenges the anthropologist. He knows something of how rules are enforced in Chinese villages. The his-torians have mapped the formal legal apparatus of the state and the conceptions on which they rested. What is yet far from clear is the rela-tionship between the various sets of norms oper-ating in the society and between different mechanisms for producing conformity to any one set of them. In such an enquiry the an-thropologist would need to range very widely, and in company; and his success would depend on his ability both to master an enormous mass of data and to encompass in his imagination the extent of a vast and complicated society.

If I were imprudent enough to try your pa-tience further I should make similar comments on the study of such general questions as reli-gious institutions and conceptions and such narrower matters as military organization and formal education. I shall in fact offer one more example, and I insist on it in order to make a case for the study of Communist China with-out necessarily getting involved in cold warfare. I refer to the communes. The fact-collecting is difficult; it calls for an ingenuity quite outside the normal repertory of anthropological talents; but here as elsewhere I lay less stress on tech-niques than on the importance of solving prob-lems. The writings on the Chinese communes usually give pride of place to questions of eco-nomic efficiency and the fate of the family, but there are broader issues. What are the limits to massive 'social engineering'? To what extent can pre-existing modes of behaviour re-assert themselves within institutions deliberately de-signed to exclude them? (There is, in this con-nection, a lot to be said on the emergence of the 'production brigade' as a possible retreat from the commune to former social units.) What consequences flow from the imposition of a mechanical social equality on systems pre-viously relying for their order on social in-equality? To what extent do the communes seal off local communities from the political centres of society? I believe that an anthropologist can properly ask and help to answer questions like these.

In studies of the sort I have sketched I sug-gest we can see some of the characteristics of the social anthropology of the sixties. Our sub-ject changes from year to year, although we may mask the gradual transformation by for-getting what we said ten years ago and by stressing the continuity from the founding fathers. British social anthropology is dissolv-ing by being no longer exclusively British and by becoming more closely attuned to voices speaking from foreign lands. The French, who taught us much to begin with, are again read-ing us some lessons. The Americans, whom we thought we had domesticated in Chicago, are bombarding us with new kinds of studies and ideas. In the sixties, taking up the problems springing from an expanding subject, we shall apply them more and more to complex societies. So that if a man says that he is interested in oriental civilization he is so far from being a deserter from the cause as to be an agent of its advancement. He is running ahead and not away. And in the process he will be engaged in activities unsanctioned by the sacred tradition which stretches all the way back to, say, 1922. One unconventional activity will be close cooperation with scholars in other fields, not because co-operation is a good thing in itself, but because it is a condition for the transfer to our subject of some of the intellectual excitement being aroused outside our frontiers. To have caught a glimpse of the possibilities inherent in the Chinese record, to have sensed the opportunities stored up in local gazetteers and genealogy books, to know that the historians are looking for anthropological help in their attempt to analyse a vast and long-enduring civilization, is to recognize the early stage of a new venture in our subject.[8]

To come closer to the end of my oblique tribute to Malinowski I want briefly to discuss a different side of the expansion of social anthropology. If we think of ourselves not only as promoters of research and new ideas, but also as teachers, we shall discover, I suggest, that there are drawbacks in the way we have been going about our business. There is an honourable minority in our ranks (in which alas I cannot claim membership) which, during the last few years, has been pressing for a reappraisal of our educational role. Now, when university education seems about to expand, the majority must surely realize that our teaching must undergo some change. We have tended to treat the undergraduate reading social anthropology as though he were offering himself as a potential professional. We have been tempted to measure his achievements by the extent to which he could make himself resemble a research worker eager for the field. And we shall not be able to do better for the next generation of undergraduates unless we can plan for a subject to be taught which will give them an intellectually satisfying view of their world without leaving most of them, as they are capped and gowned, with the feeling that they are failed field workers.

How this may be done I cannot discuss here, but I shall try to establish one principle by alluding to a subject with which social anthropology is held by some heretics to have a close connection. I mean anthropology. In this country anthropology as a teaching subject has lost

its unity, although in professional circles kind words of solidarity are exchanged between what are called the branches. And we are characteristically astonished when, as is outstandingly the case with Professor Forde, we find a man with the encyclopaedic knowledge and mental stamina to contain the subject as a whole under one skull. In the United States, in contrast, anthropology flourishes in the undergraduate schools; it is thought of as a unity; people are trained to teach it as one subject; and it succeeds in doing what must be done for the education of American undergraduates: it provides them with a set of humanistic studies to help make up deficiencies in their high school education and prepare them intellectually both for the professional training of the graduate schools and for non-academic careers. The nature of our undergraduate schools is changing and we too shall need to consider groupings of subjects which will serve to educate rather than train. I can think of an ideal combination which would dissolve the present structure of anthropology and sociology at the undergraduate level in order to teach people how to think about society and civilization both historically and sociologically. In such a combination oriental societies would appear, and I would hope that some social anthropologists would be able to teach them. But in order to do so they would need to be better orientalists than we now are. In the case of China they would have to acquire a knowledge of the literature which went beyond an acquaintance with a few field work monographs, the exploits of Judge Dee, and the more esoteric passages of the integral translation of *The Golden Lotus*.[9]

NOTES

1. The third Malinowski Memorial Lecture given at the London School of Economics and Political Science, under the chairmanship of Professor Raymond Firth, 30 October 1962. I am indebted to Mrs. H. M. Wright for help with some of the Chinese sources to which I have referred, and to Professor G. W. Skinner and my wife for critical comments on early drafts of the lecture. I have not attempted in this published version to meet all the criticisms and answer all the questions raised by colleagues, but I have added a few afterthoughts in the notes.

2. In 1944 Radcliffe-Brown wrote: 'In the last ten years, field studies by social anthropologists have

been carried out on a town in Massachusetts, a town in Mississippi, a French Canadian community, County Clare in Ireland, villages in Japan and China. Such studies of communities in "civilized" countries, carried out by trained investigators, will play an increasingly large part in the social anthropology of the future.' 'Meaning and Scope of Social Anthropology', in M. N. Srinivas, ed., *Method in Social Anthropology, Selected Essays by A. R. Radcliffe-Brown*, Chicago, 1958, p. 100. And of the famous passage in 'On Social Structure' where communities emerge as societies: *Structure and Function in Primitive Society*, London, 1952, pp. 193 f.

Professor Leslie White was another anthropological visitor and advisor to China in the thirties. Since he spoke from an American platform his recommendations ranged very widely, but in so far as field research in 'social or cultural anthropology' on Han Chinese was concerned, he laid the emphasis, as did his British counterparts, on local communities. See 'Some Suggestions for a Program in Anthropology in China', *The Chinese Social and Political Science Review*, Peiping, vol. XXI, no. 1, April 1937, pp. 127, 131. At p. 128 White refers to the possibilities of library studies, but they are of a vaguely cultural character and seem to bear very little on the kinds of historical problems I touch on later in this lecture.

3. *Report of the Sub-Committee on Oriental, Slavonic, East European and African Studies*, University Grants Committee, H.M.S.O., London, 1961. Some of my sinological friends have suggested to me that it is important to make clear a distinction between two kinds of opposition to the Hayter report on the part of orientalists. Some orientalists spurn the advances of the social scientists. They will have none of them. Others, while welcoming cooperation, are worried lest the 'training' in orientalism given, under the pressure of new fashions, to social scientists be superficial. My friends, needless to say, are in the second camp; I understand their anxiety, but I hope that it does not inhibit tendencies to experiment with the new human material being offered them.

4. For a sociologist's charitable view of the role of field work in British social anthropology see D. G. MacRae, 'The British Tradition in Social Anthropology', *Ideology and Society*, London, 1961, p. 35.

5. *Elements of Social Organization*, p. 18. In dealing summarily with the views of anthropologists on their possible contribution to the study of complex societies, I have certainly not paid enough attention to the gap between general pronouncement and particular recommendation or practice. Firth, who gave us 'micro-sociology', has been responsible for promoting a number of wide-ranging studies in Asia. His plans for research in Malaya, for example, show how he has balanced small-scale with large-scale inquiries in an attempt to provide for the study of an exceedingly complicated society (see his *Report on Social Science Research in Malaya*, Govt. Printing Office, Singapore, 1948, especially pp. 27-38). Malinowski, in his last field work, seems to have tried to achieve something much broader than the work for which we remember him. Irving Rouse, 'The Strategy of Culture History', in A. L. Kroeber, ed., *Anthropology Today*, Chicago, 1953, p. 61: '. . . there have also been attempts to record the nature of the culture during successive periods by combined use of historical documents, recollections of informants, and participant observation. This was Malinowski's objective in the study of Oaxaca markets which he was making at the time of his death.' Cf. Bronislaw Malinowsky (*sic*) and Julio de la Fuente, *La Economía de un Sistema de Mercados en México* (= *Acta Anthropologica*, Epoca 2, vol. I, no. 2), Mexico, 1957.

6. May I draw the attention of non-anthropologists to L. P. Mair, *Studies in Applied Anthropology*, London, 1957? This book offers the clearest statement I know of what social anthropologists can and cannot do when they give their minds to practical affairs. It is sometimes asserted (and in fact the statement was made by a sinologue immediately after this lecture was given) that anthropologists are free of the impulse to do good which sociologists have built into them by virtue of the history of their subject. Certainly, British social anthropology has always harboured ambitions to be of use. Malinowski and Radcliffe-Brown are vividly remembered by colonial administrators who know little of their theoretical work. I quote a mandarin of the present senior generation: '. . . the moral sense of the satisfaction it offers to the desire to make some addition to human welfare which every social scientist worth his salt carries within him.' (Professor Meyer Fortes, writing in the Preface, p. 8, to Fernando Henriques, *Family and Colour in Jamaica*, London, 1953.)

7. Dr. Bailey and Dr. Mayer have kindly shewn me how they see the role of the social anthropologist in the study of India. (See F. G. Bailey, 'The Scope of Social Anthropology in the Study of Indian Society', and Adrian C. Mayer, 'System and Network: An Approach to the Study of Political Process in Dewas', both in I. N. Madan and Gopala Sarana, eds., *Indian Anthropology, Essays in Memory of D. N. Majumdar*, Bombay, 1962.) Their ambitions in the Indian context are certainly lower than mine in the Chinese, but they are thinking about a country in which other kinds of social scientist are also busily at work.

8. It is clear that anthropological ideas have influenced sinology; American work sometimes bears Redfield's mark; Professor W. Eberhard often writes on the basis of anthropological principles; Granet, to take an earlier example, acquired much through his Durkheimian connections. I am here looking forward to a closer correlation of interests. Of course, it could be objected to my line of reasoning that young anthropologists who are trained sinologically would, because of the nature of their investment, become less mobile than anthropologists are traditionally supposed to be—they would study no society other than China, and so fail to acquire that balance which is said to come from a close acquaintance with societies of different kind and region. While I agree that the danger exists and must be guarded against, I also think that it is not confined to oriental anthropology. Parochial concentration can develop in more conventional fields of anthropological study. A corner of Africa is no less stultifying than China.

9. Until I was on the point of sending this lecture to the printer I had not seen Clifford Geertz's paper 'Studies in Peasant Life: Community and Society', in B. J. Siegel, ed., *Biennial Review of Anthropology 1961,* Stanford, California, 1962. Geertz touches on a number of the points I raise and provides a guide to what anthropologists have been writing in recent years on 'peasant' organization and culture. It is useful to have an American statement of some of the problems involved in studying civilization from the anthropological standpoint.

15

FUNCTIONALISM, REALPOLITIK, AND ANTHROPOLOGY IN UNDERDEVELOPED AREAS

ROBERT A. MANNERS

INTRODUCTION

POINT Four, technical aid, and the facts of "economic cooperation" have added a new and somewhat urgent dimension to the old anthropological interest in the phenomena of acculturation and culture change. A number of anthropologists have shifted from the largely theoretical examination of the conditions and consequences of culture contact to endeavors of a programmatic and practical nature. This is not to say, of course, that applied anthropology is itself brand new or that Mr. Truman is the putative father of even the American variety. But it is apparent that the recent efforts of this country and of the United Nations to introduce radical changes in underdeveloped areas through technical assistance, health, education and a host of other programs have involved even greater numbers of anthropologists than were utilized by the British and others in their colonial activities over the past few decades.

The crucial distinction between most of the older acculturation studies and the recent efforts of anthropologists is that the former had been occupied primarily with description—or even analysis—of the *consequences* of one kind of culture contact or another, while the latter are concerned primarily with *instruction* of administrators and other agents of enforced culture change in the best ways of introducing the new elements with the least difficulty. In her UNESCO handbook on *Cultural Patterns and Technical Change,* Margaret Mead specifies the practical value of anthropological research in assistance programs (1953). The aim of the study which led to the publication of this book, she says, was to discover "the ways in which changed agricultural or industrial practices, new public health procedures, new methods of child and maternal health care, and fundamental education can be introduced so that the culture will be disrupted as little as possible and so that whatever disruption does occur can either be compensated for, or channeled into constructive developments for the future". Therefore, the anthropologists offer their findings for the use of "experts, policy makers, specialists, technicians of all sorts, chiefs of missions and teams, members of ministries of health, education, agriculture, and industrial development in countries actively seeking to guide technological change—all those who are immediately concerned, at any level, with purposive technological change".

Some recent research efforts have attempted to improve the accuracy of prediction in introduced culture change by actual experimentation. In these controlled studies, the new elements are introduced under the watchful guidance of the experimenters who then record the changes in the culture which follow. . . . They thus endeavor to demonstrate the precise effects of

From *América Indígena,* 16 (1956): 7–33. Copyright © 1956 Instituto Indigenista Interamericano. Reprinted by permission of the publisher and the author. Robert A. Manners is Professor of Anthropology at Brandeis University.

the introduction of new technological, educational, and health practices into a "cultural community" whose prior circumstances are well known. The assumption behind these inquiries and behind the employment of anthropological advisers in the many programs of foreign aid now being undertaken is, of course, that detailed knowledge of a culture permits prediction of some of the reactions to and the effects of introduced changes. If one accepts the premise that there is a need for aid and that such aid should be introduced with the least possible disruption of community and individual adjustment and stability, then the anthropologist *seems* fairly well equipped to act as an adviser in these matters.

Malinowski has defended the anthropologist's practical efforts in colonial administration with the assertion that "social engineering is simply the empirical aspect of social theory". It is not my purpose here to question the propriety of the social scientist's functioning in practical matters where his special knowledge may be of use to administrators. But it does not, as Gluckman and others have already pointed out, follow that his understanding offered as advice will necessarily influence the policies of the administrator or that it will actually produce effects which are of benefit to the majority of the people in the contacted community. In fact, it has been suggested that for the colonial situation, at least, the results may be just the opposite—that the anthropologist's professional advice may, if used at all, serve to facilitate the manipulation of the local population in violation of their own immediate interests.

To the degree that contemporary programs of foreign aid are concerned with mass elevation of the standard of living of peoples of underdeveloped areas, the anthropological advisers to these programs may stand on higher ethical eminences than their colonial office colleagues who, in effect, lend their talents and their knowledge to the prosecution of an unhampered exploitation. Unfortunately, however, for the peace of mind of those anthropologists involved in the new assistance endeavors, there has been more than a suggestion that the aims of Point Four and other technical, health and educational programs are themselves "tainted" by self interest or non-altruistic political considerations. For example, in a review of J. E. Bingham's *Shirt-Sleeve Diplomacy,* Clarence R. Decker observes that ". . . the 'integration' of technical cooperation and political and military strategy all

strongly suggest that Point Four is already the stepchild of a revived old-fashioned power diplomacy. . . [there is a fear that] *real-politik* has been reinstated as the sole basis of our diplomacy".

In his speech to Congress on June 24, 1949, President Truman himself observed that one of the chief purposes of "technical assistance [was to] create conditions in which capital investment can be fruitful". Paul Sweezy, taking his lead from Mr. Truman's description, concludes that the object of Point Four "is pretty clearly the encouragement and protection of American foreign investments, not the balanced development of backward countries". Later on, I shall return to this topic, but at the moment it seems proper to suggest that the "goal" of improved living standards is likely, in assistance programs, to be forced to accommodate itself to the practical considerations of economically and politically wise investments. In effect, then, the "global potlach" is encumbered by political and economic strings. I suppose there is nothing intrinsically objectionable about such arrangements. I merely raise the point to suggest that the role of the anthropological adviser to aid programs may in essence be not unlike the role of his colonial office prototype. If aid should in any way be tied to practical economic and political considerations of the aiding countries, it must follow that the anthropologists will play an auxiliary role to that of the administrator and the goals will be set for him by these considerations. Within these limits, as within the limits imposed upon anthropologists in the employ of conventional colonial administrations, the adviser functions largely to predict the possible consequences of policy. He can never determine the policy itself. For if major policies arise out of the deeper necessities of power-political and economic considerations, it is unlikely that they will be deflected or drastically renovated to accommodate to the anthropologist's cautious *caveats*.[1]

This is not to say, of course, that the anthropologist serves no function to the agencies involved in the introduction of culture changes on a world-wide scale. His very employment refutes such a view. Anthropologists can and do inform on many matters involving customs, taboos, social forms and the like. Unquestionably their advice is often considered in the tactics of introducing new elements into a culture. But where grand strategy inevitably involves the precipitation of conflict and disruption, and where these disturbing potentialities may also be envisaged by the anthropologist, it is hardly likely that his advice on these matters could lead to abandonment of the project itself. Thus, the anthropologist may, for example, suggest that it would be unwise to make a frontal attack on exchange marriage or on polygyny, and the administrators of the program may decide it would be best, therefore, to overlook these practices for the time being. On the other hand, should the anthropologist advise that a landless peasantry could be won over to support a program of agricultural assistance by the gift of individual plots of farm land or by some pattern of collectivization, the realities of the program would probably doom the suggestion as unworkable. The real role of the anthropologist involved in technical and other assistance programs, then, emerges—like that of the colonial office technician—as one of prediction of cultural resistances.

The anthropologist, as professional student of the problems of acculturation and culture change, has acquired a vested interest in this realm of forecasting. Fantastic numbers of books and articles have been written dealing with the phenomena of culture change, with the origins, the reactions, the resistances and the consequences of cultural innovation. In the examination of these phenomena, writers and researchers have employed a number of concepts, some of which I shall examine in the sections which follow. Among these are the concepts of integration and disintegration, of social organization and disorganization, of rapid and enforced vs. gradual and guided acculturation, of cultural anomie, of dynamic and static cultures, of the strength of custom, of resistance to change, of differential or selective acceptance, of the functional interrelationship of the parts, and so on.

CULTURAL INTEGRATION AND INDIVIDUAL RESISTANCE AS FACTORS IN CHANGE

The more "highly integrated" cultures have sometimes been compared with a delicate watch-like mechanism. It has been suggested that the sudden introduction of new elements into such a culture acts very much like the dropping of a grain of sand into the delicate works of the watch. The watch runs erratically, or the culture becomes disorganized, anomic. Less deli-

cately balanced cultures, it is said, tend to assimilate change better if the change itself is not too "radical" or too sudden. By and large, however, there is wide agreement among many anthropologists that all changes should be introduced into cultures with extreme care since any change will be likely to have repercussions which may be felt throughout the culture. Since change inevitably implies some degree of disruption—even in societies which are not so "well-integrated"—it follows that almost any introduced change may result in "social disorganization". The more "highly integrated" the culture, the more profound the disruptive effects of innovation, and the greater the consequent disorganization.

This is only one of many problems that must be faced by the agents of guided or enforced culture change. Not only is the delicately-balanced cultural mechanism liable to disoragnization in change, but the even more delicately-balanced carriers of the culture are likely to sense the disorganizing potential of the change and, therefore, to *resist* it. This type of response is sometimes described as an unwillingness or reluctance to accept innovation. It is suggested that most beliefs, customs and practices exert a conservatizing influence on culture, that there is a "natural" tendency to react against acceptance of any kind of change. There is a sizable body of data which suggests that cultures are *normally* conservative, that people—anywhere—are suspicious of change, feel at ease in the presence of the customary and uncomfortable when confronted by the new. If this be so, then the anthropological advisers in assistance proprams have, on one level, a fairly easy job. They can make the blanket prediction that all change will disorganize, all change will be resisted—and predict themselves out of a job. But obviously the matter is not quite so simple. It appears that some parts of culture are "more resistant to change than others"; that some changes are more or less disruptive of the total culture than others; and that some segments or groups of individuals within a society demonstrate different degrees of resistance to change. In practice, then, the administrator and the anthropologist understand these differences and are prepared to consider them in introducing change.

Understanding and consideration, however, may in themselves have small impact on policy. Since, in their local aspects, assistance programs are ostensibly non-political in character, they must conduct their activities within the framework of an existing sociopolitical structure. Thus, health, education and technical assistance must be proferred not only with a minimal "disorganizing" effect on the general cultural situation, but these must not be permitted either to alter the social and political *status quo ante*.

Wherever possible, then, aid is channeled through existing political and administrative agencies within the underdeveloped area. Thus, the official disinclination of the assisting agencies to interfere with political and social arrangements lends moral and material support to the groups in political power. In this sense, the technical, educational, hygienic and other changes which are introduced function to *strengthen* the *status quo*. If they did not they would be resisted by the controlling elements; no group in a position of political dominance is likely to relinquish that position willingly. And the very changes whch may be welcomed by the group in power may be resisted by others in the society.

COLONIALISM AND THE ETHNOGRAPHER

In this connection, however, it has been suggested that the patterns of intervention involved in technical assistance differ radically from those practiced during more than 400 years of colonial penetration. The predatory behavior of pre-assistance times included specific exploitative and control aims. Contact was ordinarily undertaken with the object of procuring raw materials, providing markets, or opening areas for profitable investment of capital. Where expediency demanded at least nominal preservation of pre-existing political forms, these were preserved. Where they, or concomitant patterns of social organization, interfered with the primary exploitative aims of the intrusive power, they were modified, revamped or swept aside. Sometimes, of course, mistakes (acts which slowed up exploitation) were made and new methods had to be explored. Eventually it became apparent that the trained ethnographer, as well as the colonial administrator and the missionary, might be profitably employed in the pursuit of the practical ends. The Netherlands, France, Great Britain and other colonial powers consulted with and employed anthropologists in the interest of "understanding the native cultures", for "understanding", it was felt, might reduce

friction, minimize violations of local customs, beliefs, traditions and deeply-held values. Then one could get on with the job.

But the goals of the job and the contact itself implied radical changes in pre-existent cultural patterns. If, as Tylor has asserted, "The savage is firmly, obstinately conservative", and as Malinowski has more recently affirmed, ". . . conservatism is the most important trend in a primitive society. . ." then the intruding culture could expect resistance to the changes which it was "forced" to introduce. But if a way could be found to achieve the desired practical results without at the same time producing profound changes in the old way of life, then the job could proceed with greater smoothness and with fewer resistances. Anthropologists could tell administrators when they might go ahead or where they must go easy; or administrators could be trained so that they would themselves be able to function with anthropological knowhow. However, all parts of a culture, as Malinowski himself insisted and taught, fit together. If you introduce change in any part, contingent changes of varying intensity will make themselves felt throughout the culture.

This posed a dilemma for one of the world's outstanding anthropologists and advisers in problems of colonial administration. If all parts of a culture are interrelated, how does one prevent or even minimize the radiation effects of, let us say, the change from a subsistence economy to a subsistence-plus-cash economy? Or does one, recognizing the interrelationship of the parts, oppose the introduction of this change because it threatens to have disruptive effects on the family structure, marriage, internal political and social relations, the unity of the clan and so on? To ask the question is to answer it. If it was cash crops—or mines—or mills—or factories that one wanted introduced, they were introduced, no matter the consequences, no matter the plaintive jeremiads of the perceptive ethnographer. Because Malinowski's functional view of culture—which stresses the interrelationship of its parts—cannot be reconciled with his applied anthropological point of view—which suggests that change may proceed by a process of quarantining those elements which should not be disturbed—he was forced to fabricate an unreal cultural system. Contact produces conflict and disorganization, and true cultural communities can not, by definition, be improperly integrated or disorganized. Hence cultures in conflict, or cultural communities under contact are in a sense not true cultures. Only those parts of them which involve interrelationships among the native population constitute the true cultural community. The personnel of the contacting culture do not fit into the native organization, and must not, therefore, be reckoned a part of the native culture.

Malinowski apparently refused to apply to the contact situation his awareness of the fact that, while it is perfectly true that cultures can not be disorganized and remain viable, they are constantly undergoing alterations in the level or kind of their organization without disappearing. True cultural disorganization can at most be but a temporary thing. It must eventuate almost immediately in a new kind of organization or in the death of the culture itself. Exploitative contact appears severely disorganizing only if we assume some arbitrary and utterly unrealistic ideal of organization. If, on the other hand, we consider the changes wrought under this type of contact only an intensified manifestation of an inherent process in culture, we may look upon the result—*ethical considerations aside*—as a new level of organization or as reorganization. New experiences, new problems and new frustrations on a massive scale accompanied the changes introduced in the African cultures which were Malinowski's chief concern. But those cultures that did not die became reorganized—even though reorganization probably involved more personal hardship, insecurity and anxieties than had pre-contact organization. These were still valid cultures, although involved in contact and new forms of conflict, and although there had been serious alterations in the old way of life.

Malinowski's formulations seem to have solved to his satisfaction the seemingly insoluble contradiction between his functionalism and his applied anthropology. He found it possible to admonish the administrator against tampering with the native custom of bride-price or exchange marriage while, at the same time observing that the colonial office had levied a hut or poll tax on the natives which effectively removed the young men to labor-scarce areas. The native culture—i.e., the life in the village —remained integrated, organized and relatively conflictless. It continued to include bride-price, mother-in-law taboos and buttered umbilici. The forms of social relations in the native village—having been rescued by the anthropologist—seemed almost the same as they had been before. Because, as Gluckman so clearly points out, Malinowski does not see the contactors and the contacted as part of the same "social field", he can almost assume that a substantial part of the village culture remains the same despite the profound consequences unleashed, let us suppose, by the opening of a new gold field 500 miles away.

In point of fact, however, Malinowski does not quite assume that the culture of the village has been unaffected by the poll tax and the opening of the mine. Such a position would be patently absurd. What he does maintain is that while the contact induces changes in the tribal culture, *description* of the latter should not include reference to the contactors as integral and functioning parts of the native culture. This kind of reasoning, then, justified Malinowski in assuming that important segments of tribal culture might in part be insulated from the consequences of contact—since contact and its agents originate or lie outside of the tribal or village unit. If such a view were accurate, then it would be proper to say that an ethically-oriented and autonomous anthropologist could implement certain practices which would, in effect, maintain the cultural status quo in the face of outside changes. Or, at the very least, the anthropologist and the administrator might insure that novelty be introduced so subtly as scarcely to be noticed or felt. There are, however, at least two basic errors involved in these assumptions. The first of these, as I have already suggested, is the assumption that the tribe itself is the only realistic unit of integrated cultural interaction, even under circumstances of intense contact. Malinowski and others seem, in this case, to be saying that a cultural community cannot include diverse and conflicting ethnic groups. Or, by extension, that when a community becomes internally heterogenous or conflict-ridden it is "disorganized" and hence ceases to be an authentic and integrated cultural community. The second is the assumption, equally invalid, that the anthropologist is either autonomous or policy-significant.

And in this connection Firth remarks that: "The conditions in which the problems are set for him are not within the discretion of the anthropologist to vary. He cannot change the broad lines of policy—legal, administrative, economic, religious, educational—even though his researches may lead him to think that they are unsuitable to native needs."

AMERICAN ANTHROPOLOGISTS AND THE "UNDERDEVELOPED" AMERICAN INDIAN

Some of the errors which flow from these or related assumptions about culture and the role of the anthropologist in introduced culture change are, I believe, expressed in the writings of a number of American ethnologists who have dealt with the problems of our native Indian populations, particularly some of those in the southwest. Among these writers there is evident a strong belief that many aspects of these cultures may—and should—be retained by their bearers. If it were true that these cultures could perpetuate themselves as enclave isolates, free of contact with or dependence upon "outside" forces, then, of course, it would be justifiable—possibly desirable—so to maintain them. But this is no longer feasible. Whether they wish it or not, they have become involved in many ways, in many forms of clear material dependence, with the white culture which has surrounded and even infiltrated their tribal areas. To assert that it would be desirable for the Hopi, or the Navaho, or any other group to hold on to the "old ways" in the face of the assaults upon them which have effectively destroyed the material base which made them possible, is to assert a wish which is contrary to reality and to the possibilities of reality.

This position suggests, moreover, that the Indians themselves are wholeheartedly in favor of perpetuation of the old; and this has not been conclusively demonstrated. On the other hand, it would be an equally invalid oversimplification to assert that *all* of the Indians favor the kind of total change which would absorb them completely into white American culture. There are many who fear such an eventuality —with good reason—given the experience of Indians under the conditions of minority discrimination and prejudice which still prevail in most parts of the country. Others, too, would resist absorption because the "old ways" still provide them with subsistence and a sense of security. But the decision to accept or reject no longer lies with them, and their wishes are almost irrelevant. The American Indians, like "underdeveloped peoples" the world over, have been involved; new needs have been implanted,

and the means for gratifying these needs have been revealed to them. In the process of satisfying the new needs they are becoming involved in new forms of economic and social behavior, and these must inevitably affect all other aspects of their culture. To resist these efforts by throwing a magic circle around art, technology, education, and family, etc., and saying, in effect: "Do not touch", is to deny the interrelationship of the parts. The anthropological consultant—whether he be retained by the Bureau of Indian Affairs or the administrators of technical assistance programs in Latin America, Africa, or the Near East—who suggests the feasibility of such a program is, it seems to me, somewhat less than realistic.

But the position I am here presenting is itself open to the accusation of over-simplification unless I qualify it further. I am not, of course, suggesting that when the first trader, trapper, or missionary enters an area and hands out iron pots, iron axes or Bibles that he causes the economic, social and ritual organization to crumble and the native language to disappear. I am merely asserting that introduction of these and related elements sets in motion a process or series of processes whose results are felt in other parts of the culture; that these consequences, though not readily predictable in detail, are bound to follow some such radiant pattern; and that no amount of advice, consultation, precaution or admonition can appreciably frustrate or alter the side-effects of introduced changes. A committee of experts convened by UNESCO has declared their recognition of these consequences as follows: "The effort to extend the benefits of industrialization and technological advances to all peoples must inevitably be accompanied by profound cultural dislocations."

In short, it is the contact and the nature of the contact along with the changes it presents which determine the total cultural effect. It is not the wishes of the contacting group or of those contacted which can make this selective determination. From this it does not necessarily follow that we can predict with accuracy the pattern of cultural radiation or the side-effects of contact even when we know well the details of the contact and the cultural superstructure on which it has impinged. But it does follow that the anthropologist's advice to "go easy" with the family structure, the religion, the taboos against this or that are of doubtful

practical value in the face of the massive dynamism which may be unleashed by the introduction of the iron axe, the bulldozer, insecticides
and work for wages.

THE ANTHROPOLOGIST AND
ALTRUISTIC INTERVENTION

This brings us back to the important question: whether programs of intervention in
underdeveloped areas which are altruistically
motivated are to any degree handicapped by
the necessities which govern contact guided by
aims of exploitation and profit. Are not the
technical, health, educational and other agents
of assistance programs free to perform their
jobs without regard for the interests of the
"investors" who support their activities? And
would they not, under such circumstances, be
in a far better position to observe the cautions
and make use of the advice that the anthropologist is prepared to give?

The answer to the first of these questions
is exceedingly complex. However, it merits
some consideration here, for it suggests that a
contact which imports the material, educational,
medical and nutritional impedimenta of advanced western civilization in a spirit of benevolent selflessness will be followed by results
which differ profoundly from those which en-
sue when these elements are introduced as the
baggage of self-interest. To an important degree this may actually be the case; and it would
be demonstrably absurd to deny it. On the
other hand, it would be equally absurd to
overlook the many and growing similarities
between the earlier forms of intrusion and those
which, like Point Four, appear to have been
otherwise motivated. Present political and economic realities, like those of the past, make
their own demands. Not only are the areas for
technical assistance, educational and other programs determined by these realities, but the
nature and extent of assistance is itself limited
by the same imperatives. Speaking of South
Asia, Werner Levi notes that: ". . . United States
loans to this region are bound to have strings
attached also; at least, I doubt whether loans can
be granted in a completely altruistic manner. I
think altruism is too much to ask in international
relations. If the U. S. even on a governmental
basis makes loans, it will tie them in with some
sort of political policy . . ."

It is illuminating also to examine President
Truman's inaugural address launching Point
Four in January of 1949 and the restatement
of the aims of technical assistance enunciated
in the message to Congress just five months
later. In January, Mr. Truman said: "The old
imperialism—exploitation for foreign profit—
has no place in our plans." On June 24th of
the same year he specified the conditions of
assistance in greater detail than he had in the
initial statement. And it hardly follows from
even a cursory examination of the later statement that the "new" differs very radically from
the "old imperialism" with respect at least to
its economic aims. For the June message re-
emphasizes that the main purpose of "technical
assistance [is to] create conditions in which
capital investment can be fruitful". Mr. Truman also urged that "private sources of funds
[in addition to those furnished by such public
agencies as the Export-Import Bank and the
International Bank for Reconstruction and De-
velopment] must be encouraged to provide a
major part of the capital required". To make
the project even more attractive to investors,
Mr. Truman added two additional incentives.
The first of these was contained in the proposal that there be "special treaties guaranteeing
equal and non-discriminatory treatment to
American capital"; and the second that there
be instituted a plan for "government insurance
to private investors against the special risks of
foreign investment".

But Point Four, it may be protested, is not
the only program of aid being extended by this
country to underdeveloped areas. Perhaps programs that are under the guidance of the UN,
FAO, ILO, UNESCO, WHO, and other agencies of
a more-or-less international complexion are not
governed by the same considerations as are
those which govern American assistance delivered under the MSA or one of its successors.
Jacob Viner makes a pertinent observation. The
United States, he notes, is participating in its
own aid programs and in multi-national programs as well ". . . but the bulk of our aid is
granted by us directly to the recipient countries." And Eugene Staley in his analysis of the
Future of Underdeveloped Countries says: "The
U. S. share of the subscribed capital of the
International Bank is 35 per cent. The U. S.
has contributed about 60 per cent in the first
few years of the 'expanded program' of United
Nations technical assistance. The 12 million
dollars provided by the U. S. in 1952 for this
program and the somewhat smaller amount

contributed in 1953 *are but small fractions of the amounts the U. S. has been spending directly in its bilateral* [as opposed to multilateral] *Point Four program*" (emphasis added). Thus, the United States is clearly the most important contributor in both bilateral and multilateral programs of assistance; and our bilateral operations involve far greater sums than are expended in our generous contributions to the UN and related agencies.

If we may judge from the "practical" conditions enunciated to justify the expenditures of Point Four, we may, I believe, assume also that certain practical benefits are expected to follow from investment in *any* assistance program abroad, even when it is part of an "internationally" co-operative endeavor. Earlier I referred to a statement by Clarence Decker regarding the *realpolitik*-al nature of our assistance endeavors. Viner is even more pointed: "As long as strategic and military considerations continue to be important, we cannot surrender to the United Nations, which includes the Iron Curtain countries, 'neutralist' countries, and border-line countries . . . the decision as to how and for what purposes our aid is to be allotted."

Stringfellow Barr finds that under the first years of the United Nations: "American aid . . . was going not where suffering was most acute but where cold war politics directed it . . . our programs of economic aid, technical assistance, or whatever they might at any given moment be called, were doomed to become one facet of our foreign policy . . . any economic aid that could not be fitted into our military policies became either a pittance or an immoral handout."

It is, of course, not my desire in introducing these observations to reflect upon the morality of assistance given with ulterior motives of a practical strategic, military, economic or political color. For purposes of this discussion it is, it seems to me, only necessary to suggest that the motivation itself governs who gets help as well as what, how and how much will be offered. If this be so, one might logically expect that aid will be withheld from those areas where no advantages are anticipated—no matter how grave the need—and denied to people of governments which refuse to fulfill the "practical" conditions upon which the offer of assistance is predicated. Where such offers are extended by or in the name of the "western bloc" or by and in the name of the "Soviet

bloc" we may be justified in assuming that there is involved more than a tacit assumption of a *quid pro quo.*

CONSERVATISM AND FUNCTIONALISM

Favoring the preservation of "some of the old ways", as I have already suggested, is not only a denial of the basic anthropological conception of the functional interrelationship of a culture's "parts" but is a doctrine of conservatism as well. While there is no question that cultural or any other kind of conservatism is the privilege of any one, anthropologist or not, it should, I must emphasize, be recognized for what it is.

In an article on "The Metaphysics of Conservatism" Gordon K. Lewis observes that the vocabulary of conservatism—the pleas to proceed with caution, to eschew violence to tradition, to cherish the past—offers us, ". . . when all the sound and fury are over . . . nothing much more than the defense of the present order. . . ." If it is the present order which the anthropologist defends when he is concerned over the consequences of change, he should be aware of this. If he opposes the "present order" as inadequate, or unjust, or stifling for any moral or ethical reasons of his own choosing, and is therefore willing to see it supplanted, he must as well be willing to recognize the pervasive after-effects which will follow changes in the "present order". If he wishes strongly to preserve some of the old ways and the old values of a culture, he will find that the means to preservation of the parts may inevitably be preservation of the whole. Thus, the anthropologist's high regard for a religious rite, or for a type of family or clan organization, or for certain systems of co-operative endeavor—however admirable or desirable these may be— could conceivably promote his opposition to a technical assistance program which, by functional radiation, may threaten these cultural forms.

CULTURAL RELATIVISM AND ENFORCED CULTURE CHANGE

It is curious to note how many of the anthropologists who espouse the preservation of some of the old ways in terms of their essential "validity" do thereby implicitly abandon the very relativity which they offer in defense of the espousal. Not only is their willingness to accept change and improvement in some *material* conditions a denial—and, I would agree, a most salutary denial—of the doctrine of absolute cultural relativism, but their championing of the parts to be preserved suggests that these parts are to be more highly regarded than those which threaten, under change, to supplant or alter them.

The widespread anthropological resistance to change stems understandably from this non-relativistic evaluation in which many anthropologists are constantly—if resistantly—indulging. They are always running into items and practices which seem well worth preserving. It is therefore inevitable that they should actively advocate such preservation. It would be foolish to deny that there is much "good" in underdeveloped areas which will be replaced as they develop by much that is "bad". But nostalgia and a sincere concern for those cultural devices which seem good and desirable are unlikely to prevail against the profoundly disturbing forces of industrialism and a money economy.

This is not to say that the effects of such involvement need be or will be everywhere the same. They will not. But the dream of perpetual pluralism needs serious recasting in the light of our experience and observation. Much that we may cherish will inevitably be lost. We only hope that the larger gains to humankind will amply compensate for these losses which are adjunct to the course of introduced culture change.

At least a part of the world's cultural pluralism is today the pluralism of inequality, of differentials in wealth and access to the advantages of wealth. Few anthropologists would argue for the preservation of these pluralistic inequities. But even the pluralism which is the product of diverse cultural histories is declining under the impact of increasingly similar forces. Pluralism without gross inequality may add an interest, a zest and a potential source of perennial enrichment to the future citizens of the world. But the ironical reality appears to be that as the mechanisms for capitalizing these cross-fertilizing potentialities become increasingly effective—that is, as communication and non-evaluative tolerance improve—the differences diminish; and world culture moves at least in the direction of a broad sameness, perhaps, in Browning's poignant phrasing, towards a "common greyness".

DIFFERENTIAL ACCULTURATION AND ACCEPTANCE

Among the ethical and moral biases embraced by some anthropologists engaged in assistance programs is the bias in favor of the assumption, as I have stated earlier, that culture changes are, *per se,* unsettling to the people involved. Because changes in the way of life are upsetting, the beneficiaries of assistance programs are likely to resist them. Thus the go-slow admonition of the anthropologist may be doubly-grounded in the pragmatics of program implementation and a concern for the emotional stability of the people. Here is a curious dilemma on the horns of which many anthropologists might be indefinitely impaled were it not for the fact that the administrators are charged with the responsibility for getting changes introduced, come what anomic consequences may come. If anthropologists were to subscribe rigidly to the related doctrines of relativism and the anomic effects of change they would have to oppose any program of assistance whatsoever. But few anthropologists are even theoretically so committed, and certainly none of those involved in aid programs are practically so committed.

Perhaps this is so because anomie and resistance to change turn out to be neither so dependable nor so widespread as has sometimes been suggested. In practice, anthropologists commonly recognize that there are differentials in the rate and manner of acceptance of change. Sometimes it is said that people will accept change more readily in the material than in the non-material realm; or that differential acculturation may be seen in the greater resistance to changes in the "costumbres" than to changes in other parts of the culture. Or it may be asserted that since no culture is completely static anyway, it might be useful and decent to engage in some judicious and selective manipulation by way of hastening an inherent dynamism. It is deemed far better to exercise scientific and humane guidance over the process than to permit it to proceed whimsically and anarchically to the detriment of the "developing" peoples.

In point of fact, then, cultures do change, and people are not inevitably resistant to change, and virtually all anthropologists would agree. Whether some people are more congenial to change than others, or whether changes are more acceptable in certain parts of culture than in others is still debatable. Speaking of Mexico, Beals says, "In the main the Mexican Indian does not have sharp rejection patterns to those things which have 'practical' value." Somewhat later he suggests what he may mean by practical value when he states: "You get periods of rejection when they don't take any European culture. These are associated with a period of unpleasant (sic) relationships between Indian and white. When you get . . . more rapid acculturation coming in, it generally marks an improvement in relations. These are cases in which the government tries to do something constructive for the Indian rather than simple exploitation of him."

Two non-anthropological experts in the field of underdeveloped areas concur in Beals' view that cultures do not necessarily resist change . . . even change of a profound nature . . . that entrenched attitudes or values can even be swept aside or replaced. Although they do not concern themselves with the possible costs of rapid and enforced change, they do imply a profound shift in values which sometimes makes change and acceptance of change immediately sequential. Speaking of the pre-revolutionary period in Russia, Gerschenkorn says: ". . . how quickly in the last decades of the past century a pattern of life that had been so strongly opposed to industrial values and that tended to consider any non-agricultural economic activity as sinful and unnatural began to give way to very different attitudes". And Lamb notes, for the post-revolutionary period, how quickly the Russians have come to know that "The industrial revolution is today a complex entity which can be exported to the backward areas of the world, set up there and made to run. . . They have drawn into their industrial society over a hundred peoples living within the borders of the Soviet Union and altered their traditional way of life."

In studying the patterns of resistance and acceptance demonstrated by the peoples of "underdeveloped" areas in the face of directed attempts to change their ways, Charles J. Erasmus finds that "practical" and perceivable advantages speed acceptance. "In agriculture, for example, the introduction of improved plant varieties (higher yielding or more disease-resistant) which result in a greater profit to the farmer has repeatedly resulted in spectacular success stories."

And Ralph Beals, in an article dealing with the people of the Ecuadorian village of Nayon, observes that "Many members of the group have accepted major shifts in the socio-cultural system with little difficulty and look forward to additional changes."

As illustrations of the prevailing view that elements of material culture are more readily accepted than the non-material, I quote briefly from Barnett's analysis of innovation. He finds that "new tools, appliances, house and dress style" are more readily adopted than non-material elements because, "on the whole they create fewer, and in many cases not any, social complications". This somewhat oversimplified statement which attributes conservatism in culture to a fear of "social complications" is slightly less mystical—but hardly more analytical or illuminating—than the assumption entertained by Malinowski and others about the "natural" conservatism of primitive and "backward" peoples.

Another and highly sensitive observer, the artist-anthropologist, Covarrubias, suggests not only that change may be acceptable to a people but that it may even be accepted within that most non-material part of their culture, their religion. Of the Balinese, he says: ". . . [they] have been extremely liberal in matters of religion. Every time a new idea was introduced into the island, instead of repudiating it they took it for what it was worth and, if they found it interesting enough, assimilated it into their religion. . ." On acceptance and conservatism generally, he has this to say: "The Balinese are extremely proud of their traditions, but they are also progressive and unconservative, and when a foreign idea strikes their fancy, they adopt it with great enthusiasm as their own."

In general there appears to be some evidence for the view that in an "unforced" acculturational situation those elements and ideas will be most readily accepted which hold out a promise of benefit to the acceptors. In the forced situation, the same general rule would hold true theoretically but would be largely inoperative in practical terms since *adoption* and not acceptance (implying volition and positive affect) is the purpose. Here again it seems reasonable to insist that the anthropologist, with all of his knowledge of the "delicate balance" of a culture—of what it may accept or reject—can be of small practical value to the administrator confronted with the job of foisting changes on a people "for their own" (or someone else's) sake.

ACCEPTANCE AND THE LOCAL HIERARCHY

Few—if any—of the present assistance programs are concerned with peoples in truly primitive, undifferentiated and homogeneous communities. In terms of social organization, the aid-receiving countries are complex and hierarchically structured. Under these circumstances, introduced changes which benefit certain segments of the community may bring little or no improvement in the condition of others. If aid is extended by or under the aegis of the "western democracies", it must be offered under the conditions imposed by their traditional and our Constitutional regard for property rights. Forcible expropriation can play no part in programs aimed at economic betterment. The western nations cannot, as can the nations of the Soviet Bloc, *promise* land confiscation without compensation, followed by redistribution to the landless agricultural workers. In most of the "backward" world redistribution *after legal condemnation and purchase* with adequate compensation to the landlords is admittedly impracticable. This is one of the more serious dilemmas confronting the assistance programs of the West, and it is one which, we may note, gives to the West's Soviet Bloc competitors one of their most powerful propaganda weapons. Hakim puts his finger on the significance of this fact when he speaks of the enthusiasm with which land redistribution changes would be accepted in agrarian cultures. ". . . The landless agricultural workers and share tenants of underdeveloped countries would not fail to welcome assistance to implement a program of land reform which would give them land and would set them up as independent farmers. In fact, the peasant class has more than once been won over by movements which make precisely such promises (sic)." An aid program which fails to take this kind of step, he adds, is only likely to "leave the majority of the people in poverty". If the aid program cannot include plans for immediate and basic land reforms it will do little good for the anthropologist to protest that there will be cultural resistance to the program or apathy on the part of the landless agriculturalist. He may know, as Linton cogently

observes, that the benefits offered will not help those most in need of assistance, that the very social structure of the community must in some respects be altered before the aid will reach those most in need of it. But even if he knows this truth and suggests the consequences of ignoring it, it is hardly likely that the plan can be tailored to meet his objections.

"Many colonial peoples and the sharecroppers and tenants who form a large part of the population in even independent 'backward' nations know from sad experience that, every time their income increases, so do their taxes and rents. After each advertised economic advance they find themselves with very much the same standard of living they had before they underwent the trouble and uncertainty involved in practicing new techniques.

"One also finds that the members of the average peasant community view any attempts to improve their economic condition which originate with their rulers with considerable and not unjustified suspicion. This holds whether the rulers are foreign imperialists or a native upper class. The peasant feels that anything which his rulers offer as a chance to improve his condition is probably more to their advantage than to his own. Since his rulers have always mulcted him in the past, he assumes that they will continue to mulct him in the future" (Linton).

Hakim sees the pattern as a "tendency of the Western powers . . . to bolster up existing feudal and reactionary regimes rather than to help the progressive forces in opposition to them". He finds this situation paralleled closely by the programs of the "governments of . . . advanced countries [which deal] with colonial and semi-colonial territories". For these "have sought to win over a small minority group or class, strengthen it in its domination over the people, and allow it to reap the benefits of economic development, while the majority of the people remain in poverty and degradation".

In these observations is revealed one of the many distressing but significant parallels between the "old imperialism" and the current assistance programs which are—perhaps not improperly—imbedded in considerations of a power-political nature. Under the old imperialism the agricultural laborer was exploited for the benefit of the imperial investor and his local agents. Under the existing patterns of aid, and without the basic land reforms that would be required to make them significantly different, he many continue to suffer the same kind or degree of exploitation. The very pattern of western assistance insures the preservation of the socio-economic *status quo*. To violate the status quo and the present system of drastic exploitation which prevails so widely in much of the under-developed agrarian areas of the world would demand measures which are either financially infeasible or clearly contradictory to our concern for the sanctity of property. Thus, under the old imperialism and under the new assistance programs the picture for the more depressed segments of populations of "backward" areas continues to be a gloomy one. The role of the anthropological adviser must thus remain pretty much what it has been before—namely, that of helping the administrator "to make wise decisions" (Evans-Pritchard) but within the context of a broad policy over which he has no control and which clearly determines the larger cultural consequences of contact. The anthropologist may predict that complex cultures will be divided in their reaction to contact and assistance. Those who benefit may be happy to accept the aid. Those members of the same community who may not benefit may resist. In a certain sense, *this* is a far more dependable and predictable pattern of "resistance to culture change" than the more-frequently-referred-to conflict between acceptance of material and non-material elements.

But what of fairly homogeneous societies which appear illogically to resist the introduction of changes calculated to improve their economic conditions? Isn't this kind of resistance, one is asked, good evidence for the assertion that cultures "normally resist change?" The charge, as Linton says, has often been levelled at "our own reservation Indians". He finds the evidence unconvincing. "Government experts will tell them how to breed cattle or to get better crops by scientific methods, but they will go on as they are. If one follows back the history of the dealings of our Indians with the United States Government, it is easy to understand the reason for such apathy. Tribe after tribe made a real effort to copy white ways when they were placed on reservations. They saw that the old life was ended and did their best to adapt. However, whenever a tribe got a communally-owned cattle herd which could be a valuable source of income, stockmen who wanted the range brought pressure in Washington, and the tribe suddenly found its herd sold and the money 'put in trust'. If a

tribe developed an irrigation project and brought new lands under cultivation, presently an excuse would be found for expropriating this and moving the tribe to a still more submarginal territory. The Indians were frustrated and puzzled by changing government policies, in which the only consistent feature was that they always lost, and settled back into apathy and pauperism."

This kind of historical referrant would, it seems, give us a more satisfactory explanation of some of the forms of "cultural resistance to change" than such an assumption, let us say, as Laura Thompson's thesis of a "logico-aesthetic integration" whose delicate balance might be upset by change. It is, she says, to the preservation of this balance, somehow felt or understood by the people themselves, that they devote their energies when they fight off changes. Linton views the matter differently, tells us that many groups do not resist change but, on the contrary, appear to accept and even welcome it when it promises to bring them benefits.

THEORETICAL ORIENTATION AND PRACTICAL AID

The question may now be asked whether, in view of the apparent differences in theoretical approach to the problem of culture change, certain anthropologists may be of more practical value in assistance programs than others. Is not the anthropologist who is acquainted with the facts of possible past frustrations, or with the different attitudes expressed or felt by the various groups or classes in a society, likely to be more useful to the administrator who is implementing a program already decided upon than the anthropologist who is wary of any change because he sees change itself as a threat to the stability and the balance of a culture? If the analysis made so far is at all valid, the answer must be a pessimistic and virtually unqualified no. To the anthropologist who advises caution and is worried about the effects of any change, the administrator must answer roughly that the ends are calculated to justify the means —and the ends are a complexly woven fabric of "improved living standards" and "practical diplomatic, strategic, political" goals in a time of tension and world crisis. And to the anthropologist who may stress differential class reaction to or desire for change, or who points to the past sins of industrialized nations as a clue to a generalized response of suspicion in the present, the administrator must offer the same answer and proceed in the same way to the same desired ends.

CONCLUSIONS

Speaking of the Island of Bali, Covarrubias says: ". . . the power of our civilization to penetrate can no longer be ignored. It would be futile to recommend measures to prevent the relentless march of Westernization; tourists can not be kept out, the needs of trade will not be restricted for sentimental reasons. . . To advocate the unconditional preservation of their picturesque culture in the midst of modern civilization would be the equivalent of turning Bali into a living museum, putting the entire island into a glass case for the enjoyment of hordes of tourists".

The anthropologists who have assisted colonial administrators, and those who are presently engaged as advisers in uninational or multinational programs of assistance, have not been and are not being charged with the responsibility for stemming the penetration of "our civilization". On the contrary, their job under the old colonialism and under the new assistance programs is one of aiding in the "relentless march of Westernization". They have been asked to advise in order to facilitate that penetration which is, in one form or another, deemed inevitable or necessary. The aims of penetration under modern colonialism were clearly and unequivocally mercenary, and the means to achievement were patterned—in somewhat varying ways, it is true—along lines which seemed most likely to maximize these aims. The aims of contemporary assistance programs are in part altruistic, in part practical in the political as well as the economic sense. The patterns of distribution of current assistance programs reflect the prepotent significance of the political and economic considerations.

The anthropologist under colonialism as well as the anthropologist who assists in the conduct of aid programs advises on areas of cultural sensitivity and suggests which tactics may best insure achievement of the strategic goals of the administrator or the assistance mission. In both cases the grand strategy is imposed from above

and the tactics are accommodated to the goals. If the anthropologist feels that he must explain his participation in either type endeavor, he may say that the programs are going forward anyway, and anything he can do to ease the "cultural shock" to the objects of penetration is ethically and morally justifiable. Since most anthropological workers in the colonial and "underdeveloped" vineyards are modest fellows, it may well be that this relatively minor aid is all that they would claim to provide.

But they must then, as Gluckman points out, be prepared to accept the full implications of their "minor" activities. Having identified themselves with the project, they have become identified with the goals of the project. I have tried to suggest what some of the less obvious correlates may be. Far more is involved, it seems to me, than simple easement of the "shock of accommodation". If, by their participation, the applied anthropologists are contributing in *any* measure to the achievement of the goals of colonial or assistance programs, they are contributing to one of the most profound cultural developments of our time. It is in this context, and in the context of the controlling cultural dynamics of which I spoke earlier, that they must evaluate their participation in and their contributions to such programs.

Until that distant day when the cultural interests of a world community may conceivably allow non-political solutions of social and economic problems, these contributions will, I believe, have small influence over patterns of culture change in underdeveloped areas undergoing contact. Perhaps the best that the applied anthropologists—and the rest of us—may do between now and then would be to try to illuminate the very nature of those cultural processes which restrict the part played by the "scientist of man" on behalf of man in "backward" areas.

NOTES

1. M. Fortes reflects on the role of the anthropologist in the colonial situation with arresting pessimism when he observes: "The central problem of colonial development, from an anthropologist's point of view, is that of changing the system as a whole. . . *This is essentially a political question*" (emphasis added).

16

SOME CRITICISMS
OF CULTURAL RELATIVISM

PAUL F. SCHMIDT

THE term "cultural relativism" has become a convenient label for our times covering some positive insights and some outright errors. Like any name it means different things to different people. My concern in this paper is to point out what I take to be some of its insights and errors. Most of its errors seem to me to result from some crucial ambiguities. Until these are distinguished it is impossible to evaluate its claims. What are some of these claims and their ambiguities?

Melville Herskovits in his well-known book, *Man and His Works,* tells us that "Evaluations are relative to the cultural background out of which they arise." Now this seems to be a statement about value judgments (evaluations), but on the next page he says that "Even the facts of the physical world are discerned through the enculturative screen, so that the perception of time, distance, weight, size, and other 'realities' is mediated by the conventions of any given group." This leads to my first question: Are factual judgments as well as value judgments relative to cultural background, or are only value judgments so affected? His position on these points remains unchanged in the abridged revision of 1955 entitled *Cultural Anthropology*.

Let us first consider the broader claim: both factual and value judgments are relative to the cultural background. The claim made is still ambiguous. For the meanings of the expressions "relative to" and "cultural background" remain unclear. To take the second expression first, it is true, for example, that human beings if they are to indulge in factual and value investigations have to select and agree upon certain conventions of language and the use of certain descriptive categories. But surely it is

From *Journal of Philosophy,* 52 (1955):780–791. Copyright © 1955 by Journal of Philosophy. Reprinted by permission of the publisher and the author. Paul F. Schmidt is Professor of Philosophy, Oberlin College.

not this part of one's "cultural background" that affects our factual and value judgments. For it is a truism that our judgments are made in terms of some language, and that various languages are in use in different cultures. If we should encounter a dependence upon such backgrounds we could easily construct, by stipulative definitions, a cross-cultural language to overcome this situation.

What is it, then, in the "cultural background" that Herskovits sees as affecting our perceptions of time, distance, weight, and so on? He seems to suggest that such judgments are affected by certain beliefs, held by persons in a culture, which constitute the world-view of the culture. They constitute the "climate-of-opinion" or ultimate presuppositions, uncritically, almost unknowingly, accepted.

Now, if our factual judgments are so conditioned, then the whole basis of objective investigation and empirical verification in the sciences is destroyed. Science then becomes the kind of myth-making we have witnessed in "Soviet biology" and "Deutsche anthropology."

This point brings us to the ambiguity in the phrase "is relative to" and indicates that what it means in this context is a relativity of truth. The truth of a factual judgment is conditioned by ("is relative to") the beliefs of a world-view ("cultural background").

On this interpretation the theory destroys its own basis. It is intended to be an empirical truth of anthropology and sociology holding for all cultures, but it destroys the basis for the objectivity which is required to make meaningful assertions that are cross-cultural. It destroys objectivity because the frame of reference for measurement in each culture is somehow peculiarly "true" for that culture and no over-arching or inter-cultural standard is available to objectively adjudicate inconsistent reports. Thus the cultural relativist cannot have it both ways: he cannot claim that the truth of factual judgments is relative to their cultural background and at the same time believe in the objectivity of sociological and anthropological investigations.

Let us take for granted, then, that cultural relativism does not hold that the truth of factual judgments is determined by, or tested by, any cultural considerations whatsover but by the relevance of evidence ascertainable by scientific method which is trans-cultural. I considered this broad sense because sometimes social scientists seem to fall into employing it. In fact, lest you fear I have wasted your time, I cannot resist one more quotation from Herskovits embodying the broad sense. He gives the principle of cultural relativism as follows: "Judgments are based on experience, and experience is interpreted by each individual in terms of his own enculturation" and "Enculturation is in essence a process of conscious or unconscious conditioning, exercised within the limits sanctioned by a given body of custom." Now these statements just bristle with difficulties. (1) Does he mean in the first quote *all* judgments including this one? If so its objective truth is destroyed, because anyone else could claim the denial of this quote as based on his enculturation and no way is left to empirically test and settle the assertion or denial. (2) What does he mean by the phrase "based on"? To give an explicit meaning to such processes of derivation has eluded philosophers and methodologists from David Hume to the present. (3) Doesn't the inclusion of unconscious as well as conscious conditioning in the second quote render the hypothesis *"ad hoc"* because such unconscious conditioning is unverifiable? The history of science has taught us that such unverifiable hypotheses are intolerable in a scheme that claims to test the empirically true from false.

We turn now to an analysis of the limited thesis restricting cultural relativism to value judgments. Herskovits' statement was: "Evaluations are relative to the cultural background out of which they arise." What does the term "relative" mean in this context? It may mean: (1) that evaluations are made by different human beings; a truism, for so far as I know human beings do all the judging. Or (2) that persons or cultures manifest diverse value judgments, which seem to be an empirical fact unrelated to their justification. I shall call this the fact of cultural relativism. Or (3) that value judgments are not susceptible of any justification but rather are rationalizations of *de facto* preferences. Or (4) that there are or there can be no value judgments that are true, that is, ob-

jectively justifiable, independent of specific cultures. This last meaning seems to be the one that Herskovits attaches to cultural relativism as a theory about values. I shall call this the thesis of cultural relativism. The principal confusions in cultural relativism revolve around what I call the fact and the thesis. Let us draw out some logical consequences from this distinction. First, I wish to assert now and reaffirm later that I think the fact of cultural relativism is a well established empirical truth and we are indebted to anthropology and sociology for its establishment, although I can't resist remarking that it was known by the Sophists of the fifth century B.C. in Athens. I do not see how anyone can reject the fact of cultural relativism. I want this point to be very clear.

It further follows from this distinction that the fact of cultural relativism is perfectly compatible with the view that some values hold true for all cultures or at least are cross-cultural. Such non-relative values I am going to call "cultural invariants," borrowing the term invariance from relativity physics. I avoid the use of terms like "absolutes" or "universals," for they are so loaded with diverse connotations as to be worthless.

At this point I wish to emphasize the following conclusions, some of which will be further substantiated when we deal next with the thesis of cultural relativism. (1) The fact of cultural relativism does not imply the thesis; hence the thesis of cultural relativism will have to be established by further evidence. (2) The fact of cultural relativism is perfectly compatible with the claim to cultural invariants, so the sociologist need not and cannot object on this ground to culturally invariant theories of value. (3) The fact of cultural relativism is a factual judgment about values, not a value judgment. It says something about what is the case, not about what ought to be.

Let us now look at the thesis of cultural relativism. It maintains that no value judgments are objectively justifiable independent of specific cultures. Some authors seem to think that the fact establishes the thesis as an inductive generalization. That it may suggest it is true, but the observation of such diversity does not constitute evidence concerning the status of justification for value judgments.

Second, the thesis of cultural relativism is a factual hypothesis about values, not itself a value judgment. This distinction is an instance of a general distinction made in value theory between what is and what ought to be, or between factual judgments and value judgments. The recognition of the difference in meaning between the statement "x is the case" and "x ought to be the case" is fundamental. The easiest way I know to show this difference in meaning is to ask a person if he would accept the following statement as meaningful: "x is the case but x ought not to be the case." If "ought" means the same as "is" this statement is self-contradictory. The statement "x is the case" is a descriptive statement which is falsified by factual evidence contradictory to what it asserts. The statement "x ought to be the case" is a prescriptive statement which is not falsified by factual evidence showing that "x is not the case." The thesis of cultural relativism is a descriptive statement about the fact that no values are objectively justifiable independent of specific cultures. Now I hold the view that this intrinsic difference in meaning between "is" and "ought" has as a consequence that one cannot derive what ought to be solely from what is the case. By "derive" I mean that the statement to be justified contains predicates (appraisal terms) of a different kind from the predicates contained in the justifying statements such that the former cannot be obtained from the latter alone. Nevertheless "what is the case" is often relevant to our determination of "what ought to be." The occurrence of a value judgment in a particular culture can suggest a value which may be objectively justifiable, but we cannot derive it from such occurrences.

Why is this distinction so important to a discussion of the thesis of cultural relativism? Its importance lies in the fact that the thesis is supposed to provide us with a basis for what we ought to do; that is, to provide prescriptive as against descriptive information. In other words, to provide us with a value theory. It is at this point that ethical thinkers and thinking become involved. In support of this confusion I quote Herskovits: "For cultural relativism is a philosophy which, in recognizing the values set up by every society to guide its own life, lays stress on the dignity inherent in every body of custom, and on the need for tolerance of conventions though they may differ from one's own." The terms ought, right, and good do not explicitly occur but the statement is loaded with value judgments such as: (1) one ought to recognize the values set up by every society (some cultures do not do so); (2) every body of cus-

tom has dignity and value (but are all equal in dignity and value?); (3) one ought to be tolerant of conventions even though they differ from one's own (but some cultures are intolerant of tolerance). If these value judgments are not implicit in Herskovits' statement I hope someone will provide me with another interpretation. I shall take up shortly what I think are some of the consequences of these value judgments.

This passage is modified in the abridged revision of 1955. It now reads: "For cultural relativism is a philosophy that recognizes the values set up by every society to guide its own life and that understands their worth to those who live by them, though they may differ from one's own." The implicit value judgments are almost eliminated in favor of cultural relativism as a methodological principle as explained in the last two paragraphs of this paper. Herskovits almost seems to see the difficulty in his earlier view, except that in the next sentence he concludes: "the relativistic point of view brings into relief the validity of every set of norms for the people who have them, and the values these represent." And on the next page he slips right back to the earlier position when he says: "The very core of cultural relativism is the social discipline that comes of respect for differences—of mutual respect. Emphasis on the worth of many ways of life, not one, is an affirmation of the values in each culture." Worse yet, he actually distinguishes three different aspects of cultural relativism—methodological, philosophical, and practical—which correspond to what I call the method, the thesis as factual hypothesis, and the thesis as value theory; the first and last to be discussed shortly. Having made this important distinction he goes on to assert that the three aspects constitute a logical sequence. Hence the following logical criticism is entirely in order.

If the thesis of cultural relativism is explicitly affirmed by the anthropologist to be a factual hypothesis, then it follows that no value judgments about what ought to be can be derived from it. For to do so is to try to derive an ought from an is. Thus the factual hypothesis could be true and be compatible with a variety of value theories about what is right and good. This exposes the sense in which as a descriptive hypothesis it has something to say about the origin or status of values in cultures or about the justification for value judgments, but cannot justify prescriptive judgments. Let me bring this into focus with a simple example. As a descriptive hypothesis the thesis could be and was held by the Nazis who believed it right to kill Jews and by Americans who believed it wrong. It could be held consistently by Christian, Mohammedan, Buddhist, and atheistic thinkers, each maintaining value judgments incompatible with those held by the others. Thus knowledge of and belief in cultural relativism are compatible with diverse value theories and do not, as Herskovits thinks, imply specific value judgments.

If, on the other hand, the thesis of cultural relativism is implicitly taken as a value theory rather than as a descriptive hypothesis, then it is subject to the kind of analysis and criticism appropriate to value theories. Let us note that in order to turn the descriptive hypothesis into a value theory, an implicit value assumption connecting the two is required; something to the effect that "whatever value judgments are made by a majority of persons in culture A constitute the justification for what value judgments ought to be made by persons in culture A." But it must be pointed out that this assumption is not contained in the thesis of cultural relativism as a descriptive hypothesis, for it is a prescriptive statement. It is often supposed to be there but on analysis is not. You simply cannot derive value statements unless you have some value assumptions, at least one. I do not herein face the question as to how such prescriptive statements are obtained.

An even more serious difficulty results from taking the thesis as a value theory. It reads roughly as follows: "In every case the rightness of any act or goodness of any thing for a member of culture A is justified by reference to what in fact is considered right or good in culture A." Now, this is a value theory implying prescriptive judgments and as such is subject to the thesis. But that thesis as now interpreted tells us that any value judgment is justified only with reference to a particular culture and has no inherent objectivity for other cultures. Hence the thesis of cultural relativism taken as a cross-cultural value theory falls as a victim of its own meaning. It has cut down its own claim to objectivity as a prescriptive theory that holds cross-culturally. It holds only for those cultures which contain a majority of persons who assert it. For another culture that denied cultural relativism as a prescriptive theory, the denial would be justified. Taken as a cross-cultural prescriptive theory it is self-defeating.

Another form of cultural relativism as a value theory that avoids the ethnocentrism of the previous position and its self-defeating character attempts to extract certain value judgments from the attitudes which may be connected with a knowledge of diverse cultural practices. I shall discuss some examples shortly. The critical point is the erroneous inference from de facto attitudes belonging to the frame of reference of anthropological investigation to prescriptive judgments which are somehow "superior" because of their source in anthropological thought. We must not confuse the source or cause of such prescriptions with their ethical justification.

In the face of such logical analysis some cultural relativists are ready to admit it cannot hold cross-culturally, so I must go on to point out one practical consequence which flows from the interpretation of cultural relativism as a value theory—a consequence which will, I think, lead one to reject the theory. Notice that I am not saying that cultural relativists advocate this consequence. Most would in fact abhor it. Nor am I saying that this consequence refutes the theory. We now suppose that this value interpretation is correct. For our example let us consider the recent war with Germany. The Nazi thinks that it is right for him to exterminate Jews, condemn without trial, appropriate foreign lands and kill resisting foreign persons, violate international law, etc. Why is it right for him to think and act thus? Because these are the accepted value judgments of his culture. Hence it is right for him to follow them. The American thinks that the opposites of the above value judgments are right. Why? Because in the United States these are the accepted value judgments. Are there any cross-cultural prescriptive principles to which both sides could appeal to settle their ethical disagreement? No. Each side can legitimately on this theory claim it is right and both sides can be asserting true propositions. The result often is a power struggle. That side which wins the fight is right since its culture becomes predominant. Ethical disagreements are not solved by cultural relativism as a value theory but rather one or the other party is dissolved, liquidated. On this supposition does it make any sense for a person in one culture to tell a person in another culture that he is wrong? No. Wrongness and rightness have meaning only within a culture, not between. Your statement as an American is theoretically meaningless nonsense to him as a Nazi. On this supposition does it make any sense to have war criminals (so called) tried? No. Such action is the grossest hypocrisy and propagandistic *tour de force,* a sheer fake. Now I want to make it very clear that I do not think these consequences prove the theory is false, but I do insist that anyone who holds the theory be prepared to accept these consequences, and I think very few are. It is not here claimed that such a power struggle always results. In fact, it is only fair to mention that cultural relativism taken as a value theory can also lead to unification and harmony between two cultures if they can discover certain common value premises in each which will provide a basis for resolving their differences.

Some social scientists who have been made aware of the possible power struggle consequences of the thesis of cultural relativism as a value theory, with its attendant lack of a basis for making value judgments that are meaningful in different cultures, have resorted to a distinction between the anthropologist as scientist and as citizen. As scientists they wish to maintain the truth of the thesis, but as citizens they desire a basis for righteous condemnation of acts perpetrated in other cultures. This dualism has the effect of separating the knowledge of science from the knowledge of the citizen, for what is supposed true in science is supposed false for the citizen. This makes scientific knowledge irrelevant to social action. The distinction also implies that the basis on which the righteous condemnation of the citizen is based is not scientific knowledge, thus opening the door for the use of mythical insights of various pernicious sorts. A fact that is true is just as true for a scientist as it is for that same person as citizen. I do not think that those persons who have resorted to this dualism have squarely faced the consequences of it. If they had they would have rejected it.

We must now turn to a consideration of another claim made for the thesis of cultural relativism. Herskovits and others think that the thesis provides an objective justification for the value judgment that tolerance is good. I think this view is mistaken. Consider first the supposition that either the fact or the thesis as a descriptive assertion is true. From either of these one cannot derive the value judgment that tolerance is good, because it would involve the derivation of an "ought" from an "is." Second, suppose that the thesis as a value theory is true. Does it imply that tolerance is good? No; because the value judgment "tolerance is bad" can be accepted by culture *A,* and hence is right for culture *A,* regardless of what other

cultures accept. Either judgment is logically and factually consistent with the thesis as a value theory. As a matter of fact I think the value judgment "tolerance is good" is correct, but it requires another foundation.

I should like at this point to summarize my analyses and criticisms of cultural relativism. (1) What I call the fact of cultural relativism is a true empirical statement with a mass of well-founded evidence behind it. (2) The thesis as a descriptive hypothesis may be true but the fact of cultural relativism is not evidence for the thesis. (3) Neither the fact nor the thesis implies anything whatsoever concerning what is right or good because we cannot derive an "ought" from what "is." (4) The fact and the thesis are compatible with diverse value theories. (5) The thesis as a value theory must be rejected because its meaning implies its own refutation as a cross-cultural value theory. (6) The value interpretation of cultural relativism can lead to a power struggle. (7) Neither the value interpretation nor the factual formulations imply the judgment "tolerance is good."

My criticisms thus far have been negative. What positive knowledge do we have that is incompatible with the thesis of cultural relativism?

First, I want to notice some empirical data that suggest the existence of trans-cultural values in opposition to the fact of diversity. These data have been gathered by some social scientists about cultures and consist of certain stresses and needs that are invariant with respect to different cultures. A. H. Leighton, in his book *Human Relations in a Changing World,* gives a list of basic stresses. Their avoidance is a positive need for all cultures. The following are a sample: (1) threats to life and health; (2) discomfort from pain, heat, cold, fatigue; (3) loss of means of subsistence; (4) deprivation of sexual satisfaction; (5) isolation; and (6) threats to children. D. F. Aberle and others, in an article on "The Functional Prerequisites of a Society," give some of the following: (1) sexual recruitment; (2) shared cognitive orientations and values; and (3) the effective control of disruptive forms of behavior. The demand for satisfaction of these needs leads to certain value judgments that are invariant for all cultures, such as: one ought to provide so far as possible the means to health; or, sexual satisfaction in some form is good. I am prepared to admit the likelihood of such invariant needs for cultures, but I think that a fallacy is involved in the transition from these needs to value judgments concerning their rightness or goodness. These needs seem to me to be facts that are invariant for cultures in contrast to other facts that are relative, but both are facts. In order to derive value judgments from these needs I think one depends on a value assumption to the effect that "the basic needs of mankind ought to be realized in so far as possible in every culture." With this assumption, these invariant needs do imply value judgments, but I do not think that this value assumption can be derived from the existence of these needs. Nevertheless I would accept the assumption on other grounds. If one grants this assumption and the existence of such invariant needs, it follows that the thesis of cultural relativism is false, for it makes a claim about the relativity of justification for all values. Granting this value assumption and invariant needs we can derive cross-cultural value judgments.

If the case for cultural relativism is as weak as I picture it we may well wonder why it has been so persuasive in the modern world. Two points are relevant. The first explanation can be found by exposing a false dichotomy. This dichotomy takes the rough form: either value judgments are subjective and relative or they are transcendent and absolute. Such transcendent and absolute values are ordinarily conceived as holding true regardless of different contexts and consequences and are often conceived as imposed by some deity. Now, the fact of cultural relativism so ably demonstrated by anthropology tends to raise a good deal of scepticism concerning the existence of such absolute and transcendent values. From this situation, social scientists have easily fallen into the position that the remaining alternative is true. This conclusion would be true if this were a genuine dichotomy and the inferences are valid, but neither is the case. A genuine third alternative maintains the objectivity of value judgments but rejects the source of such objectivity in some transcendent realm, locating it, rather, in the projection of human ideals. It recognizes the relation of such judgments to a context and in this special sense the judgments are relative. But such contexts are present in different cultures, so the judgments are cross-cultural. The point is that the relation of a judgment to a context does not imply its lack of objectivity. Such a value theory can admit the fact of cultural relativism, in fact, employ it fruitfully in the specification of the conditions surrounding a context in which a moral decision has to be made. Herskovits makes a distinction between "absolutes" and "universals," rejecting the former and allowing the latter. But his universals are not my contextually objective values. His "universals" are descriptive statements concerning the fact that every culture has some moral code, aesthetic preference, and standard of truth. Besides being rather vacuous of specific content, these universals are only descriptive, not prescriptive, so the old problem remains.

The second factor and I think the key explanation that has contributed to the misinterpretation of cultural relativism as a value theory stems from its genuine success as a methodological tool in the study of cultures. The anthropologist seeks to understand cultures different from his own. Such understanding, if it is to count as objective data, must be free from one's own personal or cultural bias. Cultural relativism as a methodological principle prescribes that the anthropologist refrain from making cross-cultural evaluations at the outset of his investigation. Instead he should attempt to become a part of the culture under study, accept its values, traditions, and beliefs in order to achieve a full "inside" understanding. At the end, cross-cultural evaluations may be in order. Such has been the actual practice of great anthropologists like Malinowski. Let us call this meaning the method of cultural relativism.

As a methodological principle, it is prescriptive in meaning, asserting how one ought to proceed in investigation. Its genuine success has led social scientists into the error of supposing that it is prescriptive in the ethical sense. These two senses of prescriptive meaning must be kept separate. Further, we cannot infer an ethical prescription from a methodological prescription. Hence, we must also conclude that the method of cultural relativism fails to establish the thesis of cultural relativism. Such are some of the confusions involved in the concept of cultural relativism.

17

OBSERVATION AND GENERALIZATION IN CULTURAL ANTHROPOLOGY

JESSIE BERNARD

THE methods of cultural anthropology have in some instances become almost identified with objectivity. On the other hand, the unchecked nature of most anthropological observation has also been challenged. The question arises very naturally: Just how scientific are the methods of observation and generalization in cultural anthropology?

With respect to the first step in any science, accurate observation of the phenomena, the physical sciences have found the human organism very inadequate. Increasingly, therefore, instruments replace human sense organs. The scientist becomes more and more an inventor of techniques which will do his observing for him and also a reader and interpreter and generalizer of the records which his instruments deposit. Anthropologists have found the camera and the sound recorder valuable tools for accurate observation. But so far the volume of observation objectively recorded is relatively small, and unfortunately the thing usually recorded—physical or material culture—is often the sort easiest to observe and report on objectively even without such instruments. Such phases of nonmaterial culture as ritual, literature, songs, dances, etc., can also be observed and reported objectively either with or without instruments. But when the cultural anthropologist turns to methods, patterns, personality, temperament, structure, and other intangibles, he cannot rely on instruments—at least he has not done so—and his observations are therefore subject to challenge by anyone who cares to disagree with him.

As to generalization, here again cultural anthropology is at a disadvantage. The first great school of generalizers in the nineteenth century—Tylor, Spencer, Bachofen, Morgan, Lub-

From *American Journal of Sociology,* 50 (1945): 284–291. Copyright © 1945 by the University of Chicago Press. Reprinted by permission of the publisher and the author. Jessie Bernard is Professor of Sociology, Pennsylvania State University.

bock, Letourneau—transformed the field of antiquities into the field of scientific anthropology precisely because they did generalize the quaint and curious phenomena about preliterate peoples which travelers, missionaries, and they themselves had reported. The form which their generalizations took—that of evolutionary stages—did not suit the twentieth-century anthropologists. And for a while the straw man of fixed and unvarying evolutionary stages was a favorite whipping-boy. There then arose the school of field investigators who reported as carefully and accurately as they could the mortuary rites of preliterate peoples or their art or their language or their family system but who refused to draw any generalizations at all. This antigeneralization period culminated around 1920. Lowie's *Primitive Society* may be said to mark the turning-point. Although it decries the generalizations of the evolutionary school, it is nevertheless full of generalizations of a different kind. Since that time, generalization has returned to cultural anthropology, sometimes acknowledged, sometimes *sub rosa*.

It is the purpose of this article to analyze some of the observations and generalizations of one particular study, Margaret Mead's *Sex and Temperament in Three Primitive Societies,* as an illustration of some of the pitfalls to which current generalizations in cultural anthropology are subject. Miss Mead is one of the most prolific and influential of American anthropologists. Her works are widely read and cited. I am certainly not challenging her integrity as a scientist nor am I attacking her conclusions, which are very congenial to me. I am merely pointing out how vulnerable cultural anthropology is when it leaves the field in which objective observation is possible or when it generalizes on the basis of data gathered without instruments.

It is the essence of scientific method that everyone, whether he likes it or not, must agree with the observations obtained by it. That is the advantage of instruments. Everyone must accept their record. Indeed, scientific method might be defined as a procedure which obliterates any personal idiosyncracies. We may insist that the water is cold, but if we agree to call 100 degrees warm, then the thermometer overrides us. We may say that the room is dark, but the contraction of our pupils which the instrument records proves that it is light. One reason the physical sciences have advanced so much more rapidly than the social sciences is that our physical bodies are so much more standardized than the social aspects of our personalities. Heat is hot to everyone; cold is cold to everyone. Human flesh is made that way. But—until we have techniques and instruments which standardize our mental reactions as much as our physical ones—beauty is not beauty to everyone, nor is masculinity or femininity the same to everyone.

It will be recalled that in *Sex and Temperament* Miss Mead describes three preliterate cultures: the Arapesh, the Mundugumor, and the Tchambuli. Her conclusions on the basis of her observations are that the Arapesh as a whole are maternal and feminine in temperament; that the Mundugumor are ruthless, aggressive, and positively sexed—and that among the Tchambuli there is "a genuine reversal of the sex attitudes of our own culture, with the woman the dominant, impersonal, managing partner, the man the less responsible and the emotionally dependent person" (p. 279). Would everyone who saw what Miss Mead saw agree with the observations upon which she based these conclusions?

Would Terman, for example, consider men who recently indulged in headhunting (pp. 242-43), who conduct the intertribal trade with outsiders (p. 254), who are constantly on the verge of fighting among themselves (pp. 254, 262, *passim*), as effeminate? Would Terman, viewing moving pictures of the Tchambuli, agree with Miss Mead that these men were not masculine in temperament?

And, conversely, would everyone agree that women who devoted themselves cheerfully, happily, and efficiently to feeding and nursing children, growing and cooking food, to plaiting mosquito nets, women whose attitudes toward men were kindly, tolerant, and appreciative (p. 255), were masculine? I for one found myself constantly confused between the facts Miss Mead reported and the interpretations she made of them. I would not consider Tchambuli men effeminate on the basis of the data she

presents, nor do the women she describes seem masculine.

Throughout her description of the Tchambuli, Miss Mead applies to men adjectives and terms which we usually apply to women, and vice versa. These tend to predispose us to accept her conclusions, but in a purely scientific sense these must be discounted because they are not objective. For example:

In their [the women's] energetic friendly activity there is an air of solidarity, of firm cooperation and group purpose, which is lacking in the gaily decorated ceremonial houses along the shore, where each man sits down daintily in his own place and observes his companions narrowly [p. 239].
. . . the men moving self-consciously, abashed to eat, among the crowds of smiling, unadorned, efficient women . . . [p. 241].
Walinakwon was beautiful, a graceful dancer, a fluent speaker, proud, imperious, but withal soft-spoken, and resourceful [p. 253].
The men make a gala occasion of these latter shopping-trips; . . . have a very orgy of choice such as a modern woman with a well-filled purse looks forward to in a shopping-trip to a big city. . . . He has . . . to wheedle the items of the price from his wife. . . . Real property . . . one receives from women, in return for languishing looks and soft words [p. 254].
. . . masculine charming, graceful, coquettish dancing attention [p. 264].

What, scientifically, does sitting "daintily" mean? Would we all agree that the men sat "daintily"? Would we all agree from motion pictures that the men were "abashed" to eat among the women? Would we all agree that men "wheedled" things from women with "languishing" looks?

Miss Mead is like the novelist who tells the reader rather than shows him what his characters are like. And the behavior of the characters often belies her descriptions. To illustrate, she contrasts the men and women as follows:

Tchambuli women work in blocks, a dozen of them together, plaiting the great mosquito-bags from the sale of which most of the *talibun* and *kina* are obtained. They cook together for a feast, their clay fire-places . . . set side by side. Each dwelling-house contains some dozen to two dozen fire-places, so that no woman need cook in a corner alone. The whole emphasis is upon comradeship, efficient, happy work enlivened by continuous brisk banter and chatter. But in a group of men, there is always strain, watchfulness, a catty remark here, a double entendre there: "What did he mean by sitting down on the opposite side of the men's house when he saw you upon this side?" "Did you see

Koshalan go by with a flower in his hair? What do you suppose he is up to?"

Jolly comradeship, rough, very broad jesting and comment are the order of the day [among the women]. . . . And whereas the lives of the men are one mass of petty bickering, misunderstanding, reconciliation, avowals, disclaimers, and protestations accompanied by gifts, the lives of the women are singularly unclouded with personalities or with quarreling. For fifty quarrels among the men, there is hardly one among the women. Solid, preoccupied, powerful, with shaven unadorned heads, they sit in groups and laugh together . . . [p. 257].

The Tchambuli dwelling-house . . . presents the curious picture of the entire centre firmly occupied by well-entrenched women, while the men sit about the edges, near the door, one foot on the house-ladder almost, unwanted, on suffrance, ready to flee away to their men's houses, where they do their own cooking, gather their own firewood, and generally live a near-bachelor life in a state of mutual discomfort and suspicion [pp. 247–58].

Each man stands alone, playing his multiplicity of parts, sometimes allied with one man, sometimes with another; but the women are a solid group, confused by no rivalries, brisk, patronizing, and jovial. They feed their male children, their young male relatives, on lotus-seeds and lily-roots, their husbands and lovers upon doled-out pellets of love [pp. 263–64].

If we discount the nonscientific adjectives and concentrate on the actual behavior described, which we may accept as objective observation, would we all draw the same conclusions as those she draws? Is cheerful working together, for example, a masculine trait? With some slight modifications, Miss Mead's description of Tchambuli women preparing for a feast would apply equally well to a group of women preparing a church social in the Middle West. Are strain and watchfulness feminine traits? They are very characteristic of American businessmen, whom no one would characterize as effeminate. Miss Mead tells us that quarrels are fifty times more numerous among men than among women in Tchambuli culture. Are they fifty times more numerous among women than among men in our culture? The picture of the household in which women are dominant and men on suffrance, ready to flee, does not strike one as so very different from many households in our own culture. Men flee the woman-dominated household here, too, as the wives of transients, hoboes, club men, and even businessmen could testify.

There is still another source of confusion in Miss Mead's method. In characterizing a culture, should one judge by the theory of the culture or the actual behavior of the people? Miss Mead tells us that, theoretically and legally, men are dominant among the Tchambuli but that actually the women dominate, thus producing much confusion (pp. 264, 270–71). Is this not equally true of our own culture —or almost any other culture, for that matter? Formally men are dominant in our culture. Actually, however, if we are to believe most of the commentators on our culture, a situation similar to that of the Tchambuli obtains among us, that is, one in which women really dominate.[1] The formulation of sex relations in both Tchambuli culture and in our own is in terms of a dominant male and a subservient female. Yet Miss Mead tells us that the Tchambuli formulation of sex attitudes contradicts our usual premises (p.288). It is not the formulation of sex attitudes among the Tchambuli which contradicts ours; it is the actual behavior of Tchambuli women which contradicts our formulation of sex attitudes. But, then, so does the behavior of American women, a great many of whom are of a "dominating, organizing, administrative temperament, actively sexed and willing to initiate sex-relations, possessive, definite, robust, practical and impersonal in outlook" (p. 288). In other words, both among the Tchambuli and among us, the theoretical picture is quite different from the actual situation, and it is therefore not correct to compare the actual behavior of Tchambuli women with the theory of our culture and to conclude that Tchambuli women are masculine in temperament any more than American women are. In brief, there is no scientific proof in Miss Mead's account of the Tchambuil of "a genuine reversal of the sex attitudes of our own culture." The cultures are similar in theory; and, for all we know, similar in practice too.

Miss Mead's observations of the Arapesh and of the Mundugumor establish beyond all doubt that some cultures create gentle personalities and other cultures violent ones. But when she (1) characterizes the gentle culture of the Arapesh as, in our meaning of the term, effeminate and the violent one of the Mundugumor as masculine and when she (2) states that neither the Arapesh nor the Mundugumor differentiate the sexes on the basis of temperament (p. 279), her data do not always convince the reader of her conclusions.

For the most part the Arapesh are non-aggressive and co-operative and have a cherishing attitude toward children. But would the imper-

sonal observer of motion pictures of Arapesh
life consider everyone effeminate? Our own culture might be described as follows:

Aggression is frowned upon. Theoretically every
man is supposed to look upon every other man as
his brother. If one cheek is struck, the other should
be bared. War is hated and accepted only if under
attack. The prevailing attitude is pacifistic. Nevertheless, just as the Arapesh have the institution of
the *buanyin* to train leaders in competition and
aggression, so this culture has business and politics
which foster competition and thus furnish leadership. When a woman has a baby the father paces
the floor anxiously and nervously, often in worse
condition than the mother. When the calm, efficient
woman nurse announces that the child is born, the
men sometimes collapse.[2]

An outsider might conclude that our culture
is essentially effeminate and maternal, like the
Arapesh. And yet most of us would not agree.

But one might state that, although the theory
of our culture is co-operative and nonaggressive,
actually it is fiercely aggressive, crime and law-
nessness being rampant. The sharp competition
among women for men renders every mar-
riageable young woman the natural enemy of
every other. Without doing violence to many
undoubted facts, one might draw a picture that
would not look very different from Mundugumor culture. And yet most of us would not
characterize our culture as essentially masculine.

Miss Mead tells us that neither the Arapesh
nor the Mundugumor differentiate the sexes
temperamentally (p. 279), and yet in each case
the women differ from the men. Among the
Mundugumor, little girls are made desirable to
others, they are dressed up and decorated (p.
199), physical hazing is less among them
(p. 205), they are not taught to use weapons
(p. 210), they are rarely used as hostages
(p. 211), married women have fewer affairs
than married men (p. 219), etc. As a result
of their somewhat gentler rearing,

there are sometimes twelve or fifteen women in a
compound, and the tendency, in the absence of
fixed rules of conduct between them, is towards
forming shifting alliances within which the degree
of enmity is at least less than it is towards the
other parties or trios. All of this provides a ground-
plan that makes it possible for a group of girls to
sit about quietly talking or making grass skirts
without the restrictions imposed by an insistence
upon avoidance, jesting, or shyness. The very little
girls follow their older sisters about, and imitate
this cheerful behaviour [p. 209]. . . . [Women] are
believed to be just as violent, just as aggressive, just
as jealous [as men]. They simply are not quite as

strong physically. . . . For these reasons, although
women choose men as often as men choose women,
the society is constructed so that men fight about
women, and women elude, defy, and complicate
this fighting to the limit of their abilites [p. 210].

Strangely enough, among the gentle, effeminate
Arapesh, "brawls and clashes between villages
do occur, mainly over women" (p. 23). Is it
only because men are stronger than women
that it is always men who fight over women
and never the women who fight over men? Why
is it always the men who engage in the wars
and brawls?

A similar argument might be made in the
case of the Arapesh to show that they do make
a distinction between the temperaments of men
and women. Of the violent Amitoa, for example, the Arapesh "say in one breath that she
should have been a man because she liked action and as a man she would have had more
scope, and in the next that as a man she would
have been undesirable, a quarreller and a fo-
menter of trouble" (p. 152). Would such a
thought have occurred to people who really
made no temperamental distinctions between
the sexes?

If there is such a thing as what we in our
culture call an effeminate temperament, then,
according to Miss Mead, the Arapesh men and
the Tchambuli men ought to be very similar,
since both are patterned after what we call
a feminine mold. But they are not. Arapesh
men are "gentle, unacquisitive, and cooperative" (p. 30), whereas Tchambuli men are
quarrelsome, bickering, strained, and "catty"
(p. 257). Similarly, Mundugumor women and
Tchambuli women ought to be alike, since
both are, according to Miss Mead, masculine in
temperament. Here again, we find them different. Tchambuli women nurse their babies generously, willingly attend their needs, wean them
casually and carelessly, feed them whenever they
cry, etc. (pp. 248–49). Mundugumor women
nurse their children grudgingly, wean them
harshly, and reject them in general (pp.
195–200).

So far we have argued that Miss Mead's
characterizations of preliterate peoples in terms
of feminine, masculine, and reversed traits are
not scientific in the sense that everyone observing the same data would agree with her.
We now advance another step and present the
thesis that, even accepting Miss Mead's observations as valid, one can come to exactly
opposite conclusions to those she arrives at. For

example, Miss Mead concludes that temperament is not sex-linked (pp. 164, 280, 282, *passim*) but that it is overwhelmingly cultural. A skeptic, accepting her data, might argue to the contrary: that the reversion of cultural roles among the Tchambuli violated the natural masculine temperament to such a degree that the men were prone to neuroticism. For, as she informs us, Tchambuli "men are the conspicuous maladjusts, subject to neurasthenia, hysteria, and maniacal outbursts" (p. 275). She found more neurotic males than in any other primitive culture she has studied (p. 307).

Miss Mead, further, tells us that "we are forced to conclude that human nature is almost unbelievably malleable, responding accurately and contrastingly to contrasting cultural conditions" (p. 280). One might argue, again on the basis of her own data, that even culture cannot change inherited temperament. One might cite the case of Ombléan, the Mundugumor man, who "was gentle, cooperative, responsive, easily enlisted in the causes for others" (p. 229) or the case of the Arapesh leader Nyelahai (p. 147), who was a "loud-mouthed, malicious man, who took delight in the sorcery traffic, and went up and down the country-side abusing his neighbors." Miss Mead frequently speaks of persons who are temperamentally ill at ease in their cultures. There are, apparently, very clear-cut limits to what culture can do to certain temperaments. It would be interesting to know what, precisely, these limits are.

My own prejudices lead me to accept Miss Mead's conclusions in general. But I recognize that I accept them only because I want to and not because she has proved them. How could one set up a scientific study to test her generalizations? First of all, of course, there must be some clear-cut definition of terms. What do we mean by "temperament"? Do we mean acquired traits like "bravery, hatred of any weakness, of flinching before pain or danger" (p. 286), or "easy unashamed display of fear or suffering" (pp. 286–87), or co-operativeness, responsiveness, mildness, etc.? Obviously, if we define temperament in such terms, there can be no question of cultural conditioning. Not even the most confirmed believer in innate characteristics would, I believe, argue that these traits were inherited. So far as aggression and passivity in sex are concerned, Sumner long ago pointed out that the mores are also compulsive, so that if the mores prescribe that women as well as men shall be the aggressors, as Mundugumor mores

do, then we can expect human behavior to conform to them. But these are not matters of temperament so much as of mores.

If by temperament we mean some organic quality of the personality such as those formerly labeled "choleric," "phlegmatic," "melancholic," and "sanguine," the problem is somewhat different. These four terms refer to two personality axes. In one the gradient is from choleric to phlegmatic; in the other, from melancholic to sanguine. The Arapesh seem to be on the phlegmatic-sanguine side; the Mundugumor, on the choleric. No one, so far as I know, ever claimed a sex bias in these temperamental types in our own culture. Women as well as men have about as good a chance to be one as another. If among the Tchambuli the men tend to be choleric and the women phlegmatic, that is an interesting fact, but not one reversing the situation among us.

At any rate, once temperament is defined, the next step is to measure it. Basal metabolism tests might offer a starting point. Indices of glandular functioning might be included. Tests of interests might offer a supplementary insight. Actual activities, such as head-hunting, war, raids, inter-tribal trade, cooking, and care of children might be scaled in terms of degree of action or sedentariness. Frequency of sexual aggression might well constitute one element in such a battery of measurements. With such a set of measures one might then apply them specifically to the Arapesh, the Mundugumor, and the Tchambuli. Assuming reliable and valid instruments, we would then all have to agree on the results obtained.

What one misses most in Miss Mead's descriptions are just such measures, and when they do appear one jumps upon them avidly. For example, she tells us that only 4 per cent of the Mundugumor men achieve the ideal of their society (p. 174); in another place, 1 per cent of the total community (p. 186). Since there are only a thousand Mundugumor in all (p. 169), this means that there are only about ten men who really embody the cultural pattern. In other words, they are, roughly, almost three standard deviations away from the average. It would be worth knowing how many unaggressive nephews (p. 174) there are on the other end of the distribution, how many "sheep" there are, "to whom pride, violence, and competitiveness do not appeal" (p. 226). The same goes for the Arapesh. In brief, what we really hunger for is not only the fascinating cases that

Miss Mead presents so well but also frequency distributions, measures of deviation and dispersion, etc.[3]

If we had such measures, we might then conclude that culture can take any human type within, let us say, two or two-and-a-half standard deviations from the average and mold it to conform to either a "choleric" or a "phlegmatic" pattern. Those who are beyond two or two-and-a-half standard deviations from the mean cannot be so molded. They are the "deviants" in Miss Mead's terminology. With such measures also we could test her statement that there are no temperamental differences between the sexes among the Arapesh and the Mundugumor. Whatever the difficulties and the drawbacks to such an approach—and they are admittedly great—it would have the advantage of scientific objectivity, and the skeptic would have to accept the generalizations based upon them.

Could it not be argued that bravery, aggressiveness, etc., are not, even in our culture, specific to one sex but that the modes and circumstances of displaying them are. Thus women are not required to be brave in the presence of mice or worms or bugs; but we do demand that they be brave in childbirth, illness, the presence of death, and other personal relationships. We do not allow them to express their aggressiveness directly, yet there are many "lady-like" ways of being aggressive. Emily Post tells us that a girl may not openly chase a man, but, if she is catlike about it, no one will object. The old definition of courtship—"you chase a girl until she catches you"—as well as smoking-room jokes illustrate the fact that, whatever the theory of our culture may be about the feminine temperament, actually we do recognize it as aggressive in its own way.

The chief temperamental differences between the sexes in our culture might be summarized as follows. Because women are smaller and weaker (kinetically, not vitally) than men, because in general their basal metabolism is lower, their interests and occupations tend to be more sedentary than those of men. As a result of these facts, men tend to dominate in the economic and political spheres; but women

tend to be dominant in the family and social life. Most of the acquired temperamental differences of the sexes may be traced back to these foundations. There is not much about the Arapesh, the Mundugumor, or the Tchambuli which this description would violate.

SUMMARY

Both the methods of observation and the methods of generalization in cultural anthropology are vulnerable from a scientific point of view when they leave those aspects of culture which may be observed through instruments. What is urgently needed is the invention and application of instruments for purposes of observing these nonmaterial and psychosocial aspects of culture. These points are illustrated herein by references to Miss Mead's study of sex and temperament in primitive cultures.

NOTES

1. All comparisons of preliterate cultures with our own presupposes that we know our own culture. But this is by no means to be taken for granted. Miss Mead's references to our culture do not always coincide with my own observations. Until we have just as scientific descriptions of our own culture as of other cultures, such comparisons are highly vulnerable.

2. Mark May, *Social Psychology of War* (1943), p. 40.

3. It was a great advance when anthropologists began to disabuse us of the idea of dead-level-of-conformity which the old students of primitive peoples had given us. Miss Mead's descriptions of nonconformists are most enlightening. If we could now combine the two approaches by measuring conformity and nonconformity, our knowledge would be greatly enhanced. Miss Mead herself seems somewhat troubled by her lack of true measures of conformity and nonconformity and apologizes for the emphasis she places on nonconformity (p. 122). She justifies herself on the ground that she cannot forever go on recording the usual pattern of life. But if she had a technically efficient instrument, it would be a simple matter to tally these day-by-day activities and thus give us a more meaningful background for her presentation of nonconforming behavior.

18

RESIDENCE RULES

WARD H. GOODENOUGH

DETERMINING a community's rule or rules of residence in marriage has long been established as a basic requirement for any satisfactory descriptive account of its social system. That residence practices are important determinants of the various forms of family and kinship organization has long been postulated by ethnologists and recently been given impressive statistical documentation by Murdock.

Needless to say, studies such as his are dependent upon the reliability with which ethnographic facts are reported and interpreted. Ethnologists now take it for granted that a reliable report of residence customs is based on a house by house census of the community studied. When we read that such a census reveals a given ratio of residence types, I think most of us feel secure in what we regard as reliable information.

It was quite a shock, therefore, when I recently found myself differing considerably with John Fischer about the incidence of residence forms in a community on Truk (Romonum Island) where we both collected data within the space of three years. Our respective tabulations appear [below].[1]

Type of Residence	Goodenough		Fischer	
	Cases	Percent	Cases	Percent
Matrilocal	46	71	36	58
Patrilocal	1	1.5	20	32
Avunculocal	10	15	0	—
Neolocal	4	6	6	10
Other arrangement	3	5	0	—
Ambiguous	1	1.5	0	—
Total	65	100	62	100

On the basis of my figures we would not hesitate to classify Trukese society as essentially matrilocal, since nearly three-quarters of the married couples are apparently living in matrilocal residence. On the basis of Fischer's fig-

From *Southwestern Journal of Anthropology*, 12 (1956): 22–37. Copyright © 1956 by the Department of Anthropology, University of New Mexico. Reprinted by permission of the publisher and the author. Ward H. Goodenough is Professor of Anthropology, University of Pennsylvania.

ures, with little more than half the married couples in matrilocal residence and almost a third living patrilocally, I would myself be inclined to classify Trukese society as bilocal. In short, two censuses of the same community within three years result in differences of a magnitude sufficient to suggest a different classification of its residence customs. Fischer's and my conclusions were both based on accepted census procedure. Either there were radical changes in residence practice and physical shifts of household accordingly in three years' time or we were honestly interpreting similar census data in very different ways.

As to the first alternative, Fischer's census reveals a move by an entire extended family group from one location to another (a practice for which there is ample past precedent), a shift in residence of several people as a result of the consolidation of two related lineages (a move that was already planned when I was on Romonum), and the residential separation of a segment of Romonum's largest lineage from its parent body, together with segments of two other lineage groups. Whether these three segments form one extended family is not clear from Fischer's census. His notes also reveal seven marriage dissolutions, three by death and four by divorce, and six new marriages. In order to ascertain whether the difference in our figures was a result of these changes or due to differences of interpretation, I have classified the residences in Fischer's census in accordance with the same principles which I used with my own data. The results for a total of sixty married couples [2] are as follows: 40 cases (67%) in matrilocal residence, 9 cases (15%) in avunculocal, 4 cases (7%) ambiguously in matrilocal or avunculocal, 1 case (1%) in patrilocal, 3 cases (5%) in neolocal, and 3 cases (5%) in some other arrangement. With due allowance for the ambiguous seven percent, the results are virtually identical with those based on my data of three years earlier. Considering the numerous shifts which had taken place, involving sixteen couples in addition to those whose marital status changed as already noted, the consistency of the percentages obtained for the two censuses is remarkable.

Only one interpretation is possible. The differences in Fischer's and my results cannot be attributed to differences in the raw census data. They arise from an honest difference in how to interpret the data.

The most obvious point at which we might differ in our respective interpretations would appear to be on the distinction between patrilocal and avunculocal residence. Indeed, in my own published report on Trukese social organization, I used the term patrilocal where I might better have used avunculocal. But Fischer reports avunculocal residence for another island in the Truk area, and, in any case, confusion of avunculocal with patrilocal residence could not account for the significant difference between his and my reported incidence of matrilocal residence. Here, indeed, is a serious matter. Two trained anthropologists seem unable to agree as to what is and what is not a case of matrilocal residence. Yet few ethnological concepts have been more precisely defined than those pertaining to residence. How, then, is it possible for us to disagree?

One possibility is that we used different kinds of additional information about Trukese society as a basis for interpreting the census data. If this is true, it means that residence forms cannot be reliably determined from the usual type of census information collected by ethnographers. A second possibility is that the established definitions of residence forms are so phrased as to make unclear how they should be applied to the enumeration of individual residences. Thus, without being aware of it, we might actually be using different concepts of residence at the applied level though starting in the abstract with similar ones.

We shall see that both of these factors have been at work. Fischer and I have been using different kinds of additional data to interpret the census material and we have also been working in practice with somewhat different concepts of residence.

Few concepts in ethnology are more clearcut and seemingly straightforward than are those pertaining to residence. Moreover, we have yet to develop methods which rival in sophistication those already established for empirically determining patterns of family and kin organization. If these concepts and methods are still wanting, we are confronted with a serious challenge. Their reconsideration would appear to be in order.

First, there is the question of the adequacy of census data alone as a basis for determining a society's residence rules. In considering it, I would like to turn from Truk for a moment and use the Nakanai people of New Britain Island in Melanesia for illustrative purposes.

Nakanai communities are made up of several hamlets, which are clustered closely together. Each hamlet's site is said to be the property of the matrilineal descendants of its founder or co-founders, but a census showed no consistent pattern of residence with respect to hamlet. Each hamlet had a group of relatives as its nucleus, but the genealogical relationships between them were of every conceivable kind. Now it ultimately turned out that there is indeed a pattern, that a man regularly brings his wife to live in the hamlet where his father is residing. He and his wife remain there until his father dies. If his father moves elsewhere, they move with him. When the father dies, the couple may continue to reside as before, particularly if the father was without sister's sons or if the husband has no matrilineal association with any hamlet in his father's village. More often, however, the couple removes to the hamlet in which the husband's immediate matrilineage has hereditary land rights, or to one where there is a concentration of his male sibmates.

Several things obscure this pattern. Since many people die before their children marry, a man is likely to start residing with a father-substitute, who may be his father's brother, mother's brother, older brother or parallel cousin on either side, cross-cousin, step-father, or older sister's husband, whoever among them took charge of feeding him as a child and/or negotiating his marriage. The number of cases in which a man and his wife are actually residing in the hamlet of the groom's father or maternal uncle are relatively few. All of the older men and many of the younger have no living fathers or uncles. One man, for example, has taken his two wives to live where no other man of his sib is represented and where his father never resided at any time. His own brother is residing elsewhere, in the hamlet with which their father was associated. The man in question resided there formerly and moved to the present hamlet after a quarrel. On the face of it, his is a case of neolocal residence.

But from the genealogies we learn that his mother's brother and mother's mother's brother were associated with this hamlet, though they had died long before he moved there. Thus his apparent neolocal residence actually conforms to the pattern of a move from patrilocal to avunculocal residence, for he is now living where his mother's brothers would be, if he had any.

Furthermore, no amount of census data would reveal that residences with parallel cousins and brothers-in-law were residences with father-substitutes and hence in conformity with patrilocal principles. So frequently is the pattern obscured by the death of close relatives that our census data from Nakanai with its record of sib membership and living close kinsmen proved useless by itself for analyzing residence. The pattern began to emerge only after analysis of the genealogical data, where the dead had equal weight with the living and where questions about where a man lived elicited a list of two or more hamlets rather than just one. When I then redrafted my genealogical charts by hamlet rather than by sib, the essentially patri-avunculocal character of residence in Nakanai became finally apparent. With only census data to work with, the Nakanai must have remained one of those so-called "loosely structured societies" so frequently reported for Melanesia. We are confronted with the unavoidable conclusion, then, that careful census data, though indispensable to ethnographic insight, are not in themselves clear evidence of a society's residence rules, and that reports of residence based directly on such evidence alone are scientifically unreliable.

It is clear, then, that more than census data may be needed for even the semblance of pattern in residence to emerge. It is also clear that after a pattern does emerge, interpretation of particular residences with respect to that pattern requires additional sociological and cultural information. With the Nakanai, for example, it is important to know whether the husband's father is living or dead. If he is dead, did he die before or after the husband got married? If he died before, who acted as father-substitute for the husband? Is the father-substitute living or dead? Are the husband's uncles living or dead? Where do or did they reside? Where does the husband's lineage have land? These are the sociological facts which we must know. Behind them are the cultural facts from

which we learn their relevance: the nature of the father-son relationship in Nakanai, the father's responsibility for his son's passage into marriage, which requires paying a bride-price. As long as the father lives he assumes at least nominal responsibility for these things, however much of the burden is, in fact, carried by other kinsmen. When the father dies, these responsibilities are formally assumed by someone else. Just who else depends on a great many considerations which we need not go into here. Whoever that person is, however, he is likely to become a father-substitute as far as future residence decisions are concerned. Residence with him is, therefore, an expression of the patrilocal principle regardless of what the actual genealogical tie with him may be, or kinship term used for him. Once we understand this, we discover that most Nakanai men who live to marry spend some time in what I regard as patrilocal residence, many ultimately going on to what I regard as avunculocal residence in the hamlets associated with their respective matrilineal lineages.

It should by now be clear that the determination of residence rules poses two different problems. The first problem has to do with recognizing the pattern of residence in a society. We have seen that census data alone may not be sufficient for this. The second problem has to do with classifying the residence of individual couples. We have here seen how essential are sociological and cultural data apart from census and genealogical materials in order to know whether individual cases do or do not conform to the pattern discerned. Such information, moreover, may serve to show how cases which appear to conform to one pattern really conform to another. This brings us back to the problem as it appeared in Truk where Fischer and I, both aware of the presence of patrilocal and matrilocal forms, cannot agree on which is which in specific cases. Even where we agree as to what the patterns are, we cannot agree as to what cases conform to them. In this instance, the same sociological and cultural data were available to both of us. Where we differed was in regard to what aspects of it we considered relevant for classifying a couple's residence. This difference, I believe, may have stemmed in part from a different resolution of ambiguities which arise when we try to apply our residence concepts. Let me illustrate the problem with an example from Truk.

At the time of my census, I encountered a household in which there resided an elderly man with his second wife, and his three sons by his first marriage. The eldest son was married, and his wife resided there too. The composition of this household was typical of that of a patrilocal extended family. The natural thing to do, therefore, would be to count the two married couples as two cases of patrilocal residence. In doing this, we are taking as our criterion for classification the type of extended family which the household presents as indicated by the relationships between its members. In this instance, both couples are residing in outward conformity with the pattern of a patrilocal extended family and are each, therefore, presumably in patrilocal residence.

Here, of course, we have operationally defined residence forms in terms of conformity with household patterns as defined by genealogical connections between the household members. But if we take as our criterion of patrilocal residence the fact that the bride has removed on marriage "to or near the parental home of the groom," to quote Murdock's definition, then the pattern of household composition is no longer a reliable basis for classifying individual residence. We must know who moved where at the time of marriage. When we ask about this in relation to the above Trukese household, we learn that both present wives moved into the house from elsewhere, their husbands already residing there, and the patrilocal picture is reinforced. On the basis of this definition of patrilocal residence there is no apparent need to seek further information. Certainly the son's case is clear. He lived here with his parents and when he married he brought his wife to his parents' home.

But let us now look at some additional facts. The father's first wife belonged to a matrilineal lineage which owns the house and land in which this extended family lives. Nearby is another house in which lives a lineage sister of the dead first wife with her husband and children. We discover that the women of this lineage have lived here together with their husbands in a hamlet cluster and that the father moved here in matrilocal residence with his first wife. His sons belong to the owning lineage. When his first wife died, this lineage allowed him to continue to be with his children. When his son married, he brought his wife not to his father's house but to his own matrilineal lineage's place

of localization. The house in which his father was residing was available to him because he had no sisters living there. Had he had sisters there, he would have had to build a separate house, for adult brothers and sisters may not sleep under the same roof. Now, if all the men in a matrilineal lineage brought their wives to live on their lineage land, the result would be an avunculocal extended family. Our seemingly perfect example of a patrilocal extended family turns out to be the result of an initial matrilocal residence by the father (subsequently filiolocal) and an avunculocal residence by the son. But the son's residence is recognizable as avunculocal only when we see what would be the alignments which would result if everyone were residing in the same relationship to their matrilineal kin groups as he.

This example shows that we have a genuine problem when we try to apply our residence concepts to classifying individual marriages for purposes of statistical analysis. Our concepts, which in the abstract appear so precise, become very slippery when we try to use them in this way. If we stop to take into account the context in which these concepts were developed, I think both the reason for the problem and its solution become clear.

Our concepts have been designed for the purpose of classifying prevailing or ideal usages in different societies as a means of grouping these societies for comparative purposes. To do this it is necessary for the usages in question to have been adequately described beforehand. The concepts belong to the same order of abstraction as do such linguistic rubrics as "agglutinating" or "inflecting," which cannot be applied intelligently until the grammatical processes have first been analyzed in other terms. Concepts used for comparative purposes, moreover, must be based on criteria which are independent of any particular culture. That is why we define types of residence in terms of physical alignments of persons differentiated by genealogical (biological) considerations. The criteria are of necessity extra-cultural.

It is, therefore, a procedural fallacy to use these concepts as a basis for classifying the residence choices of individual members of a society. They do not choose on the basis of criteria which are outside their culture, which exist only in the heads of anthropologists. They choose on the basis of the criteria which are provided by their particular culture and which may be quite different—indeed probably are—from those used by the anthropolgist in classifying their culture. This means that if I wish to apply the label "patrilocal" to one of the real choices within a culture, I must recognize that it means something different from patrilocal residence in the context of ethnological comparison. I must explain what I mean by the term in the context of individual choice. But I must do more than this.

Whatever may be the purposes of an ethnographer in describing a culture, he has the duty of describing it in terms which fit the phenomena. If he is going to describe residence, for example, he cannot work with an *a priori* set of residence alternatives, albeit he has defined them with the utmost care. He has to find out what are the actual residence choices which the members of the society studied can make within their particular socio-cultural setting. The only way he can do this is to construct a theory of their residence behavior in accordance with the scientific canons of theory construction. This means that he must try to conceive categories of residence and criteria of choice which give the simplest and most accurate account of their behavior. He must try to validate them by using them to predict the future residence choices of betrothed persons, or by predicting where pairs of persons would live if they were married to each other and seeing whether his predictions agree with those which members of the society would also make for such hypothetical marriages. Once he has isolated what are the several residence choices provided by the culture, he is in a position to ascertain their order of precedence and conditions under which the order of precedence changes. Anything less than this cannot claim to be an adequate description of a society's residence rules. Once such a description has been made, one can put whatever labels one wishes on the categories isolated, just as in linguistics once a phoneme has been isolated and described the asignment of an alphabetical symbol to it is a matter of convenience. Working with such descriptions, moreover, the comparativist can see clearly what he is doing when he classifies cultures in accordance with the concepts appropriate to his enquiry.

Let us consider, then, what are the categories of residence choice as I understand them to exist in Truk. Let us see what lies behind the labels which I used without explanation in the tabulations at the beginning of this paper. Let us dispense with the labels entirely for the time being and thus avoid any possibility of further nominalistic confusion.

In my published report on Truk, I indicated that the cornerstone of its social structure is the property-owning corporation, which, because it perpetuates its membership by a principle of matrilineal descent and is a segment of the community rather than being widely extended across community lines, I chose to call a lineage. No individual can exist independent of some lineage affiliation. If he goes to another community he must either affiliate with one of its lineages or remain outside the community pale without food, shelter, or protection. If it has enough adult members and access to a suitable site, a lineage has its own dwelling house (or cluster of houses) which is regarded as the place where it is physically located. A large lineage may contain two or even three separately localized sublineages. Lineages may move from one site to another as they gain right of access to different plots of land; house sites are not regarded as permanent. There are several ways in which a lineage may have right of access. It may itself own the ground under full or provisional title; one of its members may hold personal title to the ground; or a sublineage may be the owner. A lineage may also be localized on land which belongs to a man who has married into it. When this happens, the understanding is invariably that the man's children, who are members of the lineage, have received the land in gift from their father, so that in localizing here the lineage has moved, in effect, to land belonging to one of its members. With the tendency nowadays for the lineage to be localized in a cluster of smaller houses instead of a single large one as in former times, the site may consist of several adjacent plots under separate ownership; but each case will conform to the pattern above—three adjacent plots, for example, being held by the lineage, one of its members, and one of its husbands respectively. The need for juggling of this kind has also been increased on Romonum Island with the movement of all house sites to the beach, during the decade before World War II. The point of importance to note, however, is that a man who is living on land which he got from his father is in all probability not living in the extended family associated with his father's lineage, but in that associated with his or his wife's. Let us now see what are the possible choices of residence open to a married couple within this setting.

The first thing to note is that the choice is always between extended family households. Couples do not go off and set up in isolation by themselves. The only exceptions to this are native pastors and catechists whose residence is determined by their occupation. (They find it necessary, however, to try to make some arrangements for domestic cooperation with a neighboring household.) The important question for a married couple, then, is: to what extended families does it have access? It has access by right to the extended family associated with the lineage of either the bride or the groom. A member of a lineage which is not localized becomes a dependent of his or her father's lineage for purposes of shelter. The extended families associated with the wife's father's lineage and husband's father's lineage form, therefore, a pair of secondary possibilities for choice of residence. At any one time, however, a couple has but two alternatives: on the one hand the wife's lineage or, if it is not localized, then her father's lineage, and on the other hand the husband's lineage or, if it is not localized, then his father's. Other things being equal, as long as one party to the marriage belongs to a lineage which is localized, this lineage will be chosen before joining the other's father's lineage. Resort to a father's lineage of either spouse is, therefore, a fairly rare occurrence. Other things being equal, moreover, a couple will regularly choose to live with the extended family associated with the wife's lineage rather than that associated with the husband's. It is regarded as proper for one's children to grow up in the bosom of their own lineage in close association with their lineage "brothers" and "sisters," with whom they are expected to maintain absolute solidarity, no matter what the circumstances, for the rest of their lives. Given matrilineal descent as the principle of lineage membership, regular residence with the extended family associated with the husband's lineage would keep lineage brothers separated from one another until adulthood and lineage sisters would not normally live and work together either as children or adults. Choosing to reside with the wife's localized lineage, therefore, is consistent with the high value placed on lineage solidarity.

But what are the considerations which make other things unequal? Under what circumstances

do people regularly choose in favor of the husband's localized lineage even though the wife's lineage is localized? And under what circumstances do couples prefer to reside with a wife's father's lineage household rather than the household associated directly with the husband's lineage? What are the factors, in short, which favor a husband instead of his wife and a secondary instead of a primary affiliation?

Most instances of residence with the husband's lineage household occur in cases where the wife's lineage is not localized because it does not have enough adult women to run a separate household or lacks access to suitable land. But there are other circumstances favoring such residence. Ultimate responsibility and authority in a lineage is vested in its adult men. If residence with the wife's kin would take the husband too far away from where his own lineage house is located, it may appear advisable for him to bring his wife to live at the latter place. As the physical distance between the husband's and wife's lineage households increases and as the importance of the husband in his lineage affairs increases, the greater the likelihood that residence will be with the husband's kin. Where the husband or his lineage is in a position to provide the children with far more land than the wife's lineage, and at the same time the husband and wife come from communities too widely separated to make it possible to reside in one and maintain the land in the other, residence will be with the husband's kin. If the husband's lineage will soon die out, so that his children will take over its lands, these children may organize as a new lineage temporarily operating jointly with the survivors of their father's lineage. Such of these children as are women may bring their husbands into what may be regarded either as the wife's or wife's father's localized lineage (the former as one looks to the future, the latter as one looks to the past).

Finally, it may happen that a young couple may be requested to reside with elder relatives in a household in which they do not have any *right* to live. In Fischer's census, for example, I note the case of an elderly man residing with his wife's localized kin group. He and his wife have no children. Nor are there junior kin in his wife's lineage who do not have greater responsibilities to others in the household (judging from my genealogical data). Living with them are this old man's sister's daughter and her newly acquired husband. As head of her lineage, the old man has obviously pulled her into this household with the consent of his wife and her kin (who are thus relieved of undue responsibility). She has no other reason for being there, and the arrangement will terminate when either the old man or his wife dies. Temporary arrangements like this one, made for mutual convenience and with the consent of those concerned, may be on the increase today. I suspect, however, that one hundred years ago they would also have accounted for the residence of up to five percent of the married couples.

The foregoing, then, are the considerations which I believe the Trukese have in mind when they decide where they are going to live. By postulating them, I am able to give a straightforward accounting of Trukese residence behavior as I experienced it. I find, moreover, that they make the results of the many residential and marital changes revealed in Fischer's census thoroughly intelligible, a fact not without significance for the validity of this view of Trukese residence behavior.

If we accept as valid the formulation of their residence principles presented here, then it is clear that in making their residence decisions the Trukese do not choose between living with the parents of the husband or the parents of the wife. With what parents, if any, a couple resides is a fortuitous by-product of a choice made with other considerations in mind. While there may be specific inquiries for which we might find it desirable to ascertain the frequency with which different parent-child residential alignments occur in Truk, such alignments have nothing directly to do with Trukese residence rules nor are they descriptive of them. Truk is, therefore, in obvious contrast with Nakanai, where couples choose to live in the hamlet where the husband's father resides, regardless of the latter's reason for being there.

It should also be clear that while land-ownership in Truk is a factor which limits the number of sites where a lineage can be localized as an extended family, individual couples are concerned with what extended family they will join, not with whose land they will live on (except in the case of inter-community or inter-island marriages as already noted). To use land ownership as a basis for differentiating types of residence choice, therefore, seems to me to be artificial.[3] Undoubtedly there are societies, however, where land plays a more direct role in the residence choices of individual couples.

Since it is extended families between which the Trukese choose, we may list the types of residence which are descriptive of the possibilities inherent in their social structure as follows:

1. Residence with the extended family associated with the wife's lineage.
2. Residence with the extended family associated with the husband's lineage.
3. Residence with the extended family associated with the wife's father's lineage.
4. Residence with the extended family associated with the husband's father's lineage.
5. Residence by arrangement with a specific kinsman in an extended family in which one is otherwise without residential right.
6. Residence independent of any extended family—only a hypothetical possibility until recent times, now involving church officials and a few persons seeking to break with traditional ways.

In discussing residence rules in my earlier report on Trukese social structure, I lumped types one and three above under the heading "matrilocal" and referred to types two and four together as "patrilocal," using these terms in a sense equivalent to that for which Adam has coined the expressions "uxorilocal" and "virilocal."

This brings us to the problem facing the comparativist. Granting that these are the types of residence inherent in Trukese social structure, by what means are we to equate them with the very different possibilities inherent in Nakanai social structure or that of any other society?

To solve this problem we must have a system of residence classification into which the types belonging to any and every particular culture can be readily fitted. The typology already established, taking as its criteria the several possible alignments of primary and secondary relatives in spatial proximity, is in every respect ideally suited for this purpose. The only thing that has been wrong with it has been the improper use made of it in ethnographic description. But this does not answer the question of how we are in practice to go about fitting the types we get for a specific culture into these types we use for comparative purposes.

Since the comparative system is based on alignments of primary and secondary kin, we must examine each cultural type that emerges in ethnographic description to see what alignments it would logically produce under the ideal conditions in which all couples choose it and everyone has a full complement of living kinsmen. Let us apply this procedure to the first four types we have established for Truk and see what happens.

Type 1. If everyone lived with the extended family associated with the wife's matrilineage, the result would be an alignment of matrilineally related women with their husbands; the mother-daughter link would stand out.

Type 2. If everyone lived with the extended family associated with the husband's matrilineage, the result would be an alignment of matrilineally related men with their wives; the link would be between mother's brother and sister's son.

Type 3. If everyone lived with the extended family associated with the wife's father's lineage, the result would be an alignment of women whose fathers belonged to the same matrilineage. Strange as this grouping may appear, the Trukese have standard expressions for this kind of relationship; the women would all be *pwiipwi winisam*, "siblings through fathers," or *jëfëkyren eew cëk sööpw*, "heirs (as distinct from members) of the same lineage."

Type 4. If everyone lived with the extended family associated with the husband's father's lineage, the result would now be a similar alignment of men who were *pwiipwi winisam*, whose fathers belonged to the same matrilineage. The link would be through father's brother, father's mother's brother, father's mother's mother's brother, etc.

Notably absent from the alignments of kin possible are groupings of patrilineally related men with their wives and of patrilineally related women with their husbands. Such alignments could result only by having everyone in Truk resort to residence type 5, living by special arrangement in an extended family in which they were without residential rights, and doing so in relation to the same set of relatives. It appears, therefore, that as long as extended families based on matrilineal lineages remain the object of residential choice in Truk, no matter what changes occur in the preference given to affiliation through the husband or wife, there cannot develop extended families containing systematic

alignments of patrilineally related men or women. Such can only arise through a cultural change of a more profound nature: a change in the object of choice itself, so that, for example, couples no longer see the choice as one between localized lineages but as one between the husband's and wife's parents (wherever they may be residing).

Trukese residence types 1 and 2 are clearly best regarded as equivalent to the matrilocal and avunculocal types of comparative ethnology. By analogy it is possible to regard types 3 and 4 as the logical counterparts of amitalocal and patrilocal residence in a society where localized matrilineal kin groups are the objects of residential choice. The comparable analogues of matrilocal and avunculocal residence will be equally peculiar in a society where the objects of choice are localized patrilineal groups.

These considerations led me to list the incidence of type 4 under the patrilocal heading in the tables at the beginning of this paper. In view of the general association of patrilocal residence with the systematic alignment of patrilineally related men, such practice may lead only to further confusion and for this reason be unwise. The point remains, however, that patrilocal residence in this more usual sense can occur in Truk only following upon a fundamental change in its cultural principles governing the object of residential choice. After such change, Truk would necessarily be a different society for purposes of comparative study, whose residence principles would have to be worked out anew within the framework of its now different social system. The residence types that would fit that system would resemble those which fit its present one no more closely than do those of any other society. While we may balk at calling residence type 4 patrilocal because of the groove in which our thinking about residence has long slid, there is no logical reason for not doing so. Within the framework of Trukese culture as it is presently organized, type 4 is the structural analogue of what in other social systems we would not hesitate to call patrilocal residence.

It has been my immediate purpose in this paper to examine the problem of reliability in ethnographic reporting as it relates to customs of residence in marriage. In doing so, I have necessarily touched on matters which have significance for the study of culture generally. In concluding this discussion, therefore, it may be well to say something directly about them.

We noted first that census data of the usual kind are not sufficient for a reliable formulation of residence customs. We needed additional information. The additional information needed was different for the two societies examined. What was relevant in one was irrelevant in the other. We saw, moreover, that there is no *a priori* way of deciding what of all the possible kinds of information will be relevant; this is a matter to be determined in the light of all the other things an ethnographer is learning about the society he is studying. Every ethnographer knows that as he keeps learning and trying to find order in what he learns, he eventually arrives at a way of viewing his material such that a coherent structure emerges. This is just another way of saying that cultural description is the formulation of theory of a complex sort by which we seek to account for what we observe and what our informants tell us. It is this fact, so much a part of our everyday professional experience, whose significance for ethnographic method I think we have tended to overlook—an oversight which seems to be responsible for many discrepancies in ethnographic reporting of the sort illustrated here. I think we have tended to regard theory as beginning at the comparative or cross-cultural level and to see the methodology of ethnographic description as largely a matter of accurate recording and truthful reporting. I trust that Fischer's and my experience is sufficient to show that being a careful and honest reporter is only the beginning. One must be a theoretician as well.

But here again our disciplinary bias has done us a disservice. Since we have tended to regard theory as belonging to the domain of comparative study and have looked on ethnography as the means by which we obtain data to support or refute the kinds of propositions which have preoccupied the various schools of comparativists, we have consequently been inclined to try to order our data within the conceptual framework of comparative study. Thus we are inclined to feel that we have made a descriptive ethnographic statement when we say that residence in a society is prevailing patrilocal, when what we are really saying, of course, is that the society has residence customs of a nature undisclosed but such that we feel they ought to be classified as patrilocal for comparative purposes. Thus we confuse the role of the ethnographer with that of the ethnologist. In view of the problem discussed here, it appears that this can be our undoing.

For this reason I have tried to show that what we do as ethnographers is, and must be kept, independent of what we do as comparative ethnologists. An ethnographer is constructing a theory that will make intelligible what goes on in a particular social universe. A comparativist is trying to find principles common to many different universes. His data are not the direct observations of an ethnographer, but the laws governing the particular universe as the ethnographer formulates them. It is by noting how these laws vary from one universe to another and under what conditions, that the comparativist arrives at a statement of laws governing the separate sets of laws which in turn govern the events in their respective social universes. Although they operate at different levels of abstraction, both ethnographer and comparativist are engaged in theory construction. Each must, therefore, develop concepts appropriate to his own level of abstraction, and in the case of the ethnographer to his particular universe. When we move from one level to the other we must shift our conceptual frameworks in accordance with systematic transformation procedures. Short-cutting in this has, I think, been another major reason for imprecision in our researches.

Despite such imprecisions, comparative study has managed to go forward to a remarkable degree. It is precisely because of the advances there made that we are now having to take serious stock in such matters as ethnographic reliability. I think, in this regard, that we are reaching a point comparable to that reached by linguists a short generation ago. Linguistics, with its already monumental achievements in comparative philology, took a great step forward as a science because linguists recognize that every language presents a new structure unlike any other, and that only by developing rigorous methods for arriving at precise theoretical statements of these structures would it be possible significantly to advance farther the study of language in general. I think we may be coming to a point where substantial progress in cultural anthropology will likewise require concentrating on descriptive ethnography as a legitimate scientific end in itself.

NOTES

1. J. L. Fischer, *Native Land Tenure in the Truk District* (Mimeographed, Civil Administration,

Truk), p. 23. My own figures, hitherto unpublished, are taken from field notes collected in 1947 by Dr G. P. Murdock and myself as members of the research team from Yale University in the Coordinated Investigation of Micronesian Anthropology sponsored by the Office of Naval Research and the Pacific Science Board of the National Research Council.

2. My total of sixty as against Fischer's sixty-two apparently results from the fact that he included some widowed persons in his count. The three men widowed since the time of my census were all still residing as they had been, in each case matrilocally. I am able to use his census material because of the information in my own notes about all of the individuals concerned.

3. Fischer, recognizing that additional sociological information was needed to interpret the residence picture, decided to use information about who now held the land and from whom they had gotten it, collecting this information when he made his census. This *a priori* decision on his part is one of the differences between us in interpreting the residence situation.

PART IV Functionalism, Evolution, and History

19

CONFLICT AND CONGRUENCE IN ANTHROPOLOGICAL THEORY

LINTON C. FREEMAN

WHATEVER their particular science, scientists have a way of getting themselves classified according to some theoretical position. Thus, we call ourselves (or others call us) evolutionsts, or neo-evolutionists, or structural-functionalists, or ideal-typologists, or some other theoretical name. And for the most part we accept these epithets—even with pride—for each of us is proud of his theoretical position; and we can always see the error in the other fellow's ways. The members of any theoretical "school," then, are quick to criticize the theoretical efforts of the "opposition." But this report will attempt to show that critics are often ready to reject whole theories in toto, merely because they cannot accept the assumptions implicit in their presentation. Various seemingly conflicting theories are, in certain fundamental aspects, congruent, or at least complementary, but certainly not in basic conflict.

Perhaps the best place to begin is by asking, "What is a scientific theory?" For the relatively undeveloped theories of the social sciences, we can answer that a theory is the expression of a set of hunches about which things go together in the world of our experience. Clearly, this is an over-simplified and highly informal definition of theory, but it will give us a point from which we can start our discussion. The important thing to note about this definition is that it includes not only hunches or hypotheses about the world, but their expression as well. And this is where the problems arise, for it is in the linguistic expression of a theoretical system that its assumptions can be found, and it is these assumptions which lead to the conflict.

Whitehead has said that, "It often happens . . . that in criticizing a learned book of applied mathematics, or a memoir, one's whole trouble is with the first chapter, or even with the first

page. For it is there, at the very outset, that the author will probably be found to slip in his assumptions." Very often it is these assumptions, and not the substance of an author's work, with which his critics are at odds. But since a theory is designed primarily to organize knowledge, its hypotheses—not its assumptions—are its most significant elements.

The assumptions which color the expression of a theory are of two sorts. In the first place, the statement of a theory reflects the methodological assumptions of its author. It may be stated, for example, in the language of functionalism, or the jargon of causality, or the symbolic notation of mathematics. Thus, one biologist might say that the operation of the heart is functional for the maintenance of human life. Or another, that stoppage of the heart causes death. And a third might state the same proposition:

$$(\Delta P)[L(P) \equiv H(P)],$$

which can be read, "For any person, he is a living person if, and only if, he is a person with an operating heart." Each of our biologists is making the same assertion about an empirical covariation, but their methodological assumptions and hence their languages differ; and we may get the impression that they are saying quite different things.

Secondly, the theories of a given time and place are stated in such a fashion that they reflect the *Weltanschauung*—the basic philosophy—of the culture in which they emerge. Thus, Rousseau and Morgan may introduce similar hypotheses about the interrelationships among variables in the empirical world, but these will be placed in very different evaluative settings. Rousseau will tell the tale of the vast degeneration of mankind while Morgan will suggest man's colossal progress. So again, the illusion is created that entirely different schemes are being presented.

Typically, members of one theoretical "school" are ready to reject the theories of an-

From A. F. C. Wallace (Ed.), *Men and Cultures*. Philadelphia: University of Pennsylvania Press, 1960. Reprinted by the permission of the publisher and the author. Linton C. Freeman is Professor of Sociology, Syracuse University.

other on the basis of their assumptions alone, without ever a glance at their hypotheses. Today, for example, we find ourselves in a cultural setting in which science is, in and of itself, a Good Thing. We are enamoured of the rational-empirical model, and we are quick to reject theoretical schemes which smack of any other basic philosophy. Any theory which includes a suggestion of evaluative criteria is immediately suspect. So we build our theories around an attempt to avoid evaluation and condemn our more value-ridden forebears.

Less consensus, however, exists with reference to methodological assumptions. For today we can still find evolutionists like White and Childe, who view scientific anthropology as a search for diachronic relationships, structural-functionalists like Bennett and Levy, who view scientific anthropology as a search for synchronic relationships, and culture historians like Mead, who try to avoid viewing scientific anthropology at all. It is among proponents of these three schools of thought that conflicts in theory exist. Such conflicts, however, are centered around methodological assumptions; let us glance briefly at some of their hypotheses and see to what extent real differences in theory do obtain.

To illustrate evolutionism we shall look to the theory of E. B. Tylor. In Tylor's work we find evolutionism in its purest form; it includes not only the search for diachronic relationships, but the use of evaluative criteria as well. Tylor lived and wrote in a period and place where the dominant theme of the culture was progress. People looked about them—at the technological advancement, the political enlightenment, the economic expansion—and they were convinced that they lived in the Best of All Possible Worlds and that it was getting better day by day. A general spirit of social and spiritual improvement was in the air. And Tylor was swept up in the current. So his interest in and thoughts concerning man's social life were built around the concept of evolution.

Tylor used the concept of "evolutionary stages of human life" to organize his thinking about society. He defined three such stages: savage, barbaric, and civilized. The savage stage is characterized by small settlements, a hunting and gathering economy, and simple wood, stone, or bone tools. When the members of a society "rise" into the barbaric stage they develop agriculture or herding. In this stage there are settled villages, governmental organizations, and the beginnings of metal craft. Civilized life begins with writing. It includes extensive trade with other societies, bilateral reckoning of descent, formalization of government and jurisprudence, specialization, and the development of social classes.

Thus, in proposing these three stages in the development of civilization, Tylor outlined several criteria characteristic of each stage. Some characteristics which appear at earlier stages (say small settlements) disappear and are replaced by others (settled villages) at later stages, while others are cumulative—that is, they emerge at a given level of development and continue to appear at each successive level (metal craft appears at the barbaric stage and continues on into civilization). Thus, to rid this scheme of its evaluative connotations, we find that Tylor was talking of variables when he described his characteristics. For example, the variable occupational specialization has two values: (1) no specialization, and (2) specialization. Just so, settlement pattern as a variable has thre values: (1) small bands or hamlets, (2) settled villages, and (3) urban centers or cities. And furthermore, if we reinterpret Tylor's stress upon evolutionary stages, we find that he has suggested a characteristic relationship among his variables. He has proposed, for example, that a change in settlement pattern will be accompanied by a change in occupational specialization—that, in fact, settlement pattern and occupational specialization vary together, and that they are correlated with all the other variables: tool types, social organization, subsistence economy, and the like. In short, Tylor has proposed a specific interrelationship among a set of societal variables.

The general viewpoint of the functionalists was summarized by Malinowski when he defined culture as ". . . an integral in which the various elements are interdependent." The basic hypothesis here is that, given the presence of a particular element in a society or culture, certain other elements will also be present. Bennett and Tumin specify this hypothesis by suggesting that a certain form of economic structure (e.g., industrial economy) will be associated with a certain form of social organization (e.g., lack of strong familism). They assert that a certain population size will be associated with a certain form of economic structure, and a certain amount of trade with a certain social structure. And Levy suggests further that the amount of occupational stratification will be associated with the complexity of the society, and the amount of specialization with the presence of classes.

The approach of the structural-functionalists, then, is synchronic. Instead of looking for stages in the "progress" of a society, they seek to find associations among cultural elements at a given time. Thus, they hypothesize that a society with a large population will have an industrial economy, and conversely, one with a small population will probably lack industry. So again, they are describing variables, and again they are suggesting association among these variables.

We have seen that both the evolutionists and the structural-functionalists propose that a set of societal variables are interrelated. Furthermore, these are, for the most part, the selfsame variables. Both, for example, propose that size, specialization, social organization, economic structure, amount of trade, and the like are associated. Their difference, then, rests in the diachronic approach of the evolutionists versus the synchronic view of the structural-functionalists. But how different are these approaches? If, as the evolutionists propose, one "stage" of society follows another, the elements at any given level must change together into those typical of the next level. Hence, these elements are interdependent, and the functionalists are correct. And if, on the other hand, certain elements in a culture or society imply others, as the structural-functionalists would have us believe, then any change must involve the transformation from one functionally interrelated set to another. This implies an ordered series of types of society and, therefore, the evolutionists are right. Each of these schemes, then, implies the other; the structural-functionalists stress patterns, and the evolutionists stress change, but they are both talking about the same thing: a set of socio-cultural variables which vary together—an interrelated set of cultural characteristics. So, fundamentally, when it comes to their hypotheses, there is no conflict between these two theories, there is only congruence.

The work of the culture historians has, for the most part, stressed differences rather than similarities among cultures. Clearly, this approach is not congruent with the two just described. But even the works of such noted proponents of the historical approach as Kroeber and Lowie are not entirely free from hypotheses about regularities among cultures. Thus, Kroeber has suggested ". . . that among primitive peoples society is structured primarily on the basis of kinship," while ". . . successful technological and political developments . . . characterize the more complex civilizations." And Lowie's book abounds with distinctions drawn between "primitive" and "civilized" societies. He has summarized these distinctions by saying that:

. . . certain cultural traits apepar to be organically linked, so that one of them renders the presence of another more probable or, on the contrary, may tend to exclude it. In some instances the nature of the correlation is clear to us; in others we merely recognize its reality and suspect that some intermediate link eludes us. Thus we readily see why pigs do not go with pastoral nomadism and why pottery accompanies a sedentary life.

Thus, the culture historians are describing the same association among the same variables as did the evolutionists and the structural-functionalists. In this case, the emphasis is upon the unique in a given culture, but comparisons are made and hypotheses concerning regularities are always just beneath the surface. All of these schools, the evolutionists, the structural-functionalists, and the culture historians are expressing the same hypotheses in different linguistic guises. Their methodological assumptions differ, but when we look to their hypotheses their conflict disappears—they become congruent—a single theory of socio-cultural form and process.

A. Structure and Function

20

LIMITS TO FUNCTIONALISM
AND ALTERNATIVES TO IT IN ANTHROPOLOGY

I. C. JARVIE

FUNCTIONALISM in anthropology has at least two components. It is, first of all, a theory of how societies *work*. Second, since it conceives of societies working in certain ways, it prescribes a method for their study. As the method stems from the theory of how they work, one would naturally expect that the two stand or fall together. This is not the case. On the contrary, the whole stormy history of functionalism derives much of its tension from attempts to split them apart. Critics have pointed out that the theory behind functionalism is conservative, restrictive, or even demonstrably false. Defenders of the faith have again and again pointed to the splendid and undeniable achievements of functionalist anthropology. Yet it seems never to have been seen that the criticisms could be accepted without in any way damaging the methodology; the separation could be made.

In this paper I begin by discussing the logical and substantial limits to functionalism, then I enquire into why it was accepted in the first place, and why it continues to be accepted. Finally, I consider some of the alternatives and how far they are to be accepted.

From Don Martindale (Ed.), *Functionalism in the Social Sciences,* No. 5 in a series of monographs sponsored by the American Academy of Political and Social Science. Copyright © 1965 by the American Academy of Political and Social Science. Reprinted by permission of the publisher and the author. I. C. Jarvie is Associate Professor of Philosophy, York University, Toronto.

The limits to functionalism are, I shall argue, its lack of explanatory power, its unsatisfactoriness as explanation, and the constricting effect of its assumptions about the nature and working of social systems. Its merits are mainly heuristic. Alternatives to it should incorporate the heuristic but aim at more realistic assumptions about the social system as well as at genuine and satisfactory explanations. After describing functionalism, I shall proceed to its logical and substantial limits. These limits being clearly set out, the question will arise: How did functionalism come to be accepted, and how does it continue to be accepted? Finally, I shall discuss alternatives to it.

PRELIMINARIES

To start with, what is functionalism? As a rough first approximation we can say it is a method of explaining social events and institutions by specifying the *function* they perform. Such specifications of function are considered explanatory because of a cluster of theoretical assumptions about the way societies work. So much for an abstract formulation; to explain the matter properly some detailed examples are called for.

Most discussions of functionalism—and despite its dominance, much heart-searching about it does go on—begin, understandably, with an attempt to survey and sort out the different connotations of the word "function." Merton set the trend, and he was followed by Firth, Nadel, Martindale, and others. As a variant to this procedure here are four examples of uses of the word in social anthropological statements. They should sufficiently clarify the meaning of "function," at least for the purposes of this discussion.

(1) It is one *function*, we could say, of first-fruit ceremonies which forbid the consumption of new produce before the ceremony, to prevent premature dissipation of food stocks.

(2) It is a *function* of marriage, we could say, to ensure the legal continuity of a line of descent: marriage is a contract in which one family gains rights over a woman's child-bearing capacities and calls her offspring theirs.

(3) It is among the *functions* of incest rules, we could say, to encourage men to seek women outside their group and thus enlarge it by recruitment, and at the same time to prevent internal jealousies over women within the group: men quarreling over the possession of their sisters or their mother.

(4) It is one *function*, we can say, of the leopard-skin chief among the Nuer to settle feuds.

These are examples of what probably would be agreed to be explanations typical of those found in the functionalist literature of anthropology. My formulations are already loaded in that I write "a function," "one function," and the like, instead of "the function." When I was an undergraduate we would be set essay topics like: "What is the function of cross-cousin marriage?" Only rarely would we be set: "What is the functional explanation of marriage?" This might seem to indicate interest in functions rather than explanations. Anthropologists might reply that in asking for and specifying functions they make no claims to be explanatory. But it is easy to show that the only reason anthropologists became interested in functions was because they were thought to be enlightening explanations. The question being asked in this paper is: Are they enlightening explanations or, indeed, explanations at all? The difficulties that have to be overcome in answering these questions are considerable. For instance, all the statements above are so obviously *true* that one has to begin by giving assurances all round that in saying that they are not explanations at all one is denying neither their truth nor their importance and interest. Second, anthropologists have been accustomed for such a long time

to regard these functionalist statements as genuine explanations, and they have done so on what seemed like such impeccable and authoritative assurance, that these habits of thought tend to prevent them from considering criticisms of functionalism objectively.

The criticisms of functionalism are, I hope, objective. There seem to be insuperable logical and methodological reasons why such statements as are listed above are not explanations. They *are* answers to questions of the form: "What functions has such-and-such?" But the interest of studying such questions turns entirely on the interest and importance of functions. So this latter question cannot be evaded by the most hard-headed defender of functionalism. Insofar as anthropology is functional, to raise the question of the validity of functionalism is implicitly to raise the question of the validity of anthropological theories. And to refuse to discuss the former is to refuse to discuss the latter.

My strategy now will be to outline in the next two sections the logical and substantial criticisms of functionalism.

LOGICAL AND METHODOLOGICAL LIMITS

A deductive explanation is a valid inference with a statement describing the state of affairs to be explained—the *explicandum*—as its conclusion. It is usual to divide the statements which constitute the premises of the inference, and which, so to speak, do the explaining—the *explicans*—into statements of theory and statements of fact—or "initial conditions" in physicists' and methodologists' usage. The presence of statements both of theory and of fact is not logically necessary, of course, since we could equally well put the *explicandum* in as its own premise. The inference then would certainly be valid, because it would have the same statement as premise and conclusion and any statement can always be derived from itself. Such an explanation, let us write it:

explicans	People go to church
explicandum	∴ People go to church

is called "circular" and is obviously not the sort of thing we want. So, clearly, this first purely logical characterization of the nature of explanation is not adequate. It is not enough to demand a deductive explanation; we also ask that the explanation be *satisfactory*. Now by satisfactoriness we mean, roughly, the opposite of circular. A satisfactory explanation is one that says more than a circular explanation, that is, the *explicans* contains statements which go beyond what is to be explained. We call this the requirement of independence. The fact that the statements of the *explicans* go beyond those of the *explicandum* means .that we can test the truth of the *explicans* independently of the *explicandum*. If we explain "people go to church" by "people believe in God," we know that we can test people's belief in God independently of their church-going. On top of this, all scientific explanations should, of course, be empirically testable. It will be my contention that not only does functional explanation not satisfy the demand for satisfactory explanation, it does not even satisfy the demand for logical validity of the derivation.

Let us consider the problem: Why do people go to church? The *explicandum* is the factual statement, "people go to church." This is a very vague, and possibly even false, statement. But if we decide to explain it, then we take it as true by assumption. We now have a conclusion and we want a valid inference which will entail —or explain—that conclusion. We find that the simplest such inference is where we write "people go to church" as premise. The conclusion then certainly follows logically, but we do not feel that this "explanation" has taken us very far. So we proceed to try to find something better.

Durkheim tells us that going to church is a way of expressing and reinforcing social solidarity. Now how are we going to make that into a premise in the explanation of "people go to church"? Logically we should write:

(x) People in all societies must express and reinforce their social solidarity;
(y) The only way to do so in this society is by going to church;

and then think to write: therefore:

(c) People go to church.

This may be logically in order, but it is hardly acceptable functionalist anthropology. The problem lies not in the theory, (x), contentious though that may be, but in the absurd initial condition (y), which allows "only" one way of expressing social solidarity. Clearly social solidarity can be "expressed" in a number of ways.

But unless the word "only" appears in (y) the inference will not be valid. If, for example, we weaken (y) into:

(y') Going to church is one possible way of expressing social solidarity,

then if people do not go to church it does not follow that they are not expressing their social solidarity—since they may be doing it in some of the other "possible" ways. Now it is a defining property of valid inference that if the premises are true the conclusion must be true, and if the conclusion is false at least one of the premises must be false also. But here with (y') we have a case where the following three statements are compatible:

(x)	People in all societies must express and reinforce their social solidarity	TRUE
(y')	Going to church is one possible way of expressing social solidarity	TRUE
(c)	People go to church	FALSE or TRUE

Whether (c) is true or false, it does not clash with (x) and (y'); therefore the derivation is not valid because a counterexample, an inference of the same form with true premises and false conclusion, can be constructed, since (y') covers only some possible cases. Thus if church-going is only one possible way of expressing social solidarity, it does not follow that church-going is explained by the need to express social solidarity. We can only conclude that

(c') In some societies some people may go to church.

At the very most, the expression of social solidarity constitutes one possible explanation of church-going. There may be others. Again, if we weaken (y) into

(y'') all church-going expresses social solidarity

we get no further. From (x) together with (y'') we cannot derive "people go to church"; we can only derive some statement like

(c'') all societies which have church-going members express their social solidarity; those that do not have church-going members may express it in other ways.

Only if the word "only" appears can we make

an inference from which we can deduce "people go to church." Thus to make functionalism a valid explanation, we must strengthen it unacceptably.

Let us look at a more complicated and realistic example:

(*x*) People in all societies must express and reinforce their social solidarity
(*p*) All societies have ritual foregatherings
(*q*) All ritual foregatherings express and reinforce social solidarity
(*r*) Church-going is a ritual foregathering

It is interesting to note that we cannot deduce from these premises the conclusion:

(*c*) People go to church

We can only deduce:

(*c'''*) When people go to church they are expressing their social solidarity

But is that an explanation of why people go to church? It may be an explanation of one of the things they are doing in going to church, but unless it is the *only* thing they are doing when going to church, it may not have pinpointed their *reasons* for going to church. Their reasons for going to church may have very little to do with what they are doing in going to church. I shall take up this point later. But in any case, unless the explanation is made valid, the functionalist theories explain nothing; they have no explanatory power.

So much, then, for validity. What now about satisfactoriness? Even given that functional explanations can have their logical gaps rectified, are they satisfactory? My contention would be that they are not.

Pocock makes this point inadvertently when he remarks with apparent approval that functionalism does not go beyond the known facts in its explanations. He is thinking of how it avoids historical conjectures, of course, but I think we can use this remark as a springboard for criticism. A theory makes a satisfactory explanation when it is not circular, not *ad hoc*, and is testable independently of the facts it is intended to explain. But a functional theory does not go beyond the facts it intends to explain; therefore a certain tinge of circularity, or of *ad hoc*-ness, is an inevitable consequence. To be told that the function of church-going is to express and reinforce social solidarity and that the

main test of the desire to express and reinforce social solidarity is church-going is to get into a circle which cannot be broken in favor of a "deeper" explanation. Circular, or *ad hoc*, or nonindependently testable explanations do not tell us anything new; they are methodologically unsatisfactory.

The logical criticisms I have put forward are, I think, the most important. Logic being trivial, if its rules are not obeyed, what violates it cannot even be trivially true.

SUBSTANTIVE LIMITATIONS

Functionalism is sometimes conceived of as a way of studying societies, a *method;* sometimes as a theory about how societies *work*. My criticisms in the previous section have been directed at the logical and methodological faults of the functionalist account of how societies work. I now want to come on to substantial criticisms of this account of how they work, in the course of which we will come to functionalism as a method. A great many criticisms of a substantial nature have been levelled at the theories of functionalism. Levy has explored their teleological character, and his account has been elaborated by Merton and Emmet. Several authors have argued—especially Leach and Gellner—that functionalism, because of its circular reflection back on itself, explains only unchanging social systems where the parts happen to link up into a self-explaining system. This criticism has been elaborated into the suggestion that societies are being conceived of as coherent and consistent wholes, "seamless" as Macrae calls them, and that this is unrealistic. Indeed in Malinowski this seamless idea is virtually explicit. And I suppose the criticism could be answered by saying that the assumption is a working assumption for purposes of simplification and no more a disadvantage than was the model of perfect competition in a perfect market in economics.

To this list of criticisms I want to add one more point. This is a mixture of criticsm and rescue. I believe that, while these functional theories are not explanations, they are important and interesting. They are important and interesting, I would contend, mainly because they answer the interesting questions: what feedback and side-effects do these various customs and institutions have in their society? What side-effects does marriage have; does going to church have; do first-fruit ceremonies have; do incest rules have; do leopard-skin chiefs have? People get married because they want to; this has certain effects. First-fruit ceremonies implement certain superstitions; they also have certain incidentally beneficial effects.[1] Incest rules, too, are usually bound up with superstition, but they have socially advantageous effects as well. In other words, functionalist theories draw attention to the unintended consequences of actions. But can the side-effects of an event explain that event? The explanation of social actions and institutions is one of the main tasks of social science; accounting for the unintended outcome of actions within the institutional set-up is possibly the other one. If we ask: "What are the nutritional side-effects of first-fruit ceremonies?" the answer will be that they encourage people to eat the last of their old food stocks and thus to conserve their new stocks and make them last longer. Thus people are better fed for longer than they would otherwise be. All this is to draw attention to side-effects or consequences, and it is clear that while these are enlightening, they do not explain the institutions. They do, of course, contribute to the explanation of how the society as a whole works.

But to return to the substantial objections to functionalism. If the assumptions about the nature and development of societies are dropped, and functionalists turn their theory into a research guide, all such objections—and the logical ones as well—fall away.

At this stage we can split functionalism in two: the theory that every action or institution has a function or functions, and the theory that societies are well integrated, well adjusted, and "seamless." The first assumption depends upon the second; it is because societies are seamless that all actions and institutions have a function. The first theory asserts the *existence* of functions: "There exists a function for all events and institutions." The second theory makes a factual assertion about the character of existent societies: "Present societies contain no nonfunctional elements." The first is useful but unfalsifiable; the second is restrictive and false.

Insofar as functionalism assumes a well integreated, efficiently adjusted, and "seamless" society, it is taking on the character of a metaphysical theory; that is, a theory that cannot be shown to be false. A theory which clashes with no possible experience. If a theory clashes with no possible experience, it is compatible with all possible experiences and thus has no power to explain any particular statement of experience. It is also immune to attack. Functionalism asserts: "There exists a function for every action and institution," and, of course, failure to find such a function does not refute the theory; it only spurs one to further searching. It is here that metaphysical functionalism becomes a useful heuristic. For in order to justify this further search, one does not have to prove the truth of "there exists a function for every action and institution." All one needs do is show that such a search might be fruitful. It may not turn out to be fruitful, but it is worth a try.

On the other hand, the theory that existing societies are perfect and seamless is falsifiable and, I suppose, in societies undergoing radical change, manifestly falsified. How, then, are we to make sense of a theory which can be divided into two parts, the first dependent on the second, the second false, the first unfalsifiable, the second useless, the first to be accepted? My answer is this. The search for functions has manifestly been fruitful. Hitherto unnoticed facts and connections in societies, refutations of common sense or previous theories, have been uncovered by those carrying out the functionalist program. This is fruit enough. But the false belief in seamless societies must be given up. We are thus left with the unsupported metaphysical theory that functions exist. My own preference would be to say: "Some actions and institutions have nonobvious connections with others. Do not forget to look for these." Thus the metaphysic can be turned into a harmless heuristic, and the false theory of seamlessness can be dropped.

THE APPEAL OF FUNCTIONALISM

The various criticisms of functionalism I have listed were surely not difficult to understand or anticipate. This then poses two problems: Why was such a flawed theory as functionalism adopted in the first place; and why, now that so much has been written on its defects, does it continue to flourish more or less unaffected? I think these two problems—why it was accepted and why it continues to be accepted—are separable. The answer to the first one is different from the answer to the second. Roughly, the theory was accepted in an inductivist-synchronic revolt against the speculation and diachronic interests of previous anthropology. It is sustained for quite different reasons, the principal among which, I would guess, being its manifest fruitfulness as an heuristic or methodology, and its metaphysical immunity.

Anthropologists were offered a very good reason for taking on functionalism. Malinowski, its initiator, was extremely hostile toward nineteenth-century anthropology and its technique of explaining present-day primitive societies by means of conjectures about their previous state and what might have happened since then. He objected to this historical guessing or reconstruction—that it was speculative, incapable of test, and more likely false than true. The explanation of social events had to be grounded in something better than this.

He came on functionalism, I believe, during a formative field work experience which caused him to discover that societies can be understood as interconnected and rational systems, not requiring reference to alleged past states of affairs to account for their characteristics and workings. In other words, I think functionalism's real appeal lay in the fact that it replaced and superseded something else which was thought to be faulty. Indeed, I have conjectured [elsewhere] that functionalism came first, and the criticisms of previous practice followed.

The appeal of functionalism undoubtedly consisted partly in that it prescribed explanations which required only the known and observable facts. Conjectures and history, both of which went beyond the observable facts, were unnecessary. All the parts of society could be explained by reference to their relations to the other parts. What could be more appealing to the empiricist conscience? Functionalism was a theory of society which demanded only a thorough and firsthand investigation of that society in order to understand it. No conjecture or imagination was required. Malinowski, in explaining to himself odd aspects of the Trobriand society, found he was explaining one bit in terms of another. Thus he came to the theory that all societies must be such that they can be explained in terms of themselves. His particular theory relied on postulating basic social needs, but we can ignore that here. His theory was commonsense and empiricist; it was intimately tied up with a technique, empirical observation, which was gaining a vogue, and it intimated that those who underwent the experience of applying this technique would undergo an enlightenment, similar to that promised

by psychoanalysis or the sociology of knowledge; you would be set free from bias and be in contact with the truth.

Malinowski's initial idea was that societies are like macro-organisms having macro-organic biological needs in much the same way that organisms have biological needs. The function of social institutions was principally to satisfy the macro-biological needs. Radcliffe-Brown put forward a slightly different idea, based on a mechanical analogy, stressing the "structure" of society in analogy to the mechanical "structure" of the body. Every part of such a structure, according to Radcliffe-Brown, was interlocked and interconnected, directly or indirectly, with every other bit. To see it as a whole, and exhibit the interlocked working of its various parts, was the job of the anthropologist. Radcliffe-Brown himself used the metaphor of taking a time-slice or cross-section of a society and thus exhibiting its underlying organization and interrelatedness.

In so saying, Radcliffe-Brown was already indicating the attention functionalism was increasingly to pay to the unchanging underlay of society. But in societies where everything, including the underlay, was undergoing change, the explanatory value of such frozen time-slices was bound to be limited. In a Heraclitian social universe, Radcliffe-Brown's appeal to structure was in vain. Also, Radcliffe-Brown was implicitly abandoning the concept of the "needs" of societies and persons as being not explanatory: they amounted to little more than the definition of what conditions were required to be satisfied if the society was to survive at all. The situation is much as if in economics, instead of plotting the price mechanism at work on graphs, we simply took supply and demand figures at one instant and tried to explain the economic system with the help of such models.

But despite the force, and indeed obviousness, of these criticisms, nine years since the death of Radcliffe-Brown there has been little noticeable retreat from functionalism. My explanation of this is that its practitioners could not separate functionalism from the results they had produced with its help. They rightly attributed their success to functionalism and therefore felt it must be the critics who were wrong: anthropologists could not deny or run down their own successes. To this I add an earlier point: that functionalism as fruitful heuristic is based on the metaphysical or unfalsifiable formulation of functionalism—the formulation, that is, which makes it compatible with all possible experience. Indeed most experience can easily be interpreted as giving it support. Recalcitrant experience can always be dismissed as not sufficiently explored or understood. Ability to absorb all experience, irrefutability, is often taken to be a virtue, to indicate truth. This is an error. "Irrefutable" merely means not open to criticism. But still, irrefutable statements can clash with other irrefutable statements, and because neither is criticizable we cannot know whether either or both may be false. Thus despite the rising tide of antifunctionalist criticism, the citadel holds firm. The old guard and the new are equally strong in their conviction that they need have no regard for these criticisms.

And indeed it is difficult to deny the brilliance and profundity of the achievements of social anthropology. To do so would be foolish. One has to begin, I think, with a reassurance that to attack functionalism as theory is not to undermine it as heuristic or methodology, or to denigrate results obtained by authors who have accepted it as their theory or heuristic. My guess would be that it was responsible for these results mainly as heuristic but that the heuristic can be split off quite cleanly from the theory and continue to be accepted. But even the theory could possibly have been responsible for the results: false theories can sometimes let people achieve correct results. But this is no argument to show their nonfalsity and that their replacement had better be effected.

So although both the original acceptance and the continued acceptance of functionalism are explicable, the explanation is not sufficient to justify functionalism as a theory. Instead, it seems to me that the criticisms of functionalism are so serious that it must be renounced as an ideology: it has practical and logical limitations which are most serious. On the other hand, its heuristic components—field work and the suggestion that, as societies are ordered systems with, more likely than not, some rationality behind any of their parts, interconnections should be sought—should be retained. But for some reason or other such a suggestion provokes anthropologists to rage. They throw around accusations of armchair advice and so on. My only comment is that substantial and logical criticisms are criticisms wherever they come from, and must either be answered or met. Their truth and force are quite independent of their source, however hard that may be to stomach. Defensive tactics based on vague suggestions that critics who have no field experience cannot be

taken seriously are obscurantist. The field is not a form of mystical enlightenment. If field experience feeds one with arguments which answer the criticisms, let us have them out in the open for discussion. Otherwise the next move lies with the anthropologists. They have theories which have been challenged. Either they can answer the challenge, or else they must abandon those theories.

ALTERNATIVES TO FUNCTIONALISM

For a concluding section I want to discuss briefly in the light of the previous analysis some points in connection with the alternatives there are to functionalism. At the beginning of this paper I said functionalism was both a method and a theory of how societies work. As a theory of how societies work, it seems to me superseded: this is far from being the case with it as a method. And I have already argued that even though the rationale of this method stems from the discredited theory of how societies work, it can still be adhered to independently of that theory. First, a method is to be judged by results, not merely by its rationale. Second, a completely different rationale can be given for the success of functionalist method. This completely different rationale, which I would call situational logic, is an extension or generalization of the method of economics to the study of society in general. It is the view that the only known way to explain social life is to envisage the situation as it is faced by the individual, and attempt to reconstruct those factors in that situation, including his own beliefs and proclivities, which led him to act in the way he did. Of course there may be an interesting contrast between the situation as it was and as the actor *thought* it was. But anyway, here is a rationale for functionalist method. Try to understand how the society is set up and what happens here if an actor does that there. Thus will the functionalist method bear fruit. So this is one alternative to functionalism. To a considerable extent this method is embodied in what is somewhat portentously called "action theory." And ideal-typical analyses tend to be involved in all this, too.

What I think must be seen is that although functionalism has limits, these are specific, and it should not be rejected wholesale. On the contrary, its important methodological insights should be incorporated into whatever comes to replace it.

In discussing alternatives to it, we must separate two problems: a new theory and a new method. As far as a new theory is concerned, we want one that at least does its methodological job of answering the questions is it supposed to answer. As far as a new method is concerned, first it is not clear that one is required, nor is it clear what it is for. Functionalism provides us with a method of studying society. But men do not study things: they study problems. One extra fault of functionalism is that it tends to concentrate attention on one kind of problem, interrelatedness—not necessarily the most important or most interesting. Second, there is really no single method of studying problems. One must familiarize one's self with the problem, make an attempt at a solution, criticize one's attempts, and so on, of course. But solutions are acts of creation and sometimes they come and sometimes they do not; there is nothing any method can do for us. Getting theories, or the psychology of knowledge, seems to me to be a topic on which methodology can have nothing much to say. Any method or technique—from staring at collections of facts and trying to induce, to gulping coffee while burning the midnight oil—which suits the individual, is to be endorsed. And we all know that there is no technique which *always* helps us to solve our problems; otherwise we would not be left with unsolved ones.

The functional method of studying society, then, must apply to some other part of the scientific process. My suggestion is that it is very helpful in testing solutions to problems, once we have such solutions. It insists on taking things in their context and not in isolation, and generally emphasizes the difficulty of getting at the truth. This method is so general and so true that any alternative method should, I think, be rejected. But, of course, most alternative methods will pretend to be roads to solutions and not to tests, and will be rejected. We are interested in exploring and testing our theories for falsity; this can be looked at either as the most we can do, or as the very great deal we can do, depending on one's attitude.

Various alternative methods are available. Action theory and the employment of models and ideal types, are among them. What seems to me more important than animadverting on their relative merits is to point out that greater attention must be given to the formulation of problems in social science. When a problem has been formulated properly, it should be possible to envisage what kind of solution to it will be required. "What is the function of marriage?" is not, for example, properly formulated, since the word "function" is so ambiguous and the word "the" is so specific. The problems must be separated: Why do people get married? what side-effects does the institution of marriage have? why do people approve of and sustain the institution of marriage? The effect of these reformulations is always, as in economics, to direct attention: the first, to why *people* do things, why they think they do things, why they say they do things, and so on; the second, to the nonintended repercussions their actions have through the institutional network. This method has been named situational logic and seeking the unintended consequences of individual actions. As such it incorporates the other alternative methods. It has been criticized mainly because it was thought to exclude things that sociologists want to include, but I have yet to come across an argument which demonstrates this. Mostly, it seems to me, what is thought to be excluded is in fact included, especially laws about societies. For example, the criticism that situational logic is a reductionism and would exclude laws of human society is easy to rebut. Despite occasional loose formulations, situational logic sees institutions as irreducible parts of the situation. And along with institutions must go any known laws governing institutions, and like institutions themselves these laws need not be reducible to laws about individuals, and so they would be autonomously admissable into a situational logic analysis.

In the end, though, the main point about alternatives to functionalism is that they must not succumb to the faults functionalism has been criticized for, namely, validity as explanations, in a logical sense, and they must not utilize theories that are manifestly and demonstrably false, or make belief in metaphysical theories of society mandatory; such theories can always be accepted innocuously as heuristic rules.

NOTES

1. Nonbeneficial effects, too. First-fruit ceremonies may prevent one from eating *fresh* food, and this could have deleterious effects.

21

FUNCTIONAL ANALYSIS OF CHANGE

FRANCESCA CANCIAN

FUNCTIONAL analysis is frequently criticized as being of little use in describing and predicting change. At the same time, many social scientists interested in investigating change hesitate to give up the functional approach. It has been fruitful in many empirical studies and crucial in many of the attempts to construct general theories of behavior.

Fortunately, a philosopher has come to the aid of social scientists on this confused issue. Ernest Nagel presents a formal definition of functional systems based on Merton's essay, "Manifest and Latent Functions." Nagel does not explicitly consider the problem of functional analysis of change. His formal definition of a functional system, however, provides a basis for outlining several specific ways in which functional analysis can be used to study change, and for concluding that most of the arguments about the static nature of such analysis are based on semantic confusion and unimaginative and incorrect methods.

The following discussion (1) summarizes Nagel's extensive formal definition of a functional system, (2) considers some of its methodological implications, (3) outlines the ways in which functional analysis, so defined, can deal with change, (4) answers some of the critics who charge that functional analysis cannot adequately treat change, and (5) presents two examples of investigation of change by means of functional analysis.

A DEFINITION OF "FUNCTIONAL SYSTEM"

To Nagel, functional analysis is distinguished by the use of a particular model, the model of a directively organized or functional system. A

From *American Sociological Review,* 25 (1960): 818–827. Copyright © 1960 by the American Sociological Association. Reprinted by permission of the publisher and the author. Francesca Cancian is an Assistant Professor at Cornell University where she teaches sociology.

"model," here used in a very broad sense, is a set of general relationships. A model is useful if the relationships posited in it "fit" the data in the sense of parsimoniously yielding accurate and relevant predictions. The model of a functional system consists of a fairly complex set of properties or relationships. Two simpler models are described below for purposes of clarification and contrast.

The simplest and most general system model posits interdependence of elements within a certain boundary, that is, the interdependence has a specific referent. The model for such a *simple* system may be expressed as $x=f(y)$: one property is the function of another. This is the type of system implied by using "function" in the mathematical sense. Empirical examples are: the volume of gas at a constant temperature varies inversely with its pressure; the rate of suicide varies inversely with the strength of the collective conscience; presence of male initiation rites is associated with household composition.

These types of statements, using the model of a simple system, do not necessarily lead to predictions of either change or stability. Unless the state of part of the system at some future time is known, the future state of the system cannot be predicted. For example, to predict the suicide rate in two years hence, one would have to know the strength of the collective conscience at that time.

Certain properties can be added to the definition of a simple system so that, by definition, predictions of change or stability can be made on the basis of present knowledge. In a *deterministic* system, as defined by Nagel, the properties of the system at one time are a function of its properties at a certain previous time. Since it may be inconvenient to observe the whole set, one attempts to find the smallest number of properties or variables "such that the specific forms of *all* the properties . . . at any time are uniquely determined by these n properties at that time." Nagel cites the mechanics of bodies, the several dimensions of which can be neglected, as an example of a deterministic system:

Thus, in the case of a freely falling body, it suffices to know (in addition, of course, to the laws of motion) the position and momentum of the body at some initial instant, in order to be able to calculate its position and momentum (and accordingly other properties of the body, such as its kinetic energy, which are definable in terms of these co-ordinates) at any other instant.

If one knows the present values of certain key variables and the stability or rates of change of these variables, then one can predict the values of these variables, and many others, at any future time.

If one treats a social system as a deterministic system, certain types of statements may be made. For example: since a society is integrated at the community level and is beginning to develop irrigation, it can be predicted on the basis of laws of sociocultural development that it will develop cities and a national level of socio-cultural integration within the next two centuries; since the present questionnaire responses of a small, task-oriented group show little agreement on role differentiation, it can be predicted on the basis of laws of progressive consensus on role differentiation that the responses will show more agreement after five meetings.

A deterministic system is a simple system —with the added restriction that the properties of the system at one time are a function of its properties at a previous time. A *functional* system is a deterministic system—with the added restriction that certain properties of the system are maintained despite potentially disruptive changes in the system or the environment or both.

A functional system, according to Nagel's definition, is made up of two types of variables: G's and state co-ordinates. G is the property of the system that is maintained or is stable. State co-ordinates determine the presence or absence of G. The values of the state co-ordinates may vary to such an extent that the maintenance of G is threatened, but when one exceeds the "safe" limits for G, the other(s) compensates and G is maintained. Some of the state co-ordinates may lie outside the system boundary, that is, in the environment. Such a system of G and state co-ordinates may be called functional with respect to G and the state co-ordinates may be described as having the function of maintaining G.

For example, a small, task-oriented group could be treated as a functional system. Let G be the solution of the group's task or problem. Let the state co-ordinates be task-oriented activity and emotionally-supportive activity. If these three variables can be usefully treated as a functional system, then: (1) problem solution is dependent on task-oriented activity and emotionally-supportive activity; (2) at certain times, there will be such a preponderance of task-oriented activity that problem solution will be threatened because of decreased motivation or resentment over following others' suggestions—at these times emotionally-supportive activity will increase and problem solution will no longer be threatened; (3) at certain times, there will be such a preponderance of emotionally-supportive activity that problem solution will be threatened —at these times task-oriented activity will increase to maintain problem solution or G.

It should be noted that, by definition, more than one state of the system leads to maintenance of G. Thus, in the preceding example, eventual problem solution might result from both: initially high task-oriented activity and low supportive activity, followed by increased supportive activity; and initially low task-oriented activity and high supportive activity followed by increased task activity. In a functional system there is more than one combination of the values of certain parts of the system which will result in the same trait or will have the same consequences (maintenance of G). This is one way of stating the familiar notion of functional equivalents.

It should also be noted that stability of G is not *assumed* in a functional analysis. On the contrary, it is assumed that the environment or parts of the system or both are changing so much that it is impossible for G to persist unless there are specific mechanisms within the system to compensate for these changes. It is therefore inappropriate to use this system model if the environment and the system are treated as constant, or if there is no state of the system which threatens the maintenance of G.

The definition of "functional" as "fulfilling a basic need" does assume that there is no state of the system which threatens the maintenance of G. This definition is therefore inappropriate according to Nagel's concept of a functional system. Functional analysis, as here defined, does not assume that G (some need) is stable and then explain the existence of state co-ordinates in terms of their efficiency in fulfilling this need.

Rather, functional analysis shows that G is or is not maintained because certain state co-ordinates do or do not compensate for each other's variation. An example of a *non*-functional proposition is that religion and related institutions are maintained because of a need for the meaningfulness of life to be maintained, while a *functional* analysis would propose that the meaningfulness of life is maintained because of the interaction of religion and other institutions.[1]

Thus far, no specific attention has been given to the limits on possible variation of the values of state co-ordinates. Three limits on the values of the variables determining G should be considered. First, there are limits dictated by physical reality. To return to our former example, the amount of task-oriented activity possible in a given time period is limited by the number of people in the group and the number of messages that can be communicated within that time. Second, within the limits of physical reality, there are limits determined by the definition of the system under consideration. If a property is used to define a system, one cannot analyze conditions under which this property disappears, unless a different definition is used. For example, if one wishes to study the relations among interaction, role differentiation, and cohesion *within social systems,* and a social system is defined by a certain amount of interaction, there cannot be less than this amount of interaction.

Within these two types of limits there is a third which is the most relevant to this discussion. This is the limit beyond which compensation is impossible and G ceases to exist. In our previous example, it seems reasonable to assume that if either supportive activity or task-oriented activity increases or decreases beyond a certain point, no possible adjustment can result in maintenance of G or problem solution. Thus, if task-oriented activity exceeds certain limits, some of the group members may become so hostile or uninterested that no future supportive activity can regain their cooperation. Solution of the group's problem becomes impossible and the group can no longer be considered a functional system with respect to the G of problem solution.

This discussion of limits leads to a way of conceptualizing the potential stability of a given G in a given functional system. The persistence of G depends upon the amount of discrepancy between two ranges: the range of possible variation for each state co-ordinate and the range of variation that can be compensated for by variation in other state co-ordinates. G becomes less stable as the discrepancy between these two ranges increases.

In sum, a functional system is one that satisfies the following conditions: (1) the system can be analyzed into a set of interdependent variables or parts; (2) the values of some of these variables—state co-ordinates—determine whether or not a certain property G will occur in the system; (3) there are certain limits on the variation of the values of state co-ordinates such that variation within the limits will be followed by a compensating variation of other state co-ordinates, resulting in the maintenance of G; (4) variation beyond these limits will not be followed by a compensating variation of other state co-ordinates and G will disappear.

This definition of functional systems is neither complete nor without problems of its own. However, it should suffice to show that there is no logical reason why a functional analysis cannot be useful in investigating change. There are several ways in which functional analysis can be so used. For example, the presence or absence of G can be predicted if one knows whether or not the state co-ordinates are exceeding the limits within which compensation is possible. Or, G itself can be a cycle or a rate of change. And there is no empirical reason why functional analysis cannot be used to investigate change if some phenomena fit the model of a functional system and if one can assume that they will continue to fit in the future.

Before proceeding, it should be noted that Nagel's definition of functional analysis does not include all of the many meanings ascribed to the term function. Therefore, caution should be maintained in generalizing the finding that functional analysis, as conceived by Nagel, can be used to investigate change. Functional analysis has been so broadly defined that one sociologist [Kingsley Davis] concludes that the term is "synonymous with sociological analysis." Nagel's definition elaborates and clarifies the type of "functional analysis" used, for example, by the sociologist Parsons, the anthropologist Leach, and the linguist Martinet. This definition, of course, excludes all modes of analysis that do not meet the four criteria specified above. Semantic difficulty could be largely eliminated by clear definitions of the different types of "functional analysis" and consensus on terminology. In the meantime, the special definition presented here may help to avoid semantic confusion.

A BASIC METHODOLOGICAL RULE

Nagel's formalization of functionalism provides a basis from which many useful methodological rules and terminological distinctions can be drawn, including some of those pointed out by Firth, Levy, Merton, and others. One rule, which has frequently been stated, is the importance of specifying the system and the G(s) in relation to which the state co-ordinates are functional. This rule is crucial to successful functional analysis of change (or stability) and deserves special attention. As Nagel points out in his comment on Merton's discussion of the ideological implications of functional analysis:

Functional analyses in all domains, and not only in sociology, run a similar risk of dogmatic provincialism which characterizes some analyses in sociology, when the relational character of functional statements is ignored, and when it is forgotten that a system may exhibit a variety of G's or that a given item may be a member of a variety of systems.

Specification of the system(s) and the G(s) under consideration is especially important when a plurality of systems and G's are involved. A sub-system may be functionally organized with respect to a G while the larger system is not. Or one may be interested in several G's and the conditions for maintaining some of the G's may preclude maintenance of others, that is, the range of values of a state co-ordinate that maintains G_1 may cause G_2 to disappear.

The importance of these distinctions becomes more apparent if one considers the definition of such terms as "equilibrium" and "functional unity." Equilibrium means the maintenance of G. G can be a stable state, for example, corruption of city government, or allocation of reward according to evaluation of performance; or it can be a stable rate of change, for example, accelerating rate of technological innovation, or decreasing interpersonal communication in pre-psychotics; or it can be a cycle or series of states, for example, change from a conservative power elite to an opportunistic

elite and then again to a conservative elite, or change from feudalism to capitalism to communism. If only one G is being considered, equilibrium can be clearly defined. If a plurality of G's or subsystems or both is being considered and they are ranked on a scale, then the degree of stability of each G in each subsystem can be weighted and some general notion of the equilibirum of the total system can be defined. It is possible, however, that the G's and the subsystems cannot be ranked. In such a case, it would be meaningless to specify a general state of equilibirum if some G's in some subsystems are maintained while others are not. It would also be meaningless to discuss conditions of equilibrium for the system as a whole if the conditions for maintaining some G's preclude the maintenance of other G's.

A similar argument applies to the definition of the function of a phenomenon as "the contribution it makes to the total social life as the functioning of the total social system."

Such a view implies that a social system . . . has a certain kind of unity. . . . We may define it as a condition in which all parts of the social system work together with a sufficient degree of harmony or internal consistency, i.e., without producing persistent conflicts which can neither be resolved nor regulated.

To translate this statement by Radcliffe-Brown into our terminology, the postulate of functional unity means that the conditions for maintaining a specified set of G's in the system under consideration are not mutually exclusive or are mutually supportive. If no particular G's are specified, then "functional unity" would mean that no persistent properties conflict with each other. It seems very doubtful that functional unity, in this latter sense, characterizes many social systems. In addition, treating a social system as a functional unity without specifying the G's so unified results in a vague analysis and one that allows for no internal source of change. It is this use of functional unity that best merits Geertz's criticsm of the adequacy of the functional approach in dealing with social change: "The emphasis on systems in balance, on social homeostasis, and on timeless structural pictures, leads to a bias in favor of 'well-integrated' societies in a stable equilibrium and to a tendency to emphasize the functional aspects of a people's usages and customs rather than their dysfunctional implications."

METHODS OF USING FUNCTIONAL ANALYSIS TO INVESTIGATE CHANGE

On the basis of the foregoing discussion, a more precise delineation of the resources and limitations of functional analysis in investigating change can be made. The definition of different types of systems change itself raises complex problems which cannot be discussed here. However, one set of definitions is important to the problem of the functional analysis of change, namely, the distinction between change *of* and *within* the system.

Change *within* the system refers to change that does not alter the system's basic structure. In a functional system, this means changes in state co-ordinates for which compensation is possible. G and the relationship between state co-ordinates remain the same. Change *of* the system is any change that alters the system's basic structure. In a fuctional system, this includes disappearance of G, the appearance of new state co-ordinates or the disappearance of old ones, and change in the range of variation of state co-ordinates for which compensation is possible.

The ways in which change is incorporated in functional analysis now may be specified. Their justification lies in the definition of functional systems and in the consequent possibility of ordering systems hierarchically and of treating (sub)systems as state co-ordinates maintaining G's in a more inclusive system.

(1) *Disappearance of G can be predicted as the result of failure to meet conditions of equilibrium.* Disappearance of G means change *of* the system. State co-ordinates exceed the limits within which compensation is possible and the functional system breaks down.

(2) *If G is defined as a stable rate of change or a moving equilibrium, a stable rate of change can be predicted as the result of fulfillment of the conditions of equilibrium.* In this case, state co-ordinates do not exceed the limits within which compensation is possible and G—a steady rate of change—is maintained.

(3) *Compensating changes in the values of state co-ordinates can be predicted as the result of an "initial" variation in other state co-ordinates that threaten the maintenance of G.* This is change *within* the structure of the system and

it must, by definition, be possible in a functional system.

(4) *Systems can be treated as subsystems, that is, as state co-ordinates maintaining a G in a more inclusive system. Compensating changes in subsystems can be predicted as the result of an "initial" variation in other subsystems that threaten the maintenance of G.* In this case, change *of* a subsystem is change *within* a more inclusive system. In other words, what is a G from the point of reference of the subsystem is a state co-ordinate from the point of reference of the more inclusive system. Thus, the disappearance of G, as depicted in (1) above, could be treated as the variation of a state co-ordinate in a more inclusive system.

These four methods can be used under the following conditions: first, if it can be assumed that a set of phenomena form a functional system; second, if information about an "initial" change in a state co-ordinate can be obtained; and, third, if there is information about whether this change is within or outside of the limits governing the possibility of compensation. If one is interested in predicting when an "initial" change will occur and whether or not it will be confined to such limits, he might use the model of a deterministic system (if x occurs at one time, then y will occur at some future time) or of a simple system (if x then y). These two models may also be used to predict the ramifications of the disappearance of G.

CRITICISMS AND EXAMPLES

If functional analysis can be used to investigate change in these various ways, why has it seldom been so used and why have certain critics adamantly asserted its inherent static bias? There are several cases, in fact, in which these methods of analyzing change have been employed, as the examples presented below indicate. Both the critics and proponents of functional analysis, however, often fail to see the potential of this model, and the critics frequently misconstrue the aims of the analyses which they attack.

Functionalists themselves have often invited severe criticism. The concepts of moving equilibrium and of hierarchically ordered systems are rarely used, eliminating in most instances two of the four ways of studying change functionally. Many investigators do not attempt to formulate their analyses in terms of state co-ordinates—variables that are essential to the maintenance of some G and that can vary only within certain limits if G is to be maintained. In this case, none of the four methods of analyzing change can be used. There is no predictive power for change *or stability* in the statement, "the function of x is to maintain G," unless it implies that G will cease to exist if x and its functional equivalents are terminated or if certain limits are exceeded.

Failure to state functional studies in precise form, along with lack of specification of G, the state co-ordinates, and the system under consideration, results in inadequate analysis of both change and stability. If a functional analysis has been refined to the point where it provides an adequate explanation of stability, then it will always imply certain predictions about change; if the conditions of equilibrium are specified, the prediction can be made that change will occur when these conditions are not met.

However, lack of precision characterizes functionalists and non-functionalists alike and is often unavoidable in exploratory studies. In any case, most of the critics who claim that a static bias inheres in functionalism stress neither the necessity of precise analysis nor the use of moving equilibria and hierarchically ordered systems. Instead, they focus their attack on the defining attribute of functional systems, that is, the maintenance of a certain state of the system (G) or equilibrium.

Among anthropologists, one of the strongest criticisms has been made by E. R. Leach in the theoretical sections of his book, *Political Systems of Highland Burma.* Like many other anthropologists, he assumes that functional analysis is inherently static and, *also,* that adequate descriptions of societies must be made in functional terms. Thus Leach states: "In practical field work situations the anthropologist must always treat the material of observation *as if* it were part of an overall equilibrium, otherwise description becomes almost impossible." But elsewhere he writes: "While conceptual models of society are necessarily models of equilibrium systems, real societies can never be in equilibrium." Firth seems to agree with this view when he comments that "the necessary equilibrium of the model as a construct means that essentially it is debarred from providing in itself a dynamic analysis." Given these two assumptions, Leach appears to infer—validly—that functional

analyses have been extremely inadequate in investigating change and that major alterations in methodology will have to be made before the situation improves.

But both assumptions are invalid. The first, the assumption that social and cultural systems *must* be treated as if they were in equilibrium, ignores a possibility noted above. Functional system models may be preferable, but a simple or deterministic system model may also be used. The applicability of a functional model cannot be assumed *a priori.* The model should be applied in cases where it seems useful to treat specific states or parts of the system as G's and state co-ordinates. If the G's and state co-ordinates cannot be specified, the analysis will result in a great deal of confusion (and possibly some very productive hints for further research).

Secondly, an equilibrated or functional system need not be static unless "change *within* the system" is subsumed under the term "static." Moving equilibria may be used. Or systems and subsystems may be differentiated with subsystems treated as state co-ordinates and therefore, by definition, as changing. In addition, *using* the model of a functional system does not imply that the system *is* in equilibrium, that G is being maintained. Specification of the conditions necessary to maintain G may explain why G is not being maintained. Thus Leach's criticism, at least in part, seems to be based on false premises.

If the criticisms in the theoretical sections of Leach's study are misleading, elsewhere in the volume Leach himself refutes the proposition that functional analyses are necessarily static. In the following brief (and incomplete) outline of his examination of cyclical political change in Kachin society an attempt is made to translate Leach's presentation into our terminology (G's, state co-ordinates).

Leach isolates certain political systems, among them the democratic (*gumlao*) and aristocratic (*gumsa*), and treats them as subsystems of Kachin society. Certain basic norms of this society are interpreted as the G of the larger system, and the different political subsystems as state co-ordinates. Leach also treats each political subsystem as itself a functional system. He specifies the conditions of equilibrium in each of the subsystems and demonstrates that these conditions cannot be met for long periods of time if the basic norms of Kachin society are to be maintained. The result is a cyclical set of changes of the political systems *within* the larger Kachin social system. Political subsystems (state co-ordinates) change but the basic norms (G) are maintained.

A *gumsa* political state tends to develop features which lead to rebellion, resulting, for a time, in a *gumlao* order. But a *gumlao* community, unless it happens to be centered around a fixed territorial centre. . . , usually lacks the means to hold its component lineages together in a status of equality. It will then either disintegrate altogether through fission, or else status difference between lineage groups will bring the system back into the *gumsa* pattern.

Leach shows how an aristocratic political system prospers and is maintained until it begins to undermine the Kachin norms concerning obligations towards one's wife's family. At this point, either the aristocratic system or Kachin society must disintegrate since one type of marriage system is essential to the aristocratic political system while a conflicting marriage system is "the crucial distinguishing principle of modern Kachin social structure." Leach's evidence indicates that Kachin society is a functional system with respect to this marriage system. When the marriage system is threatened by the aristocratic system, the latter disintegrates, becomes democratic, and the marriage system is maintained. A similar reversal of the political order occurs when a democratic political system reaches the point of conflicting with the basic Kachin norm of higher status for the wife's family than for the husband's family. Thus, despite his criticism of structural-functional analysis, Leach's presentation of cyclical change in Kachin society can be seen as a demonstration of the dynamic potential of such analysis.

The criticisms made by some sociologists are much more sweeping than those voiced by Leach, and seem to call for the abandonment of functional analysis rather than its refinement. Critics such as Dahrendorf and Hield appear to start with two assumptions: first, that functional systems must be static; second, that the G's used in functional analysis must be the values and norms that characterize the majority of the members of the group, often including those of the social scientists themselves. For example, Dahrendorf attacks "the sense of complacency with—if not justification of—the status quo, which by intention or default pervades the structure-functional school of social thought." He also asserts that analyses of this "school"

cannot deal with change, and since he rejects "the entirely spurious distinction between 'change within' and 'change of societies,' " he charges in effect that no type of change can be incorporated into a functional analysis. The discussion above should suffice to disprove this charge.

Hield makes similar criticisms: "The 'structural functional' orientation is a set of methodological tools for the study of social control, deviance, and 're-equilibration.' " Again: "Where deviance presents itself, the theoretical concern is with the processes involved in restoring or re-equilibrating a condition of equilibrium or social control." And: "The study of change has thus been obscured by the formulation of theoretic constructs stressing order and stability."

These criticisms have a certain validity *if* functional analysis is limited to the definition of G's in terms of a static system of shared values. The several examples presented above show the different possible definitions of G and thus of equilibrium. G may be a moving equilibrium, a state of conflict, a set of values characterizing a deviant group, or it may have nothing to do with values as, for example, in the case of an annual increase of gross national product.

These critics, then, incorrectly define equilibrium or G because they identify the inherent properties of functional analysis with the particular way such analysis has been used by many social scientists. More specifically, they attack the approach exemplified by Talcott Parsons and assume that this approach exhausts the analytic potentialities of functionalism.

Parsons has devoted a considerable part of his work to answering the Hobbesian problem of order. He defines the social system in terms of shared values: "Analytically considered, the structure of social systems as treated within the frame of reference of action, *consists* in institutionalized patterns of normative culture." Parsons assumes the stability of values to "provide a reference point for the orderly analysis of a whole range of problems of variation which can be treated as arising from sources *other* than processes of structural change in the system." If shared values define the system, it is difficult to treat major conflict and deviance in the area of values as part of the system. And if one assumes stability of values, major structural change *of* the system is excluded, by definition.

Thus Parsons' explicit strategy is to hold

constant values and the basic structure of the system. It is extremely difficult validly to criticize a theorist's strategy, since its usefulness can be tested only by comparing prolonged research using one strategy with similar research using another and by assessing the results. Some kind of strategy is necessary and something must be held constant.

Parsons, like Leach, treats certain aspects of the larger system as G's and then analyzes changes in subsystems or state co-ordinates. "Structural change in subsystems [state co-ordinates] is an inescapable part of equilibrating process in larger systems."

A final example of the dynamic possibilities of functional analysis is provided by Parsons and Smelser's study of structural change of the economic subsystem. The first step in their analysis of differentiation of ownership from control in the American economy "is to define the appropriate systems and subsystems clearly and consistently as points of reference." Relevant subsystems are defined and ranked and the relations between them are specified. But their main goal is to construct "a general model which in its outline applies to changes in the institutional structure of *any* social system." Their procedure involves, first, a definition of the conditions of equilibrium necessary for no differentiation of ownership and control in the economy, on the one hand, and, on the other, for such differentiation; second, the postulation of a sequence of conditions that will produce a change from no differentiation to differentiation; third, a demonstration of why this sequence of conditions will occur, given the relationships between subsystems.

The analysis by Parsons and Smelser of the relationships between subsystems specifies the conditions necessary to maintain a certain state of the economy. For example, specified combinations of an appropriately motivated labor force, a certain degree of encouragement of enterprise, and certain wage levels are necessary to maintain a differentiated economic system. Parsons and Smelser also describe the possible relationships between subsystems *whether or not* these relationships result in equilibrium. In other words, the model of a simple or deterministic system is used, and the analysis is focused on the repercussions of an "initial" change on other parts of the system, regardless of whether this change lies within the limits of possible compensation. If these repercussions are known, then the state of the system at future times can be predicted—it is a deterministic system. If the repercussions satisfy the conditions of a new equilibrated or functional system, then a new stable state can be predicted.

Parsons and Smelser focus on an initial change which carries especially important implications for the rest of the system because of the relationships between subsystems, namely, "withdrawal of labour input in response to dissatisfaction with mode of employment and an increased demand for productivity." This initial change violates the conditions of equilibrium of the undifferentiated economy. They then specify the sequences of conditions that must occur if a differentiated economy is to be established and maintained. For example, at an early stage it must be possible "to try out ways of exercising managerial responsibility effectively outside the direct control of the owner-groups," and at a later stage the innovations must be institutionalized and rewards must be allocated according to conformity to past innovations rather than the development of new ones. (These sequences are based on a general theory of the process of structural change in systems of action.) Partially on the basis of their previous analysis of the structure of the economy, it is shown how the ramifications of the initial change result in a state of the system which maintains structural differentiation in the economy.

The analyses of change by Parsons and Smelser and by Leach, as well as the less developed examples presented above, show some of the ways in which functional analysis can be used to investigate change. Further progress in the analysis of change does not require abandoning the model of a functional system. Rather, the need is for further specification of alternative functional models, clarification of the logical possibilities of different models, and development of theories, empirical generalizations, and procedural rules which will enable the investigator to choose the model or models best suited to his problem.

NOTES

1. This point would be clearer if functional systems had not been differentiated from simple and deterministic systems. A functional system state-

ment can be reduced to a series of simple and deterministic system statements, and this reduction demonstrates that one cannot infer causation from functional statements any more than from state-ments of mathematical function or correlation. Such a reduction is not made here because the purpose of this paper is to determine whether or not functional analysis can be useful in studying change.

22

FUNCTION AND CAUSE

RONALD PHILIP DORE

KINGSLEY DAVIS has argued that we should abandon the notion that functionalism is a special form of sociological analysis. It *is* sociological analysis, albeit occasionally clouded by misleading terminology. In at least one reader the effect of his thoughtful and wide-ranging paper was to stimulate reflection on our notions of function and cause and on the relations between them. The starting point of these reflections was the question: Does not Professor Davis' argument rest on a special and hardly universal view of what sociological analysis is or should be?

At one point he commends functionalism as having "helped to make a place in sociology and anthropology for those wishing to explain social phenomena in terms of social systems, as against those who wished to make no explana-tion at all, to explain things in terms of some other system or to plead a cause." Sociological analysis, in other words, is the explanation of social phenomena in terms of social systems. But surely cause-pleading, explanation in terms of other systems and so on are not the only alternatives. There is another position, equally sociological, equally analytical, which holds that sociologists should search for regularities in

From *American Sociological Review,* 26 (1961): 843–853. Copyright © 1961 by the American So-ciological Association. Reprinted by permission of the publisher and the author. Ronald Philip Dore teaches sociology at the London School of Economics.

the concomitant occurrences of social phenom-ena, seek to induce causal laws from such reg-ularities and seek eventually to order such laws into comprehensive theory. According to this view, systematic theory (a logically con-sistent body of causal laws) is the end product of a long search for causal relations, not a heuristically useful starting point.

This, perhaps, betrays a preference for "neat single propositions whose validity is proved but whose significance is not," a preference which Professor Davis condemns as "scientific ritualism." It is comforting to reflect that in the natural sciences at least we would not have got far without our ritualists. Newton in devel-oping his systematic theory of mechanics owed a good deal to Galileo's neat single proposition about the rate of acceleration of falling bodies.

The difference between these two views which we might characterize as the system approach and the piecemeal approach is not identical with the often imputed distinction between functional and non-functional analysis, but it does seem to be true that only the system ap-proach encourages the use of the concept of function. The piecemeal approach is quite clearly bent on looking for causal relations. The system approach finds the concept of cause and causal law difficult to apply, and often finds functions easier to handle.

Perhaps the best way to justify this asser-tion would be to analyse closely the relations between the concepts of function and of cause.

Let us take as starting point the question: In what ways can a statement about the function of an institution, a pattern of behavior, a role, or a norm be translated into a statement about causal relations?

FUNCTION—EFFECT

In the first place it is fairly obvious that "the function of X is to maintain Y" implies that X has some kind of causal influence on Y, and it is presumably this kind of "translation" Professor Davis had in mind when he denied that functional relations are non-causal. But an analysis of "causal influence" leads to difficulties. Can we say: "The assertion that, say, the system of stratification has the function of making the division of labor possible implies that among the causes of the division of labor is the system of stratification?" Obviously not if "the causes of the *origin* of the division of labor" is intended. We have to say something like "the causes of the persistence of the division of labor." This suggests that while one can legitimately ask the function of an institution, one cannot ask for the *cause* of an institution; one has to specify cause of origin or cause of persistence. It will be argued later that what this really amounts to is that one can legitimately ask only for the causes of *events*. Let us assume this argument for the moment and formulate this particular relation between function and cause as follows: "Institution X has the function of maintaining institution Y" implies that the recurring events referred to as institution X are among the causes of other events integral to the institution Y (or, can be related by causal laws to other events integral to institution Y).

FUNCTION—CAUSE

But this is not the kind of causal relationship implied when it is said that an institution is "explained" in terms of its function. Here (less often explicitly than implicitly as a result of the ambiguities of the word "explain") the transition is suggested not from function of X to the causes of something other than X, but from the function of X to the causes of X itself. When and how may this kind of transition be made?

A small boy's examination of the interior of a watch may lead him to conclude that the function of the balance spring is to control the movement of the balance wheel. He would have little difficulty in using his functional insight to arrive at a causal explanation of the spring's presence—it is there because the man who made the watch realized a need for something to control the movement of the wheel, and the process of ratiocination which ensued led him to put in the spring.

Sociologists are not always precluded from making the same kind of transition from function of X to cause of X. Human institutions are now purposefully designed on a scale rarely attempted before. An analysis of the functions of the Chinese communes leads easily to an explanation of the causes of their existence, for they were created by historically identifiable persons to perform these functions and there may well be minutes of committees which record the process of invention with constant reference to their intended consequences, both those which were to be manifest to the communed Chinese and those which were to be latent to them and manifest only to their leaders.

Perhaps more common is the case where human purpose, based on an awareness of function, is a causal factor not so much in the initiation of an institution as in its growth and development. The Roman circus started well before emperors realized the salutary political functions it shared with bread. It was not until the third century B.C. that, as Radcliffe-Brown has pointed out, the Chinese sociologist, Hsun-Tse, realized the latent psychological and social functions of ancestral rites, but his discovery certainly prompted later Confucian scholars to encourage the deluded masses in a continued belief in the reality of the manifest functions of those rites. Nowadays, with sociologists busily ferreting out latent functions in every nook and cranny of society and their writings gaining general currency, latent functions are not likely to stay latent for long. Here indeed is the complement of the self-fulfilling prophecy— the self-falsifying assertion. The sociologist who contends that X has such and such a latent function in his own society in fact makes that function manifest. The intervention of human purpose to preserve institutions so that they may continue to fulfill their *once* latent functions is likely to occur more frequently as a result.

However, modern sociologists still probably

have less direct influence in moulding the institutions of their society than Hsun-Tse had in his, and in any case most sociologists are not imputing such a causal chain when they imply a connection between latent function of X and cause of X. Merton, for instance, clearly is thinking of something else when he speaks, apropos of the Hopi rain dances, of the analysis of their latent function as an *alternative* to describing their persistence "only as an instance of 'inertia,' 'survival' or 'manipulation by powerful subgroups.'"

How then, without reference to human awareness of functions, can a statement about the function of an institution be translated into a causal statement about either the origin or the persistence of that institution?

SOCIETAL INTEGRATION

One way is to postulate an immanent tendency, universal in human societies, for the parts of the society all to be functionally integrated in the whole. Given such a tendency the function of an institution is its *raison d'être* and hence its cause. The logical grounds for such a postulate seem to be two. First there is the complementarity of roles and institutions; the role of wife implies the role of husband; the specialization of the executive to executive functions implies separate institutions for legislation and litigation, and so on. Such complementarities, however, are of limited range. Let an integrationist try his hand, for instance, at specifying the chains of complementarity which might link the institution of Presidential elections with that of the burlesque show. The second basis for belief in the integration of societies rests on the supposed integration of the human personality. Since the same individual occupies numerous roles in a variety of institutional contexts and since all individuals are subject to a craving for consistency, it follows that all the institutions of a society must be permeated by the same value preferences, the same modes of orientation to action, the same patterns of authority, the same worldview, the same sense of time, and so on. But how valid is the assumption of the consistent personality? Which of us, sophisticates that we are, could confidently claim that he has never been guilty of preferring value A to value B in one situation and reversing his preference in another? And even if this were not so, this

argument would create an a priori expectation of social integration only in the case of very simple societies. In such simple societies the number of roles is limited. Every individual in the society may occupy at some stage of his life a high proportion of the total number of roles. In such a society integrated personalities might make for integrated institutions. But this is not the case in large complex societies, segmented into regional and class sub-cultures with specialized personality types and offering a vast multiplication of roles only a tiny fraction of which any one individual will ever find himself performing.

Obviously there are no grounds for expecting such societies to be perfectly integrated. To quote Professor Davis again, "It would be silly to regard such a proposition as literally true." And one might add that modification of the proposition from "always perfectly" to "usually somewhat" integrated (a) destroys the possibility of its empirical falsification and (b) destroys its value as an automatic means of transition from function to cause.

EVOLUTIONARY SELECTION

There remains, however, at least one way in which the sociologist may move on from function to cause—by means of the notions of adaptation and selection developed in the theories of biological evolution. To take the example of stratification and the division of labor, the hypothesis would have to go something like this: for various reasons some societies which began the division of labor also had, or developed, a system of unequal privileges for different groups, others did not. Those which did functioned more efficiently as societies; perhaps they bred more rapidly than, acquired resources at the expense of, and eventually eliminated, the others. Perhaps (and this is an extension of the concept of selection not available to the biologist) their obvious superiority in wealth, power, the arts, standard of living, etc., induced the others to imitate their institutions wholesale, including the principle of stratification; or just conceivably (though here we slip "human awareness" back into the causal chain) the others bred sociologists who noted the importance of stratification to the superior societies and urged its adoption specifically. At any rate, by one, or a combination, of these processes it now happens that all societies with a division of labor have a system of stratification.

It is an unlikely story, but it seems to be the the only kind of story which will make a statement about the latent function of X relevant to a causal explanation of X. And even this, of course, is not a complete causal explanation. The "various reasons" why some societies had stratification in the first place still need to be explained. For the biologist the place of these "various reasons" is taken by "random mutation" and some sociologists, too, are prepared to probe no further.

But often the sociologist can thing of specific "various reasons" which eliminate randomness. Dennis H. Wrong, in his assessment of Davis and Moore on stratification, suggests, for instance, that when the division of labor takes place certain groups acquire greater power in the society by virtue of that division and consequently arrogate to themselves a larger share of material and other rewards. And in this case, if this hypothesis concerning one of the "various reasons" for the development of stratification in *a* society is historically validated, or accepted on the basis of what we know in general of human nature, then it could equally explain the development of stratification in any and all societies. The adaptive superiority of stratification due to its function in making the division of labor workable *may* still be relevant, too, but it is only one of a number of possible causal chains, the relative importance of which can only be assessed in the light of the historical evidence.

In any case, if one is looking for the causes of (either the origination or the continuance of) X, it is better to look for causes as such; looking for the functions of X is never a necessary, and not always even a useful, first step.

In point of fact we know from historical evidence that this evolutionary argument relating function to cause is irrelevant to certain social institutions which sociologists describe. The American boss-directed political machine, for instance, is said by Merton to have the functions of providing a centralization of power, of providing necessary services to those who need help rather than justice, of organizing essential, but morally disapproved, sectors of the economy etc., and as such contributes to the maintenance of the social system as a whole. However, we know that the boss-system developed long since the United States was in direct and aggressive competition with other social groups for resources; we know from historical evidence that there has been no process of selective weeding out of societies involved.

In such cases one can still appeal to a weakened form of the evolutionary argument to relate function to cause by defining causally important conditions not for the original development of the institution but for its later transmission. It would have to go something like this: if the boss-system had not had these effects and so contributed to the smooth working of society, nor had these effects been neutral with respect to the smooth working of society, but had, on the contrary been positively detrimental to society's smooth working, people would have stopped doing it. In other words the fact that this feature was *not dysfunctional* to the workings of the society is a necessary condition of its present existence. It is also a necessary condition that all members of the society were not eliminated by an epidemic of bubonic plague. One could think of many more such negatively defined necessary conditions, all of which play a part, but only a small part, in a full causal explanation.

SUMMARY

This seems to exhaust the possible methods by which assertions about the functions of X can be involved in assertions about the causes of the (origin or continuance of) X. The sociologist may not be the least bit interested in any of them. Having discovered that, say, social stratification has the function of making the division of labor workable, he may be content with saying just that—and with perfect justification provided he concedes that he has said nothing about *why* societies are stratified. He may go on to point a corollary of his assertion —that if stratification were abolished the division of labor would become unworkable. This is, indeed, an eminently useful social activity and the kind of analysis which can properly precede attempts at social reform. It is also, incidentally, the kind of activity in which a good many social anthropologists in particular have been professionally engaged in colonial administrations. The practical need to assess the probable effects of changes in institutions wrought by colonial policy has provided an important application of functional analysis which perhaps explains (causally) why so many anthropologists have been content with functional analysis as a legitimate final goal of their activities.

We may sum up the argument so far as follows:

1. In a not very clearly defined way the suggestion that institution X has the function of maintaining Y implies some causal influence of X on Y.

2. Assertions about the functions of an institution X are relevant to assertions about the causes of the origin or the persistence of that same institution X if, and only if: (a) one assumes that the function is manifest to the present actors in, to the present upholders of, or to former upholders or inventors of the institution in question, and as such has played a part in their motives for performing, or inducing others to perform, the institutionalized behavior involved; (b) one postulates an immanent tendency for the functional integration of a society; (c) one postulates an adaptive superiority conferred by the institution which permitted it, having developed in one society, to spread to others.

These ideas are not particularly new. The reason why they need reiterating is, it seems, largely because of the ill-defined relation between function and cause suggested by the first of our two propositions. It is the main business of this paper to try to improve the definition of that relation and, in the course of doing so, to make a few pertinent remarks about the use of analogies from natural science.

SYSTEM AND EVENT

Let us first examine the concept of system. "How else can data be interpreted," said Professor Davis in his paper, "except in relation to the larger structures in which they are implicated? How can data on the earth's orbit, for example, be understood except in relation to a system in which they are involved—in this case the solar system or the earth's climatic system?" Is this, however, a good analogy? There are indeed systems in nature, such as the solar system, the parts of which are in continuous interaction with each other in such a way that causal laws, expressed in the form of differential equations, allow one to predict one state of the system from another prior or later state. In human societies, however, though the money market might be somewhat similar, such systems are rare. Social systems (in the Parsonian manner) are not analogous in that the parts are not *simultaneously* affecting each other in the way in which the sun and the moon simultaneously affect each other by their gravitational attraction. The mutual relation of, say, the system of socialization to the system of political control is mediated by the personality structure, and as such it is a relation which requires a long time interval to work through the whole causal sequence. Parents may well train their children today in ways which are "significantly congruent" with the ways in which they behave politically today, but, in the other direction, the way in which they now behave politically is affected by the way in which they were trained, not today but a generation ago.

The analysis of systems such as the solar system can dispense with the notion of cause in favor of function—but this, be it noted, is strictly the mathematician's function, not that of the sociologist or of the physiologist. It is not, however, impossible to apply the concept of causal law and causal event to such systems, and to do so might help to elucidate the nature of the distinction we have earlier made between the causes of the origin of, and the causes of the persistence of, institutions. If we are to give a causal explanation of the movement of the moon between 10:00 P.M. and 10:05 P.M. tonight, we would need to refer to the simultaneous events of the movements of the earth and the sun, etc., relating them to it by Newton's law of gravitation. We should also have to mention a previous event—the moon's motion at the point immediately prior to 10:00 P.M.—and relate it to the event in question (its movement between 10:00 and 10:05 P.M.) by means of Newton's first law of motion concerning momentum. Having started on this track we can regress almost indefinitely from event to event back through time (chopping our time continuum arbitrarily into "events"), the moon's velocity at any particular moment being affected by its velocity the preceding moment, until we get to an earlier traumatic event, namely the moon's supposed wrenching off from the earth. In the whole of this process it is only events which we relate to each other by causal laws and only of events that we ask: what are their causes? Similarly—and this is the point of the example—when we talk of "the cause of the origin of an institution" and "the cause of the persistence of an institution" we are in both cases asking for the causes of events—in the first case the causes of the particular once-and-for-all events associated with the origin of the institution, and in the second of the recurring events which *are* the institution.

In the light of this view of causal relations, let us now look at the analogy between physiology and sociology often invoked by those who favor sociological explanation in terms of systems. It is often asserted that because the physiologist leaves questions concerning the origin of the heart to the student of evolution and concentrates on tracing its functions as it at present exists, he is not concerned with causes. But this is surely not so. "The function of the heart in the human being is to pump blood" implies "The cause of the flow of this blood at this time is the pump of that heart then" and this is as much a causal assertion as "one of the reasons why animals have hearts is because when random mutation produced the first primitive heart its possessors gained the ability to out-breed the heartless."

Physiologists and students of evolution have achieved a division of labor which is not formalized among sociologists. Consequently, among sociologists the search for an "explanation" of an institution is often ambiguous. "Why is there a system of unequal rewards in this society?" may be answered by some "because parents tell (this parent and this parent told) their children that some positions in society are more worthy of respect than others, and because employers pay (this employer and this employer paid) more for some kinds of work than others, etc." This is the "physiological" explanation of the recurring events of rewarding particular people with particular acts of deference and so on which is what we mean by stratification. Alternatively the answer might be "because with the division of labor some groups became more powerful and arrogated privileges to themselves, or because differentiated societies which had systems of stratification proved more successful than those which didn't,"—the "evolutionary" explanation of the particular events which led to the institutionalization of certain patterns of behavior.

INSTITUTIONS

It will be noted again that whichever way the question is taken it can be handled as if it were a question about particular events. It is the chief assertion of this paper that ultimately these are the only terms in which causal questions can be framed. But if this is the case,

what then is the relation between the particular events observed by the sociologist and his concepts such as stratification, marriage, or socialization—concepts of "institutions," "norms," "behavior patterns?" Is it not exactly the same as the relation between a particular human heart and *the* human heart for the physiologist? The physiologist's statement that "the function of the heart is to pump blood" is a summary generalization of statements about the causal relations between the particular events of heart-pump and blood-flow in particular human bodies—events which nowadays recur more than two billion times a second. If the sociologist's statements are to have any empirical reference it is difficult to see how they can be different from this; how, that is to say, the relation between "John kisses Mary" and "courtship," or between "farmer George touched his cap to the lord of the manor" and "stratification" can be other than the relation between "the pump of this heart" and "the pump of the human heart."

Even sociologists who accept this are often tempted to forget it, partly because while any single heart-pump is very much like another, kisses can vary greatly in intensity, passion, and significance. This is also the reason why it is more important that the sociologist should *not* forget it; it matters very little to the physiologist if he forgets that his abstract human organ is a generalization from particular organs in particular people *because* they are all very much alike.

If it be accepted that the sociologist's "institutions" are summary generic terms for classes of particular recurring events, then it follows that his statements about the functional interrelations of institutions are generalizations about the causal relations between these recurring events. In other words that "the system of stratification functions to make the division of labor workable" is a generalized summation of a number of lower order generalizations to the effect that, for instance, "men submit to a lengthy medical training because they have the prospect of greater rewards" etc., which are themselves generalizations from statements of particular events ("Jack submitted . . . because he had . . .").

We might emphasize this assertion that statements about the functional relations between institutions are *only* generalizations about relations between particular events by means of a mathematical analogy (offered only, it might be added, as a didactic illustration and not as a proof). If it is granted that events like "John (unmarried) passionately kisses Mary (unmarried)" (a) are summarily referred to by such a term as "romantic courtship" (Σa); and events like "John (married) hits Mary (married)" (b) are summarily referred to by such a term as "pattern of marital maladjustment" (Σb), then the statement "patterns of courtship affect patterns of marital adjustment" is a summary of statements of the nature "the way John kissed Mary then affects the way he hits her now," and as such is a statement of the nature Σab, *not* of the nature Σa x Σb.

SOCIAL FACTS AND REDUCTIONISM

Some sociologists would part company at this point. They might agree with the above view of the logical nature of constructs like "institution," "behavior pattern" etc., but still hold that there *is* a Σa x Σb kind of sense in which institutions can be related over and above the relations of the particular events they describe. It is difficult to see how this can be so. More consistent is the position of those who would hold that concepts like institutions are not, or are not only, generalizations about recurring events. Such arguments might well appeal to the Durkheimian characterization of norms and institutions as "social facts." But the position outlined above is in no way incompatible with one interpretation of the Durkheimian view. It is undoubtedly true that the members of a society do have reified concepts of, say, "marriage," "romantic love," "filial conduct" which are both more than and less than generalizations concerning particular relations between particular people. But these reified concepts are part of the *data* of sociology. Having a concept of marriage is (though normally less easily observed) as much an event in society as having a quarrel with one's wife and susceptible of the same kinds of quesions and explanations. There is no more reason for the sociologist to adopt for his thinking *about* society the terms used for thinking *in* society (to take, in other words, his analytical tools straight out of his data) than there is for a carpenter to use nothing but wooden saws.

The point might be made clearer if it is stated in the terms of Maurice Mandelbaum's discussion of "societal facts." His argument that societal facts are not reducible to statements concerning the actions of individuals rests on an identification of what one might call "societal (or cultural) concepts" with "sociologists' concepts." One can agree with his formulation—that there is a language S, in which concepts like marriage, the banking system, the Presidency, etc., appear; that there is another language P in which we refer to the thoughts and actions of individuals; and that sentences in S cannot be translated wholly into P because some of the thoughts and actions of individuals consist of *using* S. But the contention here is that the sociologist should be speaking in a different language—meta-SP if one likes—which certainly resembles S and was developed from S but is an artificial creation for the purpose of analyzing causal relations in society and can only be effective for this purpose if it *is* reducible to P (including all the necessary concepts of S—the words spoken and the thoughts thought by individuals—which P must incorporate). Another way of putting it would be to say that Mandelbaum's arguments that societal facts are not reducible to facts about individuals are really arguments to show that *language* is a necessary part of the sociologist's data for which there can be no substitute. And no one would wish to quarrel with that.

The position outlined above is part of the thesis of "methodological individualism," the brief debate about which seems to have died down without much interest being shown by professional sociologists. The methodological individualist doctrine which holds that all sociological laws are bound to be such as can ultimately be reduced to laws of individual behavior is a hard one to refute, but one which few sociologists find attractive. The reason is perhaps this: the examples we have given of the particular causal relations actually implied by statements of the functions of institutions were of the type: "Jack became a doctor because of the prospect of . . ." "The way John kissed Mary then affects the way he hits her now." All imputations of a causal relation imply a causal law. In these cases the relevant laws are laws of individual behavior—"an individual of such and such training in such and such circumstances will orient present actions to remotely deferred gratifications," "behavioral dispositions towards individual others built up under the stress of strong biological urges tend to be modified after the satiation of those urges" might be examples. These can be stated in purely behavioral terms. Nevertheless when they are so stated the possibility of further reduction to laws of psychological processes becomes apparent. Psychological reductionism has never appealed to sociologists; it has usually been conceived as a threat to the integrity and importance of sociology. It is difficult to see why. It would be as absurd to argue that because all the laws of social behavior might ultimately be reducible to psychological terms sociologists should give up sociology and take to psychology, as to hold that chemists should all abandon chemistry since their laws might ultimately be reduced to laws of physics. The antipathy towards the reductionist thesis exists, however, and sociologists have for a long time been intermittently fighting a losing battle to prove (to themselves, it seems, since no one else seems to have been particularly interested) that there *are* irreducible sociological laws *sui generis*. Is not the resort to "function" in part a continuation of this warfare by more diplomatic means?

Professor Davis noted that in their studies of social change functionalists behave no differently from other sociologists who claim to be opposed to functionalism. Now, studies of social change are explicitly looking for causes—for the causes of the particular events associated with the origination and changing of institutions. To keep one's nose equally on the scent for causes in the analysis of stable systems, however, involves constant reference to the recurring events which make up the institutional units under study and poses the problem of the kind of reductionism outlined above. The concept of function offers an escape; it blurs the precise causal relations imputed and yet descriptions in terms of functions seem somehow to be causal; it makes it easier for institutions to be treated as ultimate units without constant reference to the empirical content of such concepts; in this way the sociological integrity of sociology is preserved and grand theory concerning social systems becomes possible.

VARIOUS SOCIOLOGIES

What, then, of functional*ism*? It is, as Kingsley Davis points out, a name for a variety of methodological and philosophical (following Davis, following Radcliffe-Brown, though "moral" might be more apposite positions). It might be useful to elucidate these positions

with reference to the two main theses of this paper. These theses are: (1) There is a difference between questions about the functions of an institution and questions about the cause(s) of (the particular once-and-for-all events leading to the origin of, or the recurring events which make up) that institution, and answers to the first kind of question are relevant to answers to the second kind of question only (legitimately) via human motives or evolutionary selection, or (illegitimately) by use of the postulate of necessary integration. (2) Questions about the functions of an institution logically imply questions about the effects of recurring particular events which make up that institution as causes of other recurring particular events.

Functionalists, then, could be any of four types of sociologists. Type (a) sociologists easily accept both of these propositions but find the concept of function useful because they are chiefly concerned with the way in which changes in one institution in a particular society would affect other institutions, for example, the social reformer or the colonial anthropologist. Type (b) sociologists accept both of these propositions but hold the philosophical view that sociologists should concern themselves only with the kind of causal relationships which have a direct bearing on the equilibrium of the social system (i.e., are [eu]functional or dysfunctional) and not with other causal chains which, being in this special sense "non-functional," are "pragmatically unimportant."

It is this particular philosophical view with its implication that "stability is all," together with the fact that functionalists of type (a) have usually tended in practice to give reasons for pessimism about the possible scope of social reform, which provide the basis for the charge of functionalist conservatism. Type (c) sociologists are mainly concerned to construct models of social systems and either deny the second of these propositions or occasionally ignore its implications in order to reduce the difficulties of their task. Type (d) sociologists would deny the first of these propositions (usually, specifically the charge that the postulate of necessary integration is illegitimate) and, in giving a description of the functions of an institution, would imply that this is also, automatically, a causal explanation of that institution.

A number of alternative positions are possible if these two propositions are accepted. There is the piecemeal approach, outlined at the beginning of this paper, which suggests that sociologists should concern themselves with searching for regularities in the concomitant occurrence of social events with a view to inducing causal laws which might ultimately be ordered in some systematic theory. There is the historical approach which is largely concerned with discovering the causes of the particular once-and-for-all events which explain the origins of institutions. There is the static approach which concentrates on societies which have been stable over long periods of time and seeks for the causal relations between the recurring events which make up their institutions. There is still possible scope for the model-system approach in so far as it seeks to build up a pattern of causal relations such as might pertain to an ideal and entirely stable society, without having recourse to the short cut of functionalists variety (c). There is, finally, the "issue" approach, the virtues of which have recently been argued with much vehemence by C. Wright Mills. This involves starting from practical questions which actually worry people, such as "who is likely to plunge us into a world war," and using for the purpose of elucidation questions about the causes of recurring institutionalized events—so that by knowing why people do things we shall be in a better posi-

tion to know how to stop them; questions about the once-and-for-all causes—so that by knowing how things got the way they are we shall be in a better position to judge whether that is the way they ought to be; and questions about functions of institutions—so that we would have a better idea of what we would be up against if we tried to change them. All kinds of questions are asked not as ends in themselves but as means to eliciting guides for judgment and action. This is not, perhaps, a scientific pursuit in the way that the other approaches outlined above are scientific, though it is one that has intermittently occupied a great many sociologists of repute.

The differences between these various positions are in part methodological—differences concerning the truth of the two propositions enunciated earlier. In part they are moral differences about the proper scale of priorities which should guide the sociologist's use of his time. About the methodological issues there is legitimate ground for dispute. But about the "oughts" implied in these various positions, we can only preach at each other. It would be sad if we stopped preaching, but let us try to keep our sermons and our methodological discussions separate.

23

ON SOCIAL STRUCTURE

S. F. NADEL

PERHAPS I should have called this book *Towards a Theory of Social Structure* or even *Thoughts on a Theory of Social Structure,* to indicate more faithfully its experimental nature. Also, much of it is of the clearing-the-decks type; and though this is a task both necessary and, I think, profitable, it cannot be claimed to pro-

From S. F. Nadel, *The Theory of Social Structure* ("Preliminaries"). Copyright © 1957, Cohen and West, Ltd.; © 1964, The Free Press. Reprinted by permission of the publishers. At the time of his death in 1956, S. F. Nadel held the post of Professor of Anthropology at the Australian National University.

duce a great deal in the way of final answers or definitive solutions.

Even the word 'theory' which appears in the title needs to be placed in the right perspective. Broadly speaking, we mean by a theory a body of interconnected propositions (hypotheses, generalizations) concerned with a particular problem area and meant to account for the empirical facts in it. Now in fully-fledged scientific theories 'accounting for' means 'explaining'. In this sense the interconnected propositions or generalizations are such that 'observable consequences logically follow' (R. B. Braithwaite). Differently put, they are such that the empirical facts within the range covered by the theory are deducible from it, so that their being what they are is predicted (by the theory) and understood (in the light of the theory). Needless to say, only the most advanced sciences have reached this level of explanatory theory-building. But 'theory' can also be understood in another, less ambitious sense, namely as a body of propositions (still interconnected) which serve to *map out* the problem area and thus prepare the ground for its empirical investigation by appropriate methods. More precisely, the propositions serve to classify phenomena, to analyse them into relevant units or indicate their interconnections, and to define 'rules of procedures' and 'schemes of interpretation' (Felix Kaufman). 'Theory' here equals conceptual scheme or logical framework; and it is in this sense that the present enquiry can be said to aim at a 'Theory'. Actually, in one or two places I shall also advance what amount to explanatory hypotheses. But they are presented incidentally, because the run of the argument leads in that direction, and not in any sense as crucial points in the 'theory'.

So much by way of introduction. Turning now to my proper subject I can do no better than take my lead from the statement, recently made by a prominent anthropologist (Meyer Fortes), that 'notable advances have been made in the theory of social structure of homogeneous societies. . . . By comparison theories about culture are unsystematic and unco-ordinated.' I do not wish to go into the latter assertion (which can, I think, easily be disproved). But I would suggest that, in anthropology, the very concept of social structure is still in a sense on trial. At least discussions about it still tend to be polemical (the passage just quoted being an example). This may seem surprising considering that in the sister-discipline, sociology, the concept gained wide currency almost from the start. The term appears already in the writings of Herbert Spencer and Durkheim, and is rarely left unmentioned in modern literature. But there it is mostly used in a broad and almost blanket fashion, referring to any or all features contributing to the make-up of societies; it thus becomes simply a synonym for system, organization, complex, pattern, type, and indeed does not fall very short of 'society as a whole'. Take these examples: 'Social Structure is the web of interacting social forces from which have arisen the various modes of observing and thinking. . . .' (K. Mannheim). The study of 'social

structure is concerned with the principal forms of social organization, i.e. types of groups, associations and institutions and the complex of these which constitute societies. . . . A full account of social structure would involve a review of the whole field of comparative institutions' (M. Ginsberg). 'Group structures' represent the kind of reality 'into which we are born and within which we find work and recreation, rewards and penalties, struggle and mutual aid. . . .' All 'the various modes of grouping . . . together comprise the complex pattern of social structure. . . . In the analysis of the social structure the role of the diverse attitudes and interests of social beings is revealed' (R. M. MacIver and C. H. Page).

In anthropology, on the other hand, the introduction of the term went together with the attempt to give it a narrower and precise definition. We owe both to Radcliffe-Brown, whose students and followers have further developed and partly redefined the concept. But again, several anthropologists still prefer the broader, unspecific meaning of 'social structure', while others—especially in America—omit the term altogether, e.g. Linton in *The Study of Man* or Lowie in his *Social Organization*. One prominent anthropologist, Kroeber, explicitly questions its usefulness, stressing, perhaps a little intolerantly, the vagueness with which it tempts its users: ' "Structure" appears to be just yielding to a word that has a perfectly good meaning but suddenly becomes fashionably attractive for a decade or so—like "streamlining"—and during its vogue tends to be applied indiscriminately because of the pleasurable connotation of its sound.'

If there are instances suggesting that the anthropologist can well do without an additional concept of so fluid a connotation, a case has also been made out for precisely this broader use. Thus Firth points out that 'any science must have a budget of terms of general application, not too closely defined, and . . . structure may be one of them'. This is a weighty and persuasive argument; even so I shall, in the present discussion, take the opposite standpoint. I shall do so essentially heuristically, with a view to assessing the fruitfulness of the concept *if it be narrowly defined*. Nor is it difficult to defend this standpoint. It will hardly be denied that the addition of a new term to a technical vocabulary already well provided with rough equivalents cannot but suggest that it has a specific connotation, referring to a range of

problems or to methods of enquiry not previously isolated or perceived. In the case of a
word like 'structure', which has a well-defined
meaning in other disciplines, this seems doubly
true. And ideally, considering scientific economy
and consistency, the acceptance of any new
terms might well be made subject to these conditions. Let us therefore apply these conditions
and treat 'social structure' in this sense, as a
novel and specialized conceptual tool the fruitfulness of which it is worth exploring.

Equally, this task of exploration is neither
unwarranted nor redundant. For even among the
scholars who present us with a clear-cut definition of social structure, there is little agreement, at least on the level of verbal formulation.
All the students of social structure are agreed
that in studying 'structure' we study essentially
the interrelation or arrangements of 'parts' in
some total entity or 'whole'. They are agreed,
further, that the adjective 'social' specifies the
character of that 'whole'—which is 'society' or
any of its subdivisions, and not 'culture' and
any of its sectors or provinces: which distinction is by now too well established to need
further comment. We might only add that one
or two scholars also employ the concept of
structure in the latter sense. Thus Herskovits
means by 'structure of culture,' somewhat
naively, the progressive combination of 'traits',
in complexes, areas and patterns. Bateson applies the same phrase, on a much more sophisticated level, to the 'logical' order (in terms
of 'premises' or 'underlying assumptions') discernible in the modes of behaviour typical of a
people. More recently, Feibleman has advanced
a similar view, equating the 'structure of culture' with the 'common axiom sets' from which
'all manifestations of a culture can be deduced'.

Now as regards the concept of structure applied to 'society', though there is no dispute
about the total entity whose division into parts
is taken as the subject matter of structural
studies, on the nature of the parts themselves
views differ widely. Indeed, the variety of views
gives rise to considerable confusion. Let us look
at some of them.

Radcliffe-Brown in one of his more recent
contributions, explains that 'the components of
social structure are human beings', the structure itself being an 'arrangement of persons in
relationships institutionally defined and regulated'. There is a more recent definition still,
which is interesting because its circularity betrays the difficulties inherent in the conceptualization of social structure: this is now said
(Radcliffe-Brown) to be made up of 'human
beings considered not as organisms but as occupying positions in social structure'. Eggan finds
the components or units of social structure in
the inter-personal relations, which 'become part
of the social structure in the form of status positions' occupied by individuals. Evans-Pritchard
restricts social structure to the interrelations of
groups, explicitly excluding inter-personal relations. Fortes once more accepts the latter as
'elements' of social structure, adding that they
are reached through abstracting 'the *constant*
features in the pattern of organization of all
activities in which (the relation) is significant',
But he also maintains that social structure
contains 'parts and relations of diverse nature
and variability' and pertains to 'social events
and organizations' as their '*variable*' aspect. For
Leach, social structure (in so far as 'practical
situations' are concerned) 'consists of a set of
ideas about the distribution of power between
persons or groups of persons'. Finally, the latest
edition of *Notes and Queries on Anthropology*
advances the all-too-catholic definition of social
structure as the 'whole network of social relations in which are involved the members of a
given community at a particular time'; while
Lévi-Strauss *per contram* holds that social structure 'can by no means be reduced to the ensemble of social relations to be described in a
given society'.

It will be agreed, I think, that there is little
to be gained from trying to reconcile these
various conceptions. Let me, therefore, begin
at the beginning and examine afresh the meaning which can usefully and logically be assigned
to 'social structure'. I propose to proceed strictly
operationally, that is, I shall attempt to specify,
at every stage, the 'operations', observational
or cognitive, which underlie any term used; and
I hope that this procedure will not be regarded
as unduly painstaking and circuitous or, for that
matter, as belabouring the obvious.

I shall on occasion also employ a system of
notation which I am attempting to develop,
mainly on the basis of familiar symbols borrowed from mathematics and symbolic logic.
I shall do so not in order to give a more 'scientific' appearance to my exposition, but because
I firmly believe that social analysis in its present stage can profitably make use of such forms
of notation, and is ready for them. Their purpose, to begin with at any rate, would be to
help in demonstrating certain complicated

situations more simply and accurately than can be done by verbose descriptions. This is obviously only a beginning, though I hope a promising one. And no part of social analysis seems more appropriate for making a start than the analysis of social structure which, as we shall presently see, is focused upon formal features and relations, that is, upon the kind of phenomena with which mathematics and logic pre-eminently deal.

Perhaps there is more to be said in defence of this new departure. It has been argued [by R. K. Merton] that sociological exposition and interpretation cannot help being 'highly discursive'; for 'sociology has few formulae, in the sense of highly abbreviated symbolic expressions of relationships between sociological variables'. If so, a system of symbolic expressions, even in the form of a mere notational system, must help towards a sharper and more concise manner of exposition. To be sure, the technique of notation will not by itself produce significant 'formulae'; it does not automatically procure a fuller insight into the 'relationships between sociological variables'. It only equips us with a new tool for demonstrating them, if or when they are discovered. But let us not minimize the usefulness of this equipment. New tools have been known to facilitate new discoveries. They certainly produce, in those who use them, a new attitude, a new way of looking at the material to be handled: which is probably the decisive step.

I

We begin with the most general definition of 'structure', which underlies the use of the term in all other disciplines. There structure is a property of empirical data—of objects, events or series of events—something they exhibit or prove to possess on observation or analysis; and the data are said to exhibit structure inasmuch as they exhibit a definable articulation, an ordered arrangement of parts. Indicating articulation or arrangement, that is, formal characteristics, structure may be contrasted with *function* (meaning by this term, briefly, adequacy in regard to some stipulated effectiveness) and with *content, material* or *qualitative character*. The former contrast is too familiar to need illustration; the latter has a wide application in psychology, linguistics, and logic.

It should be noted in passing that in two instances at least 'social structure' is explicitly denied to have the character here envisaged, that is, to be a feature of 'empirical reality.' . . . For the sake of completeness, we should add a third dichotomy to the two mentioned, i.e. *structure* and *process;* but this point, too, may at this stage be disregarded.

While the separation of structure from function implies a divergence of viewpoint and interest, the separation of structure from content, material, and qualitative character implies a move to a higher level of abstraction. For when describing structure we abstract relational features from the totality of the perceived data, ignoring all that is not 'order' or 'arrangement'; in brief, we define the positions relative to one another of the component parts. Thus I can describe the structure of a tetrahedron without mentioning whether it is a crystal, a wooden block, or a soup cube; I can describe the arrangement of a fugue or sonata without making any musical noises myself; and I can describe a syntactic order without referring to the phonetic material or semantic content of the words so ordered.

This has an important consequence, namely that structures can be transposed irrespective of the concrete data manifesting it; differently expressed, the parts composing any structure can vary widely in their concrete character without changing the identity of the structure. Our definition should thus be rephrased as follows: structure indicates an ordered arrangement of parts, which can be treated as transposable, being relatively invariant, while the parts themselves are variable. This definition, incidentally, fully corresponds to the one logicians would apply in their field: there too one speaks of an 'identical structure' in the case of any 'abstract set' which 'may have more than one concrete representation', the latter being potentially 'extremely unlike in material content' (M. R. Cohen and E. Nagel).

Now to translate all this into the language appropriate to the analysis of societies. There is an immediate difficulty; for it is by no means easy to say precisely what a 'society' is. But whatever we may wish to include in a sophisticated definition of society, certain things are clear and can be stated quite simply. To begin with, societies are made up of people; societies have boundaries, people either belonging to them or not; and people belong to a society in virtue of rules under which they stand and which impose on them regular, determinate ways of acting towards and in regard to one another. Conceivably, in theory, there might be as many such ways of acting as there are situations in which people meet, practically an infinite number. But we are here speaking of ways of acting governed by rules and hence in some measure stereotyped (or rendered 'determinate'). And of the ways of acting so understood it is true to say that they are finite and always less numerous than the possible combinations of people: which means that the same ways of acting are repetitive in the population. We need only add that these ways of acting are repetitive also in the sense that they apply to changing or successive populations.

Let me expand this a little. For 'determinate ways of acting towards or in regard to one another' we usually say 'relationships', and we indicate that they follow from rules by calling them 'institutionalized' or 'social' (as against 'private' or 'personal') relationships. We identify the mutual ways of acting of individuals as 'relationships' only when the former exhibit some consistency and constancy, since without these attributes they would merely be single or disjointed acts. But what is constant or consistent is not really the concrete behaviour, with its specific quality or content. If it were so, the individuals involved in any relationship would have to act *vis-à-vis* one another always in precisely the same manner. Now we may disregard that inevitable variability which comes into play when actions, even though intended to be identical, are repeated on different occasions and in varying circumstances. There remain a few approximations to the kind of relationship which would produce the same uniform behaviour throughout. They are exemplified in relationships which are strictly utilitarian and revolve upon a single purpose, such as the relationship between fellow workers, between shopkeeper and customer, perhaps between teacher und pupil.

Most relationships, however, lack this simple constancy or uniformity. Rather, the *concrete* behaviour occurring in them will always be diversified and more or less widely variable, intentionally changing with the circumstances; it will be constant or consistent only in its *general character,* that is, in its capacity to indicate a certain type of mutuality or linkage. We may still say of persons in a given relationship that they act towards each other 'always

in the same manner'; but 'manner' should be in the plural, and 'the same' understood very broadly. It is in virtue of this general character or broad 'sameness' that we regard a whole series of genuinely varying ways of acting as adding up to a single ('constant', 'consistent') relationship. Conversely, any relationship thus identified (and, incidentally, named as aptly as is possible) is understood to signify such a whole series subsumed in it.

Thus we take 'friendship' to be evidenced by a variety of mutual ways of acting, perhaps visible on different occasions, such as help in economic or other crises, mutual advice on various matters, efforts to be together, certain emotional re-responses. A 'respect relationship' will imply manners of greeting, a particular choice of language, advice sought and given, services offered and expected, etc. The parent-child relationship similarly includes actions exacting respect, behaviour indicative of love and care, and acts of a disciplinary or punitive kind. To say it again, the large majority of social relationships are of this inclusive and serial type (which Gluckman calls 'multiplex'). Differently expressed, each relationship has a whole range of 'concrete representations', implying them all. Thus, in identifying any relationship we already *abstract* from the qualitatively varying modes of behaviour an invariant relational aspect—the linkage between people they signify.

This can be shown symbolically by indicating the diverse *modes* of behaviour by small letters (a to n), the *condition* 'towards' or 'acting towards' by the sign ':', and the implicitness of the modes of behaviour in the relationship by the logical sign for *implication,* ' $\supset$ '; we further indicate the fact that a relationship rests not on a single 'way of acting' but on a whole range or series by the mathematical symbol for 'series', Σ. Thus, when we say of any two persons A and B that they stand in a particular relationship r which, for the sake of simplicity, we will assume to be a strictly symmetrical one, we mean that

(1)   A r B, if
A (a, b, c . . . n): B, and *vice versa;*
∴ $r \supset \Sigma$ a . . . n.

Firth holds very similar views on the process whereby we identify social relationships, or 'infer' them from some observed sequence of acts: 'We see sufficient elements of likeness to allow us to attribute identity, to abstract and generalize into a type of social relation'. Let us note, however, that this abstraction and generalization does not go very far. We still need to distinguish relationships or types of relationships qualitatively, by their content of aims, emotions, etc. It is thus that we speak of friendship as against love or loyalty, separate respect from reverence or servitude, or distinguish between relationships having an economic, political, religious or perhaps purely emotive significance.

It is clear, on the other hand, that all relationships, through the linkage or mutuality they signify, serve to 'position', 'order' or 'arrange' the human material of societies. And considering what we said before about the repetitiveness of relationships in the population, it follows that they do satisfy the criterion of invariance implicit in the concept of structure. They do so in the sense that every relationship has its several 'concrete representations' also in the widely varying individuals who may, at any time, be linked or positioned in the stated fashion.

But relationships are not irregularly repetitive, and the individuals acting in them not variable at random. (We may ignore relationships occurring fortuitously, for example, owing to sympathies or antipathies which happen to affect people: they do not concern us to any great extent since social enquiry is *ex hypothesi* about regularities, not accidents.) Rather, the recurrence of relationships is once more circumscribed by rules, the same set of rules which determines the 'ways of acting' of people towards one another. It is part of these rules that they also specify the type of individuals— any individual satisfying certain conditions or placed in certain circumstances—who can or must act in particular relationships. Expressed more simply, individuals become actors in relationships in virtue of some brief; which brief is obviously as invariant as the relationships that hinge on it. And instead of speaking of individuals 'being actors in virtue of some brief', we usually speak of individuals enacting *roles*.

This will become clearer a little later. At the moment only one further thing needs saying. Though relationships and roles (more precisely, relationships in virtue of roles) 'arrange' and 'order' the human beings who make up the society, the collection of existing relationships must itself be an orderly one; at least, it must be so if the ordered arrangement of human beings is indeed a total arrangement, running through the whole society. Think of a piece of polyphonic music: any two tones in it are positioned relative to one another by the intervals they describe; but the total design or structure of the piece clearly lies not in the mere presence and collection of all these intervals but in the order in which they appear. Though this analogy has drawbacks, it illustrates the point I wish to make if for intervals we read relationships and for musical structure, social structure.

Oddly enough, this question has rarely been raised, as a question. Most writers on social structure seem content to indicate that it is composed, in some unspecified manner, of persons standing in relationships or of the sum-total of these. Only Lévi-Strauss goes further, insisting that the mere 'ensemble' of existing relationships does not yet amount to 'structure' (see above, p. 00). Like myself, he thus stipulates a further 'order', over and above the one implicit in the relationships, and interrelating the latter. Let us note that this is not merely a two-level hierarchy of, say, first-order relations (linking and arranging persons) and second-order relations (doing the same with relationships). We are dealing here with differences in kind; the orderliness *of* a plurality of relationships differs radically from the ordering of a plurality of individuals *through* relationship. And whatever the precise nature of the former, we can see that it must correspond to something like an overall system, network or pattern.

We may break off at this point. We now have all the terms needed for a definition of social structure, and we may put it this way: We arrive at the structure of a society through abstracting from the concrete population and its behaviour the pattern or network (or 'system') of relationships obtaining 'between actors in their capacity of playing roles relative to one another' (T. Parsons).

Though this and similar definitions are basically correct (and must be so if our reasoning has been correct) they conceal serious methodological difficulties; for a satisfactory theory of social structure on this basis presupposes an adequate theory of roles, and none has yet been advanced in any systematic fashion. As a next step, therefore, I propose to make this attempt. But a few comments are still needed to complete this preliminary discourse.

II

(i) First, let me stress that the phrase 'playing roles relative to one another' in our definition of social structure does not merely mean 'playing roles *vis-à-vis* one another'; that is, we are not restricting social structure to face-to-face relationships or situations. This viewpoint hardly needs justifying. I mention it only because in using the conventional phraseology (or one not too clumsy) one is apt to give the impression of considering primarily face-to-face situations. Relationships other than face-to-face do pose certain special technical problems such as appropriate machineries of communication. But the reliance, on the part of the society, on face-to-face relationships equally involves technical difficulties, now concerning facilities for the necessary physical propinquity of the actors. I shall disregard both questions, which refer to the prerequisite conditions of social structures rather than to social structure as such.

(ii) It might seem that the approach here proposed, starting from the concepts of roles and role-playing actors, must miss a whole province or aspect of social structure, namely that formed by the ordered arrangements of sub-groups and similar subdivisions of society. We may take it for granted that any society does contain within it a number of smaller and simpler replicas of itself, which we conventionally call sections, segments, sub-groups etc. Their presence and arrangement clearly represents as much an 'articulation' as does the division of society into role-playing actors. Which seems to suggest that our definition of social structure is incomplete and that, in order to make it complete, we have to mention not only relationships between actors or persons but also the interrelations between sub-groups. But this juxtaposition is deceptive in spite of the near-coincidence of the terms 'relationship' and 'interrelation'. The latter (applied to groups) is not a counterpart or parallel of the former (applied to persons), as even a cursory glance will show; for while the relationship of persons implies interaction between them, behaviour of one towards or in regard to the other, groups of which we say that they are interrelated do not interact or behave as such,

collectively, save in relatively few, special cases. Rather we must look at the situation in a different way.

Sub-groups, like that widest group the 'society at large', are made up of people in determinate, stable relationships. And any group is characterized by the kinds of relationships that occur between the people in question, holding them together. Now inasmuch as sub-groups are discrete entities, bounded units, at least certain of these characteristic relationships must be equally bounded, that is, they must come to an end somewhere, their cessation demarcating the boundaries of the group. From this point of view, then, we might describe sub-groups as areas of bounded relationships. But inasmuch as they are also subdivisions of a wider collectivity and not isolated, self-sufficient units, the bounded relationships must themselves be interrelated. In other words, they must exhibit or fit into the overall network or pattern we spoke of before. The interrelation of sub-groups is therefore only a special case of the relatedness or 'orderliness' of relationships, and our definition of social structure both covers it and will logically lead us to it.

For the sake of completeness I ought to add this further remark, if only in parenthesis. In a somewhat different frame of reference the bounded unity of groups (and of society at large) can be demonstrated more simply by the criterion of *co-activity,* i.e. by indicating the particular co-ordinated activity (or activities) which would hold between all persons in the human aggregate claimed to constitute a group. This is the criterion I in fact adopted in a previous study. But though satisfactory in that context, the criterion is less so in the present one. For it is clear that a single embracing co-activity cannot always be translated into a single, equally embracing, relationship. This is feasible only if either the co-activity involves no differentiation in the position of the participants (so that ArB equals BrC . . . *ad inf.*), or the relationship considered is of a highly general kind (e.g. the 'fellowship' of fellow tribesmen or citizens, the 'kinship' of a group based on descent). But usually the former condition will be inapplicable or the latter too uninformative, and the embracing co-activity will need to be broken up into a series of distinct relationships in accordance with the different parts played by the participants. Thus, from the present viewpoint, directed as it is upon relationships, the more devious definition of group unity quoted above proves the only possible one.

(iii) I must now explain that the two terms, 'network' and 'pattern', are not meant as synonyms. Rather, they are intended to indicate two different types or perhaps levels of overall structuring with which we shall meet throughout this discussion but for which, frankly, I have not been able to find very satisfactory terms. The best way I can describe them is by saying that one type of structuring is abstracted from *interactions,* the other from *distributions.* The latter may in turn apply to a variety of things— to concrete populations, to persons in their roles, as well as to relationships and sub-groups. The terms 'network' and 'pattern' are meant to indicate this distinction primarily in regard to relationships.

Thus I shall mean by 'pattern' any orderly distribution of relationships exclusively on the grounds of their similarity and dissimilarity. It is best exemplified (there are other, less clearcut examples) by societies of the type Durkheim calls 'segmental', i.e. societies characterized by the repetition of like aggregates in them', the 'aggregates' being, for instance, clans, lineages, age sets or social strata. Let me explain this more fully. Since any group or sub-group consists of an area of bounded relationships it follows that, if the sub-groups are repetitive, the relationships characterizing them will be distributed in a similarly repetitive manner. That is to say, the relationships will occur within each of the like units (or 'aggregates') but not outside or between them, disappearing or being replaced by different relationships at the group boundaries. Think of the particular fellowship linking age mates and age mates only; of the economic and ritual collaboration valid within (but not without) descent groups; or of the intercourse on an equal footing restricted to members of the same social stratum. We can visualize this discontinuous but repetitive distribution by representing the clusters of identical relationships (*r*) in the sub-groups, as against the relationships occurring at their boundaries (B*r*), in some such fashion:

$$
\begin{bmatrix} rrr \\ rrr \\ rrr \end{bmatrix} \begin{matrix} \mathrm{B}r \\ \mathrm{B}r \\ \mathrm{B}r \end{matrix} \begin{bmatrix} rrr \\ rrr \\ rrr \end{bmatrix} \begin{matrix} \mathrm{B}r \\ \mathrm{B}r \\ \mathrm{B}r \end{matrix} \begin{bmatrix} rrr \\ rrr \\ rrr \end{bmatrix}
$$

I suggest, then, that such distributive arrangements warrant special recognition, and that 'pattern' is an apt description. At the same time I do not propose to deal with them specifically in the subsequent discussion. Rather, I shall treat them as an unproblematic and relatively elementary aspect of social structure. They are unproblematic because there really is nothing further to be said about these patterns once we have described the repetitive distribution in question. And they are relatively elementary because a distributive order is the simplest kind of order, involving a very low level of abstraction. But we must note this. The distributive pattern never stands by itself; for if the respective subdivisions are in fact such, i.e. *components* of a society, then they must also be linked by certain interactions and by interrelations based on these: else they would not add up to one society (in which there must be behaviour 'towards and in regard to one another'). Thus the 'pattern' will go together with a 'network', and it is from the combination of the two that genuine problems will arise, the sort of problems we have in mind when we talk about the interpendence of group segments, about 'social symbiosis', or about the cohesion and integration of any 'society at large'.

By 'network', on the other hand, I mean the interlocking of relationships whereby the interactions implicit in one determine those occurring in others. Firth has recently commented on the fondness of anthropologists for metaphors like 'network', though he concedes the usefulness of this 'image' which allows us to visualize the relations between persons as 'links' and 'lines'. Obviously, the network talked about by anthropologists is only a metaphor. But it has been used very effectively also by others, e.g. by physicists, engineers and neurophysiologists. They speak, for example, of communication networks or of the networks of nerve cells and paths. Let me stress that I am using the term in a very similar, technical sense. For I do not merely wish to indicate the 'links' between persons; this is adequately done by the word relationship. Rather, I wish to indicate the further linkage of the links themselves and the important consequence that, what happens so-to-speak between one pair of 'knots', must affect what happens between other adjacent ones. It is in order to illustrate this interrelatedness or interlocking of the relationships (each a 'link' between two 'knots'), that we require an additional term, and 'network' seems the most appropriate.

To mention another recent use of this metaphor. Barnes employs it to illustrate a particular kind of 'social field', constituted by relationships which spread out indefinitely rather than close in, as it were, and hence do not 'give rise to enduring social groups'. This spreading-out follows roughly the schema ArB, BrC, CrD . . . , though any one person may have relationships with several other persons and the 'other persons' may conceivably also maintain relations among themselves. A paradigm is friendship, each person seeing 'himself as at the centre of a collection of friends', who in turn have further friends and may or may not be friends with each other. This picture comes close to the one I have in mind, though it represents a special and simpler case. For Barnes's 'network' does not predicate more than that certain relationships interlock through persons participating in more than one relationship; I visualize a situation in which this interlocking also bears on 'what happens' in the relationships and hence on their effective interdependence. For Barnes, the important thing is the dispersal of the relationships, and the open-ended character of the network; for me, its coherence and closure, that is, its equivalence with a 'system'.

(iv) Let me, in conclusion, say a little more about 'distributive patterns', more precisely about one particular type. It occurs when a society is so constituted that it contains a fixed number of subdivisions, of whatever kind. The fixed number only indicates the high degree of constancy characterizing the 'pattern'; and examples are of course familiar—societies having a moiety system, or six phratries (like the Zuni), four castes (like classical India), or so-and-so many age grades.

We might add that similar fixed numerical arrangements may apply also to the actors expected to fill particular roles or, more generally, to the population composing classes of people or sub-groups in the society. A club or association with a fixed membership and, perhaps, one President, two Vice-Presidents, and three Members of Council, is a simple illustration. More sophisticated examples will be found in Simmel, who paid special attention to this aspect of social structure, considering it highly relevant. Recently, from a somewhat different point of view, Lévi-Strauss has touched upon the same issue. He has in mind not a numerical arrangement fixed, i.e. kept invariant, by explicit social rules, but one exhibiting a purely statistical (and approximate) invariance. This would be the case, if I may choose my own examples, where we find that the size of clans varies round a mean number, which is maintained by fission (if clans grow too large) or fusion (if they grow too small); or again, we might find that the ruling class in a stratified society always approximates to, say, ten per cent of the population.

Now what is sociologically relevant in such numerical arrangements, whether they apply to persons in roles, to the population of sub-groups or to the number of the sub-groups themselves, is not the distributive pattern as such. Once more, considered by itself, it represents an unproblematic and elementary form of structuring. It becomes interesting and important only through its implication of interdependence between the persons or sections so numbered, that is, when it goes together with some differentiation and interlocking of their respective 'ways of acting' and hence with a 'network' of relationships. Thus the numbered set of phratries or castes may be so conceived that each has specific duties, secular or ritual, towards all others; a dual segmentation of the society, perhaps even the presence of two Vice-Presidents in an association, may serve to canalize and balance opposition; and the invariant population of clans or ruling classes may represent the optimum size for the particular activities assigned to these segments. Here we have a whole range of significant problems, and problems still in need of further study. They concern the extent to which these and similar forms of interdependence and integration depend on particular numerical arrangements or, conversely, the extent to which the numerical invariance facilitates (or the opposite) aimed-at possibilities of interaction. But these are essentially questions of adequacy, of the appropriateness of means to ends, that is, of *function*, and hence beyond the scope of this discussion.

B. Evolution

24

EVOLUTION:
SPECIFIC AND GENERAL

MARSHALL D. SAHLINS

IT seems to us that Huxley has been pre-mature in congratulating evolutionary biology on its explicit recognition of the difference be-tween divergence and progress. Despite Hux-ley's own efforts to make the distinction, and despite the fact that the distinction may well strike a biologist as commonplace should he pause to consider it, it is nevertheless not gen-erally explicated by prominent biologists, and judging from confusion about the character of life's evolutionary progress in recent literature, it is perhaps not fully understood. On the other hand, the distinction has long existed in the literature of evolutionary anthropology. E. B. Tylor, in the opening chapter of *Primitive Cul-ture,* laid out the study of cultural evolution both "stage by stage" as well as "along its many lines." Yet in this, as in so much else, twentieth-century anthropology did not heed Tylor's advice. The dual character of the evolu-tionary process was not recognized, and this failing has become the very heart of current confusion and polemical controversy about such terms as "unilinear," "multilinear," and "uni-versal" evolution, as well as about the difference between "history" and "evolution."

It appears almost obvious upon stating it

Reprinted from Marshall D. Sahlins and Elman R. Service, Eds., *Evolution and Culture* by permis-sion of the University of Michigan Press. Copyright © by the University of Michigan Press 1960. Mar-shall D. Sahlins is Professor of Anthropology, University of Michigan.

that in both its biological and cultural spheres evolution moves simultaneously in two direc-tions. On one side, it creates diversity through adaptive modification: new forms differentiate from old. On the other side, evolution generates progress: higher forms arise from, and surpass, lower. The first of these directions is Specific Evolution, and the second, General Evolution. But note that specific and general evolution are not different concrete realities; they are rather aspects of the same total process, which is also to say, two contexts in which we may place the same evolutionary things and events. Any given change in a form of life or culture can be viewed *either* in the perspective of adap-tation *or* from the point of view of overall prog-ress. However, the context is very important: a difference in taxonomy is required in examining these two aspects of evolution. Concerned with lines of descent, the study of specific evolution employs phylogenetic classification. In the gen-eral evolutionary outlook emphasis shifts to the character of progress itself, and forms are classed in stages or levels of development with-out reference to phylogeny.

SPECIFIC AND GENERAL BIOLOGICAL EVOLUTION

Life inevitably diversifies. It does so because it is perpetuated by reproduction and inheri-tance, so that adaptive changes are transmitted only in lines of descent. Thus in evolving—which is to say, moving in the direction of increasing use of the earth's resources or increasing transformation of available energy—life necessarily differentiates into particular (breeding) populations, each adjusted to the exploitation of a given environment. This is the specific aspect of life's evolution, the familiar origin and ramification of species. The much-lauded "modern synthetic theory" of biology, unifying genetic principles with natural selection, is devoted to the unraveling of specific evolution.

The perspective required for understanding specific evolution is a phylogenetic one. We are interested in how one species grows out of another and how the new species gives rise to still other species. We are interested in the precise historical and genetic relations between species, and want to show these connections as well as to explain them by reference to natural selection. Thus we trace out the branching and rebranching of lineages, relating each new line to its ecological circumstances. Inasmuch as our perspective is phylogenetic, so is our taxonomy. While biological taxonomy was not originally phylogenetic, it has come to be primarily so used, indicating again that the decisive concern of evolutionary biology remains specific evolution.

Adaptive specialization of populations is an inevitable aspect of life's evolution, and *advance* is a normal concomitant of adaptive specialization. In the context of specific evolution "advance" means that by adaptive modification the population is enabled to maintain or better itself in the face of a threat induced by changing environment or that it is enabled to exploit the same environment more effectively than before. In any case, in the specific perspective advance is characteristically *relative*—relative to the environmental circumstances. This can be illustrated by looking at adapting species in terms of structure and functioning.

Specific advance is manifest both in improved structure and improved functioning of members of an adapting population, although improved structure usually receives greater attention because it is more easily observed or (for fossils) deduced. There are many possible kinds of functional improvements: in vision, smell, speed, or in temperature control, and so on. Likewise there are many possible kinds of concomitant structural improvements: changes in limb structure, in the brain, in the eyes, the development of claws, fins, fur, and the like.

But that which is a significant improvement for one species need not be so for another, for they may be adjusting to radically different environments or in radically different ways to the same kind of environment. For some forms in some habitats, increase in size is an adaptive advance. for others, decrease in size is selectively advantageous, and so with all other characteristics. Therefore, no one organism, however high in general standing, has a monopoly on or even necessarily more kinds of adaptive advances than any other. A "higher species," in other words, is not in every respect more "advanced" than a lower: man's color vision may be superior to that of the fish, but he cannot swim as well, nor for that matter is his eyesight the most perfect in the animal kingdom. Moreover, higher organisms are not inevitably more perfectly adjusted to their environments than lower. On the contrary, many higher species die out while lower forms continue to survive in their particular niches for eons. Higher forms are often more generalized, less specialized (adapted) for any particular niche, than lower.

Adaptive improvement is relative to the adaptive problem; it is so to be judged and explained. In the specific context each adapted population is adequate, indeed superior, in its own incomparable way. Considering life's evolution phylogenetically we can be only biological relativists. At this point the cultural anthropologist will probably be unable to refrain from linking the famous axiom of cultural relativism with a specific perspective on cultural change. Such would be a correct historical inference: the philosophy of cultural relativism was elaborated precisely by the historical-particularist school which dominated American anthropology through the first half of this century. But to pursue this further now is to anticipate a later discussion.

In sum, specific evolution is the phylogenetic, adaptive, diversifying, specializing, ramifying aspect of total evolution. It is in this respect that evolution is often equated with movement from homogeneity to heterogeneity. But general evolution is another aspect. It is the emergence of higher forms of life, regardless of particular lines of descent or historical sequences of adaptive modification. In the broader perspective of general evolution organisms are taken out of their respective lineages and grouped into types which represent the successive levels of all-round progress that evolution has brought forth.

Let us first illustrate the difference between

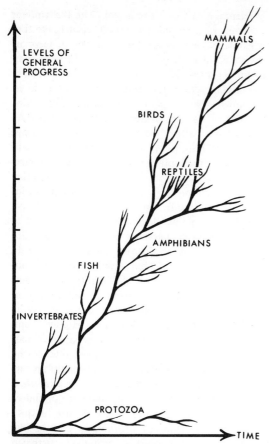

LEVELS OF
GENERAL
PROGRESS

MAMMALS

BIRDS

REPTILES

AMPHIBIANS

FISH

INVERTEBRATES

PROTOZOA

TIME

DIAGRAM 1. *Diversity and progress among major lineages of animal life (schematized)*

general and specific evolution with a diagram (Diagram 1). Suppose it is possible to plot the phylogenetic origins of the major lineages of animal life. A good way of doing this graphically would be in the shape of a climbing vine —not a tree, for there is no trunk, no "main line"—each larger branch of the vine representing a major divergence of life through time, and smaller branches representing diversification of major lineages. But the vine has a dimension of height as well as a temporal extension of branches. Suppose that the height is "evolutionary height," that is, that the distance of any form from the base indicates degree of over-all progress according to some agreed-upon criterion. A series of horizontal lines could then be drawn across the vine, with the vertical intervals between them indicating levels of general progress through time. Thus on the diagram, life's evolution is depicted in its lateral, branching dimension as well as in its vertical, progressive one.

The difference between specific and general evolution can also be illustrated by reference to a familiar group of animals, the primates. The primates are customarily divided into four broad formal categories: prosimian, New World monkeys, Old World monkeys, and hominoid. Each of the latter three, according to Simpson, originated from a different line of prosimian, not one developed out of another. Phylogentically or specifically, the study of primates consists of tracing the early prosimian radiation, determining how, when, and why each of the other types specialized out, and following the further course of divergence within each line. But it seems obvious and is usually implicitly accepted that the four types of primates, especially their recent representatives, can be arranged to indicate levels of general progress. The hierarchy of over-all standing is, of course: prosimian, New World monkey, then Old World monkey, with hominoid as highest. Although the sequence is a violation of phylogeny, it aids in understanding other consequences of evolution. The hierarchy is commonly used to illustrate general progress in intelligence, social life, and a number of other features. Moreover, a check of history reveals that the levels represented by selected recent specimens are indeed successive. The implication of the last statement deserves to be made explicit: in the taxonomy of general evolution a modern representative of a stage is as "good," i.e., as indicative of the level, as the original and probably extinct representative.

As with the primates, so with life forms in general: a man is more highly developed than a mouse, a mouse than a lizard, a lizard than a goldfish, a goldfish than a crab, a crab than an amoeba. All of these are contemporary, no one is ancestral to the other; they are present termini of different lineages. In what sense can we speak of evolutionary development of one over the other? To anticipate again, the same question appears when we look at contemporary cultures. Eskimo, Sioux Indian, and English culture all exist at the same time and are unrelated to each other. What are the criteria for deciding which is higher on the evolutionary scale, and which lower?

Before an answer can be suggested, another distinction is required. Anyone will recognize the taxonomic shift that occurs in moving from specific to general evolution, a shift from phylogenetic categories to levels of development respectively. But another more subtle shift has also occurred: that is, from species or populations as such to particular organisms as such. In specific evolution the unit of study is the population, the species as a whole, which evolves or differentiates into new kinds of populations. The well-known biological definition of specific evolution, a change in gene frequencies, is a statement explicitly about the structure of a population. In moving to general evolution, however, the concern becomes forms *qua* forms, typical organisms of a class and *their* characteristics. The general taxonomic category, the level, refers to a class of organisms of a given type. It is accurate to say that specific evolution is the production of diverse species, general evolution the production of higher forms.

The difference is not a semantic nicety; it becomes decisive for determining criteria of general progress. It must be recognized that the evolutionary success of a species is often accomplished at the expense of higher development of its individuals. In many situations a species is better maintained by utilizing available energy to produce more of its kind rather than a smaller number of more highly developed specimens (something like modern "higher" education). Specific and general evolution can thus be at cross-purposes, and a measure of the success of a species is not necessarily one of the degree of general development of the particular organisms involved.

Now to a most important point: to embrace general evolution is to abandon relativism. The study of all-round progress requires criteria that are absolute, that are relevant to all organisms regardless of particular environments. The development of higher organisms can be conceived in functional, energy-capturing terms: higher forms harness more energy than lower. Or the criteria of general progress may be structural, the achievement of higher organization.

One common notion of progress can be dismissed out of hand. Most of us have a tendency to equate progress with *efficiency,* which is not altogether surprising because this idea is peculiarly appropriate to a competitive, free-enterprise economy. But an organism's thermodynamic efficiency is not a measure of its general evolutionary status. By efficiency we usually mean some ratio of output to input; thus in rating a machine's efficiency we divide the output of work by the input of energy. Analogously, a measure of the thermodynamic

efficiency of a living thing would be the amount of energy captured and used relative to the organism's own expenditure in the process of taking it. But suppose we know the efficiency of an organism as an energy-capturing machine; the use to which the efficiency is put remains unknown. Is it put into build-up and maintenance of its organization? Not necessarily. As pointed out before, the energy taken can be put into the build-up of higher structures *or* into more numerous offspring, each of which concentrates a relatively low amount of energy. The implication is inescapable: an organism can be more efficient than another and yet remain less highly developed.

The difference between higher and lower life forms, it seems to us, is not how efficiently energy is harnessed, but how much. Thermodynamic achievement is the ability to concentrate energy in the organism, to put energy to work building and maintaining structure. Living things take free energy from nature, use it, and dissipate it. In the long run dissipation equals capture, or in terms of entropy, exceeds it—the entropy in the environment in which an organism has lived and died is greater after than before the process. But while alive the organism is trapping energy and transforming it into a higher state, that of protoplasm and its upkeep. It is the amount so trapped (corrected for gross size of the form) and the degree to which it is raised to a higher state that would seem to be the evolutionary measure of life; that would seem to be the way that a crab is superior to an amoeba, a goldfish to a crab, a mouse to a goldfish, a man to a mouse. We put all this in quite qualified form because we lack any competence in physical biology, and do not know how to specify the operations required to ascertain this measure. "A man's reach should exceed his grasp."

But the ability to calculate general progress hardly need remain limited because of our ignorance. General progress can be stated in other, more well-known terms: in terms of organization. Thermodynamic accomplishment has its structural concomitant, greater organization. The relation between energy-harnessing and organization is reciprocal: the more energy concentrated the greater the structure, and the more complicated the structure the more energy that can be harnessed. What is meant by "greater," "higher," or "more complicated" organization? The connotations of these terms are embraced within another, even more formidable one: "level of integration."

The idea of level of integration can be broken down into three aspects. An organism is at a higher level of integration than another when it has more parts and sub-parts (a higher order of segmentation); when its parts are more specialized; and when the whole is more effectively integrated. Thus general progress in life proceeds in the development of specialized organs and organic subsystems, such as digestive, respiratory, reproductive, and the like, and also in the development of special mechanisms of integration, such as the central nervous system and the brain. When organisms are compared on this basis, over-all progress is clearly seen in the evolutionary record.

And there are still other yardsticks of life's general progress. These are again functional but not put thermodynamically. Huxley's phrase, "all-around adaptability," sums them up. Higher organisms are freer from environmental control than lower, or more precisely, they adapt to a greater variety of particular environments while less bound to any limited niche. It may be that this can also be expressed in terms of greater mobility: higher forms have more, and more complex, motions than lower. More developed organisms are more intelligent also, which is perhaps again only another way of saying that they have more complex motions. Finally, and related to all these aspects of all-round adaptability, higher forms have greater dominance ranges than less developed types.

To recapitulate: specific evolution is "descent with modification," the adaptive variation of life "along its many lines"; general evolution is the progressive emergence of higher life "stage by stage." The advance or improvement we see in specific evolution is relative to the adaptive problem; it is progress in the sense of progression a long a line from one point to another, from less to more adjusted to a given habitat. The progress of general evolution is, in contrast, absolute; it is passage from less to greater energy exploitation, lower to higher levels of integration, and less to greater all-round adaptability. Viewing evolution in its specific context, our perspective and taxonomy is phylogenetic, but the taxonomy of general evolution crosscuts lineages, grouping forms into stages of over-all development.

SPECIFIC AND GENERAL CULTURAL EVOLUTION

Culture continues the evolutionary process by new means. Since these cultural means are unique, cultural evolution takes on distinctive characteristics. But still culture diversifies by adaptive specialization and still it successively produces over-all higher forms. Culture, like life, undergoes specific and general evolution.

The cultural anthropologist surveying the ethnographic and archaeological achievements of his discipline is confronted by variety if nothing else. There are myriads of culture types, that is, of the culture characteristic of an ethnic group or a region, and an even greater variety of cultures proper, of the cultural organization of given cohesive societies. How has this come about? In a word, through adaptive modification: culture has diversified as it has filled in the variety of opportunities for human existence afforded by the earth. Such is the specific aspect of cultural evolution. One of the best statements it has received belongs to Herbert Spencer, who, ironically, is commonly and pejoratively categorized today as a "unilinear" evolutionist.

Like other kinds of progress, social progress is not linear but divergent and re-divergent. Each differentiated product gives origin to a new set of differentiated products. While spreading over the earth mankind have found environments of various characters, and in each case the social life fallen into, partly determined by the social life previously led, has been partly determined by the influences of the new environment; so that multiplying groups have tended ever to acquire differences, now major and now minor: there have arisen genera and species of societies.

That culture is man's means of adaptation is a commonplace. Culture provides the technology for appropriating nature's energy and putting it to service, as well as the social and ideological means of implementing the process. Economically, politically, and in other ways, a culture also adjusts to the other cultures of its milieu, to the superorganic part of its environment. . . . Cultures are organizations for doing something, for perpetuating human life and themselves. Logically as well as empirically, it follows that as the problems of survival vary, cultures accordingly change, that culture undergoes phylogenetic, adaptive development.

The raw materials of a culture's phylogenetic development are the available culture traits, both those within the culture itself and those that can be borrowed or appropriated from its superorganic environment. The orienting process of development is adaptation of these traits to the expropriation of nature's resources and to coping with outside cultural influence. In this orienting, adaptive process elements within a culture are synthesized to form new traits, an event we call "invention," and items made available from the outside are incorporated, a process we call "diffusion," or sometimes, "acculturation."

It is time we took stock of the specific evolutionary sophistication of our discipline. The culturological study of the mechanics of invention, diffusion, and cultural adaptation in general—including cultural ecology—is fairly well advanced. We need not bow before Huxley's invidious comparison of our understanding of cultural evolution and the "triumphant synthesis" of (specific) evolutionary biology. The synthesis exists in anthropology; it remains only to make it intellectually triumphant.

New cultural traits arising through adaptation can be considered adaptive advances. In this they are similar to structural and functional advances in species, although they are quite different in content. A cultural advance may appear as an innovation in kin reckoning, a "Dionysian" war complex, the elaboration of head-hunting, the development or the redefinition of the concept of mana, or any of a host of other things. Even an efflorescence of stone statuary can be viewed in an adaptive context (among others), as we suggested recently for the stone heads of Easter Island:

The earliest Easter Islanders arrived from the central Polynesian hearth with a ramage organization [in Fried's terms, "ranked lineages"] and a tradition of image carving. The organization was suited to and reinforced by communal labor and specialized production [in utilitarian spheres]. Environmental features of the new home largely precluded the use of communal and specialist labor in subsistence production. As a result, these efforts were channelled into an esoteric domain of culture. Perhaps facilitated by a tradition of carving, a limited amount of wood [yet] the availability of easily worked tuff, the canalization toward esoteric production took the particular direction that resulted in the renowned stone heads of Easter Island.

To cite further examples is unnecessary: recent years have witnessed an abundance of studies demonstrating that special cultural features arise in the process of adaptation. This is the kind of work in which Julian Steward has pioneered.

We are, unfortunately, still accustomed to speak of cultural adaptive modifications such as Easter Island stone images—or Australian section systems, Eskimo technical ingenuity, Northwest Coast potlatching, or Paleolithic cave art —as "cultural bents," manifestations of "cultural interest" or "cultural outlook." But to what purpose? Our understanding has not been enhanced (as usual) by restatement in anthropomorphic terms. In the evolutionary perspective these "bents" are adaptive specializations. So considered they can be interpreted in relation to selective pressures and the available means of maintaining a cultural organization given such pressures.

Adaptive advance is relative to the adaptive problem. In this context a Grecian urn is not a thing of beauty and a joy forever: it is not higher, or better, than a Chinese vase or a Hopi pot; among languages, suffixing tendencies are not more advanced than prefixing; Eskimo kin terminology is no higher than Crow; neither Eskimo nor Crow culture is more developed than the other. *Viewed specifically,* the adaptive modifications occurring in different historical circumstances are incomparable; each is adequate in its own way, given the adaptive problems confronted and the available means of meeting them. No one culture has a monopoly on or even necessarily more kinds of adaptive improvements, and what is selectively advantageous for one may be simply ruinous for another. Nor are those cultures that we might consider higher in general evolutionary standing necessarily more perfectly adapted to their environments than lower. Many great civilizations have fallen in the last 2,000 years, even in the midst of material plenty, while the Eskimos tenaciously maintained themselves in an incomparably more difficult habitat. The race is not to the swift, nor the battle to the strong.

When we look at the specific aspect of culture's evolution we are cultural relativists. But this is not justification for the extension or the distortion of the relativist injunction that says "progress" is only a moral judgment, and all "progress," like all morality, is therefore only relative. Adaptive advances considered as such are relative. Like morals they are to be judged as more or less effective specializations. But general progress also occurs in culture, and it can be absolutely, objectively, and nonmoralistically ascertained.

So far specific cultural evolution has been treated much like specific biological evolution, often in identical terms; but there are also important differences. The fundamental differences stem from the fact that cultural variation, unlike biological, can be transmitted between different lines by diffusion. Separate cultural traditions, unlike separate biological lineages, may converge by coalescence. Moreover, partial phylogenetic continuity sometimes occurs between successive general stages of cultural evolution as backward cultures, borrowing wholesale the achievements of higher forms, push on to new evolutionary heights without recapitulating all intermediate stages of development. By contrast, each new adaptive step is a point of no return for biological populations; they can only (at best) move forward to that full specialization which is ultimately the (dead) end of further progress. In the same connection, replacement of a less highly developed by a more progressive cultural form can be accomplished by diffusion or acculturation, which has the advantage for people that a higher culture may dominate without total destruction of the population, or even loss of ethnic or social integrity, of the lower. In the chapters to follow these unique qualities of cultural evolution are examined in detail.

While convergence by diffusion is common in specific cultural evolution, so is parallel independent development, as anthropology has learned well after years of controversy over "diffusion versus independent invention." Perhaps parallel, independent development—the consequence of similar adaptation to similar environment—is more common in culture than comparable phenomena seem to be in life because of the limitation on variation imposed by the generic similarity and unity of humanity, the "psychic unity of mankind." In any case, a professional anthropologist can immediately bring to mind a host of parallelisms or "regularities," as Steward calls them, in cultural evolution. Steward, incidentally, virtually equates parallelism with his term, "multilinear evolution," and, furthermore, asserts that multilinear evolution is anthropology's only road to profitable, albeit limited, evolutionary generalization. We have something to say about this in the concluding section of the chapter.

Specific evolution is not the whole of cultural evolution. Culture not only produces adaptive sequences of forms, but sequences of higher forms; it has not only undergone phylogenetic development, but over-all progress. In brief, culture has evolved in a general respect as well as a specific one.

General cultural evolution is the successive emergence of new levels of all-round development. This emergent process, however, is not necessarily a historically continuous, phylogenetic one, for new levels of general standing are often achieved in unconnected (or only partially connected) cultural traditions. The relation between general and specific cultural evolution can thus be depicted as we have done before for comparable aspects of biological evolution. *Mutatis mutandis,* Diagram 1 will serve for both —with the proviso that various culture lines may cross at many points to indicate convergence by diffusion.

The general perspective on cultural evolution has been labelled, by its critics, "universal evolution." Readers other than anthropologists may find this difficult to believe, but the very term "universal" has a negative connotation in this field because it suggests the search for broad generalization that has been virtually declared unscientific (!) by twentieth-century, academic, particularistic American anthropology. Correlatively, "universal evolution" is criticized on the grounds that it *is* universal, i.e., so general as to be vague, obvious, or simply truistic. We hope the reader, then, will pardon us for a rather long digression concerning the scientific value of the study of general evolution.

The objectives of general evolutionary research are the determination and explanation of the successive transformations of culture through its several stages of over-all progress. What progressive trends have emerged in warfare, for example, or in economy, in political institutions, or in the role of kinship in society? As the questions we ask are not posed in terms of adaptive modification, neither will our explanations be. In other words, studies of specific and general evolution lead in different directions, as has evolution itself.

Let us take for an example the evolutionary analysis of war. Considered phylogenetically or specifically, variations in warfare are related to the selective circumstances operating on the cultures involved. In this way we examine and explain the development of warfare among Plains Indians in the nineteenth century, or why it differs from war among California Indians or the Iroquois. Each type of warfare thus considered is a unique, historic type, to be interpreted with reference to its particular historical-ecological circumstances. Using a general perspective, however, we classify types of warfare as representatives of stages in the over-all development of that aspect of culture, and then trace the progressive trends in was as they unfold through these successive stages. (Incidentally, anyone can see from the example we have chosen that "progress" is not here equated with "good.") The progressive trends discovered might include such things as increase in the scale of war, in the size of armies and the numbers of casualties, in the duration of campaigns, and the significance of outcome for the survival of the societies involved. These trends find their explanation not in adaptation but by reference to other developments accompanying them in the general progress of culture, such as increasing economic productivity or the emergence of special political institutions. Our conclusions now are of the form: war changes in certain ways, such as increases in scale, duration, etc., in proportion to certain economic or political (or whatever) trends, such as increasing productivity. It is obvious that the evolution of war has involved both diversification and progressive development, and only the employment of both specific and general perspectives can confront the evolutionary whole.

Distinguishing diversification from progress, however, not only distinguishes kinds of evolutionary research and conclusions, it dissipates long-standing misconceptions. Here is a question typical of a whole range of such difficulties: is feudalism a general *stage* in the evolution of economic and political forms, the one antecedent to modern national economy? The affirmative has virtually been taken for granted in economic and political history, and not only of the Marxist variety, where the sequence slave-feudal-capitalist modes of production originated. If assumed to be true, then the unilineal implications of the evolutionary scheme are only logical. That is, if feudalism is the antecedent stage of the modern state, then it, along with "Middle Ages" and "natural economy," lies somewhere in the background of every modern civilization. So it is that in the discipline of history, the Near East, China, Japan, Africa, and a number of other places have been generously granted "Middle Ages."

But it is obvious nonsense to consider feudalism, Middle Ages, and natural economy as the *general stage* of evolution antecedent to high (modern) civilization. Many civilizations of antiquity that antedate feudalism in its classic European form, as well as some coeval and some later than it in other parts of the world, are more highly developed. Placing feudalism between these civilizations and modern nations in a hierarchy of over-all progress patently and unnecessarily invalidates the hierarchy; it obscures rather than illustrates the progressive trends in economy, society, and polity in the evolution of culture. Conversely, identifying the specific antecedents of modern civilizations throughout the world as "feudalism" is also obviously fallacious and obscures the historic course of development of these civilizations, however much it may illuminate the historic course of Western culture.

Is not Marx [in the *Communist Manifesto*] in reality beginning with an analysis of the social development of Western Europe and the countries brought from time to time within its orbit from the Dark Ages to the growth of an advanced system of Capitalism, and then trying to apply the results achieved by this analysis to human history as a whole? May not the first of these steps be valid, and the second invalid . . . Were the Dark Ages really an advance over the Roman Empire? Civilisation for civilisation, can anyone possibly believe that they were? (Cole)

Feudalism is a "stage" only in a *specific* sense, a step in the development of one line of civilization. The stage of general evolution achieved prior to the modern nation is best represented by such classical civilizations as the Roman, or by such oriental states as China, Sumer, and the Inca Empire. In the general perspective, feudalism is only a specific, backward form of this order of civilization, an underdeveloped form that happened to have greater evolutionary potential than the others and historically gave rise to a new level of achievement. There is nothing unusual in evolutionary "leapfrogging" of this sort. The failure to differentiate these general and specific facets of the development of civilization can only be a plague on both houses of evolutionary research and a disgrace to the whole evolutionary perspective.

The reader may well feel disturbed, if not deceived, by the preceding discussion. How can an exposition of the course of evolution arbitrarily rip cultures out of the context of time and history and place them, just as arbitrarily, in categories of lower and higer development, categories that are presumed to represent *successive* stages? We are confronting the taxonomic innovation that is required for the study of general evolution.

Perhaps it will help to point out that in biological evolution new forms of low degree are arising all the time, such as new forms of bacteria; in other words, the specific evolution of lower forms does not stop when they are by-passed by higher forms. It follows that the later form is not necessarily higher than the earlier; the *stages* or *levels* of general development are successive, but the particular representatives of successive stages need not be. To return to feudalism, it represents a lower level of general development than the civilizations of China, ancient Egypt, or Mesopotamia, although it arose later than these civilizations and happened to lead to a form still higher than any of them.

The fundamental difference between specific and general evolution appears in this: the former is a connected, historic sequence of forms, the latter a sequence of stages exemplified by forms of a given order of development. In general evolutionary classification, any representative of a given cultural stage is inherently as good as any other, whether the representative be contemporaneous and ethnographic or only archaeological. The assertion is strengthened very much by the knowledge that there is a generic relation between the technical subsystem of a culture and the social and philosophical subsystems, so that a contemporaneous primitive culture with a given technology is equivalent, for general purposes, to certain extinct ones known only by the remains of a similar technology.

The *unit* of general evolutionary taxonomy, it should be noted, is a cultural system proper, that is, the cultural organization of a sociopolitical entity. A *level* of general development is a class of cultures of a given order. But what are the criteria for placing particular cultures in such classes, for deciding which is higher and which lower?

In culture, as in life, thermodynamic accomplishment is fundamental to progress, and therefore would appear useful as a criterion of emergent development. It is well known that revolutionary all-round advance occurs when and where new sources of energy are tapped, or major technological improvements are applied to already available sources. But here we enter a caveat similar to that brought up in connection with the thermodynamic development of life: general progress is not to be equated with thermodynamic *efficiency*.

Technological innovation can raise efficiency, i.e., increase the amount of energy captured per unit of human energy expended, yet still not stimulate the progressive development of a culture. Whether or not, or to what extent, a gain in productive efficiency is actually employed in the build-up and maintenance of higher organization depends on local selective circumstances. An increase in efficiency may not be directed toward any advance whatsoever if the existing adaptation cannot accommodate it or the selective pressures remain insufficient to induce it. A people may adopt a technological innovation that theoretically might double output, but instead, they only work half as long (twice as efficiently) as they used to. Such, indeed, is a common outcome of the imposition, however "well-meaning," of Western technology the world over. Or, as Harris has pointed out, a gain in efficiency can as well be put into increasing population as into more goods and services, means of communication, new political systems, or the promulgation of transcendental philosophies, and so forth. A continuation on this course will eventually lead to an expansion of population beyond available social means of organizing it. In an open environment the society will fission into two or more societies, each at a relatively low level of cultural organization, rather than producing one cultural system of a high order of development. Progress is not the inevitable outcome of efficiency.

It seems to us that progress is the total transformation of energy involved in the creation and perpetuation of a cultural organization. A culture harnesses and delivers energy; it extracts energy from nature and transforms it into people, material goods, and work, into political systems and the generation of ideas, into social customs and into adherence to them. The total energy so transformed from the free to the cultural state, in combination perhaps with the degree to which it is raised in the transformation (the loss in entropy), may represent a culture's general standing, a measure of its achievement.

The reader will surmise from the qualified phraseology that we are once more on uncertain ground. It is hardly consolation that we share this unenviable position with our colleagues; it does not appear that any satisfactory and usable method of quantifying the thermodynamic achievements of different cultures has been developed—or even that, with a few exceptions, any one is very much concerned. Perhaps a start can be made by estimating the total mechanical energy delivered per year by a society. Among primitives, where human beings are usually the sole form of mechanical energy, the calculation would be relatively simple: population size multiplied by average manpower (in energy units) over the year. In societies using nonhuman mechanical energy as well as human, the two are added together—statistics of the amount of nonhuman mechanical energy of many modern societies are avilable.

Although there is a lack, for the moment, of ready estimations of cultural progress in energy terms, the attempt to measure general standing need by no means be abandoned. There are good structural criteria. As in life, thermodynamic achievement has its organizational counterpart, higher levels of integration. Cultures that transform more energy have more parts and subsystems, more specialization of parts, and more effective means of integration of the whole. Organizational symptoms of general progress include the proliferation of material elements, geometric increase in the division of labor, multiplication of social groups and subgroups, and the emergence of special means of integration: political, such as chieftainship and the state, and philosophical, such as universal ethical religions and science. Long ago, Spencer described all this in painstaking, if not always accurate, detail. Although many social scientists deny that the idea of "progress" is applicable to culture, how can it be denied in the terms we have just stated it? As Greenberg remarks—despite the fact that he rejects the term "progress," after having defined it morally— a theory

. . . which regarded all species as interconnected but which posited some mammalian form as the primeval ancestral type, whence descended in one line all the other vertebrates, in another the ancestor of all non-vertebrate phyla, with Protozoa first appearing in a very recent period, would not be adjudged a representative evolutionary theory.

Similarly, culture has not fallen from evolutionary heights; it has risen to them.

The social subsystem of cultures is especially illustrative of progress in organization, and it is often used to ascertain general evolutionary standing. The traditional and fundamental division of culture into two great stages, primitive and civilized. is usually recognized as a social distinction: the emergence of a special means of integration, the state, separates civilization from primitive society organized by kinship.

Within the levels *societas* and *civitas,* moreover, further stages can be discriminated on criteria of social segmentation and integration. On the primitive level, the unsegmented (except for families) and chiefless *bands* are least advanced —and characteristically, preagricultural. More highly developed are agricultural and pastoral tribes segmented into clans, lineages, and the like, although lacking strong chiefs. Higher than such egalitarian *tribes,* and based on greater productivity, are *chiefdoms* with internal status differentiation and developed chieftainship. Similarly, within the level of civilization we can distinguish the *archaic* form—characteristically ethnically diverse and lacking firm integration of the rural, peasant sector—from the more highly developed, more territorially and culturally integrated *nation state,* with its industrial technology.

General progress can also be viewed as improvement in "all-round adaptability." Higher cultural forms tend to dominate and replace lower, and the range of dominance is proportionate to the degree of progress. So modern national culture tends to spread around the globe, before our eyes replacing, transforming, and extinguishing representatives of millennia-old stages of evolution, while archaic civilization, now also falling before this advance, even in its day was confined to certain sectors of certain of the continents. The dominance power of higher cultural forms is a consequence of their ability to exploit greater ranges of energy resources more effectively than lower forms. Higher forms are again relatively "free from environmental control," i.e., they adapt to greater environmental variety than lower forms. (By way of aside, the human participants in this process typically articulate the increasing all-round adaptability of higher civilizations as increase in their *own* powers: the more energy and habitats culture masters, the more man becomes convinced of his own control of destiny and the more he seems to proclaim his anthropocentric view of the whole cultural process. In the past we humbly explained our limited success as a gift of the gods: we were *chosen* people; now we are *choosing* people.)

General cultural evolution, to summarize, is passage from less to greater energy transformation, lower to higher levels of integration, and less to greater all-round adaptability. Specific evolution is the phylogenetic, ramifying, historic passage of culture along its many lines, the adaptive modification of particular cultures.

SOME IMPLICATIONS

We should now like to relate the distinction drawn between specific and general evolution to current scholarly views of evolution, particularly to anthropological views.

But first a word about terms: "specific evolution" and "general evolution" are probably not the best possible labels for the adaptive and over-all progressive aspects of the evolutionary process. Friends and colleagues have suggested others: "lineal," "adaptive," "special," "particular," and "divergent" have been offered for "specific"; "emergent," "progressive," or "universal" for "general." All the alternatives we judge to be somewhat inadequate, for one reason or another, although some were occasionally used in the preceding discussion. In a recent publication, Greenberg distinguishes "transformism" from "advance" in evolution, which seems to correspond to our "specific" and "general." The reader is free to adopt any of the alternatives. The terms are not the issue; the issue is empirical realities.

. . . when we define a word we are merely inviting others to use it as we would like it to be used . . . the purpose of definition is to focus argument upon fact, and . . . the proper result of good definition is to transform argument over terms into disagreements about fact, and thus open arguments to further inquiry. (Mills)

In biology, the differentiation between general and specific aspects of the evolutionary process has not recently been of great concern. Modern evolutionary biology has chosen to confine itself to the phylogenetic course of life; as noted before, the heralded "modern synthetic theory" is wholly devoted to this. The true "triumphant synthesis" which would unify the particular and general facets of evolution does not exist in biology.

Yet failure to distinguish specific and general evolution, it seems to us, has occasioned some confusion in biology about the nature of evolutionary progress. All-round progress is not detached from relative, specific progression, which apparently leads many biologists, even eminent ones such as Simpson, to virtually deny that progress is a general consequence of evolution. In fact, in a recent article Simpson insists that evolution is only "historical" (i.e., specific) and denies that comparative anatom-

ical studies (i.e., general evolution) are evolutionary at all:

In comparative anatomy some such sequence as dogfish-frog-cat-man is still frequently taught as "evolutionary," i.e., historical. In fact the anatomical differences among those organisms are in large part ecologically and behaviorally determined, are divergent and not sequential, and *do not in any useful sense form a historical series.* The same objection applies with perhaps even greater force to studies of behavior which state or assume an evolutionary (historical) sequence in, for instance, comparison of an insect ("invertebrate level"), a rat ("primitive mammalian level"), and a man. (Emphasis ours.)

Simpson is not willing to rise above the phylogenetic perspective that dominates biology today. The cultural anthropologist will recognize current biological dogmas such as "all progress is relative"—which is false—and "historically divergent forms defy sequential classification by levels of development." They are precisely the dicta that have held back the study of general cultural evolution for the last sixty years. It is almost as if biologists have fallen before a sterile "cultural analogy."

Julian Huxley should be exempted from this stricture, for he has long insisted on separating the over-all progressive from the divergent trends in evolution. Indeed, Huxley considers the former far more important than diversity, which he characterizes as, "a mere frill of variety . . . a biological luxury, without bearing upon the major and continuing trends of the evolutionary process." When one considers how much thought, effort, expense, and interest is now vested in biology on a "mere frill of variety," Huxley's assertion is really startling, if not revolutionary. But it is not our intention to begin revolutionary agitations, particularly in what is not our own fatherland.

The traditional evolutionary concerns of anthropology have been precisely the reverse of those in biology, for until recently general evolution rather than specific has occupied first place in evolutionary anthropology. The way the great nineteenth-century cultural evolutionists, Tylor, Spencer, and Morgan, classified and considered cultures indicates that they were principally interested in general progress. Their procedure was to determine *stages* of development and to exemplify them with contemporaneous cultures.

For this reason alone it would be difficult to support the charge that evolutionary theory was grafted wholesale from biology onto culture, or that it was only "biological analogy." It also seems grossly inaccurate, however frequently it is done, to characterize the perspective of the anthropological pioneers as "unilinear," which is the idea that every culture in particular goes through the same general stages. The locus of unilinear evolutionism is not in anthropology, but, as we have seen with respect to the problem of feudalism, in "crude Marxism" (this phrase is a kind of current redundancy) and Bourgeois History . . . strange bedfellows. Considering only their procedures and obvious objectives—and not what they or others have said *ad hoc* about these—the nineteenth-century anthropological evolutionists should be acquitted of the unilinear charge, once and for all. Because the specific aspect of evolution was not given much attention does not warrant a criticism which says, in effect, that it was lumped with the general, thus yielding unilinear evolution. The error, if any, was omission not commission. And even so, we recall Spencer's words, "Like other kinds of progress, social progress is *not linear* but divergent and re-divergent" (our emphasis).

But they are dead, and it probably doesn't matter too much if exonerated or not. What progress has evolutionary anthropology made since the nineteenth century? The current revival of evolutionism in anthropology is, with the exception of White, decisively specifically oriented. By and large, it is particularistic and historically oriented, as anthropology in general has been throughout our century. Steward's "multilinear evolution" is now widely accepted and respectable. This is a gain, for as a platform, multilinear evolution conceivably embraces all of the specific trends in cultural evolution. But at what cost shall we secure this gain? In practice, Steward confines his attention to "regularities," which is to say, parallel developments in unrelated cultural lines, and at the same time belabors any more general evolutionary concerns. If anthropology continues on this theoretical course, then it can only fail to cope with the larger problem of the origin of diversity, not to mention the whole field of general evolution. Thus the total effect of widespread approval of Steward's position will mean undue limitation, a continuation of the reaction against the nineteenth century.

The historical orientation of twentieth-century American anthropology and of much of its current evolutionism has occasioned a rich con-troversy in recent years about the relation between "history" and "evolution." A set of interconnected issues are involved: (1) Is evolution to be concerned with historical developments in particular cultures or not? (2) Is environment a relevant, variable factor in the explanation of evolution or an irrelevant, constant factor? (3) Is evolution "history," or are these different real processes? The chief antagonists in the controversy are Kroeber, Steward, and White.

White distinguishes history as unique sequences of events located in time and space, whereas evolution is the progression of forms not considered in reference to specific times and places:

In the evolutionist process we are not concerned with unique events, fixed in time and place, but with a *class* of events without reference to specific times and places . . . The historian—devotes himself to a specific sequence of particular events; the evolutionist, to a sequence of events as a general process of transformation.

Since evolution does not deal with specifics, since it is concerned with classes of cultural forms, culture is considered as a whole and particular environments are not relevant, in White's view:

The functioning of any particular culture will of course be conditioned by local environmental conditions. But in a consideration of culture as a whole, we may average all environments together to form a constant factor which may be excluded from our formula of cultural development.

Not many accept White's attempt to distinguish history from evolution; many profess not to understand it. Perhaps that is why White is labelled a "neoevolutionary," although, as he says, all he states is the general evolutionary perspective of the nineteenth century.

Kroeber, in an exchange with White, insists that evolution is primarily the historic process, and that historians "do" evolution. Murdock goes Kroeber one better: "The only cultural processes are historical," he writes. And ten years later, ". . . evolution consists of real events, not of abstractions from events, so that evolutionary development is historical in the strictest and most literal sense." Likewise, for Steward (multilinear) evolution is concerned with, "significant parallels in culture *history* . . . *inevitably* concerned with historical reconstruction" (emphasis ours). In turn, parallel development is parallel adaptation to *environment;* environmental considerations are indispensable.

The distinction between general and specific evolution is relevant to—and we think, resolves —the debate. The historic development of particular cultural forms is specific evolution, phylogenetic transformation through adaptation. Environment, both natural and superorganic, is obviously essential to the understanding of such processes. The progression of *classes* of forms, or in other words, the succession of culture through stages of over-all progress, is general evolution. This process is neither phylogenetic nor as such adaptive; consequently, environment is "constant," or better, irrelevant. That process which Kroeber labels "history," Steward, "multilinear evolution," and Murdock, "evolution," is the specific aspect of the grand

evolutionary movement; that which White names "evolution" is the general aspect. Adopting the grand-movement perspective suggested here, evolution is in one respect "history," but in another not; in one aspect it involves particular events, but in another classes thereof; in one respect environment is relevant, but in another it is to be excluded from consideration. Each of the participants in the controversy is in one respect "right" but in another "wrong"—from our standpoint.

And, if we may be permitted to press home the implications, it seems to us then that evolutionism is the central, inclusive, organizing outlook of anthropology, comparable in its theoretical power to evolutionism in biology. ". . . the great principle that every scholar must lay firm hold of . . ."

25

MULTILINEAR EVOLUTION: EVOLUTION AND PROCESS

JULIAN H. STEWARD

THE MEANING OF EVOLUTION

CULTURAL evolution, although long an unfashionable concept, has commanded renewed interest in the last two decades. This interest does not indicate any serious reconsideration of the particular historical reconstructions of the nineteenth-century evolutionists, for these were quite thoroughly discredited on empirical grounds. It arises from the potential methodological importance of cultural evolution for contemporary research, from the implications of its scientific objectives, its taxonomic procedures, and its conceptualization of historical change and cultural causality. An appraisal of cultural evolution, therefore, must be concerned with definitions and meanings. But I do not

wish to engage in semantics. I shall attempt to show that if certain distinctions in the concept of evolution are made, it is evident that certain methodological propositions find fairly wide acceptance today.

In order to clear the ground, it is necessary first to consider the meaning of cultural evolution in relation to biological evolution, for there is a wide tendency to consider the former as an extension of, and therefore analogous to, the latter. There is, of course, a relationship between biological and cultural evolution in that a minimal development of the Hominidae was a precondition of culture. But cultural evolution is an extension of biological evolution only in a chronological sense (Huxley). The nature of the evolutionary schemes and of the developmental processes differs profoundly in biology and in culture. In biological evolution it is assumed that all forms are genetically related and that their development is essentially divergent. Parallels, such as the development of flying, swimming, and warm blood, are superficial and fairly uncommon. These latter, moreover, are generally considered to be instances of convergent evolution rather than true parallels. In cultural evolution, on the other hand, it is assumed that cultural patterns in different parts of the world are genetically unrelated and yet pass through parallel sequences. Divergent trends which do not follow the postulated universal sequence, such as those caused by distinctive local environments, are attributed only secondary importance. Such modern-day unilinear evolutionists as Leslie White and V. Gordon Childe evade the awkward facts of cultural divergence and local variation by purporting to deal with culture as a whole rather than with particular cultures. But Childe quite explicitly distinguishes biological from cultural evolution by stressing the divergent nature of the former and the operation of diffusion and the frequency of convergence in the latter. It is interesting that such history as is implied in cultural relativism is rather similar to that of biological evolution: the variations and unique patterns of the different areas and subareas are clearly conceived to represent divergent development and presumably an ultimate genetic relationship. It is only the complementary concept of diffusion, a phenomenon unknown in biology, that prevents cultural relativism from having an exclusively genetic significance, like that of biological evolution.

Analogies between cultural and biological evolution are also alleged to be represented by two attributes of each: first, a tendency toward increasing complexity of forms and, second, the development of superior forms, that is, improvement or progress. It is, of course, quite possible to define complexity and progress so as to make them characteristic of evolution. But they are not attributes exclusively of evolution; they may also be considered characteristics of cultural change or development as conceived from any nonevolutionary point of view.

The assumption that cultural change normally involves increasing complexity is found in virtually all historical interpretations of cultural data. But complexity in biology and culture differ. As Kroeber states: "The process of cultural development is an additive and therefore accumulative one, whereas the process of organic evolution is a substitutive one." It is on the question not of complexity but of divergence that the relativists and evolutionists differ. According to the latter, cumulative change follows parallel trends, whereas, according to the former,

it is ordinarily divergent, though sometimes it is convergent and occasionally it is parallel.

Although complexity as such is not distinctive of the evolutionary concept, an allied concept might be considered to distinguish both biological and cultural evolution from nonevolutionary cultural-historical concepts. This is the concept of organizational types and levels. Whereas relativism seems to hold that a rather fixed and qualitatively unique pattern persists in each cultural tradition, despite cumulative changes which create quantitative complexity, it is implicit in the evolutionary view that development levels are marked by the appearance of qualitatively distinctive patterns or types of organization. Just as simple unicellular forms of life are succeeded by multicellular and internally specialized forms which have distinctive kinds of total organization, so social forms consisting of single families and lineages are succeeded by multifamilial communities, bands, or tribes, and these, in turn, by state patterns, each involving not only greater internal heterogeneity and specialization but wholly new kinds of overall integration. Thus evolutionism is distinguished from relativism by the fact that the former attributes qualitative distinctiveness to successive stages, regardless of the particular tradition, whereas the latter attributes it to the particular tradition or culture area rather than to the development stage.

This brings us to the question of progress, which is the second characteristic attributed to both biological and cultural evolution. Progress must be measured by definable values. Most of the social sciences are still so ethnocentric, especially in their practical applications, that value judgments are almost inescapable. Even the "Statement on Human Rights" (1947) offered to the United Nations by the American Anthropological Association clearly reflects the American value placed upon individual rights and political democracy. This or any other criterion of value, however, certainly does not imply evolution. In fact, the concept of progress is largely separable from evolution, and it may be approached in many ways. Kroeber, who is by no means an evolutionist, suggests three criteria for measuring progress: "the atrophy of magic based on psychopathology; the decline of infantile obsession with the outstanding physiological events of human life; and the persistent tendency of technology and science to grow accumulatively." These values are not absolute in a philosophical sense; they are "the ways in which progress may legitimately be considered a property or an attribute of culture." By definition, then, it is possible although not necessary to regard progress as a characteristic of any form of cultural change, whether it is considered evolutionary or not.

We must conclude that cultural evolution is not distinguished from cultural relativism or historical particularism by any essential similarity of its developmental scheme with that of biological evolution, by the characteristic of increasing complexity, or by the attribute of progress. This is not to say, however, that evolution lacks distinctive features. The methodology of evolution contains two vitally important assumptions. First, it postulates that genuine parallels of form and function develop in historically independent sequences or cultural traditions. Second, it explains these parallels by the independent operation of identical causality in each case. The methodology is therefore avowedly scientific and generalizing rather than historical and particularizing. It is less concerned with unique and divergent (or convergent) patterns and features of culture—although it does not necessarily deny such divergence—than with parallels and similarities which recur cross-culturally. It endeavors to determine recurrent patterns and processes and to formulate the interrelationships between phenomena in terms of "laws." The nineteenth-century evolutionists are important to contemporary studies more because of their scientific objective and preoccupation with laws than because of their particular substantive historical reconstructions.

Cultural evolution, then, may be defined broadly as a quest for cultural regularities or laws; but there are three distinctive ways in which evolutionary data may be handled. First, *unilinear evolution,* the classical nineteenth-century formulation, dealt with particular cultures, placing them in stages of a universal sequence. Second, *universal evolution*—a rather arbitrary label to designate the modern revamping of unilinear evolution—is concerned with culture rather than with cultures. Third, *multilinear evolution,* a somewhat less ambitious approach than the other two, is like unilinear evolution in dealing with developmental sequences, but it is distinctive in searching for parallels of limited occurrence instead of universals.

The criticial differences between these three concepts of evolution have not been recognized, and there is still a general tendency to identify any effort to determine similar form and process in parallel developments with nineteenth-century unilinear evolution and thus categorically to reject it. The Marxist and Communist adoption of nineteenth-century evolutionism, especially of L. H. Morgan's scheme, as official dogma, has certainly not favored the acceptability to scientists of the Western nations of anything labeled "evolution."

UNILINEAR EVOLUTION

There is no need to discuss the validity of the nineteenth-century evolutionary schemes, for their vulnerability in the face of twentieth-century archaeological and ethnographic research has been amply demonstrated. Although no effort has been made to revise these schemes in the light of new empirical data concerning the history of individual cultures—which itself is a somewhat remarkable fact—it does not necessarily follow that L. H. Morgan and his contemporaries failed completely to recognize significant patterns and processes of change in particular cases. The inadequacy of unilinear evolution lies largely in the postulated priority of matriarchal patterns over the other kinship patterns and in the indiscriminate effort to force the data of all precivilized groups of mankind, which included most of the primitive world, into the categories of "savagery" and "barbarism." The category of "civilization," however, involved a less sweeping generalization for the simple reason that civilization was thought of largely in terms of the Near East, the northern Mediterranean, and nothern Europe. Other areas which achieved civilization, particularly the New World, were far less known and have been accorded less attention.

In other words, whereas the historical reconstruction and the deductions derived therefrom were largely wrong as regards early stages of cultural development because they failed to recognize the many varieties of local trends, the analyses of civilization contain many valuable insights because they are based more specifically upon developments which occurred first in Egypt and Mesopotamia and later in Greece, Rome, and northern Europe. Although comparisons with other areas, particularly with the Americas but also with India and China, left much to be desired so far as forms, functions, and developmental processes of civilization in general are concerned, the conclusions may nonetheless be valid under limited circumstances. Thus Henry Maine's insights concerning the processes involved in development from a kin-based society to a territorial, state society undoubtedly throw light on cultural development in many areas, though not necessarily on all. Such categories as "kin-based" and "state" are too broad; distinctions between particular, though recurrent, types within these categories are needed.

There are probably many developmental forms and processes discussed by the evolutionists which have validity, provided that they are considered qualities of particular cultural traditions rather than universal characteristics of culture. The extremely illuminating analyses that V. Gordon Childe and others have given us of cultural development in the eastern Mediterranean and Europe probably would find certain rather precise parallels in other world areas if a truly comparative study were made. Significantly, however, Childe's approach to evolution on a wider scale has entailed a retreat into broad generalizations.

UNIVERSAL EVOLUTION

Universal evolution, which is represented today principally by Leslie White and V. Gordon Childe, is the heritage of nineteenth-century unilinear evolution, especially as formulated by L. H. Morgan, in the scope of its generalizations but not in its treatment of particulars. Aware that empirical research of the twentieth century has invalidated the unilinear historical reconstructions of particular cultures, which constituted the essential feature of nineteenth-century schemes, White and Childe endeavor to keep the evolutionary concept of cultural stages alive by relating these stages to the culture of mankind as a whole. The distinctive cultural traditions and the local variations—the culture areas and subareas—which have developed as the result of special historical trends and of cultural ecological adaptations to special environments are excluded as irrelevant. White states: "We may say that culture as a whole serves the need of man as a species. But this does not and cannot help us at all when we try to account for the variations of specific culture. . . . The functioning of any particular culture will of course be conditioned by local environmental conditions. But in a consideration of culture as a whole, we may *average all environments together* to form a constant factor which may be excluded from our formulation

of cultural development" (Steward, italics mine). Childe reconciles the general and particular in much the same way. He writes that "all societies have lived in different historical environments and have passed through different vicissitudes, their traditions have diverged, and so ethnography reveals a multiplicity of cultures, just as does archaeology." Childe finds that consideration of the particular is a "serious handicap if our objective is to establish general stages in the evolution of cultures," and, therefore, in order to "discover general laws descriptive of the evolution of all societies, we abstract . . . the peculiarities due to differences of habitat." Diffusion must also be discounted, because any society must be in a position to accept diffused technological and social features. At the same time, while local developments within each general stage are largely divergent, the concept of evolution is salvaged by assuming that diffusion brings technological and social features to all societies, thus convergently re-creating the required patterns. This rather involved effort to enlist diffusion in order to offset divergent evolution is based empirically almost exclusively upon Old World data. How Old World and New World parallels would square with such reasoning Childe does not say.

It is interesting that White's theoretical discussions make no reference to his own extensive and detailed studies of the Pueblo Indians and that Childe's superb knowledge of developmental patterns and processes which are disclosed in the archaeology of the Near East and Europe becomes almost an embarrassment in his theoretical discussions. Childe's insights into the cultural development of these two areas are most illuminating, but he merely confuses the two areas when he endeavors to fit them into simplified developmental stages.

It is important to recognize that the evolutionism of White and Childe yields substantive results of a very different order from those of nineteenth-century evolution. The postulated cultural sequences are so general that they are neither very arguable nor very useful. No one disputes that hunting and gathering, which is Childe's diagnostic of "savagery," preceded plant and animal domestication which is his criterion of "barbarism," and that the latter was a precondition of large populations, cities, internal social differentiation and specialization, and the development of writing and mathematics, which are characteristics of "civilization."

If one examines universal evolution with a view to finding laws or processes of development rather than examining it merely in terms of a sequential reconstruction of culture, it is also difficult to recognize anything strikingly new or controversial. The generalization that culture changes from the simple to the complex and White's "law" that technological development expressed in terms of man's control over energy underlies certain cultural achievements and social changes have long been accepted. Childe's transfer of the Darwinian formula to cultural evolution also will not evoke challenge. Variation is seen as invention, heredity as learning and diffusion, and adaptation and selection as cultural adaptation and choice. It is certainly a worthy objective to seek universal laws of cultural change. It must be stressed, however, that all universal laws thus far postulated are concerned with the fact that culture changes —that any culture changes—and thus cannot explain particular features of particular cultures. In this respect, the "laws" of cultural and biological evolution are similar. Variation, heredity, and natural selection cannot explain a single life-form, for they do not deal with the characteristics of particular species and do not take into account the incalculable number of particular circumstances and factors that cause biological differentiation in each species. Similarly, White's law of energy levels, for example, can tell us nothing about the development of the characteristics of individual cultures. We may deduce from the data of both biological and cultural evolution that new organizational forms will appear in succession, but the specific nature of these forms can be understood only by tracing the history of each in great detail.

The problem and method of universal evolution thus differ from those of unilinear evolution. Right or wrong, the nineteenth-century evolutionists did attempt to explain concretely why a matriarchy should precede other social forms, why animism was the precursor of gods and spirits, why a kin-based society evolved into a territorial-based, state-controlled society, and why other specific features of culture appeared.

MULTILINEAR EVOLUTION

Multilinear evolution is essentially a methodology based on the assumption that significant regularities in cultural change occur, and it is concerned with the determination of cultural laws. Its method is empirical rather than deductive. It is inevitably concerned also with historical reconstruction, but it does not expect that historical data can be classified in universal stages. It is interested in particular cultures, but instead of finding local variations and diversity troublesome facts which force the frame of reference from the particular to the general, it deals only with those limited parallels of form, function, and sequence which have empirical validity. What is lost in universality will be gained in concreteness and specificity. Multilinear evolution, therefore, has no a priori scheme or laws. It recognizes that the cultural traditions of different areas may be wholly or partly distinctive, and it simply poses the question of whether any genuine or meaningful similarities between certain cultures exist and whether these lend themselves to formulation. These similarities may involve salient features of whole cultures, or they may involve only special features, such as clans, men's societies, social classes of various kinds, priesthoods, military patterns, and the like.

It may be objected that a limited formulation which postulates that some special feature—let us say a clan—has developed in two or more cultures independently for the same reasons cannot be considered evolution. We thus return to definitions. If evolution can be considered an interest in determining recurrent forms, processes, and functions rather than world-embracing schemes and universal laws, the many efforts to make scientific generalizations, whether they deal with synchronic, functional relationships or with diachronic, sequential relationships and whether they embrace few or many cultures, are methodologically akin to evolution. The nineteenth-century evolutionists were deeply interested in making generalizations.

THE METHOD OF MULTILINEAR EVOLUTION

PARALLELISM AND CAUSALITY

An implicit interest in parallelism and causality has always been present in cultural studies, and it seems to have increased during the last two decades. It would be quite surprising, in fact, if anyone held so tenaciously to the logical implications of the relativist position as to claim that understandings derived from the analysis of one culture did not provide some insights as to form, function, and process in others. The difficulty is in raising these insights from the level of hunches to that of explicit formulations. Postulated parallels and recurrent cause-and-effect relations are regarded with suspicion. They may be questioned on empirical grounds; and the inherent difficulty of deriving cultural laws may be attacked on philosophical grounds. The methodology of cultural studies thus remains predominantly that of historical particularizing rather than of scientific generalizing.

A genuine interest in parallels, however, has been clearly expressed by many scholars who have made outstanding contributions within the framework of the so-called "Boas school." Thus Lowie, who was unsparing of L. H. Morgan's unilinear reconstruction, not only recognizes independent invention and parallel development in many features, such as moieties, dual systems of numbers, messianic cults, and others, but he is quite prepared to accept a kind of necessity in cultural development to the extent that certain cultural achievements presuppose others. "If a tribe practices metallurgy it is clearly not on the plane of savagery; only stockbreeders and farmers forge metal." But he denies that cultures can be graded on the basis of metallurgy because the Africans, for example, were metallurgists but lacked other features of more developed civilizations. Although Lowie cannot accept Morgan's unilinear evolution, he is in accord with most of the profession in accepting such generalizations as universal evolution has to offer, and moreover, he is something of a multilinear evolutionist. Who, then, is more of an evolutionist, Lowie or White?

American anthropologists have traditionally assumed that there were Old World and New World parallels in the invention of farming, stockbreeding, ceramics, metallurgy, states, priests, temples, the zero and mathematics, writing, and other features. It would perhaps be going too far to say that this makes them multilinear evolutionists. When the question of parallel cultural causality arises, these similarities are held to be only superficial or to represent convergent evolution, or else it is said that the historical and functional relationships involved are as yet too imperfectly understood to permit formulation in terms of cross-cultural regularities. Nevertheless, many persons have recognized such a deep significance in these parallels that they believe diffusion must have occurred between the hemispheres, while others

have attempted to formulate Old and New World sequences in terms of comparable developmental periods.

Kroeber did not hesitate to conclude from the numerous parallels in different parts of the world that "culture relations or patterns develop spontaneously or from within probably more frequently than as a result of direct taking-over. Also, the types of culture forms being limited in number, the same type is frequently evolved independently. Thus, monarchical and democratic societies, feudal or caste-divided ones, priest-ridden and relatively irreligious ones, expansive and mercantile or self-sufficient and agricultural nations, evolve over and over again." Elsewhere, I have called attention to statements by Lesser, Boas, Kidder, and others that cross-cultural understandings in terms of laws, regularities, or parallels—those who object to calling these "laws" may use some other term—are a major objective of anthropology. This list could be extended to include a substantial portion of the profession.

The determination and analysis of parallels as a methodological objective of multilinear evolution need not be carried out on a purely cultural level. Leslie White has argued so cogently in favor of understanding cultural change in strictly culturological terms that the impression may stand that culturology and evolution are synonymous. It is beyond the scope of this paper to argue the matter. But I must insist that White's elimination of both the human and the enviromental factors is an aspect of his concern with culture rather than with cultures. I have endeavored in various studies to demonstrate how cultural-ecological adaptations—the adaptive processes through which a historically derived culture is modified in a particular environment—are among the important creative processes in cultural change. There are certain problems in which man's rational and emotional potentials are not a zero factor in the equation. Thus Kluckhohn suggests: "If a tribe's customary outlet for aggression in war is blocked, one may predict an increase in intratribal hostility (perhaps in the form of witchcraft) or in pathological states of melancholy resultant upon anger being turned inward against the self." This psychological attribute of human beings which channels aggression in certain ways may be a significant factor in the formulation of certain cultural parallels. For example, among the Iroquois and their neighbors, war captives were adopted as members of the captor's family, then tortured and killed. Raymond Scheele has suggested that this pattern provides a means of diverting latent hostilities against kin to members of an alien group. A similar pattern is found among the Tupinamba of South America and among tribes in other parts of the world. Although the psychological premises and the cultural manifestations may be open to question, the data suggest a useful cross-cultural formulation of certain modes of behavior.

The kinds of parallels or similarities with which multilinear evolution deals are distinguished by their limited occurrence and their specificity. For this reason, the outstanding methodological problem of multilinear evolution is an appropriate taxonomy of cultural phenomena.

CULTURAL TAXONOMY

Any science must have precise means of identifying and classifying the recurrent phenomena with which it deals. It is symptomatic of the historical rather than the scientific orientation of cultural studies that there are few terms designating whole cultures or components of cultures which may be employed cross-culturally. "Plains culture," "East African cattle culture," "Chinese civilization," and the like designate culture areas which are conceived as unique patterns and complexes of elements. A great many sociological terms, such as "band," "tribe," "clan," "class," "state," "priest," and "shaman," are used to describe features which are found repeatedly in generically unrelated cultures, but they are much too general even to suggest parallels of form or process. The most precise terms designate very special technological features, such as "bow," "atlatl," or "ikat weaving." Such features, however, generally imply no large patterns, and the only inference ordinarily drawn from their distributions is that diffusion has taken place.

The present status of cultural taxonomy reveals a preoccupation with relativism, and practically all systems of classification are fundamentally derived from the culture-area concept. Basically, the culture area is characterized by a distinctive element content, which, on a tribal level at least, constitutes the shared behavior of all members of the society. Classification may give equal weight to all elements, as in Klimek's statistical handling of the culture-element lists which were compiled in the

University of California survey of western tribes or as in the midwestern or McKern method of classifying archaeological complexes. The former yields culture areas and subareas; the latter gives categories of associated elements, which of themselves are placed neither in time nor in space. Following Wissler, culture area classifications have tended strongly to emphasize economic features, although not all postulate so close a relationship between culture and environment as Wissler, and noneconomic traits receive emphasis which varies with the individual scholar and which may lead to a diversity of classificatory schemes for the same data. Thus South America has been grouped into five areas by Wissler, eleven by Stout, three by Cooper and by Bennett and Bird, four by the *Handbook of South American Indians* (Steward), and twenty-four by Murdock. Each gives primacy to features of interest to the individual. All these classifications are particular to the data of South America. None endeavors to recognize in any of the three to twenty-four areas structural or developmental features which are common to areas outside South America.

Classification of cultures in terms of value system or ethos has essentially the same basis as that of culture areas. Such classifications all presuppose a common core of shared culture traits which cause all members of the society to have the same outlook and psychological characteristics. Benedict's concept of pattern, Gorer's and Mead's concept of national character, and Morris Opler's concept of themes derive from a taxonomic approach that is basically like that of Wissler, Kroeber, Murdock, Herskovits, and others.

If a taxonomic system is to be devised for the purpose of determining cross-cultural parallels and regularities rather than of stressing contrasts and differences, there is needed a concept which may be designated "culture type." The difficulty of empirical determination of significant types has constituted the principal obstacle to a systematic search for regularities and parallels. By the present definition, a culture type differs from a culture area in several respects. First, it is characterized by selected features rather than by its total element content. Since no two cultures are quite alike in their element totality, it is necessary to select special constellations of causally interrelated features which are found among two or more, but not necessarily among all, cultures. Second, the selection of diagnostic features must be determined by the problem and frame of reference. Conceivably, any aspect of culture may be attributed primary taxonomic importance. Third, the selected features are presumed to have the same functional interrelationship with one another in each case.

Illustrative of cultural types are Wittfogel's "oriental absolute society," which exemplifies cause-and-effect regularities between a special kind of sociopolitical structure and an irrigation economy; the present author's "patrilineal band," which is characterized by certain inevitable relationships between a hunting economy, descent, marriage, and land tenure; Redfield's folk society, which has certain general features common to many, if not most, societies at a simple development or integrational level and which reacts to urban influences—at least to influences of the modern industrial type of urbanism—according to postulated regularities; and a feudal society, which once characterized both Japan and Europe, where it exhibited similarities in social and political structure and economy.

These few, illustrative types make economic and sociological features primary because scientific interest is widely centered in such features and because socioeconomic structure has therefore been more broadly examined and more readily formulated than other aspects of culture. Economic patterns are generally ascribed considerable importance because they are inextricably related to social and political patterns. Certain aspects of religion, however, are also included in Redfield's types. In an elaboration of Wittfogel's irrigation societies, the author has tentatively formulated developmental types which include not only social and political patterns but also technological, intellectual, military, and religious features that mark successive areas in the history of these societies.

A taxonomic scheme designed to facilitate the determination of parallels and regularities in terms of concrete characteristics and developmental processes will have to distinguish innumerable culture types, many of which have not as yet been recognized. A methodology like that of White and of Childe which ignores local particulars and deals only with world stages will not serve the purpose we have in mind. A stage of hunting and gathering, for example—or of savagery, to use the evolutionists' term—is far too broad a category. The functional relations and cultural-ecological adaptations which led to a patrilineal band, consisting of a localized lineage, were very different from those which produced a nomadic, bilateral band composed of many unrelated families. But these are only two of many types of hunting and gathering societies which developed as the result of particular cultural-historical and cultural-ecological circumstances. There are also types characterized by dispersed family groups, such as the Shoshoni and Eskimo, and by cohesive tribelets, such as those of California. Moreover, it does not at all follow that all hunters and gatherers are classifiable into types which have cross-cultural significance. Many may be unique, except as some limited feature of their culture parallels a similar feature of another culture—for instance, the development of clans.

Since hunting and gathering tribes fall into an undetermined number of cultural types, any larger developmental scheme cannot with certainty take any type as representative of a universal early stage, except in characteristics that are so general as to signify nothing concretely about any particular culture. The absence among hunters and gatherers of dense and stable population, of large permanent towns, of social classes and other kinds of complex internal specialization, of priesthoods, group ceremonialism, money, investment, writing, mathematics, and other characteristics of "civilized" people is to be expected. The particular forms of marriage, family, social structure, economic co-operation, socioreligious patterns, and other features found among these primitive societies differ in each type. Consequently, the objective is to ascertain the detailed processes by which hunters and gatherers were converted into farmers or herdsmen and these latter into more "civilized" people, and it is necessary to deal with particular types.

Among the farming cultures there is also a large variety of cultural types which have not been systematically classified with reference to problems of cross-cultural parallels or formulations of causality. Irrigation civilizations have received considerable attention. But the term "tropical forest agriculture" still refers merely to those who farm in the tropical rain forests rather than to specific crops, methods of farming, markets, and related cultural features. Possibly the culture areas of the rain forest in the Old and New World, including both the Mediterranean and the northern hardwood forests, developed indigenous unique culture types. It is more likely that significant parallels between such areas would be disclosed if they were compared with reference to environment, technology, and era of development.

At present, interest in parallels centers in the development of Old and New World civilizations. The parallels are striking and undeniable. They include the independent development—independent, that is, according to most but not all anthropologists—of an impressive list of basic features: domesticated plants and animals, irrigation, large towns and cities, metallurgy, social classes, states and empires, priesthoods, writing, calendars, and mathematics. Although there is still considerable tendency to stress the distinguishing features of each center or tradition and thus to view each as a culture area rather than as a culture type, interest in function and processes is gradually leading toward the use of comparable terminology. Instead of narrow technological terms like "Old Stone Age," "New Stone Age," and "Bronze Age," such potentially typological terms as "Formative," "Florescent" or "Classical," and "Empire" or "Fusion" are being used for the New World. For Old World development, Childe has introduced partially equivalent terms, such as "Urban Revolution." I think it is safe to predict that as interest centers more and more upon the functional interrelationship of cultural features and upon the processes by which cultures are adapted to a variety of environments, a taxonomy suggesting significant parallels will appear.

The conceptual basis of multilinear evolutionary taxonomy is no less applicable to contemporary trends of cultural change than to pre-Columbian changes. Today, the many distinctive varieties of native culture areas of the world—and these include whole nations, subcontinents, and continents, such as China, India, Southeast Asia, Africa, and Latin America—are being strongly affected by industrialization which diffuses primarily from Europe and America and secondarily from subcenters created in all continents.

Whether the particular features of industrial developments—the mechanization of farm and factory production, the cost accounting methods, corporate and credit financing, and the national and international systems of distribution and marketing—are considered to be a single world development or a number of quasi-independent growths from a general industrial basis, there appear to be rather striking parallels in the consequences of the diffused features. These parallels are classifiable in terms of trends toward the production of cash commodities, purchase of manufactured articles, individualization of land tenure, appearance of a cash-based rationale in values and goals, reduction of the kinship group to the nuclear family, emergence of middle classes of business, service, and professional personnel, sharpening of interclass tensions, and rise of nationalistic ideologies. All these are features which also characterize the peoples of Euro-American nations. But it would be too simple an explanation to say that these features were also merely diffused from Europe. Detailed study of native populations discloses processes which made the development of these features inevitable, even in the absence of sustained, face-to-face contacts between the native populations and Europeans which could introduce new practices and a new ethic. There is good reason to believe that the very fundamental changes now occurring in the most remote parts of the world are susceptible to formulation in terms of parallels or regularities, despite various local overtones which derive from the native cultural tradition. Although no very deliberate effort to formulate these regularities has yet been made, considerable contemporary research is directly concerned with modern trends, and the substantive results are probably sufficiently detailed to permit preliminary formulations.

Not all parallels need be based essentially upon a developmental sequence. Thus Redfield's postulated regularities in the changes of a folk society under urbanizing influence can hardly be called "evolution." However, it is our basic premise that the crucial methodological feature of evolution is the determination of recurrent causal relationships in independent cultural traditions. In each of the cultural types mentioned above, certain features are functionally related to others, and time depth or development is necessarily implied; for, regardless of which features are considered causes and which are considered effects, it is assumed that some must always be accompanied by others under stipulated conditions. Whether it requires ten, twenty, or several hundred years for the relationship to become established, development through time must always take place. Therefore, parallel developments which require only a few years and involve only a limited number of features are no less evolutionary from a scientific point of view than sequences involving whole cultures and covering millenia.

CONCLUSIONS

Cultural evolution may be regarded either as a special type of historical reconstruction or as a particular methodology or approach. The historical reconstructions of the nineteenth-century unilinear evolutionists are distinctive for the assumption that all cultures pass through parallel and genetically unrelated sequences. This assumption is in conflict with the twentieth-century cultural relativists or historical particularists, who regard cultural development as essentially divergent, except as diffusion tends to level differences. This disagreement concerning fundamental historical fact is reflected in cultural taxonomy. The major categories of the unilinear evolutionists are primarily developmental stages applicable to all cultures; those of the relativists and particularists are culture areas or traditions. The difference in point of view also involves the very logic of science. The evolutionists were deductive, a priori, schematic, and largely philosophical. The relativists are phenomenological and esthetic.

Twentieth-century research has accumulated a mass of evidence which overwhelmingly supports the contention that particular cultures diverge significantly from one another and do not pass through unilinear stages. Since this basic fact of cultural history is no longer a matter of major controversy, those who have sought to keep the tradition of nineteenth-century evolution alive have been forced to shift their frame of reference from the particular to the general, from a universal scheme into which all individual cultures may be fitted to a system of broad generalizations about the nature of any culture. They concede that particular cultures have distinguishing features caused by divergent development in different areas as well as by the stage of development, but they now profess to be interested in the evolution of culture generically considered and not of cultures. Their reconstruction of world culture history is, as a matter of fact, made in such general terms as to be quite acceptable to everyone. No one doubts that hunting and gathering preceded farming and herding and that the last two were preconditions of "civilization," which is broadly characterized by dense and stable populations, metallurgy, intellectual achievements, social heterogeneity and internal specialization, and other features.

Because the weight of evidence now seems to support divergent cultural development, the proposition that there are significant parallels in cultural history is regarded with suspicion. Nonetheless, probably most anthropologists recognize some similarities in form, function, and developmental processes in certain cultures of different traditions. If interest in these parallels can be divested of the all-or-none dogma that, because cultural development is now known not to be wholly unilinear, each tradition must be wholly unique, a basis may be laid for historical reconstruction which takes into account cross-cultural similarities as well as differences. The formulation of the similarities in terms of recurring relationships will require a taxonomy of significant features. Taxonomy may be based upon few or many features and upon a varying number of different cultures. The developmental formulation may involve long or short historical sequences.

For those who are interested in cultural laws, regularities, or formulations, the greatest promise lies in analysis and comparison of limited similarities and parallels, that is, in multilinear evolution rather than in unilinear evolution or universal evolution. Unilinear evolution is discredited, except as it provides limited insights concerning the particular cultures analyzed in detail by the nineteenth-century students of culture. Universal evolution has yet to provide any very new formulations that will explain any and all cultures. The most fruitful course of investigation would seem to be the search for laws which formulate the interrelationships of particular phenomena which may recur cross-culturally but are not necessarily universal.

26

ON THE EVOLUTION OF
SOCIAL STRATIFICATION AND THE STATE

MORTON H. FRIED

The evolutionists never discussed in detail—still less observed—what actually happened when a society in Stage A changed into a society at Stage B; it was merely argued that all Stage B societies must somehow have evolved out of the Stage A societies.—
E. R. LEACH

To some extent E. R. Leach's charge, which relates to the evolution of political organization, is unfair. The climate in which pristine systems of state organization took shape no longer exists. The presence of numerous modern states and the efficiency of communications have converted all movements toward state level organization into acculturation phenomena of some degree. In fact, it seems likely that the only true pristine states—those whose origin was *sui generis,* out of local conditions and not in response to pressures emanating from an already highly organized but separate political entity—are those which arose in the great river valleys of Asia and Africa and the one or two comparable developments in the Western Hemisphere. Elsewhere the development of the state seems to have been "secondary" and to have depended upon pressures, direct or indirect, from existing states. Where such pressures exist, the process of development is accelerated, condensed, and often warped, so that a study of contemporary state formation is a murky mirror in which to discern the stages in the development of the pristine states.

Further, the conditions of emergence of rank and stratification as pristine phenomena are similarly obscured when the impetus to change is the introduction of aspects of a market economy, money as a medium of exchange, rationalization of production, and the transformation of labor into a commodity. It would be extremely gratifying to actually observe societies in transition from "Stage A"

From Stanley Diamond (Ed.), *Culture in History: Essays in Honor of Paul Radin.* Copyright © 1960 by the Columbia University Press. Reprinted by permission of the publisher and the author. Morton H. Fried is Professor of Anthropology, Columbia University.

(egalitarian organization) to a "Stage B" (rank society) and from there to a "Stage C" (stratification society) and finally from that stage to a "Stage D" (state society). Indeed, some of these observations have been made, though no one has yet been able to follow a single society or even selected exemplars from a group of genetically related societies through all these stages. Instead a variety of unrelated societies are selected, each representing one or another of the several possible transitions. Mr. Leach himself has contributed one of the most valuable of the accounts dealing with this matter in his analysis of the movement from *gumlao* to *gumsa* organization among the Kachin of northern Burma.

Following leads supplied in the data of such accounts as that of Leach, just mentioned, of Douglas Oliver, and others, it is our intention to discuss in detail the things which it seems to us must have occurred in order to make the previous transitions possible. Since the data are largely contemporary, the statements are to be viewed as hypotheses in their application to pristine situations beyond even archaeological recall.

Here then is what we seek to accomplish: (1) to suggest some specific institutional developments, the occurrences of which are normal and predictable in viable societies under certain conditions, and in the course of which the whole society perforce moves into a new level of socio-cultural organization; (2) to suggest some of the conditions under which these institutional developments occurred and came to florescence; (3) to indicate as a by-product, that the movement occurs without conscious human intervention, the alterations taking place slowly enough and with such inevitability that the society is revolutionized before the carriers of the culture are aware of major changes.

In approaching this task, it seems wise, if only to head off needless argument, to deny any intention of supplying a single master key to a lock that has defied the efforts of great talents from the time of the Classical civilizations to the present. It seems obvious that other sequences of events than those sketched here could, under proper circumstances, have had similar results. Indeed, the writer is eager to entertain other possibilities and hopes hereby to stimulate others to offer counter suggestions. It will also be obvious to the reader that substantial trains of thought herein stated are merely borrowed and not created by the writer. The recent strides in economic anthropology, and I refer primarily to the work of Polanyi, Arensberg, and Pearson, the clarification of some basic concepts in the study of social organization, and the incentives provided by a seminal paper by Paul Kirchhoff (1935) have all been combined in the present effort.

THE NON-RANK, NON-STRATIFIED SOCIETY

Every human society differentiates among its members and assigns greater or less prestige to individuals according to certain of their attributes. The simplest and most universal criteria of differential status are those two potent axes of the basic division of labor, age and sex. Beyond are a host of others which are used singly or in combination to distinguish among the members of a category otherwise undifferentiated as to sex or age group. Most important of the characteristics used in this regard are those which have a visible relation to the maintenance of subsistence, such as strength, endurance, agility, and other factors which make one a good provider in a hunting and gathering setting. These characteristics are ephemeral; moreover, the systems of enculturation prevalent at this level, with their emphasis upon the development of subsistence skills, make it certain that such skills are well distributed among the members of society of the proper sex and age groups.

The major deviation from this system of subsistence-oriented statuses is associated with age. However, it makes no difference to the argument of this paper whether the status of the old is high or low since the basis of its ascription is universal. Anyone who is of the proper sex and manages to live long enough automatically enters into its benefits or disabilities.

Given the variation in individual endowment which makes a chimera of absolute equality, the primitive societies which we are considering are sufficiently undifferentiated in this respect to permit us to refer to them as "egalitarian societies." An egalitarian society can be defined more precisely: it is one in which there are as many positions of prestige in any given age-sex grade as there are persons capable of filling them. If within a certain kin group or territory there are four big men, strong, alert, keen hunters, then there will be four "strong men"; if there are six, or three, or one, so it is. Eskimo society fits this general picture. So do many others. Almost all of these societies are founded upon hunting and gathering and lack significant harvest periods when large reserves of food are stored.

There is one further point I wish to emphasize about egalitarian society. It accords quite remarkably with what Karl Polanyi has called a reciprocal economy.

Production in egalitarian society is characteristically a household matter. There is no specialization; each family group repeats essentially similar tasks. There may be individuals who make certain things better than do others, and these individuals are often given recognition for their skills, but no favored economic role is established, no regular division of labor emerges at this point, and no political power can reside in the status (Leacock). Exchange in such a society takes place between individuals who belong to different small-scale kin groups; it tends to be casual and is not bound by systems of monetary value based upon scarcity. Such exchanges predominate between individuals who recognize each other as relatives or friends, and may be cemented by such procedures as the provision of hospitality and the granting of sexual access to wives.

Within the local group or band the economy is also reciprocal, but less obviously so. Unlike the exchange between members of different local groups which, over the period of several years, tend to balance, the exchanges within a group may be quite asymmetrical over time. The skilled and lucky hunter may be continually supplying others with meat; while his family also receives shares from the catch of others, income never catches up with the amounts dispensed. However, the difference between the two quantities is made up in the form of prestige, though, as previously mentioned, it conveys no privileged economic or political role. There frequently is a feeling of transcience as it is understood that the greatest hunter can lose his luck or his life, thereby making his family dependent on the largesse of others.

In all egalitarian economies, however, there is also a germ of redistribution. It receives its simplest expression in the family but can grow no more complex than the pooling and redisbursing of stored food for an extended family. In such an embryonic redistributive system the key role is frequently played by the oldest female in the active generation, since it is she who commonly coordinates the household and runs the kitchen.

THE RANK SOCIETY

Since a truly egalitarian human society does not exist, it is evident that we are using the word "rank" in a somewhat special sense. The crux of the matter, as far as we are concerned, is the structural way in which differential prestige is handled in the rank society as contrasted with the way in which egalitarian societies handle similar materials. If the latter have as many positions of valued status as they have individuals capable of handling them, the rank society places additional limitations on access to valued status. The limitations which are added have nothing to do with sex, age group, or personal attributes. Thus, the rank society is characterized by having fewer positions of valued status than individuals capable of handling them. Furthermore, most rank societies have a fixed number of such positions, neither expanding them nor diminishing them with fluctuations in the populations, save as totally new segmented units originate with fission or disappear as the result of catastrophe or sterility.

The simplest technique of limiting status, beyond those already discussed, is to make succession to status dependent upon birth order. This principle, which is found in kinship-organized societies, persists in many more complexly organized societies. At its simplest, it takes the form of primogeniture or ultimogeniture on the level of the family, extended family, or lineage. In more complex forms it may be projected through time so that only the first son of a first son of a first son enjoys the rights of succession, all others having been excluded by virtue of ultimate descent from a positionless ancestor. There are still other variants based on the theme: the accession to high status may be by election, but the candidates

may come only from certain lineages which already represent selection by birth order.

The effects of rules of selection based on birth can be set aside by conscious action. Incompetence can be the basis for a decision to by-pass the customary heir, though it would seem more usual for the nominal office to remain vested in the proper heir while a more energetic person performed the functions of the status. A stategic murder could also accomplish the temporary voiding of the rule, but such a solution is much too dangerous and extreme to be practical on the level which we are considering. It is only in rather advanced cultures that the rewards associated with such status are sufficient to motivate patricide and fratricide.

Whether accomplished by a rule of succession or some other narrowing device, the rank society as a framework of statuses resembles a triangle, the point of which represents the leading status hierarchically exalted above the others. The hierarchy thus represented has very definite economic significance, going hand in hand with the emergence of a superfamilial redistributive network. The key status is that of the central collector of allotments who also tends to the redistribution of these supplies either in the form of feasts or as emergency seed and provender in time of need. Depending on the extent and maturity of the redistributive system, there will be greater or lesser development of the hierarchy. Obviously, small-scale networks in which the members have a face-to-face relationship with the person in the central status will have less need of a bureaucracy.

In the typical ranked society there is neither exploitative economic power nor genuine political power. As a matter of fact, the central status closely resembles its counterpart in the embryonic redistributive network that may be found even in the simplest societies. This is not surprising, for the system in typical rank societies is actually based upon a physical expansion of the kin group and the continuation of previously known kinship rights and obligations. The kingpin of a redistributive network in an advanced hunting and gathering society or a simple agricultural one is as much the victim of his role as its manipulator. His special function is to collect, not to expropriate; to distribute, not to consume. In a conflict between personal accumulation and the demands of distribution it is the former which suffers. Anything else leads to accusations of hoarding and selfishness and undercuts the prestige of the central status; the whole network then stands in jeopardy, a situation which cannot be tolerated. This, by the way, helps to explain that "anomaly" that has so frequently puzzled students of societies of this grade: why are their "chiefs" so often poor, perhaps poorer than any of their neighbors? The preceding analysis makes such a question rhetorical.

It is a further characteristic of the persons filling these high status positions in typical rank societies that they must carry out their functions in the absence of political authority. Two kinds of authority they have: familial, in the extended sense, and sacred, as the redistributive feasts commonly are associated with the ritual life of the community. They do not, however, have access to the privileged use of force, and they can use only diffuse and supernatural sanctions to achieve their ends. Indeed, the two major methods by which they operate are by setting personal examples, as of industriousness, and by utilizing the principles of reciprocity to bolster the emergent redistributive economy.

Despite strong egalitarian features in its economic and political sectors, the developing rank society has strong status differentials which are marked by sumptuary specialization and ceremonial function. While it is a fact that the literature abounds in references to "chiefs" who can issue no positive commands and "ruling classes" whose members are among the paupers of the realm, it must be stated in fairness that the central redistributive statuses *are* associated with fuss, feathers, and other trappings of office. These people sit on stools, have big houses, and are consulted by their neighbors. Their redistributive roles place them automatically to the fore in the religious life of the community, but they are also in that position because of their central kinship status as lineage, clan, or kindred heads.

FROM EGALITARIAN TO RANK SOCIETY

The move from egalitarian to rank society is essentially the shift from an economy by reciprocity to one having redistribution as a major device. That being the case, one must look for the causes of ranking (the limitation of statuses such that they are fewer than the persons capable of handling them) in the conditions which enable the redistributive economy to emerge from its position of latency in the universal household economy, to dominate a network of kin groups which extend beyond the boundaries of anything known on the reciprocal level.

Though we shall make a few suggestions relating to this problem, it should be noted that the focus of this paper does not necessitate immediate disposition of this highly complicated question. In view of the history of our topic, certain negative conclusions are quite significant. Most important of all is the deduction that the roots of ranking do not lie in features of human personality. The structural approach obviates, in this case, psychological explanations. To be precise, we need assume no universal human drive for power in comprehending the evolution of ranking.

It is unthinkable that we should lead a reader this far without indicating certain avenues whereby the pursuit of the problem may be continued. We ask, therefore, what are the circumstances under which fissioning kin or local groups retain active economic interdigitation, the method of interaction being participation in the redistributive network?

In a broad sense, the problem may be seen as an ecological one. Given the tendency of a population to breed up to the limit of its resources and given the probably universal budding of kin and local groups which have reached cultural maxima of unit size, we look into different techno-geographical situations for clues as to whether more recently formed units will continue to interact significantly with their parent units, thereby extending the physical and institutional range of the economy. Such a situation clearly arises when the newer group moves into a somewhat different environment while remaining close enough to the parent group to permit relatively frequent interaction among the members of the two groups. Given such a condition, the maintenance of a redistributive network would have the effect of diversifying subsistence in both units and also providing insurance against food failures in one or the other. This is clearly something of a special case; one of its attractions is the amount of work that has been done upon it by another student of the problem (Sahlins).

It is possible to bring to bear upon this problem an argument similar to that employed by Tylor in the question of the incest taboo, to wit: the redistributive network might appear as a kind of random social mutation arising out of nonspecific factors difficult to generalize, such as a great personal dependence of the members of the offspring unit upon those they have left behind. Whatever the immediate reason for its appearance, it would quickly show a superiority over simple reciprocal systems in (a) productivity, (b) timeliness of distribution, (c) diversity of diet, and (d) coordination of mundane and ceremonial calendars (in a loose cyclical sense). It is not suggested that the success of the institution depends upon the rational cognition of these virtues by the culture carriers; rather the advantages of these institutions would have positive survival value over a long period of time.

We should not overlook one other possibility that seems less special than the first one given above. Wittfogel has drawn our attention on numerous occasions to the social effects of irrigation. The emergence of the superfamilial redistributive network and the rank society seem to go well with the developments he has discussed under the rubric "hydro-agriculture," in which some supervision is needed in order to control simple irrigation and drainage projects yet these projects are not large enough to call into existence a truly professional bureaucracy.

It may be wondered that one of the prime explanations for the emergence of ranking, one much favored by notable sociologists of the past, has not appeared in this argument. Reference is to the effects of war upon a society. I would like in this article to take a deliberately extreme stand and assert that military considerations serve to institutionalize rank differences only when these are already implicit or manifest in the economy. I do not believe that pristine developments in the formalization of rank can be attributed to even grave military necessity.

THE STRATIFIED SOCIETY

The differences between rank society and stratified society are very great, yet it is rare that the two are distinguished in descriptive accounts or even in the theoretical literature. Briefly put, the essential difference is this: the rank society operates on the principle of differential status for members with similar abilities, but these statuses are devoid of privileged economic or political power, the former point being the essential one for the present analysis. Meanwhile, the stratified society is distinguished by the differential relationships between the members of the society and its subsistence means— some of the members of the society have unimpeded access to its strategic resources while others have various impediments in their access to the same fundamental resources.

With the passage to stratified society man enters a completely new area of social life. Whereas the related systems of redistribution and ranking rest upon embryonic institutions that are as universal as family organization (*any* family, elementary or extended, conjugal or consanguineal, will do equally well), the principles of stratification have no real foreshadowing on the lower level.

Furthermore, the movement to stratification precipitated many things which were destined to change society even further, and at an increasingly accelerated pace. Former systems of social control which rested heavily on enculturation, internalized sanctions, and ridicule now required formal statement of their legal principles, a machinery of adjudication, and a formally constituted police authority. The emergence of these and other control institutions were associated with the final shift of prime authority from kinship means to territorial means and describes the evolution of complex forms of government associated with the state. It was the passage to stratified society which laid the basis for the complex division of labor which underlies modern society. It also gave rise to various arrangements of socio-economic classes and led directly to both classical and modern forms of colonialism and imperialism.

THE TRANSITION TO STRATIFIED SOCIETY

The decisive significance of stratification is not that it sees differential amounts of wealth in different hands but that it sees two kinds of access to strategic resources. One of these is privileged and unimpeded; the other is impaired, depending on complexes of permission which frequently require the payment of dues, rents, or taxes in labor or in kind. The existence of such a distinction enables the growth of exploitation, whether of a relatively simple kind based upon drudge slavery or of a more complex type associated with involved divisions of labor and intricate class systems. The development of stratification also encourages the emergence of communities composed of kin parts and non-kin parts which, as wholes, operate on the basis of non-kin mechanisms.

So enormous is the significance of the shift

to stratification that previous commentators have found it essential that the movement be associated with the most powerful people in the society. Landtman, for example, says: "It is in conjunction with the dissimilarity of individual endowments that inequality of wealth has conduced to the rise of social differentiation. As a matter of course the difference as regards property in many cases goes hand in hand with difference in personal qualities. A skilful hunter or fisher, or a victorious warrior, has naturally a better prospect of acquiring a fortune than one who is inferior to him in these respects."

If our analysis is correct, however, such is definitely not the case. The statuses mentioned by Landtman are not those which stand to make great accumulations but rather stand to make great give-aways. Furthermore, the leap from distribution to power is unwarranted by the ethnographic evidence.

There are unquestionably a number of ways in which secondary conditions of stratification can emerge. That is, once the development of stratification proceeds from contact with and tutelage by cultures which are at the least already stratified and which may be the possessors of mature state organization, there are many specific ways in which simpler cultures can be transformed into stratified societies. The ways which come quickest to mind include the extension of the complex society's legal definitions of property to the simpler society, the introduction of all-purpose money and wage labor, and the creation of an administrative system for the operation of the simpler society on a basis which is acceptable to the superordinate state. Often the external provenance of these elements is obvious in their misfit appearance. A sharper look may reveal, indeed, that the stratified system is a mere façade operated for and often by persons who have no genuine local indentities, while the local system continues to maintain informally, and sometimes in secrecy, the older organization of the society. Put more concretely, this means that "government" appointed chiefs are respected only in certain limited situations and that the main weight of social control continues to rest upon traditional authorities and institutions which may not even be recognized by the ruling power.

An excellent climate for the development of stratification in a simple society can be supplied in a relatively indirect way by a society of advanced organization. Let us take the situation in which a culture has no concept of nuclear family rights to land. The economy is based upon hunting, trapping, and fishing, with the streams and forests being associated in a general way with weakly organized bands which have a decided tendency to fragment and reconstitute, each time with potentially different membership. Subvert this setup with an external market for furs and a substantial basis for stratification has been laid. This system, like the direct intervention of a superordinate state, also seems to have certain limitations for there is ample evidence that the development of private property in such a system as that just mentioned is confined to trapping lines and does not extend to general subsistence hunting and fishing in the area.

Another situation that bears study is one in which important trade routes linking two or more advanced societies traverse marginal areas in which simple societies are located. Certain geographical conditions make it possible for the relatively primitive folk to enhance their economies with fruits derived from the plunder of this trade or, in a more mature system, by extorting tribute from the merchants who must pass by. The remoteness of these areas, the difficulty of the terrain and the extreme difficulties and costs of sending a punitive force to pacify the area often enables the simpler people to harass populations whose cultural means for organized violence far exceeds their own. Be this as it may, the combination of the examples of organization presented by the outposts of complexly organized societies and the availability of commodities which could not be produced in the simple culture may combine to lay the basis for an emergence of stratification. Precisely such conditions seem partially responsible for the political developments described for the Kachin.

None of this seems to apply to the pristine emergence of stratification. As a matter of fact, it is not even particularly suggestive. There is, however, one particular ecological condition that appears in highland Burma which also has been noted elsewhere, each time in association with rather basic shifts in social organization paralleling those already sketched in the previous section of this paper. We refer to the shift from rainfall to irrigation farming, particularly to the construction of terraced fields. This is admittedly a restricted ethnographic phenomenon and as such it cannot bear the weight of any general theory. It is the suggestive character of these developments and the possibility of extrapolating from them to hypothetical pristine conditions that makes them so interesting.

In brief, the shift to irrigation and terracing is from swiddens or impermanent fields to plots which will remain in permanent cultivation for decades and generations. Whereas we have previously stressed the possible role of hydro-agriculture in the transition from egalitarian to rank society, we now note its possible role in the transition to stratification. This it could accomplish by creating conditions under which access to strategic resources, in this case land and water, would be made the specific prerogative of small-scale kin groups such as minimal lineages or even stem families. Through the emergence of hydro-agriculture a community which previously acknowledged no *permanent* association between particular component units and particular stretches of land now begins to recognize such permanent and exclusive rights. Incidentally, the evidence seems to indicate that the rank-forming tendencies of hydro-agriculture need not occur prior to the tendencies toward stratification: both can occur concomitantly. This in turn suggests that we must be cautious in constructing our theory not to make stratification emerge from ranking, though under particular circumstances this is certainly possible.

A point of considerable interest about hydro-agriculture is that it seems to present the possibility of an emergence of stratification in the absence of a problem of over-population or resource limitation. We need a great deal of further thought on the matter. Studies of the last two decades, in which a considerably higher degree of agricultural expertise on the part of the fieldworkers has been manifested than was formerly the case, have increasingly tended to show that hydro-agriculture does not invariably out-produce slash and burn and that, other things being equal, a population does not automatically prefer hydro-agriculture as a more rationalized approach to agricultural subsistence. Here we can introduce a factor previously excluded. The hydro-agricultural system invariably has a higher degree of settlement concentration than swiddens. Accordingly, it would seem to have considerable value in the maintenance of systems of defense, given the presence of extensive warfare. Here, then, is a point at which military considerations would seem to play an important if essentially reinforcing role in the broad evolutionary developments which we are considering.

The writer is intrigued with another possibility for the emergence of stratification. Once again, the conditions involved seem a little too specific to serve the purpose of a single unified theory. It requires the postulation of a society with a fixed rule of residence, preferably one of the simpler ones such as patrilocality/virilocality or matrilocality/uxorilocality, and a fixed rule of descent, preferably one parallel to the residence rule. It further postulates a condition of population expansion such that, given slash and burn agriculture, the society is very near the limits of the carrying capacity of the system. Such conditions are very likely to develop at varying speeds within an area of several hundred miles due to obvious imbalances in reproductive rates and to microecological variation. Now, as long as there is no notable pressure of people on the land, deviation in residence and even in descent will be expectable though quite unusual and lacking in motivation. As the situation grows grave in one area but remains relatively open in another, there may be a tendency for a slight readjustment in residence rules to occur. For example, in a normally virilocal society, the woman who brings her husband back to her natal group transgresses a few customary rules in doing so but presents her agnates with no basic problems in resource allocation since she, as a member of the agnatic group, has her own rights of access which may be shared by the spouse during her lifetime. The complication arises at her death when her husband and all of her children discover themselves to be in an anomalous position since they are not members of the kin community. Where local land problems are not severe and where such breaches of the residence pattern are yet uncommon, it is not unlikely that the aliens will be accepted as *de facto* members of the community with the expectation that future generations will revert to custom, the unorthodox switch of residence fading in memory with the passage of time. Here we have a crude and informal *ambil-anak*. But as the local community enters worsening ecological circumstances and as the exceptional residence becomes more frequent, the residence and descent rules, particularly the latter, assume greater and greater importance. As the situation continues, the community is slowly altered, though the members of the community may be unable to state exactly what the changes are. The result, however, is clear. There are now two kinds of people in the village where

258   FUNCTIONALISM, EVOLUTION, AND HISTORY

formerly there was only one. Now there are kernel villagers, those who have unimpaired access to land, and those whose tenure rests upon other conditions, such as loyalty to a patron, or tribute, or even a precarious squatter's right.

THE STATE SOCIETY

The word should be abandoned entirely . . . after this chapter the word will be avoided scrupulously and no severe hardship in expression will result. In fact, clarity of expression demands this abstinence (Easton).

The word was "state" and the writer, a political scientist, was reacting to some of the problems in his own field in making this judgment, but it does look as if he was pushed to drastic action by the work of some anthropologists in whose hands the concept of state lost all character and utility, finally ending as a cultural universal. E. Adamson Hoebel, one of the few United States anthropologists to make a serious specialization in the field of law and the state, formerly introduced students to this question by remarking that

where there is political organization there is a state. If political organization is universal, so then is the state. One is the group, the other an institutionalized complex of behavior.

In a revision of the same book after a few years, Hoebel's treatment of the subject seems to indicate that he is in the process of rethinking the matter. His summary words, however, repeat the same conclusion:

Political organization is characteristic of every society. . . . That part of culture that is recognized as political organization is what constitutes the state.

This is a far cry from the approach of evolutionists to the state as exemplified in Summer and Keller:

The term state is properly reserved for a somewhat highly developed regulative organization. . . . It is an organization with authority and discipline essential to large-scale achievements, as compared with the family, for example, which is an organization on the same lines but simpler and less potent.

Without making a special issue of the definition of the state (which would easily consume the entire space of this article, if not the volume) let me note one used by the jurist Léon Duguit which conveys the sense most useful to the point of view of this paper:

En prenant le mot dans son sens le plus général, on peut dire qu'il y a un État toutes les fois qu'il existe dans une société donnée une différenciation politique, quelque rudimentaire ou quelque compliquée et developée qu'elle soit. Le mot État designe soit les gouvernants ou le pouvoir politique, soit la société elle-même, ou existe cette différenciation entre gouvernants et gouvernés et ou existe par là même une puisance politique.

The difference between Hoebel and Duguit seems to be in the clear statement of power. Reviewing our own paper in the light of this difference we note our previous emphasis on the absence of coercive economic or political power in the egalitarian and rank societies. It is only in the stratified society that such power emerges from embryonic and universal foreshadowings in familial organization.

The maturation of social stratification has manifold implications depending on the precise circumstances in which the developments take place. All subsequent courses, however, have a certain area of overlap; the new social order, with its differential allocation of access to strategic resources, must be maintained and strengthened. In a simple stratified society in which class differentials are more implicit than explicit the network of kin relations covers a sufficient portion of the total fabric of social relations so that areas not specifically governed by genuine kinship relations can be covered by their sociological extensions. The dynamic of stratification is such that this situation cannot endure. The stratified kin group emphasizes its exclusiveness: it erodes the corporative economic functions formerly associated with stipulated kinship and at every turn it amputates extensions of the demonstrated kin unit. The result of this pruning is that the network of kin relations fails more and more to coincide with the network of personal relations. Sooner or later the discrepancy is of such magnitude that, were non-kin sanctions and non-kin agencies absent or structured along customary lines only, the society would dissolve in uncomposable conflict.

The emergent state, then, is the organization of the power of the society on a supra-kin basis. Among its earliest tasks is the maintenance of general order but scarcely discernible from this is its need to support the order of stratification. The defense of a complete system of individual statuses is impossible so the early state concentrates on a few key statuses (helping to explain the tendency to convert any crime into either sacrilege or *lèse majesté*) and on the basic principles of organization, e.g., the idea of hierarchy, property, and the power of the law.

The implementation of these primary functions of the state gives rise to a number of specific and characteristic secondary functions, each of which is associated with one or more particular institutions of its own. These secondary functions include population control in the most general sense (the fixing of boundaries and the definition of the unit; establishment of categories of membership; census). Also a secondary function is the disposal of trouble cases (civil and criminal laws moving toward the status of codes; regular legal procedure; regular officers of adjudication). The protection of sovereignty is also included (maintenance of military forces; police forces and power; eminent domain). Finally, all of the preceding require fiscal support, and this is achieved in the main through taxation and conscription.

In treating of this bare but essential list of state functions and institutions the idea of the state as a universal aspect of culture dissolves as a fantasy. The institutions just itemized may be made to appear in ones or twos in certain primitive societies by exaggeration and by the neglect of known history. In no egalitarian society and in no rank society do a majority of the functions enumerated appear regardless of their guise. Furthermore there is no indication of their appearance as a unified functional response to basic sociocultural needs except in those stratified societies which are verging upon statehood.

THE TRANSITION TO STATE

Just as stratified society grew out of antecedent forms of society without the conscious awareness of the culture carriers, so it would seem that the state emerged from the stratified society in a similar, inexorable way. If this hypothesis is correct, then such an explanation as the so-called "conquest theory" can be accepted only as a special case of "secondary-state" for-

mation. The conquests discussed by such a theorist as Franz Oppenheimer established not stratification but super-stratification, either the conqueror or the conquered, or perhaps even both, already being internally stratified.

The problem of the transition to state is so huge and requires such painstaking application to the available archaeological and historical evidence that it would be foolish to pursue it seriously here. Let us conclude, therefore, by harking back to statements made at the outset of this paper, and noting again the distinction between pristine and secondary states. By the former term is meant a state that has developed *sui generis* out of purely local conditions. No previous state, with its acculturative pressures, can be discerned in the background of a pristine state. The secondary state, on the other hand, is pushed by one means or another toward a higher form of organization by an external power which has already been raised to statehood.

The number of pristine states is strictly limited; several centuries, possibly two millennia, have elapsed since the last one emerged in Meso-America, and there seems to be no possibility that any further states of the pristine type will evolve, though further research may bring to light some of the distant past of which we yet have no positive information. In all, there seems to have been some six centers at which pristine states emerged, four in the Old World and two in the New: the Tigris-Euphrates area, the region of the lower Nile, the country drained by the Indus and the middle course of the Huang Ho where it is joined by the Han, Wei, and Fen. The separate areas of Peru-Bolivia and Meso-America complete the roster.

If there is utility in the concept of the pristine state and if history has been read correctly in limiting the designation to the six areas just enumerated, then we discover a remarkable correlation between areas demanding irrigation or flood control and the pristine state. Certainly this is no discovery of the author. It is one of the central ideas of Wittfogel's theory and has received extensive treatment from Julian Steward and others. The implication of the "hydraulic theory" for this paper, however, is that the development of the state as an internal phenomenon is associated with major tasks of drainage and irrigation. The emergence of a control system to ensure the operation of the economy is closely tied to the appearance of a distinctive class system and certain constellations of power in the hands of a managerial bureaucracy which frequently operates below a ruler who commands theoretically unlimited power.

It is an interesting commentary on nineteenth-century political philosophy that the starting point of so many theories was, of necessity, the Classical world of Greece and Rome. According to the present hypothesis, however, both of these great political developments of antiquity were not pristine but secondary formations which built on cultural foundations laid two thousand years and more before the rise of Greece. Furthermore, it would seem that the active commercial and military influences of the truly ancient pristine states, mediated through the earliest of the secondary states to appear in Asia Minor and the eastern Mediterranean littoral, were catalysts in the events of the northern and western Mediterranean.

CONCLUSION

The close of a paper like this, which moves like a gadfly from time to time, place to place, and subject matter to subject matter, and which never pauses long enough to make a truly detailed inquiry or supply the needed documentation, the close of such a paper requires an apology perhaps more than a conclusion.

I have been led to write this paper by my ignorance of any modern attempt to link up the contributions which have been made in many sub-disciplines into a single unified theory of the emergence of social stratification and the state. That the theory offered here is crude, often too special, and by no means documented seems less important than that it may be used as a sitting duck to attract the fire and better aim of others.

27

LANGUAGE AND EVOLUTION

JOSEPH H. GREENBERG

THE great achievement of Darwin in the *Origin of Species* was to establish on a firm and generally accepted basis the interpretation of differences among species as arising gradually through processes of change from other species rather than once and for all by an original creative act. Of the factors of change by which new species might develop, the most prominent in Darwin's theory, but by no means the only one, was the perpetuation through natural selection of those variations best suited for survival in the struggle for existence. As has often been noted, the theory that species evolve in the course of time was not invented by Darwin. It

was, indeed, a familiar notion to the biologists of the preceding half-century but it was not until the careful and impressive marshalling of evidence in its behalf by Darwin in his classic work, and, in particular, the advancement of natural selection by him as an explanatory principle that it became plausible to more than a minority of biological scientists.

In view of these historical developments, any consideration of Darwinian evolution must carefully distinguish the theory that species develop from other species, which is an assertion concerning the history of life-forms, from the theory of natural selection which asserts that natural selection has played a major role in producing this result. The specification and analysis of such ambiguities assumes crucial importance when the term evolution is applied to a set of phenomena as radically different from the biological as language.

From Betty Meggers (Ed.), *Evolution and Culture: A Centennial Appraisal.* Copyright © 1959 by the Anthropological Society of Washington. Reprinted by permission of the publisher and the author. Joseph H. Greenberg is Professor of Anthropology, Stanford University.

There is a further ambiguity lurking in the phrase "theory of evolution," partly allied to the distinction just mentioned, but of even more fundamental importance. In the first of two senses of evolution, which in this aspect may be called tranformism, it may be contrasted with creationism as the opposing doctrine. In the second sense, which is quite distinct, it may be considered synonymous with advance or progress.

The transformationist meaning of evolution arises from the considerations involved in any class of phenomena in which the investigator is confronted with the existence of a variety of kinds or species. In such instances, there are two alternative types of theories to account for the existence of distinct kinds. According to the creationist view, each kind is a fixed type that can only vary within certain fixed bounds in the entire course of its existence. Each kind is defined by reference to certain constant and unchanging characters that constitute, in the terminology of scholastic logic, its essential or definitional predicates. Variations may occur with respect to the other characters, which are therefore accidental rather than essential. Further, this essence is a formal cause which explains the existence of the species.

Differences among species are explained according to this doctrine as issuing from distinct creative acts. Species can be created or destroyed but they cannot, by changing their essential characteristics, give rise to other and new species. It is not necessary that all kinds should have been created at the same time or that all should survive indefinitely. When confronted with fossil evidence indicating that the species of different geological epochs were, in general, different the creationist necessarily denied that any links of development connected similar but distinct species in successive periods. The theory adopted was that called "catastrophism," namely that by a series of cataclysms, earlier species had been destroyed and were replaced by more recent ones through new creative acts.

The evolutionary theory of transformation of species, as opposed to creationist beliefs, maintains that there are no fixed bounds to specific change. Therefore earlier species give rise to later ones by a process of developmental change. The fact that, in the instance of life-forms, species fall into coherent larger groupings, the genera, and that these in turn may be grouped into distinct families, and so on, in an ordered hierarchy receives its distinctive transformationist explanation. Such groupings had long been noted and had been codified by Linnaeus in his great systematic work, which appeared more than a century before Darwin's *Origin of Species.* According to transformationist theory, those species that belong to the same genera are the differentiated descendants of a single ancestral species, their resemblances being explained as the result of common descent. The resemblances among those genera which belong to the same family are explained in turn by the theory that the species ancestral to each genus are the descendants of a still earlier species ancestral to the family as a whole, and similarly with larger and higher groupings. Fossil forms are, then, either such ancestors of existing groupings or additional lines of descent from them which have become extinct without leaving descendants.

The model of evolution that thus emerges is a branching tree, the varieties of today are like twigs which, as they sprout, become the species of tomorrow. These in turn likewise put forth new twigs, some of which perish while others survive and produce new differentiated descendants. Hence the transformationist theory may fittingly be called that of branching evolution.

The creationist and transformationist views are not merely two philosophic theories between which the observer chooses on the basis of predilection or metaphysical inclination. Given sufficient data we can decide between them for any particular group of phenomena. Thus the theory of catastrophism posited by the creationists was eventually abandoned because it was not supported by the geological evidence. Further, it was the ability of the transformationist theory to account for the coherence of generic and higher classificational groups which, it appears, first aroused in Darwin the conviction that species were not fixed, unchangeable types. For being struck by the number of distinct species on certain islands, which in the creationist view would be separate creations, and at the same time by their resemblance to the species of the nearest mainland, the theory forcibly presented itself to Darwin that whether by migration or whether by geographical continuity at a former period when a land bridge existed, what was originally the same species on island and mainland must during the subsequent period of isolation have developed into separate but related species. This would explain at once their distinctness and their close resemblance, both of which, as Darwin noted, are inexplicable by the creationist theory.

What is urged here is not that the evolutionary transformationist view is necessarily the correct explanation as opposed to the creationist in every instance, but that the question can be decided on the basis of certain kinds of evidence and that, in the case of biological species, this evidence was decisive in favor of the transformationist theory.

The foregoing definition of evolution as transformation of species, in which meaning it is the logical opposite of creationism, is to be distinguished from evolution in the sense of progress in the course of evolutionary change. Because of the ethical implications of the term "progress," it might be better to employ the word "advance" for purposes of scientific discussion. By advance will be meant the theory that more complex, internally differentiated and efficiently adapted forms make their appearance in general in the later stages of evolutionary change. The ethical judgment that this occurs and is good may be called the doctrine of progress.

The distinctness of the theories of evolution as tranformism and evolution as advance is indicated, among other evidences, by the fact that certain scientists have held one while rejecting the other. As was pointed out by the eminent geologist Lyell, who distinguished these two theories by the names "transmutation" and "progress," it is quite possible to hold the creationist and progressive views at the same time. For example, those biologists in the earlier part of the nineteenth century who adhered to the catastrophic version of creationism maintained that each successive creation marked an advance over the previous one in the sense described above.

The particular mechanism of evolutionary change to which Darwin attached major significance and whose plausibility was a primary factor in the spectacular success of his theory was, of course, natural selection. Now, as Darwin states repeatedly, the descendants of a particular life-form are, through the agency of natural selection, likely to be more efficient than their ancestors. There is, therefore, implicit in the notion of natural selection, the theory of the inevitability of continuous advance in the series of life-forms. It is true, moreover, as an empirical fact, that the paleontological evidence, as we go back in time becomes increasingly confined to forms of simple and relatively un-

differentiated structure and of limited range of adaptation to environment. It was precisely one of the recommendations of the theory of natural selection that it helped to make this temporal advance intelligible.

However, it is a well-known fact of the history of biology that the status of natural selection as a major factor in evolution has been less secure than the acceptance of the reality of evolution in the sense of transformation of species. Likewise the concept of advance has tended to remain a vague and generally unsatisfactory notion to many biologists. Thus George G. Simpson states, "Whether recent man is to be considered more complex and more independent than a Cambrian trilobite will be found subject to qualification and definitions." Among the difficulties here are that efficiency of adaptation is always relative to a particular environment while the environment itself changes in the course of time, and that there are many scales of efficiency so that, of two species compared, one may have superiority in one respect and the other in some other respect and these scales are, strictly speaking, incommensurable. For these reasons the definition of evolution as transformation appears to be more fundamental than the definition in terms of advance.

It is one of the contentions of this paper that the theory of evolution as transformation applies *mutatis mutandis,* and with relatively minor modifications both to linguistic and biologic change. This agreement was noted both by biologists and linguists in the period immediately following the publication of *Origin of Species.* Thus Darwin himself remarks in *The Descent of Man,* a later work, that "the formation of different languages and of distinct species and the proofs that both have been developed through a gradual process are curiously parallel."

In linguistic science, the creationist view is represented by the Biblical account of the Tower of Babel, according to which all language differences were created at the same time by the confusion of tongues. This theory was superseded by the transformationist account much earlier than in the instance of biology. Thus Max Mueller, an outstanding linguistic scholar contemporary with Darwin, in spite of his opposition to Darwin's views regarding the animal descent of man, was able to say that "in language, I was a Darwinian before Darwin," while August Schleicher, another leading linguist of the period, in a published lecture "Die

Darwinsche Theorie und die Sprachwissenschaft" (1863), spelled out this parallel in detail.

The event that marks most clearly the triumph of transformism over creationism in linguistic science was the recognition that the resemblances among the languages we now call Indo-European are to be explained as a result of common inheritance with differential change from an extinct ancestral form of speech. The acceptance of this theory is usually, but somewhat arbitrarily, dated from a statement by Sir William Jones substantially to this effect in 1786. In fact, both in the case of the Semitic and Finno-Ugric languages, this explanation had been current even earlier. Thus the recognition of transformism in linguistics substantially antedates the first modern statement of this theory in biology by Lamarck in 1801.

Probably the chief factor in the early acceptance of this type of explanation in linguistics as compared with biology is the vastly more rapid change in language. The common-sense objection to transformism in biology, namely, that actual changes in species had never been observed in historic times and that, to all appearances, species were fixed types, appears to have been the most powerful single factor in the general rejection of evolution by biologists in the period preceding Darwin. Language, within the realm of individual experience and unaided by records of its past, seems fixed no doubt, but not to the same degree. Older people can recall vocabulary items and idioms which were current in their youth but are no longer heard. On occasion, they may even have noted phonetic changes. Thus the older generation of New Yorkers remembers when the *oi* dipthong in such words as "hurt" was general and accepted among educated speakers and has witnessed its replacement, at least among educated speakers, within an individual life-span.

These changes, apparently small within the lifetime of a single person, display powerful cumulative effects in periods of time well within the scope of written records. Thus, Anglo-Saxon exhibits differences from modern English comparable with those of modern German. If Anglo-Saxon and modern English were spoken contemporaneously they would undoubtedly rank as separate languages. It was possible, then, actually to observe in this historically well-attested instance the change of one language into another.

In general, languages ancestral to existing groups of genetically related languages, which would correspond to the fossil evidence of biology, take us back to periods before the existence of written records. However, in the well-known instance of Latin, there are abundant records of a language, which through a series of locally different variants, has given rise to the existing diversity of Romance local dialects and standard languages. In view of these known facts, it was not too audacious a step to assume that in similar fashion an ancestral language had once existed bearing the same relation to the existing branches of Indo-European that Latin held in relation to Romance speech-forms. It became a mere historical accident that Latin was attested in written form whereas the Indo-European Ursprache, which was spoken before the existence of writing in the area of its occurrence, could not be known through direct evidence of this kind.

The nature of the parallel between the evolution of languages and species, which so struck both linguists like Mueller and Schleicher and natural scientists like Darwin and Lyell, refers to the conception of evolution as transformation of kinds. The transmission of physical characters by the genetic mechanism corresponds to the transmission of language from one generation to the next or one population to another by learning. In both cases, variations arise, some of which are perpetuated. In both instances geographic isolation, whether complete or imperfect, leads to the perpetuation of locally different variants. Difficulties of determining where a variety ends and a species begins, difficulties that were important factors in Darwin's disillusionment with the creationist theory, resemble the linguist's difficulties in defining language as opposed to dialect. Ultimately these variant descendants became distinct enough to be ranked indisputably as separate languages or species. The parallelism is further indicated by the metaphor of the branching tree common to both disciplines.

The status of transformist explanations of linguistic similarities was further enhanced by the successful reconstruction of essential features of the ancestral language through systematic comparison of features of the descendant languages, notably in the instance of Indo-European where, as is the rule, the ancestral language was not known from written records. This enterprise received a great impetus through the discovery, which was not long in coming, that in certain respects, particularly in regard to the sound system, changes were not haphazard but rather showed a surprising degree of regularity. This discovery of the regularity of sound changes, first announced in the specific instance of the consonantal changes of Germanic as compared to Sanskrit, Greek and Latin by Rask (1818) and Grimm (1822) and which came to be known as Grimm's law, aided greatly in making comparative linguistics the most systematic in its method and reliable in its results of all the reconstructive historical sciences dealing with man in his sociocultural aspects.

Just as transformism is the analogue of genetic relationship, so the creationist view of fixed species is implied in the use of classificational criteria with typological rather than genetic validity. Typological classifications have their legitimate uses provided it is made clear that they have no necessary historical implications. The distinction between genetic and typological classification rests on the criteria employed in classification, and here again there is a parallel between biology and linguistics. In the terminology of biology, we wish to distinguish between homologies, or similarities that are the outcome of true common descent, and analogies which result from convergence, generally through similarity of function, and which are irrelevant to genetic classification.

In language it is characteristically resemblances involving sound without meaning or meaning without sound that provide the basis for typological classifications. An example of the former is a classification of languages into tonal and non-tonal, in which all languages will fall into one class or the other regardless of the presence or absence of concrete sound-meaning resemblances. For example, the tone language of West Africa, Southeast Asia and indigenous Mexico will fall into one typological class and even languages closely related to any of these will be in the other non-tonal group if they differ in regard to the particular typological criterion employed. An example of a criterion of meaning without sound is the use of sex gender as a principle of language classification: in certain languages there are morphemes, that is sequences of sound, with the meaning "masculine" and "feminine," while in the non-sex gender languages they are absent.

The use of any such criteria for supposed genetic classfication—and they continue to be widely employed in certain areas—requires the unstated assumption that certain features like the essential as opposed to the accidental attributes of the creationists, are fixed and define the species or, in this instance, the language family. Thus when a writer on southeast Asia states that Annamite cannot belong to the Austroasiatic family of languages because it is tonal whereas the other recognized members of the family are not, he is assuming that a non-tonal language can never evolve into a tonal one. If this statement were true, we would have two or more languages at the beginning and each would have as one of its essential attributes tonality and non-tonality and would be incapable of losing tonal structure if it possessed it or acquiring it if it did not. This is the precise analogue of the notion of fixed species.

What decides the case for real historical connection is the existence of resemblances in both sounding and meaning, such as exist between English and German in basic vocabulary and specific morphemes with grammatical function. Cognate forms are therefore the methodological equivalent of homologies in biology. Because of the arbitrariness of the relation between sound and meaning in language, in that any sequence of sounds is capable of any meaning, these provide a precise parallel to the non-adaptive character of biology.

It seems, at first blush, a much more important thing to say regarding a language that it is tonal or has gender than that the word for "nose" is *Nase* and this perhaps accounts for the persistence of such criteria which, on the face of it, seem to involve more impressive resemblances. Darwin, in his discussion of the criteria of biological classification, notes likewise that it is not the functionally important characters that are significant for classification but rather an accumulation of apparently trivial non-adaptive details:

It might have been thought (and was in ancient times thought) that those parts of the structure which determined the habits of life and the general place of each being in the economy of nature would be of high importance in classification. Nothing could be more false.

Once it is realized that a classification based on gender or non-gender is similar in principle to a biological classification into flying and non-flying animals and that a Semitic language which ceases to be triliteral does not cease to be a Semitic language by descent any more than a bat ceased to be a mammal when it began to fly, then typological classification can resume its legitimate place without giving rise to the confusions that have marked this type of endeavor in the past.

The distinction between the fact of evolution as specific change and the mechanism of survival of the fittest was pointed out in an earlier section of this paper. Darwin himself extended the parallel between language and biology in this instance also. The new linguistic forms that arise continually in any language community are likened to variations, only the fittest of which survive and become incorporated in the linguistic heritage. Again Lyell (1863) in his elaborate comparison of languages to biological species, notes the spread of specific languages over wide areas followed by their later differentiation into separate languages and the extinction of the other languages spoken in these territories. This sequence of events resembles closely the biological processes of adaptive radiation and extinction of species. Natural selection as applied to language would then involve an intralinguistic struggle for survival among forms within the language and a battle among languages in which some spread and produce descendants while others perish.

Regarding the intralinguistic struggles, linguists would probably agree that many changes are functionally indifferent and that while certain changes make for greater efficiency there are likewise certain outcomes of normal linguistic processes of change, such as grammatical irregularities and semantic ambiguities, which are functionally negative. Taking linguistic change as a whole, there seems to be no discernible movement toward greater efficiency such as might be expected if in fact there were a continuous struggle in which superior linguistic innovations won out as a general rule.[1]

Similarly, it can be seen that one language succeeds another, not because it is more advanced as a language, but for extra-linguistic reasons of military, economic or cultural superiority of its speakers. Nor has any people ever perished because of the inadequacy of its language. This is not to say that there are not important differences between languages that have been the object of literary cultivation and those that have not, or those which possess an extensive technical vocabulary and those lacking in this regard. However, such differences are but a reflection of non-linguistic differences. They affect nothing basic in the language itself; any language is capable of literary elaboration or technical expansion if non-linguistic circumstances encourage or require it.

Any attempt to show the existence of evolutionary advance in language development must rest on a typological basis. The linguistic typology prevalent in the nineteenth century which in its most common version involved a threefold classification into isolating, agglutinative and inflective is an instance of such a typology. For such a typological analyisis to prove the existence of evolutionary advance in language requires, in addition to a methodologically valid typological procedure, the proof of two further premises. The first of these is that, when the types are arranged in some given order, it can be demonstrated or at least made probable that there was once a time in which all languages belonged to the most "primitive" of these types. Following this, there should be a stage in which the next most advanced type existed alongside survivals of the earliest type, and so on. This is similar to the requirement that for stone tools to be considered a more primitive stage of technology than metal tools we must demonstrate that there was once a period in which stone tools existed while metal tools had not yet made their appearance.

The other requirement is a proof that the criteria employed in distinguishing the typological classes are not irrelevant to the actual uses to which language is put so that the criteria for the more advanced types involve characteristics that can be shown in some manner to be adaptively superior to the criteria which distinguish languages lower on the scale of evolutionary advance.

The well-known nineteenth century typology alluded to above was in its most commonly accepted form considered by almost all of its adherents to be a typology of evolutionary advance. In fact, this typology failed on all three grounds mentioned. It was not a methodologically valid typology, since the criteria were never clearly stated in such a manner that they might be applied reliably to all languages. Further, there was no proof of the chronological sequence concerned and there was no proof that isolating languages, such as Chinese, were any less efficient in expressing thought than inflective languages such as Sanskrit.

Those who posit a number of stages in the development of thought and endow these stages with historical reality in addition to conceptual validity, will generally seek support from the data furnished by language. That is, they will tend to see in language at once the reflection of various stages of mental development and a kind of evidence in language, by this very fact, of the validity of their analogies. Implicit in all such attempts is a typology defining these stages and such a typology must satisfy the requirements discussed above. One example is the approach of Levy-Bruhl (1910) which in setting up two polar types of mentality, pre-logical and logical, uses evidence from language in support of this thesis. His attempts and those of similarly oriented writers have generally used linguistic evidence in such a fashion that virtually all linguists find them unconvincing. The issue is, however, of some significance because in certain other disciplines the naivete of such employment of linguistic evidence is not always realized.

From the discussion thus far it may seem that the positive contribution of Darwinism to linguistic science is minimal. Our results might be summarized as follows: The concept of evolution can be analyzed as involving two major but independent components. The first of those, the notion of transformation of kinds, is valid but was well established in linguistics prior to Darwin. The second component, that of progress or advance, is not valid in the instance of language and its application whether under the flag of Darwinism or under other influence has led to no positive results.

Yet one question remains—the origin of language itself in the evolutionary process— and it is precisely the success of Darwin's ideas in the biological science that makes this problem in the end unavoidable not only for linguistics, which it would appear chiefly to concern, but for the other sciences that deal with man as well. For, by any definition of emergence, language is a major instance of the appearance of something essentially new in the course of evolution comparable in its significance only to such other basic emergents as life itself or intelligent behavior.

Darwin himself sought to bridge the gap by showing that human language is but a further elaboration of germs already found in animal behavior. Max Mueller, on the other hand, saw the difference as so great that he rested his argument against the possibility of human descent from other animals on the possession of language by man:

. . . it becomes our duty to warn the valiant disciples of Mr. Darwin that before they can claim a real victory, before they can call man the descendant of a mute animal, they must lay regular siege to a fortress which is not to be frightened into submission by a few random shots; the fortress of language, which as yet stands untaken and unshaken on the very frontier between the animal kingdom and man (1873).

Today, presumably, no scientist would accept this as a refutation of the Darwin theory. We distinguish between the evidence for the truth of a fact and the theories designed to account for the fact. If the linguist cannot furnish a satisfactory theory of the origin of language, this does not invalidate the other evidence for the descent of man from forms of life that did not possess symbolic behavior. It rather poses a problem for the sciences dealing with man to explain how language could have arisen in the course of evolutionary development.

The fundamental role of language in making possible that accumulation of learned behavior which we call culture and which is the distinctively human mode of adjustment is appreciated by all anthropologists and social scientists in general. At the present time, however, it is probably more usual to phrase this difference between man and other species in terms of symbolic as distinct from merely sign behavior, with the understanding, no doubt, that language is by far the most important type of human symbolic behavior. It would seem, however, that this view of language as merely one, even if the most important kind of symbolic behavior, tends to obscure the particular and unique functions of linguistic compared to other types of human symboling. Among non-linguistic human symbols we may distinguish first certain individual symbols. Some of those are found in every human community. An example is the sending of flowers at a wedding, which would be generally stated to have a symbolic significance. It is true that only human communities have symbols of this kind, but they are clearly isolated in that they do not fit into any system of multiple related smbols. A more elaborate instance of a non-language symbol is a set of traffic lights since this is a system of several symbols, red, green, and it may be, amber. However, in distinction to language, the number of messages is finite and, indeed, extremely small.

The subordinate stauts of such symbols in respect to language is of a more fundamental nature than their mere isolation or finiteness, for it is a subordinate status shared even with such elaborate and infinite systems as those of mathematics. Language has a unique role which results from its generality of reference and ontogenetic priority in the life history of the individual. For example, in descriptions of Navaho religion we learn that certain colors symbolize certain cardinal directions, i.e. black symbolizes north. We take this to be a direct explanation of the symbol, but in fact we have described it by another symbol, the Navaho word for "north." If we do not know what this means we may translate into English. The infinite regress of explaining symbols by other symbols must have a conclusion, the point at which understanding is reached. If this is itself a symbol system it is always some language, which is thus the ultimate level of explanation. If this also fails we must resort to non-symbolic behavior such as pointing or the like. This even applies to such complex and elaborate systems as mathematics. We all learn some language before we learn mathematics and mathematics is ultimately explainable in ordinary language but not vice versa.

It is conceivable in certain instances that a non-linguistic symbol might be learned without language actually being employed. Thus, by standing on a corner and noting the events associated with the different traffic signals an observer might discover the system involved. It is unlikely that the reasoning involved could be carried out before language was mastered. I do not believe that any fond parents of a pre-language child would risk the experiment. Even if such learning were possible, it would still be true that such a system could not occur in a community without language and that verbal behavior figured indispensably in its invention, its establishment, and the diffusion of the necessary knowledge concerning it in the community. In other words, non-linguistic symbols always arise through some kind of concerted action and pre-arrangement which depends on language. To cite another illustrative example, the symbol system "one if by land and two if by sea," which functioned in connection with the ride of Paul Revere, was a pre-arrangement agreed on by means of language. The relevance of these considerations in the present connection, is that since all other symbols have language as a precondition, the evolutionary problem of the origin of symbolic behavior resolves itself into the problem of the genesis of language. Once language exists, the conditions for the existence of the other kinds of symbols are fulfilled.

The question then, which will be considered here in only a few of its numerous aspects, is the difference between sign behavior, which is pre-linguistic intelligent behavior, and linguistic behavior, which is behavior mediated by the symbol system we call language. We may define a sign, A, as a state of affairs that is evidence to an organism of another state of affairs, B, not simultaneously experienced but associated with it by temporal contiguity in the past. Then A is a sign of B, or we may say that A means B. In these terms, classical or instrumental conditioning is easily restated in the language of sign theory. In the instance of Pavlov's experiment, the bell (A) is a sign of food (B) to the dog. That this relation indeed holds is indicated to the observer by the organism's response of salivation to the conditioned stimulus. Thus salivation itself becomes a sign to the observer that the bell is a sign of food for the dog. In such cases, we may say that the bell as a sign has a meaning functionally equivalent to a sentence in language such as "food will be offered." Such a sign, which is equivalent to a sentence in language, may be called "complete."

The difference between sign and symbol is usually described in terms of the arbitrariness and conventionally of the latter. However, the connection between the bell and the food is conventional also and the two are without causal connection. For sign behavior all that is required is that the sign and thing signified should have been regularly associated in the previous experience of the organism. In many discussions of language learning, the symbolic counterpart of the sign is some single word, which is isolated from its context in a sentence and is therefore incomplete. The question is then raised how this word becomes associated with the thing it signifies. The paradigm is still that of sign learning and this is not disguised by the superficial difference that the physical sign vehicle is a sequence of articulate sounds. This is no doubt a stage in the human acquisition of language. In principle it would appear that animals are capable of such responses. It should also be obvious that the fact that a parrot speaks or responds to what to the human is a whole sentence does not make it any the less a single sign.

The difference between a symbol such as a sentence and sign such as the bell of Pavlov's experiments is that the symbol analytically specifies the situation to which it refers. Particular parts of the sentence refer to particular aspects of the situation, whereas the bell is a unitary sign for an unanalyzed situation. The meaning of a sentence cannot be explained in every instance by past experience in which, like the bell, it has been associated with the state of affairs it describes. When we have mastered language, we can respond appropriately to a sentence we have never heard before and which cannot therefore have any association with our experience, or we can construct such a novel sentence.

How is this feat accomplished? The key, I believe, is the first postulate of Bloomfield's set, that in every speech community some utterances are partly alike both phonetically and semantically. For example, the utterances "Take the apple!" and "Take the banana!" are partly alike in sound and meaning. What is different phonetically between the utterances refers to what is different about the two situations and what is the same refers to what is constant. If we now take the sentence "Drop the apple!" the contrast between this situation and the one correlated with "Take the apple!" confirms our analysis of "take." All this has doubtless been facilitated by experience during the period in which the child learns such words as "apple" and "banana" as isolates, not yet as parts of symbols, i.e. sentences. The evidence that analysis has taken place is the ability, having the three sentences, "Take the apple!" "Take the banana!" and "Drop the apple!" now to understand or reproduce the new sentence "Drop the banana!" without previous experience of it. It is this power that language posseses of analyzing experience and then combining the parts isolated by analysis into new syntheses that enables us to talk of past and remote future experience, to entertain hypotheses, tell lies and talk grammatical nonsense. Initially, however, there must have been coordination between linguistic and non-linguistic events in the experience of the learner. Let us imagine a community of schizophrenics each continually verbalizing in detached fragments having no reference to the immediate situation, with no internal sequential

connections nor with connections to what others are saying! Then it is obvious that even the most talented observer unacquainted with this language could never acquire it by considering the linguistic behavior of its speakers.

The rules by which novel utterances are understood or constructed involve an analysis into classes of words and smaller meaningful units, rules of combination and rules of semantic interpretation. This analysis is what is called grammar. The ability to carry out grammatical analysis would then seem to be one of the things that distinguishes man from other animals. It involves what for want of a more suitable term might be called "multiple abstraction." At the same time that the learner abstracts one element from its context and associates it with some aspect of the situation, he is likewise analyzing other parts of the utterance in similar fashion. We might therefore call language a 3-ring, or more accurately an n-ring abstractional circus since there is no upper limit to the length of sentences. To carry all this out, man must moreover compare what is in his immediate experience with past sentences and the situations associated with them.

It would seem then that, as might have been anticipated, language does involve a new skill of which other animals are incapable. Yet, this skill can still be understood as a stage that depends on the sign skills occurring in pre-language behavior. It is hoped that the present analysis of the basic essentials of symbolic behavior, while it renders full justice to the status of language as an evolutionary emergent, may also serve to make this emergence appear understandable so that, even as Darwin believed, no conceptually unbridgeable gap separates man from his non-human ancestors.

NOTES

1. Almost alone among linguists, Jespersen maintains that linguistic change is in the direction of greater efficiency. His examples, practically all drawn from Indo-European, suggest a particular drift in regard to structural changes in that family rather than a universal linguistic process.

C. History

28

HISTORY AND SCIENCE IN ANTHROPOLOGY

MARC J. SWARTZ

THE basic issues which this paper will be concerned with are: how has history been defined, what has been asked about history, and what sort of answers have been found. These questions may also be stated as: what is the nature of historical theory (since "theory" here will mean any set of definitions, assumptions, and operating hypotheses) and how do different theories affect what may "be done" with history.

In order to gain perspective on these questions, we will first examine the positions of a number of different anthropologists vis-à-vis these issues. The theorists included here have been chosen because their positions represent the basic stands that have been taken in anthropology on these problems.

Franz Boas has long been cited as the prime example of the "antitheoretical" view in anthropology. This tag has been so much used that it has led some to accept the naive position Boas himself held, namely that an "anti" or "non" theoretical position is in fact possible, even that "pure fact" can be collected without the least interference from theory. That Boas held this position is understandable since he viewed theory as being made up of deduction which was a matter of "unbridled imagination and

From *Philosophy of Science*, 25(1): 59–70. Copyright © 1958 by the Williams and Wilkins Company, Baltimore, Md. 21202, U.S.A. Reprinted by permission of the publisher and the author. Marc J. Swartz is Professor of Anthropology and African Studies, Michigan State University.

wild conjecture." He was reacting to the unilinear evolutionists and the extreme diffusionists. When he said that deduction (as applied to social evolutionists) was for "armchair philosophers" he was striking a blow for a more empirical anthropology. Unhappily, all the consequences of his position were not so salubrious, for he anathematized all explicit theory for many of his followers and theory still holds a somewhat dubious aura for some in the field. This is despite the fact that Boas himself was the fountainhead of an elaborate, albeit implicit, theory. Since this theory is greatly concerned with history, we will examine it.

Any theory of history must include a definition of the concept "history." Since Boas never made his theory explicit, his definition has to be gleaned from a number of his writings, but I think the following makes his position rather clear. "In order to understand history it is necessary to know not only how things are, but how they came to be." "If we try to understand what the people are at the present time, we have to inquire into their descent. We must consider the climactic and geographic changes that have occurred. All these have no relation to the laws that may govern the inner life of society. They are accidents. Culture can be understood only as an historical growth. It is determined to a great extent by outer occurrences that do not originate in the inner life of the people." (Part of culture history is in finding out how) "the whole of an indigenous culture in its setting among neighboring cultures builds up its fabric."

Boas, then, holds "history" to be a concept referring to dynamic processes (note plural) that occur over time, that these processes may be, in some aspects, unique, and that they need not be entirely from within the complex of inter- and intra-human phenomena. This is what "history" is for Boas, and having seen what it "is" for him we have a beginning toward finding out what he can ask about it and what answers he is likely to find. In doing this we should bear in mind his statement that "Culture can be understood only as an historical growth." I think it will develop that while he holds that culture can be understood *only* as historical growth, that history alone is not enough for full understanding and that history is seen by Boas as a necessary but not a sufficient condition for the understanding of culture.

Since Boas sees history as unique processes or phenomena which occur over time, or, to put it somewhat differently, as how the present state of affairs arose, it is not surprising that he was much concerned with the tracing of the various aspects of culture to their earlier sources. He holds that we can get only indirect evidence on history, but that we must gather such evidence as is pertinent for the answering of the main *historical* question, viz., by what series of unique events did the present (cultural) situation arise. Before we can proceed with his theory and develop more fully the questions he asked and the sort of answers he expected, we must know by what canons he chose the material of his inquiry. From his insistence that history contains many separate processes we would expect that his investigations would be concerned with the development of the several separate aspects of culture each as an independent object of study. He puts it "(my work in) unraveling the historical development of social organization, secret societies, spread of art forms, . . . and of folk tales is for the enlightenment of problems concerned with . . . the history of a culture back into earlier times." From his position on the unique character of many of these processes, his constant efforts to obtain detailed and exhaustive data on the problem being considered is to be expected, for if an event is unique we can learn nothing about it by appealing to other events which fit the same general category. Only through the collec-

tion of all the data there is about a unique event or process can we truly understand it.

Boas realized, however, that there were certain limitations on the kind of data that could be collected about a given topic. In seeking for "how things came to be" there was, he knew, some data of the highest significance which could not easily be found. Since he held that "the causal conditions of cultural happenings lie always in the interaction between individual and society," it is not difficult to understand that the reconstruction of history among groups with no documents to tell us about specific individual interactions with society in connection with a given past event should be an insurmountable task for history. It is at this point that he is forced to bring in science, which for him is the stating of similarities or regularities in recurrent processes. He held that through studies of current acculturation phenomena we might be able to gain understanding of the dynamics of culture. He is committed to supplementing history (as he defines it) with the regularities of individual-society interaction for the understanding of culture since it is only through the application of established regularities about such phenomena that he can fill the gap left by the impossibility of recovering this data from the past. Boas thought it much easier to establish dissemination than to follow up development due to inner forces, since he thought the data for the latter sort of study much more difficult to obtain. He says: "They may, however, be observed in every phenomenon of acculturation in which foreign elements are remodeled according to the patterns prevalent in their new environment, and they may be found in the peculiar local developments of widely spread ideas and activities. The reason why the study of inner development has not been taken up energetically, is not due to the fact that from a theoretical (!) point of view it is unimportant, it is rather due to the inherent methodological difficulties."

It appears from the above that the "interaction of man with society" is not thought by Boas to be in the class of unique or non-repetitive, non-regular events available only to exhaustive individual study. We may formulate generalities about these but we can find out about most other events in history only by studying the specific events. He holds to this position as it applies to that part of the history of an event which deals with dissemination or diffusion, as is indicated by his adamantine stand against those, like Smith, who tried to gain understanding of some particular diffusion by referring to statements about a class of allegedly similar diffusions, as well as by his own careful and detailed investigations of the spread of a given aspect of culture.

Having seen something of Boas' theory, let us examine the questions which Boas set out to solve by the study of history. His works are filled with questions like "In a group of folk-tales which character—raven, mink, coyote, blue jay—plays the trickster," revealing his interest in the specific and the unique. He used the answers to questions like the above to find out about the diffusion of the tales and thereby something about the history of the culture that contained the tales. He maintained that it was not enough for proof of historical contact be-tween peoples to make a catalogue of similar traits in their cultures, but that the similar traits must be shown to be similarly related. It was in establishing the similar relations between similar traits that the vast amounts of detail had to be brought to bear.

For Boas the most important question that history could answer was what happened to make a particular, unique culture the way he found it. By the detailed examination of diffu-sion he hoped to establish the unique processes by which the several aspects of a culture came to their present status and his work is centered around doing this. However, diffusion for him was not, in itself, all of the process by which an existing state was brought into being. It might even be said that evidence for the diffu-sion of a trait was only to establish the stimulus for the internal dynamics of the culture and Boas, holding these as difficult to study, left them for other workers. Nonetheless, he seems committed to the position that a full under-standing of culture is not forthcoming without the establishment of regularities of internal dy-namics since history by itself—in Boas' position —can tell us only what was presented to a culture and not how it was accepted, integrated, and changed. Boas recognized clearly the need for the establishment of such regularities. He says: "While on the whole the unique character of cultural growth in each area stands out as a salient element in the history of cultural devel-opment, we may recognize that typical paral-lelisms do occur. We are, however, not so much inclined to look for similarities in detailed cus-toms but rather in certain dynamic conditions which are due to social or psychological causes that are liable to lead to similar results." As I have said, he himself avoided the problems of the establishment of regularities by labeling this endeavor "methodologically difficult" but in so doing he diminished his ability to gain the understanding he sought. He says "The idea that the phenomena of the present have developed from previous forms with which they are genet-ically connected . . . knit together groups of facts that had hitherto seemed disconnected," but he has only provided himself with a means for investigating the "genetic connections" of forms while avoiding the study of the "develop-ment" of the forms out of what may be an aversion to the establishment of regularities. Regardless of the reason for his neglecting the search for regularities, I maintain that his posi-tion commits him to the investigation of dynam-ics and to the inability to investigate these as recurrent, regular phenomena—science to him.

Whatever the ability of Boas' scheme to solve the basic problems he set out to illuminate, his general conception of the role of history as a device to be used in the understanding of cul-tures as they now are is very widely shared. To take as an example just one of the many who hold this view, Lowie says "the explanation of a cultural phenomenon will consist in referring it back to the particular circumstances that pre-ceded it." However, concurrence on this view of history is not universal among anthropol-ogists, or even among American anthropologists. Leslie White maintains that far from giving us any generic understanding of a culture as it now is, history can only tell us a few specific things. White proceeds from a far less inclusive definition of history than did Boas, so this is to be expected. For White, history is only "con-cerned with events in their temporal aspect." Boas divides explanations of culture into his-tory and science but White separates them into three different parts or conceptual schemes. These are history, evolution, and formal-func-tional analysis. He holds that phenomena may be referred to any one of three schemes but that each one is peculiarly equipped for an-swering certain questions and not for others. If we are interested in a phenomenon as the emergence of a form out of previous forms, we are making an evolutionary study. When we wish to know how a process works and what its structure is, we are involved in a formal-functional study. Only when we ask when a phenomenon originated, who was party to its origination, and where it has diffused from its point of origin are we asking historical questions. In this respect White, like Boas, is very emphatic in pointing out that history is concerned with the uniqueness of events, while evolution is concerned with their similarity. "The interest (of history) is always focused upon the unique event of a specific time and place."

In cultural processes the scope of history is put forth by White as follows: "Whether it be firearms, porcelain, the potter's wheel, the calculus—or what not, the custom has a history. It originated at a certain time and place, and diffused subsequently to certain places at definite times." But the history of a process, by his definition is not enough. We must also have the evolutional and formal-functional analysis of the process before we can fully understand it. "One type of interpretation is as legitimate and as necessary as another. All three are essential if the science is to be well balanced and complete."

White differs from Boas as concerns the inclusiveness of the concept 'history' and as to the number of conceptual schemes involved in the understanding of culture (as well as on very many other things not immediately relevant here), but on three major issues the two agree. First, they both define history as concerned with unique events and second, they jointly view history as concerned with time sequences even though their emphases differ. Third, though White is more explicit, they both maintain that historical knowledge is not enough and that it must be supplemented by knowledge of non-unique regularities. Of course White and Boas are greatly at odds about how these regularities are to be established. Boas exudes caution, even timidity where generalizations are concerned and holds that "we must recognize the fact that before we seek for what is common to all culture, we must analyze each culture by careful and exact methods; (Intro. to publ. of the Jesup No. Pacific Exped., Vol. 1 1898–1900, p. 4)" while White blusters into generalities with a certain scorn for the empirically oriented. He tells us that "the basic principles, the great generalities of science, are not arrived at inductively. . . ."

Despite the immense differences, both Boas and White agree that history alone, while necessary is not sufficient for the full understanding of culture; that the questions which history can answer are essential but that they are not the only ones which require replies. There are, of course, many who dissent from this view of the role of history as being intimately concerned with unique events and/or time sequence and who variously do not concur that these two aspects are of paramount importance. We will now examine the theories of history of some of these dissenters.

A. L. Kroeber is most explicit in his definition of "history" as regards time sequence and his position is very different in emphasis from that of both White and Boas in this (and many other) regards. Kroeber says "I suggest as the distinctive feature of the historical approach, in any field, not the dealing with time sequence —though that almost inevitably crops out where historical impulses are genuine and strong— but an endeavor at descriptive integration." In the exposition of the concept "descriptive integration" we get, at once, an insight into Kroeber's position on history and some beginning [insight] into the differences between his theoretical approach and aims and those of the previous two theories. "By descriptive," he says, "I mean that the phenomena are preserved intact as phenomena, so far as that is possible; in distinction from the approach of the nonhistorical sciences, which set out to decompose phenomena in order to determine processes as such. History of course does not ignore process, but it does refuse to set it as its first objective. Process in history is a nexus among phenomena treated as phenomena, not a thing to be sought out and extracted from phenomena. Historical activity is essentially a procedure of integrating phenomena as such; scientific activity is essentially a procedure of analysis, of dissolving phenomena in order to convert into process formulations."

From all the above a number of important aspects of A. L. Kroeber's theory follow or at least are foreshadowed. The major part played by the concept 'pattern' in Kroeber's theory is of course necessitated by his notion 'descriptive integration.' Kroeber, indeed, utilizes 'pattern' as one of his most powerful tools of 'historical' (in his sense) analysis and it is in the development of this concept that one of his sharpest differences from Boas appears. To Kroeber, pattern is the organization of events into systems or manifestations of order. He says a culture pattern is "a system [which] . . . bears in itself certain specific potentialities and also specific limitations, which enable it, even compel it, barring catastrophe from outside to realize or fulfill itself to the terminus of these potentialities, but not to go beyond them."

Pattern, then, is for Kroeber itself a moving and dynamic force. Though he accounts himself, and is, more concerned with bringing together phenomena into a coherent body, i.e., descriptive integration of events into patterns, than he is with process, still he does deal with processes and the dynamic unit for this is the pattern. In *Configuration of Culture Growth* he speaks of the "life cycle" of culture patterns, ascribing to the patterns "growth," "realization," "exhaustion," and "death" (page 91) or "growth," "saturation," and "exhaustion" (page 13). How different this is from Boas who has the individual at the basis of process. If this important difference needs any further emphasis, Boas can be quoted as saying "it seems hardly necessary to consider a mystic entity that exists outside of its individual carriers and *that moves of its own force*" (italics mine). White, with his disregard of the individual and constant explanation of culture in terms of energy applied through technology as a *ding an sich* in the shaping of culture, is quite close to Kroeber in this respect.

The Kroeber conception of an outside force in culture, an enteleky, 'wave of the future,' or elan vitale type force, gives him an approach to history quite unlike that of Boas. Both Kroeber and Boas as well as White see history as unique events, but Kroeber in disallowing the individual frees himself from the need to supplement historical explanations with statements of regularities. It is true that Kroeber speaks occasionally of the possibility of science entering into cultural explanations but on these rare occasions it is clear that any regularities found would only add frills to the historical study which is, in itself, complete. Boas, if his position is consistently held, has only half an explanation when he has the historical material. To achieve the full understanding of cultural phenomena, in the Boasian scheme one must know *how* the phenomenon occurred as well as that it did occur and to do the former, regularities in the interaction of the individual and society must be established.

This last brings out another important difference between Kroeber on the one hand and Boas (and also White) on the other. This difference is one of aim. Boas and White both use history as a part of an effort to establish explanations for cultural phenomena. Boas always asks what were the antecedents of the present state and this with some statements about the dynamics of the change would explain the new state. White uses historical studies in conjunction with evolutionary and formal-functional studies to demonstrate that his principle of technological determinism explains cultural phenomena. Kroeber does not attempt explanation. The main import of his repeated avowal of greatest concern with phenomena rather than process seems to be that he is mainly seeking to show how things are and how they got to be the way they are. Kroeber strives to put things into order systems, to descriptively integrate, not to explain the present state of things.

The Kroeber position differs from both White and Boas in the role of historical material in the understanding of culture and in the definition of history as necessarily involving time sequence, but it does agree in having history composed of unique events. Such agreement is far from universal, there being two major theoretical positions which have history composed of recurring events. These two are the diffusionist and unilinear evolutionist viewpoints. An example of the latter is L. M. Morgan.

Morgan contended that the condition of mankind was essentially the same at any given stage in his universal developmental scheme. This being his position, history stands not as a series of unique events but rather as events which, at least grossly, are the same in every group as they are for another group that has passed through the same developmental stage.

Historical material has a somewhat ambiguous role in the schemes of Morgan and other universal evolutionists. While the material originally may have had some part in the formation of Morgan's scheme, it does not seem to be used either to explain cultural phenomena or to be drawn together into integrated patterns. Rather, as is somewhat true of White, the data of history are employed as examples of the developmental stages and far from the data modifying the theory, one may say that the theory modifies the data. For example, Morgan uses his theory to tell us that Greece and Rome *must* have had a matrilineal kinship system prior to their historically known patrilineal system. This is so not because there is evidence on Greece and Rome to indicate confirmation of Morgan's hypothesis that matrilineal systems always precede patrilineal, but rather it is so because Morgan's position is that matrilineal systems always precede patrilineal, and Greece and Rome are known to have had patrilineal systems.

While the diffusionists were in many ways different from evolutionists like Morgan, they closely resembled them in using historical data in very much the same way and viewing history as a series of recurrent, unique events. The *Kulturkreise* as represented by Graebner and Foy had the same six to eight basic blocks of culture diffusing to all the peoples on the earth so that at a given 'circle' the history of any group is basically the same as that of any other.

Another diffusionist, Ratzel, has a largely different position from the Viennese above, but he also views history as composed of recurrent events. He postulated that there was a primeval period of very intensive migration with much crossing and recrossing of the earth with attendant contacts between the different cultural groups. These contacts brought about a universal leveling of cultures so that the history of one group is, at least for a period of time, the same as the history of another. Because of this postulated period of migration and contact it was not necessary to use historical material to demonstrate the occurrence of a diffusion. We might say of Ratzel that his explanations are from the "historical unity" of man, although, of course, he supplemented his diffusion with a recognition of the effect of environment.

So far, to sum up, we have considered four basic positions on the theory of history. The first of these holds history to be a sequence of unique events and as such these must be recovered for each case. History is here not the entire explanation of culture since it can tell us only the events which have preceded the present state of affairs. In order to gain full understanding we must also have knowledge of the regularities which are present in the dynamics of culture since these dynamics occur through individuals and cannot often be recovered as historical data. In this theory, history is conceived as necessarily involving time sequence and (it might be added) while this sequence may not necessarily be a causal one, it is usually one in which the relation of an antecedent-consequent obtains.

The second main theoretical position converges with the first insofar as history is conceived as a series of unique events. This position differs from it, however, in that history does not necessarily involve time sequence but does always involve the pulling together of events into ordered patterns or systems. This last, descriptive integration, is a goal in itself and the historical material is not necessarily used to explain cultural phenomena. This position, like a somewhat minor one between it and the first, sees the dynamics of culture in a force outside of the individual. Any explanation that might be made from this position is done with recourse to extra-historical or scientific material.

The third position is that history is not unique, but recurrent and that the material of history is more to be used as examples than as in either an explanation of phenomena or a descriptive integration. Some holders of this position would contend that the historical data are used as a test of their theories. Insofar as this is true, it is more or less distinctive of this position, for in the first theory as represented by Boas, history is conceived as a partial explanation of phenomena and not as test of any theory. It might cogently be argued that Boas used history to test the hypothesis that the present is derived from the past, but certainly he did not think of it in that way.

A fourth basic position which has not been presented is that history is irrelevant to the understanding of cultural phenomena and as such need not be considered.

Another way of classifying the uses of history would be to divide them as follows. First there are those writers who conceive of history as the unfolding of a uniform force which has been postulated on *a priori* grounds. This would include the unilinear evolutionists with their psychic unity and the diffusionists with their historic unity. Next are those who conceive of history as a series of events, each one causally related to the next. This position includes Boas with the qualification that the nature of the causal relation between events is not to be discovered from historical material. Third are those who define history differently than the first two and see history as statements of ordered phenomena and consider the task of history not that of explaining phenomena but rather of displaying them in a descriptive system.

I would like now to raise some general considerations on the nature of historical theory and the use of historical material. First I would like to comment on the theories of history which contend that it is a series of unique events. Obviously such a contention is warranted since the events of history are different in many ways, so the question is not one of validity but rather of something else. The traditional argument for viewing historical events as unique is that each occurrence is completely singular and that only the concatenation of certain never-to-be-repeated events will contribute to the specific phenomenon in which the historian (anthropologist) is interested. On the other hand it is argued that while events are never identical since if they were they would be co-extensive, still they are similar in enough ways so that similar events in similar concatenations result in similar effects. This argument seems to resolve itself into a question of interest, i.e., whether the anthropologist wishes to understand a particular culture or to formulate general rules which will guide him in understanding something broader than a single culture whether it be 'historical pressures,' 'principles of culture change,' or whatever. It is my contention that this is not the case, that the question of whether historical events should be viewed as unique or similar is not a function solely of the interest of the worker. Rather I will contend that in either case, i.e., both when the author is concerned with understanding a single culture and when his concern is more broad, the events of history are not, in fact, viewed as unique and that assumed general principles or statements of empirical regularity always enter into the exposition, though usually implicitly.

First it has become almost bromidic that the observer abstracts and selects from the phenomena he is studying and that this selection is not gratuitous but rather is guided. This guiding, so to speak, is on the basis of certain hypotheses which the researcher holds, perhaps implicitly, about what is important or meaningful or basic. These hypotheses are general statements and since they are always employed in observation they force the use of generalizations into historical inquiries. Further than this, the anthropologist must always evaluate his data, interpret the precise meaning of verbal or written information, and/or pass on the authenticity of records and other material. To do this he must, and always does, have canons of criticism and these, too, are of the nature of laws or statements of regularity. I do not maintain that there is no difference between viewing history as a series of unique events antecedent to the specific phenomenon under consideration and viewing history as a series of similar events leading to similar phenomena,

but that the main difference is in scope and that in both the general principles must, are, and have always been employed.

The second point I would like to take up concerns the two main uses of historical data, viz., explanation and descriptive integration. In *both* general principles and lawlike propositions must be brought to bear so that those who believe they avoid the use of generalities by shunning causal explanations are, I contend, mistaken. The process of abstraction and that of selection are certainly as omnipresent in descriptive integration as in any other type of human observation and while it is true that by avoiding any explanation it is not necessary to assume any laws of causal dependence, so that one type of general statement is avoided, another is put in its place. This is some sort of an assumption about what constitutes an ordering of events and this is certainly as broad as any assumption about causality. There is, however, one essential difference between the two types of assumptions. The causal assumptions may be tested against reality by prediction whereas those concerned with what constitutes an ordering of events can never be empirically tested. Whether this last is undesirable or not is a question of values, but those taking this position should be aware that any formulation of an ordering of events will have the same validity as any other and that this price is paid not for getting rid of all lawlike statements but only of one sort.

My basic contention, then, is that whether history is conceived of as a unique series of events or as a series of similar events, and whether the data of history is used for explanation or for descriptive integration, the use of generalities, statements of empirical regularity, cannot be avoided though they can, of course, remain implicit. That more fruitful results would be forthcoming if the generalities used by those of us who work with history were made explicit and tested, seems a point which does not need to be labored.

Let us examine for a moment the nature of generalities which are used in historical explanations such as those Boas wished to make, the Evolutionists proposed, and even Kroeber essays. It has already been pointed out that all of these involve statements of regularity. Now we will show that they all, excluding Kroeber, have or attempt the same *type of* statements. This asserts that where an event of a specified kind C occurs at a given time and place, an event of a specific kind E will occur at a place and time which is related in a specified manner to the place and time of the occurrence of the first event (symbols "C" and "E" suggest cause and effect which are often, but not always, applied to events related by a law of the above kind). We have seen that Boas maintained that the part of the regularity involving the relation of the first (in time) and the next event had to be determined by means other than those of history. In this he demonstrates his impressive sophistication, but others have not followed him in this and maintain only the first part of his position, namely that culture can be understood completely through the examination of events in time and without any reference to material outside of these events. Hume has pointed out the untenability of attempting to reveal that one event produced another by an intensive examination of the two events. The untenability of such an attempt lies in the necessity of assuming some sort of connection or dependence between events. This is usually referred to as "dynamics" or process and as Boas recognized, these two are not ascertainable by the examination of sequences of past events. As Hempel puts it, "to speak of empirical determination (in history) without reference to general laws means to use a metaphor without cognitive content."

Kroeber presents a position somewhat different than those proposing to explain culture solely by the examination of a series of events. He maintains that change in culture come about through the unfolding of elements in the composition of culture. This sort of an explanation (which is in many ways like that of the unilinear evolutionists and the diffusionists) on the basis of some force inherent in culture, some entelechy, is only metaphoric since it provides us with no mechanisms or principles for exploration. To quote Hempel again, "Accounts of this type are based on metaphors rather than laws. They convey pictorial and emotional appeals instead of insight into factual connections. They substitute vague analogies and intuitive plausibilities 'for deduction from testable statements.' "

In summary, my position is that regardless of the use of historical data, the assumption of regularities and general principles is always involved. Causal explanations on the basis of historical data differ only slightly from so-called pure descriptions since both involve many of the same elements. The distinction generally held between history and science as differing in the use of general statements and the application of law-like principles is held here to be a specious one since both are entirely dependent upon general statements and "good" history like "good" science will make explicit the general propositions that it uses and will seek confirmation for them. Some history is not "good" history just as some science is not "good" science but this does not in any way affect the identity of the two.

One, then, is led to agree with the philosopher Nagel when he says: "Neither can historical study dispense with at least a tacit acceptance of universal statements of the kind occurring in the natural sciences. . . . In brief, history is not an ideographic discipline."

29

SOME ISSUES
IN THE LOGIC OF HISTORICAL ANALYSIS

ERNEST   NAGEL

ACCORDING to Aristotle, poetry, like theoretical science, is "more philosophic and of graver import" than history, for the former is concerned with the pervasive and universal, and the latter is addressed to the special and the singular. Aristotle's remark is a possible his-

From *Scientific Monthly,* 54 (March, 1952): 162–169. Reprinted by permission of the publisher and the author. Ernest Nagel is Professor of Philosophy, Columbia University.

torical source of a widely held current distinction between two allegedly different types of sciences: the nomothetic, which seek to establish abstract general laws for indefinitely repeatable processes; and the ideographic, which aim to understand the unique and nonrecurrent. It is often maintained that the natural sciences are nomothetic, whereas history (in the sense of an account of events) is ideographic; and it is claimed in consequence that the logic and conceptual structure of historical explanations are fundamentally different from those of the natural sciences. It is my aim here to examine this and related issues in the logic of historical analysis.

I

Even a cursory examination of treatises in theoretical natural science and of books on history reveals the prima facie difference between them, that by and large the statements of the former are general in form, and contain few if any references to specific objects, places, and times, whereas the statements of the latter are almost without exception singular and replete with proper names, dates, and geographic specifications. To this extent, at least, the alleged contrast between the natural sciences as nomothetic and history as ideographic appears to be well founded.

It would, however, be a gross error to conclude that singular statements play no role in the theoretical sciences or that historical inquiry makes no use of universal ones. No conclusions concerning the actual character of specific things and processes can be derived from general statements alone; and theories and laws must be supplemented by initial or boundary conditions when the natural sciences attempt to explain any particular occurrence. Nor does the familiar and often useful distinction between "pure" and "applied" natural science impair the relevance of this point. For, clearly, even the pure natural sciences can assert their general statements as empirically warranted only on the basis of concrete factual evidence, and therefore only by establishing and using a variety of singular statements. And there are branches of natural science, such as geophysics and animal ecology, that are concerned with the spatiotemporal distribution and development of individual systems. It follows, in short, that

neither the natural sciences taken as a whole nor their purely theoretical subdivisions can be regarded as being exclusively nomothetic.

Neither can historical study dispense with at least a tacit acceptance of universal statements of the kind occurring in the natural sciences. Thus, although the historian may be concerned with the nonrecurrent and the unique, he selects and abstracts from the concrete occurrences he studies, and his discourse about what is individual and singular requires the use of common names and general descriptive terms. Such characterizations are associated with the recognition of various kinds or types of things and occurrences, and therefore with the implicit acknowledgment of numerous empirical regularities. Again, one phase of a historian's task is to establish the authenticity of documents and other remains from the past, the precise meaning of recorded assertions, and the reliability of testimony concerning past events. For the effective execution of this task of external and internal criticism, the historian must be armed with a wide assortment of general laws, borrowed from one or the other of the natural and social sciences. And, since historians usually aim to be more than mere chroniclers of the past, and attempt to understand and explain recorded actions in terms of their causes and consequences, they must obviously assume supposedly well-established laws of causal dependence. In brief, history is not a purely ideographic discipline.

Nonetheless, there is an important asymmetry between theoretical and historical sciences. A theoretical science like physics seeks to establish both general and singular statements, and in the process of doing so physicists will employ previously established statements of both types. Historians, on the other hand, aim to assert warranted singular statements about the occurrence and interrelations of specific actions; and though this task can be achieved only by assuming and using general laws, historians do not regard it as part of their task to *establish* such laws. The distinction between history and theoretical science is thus somewhat analogous to the difference between medical diagnosis and physiology, or between geology and physics. A geologist seeks to ascertain, for example, the sequential order of geologic formations, and he is able to do so by applying various physical laws to the materials he encounters; it is not the geologist's task, qua geologist, to establish the laws of mechanics or of radioactive disintegration that he may employ.

The fact that historical research is concerned with the singular, and seeks to ascertain the causal dependencies between specific occurrences, does not warrant the widespread contention that there is a radical difference between the logical structure of explanations in the historical and the generalizing sciences. I shall consider only one specific argument to support the claim that there is such a difference. It has been said that there is a demonstrable *formal* difference between the "general concepts" of the theoretical sciences and the "individual concepts" assumed to be the goals of historical inquiry. Concepts of the first kind are alleged to conform to the familiar logical principle of the inverse variation of the extension and intension of terms: when a set of general terms is arranged in order of their increasing extensions, their intensions decrease. But quite the reverse is said to be the case for the individual concepts of historical explanations, since the more inclusive the "scope" of such a concept, the richer and fuller is its "meaning." Thus, the term "French Enlightenment" is claimed to have not only a more inclusive scope than the term "the life of Voltaire," but also to possess a fuller intension.

But this is simply a confusion, derived in part from a failure to distinguish the relation of *inclusion* between the extensions of terms, from some form of *whole-part* relation between an instance of a term and a component of that instance. Thus, the French Enlightenment may be said to "contain" as one of its "components" the life of Voltaire; and it is doubtless correct to maintain that the term "French Enlightenment" is "richer in meaning or content" than the term "the life of Voltaire." But the *extension* of the term "French Enlightenment" does *not* include the *extension* of the term "the life of Voltaire," so that the logical principle under discussion cannot be significantly applied to these terms.

More generally, there appears to be no good reason for claiming that the general pattern of explanations in historical inquiry, or the logical structure of the conceptual tools employed in it, differs from those encountered in the generalizing and the natural sciences. The explanatory premises in history, as in the natural sciences, include a number of implicitly assumed laws, as well as many explicitly (though usually incompletely) formulated singular statements of initial conditions. The tacitly assumed laws may be of various kinds. They may be statements of regularities well attested in some special science, or they may be uncodified assumptions taken from common experience; they may be universal statements of invariable concomitance, or they may be statistical in form; they may assert a uniformity in temporal sequence, or they may assert some relation of coexistent dependence. The singular statements of initial conditions are of comparable variety, and although the truth of many of them is often incontrovertible it is frequently highly conjectural. Indeed, the relevance of such singular statements to the specific problems under investigation, as well as their truth, are questions upon which historians are often undecided or unable to achieve unanimity. There are, in fact, several problems in this connection that are of much concern to historical research, although they are not without relevance to other branches of social science as well. I therefore turn to consider briefly some of the real and alleged difficulties that plague the pursuit of historical knowledge.

II

It is a platitude that research in history as in other areas of science selects and abstracts from the concrete occurrences studied, and that however detailed a historical discourse may be it is never an exhaustive account of what actually happened. Curiously enough, it is the very selectivity of history that generates many of the broader questions relating to the nature of historical inquiry and is sometimes made the occasion for wholesale skepticism concerning the possibility of "objective" explanations in historical matters. Since a historian exercises selection in choosing problems for study, and also in his proposed solutions to them, it will be convenient to examine some of the relevant issues under these two heads.

1) Historians do not all concern themselves with the same things, and there are undoubtedly many past events that have received attention from no historian. Why does one historian occupy himself with ancient Greece, another with modern Germany, still another with the development of legal institutions in the American colonies, a fourth with the evolution of mathematical notation, and so on? Is there some general feature which differentiates those oc-

currences that are of concern to historians from those that are not? And, above all, is a historian prevented from giving a warranted or objective account of things because of his initial choice of a limited problem?

It is clear that there is no uniform answer to the first of these queries, for in historical inquiry as in other branches of science a variety of circumstances may determine what problems are to be investigated. It may be individual preference and endowment, controlled by education and the influence of teachers; it may be professional obligation or the desire for financial gain; it may be national pride, social pressure, or a sense of political mission. Historians of ideas have given some attention to this matter, and have uncovered interesting data concerning stimuli to specific investigations. But there is no prima facie reason to believe that, because a historical inquiry begins with a specific problem, or because there are causal determinants for his choice, a historian is in principle precluded—any more than is a natural scientist—from rendering an adequate account of the subjects he is investigating.

Many writers maintain, however, that the selectivity of history is peculiar in that the historian is inescapably concerned with "value-impregnated" subject matter. Thus, according to one influential view, an individual or process can be properly labeled as "historical" only if it is "irreplaceable," either because it uniquely embodies some universally accepted cultural value or because it is instrumental to the actualization of such a value. In consequence, the supposition that historical inquiry can ignore theoretical value relations is said by some writers to involve a self-deception, whereas other commentators have concluded that unlike the physical sciences "history is violently personal," since "stars and molecules have no loves and hates, while men do." There is, however, no basis for the claim that historical study is addressed exclusively to value-impregnated occurrences, unless indeed the word "history" is arbitrarily redefined so as to conform with the claim. For, although undoubtedly much historical inquiry is concerned with events that may be so characterized, there are also many investigations commonly called "historical" that are not of this nature—for example, inquiries into the development of the stars, biological species, and much else. More generally, there appears to be no warrant for any of the various claims that the occurrences studied by historians are distinguished by some inherent differentiating feature from those that are not. Moreover, even when a historian is concerned with admittedly value-impregnated subject matter or with occurrences manifesting various passions, it by no means follows that he must himself share or judge those values or passions. It is an obvious blunder to suppose that only a fat cowherd can drive fat kine. It is an equally crude error to maintain that one cannot inquire into the conditions and consequences of values and evaluations without necessarily engaging in moral or aesthetic value judgments.

There is also the broad question whether historical inquiry is inevitably guilty of distorting the facts because it is addressed to limited problems and is concerned only with certain selected materials of the past. The supposition that it is entails the view that one cannot have competent knowledge of anything unless one knows everything, and is a corollary to the philosophic doctrine of the "internality" of all relations. It will suffice here to note that, were the doctrine sound, not only would every historical account ever written be condemned as a necessarily mutilated and distorted version of what has happened, but a similar valuation would have to be placed on all science, and indeed on all analytical discourse. In short, the fact that inquiry is selective because it originates in a specific and limited problem places the historian in no worse position than it does other scientists with respect to the possibility of achieving what is commonly characterized as objectively warranted knowledge.

2) Historical inquiry is selective not only in its starting point; it is also selective in proposing solutions to its problems. A variety of skeptical doubts about the possibility of an objective history has been expressed in consequence.

One such expression takes the form that, in view of the inexhaustibly numerous relations in which a given event stands to other events, no account can ever render the "full reality" of what has occurred. Accordingly, since every historical account covers only a few aspects of an occurrence and stops at some point in the past in tracing back its antecedents, every proposed explanation of that occurrence is said to bear the mark of arbitrariness and subjectivity. Part of this objection can be summarily dismissed with the reminder that it is never the task of any inquiry initiated by a specific problem to *reproduce* its subject matter, and that it would be a gratuitous performance were a historian in the pursuit of such a problem to formulate "all that has been said, done, and thought by human beings on the planet since humanity began its long career." Not only is the bare fact that inquiry is selective no valid ground for doubting the objectively warranted character of its conclusions; on the contrary, unless an inquiry were selective it would never come near to resolving the specific question by which it is generated.

However, the objection under discussion also rests on another misconception: it in effect assumes that since every causal condition for an event has its own causal conditions, the event is never properly explained unless the entire regressive series of the latter conditions are also explained. It has been maintained, for example, that

A Baptist sermon in Atlanta, if we seek to explain it, takes us back through the Protestant Reformation to Galilee—and far beyond in the dim origins of civilization. We can, if we choose, stop at any point along the line of relations, but that is an arbitrary act of will and does violence to the quest for truth in the matter (C. A. Beard).

But is there any violence to the truth? Is B not a cause of A simply because C is a cause of B? When some future position of a planet is predicted with the help of gravitational theory and information about the initial condition of the solar system at some given time, is there ground for skepticism simply because the assumed initial conditions are in turn the outcome of previous ones? These are rhetorical questions, for the answers to all of them are obviously in the negative. Moreover, precisely what is the problem in connection with the Baptist sermon in Atlanta? Is it why a given individual delivered it at a stated time and occasion, or why he chose a particular text and theme, or why that occasion happened to arise, or why Baptists flourish in Atlanta, or why they developed as a Protestant sect, or why the Protestant Reformation occurred, or why Christianity arose in antiquity? These are all quite different questions, and an adequate answer for one of them is not even relevant as a proposed solution for the others. The supposition that, when a problem is made definite a regressive chain of answers must be sought if any one answer is to be objectively warranted, is patently self-contradictory. On the other hand, the fact that one problem may suggest another, and so lead to a possibly endless series of new inquiries, simply illustrates the progressive character of the scientific enterprise; that fact is no support for the claim that unless the series is terminated, every proposed solution to a given problem is necessarily a mutilation of the truth.

Skepticism concerning the possibility of objectively warranted explanations in human history takes a more empirical turn when it bases its negations on the influence of personal and social bias upon such inquiry. The doubt embodied in the *aperçu* that history is written by the survivors is by no means a novelty; but in recent years it has been deepened and given a radical form by many sociologists of knowledge. According to some of them, all thought is conditioned and controlled by the "existential situation" in which it occurs; and, especially when thinking is directed to human affairs, the interpretation of observed facts, the selection of problems for inquiry and the methods employed for resolving them, and the standards of validity accepted are all functions of the thinker's unconscious value commitments and world outlook, his social position, and his political and class loyalties. Every cognitive claim concerning matters of vital human interest is therefore said to be valid only within the particular social setting in which it emerges; and the belief that it is possible to obtain explanations that are "true" for everyone, irrespective of his position in a given society, is declared to be part of the self-deception (or "ideology") of a culture.

There appear to be four distinct issues raised by this form of skepticism. In the first place, the choice of particular problems for study, especially inquiries into human affairs, is undoubtedly controlled by the character of a given culture, and sometimes by the status of the student in that culture. An investigation of traffic problems is not likely to be made in an agricultural society, and a man's interest in labor history may very well be causally related to his social position. But, as has already been seen, this form of selective activity on the part of an inquirer does not necessarily jeopardize the objectivity of his findings.

In the second place, no inquiry takes place in an intellectual vacuum, and every investigator approaches his task with information and guiding ideas derived in large measure from his culture. But it does not follow from this circumstance alone that the conscious and unconscious value commitments associated with the social status of an investigator inevitably influence his acceptance of one conclusion rather than another. The preconceptions he brings to the analysis of a given problem may be neutral to all differences in social values, even when that problem is concerned with human affairs. And, in point of fact, there are many questions in the social as well as in the natural sciences upon which there is complete agreement among students, despite their different social positions and loyalties.

It is undoubtedly the case, in the third place, that the standards of validity operative in an inquiry are *causally* related to other cultural traits, and that social status, class and national bias, and general world perspectives frequently influence what conclusions a man accepts. For example, the degree of precision currently demanded in experimental work is certainly not independent of the current state of technology; and a comparison of Southern and Northern histories of the period of reconstruction following the American Civil War makes amply clear the force of sectional and race bias. This is an area of study that has not yet been systematically exploited, although sociologists of knowledge have already illuminated the genesis of many ideas and the manner in which social pressures enforce their acceptance. In any event, biased thinking is a perennial challenge to the critical historian of human affairs; and research into the causal determinants of bias is of undoubted value for recognizing its occurrence and for mitigating if not always eliminating its influence. The very fact that biased thinking may be detected and its sources investigated shows that the case for objective explanations in history is not necessarily hopeless. Indeed, the assertion that a historian exhibits bias assumes that there is a distinction between biased and unbiased thinking, and that the bias can be identified—for otherwise the assertion would at best be simply futile name-calling. In consequence, it is possible, even if frequently difficult, to correct the bias and to obtain conclusions in better agreement with the evidence. Accordingly, if doubt concerning the objectivity of a historical explanation is based on considerations relating to the causal influence of various social factors upon the evaluation of evidence, it is often salutary and well taken; but it does not entail a wholesale skepticism concerning the possibility of such explanations.

This brings me to the final issue. It is sometimes argued that the social perspective of a student of human affairs is not only causally influential upon his inquiry, but is *logically* involved both in his standards of validity as well as in the meaning of his statements. And it is also maintained that one must therefore reject the thesis that "the genesis of a proposition is under all circumstances irrelevant to its truth" (K. Mannheim). On the other hand, the radical skepticism concerning objective explanations of human affairs that results is qualified by the further claim that a "relational" type of objectivity can nevertheless be achieved. Thus, students who share the same social perspective and employ the same conceptual and categorical apparatus will allegedly arrive at similar conclusions on any problem when the standards characteristic of their common perspective are correctly applied. And students operating within different social perspectives can attain objectivity in a "roundabout fashion" by construing their inevitable differences in the light of the differences in the structures of their perspectives.

There are, however, grave factual and dialectical difficulties in these several claims. There is no factual evidence to show that the "content and form" of statements, or the standards of validity employed, are *logically* determined by the social perspective of an inquirer. The facts commonly cited establish no more than some kind of causal dependence between these items. For example, the once much-publicized view that the "mentality" or logical operations of "primitive" social groups are different from those typical of European civilization—a difference that was once attributed to institutional differences in the societies compared—is now generally recognized to be without foundation. Moreover, even the most extreme proponents of the sociology of knowledge admit that there are many assertions (those usually mentioned come from mathematics and the natural sciences) which are neutral to differences in social perspective and whose genesis is irrelevant to their validity. Why cannot assertions about human affairs exhibit the same neutrality? If, as no one seems to doubt, the truth of the statement that two horses can in general pull a greater load than either horse alone is logically independent of the social status of the one who asserts it, what inherent social circumstance precludes such independence for the statement that two laborers can in general dig a ditch of given dimensions more quickly than either laborer working alone?

Second, what is the logical status of the

claim that social perspectives enter essentially into the content and warrant of all assertions about human affairs? Is the claim itself meaningful and valid only for those occupying a certain social status? In that case, its validity is narrowly self-limited, no student with a different social perspective can properly understand or evaluate it, and it must be dismissed as irrelevant by most inquirers into social questions. Or is the claim peculiarly exempt from what it asserts, so that its meaning and truth are not logically dependent upon the social status of those who assert it? In that case, then, there is at least one conclusion about human affairs which may be "objectively valid" in the usual sense of this phrase; and if there is one such conclusion, there is no clear reason why there may not be others.

Finally, the relational type of objectivity which the claim admits as attainable is nothing other than objectivity in the customary sense, which the claim appears to deny as possible. A translation formula which renders the "common denominator" of seemingly diverse conclusions stemming from differing social perspectives, cannot in turn be "situationally determined" in the sense under dispute. Indeed, the search for such formulas is but a well-known phase of theoretical research in all areas of inquiry. It is a search for objective invariants in numerically and qualitatively distinct processes; and when the quest is successful, as it often is, it terminates in laws of greater or less generality, with whose help what is relevant to the occurrence of an event or to the continuance of a process can be distinguished from what is not.

In brief, therefore, although the historian is undoubtedly selective in the conduct of his inquiries, and although personal and social bias frequently color his judgment and control what conclusions he accepts, none of these facts precludes the possibility of warranted explanations for the events he studies.

III

The elimination of theoretical objections to the possibility of warranted explanations in history obviously does not ensure the realization of that possibility. As a matter of fact, there are serious obstacles, other than those already mentioned, which frequently do obstruct the quest for such explanations.

The search for explanations is directed to the ideal of ascertaining the necessary and sufficient conditions for the occurrence of phenomena. This ideal is rarely achieved, however, and even in the best-developed natural sciences it is often an open question whether the conditions mentioned in an explanation are indeed sufficient. Most historical inquiry is even further removed from this ideal, since the full circumstances are often quite complex and numerous and are usually not known. Historians therefore frequently cite only what they regard as the "main," "primary," "principal," "chief," or "most important" causal factors and cover their ignorance of the others by the convenient phrase "other things being equal." To mention but one example, the "main" cause of America's entrance into the first world war is declared by one careful student to be Germany's adoption of an unrestricted submarine warfare, though the factor cited is not assumed to be sufficient for producing the effect.

The "weighting" of causal factors in respect to their "degree of importance" is sometimes dismissed as essentially "arbitrary" and "meaningless"—partly on the ground that there is no warrant for selecting one occurrence as the cause of a given event rather than some prior cause of that occurrence (for example, since unrestricted submarine warfare was Germany's response to the British blockade, this latter occurrence is allegedly as much the cause of America's entrance into the war as is the former), and partly on the ground that no verifiable sense can be attached to such characterizations as "chief" or "most important" in connection with causal factors. It must be admitted that the natural sciences do not appear to require the imputation of relative importance to the causal variables that occur in their explanations; and it is easy to dismiss the question of whether there is any objective basis for such gradations of variables, with a peremptory denial on the ground that, if a phenomenon occurs only when certain conditions are realized, all these conditions are equally essential, and no one of them can intelligibly be regarded as more basic than the others. And it must also be acknowledged that most historians do not appear to associate any definite meaning with their statements of relative importance, so that the statements often have only a rhetorical intent, from which no clear empirical content can be extracted. Nevertheless, we often do make such claims as that broken homes constitute a more important cause of juvenile delinquency than does poverty, or that the lack of a trained labor force is a more fundamental cause of the backward state of an economy than the lack of natural resources. Many people might be willing to admit that the *truth* of such statements is debatable, but few would be willing to grant that they are totally without *meaning* so that anyone who asserts them is invariably uttering nonsense.

It is desirable, therefore, to make explicit what such statements may be intended to convey. In point of fact, ascriptions of relative importance to determinants of social phenomena appear to be associated with a variety of meanings, some of which I shall try to distinguish. If A and B are two adequately specified factors upon which the occurrence of a phenomenon C is supposed to depend in some fashion, the statements I wish to consider will be assumed to have the schematic form "*A* is a more important (or basic, or fundamental) determinant of *C* than is *B*."

1) A and B may both be necessary for the occurrence of C, though perhaps their joint presence is not sufficient for that occurrence. Then one sense in which A might be said to be a more important determinant of C than is B is simply this: variations in B occur infrequently and may be neglected for all practical purposes, whereas variations in A, with consequent variations in C, are quite frequent and perhaps uncontrollable. Thus, suppose that dislike of foreigners and need for economic markets are both necessary conditions for the adoption of an imperialist policy by some country; but suppose that xenophobia in that country varies little if at all during a given period, whereas the need for foreign markets increases. In this first sense of more important, need for foreign markets is a more important cause of imperialism than is dislike of foreigners.

2) But there is another though more difficult sense of more important. Assume again that A and B are both necessary for the occurrence of C. But suppose that there is some way of specifying the magnitude of variations in A, B, and C, respectively, and that, although changes in one may not be comparable with changes in another, the changes within each item are comparable. Suppose, further, that a greater change in C is associated with a given proportional change in A than with an equal proportional change in B. In that event, A

might be given a more important rank as a determinant of C than is assigned to B. For example, assume that a supply of coal and a trained labor force are both necessary for industrial productivity; but suppose that, say, a 10 per cent variation in the labor force produces a greater alteration in the quantity of goods produced (as measured by some convenient index) than does a 10 per cent variation in the coal supply. Accordingly, the availability of a trained labor force could be said to be a more important determinant of productivity than the availability of coal.

3) Suppose now that the joint presence of A and B is not necessary for the occurence of C, so that C can occur under conditions A and Y, or under conditions B and Z, where Y and Z are otherwise unspecified determinants. In this case, also, there is a sense of more important analogous to the first sense mentioned above. More explicitly, the frequency with which the first condition B and Z are realized may be small when compared with the frequency of the realization of A and Y; and this possibility may then be expressed by saying that A is a more important determinant of C than is B. Thus, assume that automobile accidents occur either because of negligence or because of mechanical failure; and suppose that the frequency with which there is such failure that leads to accidents is very much less than the frequency with which carelessness terminates in accidents. In that case, negligence may be said to be a more important cause of accidents than is mechanical failure.

4) Assume, again, that the joint presence of A and B is not necessary for the occurrence of C; and suppose that the relative frequency with which C occurs when the condition A is realized but B is not is greater than the relative frequency of C's occurrence if B is realized but A is not. It is such a state of affairs which is sometimes intended by the assertion that A is a more important determinant of C than is B. For example, a statement such as that broken homes are a more fundamental cause of juvenile delinquency than is poverty is frequently best interpreted to mean that the relative frequency of delinquency among juveniles coming from broken homes is much greater than among children coming from homes marked by poverty.

5) One final sense of more important must be mentioned. Suppose that a theory T is formulated with the help of A as a fundamental

theoretical term; and suppose that T can account for the phenomenon C when T is supplemented by appropriate data which involve reference to B. In consequence, though reference to B is essential for explaining C with the help of T, reference to B is not always necessary when T serves to explain phenomena other than C. Accordingly, since the range of phenomena which fall within the province of T (and therefore within the range of application of A) is more inclusive than the phenomena for which B is relevant, A may be said to be a more basic determinant of C than is B. Something like this sense of more basic appears to be intended by those who claim that the social relations that govern the production and distribution of wealth constitute a more basic determinant of the legal institutions of a society than do the religious and moral ideals professed in that society.

Other senses of more important or more basic can undoubtedly be distinguished, but the five here mentioned appear to be those most frequently used in discussions of human affairs. It is essential to note that, although a definite meaning may thus be associated with ascriptions of greater importance to assumed determinants of social processes, it does not follow that the available evidence does in fact warrant any given assertion of such a claim. Accordingly, even when a historian does intend to convey a verifiable content by such assertions, it is doubtful whether in most cases they are actually supported by competent evidence. There is next to no statistical material bearing on the relative frequency of occurrence of the phenomena of special concern to students of human affairs. Historians are therefore compelled, willy-nilly, to fall back upon guesses and vague impressions in assigning weights to causal factors. There are often wide divergences in judgment as to what are the main causes of a given event, and one man's opinions may be no better grounded than another's. Whether this defect in current causal imputations in historical research can eventually be remedied is an open question, since the probable cost of remedial measures in terms of labor and money seems staggering. Meanwhile, however, a judicious skepticism concerning the warrant for most if not all judgments of relative importance of causal factors (among those assumed to be relevant to an event) appears to be in order.

Doubtless the basic trouble in this area of inquiry is that we do not possess at present a generally accepted, explicitly formulated, and fully comprehensive schema for weighing the evidence for any arbitrarily given hypothesis so that the logical worth of alternate conclusions relative to the evidence available for each can be compared. Judgments must be formed even on matters of supreme practical importance on the basis of only vaguely understood considerations; and, in the absence of a standard logical canon for estimating the degree in which the evidence supports a conclusion, when judgments are in conflict each often appears to be the outcome of an essentially arbitrary procedure. This circumstance affects the standing of the historian's conclusions in the same manner as the findings of other students. Fortunately, though the range of possible disagreement concerning the force of evidence for a given statement is theoretically limitless, there is substantial agreement among men experienced in relevant matters on the relative probabilities to be assigned to many hypotheses. Such agreement indicates that, despite the absence of an explicitly formulated logic, many unformulated habits of thought embody factually warrantable principles of inference. Accordingly, although there are often legitimate grounds for doubt concerning the validity of specific causal imputations in history, there appears to be no compelling reason for converting such doubt into wholesale skepticism.

30

INDIAN-EUROPEAN RELATIONS IN COLONIAL LATIN AMERICA

ELMAN R. SERVICE

THE degree to which aboriginal racial and cultural traits are retained in modern Latin America varies greatly from region to region. Southern South America, including most of Argentina and all of Uruguay, is a great expanse of almost purely European settlement. Costa Rica, some parts of coastal Brazil, and most of the Antilles are also largely non-Indian in both race and culture. Other parts of Latin America are populated primarily by descendants of an early mixture of Indians and Europeans who live in essentially European-style communities, retaining only a few discrete traits of aboriginal culture. Paraguay and much of interior rural Brazil are the best examples of this type; but some of Western Argentina, middle Chile, lowland Peru, interior Central America, and parts of Venezuela and Colombia are also of this mixed Indian-European, or *Mestizo,* type of population. A third category is found most strikingly in the highlands of Bolivia, Peru, Ecuador, Mexico, and Guatemala, where there are huge rural populations of pure Indian descent. Despite their long submission to the national political systems and many important modifications in the organization of their cultures, they tend to retain certain elements of the aboriginal traditions as well as a rather distinctive ethos. I shall refer to these three kinds of regions as Euro-America, Mestizo-America, and Indo-America.

The racial and cultural characteristics of these modern Latin American regions clearly are correlated with variations in the nature of the relations of Indians and Europeans in the early period of European colonization. It is possible to view the different kinds of Indian-European relations from either of two perspectives. One may see the variations as caused by the differing policies, actions, and institutions

From *American Anthropologist,* 25: 411–423. Copyright © 1955 by the American Anthropological Association. Reprinted by permission of the publisher and the author. Elman R. Service is Professor of Anthropology, University of Michigan.

of the Europeans; or, conversely, one may choose to emphasize the great diversity in aboriginal cultures to which the Europeans were forced to adjust. The emphasis here is the latter—which is probably not surprising to anthropologists—but, inasmuch as historians, geographers, and other nonanthropologists are likely to choose the former approach, it seems necessary to devote a few preliminary pages to the argument that the policies and institutions of the colonists varied greatly from one region to another as *responses* to the problems created by the extensive differences in the native cultures which they encountered. The second part of the article is devoted to an evaluation of these cultural differences in order to isolate the particular characteristics which were of most direct significance in creating the conditions which resulted in the survival of great numbers of Indians in Indo-America, their early assimilation in Mestizo-America, and their extermination or expulsion in Euro-America. Part III is concerned with the quality of the acculturation, as such, which characterized the three areas. Sheer physical survival is, of course, a necessary condition for acculturation, but I have chosen to discuss acculturation separately because the particular aspects of native culture which account for the variations in the amount of biological assimilation seem to be different from those which directly influenced the nature of the cultural modifications.

I

It is apparent on mere inspection that there is a correspondence between three distinctly different kinds of aboriginal culture and the three modern regional types. The purest modern Indian communities are found in areas of the pre-Columbian native empires. The modern Mestizo communities are found most typically in the forested lowlands, where the aborigines lived in villages, subsisting by hunting, fishing,

LATIN AMERICA
RURAL POPULATION TYPES

Euro-America ☐

Mestizo-America ▨

Indo-America ■

and gardening. And much of the area of predominantly European occupation corresponds to the marginal lands of the widely scattered small bands of hunting-gathering Indians. Separate consideration must be given to the coastal regions of Brazil, the Guianas, and the Antilles, where great plantations were developed and Negro slaves eventually imported to work on them.

In attempting to achieve dominance over areas in the New World and to profit from their achievement, the invading Europeans had three alternatives with respect to their actions toward the natives. They could exploit them by means of encomienda tribute or on forced labor projects. If the Europeans could not control large communities of natives, they could make household servants and agricultural slaves of single families and individuals. If the natives were utterly uncontrollable, the Europeans could only exterminate them or drive them from the area of settlement. The first of the three alternatives was always preferable, but the actual practice was in the end determined by the culture of the Indian society itself.

As the various colonies took form, adapting to the exigencies of the local situations, there were concomitant changes in the colonists' expectations and actions which were reflected in changes in policy toward the natives. Such differing institutions as the true encomienda, which regulated native villages, the *originario* or *yanacona* of household servants, the *laboría* of Indian families who lived on Europeans' farms or ranches, and the various mission systems all had different effects on Indian acculturation. Although it should be emphasized that these varying institutions were a result rather than a cause of the colonists' distinctive relations with different kinds of Indians, a concern with the nature of these institutions and the kind of acculturation which they fostered leads in a fruitful direction precisely because it reveals so clearly the nature of the problems the colonists faced with respect to control and exploitation of the natives. It will be shown more clearly in later pages how these differing institutions can be regarded as consequences or responses to the problems posed by the varying kinds of Indian cultures.

It seems that there was actually only one important policy change which was directly responsible for a subsequent alteration in the treatment of the natives of distinct regions. This is the great difference in Spanish action against the Indians of the Greater Antilles as compared to the policy used in the later colonization of the mainland. After the famous "destruction of the Indies" the clergy had increasing influence on Crown policy, and the resulting changes in regulations gave the Indians of the mainland greater protection. In this case it is clear that the policy change must be considered in comparing the early relations of the Indians and Spaniards in the Indies with those prevalent subsequently in the continental areas. But the later changes in Crown policy, such as, for example, the imposition of the so-called "New Laws" of 1542, do not explain the three great variations in Indian assimilation and acculturation which occurred on the mainland. The laws were supposed to be applied everywhere. To be sure they were not so applied, and, when they were applied, they did not always have the same effect in different areas. Again, it was the local situation, especially the nature of the Indian cultures themselves, which created these distinctions.

The great value of comparing policy changes and their effects is that, like variations in the institutions of control, they reveal so clearly those elements which are of special significance in the local situation. The laws regulating the control of native labor in Peru, where the Crown had focused so much of its attention, were inapplicable in Chile, and, when applied in Paraguay, for example, they had unforeseen results. It was ultimately clear to the local authorities, and finally even to the *Consejo de Indias,* that the laws had to be adjusted to extreme differences in Indian society.

It might seem that there were certain kinds of distinctions among the Europeans themselves which in some measure could help account for variations in Indian-European relations in different regions. The Portuguese in Brazil may be seen as having had different policies and perhaps a somewhat different culture from the Spaniards in the rest of Latin-America. Differences in the culture of colonists from the north as opposed to colonists from the south of Spain also have been suggested as being of significance. Perhaps most appealing of all is the notion that the distinctive policy of the mission systems created an acculturational situation in the regions they dominated which was quite different from that of the area dominated by encomenderos and the civil power. It is the writer's belief, however, that none of these factors was of primary importance.

The policies of Spain and Portugal may have differed somewhat, but not enough to be considered as dominant influences on the nature of Indian acculturation in Latin America. Certainly one of the strongest impressions gained from reading documents from the early colonial period is that the aims and means of the newcomers were practically identical on the widely separated regions. It is quite clear that the settlers of Costa Rica, São Paulo, Paraguay, New Mexico, the Amazon Basin, or Chile wanted gold, tribute, and control of Indian labor just as avidly as did those of Mexico or Peru. More obvious and more important, however, is the fact that there is no correlation between kinds of policy (and native-European relations) and areas of Portuguese or Spanish control. And, we might add, our category "Mestizo-America" includes areas of both Portuguese and Spanish settlement. Even many modern rural communities in Brazil are very similar to those of Paraguay, an area settled by Spaniards. Similarities in habitat and in aboriginal culture seem to have overridden any distinction that could be made between Spaniards and Portuguese.

It is entirely possible that cultural distinctions among the Spanish colonists themselves were of greater magnitude than those distinguishing the general population of Spain from the people of Portugal. But, inasmuch as no one group of early colonists came from a single area of Spain, this consideration is of little value to us.

It is obvious that Indian-European relations in the various missions were not the same as those in the encomiendas. While the rules observed by the missions were exactly the same as most of the "New Laws" of 1542 which were designed to apply to the village encomiendas, the actual consequences of their application in the missions turned out to be radically different. A reason usually given is that the missions rigidly observed many of the protective measures which the encomenderos found it expedient to ignore. A much more important factor, however, and one which affected the observance of those very protective measures, was that the missions operated with a very different type of Indian society, and under very different circumstances. The Indians sheltered in the missions were not the sedentary, intensive agriculturalists of the type exploited most effectively by the encomiendas. They were, instead, most typically the broken remnants of less developed tribes which had fled from their homelands. Many of the missions also had a quasi-military purpose, having been located by the Crown to serve as buffer settlements in otherwise unprotected border areas. Their defensive function increased the rigidity of the controls exercised over the Indians.

To a considerable extent, the official Church in the New World had functioned as the "other arm" of the mother states, serving the purposes of Crown authority and conflicting with the local authorities and encomenderos only to the degree that these failed to support the imperial aims. The aims of the empire, of course, often conflicted with those of local powers. The Spanish Crown, for example, feared that a class of hereditary feudal-like nobles might become too powerful and, especially in later times, that local political entities would develop into "nations" and gain political autonomy. This is one of the reasons why the Spanish Crown tried to protect the Indians against the more predatory encomenderos. The humanitarian laws regulating treatment of the natives were not actually hypocritical, as they have been so often judged, but were politically expedient and intended to be effective. It might also be added that Indians were viewed by the Crown as a "natural resource" which it was important to protect by conservation measures rather than to allow them to be destroyed by short-sighted exploitation.

The clergy frequently complained to the Crown authorities of cruelties committed against the Indians. Finally the religious brotherhoods, most notably the fervent Jesuits and Capuchins, both products of the great Catholic reform movement, were granted permission to try their hands at converting the Indians in areas where they would be free of the local civil authority and the encomenderos, and could at the same time aid the Crown in consolidating control over the area.

It is important to note that, despite Crown support, the missions were not effective *rivals* of the New World colonists for control of the Indians. They were granted jurisdiction in remote areas and gathered together Indians who were not accessible to the colonists. In fact, it could be argued that the unexpectedly successful missions, especially those of the Jesuits, owed much of their success to the activities of slavers, who, in a literal sense, drove the Indians into the missions for refuge. This is clearly so in the Amazon region and in Paraguay, but it could also be said that the development of mining in the Parral area of Mexico had so intensified the search for captive labor

that it caused a great many refugees to move toward the west coast, thus insuring the success of the missions there.

The varying patterns of European-Indian relations which laid the basis for the three broad categories of Indian acculturation had already been established by the time the missions became fully operative in the seventeenth century. The success of the mission fathers in controlling their Indians, therefore, had little influence in establishing the racial and cultural basis of the colonies themselves, for not only were the missions located in remote areas, but they were fairly effectively sealed off from contact with outsiders. Later, when the control of the autonomous missions was abolished, the Indians had to adjust to essentially Europeanized conditions or flee, and most of them chose this latter course.

The ultimate fate of the Jesuits illustrates their dependent position. When it was finally recognized that the missions had succeeded in controlling large numbers of Indians and were presumed to be growing wealthy, the civil power was mustered against them. The colonies had by this time expanded to a point which enabled them to take care of their own frontiers, and the mission areas were no longer so inaccessible or so difficult to utilize. It was largely for this reason that the "Imperial Jesuits," the most powerful and successful of all, were expelled from the New World, first by the Portuguese in 1759 and then by the Spanish in 1767.

II

The European colonists were faced with truly remarkable cultural and demographic differences among the Indians they encountered in the New World. The inhabitants of the Mesoamerican and Andean highlands, the "high culture" areas, numbered in the millions and were densely settled, often in large communities or even cities. Their agriculture was intensive and stable, and the economy was controlled by highly organized theocratic states. In the lowland regions the population density was not nearly so great, nor were the villages large. Food production was based on slash-and-burn horticulture, so that the villages were not stable, although some of the lowland peoples in especially favorable areas, the so-called "circum-Caribbean" tribes, had achieved some intervillage confederations or realms and had developed incipient political and religious states. The Indians who sparsely populated the plains of Uruguay, Argentina, and northern Mexico depended on hunting and gathering. They lived a relatively nomadic life with no permanent social organization larger than the extended family.

It is suggestive that the regions of greatest European success in controlling the natives were in the highlands, where the Indians also have survived most completely as racial and cultural entities incorporated into the modern nations. Spanish culture was in many important structural aspects quite similar to these "high cultures," both being based on intensive agriculture and the exploitation of a huge class of agricultural laborers. Political and religious aspects of both cultures not only had local manifestations but also were organized into hierarchical bureaucracies. But the resemblance of Iberian culture to that of the Indians of the lowland areas was less, for the lowland horticulturists lacked a developed economic, political, and religious state. Iberian culture was even more distinct from that of the marginal hunters and gleaners. A logical suggestion, then, might be: the more alike the conquerors and conquered, the more simple and easy the adjustment will be, other things being equal. The less difficult and disruptive the adjustment, the more likely are the conquered people to survive, preserving at least the local basis of their native social organization and cultural forms.

This proposition possibly contributes to our general understanding of the situation in Latin America, but we need in addition a fuller analysis of the interplay of specific factors and some sort of a test of the relative importance of these factors. From the point of view of the needs of the Europeans, certain attributes of Indian culture were more significant than others. Of course single features such as presence or absence of intensive agriculture, a certain population density, stability and size of communities, specialization of labor, public works, kinds of political and religious state institutions, and so on, do not arise independently of each other. The present attempt to establish a priority of one factor over another is not to deny their real interrelationship but merely to suggest that certain of them had more direct relevance to the actions of the conquerors than others.

The varying characteristics of native culture which influenced the actions of the colonists must be judged largely in terms of their effect on the means used in the subjugation and control of the natives as a labor force, for this was the primary need which governed the actions of the Europeans. All the different kinds of encomiendas were used explicitly to gain such control. Once the brief initial period of ransacking the Indian treasurehouses was over, control of Indians was requisite first for tribute in food, and second for handicrafts for trade. When mining began, and trade was increased, an even larger labor force was essential.

If Indians were to be exploited for tribute and labor the technology of the society would have to be adequate to the production of surpluses in food above the needs of the food producers. Here would seem to be one of the most significant differences between the highland cultures and those of the lowlands. In the Andes and in Mexico native agriculture was sufficiently intensive and efficient to support both the Spaniards and a native labor corps which could engage in petty manufacturing, mining, and transportation, as it had previously supported native nonagricultural classes of bureaucrats and artisans and part-time labor on public works. Furthermore, the highland production supported a dense population and large-sized communities, which meant not only that a sufficient percentage of the population was available for work but also that the sheer size of the labor force was very great within one small area. The lowland horticultural peoples, on the other hand, did not consistently produce a sufficient surplus for a permanent labor force, nor was the basic population so numerous. It should go without saying that the marginal tribes offered much less.

There was a further difference in the economies of the three kinds of tribes which was of considerable significance. The great productivity of the highlands technology involved interdependence among specialized ecological zones. The functioning economy was very large as a unit and very complex. An individual family or even a group of families could not reproduce this economy and subsist in isolation. The density of the population also limited the number of refuge areas within the highlands region. This meant that the Spaniards had comparatively little difficulty in controlling the natives, in contrast to the lowlands where "escaping Indians" seem to have been one of the greatest difficulties the Europeans faced. One of the striking characteristics of the early colonial period in the Mexican and Andean highlands was the great amount of vagrancy in the Indian population. Displaced Indians in those regions did not typically become "wild," although a few did, but usually floated around like hoboes within the confines of the colony.

There is another sense in which the high productivity in the highlands was related to ease of Spanish control, though less directly. This productivity was the basis for the development of a native bureaucratic state which had both theological and civil aspects. The manipulation of this kind of controlling mechanism was not unfamiliar to the conquerors, and they quickly placed themselves at the top of the hierarchy and governed the mass of the population through native intermediaries in the lower echelons of the bureaucracy.

In the tropical forests some of the coastal peoples of the circum-Caribbean type had a more intensive and productive economy than did the true tropical forest peoples of the interior, although it was based on essentially the same technology. But despite the fact that they had an inchoate state apparatus, they were not as controllable as the highland societies, for they could retreat to the great inland regions and subsist, though less efficiently, with the same techniques of horticulture, hunting, and fishing that they had used in their homeland. The marginal peoples had even greater freedom of movement. In fact, they were able to raid and harass the Europeans as well as escape them, so much greater was the self-sufficiency and consequent mobility of their small social units.

Control of Indians in the lowlands thus meant capture and enslavement of individual Indians. In the early years of lowland settlement the encomienda was attempted in a few places, but it quickly failed. Because the Indian villages were small, scattered, and mobile the encomendero literally had to live among his Indians to govern them, and the agricultural practices had to be Europeanized considerably to increase production.

Of all the lowland countries in which the encomienda was tried, it worked best in Paraguay for several special reasons, of which the most important was that the natives did not have the same opportunities to flee as in other areas. The Guaraní Indians of central Paraguay were cut off on the south, west, and northwest by arid wastelands and by the mobile warlike tribes of those regions. At first some of the

Guaraní moved to the east, but they soon became victims of the *mamelucos,* slave raiders of São Paulo. Thus, from the very first the Spaniards were much more truly the "protectors" of the Indians in Paraguay than elsewhere, and the Indians were less inclined to flight. Even under these favorable circumstances, the encomiendas of village Indians were very small and within a few generations had dwindled to near extinction because the Spaniards and the later mestizos found a more effective economic use for the Indians in their own households and in private agricultural holdings than as producers of tribute.

From the earliest years of the settlement in Paraguay, the Spaniards found themselves engaged in a struggle for existence rather than wealth, as did the colonists of other lowland areas. They mixed European techniques, crops, and domestic animals with the most feasible native crops and techniques, and took complete personal charge of the agricultural economy. Labor was obtained to some extent, as during harvests, or in erecting a public building, by levies on the villages (the *mita*), but the basic year-round subsistence labor was controlled by a system of quasi-slavery, the *originario-encomienda* (sometimes called the *yanacona*). This system began as the Spaniards took native women as concubines and house-servants. Later, as tribute from the encomienda villages dwindled and the Spaniards acquired their own private lands, whole families of natives were attached as servants and farm laborers to the Spanish households. The Europeans had complete control and supervised every aspect of the lives of their "slaves." Naturally, both race mixture and cultural assimilation followed rapidly.

In other lowland regions there was usually greater difficulty in controlling the Indians. In the Amazon Valley the Indians had a much better chance to escape, and outright slavery thus developed sooner. By the time large-scale plantations were possible in some of the coastal regions, the Indians were so few and so difficult to hold that they had to be augmented with Negro slaves.

We might here briefly consider some of the implications of the importation of Negro slaves. While parenthetical to our main discussion, this digression may serve to highlight the nature of the difficulties that the Europeans faced in trying to control the Indians of the lowland areas. As long as Indians were used in small numbers on the family farms of the Europeans, they could apparently be kept under control. The plantation system, however, involved a much larger number of workers, and the difficulty of preventing their escape was tremendously increased. Possibly, too, certain paternalistic practices had to be abandoned in favor of increased control and greater production, resulting in a depersonalized and more unpleasant life for the slaves. And under the household system the continual mestization of the Indians created a need for replenishing the labor supply with new slaves, which were increasingly harder to capture as the Indians withdrew farther and farther and as the missions took in more and more of them.

Many explanations of the need for importation of Negroes have been offered: they were inherently stronger and better workers than the Indians; they were constitutionally better equipped to withstand European diseases; they were accustomed to a slave-like existence under their native African ruling states; they were skilled on a higher technological level. The problem of the *control* of an adequate number of laborers is an important one which is often overlooked. The Negroes were far from their homeland, in a strange environment, speaking languages alien to the natives of the hinterlands. They had not established a social and economic organization among themselves which would enable groups of them to survive in the interior were they to escape. The Indians did not have these disadvantages to the same degree, even when they had been transported long distances. In later years, after the Negroes had become accustomed to the new environment and had achieved something like a common culture and organization which could aid their autonomous survival, many of them did escape to the jungles, where some of their descendants survive today, utilizing many American Indian techniques.

The cotton plantations of the South Seas which arose during the cotton scarcity caused by the American Civil War provide an interesting parallel case. The huge plantations which were established in the Fijian Islands had a great deal of difficulty in securing labor because the local Fijians could and did disappear into the interior mountains to survive quite easily. "Blackbirding" solved this difficulty. Melanesians from far-away islands, like the New Hebrides, could be more easily controlled in Fiji, a new environment peopled with strangers or enemies. Certainly the racial or constitutional differences between Fijians and the inhabitants of the New Hebrides were not significant in this instance. Neither need we here apply Benedict's reasoning . . . on Latin American Indian acculturation and argue that the Fijians resisted because they were "freedom-loving" or more "democratic" than the other Melanesians. Removal of a people from a known habitat to an unknown one reduces the likelihood of successful escape, and this would seem to be the telling feature in each case.

This same hypothesis can be tested in several areas in Latin America where there was a variation in the mobility of tribes who lived adjacent to one another and who would have been equally subject to control (and acculturation) by the invaders had there not been this difference. The variation in the acculturation of the highland Maya and the lowland Maya may well have been due to the fact that the lowland political system had disintegrated, leaving the scattered unstable settlements of horticulturalists very difficult to control. This suggestion also seems to explain the situation in Chile. The southern Araucanians were horticulturalists and hunters of the forest, and had, along with this relatively mobile kind of economy, a huge forested region south of them in which to take refuge. The Indians of the region of Santiago, on the other hand, depended on more permanent fields, and there was no available retreat in which they could subsist. It was here that the encomiendas of Chile were established.

Similarly, the Spaniards in the American Southwest could do little with the Navaho, Apache, and Ute except defend themselves against them, whereas even the pueblos most remote from the Rio Grande settlements of Spaniards, the Zuñi and Hopi, had to accept a considerable measure of Spanish control. The Hopi, to be sure, did succeed in remaining "apostate" for a long time, but they were the most inaccessible of all the pueblos. Spanish expeditions had little difficulty in subduing them, but the Spaniards could not afford to remain in the area to keep them subjugated.

III

We have, up to this point, discussed certain aspects of three distinct kinds of Indian culture in an effort to show why the actions of the Europeans varied so greatly in different regions.

The consequences of these distinct kinds of Indian-European relations ranged from the continuing physical survival of masses of Indians in Indo-America, through rapid race mixture in Mestizo-America, to near-extermination in Euro-America. To phrase this in terms of acculturation, it could be said that the rate of acculturation varied from "very slow" in Indo-America, where the means by which Europeans controlled the Indians were indirect and not so immediately disruptive to the community and family organization, to "rapid" in Mestizo-America, where the control of Indians was accomplished by slavery or quasi-slavery—stringent and personal. In Euro-America the rate was practically "zero" because nearly all the Indians escaped control or were killed in the struggle.

More importantly, we may note three different kinds or qualities of acculturation in these areas. The marginal hunters, the lowland horticulturalists, and the highland intensive agriculturalists may be viewed as representing three different levels or stages of social evolution which are accompanied by distinct kinds of cultural institutions at each level, and which therefore present quite different possibilities for acculturation even when the acculturative influences are of equal strength. The marginal peoples had no permanent organizational institutions above the level of the extended family; their culture could be called *familial*. The lowland horticulturalists were organized into multifamily villages, and their culture thus not only was familial but also had a suprafamilial or *community* aspect. The highland peoples had in addition a multifamilial, multicommunity *state* organization and associated cultural institutions.

In the highlands the Spaniards were able to take almost immediate control of the state political and religious institutions, and thus could control the bulk of the population. The state or official aspect of the Catholic Church (as distinct from community or "folk" Catholicism) was substituted for the indigenous state religion, and the legal-political aspect of the state was altered. But the important "contact of cultures" was essentially state institution to state institution, directly affecting only a relatively small proportion of the Indian communities in the early years. The influence on the native familial culture in those communities was even more indirect. Mestization and drastic acculturation or assimilation occurred only when individual Indians or small families were removed from their villages to the homes or communities of the Europeans. This has been, of course, a continuing process since the first years of the conquest, and we must also note that some highland communities were grouped and reorganized by the Spaniards during the epoch of great population loss, thereby altering the community organization. Thus, in a sense, all three kinds of acculturational processes can be found in the highlands, but the unusual survival of so many ancient Indian communities is our chief concern with that area.

A multifamily village culture, lacking state institutions, is much less a barrier to change at the family level, for contact and control must be direct and personal. When the Indians were controlled and put to work as villages, the community organization was very quickly altered. But village institutions are suprafamilial. Their function is to integrate the families for greater cooperation and proficiency in production and in warfare. They also take over certain familial functions of economics, politics, education, and religion and thus make the family a dependent part of a larger unit, although the functions of the family in these matters are not entirely superseded. A change in village organization may alter all these interfamilial relations, but the residual, purely familial aspects of the culture are less directly affected and can survive longer.

As we have seen, in the tropical forest areas of European control, the native village organization did not protect the Indian families for very long. Since the Indians could escape easily the Europeans had to enslave them as individuals. Even in areas where the villages came more easily under European control, as in Paraguay, native production was so inadequate that the Indians were finally put to work on the Europeans' estates under European direction. After the families were stripped of their village organization, their assimilation was rapid.

The kind of acculturation which occurred in the Jesuit missions was quite different. It appears that the change at the level of village institutions was rapid, but that the fundamentals of family life were not importantly altered, even after 150 years, for after the expulsion of the Jesuits most of the Indians were able to survive in the remote jungles. I have visited some of these Indians in northern Paraguay and in the Mexican Sierra Madre Occidental, and suggest that they seem more "deculturated" than acculturated, so simple is their social and political life compared to their aboriginal state. If this is so in other areas as well, it may possibly be due to the nature of mission acculturation. The full expression of aboriginal community culture was lost in the missions, while that of the family was not. Today, because these natives live scattered in marginal areas, they have never fully recovered their village culture. The typical suprafamilial organization is the composite band, a simple compounding of families for rather ephemeral and expedient purposes, so that a complex of extended relationship bonds has no chance to crystallize. There are often no local exogamous marriage rules, and a true village organization can hardly be said to exist.

The vaunted success of the Jesuits in controlling and acculturating the natives deserves a further comment. They had little difficulty in adjusting the Indians to the missions and, conversely, the Indians had little difficulty later in readjusting to an independent existence, because of some unusual circumstances. Most of the Indians were sheltered in the missions as individuals and single families, much as refugees might be cared for in a modern "DP" camp. The communities of the Indian refugees no longer existed, and the missions represented a *substitute* for the native organization. Therefore, it cannot be said that the mission system was an acculturative influence on village institutions. The success of the Jesuits in imposing the Catholic religion was likewise not exactly a case of "acculturation." The Indians of the missions had no state religion to be changed; the Jesuits merely *added* Catholicism as a cultural overlay, just as the teaching of European instrumental music did not first involve a change or destruction of a native music, for these Indians had none. Aspects of some of these cultural overlays penetrated the familial culture, but the Indian family held its own in most other respects.

A thorough and final cultural assimilation takes place when familial institutions are changed. When the marriage customs, intrafamilial division of labor, family religious practices, relations of husband and wife and parents and children are significantly altered, each new individual, the ultimate pinpoint repository of the cultural heritage, is changed in all important respects. This also occurs, of course, as single members of a primitive society are made to give up their "old ways" and adjust themselves individually to the invading system. Familial and individual assimilation of this sort occurred to some extent in all three areas of Latin America; among the marginal Indians, however, it was the only way in which acculturation could take place. It did not occur so frequently as among the village Indians because, although marginal (i.e., familial) culture is the most vulnerable, the marginal peoples were able to escape control more easily. It follows, nevertheless, that this kind of acculturation should become more frequent as the invading culture becomes more pervasive and the alternative of retreat becomes less and less feasible. Thus the rate of assimilation (and destruction) of the heretofore independent tribal Indians of Latin America has increased greatly in recent years as modern civilization has so rapidly expanded its range and intensified its influence.

If the foregoing perspective is useful for an understanding of the processes of acculturation in colonial Latin America, it should be useful elsewhere. We have noted its relevance to conditions in the southwest of the United States, and it applies more completely to the ancient colonization of southwest China. But it is not helpful in many other kinds of situations. One particularly important qualification is that the influences resulting from the spread of modern Western industrial civilization are typically of a different order from the sort described in this article. The acculturation of the natives in Latin America and in the American Southwest and southwestern China resulted from colonization, and was closely related to institutions of personal control of dependent labor. The institutions of control in turn adapted differently to the kinds of indigenous cultures encountered, with consequent variations in the quality of acculturation. We have suggested that the rates and degrees of acculturation were most rapid and complete where control was most direct and personal. But primitive and peasant peoples today may be affected by the expansion of financial empires, and even become a part of them, without their areas being conquered or colonized and often enough without the mediation of any institutions of direct, personalized control.

31

CLOSED CORPORATE PEASANT COMMUNITIES IN MESOAMERICA AND CENTRAL JAVA

ERIC R. WOLF

ONE of the salient aims of modern anthropology, conceived as a science, is to define recurrent sequences of cause and effect, that is, to formulate cultural laws. This paper is concerned with recurrent features in the social, economic, and religious organization of peasant groups in two world areas, widely separated by past history and geographical space: Mesoamerica [1] and Central Java.[2] These have been selected for comparison, because I have some measure of acquaintance with Mesoamerica through field work, and a measure of familiarity with the literature dealing with the two areas.

The cultural configuration which I wish to discuss concerns the organization of peasant groups into closed, corporate communities. By peasant I mean an agricultural producer in effective control of land who carries on agriculture as a means of livelihood, not as a business for profit. In Mesoamerica, as in Central Java, we find such agricultural producers organized into communities with similar characteristics. They are similar in that they maintain a body of rights to possessions, such as land. They are similar because both put pressures on members to redistribute surpluses at their command, preferably in the operation of a religious system, and induce them to content themselves with the rewards of "shared poverty." They are similar in that they strive to prevent outsiders from becoming members of the community, and in placing limits on the ability of members to communicate with the larger society. That is to say, in both areas they are corporate organizations, maintaining a perpetuity of rights and membership; and they are closed corporations, because they limit these privileges to insiders, and discourage close participation of members in the social relations of the larger society.

From *Southwestern Journal of Anthropology*, 13(1): 1–14. Copyright © 1957 by the Department of Anthropology, University of New Mexico. Reprinted by permission of the publisher and the author. Eric R. Wolf is Professor of Anthropology, University of Michigan.

Outright communal tenure was once general in both areas. In Java, such tenure still survived in a third of all communities in 1927, while land in more than a sixth of all communities was still redistributed annually. Such land consisted of the community's most valuable land, the irrigated rice fields. Yet even where communal tenure has lapsed, jurisdiction over land by the community remains important. Communities may deny or confirm the rights of heirs who have left the village to inherit village lands; they may take back and issue land to someone else if a member leaves the community; or they may take back land issued if a member commits a crime. Aliens may settle in such a community as sharecroppers, but may not inherit or buy the land they work. Community members have priority in the purchase of village lands. And members do not have the right to pledge their land as security.

Estimates concerning the survival of land-holding communities in Mesoamerica tend to vary greatly. McBride estimated that in Mexico, in 1854, there were some 5,000 "agrarian corporations" in possession of 11.6 million hectares, but that in 1923 land-holding communities survived only in "certain out-of-the-way parts of the country." Tannenbaum, in turn, calculated that in 1910 about 16 percent of all Mexican villages and 51 percent of the rural Mexican population lived in "free villages," that is, villages not included in some large estate. This computation has been criticized by Simpson who follows Luis Cabrera in holding that "by the end of the Díaz regime [in 1910] . . . 90 per cent of the villages and towns on the central plateau had no communal lands of any kind." A recent estimate holds that in 1910 41 percent of land-holding communities still maintained communal tenure, though on an illegal basis. Today, there is a general tendency to maintain communal tenure on hillsides and forests, but to grant private ownership over valley bottoms and garden plots. Even in such cases, however, communities can and do prohibit the sale of land to outsiders and limit the right of members to pledge land as a security on loans. In contrast to Central Java, periodic re-allotment of land to community members seems to be rather rare in Mesoamerica.

Peasant communities in both areas show strong tendencies to restrict membership in the community to people born and raised within the boundaries of the community. The community is territorial, not kinship-based. Rules of community endogamy further limit the immigration of new personnel. These rules are characteristic of Mesoamerica; they occur only occasionally in Central Java.

Membership in the community is also demonstrated by participation in religious rituals maintained by the community. In Java, each community is charged with the maintenance of proper relations with its spirits and ancestors. The rituals which serve this function cannot be carried on by the individual. Each year the land is ritually purified (*slametan bresih desa*), the community spirit is feasted (*sedekah bum*), and offerings are made to the souls of the dead (*njadran*). The religious official—in the past usually the chief, but nowadays more often the land supervisor and diviner of the community —is looked upon as "a personification of the spiritual relation of the people to their land." In Mesoamerica, there is no evidence of ancestor worship or propitiation as such.[3] Yet each community tends to support the cult of one or more saints. The functions associated with these cults are delegated to members of the community. A man gains social prestige by occupying a series of religious offices charged with these functions; these tend to be ranked in a prescribed ladder of achievement. Often, they carry with them a decisive voice in the political and social affairs of the community. Apparently only members of the community are normally admitted to such religio-political participation.

In both areas, the community motivates its members to expend surpluses in the operation of a prestige economy. The prestige economy operates largely in support of the communal religious cult, and allied religious activities. In Central Java, where cattle are symbolic of landownership, wealth is expended conspicuously in cattle sacrifices, as well as in a large number of ritual feasts (*slametans*) offered by private individuals to ward off evil or difficulties, to celebrate special events in the life-cycle, to

mark holidays, and to emphasize stages in the production of rice. Similarly, pilgrimages to Mecca earn prestige at the cost of large stores of surplus wealth. In 1927, the cost of such a pilgrimage was estimated at 1,000 florin. In that year, 60,000 Indonesians made the voyage, spending 60 million florin in the process, "an enormous sum for so poor a country." In Mesoamerica, adult members of the community generally undertake to finance part of the cult of one or more saints, when they assume religious office. Expenditures may prove economically ruinous, though they earn great social prestige for the spender.

In both areas, we not only encounter a marked tendency to exclude the outsider as a person, but also to limit the flow of outside goods and ideas into the community. This tendency is often ascribed to "inherent peasant conservatism" or to adherence to "static needs," but may actually represent the complex interplay of many factors. Villagers are poor, and unable to buy many new goods. The goods purchased must be functional within peasant life. Peasant needs in both areas are met by marketing systems which serve only the peasantry, and which are organizationally and culturally distinct from other marketing systems within the larger societies to which they belong. Such markets also have similar characteristics. They tend to offer a very high percentage of objects manufactured by peasant labor within the peasant household. They show a high proportion of dealings between primary producers and ultimate consumers. They are characterized by small purchases due to the limited amount of consumer purchasing power. In both areas, moreover, we find regular market days in regional sequence which make for a wide exchange of an assortment of local products, probably much larger than any store-keeper could hope to keep in his store. Such markets can only admit goods which are congruous with these characteristics. The goods sold must be cheap, easily transportable, adaptable to the limited capital of the seller. Only goods such as these will reach the peasant household.

In both areas, moreover, peasant communities maintain strong attitudes against accumulated wealth. In Mesoamerica, display of wealth is viewed with direct hostility. In turn, poverty is praised and resignation in the face of poverty accorded high value. We have seen how much surplus wealth is destroyed or redistributed through participation in the communal religious

cult. In Java, there are similar pressures to redistribute wealth:

> . . . every prosperous person has to share his
> wealth right and left; every windfall must be dis-
> tributed without delay. The village community can-
> not easily tolerate economic differences but is apt to
> act as a leveller in this respect, regarding the indi-
> vidual as part of the community . . . (Boeke).

Surplus wealth thus tends to be siphoned off,
rather than to be directed towards the purchase
of new goods.

It is further necessary to point out that
closed corporate peasant communities in both
areas are socially and culturally isolated from
the larger society in which they exist. The nature of this isolation will be discussed below.
This general isolation of the peasant community
from the larger society is, however, reinforced
by the parochial, localocentric attitudes of the
community. In Mesoamerica, each community
tends to maintain a relatively autonomous economic, social, linguistic, and politico-religious
system, as well as a set of relatively exclusive
customs and practices. In Gillin's words, "the
Indian universe is spatially limited and its horizon typically does not extend beyond the limits
of the local community or region." In Central
Java, similarly, each community is a separate
sociocultural universe. Such localocentrism is a
form of "ignorance [which] performs specifiable
functions in social structure and action"
(Moore and Tumin). It serves to exclude cultural alternatives by limiting the "incentives on
the part of individuals of the groups in social
interaction to learn the ways of their neighbors,
for learning is the psychological crux of acculturation" (Hallowell). In Mesoamerica, such
exclusion of cultural alternatives is strongest in
the area of the *costumbres,* those religious and
social features of the community which—in
terms of this paper—help to maintain its closed
and corporate character. In Java, similarly,
communities show a tendency to

> . . . preserve a balance by averting and fighting
> every deviation from the traditional pattern.
> . . . when the villager seeks economic contact
> with western society, he does not enjoy the support
> of his community. Quite the contrary. By so doing
> he steps outside the bounds of the community,
> isolates himself from it, loses its moral support and
> is thrown on his own resources (Boeke).

Peasant communities in both areas thus
show certain similarities. Both maintain a
measure of communal jurisdiction over land.
Both restrict their membership, maintain a religious system, enforce mechanisms which ensure the redistribution or destruction of surplus
wealth, and uphold barriers against the entry of
goods and ideas produced outside the community. These resemblances also mark their
differences from other kinds of peasant communities. They form a contrast, for instance,
with the "open" peasant communities of Latin
America where communal jurisdiction over land
is absent, membership is unrestricted, and
wealth is not redistributed. They also contrast
with the peasant communities of a society like
pre-British Uganda where access to scarce land
was not an issue, and where local groups consisted of client families, united in temporary
allegiance to a common chief by hopes of
favors, bounty, and booty in war, yet able to
change their residence and to better their life
chances through changes in loyalties when these
were not forthcoming. Differences also appear
when the corporate communities discussed in
this paper are compared with the peasant communities of China. In China, free buying and
selling of land has been present from early
times. Communities are not endogamous and
rarely closed to outsiders, even where a single
stratified "clan" or *tsu* held sway. Constant circulation of local landowners into the imperial
bureaucracy and of officials into local communities where they acquired land prevented the
formation of closed communities. Moreover,
state controls maintained through control of
large-scale water works heavily curtailed the
autonomy of the local group. In such a society,
relations between individual villagers and individual government officials offered more security
and promise than relations among the villagers
themselves. Peasants may thus be found organized into many kinds of communities; only
some, however, live in closed corporate bodies
of the kind described here.

These casual contrasts afford another insight.
In each case, the kind of peasant community
appears to respond to forces which lie within
the larger society to which the community belongs rather than within the boundaries of the
community itself. The "open" peasant communities of Latin America "arose in response to the
rising demand for cash crops which accompanied the development of capitalism in
Europe" (Wolf). Pre-British Uganda was characterized by political instability at the top, considerable personal mobility, and frequent shifts

in personal allegiances, all of which found expression in the character of its local groups. Similarly, efforts to understand the peasant community in China purely in its own terms would be foredoomed to failure. These considerations suggest that the causes for the development of closed corporate communities in Mesoamerica and Central Java may derive from the characteristics of the larger societies which gave rise to them.

Historically, the closed corporate peasant configuration in Mesoamerica is a creature of the Spanish Conquest. Authorities differ as to the characteristics of the pre-Hispanic community in the area, but there is general recognition that thoroughgoing changes divide the post-Hispanic community from its pre-conquest predecessor. In part, the new configuration was the result of serious social and cultural crises which destroyed more than three-quarters of the Indian population, and robbed it of its land and water supply. Population losses and flight prompted colonial measures leading to large-scale resettlement and concentration of population. The new Indian communities were given rights to land as local groups, not kinship-wise; political authority was placed in the hands of new local office holders and made elective; tribute and labor services were placed on a new basis; and "the rapid growth of Indian *cofradías* (sodalities) after the late sixteenth century gave to parishioners a series of organized and stable associations with which personal and communal identification might readily be made" (Gibson). In Java, similarly, corporate peasant communities did not take shape

until after the coming of the Dutch, when for the first time the village as a territorial unit became a moral organism with its own government and its own land at the disposal of its inhabitants (Furnivall).

At the time of the Dutch conquest, there was still "an abundance of waste" in Java; slash-and-burn farming was carried on quite generally; population densities averaged only 33.9 persons per km². The closed corporate peasant community in Central Java thus represents an attempt to concentrate both population and tenure rights.

Over the greater part of Java it was only on the introduction of land revenue from 1813 onwards that villages were reduced to uniformity and their lands bound up into a closed unit, and during this

process there were numerous references to the splitting and amalgamation of villages, and to the promotion of hamlets to the status of independent villages (Furnivall).

In the two areas, then, the closed corporate peasant community is a child of conquest; but this need not always be so. The corporate community of pre-1861 Russia, the *mir*, was the product of internal colonization, rather than of foreign domination imposed by force of arms. The corporate peasant community is not an offspring of conquest as such, but rather of the dualization of society into a dominant entrepreneurial sector and a dominated sector of native peasants. This dualization may take place in peaceful as well as in warlike circumstances, and in metropolitan as well as in colonial countries.

Both in Mesoamerica and Central Java, the conquerors occupied the land and proceeded to organize labor to produce crops and goods for sale in newly established markets. The native peasantry did not command the requisite culturally developed skills and resources to participate in the development of large-scale enterprises for profit. In both areas, therefore, the peasantry was forced to supply labor to the new enterprises, but barred from direct participation in the resultant returns. In both areas, moreover, the conquerors also seized control of large-scale trade, and deprived the native population of direct access to sources of wealth acquired through trade, such as they had commanded in the pre-conquest past.

Yet in both areas, the peasantry—forced to work on colonist enterprises—did not become converted into a permanent labor force. The part-time laborer continued to draw the larger share of his subsistence from his own efforts on the land. From the point of view of the entrepreneurial sector, the peasant sector remained primarily a labor reserve where labor could maintain itself at no cost to the enterprises. This served to maintain the importance of land in peasant life. At the same time, and in both areas, land in the hands of the peasantry had to be limited in amount, or the peasantry would not have possessed sufficient incentive to offer its labor to the entrepreneurial sector. It is significant in this regard that the relation between peasant and entrepreneur was not "feudal." No economic, political, or legal tie bound a particular peasant to a particular colonist. In the absence of such personal, face-to-face bonds, only changes in the general conditions underlying the entire peasant economy could assure the entrepreneurs of a sufficient seasonal supplement to their small number of resident laborers. This was accomplished in Mesoamerica in the course of the enforced settlement of the Indian population in nucleated communities during the last decades of the 16th century and the first decade of the 17th. By restricting the amount of land in the hands of each Indian community to six and one-half square miles, the Crown obtained land for the settlement of Spanish colonists. A similar process of limiting the land frontier of the native population was introduced in Java. If access to land thus remained important to the peasantry, land itself became a scarce resource and subject to intense competition, especially when the peasant population began to grow in numbers.

With possibilities for accumulation limited to money-wages obtained in part-time employment and to occasional sales of agricultural produce or products of home crafts at low prices, peasant agriculture remained needs dependent on the expenditure of labor, a labor furnished by growing numbers of people living off a limited or decreasing amount of land. The technology of the peasantry thus remained labor-intensive, when compared with the capital-intensive and equipment-intensive colonist enterprises. Peasant technology is often described as "backward" or "tradition-bound," in disregard of many items such as second-hand Singer sewing machines, steel needles, iron pots, nails, tin-cans, factory-woven goods, aniline dyes and paints, etc. which may be found in the peasant inventory. It is backward only because the peasant is a captive of the labor-intensive technology with which he must operate. He must always weigh the adoption of a new good against the balance of his resources. This balance includes not only financial or technical resources, but also "resources in people" to whom he must maintain access by maintaining proper cultural behavior. These human relations he could only disregard at the price of sharply increasing life risks. The labor-intensive technology in turn limits the amounts and kinds of technological change and capitalization which he can afford, as well as his consumption and his needs.

The social and economic dualization of post-conquest Mesoamerica and Java was also accompanied in both areas by dualization in the administrative sphere. By placing the native communities under the direct jurisdiction of a special corps of officials responsible to the home government rather than to officials set up by the colonists, the home government attempted to maintain control over the native population and to deny this control to the colonists. By granting relative autonomy to the native communities, the home government could at one and the same time ensure the maintenance of cultural barriers against colonist encroachment, while avoiding the huge cost of direct administration. Thus, in Mesoamerica, the Crown insisted on the spatial separation of native peasants and colonists, and furthered the organization of the native population into nucleated communities with their own relatively autonomous government. It charged these native authorities with the right and duty to collect tribute, organize corvée labor and to exercise formal and informal sanctions in the maintenance of peace and order. In Java, the government relied from the beginning on the coöperation of the autonomous communities, by making use of the traditional channels of intermediate chieftainship. Administrative "contact with village society was limited to a minimum" (Kroef). After a perod characterized by emphasis on individualism and distrust of native communalism during the second half of the 19th century, the Dutch administration reverted to reliance on the closed corporate peasant community at the beginning of the 20th century.

Once the dualized system of administration began to operate, however, the colonists themselves found that they could often use it to their own advantage. In Central Java the sugar industry has preferred to rent land in block from native villages, and to draw on the total supply of labor in the village, rather than to make deals with individual villagers. Since sugar can be rotated with rice, such rental agreements have usually specified that sugar cultivation by the colonist enterprise could be followed by food production on the same land by native peasants in an orderly rotational cycle. Thus

the sugar cultivation of the estates and the rice and other cultivations of the population are, as it were, co-ordinated in one large-scale agricultural enterprise, the management of which is practically in the hands of the sugar factory (Kolff).

In the last years before World War II, the total area of land rented from native corporate communities did not exceed 100,000 hectares or 3 percent of irrigated rice land. In boom years it might have been 6 percent. But sugar production was concentrated in Central Java, and there covered a large part of the arable area. I have argued elsewhere that a somewhat similar symbiotic relation between corporate peasant community and colonist enterprise can be discovered in Mesoamerica. There even the voracious haciendas reached a point in their growth where absorption of corporate peasant communities into the estates put too great a strain on the control mechanisms at their disposal, and where they found systematic relations with such communities on their borders beneficial and useful.

Within the native sector, administrative charges in both areas were thus placed largely on the community as a whole, and only secondarily on the individual. This was especially true of tribute payments and labor services. In Central Java the demands on land-holders became so great

that land-holding was no longer a privilege but a burden which occupants tried to share with others. . . . Again, in many parts of Java, the liability to service on public works was confined by custom to land-holders; and, as officials wished to increase the number of hands available for public works, and the people themselves wished to distribute and reduce the burden of service on such works, it was to the interest of both officials and land-holders that the occupation of land should be widely shared. This encouraged communal possession and obliterated hereditary social distinctions (Furnivall).

In Mesoamerica also, tribute and labor charges were imposed on the whole community during the 16th and 17th centuries. Only around the beginning of the 18th century were they charged to individuals. The constant decrease of the Indian population until the mid-17th century, the flight of Indians into remote refuge-areas, the exodus of Indians to the northern periphery of Mesoamerica and to permanent settlements on colonist enterprises all left the fixed tribute-payments and corvée charges in the hands of the remnant population. It is reasonable to suppose that these economic pressures accelerated tendencies towards greater egalitarianism and levelling, in Mesoamerica as in Java. It is possible that the disappearance of status distinctions between nobles and commoners and the rise of religious sodalities as dispensers of wealth in religious ceremonial were in part consequences of this levelling tendency.

It is my contention that the closed corporate peasant community in both areas represents a response to these several characteristics of the larger society. Relegation of the peasantry to the status of part-time laborers, providing for their own subsistence on scarce land, together with the imposition of charges levied and enforced by semi-autonomous local authorities, tends to define the common life situation which confronts the peasantry of both societies. The closed corporate peasant community is an attempt to come to grips with this situation. Its internal function, as opposed to its external function in the social, economic, and political web of the dualized society, is to equalize the life chances and life risks of its members.

The life risks of a peasantry are raised by any threat to its basic source of livelihood, the land, and to the produce which is raised on that land. These threats come both from within and without the community. Natural population increase within the community would serve to decrease the amount of land available to members of the community, as would unrestricted purchase and hoarding of land by individual community members. Thus, as long as possible, closed corporate peasant communities will tend to push off surplus population into newly-formed daughter villages. More importantly, however, they will strive to force co-members to redistribute or to destroy any pool of accumulated wealth which could potentially be used to alter the land tenure balance in favor of a few individual families or individuals. Purchase of goods produced outside the peasant sector of society and their ostentatious display also rank as major social threats, since they are prima facie evidence of an unwillingness to continue to redistribute and destroy such accumulated surplus. They are indications of an unwillingness to share the life risks of fellow villagers according to traditional cultural patterns. Among most peasant groups, as indeed among most social groups anywhere, social relations represent a sort of long-term life insurance. The extension of goods and services at any given moment is expected to yield results in the future, in the form of help in case of threat. Departure from the customary distribution of risks, here signalled by a departure from the accepted disposal of surpluses, is a cause for immediate concern for the corporately organized peasantry, and for its immediate opposition. Similarly, unrestricted immigration and unrestricted purchase of land by outsiders would both serve to decrease the amount of land available to community members, as it would endanger the pattern of distribution of risks developed by community members over time. Hence the maintenance of strong defenses against the threatening outsider. It must be emphasized that these defenses are required, because the closed corporate community is situated within a dualized capitalist society. They are neither simple "survivals," nor the results of "culture lag," nor due to some putative tendency to conservatism said to be characteristic of all culture. They do not illustrate the "contemporaneousness of the non-contemporaneous." They exist, because their functions *are* contemporaneous.

This is not to say that their defensive functions are ultimately adequate to the challenge. The disappearance of closed corporate peasant communities where they have existed in the past, and the lessening number of surviving communities of this type, testify to the proposition that in the long run they are incapable of preventing change. Internal population surpluses can be pushed off into daughter villages only as long as new land is available. Retained within the boundaries of the community, they exercise ever-increasing pressure on its capacity to serve the interests of its members. The corporate community may then be caught in a curious dilemma: it can maintain its integrity only if it can sponsor the emigration and urbanization or proletarianization of its sons. If the entrepreneurial sector is unable to accept these newcomers, these truly "marginal" men will come to represent a double threat: a threat to their home community into which they introduce new ways and needs; and a threat to the peace of the non-peasant sector which they may undermine with demands for social and economic justice, often defended with the desperation of men who have but little to lose.

Secondly, while the closed corporate peasant community operates to diminish inequalities of risks, it can never eliminate them completely. Individual member families may suffer losses of crops, livestock, or other assets through accident or mismanagement. Some member families may be exceedingly fertile and have many mouths to feed, while others are infertile and able to get along with little. Individuals whose life risks are suddenly increased due to the play of some such factor must seek the aid of others who can help them. Some of these risks can be met through the culturally standardized social relations of mutual aid and support; some, however, will strain these relations beyond their capacity. Individuals may then in desperation seek aid from members of their community or from outsiders whose aid is tinged with self-interest. It would seem that even the most efficient prestige economy cannot be counted on to dispose of all surplus wealth in the community. Pools of such wealth tend to survive in the hands of local figures, such as political leaders, or nobles, or usurers, or store-keepers. Such individuals are often exempt from the everyday controls of the local community, because they occupy a privileged position within the economic or political apparatus of the larger society; or they are people who are willing to pay the price of social ostracism for the rewards of a pursuit of profit and power. Such individuals offer the needy peasant a chance to reduce his risks momentarily through loans or favors. In turn, the peasant in becoming their client, strengthens the degree of relative autonomy and immunity which they enjoy in the community. Such internal alliances must weaken communal defenses to a point where the corporate organization comes to represent but a hollow shell, or is swept aside entirely.

NOTES

1. In this paper, the term is used as short-hand for Mexican and Guatemalan communities which conform to the configuration discussed.
2. Central Java is a region of rice-growing nucleated villages with a tendency to communal land tenure. It was also the main center of commercial sugar and indigo production which promoted communal tenure and dense populations. Western Java is characterized by cattle-breeding rather than by agriculture; Eastern Java is occupied by small hamlets, scattered among individually held rice fields. Central Java is used as short-hand for Javanese communities which conform to the configuration discussed.
3. I should like to express a guess that further field work might reverse this statement. It is possible, for instance, that the cemetery plays a much greater symbolic role in Mesoamerican life than is generally suspected. The Mazatec of the Papaloapan River valley, about to be resettled, took great care to transfer the bones of their dead from their old to their new villages (Pozas, personal communication). The annual feast of the dead may have more communal function than is generally assumed.

PART V Culture and Personality

32

THE INFLUENCE OF LINGUISTICS
ON EARLY CULTURE AND PERSONALITY THEORY

DAVID F. ABERLE

I. INTRODUCTION

IN this essay I shall try to describe the impact of linguistics on early writing in the field of culture and personality: to discuss why language was used as a model for theories of culture, what assumptions about culture were made by extension from this model, and what difficulties arose from these assumptions. Although I shall largely restrict my attention to Ruth Benedict and Edward Sapir, many of the comments I make have a far wider applicability, not only to other theorists in the field of culture and personality, but to many current approaches to cultural theory in general.

The topic is appropriate for an essay in honor of Leslie A. White, both because of his interest in the history of anthropological theory and because the first known paper entitled "Personality and Culture" was written by White [in 1925]. It was a plea for the use of cultural (including in that term what some would call social and situational) variables, to replace the physiological and neurological variables which were then prominent in many texts in academic psychology. It contained no word of the impact of personality on culture. By the time the reader has finished the present essay, he may feel that it has returned to White's position.

I shall be primarily concerned with Benedict and Sapir, although Franz Boas will also receive some attention. The period under analysis stretches from 1911 and the first volume of the *Handbook of American Indian Languages* (Boas, 1911) to 1938 and the last of Sapir's publications in the field of culture and personality.

From Gertrude E. Dole and Robert Carneiro (Eds.), *Essays in the Science of Culture.* Copyright © 1957 by the Thomas Y. Crowell Company. Reprinted by permission of the publisher and the author. David F. Aberle is Professor of Anthropology, University of British Columbia.

II. BACKGROUND

It seems fairly evident that Boas and many of his followers rejected most of the theoretical currents in cultural and social science of the times. (The reasons for the rejection fall outside the scope of this paper.) There have been many comments on the Boasians' hostility to, or neglect of cultural evolution. Such works as Lowie's *History of Ethnological Theory* (1937) and Benedict's lectures on anthropological theory as I heard them in 1940–41, indicate that French sociology as represented by Durkheim, and Lévy-Bruhl was also rejected or was accepted only in the form of piecemeal propositions. Functionalism in the manner of Radcliffe-Brown or of Malinowski was similarly unacceptable. Thurnwald's theoretical work seems to have made no impact, and there is no evidence that German sociology as represented by Weber received any significant attention during the years under discussion. The rejection or neglect of these various theoretical positions occurred in some instances prior to the development of culture and personality as a field; in other cases rejection accompanied the development of the field of culture and personality. Such orientations meant that during the period under discussion, most of the currents of theory which made it possible to think of culture as an organization, as a system, either synchronically or diachronically, made no headway among the Boasians. In spite of individual exceptions to this generalization, it seems to me to be true on the whole.

In what terms, then, was culture to be analyzed? Boas and his followers considered that it was to be seen as a result of two factors, an historical factor and a psychic one. As for history, no culture can be understood solely by reference to its current situation. As a result of the accidents of history, it has had contacts with a variety of other cultures. These other cultures provide the pool of potential cultural material on which a culture can draw. Since there is no general basis for predicting what cultures will have contact with what others, the historical factor has an accidental and fortuitous character. With respect to the psychic factor (hereafter called psyche), there are qualities of men's minds—whether general tendencies to imitate or specific attitudes held by a particular group—which determine whether or not any available cultural item will be borrowed. Although contacts are unpredictable, the laws of psychology may account for acceptance and rejection. Hence the laws of culture are psychological laws. Thus culture is an emergent only in the sense that it is an historical precipitate, something more than a situational product. This position is represented by such writings as Boas' 1930 essay on social science methodology, Sapir's focus in 1916 on historical and psychological explanations of culture in the introduction to *Time Perspective,* and Benedict's remarks on history and psychology in *Patterns of Culture.* For all three writers the question was, how much is to be explained by history and how much by psyche. Under these circumstances, of course, problems of history and historical reconstruction were seen as particularly important. Although the sequence of culture contacts might be planless, history and the study of diffusion would tell us what the sequence was. And psychological problems were important, since a grasp of psychological principles would explain the selection of traits from the pool made available by contacts. This was the opening wedge for students of culture and personality.

As it happens, these and other orientations toward cultural phenomena proved particularly stimulating for the development of descriptive linguistics. The history-psyche dichotomy was absorbed without difficulty. The section on linguistic drift in Sapir's *Language* (1921) makes it quite clear that for Sapir drift is to be understood both in terms of long-range directional trends (history) and in terms of such factors as speakers' needs for pattern congruence, resulting in extension of one linguistic form at the expense of another, needs for pattern maintenance, and so on (psyche). Hence the analysis of language could go on within the context of Boasian assumptions about culture.

Parenthetically, this seem to me to account for the seeming paradox that Sapir, working successfully with language, "the most massive and inclusive art we know, a mountainous and anonymous work of unconscious generations," could nevertheless deny the concept of the superorganic. He maintained that cultural phenomena stand in the same relationship to psychology as geological phenomena do to physics: it is not that the laws of physics do not apply to geological formations, or the laws of psychology to cultures, but that they do not account "conceptually," but only "concretely" for the particular phenomena encountered (a mountain range, a culture): that is, they explain, say, the fact of folding in a mountain range, but not the existence or particular form of that range. Nowhere is there evidence that he placed any reliance on cultural or social laws—only in particular congeries of materials and the underlying psychological laws. Sapir could work in this way with language; difficulties, we shall see, arose when culture was thus viewed.

Yet Boasian negativism and particularism proved very fruitful in the development of descriptive linguistics. Boas rejected oversimple theories of the development of language and categorization of language, and waged war against ethnocentric models for the analysis of language. By insisting that the phonology and morphology of every language must be analyzed uniquely in their own terms, he provided the critical key for the linguistic study of "exotic" languages. The value of this strategy was amply manifest as early as 1911, with the publication of Part I of the *Handbook.*

We have already seen that Boas and his followers rejected a variety of possible approaches to culture—of analogies for thinking about culture: the analogy of biological evolution, the analogy of the biota, the analogy of the functioning organism. Given a striking early success in one field of cultural analysis, linguistics, it would appear natural that the analogy adopted would be that of language. I am not arguing that the approach to language developed in independence of thinking about culture and was then applied to culture. Rather I am saying that certain general assumptions made about culture, including language, proved particularly fruitful for work in linguistics, and that success and more detailed theoretical development in linguistics made the extension of assumptions derived from linguistics to total culture exceedingly tempting. Indeed, until very recently most of the parallels drawn between language and total culture have begun with language and been extended to culture: it is far commoner to find sentences which say, "As in language, so in culture," than to find those which say, "As in culture, so in language." [1]

III. THE LINGUISTIC ANALOGY

It is now necessary to select for discussion certain salient characteristics of language as viewed by Boas and Sapir (and indeed by many other linguists) and to show that parallels were drawn, explicitly and implicitly, between language, in these respects, and total culture. In this way the significance of the linguistic model for cultural theory can be demonstrated. It should be said that this is *not* an effort to present the most recent and sophisticated views on these subjects, but rather to represent the point of view both of Sapir, a linguist, and of Benedict, a nonlinguist, during Sapir's life and the first half of Benedict's professional career. The truth of the propositions about language is not critical, although many of them would be considered valid by linguists today. I shall list seven features of language and seven corresponding cultural analogies, commenting critically on some of the analogies. Part *a* of each of the following numbered paragraphs will deal with language, part *b* with cultural parallels, and part *c* with criticism.

1a. Language is characterized by the fact that it selects a small number of actualizations from a large number of possibilities. The range of phonetic possibilities is enormous, but only a small number of phonemes is actually used by any language. The range of grammatical principles is also vast, but the principles used in any given language are few.

1b. By the same token, culture is selective. No given culture utilizes more than a tiny fraction of the total range of known human behavior.

It is in cultural life as it is in speech; selection is the prime necessity. In culture . . . we must imagine a great arc on which are ranged the possible interests provided either by the human age-cycle or by the environment or by man's various activities. A culture that capitalized even a considerable proportion of these would be as unintelligible as a language that used . . . [all the known sounds]. Its identity as a culture depends upon the selection of some segments of this arc. Every human society everywhere has made such selection in its cultural institutions. Each from the point of view of another ignores fundamentals and exploits irrelevancies. One culture hardly recognizes monetary values; another has made them fundamental in every field of behavior. In one society technology is unbelievably slighted even in those aspects of life which seem necessary to ensure survival; in another, equally simple, technological achievements are complex and fitted with admirable nicety to the situation (Benedict).

1c. Benedict's use of the linguistic analogy is explicit in this passage. She argues that selection is necessary in culture, as in language, for coherent interaction to occur. It is perfectly true that there must be limitation in cultural "form" and "vocabulary" for any group in direct communication. But as total cultures become more complex and heterogeneous, as groups become more differentiated, the over-all set of patterns for a complex culture can be exceedingly elaborate, to the degree that it is hard to see any limits for that *total* culture set by selectivity alone. In the contemporary United States, or in eighteenth-century India, how much of the total cultural complex is determined by a selectivity based on a need for coherent interaction?

This, however, is not the basic problem posed by the analogy. Linguistic selectivity is based on the fact that random sound-production would make communication impossible. The question of *which* sounds are selected is fundamentally unanswerable for any particular language, except in terms of a prior state plus change over time. We do not, and need not try to account for the origins of a particular selection, but need only acknowledge its existence. To adopt such a position for total cultures is almost too easy a path. Benedict seems to tell us that cultures select so as not to be unintelligible or chaotic, that we know the range of materials from which they select, as we know the range of sounds from which languages select, and that we know what they have selected—and that the inquiry can stop there.

This point of views ignores the fact that selection in cultures is not simply a reduction in random behavior, that on the contrary it has other important adaptive functions in addition to making face-to-face relationships intelligible. Benedict denies this: some cultures, she says, do not trouble to work on their technology; others do. This view is not sufficient. In linguistics, given the prior state of a language, the linguist can sometimes account for a later stage on the basis of the accommodations of elements to their internal environment. But with cultures, elements accommodate not only to one another but to the external environment. If a group is located in an environment where agriculture is possible, and is then driven into one where agriculture is impossible, then the "selection" of hunting and gathering as a primary basis for subsistence is not surprising, nor is it based on the need for reduction of random behavior. If a nonagricultural group is living in an environment where agriculture is possible, and is exposed to agriculture, then in most instances it must either "select" agriculture or face expulsion from the area through intercultural competition. Selection in culture, then, rests on factors which go well beyond the issue of reduction of random behavior. It is not adequate to document the fact of selection and the nature of the selection, and to treat it as arbitrary but interesting.

2a. Language is patterned. Indeed a treatment of the traits of a language is meaningless without a consideration of their arrangement. Similarly, elements cannot be adequately analyzed except in the context of the pattern of which they form a part.

2b. Culture is patterned; traits can be understood only by reference to their arrangement, and cannot be understood apart from their context. Sapir makes the link between language and culture explicit—as well as telling us that language is the most helpful model for understanding cultural patterning. In an essay written in 1929 Sapir says that both language and culture are patterned, but culture patterns are harder to grasp; so language will show the way.

3a. Some of the most important linguisitic patterns are unconscious ones: the speaker does not recognize them except under very special circumstances.

3b. Some of the most important cultural patterns are unconscious—or the "real" basis for their formation is unconscious. In this area Sapir does not so much assert the utility of linguistics for an understanding of total culture, as handle both language and other behavior under the same rubric, in "The Unconscious Patterning of Behavior in Society."

Boas' views on this matter are of particular interest because they show so early a concern with the utility of linguistics for an understanding of culture. He wrote, "Linguistic phenomena never rise into the consciousness of primitive man, while all other ethnological phenomena are more or less clearly subjects of conscious thought." Linguistic categories are one such area of unconscious thought. Other cultural categories, which bring together rules of etiquette, objects viewed with disgust, attitudes toward modesty, and the like, may, like linguistic categories, originate in similarly unconscious fashion.

It seems necessary to dwell upon the analogy of ethnology and language in this respect, because, if we adopt this point of view, language seems to be one of the most instructive fields of inquiry in an investigation of the formation of the fundamental ethnic ideas. The great advantage that linguistics offer in this respect is the fact that, on the whole, the categories which are formed always remain unconscious, and that for this reason the processes which lead to their formation can be followed without the misleading and disturbing factors of secondary explanations [what today would be called rationalizations], which are so common in ethnology, so much so that they generally obscure the real history of the development of ideas entirely (Boas).

The unconscious patterns found in language, then, will help us to understand the patterning of culture, where, for one reason or another, the patterns or their underlying rationale (as opposed to actor's explanation) are more difficult to grasp.

4a. Every language is a unique configuration. There are no general categories for the analysis of all languages. (I do not wish to make this position ridiculous. Phonology, grammar, and syntax are, of course, properties of all languages, as Boas, Sapir, and all other linguists would insist. But no specific phonology, grammar, or syntax is found in all languages; no categories such as the dative, sex gender, mood, tense are general phenomena.) The fundamental process of analysis must be to find the system of categories in the language in question and to describe it. By the same token, the unique configurations thus discovered cannot be compared point for point, but only as wholes (except when we are considering related languages).

This position is well represented in Boas' introduction to the *Handbook* and in Sapir's *Language.* In this connection, I do not wish to imply that linguists do not in fact compare languages or parts of languages typologically. Indeed Sapir made such comparisons. Nevertheless, there was a prevalent attitude among this group of theorists that different languages were fundamentally non-comparable.

4b. Every culture is a unique configuration. There are no general categories for analysis, in the same sense that there are none for languages. The process must be to discover and describe the unique cultural configuration. Comparison must utilize cultural wholes.

I can find no passage in Benedict or Sapir which makes explicit use of a parallel between language and culture in this respect, but can only show that Benedict's attitude toward culture is similar to that expressed by Sapir and Boas toward language in the citations provided above. For Benedict, Zuni, Kwakiutl, and Dobu cultures "are not merely heterogeneous assortments of acts and beliefs." "They differ from one another not only because one trait is present here and absent there, and because another trait is found in two regions in two different forms. They differ still more because they are oriented as wholes in different directions. They are travelling along different roads in pursuit of different ends, and these ends and these means in one society cannot be judged in terms of those of another society, because essentially they are incommensurable." Furthermore, I cannot document my assertion that for Benedict general categories for comparing parts of cultures with one another were of trivial importance, save by stating that she conveyed this impression both in her course on anthropological theory and in her various area courses. I think, however, that many of my readers will recognize both the idea of the inutility of part-comparisons and the parallel idea of cultural incommensurability as being a part of the spirit of the times. I believe that the prestige of the linguistic analogy made such ideas far more comfortable for cultural theorists than would otherwise have been the case.

4c. The difficulty with the assumption of "incommensurability" is that, if it is taken literally, scientific work becomes impossible. If two objects or events are truly incommensurable, then no further statements can be made about them in the same universe of discourse. The less imposing claim that two objects or events (in this instance two cultures) can only be compared "as wholes" can be an almost equally serious stumbling block, although it need not be. It may mean that only attributes of each total system can be compared usefully, and that attributes of parts of the system which do not apply to the whole cannot be so usefully compared. If that is what is meant, the scientist's task is to develop a systematic list of attributes for the comparison of the wholes. But what seems to have happened in the case of cultures treated by Benedict and Sapir is the "comparison" of nonsystematic descriptions of certain cultures. All that emerges is some governing principle—dominant pattern, ethos, or what have you, like the Apollonian label, which is "compared with"—that is, described in the same work as—another such principle, say Dionysian. In the case of language,

the insistence on incommensurability or on comparison of wholes, then, resulted in the emergence of descriptive linguistics, but in the case of culture it had the effect of retarding the development of general frameworks for the comparison and contrast of cultural systems.

5a. Languages change through "drift." Drift has three characteristics which are important for present considerations. First, although inspection of historical tendencies tells us the direction of drift (say, toward positional emphasis in English), there is no a priori basis for predicting the direction of drift. Second, changes are consistent, not random, so that the result of change is not chaos but either the "same" pattern with different content, or a shift to a different pattern. Third, change frequently gives rise to greater consistency: out of several available patterns one is chosen for dominant emphasis.

> The linguistic drift has direction. . . . What is the primary cause of the unsettling of a phonetic pattern and what is the cumulative force that selects these or those particular variations of the individual on which to float the pattern readjustments we hardly know. . . . It is obvious that a language cannot go beyond a certain point in this randomness. Many languages go incredibly far in this respect, it is true, but linguistic history shows conclusively that sooner or later the less frequently occurring associations are ironed out at the expense of the more vital ones. In other words, all languages have an inherent tendency to economy of expression. . . . Thus analogy not only regularizes irregularities that have come in the wake of phonetic processes but introduces disturbances, generally in favor of greater simplicity or regularity, in a long established system of forms. These analogical adjustments are practically always symptoms of the general morphological drift of the language. . . .

5b. Cultures also change through drift. The reasons why they drift the way they do are either unimportant or incomprehensible, but the result is often greater consistency.

In discussing the development of styles of writing, Sapir said in 1921, "It is not otherwise with language, with religion, with the forms of social organization. Wherever the human mind has worked collectively and unconsciously, it has striven for and often attained unique form. The important point is that the evolution of form has a drift in one direction, that it seeks poise, and that it rests, relatively speaking, when it has found this poise." "The drift of culture, another way of saying history, is a complex series of changes in society's selected inventory—additions, losses, changes of emphasis and relation." Sapir continues by saying ". . . we shall do well to hold the drifts of language and of culture to be non-comparable and unrelated processes." But here he is not rejecting the analogy of drift as such, but the idea that the drift of a particular language is related in any causal or functional way to the drift of the culture associated with the speakers of that language: he is saying not that we cannot speak of cultural drift on the analogy of linguistic drift, but that the two processes do not go on *pari passu*.

Benedict makes the analogy explicit in her "Configurations of Culture in North America" (1932).

It is, however, the reality of such configurations that is in question. I do not see that the development of these configurations in different societies is more mystic or difficult to understand than, for example, the development of an art style. Many cultures have never achieved this thoroughgoing harmony. There are peoples who seem to shift back and forth between different types of behavior. . . . But the fact that certain people have not . . . [achieved consistency], no more makes it unnecessary to study culture from this angle than the fact that some languages shift back and forth between different fundamental grammatical devices in forming the plural or in designating tense, makes it unnecessary to study grammatical forms.

Both Sapir and Benedict, then, made explicit analogies between linguistic drift and cultural process. Benedict did not, of course, argue that *all* cultures showed a drift toward consistency, but in discussing this drift, she compared it with linguistic drift. I cannot point out further explicit comparisons between linguistic and cultural drift made by Benedict and Sapir, but it is worthwhile quoting one key passage in which Benedict makes use of the concept of cultural drift.

The cultural situation in the Southwest is in many ways hard to explain. With no natural barriers to isolate it from surrounding peoples, it presents probably the most abrupt cultural break that we know in America. All our efforts to trace out the influences from other areas are impressive for the fragmentariness of the detail; we find bits of the weft or woof of the culture, we do not find any very significant clues to its pattern. From the point of view of the present paper this clue is to be found in a fundamental psychological set which has undoubtedly been established for centuries in the culture of this region, and which has bent to its own uses any details it imitated from surrounding peoples and has created an intricate cultural pattern to express its own preferences. It is not only that the understanding of this psychological set is necessary for a descriptive statement of this culture; without it the cultural dynamics of this region are unintelligible. For the typical choices of the Apollonian have been creative in the formation of this culture, they have excluded what was displeasing, revamped what they took, and brought into being endless demonstrations of the Apollonian delight in formality, in the intricacies and elaborations of organization.

Discussion of several features of this quotation must be deferred. The noteworthy point for present purposes is that Benedict treats cultural drift as an autonomous process. She considers it important to discover the nature of the fundamental configuration and to describe the direction of the drift (toward a more and more harmonious Apollonian pattern), but she does not ask why the drift takes a particular direction. This corresponds exactly to the linguist's attitude toward linguistic drift.

5c. The criticism of the concept of cultural drift as used by Benedict and Sapir is identical with the criticism of the concept of selectivity (*1c* above), since the two concepts are closely allied. For example, there is no mention of the environmental, technological, and economic factors which might account for a portion of the selective nature of the drift. Benedict seems to feel no need to mention them—just as it would be unnecessary in linguistics to inquire why one pluralizing device was winning out over others, provided one could demonstrate that one such device was in the ascendancy. Benedict seems to see all the cultural apparatus of the Plains, of the Circumpueblo area, and of the Colorado River, as available to the Puebloans—who either refused to take it on or transformed it, because they had an Apollonian bent. She does not point out the significance of ecology: that the Puebloans occupied reusable agricultural land, which they had to defend, had a culture primarily based on agriculture, irrigated their lands, did not have dense herds of buffalo immediately available in their area, etc., whereas the Plains Indians did have such herds, could use the horse efficiently to hunt them, occupied non-agricultural or marginally agricultural lands, and found predation easy and defense of a sharply delimited area unnecessary. The facts of ecological succession or ecological adaptation in the Pueblo area are not treated as important. It should be noted, however, that when she wrote, Southwestern archeologists tended to make more of a mystery of the origins of Southwestern culture than would be the case today.

6a. No language is inherently "superior" or "inferior" to another as an adaptive or an expressive vehicle: in terms of morphology all languages are potentially capable of carrying the same informational "load," although a given language may not have the lexicon for certain messages, if these messages are not required. Even though it may be possible to speak of grammatical complexity or simplicity, there is no association between complexity and communicative capacity. One language is no more "primitive" than another—either in the sense of being simpler, or in the sense of representing an earlier, less developed stage of communication.

6b. As adaptive systems, cultures cannot be described as "superior" or "inferior" nor called "simple" or "complex" or "primitive" or "civilized" except by putting the words in quotes.

6c. There is a sense in which cultural relativism is a valid position: science does not provide answers to questions of ultimate values. There is no scientific sense in which we can say that nineteenth-century American culture is "better" than Plains Indian culture. But again the question of adaptation arises when we consider total cultures, in a way that it does not when we consider linguistic phonology and morphology. American English may not be a superior communicative device compared with Omaha. But plough agriculture and its accompaniments are superior *as an adaptation in the American prairies* to buffalo hunting and gathering: American culture successfully competed with and annihilated Plains culture when the two attempted to utilize the same environmental niche.

Cultures can be ranked with respect to energy utilization, and there are associations between energy utilization and other features of culture (White, 1949). But even when languages are ranked with respect to complexity (for example, Greenberg, 1954), no special corollaries have been discovered. Cultures can be ranked with respect to the number of role systems, the elaboration of the division of labor, the size of the group integrated within one cultural system, and so on. There are no parallels in linguistic systems.

In sum, the morphology of any given language is equivalent to any other as a communicative device. But although any culture may be an adequate—that is, a feasible—adaptation for a particular environment, it is frequently possible to say quite straightforwardly whether a hunting and gathering, or an agricultral economy will be competitively superior in a particular setting. As in the case of selection and drift, the analogy between language and culture breaks down insofar as adaptation and ecological, technological and economic considerations do not have linguistic analogues. (In fact, however, there are analogues for communication systems, though not for natural languages.)

7a. The grammar and phonology of a language analyzed by a linguist consist of the shared speech-patterns of a speech community. They are derived by analyzing the patterns of speech of a series of individual speakers and factoring out the shared patterns from the various idiolects. We do not derive the dative from speaker A and the accusative from speaker B. The idiolect is, loosely speaking, isomorphic with the language. This proposition I regard as so fundamental to linguistic research as to require no documentation.

7b. A culture consists of the shared behavior of the members of a group.[2] It also is derived by examining the behaviors (including descriptions of behavior, conversation, etc.) of the members of a group and factoring out the shared patterns from the various idiosyncratic behaviors. The outlook of the individual—his cultural idiolect—is isomorphic with the culture. Although, as I think I can later show, this outlook pervades the work of Sapir and Benedict (See Section IV), I cannot demonstrate that the linguistic analogy was used in this connection. I believe that no such analogy was used precisely because the assumption here was entirely implicit: no other view of culture was imagined.

7c. This, of course, although an implicit analogy, is the most critical misapplication of the linguistic model. There are *three* terms in fact to a consideration of linguistic materials: idiolect, language (or dialect), and system of communications. People do not *share* a system of communication, they *participate* in it, precisely because they occupy *different* positions in the communications chain. The organization of a communications system is different in kind from the organization of an idiolect or a dialect; it has no isomorphism with either.

There are three corresponding terms for the analysis of a culture: cultural idiolect, shared culture, and cultural system. And cultural system, again, is a matter in which individuals participate. It is not a matter of sharing. This distinction is easily obscured in the most primitive cultures, since to some degree every member *knows* about the cultural behavior involved in other roles, but the distinction is still there. Even the cultural *system* of a simple Shoshonean group involves relationships of asymmetry and reciprocity. It involves the interaction of, not the sum of, the cultural behavior of males and of females, of children and adults and aged.

If the insistence on *shared* behavior is maintained in the analysis of complex cultural systems, confusion arises rapidly. It leads to an insistence that it is nonsense to speak of American culture, since so many groups have such different beliefs, ideologies, and habits. Alternatively, it leads to a definition of an American culture which consists only of those things which all, or almost all, Americans share: belief in the ballot box, knowledge of American English, use of cash, etc. But it is precisely the interlocking of *different* cultural items *not* uniformly diffused through the population which permits American culture to function as a system: for example, the relationship between mathematics, engineering, and mechanical skills that makes a factory possible. Indeed, it is a requisite for the functioning of a highly differentiated cultural system that the members who participate in the system *cannot* share all the items that make up the culture complex.

It is here that linguistics, which could proceed using only history and psyche for the analysis of linguistic phenomena, was utterly misleading as an analogy for the understanding of culture. The inability of the Boasians to come to terms with cultural *systems,* masked by the success of linguistics, led to difficulties which have plagued the development of culture and personality theory ever since—and indeed the development of cultural theory.

IV. EARLY CULTURE AND PERSONALITY THEORY

It now becomes necessary to shift to a chronological treatment of essays by Sapir and Benedict in the area which has become known as "culture and personality." As a preliminary, there are a few points that I should like to clarify.

First, I am *not* attempting to make a critique of descriptive or comparative linguistics, of Sapir as a linguist, of the Whorfian hypothesis,

or anything of the sort. I do not assert that the linguistic model was the sole source of the approach to culture of Boas, Benedict, and Sapir. Nor am I saying that *all* analogies between language and total culture are false and misleading. Indeed it is true that language and culture are patterned, are selective, involve unconscious elements (elements of which speakers or members of the culture are unaware), and so on. I have tried to make clear the particular points at which I consider the analogies to be misleading, incorrect, or incomplete. Nor do I claim that there is no value in the work of Benedict or Sapir, or that an understanding of an individual's organization of the cultural materials available to him is valueless. I would claim, however, that the unwillingness or inability to come to grips with culture as a system in any sense except a set of congruences analyzed from the point of view of the actor in the system was a serious source of confusion in culture and personality theory.

I would not argue that Benedict and Sapir were incapable of analyzing cultural systems as such. Sapir's 1915 essay on Northwest Coast social organization and Benedict's "Marital Property Rights in Bilateral Society" alone would refute such a suggestion. I would claim, however, that this was not the approach that either one found most congenial, and that the central tendency of their work is correctly described in this essay. This tendency is manifest in their concern for ritual, mythology, folklore, ideology, and style, and in their relative lack of interest in economics, political systems, and the organization of kinship relationships. In this section I shall no longer be concerned with establishing the use of a linguistic model, but instead with some of the problems raised by cultural theory, and by culture and personality theory, developed in the context of the assumptions mentioned in Section III.

By 1916, in his *Time Perspective,* Sapir had already divided the universe of explanation of cultural phenomena into historical and psychological factors or explanations. This dichotomy persisted throughout his professional career, although the weight which he was disposed to give to psychological versus historical factors varied from time to time. It should be said that sometimes Sapir uses the word "psychological" to refer to explanations based on the immediate operation of men's minds. Such explanations of cultural phenomena he always eschewed. Culture was always to be explained in part historically, but increasingly, psychological factors operating through time rather than immediately, were invoked.

In *Time Perspective* Sapir shows his concern with meaning rather than with function and system: "If any general point should have come out more clearly than another in the course of our discussion, it is the danger of tearing a culture element loose from its psychological and geographical (i.e., distributional) setting." A reply to an article of Dewey's published in 1916 displays his historical bias and his rejection of culture as a system: "Each of the aspects of social life, say philosophy, or music or religion, is more definitely determined in form and content by the past history of that aspect . . . than by its co-existence with the other aspects of that life." There is, however, a foreshadowing of the position he was to take in "Culture, Genuine and Spurious": "A constant but always very imperfectly consummated tendency is present towards the moulding of these more or less distinct strands into a fabric; countless modifications and adaptations result, but the strands nevertheless remain distinct."

By 1917, it was to meaning that Sapir turned for understanding unsolved anthropological problems: an understanding of symbol-formation in the unconscious, he felt, would prove "indispensable for an approach to the deeper problems of religion and art," presumably because psychoanalysis affords some possibility of understanding the phenomena of the mind as an organized whole—unlike academic psychology.

A review of Lowie's *Primitive Society* in 1920 contains a rejection of evolutionism and of "psychological" explanations. The psychology to which he objects, however, is the tendency to explain institutions as arising out of universals of the human mind. Indeed Sapir puts evolutionism in the class of psychological explanations, presumably basing this criticism on certain elements in Morgan's and Bastian's thinking, although they are not mentioned. Evolutionism is psychological for Sapir because he sees it as a tendency to view cultural phenomena as arising from "germs of thought" operating under similar conditions. His answer to these approaches is Lowie's particularistic, diffusion-based historicism: ". . . what if a widespread social feature . . . can be shown . . . to be not the immediate and universal psychological repsonse that we would have it, but an originally unique, local phenomenon that has gradually spread by cultural borrowing over [a]

continuous area?" Nevertheless, it was to psychology in history that Sapir turned for his explanations, and indeed had already turned, in "Culture, Genuine and Spurious," which was begun by 1919 and published in full in 1924.

This essay is crucial for the understanding of the developement of culture and personality theory. Sapir begins by distinguishing three views of culture. One is the layman's—the view which uses culture as a synonym for education and refinement of taste. Another is the traditional ethnological view: "any socially inherited element in the life of man, material and spiritual" is cultural. Sapir wishes to add to these his own view, which is culture as a world outlook. His view "aims to embrace in a single term those general attitudes, views of life, and specific manifestations of civilization that give a particular people its distinctive place in the world. Emphasis is put . . . on how what is done and believed functions in the whole life of that people, on what significance it has for them." "Culture thus becomes nearly synonymous with the 'spirit' or 'genius' of a people," but these terms, Sapir says, are psychological, whereas "culture includes . . . a series of concrete manifestations" of this spirit.

In a sentence Sapir now states the core conception of Benedict's *Patterns of Culture*. "A mode of thinking, a distinctive type of reaction, gets itself established, in the course of a complex historical development, as typical, as normal; it serves then as a model for the working over of new elements of civilization." Here we have a gifted linguists' understanding of cultural development, after the model of language: a pattern —like affixing—gets somehow established; the pattern is an orientation toward the world, not a system of relationships among culture traits or among social roles; new items are accommodated to that pattern. There is no need to explain the source of the pattern.

As examples he uses French and Russian culture. In the case of the French he focuses on such characteristics as "clarity, lucid sytematization, balance, care in choice of means, and good taste" and finds reflections of French "genius" in the nature of aesthetic movements, the quality of musical style, attitudes toward religion, and "the strong tendency to bureaucracy in French administration." One can be impressed with the intuitive flash which allies bureaucracy and musical style, but the treatment of these two elements of culture on the same level and in the same terms makes sense

only in the light of Sapir's avowed view of culture as "general attitudes." Sapir's statement
may dazzle, but it begs more questions than it
raises as to the nature and sources of the
characteristics of French bureaucracy, and I
cannot in fact imagine what next steps should
be taken, in the light of Sapir's statement, to
understand the phenomenon. This tendency to
bring together many institutional areas under
one configurational rubric, without a proper
understanding of the systematic character of
any of the areas involved, was to be a source
of confusion in culture and personality theory
for several decades: the inability to separate a
cultural system from an individual outlook—or
in my earlier terms, to separate the analogue
of a communications system from the analogue
of a language.

Sapir's interest in configuration, expressed
in "Culture, Genuine and Spurious," developed
as a preoccupation with a drive toward formal
elegance in culture—a "form libido" as he once
called it. Meantime his interest in the source
of configurations made him increasingly concerned with psychology, and specifically with
psychoanalysis. The concern with a drive toward
form arises again in an essay on "Anthropology
and Sociology" (1927), where it is introduced
to explain parallel developments that do not
rest on diffusion. "We can only glance at a few
of these formal convergences . . . which we believe to be of common interest to anthropology,
to sociology, and to a social psychology of
form which has hardly been more than adumbrated." He compares the internal solidarity and
external hostility of Naga clans, Northwest coast
villages, and modern nations. "In each case a
social group-pattern—or formal 'image,' in psychological terms (clan, nation)—so dominates
feeling that services which would naturally flow
in the grooves of quite other intercrossing or
more inclusive group patterns . . . must suffer
appreciable damage." Here Sapir makes the
attitudes of individuals, shared to be sure, account for social forms. But clearly this analysis
will not long prove satisfactory: he will eventually be driven to account for the kinds of
feelings by finding out more about the kind of
persons involved. There is a further and more
elaborate treatment of form libido with reference to the neat arrangements of clans, band
camps, and the like, in various primitive societies,
and the analogy from Sapir's views of linguistic
process is evident. More important for culture
and personality theory is Sapir's concern with

"the possible transfer of a psychological attitude
or mode of procedure which is proper to one
type of social unit to another type of unit in
which the attitude or procedure is not so clearly
relevant." This point of view has its parallel
in Sapir's comments on "analogical adjustments
in language," quoted earlier.

An example of pattern transfer is to be found
in the Roman Catholic Church bureaucracy,
which is probably a

carry-over of the complex structure of Roman civil
administration. That the Jews and the evangelical
Protestant sects have a far looser type of church
organization does not prove that they are, as individuals, more immediately swayed by the demands
of religion. All that one has a right to conclude is
that in their case religion has socialized itself on a
less tightly knit pattern, a pattern that was more
nearly congruent with other habits of their social
life.

Apparently the Protestants just lost their
bureaucratic habits. Whatever this example and
the earlier one prove about the social process,
they seem to me to indicate that for Sapir the
presence, absence, and form of institutions are
to be explained in terms and their congruence
with a particular world view of the members
of the society in which they appear (or do not
appear). Sapir sums up by saying that he sees
a "germ of a social philosophy of values and
transfers that joins hands in a very suggestive
way with such psychoanalytic concepts as the
'image' and the transfer of emotion." By 1927,
then, Sapir was building analogies not just between language and culture, but between personality processes and culture.

The full tide of Sapir's use of personality
psychology, however, comes in the essays published between 1932 and 1938. The analysis of
his writings during this period can focus only
on some features of his thinking which are
particularly relevant for present purposes and
cannot do justice to the entirety of his thought.
(Thus I must pass by his pungent and still
useful criticisms of psychoanalytic approaches
to primitive data.) These essays are increasingly
concerned with grasping the organization of the
individual's private world. Sapir points out, for
example, that two individuals of ostensibly similar social position may live in quite different
perceived worlds. He becomes increasingly concerned with what he regards as the failure of
standard ethnographies—not merely their failure
to deal with the world outlook of various cul-

tures, but their unwillingness to treat of individual variation in outlook.

In 1932 Sapir says, "The more closely we study this interaction [of systems of ideas which characterize the total culture and systems established in individuals], the more difficult it becomes to distinguish society as a cultural and psychological unit from the individual who is thought of as a member of the society to whose culture he is required to adjust." "Personality organizations . . . at last analysis are psychologically comparable with the greatest cultures or idea systems. . . ." The isomorphism between personality system and cultural system has now become an explicit element in his theoretical approach. By 1934, in his essay entitled "Personality," he writes:

The socialization of personality traits may be expected to lead cumulatively to the development of specific psychological biases in the cultures of the world. Thus Eskimo culture, contrasted with most North American Indian cultures, is extraverted; Hindu culture on the whole corresponds to the world of the thinking introvert; the culture of the United States is definitely extraverted in character. . . . Social scientists have been hostile to such psychological characterizations of culture but in the long run they are inevitable and necessary.

By 1932, then, the direction of drift is determined by the cumulative bias of socialization.

By 1934 the revolt against cultural process as such has become explicit. In "The Emergence of a Concept of Personality in a Study of Cultures" we find:

. . . if we are justified in speaking of the growth of culture at all, it must be in the spirit, not of a composite history made up of the private histories of particular patterns, but in the spirit of the development of a personality. The complete, impersonalized 'culture' of the anthropologist can really be little more than an assembly or mass of loosely overlapping idea and action systems which . . . can be made to assume the appearance of a closed system of behavior. . . . The anthropologist should not fear the "concept of personality, which must not . . . be thought of . . . as a mysterious entity resisting the historically given culture but rather as a distinctive configuration of experience which tends always to form a psychologically significant unit and which, as it accretes more and more symbols to itself, creates finally that cultural microcosm of which official 'culture' is little more than a metaphorically and mechanically expanded copy."

Acceptance of his view, says Sapir, will force the consideration of new problems, and especially of problems of socialization practices. He suggests the study of a child's acquisition of culture patterns from birth until ten years of age, to see how, and out of what materials, the child forms a significant world. "I venture to predict that the concept of culture which will then emerge, fragmentary and confused as it will undoubtedly be, will turn out to have a tougher, more vital, importance for social thinking than the tidy tables of contents attached to this or that group which we have been in the habit of calling 'cultures.' " Culture, finally, becomes unreal for Sapir: it is only a convenient and fallacious way of talking about the sum of individual behavior. Its causes are to be sought in socialization patterns.

This view becomes even clearer in "Why Cultural Anthropology Needs the Psychiatrist" (1938):

To the extent that we can . . . speak of causative sequences in social phenomena, what we are really doing is to pyramid, as skillfully and as rapidly as possible, the sorts of cause and effect relations that we are familiar with in individual experience, imputing these to a social reality which has been constructed out of our need for a maximally economical expression of typically human events. It will be the future task of the psychiatrist to read cause and effect in human history. He cannot do it now because his theory of personality is too weak and because he tends to accept with too little criticism the impersonal mode of social and cultural analysis which anthropology has made fashionable.

We have gone, then, from the analogy of language and culture, to the germ of *Patterns of Culture* found in "Culture, Genuine and Spurious," to the idea of cumulative drift dominated by a pattern somehow selected and established; from there to the equating of psychological forces (image, transfer) with social forces, and finally to a search in personality development for the source of the forces—the basis of the drift. Culture and personality have been made isomorphic at last, in the same degree that idiolect and dialect are for the linguist. And throughout these last essays runs a fatigue and disgust with the *membra disjecta* of traditional ethnography divorced from cultural theory. From rejection of cultural systems, we have come at last to the individual as the source of, or the homologue of the cultural pattern.

Treatment of Benedict's work will be somewhat briefer—not that she is a less significant figure, but because some of the major points to be discussed have already been dealt with in Section III. Furthermore, in Sapir's case I have dealt with writings published from 1916 to 1938, whereas in Benedict's, I attempt to cover only the years 1922–34, and especially 1928–34. A rounded treatment of Benedict's thought should follow through to her last works, but the interest in this paper is not the intellectual life of particular theorists; it is the development of a trend in theory.

Benedict's two earliest publications, "The Vision in Plains Culture" (1922) and "The Concept of the Guardian Spirit in North America" (1923) are concerned with showing the "non-organic" quality of various religious trait complexes: the lack of necessary connection among the traits. After the fact we can see that she is also showing how each particular exemplification of the vision or the guardian spirit is related to some general feature of the culture in question. Indeed, the paper on the vision quest has the germ of the approach of *Patterns of Culture*: "The ritualistic system of the Blackfoot, then, offers a perfect example of the enormous formative power of a once-established pattern, and its tendency toward indefinite self-complication."

The positive stress on configurations, rather than the emphasis on the lack of organic quality of a trait complex, becomes a dominant note in "Psychological Types in the Cultures of the Southwest" (Benedict, 1930).[3] (The key passage of this paper has already been discussed in Section III.) Benedict saw the Apollonian ethos as a "psychological set" at this time. She says of the various Southwestern groups she has described,

these cultures, though . . . made up of disparate elements fortuitously assembled from all directions by diffusion, are none the less over and over again in different tribes integrated according to very different and individual patterns. The order that is achieved is not merely the reflection of the fact that each trait has a pragmatic function that it performs. . . . The order is due rather to the circumstances that in these societies a principle has been set up according to which the assembled cultural material is made over into consistent patterns in accordance with certain inner necessities that have developed within the group.

History and psyche again! Diffusion provides the content; configuration determines the organization. As a trait is borrowed, quite frequently it "is reworked to express the different emotional patterning characteristic of the culture that has adopted it."

So the inner necessity is not a matter of systematic organization, but of psyche, of emotionally necessity—of *Weltanschauung*. She goes on to make the assumption of individual-culture isomorphism: "Cultural configurations stand to the understanding of group behavior in the relation that personality types stand to the understanding of individual behavior." In psychology, it is now recognized that behavioral items only make sense in the context of personality configuration:

If this is true in individual psychology where individual differentiation must be limited always by the cultural forms and by the short span of a human lifetime, it is even more imperative in social psychology where the limitations of time and of conformity are transcended. The degree of integration that may be attained is of course incomparably greater than can ever be found in individual psychology. Cultures from this point of view are individual psychology thrown large upon the screen, given gigantic proportions and a long time span.

The configurations of particular cultures cannot be explained by reference to general human nature:

Another and greater force has been at work that has used the recurring situations of mating, death, provisioning, and the rest almost as raw material and elaborated them to express its own intent. This force . . . we can call within that society its dominant drive.

She concludes:

These dominant drives are as characteristic for individual areas as are house forms or the regulations of inheritance. We are too handicapped yet by lack of relevant descriptions of culture to know whether these drive-distributions are often coextensive with distributions of material culutre, or whether in some regions there are many such to one culture area defined from more objective traits.

Although Benedict here suggests the possibility of some ecological fit of her configurations, she does not develop the idea. Indeed, as I have shown, the "Psychological Types" paper expresses some astonishment at the differences of psychological orientation between the Pueblos and the Plains, without ever adverting to the gross technological, economic and environmental differences between them for an explanation. Nevertheless, she does not fall back on socialization patterns to account for the configurational drives. She takes essentially the position I have ascribed to the linguist: she observes the pattern and its power to rework materials over time, but does not attempt to account for differences of patterns between cultures.

From a theoretical point of view, *Patterns of Culture* is simply an elaboration of "Psychological Types" and "Configurations of Culture." Again we find the history-psyche dichotomy.

The difficulty with naive interpretations of culture in terms of individual behavior is not that these interpretations are those of psychology, but that they ignore history and the historical process of acceptance or rejection of traits. Any configurational interpretation of cultures also is an exposition in terms of individual psychology, but it depends upon history as well as upon psychology. It holds that Dionysian behaviour is stressed in the institutions of certain cultures because it is a permanent possibility in individual psychology, but that it is stressed in certain cultures and not in others because of historical events that have in one place fostered its development and in others have ruled it out. At different points in the interpretation of cultural forms, both history and psychology are necessary; one cannot make the one do the service of the other (Benedict, 1934).

For Benedict, as for Boas and Sapir, the distinctive thing about a culture is not that it is a system organized in a different way from an individual personality, but that it has a history—that it is an accretion—that it is not and cannot be created *de novo* in each generation. The protest is against *immediate* psychological explanation, not against psychological explanation. Only, psychology is not enough; a series of unknown accidents have determined the selective principles operating in any given culture, the accidents of history.

But for Benedict, the nonlinguist, the ontogenetic considerations which began to concern Sapir at the end of his life remained insignificant. Sapir, who did not ask the source of positional emphases in English, did ask for the source of Eskimo extraversion—in the cumulative biases of socialization. Benedict, the nonlinguist, maintained the linguist's position to a considerable degree—to locate the pattern and demonstrate its effect, but not to ask for its source. Mead has justly observed that even in Benedict's last book, *The Chrysanthemum and the Sword,* child-rearing was a relatively unimportant element in the presentation.

V. THE "CULTURE" OF CULTURE AND PERSONALITY

To use a model of culture based on the analogue of language is not necessarily wrong, but it is frequently incomplete and misleading. In linguistics it is not wrong to analyze a language as a phonological or morphological system, to profess ignorance as to the origins of grammatical devices or drift tendencies, nor is it wrong to write grammars. By the same token, it is not wrong to examine the ideas, attitudes and values of members of a society, nor to show the harmonies among these orientations and the ways in which they seem to govern behavior in several spheres of life. It would be wrong, however, to write a monograph entitled "The Communications Network among the Bathonga" which referred only to phonology, morphology, and lexicon and which did not discuss who communicates with whom, when, and about what. A description of a language may be essential to understand the content of communication, but it does not provide information about the network of communication. This network is participated in, not shared by the members of the group. In the same way, the most important systematic characteristics of culture, such as the relationships between technology and environment, between the product of this interaction and economic structures, between these structures and political units, and so on, do not emerge from a description of a set of value-orientations. They cannot. These are two different types of systems. When they are confused (for the cultural system I have mentioned cannot be ignored by even the hardiest psychologizer), the confusion seems to drive theorists to various sorts of efforts at solution—none of them satisfactory.

The first solution is that of obfuscation: of attempting to obliterate the difference between individual and culture, sometimes by maintaining that they are isomorphic, sometimes by maintaining that they are an identity, sometimes by claiming that cultures are just like individuals except that they have longer histories. Benedict's position lies somewhere in this range. This solution destroys the field of culture and personality by providing it with nothing to relate to anything else. To the degree that culture and personality are identical, there is no interaction between them.

The second solution arises out of the feeling that there is something to explain, and not merely to document. It involves an effort to explain the sources of the configurations (again, remember, value-attitudes) which are seen as straining for expression and dominating new cultural materials in a given culture. In the long run, it is not intellectually very satisfying simply to maintain that the configurations result from the vagaries of history. The temptation is then to turn to socialization patterns, to the early patterning of personality, as a source of the cultural configuration. To this solution Sapir turned toward the end of his life, although he cannot be said to have adopted it wholeheartedly or without qualification. This solution is reductionist. It assumes that the cultural order can be explained by the orientations of its component individuals, which creates a special kind of problem, since the issue of why the individuals continue to share the same orientations must arise again. (The same problem can arise from the "isomorphic" view.)

The third solution denies that there is a problem. It is the "chicken and egg" solution. Its proponents point out that no individual is born outside a culture. The individual is born in a culture, is socialized to find it congenial (or perhaps to find it uncongenial), and therefore strives to maintain it (or change it). The circle is complete, and therefore, it is said, the question of where to break into it for descriptive purposes is arbitrary. Oddly enough, however, those who maintain this view either "break" the circle at the point where the child's socialization starts, or stress the importance of socialization for perpetuation or change.

Now, in fact, it is becoming increasingly apparent that we cannot find cases where changes in socialization, occurring prior to other major changes in a cultural system, have resulted in such changes. On the other hand, myriad other sources of cultural change press for attention. And finally, it seems highly reasonable to regard socialization changes as responses to other changes. Therefore the point at which we should break into the "circle" is the description of the on-going adult system of relationships in its ecological context. This will "explain" socialization. Socialization itself explains the how, not the why of stability and never explains major features of change. It may account for the nature of adjustment to or resistance to change. The third solution, which attempts to do away with the problem, eventually betrays its psychologistic bias.

It might appear from what has been said that this essay is an effort to destroy the entire area of culture and personality studies as a legitimate field of scientific enquiry. The intention, however, is rather to give to the field a properly delimited sphere of endeavor, within which there is ample room for adequate research. The viable core of culture and personality studies is the analysis of the impact of the cultural system (*not* of a *Weltanschauung* alone) as a technological, economic, or political organization on the individual through the mediation of socialization patterns and as that organization affects him in his adult life. This analysis must be carried out in terms appropriate to personality theory—whether in terms of drives, defenses, cognitive orientations, motives or of personality theory not yet available. Essentially, although my language differs from his, I am proposing a field of endeavor very like that outlined by White in 1925.

As White then said, and as Mead and others have often said, the variations in cultural systems promise us a greater opportunity to measure the impact of various factors on the development and functioning of personality than any laboratory setting imaginable in the present cultural order. The adaptation of personality systems, as realities in their own right, to cultural systems, as realities in their own right, is a subject of no small interest and importance for personality theory. It also has its special interest for anthropology. This adaptation does not account for the content, organization, or process of change of a culture, but it does tell us something of the "physiology" of a culture—of how culturally relevant incentives and inhibitions are produced in persons. There is also some reason to believe that an understanding of the dynamics of modal personality types (themselves the products of cultural systems) may assist us in the study of expressional devices in different cultural systems—matters of ritual idiom, gesture, some features of art style, recreation, and the like. Some research in this area looks promising, but too little objective work is yet available for a definite judgment. Unfortunately, the earlier work in culture and personality tended to reduce all aspects of culture except those obviously related to the biological survival of the individual organism to expressional elements, and hence to lapse into one or another of the confusions discussed above.

In sum, culture and personality theory developed in the vacuum created by the rejection of perspectives which saw culture as a system, either synchronically or diachronically. This theoretical approach rested in part on an analogy between total culture and language. Benedict and Sapir were among the earliest proponents of this view of culture, but the explicit and implicit assumptions they employed remain with us and trouble us today. Indeed the temptation to fall back on the linguistic model in other forms than those I have mentioned arises again and again, whenever culture seems too perplexing. A viable study of culture and personality, capable of dealing with cause and effect in definite terms, will be built on an appropriate model of culture, which represents it as an organized, symbolically mediated mode of adjustment of human groups to their environment. But needless to say, the personality investigations which proceed within this context must similarly be built on a frank recognition of personality systems, and on an appropriate and sophisticated personality theory and methodology of study. For if culture is not a macrocosm of personality, neither is personality a microcosm of culture.

NOTES

1. To avoid confusion, I should say at this point that although I must speak of "language and culture," I do not regard language as noncultural or culture as nonlinguistic. I am speaking of language as it is analyzed by linguists, and of culture as including linguistic behavior—but linguistic behavior viewed as a communicative device rather than as a set of phonological and morphological principles.

2. By the "shared" speech patterns of a speech community, I refer to patterns of phonology or morphology found in similar or nearly identical form in the speech of each member of the community. By "shared" behavior I refer to linguistic or nonlinguistic activities manifest in similar or near-identical form by each member of the group. It may be objected that no one *really* meant that the patterns were shared by *all* members of the group, that obviously there are at a minimum age and sex differences; to this the reply must be made that the problem was not dealt with in sufficiently explicit a fashion. It may also be claimed that by "sharing" some theorists refer to common understandings, not common behavior. Again, there has not been sufficient care to make this explicit, if that is the intention.

3. This paper was delivered in September of 1928 but published in 1930. There are a number of parallels between it and Sapir's 1928 paper on religion. These and other parallels led me to be concerned with the question of when Sapir and Benedict began to use each other's work. I am much indebted to Margaret Mead for information on this score. She informs me that Benedict wrote her paper on the vision quest before she met Sapir, and probably before she had read "Culture, Genuine and Spurious." From 1922 on they did work closely together and influenced each other. There is a good deal of correspondence between 1922 and 1926, and Sapir visited New York fairly often during part of this period, since his first wife was then ill and in New York. [Margaret Mead's *An Anthropologist at Work, Writings of Ruth Benedict*, appeared in 1959, too late for me to use in revising this paper, which had gone to the editors in final form in October of 1958. Sapir's comments on some of Benedict's work, Benedict's on Sapir's, and Mead's elucidation of the background of *Patterns of Culture* would have made it possible to deal with certain major differences between Sapir's and Benedict's theoretical positions. Here, however, my primary interest is in their similarities.]

33

PERSONALITY
AND SOCIAL STRUCTURE

BERT KAPLAN

ONE of the more dramatic phenomena in social science during the past decade has been the tremendous development of interest in the field of research and theory concerning the relationships between personality and social systems. Although sociologists like G. H. Mead, E. W. Burgess, and C. H. Cooley, to mention only a few, made significant contributions in this field, it was not until recent years that interest in it became general. The main theoretical and empirical issues within it are not easy to determine and the fact that a great many sociologists as well as anthropologists and psychologists are concerned with this area does not mean that they are all focused on the same issues. Probably the main sub-area is what has come to be known as the culture and personality field. This field has been mainly dominated by anthropologists and by studies of national character and of modal personality in nonliterate societies (47, 58, 41). Both sociologists and psychologists, however, have recognized its relevance for their problems and have not only applauded from the sidelines, but have integrated its empirical findings and conceptions into their own theories and teaching. However, the culture and personality area does not encompass the whole field. Since sociologists have tended to define the term personality rather broadly, frequently as being synonymous with the individual, and there has been little clear consensus as to the meaning of social structure, the writings under the heading of personality and social structure have ranged widely, going from such broad problems as the relationship of the individual to society to more narrow ones involving specific kinds of behavior and small-group structure. One result is a considerable amount of misunderstanding and faulty communication, especially when the parties to the discussion are from different disciplines.

In the present chapter no attempt will be made to consider all of the different frameworks which have been utilized, nor shall research under any particular framework be reviewed comprehensively. Instead, attention will be focused on a limited number of issues which are believed to have been of special importance during the past decade. The concept "personality" will be used throughout in a more narrow sense than is frequently the case, and will in general coincide with the implicit definitions of the psychiatrist, the psychoanalyst, and the clinical psychologist in which the idea of motivation or of need-disposition is central. The term social structure will also be assigned a relatively narrow meaning and will be used to indicate the over-all organization of social institutions and other components of the social system. In other words, we shall be concerned with "the social structure" rather than with specific kinds of "social structuring." In addition no systematic distinction will be maintained between social and cultural systems, and social and cultural components will be regarded as elements of a single system.

The main focus of this chapter will be on the role of personality in the maintenance and proper functioning of social systems. This focus may be distinguished from the more usual one of the impact of the social system on personality, although, as we shall see, they are not completely separate. We shall consider first a number of conceptions concerning the part which personality plays in social systems; secondly, some of the ways in which it is thought that personality acquires a shape that is appropriate to the role it plays; and, finally, we shall discuss a number of empirical and methodological issues which are relevant to these and other questions in the culture and personality area.

THE PLACE OF PERSONALITY IN SOCIAL FUNCTIONING

It seems possible to distinguish three ways in which personality has been thought to function in or influence social systems: as a determinant of social institutions, as an integrating link between social institutions, and, finally, as a support for social institutions by guaranteeing appropriate behavior and minimizing disrupting deviant behavior.

PERSONALITY AS A DETERMINANT OF SOCIAL INSTITUTIONS

At present this viewpoint is in general disrepute among social scientists. Geza Roheim has perhaps been the principal exponent of Freud's primal-horde theory in which society, represented by the totem, emerged as a result of the rebellion of the sons against their father. In killing him, however, they introject his image which becomes, as the superego, the basis for law and order. Roheim (96, 97) gave rich documentation to the belief that religious ritual and mythology received their form and content from variants of the childhood neurosis surrounding the Oedipus complex. In this respect he and a host of other psychoanalytic writers have anticipated Kardiner when he suggests that the secondary institutions of a culture are determined by basic personality constellations. The difference is that Roheim and the early psychoanalytic writers emphasized the universality of the personalty processes involved, i.e., the Oedipus complex, while Kardiner introduced the idea that these processes varied from group to group. Roheim undoubtedly had an important point when he sought to demonstrate the existence of panhuman personality processes. However, it would seem difficult to derive the astonishing diversity of cultural forms from these basically similar processes. In addition it is possible that myths and religious rituals might reflect key personality processes but that components of other social institutions would not.

A number of writers on the subject of national character have suggested, although often not explicitly, that important social institutions are reflections of personality forces. Thus in Gorer's analysis of Americans (26), political systems, dating patterns, and certain economic practices are regarded as emerging from feelings about authority, uncertain self-esteem, and the need for love, respectively. Similar interpretations are made for the Great Russians (27) and the Japanese (25). The same kind of analysis is to be found in the writings of Mead (76), La Barre (61), and others.

Although, as Inkeles and Levinson (47) point out, many social institutions are historical residues from periods long past and it is therefore not possible to establish causal connections with any assurance, it does not seem necessary to exclude the possibility that modal personality processes do have a dynamic role, taken together with other forces, in determining the form of particular institutions. Fromm (20, 21) in his analysis of "character" in our own society has discussed the situation in which large numbers of individuals transcend the values of their society and become "free and productive" in influencing "morality" so that it reflects their own nature and potentialities. Lynd (67) takes a similar view, emphasizing that man's biology imposes certain needs and rhythms on him, and that he consequently must shape social institutions which will be congenial rather than alien to them. Riesman's "autonomous" man (95) is also independent and value producing.

Barnouw (6) has given an interesting analysis of the part which personality can play in historical processes. By contrasting the course of acculturation of the Wisconsin Chippewa with that of neighboring tribes such as the Dakota and Cheyenne he attempts to show that differences were related to personality differences among the groups. Although the brief personality analyses presented are not particularly convincing, the theory that modal personality patterns play a significant role in historical events seems important and one wishes that historians would take note of it.

PERSONALITY AS A FACTOR IN THE INTEGRATION OF SOCIAL INSTITUTIONS

The principal exponent of this point of view has been Abram Kardiner (53, 54, 55). He theorizes that certain aspects of a culture which he calls "primary institutions," and which consist for the most part of child rearing practices, exercise a crucial role in the formation of the personality characteristics of members of the group. Since the effect of these primary institutions is felt by all children in the group, the resulting adult patterns will be shared ones.

These shared personality characteristics, known as the basic personality structure, in turn have a crucial effect on certain other aspects of the culture, namely, the secondary institutions. The basic personality structure serves as a link between different social institutions and is regarded as one of the main bases for the integration of culture. This theory has been subjected to a number of tests, the main ones being the Alorese study reported by Du Bois (18) and the research of Whiting and Child (114). The Kardiner-Du Bois study actually provided a test for only the first part of the theory, namely, that adult personality constellations are caused by child rearing practices. This study is discussed below.

The Whiting and Child research constitutes a more direct test of the "personality integration of culture" theory. This study attempted to test the theory that a relationship existed between culturally patterned child rearing practices and personality. Instead of making direct observation of personality characteristics, Whiting and Child considered that belief systems relating to illness and death could be regarded as indices of these characteristics. In a sophisticated and relatively precise way these writers described a number of variations in each of five areas of child training, those dealing with oral, anal, and sexual behavior as well as dependence and aggression. It was hypothesized that particular kinds of training in each of these areas would lead to certain personality characteristics which in turn would be reflected in the belief systems. For example, especially gratifying or frustrating experiences in any of these areas would lead to "fixations," or lifelong preoccupations that would influence the belief systems. Child-rearing practices and belief systems were examined in 75 cultures, a work constituting one of the first major uses of the Cross-Cultural Files (for others, see Murdock, 82, and Horton, 43). The authors conclude that there was confirmation of the general hypothesis that child training practices are related to explanations of illness and therapeutic practices. Although their argument that this relationship occurs through the mediation of personality variables is convincing, the possibility exists that the basis for this relationship lies in some third factor. However, the conclusions are quite startling and suggest that the more usual theory of social integration in which social institutions are thought to be related to each other in terms of the functions of each in the maintenance of the whole may

not be the only or even the best model for understanding social integration. Sapir (99) has suggested that the relationship between various aspects of a social pattern are frequently of an unexpected, subtle, and symbolic nature and are not comprehended by any single theoretical scheme. It seems possible, then, that there is more than one basis for social integration and that some institutions are connected to each other in a totally different way than others are. Thus the theory of personality integration of cultural institutions need not be regarded as contradicting the structural-functional approach.

PERSONALITY AS A SUPPORT OF THE SOCIAL SYSTEM

Since sociocultural systems can be said to exist concretely only in individuals (100, 15, 58) their maintenance is dependent on the support and compliance of individuals. That is, the individuals who are the carriers of culture must perform willingly. The development in a group's members of personality characteristics which insure this willingness to participate may be regarded as the primary task of the socialization institutions. Inkeles and Levinson (47) speak of the situation of "ideal congruence" as involving the maximum degree of compatibiliy between personality traits and social requirements. They say that:

Insofar as the relevant traits of character are modally present in the population of any society, the chances are increased that culturally and structurally important goals will be aspired toward and implemented by the society's members, thus in significant degree ensuring the continued effective functioning of the social system (page 1006).

Inkeles and Levinson emphasize the importance of "modal" personality, that is, of the regularities in the personalities of members of a group which can be ascribed to the sociocultural system pattern. In their discussion of congruence they focus for the most part on the relation of those modes to societal functioning.

It is obvious, however, that "ideal" congruence does not always exist and perhaps never does. Inkeles and Levinson speak of two types of noncongruence, that induced by institutional change when relatively well-established modal personality types exist and that occurring in a stable society when there is a large influx or immigration of a personality type different from the ones most prevalent in the society. Both of these situations present opportunities for crucial empirical research to determine the extent to which either character type or institutional pattern changes radically. That is, when there is noncongruence of either type it becomes possible to follow, although it may take a number of years or even generations, the vicissitudes of change in either social system or personality types or both. Present-day Soviet Russia is a good example of noncongruence and a number of workers have been studying it.

Dicks (16, 17) has contributed important empirical findings which demonstrate this noncongruence in Soviet Russia. He finds that the traditional Russian oral personality traits are not appropriate to the Soviet system and that important strains result. He notes, however, that a new personality type has emerged which is characteristic of the leaderships and is predominantly "anal." This "type" appears to be an overreaction, or a swing which is too far in the opposite direction and is also noncongruent. The two prevalent personality types exert opposing influences on the social system and both appear to give rise to chronic tension, frustration, and malaise.

Inkeles (46) has described changes of child-rearing values in three generations of Russians in the direction of providing more appropriate adaptations to the changed social conditions and suggests that similar changes probably operate at the personality level. One interesting conclusion which can be drawn from observations of noncongruence such as that existing in the Soviet Union is that the social system as a whole nevertheless persists. Even drastic noncongruence does not seem to disrupt the society's functioning. This should warn us against being too certain of the dependence of societal functioning upon the support of particular personality characteristics. Noncongruence undoubtedly results in strain among individuals, and in inefficiency in the social system, but so long as the necessary tasks get done it is not fatal or perhaps even serious. As Parsons suggests (92) the system of positive and negative sanctions stands as a second line of defense when appropriate motivations fail to develop, and the required behavior can be elicited by these mechanisms. Although Inkeles and Levinson point out that the effectiveness of sanctions can be increased by certain personality characteristics, it is probable that sanctions do not depend entirely on the existence of such characteristics.

ROLE AND PERSONALITY

One of the most significant theoretical trends in sociology during the past decade has been the concentration on the concept of role as the mediator between societal requirements and individual behavior. This concept has in most serious theoretical attempts come to assume the position of a cornerstone without which many conceptual structures would be unstable. This is primarily because of the importance of the role for the social system. To quote Parsons (88)

Roles are from the point of view of the functioning of the social system, the primary mechanisms through which the functional prerequisites of the system are met. There is the same order of relationship between roles and functions relative to the system in social systems as there is between organs and functions in the organism (page 115).

Baldwin (5) has suggested that for many "role" is a descriptive concept and refers simply to certain uniformities of behavior in a particular class of individuals, i.e., "the cowboy" or "the Bostonian." Used in this sense the "role" does not have any functional significance in maintaining the social system. The concept has also been used in an explanatory sense, as, for example, when it defines the expectations of people in general about appropriate behavior for individuals occupying a certain position. We follow the second usage.

While appropriate role behavior can be elicited through the operation of a system of positive and negative sanctions or rewards and punishments, it may also be encouraged by the development of motivations that will guarantee proper behavior without the application of external sanctions. We have suggested above that in the absence of relevant motivations external sanctions may insure the requisite performances. One thinks of a society in which slaves do most of the necessary jobs under threat of punishment. However, this does not seem to be the typical situation. In most known societies participation is voluntary and individuals seem predisposed to fill the available roles. External sanctions, it seems, are of secondary importance in behavioral conformity and come into force mainly in relation to deviance and in cases where some kind of failure of the socialization process has occurred.

American social scientists have placed great

emphasis on the theory that a role, once occupied, exerts a strong formative influence on its occupant. Newcomb (85), for example, has taken the position that many role assignments are made on the basis of visible characteristics which individuals possess but that once the role has been assigned its occupant usually acquires still other characteristics which add to his fitness. These new characteristics, or "acquired motive patterns" as Newcomb calls them, develop chiefly because the role becomes an important element in the individual's self picture (23). Thus the new boss comes after a short time to think of himself as a boss and a new ego-identity, to use Erikson's term, is established. Subsequently, the need to maintain this new self picture involves a host of new goals or motives. Waller's study of the teacher (112) provides a good example of this process (68).

Merton's (79) analysis of the bureaucratic personality provides an excellent illustration of the way in which tendencies which may be only slight when the individual first assumed a role become important after he has been in it for a number of years. The "personality" pattern of the bureaucrat thus comes to be, in an important sense, organized around his role in the bureaucracy. However, the increased fitness of the individual for his role is not the only consequence of this development. It has negative effects as well. Using Veblen's term "trained incapacity" and Warnotte's "professional deformation," Merton describes the way in which the bureaucrat because he becomes *too* "methodical, prudent and disciplined," actually is *unfit*, to a certain degree, for his office. In the process of leaving a margin of safety and becoming specially efficient there is a transference of focus from aims to means, the latter becoming ends in themselves. It is clear from this example that the influence of role on personality is not necessarily in the direction of creating increased fitness. The effect may be just the opposite. In addition it is probable that some of the effects of role have little or no relevance to the dimension of "fitness." The main point is that it seems likely that many of the influences roles exert on personality are random to the idea of efficiency in role performance. In the present climate of opinion in the social sciences, which tends to assume that there is a rather close fit between personality and social structure, this is a somewhat radical hypothesis. Gerth and Mills (23), for example, express the common viewpoint that although character

structure is anchored in the organism, "it is formed by the particular combination of social roles which the person has incorporated from out of the total roles available to him in his society." The view we have suggested is that the fit is less close than is generally thought and occurs through a few main links rather than through myriad minor ones.

A second reason that individuals are frequently found to have personality traits which are appropriate to the roles they occupy resides in the fact that there is a considerable amount of role recruitment and self-recruitment. To some degree individuals seek roles that are most congenial to them. Henry's (38) study of the personality characteristics of successful American business executives is relevant to this point. Using interviews and projective tests, principally the Thematic Apperception Test, he found that to a remarkable degree the one hundred individuals studied had certain characteristics in common. It seemed to Henry that these characteristics were a minimum requirement for success and that the absence of them was coincident with failure within their organizations.

The characteristics found by Henry were strikingly appropriate to the requirements of the executive position. However, as Henry points out:

The extent to which such reshaping of the adult personality is possible, however, seems limited. An initial selection process occurs in order to reduce the amount of time involved in teaching the appropriate behavior. Those persons whose personality structure is most readily adaptable to this particular role, tend to be selected to take this role. Whereas those whose personality is not already partially akin to this role are rejected (page 286).

To this we would add that it is obvious that individuals with the above described characteristics would seek executive positions and would be relatively successful in doing so. Newcomb's suggestion (85) to the effect that, "we should expect to find more uniformity in personality on the part of those holding the same achieved positions, than on the part of those holding the same ascribed position," is applicable here, as is the concept of "anticipatory socialization."

From the point of view of a systematic theory of the formative influence of roles or social systems on personality, however, the two kinds of relationships just discussed, namely, those resulting from random effects of role and those resulting from recruitment and self selection, are of only secondary interest. These relationships do little to clarify the mechanism by which personality is systematically shaped into socially appropriate patterns. The question of chief theoretical interest in the present chapter is not whether role influences personality or the behavior of individuals but whether the role or other units of the society systematically produce in individuals particular motivational and other components of personality which induce conformity to role and societal requirements. There is an implication in much theoretical work in this field of study that since role behaviors vary widely, there is a corresponding variability at the personality level which serves to explain the behavioral differences. The most usual statement is that role requirements become "internalized" and are transformed into individual motives. Thus what was originally a unit of the social system, the role expectation, becomes a component of the personality or self system. This view is reflected in the expectation that particular personality patterns will be found among individuals in various roles. Linton (66) has introduced the concept "status personality" to indicate this idea. He says that "all societies assume that the individuals who occupy certain positions in their systems of organization, will as a group, show personality norms differing from those of individuals in certain other positions." Although Linton does mention the possibility that the "status personality" is a cultural fiction which results from the confusion of similarities in role *behavior* with similarities in *personality,* and treats the matter as an open question to be clarified by empirical research on the personalities of individuals in various status groups, the concept has received widespread and somewhat uncritical acceptance.

Parsons has suggested in his analysis of the American professional (87) that the same motives are not necessarily present in all individuals who are playing the same role. He states, although it is not clear whether it is on the basis of any empirical study:

Indeed there is little basis for maintaining that there is any important broad difference of typical motivation in the two cases (doctors and businessmen), or at least any of sufficient importance to account for the broad differences of socially expected behavior (page 196).

Also the recurrent patterns of behavior which are required for institutional functioning may have different meanings in different personalities.

The social problem is to get the patterns (of behavior) whatever their functional significance to the person. . . . It does not matter whether there are important differences among types of personality possessing this need-disposition as long as it exists. Moreover it does not even matter greatly whether the dominant sub-integrations of need-dispositions are not directly gratified . . . as long as the personality systems allow them to carry out the action without more than a certain amount of strain and as long as there are . . . institutions capable of absorbing and tolerating the repercussions of the strain (93, page 158).

Parsons suggests that the crucial personality variables underlying role behavior are an identification with the moral order, a respect for legitimate authority, and a feeling of "disinterested" obligation to live up to expectations in his variously defined roles. This is a crucial idea that has general applicability for the whole culture-personality field. Thus, for example, if the Zuni "ideal personality" requires nonaggressive behavior, the motivational component involved in nonaggressive behavior which conforms to this pattern is not necessarily "lack of aggression," but rather may be compliant and conforming tendencies in the individual. With this possibility it is not necessary that the social system create different motivational patterns for each of the roles contained within it. It suggests instead that the motivations toward conformity and toward acquiescence to legitimate authority are among the chief points of contact between social structure and personality.

As Parsons and Shils say (93):

In most cases, individuals perform role functions in the division of labor which do not, as such, completely and directly gratify any specific need-disposition or any set of the need-dispositions of their personality system. It is the nature of instrumental action that it should be this way. Conformity with the role-expectations is possible, however, either through a generalized need-disposition to conformity or through instrumental orientations (page 152).

It is possible to inquire more closely into the nature of personality characteristics upon which conformity is based. The "respect for legitimate order" seems to be just one of such characteristics. It may itself be divided into two types, that which derives from the "internalization" of a more or less stable set of traditional values and that which involves simply the moral orientation, that is, the desire to do what is good and right without, however, the commitment to any particular set of ideas about what is good or right. From the first of these ideas we derive our theories of the superego; the second is closer to what White (113) has called "the mature conscience" and Erikson (19) has called the "humanization of conscience." It is clear that both types sustain conformity.

For the most part, social scientists have accepted the theory of the psychoanalysts that the value system internalized as the superego forms the chief basis for conformity. In recent years it has become apparent that a second main basis exists as well. We refer to what Riesman (95) has called "other directedness." In a society which is becoming increasingly characterized by normlessness, sociability and the orientation toward acceptance and popularity have become important bases for conformity. Here also the orientations provided by the group become coercive in their influence.

The "marketing orientation" described by Fromm (21) is a related personality trend. Individuals with this orientation are dependent upon others for acceptance and status. In order to win the acceptance the individual "becomes" the kind of person who is in the greatest demand. He tries to be as "attractive" as possible and in Fromm's terms says, "I am as you desire me." This behavior is extraordinarily plastic and flexible, shifting with the "requirements of the market." As Fromm says:

. . . its very nature is that no specific and permanent kind of relatedness is developed, but that the very changeability of attitudes is the only permanent quality of such orientation. In this orientation those qualities are developed which can best be sold . . . the premise of the marketing orientation is emptiness, the lack of any specific quality which is not subject to change since any persistent trait of character might conflict someday with the requirements of the market (page 77).

Since for the most part role requirements specify desirable behavior but do not specify the motivations for it, this arrangement works well in insuring conformity. However, this concept is more applicable when the roles are functionally specific than when they are functionally diffuse, to use Parsons' terms (88).

Baldwin (5) in his analysis of the psychological mechanisms underlying behavioral uniformities distinguishes two types of compliance. In one of these the compliant behavior is instrumental to the achievement of some reward or avoidance of a punishment. Baldwin, however, believes that the two bases for compliance which we have discussed above, that is, compli-

ance out of a sense of duty and compliance to fulfill the expectations of some other person, are consummatory in nature and require no cognition of reward in order to be executed. He says:

Compliance to a cognized rule is a general mechanism permitting very great flexibility. The rule may change, it may hold only on odd numbered weeks, it may hold only when one is elected to a role. If it is intellectually clear, then compliance can occur. This mechanism is therefore most suitable for those social uniformities which require flexibility (page 23).

Baldwin suggests that compliance is possible only for voluntary behavior and cannot be elicited against the will of the actor; hence the special requirement that it be based on the motivational dispositions of the actor.

Parsons and Shils (93) make the related point that the

. . . need to be approved and esteemed is . . . a fundamental motivational basis for the acceptance of socially necessary disciplines. There is a sense in which, paradoxical as it may seem, the core of the reward systems of societies is to be found in the relevance of this element of the motivation of individuals. What people want most is to be responded to, loved, approved, and esteemed. If, subject, of course, to an adequate level of physiological need-gratification, these needs can be adequately gratified, the most important single condition of stability of a social system will have been met (page 150).

These bases of conformity are related in various ways to the systems of positive and negative sanctions operating in a society. The latter may be regarded as direct social mechanisms for inducing appropriate role behavior. Their success, however, as Inkeles and Levinson (47) suggest, is dependent upon the responsiveness of individuals to them. In discussing the relationship of personality to *positive* sanctions, which are defined as the rewards offered for effective behavior, they suggest that the effectiveness of such sanctions depends on the motivations of individuals to attain them.

In our own society a major *positive* sanction is money, which may be regarded as an all-purpose reward capable of satisfying a wide variety of different needs for gratification. Most frequently, however, it is regarded as a means of attaining "success." Financial and social success as rewards can be most meaningful when the main basis for conformity is of the "other directedness" or "market orientation" variety but will probably not be relevant if the moral orientation is prevalent. Inkeles and Levinson distinguish congruence between motivational trend and sanction from a second type of congruence in which other psychological traits affect the "instrumental adequacy" of the individual. Thus in a society where accumulation of wealth is rewarded by recognition, the "tendency to be penurious" increases one's chances of achieving the proffered reward. While such characteristics undoubtedly help explain individual differences in achieving rewards, it does not seem necessary that they be modal in a group, for the reason that the proffered rewards do not actually have to be achieved in order to function as motivators. In fact if everyone in the group could actually reach them, their attraction would probably be much diminished. The fact that rewards are partly out of the reach of most of those striving for them may result in strain, but this does not necessarily interfere with the efficient functioning of the social system.

It is more difficult to say what type of positive sanction is most closely associated with the moral orientation we described above since moral behavior does not require an extrinsic reward. As Baldwin (5) says: "There may be people who want to comply with a rule. For them the reward or sanction is psychologically unnecessary." It seems likely that negative sanctions are most important here. A number of writers have classified cultures as "guilt" or "shame" cultures (94) according to whether the main nonphysical sanctions are aimed at one or the other of these feelings. Although in actual practice it is sometimes rather difficult to make a sharp distinction between these two processes (42), one might expect that the moral orientation would fit the traditional society in which the member's own guilt over real or imagined deviancy would serve as the main sanction. The term "sanction" has a somewhat different meaning when used in this way since it stems from the individual rather than from others. In the society in which "other directedness" or the "marketing orientation" is the chief motivation for conformity we might expect that "exposure" and shaming along with rejection, failure, and withdrawal of love would serve as the most important sanctions.

The principal point made here is that a few types of motivational dispositions can provide the impetus for a wide variety of role behavior. Where most contemporary theorists have emphasized the formative effects of a particular set of role expectations and have suggested that a high degree of role differentiation results in a similar degree of differentiation at the personality level, it seems possible that adequate fulfillment of role expectations does not require this differentiation. This is not to deny the fact that such personality differentiation takes place. Roles undoubtedly do exert an influence on personality in the way Newcomb and others have indicated. This influence, however, is largely an accidental by-product rather than a crucial dynamic force explaining conformity, and it may or may not have functional consequences. While such by-products may have an important positive or negative effect on the ways in which roles are played, from the point of view of a theory dealing with the shaping of personality by society so that it will have an appropriate form, the direct influence of role on personality seems largely nonsystematic and secondary in importance. One might speak of the "unanticipated consequences" of role participation. The same thing might be said about role conflict. From the point of view of understanding mental health problems, role conflicts are undoubtedly of great importance. Most writers on the subject of personality and social structure have inclined toward the position that personality "strains" are "undesirable," functionally speaking. Except when the strains are very extreme it is unlikely that this is true. Social systems function by and large with little regard to the strain or comfort of their members so long as appropriate behavior is forthcoming. This opinion applies to strain resulting from role conflict (105, 22, 44, 4), to strain arising from the lack of congruence between role expectations and personality dispositions (106, 101, 3), and to strain resulting from the futile striving for proffered rewards. As Parsons (88) says:

From the point of view of functioning of the social system it is not the needs of all the participant actors which must be met nor all the needs of any one but only a sufficient proportion of a sufficient fraction of the population. It is indeed a very general phenomenon that social forces are directly responsible for injury to or destruction of some individuals and some of the wants or needs of all individuals and though this may be reduced it is highly probable that it cannot be eliminated under realistic conditions (page 28).

THE DEVELOPMENT OF SOCIALLY APPROPRIATE
MOTIVATIONS

Our problem here is somewhat more limited than that usually proposed. Instead of being concerned with the effect of social institutions on personality we shall be interested only in those systematic effects which foster efficient institutional functioning. We have suggested the theory that a very small number of powerful and widespread motivational patterns serve to explain conformity to a great variety of role requirements. These may be regarded as the absolutely necessary and minimum requirements for institutional functioning. A large number of other personality characteristics may contribute to the niceties of the situation but are perhaps dispensable.

The process by which personality comes to have this appropriate shape is ordinarily referred to as socialization. The most prevalent theory of socialization is that the early care of children is socially patterned in such a way that the appropriate adult personality characteristics are produced (19). This belief rests heavily on the psychoanalytic theories which hold that the early years of life are crucial in personality development. To a very large extent research in the field of culture and personality has been focused on the problem of linking child-rearing practices to adult personality patterns. This focus has been deplored by many (86, 41) who suggest that decisive influences may come in middle childhood and later.

Our concern here is with the extent to which these socialization practices have as their manifest or latent function the creation of personality characteristics that produce conformity to desired norms and role requirements. While most culture-personality studies have attributed such a function to child-rearing patterns, actual empirical demonstrations or convincing theoretical expositions are rare. Of the empirical studies the work of Allison Davis and his colleagues (14) is most germane. These writers have documented in convincing fashion the existence of different patterns of child rearing in two social classes among American Negroes. A number of aspects of the child-rearing patterns they described can be interpreted as helping to develop personality characteristics which will fit the social institutions and normative expectations of the society. Merton and Kitt (80) have referred to the kind of training in which parents prepare their children for membership in groups that are somewhat higher on the hierarchical social scale than their own groups as "anticipatory socialization."

Aberle (2) has recently discussed the question of the child-rearing practices. He makes a plea for research which will show how the pattern of socialization is related to the configuration of other social institutions and rejects the view that socialization practices aim simply at reproducing the personality characteristics of the socializing agents. Aberle explores the relations of these practices to various aspects of the social system, and also of various aspects of the socialization pattern to the social system. He concludes that there may be a broad network of relationships among a number of different aspects of the social system and socialization practices. At a number of points the type of relationship he suggests involves the training of children for adult roles. On the other hand components of certain institutions such as religious rituals seem to reinforce socialization patterns. Erikson (19) makes a similar point when he states "child training to remain consistent must be imbedded in a system of continued economic and cultural synthesis."

Murphy (83) has addressed himself to the problem of how social uniformity is created. He rejects as "naive" and simplistic the view that the child "takes over" the culture from his parents and suggests that certain processes in the child such as the demand to be admitted, to be loved and respected as a member of the group, the protest against exclusion on the grounds of immaturity and the rebellion against interference with his primitive impulses indicate that the "young absorb a good deal of their familial culture" partly because they want to, partly because they have to. "There is no simple osmosis of the prevalent social usages from old to young; there is a mixture of love-feast and battle royal." While indicating that the young learn to act, perceive, and value as their elders do, Murphy suggests that we still have only the vaguest understanding of *how* this learning takes place. In his analysis of the *how* of socialization he emphasizes the principle of "anchorage" of perceptions to what is pleasing and satisfying. To the developing child it is most satisfying to do, see, and value as others around him are doing. Thus socialization is in part based on "collectively experienced and collectively reinforced autisms." In addition a secondary set of controls in the form of "conscience" comes about through the child's identification with the strong and authoritative figures in his life. Finally, external controls reinforce the two bases of social conformity when the purely personal autisms become too prominent. Conformity thus depends "partly on authority and partly on eager acceptance."

One of the main foci of the vast and complex theoretical systems that have been built by Talcott Parsons and his collaborators (87, 88, 89, 90, 91, 92) has been analysis of the socialization process. This theory which is perhaps the most elaborate and sophisticated analysis of the relationship between personality and social strutcture to date has not yet been completely absorbed by workers in the social sciences. Our treatment here is intended to present only a few elements of the theory and does not make any pretense of being a systematic account of the whole.

Parsons suggests that personality and society may be regarded as independent systems, neither of which "provides the premises from which the major characteristics of the other, or of action in general, can be derived." The individual is therefore not the unit of the social system, but a separate system which interacts with it, the basic unit of the former being the status-role. Parsons distinguishes a third system, the culture, which refers to the system of meanings that give the individual a stable orientation to the objects with which he is interacting. Action is understandable only when all three systems are involved, the personality system providing the motivational energy and orientation, the cultural system providing the value orientation, and the social system the structure of the situation. These three kinds of orientations of the actor to the situation of action allow us to understand the modes of action which he selects.

The participation of the individual in the social system is organized and structured by certain role-status positions or sets of expected behaviors and must be regularized through the development of appropriate and stable motivations. These role units, which on the one hand are parts of the social system, may also become parts of the personality. This is referred to as the interpenetration of the two systems. The penetration of the third system, the cultural, subjects the other two to certain constraints and adds stability to the interactive process. The three components of the cultural system are the cognitive, cathectic, and evaluative. The concept of internalization has been somewhat broadened so that cognitive and cathectic orientations as well as moral standards are considered to be incorporated into the personality. This has the effect of viewing self-object images and characteristic affective modes as emerging from the social situations in which the individual participates. As Parsons points out, this represents a more comprehensive treatment of what the personality takes over from the outside than is given in psychoanalytic theory, where only the internalization of moral standards is given conceptual status.

The relationship between personality and social systems is seen to reside in the fact that the need-dispositions of the former and the role expectations of the latter were both derived from the same patterns of value orientation. The cultural system is on the one hand internalized and becomes a main part of the personality and on the other hand is institutionalized and becomes part of the social system. This development leads to a certain degree of structural isomorphism between personality and the social system which makes it possible for many analytic categories, i.e., the pattern variables, to be applied to both, and is the basis for the compatibility of action to both systems simultaneously. Internalization, or socialization as it is frequently referred to, consists of the acquisition of new patterns of orientation. These patterns, which emerge from the successive interactive systems in which the individual participates, consist primarily of the reciprocal role relationships which were stabilized in the interactive systems.

The crux of the Parsons theory, insofar as it concerns relations between personality and social structure, appears to reside in the concept of the penetration of the cultural system into both the personality and social systems. It is this concept which we wish to examine critically. Parsons (92) considers internalization as a process by which cultural elements can be transmitted with minimal change from one system to another. This transmission is regarded as basic. "Only in a figurative sense does an actor *have* patterns of value-orientation. In a strict sense he *is,* among other things, a system of such patterns" (93). Parsons addressed himself to the question we have raised in his paper, "The superego and the theory of social systems" (89). There, discussing Freudian theory, he states:

. . . the cognitive definition of the object world

does not seem to have been problematical for Freud. He subsumed it under external reality in relation to which ego functions constitute a process of adaptation. He failed to take explicitly into account the fact that the frame of reference in terms of which objects are cognized and therefore adapted to, is cultural and thus cannot be taken for granted as given but must be internalized as a condition for the development of mature ego functioning (page 18).

It is the broadness of the way the concept of internalization is used about which we have strong reservations.

Can values have potent influences on behavior even if they are not internalized? It does seem possible to go a very long distance toward explaining behavior which is congruent with the sociocultural system without invoking the concept of internalization. Given an individual who has developed either of the two main motivational tendencies we have discussed above, the desire to behave morally or the desire to please others, we can see that he has the problem of knowing what behavior will be satisfactory. The cultural orientations will serve as quite elaborate guides detailing what is good or bad, and what kinds of behavior are generally regarded as pleasing. The individual need merely act in terms of these orientations. Conformity involves an *acquiescence* in and *approval* of the validity of the value orientations and belief systems and an acceptance of the desirability of acting according to them.

We do not believe that such acquiescence necessarily involves "internalization." Spiro (104) has said that "once something is learned it is no longer external to the organism but it is 'inside' the organism and once it is 'inside,' the organism becomes a biosocial organism determining its own behavior as a consequence of the modifications it has undergone in the process of learning."

We believe that this view of learning fails to distinguish between learning to *do* something and learning *about* something. The learning of cognitive and evaluative orientations may involve the development of representations or maps of the cultural state of affairs. These are not tendencies to action but simply guides to the nature of the world in which one lives that one may or may not act in terms of. What is learned is not, for example, the value itself but simply that the value exists and that it is deemed important by respected members of the group to which one belongs.

Lewis (65) has called attention to the fact that his distinction between the private and public aspects of personality is related to Mowrer's two-factor theory of learning (81). Mowrer's sign learning is thought to be relevant to the "private" personality while solution learning leads to either "private" or "public" personality.

The crucial situation for determining whether cultural orientations are internalized or not occurs when the individual changes his allegiance from one group to another. If, for example, the value orientations of the first group persist in the individual and continue to determine his behavior we can agree that internalization has occurred. If, however, he is able to renounce, in a real sense as well as verbally, his former values along with the group, and accept a new and perhaps contrasting set as binding on his behavior, it seems appropriate to question whether there has been any real internalization. It would perhaps be more correct to apply the concept of "reference group behavior" (80) and predict that the values which will be most significant for the behavior of an individual are those of the group to which he belongs, of which he identifies himself consciously or unconsciously as a member. We do not wish to imply that internalization does not take place nor that it is unimportant. It does seem, however, that its scope may be limited and that some values remain "external" at least in the sense that when the individual changes his group identification he abandons them. In addition the fact that actual internalization occurs and is important does not signify that the whole of the cultural pattern is internalized. The actual extent to which it is is a matter for empirical investigation. Bettelheim's observations (10) of inmates of Nazi concentration camps gives some relevant evidence. He noted that most of the older prisoners abandoned the aim of maintaining themselves as the same kind of persons they were when they entered the prison camp. They accepted the reality of the prison camp and tried to adapt to it, behaving in terms of the values of the prison camp, identifying with their guards and actually adopting their attitudes toward other prisoners.

SOME EMPIRICAL AND METHODOLOGICAL ISSUES

In the remainder of this chapter our attention will be turned to what has become known as the field of "culture and personality." After a brief attempt at providing the immediate historical context we shall discuss some representative empirical studies and theoretical analyses with respect to three issues which we believe have been of salient importance in the work of the last decade. The three issues are: (a) how is personality to be studied in cultures other than our own, (b) how are the culture and personality concepts best defined and what order of relationship is conceived to exist between the two concepts, and (c) to what extent is the modal personality approach justified and adequate. We do not suggest that these issues comprehend all of the research in the culture-personality area. One or the other of them, however, is involved in almost every culture-personality study.

THE HISTORICAL BACKGROUND

The most significant influences of the last decade in the culture-personality field came through the work of Ruth Benedict, Margaret Mead, and Abram Kardiner. Benedict's *Patterns of Culture* (9) was perhaps the single most influential work and has dominated the thinking about culture-personality relations of the great majority of sociologists, psychiatrists, psychologists, anthropologists, and educated laymen, and to a considerable extent continues to do so at the present time. The entire work pointed in impressive fashion to the diversity of cultural forms and the plasticity of human nature and also pointed out the fallacy of ethnocentrism.

Margaret Mead's work during the 1930's also was tremendously effective in documenting the astonishing extent of cultural diversity (72, 73, 74, 75). She suggests that this cultural diversity is accompanied by a similar diversity of personality traits of a very fundamental nature.

Abram Kardiner (53, 54, 55) was the third great influence on the culture-personality field. In addition to the theory of cultural integration through personality structure which we have discussed above, Kardiner introduced the concept of basic personality structure and it is through this concept that he has had his greatest influence. This concept came to be very widely used, although without the specific theoretical meanings assigned to it by Kardiner. Instead it stood for the belief that individuals in a society, with the exception of a few deviants, would have a particular constellation of personality traits in common by virtue of their exposure to similar experiences as young children. This

shared personality constellation also was known as the "modal personality" and in an important sense the two terms came to dominate the culture-personality scene. This concept achieved such overwhelming acceptance that most workers in the field defined their research task as the discovery of the "basic" or "modal" personality constellations and their relationship to the child-rearing institutions in the culture under study.

The conceptions of Benedict, Mead, and Kardiner emphasizing the plasticity of human nature dominated theories and research to an amazing extent and had almost complete and universal acceptance. They provided the unified and simplified conceptions which made it possible for large numbers of people to understand the importance of cultural factors in personality development and to initiate a large quantity of important research on personality in every part of the world. Yet one cannot help feeling that the very forcefulness and appeal of their arguments led to a premature stabilization of culture-personality theory. Their theories became a kind of orthodoxy which tended to prevent the development and presentation of alternate points of view.

HOW IS PERSONALITY TO BE STUDIED

The past decade has seen the flowering of a completely new kind of study in the social sciences, the empirical study and description of personality in nonliterate and non-Western societies. Under the influence of pioneer studies by Du Bois (18), Hallowell (29, 30, 31), and J. Henry (34) the attention of anthropologists and psychologists turned to the determination of the personality characteristics of various exotic peoples, not by inference from cultural institutions, nor by observation of behavior, but through the use of the standard techniques in the armamentarium of the clinical psychologist and the psychiatrist.

A number of studies, including those by Gladwin and Sarason (24), Lessa and Spiegelman (64), W. E. Henry (37), and Mead (77), have sought to investigate the usefulness of these techniques in ethnographic work although from our point of view in an inappropriate manner. Lessa and Spiegelman, for example, present an analysis of a series of Ulithian Thematic Apperception Tests with the aim of judging the proposition that "thematic test material can reflect the culture as a whole and specifically that it can shed light on the nature of the basic personality structure of the people of Ulithi Atoll." One wonders why a procedure for studying personality should be used to learn about the culture and evaluated in terms of this criterion. The authors ask: "From the point of view of the anthropologist . . . how useful is the method? Is it worth the ethnographer's time to gather test material routinely . . . ?" They conclude that "Little new was added to what the ethnographer already knew about the culture, yet the test results seemed to provide an independent verification of what was observed in the field. Using different materials and separate approaches it was possible to arrive at essentially similar conclusions."

In general, there is little excuse for the psychologist to abandon his own task, that of personality description, and use his materials for cultural analysis. In this case the description of personality suffers by being vague and undifferentiated and the description of the cultural pattern is equally diffuse and stereotyped. As Wallace (111) points out, "The results well illustrate the principle that the best way to describe a culture is the old-fashioned ethnographic way. . . ."

The somewhat violent controversy over whether projective tests are useful to the anthropologist, which was the topic of a symposium in the *American Anthropologist* (35), can be simply resolved by asking what the purposes of the anthropologist are (78, 32, 39). If one of his purposes is to describe the prevalent personality characteristics of the people he is working with, he cannot avoid considering how he can do this. There can be little doubt that, at least in our own culture, projective tests have an important role to play in the comprehensive personality study, and evidence is accumulating that they work in a similar way in many other cultures as well. We can only agree with Jules Henry when he states that "Were I to go into the field tomorrow to study a culture, I would not use the Rorschach test." However, if one of Henry's purposes in going into the field was to study personality he would be very foolish not to consider seriously, at least, whether projective techniques could help him in his task.

William Henry attempted as one of the Studies in Indian Education a similar evaluation of the Thematic Apperception Test. His study is worthy of note because it constitutes one of the first applications of the test in nonliterate societies. He was able to show quite conclusively

that it gave very similar results to those of the Rorschach, Life History, figure drawing, and a battery of other tests. In addition, on the basis of Thematic Apperception Tests, Henry attempted a description of certain aspects of Hopi and Navaho society, especially those which were relevant to the personality development of children. He found that his descriptions were in essential agreement with the published materials on the two societies and that experts, familiar with the cultures and the literature describing them, were of the opinion that his inferences were essentially correct. Here again we must question the appropriateness of evaluating the TAT in terms of its ability to develop correct pictures of the culture.

Henry's development of a special set of TAT cards set a trend in the use of TATs that is now widely followed. He believed, and others did after him, that the Murray TAT provided scenes which were too exotic, strange, and incomprehensible for subjects in nonliterate societies to utilize for the purpose of self-expression and projection. Our own experience indicates that is not necessarily the case. In a study of Navaho and Zuni young men (50, 109) both the Murray pictures and a specially designed set of pictures drawn by Indian artists were administered to about thirty subjects. Contrary to expectations, the Murray set yielded stories which were far superior in interest and psychological significance to those elicited by the specially designed Indian set. While one would not wish to generalize from this one piece of research, it does suggest that stimulus materials coming from another culture, which are only partly understood, may be helpful in breaking down the concrete attitudes that are so fatal to the operation of projective techniques.

Mead (77) presents and discusses the analyses by five Rorschach workers of a record of an Arapesh man collected in the early 1930's. Mead states that the Rorschach did not reveal anything about the culture which she did not already know. She does say, however, that its contribution was much greater when she turned "from the question of cultural illumination to the question of individual character formation" and since this is, as we have suggested, the test's appropriate area of application, we can regard her judgment about the test as positive. However, as we compared the Rorschach protocol with the rich life history and interview materials which are presented in the same volume, it seemed justifiable to question the usefulness of the test. The Arapesh Rorschach protocol was a lengthy document apparently rich in symbolic and expressive content. Nevertheless, the meaning of the responses is cryptic and difficult to comprehend, although they give one the strong conviction that important areas of personality are involved in them. We feel about the record much as we do about cryptic records in our own society, namely, that they are extremely personal documents in which many of the responses have quite private meanings or emotional contexts which are only incompletely indicated in the responses themselves. In consequence some further exploration with the subject himself is necessary, much in the manner in which the psychoanalyst explores the meaning of a dream. This approach seems especially important in exotic cultures where the actuarial approach used by most present-day Rorschach workers breaks down completely in the absence of extensive norms.

The difficulty of adequately interpreting the Arapesh Rorschach raises the general problem of whether collecting Rorschachs in nonliterate societies really meets a serious need in the important business of personality study or is merely a form of boondoggling which satisfies a relatively idle though by no means culpable curiosity about what Rorschachs in exotic cultures look like. We have a certain amount of faith that the former is the case at least in some societies, although on the whole we believe that there is a considerable variation from culture to culture in the optimal approach to the study of personality. The understanding of this variation is an extremely important problem for culture and personality workers. In this connection the writer's project of assembling, reproducing on Microcards, and distributing personality materials which have been collected in nonliterate and non-Western societies offers the promise of being useful.

The majority of studies in the culture and personality area have been concerned with exploring the sociocultural determinants of personality in particular societies. For the most part this work has required the delineation of modal personality trends, although in some instances particular isolated personality characteristics were studied (29). Inkeles and Levinson (47) have discussed the methodology of modal personality studies in detail and have described three typical procedures: the personality assessment of individuals, the study of collective adult phenomena, and the study of child-rearing systems. For the first type they point out the dilemma created by the need for studies of large representative samples, even in relatively small societies, and the need for "clinical" studies in depth which ordinarily require many hours of work. They suggest that brief clinical-assessment procedures such as projective techniques and semistructured clinical interviews provide partial solutions which permit moderate-sized samples of about fifty to a hundred cases but which achieve considerable penetration in depth. Henry and Spiro (36) have recently reviewed projective test studies and Gottschalk, Kluckhohn, and Angell (28) have reviewed the use of personal documents in social science.

The chief problem, however, is not the collection of adequate personality materials but their analysis and conversion into modal personality statements. It is probably correct to say that psychologists can collect more data than they can reliably and validly interpret. Two approaches seem possible. One is the scoring of protocols in terms of a number of predetermined categories; the other is the development of separate personality descriptions of each subject followed by an attempt to determine the elements which are common to all or most of the individual studies (13, 56, 50, 52). As one who has worked extensively with the second method, the writer can testify to its difficulty. In both the Hutterite and the Navaho-Zuni studies extensive case descriptions were constructed, but the very rich characterizations of the separate individuals dwindled to a very small number of relatively uninteresting modal statements. One gained the impression that more could be learned about the personality of the Hutterites, Navaho, or Zuni from any one of the case records than from a summary of a hundred and twenty case records. For example, (50) of 280 separate themes in the personality descriptions of 14 Navaho young men, only 15 themes were found in more than one third of the individual cases while 181 themes were found to hold for only one person. Only four themes held for more than half of the sample. The main difficulty with this kind of analysis is that we cannot be certain about the independence of the 280 themes. If some of them had been combined, as they might very well have by another worker, the number of modal themes might have been different.

These difficulties are not insurmountable. They simply require that substantial resources of time and talent be mobilized at the analysis of data phase of the culture-personality study. In fact, substantial resources are needed in every phase of studies of modal personality. The data collection phase should provide for twelve to twenty hours of study with each subject if there is any intention that the studies be comprehensive. Personality data can be collected in much less time, but it is a misapprehension that anything resembling a complete picture can be gained by the administration of a single projective test. Projective tests have an important, perhaps essential, role in personality studies, but they do not necessarily play the most important role and certainly the data they yield can be understood properly only in the context of the life history and information about the actual functioning of the individual in the social groups to which he belongs. Incomplete personality pictures may in some cases be worse than none at all if they are misleading and their meaning is misinterpreted.

The problem of what procedures are most fruitful in other societies is one which has barely been studied but which is absolutely basic for the culture-personality field. On the basis of materials which have been collected in perhaps thirty cultures, it is possible to say that techniques like the Rorschach, the TAT, and the life history work better in some groups than in others, and that in some they seem to be almost useless.

The greatest part, by far, of the personality studies in nonliterate societies have been conducted by anthropologists, although some psychologists have participated in them at the stage of data analysis. In one sense this has been unfortunate since the study of personality is a vastly complicated and difficult business, calling for the utmost in interpersonal skills, psychological sophistication, and creativity. Although anthropologists have very often been able to collect quite interesting materials on personality, they have by and large functioned very much at the level of the psychological technician, who can collect very valuable materials if he is told what to do but whose work frequently lacks understanding, flexibility, and depth. This is not meant as a criticism of anthropologists who have worked in the culture-personality field. The problems of discovering how to do adequate personality studies in a wide range of socio-cultural systems are so difficult, however, that they require the concerted efforts of a large number of highly trained and creative specialists in personality study.

The second kind of procedure frequently used for the delineation of the modal personality is the study of collective adult phenomena. This method involves the analysis of materials such as myths, folk tales, literary works, and folk products like popular songs and movies regarded as deriving from modal personality patterns. The analyses by Bateson (7) and Kracauer (60) of German movies, by McGranahan and Wayne (69) of German and American plays, by Wolfenstein and Leites (115) of American movies are a few examples of such studies. In discussing these and other ethnographic materials, including rituals and ceremonial dances as well as some observed regularities in collective behavior which are frequently called cultural themes or "plots," Inkeles and Levinson say that there is often good reason to believe that these materials do reflect modal personality trends. They raise the question, however, of the representativeness of the particular sample of data which is being studied and say that this method cannot tell with any conclusiveness what range and varieties of modal personalities actually exist in a society. The additional point may be made that this kind of analysis often involves circularity, since the modal personality characteristics are supposed to explain the ethnographic materials from which they were inferred.

These points would seem to hold also for the method of inferring personality patterns from a knowledge of child-rearing patterns (8, 54, 55, 27). In all but a very few of these studies the confidence in such inferences has been so great that no studies of individuals have been thought necessary. Kardiner's analysis of the Alorese materials is a notable exception, but even here Kardiner gives the empirical materials much lower status than the inferred characteristics. It is obvious that this method is prejudicial to the question of whether a modal personality does indeed exist since it allows no other possibility. Both Klineberg (57) and Inkeles and Levinson (47) have emphasized the importance of the study of individuals in research on modal personality.

SOME PROBLEMS OF DEFINITION
AND METHODOLOGY

The avowed purpose of most culture and personality studies during the past decade has been the illumination of the relationship between them. The achievement of this aim has been seriously hindered by a considerable degree of confusion and disagreement about the meanings of these two terms and the kind of relationship between them which is contemplated. In this section we shall discuss a number of definitional and conceptual issues which we believe have been implicitly involved in almost every theoretical and empirical work in this field during the last several years.

Perhaps the most important of these issues concerns the distinctions or the lack of them between the terms culture and personality. The most prevalent viewpoints seem to de-emphasize any distinctions. Culture and personality are thought to be so intimately related and so interdependent that the use of the two terms implies a false and artificial dichotomy. Spiro, for example, entitles his paper (104) "Culture and Personality: The Natural History of a False Dichotomy," being critical of the idea that the terms culture and personality refer to different kinds of phenomena, and also of the notion that the purpose of research and theory in this field is to build conceptual bridges between the two (11). He believes that the culture and personality "problem" is created by this false dichotomy. Spiro states that culture exists within individuals and is the product of the individual's interaction with his fellows. Since he also defines personality as the product of one's interactions with other individuals it is not surprising that he speaks of the "personality-culture" and concludes that the term personality can be substituted for the term culture in certain kinds of analysis.

It is clear that definitional problems are of key importance in these matters. Perhaps a more fundamental matter, however, is whether the worker wishes to make a distinction between the two concepts or not, for it seems that there is enough variability of definitions among authorities in these fields that each worker can choose the ones which best suit his purposes. Our own belief in this matter is that dedifferentiation serves no useful purpose but on the contrary makes it very difficult to formulate meaningful empirical research. The refusal to distinguish clearly between culture and personality leaves research with no immediate aim, since if one is not dealing with two distinguishable entities or systems there is no possibility of studying the extent or nature of

their relationship. The fact that there can be no personality apart from human society does not mean that it may not be valuable for some purposes to study them as separate systems. Certainly one would not wish sociologists to abandon their focus on social systems or psychologists their focus on the individual.

Hand in hand with the "culture-in-personality" approach has gone the often stated belief that both culture and personality are abstractions from the same behavior and are, at most, two different ways of looking at the same thing (58). If such be the case the two terms and the distinctions between them are, as Smith (103) puts it, "figments of the scientific imagination." The distinction to us is not an arbitrary one but arises out of the fact that some behavior requires the culture concept for its explanation while other behavior requires the personality concept. It is probably true that almost all behavior must in some sense be explained by the interactions of both sociocultural and personality systems. However, what is significant is not that both systems participate, but that in most behavior the influence of one or the other is preponderant and in some the influence of one or the other is almost imperceptible. It is, as we understand it, one of the main tasks of culture-personality inquiry to determine the extent of overlapping influence by both systems and the particular areas in which it occurs.

One of the most confusing consequences of the failure to distinguish between the behavioral referents of the two concepts has been the discussion of certain cultural phenomena as if they were personality characteristics. This makes most of the questions with which culture-personality workers have been concerned both meaningless and tautological. As Inkeles and Levinson say: "To define national character as more or less synonymous with the sum of learned cultural behavior makes any effort to relate culture to character largely an effort to relate culture to itself."

The logic of this situation is closely dependent on the way in which the concepts are defined. Many social scientists tend to expand the meaning of personality so that it becomes roughly synonymous with the individual. The same writers frequently complain that the personality concept is too "global" and should be replaced by sub-concepts with more precise meanings. It is probably not feasible to set any exact limits on what we will regard as personality. However, one can apply to certain processes such as belief systems, attitudes, values, and sentiments, which Inkeles (45) has termed the "social personality," the terms peripheral, outer (in the sense of Lewin's onion model), temporary, and phenotypic. It seems incorrect and unsound to emphasize these processes when discussing personality but to ignore the genotypic, central, inner processes which psychologists whose specialty is personality study ordinarily regard as the "core" of personality. Sanford (98) has recently said:

... with respect to the kind of motives I have called most interesting and particularly important one might say that they tend to be deep, inner, hidden, basic, central, genotypic, resistant to change, and originating early in the life of the individual.

With respect to the Parsons and Shils (93) definition of personality as the "organized system of the orientation and motivation of one individual actor" we might suggest that the "orientation" aspects of personality may be characterized as peripheral while the "motivational" aspects are central. The point is not that the former are unimportant but that it is useful to distinguish them from the motivational processes and that this distinction tends to break down if both are subsumed under a single heading. Lewis' distinction (65) between private and public personality is relevant. He indicates that much misunderstanding arises out of the fact that the anthropologist is interested primarily in the relations between the public personality and culture while the psychologist is mainly concerned with private personality.

One other definitional problem deserves some attention. Personality may be defined in terms of patterns of behavior or in terms of patterns of inner processes (71, 65). Since the proponents of the inner processes type of definition tend to agree that the inner processes are known only insofar as they are inferred from observed behavior, and the proponents of the behavioral definition for the most part accept the existence of the inner processes as intervening variables which are required to explain observed behavior, it would appear that the differences between the two viewpoints might be of only minor importance. It seems to us, however, that the possibility of making an adequate distinction between the concepts of personality and culture is dependent on defining the former in terms of inner processes rather than behavior.

When the latter type of definition is used, personality tends to become synonymous with culture since there is usually no criterion available for the isolation of those behaviors which are most relevant to personality from those which refer primarily to culture. Thus the behavioral definition best suits the purposes of workers who prefer to break down the conceptual distinctions, while the inner processes definition helps those who would sharpen the distinctions.

STUDIES OF MODAL PERSONALITY

To a very considerable extent studies of modal personality and national character have proceeded under the assumption that something like a modal personality does exist and that the main tasks of the researcher are to describe the modal constellation and discover its genesis in the social pattern or, more usually, in the child-rearing institutions. This research model has, as we have suggested above, been somewhat confused by the failure of many workers to maintain the distinction between personality and cultural processes. When modal personality is defined as synonymous with the sum total of learned cultural behavior there can be no question of its "existence." Smith (103) expresses this when he says:

If in fact the members of a definable social group share a set of traditional behavior patterns that warrant designation as a culture or sub-culture, by the same token these patterns (having no existence apart from behaving persons) cannot fail to be integrated into the personalities of the members. . . . The "existence" of modal personality and status personality is no more controversial than the existence of culture and statuses. At most these are merely alternatives of organizing the same data (page 60).

Since we have maintained that personality should be regarded as a separate system which is not synonymous with nor reducible to the cultural system, the existence of modal personality constellations is for us a real problem that is not solved automatically by the knowledge of the existence of cultural regularities. Two main criteria for the acceptance of the existence of a modal personality pattern may be applied. One is that some degree of homogeneity within the group is required, and the second is that the characteristics with respect to which there is homogeneity should vary from group to group.

The Alorese study reported by Du Bois (18)

and Kardiner (54, 55) which was described above is, in many respects, the most important study of modal personality that has been done. Although Kardiner claimed that the personality constellation which he derived from Alorese child-rearing patterns was found in the seven autobiographies he examined and was "almost identical in essence" to the conclusions that Oberholzer derived from the Rorschach data, he failed to support these judgments with the appropriate objective analyses. At a number of points at which Kardiner or Oberholzer claimed to find close agreement, we could only with great difficulty see any similarity whatsoever, and a number of the successes claimed by Kardiner were instances in which the adult constellations noted in the Rorschach test could be explained by the personality dynamics inferred by Kardiner. Since the chief dynamic factor was maternal deprivation, it would undoubtedly be possible to link a wide variety of adult constellations to it. In addition there was considerable variation among both the autobiographies and the Rorschachs. It seems to us that the issue which Kardiner closed so finally was not really decided by this study and that it requires replication with the same data but using the more rigorous methods which are easily available in present-day social science. Kardiner said that "We may not in the future be obliged to study each culture with the thoroughness that we did the Alorese. The conclusions reached there will stand." In our opinion the Alorese study was only a beginning. Although it pointed the way by being the first serious well-conceived culture-personality study, and substantial resources and energies went into its consummation, these were but a fraction of those needed for an adequate study.

The Indian Education Research Project conducted jointly by the Committee on Human Development of the University of Chicago and the Bureau of Indian Affairs, in which studies of children were carried on in five cultures, is perhaps the most extensive of all of the culture-personality projects during the past decade. The five cultures studied were the Sioux by MacGregor (70), the Hopi by Thompson and Joseph (107), the Navaho by Kluckhohn and Leighton (59) and Leighton and Kluckhohn (63), the Papago by Joseph, Spicer, and Chesky (49), and the Zuni by Adair and Leighton in a still unpublished report. In addition Thompson (108) and Havighurst and Neugarten (33) have made some cross-cultural comparisons. It is not possible to deal adequately with this extensive series of studies in a few paragraphs. Methodologically, however, the studies all involved more or less orthodox ethnographic descriptions and in addition quite lengthy series of personality materials, including projective tests, autobiographies, and a number of miscellaneous tests designed to tap values and attitudes. These materials were used first to develop an over-all characterization of the personality of children in the society and second, a series of descriptions of individual children. Finally, in a relatively unsystematic way certain connections between the societies and the personality traits were made. With a few exceptions this procedure was less productive than might have been hoped. In part this was the result of a paucity of theoretical orientation; in part the relative sparseness of the personality findings was involved. Thompson's comparison (108) of the Rorschach perceptions of the Hopi, Navaho, and Papago does provide valuable evidence of the diversity of the three groups in this area, and the still unpublished comparison of the Rorschach findings in the five societies should add to the contribution of the project. In general we might say that the Indian Education studies do not add appreciably to our knowledge of the homogeneity or diversity of personality characteristics within societies but do suggest while not being completely convincing that personality differences between societies do exist.

Another typical culture-personality study is that of Gladwin and Sarason, *Truk: Man in paradise* (24). Gladwin described his purpose as that of determining whether two orders of data (psychological and ethnographic) were congruent. The conclusion was that on the whole the two pictures were congruent and that where discrepancies existed they could be explained by Sarason's ignorance of certain facts about the culture, without which it was not possible to understand the response.

How may this congruence be interpreted? The most likely explanation is that Gladwin was a keen enough observer to note the same personality characteristics reflected in everyday behavior which Sarason saw in the projective test material. Gladwin, however, focused primarily on an ethnographic description and it seems likely that the congruence also means that Sarason's personality descriptions fit the cultural facts as Gladwin knew them. Because both of these factors entered into the congruence it is difficult to say whether this study has actually demonstrated anything of importance for culture-personality theory, even though it makes a creditable contribution to a better understanding of the technique of personality study in nonliterate societies.

Since Gladwin set out to do a culture-personality study, it is appropriate to ask how he got off the track. Very early in his discussion (page 22), Gladwin equates "cultural determinants" with "life experience" and defines his task as exploring the relationship between "personality" and the "life experience." In a review of this work, Schneider (102) has made the point that the focus on "proximal" events in the life experiences of the Trukese makes it impossible to "sort the temporally stable and structurally crucial determinants (of personality) from those which are transient and, from the point of view of the culture, peripheral."

One of the most original and methodologically sophisticated attempts to delineate modal personality characteristics in a rigorous way was Wallace's (110) study of the Rorschachs of the Tuscarora Indians. In a more or less arbitrary way, he established limits (one standard deviation on either side of the mode) around the central tendencies of scores of Rorschach variables. He asserted that those subjects who fell within those limits on all 21 of the variables could be said to possess the Tuscarora "modal personality." Wallace was then able to compare the number of Tuscarora Indians who had the Tuscarora "modal personality" with Ojibwa Indians who did. He found that 37 per cent of the Tuscarora were "modal" and that only 5 percent of the Ojibwa fell within the Tuscarora mode. This difference is a statistically significant one. Twenty-eight per cent of the 102 Ojibwa Rorschachs fell in the Ojibwa modal class. Although the definition of the limits of the modal class was somewhat arbitrary and a shift in those limits would cause a different number of individuals to fall in the modal class, the evidence does indicate rather conclusively that the Rorschachs of the two groups are different. It is difficult to decide whether the limits of the modal class which were set by Wallace are too wide or too narrow. However, if the present figures are accepted as representing something like the actual situation the relatively small percentage of cases in the groups which were found to be modal is of great interest. They seem to call for a new variety of theory that could explain how only a minority of individuals in a society, *rather than a majority,* comes to respond positively to the cultural pressure toward uniformity of personality.

The cross-cultural study occupies an important place in the culture-personality field since it offers possibilities of control of variables analogous to those of the laboratory experiment. For example, we could not really be convinced that a personality trait or pattern found commonly in a particular group was related to sociocultural factors unless it was also shown that the same trait or pattern was not found in the absence of these factors. By implication all studies of modal personality fall into the category of cross-cultural research since they suggest that the resultant personality picture is different from that found in other societies. However, it is very rare to find a research report that makes explicit comparisons. A number of cross-cultural studies have been conducted (12, 48, 1, 51, 111), but the research possibilities have only been touched on.

In general these studies reveal a number of moderately sized differences which may be taken as evidence for the existence of a cultural influence on personality. However, one is struck by the fact that in almost every case reactions within the groups were quite variable. Kaplan (50, 51) attempted to set up a direct test of the modal-personality thesis, utilizing projective test materials from four cultures in the American Southwest, the Navaho, Zuni, Mormon, and Spanish-American. He described the variance of Rorschach scores both within and among the four cultures and set up several sorting tests to see whether test protocols could be sorted into four appropriate groups and then whether they could be matched to protocols which had already been sorted. The results indicated that differences in Rorschach scores among the four groups were present although in every case the variability within the groups was large and the overlap between the groups very great. In his comparison of Navaho and Zuni TATs (unpublished manuscript) he found that

in these two relatively small samples we find considerable variability of personality, with only a few characteristics being really widespread in the groups. However, there are many small clusters of individuals within each of the cultures which have characteristics in common. In many of these cases no similar clusters are found in the other cultures. Differences between the cultures do exist and are fairly numerous, demonstrating the effect of culture on personality quite conclusively. However, the differences are far outnumbered by the similarities, so that we may justifiably conclude that the two cultures were more alike than different with respect to personality.

The influence of culture on personality does not appear to create a common personality configuration in its members, but instead tends to foster a variety of personality tendencies in small groups or clusters of individuals while leaving many aspects of personality free to vary without respect to group membership.

The studies reviewed above and others, such as those of Lantis (62), Lewis (65), and Honigmann (40), do not in general provide conclusive evidence with regard to the modal-personality hypothesis. They do indicate that societies differ somewhat in the personality characteristics that are found most frequently in them but in the absence of adequate cross-cultural studies it is difficult to say how great these differences are. In addition, most of the studies suggest that personality variability within societies is very large. This heterogeneity indicates that the very simple model which has been utilized in the culture and personality field of a modal type around which all but a few deviants tend to cluster may be an incorrect one and that simplistic theories which are closer to the actual empirical findings will have to be developed. The past decade in the culture and personality field may in one sense be regarded as a moving away from the simple theories of cultural determinism to more sophisticated and elaborate as well as less confident theories about the nature and extent of personality diversity in different societies and of homogeneity within societies. The suggestion of Inkeles and Levinson (47) that societies may have multiple modes rather than a single one is a movement in this direction. Gardner Murphy's statement (84) perhaps best sums up the situation:

The conception of the almost limitless flexibility of human nature has been encouraged greatly by the observations of anthropologists, who have taught us to be skeptical regarding the picture of a uniform essential nature. Our psychological methods of analysis have arisen in the western world; anthropologists offer observations which appear to suggest that very different kinds of human nature can be organized and cultivated in different cultural areas. Quite aside from what the anthropological observers themselves have to say, which is often more cautious and critical than what their readers have to say, there seems to be much to suggest that people may become almost anything. Human beings may be essentially gentle and cooperative, like the mountain Arapesh described by Margaret Mead (1937), or savagely competitive, like the Manus of the Admiralty Islands; they may be intensely in-dividualistic, like the plains Indians described by Ruth Benedict (1934), or intensely group minded, like the Pueblo Indians of the Southwest. . . .

Actually, it seems from the vantage point of 1954 that these anthropological studies have been much overinterpreted. . . . As in so many other cases, many psychologists were caught for a while in a dream induced by the fascinating nature of the new material, for which they had no adequate conceptual framework, and sometimes by the desire to separate the social life of man as widely as possible from the life of his humbler brethren of the mammalian genera. . . . Men do not behave like cedars, earthworms, cats, or elephants; they behave like men. All cultures work with raw human material; in every culture the educative process fails when it stretches human nature too far. We are very flexible, but not putty for the window mender, nor clay for the potter (pages 628, 629).

SUMMARY CONCLUSIONS

This paper has been concerned mainly with two different but related issues that may be said to dominate the field of personality and social structure at the present time. One of these issues, which has been the principal focus of the second part of the chapter, is the nature of the relationships between societal systems and personality. While methodological problems occupied most of our attention, the issue behind them had to do with the extent of the influences of sociocultural systems on personality. The empirical question which has still to be investigated adequately is whether essentially different kinds of "human nature" are created either as a result of the varying conditions of development and existence in the world's societies or in order to satisfy the diverse requirement for participation in and support of these societies. It has undoubtedly been clear that our prejudices in this matter are in favor of the view that human nature is solidly anchored in a biological organism and that personality characteristics resulting from human biology overshadow in importance the special characteristics attributable to the particular social patterns in which development occurs. According to this view the study of the characteristics of the species, man, is a primary task which can, however, be accomplished only when the exact nature and extent of the variability of personality according to social patterns is understood.

The first part of the paper was concerned with the requirements sociocultural systems make on personality. The necessity that con-

formity and compliance to differing social requirements be voluntary and individually
motivated appears to be at odds with the above
conception. It was shown, however, that the
quite diverse behaviors of individuals in different societies do not necessarily have their basis
in similarly varying personality characteristics.
Instead, the key to the diversity of behavior
was seen to lie in the existence of any one of
a small number of motivational tendencies
which could be found in any society in the
world.

REFERENCES

1. ABEL, THEODORA M., and HSU, F. L. K., "Some aspects of the personality of Chinese as revealed by the Rorschach Test," *J. Proj. Techniques,* Vol. 13 (1949), pp. 285–301.

2. ABERLE, D. F., "Social system and socialization," Paper delivered at Conference on Cross-Cultural Research on Personality Development, Kansas City, Mo., May, 1955.

3. ABERLE, D. F., and NAEGELE, K. D., "Middle-class fathers" occupational roles and attitudes toward children," *Amer. J. Orthopsychiat.,* Vol. 22 (1952), pp. 366–378.

4. ACKERMAN, N. W., "Social role and total personality," *Amer. J. Ortho-psychiat.,* Vol. 21 (1951), pp. 1–17.

5. BALDWIN, A. L., *The psychological process underlying behavioral con-formity,* Paper delivered at Conference on Cross-Cultural Research on Personality Development, Kansas City, Mo., May, 1955.

6. BARNOUW, V., "Acculturation and personality among the Wisconsin Chip-pewa," *Amer. Anthrop.,* Vol. 52 (1950), Pt. 2, Memoir 72.

7. BATESON, G., "Cultural and thematic analysis of fictional films," *Trans. N. Y. Acad. Sci.,* Ser. II, Vol. 5 (1943), pp. 72–78.

8. BATESON, G., and MEAD, MARGARET, *Balinese character: A photographic analysis,* New York, N. Y. Acad. of Sci., 1942.

9. BENEDICT, RUTH, *Patterns of culture,* Boston, Houghton Mifflin, 1934.

10. BETTELHEIM, B., "Individual and mass behavior in extreme situations," in T. M. Newcomb and E. L. Hartley (eds.), *Readings in social psychology,* New York, Henry Holt, 1947, pp. 628–638.

11. BIDNEY, D., "Toward a psychocultural definition of the concept of person-ality," in S. S. Sargent, and Marian W. Smith (eds.), *Culture and per-sonality,* New York, The Viking Fund, 1949, pp. 31–52.

12. BILLIG, D., GILLIN, J., and DAVIDSON, W., "Aspects of personality and culture in a Guatemalan community: Ethnological and Rorschach ap-proaches," *J. Personal.,* Vol. 16 (1947–1948), pp. 153–187, 326–368.

13. CAUDILL, W., "Japanese American personality and acculturation," *Genet. Psychol. Monogr.,* Vol. 45 (1952), pp. 3–102.

14. DAVIS, A., and HAVIGHURST, R. J., "Social class and color differences in child rearing," *Amer. Soc. Rev.,* Vol. 11 (1946), pp. 698–710.

15. DE LAGUNA, GRACE A., "Culture and rationality," *Amer. Anthrop.,* Vol. 51 (1949), pp. 379–391.

16. DICKS, H. V., "Personality traits and national socialist ideology," *Hum. Relat.,* Vol. 3 (1950), pp. 111–154.

17. DICKS, H. V., "Observations on contemporary Russian behaviour," *Hum. Relat.,* Vol. 5 (1952), pp. 111–175.

18. DU BOIS, CORA, *The people of Alor,* Minneapolis, Univ. of Minn. Press, 1944.

19. ERIKSON, E. H., *Childhood and society,* New York, Norton, 1950.

20. FROMM, E., *Escape from freedom,* New York, Farrar and Rinehart, 1941.

21. FROMM, E., *Man for himself,* New York, Farrar and Rinehart, 1947.

22. GARDNER, B. B., and WHYTE, W. F., "The man in the middle: Position and problems of the foreman," *Appl. Anthrop.*, Vol. 4 (1945).

23. GERTH, H., and MILLS, C. W., *Character and social structure*, New York, Harcourt, Brace, 1953.

24. GLADWIN, T., and SARASON, S. B., *Truk: Man in paradise*, New York, The Viking Fund, 1953.

25. GORER, G., "Themes in Japanese culture," *Trans. N. Y. Acad. Sci.*, Ser. II, Vol. 5 (1943), pp. 106–124.

26. GORER, G., *The American people*, New York, Norton, 1948.

27. GORER, G., and RICKMAN, J., *The people of Great Russia*, London, Crosset Press, 1949.

28. GOTTSCHALK, L., KLUCKHOHN, C., and ANGELL, R., *The use of personal documents in history, anthropology, and sociology*, New York, Soc. Sci. Res. Council, Bull. 53, 1945.

29. HALLOWELL, A. I., "Aggression in Salteaux society," *Psychiatry*, Vol. 3 (1940), pp. 395–407.

30. HALLOWELL, A. I., *The Rorschach Test as a tool for investigating cultural variables and individual differences in the study of personality in primitive societies*, Rorschach Res. Exch., Vol. 5 (1941), pp. 31–34.

31. HALLOWELL, A. I., "The Rorschach technique in the study of culture and personality," *Amer. Anthrop.*, Vol. 47 (1945), pp. 195–210.

32. HARDING, C. F., "A plea for an anthropological approach to the study of personality," *Human Org.*, Vol. 12 (1953), pp. 13–16.

33. HAVIGHURST, R. J., and NEUGARTEN, BERNICE L., *American Indian and white children: A sociopsychological investigation*, Chicago, Univ. of Chicago Press, 1955.

34. HENRY, J., "Rorschach techniques in primitive cultures," *Amer. J. Orthopsychiat.*, Vol. 11 (1941), pp. 230–234.

35. HENRY, J. "Symposium on: Projective testing in ethnography," *Amer. Anthrop.*, Vol. 57 (1955), pp. 245–247.

36. HENRY, J., and SPIRO, M. E., "Psychological techniques: Projective tests in field work," in A. L. Kroeber (ed.), *Anthropology Today*, Chicago, Univ. of Chicago Press, 1953, pp. 417–429.

37. HENRY, W. E., "The thematic apperception technique in the study of culture-personality relations," *Genetic Psychol. Mono.*, Vol. 35 (1947), pp. 3–135.

38. HENRY, W. E., "The business executive: The psycho-dynamics of a social role," *Amer. J. Soc.*, Vol. 54 (1949), pp. 286–291.

39. HENRY, W. E., "Psychological tests in cross-cultural research," Paper delivered at Conference on Cross-Cultural Research on Personality Development, Kansas City, Mo., May, 1955.

40. HONIGMANN, J. J., *Culture and ethos of Kaska society*, New Haven, Yale Univ. Publications in Anthrop., No. 70, 1949.

41. Honigmann, J. J., *Culture and personality*, New York, Harper, 1954.

42. HORNEY, KAREN, *New ways in psychoanalysis*, New York, Norton, 1940.

43. HORTON, D., "The functions of alcohol in primitive societies: A cross-cultural study," *Quart. J. Stud. Alcohol*, Vol. 4 (1943), pp. 199–320.

44. HUGHES, E. C., "Dilemmas and contradictions of status," *Amer. J. Soc.*, Vol. 50 (1945), pp. 353–359.

45. INKELES, A., "Some sociological observations on culture and personality studies," in C. Kluckhohn, H. A. Murray, and D. M. Schneider (eds.), *Personality in nature, society, and culture*, 2nd ed., New York, Knopf, 1953, pp. 577–592.

46. INKELES, A., "Social change and social character: The role of parental mediation," *J. Soc. Issues*, Vol. 11 (1955), pp. 12–23.

47. INKELES, A., and LEVINSON, D. J., "National character: The study of modal personality and sociocultural systems," in G. Lindzey (ed.), *Handbook of social psychology,* Cambridge, Addison-Wesley, 1954, pp. 977–1020.

48. JOSEPH, ALICE, and MURRAY, VERONICA F., *Chamorros and Carolinians of Saipan: Personality studies,* Cambridge, Harvard Univ. Press, 1951.

49. JOSEPH, ALICE, SPICER, R. B., and CHESKY, JANE, *The desert people: A study of the Papago Indians,* Chicago, Univ. of Chicago Press, 1949.

50. KAPLAN, B., "The modal personality hypothesis tested in four cultures," Unpublished doctoral dissertation, Harvard Univ., 1949.

51. KAPLAN, B., "A study of Rorschach responses in four cultures," *Pap. Peabody Museum of Arch. and Ethnol.,* Harvard Univ., Vol. 42 (1954), 2.

52. KAPLAN, B., and PLAUT, T., *Personality in a communal society: An analysis of the mental health of the Hutterites,* Lawrence, Social Science Studies, Univ. Kansas, 1956.

53. KARDINER, A., *The individual and his society. With a foreword and two ethnological reports by R. Linton,* New York, Columbia Univ. Press, 1939.

54. KARDINER, A., "The concept of basic personality structure as an operational tool in the social sciences," in R. Linton (ed.), *The science of man in the world crisis,* New York, Columbia Univ. Press, 1945, pp. 107–122.

55. KARDINER, A. (with the collaboration of R. Linton, Cora Du Bois, and J. West), *The psychological frontiers of society,* New York, Columbia Univ. Press, 1945.

56. KARDINER, A., and OVESEY, L., *The mark of oppression: A psychological study of the American Negro,* New York, Norton, 1951.

57. KLINEBERG, O., *Tensions affecting international understanding,* New York, Soc. Sci. Res. Council, Bull. 62, 1950.

58. KLUCKHOHN, C., "Culture and behavior," in G. Lindzey (ed.), *Handbook of social psychology,* Cambridge, Addison-Wesley, 1954, pp. 921–976.

59. KLUCKHOHN, C., and LEIGHTON, DOROTHEA, *The Navaho,* Cambridge, Harvard Univ. Press, 1946.

60. KRACAUER, S., *From Caligari to Hitler,* Princeton, Princeton Univ. Press, 1947.

61. LA BARRE, W., "Some observations on character structure in the Orient: The Chinese," *Psychiatry,* Vol. 9 (1946), pp. 375–395.

62. LANTIS, MARGARET, "Nunivak Eskimo personality as revealed in the mythology," *Anthrop. Pap. Univ. Alaska,* Vol. 2 (1953), pp. 109–174.

63. LEIGHTON, DOROTHEA, and KLUCKHOHN, C., *Children of the people,* Cambridge, Harvard Univ. Press, 1947.

64. LESSA, W. A., and SPIEGELMAN, M., *Ulithian personality as seen through ethnological materials and thematic test analysis,* Berkeley, Univ. of Calif. Publications in Culture and Society, 2, 1954.

65. Lewis, O., *Life in a Mexican village: Tepoztlan restudied,* Urbana, Univ. of Illinois Press, 1951.

66. LINTON, R., "Problems of status personality," in S. S. Sargent and Marian W. Smith (eds.), *Culture and personality,* New York, The Viking Fund, 1949, pp. 163–173.

67. LYND, R. S., *Knowledge for what,* Princeton, Princeton Univ. Press, 1946.

68. McCLELLAND, D. C., *Personality,* New York, Dryden Press, 1954.

69. McGRANAHAN, D. V., and WAYNE, I., "German and American traits reflected in popular drama," *Hum. Relat.,* Vol. 1 (1948), pp. 429–455.

70. MacGREGOR, G., *Warriors without weapons,* Chicago, Univ. of Chicago Press, 1946.

71. MacKINNON, D. W., "The structure of personality," in J. McV. Hunt (ed.),

Personality and the behavior disorders, New York, Ronald Press, 1944, pp. 3–48.

72. MEAD, G. H., *Mind, self, and society,* Chicago, Univ. of Chicago Press, 1934.

73. MEAD, MARGARET, *Coming of age in Samoa,* New York, Morrow, 1928.

74. MEAD, MARGARET, *Growing up in New Guinea,* New York, Morrow, 1930.

75. MEAD, MARGARET, *Sex and temperament in three primitive societies,* New York, Morrow, 1935.

76. MEAD, MARGARET, *And keep your powder dry: An anthropologist looks at America,* New York, Morrow, 1942.

77. MEAD, MARGARET, *The Mountain Arapesh. Vol. V: The record of Unabelin with Rorschach analysis,* New York, Anthrop. Pap. Amer. Mus. of Nat. Hist., 1949.

78. MENSH, I., and HENRY, J., "Direct observation and psychological tests in anthropological field work," *Amer. Anthrop.,* Vol. 55 (1953), pp. 461–480.

79. MERTON, R., *Social theory and social structure,* Glencoe, Ill., The Free Press, 1949, pp. 151–160.

80. MERTON, R., and KITT, A. S., "Contribution to the theory of reference group behavior," in R. Merton and P. F. Lazarsfeld (eds.), *Continuities in social research,* Glencoe, Ill., The Free Press, 1950, pp. 40–105.

81. MOWRER, O. H., *Learning theory and personality dynamics,* New York, Ronald Press, 1950.

82. MURDOCK, G. P., *Social structure,* New York, Macmillan, 1949.

83. MURPHY, G., "The internalization of social controls," in M. Berger, T. Abel, and C. H. Page (eds.), *Freedom and control in modern society,* New York, D. Van Nostrand, 1954, pp. 3–17.

84. MURPHY, G., "Social motivation," in G. Lindzey (ed.), *Handbook of social psychology,* Cambridge, Addison-Wesley, 1954, pp. 601–633.

85. NEWCOMB, T. M., *Social psychology,* New York, Dryden Press, 1950.

86. Orlansky, H., "Infant care and personality," *Psychol. Bull.,* Vol. 46 (1949), pp. 1–48.

87. PARSONS, T., *Essays in sociological theory,* Glencoe, The Free Press, 1949, pp. 185–200.

88. PARSONS, T., *The social system,* Glencoe, Ill., The Free Press, 1951.

89. PARSONS, T., "The superego and the theory of social systems," *Psychiatry,* Vol. 15 (1952), pp. 15–25.

90. PARSONS, T., "Psychology and sociology," in J. Gillin (ed.), *For a science of social man,* New York, Macmillan, 1954, pp. 67–101.

91. PARSONS, T., BALES, R. F., and SHILS, E. A., *Working papers in the theory of action,* Glencoe, Ill., The Free Press 1953.

92. PARSONS, T., BALES, R. F., and collaborators, *Family, socialization and interaction process,* Glencoe, Ill., The Free Press, 1955.

93. PARSONS, T., and SHILS, E. A., *Toward a general theory of action,* Cambridge, Harvard Univ. Press, 1951.

94. PIERS, G., and SINGER, M. B., *Shame and guilt: A psychoanalytic and a cultural study,* Springfield, Ill., Charles C Thomas, 1953.

95. RIESMAN, D., *The lonely crowd,* New Haven, Yale Univ. Press, 1950.

96. ROHEIM, G., "The origin and function of culture," *Nervous and Mental Disease Mono.,* Vol. 63 (1943), pp. 1–107.

97. ROHEIM, G., *Psychoanalysis and anthropology,* New York, International Univ. Press, 1950.

98. SANFORD, N., *Surface and depth in the individual personality,* Presidential address, Div. Eight of the Amer. Psychol. Assoc., San Francisco, Sept., 1955.

99. SAPIR, E., "The emergence of the concept of personality in the study of culture," *J. of Soc. Psychol.*, Vol. 5 (1934), pp. 408–415.

100. SAPIR, E., "Cultural anthropology and psychiatry," in D. G. Mandelbaum (ed.), *Selected writings of Edward Sapir in language, culture and personality*, Berkeley, Univ. of Calif. Press, 1949.

101. SCHNEIDER, D. M., "Social dynamics of physical disability in army basic training," *Psychiatry*, Vol. 10 (1947), pp. 323–333.

102. SCHNEIDER, D. M., "Review of T. Gladwin and S. Sarason, *Truk: Man in paradise*," *Amer. Anthrop.*, Vol. 57 (1955), pp. 1098–1099.

103. SMITH, M. B., "Anthropology and psychology," in J. Gillin (ed.), *For a science of social man*, New York, Macmillan, 1954, pp. 32–66.

104. SPIRO, M., "Culture and personality: The natural history of a false dichotomy," *Psychiatry*, Vol. 15 (1951), pp. 19–46.

105. STOUFFER, S. A., "An analysis of conflicting social norms," *Amer. Soc. Rev.*, Vol. 14 (1949), pp. 707–717.

106. STOUFFER, S. A., SUCHMAN, E. A., DIVINNEY, L. C., STAR, SHIRLEY A., and WILLIAMS, R. M., *The American soldier: Adjustment during army life*, Princeton, Princeton Univ. Press, 1949.

107. THOMPSON, LAURA, and JOSEPH, ALICE, *The Hopi way*, Chicago, Univ. of Chicago Press, 1944.

108. THOMPSON, LAURA, "Perception patterns in three Indian tribes," *Psychiatry*, Vol. 14 (1951), pp. 255–263.

109. VOGT, E. Z., "Navaho veterans: A study of changing values," *Pap. Peabody Museum of Arch. and Ethnol.*, Harvard Univ., Vol. 41 (1951), 1.

110. WALLACE, A. F. C., *The modal personality structure of the Tuscarora Indians as revealed by the Rorschach test*, Smithsonian Inst., Bur. of Amer. Ethn., Bull. 150, 1952.

111. WALLACE, A. F. C., "Review of Ulithian personality as seen through ethnological materials and thematic test analysis," *Amer. Anthrop.*, Vol. 57 (1955), pp. 392–393.

112. WALLER, W., *The sociology of teaching*, New York, Wiley, 1932.

113. WHITE, R. W., *Lives in progress*, New York, Dryden Press, 1952.

114. WHITING, J. W. M., and CHILD, I. L., *Child training and personality*, New Haven, Yale Univ. Press, 1945.

115. WOLFENSTEIN, MARTHA, and LEITES, N., *Movies: A psychological study*, Glencoe, Ill., The Free Press, 1950.

34

BEHAVIORAL EVOLUTION
AND THE EMERGENCE OF THE SELF

A. IRVING HALLOWELL

THE advent of Darwinism helped to define and shape the problems of modern psychology as it did those of anthropology. An evolution of mind within the natural world of living organ-

From Betty Meggers (Ed.), *Evolution and Anthropology: A Centennial Appraisal*. Copyright © 1959 by the Anthropological Society of Washington. Reprinted by permission of the publisher and the author. A. Irving Hallowell is Professor Emeritus of Anthropology, University of Pennsylvania.

isms was envisaged. Now a bridge could be built to span the deep and mysterious chasm that separated man from other animals and which, according to Descartian tradition, must forever remain unbridged. Darwin (1871, 1873) himself explicitly set processes of reasoning, long considered an exclusively human possession, in an evolutionary perspective and advanced an evolutionary interpretation of the facial and postural changes of man when expressing emotion. He argued that mental differences in the animal series present gradations that are quantitative rather than qualitative in nature. Although Darwin was later accused of gross anthropomorphism by his critics, nevertheless, he stimulated others to think and write about mental evolution. Romanes (1883) coined the term "comparative psychology" and it was not long before a phylogenetic dimension had been added to the program of scientific psychology.

In its early stages, however, comparative psychology had little interest for anthropologists. In reaction against anecdotalism, more rigorously controlled observations were demanded by psychologists and lower mammals, like the rat, and insects, too, became preferred laboratory subjects. The results of these observations, even though highly reliable, did not throw much light on the phylogenetic roots of human psychology. Laboratory studies of infrahuman primates, like chimpanzee, initiated by Köhler and Yerkes, only developed to a point where they engaged anthropological interest in the twentieth century. The pioneer field studies of C. R. Carpenter were undertaken even later and the first publication came in 1934. Even today, as Nissen points out, "of the 50-odd living genera of primates, only a very few have been studied to any extent in regard to behavior: man, chimpanzee, the macaques, and cebus monkeys."

The most immediate impact upon anthropology of the evolutionary idea in the early post-Darwinian period of the nineteenth century is a familiar story. Physical anthropologists began to pursue problems in the area of morphological evolution, while archeologists and ethnologists attempted to apply the evolutionary theory to cultural development. Since it was assumed that processes of evolution were not confined to the organic sphere alone, a psychological question arose: Had not mental as well as cultural evolution taken place in the course of man's long struggle upward from savagery to civilization? Could it not be shown

that in the cultures of primitive peoples there was mirrored a reflection of primitive mind? J. G. Frazer was among those who explicitly linked this problem with the generic question of mental evolution since he adhered to the recapitulation theory. He thought that not only ethnographic data were relevant but likewise studies of the ontogenetic development of the child and of patients in mental hospitals. He said that "this comparative study of the mind of man is thus analogous to the comparative study of his body which is undertaken by anatomy and physiology." But when unilinear stages of cultural evolution were rejected by most twentieth century anthropologists, the notion of "primitive mind," as applied to nonliterate peoples, collapsed with them; the conclusion was drawn that culture change and development in *Homo sapiens* is not primarily linked with an evolution in mentality. And outside of anthropology the more inclusive concept of mental evolution, in so far as it was linked to the theory of recapitulation, became generally defunct with the rejection of this theory by biologists. Thus the psychological dimension of evolution, which to Darwin himself was an integral part of the total evolutionary process and of vital significance for our comprehension of man's place in nature, fell upon evil days. It is true that animal psychologists continued to investigate some problems comparatively; but special areas of investigation, such as learning behavior in rats, emerged into the foreground while a primary focus on evolutionary questions as such receded. Schneirla, in a review of trends in comparative psychology, emphasizes the fact that "most American animal psychologists at present seem to be really non-evolutionary minded, in the sense that they show no special zeal to find how man differs mentally from lower animals and vice versa, but rather focus strenuously on general problems without much attention to phyletic lines." Yet, as Nissen says, "one of the weakest links in the sciences dealing with evolution, the one most needing to strengthen its facts and theoretical framework, is that dealing with behavior."

Among anthropologists a paradoxical situation developed in the early decades of this century. Evolution, once so *inclusively* conceived, was reduced, in effect, to investigations in the area of physical anthropology. But physical anthropologists concerned themselves with morphological problems, not behavior. At the same time cultural anthropologists became more and more completely culture-centered. Culture, although assumed to be acquired in a learning process, was abstracted and studied as such. Culture traits, complexes and patterns became key terms. In effect, this preoccupation with culture led to a *re*-creation of the old gap between man and the other primates which it was once thought the adoption of an evolutionary frame of reference would serve to bridge. The repeated emphasis given to speech and culture as *unique* characteristics of man sidestepped the essence of the evolutionary problem. For unless culture and speech be conceived literally as *sui generis* phenomena, they must be rooted in behavioral processes that can no more be considered apart from the general framework of behavioral evolution than the distinctive structural characteristics of man can be considered apart from morphological evolution. Without the establishment of the nature of such linkages, the question arises: How far has the emphasis given to distinctive attributes of man advanced our understanding of man's evolutionary position in the animal series beyond the descriptive epithets of an earlier day? One thinks of such characterizations of man as the rational animal, the tool-making animal, the cooking animal, the laughing animal, the animal who makes pictures, or *animal symbolicus*. All these characterizations stress man's differences from other living creatures. Like the criteria of culture and speech, they emphasize discontinuity rather than the continuity that is likewise inherent in the evolutionary process.

A statement made by Carpenter a few years ago clearly articulates an opposition to any such sharp descriptive dichotomization between man and other primates. He said he found untenable a number of assumptions that seemed acceptable to many of his colleagues. One of these was "that the phenomena known as 'mind,' language, society, culture and 'values' exist exclusively on the level of human evolution." And Hebb and Thompson say that "exposure to a group of adult chimpanzees gives one the overwhelming conviction that one is dealing with an essentially human set of attitudes and motivations." Thus, while continuous lip service has been rendered the idea of evolution by cultural anthropologists, the statements of Carpenter and Hebb should remind us that there remain crucial evolutionary questions that transcend the old problem of unilinear stages of cultural development and the kind of problems which have been dealt with by physical anthropologists. These questions are difficult ones because they must be approached indirectly. They concern the functional dimensions of a human existence viewed in the perspective of an evolution of behavior that cannot be directly observed at successive stages in time. They involve psychological structures which, since they function as intervening variables, have to be inferred. Nevertheless, these problems have to be faced sooner or later for functional or behavioral criteria frequently have been invoked in dealing with problems of human evolution without sufficient discussion of all the psychological implications involved.

Some years ago Clark, referring to the question of the zoological classification of the Australopithecines, said that "taxonomic difficulties of this sort, of course, are bound to arise as discoveries are made of fossils of a seemingly transitional type, and with the increasing perfection of the fossil record, probably the differentiation of man from ape will ultimately have to rest on a functional rather than an anatomic basis, the criterion of humanity being the ability to speak and make tools." But effective use of such criteria is hardly a simple matter. We cannot depend on the evidence from human paleontology and archeology alone. Insofar as speech is concerned, the day is past when it was thought that reliable inferences could be made from brain anatomy. Can we assume, for example, that speech as observed in *Homo sapiens* possesses properties as a system of communication that can be treated as a phenomenal unity in evolutionary perspective? How far can it actually be projected into the past? Do we not have to know more than we do now about the properties of non-linguistic systems of communication at sub-human levels in order to understand the position of speech in behavioral perspective?

Recently, Hockett has identified seven universal properties of human language and compared them with the available data on nonhuman systems of communication. What is striking is the high degree of overlapping he found. This suggests that the combination of properties that characterize speech did not arise full blown. Consequently, Hockett is led to suggest a tentative evolutionary reconstruction. The latter, of course, is not concerned in any way with the development of speech forms within *Homo sapiens*. This kind of evolutionary inquiry, focused on the discovery of "primitive languages," has proved as fruitless as attempts to discover evidence for a "primitive mind" in our species.

If tools are taken as an index of a human status, considerable preliminary analysis will also be required to make this criterion reliable. Man has long been defined as the "tool maker." Recently Oakley has tried to be much more precise than others have been. Yet an English biologist, Pumphrey, has remarked that " 'Subman, the Implement Maker' would have been a more accurate if less impressive title at least for the first half of his book," *Man, the Tool Maker*. Pumphrey sees "no valid reason for assigning intellect to a maker of implements"—"the web of a garden-spider and the nest of a chaffinch are highly fabricated implements"—whereas genuine tools, which he thinks cannot be assigned to early members of the Hominidae, "were made in order to *make* something else with them." While the tool concept does possess a generic unity if some very broad adaptive function is implied, without further analysis it is not very useful for making distinctions in an evolutionary frame of reference. When Bartholomew and Birdsell say that "in contrast to all other mammals, the larger arboreal primates are, in a sense, tool-users in their locomotion" since, "as they move through the maze of the tree tops, their use of branches anticipates the use of tools in that they routinely employ levers and angular movements," this is a very broad interpretation of tool-using. These authors draw the conclusion, moreover, that "protohominids were dependent on the use of tools for survival."

There is ample evidence that both biologists and psychologists have had their own difficulties in dealing with the question: what constitutes tool-using? And because the phenomenon of tool-using is not confined to the primates alone, it is necessary to understand the varying factors that underlie what has been called tool-using in other animals in order to interpret properly the phenomenon of tool-using in the behavioral evolution of the primates and the differential factors that made tool-making possible as a unique development within the hominids.

In psychological experiments with infra-hominid primates "instrumentation," as it is usually called, includes piling up boxes to secure food, the manipulation of sticks to achieve a similar goal or pole vaulting! What is interesting is that high proficiency in instrumentation under laboratory conditions appears to be a function of previous experience in related situations.

In these cases, however, it is individual learning rather than social learning that is involved in tool-using of this order. Sultan's success in "making" a tool was a unique individual achievement. While there would seem to be no question about the capacity of some primates to use tools as a means of achieving a desired goal when sufficiently motivated, this potentiality alone is only one of the necessary prerequisites to a more highly developed stage of tool-using. Moreover, it seems quite likely that, under natural conditions, some rudimentary habits of tool-using in the narrower, rather than the broadest sense, may have been individually learned and socially transmitted in subhominid or early hominid groups. If so, this would exemplify what I have called a *proto-cultural* stage. Nevertheless, the conditions operative at such a stage in primate groups are not in themselves sufficient to account for the still more advanced level of *tool-making*. If the latter is invoked as a functional criterion of a human status, we need to do more than differentiate between tool-using and tool-making. We must ask whether tool-making presupposes a higher order of psychological structuralization and functioning than tool-using; whether it implies a social system different from that of infra-hominid primates; or a different system of communication. Since tool-making as observed in *Homo sapiens* is a skilled act, learned in a social context where speech exists, and is usually performed with reference to a purposeful use at some *future* time, must we not make up our minds, when interpreting the archeological evidence, whether tool-making necessitates a sense of self-orientation in time, and whether it presupposes an institution of property that assures continued control over the tool in the interval?

When we have direct evidence of the persistence of characteristic techniques of manufacture and tool styles, as well as evidence of innovation or invention (i.e., a tool-making tradition), we then have indices of a human level of cultural adaptation. But this involves far more than tool-making per se or social transmission. The more perplexing evolutionary problem arises in cases where the material evidence is more ambiguous. Here, our assumption about all the conditions that make tool-making possible becomes crucial.

Oakley has discriminated six stages in the development of tool-using and tool-making in the *Hominidae*. "Regular tool-making with marked standardization" does not appear until the fourth stage, at which point the precursors of *Homo sapiens* are definitely involved. Oakley captions his tabulation "Six Levels of Culture on the Basis of the Use and Making of Tools." Since he has expressed the opinion that ". . . though man's Pliocene ancestors were not tool makers, they were tool-users . . ." and does not think it necessary to assume that the earliest hominid tool users, or even tool makers, possessed speech, I have suggested that the evolutionary picture would be clarified if we characterized the first two stages of Oakley's scheme as *protocultural,* rather than cultural.

This brief discussion of speech and tools as functional criteria of a human status has indicated some of the preliminary difficulties met with in applying them. The evolutionary problem becomes even more complex if, to begin with, we attempt to operate with the concept of culture as the criterion of a human status —that "complex whole" of Tylor's classic definition which, he said, was acquired by individuals as members of society. How can we apply such an abstract generic concept, derived from empirical observations of a very concrete nature in any meaningful analysis of the developmental aspects of human evolution and adaptation? Wissler tried to solve the problem by assuming the phenomenal unity of what he called a "universal pattern" of culture. His solution was reductionistic. He projected this pattern—including speech—full fledged from the properties he conceived the "germ plasm" to possess. "The pattern of culture is just as deeply buried in the germ plasm of man as the bee pattern in the bee," he said; "the human pattern . . . is a part, if not the whole, of man's inborn behavior . . . man builds cultures because he cannot help it, there is a *drive* in his protoplasm that carries him forward even against his will." Wissler, however, did not specify any particular genus or species of the *Hominidae.* He did not say whether the same universal pattern for culture was embedded alike in the genes of *Pithecanthropus* as well as *Homo* and, at the time he wrote, the problem presented by the Australopithecines had not yet arisen.

Even aside from Wissler's lack of generic or specific identification he seems to have assumed a closer connection between genes and behavior than is warranted by the biological evidence. Schneirla, for instance, has pointed out that ". . . the gaps between genes and somatic characters are great; those between genes and behavior, which are greater still, can

be bridged only by studies directed at understanding the intervening variables and their interrelationships. Earlier notions of a one-to-one relationship between these agencies and their effects have fallen away before advances in physiological genetics." It appears dubious whether any reductionistic approach to the question of the evolutionary roots of culture can be any more fruitful than "preformistic" theories in biology.

At present the whole evolutionary problem is further complicated by the fact that since morphological rather than behavioral characteristics furnish the traditional criteria for zoological classification, the hominid status given the Australopithecines has undermined the common use many of us have been making of the terms "man" and "human." Clark has reminded us that "these terms may not properly be used as though they were equivalent to the zoological terms *Homo* and *Hominidae* or to the adjectival form 'hominid.' . . ." What becomes then of such familiar correspondences as man: speech: tools: culture: human? Taking the paleontological evidence into account, with what members of the *Hominidae* except *Homo sapiens* can we unequivocally link the kind of cultural mode of adaptation that corresponds in *all* respects to what we know from direct observation and experience? With *Homo neandertalensis,* probably. But is there not more than a shadow of doubt about the other genera? Even if they are not considered to be in our direct ancestral line, the discovery of the African ape-men has served to bring structural and behavioral questions into a new evolutionary focus. What is particularly significant is the evidence that modification in posture was probably the most important initial step in hominid evolution and that expansion of the brain took place much later. Thus instead of the "emergence" of a characteristic combination of morphological traits that can be labelled "man," it appears that basic "human" traits were independently developed in a longtime evolutionary sequence. As Howells has said,

Heretofore we have been given to talking about "the appearance of man"—the tyranny of terminology—as if he had suddenly been promoted from colonel to brigadier general, and had a date of rank. It is now evident that the first hominids were smallbrained, newly bipedal, proto-Australopith hominoids, and that what we have always meant by "man" represents later forms of this group with secondary adaptations in the direction of large brains and modified skeletons of the same form.

Analogically, it is equally doubtful whether we should any longer talk in terms of the "appearance of culture," as if culture, too, along with "man" had suddenly leaped into existence. For if we do, we may unwittingly find ourselves in the *anti-evolutionist* camp. If the ancestral hominids were at all like the Australopithecines, it seems unlikely that they could have had a system of communication that was fully the equivalent of human speech, and it is difficult to interpret their osteodontokeratic implements as evidence of a fully developed tool-making tradition. In the light of our present knowledge, we cannot attribute speech and a cultural mode of adaptation to all the *Hominidae.*

Thus, instead of assuming that culture possesses a phenomenal unity from the start and trying to identify its existence in the past, it seems more fruitful to consider certain aspects of behavioral evolution that are non-cultural in nature, but which are among the indispensable conditions that made cultural adaptation possible in the later phases of hominid evolution. The most important of these conditions are sociopsychological in nature. Our empirical data are derived from observation on sub-hominid primates in their natural habitat or under laboratory conditions, for deductions from comparative behavior are as methodologically legitimate as those from comparative anatomy.

Social systems are not unique to *Homo sapiens.* And, even at this highly evolved level, "social structure" is now frequently differentiated analytically from culture or personality organization. Eggan, for example, has expressed the opinion that "the distinction between society and culture, far from complicating the procedures of analysis and comparison, has actually facilitated them." He goes on to say that "social structure and culture patterns may vary independently of one another, but both have their locus in the behavior of individuals in social groups."

In approaching the socio-psychological dimension of primate evolution, a distinction of the same order is useful. Life in structured social groups is characteristic of primates and long antedated anything that can be called a cultural mode of adaptation among the more advanced hominids. Social structure can thus be treated as an independent variable in this perspective. While at the highest level of primate behavioral evolution there are no organized societies without culture (or the reverse), at lower levels there were societies without culture.

In developmental perspective a necessary locus and an indispensable condition for a cultural system is an organized system of social action. It likewise seems reasonable to assume that systems of social action at lower primate levels require some system of communication for their operation. To characterize such a system as "language" is ambiguous and even misleading without an analysis of its specific properties. On the other hand, it is difficult to imagine how a fully developed cultural mode of adaptation could operate without speech, that is, an oral system of communication having the properties with which we are familiar in *Homo sapiens.* But since this typical mode of human communication always implies a speech community, an organized social system is as necessary a condition for the functioning of human language as it is for a cultural mode of adaptation. What we can discern in primate evolution, then, is a behavioral plateau that provided the necessary context but not all of the sufficient conditions for speech and culture.

It will be unnecessary here to analyze all of the properties of infra-hominid social structures, but, broadly speaking, they present limited varieties of a single type, whereas at the highest hominid level we have a much greater range and diversification of types. The infra-hominid type of social structure is linked to the biological fact that a basic function is involved—the procreation and nurture of offspring that are helpless not only at birth, but for considerable periods afterwards. The structure of the group is determined by the roles played by adult members of both sexes towards each other and toward their offspring. In some groups there is a social gradient established by the ascendency of certain males over other males as well as females. Variants of this generic type of structure are a function of the relative number and sex of the associated adults, i.e., monogamous, polygynous or sexually communistic mateships. We can reasonably ascribe this *generic* type of social structure to the precursors of the *Hominidae,* although in what specific variant form it is difficult to say.

What a different picture we get from the one painted by Herbert Spencer and nineteenth century anthropologists who, in their speculations about social evolution were not even willing to grant early man a family structure. Spencer wrote:

We have thus to begin with a state in which the

family, as we understand it, does not exist. In the loose groups of men first formed, there is no established order of any kind; everything is indefinite, unsettled. As the relations of men to one another are undetermined, as are the relations of men to women . . . the lowest groups of primitive men, without political organization, are also without anything worthy to be called family organization: the relations between the sexes and the relations between parents and offspring are scarcely above those of brutes.

To Spencer, social evolution was super-organic evolution and actually involved an unbridged gap between man and other animals. The picture that now seems to emerge suggests that instead of the occurrence in any developmental sequence of the three variant forms of bi-parental family groups identified at the subhominid level, we have empirical evidence for the recurrence of all of them in *Homo sapiens*. However, another variant, polyandrous mateships, has been added and, instead of the best example of sexual communism being found among very primitive people, it is exemplified by the Oneida colony in nineteenth century America!

Thus, an old and basic generic type of social structure, with a limited range of sub-types, links the most evolved hominid with a pre-hominid level of behavioral development. While in *Homo sapiens* a new factor is introduced in that the evaluation of the variant types of bi-parental structure differs according to *culturally* constituted value systems, the recurrence of such structures supports their treatment as independent variables in the social dimension of primate behavioral evolution. Furthermore, the biparental type of social structure persisted throughout the extremely long period during which major morphological changes occurred in members of the primate order, including those which ultimately differentiated the *Hominidae* from the *Pongidae* and early hominids from later ones. In social behavior and organization, as well as at the structural level, there have been constancies as well as variations and novelties in primate history.

The significance of the social dimension of behavioral evolution in the primates for an understanding of the later phase of cultural adaptation has still another aspect. The dynamics of social structures of the type described, while partly determined by their biological function and the age and sex of the participating individuals, are also dependent upon social learning. Carpenter has explicitly stressed the necessity of *socialization* as a condition for the integrative

functioning of such groups. If this is the case, we may assume that the intimate relation between learning and social structure fundamental to the functioning and elaboration of cultural adaptation was well established prior to the structural changes that led to both erect posture and expansion of the brain. We can generalize even further and say that, among the higher anthropoids at least, learned habits may be socialized and transmitted even in the absence of speech. Examples would be nest building in chimpanzee and the techniques of working the drinking fountain at Orange Park, which chimpanzees learned from each other.

The social transmission of culture has sometimes been stressed as one of its chief earmarks. But to my mind it is only one of the necessary conditions of cultural adaptation rather than a distinguishing characteristic. It is a prerequisite of culture and an earmark of a *protocultural* behavioral plateau. Concepts of culture that lay primary emphasis on shared and socially transmitted behavior without qualification do not enable us to make a necessary distinction of degree between different levels of behaviorial evolution. Voegelin has made the acute observation that while there is a general agreement that all culture involves learned behavior "additional conditions are generally invoked before learned behavior is granted the status of culture," and that "if ever the converse statement were made (*that all learned behavior is culture*), it would necessarily imply that infra-human animals have culture." The fact that some animals do learn from each other in their natural state and that chimpanzees are capable of acquiring "culture traits" in social interaction with members of our species, does not mean in either case that a level of cultural adaptation has been reached. Other conditions and capacities besides learning are required.

In primate evolution, learning could not acquire maximum importance as a psychological factor in social adjustment until conditions arose in which the social transmission of acquired experience could function in social structures of wider range than the bi-parental type of family organization. In social structures of this latter type, the phenomenon of territoriality which, according to Carpenter, "reduces stress, conflict, pugnacity, and non-adaptive energy expenditure" within each group by isolating it from other groups, sets up a barrier at the same time to the integration of groups and the development of social structures of a wider range and more complex order. Offspring do not associate with parents after sexual maturity has been reached. They leave their primary group and form new ones. Individuals of two or more generations are not continuously associated in the same group during their lifetime. Consequently, conditions that permit continuity in learned habits are highly restricted. There is no way for experience to become cumulative, either spatially or temporally, beyond the narrowest range. In order for a cultural level of adaptation to be reached, structures of wider range were required as a social setting. This further step was contingent upon the development and functioning of psychological capacities that transcend those sufficient to account for the dynamics of the narrow-range social structures described. In short, the social integration of groups larger in size, more varied in personnel and characterized by a greater diversity in roles, resulting from the association of individuals of several generations, required a transformation in psychological structure for its operation.

How much these further steps in socio-psychological evolution may have been directly associated with the expansion of the cortex is difficult to say. There may well have been a critical transition, but scarcely an arbitrary "Rubicon" of 750 cc. Although we cannot trace these developmental stages by direct observation we do know what the behavioral outcome was in the most higly evolved hominid. Here, along with a greater diversification in the forms of social structure that characterize *Homo sapiens,* we are confronted with a change in their underlying dynamics. At this more advanced stage, societies function as *moral* orders. It is this fact that gives us the major key to the kind of psychological transformation that occurred.

The functioning of a social system as a moral order implies a capacity for self objectification, self identification, and appraisal of one's own conduct, as well as that of others, with reference to socially recognized and sanctioned standards of behavior. Without a psychological level of organization that permits the exercise of these functions, moral responsibility for conduct could not exist, nor could any social structure function as a moral order. Learning remains important, of course, but it now functions at a higher level. The relations between needs, motivation, goals and learning become more complex. The added moral dimension of a social system is not reducible to learned and socially transmitted habits. Patterns of incest avoidance, for example, with their manifestations of shame, guilt and anxiety, long presented a puzzling socio-psychological problem because the psychological structure that underlies them was not understood. Such patterns of avoidance do not and could not operate at a sub-hominid level where the phenomena of self awareness and moral responsibility for conduct do not exist. No wonder then that without an understanding of the nature of the psychological structure that made incest tabus possible, they were often thought to have an instinctive basis.

Further ramifications of the socio-psychological significance of self awareness in *Homo sapiens,* where we find a fully developed mode of cultural adaptation, need not be considered here since our perspective is an evolutionary one. With this problem in mind, however, the question can be raised whether the capacity for self objectification is common to all *Hominidae.* If we include the Australopithecines, I see no reason to suppose so. And, if we wish to postulate an equivalent structural and behavioral stage as being chronologically early hominoid, there is no evidence that suggests any different conclusion.

While it has been widely recognized that self awareness is a generic phenomenon in *Homo sapiens,* the psychological structure that underlies it has been seriously studied only since the rise of a more general interest in personality structure, mainly under the impact of psychoanalytic theories. The evolutionary aspects of the problem have been scarcely touched. Indeed, there have been "many psychologists of the modern period," as Asch says, "who have spoken of the individual organism as of a congeries of capacities and tendencies without a self-character." It has been pointed out, moreover, that "between 1910 and 1940, most psychologists preferred not to mention 'ego' or 'self' in their writings" (Sargent). Nowadays, ego and self are familiar terms, although the connotation given them is not standardized. However, no one uses the ego concept in any substantive sense but rather as a psychological construct useful in conceptualizing a sub-system of the total personality, objectively approached, with reference to its development, structure and functioning. If we wish to be rigorous it is best to speak of a group of ego processes or functions, although this is sometimes awkward. Ego functions have a wide range; they are intimately connected with such cognitive processes as attention, perception, thinking and judgment, because ego processes are involved in determining adjustments to the outer world in the interests of inner needs, particularly in situations where choice or decision, and hence delay or postponement of action is required.

On the other hand, the concept of self carries a reflexive connotation: "I" can think of "me." I can discriminate myself from other objects perceptually; I can conceive of myself as an object; I can develop attitudes toward myself. Thus the self is a phenomenal datum while the ego is a construct. "The self can be observed and described; the ego is deduced and postulated. The ego may be conceived in quasi-physiological terms as a sub-system of the organism. . ." (MacLeod). Furthermore, the self does not mirror the ego—the subject's capacity for self-objectification does not imply his objective knowledge of the psychodynamics of his total personality. Considered in evolutionary perspective, ego may be said to be the major "psychological organ" that structurally differentiates the most highly evolved members of the *Hominidae* from sub-hominid primates and probably other hominids of lower evolutionary rank. It lies at the core of a human personality structure as we know it in *Homo sapiens*. It permits adaptation at a new behavioral level. Since, in ontogenetic development, the beginnings of ego processes can be identified in the first half year of life, well before the acqusition of speech, we can say that while ego development occurs in a context of social interaction, in its initial stages it is not contingent upon the prior existence of either speech or culture. The underlying capacities for ego functioning must have deeper psychobiological roots. This is the area in which the evolutionary problem lies.

Heinz Hartmann, a psychoanalytic writer, has made a most illuminating suggestion as to how this problem may be approached. He says that we must not overlook important relations between animal instinct and human ego functions. His point is that "many functions, which are taken care of by instincts" in lower animals "are in man functions of the ego." We should not identify the nature and role of instincts in animals with "drives" in man. "The id, too, does not appear to be a simple extension of the instincts of lower animals. While the ego develops in the direction of an ever closer adjustment to reality, clinic experience shows the drives, the id-tendencies, to be far more estranged

from reality than the so-called animal instincts generally are. . . ." In other words, the general evolutionary trend is one in which the role of central cortical functions, acting as intervening variables, becomes increasingly important. Ego processes and functions in *Homo sapiens* would appear to represent the culmination of this trend in the primates.

Evidence then for the phylogenetic roots of the ego must be sought in the functional equivalent of ego processes and functions at lower primate levels. Although Nissen does not make the inference himself, I think that the examples he gives in support of his assertion that the higher anthropoids are "guided by a delicately balanced system of values," may be taken as evidence of the functioning of rudimentary ego processes. He says that:

The larger and stronger male chimpanzee deferring to his female companion in the division of food, even after the female is pregnant and no longer suitable as a sex partner—the animal 'punishing' the misbehavior of his cage mate and in position to inflict serious injury, but contenting himself with merely nipping him painfully—the chimpanzee refusing to expose himself to the frustration of occasional failure in a difficult problem, although he could get a desirable tidbit 50% of the time by merely continuing to make a simple and easy response—these are but a few of many instances of a finely adjusted hierarchy of values. Like man, the chimpanzee has many values only indirectly related to primary needs, as for food, sex, and knowledge.

These situations exemplify the behavioral outcome of the shift from physiological to cortical controls which laid the foundation that enabled the *Pongidae* and, no doubt, their proto-hominid relatives, to develop a new level of psychobiological adaptation. I cannot escape the impression that the group of chimpanzees at Orange Park who, seeing visitors arriving, ran quickly to the drinking fountain and, after filling their mouths with water quietly waited until the closer approach of the visitors before discharging it at them, exemplifies in a rudimentary form the integration of attention, perceiving, thinking, purposiveness and the postponement of action that are among the ego processes and functions attributed to *Homo sapiens*. Hebb and Thompson, who report this observation, do not refer to ego processes or functions but use the episode to illustrate the chimpanzees' capacity for what they call "syntactic behavior," which they consider crucial in phylogenesis. It involves an "increasing independence of the conceptual activity from the present sensory environment, and an increasing capacity for entertaining diverse conceptual processes at the same time." Among other things it "eventually makes speech possible." "At the lowest level, it is the capacity for delayed response or a simple expectancy; at the highest level, for 'building' not only a series of words but also of sentences, whose meaning only become clear with later words or sentences." To my mind, Hebbs' concept of syntactic behavior falls along the psychological dimension in phylogenesis where we must look for the rudimentary phases of ego processes and functions. At the same time, I do not think that behavioral evidence such as that cited, which appears to indicate the functioning of rudimentary ego processes, allows us to make the further inference that this behavior involves self-objectification.

The capacity for self-objectification represents a level of psychological integration that requires the operation of additional factors. While, on the one hand, self-objectification is rooted in a prior development of ego functions, on the other it is contingent upon the capacity for the symbolic projection of experience in socially meaningful terms, i.e., in a mode that is intelligible interindividually. There must be a functional integration of intrinsic symbolic processes with some extrinsically expressable means of symbolization. An extrinsic mode is necessary in order to mediate socially transmitted and commonly shared meanings in a system of social action. There must become available to an individual some means whereby inwardly as well as outwardly directed reference to his own experience and that of others, as well as to objects and events in his world that are other than self, can find common ground. The capacity for ego processes and functions must be implemented by some means of representation that transcends the intrinsic symbolic processes of the organism itself which, at a lower level, may function without articulation or extrinsic symbolization of any kind.

In evolutionary perspective there is evidence that intrinsic symbolic processes (i.e., central processes that function as substitutes for or representatives of sensory cues or events that are not present in the immediate perceptual field) occur not only in sub-hominid primates but in some lower species. But even in the higher apes the functioning of representative processes appears to be limited, as is a capacity

for ego processes. But it is difficult to know precisely what these limits are. Schneirla, making reference to Crawford's experiment on the cooperative solving of problems by chimpanzees, says that these animals "were able to learn a gestural form of communication and use it symbolically." They were enabled

to summon one another by means of self-initiated gestures such as gentle taps on the shoulder. These were truly symbolic, and not merely signals to action. The chimpanzee who tapped was presenting, in anticipation of its social effect, a special cue which had come to symbolize, i.e., to stand for meaningfully, the expected social result. The symbolic, anticipative, and directive nature of this gestural cue was indicated by the fact that, when shoulder taps were insufficient, or slow in producing cooperation, the active animal would turn to pulling alone, or might act forcibly and directly to get the second animal involved in pulling. Although it is not known how far and in what ways such gestural devices may be involved in chimpanzee group communication under natural conditions, their use is probably very limited.

Interpreted in this way, the gestures referred to may be considered a rudimentary and highly limited mode of extrinsic symbolization. Their function, of course, was imposed by the nature and circumstances of the experiment. In this framework conditions were not favorable for the perpetuation of these gestures through further social learning and transmission in a wider group.

A unique observation of the behavior of Viki illustrates the functioning in a non-experimental situation of spontaneous intrinsic representative processes, tantalizing because of their incommunicability. It is reported that Viki had an imaginary pull-toy that she sometimes imaginatively towed around on an imaginary string. She was very shy about this play. Viki could not deliberately communicate the intrinsic symbolic processes she experienced to ape or man. She could only act out her fantasy by behaving as she did. Mrs. Hayes could only observe and guess what the probable image was that lay back of her behavior. Viki herself could not abstract, objectify and project her experience in any symbolic form extrinsic to herself. Consequently, there is no reason to suppose that she could think about herself as an object playing with her pull-toy. Because there was no system of extrinsic symbolization available as a means of communication, the world that Viki and Mrs. Hayes could share was very limited psychologically. It may be that one of the major reasons chimpanzees cannot be taught to speak is that they are not capable of manipulating second order abstractions of the type necessary for extrinsic symbolization, even though lower levels of abstraction are possible for them.

Systems of extrinsic symbolization necessitate material media for the communication of meanings. Abstraction and conceptualization are required since objects or events are introduced into the perceptual field as *symbols,* not in their concrete reality. Thus systems of extrinsic symbolization involve the operation of the representative principle on a more complex level than do processes of intrinsic symbolization. In the case of *Homo sapiens,* extrinsic symbolic systems, functioning through vocal, graphic, plastic, gestural or other media, make it possible for groups of human beings to share a common world of meanings. A cultural mode of adaptation is unthinkable without systems of extrinsic symbolization.

The earliest unequivocal proof of the capacity of *Homo sapiens* for extrinsic symbolization in a visual mode is found in the cave art of the Upper Paleolithic. Here we find the graphic representation, in a naturalistic style, of such animals as mammoth, bison, rhinocerous, wild horse, etc., which could not have been present in the perceptual field of the artist. The location of the drawings in most of the caves excludes this possibility. On the one hand, this proves that the men of this period had highly accurate and vivid images of contemporary animals (intrinsic symbolization). On the other, it demonstrates their capacity to project these images and represent them in a material medium. Even when the animals themselves were not present, the drawings of them could convey to other men what was "in" the artists' "mind." This type of symbolization may be called iconic. While there is some abstraction, there is a relatively close correspondence in form between the object, the image, and the graphic representation. The symbolism of speech is typically at the opposite pole and in a different mode. Sound clusters are given a meaning content that is unrelated to the form or qualities of the objects or events represented. What I should like to emphasize here is that the same basic capacity is involved. Art forms are as indicative as are speech forms and graphic art may likewise be highly abstract. It seems to me hard to deny that the peoples of the Upper Paleolithic possessed a vocal mode of representation, although we have no direct evidence of speech. On the other hand, Viki and other chimpanzees have shown as little capacity for graphic symbolization as for vocal symbolization.

From an evolutionary point of view, the capacity for individual and social adaptation through the mediation of extrinsic types of symbolization enabled an evolving primate to enlarge his world. The immediate, local, time-and-space-bound world of other primates, who lack the capacity for dealing effectively with objects and events outside the field of direct perception, could be transcended. Speech, through the use of personal pronouns, personal names and kinship terms, made it possible for an individual symbolically to represent and thus objectify himself in systems of social action. Self-related activities, both in the past and future, could be brought into the psychological present and reflected upon. What emerged was a personality structure in which ego processes and functions became highly salient. And, with the development of speech as an oral system of symbolic communication, that likewise functioned as a primary tool in reflective thought, a higher level of ego functioning could arise—awareness of self.

The central importance of ego processes and self awareness that we find distinctive in *Homo sapiens* can be viewed from another angle. Since self consciousness involves self appraisal in relation to sanctioned moral conduct, we can see the social as well as the individual adaptive value of universal psychological processes such as repression, rationalization and other defense mechanisms. Culturally constituted moral values impose a characteristic psychological burden, since it is not always easy, at the level of self awareness, to reconcile idiosyncratic needs with the demands imposed by the self. For animals without the capacity for self awareness no such frustration can arise. In *Homo sapiens,* unconscious mechanisms may be viewed as an adaptive means that permits some measure of compromise between conflicting forces. They relieve the individual of part of the burden forced upon him by the requirements of a morally responsible existence. There seems to be little question that one of the crucial areas of individual adjustment turns upon the tolerance with which the self views its own moral status and the sensitivity of the self to feelings of anxiety and guilt.

Psychoanalysts, in particular, have come more and more to recognize that behavioral dys-functioning centers on the ego. Leopold Bellak has recently articulated the shift in focus that has occurred in psychoanalytic thinking. "The novelty in psychoanalysis," he says, "was originally its introduction of the unconscious in the sense of the unconsciousness of feelings, the unawareness of previously experienced events, the covert nature of motivations, and the hidden meaning of dreams and symptoms. Slowly attention focused on the forces responsible for this unconsciousness, notably repression." A new era, however, "dedicated to the analysis not only of the unconscious but of the ego and its defenses," was initiated with Anna Freud's book, *The Ego and the Mechanisms of Defense* (1936). So that now, "the pendulum has swung nearly full cycle, in that there is so much talk about ego psychology today that the forces of the unconscious are possibly already somewhat in disregard."

Franz Alexander, commenting on the same shift of interest, says that "mental disease represents a failure of the ego to secure gratification for subjective needs in a harmonious and reality-adjusted manner and a breakdown of the defenses by which it tries to neutralize impulses which it cannot harmonize with its internal standards and external reality." He goes on to observe that "the highest form of integrative function requires conscious deliberation. Everything which is excluded from consciousness is beyond the reach of the ego's highest integrative functions. . . . Psychoanalytic therapy aims at the extension of the ego's integrative scope over repressed tendencies by making them conscious."

Thus, in the terminology I have been using here, psychological functioning at a level of self awareness is as important for rational personal adjustment as it is for the functioning of socio-cultural systems. Furthermore, as Schneirla points out, it is an error stemming from an inadequate comprehension of the complex nature of a human level of existence to assume "that man's 'higher psychological processes' constitute a single agency or unity which is capable of being sloughed off" even under extreme provocation. On the contrary "socialized man even under stress of extreme organic need or persistent frustration does not regress to the 'brute level.' Rather, he shifts to some eccentric and distorted variation of his ordinary personality, which varies from his prevalent socialized make-up according to the degree of integrity and organization attained by that adjustment system."

Contemporary anthropologists who stress social structure as a major object of study, as well as those who emphasize culture, assume persons as role players or actors. Whether explicitly acknowledged or not, socio-cultural systems presume the functioning of individuals capable of developing a psychological structure in which ego processes function at a level where objectification of the world and objectification of the self are salient. Neither the study of social structure nor the study of cultures can in themselves fully account for the evolution of the psychological structure that makes their operation possible. What we observe in the behavior of *Homo sapiens* is the culmination and distinctive integration of processes and capacities that did not present a unified picture in the past, and which thus require analytic discrimination and investigation in a longer evolutionary perspective than is represented by *Homo sapiens* or even the *Hominidae*. A cultural level of adaptation could not arise *de novo*. Prerequisite conditions of a non-cultural order were necessary. Simple forms of learning, some socialization of the individual, an ongoing social structure based on a limited range of roles, the transmission of some group habits, and perhaps tool using may be identified as necessary but not sufficient conditions for a "human" level of existence. Granted that the existence of these conditions provided a foundation, it would appear that all of them were raised to a new level of functional integration by the psychological restructuralization that must have occurred during the course of the evolution of the *Hominidae*. Without this added factor, expressed in part by the development of extrinsic forms of symbolization, a cultural level of adaptation could not have been reached in the first place.

So far as learned behavior is concerned, its importance in relation to culture has sometimes been exaggerated, since learning in the sense of conditioning is found far down the animal scale. What seems to be significant in primate evolution is that social learning—focused upon mother-infant relations—became linked with the functioning of social structure at the sub-hominid level. But at this level *what* was learned appears to have been quantitatively limited. In the case of the howling monkeys, for example, although a dozen or more vocal signs are important in group integration, it does not seem that these are learned. In *Homo sapiens* we have a quantitative maximization of social learning that is also qualitatively distinctive.

Social learning is as essential for the development of the personality structure of the individual as it is for the maintenance and transmission of the values and goals of a socio-cultural system. But this is not all. There are psychological functions manifested at this level that transcend *what* has been learned. We find cognitive processes raised to a higher level of functioning by means of culturally constituted symbolic forms which can be manipulated creatively through reflective thought and expression. Cultural modes of adaptation, or certain aspects of them, learned and transmitted as they may be, also can be objectified, thought about, analyzed, judged and even remodelled.

The great novelty then, in the behavioral evolution of the primates, was not simply the development of a cultural mode of adaptation as such. It was, rather, the psychological restructuralization that not only made this new mode of existence possible but provided the psychological basis for cultural *re*-adaptation and change. The psychological basis of culture lies not only in a capacity for highly complex forms of learning but in a capacity for transcending what is learned; a potentiality for innovation, creativity, reorganization and change.

The psychological dimension of evolution is as crucial as morphological evolution if we wish to understand the integral unity of culture, social structure and personality organization observed in *Homo sapiens*. The unified frame of reference envisaged by Darwin and others was sound. We must continue to work within it if we are ever thoroughly to understand man's place in nature.

35

CULTURAL
AND COGNITIVE DISCONTINUITY

ULRIC NEISSER

TWENTY-FIVE years ago, Bateson (1936) suggested that *eidos,* the cognitive aspect of culture, could serve as an important focus of anthropological thought. His suggestion seems to have received little systematic attention. Perhaps the reason for this neglect lies not so much within anthropology itself as in the neighboring discipline of psychology. The "higher mental processes" have always been a part of psychology, but one who tried to follow Bateson's suggestion in the 1930's and 1940's would have found that we had little to offer him. Most studies of thinking and remembering then being conducted seemed sterile and unrewarding, and were of interest only to specialists.

Today, the situation is very different. Cognition has again become a central concern in psy-

From Thomas Gladwin and William Sturtevant (Eds.), *Anthropology and Human Behavior.* Copyright © 1962 by the Anthropological Association of Washington. Reprinted by permission of the publisher and the author. Ulric Neisser is Professor of Psychology, Cornell University.

chology, generating ideas and excitement at a relatively high rate. Perhaps we have come to the point where Bateson's proposal can be implemented. In this paper, I will first try to examine the limitations of the older approaches to cognition, and go on to discuss some of the sources of the new confidence that characterizes the field. Then I will focus on a particular expression of these trends: Ernest Schachtel's developmental theory of memory. Finally, I will outline some of the implications that this theory seems to have for the study of culture and of culture change.

In the period before 1950, experimental psychology in America was dominated by behaviorism, and particularly by the sophisticated and systematic behaviorism of Clark Hull. Of course, not all psychologists adhered to it; probably most did not. Nevertheless, theoretical issues (and research) tended to be polarized along lines dictated by its concepts. Those who were not for behaviorism were against it, with the most vocal opposition coming from the

Gestalt school. The principal business of psychology seemed to be the evaluation of the claims and counter-claims of the factions. Was learning a matter of trial-and-error, or of insight? Did it require reinforcement or not? Did thinking consist of a series of implicit, unobservable responses or was it more like the reorganization of a perceptual field? Was memory a matter of the preservation of stimulus-response bonds or storing up configurational traces?

Not all theorizing about cognition was drawn into the conflict. Psychoanalytic psychology, insulated by heavy layers of cultural and professional differences, had an independent cognitive theory. In Freud's view, learning resulted from the frustration of instinctual urges. The growing child is gradually forced into grudging acceptance of adult ways of thought, as he finds no other way to achieve even partial gratification of his needs. The primary mental process is hallucinatory wish-fulfillment. Only slowly does steady pressure from the environment generate "secondary" modes of thought. Even thereafter, cognitive activity remains in the service of the drives. Freud himself seemed more interested in the defensive uses of thought and memory than in their realistic functions. The mind was visualized as the scene of an interplay of energies. Cognitive activity was thought of as the outcome of a fierce struggle between cathexes and counter-cathexes, instincts and censors, id and ego. Such a theory could make rather little contact with the down-to-earth concepts of behaviorism. Where a rapproachment between S-R (stimulus-response, or Hullian) theory and psychoanalysis was attempted (as in the influential work of Dollard and Miller [1950]), its success was primarily in the areas of motivation and symptom formation, rather than of memory and thought.

In retrospect, these approaches to cognition share an air of unreality. Their descriptions of thought-processes appear forced and unnatural. Perhaps they seemed so even to their partisans. No matter which viewpoint is chosen, there is no neutral terminology in which to discuss cognition or symbolization. Each theory is committed to one or another form of descriptive metaphor, and all the metaphors are inadequate. The behaviorist, for example, must treat mental activity as if it were a series of responses. The responses are necessarily unobservable, as are the stimuli that instigate them and the reinforcements which strengthen them. Neverthe-less, the analogy to response processes has to be preserved if behaviorism is to deal with thinking. The Gestalt psychologist operates under an equally heavy handicap. He must treat thinking as the restructuring of a perceptual field. If this metaphor does not fit, the thought process will probably be dismissed as "unproductive" and unworthy of further study. Finally, as we have already seen, the psychoanalyst likens mental activity to the movement and dissipation of physical energies. This often puts him in the paradoxical position of being better able to explain not-thinking (repression) than thinking. None of the analogies does justice to thinking and remembering in themselves.

For a long time, most psychologists thought it was impossible to deal with cognition more directly. Introspection had been discredited; no one believed that direct descriptions of consciousness would provide a fruitful language for the study of thought. (Brain physiology offered hope of a more direct approach, but it was not sufficiently developed to be useful. Even today, we do not know the brain well enough to say much about the thought process in neural terms.) Thus, the few men who wrote about thinking or remembering as if they were real processes, to be taken seriously in their own right, were regarded by the rest of the profession with something rather like suspicion. Outstanding in this small group were Frederick Bartlett and Jean Piaget. Their work was of very great importance in preparing for the current revival of interest in cognition, and I will return to it a little later.

Recently, a new language has appeared in which cognitive processes can be described. This is the language of *information processing,* which was first developed to deal with problems in electronic communication, and has proven its value for the theory and technology of high-speed computers. It is based on the systematic exploitation of a rather simple principle: any description (or message) is itself a sequence of events. It can be considered in the context of the alternative events (statements, messages) that might otherwise have occurred, within the existing constraints. From this point of view, every statement is a choice, or a series of choices, among possibilities. These considerations lead first to a quantitive measure: the amount of information in an event can be roughly equated with the size of the range of alternatives from which it is drawn. More important for the study of cognition is that this language permits a precise description of the transformations and condensations which information can undergo. For example, the alternative events (messages) can be grouped, and a subsequent choice can be made to depend on the group to which a first message belongs. This amounts to abstracting from the message whatever property was the basis of the grouping. However elaborate the information processing may be, it can be fully specified without any reference to the "hardware" of the computer that carries it out. A single program can be run on many machines, physically very different from one another. The sequence or pattern of processes remains the same, and can be rewardingly studied in its own right. *It is thus possible to work with symbolic processes of great complexity in a relatively direct way,* without falling back on any of the classical metaphors. As psychologists have come to realize that information and its vicissitudes are the subject matter of a real and flourishing branch of science, the "higher mental processes" have been viewed in a new light. The earlier controversies about what thinking was really like (i.e., which analogy was best) have lost their force. A great deal of current research is centered around such informational concepts as "feedback," "processing hierarchy," and "strategy."

DEVELOPMENTAL SCHEMATA AND MEMORY

The availability of informational concepts is only one of the reasons for the renewed interest in cognition. A second source is the increasing influence of developmental psychology. The behaviorists and their opponents placed very little emphasis on the history and continuity of the organism. There was no stress on the cumulative growth of mental functions; mental activity was determined by the individual's past only in rather specific and isolated ways. This attitude was in sharp contrast with the explicit developmental approach stressed by Freud. Nevertheless, even psychoanalytic theory did not deal with *cognitive* development in much detail until recently. Thus, the study of mental growth remained outside the mainstream of theoretical psychology. It did not remain untouched, however. Jean Piaget, among others, has worked systematically in this area for decades. Especially relevant are *Play, Dreams, and Imitation in Childhood* (1951) and *The Origins of Intelligence in Children* (1952). I also wish to acknowledge a particularly clear exposition of Piaget's concepts in Flavell (1958).

The fundamental assumption on which any developmental approach rests is straightforward: thinking and remembering do not occur in the same way throughout life, but change as the child grows into a man. The changes are not only of content but also of method and style. For the most part, they result from the cumulative effect of the cognitive activity itself. That is, the very act of processing information causes change in the system which carries out the process. Piaget calls this change accommodation. Particularly clear examples, at the adult level, are to be found in the phenomena of perceptual learning. A piece of music that is heard for the fifth time does not sound as it did at first. Repeated experience has modified the listener; he has developed new modes of perception to cope with it. Naturally, these modes can be applied to other pieces of music in the same style. It is important to note that *both* the listener and the music he hears are altered. Accommodation is the change in him; its effect in reshaping the input is called *assimilation*.

These two reciprocal processes—assimilation of reality and accommodation to it—are stressed by Piaget as responsible for the growth of intelligence. As a baby grows into childhood, and the child to maturity, both his manner of thinking and its results undergo progressive development. The structures which are accommodated and which do the assimilating are called *schemata* by Piaget. As an example of a schema, consider the development of visual space perception. For the adult, the world always appears spatially extended, in the sense that it contains regions to which he might go or where objects might be put. To move an object is to change its position relative to him while leaving it otherwise unaltered. Some objects are nearer than others; if distant ones are obscured by things nearby they nevertheless continue to exist. Certain objects are reachable and graspable from where we sit; others will become so if we change our position. While these attributes of space appear trivial, the perceptual world of the young infant has almost none of them. Psychological space itself is a schema, a mental structure, which develops gradually. In this area, the accommodative process critically involves the child's own activities and movements. As fast as it is formed, any schema is used to assimilate new experiences, changing them to an extent that makes what come after quite incommensurable with what went before.

This does not imply that the newborn child has no schemata at all, or that he tastes reality "raw." The very structure of our sense organs is assimilative. (So is the structure of motility and response, but we cannot consider the parallel further here.) The input to the visual nervous system, for example, consists of the rapidly fluctuating activity of about 100 million receptor cells in the eye, each of which acts selectively as a result of the electromagnetic radiation that reaches it. This wealth of information is heavily condensed by processes that are ready to operate at birth. Even the youngest baby can make at least some "abstractions" about color, brightness, crude form, and rough bidimensional position. The other human sense modalities are also fundamentally assimilative; they transform reality before they make it available to the central nervous system. The subsequent accommodations (such as those by which perceptual space is developed) build on the mechanisms that are already there, integrating them into more elaborate, multi-level processing systems.

We have used spatial schemata as an example, but they are only one of the dimensions of cognitive growth. For the adult, every experience is assimilated along a great many dimensions. Cause and chance, meaning and nonsense, right and wrong, sick and well, long run and short run, easy and hard—every such mode of classification implies a highly complex process of experience and analysis, based on an enormous fund of past accommodation. What we acquire as we grow up is not merely knowledge, but habits of thought; not merely content, but process. We understand the world through, and with, the assimilative schemata.

The concept of schema is particularly interesting here because, almost thirty years ago, Sir Frederick Bartlett (1932) used it so effectively to describe certain phenomena of memory. He observed that precisely literal recall of past events almost never occurs. Whether the task is to copy a picture seen at an earlier time, to retell a story, or to describe a witnessed event, memory always reveals something of the rememberer himself. The structure of his response, its style and its pattern, reflect the schema through which the original event was assimilated. Particular parts of the original are distorted or omitted, and entirely novel elements often introduced. Bartlett's experiments showed how a myth from another culture underwent systematic change in the memories of his English experimental subjects. The original myth could not readily fit the cognitive schemata of subjects who had accommodated to a lifetime of other values and other styles of story telling.

It was Bartlett's thesis that memory consists in large measure of these schemata themselves. The past is not stored as a collection of static traces, but as an organized mass. Remembering is essentially reconstructive: what we recall depends on our ability to infer the histories of our present schemata. This constructive inference focuses on certain salient features preserved from the past, often represented by images. The direction and character of recall is based both on the specific information in the image or schema and on the "attitude" of the recalling person. To a considerable extent, the act of remembering occurs in order to justify or satisfy this attitude.

The schematic theory of memory can be significantly rephrased in Piaget's terms. Past events are retained as accommodative changes in the schema. To be preserved, an event must fit existing schemata closely enough to be assimilated, but diverge sufficiently to produce some accommodation. A later situation which is to elicit recall must itself be assimilated, through the schemata which are then operative. If these latter are not somehow congruent with the earlier ones, they will be unable to interpret or assimilate the memory that the earlier ones preserve. The result is "forgetting." In Bartlett's phrase, the recall of material from the past requires a "turning around on one's own schemata." Clearly, it must be the present schemata which turn.

Bartlett was keenly aware of the role that motives and interests played in determining what was remembered and forgotten. Only in areas of life which are culturally or personally important do schemata become articulate enough for detailed memory. His emphasis of this point brought him in contact with ethnology. A part of his book contrasts the memories of the Swazi people of South Africa with the memories of his English subjects. The Swazi could remember cattle transactions, which were important in their culture, with astonishing accuracy. A Swazi herdsman of no outstanding intellect could recall every detail of a sale that had taken place the previous year, involving a considerable number of animals. He knew the coloring of each beast, their ages, the persons from whom they had been purchased, the prices, and so on. At the same time, such a man would be pathetically inadequate in memory performances that would have been easy for Englishmen. Administrative magistrates were often frustrated by the apparent inability of the Swazi to recall specific events well enough to testify about them in court. Gregory Bateson reports similar observations among the Iatmul of New Guinea (1936). He was impressed by the great amount of rote material that the men of the Iatmul had at their fingertips in ceremonial debates. These examples show the degree to which social factors dictate the structure of cognitive schemata. By emphasizing some areas and types of cognition and ignoring others, the culture determines in large part what can and cannot be remembered.

This theory of memory is implicitly a developmental one, although Bartlett did not discuss the growth of schemata in any detail. He was primarily concerned with adult memory and its vicissitudes. On the other hand, Piaget's theory of intellectual development has clear implications for memory, which he has never made explicit. Both anticipate modern cognitive psychology, in that they concern themselves directly with information processing and make little use of the classical analogies. Information is taken in, reorganized, filtered, preserved, and perhaps distorted before it is used. The apparatus which accomplishes all this is modified as a result of its own activities, and therefore will handle subsequent input in a different way.

It remained for Ernest Schachtel (1947) to combine these two views in the context of psychoanalytic theory. In doing so, he succeeded in discarding the metaphor of forces and energies, of quasi-electrical attraction and repulsion, which made Freud's approach to cognition so cumbersome. He treats cognitive activity as existing in its own right. His work is far more than a simple sum of Bartlett and Piaget, however, for the psychoanalytic background with which he approaches the subject gives a new richness and depth to his interpretation. The problem to which he addressed himself is one that was first forcefully stated by Freud (1905): why can no one remember his early childhood?

CHILDHOOD AMNESIA

Freud saw childhood amnesia as the necessary outcome of the forces of repression. It serves to conceal the beginnings of our sexual lives. Once past Oedipal crisis, we cannot bear to think of the perverse and incestual passions which were once so strong. Any memory from infancy, no matter how innocuous the event itself might have been, would risk bringing the old and dangerous emotions to the surface again. Only painfully have we achieved an integration of personality in which these feelings play no apparent part; their rebirth might well destroy it. Therefore, a powerful counterforce keeps down all the thought, images, and affects which originated in early childhood. The repressed memories are not destroyed, but become unconscious. From their unconscious location, they exert a strong attraction on any new material that is related to them in any way. The result is the "Psychopathology of Everyday Life": motivated forgetting, slips of the tongue, and the like. The potentially dangerous ideas are both pulled from below (by the unconscious material) and pushed from above (by the censoring ego) until they slip safely out of sight.

This theory is plausible in many respects, and much of it rings true. Experience with psychotherapy does continuously confirm an intimate relation between what is forgotten and what is unacceptable to the patients. Moreover, it is not unusual for childhood memories to come to light in the course of therapy, as if a counterforce had genuinely been relieved. Nevertheless, despite these confirmations, Freud's theory of infantile amnesia has seemed less than adequate. It has almost no point of contact with any interpretation of ordinary adult remembering and forgetting; it relies on an unimpressive analogy with physical forces in opposition to one another; and it would seem to predict that a patient should readily recall his childhood years when his analysis was completed—a prediction which is never confirmed.

In his discussion of this problem, Schachtel begins by contrasting the experienced world of the child with that of the adult. In one sense, as we have seen, the child's world lacks something that the adult's possesses. Without the schemata with which the adult assimilates reality, he does not have the conviction of order and sensibleness which is one of the prizes of growing up. But just for this reason, what he perceives is far more exciting and engaging, far richer, than anything the adult will ever see. Schachtel poignantly describes the world that each of us has lost. "No Columbus, no Marco

Polo has ever seen stranger and more fascinating and thoroughly absorbing sights than the child that learns to perceive, to taste, to smell, to touch, to hear and see, and to use his body, his senses and his mind." It is not only in the realm of sensation and perception that the child lacks the schemata of the adult. He is equally unable to assimilate emotions—his own or others!—to any schema. Action and responsibility, values and mores, dependence and independence—all these are seen very differently after cognitive development than before. In all of these areas the child must accommodate to reality. The term "accommodation" has a double meaning here. In Piaget's sense, it refers to the necessary and healthy growth of mental schemata as a result of the need to assimilate what the child encounters. Schachtel stresses another interpretation. The society in which the child grows up demands that he be "accommodating" where its conventions are concerned. Relentlessly it enforces a conformity of categorization, of interpretation, and of communication. The acceptable adult must want what his fellows want, or something fairly close to it; he must see what they see, and believe in the importance of what is important to them. It is especially necessary that he speak as they speak, and as he yields to the pressure for linguistic conformity he becomes committed to that particular language's somewhat arbitrary analysis of reality.

Essentially, the experiences of childhood are incompatible with the schemata of the adult. It is no wonder, then, that the adult cannot recall them. The events, activities, and emotions of childhood were assimilated in a way that is no longer open. Years of sophisticating accommodation have made it as impossible to remember our own childhood as to fully understood anyone else's. The early years are like a forgotten dream. The simile of the dream is appropriate: our inability to remember dreams is based on the same factors. The coherent schemata of waking life have no room for their childlike illogic. It is worth noting the great individual differences in memory for dreams, as in memory for childhood experiences: not all persons are equally accommodating to society's demand.

This means that the universal amnesia for childhood is not primarily the result of anxiety or guilt, and is not based on an active process of suppression. It is, instead, a necessary consequence of the discontinuities in cognitive functioning which accompany growth into adulthood. From pre-verbal to verbal, from naive to sophisticated, from carefree to responsible, from weak to powerful—the cognitive accommodations which must accompany these transitions seem to make the past inaccessible. Schachtel finds the changes repugnant, preferring the spontaneity of the child to the stereotypy of the adult. For him, both the amnesia and its cause are a matter for deep regret. Over and over again he stresses the value of what is lost in the process of acculturation and accommodation, as if adulthood was an essentially impoverished condition. To me, his view appears one-sided. Childhood is not so simple, nor maturity so barren. Indeed, it is in the prematurely rigid schemata of early and middle childhood that the roots of adult neurosis are found. Psychotherapy does not aim at regressing the patient to the conceptual innocence of childhood, but at permitting him to grow beyond childhood. The healthy person is not the one who refuses to assimilate, but the one whose schemata are adequate to reality.

As the mental apparatus of a growing child develops, and the information handling processes become more intricate, thinking goes through a succession of stages. These are semi-stable states of accommodation, phases through which the cognitive mechanisms must evolve on the route to intellectual maturity. A child assimilates and "distorts" the world of his experience in ways characteristic of his age. As he grows up, constant necessity for accommodation results in cognitive change. This change can come about in three fundamentally different ways, which we must clarify.

The first mode of accommodation is *absorption*. Later forms of a cognitive schema may absorb earlier ones completely. This is what usually happens with repeated exposure to a piece of music. The inharmonious jumble that was experienced the first time simply ceases to exist. It cannot be perceived again and cannot be remembered. The new schema has swallowed up all the elements and interrelations of the old. Absorption is a common experience in hidden-picture puzzles. When we finally find the outline of the squirrel that the artist has cleverly concealed in the bark of the tree, we cannot lose it again; it is impossible to imagine how we could have failed to see it before. The same thing tends to happen in successful rote learning. One who knows a poem by heart usually does not recall the individual trials on which he practiced it. In a sense, he has an amnesia for them. Are they "forgotten?" Yes and no: they have a continuing effect (because they established the schema which now exists) but they cannot be individually recalled.

A second mode of accommodation might be called *displacement*. Part of the cognitive apparatus does not evolve, but continues to exist side by side with a new schema which assimilates the same environmental events in a different way. A trivial example of such dual mental functioning is the "double-take." The double-take occurs when you suddenly realize that something heard or seen a few moments ago actually had quite a different significance from that which you had, perhaps inattentively, ascribed to it. One assimilation process interpreted the event as unimportant. A second process, occurring simultaneously but unconsciously, interpreted it very differently; the double-take occurs when the second assimilation becomes conscious. More sustained instances of displacement are common among social scientists, who are able to react to a social situation either "personally" or "professionally." The behavioral results of these two ways of assimilating racial discrimination (for instance) can be poles apart.

Adequate consideration of the consequences of "displacement," in this sense, would go far beyond the intent of this paper. . . . It is possible to interpret the classical evidence for unconscious cognitive processes in these terms. Suppose that an adult has preserved the assimilative mechanisms of a four-year-old with respect to certain events; for example, situations involving sexuality. These schemata will be "unconscious" from the point of view of his organized adult awareness, but will continue to process information and control behavior. The results will be perceptual defense, forgetting of intentions, and perhaps other symptomatic phenomena. This interpretation is not far from that implied by the concept of "dissociation," but here the displacement is viewed as one possible outcome of a developmental process that will take *some* form in any case.

The third mode of accommodation is the *integrative* one. In many cases it is possible for a new schema to make use of an old one without destroying its integrity. Integration requires a step to another level of abstraction or understanding, in which outputs of the older modes of processing are only part of a more comprehensive whole. This hierarchical organization can be taken for granted in some aspects of perceptual development. We do not lose our ability to see figure and ground when we understand the three-dimensional permanence of figured objects. Moreover, their perceptual solidity is not impaired when we endow them with cultural or personal meaning. To be sure, wide individual differences exist here. Some persons see much more than others of the natural shapes and colors about them. The artist's world is filled with shapes and colors that go unnoticed by the less perceptive. He has somehow maintained—and developed!—the integrity of assimilative systems that are absorbed or displaced in the rest of us.

The foregoing analysis of the accommodative processes can be applied to the problem of childhood amnesia. Both absorption and displacement of earlier schemata must lead to "forgetting." Both types of change must almost inevitably occur as a baby becomes a child, and a child grows to adulthood. Indeed, even integration leads to a certain loss; a childish mode of functioning, somehow preserved in an adult structure, cannot be identical with its unintegrated form. However understanding a parent (or a teacher or a therapist) may be, he remains an adult. But this change of perspective is insignificant compared with the total amnesia for infancy which we all share, and which I attribute to absorption and displacement. What circumstances lead to one mode of accommodation rather than another? An adequate answer can hardly be given. It is very likely, however, that the manner in which different developmental stages are handled by environment and culture are particularly important. Displacement will tend to occur where cultural factors emphasize the discontinuity and incompatibility between different phases of development, while integration must be easier where several stages of assimilation are welcomed and used together in a consistent way. Thus we must expect a close relationship between the continuity or discontinuity of developmental patterns on the one hand, and the continuity of memory on the other.

UNIVERSAL AND CULTURAL DISCONTINUITIES

The degree to which culture controls the manner and amount of cognitive change must vary greatly. We will first consider a change for which complete integration is probably impossible in any culture. The shift from preverbal to linguistic functioning probably implies some irreversible absorption of primitive schemata. The child must accommodate and develop a large proportion of his information-processing capacity until it can deal with the spoken word. When he has done so, all of his cognitive activity will be affected. It will have become more precise, more communicable, more sequential, more articulate. Its exact form will depend on the particular language he learns, but the effects of linguistic differences are far less important than the overwhelming consequences of having a language at all. And while the rewards of language are great, there is a price. Having learned speech, the child can no longer assimilate new—or old—situations as he once did, and will forget his infancy.

It does not seem likely that the vague awareness of the first year of life can ever be fully integrated into a cognitive structure heavily influenced by language. It would follow that we cannot look forward to finding a society whose members articulately describe the first months of their lives. Of course, it is possible that a few aspects of the earliest cognitive activity can be integrated with later behavior, so that some fleeting memory is preserved. Even where this does not occur, and the early months are forgotten, we cannot say that they have no effect. On the contrary, it is just during this period that the basic accommodations are made which will dominate later life.

Although the use of language is the most obvious universal difference between the cognition of the very young child and of the adult, there are others. One that may be worth mentioning here is the change in the number of independent sources of action of which we are aware. The newborn's amorphous universe gradually crystallizes into himself and mother, or perhaps into himself and two or three outside persons. As he grows, it must come to include many more. To the extent that this growth does not take place, to the extent that an adult continues to assimilate reality with a schema that only has room for one or two actual persons, he will be mentally ill. We can expect to find illnesses centering around this cognitive failure in every culture, because none can avoid making this demand on each individual. The normal adult has to assimilate the fact that there are other people besides himself. To do so successfully must almost certainly require some cognitive absorption of the early "primary process" mechanisms, and perhaps some displacement as well.

These fundamental accommodations are well under way in the first year or two of life. The changes in language and person-perception that occur thereafter are surely relatively continuous with whatever already exists. We would not necessarily expect them to cause amnesia for more than this period. Yet, in our culture, the amnesia of childhood covers a much longer period for most persons. Individuals can be found who claim to have coherent memory back to the second year, but they are rare. The earliest systematic recollections usually seem to start at five or six, and often are postponed still later. It is possible, of course, that some innate restriction of cognitive development is operating here. Another possibility, however, is that the later amnesia results from cognitive displacements, produced by the patterns which the culture prescribes for the development of its children. Let us consider two very different examples: the distinction between higher and lower senses, and between work and play. The first of these is emphasized by Schachtel. Smell and taste, the "lower," more "animal" senses, are tabooed by Western civilization. Both are intimately linked to pleasures of the body to which our culture gives as little recognition as possible; neither provides discriminative information which our culture finds important. We find strong bodily odors disgusting, and we do not expect to identify people by their smell. As a result, we do not develop schemata which might enable us to assimilate or recall olfactory information. As adults, we pay little attention to smell. Even innate assimilative mechanisms seem to go unused, remaining unintegrated with the rest of our cognitive activity. But is this a necessary loss? Can there be cultural patterns within which smells and tastes are more explicitly schematized? The answer is probably yes. Even the rather minor differences between France and America may be significant in this respect. France is famed both for her cuisine and her perfume. To the extent that the culture emphasizes these experiences, we would expect the average Frenchman to have better discrimination of and better memory for tastes and smells than we do.

The cultural determination of such differences as that between work and play has been eloquently stated by Ruth Benedict, in her classical paper on cultural discontinuity (1938). "We think of the child as wanting to play and the adult as having to work, but in many societies the mother takes the baby daily in her shawl or carrying net to the garden or to gather roots, and adult labor is seen even in infancy from the pleasant security of its position in close contact with its mother. When the child can run about, it accompanies its parents, still doing tasks which are essential and yet suited to its powers: and its dichotomy between work and play is not different from that its parents recognize, namely, the distinction between the busy day and the free evening . . . the child is from infancy continuously conditioned to responsible social participation, while at the same time the tasks that are expected of it are adapted to its capacity. The contrast with our society is very great." When we become men, we are admonished to put away childish things—and with them, childish pleasures, attitudes, and thoughts. It is little wonder that we put away childish memories in the bargain. In terms of the hypotheses we are considering here, we would expect more continuous societies to suffer less from infantile amnesia than we do.

Many other aspects of cognitive development may well be culturally determined. Benedict herself suggested the submission-dominance dimension, among several others. We expect the child to obey, and the adult to command. Not all people make either demand. Another interesting possibility is that Piaget's observations of the development of morality, causality, and certain kinds of logical thinking may themselves be culture-bound. . . . Wherever important differences between the customary assimilations of adults and of children are the rule, we can expect relatively less recall of childhood experience. Wherever the culture makes the transition relatively continuous, and particularly where the cognitive accommodations of adulthood are consistently based on those of the child, childhood memories should be more available.

Cultural differences have another implication for Schachtel's hypothesis. Not only the thoroughness of the amnesia, but also the period that it covers should vary with the developmental pattern in the society. In America, real childishness has to end by about the seventh year of life. Older children may play, but they know what work is; they are not adults, but adult roles are clear to them; they may cry, but they know they shouldn't. Most of their play is already an imitation of adult activity, a preliminary attempt to master the roles that they know to lie ahead. Not all societies draw the line at the same age. In *Growing Up in New Guinea* (1930), Margaret Mead emphasized the discontinuity of the transition to adulthood among the Manus. In that culture, children remained extraordinarily unconcerned with the world of grown-ups until they reached ten or twelve. Till then they ran free, played all day, took little notice of adult beliefs and less of adult activity. The adults, for their part, were much too wrapped up in the business of trade and property to care what the children did. Her description is vivid. "Where the adults were a driven, angry, rivalrous, acquisitive lot of people who valued property and trade above any form of human happiness except the maintenance of life itself, the children were the gayest, most lively and curious, generous and friendly, that I had ever known." In these circumstances, coming of age involved drastic reorientation of the child's entire way of life. It would seem, then, that infantile amnesia among the Manus of that period should have been both deeper and longer than among ourselves. Not only would we expect an adult to recall very little of his early childhood, but to be relatively amnestic for what we call the latency period as well. The Manus no longer live as they did, so the hypothesis cannot be verified for them. Perhaps it can still be tested somewhere else in the world-wide laboratory of anthropology.

To the extent that the discontinuities of development are culture-bound, they can conceivably be reduced. It is not necessary that children regard adulthood as an age when they must renounce all that gives them pleasure, nor need adults think of childishness with shame or condescension. Surely, where such a choice exists, integration is preferable to discontinuity. Why does our own society so systematically choose the latter? A part of the answer lies in the very amnesia which the discontinuity produces. Parents do not know what they do to their children, because they cannot understand them adequately. What one generation has already lost, it does not hesitate to make its children lose also. Thus, paradoxically, childhood amnesia exerts a stabilizing influence on practices of child-rearing. These practices are not seen from the child's point of view by the controlling adult; that point of view is usually inaccessible to him. In technical terms, parents and society receive inadequate feedback. As a result, children are brought up primarily to suit cognitive and emotional habits of adults. When a Negro is denied the right to eat at the same counter with white persons, we stand with him in his protest, because we understand his feelings. His dignity is enough like ours that we can act together in a mutual purpose. When a child is denied the right to eat with his parents, our attitude cannot be so clear. We do not remember what such situations were like for us, so we do not know what they are like for him. No matter which side of such a question we choose, it will be a partially blind, partially mal-adaptive choice. So we do whatever is convenient and culturally prescribed. Perhaps we send him away, and in so doing help to perpetrate the discontinuity and the amnesia on another generation.

CULTURE CHANGE AND COGNITIVE DISCONTINUITY

Once a child has grown into the adult, nothing can ever change the system with which he assimilates information so radically again. His memory should be correspondingly continuous as far back as his schemata can reach, except in pathological cases. Yet, on the assumptions we have been making, *any* accommodative change in a supraordinate schema must result in some forgetting, unless it thoroughly integrates the older schemata. The greater the change, the more loss is to be expected. Minor amnesias of this kind occur very frequently. Nearly everyone has been unable to remember last night's joke on the morning after, or has forgotten to call his wife from the office. These losses are not permanent, because the schemata in question are only temporarily inaccessible. More striking amnesias are often observed when a linguistic change has altered the cognitive apparatus. Thus it is frequently observed that travelers forget all their French during visits to Germany, and all their German when they are in France. This is especially likely if they do not know either language very well in the first place.

When a drastic cognitive reorganization occurs to many people at once, it must stem from and result in other modifications in their way of life; that is, it will be part of a culture change. Putting it the other way, we can safely assume that any substantial change in culture will require accommodative cognitive change in its participants. The question is timely, for cultural changes on a broad scale are occurring all over the world. The established mores of hundreds of different societies are breaking down in the rush toward the Western twentieth century. Entire societies are trying to trade in their used ideas for new models. To some extent they will succeed in their efforts, and the old order will yield its place to the new, although such changes rarely can occur without psychological and sociological dislocation. Every cultural transformation, whether it is viable or not, will be accompanied by changes of schema, of mode of thought, that must have consequences for memory.

One practical conclusion for ethnologists is that the memories of informants for the period before a culture change will tend to be unreliable. The more acculturated an informant is, the greater the risk of misinformation. And naturally, there is a temptation to use just such persons as informants, because it is particularly easy for the ethnologist to communicate with them. It may be important to keep the mnemonic dangers of such a selection in mind. The man who gets along best with you is probably not getting along as well with his own past in the older culture.

More important theoretically is that the culture as a whole will be partially cut off from its history by the process of culture change. It will suffer from a displacement amnesia which may be very substantial, even if it cannot rival childhood amnesia for thoroughness. Old ideas, old customs, old events, old moods will be forgotten, or more likely will be subtly altered to suit the present needs of the group. What can be recalled may have some of the characteristics of screen memories: the importance of the event is actually judged by present standards, not by past ones. We would expect to find a condition very much like the classical picture of repression, in the culture as a whole as well as in single persons. Mistakes and misperceptions will occur, based on the old ways of thought; neurotic symptoms will appear, generated by a conflict which is superficially denied any present importance. Potentially useful problem solutions will not emerge, or will be rejected, if they belong in the old context rather than the new. Much that could be of great value will be lost, particularly if the culture change has come suddenly and discontinuously rather than gradually and coherently.

The antidote to amnesia is integration. If the inevitable cognitive change can be an incorporation of preceding schemata, rather than a rejection of them, then much can be preserved. Such an antidote is easier to prescribe than to administer, either between child and adult or between old culture and new. Let us at least strive to keep it before us as an explicit goal, both in education and in acculturation: that the past shall not altogether die, but shall continue to live in our understanding of the present.

PART VI Ecology

36

CULTURE AND ENVIRONMENT:
THE STUDY OF CULTURAL ECOLOGY

MARSHALL D. SAHLINS

"THE sterility of the soil in Attica," wrote Montesquieu, "established a popular government there, and the fertility of Lacedaemon an aristocratic one." We are not convinced. Yet the statement is characteristic of a main intellectual legacy in the ecological study of culture, environmental determinism, that ancient idea of "a mechanical action of natural forces upon a purely receptive humanity." From more recent forebears, notably including American field anthropologists of this century, we are heir to an opposed position, environmental possibilism, which holds that cultures act selectively, if not capriciously, upon their environments, exploiting some possibilities while ignoring others; that it is environment that is passive, an inert configuration of possibilities and limits to development, the deciding forces of which lie in culture itself and in the history of culture.

Another outlook appears. At first it was only as an offhand remark, a critical argument. Now it informs some of the best work in American archaeology and ethnology: It is an idea of reciprocity, of a dialogue between cultures and their environments. The truism that cultures are *ways of life*, taken in a new light, is the ground premise—cultures are human *adaptations*. Culture, as a design for society's continuity, stipulates its environment. By its mode of production, by the material requirements of its social structure, in its standardized perceptions, a culture assigns relevance to particular external conditions. Even its historic movement is movement along the ecologic seam it is organized to exploit. Yet a culture is shaped by these, its own, commitments: it molds itself to significant external conditions to maximize the life chances. There is an interchange between culture and environment, perhaps continuous dialectic interchange, if in adapting the culture transforms its

landscape and so must respond anew to changes that it had set in motion. I think the best anwer to the . . . controversy over which is the determinant, culture or environment, should be this: both—the answer lies at both extremes.

The significance of given environmental features, as well as their weight upon a culture, is contingent on that culture. Here is a politically developed Asiatic Society relying upon intensive double-crop agriculture. Subjected to a shortening of summer seasons by five days, it may be under critical selection. A certain isotherm becomes a threshold beyond which the system as constituted cannot be maintained. Yet the same climatic shift means little or nothing to a fishing tribe; its niche is governed by the conditions that directly concern the fishing. Similarly, coal is a relevant resource of an industrial technology, and its distribution in the ground affects the design, the external relations, even the historic fate of an industrial nation. But to a hunting-and-gathering people, to Australian aborigines, say, coal is completely irrelevant: in the ground or no, it is not part of their environment; it has no selective impact on them, unless

AUSTRALIAN ABORIGINES HIT IT RICH
Special to the *Detroit News*

Canberra, April 17 [1963]—One of the world's most primitive people—scientists say they are just passing through their stone age—will get a multimillion dollar rake-off from a big Australian mine project.

They are the aborigines on the Arnhemland Peninsula of northern Australia. They are sitting [squatting?] on one of the biggest bauxite lodes, the ore of aluminum, ever found in the country.

Because the effects of natural circumstances are thus conditional, one cannot read, with geographical determinists, from the configuration of an environment to *a* configuration of culture. On the other hand, the equally simple-minded textbook rebuttal to the effect that different cultures may emerge in similar environments—standard example: Manhattan Island 1962 *vs.*

Manhattan Island 1492—does not dispose of environmental influence. The environment-culture relation need not be one-to-one, but environment is never, thereby, a powerless term. Natural resources, when relevant to prevailing production, govern dispositions of technologies and populations; a line of rainfall, no matter that the precise line is determined from within, is, as such, a cultural boundary; topographical features are so many barriers to or routes of communication, sites for settlement, or strategic positions of defense.

The circumstances with which most peoples have to deal, moreover, are of two distinct kinds: relations are developed with two environments. Societies are typically set in fields of *cultural influence* as well as fields of *natural influence*. They are subjected to both. They adapt to both. Indeed, terms of the relation to nature may be set by intercultural relations —as when avenues of trade govern avenues of production—and terms of intercultural relations may be set by relations to nature—as when avenues of production govern avenues of trade. It is all so obvious. But until recently the discipline of cultural ecology has operated myopically as if it were biological ecology, without reference to intercultural adaptation. We have, mistakenly in my view, limited the notion of environment and the concern for selection to the geography and biology of a milieu. Research into relations between cultures has been carried on as a thing apart, mostly under the traditional head of "acculturation," and thus not so much from the perspective of adaptation as from that of assimilation. A widespread recognition that cultures act as selective forces upon one another, and with it the realization that culture contact creates complementarity, not merely similarity in structure, seems imminent. Cultural ecology has an untapped potential to provoke useful thoughts about militarism, nationalism, the orientation of production, trade, and many other specialized developments which, if they are not "acculturation" in the conventional sense, still come out of the interaction of cultures.

The dual quality of "environment" is sometimes brought home by actions of nature and of outside cultures from different directions, setting off change in different sectors of an affected culture. Just for this point, let me use the "architectural" or "layer-cake" model of a culture-system that has been popularized in evolu-tionist writings. The model holds that economic and material elements—"mode of production" or, in another view, "technology"—are basic, the decisive foundation of the cultural order, and that polity and ideology are "superstructure," resting upon and systematically reflecting material foundations. Now ordinarily the imprint of nature may be traced upwards through the cultural order—but external cultural influences may very well impress themselves from the top down. Natural circumstances directly affect technical deployment, productivity, the cycle of employments, settlement patterns, and so forth; from these points the systematic relations of base to superstructure relay impulses to the higher, political and ideological spheres. The material base adapts to nature and the superstructure to the material base. Grant that —even though it is mechanical and oversimplified. A culture, on the other hand, may come to terms with its social milieu in the first place by ideological and political adjustments—the outside cultural pressure itself is often ideological and political in the main and at first. Such has been the classic course of adaptation in primitive and underdeveloped societies opened to Western dominance. The initial revisions appear in ideology, as in conversion to Christianity, and in social-political sectors, by virtue of incorporation in a colonial realm, with radical economic change setting in derivatively or afterwards. Hence the characteristic crisis of the postcolonial period, the "inverse cultural lag" compounded of advanced political norms harnessed to an underdeveloped economy.

For decades, centuries now, intellectual battle has been given over which sector of culture is the decisive one for change. Many have entered the lists under banners diverse. Curiously, few seem to fall. Leslie White champions technological growth as the sector most responsible for cultural evolution; Julian Huxley, with many others, sees "man's view of destiny" as the deciding force; the mode of production and the class struggle are still very much in contention. Different as they are, these positions agree in one respect, that the impulse to development is generated from within. The system by one means or another is self-sustaining, self-developing. The case for internal causes of development may be bolstered by pointing to a mechanism, such as the Hegelian dialectic, or it may rest more insecurely on an argument from logic, which is usually coupled with indifference to the source of change in the presumed critical sector. In any event, an unreal and vulnerable assumption is always there, that cultures are closed systems. Cultures are abstracted from their influential contexts, detached from fields of forces in which they are embedded. It is precisely on this point that cultural ecology offers a new perspective, a counterpoise to conventional evolutionary arguments. For it shifts attention to the relation between inside and outside; it envisions as the mainspring of the evolutionary movement the interchange between culture and environment. Now which view shall prevail is not to be decided on a sheet of paper; the test as always is long-term utility. But if adaptation wins over inner dynamism, it will be for certain intrinsic and obvious strengths. Adaptation is real, naturalistic, anchored to those historic contexts of cultures that inner dynamism ignores. Perhaps it even helps explain why no agreement has ever been had on which aspect of culture takes the lead in development. The various inner dynamisms, though contradictory, have each and all been supportable because, in fact, different sectors, from the mode of production to the view of destiny, at different times are decisive—depending on the point of impact of the selective field.

The trial of the ecological perspective must, and will, be in the empirical arena. The decision rests on its success in handling the facts of this case and that, and indeed an impressive list of accomplishments, headed by the researches of Julian Steward, can already be proclaimed. And it begins to be possible to reflect upon the empirical encounter, to generalize, tentatively, about the adaptive behavior of cultures. The remainder of my remarks are in this vein.

Adaptation implies maximizing the social life chances. But maximization is almost always a compromise, a vector of the internal structure of culture and the external pressure of environment. Every culture carries the penalty of a past within the frame of which, barring total disorganization, it must work out its future. Things get functionally arranged. The present American industrial system runs on an agrarian seasonal cycle. The American educational process, legislative process, a whole host of critical activities virtually cease in summer, as if there was pressing work to be done, the harvest to be taken in. And now that in fact 90 per cent

of the population has no such obligation, the summer becomes a holiday, and industrial output is accordingly adjusted to demands of a travel and sportsminded market.

There is more to this adaptive compromise than mere contradiction between received cultural order and new conditions of existence. We see different selective pressures working at cross purposes, evoking insoluble contradictions within a culture itself. We see too that adaptive responses can have disadvantageous side effects, as the modification of one constellation of custom sets off untoward consequences elsewhere in the system. To adapt then is not to do perfectly from some objective standpoint, or even necessarily to improve performance: it is to do as well as possible under the circumstances, which may not turn out very well at all. In one of the tropical islands of Fiji, if I may draw upon personal observations, there is a great demand at present for houses of timber with galvanized iron roofs, houses that Fijians are pleased to call "European," an allegation that curiously outvalues the fact that these dwellings retain the heat and are otherwise unsuited to the native climate and mode of life. At the same time, the number of punts—the most feasible type of boat for Fijians at present and also, one might note, "European"—declines steadily in this island, which means the decline of a rare opportunity for getting some needed protein through fishing. The rise in tin-roof demand is directly related to the decline in boats: the materials for both must be purchased and carpenters rewarded, so it is a question of allocation of scarce finances. Yet, at an obvious cost in personal comfort, and possibly in health too, this peculiar pattern of desires does neutralize an adaptive dilemma. On one side, the native kinship organization with its strong ethics of mutual aid has been very much kept going in Fiji. It is still effective—no, necessary—in the subsistence sector of their lives. On the other side, the usual tendencies of individual acquisitiveness have been touched off by their involvement in copra production and world trade. Now, while the traditional norm of share-alike keeps people alive, it also weakens the producer's hand in movable things that he has purchased. Boats may just be taken outright by kinsmen in need, or, being scarce, they are frequently borrowed, and the owners saddled with maintenance costs. A tin-roof house becomes desirable, and I suspect is singularly identified with the dominant European (i.e., British) order, because it is, in the cultural nature of things, inalienable—one can neither take it home nor decently throw a relative out of his own house. So the Fijian produces copra, continues to have many relatives, fishes less than he needs to, and swelters. An adaptive perspective, goes the moral, must not presume that whatever is there is good, rational, useful or advantageous. Lots of things people do are truly stupid, if understandable, and many cultures have gone to the wall.

In fact a culture's downfall is the most probable outcome of its successes. The accomplished, well adapted culture is biased. Its design has been refined in a special direction, its environment narrowly specified, how it shall operate definitively stated. The more adapted a culture, the less therefore it is adaptable. Its specialization subtracts from its potential, from the capacity of alternate response, from tolerance of change in the world. It becomes vulnerable in proportion to its accomplishments. Alterations of the milieu are less than likely to be opportunities, more than likely disturbances. By its commitment to an external *status quo* it assigns the negative (negative selection) to environmental change.

Unfortunately, all this is probably convincing in the same measure as it is abstract. How shall we describe in detail the meaning of a cultural specialization, state precisely the mechanisms of its self-defense, assess accurately its adaptive potential? We are in thrall at the moment to organic notions of culture, like the evolutionist "layer cake" model I used before. A beginning on the critical questions can be made by capitalizing that central idea of the organic outlook: "functional interdependence." It should be possible, for example, to uncover chains of interdependent customs that terminate in components directly joined with the environment: an ancestral cult that sanctifies the patrilineal principle, small scale lineages acting as social proprietors, permanent but limited neolithic agriculture— that kind of thing. Professor Wolf remarks ... that properties of the elements within such circuits set restrictions on what may be coupled in, and prevailing relations between elements will bear just so much modification in any one of them. Yet what seems truly striking about a mature culture is not so much the organic logic of it as the idiocies of its functional connections, the irrelevancies of its structure. Things

bear upon one another that, in the nature of these things, need not do so.

I am saying that there are two kinds of functional couplings in culture, logical and idiosyncratic, and that specialized cultures may be distinguished by an overburden of the latter. The coexistence of a centralized Asiatic bureaucracy and intensive irrigation agriculture is, for an example, logically consistent, in the nature of imperatives. Bureaucracy and irrigation perform necessary services for each other. Each fits within the complementary requirements of the other. But what are we to make of this fact, so painfully familiar in American television: that the style of drama is constrained by the requirements of selling soap or underarm deodorants? The constraint, incidentally is no less compelling for its idiocy, but it is clearly of a different order than functional relations of the irrigation-bureaucracy sort. Irrelevancy is the penalty of a particular past, the structural anomaly of a specialized culture. It is only understandable, and only tolerable, in the context of its own history and the circumstances that have made history. Outside of that context, any mature culture is a monstrosity.

In the past, before World War II, American anthropologists worked from a different model of culture. It was a model of "mechanical solidarity" rather than "organic solidarity," the idea that customs of a society are more importantly alike than they are complementary. Ruth Benedict, in *Patterns of Culture,* unfolded the idea; since then many intellectual descendants and cousins of it have appeared—cultural style, cultural ethos, cultural configuration, and others. "Culture pattern" means design and Gestalt, but more, it means a common alignment of the diverse pieces of culture. It has to do with the singular and pervasive genius of a people. So among the militarist tribes of the American Plains the Dionysian element appears again and again in many different areas of culture: in their vision quests and guardian spirit beliefs, in super-machismo definition of the male role and a corollary acceptance of transvestism among those who could not live up to it, in military qualifications of leadership, suicidal pledges of revenge, in Spartan childhood training. We are confronting a cultural orientation, and although Benedict saw it artistically as a people's selection from the great arc of human-temperamental possibilities, in the harder view it looks to be selection of a different kind. The internal orientation of Plains culture was cast from the forge of ecological selection: the Dionysian pattern was hammered out in intertribal battle over access to trade posts and trade goods, horses and hunting grounds. I think that the Benedictian models ought to be revived, to be reconsidered in the light of new interests. We know already, as Benedict had observed, that an integrated pattern cuts down the capacity for change—in current usage, the adaptive potential. Innovations are either given the prevailing polarity or, if they do not lend themselves to it, are rejected.

However cultural specialization be ultimately perceived, in configurational, organic, or some other terms, many of the little devices that insulate peoples against cultural alternatives are already apparent. Among them are negatively charged ideas about conditions and customs in neighboring societies. These are well known under the head "ethnocentrism," but they have been more despised as unenlightened attitudes than they have been studied as ideological defenses. For they are "ideology" in the strict sociological sense of beliefs that prevent people from knowing what is going on in the world. One species of ethnocentric idea is specially important for this discussion, the peculiar notions that societies put out about the environments of their neighbors. The species could be called "great wall ideology," for like the Chinese wall these beliefs divide the terrain in which the received way of life is effective from the terrain in which it cannot survive, and by fantastic allegations of an outer darkness they keep people within the wall, and so committed to the traditional order. Consider, for example, the warnings solicitously tendered by Pathans of Swat State (Pakistan) to an anthropologist who was contemplating a visit to the neighboring Kohistani people: "Full of terrible mountains," they said of Kohistani territory, "covered by many-colored snow and emitting poisonous gases causing head and stomach pains when you cross the high passes, inhabited by robbers and snakes that coil up and leap ten feet into the air; with no villages, only scattered houses on the mountain tops." The noteworthy difference the anthropologist discovered between Kohistani and Pathan territories was seasonal temperatures somewhat lower in the former, a small enough matter in itself but sufficient to keep Pathan political economy from operating effectively beyond its proper border.

Adapted and specialized, mature cultures are conservative, their reactions to the world defensive. They accommodate new environmental conditions to their structures more than their structures to new conditions, absorbing fluctuations of their milieus within the prevailing order of things, so that the more they change the more they remain the same. They compensate rather than revise. And new relations to the world suggested from within remain still-born. These are manifest tendencies of primitive and modern societies alike, dramatically manifest in successful attempts to preserve the old social regime by letting slip new economic opportunities. It is organizational sabotage. It is the essence of Kwakiutl potlatch extravagances during the fur trade, as it is also of the planned obsolescence that saves industries by wasting their productive capabilities. It is the "creeping socialism" that prevents large sectors of private enterprise from falling to pieces. Anthropologists record the herculean technical efforts of the Yakut, an Inner Asian pastoral people pushed into the Siberian forest, to keep horse nomadism alive out of its element rather than switch over to a more functional economy—the Yakut went so far as to develop irrigation, but mostly to grow more winter fodder. From New Guinea comes word of an inland people moved to the coast under missionary aegis who, for forty years, have refused to learn to fish, swim, or handle canoes.

In the final defensive phases of its history, a specialized culture may reach yet greater heights of dysfunction. As normal technical and political competences fail, supernatural reserves are engaged. This foxhole propensity of man and culture we have known for some time, at least since Malinowski's famous observation that the involvement of ritual in Trobriand island fishing increases with the hazards of the enterprise —just as in America religious ikons have been enshrined on the dashboards of automobiles since the advent of overpowered engines and overcrowded highways. The same escapism comes over cultures as wholes when faced by pressures beyond practical control: preservation becomes a supernatural business and what is threatened becomes holy. Just so with some famous millennial movements, such as the American Indian Ghost Dances of the later eighteen hundred's that looked to a magical restoration of the buffalo, the land, dead customs, and dead Indians. (Perhaps modern, overdeveloped nations are showing symptoms of defensive sanctification. Social critics in America, especially the daily syndicated viewers-with-alarum, despair that our healthy respect for the past is sometimes translated into reverent superstition, our historic legacy into the tyranny of an ancestral cult. However that may be, it has been deemed advisable to insert "this nation *under God*" into the pledge of allegiance to the flag, and a fine contrast this makes to the old saw about pioneer days: "Well parson, maybe I did hew this fine farm out of the wilderness with God's help—but you should have seen it when He had it alone!" God help those who cannot help themselves!)

Yet when the question is posed: if highly specialized peoples are conservative, where do the breakthroughs occur? Our theory seems to predict that evolution should grind to a halt, which it certainly does not do. Speculation turns to the idea of "generalized cultures," those with good adaptive possibilities. We find them sometimes on frontiers, among pioneering fringes that of necessity have simplified a heritage of little use at the present juncture. Or, from the analogy of genetic drift in species, we find them among peoples suddenly reduced to small remnants by large catastrophes, a condition that might favor the rapid spread of innovations. Yet these circumstances are too rare, on the whole too insignificant, to bear the grand movement of evoltuionary variation.

We know—we take it as premise sometimes —that competition has a salutary effect on development. Even the seeming tragedy of conquest and defeat may have its phoenix aftermath. Perhaps there is room in ecological theory for some such concept as the "Hamburg effect," referring to the remarkable service performed for German industry by Allied bombers in the last war whose obliteration of entrenched handicraft business in that city finally put production on an all-out military line. The conflict created by expanding, dominant cultures seems specially critical for the creation of evolutionary potential. Throughout history, advanced cultures have displayed a special gift for generating further advance, but not so much in their developed centers as on their ethnic borders.

For the advanced societies, in displacing backward peoples or harnessing them to their own progress, become agents of a disruption that frees the backward region from the dead hand of its own past. "To make scrambled eggs, one must first crack the eggs." But hinterlands are not merely disorganized by dominant cultures, they become committed to main streams of progress as tributaries of it. Thus they are first, involved in development, and second, set politically against its historic agent. They could become, therefore, revolutionary cultures, prepared at the same time to overthrow the old order and overtop the one presently on their backs. Look closely at the so-called nativistic movements along the Melanesian and African peripheries of modern civilization: ostensibly symptoms of cultural bankruptcy, on examination they reveal themselves as capitalizations of advance. Although at certain early phases a Melanesian cargo cult has its inclinations toward a native restoration, in its jealousy of "way belong white man" and its goal of "coming inside" it turns irreversibly from tradition, and its rebellious organization of heretofore autonomous communities is, in the understanding of the most acute observers, the germ of nationalism.

In other words, advanced and dominant cultures create the circumstances for their own eclipse. On one hand, they themselves become specialized. Their development on a particular line commits them to it: they are mortgaged to structures accumulated along the way, burdened, in Veblen's phrase, with the penalty of taking the lead. On the other hand, they restore adaptability to previously stable and backward peoples within their spheres of influence. These underdeveloped orders, rudely jolted from historyless equilibrium, may now seize "the privilege of historic backwardness" and overturn their submission by taking over the latest developments of advanced cultures and pushing on from there. How many great civilizations have lived with, and finally died from, the menace of border barbarians? Of course, as is made obvious today by the struggles of new nations, it is not easy for the "barbarians," if only because progress in the hinterlands is rarely to the interest of dominant civilizations. Yet no matter how often underdeveloped peoples fail to gain evolutionary momentum, history shows that progress is not so much nourished in the strategic heights as in the fertile valleys of the cultural terrain.

Cultural progress then is an outcome of adaptation and selection. Progress, moreover, is itself adaptive, or at least the complex cultures have the greatest "all round adaptability" in Julian Huxley's words. So progress will be selected for from time to time.

Advanced cultures are distinguished by superior means of coping with the world. The improvements in productive technology that have occurred through prehistory and history, especially the several revolutions from the development of agriculture to the development of nuclear power, are the best known, but they are not alone. There have been very important improvements in the technology of mobilization, that is, in means for delivery of power, goods, persons, and messages. These particularly give advantage in intercultural relations, making it increasingly possible to base an advance on the exploitation of surrounding societies through trade, conquest, or colonial rule. The existence of one set of cultures, especially rich ones effectively exploiting their several environments, creates a niche as it were for the cultural predator that can adapt itself to the adaptations of others. (Perhaps overly impressed with the consequences of the Western Industrial Revolution, anthropologists have been wont to locate the basis of progress in breakthroughs of production, forgetting that the development of Rome, of Greece, and many other civilizations had no such ground.) Finally, there have occurred improvements in still another realm, that of protective technology: the advances in shelter, clothing, or medical techniques, for instance, that defend society against natural hazards; and those in armament that subdue cultural hazards.

It is often said that highly developed cultures are comparatively free from environmental control. But environmental influences are not really put in abeyance by cultural advance. It is rather that advance cannot be put in abeyance by environmental features. The performance of the highest cultures is least constrained by natural conditions. In a way, culture acts to repeal for humans the famous biological law of the minimum. In recent millennia especially, progressive cultures have shown great capacity to wheel and deal in the face of local natural deficiencies. On top of Mt. Everest, Westerners have lived despite the natural lack of oxygen; they have maintained themselves in outer space despite the absence of gravity. What has happened in the long habitable regions of this earth, however, is more important—for the moment. The advanced peoples have sustained imperialist probes of various kinds far beyond their traditional home base, if necessary by provisioning these outposts by the exploitation of the home base. And they maintain high levels of order and complexity at the home base by drawing in resources over long distances. The advanced cultural type is not as confined as the less advanced. It is distributed over greater ranges of rainfall, topography, soil type, whatnot, and it is engaged too with a greater external cultural diversity. A higher culture has more environment than a lower one.

Thus the rise in the first place of dominant cultures. Deploying power and personnel in a variety of zones, advanced cultures often compete successfully with the indigenous occupants of these zones for resources that have become indispensable to the developed peoples. The higher orders typically displace less developed ones in regions similar to, and available to, centers of progress. Societies more distant, and those exploiting other natural settings, are harnessed to the centers of development and thereby are partly acculturated. This closes a circle: we had seen that dominance can initiate progress; we see now that progress sets off dominance. I suggest that the Hegelian interplay of these main adaptive processes provides the momentum by which culture continuously transcends itself.

Anthropology was conceived in the first place out of the dominance power of high civilization. In those "new worlds given to the world" by the European expansion were peoples and customs that could not fail to provoke an anthropological curiosity. One hopes that anthropology and its sister human sciences will keep pace now with the accumulating consequences of dominance. To do so, the development of the ecological perspective is a first requisite. The era of world history has begun. The scale of functional dependence between societies expands, drawing together the histories of different parts of the planet. The several cultures of mankind become subcultures, subsystems, differentiated parts of a larger complex of cultural relations. Cultures cannot any longer be understood by contemplation of their navels. None is intelligible in isolation, apart from its adaptation to others in the world-cultural net. As each society's history so becomes the history of every other society, and each society becomes an environment of every other, it becomes for us common sense and necessity to learn how to interpret cultures as much from the outside, from their environmental contexts, as from their inner values.

37

THE FRONTIER IN HISTORY

OWEN D. LATTIMORE

A FRONTIER is created when a community occupies a territory. From then on the frontier is changed and shaped by the activity and growth of the community, or by the impact on it of another community. History being composed of records of growth, it is the changing of frontiers by the social growth of communities that is of primary importance for the historian.

The community whose frontier is to be studied may be a primitive band, a tribe, a nation, or a cluster of nations or states recognizable as a culture or civilization. Frontiers may be classified in many different ways, but there are two kinds that are of special interest in history. On the one hand there is the frontier between two communities that are of the same kind; on the other hand the frontier between different kinds of community. When, in the process of growth, two communities of the same kind are amalgamated, whether it be by conquest or by agreement, the change is primarily one of magnitude and only secondarily one of quality. The new unit is larger but still of the same kind, except to the extent that problems of magnitude may subsequently and secondarily contribute to changes in social and administrative institutions.

The case is not so simple when a community of one kind takes over—usually by conquest—a community differing from it in kind. If there is a great difference in social vigor and institutional strength the weaker community may be simply subsumed by the stronger; but if the difference in kind is great, while the difference in strength is not so great, the result will be a new community not only larger in numbers and occupying a greater territory, but differing in quality from both of the communities by whose amalgamation it was created. In this connection it is well to note also that when an

expanding community, in taking over new territory, expels the old occupants (or some of them), instead of incorporating them into its own fabric, those who retreat may become, in the new territory into which they spread, a new kind of society. There is much of this kind of change in frontier history, of which mention will be made again below.

There is need here to touch only lightly and in passing on the various physical kinds of frontier. It is at least necessary to mention, however, that the linear frontier as it is conventionally indicated on a map always proves, when studied on the ground, to be a zone rather than a line. A frontier line separates two jurisdictions; but whether the two communities that are set apart from each other in this way are similar in a general way like France and Italy, or notably dissimilar like India and Tibet, the maximum of difference is to be sought near the center of gravity of each country and not at the frontier where they meet. A frontier population is marginal. Where—to take a commonplace example—a frontier is emphasized by tariffs on goods exported and imported, it is normal for many people in both frontier populations to engage in smuggling. A frontier dweller's political loyalty to his own country may in this way be emphatically modified by his economic self-interest in illegal dealings with the foreigners across the border. Moreover while the motive is economic the activities cannot be limited to the economic. They inevitably set up their own nexus of social contact and joint interest. Men of both border populations, working together in this way, become a "we" group to whom others of their own nationality, and especially the authorities, are "they." To this extent it is often possible to describe the border populations on both sides of a frontier, taken together, as a joint community that is functionally recognizable though not institutionally defined. It is not surprising that the ambivalent loyalties of frontier peoples are often conspicuous and historically important.

In the early spread of a community a river may easily serve as a stopline that later becomes a political frontier. Later, with the maturing of the societies on the two sides of the river what was once a line of cleavage may become a channel of transportation drawing to itself economic activities from both of its banks, and this in turn may cause a chronic maladjustment between two societies whose political independence holds them apart from each other although their economic interests tend to merge into each other. In Europe the Rhine has a history of this kind. In Asia the Amur, until about a century ago, could almost be called a Rhine without a history. It was a majestic stream dividing puny tribes in an immense but thinly peopled land. Cross-river movement was unimportant and traffic up and down the stream negligible; but with the Chinese multiplying in Manchuria and the Russians in Siberia, with steam traffic on the river, railways converging on it and paralleling it, and industrial exploitation of natural resources beginning to proliferate, the Amur has entered on a quite different chapter of political and economic history.

For a primitive community the crest of a great mountain range may make an even more convenient stop-line than a great river; but history also modifies the significance of mountain frontiers. The Catalonian is a Spaniard; but he also has ties with the population across the Pyrenees in French territory that he does not have with other Spaniards, because his everyday speech is more closely related to the *langue d'oc* than it is to Spanish. The Alps, as "natural" frontiers, had one degree of significance for primitive man; another when European man had progressed to the engineering of roads; another when an industrialized society was able to drive railroad tunnels under the mountains; another when the internal combustion engine made the motorable road profitable; and still another when it became possible to fly right over the mountains. In Asia and other parts of the world where industrialism did not evolve locally but penetrated at a late date, the history of transportation is not infrequently dramatically reversed; there are not a few regions where the airplane has been seen before the motor car and the motor car before the railroad train. There are frontiers where technology has moved faster than political history. On their mountainous inland frontiers which can now be flown over, and which face toward Russia, which has an advanced airplane manufacturing technology, and toward China which

probably soon will have one, India and Pakistan, where the technology of flight is not well developed, confront problems not inherited from the years of British rule.

The changing significance, for changing societies, of an unchanging physical configuration which may at one time be a frontier, at another time a frontier of different significance (as when an old external frontier becomes an internal demarcation within an enlarged community), and at another time no frontier at all (as in the case of the western frontier of expansion of European man across the North American continent), leads to the axiomatic statement that frontiers are of social, not geographic origin. Only after the concept of a frontier exists can it be attached by the community that has conceived it to a geographical configuration. The consciousness of belonging to a group, a group that includes certain people and excludes others, must precede the conscious claim for that group of the right to live or move about within a particular territory; and it is probable that at the level of, say, the Australian aborigine the concept of the region or habitat is clearer than any concept of a sharply defined edge or frontier of the region. The region is a body that does not have an edge, but shades off into a margin of uncertainty, a no-man's land where other bands or communities may be encountered. Under such conditions even a well-defined range of hills may be thought of not so much as "the frontier" but rather as "the landmark beyond which, at an uncertain depth, varying from season to season, we are likely to encounter those other people with whom, if we run across them, we may perhaps fight, perhaps trade."

Truly primitive societies are "undifferentiated." They eat anything they can pluck or pick up (fruits, berries, seeds of seed-bearing grasses, nuts); anything that they can dig up (roots); anything that they can catch or kill (animals, birds, fish, reptiles, insects). Evolution from this level is by various kinds of specialization. Under the strong influence of Darwinian thinking in the nineteenth century it used to be assumed that there was a straight line of evolution through successive stages followed by all societies. The postulated series was hunter-shepherd-farmer-urban man; but the evidence does not support either the simplicity or the universality of such a succession. The Eskimo society, for example, vulgarly described as "primitive," was in fact highly specialized. True pastoral nomadism, for example, is not very early but rather late, and was probably the result of the confluence of groups who had previously been mainly hunters, and had moved out from forest into grasslands, and groups who, at the edge of the grasslands, had detached themselves from farming communities.

For an extremely regular, strongly patterned record of the processes of specialization and their consequences in the shaping of frontiers the history of China may be taken as a standard—an experimental, not an absolute standard —for estimating relative frontier values in the history of other societies and other parts of the world. In the general area of the Chinese culture, as in the general area of each of the great cultures of the Old World, we find indications from which a truly primordial undifferentiated society may be inferred, followed by the archaeological record of a New Stone Age and the beginnings of agriculture. Comparison of the record in China and elsewhere suggests a number of generalizations.

1) Early "specialization" is far from being the same thing as exclusive or nearly exclusive concentration on one activity, such as agriculture. While some communities began to depend more in quantity, and more regularly on their farming, others continued to rely more on hunting and gathering.

2) Through this kind of early, tentative specialization we can visualize the formation of two diverging types out of what had originally been a uniform society. These we may call, for convenience, "progressive" (agriculture becoming primary, hunting and gathering becoming secondary), and "backward" (hunting and gathering remaining primary, agriculture remaining secondary, in some cases not advancing beyond a desultory stage).

3) Out of this process we may further postulate the emergence of two kinds of frontier, between similar groups and between dissimilar groups.

4) In this process there was undoubtedly selective migration. The increasingly specialized groups sought out the kind of terrain that they had learned how to exploit, while the less evolved, more generalized groups remained in the kind of terrain where they knew how to live by hunting and gathering. Certainly by about the sixth century B.C. according to the ancient Chinese accounts of clashes with the "barbarians," the Chinese were in the plains and major valleys, the barbarians in hilly coun-

try with smaller valleys. This was several centuries before the Chinese had spread up the steppe margins of North China. The barbarians were probably "backward" congeners of the true Chinese. They were certainly not yet pastoral nomads. In at least one account they are described as fighting on foot, while the Chinese fought in chariots.

5) The domestication of animals was a tangential specialization. The reindeer (touching only the most distant northern periphery of the Chinese culture-area but important in the history of nomadism) was domesticated by forest hunters. Cattle and sheep were domesticated by sedentary communities. The ass was domesticated (Mesopotamian, Iranian region, North Africa) before the horse. The carriers of the use of the horse, especially the use of cavalry in war instead of the chariot, were people who spoke an Indo-European language, and only with the use of the horse in combination with the herding of cattle and sheep did the development of the full complex of true pastoral nomadism become possible. It is not clearly identifiable in Chinese history until as late as the fourth century B.C. but was earlier in Central Asia and the South Russian steppes.

6) Very early in the differentiation of specialized societies it becomes important to take note of an economic scale, ranging from extensivity to intensivity, which is of primary significance in the classification of different kinds of frontier.

a) In a truly primitive economy there is a maximum of extensivity. Social units measurable in tens of people must range over territorial units of tens or even hundreds of square miles; otherwise the game and other natural food resources will be quickly exhausted. When the social units are so small and also so widely scattered, even the "tribe" must remain a relatively loose concept.

b) Pastoral nomadism is less extensive. The territory must still be wide, but the social units can be larger and, having a facility of movement that permits concentration, when needed, as well as dispersion, the tribal organization can be very much stronger.

c) Rainfall agriculture is notably extensive as compared with intensive, irrigated agriculture, but much more intensive than pastoralism. It can support villages and even towns whose inhabitants, producing no food themselves, live on the surplus produced by the farming part of the community.

d) Irrigated agriculture is the most intensive pre-industrial economy. The food-producing units are measurable in acres—sometimes less than one acre for a food-producing family— and the urban-rural complex can be very highly developed, with cities of over 100,000 population.

By applying these generalizations the social history of China can be swiftly reviewed. The core of what later came to be China was in the loess country of the middle Yellow River. This actual core has long since become highly developed; but when flying over parts of the provinces of Ninghsia, Kansu, and Sinkiang a vivid impression can be gained of what primitive Chinese agriculture was like. Miles apart from the major oases of this area, where pockets of soft soil can be found in combination with small streams or even a little spring, miniature oases can be seen that are occupied by only three or four families or perhaps a single family. When an outlying oasis of this kind is visited, there are usually no ploughs to be found. The mattock and the spade are the primary farming tools; but with them small irrigation ditches can be dug, and this was probably done with stone tools even before the use of metal. The men often spend part of their time hunting and trapping.

In the loess core of ancient China (soft, easily worked soil; no stones; a climate in which a number of crops could be grown; enough uncertainty of rainfall to make irrigation spectacularly rewarding) there was developed from such minute nuclei as those I have described, now to be found only in fringing areas, a complex of farming practices and social organization that became capable of taking over larger and larger cultivable areas and of assimilating to itself other emergent agricultural types that were not originally identical with it.

Growing success made this increasingly recognizable "Chinese" complex more selective in spreading first into those geographical areas that it could take over without changing the trend of development of its increasingly well defined combination of technical practices and social organization. As it spread, it drove out of the most-wanted land or conquered and absorbed the tribes that it encountered. Only at a later time, when there began to be a shortage of optimum land, were the "Chinese" practices —by now more strongly developed, resourceful, and capable of raising the productivity of poorer land to a level formerly possible only on the best

land—applied to taking over the territory of the "backward" groups scattered through the blocks of hilly land, marsh, jungle or forest in the same vast continental expanse as the Chinese themselves. These groups that had lagged behind in the culture that was once that of the people who had now become "the Chinese" were increasingly assigned now to the hostile category of "the barbarians;" but they were "inner" barbarians, of the same matrix as the Chinese. Only at a still later stage did those of them who were extruded to the steppe fringe of the Chinese landscape detach themselves from the old matrix and become one of the components of the pastoral nomad society of the steppes, the "outer" barbarians.

The consequence of the bias to which the further evolution of the Chinese was now committed was the creation of two different kinds of frontier.

Southward to the Yangtze and beyond they invaded or infiltrated a terrain that was already becoming agricultural. To some extent this area was already being affected by higher cultures from the Indo-Burmese direction; but the Chinese prevailed. They first took the bigger plains and valleys. Where there was enough hilly and mountainous terrain the old tribes largely remained in the same country as the Chinese, but at higher altitudes. In Southwest China the low-altitude people are in fact an amalgam of incoming Chinese and the pre-Chinese peoples; and this kind of stratification extends far beyond China itself into the Indochinese peninsula, Thailand, and Burma, with the influences of the ancient high civilizations of China and India reaching far out over the lower levels where concentrated agriculture and big cities are to be found, but not up into the higher altitudes.

On the middle slopes in Southwest China there is a more primitive agriculture practiced by tribes that have not yet been gathered into the Chinese amalgam, with survivals of hunting and gathering economies at still higher altitudes. There are important social consequences when weaker peoples retreat in this manner before the advance of a stronger culture. They are worth a chapter of their own in social history and in the study of frontiers. In such retreats the retreating people lose, but their chiefs gain; the tribal structure is tightened up and the authority of the chiefs is enhanced. A man who would have been no more than a petty village headman if he had stayed behind

with a few of his people to be overflowed by
the incoming Chinese may, by organizing the
retreat and taking command of rearguard actions against the Chinese become a real chief,
with a degree of authority not previously known
within the retreating community.

The new character of authority seems to be
directly related to the function of the chief as
representative of his tribe, recognized by the
Chinese in order to provide institutions and
conventions for the coexistence of the Chinese
community and the tribal communities. The
fact that the Chinese make him their go-between
reinforces the power of the chief over his own
people. In this way the hereditary principle
is strengthened and a family of chiefs may
come to have a vested interest in perpetuating
the subordination of the people as a whole, in
order to sustain its own authority. A status of
this kind is quite compatible with occasional
leadership of tribal insurrections against the
dominant people. Frontier phenomena of this
kind are probably one of the origins of feudalism. They are notable in the history of Tibet
and it would be interesting to compare them
with frontier history elswhere; for instance,
the history of the Highland clans of Scotland.

On the south, then, the Chinese frontier
had an indefinite horizon of potential further
expansion and an altitudinal stratification of
remnant tribes.

On the north, the social commitment of
the Chinese to a specialized complex of agricultural practices and administrative organization created a different kind of frontier.

The rise in height from North China to the
Mongolian plateau defines a critical watershed.
South of it the streams are perennial and flow
to the Yellow River or the sea. Irrigated agriculture can be practiced and there is also a
margin of less intensive rainfall agriculture.
North of it the annual rainfall is both less and
more irregular and the streams are small, flow
inland, and die away. In a schematic way three
zones may be distinguished though locally they
are sometimes mixed up by such variations as
height, or salinity, or sand. The southern half
of the province of Jehol (with streams flowing
toward the sea) is for example an ancient zone
of nomadic and Chinese interpenetration, with
alternating dominance of the one or the other.

First there is a zone in which the farmer
must give up irrigation and take his chances
with the rainfall; the hazard is not so much
the low average rainfall as the seasonal irregularity of the rain. The farmer must be content
with a much lower yield per acre, which in turn
means larger holdings, which again means more
widely dispersed settlement. North of this there
is a zone in which a mixed economy is much
safer than reliance on cultivation alone; if
enough of the land is reserved for livestock
there will usually be enough rain for the pasture
when there is not enough for a grain crop.
Finally there is a zone where herding is the
only rational economy; though even here there
are patches where a desultory agriculture is
practiced—but on such a minor scale that if
the crop matures it is a gain, while if it fails
no serious harm is done.

When the Chinese in their northward spread
began to approach this Mongolian terrain on a
broad front, in about the fourth century B.C.,
they were driving before them various "backward" communities or groups whom they had
for centuries regarded as "barbarians" but who
were not yet true steppe nomads. If the Chinese
had gone on into the zone where irrigated farming must be abandoned they would have had to
reverse their set trend of evolution toward becoming a more and more closely settled rural-
urban people; they would have had to devolve
in the direction of becoming a more dispersed
society with a more extensive economy. Their
institutions were too strong to permit such a
change, and they tried to set a limit to their
own expansion. The zone in which they tried
to stop became the line of the Great Wall—
which in reality is a zone rather than a line,
because in various periods there were both
outlying walled fortifications and internal supplementary defenses. The "barbarians" whom the
Chinese expelled as they advanced (and many
Chinese who in later times detached themselves
from the frontier edge of the Chinese society)
went on into the steppe and were recruited into
the true pastoral nomadic society, other components of which were communities that had
emerged into the steppe from the forests of
Siberia and Manchuria, or from the fringes of
the oases of Turkistan.

Thus on the south and the north the Chinese
created two contrasting frontiers. The geog-
rapher can describe these frontiers according
to their differences of latitude, terrain, climate,
vegetation, and animal life. From the point of
view of sociology and the evolution of institutions they can be described in terms of the
alternative processes through which a society
either continues a trend of development on

which it is already launched, intensifying and sophisticating its characteristics but not changing them in kind, or diverges to a trend that will result in creating a different kind of society.

In these terms the southern frontier of the Chinese culture can be called dynamic, the northern frontier static. It is true that the northern frontier could not in fact be made permanently static; it was crossed by alternating barbarian incursions and Chinese outward thrusts attempting to subdue or discipline the barbarians; but nothing could be more static in conception than the Great Wall. We may rightly speak therefore of a frontier of inclusion on the south and a frontier of exclusion on the north.

Within these frontiers China, as the homeland of a major civilization, evolved a compartmented or cellular structure of its own—an indefinite multiplication of standardized units. Of these the smallest was the village. Its fields were grouped around it and the farmer walked out to his work; the isolated farmstead existed, but was not typical. Except in regions producing specialized commodities like silk, village handicraft produced only a very small surplus to go into trade beyond the village.

Larger in size was the district town, the center of a cluster of such villages. Here there was more handicraft production, more trade, and also a non-producing administrative staff and, where necessary, a garrison.

Still larger was the regional city, the size of the region being determined by the balance between facility of transportation, especially where rivers and canals could be used, and difficulty of transportation where the crossing of mountains sharply increased the cost of moving food and other commodities in bulk. Generally speaking the administrative province tended to coincide with a geographical region, so that the regional city was also a provincial capital; though some regions were so rich that they could support more than one large city.

Most important of all was the national capital. Given the structure of China as a whole, the national capital was of course also the center of gravity of a region. This metropolitan region was, in different periods of history, either the most important economic region, the critical strategic region, or both.

In this repetitive structure of comparable units it is important to note the topographical coincidence of urban centers and centers of gravity of rural production. In an industrial civilization we take it for granted that areas of maximum rural production may lie far from urban centers of consumption. In China, the areas of most intensive cultivation lay in concentric rings around the town and cities. This was not only because of the need of the cities for food, but because of the fecal output of the cities. The shorter the distance to which this manure had to be transported from inside the city to a field outside the city wall, the cheaper the cost of fertilization; and conversely, the shorter the distance from which food had to be transported into the city, the cheaper its cost. It is for these reasons that a Chinese walled city, looked at from the air, is seen to be surrounded not by a ring of residential suburbs, like an industrial city, but by concentric circles of dark green (right up against the city walls) and lighter and lighter green, marking with economic precision the cost of transporting fertilizer from the city.

This close reciprocity of the urban and the rural helps to explain the old regional China. There were in fact only approximations toward a national market, in such commodities as metals (especially iron), silk, and tea; salt was on the whole a regional rather than a national commodity, though sometimes it was carried to great distances. The village had a small surplus to contribute to the district town; the regional city had a larger surplus, collected from its cluster of district towns. Only small surpluses overflowed into national trade. The most important market was the regional market. To the extent that a national market existed, it depended on the ability to transport goods that were high in value compared to their bulk and weight; it was therefore more a market of luxuries than of necessaries. In the economics of transportation the cost of food was of paramount importance. In a pre-industrial civilization, when food has to be transported either by grain-consuming human porters or by grain-consuming draught-animals the margin of profit is eaten up within approximately 100 miles— the more or the less depending on whether the terrain is flat or mountainous. Really cheap transportation of food in bulk is possible only by river, canal, or sea; and this is why the Nile and the Mediterranean, the Tigris and Euphrates, the Indus and the Ganges, the Yellow River and the Yangtze (and the ancillary canals in all of these regions) played so important a part in the history of the great civilizations of the Old World.

In China as in the other great pre-industrial civilizations the most effective way of increasing food production was to apply more human labor to the land in order to cultivate it more intensively; but since the food-producers were also food-consumers, coercion had to be used in order to make them surrender enough food to maintain the great cities, leading often to the cruel paradox of chronic undernourishment among farmers. Slavery was one method of coercion; but in China the most important methods were share-cropping and the corvée. Share-cropping is a system that forces food-producers to bid against each other in offering the landlord a share of the crop (often 50 per cent and sometimes as much as 70 per cent) in exchange for permission to cultivate the land. The corveé is forced labor contributed to the district, the province, or the state for digging canals, throwing up embankments, or building roads; and both forms of coercion added emphasis to the regional compartmentation of China's economy.

By applying the foregoing criteria it is possible to state a sort of equation that is helpful in analyzing not only the regional structure of China but the structure of its frontiers. The terms of this equation are the geographical range of:

a) Unification by military action.

b) Centralization under uniform civil administration.

c) Economic integration.

Of these terms it can be said that, under conditions prevailing not only in China but over the whole of the Old World prior to the Great Navigations that opened up the oceans at the end of the fifteenth century;

a) The radius of military action was greater than that of civil administration. An inner radius reached over territories that could, after conquest, be added to the state, and an outer radius reached into territories that could be invaded, with profit in plunder or tribute, or for the purpose of breaking up barbarian concentrations dangerous to the state, but that could not be permanently annexed.

b) Civil administration tended to be stronger regionally than nationally. The solidity of the state was closely associated with the fact that similar administrations duplicated each other in region after region. In the cyclical history of the rise and fall of dynasties, even in periods of chaos at the fall of a dynasty, there would be regions that maintained their stability while the empire fell apart; and it was from these regions that it was possible to "grow back" once more to a unified state.

c) Economic integration had the shortest range. It was a function of the ability to transport bulk goods (especially food) at a profit. For many centuries, and not only in China, this meant that where transportation by water was available within an empire, linking several regions to each other, the empire that could be built was larger and more stable than where transportation depended in the main on carts, pack animals, or human porters.

Where a political frontier is also a frontier between different economic systems the importance of differences in the range of economic integration can hardly be exaggerated. On the south, the Chinese were able to keep adding new regional "compartments" to their realm because even though, at each step in distance, a new compartment contributed less and less to the feeble national market, it was at least within itself economically and administratively uniform with the other regions of the state.

On the north it was different. The farthest outlying Chinese farms had two markets: in China and among the barbarians. If they took their grain to the south they had to pass through farmland. There was no grazing on the way. The transport animals had to be quartered at inns overnight, and forage had to be bought for them. There was no profit unless the market was within 100 miles or so; though an extra distance could be travelled if the grain were turned into alcohol at an outlying distillery. (Hence the very great increase in Chinese colonizing penetration of Mongolia under the stimulus of railway building; the nearest market was no longer the nearest town, but the nearest railway station).

The barbarian market had a much greater geographical magnitude. Grain loaded on camels, who grazed at each march on the open steppe, without inn-charges, could be carried as far as 800 miles at a profit. Trade of this kind built up mutual interests between barbarians and frontier Chinese. It goes far to explain why frontier Chinese often (especially in times of political disorder and a poor market in China) attached themselves quite readily to barbarian rulers.

There is also another aspect of frontier and trans-frontier trade to be considered. As late as the time of Marco Polo (at least) the trade of the merchant who ventured beyond his own district depended delicately on the whims of potentates. Precise book-keeping was something that developed only later, as the factors of production cost, transportation cost, and forecasting of the market demand became more calculable. The distant venture was concerned less with the disposal of goods in bulk and more with curiosities, rarities and luxuries. Both the hazards and the rewards depended on the whims of armed men, capricious nobles, and arbitrary sovereigns. The merchant sought out those who could extend favor and protection. If he were unlucky he might be plundered or taxed to ruination; but if he were lucky he received for his goods not so much an economic price as a munificent largesse.

This atmosphere of ancient and even medieval trade has been overlooked by both conventional and Marxist historians. Thus Teggart in a book that is invaluable to the student of frontiers even though the word "frontier" is not in the index and neither the formation nor the functions of frontiers are discussed, in his study of what he calls "correlations" of events on the Chinese and Roman frontiers, lays great stress on "interruptions of trade" as the cause of frontier wars and invasions; but his unspoken assumption seems to be that trade was a matter of what we would now call "normal" economic supply and demand. Much more specific is a Marxist writer who, though he recognizes that Chinese goods reached the steppe barbarians partly as "tribute-gifts," also states flatly that "China in the Han epoch strenuously sought markets for the disposal of its wares. This is shown by the whole history of the trade in silk." It is extremely doubtful whether this statement can be supported by evidence convincing to an economic historian. The statement can only be based on the assumption that manufacturers made too much for the domestic market, and the surplus had to be "disposed of" in foreign trade. Such a concept misses the essential fact that the structure of the silk trade and of much other trade was more a tribute structure than a trade structure. The state in China collected a tribute of the typical products of regions. A luxury product like silk went partly into imperial warehouses and part of it was distributed as gifts to courtiers, nobles, administrative officials and, by extension, as gifts to barbarian envoys to be carried back to nomad chiefs and the kinglets of the oases of the Tarim basin. This traffic gave rise to a special kind of trade which might well be called "gift-trade"

between privileged persons. Commodities like silk got into the hands of merchants engaged in the trans-frontier trade more because they knew "the right poeple" than because they had the capital to engage in buying and selling. Indeed, envoys themselves engaged in this kind of trade as a sideline. This helps to explain why there are so many historical references to petitions (sometimes demands) by barbarians that they be allowed to "submit tribute" to China *more often*—in the first place the "gifts" of the emperor had to be more munificent than the "tribute" offered; in the second place the tribute-bearing missions offered, over and above the delivery of the tribute and the carrying back of the gifts, opportunities for privileged and profitable trade. What passed directly between the Chinese and the pastoral nomads and Inner Asian oasis communities nearest to them was then relayed on by similar methods until Chinese commodities eventually reached the Mediterranean, while products of regions far to the west entered China.

From the point of view of the fiscal good of the state it is probable that there were more differences than resemblances between the conventional views prevailing in China say two thousand years ago and the mercantilistic theories that arose in Europe during the transition from the middle ages to the era of world trade. Like the mercantilists, the Chinese welcomed the accretion of gold, much of which came from beyond the frontiers; but they did not believe in the promotion of foreign trade as a good in itself. Probably the basic view was that a flourishing condition was promoted by retaining in China what China produced; if commodities were allowed to pass over the frontier, the justification must be political rather than economic. Certainly the famous journey into Inner Asia of Chang Ch'ien (second century B.C.), which is conventionally celebrated by Western writers as the opening of the great Silk Route, was in fact undertaken for no such purpose, but for the political purpose of finding allies to turn the flank of the nomads who were harassing the Great Wall frontier.

From the point of view of a Chinese frontier administrator, therefore, the major considerations (and probably a Roman frontier administrator had much the same problems) in regulating trade with the barbarians included at least the following public and personal problems: Were goods going out in quantities that represented a drain of wealth from the territory

under his jurisdiction? Was the export of bor-
der-produced non-luxury "consumer goods" like
grain building up a tie between the people whom
he ruled and the nomads that would affect their
loyalty to the state he represented? And—the
personal element—could he make enough out of
it, through gifts, bribes, and tolls paid by
merchants to enable him to retire from the
harsh frontier to live in civilized comfort in
the metropolitan area in the cheerful assurance
that frontier stability would last for his time?

There is still another aspect of the frontier
of a great state like China that must be brought
into focus, in order to link the frontier problems of one state with those of other states.
Using a term derived from cartographical convention we may describe the advance of the increasingly standardized Chinese up to the line
of the Great Wall frontier as "vertical." In this
advance they drove before them those of the
barbarians of North China whom they did not
subordinate and absorb. As noted above, many
or most of these barbarians were congeners of
the Chinese themselves, but backward in the
sense of being less specialized in agriculture
and not having nearly as highly developed an
urban-rural complex as the Chinese already had.
These barbarians, as we know from many
chronicle notices, had for centuries had horses
and sheep, but they were not yet true pastoral
nomads—although it has long been a convention
among Chinese historians to "read back" into
earlier history the assumption that they were
pastoral nomads. Undoubtedly they were in
fact peoples with a mixed economy; they were
agricultural like the Chinese, but their agriculture was less advanced than that of the Chinese,
and they had more livestock than the Chinese.
Only when, at the edge of the true steppe, they
unmoored themselves from the last of their
agriculture and launched out into the grasslands
to live almost completely by management of
their livestock did they become true pastoral
nomads.

We know that some of the border Chinese
began to follow the same line of divergent evolution, and that it was to retain the Chinese within
China as well as to keep the new-style pastoral
barbarians out of China that the Great Wall
was built. At the same time, however, a new
and formidable development had taken place.
With the end of their vertical northward retreat
and their detachment from agriculture, the new-
style pastoral nomads of the frontier, or rather
the trans-frontier, had now a new and strategi-

cally important facility of lateral movement.
With this new mobility they could raid the
Chinese frontally; they could withdraw nimbly
when strong Chinese expeditions were sent out
against them; and they could make contact with
the other pastoral nomadic societies already
existing farther out in Inner Asia.

Frontier warfare now took on a new character. Until this time, war had been one factor
in determining what kind of system was fittest
to survive in China: it interacted with the factors of agricultural specialization, urban-rural
balance, social organization, and administrative
efficiency.

That which became "the" Chinese culture
emerged out of competition with variants that
approached less closely the forms that were
eventually to be established as the type-culture.
In this competitive evolutionary process military
successes acted in conjunction with economic
successes and organizational improvements; the
effect of war, especially in expropriating territory from more backward groups and putting
it to more efficient use was not exhaustion but
an increase in social and economic vigor.

Once the Great Wall frontier was created
war became, for the Chinese, indecisive and
exhausting. In the new kind of war the agricultural (or more properly the urban-agricul-
tural) society of China and the pastoral
nomadic society of Inner Asia could alternat-
ingly win victories over each other; but the
steppe could not be taken over by China and
made uniform with China in agricultural practices, proportion of urban to rural population
and all the other characteristics that give consistency to a culture and a civilization; nor
could the peoples of the steppe, even when they
invaded China successfully, turn its fields into
grazing lands and establish there a pastoral
society fitter to survive than an agriculturally
based society.

The nomads did have certain advantages,
however, in spite of the striking contrast between their small numbers and the mass of the
Chinese population. In pre-industrial warfare,
the mounted archer represented the maximum
concentration of mobility and fire-power. Only
rarely and when they were lucky could expeditions from China inflict real damage on the
nomads by capturing their camps and herds;
normally, there was time to move out of the
way. When the nomads attacked, on the other
hand, they attacked fixed targets; they could
raid the farmlands in the harvest season and

carry away grain, and when they succeeded in cutting the communications of a city and capturing it, the plunder was immense. Moreover they could often, by the mere threat of attack, collect a kind of blackmail or Danegeld.

In the new pattern of war, therefore, the great Chinese victories were won when the state was vigorous enough to plan and mobilize carefully and to send out expeditions that moved quickly and won at the first shock. When they could not do this, and frontier warfare was desultory and chronic, the Chinese frontier provinces were slowly drained and exhausted and the prestige of the state eroded, while the nomads profited economically, grew stronger every year, and in the rivalry between chieftains eventually produced one of the Chingis Khan stamp who could not only lead a band of warriors but impose a control of imperial sweep over a conglomeration of tribes. For about two thousand years the rule of history was to be that great Chinese dynasties were formed in the heart of the country, moved up to the frontier with a strong momentum, enrolled nomad and semi-nomad auxiliaries, struck swiftly and at long range into the steppe, and paralyzed the nomadic society with such sudden defeats that the resulting Pax Sinica lasted for two generations or more; while the great nomad conquests were preceded by decades of gradual encroachment on the Chinese frontiers, accompanied by minor warfare among the tribes themselves and between rivals for supreme leadership.

These conditions extended far beyond the Chinese frontier. The lateral mobility of the tribes enabled them to move along the whole front of the agricultural and city-building states from China to the Black Sea, probing to find the weakest spots at which to break through. It is customary to attribute the astonishing conquests of Chingis Khan simply to his military genius, but it would be more rational to point out that his genius was given its opportunity by the coincidence that at the turn from the twelfth to the thirteenth century all the great civilized states from China to the Near East were simultaneously in that phase of the cyclical rise and fall of dynasties which made them weak on their frontiers and open to nomad incursions.

It is at this point that a transition should be made from the discussion of Chinese frontier history as a type to comparison of the significance of frontiers in history as a whole. To make the needed comparisons is beyond the power of a single writer with limited ability to draw on the necessary sources. Historians deal with sources written in so many languages that the individual historian's view of culture, society, and political units tends to be language-bound. Working within the sources to which he is limited, he tends naturally toward emphasis in the peculiarity of his field of concentrated interest. The archaeologists have certain advantages, They deal with artifacts that not only are not language-bound but by their very nature lead to the classification of societies by similarity of function, not by differences of language and superstructure. Their work throws light on the essentials of economic and social structure at the artifact level of the tools used and the things produced, thus providing a material underpinning for later, chronicled records of the ways in which the products of the society were appropriated and distributed. It is not surprising that the unity of Old World cultural origins is in many ways clearer in prehistory than in recorded history.

Certain themes, however, do stand out. There was a linked chain of fortified northern frontiers of the ancient civilized world from the Pacific to the Atlantic. The earliest frontier walls appear to have been in the Iranian sector. The walled frontiers of the western Roman empire in Britain and on the Rhine and Danube faced forest, upland, and meadow tribes, not pastoral nomads; in the lateral movements of peoples outside the Roman *orbis terrarum,* the Greek οἰκουμένη and the Chinese *t'ien hsia*— all semantically equivalent terms—one of the obscure areas is the mode of interaction between forest peoples and steppe peoples; the mixed following of Attila is here an obvious focus of interest. In the Iranian-Mesopotamian-Arab world the geographical and social pattern is much more confused than on either the west Roman or the Chinese frontier, a major phenomenon being that pastoral nomads were not only excluded on the north but enclosed in blocks of desert, semi-desert, steppe, and highland country within the general sweep of civilization. Here there is a need for special comparative studies of the differences, resemblances and occasional interaction between excluded nomads and enclosed nomads.

Leaving aside their differences, however, there are similar phenomena in all of these frontier histories.[1] As in China, the range of military striking power exceeded the range of ability to conquer and incorporate; the range of uniform civil administration exceeded that of economic integration. The northern frontier at which an attempt was made to exclude the barbarians was also the limit beyond which uniform blocks of cultivated territory with a uniform complement of cities and administrative services could not be added to the state; the limit within which a standardized tribute largely in kind and not costing too much in transport could be gathered by the state and beyond which trade was essentially centrifugal, draining the state of more than it brought in.

It is remarkable how the Roman Rhine-Danube *limes* conformed to an *orbis terrarum* that could be economically integrated with the cheap water transportation of the Mediterranean and Black Sea—schematically, and on an even more grandiose scale, the combined Yangtze and Grand Canal of the Romans. The importance of the economics of transportation is emphasized by the history of the post-Roman eastward spread of the Germans against the Slavs, where the question was not simply one of military superiority but of the gradually developed ability, through use of the rivers and the Baltic ports, to integrate the conquered territory economically; this marked the transformation of an ancient frontier of exclusion into a new frontier of inclusion.

Premonitory signs of a new historical age are usually to be seen long in advance, before the preceding period has run its course. In this sense we may look on the Vikings, beginning in the eighth century, as early forerunners of the Great Navigations. They were the first (the first, at least, in the Western world) to abandon coast-hugging navigation and to strike out into the open sea, and the first to combine sea voyages with overland operations. With the Great Navigations at the end of the fifteenth century both military and economic range were enormously expanded. The Europeans now had arms decisively superior to those of any people that they encountered in Asia, Africa, or the Americas, and they had ships capable of carrying bulk cargoes. They brought back at first gold, rarities, and luxury goods, but they soon began also to bring back raw and semi-processed materials to be finished in European workshops and put back into trade again. The genesis of the industrial economy was in a number of interacting factors. The increased supply of gold and silver increased the amount of ready, easily transferable capital. Bulk transportation raised the amount of goods in trade to a new order of magnitude. The increased amount of material to be processed stimulated mechanical invention.

The result was the creation of a new kind of frontier, the overseas frontier, the varieties of which may be classified in several ways. On the one hand a European country could lay claim to a land either nearly empty or inhabited by people with no strong state, such as most of North America, Brazil, the Argentine, South Africa, Australia, and New Zealand. This land became a frontier in that it had to be defended against European rivals. The tendency was to people it with colonists from the claimant country (and sometimes also with captured or purchased slaves). Except where slavery was introduced as a new institution, and except to the extent that mercantilist theories were carried out by trying to hold back the development of manufactures, so that the colony would serve as a raw-material supplier to the ruling country, the trend in such colonies was to reproduce the economic and social institutions of the colonizing country.

On the other hand a European country would conquer all or part of a country that already had a high culture and well developed state institutions, as in India and parts of Central and South America. Here the conquerors established themselves principally as a ruling class, and thereafter tenaciously followed a policy of maintaining two differentials—the social differential between conquered and conquerors, and the economic differential between conquered country and ruling country. The introduction of advanced methods of production, such as industry, was at first avoided; later, when it was permitted, it was introduced at a level lower than that of the ruling country, so that a differential still remained.

In both kinds of overseas possession, one of the old rules of frontier history continued to operate: the new frontiers were shaped less by geographical and material conditions than by the cultural momentum and impact of those who created them. Indeed, as the industrial economy has developed, man has more and more subordinated the material environment. Until the twentieth century China and Mongolia could not be integrated, because the Chinese society could not establish itself in a non-agricultural landscape without making changes in its economic practices and social institutions that would have meant ceasing to be Chinese; but in the twentieth century, with rail, motor, and air communication, with industrial mining production in Mongolia and industrial processing of both the pastoral products of Mongolia and the agricultural products of China, both communities can be subsumed as reciprocating components of an enlarged and integrated community.

Communities with short histories, however, seem instinctively to seek to compensate for the shortness of their history by emphasizing the particularities of their society. In the United States F. J. Turner founded a school of frontier theory (which has had echoes in kindred countries like Canada and Australia) premised on the assumption that in a country like the United States, which had for the first part of its history an advancing frontier of colonization on new land, the circumstances of frontier activity have a powerful effect in shaping the society as a whole. He has been described by another American historian [H. S. Commager] as "not the historian of the frontier . . . but the historian of America who took his vantage point along the frontier."

Turner celebrates the manner in which frontiersmen emerge in a frontier environment in a passage that is of interest to all students of frontier history, because it is a description of that ambivalent "man of the border" who is to be found also on the Great Wall frontier of China, the Cossack frontier of Russia, the frontier of German advance against the Slavs:

The wilderness masters the colonist. It finds him a European in dress, industries, tools, modes of travel, and thought. It takes him from the railroad car and puts him in the birch canoe. It strips off the garments of civilization and arrays him in the hunting shirt and the moccasin. . . . Before long he has gone to planting Indian corn and plowing with a sharp stick; he shouts the war cry and takes the scalp in orthodox Indian fashion. In short, at the frontier the environment is at first too strong for the man. . . . Little by little he transforms the wilderness, but the outcome is not the old Europe, not simply the development of the old Germanic germs any more than the first phenomenon was a case of reversion to the Germanic mark. The fact is, that here is a new product that is American.

Yet the argument, so limited, will not stand up. Turner repudiates "the study of European germs developing in an American environment. Too exclusive attention has been paid by institutional students to the Germanic origins, too little to the American factors." But was it so exclusively the "American factors" that prevented the part of North America where the trend of institutional development was determined first by British settlement from becoming a mere duplicate of England? He neglects the fact that when the British landed in North America with the cultural and social baggage that they brought, they also left some behind; and included in what they left behind was the hereditary, aristocratic, landed family tied by what still remained of feudalism more closely to the crown than to the rest of England's complex of institutions. England itself was already beginning to transform itself from a society dominated by the landed nobility and gentry into a society at first commercial and then increasingly industrial; but this could be done only slowly because of the weight of vested interest. The Americans, because of the institutions they had left behind them as well as those they brought with them, and not merely because of the free land and abundant raw materials of the frontier of new settlement, were able, once they had thrown off their colonial disabilities, to move ahead in the same direction as the British, but even faster. It is this that principally accounts for the fact that the United States and Britain of to-day are so close akin but at the same time so different.

Turner, in fact, was an acute observer; but what he saw so clearly, he saw while standing on his head. In large measure, when he thought he saw what the frontier did to society, he was really seeing what society did to the frontier. That he was standing on his head accounts for the fact that he touches only glancingly on the American frontiers of the French and Spanish. (He does mention that while the British took the land of the Indian and farmed it, the French in adjoining Canada emphasized trade with the Indians.) Yet why was it that the Spanish and French frontiers in America (especially the frontier in Canada, so close geographically to New England) did not create societies more like that of the United States—except, significantly, in Canada west of Quebec, where the settlers were British? What can account adequately for the great differences, unless it be the differences in cultural momentum and impact of the Spanish and French who came to the Americas? Undoubtedly differences in the institutions of land tenure that they brought with them go far toward explaining the differences between French, English, and Spanish America.

The interest of such questions is not limited to the history of the past. There is also the future to consider. Since the first and second world wars a new period of frontier history has begun. The United States, Canada, the Western European states and Australia and New Zealand form a cluster of nations. The frontiers between them are of the sort that divide communities differing from each other in degree, but not in kind. The frontiers between them and the Soviet-Chinese-East European cluster of nations are frontiers between communities differing in kind. There is also a third cluster, of which India is the prototype, which can perhaps be best described by saying that it has the potential of becoming different in kind from both of the other two.

The frontiers between the American-Western and the Soviet-Chinese-Eastern groups are not frontiers of a Great Wall type for one very significant reason: each of these groups represents an institutional system of combined economic and social organization that is capable of taking over the entire world and making it an all-inclusive *orbis terrarum*. The Indian type does not appear to have the capacity (or the desire) to take over the *orbis terrarum*, but it does appear to have the capacity to hold the other two groups apart, and if it should be able to do that long enough, perhaps an annealing process will become possible, integrating a united world of different but reciprocating components.

In a world so constructed frontiers, frontier contacts, and trans-frontier traffic are of primary importance.

NOTES

1. Because of ignorance, I refrain from more than passing comment on pre-Columbian history in America. Reference should at least be made, however, to such phenomena as the frontier walls of the Incas and their astonishing imperial roads, which must have served economic integration as well as military unification. For lack of the horse, a pastoral nomadic society of the Eurasian type could not be created in the Americas. The standard work on the significance of the introduction of the horse is Clark Wissler, "The influence of the horse in the development of plains culture," *American Anthropologist*, N. S., 16, N. 1 (Lancaster, Pennsylvania, 1914); but his treatment is more anthropological than sociological. He notes that "the horse was a great inciter of predatory warfare which must have increased the range and intensity of operations." It is fascinating to speculate on what might have happened if the white men who brought the horse had been armed only with the bow and arrow, and if the Indians had already domesticated the sheep and the bison. An Indian steppe empire of the great plains of North America might have arisen as suddenly and dramatically as the Hsiungnu empire beyond the Great Wall of China.

38

ECOLOGIC RELATIONSHIPS OF
ETHNIC GROUPS IN SWAT, NORTH PAKISTAN

FREDRIK BARTH

THE importance of ecologic factors for the form and distribution of cultures has usually been analyzed by means of a culture area concept. This concept has been developed with ref-

From *American Anthropologist*, 58: 1079–1089. Copyright © 1956 by the American Anthropological Association. Reprinted by permission of the publisher and the author. Fredrik Barth is Professor of Social Anthropology, Universitet I Bergen.

erence to the aboriginal cultures of North America. Attempts at delimiting culture areas in Asia by similar procedures have proved extremely difficult, since the distribution of cultural types, ethnic groups, and natural areas rarely coincide. Coon speaks of Middle Eastern society as being built on a mosaic principle— many ethnic groups with radically different cultures co-reside in an area in symbiotic relations of variable intimacy. Referring to a similar structure, Furnivall describes the Netherlands Indies as a plural society. The common characteristic in these two cases is the combination of ethnic segmentation and economic interdependence. Thus the "environment" of any one ethnic group is not only defined by natural conditions, but also by the presence and activities of the other ethnic groups on which it depends. Each group exploits only a section of the total environment, and leaves large parts of it open for other groups to exploit.

This interdependence is analogous to that of the different animal species in a habitat. As Kroeber emphasizes, culture area classifications are essentially ecologic; thus detailed ecologic considerations, rather than geographical areas of subcontinental size, should offer the point of departure. The present paper attempts to apply a more specific ecologic approach to a case study of distribution by utilizing some of the concepts of animal ecology, particularly the concept of a *niche*—the place of a group in the total environment, its relations to resources and competitors.

GROUPS

The present example is simple, relatively speaking, and is concerned with the three major ethnic groups in Swat State, North-West frontier Province, Pakistan. These are (1) *Pathans*—Pashto-speaking (Iranian language family) sedentary agriculturalists, (2) *Kohistanis*—speakers of Dardic languages, practicing agriculture and transhumant herding; and (3) *Gujars*—Gujri-speaking (a lowland Indian dialect) nomadic herders. Kohistanis are probably the ancient inhabitants of most of Swat; Pathans entered as conquerors in successive waves between A.D. 1000–1600, and Gujars probably first appeared in the area some 400 years ago. Pathans of Swat State number about 450,000, Kohistanis perhaps 30,000. The number of Gujars in the area is difficult to estimate.

The centralized state organization in Swat was first established in 1917, and the most recent accretion was annexed in 1947, so the central organization has no relevance for the distributional problems discussed here.

AREA

Swat State contains sections of two main valleys, those of the Swat and the Indus Rivers.

The Swat River rises in the high mountains to the North, among 18,000 foot peaks. As it descends and grows in volume, it enters a deep gorge. This upper section of the valley is thus very narrow and steep. From approximately 5,000 feet, the Swat valley becomes increasingly wider as one proceeds southward, and is flanked by ranges descending from 12,000 to 6,000 feet in altitude. The river here has a more meandering course, and the valley bottom is a flat, extensive alluvial deposit.

The east border of Swat State follows the Indus River; only its west bank and tributaries are included in the area under discussion. The Indus enters the area as a very large river; it flows in a spectacular gorge, 15,000 feet deep and from 12 to 16 miles wide. Even in the north, the valley bottom is less than 3,000 feet above sea level, while the surrounding mountains reach 18,000 feet. The tributary valleys are consequently short and deeply cut, with an extremely steep profile. Further to the south, the surrounding mountain ranges recede from the river banks and lose height, the Indus deposits some sediment, and the tributary streams form wider valleys.

Climatic variations in the area are a function of altitude. Precipitation is low throughout. The southern, low-altitude areas have long, hot summers and largely steppe vegetation. The Indus gorge has been described as "a desert embedded between icy gravels" (Spate). The high mountains are partly covered by permanent ice and snow, and at lower levels by natural mountain meadows in the brief summer season. Between these extremes is a broad belt (from 6,000 to 11,000 feet) of forest, mainly of pine and deodar.

PATHAN-KOHISTANI DISTRIBUTION

Traditional history, in part relating to place-names of villages and uninhabited ruins, indicates that Kohistani inhabitants were driven progressively northward by Pathan invaders. This northward spread has now been checked, and the border between Kohistani and Pathan territories has been stable for some time. The last Pathan expansion northward in the Swat valley took place under the leadership of the Saint Akhund Sadiq Baba, eight generations ago. To understand the factors responsible for the stability of the present ethnic border, it is necessary to examine the specific ecologic requirements of the present Pathan economy and organization.

Pathans of Swat live in a complex, multi-caste society. The landholding Pakhtun caste is organized in localized, segmentary, unilineal descent groups; other castes and occupational groups are tied to them as political clients and economic serfs. Subsistence is based on diversified and well-developed plow agriculture. The main crops are wheat, maize, and rice; much of the plowed land is watered by artificial irrigation. Manuring is practiced, and several systems of crop rotation and regular fallow-field rhythms are followed, according to the nature of the soil and water supply. All rice is irrigated, with nursery beds and transplantation.

Only part of the Pathan population is actively engaged in agriculture. Various other occupational groups perform specialized services in return for payment in kind, and thus require that the agriculturalists produce a considerable surplus. Further, and perhaps more importantly, the political system depends on a strong hierarchical organization of landowners and much political activity, centering around the men's houses (*hujra*). This activity diverts much manpower from productive pursuits. The large and well-organized Pathan tribes are found in the lower parts of the Swat valley and along the more southerly tributaries of the Indus, occupying broad and fertile alluvial plains. A simpler form of political organization is found along the northern fringes of Pathan territory. It is based on families of saintly descent, and is characterized by the lack of men's houses. This simplification renders the economy of the community more efficient (1) by eliminating the wasteful potlatch-type feasts of the men's houses, and (2) by vesting political office in saintly persons of inviolate status, thus eliminating the numerous retainers that protect political leaders in other Pathan areas.

Pathan territory extends to a critical ecologic threshold: the limits within which two crops can be raised each year. This is largely a function of altitude. Two small outliers of Pashto-speaking people (Jag, in Duber valley, and a section of Kalam) are found north of this limit. They are unlike other Pathans, and similar to their Kohistani neighbors in economy and political organization.

The conclusion that the limits of double cropping constitute the effective check on further Pathan expansion seems unavoidable. Pathan economy and political organization re-quires that agricultural labor produce considerable surplus. Thus in the marginal, high-altitude areas, the political organization is modified and "economized" (as also in the neighboring Dir area), while beyond these limits of double cropping the economic and social system can not survive at all.

Kohistanis are not restricted by this barrier. The Kohistani ethnic group apparently once straddled it; and, as they were driven north by invading Pathans, they freely crossed what to Pathans was a restricting barrier. This must be related to differences between Kohistani and Pathan political and economic organization, and consequent differences in their ecologic requirements.

Kohistanis, like Pathans, practice a developed plow agriculture. Due to the terrain they occupy, their fields are located on narrow artificial terraces, which require considerable engineering skill for their construction. Parts of Kohistan receive no summer rains; the streams, fed from the large snow reserves in the mountains, supply water to the fields through complex and extensive systems of irrigation. Some manuring is practiced. Climatic conditions modify the types of food crops. Maize and millet are most important; wheat and rice can only be raised in a few of the low-lying areas. The summer season is short, and fields produce only one crop a year.

Agricultural methods are thus not very different from those of Pathans, but the net production of fields is much less. Kohistanis, however, have a two-fold economy, for transhumant herding is as important as agriculture. Sheep, goats, cattle, and water buffalo are kept for wool, meat, and milk. The herds depend in summer on mountain pastures, where most of the Kohistanis spend between four and eight months each year, depending on local conditions. In some areas the whole population migrates through as many as five seasonal camps, from winter dwellings in the valley bottom to summer campsites at a 14,000 foot altitude, leaving the fields around the abandoned low-altitude dwellings to remain practically untended. In the upper Swat valley, where the valley floor is covered with snow some months of the year, winter fodder is collected and stored for the animals.

By having two strings to their bow, so to speak, the Kohistanis are able to wrest a living from inhospitable mountain areas which fall short of the minimal requirements for Pathan occupation. In these areas, Kohistanis long retained their autonomy, the main territories being conquered by Swat State in 1926, 1939, and 1947. They were, and still are, organized in politically separate village destricts of from 400 to 2000 inhabitants. Each community is subdivided into a number of loosely connected patrilineal lineages. The central political institution is the village council, in which all landholding minimal lineages have their representatives. Each community also includes a family of blacksmith-cum-carpenter specialists, and a few households of tenants or farm laborers.

Neighboring communities speaking the same dialect or language could apparently fuse politically when under external pressure, in which case they were directed by a common council of prominent leaders from all constituent lineages. But even these larger units were unable to withstand the large forces of skilled fighters which Pathans of the Swat area could mobilize. These forces were estimated at 15,000 by the British during the Ambeyla campaign in 1862.

"NATURAL" SUBAREAS

The present Swat State appears to the Kohistanis as a single natural area, since, as an ethnic group, they once occupied all of it, and since their economy can function anywhere within it. With the advent of invading Pathan tribes, the Kohistanis found themselves unable to defend the land. But the land which constitutes one natural area to Kohistanis is divided by a line which Pathans were unable to cross. From the Pathan point of view, it consists of two natural areas, one containing the ecologic requisites for Pathan occupation, the other uninhabitable. Thus the Kohistanis were permitted to retain a part of their old territory in spite of their military inferiority, while in the remainder they were either assimilated as serfs in the conquering Pathan society or were expelled.

From the purely synchronic point of view, the present Pathan-Kohistani distribution presents a simple and static picture of two ethnic groups representing two discrete culture areas, and with a clear correspondence between these culture areas and natural areas: Pathans in broad valleys with a hot climate and scrub vegetation as against Kohistanis in high mountains with a severe climate and coniferous forest cover. Through the addition of time depth, the possibility arises of breaking down the concept

of a "natural area" into specific ecologic components in relation to the requirements of specific economies.

Analysis of the distribution of Gujars in relation to the other ethnic groups requires such a procedure. Gujars are found in both Pathan and Kohistani areas, following two different economic patterns in both areas: transhumant herding, and true nomadism. But while they are distributed throughout all of the Pathan territory, they are found only in the western half of Kohistan, and neither reside nor visit in the eastern half. The division into mountain and valley seems irrelevant to the Gujars, while the mountain area—inhospitable to Pathans and usable to Kohistanis—is divided by a barrier which Gujars do not cross. The economy and other features of Gujar life must be described before this distribution and its underlying factors can be analyzed.

Gujars constitute a floating population of herders, somewhat ill-defined due to a variable degree of assimilation into the host populations. In physical type, as well as in dress and language, the majority of them are easily distinguishable. Their music, dancing, and manner of celebrating rites of passage differ from those of their hosts. Their political status is one of dependence on the host population.

The Gujar population is subdivided into a number of named patrilineal tribes or clans—units claiming descent from a common known or unknown ancestor, but without supporting genealogies. There are sometimes myths relating to the clan origin, and these frequently serve as etymologies for the clan name. The clans vary greatly in size and only the smallest are localized. The effective descent units are patrilineal lineages of limited depth, though there is greater identification between unrelated Gujars bearing the same clan name than between strangers of different clans. These clans are irrelevant to marriage regulations. There is little intermarriage between Gujars and the host group.

The economy of the Gujars depends mainly on the herding of sheep, goats, cattle, and water buffalo. In addition to animal products, Gujars require some grain (maize, wheat, or millet) which they get by their own agriculture in marginal, high-altitude fields or by trade in return for clarified butter, meat, or wool. Their essential requirements may be satisfied by two rather different patterns of life—transhumance and true nomadism. Pathans differentiate persons pursuing these two patterns by the terms Gujar and Ajer, respectively, and consider them to be ethnic subdivisions. In fact, Gujars may change their pattern of life from one to the other.

Transhumance is practiced mainly by Gujars in the Pathan area, but also occasionally in Kohistan. Symbiotic relationships between Gujars and Pathans take various forms, some quite intimate. Pathans form a multi-caste society, into which Gujars are assimilated as a specialized occupational caste of herders. Thus most Pathan villages contain a small number of Gujars—these may speak Gujri as their home language and retain their separate culture, or may be assimilated to the extent of speaking only Pashto. Politically they are integrated into the community in a client or serf status. Their role is to care for the animals (mainly water buffalo and draft oxen) either as servants of a landowner or as independent buffalo owners. They contribute to the village economy with milk products (especially clarified butter), meat, and manure, which is important and carefully utilized in the fields.

In addition to their agricultural land, most Pathan villages control neighboring hills or mountain-sides, which are used by Pathans only as a source of firewood. The transhumant Gujars, however, shift their flocks to these higher areas for summer pasture, for which they pay a fixed rate, in kind, per animal. This rent supplies the landholders with clarified butter for their own consumption. Gujars also serve as agricultural laborers in the seasons of peak activity, most importantly during the few hectic days of rice transplantation. They also seed fields of their own around their summer camps for harvest the following summer.

In Kohistan there is less symbiosis between Gujars and their hosts but the pattern is similar, except that the few fields are located by the winter settlements.

The transhumant cycle may be very local. Some Gujars merely move from Pathan villages in the valley bottom to hillside summer settlements 1,000 or 1,500 feet above, visible from the village. Others travel 20 or 30 miles to summer grazing grounds in the territory of a different Pathan tribe from that of their winter hosts.

Nomads travel much farther, perhaps 100 miles, utilizing the high mountain pastures in the summer and wintering in the low plains. While the transhumant Gujars place their main emphasis on the water buffalo, the nomads specialize in the more mobile sheep and goats. Nonetheless, the two patterns are not truly distinct, for some groups combine features of both. They spend the spring in the marginal hills of Pathan territory, where they seed a crop. In summer the men take the herds of sheep and goats to the high mountains, while the women remain behind to care for the buffalo and the fields. In autumn the men return with the herds, reap the crops, and utilize the pastures. Finally, they store the grain and farm out their buffalo with Pathan villagers, and retire to the low plains with their sheep and goats for the winter.

The true nomads never engage in agricultural pursuits; they may keep cattle, but are not encumbered with water buffalo. The degree of autonomous political organization is proportional to the length of the yearly migration. Households of locally transhumant Gujars are tied individually to Pathan leaders. Those crossing Pathan tribal borders are organized in small lineages, the better to bargain for low grazing tax. The true nomads co-ordinate the herding of flocks and migrations of people from as many as 50 households, who may also camp together for brief periods. Such groups generally consist of several small lineages, frequently of different clans, related by affinal or cognatic ties and under the direction of a single leader. Thus, though migrating through areas controlled by other political organizations, they retain a moderately well-defined organization of their own.

GUJAR DISTRIBUTION

The co-existence of Gujars and Pathans in one area poses no problem, in view of the symbiotic relations sketched above. Pathans have the military strength to control the mountainous flanks of the valleys they occupy, but have no effective means of utilizing these areas. This leaves an unoccupied ecologic niche which the Gujar ethnic group has entered and to which it has accommodated itself in a politically dependent position through a pattern of transhumance. Symbiotic advantages make the relationship satisfactory and enduring. It is tempting to see the expansion of Gujars into the area as resulting from the Pathan expulsion of Kohistanis from the valley. The Kohistanis, through their own pattern of transhumance, formerly filled the niche and it became vacant only when the specialized agricultural Pathans conquered the valley bottom and replaced the Kohistanis.

But the co-existence of Gujars and Kohistanis poses a problem, since the two groups appear to utilize the same natural resources and therefore to occupy the same ecologic niche. One would expect competition, leading to the expulsion of one or the other ethnic group from the area. However, armed conflict between the two groups is rare, and there is no indication that one is increasing at the expense of the other. On the other hand, if a stable symbiotic or noncompetitive relationship may be established between the two groups, why should Gujars be concentrated in West Kohistan, and not inhabit the essentially similar East Kohistan area? The answer must be sought not only in the natural environment and in features of the Gujar economy, but also in the relevant social environment—in features of Kohistani economy and organization which affect the niche suited to utilization by Gujars.

EAST VS. WEST KOHISTAN

As indicated, Kohistanis have a two-fold economy combining agriculture and transhumant herding, and live in moderately large village communities. Although most Gujars also practice some agriculture, it remains a subsidiary activity. It is almost invariably of a simple type dependent on water from the melting snow in spring and monsoon rains in summer, rather than on irrigation, and on shifting fields rather than manuring. The Kohistanis have a more equal balance between agriculture and herding. The steep slopes require complex terracing and irrigation, which preclude shifting agriculture and encourage more intensive techniques. The size of herds is limited by the size of fields, which supply most of the winter fodder, since natural fields and mountain meadows are too distant from the winter dwellings to permit haying. Ecologic factors relevant to this balance between the two dominant economic activities become of prime importance for Kohistani distribution and settlement density.

There are significant differences in this respect between East and West Kohistan, i.e., between the areas drained by the Indus and the Swat Rivers respectively. While the Indus and the lowest sections of its tributaries flow at no more than 3,000 feet, the Swat River descends from 8,000 to 5,000 feet in the section of its valley occupied by Kohistanis. The higher altitude in the west has several effects on the economic bases for settlement: (a) Agricultural production is reduced by the shorter season and lower temperatures in the higher western valley. (b) The altitude difference combined with slightly higher precipitation in the west results in a greater accumulation of snow. The Indus bank is rarely covered with snow, but in the upper Swat valley snow tends to accumulate through the winter and remains in the valley bottom until April or May. Thus the sedentary stock-owner in West Kohistan must provide stored fodder for his animals throughout the four months of winter. (c) The shorter season of West Kohistan eliminates rice (most productive per land unit) as a food crop and reduces maize (most advantageous in return per weight of seed) in favor of the hardier millet.

These features serve to restrict the agricultural production of West Kohistan, and therefore the number of animals that can be kept during the winter season. No parallel restrictions limit the possibility for summer grazing. Both East and West Kohistan are noteworthy for their large, lush mountain meadows and other good summer grazing, and are thus rich in the natural resources which animal herders are able to exploit. However, these mountain pastures are only seasonal; no population can rely on them for year-round sustenance. Consequently, patterns of transhumance or nomadism are developed to utilize the mountain area in its productive season, while relying on other areas or techniques the rest of the year. True nomads move to a similar ecologic niche in another area. People practicing transhumance generally utilize a different niche by reliance on alternative techniques, here agriculture and the utilization of stored animal fodder. There appears to be a balance in the productivity of these two niches, as exploited by local transhumance in East Kohistan. Thus, in the Indus drainage, Kohistanis are able to support a human and animal population of sufficient size through the winter by means of agriculture and stored food, so as to utilize fully the summer pastures of the surrounding mountains. In an ecologic sense, the local population fills both niches. There is no such balance in the Swat valley. Restrictions on agricultural production limit the animal and human population, and prevent full exploitation of the mountain pastures. This niche is thus left partly vacant and available to the nomadic Gujars, who winter in the low plains outside the area. Moreover, scattered communities of transhumant Gujars may be found in the western areas, mainly at the very tops of the valleys. With techniques and patterns of consumption different from those of Kohistanis, they are able to survive locally in areas which fall short of the minimal requirements for permanent Kohistani occupation. The present distribution of Gujars in Kohistan, limiting them to the western half of the area, would seem to be a result of these factors.

A simple but rather crucial final point should be made in this analysis: why do Kohistanis have first choice, so to speak, and Gujars only enter niches left vacant by them? Since they are able to exploit the area more fully, one might expect Gujars eventually to replace Kohistanis. Organizational factors enter here. Kohistanis form compact, politically organized villages of considerable size. The Gujar seasonal cycle prevents a similar development among them. In winter they descend into Pathan areas, or even out of tribal territory and into the administered areas of Pakistan. They are thus seasonally subject to organizations more powerful than their own, and are forced to filter through territories controlled by such organizations on their seasonal migrations. They must accommodate themselves to this situation by travelling in small, unobtrusive groups, and wintering in dispersed settlements. Though its is conceivable that Gujars might be able to develop the degree of political organization required to replace Kohistanis in a purely Kohistani environment, their dependence on more highly organized neighboring areas still makes this impossible.

The transhumant Gujar settlements in Kohistan represent groups of former nomads who were given permission by the neighboring Kohistanis to settle, and they are kept politically subservient. The organizational superiority of the already established Kohistanis prevents them, as well as the nomads, from appropriating any rights over productive means or areas. What changes will occur under the present control by the State of Swat is a different matter.

This example may serve to illustrate certain viewpoints applicable to a discussion of the ecologic factors in the distribution of ethnic groups, cultures, or economies, and the problem of "mosaic" co-residence in parts of Asia.

(1) The distribution of ethnic groups is controlled not by objective and fixed "natural areas" but by the distribution of the specific ecologic niches which the group, with its particular economic and political organization, is able to exploit. In the present example, what appears as a single natural area to Kohistanis is subdivided as far as Pathans are concerned, and this division is cross-cut with respect to the specific requirements of Gujars.

(2) Different ethnic groups will establish themselves in stable co-residence in an area if they exploit different ecologic niches, and especially if they can thus establish symbiotic economic relations, as those between Pathans and Gujars in Swat.

(3) If different ethnic groups are able to exploit the same niches fully, the militarily more powerful will normally replace the weaker, as Pathans have replaced Kohistanis.

(4) If different ethnic groups exploit the same ecologic niches but the weaker of them is better able to utilize marginal environments, the groups may co-reside in one area, as Gujars and Kohistanis in West Kohistan.

Where such principles are operative to the extent they are in much of West and South Asia, the concept of "culture areas," as developed for native North America, becomes inapplicable. Different ethnic groups and culture types will have overlapping distributions and disconforming borders, and will be socially related to a variable degree, from the "watchful co-residence" of Kohistanis and Gujars to the intimate economic, political and ritual symbiosis of the Indian caste system. The type of correspondence between gross ecologic classification and ethnic distribution documented for North America by Kroeber will rarely if ever be found. Other conceptual tools are needed for the study of culture distribution in Asia. Their development would seem to depend on analysis of specific detailed distributions in an ecologic framework, rather than by speculation on a larger geographical scale.

39

TAPPERS AND TRAPPERS:
PARALLEL PROCESS IN ACCULTURATION

ROBERT F. MURPHY and JULIAN H. STEWARD

THE PROBLEM

THE purpose of this paper is to show how two cases of acculturation exemplify parallel processes of cultlre change, that is, cross-cultural though differences in outward form and substanesses of culture change, that is, cross-cultural regularities of function and causality, even though differences in outward form and substantive content are such that the acculturation might also be considered as convergent development.

As subsequent sections will show in detail, the Mundurucú of the Tapajós River in Brazil and the Northeastern Algonkians in Canada differed during precontact times in social structure, in the general nature of their culture, and in their cultural ecological adaptations. The first were tropical forest hunters and horticulturalists living in semi-permanent villages and given to warfare. The second were hunters of large migratory game and were loosely organized in nomadic bands. Despite these differences, however, both represented roughly the same level of sociocultural integration. That is, individual families were related to one another through certain supra-familial patterns—village activities in the one case and band functions in the other —but the local unit in each instance was politically autonomous.

Since this paper is essentially an illustration of methodology, it is important to stress that the concept of level does not classify cultures according to concrete and substantive form and content. Different cultures may be wholly unlike in their particulars in that they are the products of distinctive area histories or traditions and of local adaptation to environments. At the same time, the largest integrated and

From *Economic Development and Cultural Change*, Vol. 4, July, 1956. Copyright © 1956 by the University of Chicago Press. Reprinted by permission of the publisher and the authors. Robert F. Murphy is Professor Anthropology, Columbia University; Julian H. Steward is Research Professor of Anthropology, University of Illinois.

autonomous social units may be of a similar order of inclusiveness. While, therefore, similarity of level must underly formulations of cross-cultural regularities, such similarity alone does not at all imply typological identity. The aboriginal tropical forest Mundurucú and the subarctic Algonkian hunters were wholly unlike in most cultural particulars and in social structure, although both were integrated on comparable sociocultural levels.[1]

They were alike, however, in the acculturative processes to which they were subjected and in the final cultural type which is now emerging in both populations. The processes were similar in the special manner in which outside commercial influence led to reduction of the local level of integration from the band or village to the individual family and in the way in which the family became reintegrated as a marginal part of the much larger nation. The resultant culture type was similar in each case in that the local culture core contained the all-important outside factor of almost complete economic dependence upon trade goods which were exchanged for certain local produce and because the functional nature of local production, the family, and other features were directly related to this new element. The common factor postulated to have causal importance is a kind of economic activity—the collection of wild produce—which entailed highly similar ecological adaptations. While rubber production differs as greatly in particulars from fur trapping as the tropical forests differ from the subarctic barren-lands of Labrador, the result of the acculturative processes in the two cases was the independent emergence of the same type of culture, as defined in terms of level of integration and culture core. We shall use the latter term to denote the structural interrelationships of the basic institutions of the culture.

This case study should also help clarify the heuristic concept of cultural ecology, and especially to illustrate how fundamentally it differs from environmental determinism. It will be shown that total environment is in no way the decisive factor in the culture-environment relationship. In analyzing the creative processes in the adaptation of culture to environment, it is necessary to determine the crucial features in the environment that are selectively important to a culture of a particular level and a particular area tradition. In this sense, it does not matter how different the subarctic and the tropical forests are in their totality. The primary fact is that each environment afforded a resource for trade purposes which could best be exploited by individual families controlling these products within delimited territories. These products did not achieve importance until the native populations became parts of larger sociocultural systems and began to produce for outside markets in a mercantilist pattern.

The process of gradual shift from a subsistence economy to dependence upon trade is evidently irreversible, provided access to trade goods is maintained. It can be said, therefore, that the aboriginal culture is destined to be replaced by a new type which reaches its culmination when the responsible processes have run their course. The culmination point may be said to have been reached when the amount of activity devoted to production for trade grows to such an extent that it interferes with the aboriginal subsistance cycle and associated social organization and makes their continuance impossible.

NORTHEASTERN ALGONKIANS

Our discussion of the acculturation of the Northeastern Algonkians assumes that the family-owned fur-trapping territories widely reported among these Indians were post-white in origin. The supposition of Speck, Cooper, and Eiseley that such territories were aboriginal lacks support in early historical documents. Moreover, indisputable cases of post-white formation of family territories have been reported by Leacock among the Eastern Montagnais, Jenness among certain of the Mackenzie Basin Athabaskans, and Steward among the British Columbia Carrier. Leacock's study deals with the processes of development of trapping territories in greatest detail and consequently provides the most illuminating material. We shall constantly refer to it in the following delineation of the aboriginal culture core and the subsequent changes in it.

According to Leacock, the Eastern Montagnais formerly possessed very loosely integrated bands. The basic aboriginal social unit was the "multi-family" winter hunting group consisting of two to five families. These groups were nominally patrilocal, but there was considerable deviation from this pattern, and individual families readily shifted from one group to another. The continual splits and reamalgamations of these winter groups depended upon the vicissitudes of the subarctic Laborador winter. Game, never abundant or highly concentrated, became thinly scattered during severe winters. Families then had to break away from the winter multi-family group in order to exploit the country extensively. In better times, they might reassemble with a different group of families. While each of these groups had a leader, his following was ill-defined and fluctuating in membership.

Despite the frequent necessity for the winter group to split into smaller units, the Eastern Montagnais preferred to live in larger social groups, for collective hunting was generally more efficient for taking large game. Leacock's more conservative informants, in fact, regarded solitary or semi-solitary hunting as a white man's technique, and they expressly said that it was not appropriate for Indians. Moreover, in the absence of outside sources of food, which are available today, sharing of game was essential to survival since any family might be unlucky in hunting. The rigors of the environment necessitated a degree of social fluidity and amorphousness that was essential to physical survival. Owing to a number of variations in environmental factors, especially in the quantity and distribution of game, crystallization of more rigid and permanent winter groups was impossible.

The Montagnais were, however, grouped into somewhat larger units during the summer season of fishing and caribou-hunting. Each summer, several multi-family winter groups gathered together on the shores of the lakes and rivers, where they could obtain fish in some quantity. These groups, according to Leacock, did not maintain ownership of well-defined territories in native times. Each band had only a rough and generally recognized territorial locus of operations. But it would have been contrary to the interests of any one band to encroach upon the lands of other bands; for band areas represented an approximate division of resources in relation to population. But since local availability of game differed each year, it was customary that a temporarily favored band offer hospitality to one that was starving.

These "bands" had little or no formal organization. There were no band chiefs or definite mechanisms for integrating the band as a social entity. The bands existed principally upon the basis of economic reality. They had greatest functional significance during the season of hunting large, migratory animals. While both the Montagnais and the culturally indistinguishable Naskapi hunted caribou, the relatively greater reliance of the latter upon caribou probably accounts for the stronger development of band hunting territories in northern Labrador.

Leacock divides the development of the family trapping territory into three general phases. In the first stage, when the Indians were only slightly involved in the fur economy, the trapping of fur-bearing animals and trade for hardware and food-stuffs was secondary to native subsistence activities. In this stage the Indians were only partially dependent upon the trader and could still subsist on the native economy. Since the small, nongregarious and nonmigratory fur-bearing animals were not killed in great numbers by the more primitive techniques of wooden traps and firearms and since they yielded inadequate meat, the primary winter dependence was upon deer and other larger game. The Indians could devote themselves to the luxury of securing trade articles only after assuring themselves of an ample food supply.

These marginal trappers, however, rapidly became so involved in the barter system that certain western goods, such as pots, pans, knives, axes, steel traps, and firearms became necessities to them. Since these available manufactured articles were much more efficient than the corresponding native implements, the latter were rapidly displaced and knowledge of their manufacture was eventually lost. The basic process therefore was one of increasing dependency upon trade, which eventually brought the loss of many useful arts. During this early stage of dependency, the customary use of ill-defined territories by amorphous bands was still the only approximation of land ownership to be found, and bonds of intra-group dependency were still tight.

In the second period of Montagnais acculturation, the same fundamental process continued to the point where certain basic readjustments became necessary. Dependency upon the trader increased to such an extent that fur trapping became more important than hunting for subsistence. The Indian was now forced to buy the major part of his winter's provisions from the trader, and game formed only a supplemental food source. Owing to the difficulties of transporting a supply of food adequate for the entire family, the men began to leave their families at the trading post during the winter while they trapped in the company of other men. Debt obligations and credit facilities had already linked Indians with particular trading posts. The practice of leaving families at the posts throughout the winter tightened these bonds. The families depended upon the store for subsistence, and the post became the center of the trapper's social world as well as economic world.

Leacock states that during this second stage, which is typified by the present day Natashquan band of Eastern Montagnais, there is still considerable territorial shifting of fur trappers and that family trap-line tenure is temporary and unfixed. Older informants expressed a preference for collective activity, which is exemplified today by trapping in groups, lack of definite proprietary rights in trapping territories, and the sharing among the men of the trapping groups of the fur from animals shot with guns. That animals trapped were claimed by the trap owner is probably also native.

The stages outlined by Leacock, however, are not presented by her as clearly distinguishable periods during which cultural stability was achieved. They are no more than transitory phases, and the Eastern Montagnais are now, in our terminology, moving toward the culmination of the processes of change. Certain men, says Leacock, show an increasing tendency to return to the same trapping territory year after year. Within these more limited precincts, usually no more than two trappers can work together. To a certain extent, the example for this pattern has been set by the white trappers, but the Indians follow it primarily because it is the most efficient working arrangement. When a single Indian enjoys the yield and has a vested interest in the vital resource of his territory, he attempts to protect and perpetuate it by practices of fur conservation which were not native to the culture. The more conservative Montagnais trappers do not wholly approve of the new mode of work followed by their compatriots, but they respect their tenure of exclusive trapping rights to a limited region. What emerges is a system of ownership by usufruct, a system also found among the Western Montagnais and, in fact, in many other areas of the world in which controls of law and government are loose and population density is low.

As more and more Eastern Montagnais adopt this new exploitative pattern, the group as a whole increasingly acknowledges family rights to delimited fur territories. Such rights will extend over much if not most of this area, and it will undoubtedly encroach seriously upon the semi-nomadism of the more conservative Indians. Ultimately, these latter, too, will have to change. What finally emerges will be the classical family trapping territory system in which definitely limited tracts are held by the head of a family and inherited patrilineally.

In order not to confuse or oversimplify theories of the origin and development of property rights, it is important to recognize that rights to fur trapping territories mean merely customary or usufruct rights to the furs of animals within a defined area. They by no means give exclusive rights to control of and profit from the land itself and everything thereon or even to all its wild life. Anyone may pursue and kill deer or caribou on any fur area. In some instances, another may kill and take the meat of a beaver, provided only that he give the pelt to the man having exclusive rights to the furs within the territory in question.

Two basically different concepts of rights to resources within the same area co-exist, each justifiable and explainable in its own way: the right to hunt large game for subsistence purposes practically anywhere and the right to monopolize fur-bearing animals within prescribed areas. In British Columbia the provincial government recognized these differences some years ago and registered family owned trapping territories of the Carrier Indians and protected them by law while permitting moose-hunting anywhere.

This end product of acculturation is substantially Leacock's third stage. The nuclear family now becomes the primary economic and social unit, and the old bonds of inter-familial economic dependency become attenuated. The new individualism has even penetrated the nuclear family. Among the Western Montagnais, the son of a trapper owns the beaver lodges which he discovers, whereas among the most acculturated of the Eastern group, only the family head may own such a resource.

With the breakdown in interfamilial ties among the Northeastern Algonkians, the economic centers of gravity for the families are the trading posts. Leacock says:

The movement of trading posts has obviously been the most important factor determining recent shifts in the size and location of Montagnais bands. However, it would be wrong to infer from this that increasing dependence on trade has acted to destroy formerly stable social groups. The reverse seems to be closer to the truth—that the changes brought about by the fur trade have led to more stable bands with greater formal organization.

Leacock gives the Seven Islands band as an example of this post-contact development. This new "band," however, is of a different order entirely than aboriginal hunting bands, for the principal bond between the members is that they all trade at the Seven Islands trading post. They claim no band territory; in fact, all present trends are towards familial tracts and not band lands. The modern band has a chief whose principal function is to act as intermediary with the Indian Agent. Also, the Indians refer to themselves as the "Seven Islands" (derived from the name of the trading post) people, and are so called by other Indians. In the interest of taxonomic clarity it is best not to describe such an arrangement as a "band." Such a group is reminiscent of the post-white Shoshoneans of the Great Basin, who classify themselves principally by reservation, for example, Warm Springs Paiute, Burns Paiute, Owyhee Shoshoni, and so forth. Prior to the Reorganization Act, the only basis for these groupings was common residence on a reservation and representation by a spokesman, who generally attained his position partly through prestige, but probably more importantly through recognition by the Indian Agent. Since the agents preferred "cooperative" men, the chiefs often did not truly represent the Indians. These reservation people, like Leacock's Seven Islands band, had little formal structure and a very limited *raison d'etre*. The stability of these groups is almost entirely a function of their linkage to the whites, an outside factor. Among the more acculturated Eastern Montagnais, the basic socio-economic unit appears to be the nuclear family.

THE MUNDURUCÚ

We shall discuss the Mundurucú in somewhat greater detail than the Algonkians not only because they are less known ethnographically but because the special problem of acculturation toward individual families has not been adequately described for South America.

The Mundurucú have been in active contact with European civilization for the last 160 years, of which only 80 years have been spent in rubber exploitation. The following description of the pre-rubber period Mundurucú does not purport to depict the *pre-contact,* or aboriginal, Mundurucú, but refers to the middle of the nineteenth century. . . .

The Mundurucú have inhabited the gallery forests and savannah lands east of the upper Tapajós River in the state of Pará, Brazil, for at least two centuries. The savannah in this region is quite limited, and the predominant flora are the high forest and thick vegetation typical of the Amazon basin. The Mundurucú chose the open country for their villages because remoteness from the larger streams afforded some protection from river-borne enemy attack and relief from the swarms of insects which infest the river banks, while the absence of forests immediately adjoining the villages gave some security against the dawn surprise attacks favored by nearly all tribes of the region. These attacks were difficult to launch without cover. Since the Mundurucú used water transportation only slightly, isolation from the rivers was not a hardship.

It has been noted that the nineteenth century Mundurucú and Northeastern Algonkians were on the same level of sociocultural integration. The simple, loosely-structured nomadic hunting bands of the Algonkians were roughly equivalent to the semi-sedentary villages of the Mundurucú. In both instances, the local group consisted of a multi-family, autonomous community. Under certain circumstances, the various Mundurucú villages tended to integrate on a tribal level, but there were no permanent trans-village political controls. That no Mundurucú village could function in isolation, since there was inter-village marriage and periodic cooperation in warfare and ceremonialism, does not necessarily imply a higher level of integration in economic or political activities. Similarly, it can be argued that Northeastern Algonkian bands were autonomous but by no means isolated from other such units.

The Mundurucú and Algonkians were integrated on the same level, but their cultures differed structurally or typologically and in content. Patrilineal clans and moieties in Mundurucú society made kinship ties more extensive and pervasive. Village subsistence was based on slash-and-burn horticulture. Although the heavy work of clearing the forest was done by work groups consisting of all the village males, garden care and manioc processing were carried out by the women of the matrilocal extended family. The chief occupations of the men were hunting and warfare.

Leacock's reconstruction of the aboriginal society of the Eastern Montagnais shows the nuclear family to have had greater functional importance than among the Mundurucú. The Montagnais family was a relatively stable unit within the shifting and amorphous hunting bands, whereas the Mundurucú pattern was the converse. Each Mundurucú household was a stable unit composed of women and their female offspring. The Mundurucú had the seeming paradox of matrilocal extended families in a society of patrilineal clans and moieties. The men married into these extended families from similar units in the same village or from other villages. However, there was no need to integrate a husband into the extended matrilocal family of the household, because the focus of his activities was the men's house. All males upon reaching adolescence slept in the men's house, which was located on the western perimeter of the circle of houses composing the village. The females of each household prepared and sent food to the men's house to be eaten in a communal meal. The men's house was also the center of male work and relaxation. The most immediate economic tie of a man to his wife's house was that he brought his daily take of game there. Communal distribution of game, however, made this economically unimportant. Otherwise, the husband visited his household for purposes of sex, to play with the children, or to take a between-meals snack.

Marital break-ups caused no great social maladjustment. The woman and her children simply lived on in the household and took another husband. If the ex-husband was originally from the same village, he did not even have to move his hammock from the men's house. The husband and wife performed no economic tasks together, and the sexual division of labor operated mainly within the context of the village as a whole rather than the nuclear family.

The yearly cycle of activity of the pre-rubber period Mundurucú was not patterned by warm and cold seasons as in Labrador, but by rainy and dry periods. At the end of each rainy season, April on the upper Tapajós River, the trees and vegetation in each projected garden were felled by a work party composed of all the men of the village and allowed to dry out. After clearing the forest, many families went in small groups to the larger streams where fishing was good during low waters and where they could hunt the many game animals which left the interior forests to feed and drink at the streams.

After two to three months it was necessary to return to the village to burn the felled vegetation in the garden clearings before the first rains wet the forests. After the early rains had sufficiently moistened the ground, individual gardens were planted to manioc by the cooperative efforts of all the men and women of the village. Other vegetables were planted by the women of the household of the man who initiated the gardens, and who was formally considered to own it.

Maize, squash, beans, and other vegetables were harvested by January or February and eaten immediately. The root crops, including bitter and sweet manioc, matured at the end of the rainy season in new gardens. A longer period of maturation was required for root crops in replanted gardens. Bitter and sweet manioc can be harvested as needed; this natural storage made these crops invaluable for year-around subsistence.

The bitter manioc, by far the most important garden product, required considerable labor to render it edible. The tubers were grated, the prussic acid was extracted by use of the *tipití*, or basketry press, and the pulp was then toasted either in the form of the native *beijú*, a flat manioc cake, or of *farinha*, the coarse Brazilian manioc flour. *Farinha* was sold to Brazilian traders. All phases of manioc processing were carried out by the women of the extended family household, who worked together under the direction of the oldest woman of the house. The labor was divided according to specialized tasks which, however, probably contributed as much towards making the operation pleasant as efficient.

Farinha was thus a collective product in that it involved the communal labor of the village in garden clearing and manioc planting, and the efforts of the women of the household in processing. Moreover, it was sold to the traders by the village as a whole and not by individuals. In this barter the hereditary village chief represented the village, and the proceeds from the sale were divided equally among the contributing households.

Bates, the British naturalist, describes the mode in which this trade was conducted in the mid-nineteenth century, when the first small quantities of rubber were traded by the Mundurucú along with larger amounts of other produce:

They [the Mundurucú of the upper Tapajós River] make large plantations of mandioca, and sell the surplus produce, which amounts on the Tapajós to from 3000 to 5000 baskets (60 lbs. each) annually, to traders who ascend the river from Santarem between the months of August and January. They also gather large quantities of salsaparilla, india-rubber and Tonka beans in the forests. The traders on their arrival at the Campinas (the scantily-wooded region inhabited by the main body of Mundurucus beyond the cataracts) have first to distribute their wares—cheap cotton cloths, iron hatchets, cutlery, small wares, and cashaça—amongst the minor chiefs, and then wait three or four months for repayment in produce.

When rubber became the major product of Amazonia the same pattern of trade was perpetuated among the Mundurucú. All of the rubber collected was turned over to the chief, who alone negotiated directly with the trader. The merchandise given for the rubber was, insofar as could be ascertained through contemporary informants, equitably distributed to each man in proportion to the rubber he had produced. But since chiefs were commonly more prosperous than other men, it can be assumed that they did not suffer in their role of middleman. The share taken by the chief, however, was never so great as to result in truly significant wealth differences. In fact, the traders usually managed to keep the Indians in debt, and this debt was charged against the chief as the representative of the village. Tocantins, who visited the Mundurucú in 1875, published a bill presented to one chief. If this bill is typical, the Indians' indebtedness was frequently very heavy. These debts were used to force the chief to extract greater production from his followers.

As the Mundurucú depended increasingly upon trade, the chief became more subordinate economically to the trader, who manipulated him accordingly. The trader eventually was able to appoint "chiefs" to carry on the trade. An appointed chief was usually known as the *capitao*, or "captain," as distinguished from the hereditary village chief, who was called *anyococucat* or *ichöngöp*. By using the "captains" as local trade representatives, the traders were able to increase their control over the villages.

At the same time, by robbing the hereditary chiefs of their trade function, they weakened the entire structure of leadership. In time, the *capitao* displaced the hereditary chief almost entirely. To increase the prestige of the trader-appointed chief, the trader often took his protegé on his annual trip to buy supplies in Belém, where the chief's position was confirmed by the governor or some other official.

The Mundurucú dependency upon trade at first evidently increased the peacetime authority of the hereditary chief, for the villagers relied upon him to promote and secure their best interests in trading activities. The appointment of *capitaos* undermined the native chief, and initially increased the trader's control over the village. The people became confused, however, as to whether the *capitao* or the *anyococucat* should be regarded as "chief." Ill feeling towards and suspicion of the appointed chiefs began to develop, for the Indians were always aware of, although powerless to cope with, the sharp practices of the traders, and they usually assigned the *capitao* a share of the blame. Upon the latter fell the onerous task of goading the people to harder work in the rubber avenues. Since most Mundurucú do not even today consider rubber collection a congenial occupation, the role of the *capitao* must have done little to increase his popularity. During the field research among the Mundurucú, the young, bilingual trader-appointed "chief" of the village of Cabitutú was in danger of losing his life. Distrust of the trader, whom the "chief" represented, was centered upon this young man and threatened his position so greatly that he was on the verge of flight.

In later years, as will be described subsequently, individual Mundurucú Indians have tended increasingly to deal with the trader directly rather than through the "chief." For this reason, village political organization has been effectively shattered.

The white-appointed Mundurucú "chief," unlike his Northeastern Algonkian counterpart, mediated trade relations between a group of followers and the whites. After individual trading had become strongly established among one section of the Mundurucú, however, "chiefs" were chosen by the Indian Agent and by missionaries in order to control the general behavior of the Indians, and not specifically for commercial purposes. This more nearly approximates the modern Montagnais situation, although it was reached through a different sequence of functional roles and from a different aboriginal base. In both cases, the Indians themselves were very conscious that these men were not genuine chiefs in terms of aboriginal leadership patterns, and both groups apparently suspected that the white-recognized chief was promoting the interests of the white men rather than those of his own people. The new leadership patterns never became fully established. While these patterns were functional in terms of white-Indian relations, they were dysfunctional in terms of the native socio-cultural structure.

Among the Mundurucú, therefore, the integrity of the local socio-political groups was, in part, temporarily maintained by a change in the functional role of the chieftain. That the changed pattern of leadership eventually became dysfunctional resulted in part from the ecological adaptations necessary to rubber collection. These adaptations, however, did far more than contribute to the disintegration of political controls. They undercut the very economic basis of village life.

Hevea brasiliensis, the native and most common species of rubber tree, grows wild throughout the upper waters of the Amazon. It can be exploited only during the dry season, and, in the upper Tapajós River valley, the maximum length of the gathering season is from May to early December, approximately seven months. Since these trees are scattered throughout the low lands near the watercourses, they are reached by circuitous paths cut through the undergrowth. The spacing of the trees and the work involved in rubber collection generally limit the number of trees tapped daily by one man to one hundred and fifty or less. Some collectors improve their yield per tree by maintaining two or three separate avenues which they visit only every second or third day. The distribution of rubber trees is such that each avenue gives access to trees within an area of about three to five square miles. The actual size of this territory depends, of course, upon the density of the rubber trees. In some sections of the Amazon drainage wild rubber is more abundant than in others. One may travel ten to twenty miles on reaches of river where rubber is sparse without passing a single habitation, but, where rubber is more plentiful, one encounters houses at intervals of a mile or even a half-mile.

The rubber tapper must work in his avenue or avenues almost daily, and therefore must live near them. Since each tapper exploits a considerable tract of land, his physical remoteness from neighboring tappers is a matter of necessity. Thus, on the Tapajós River, which has a population of about 3,000 excluding the Mundurucú, there are only two Brazilian villages of any consequence. One of these has a population of about 700, and the other has only 150 people. The other settlements are merely hamlets consisting of a trading post and from two to seven houses. The majority of the population live in isolated houses on the river banks.

The exploitation of wild rubber is a solitary, individual occupation in that the tapping of the tree, the subsequent collection of the latex, and the final coagulation process are one-man jobs. The last phase, carried out at the end of the day, consists of solidifying the latex over a smoky fire. The simplicity and the daily time-schedule of the entire rubber process in Amazonia is such that no one can profitably leave off collection to specialize only in tapping or collection or coagulation. For similar reasons, two men do not work in the same avenue. However companionable, it would not be a practicable means of increasing production.

This brief account of how wild rubber is exploited is necessary to an understanding of changes in Mundurucú society. In the earlier contact period, the Mundurucú traded chiefly in manioc flour and wild products, and rubber was of secondary importance. Chandless' observation that in 1860 the Mundurucú of the upper Tapajós "trade in salsa and sell provisions to the parties of India-rubber makers" indicates that important trade in articles other than rubber continued at least until 1860. Shortly after this date, however, the tempo of rubber extraction in the Amazon quickened, and in 1875, as Tocantins' account shows, rubber was the most important Mundurucú product.

With the advent of the rubber trade, Mundurucú acculturation entered its second stage. During the first, when trade in manioc flour and certain wild products predominated, the hereditary chief mediated between the traders and his people, aboriginal social patterns were largely unchanged, and warfare was still vigorously prosecuted, frequently under the sponsorship of traders and colonial authorities. During the second stage, which lasted until 1914, warfare abated, the size of villages decreased owing to migration and European-introduced diseases, and the position of the hereditary chief was weakened by the imposition of appointed

"chiefs." The period was characterized by a "loosening" of integration rather than by a change in mode of integration, or structure.

Work in the rubber avenues in the latter half of the nineteenth century did not upset the annual subsistence cycle as much as might be expected. Whereas many people had formerly left their villages during the dry season to hunt and fish along the streams, they now left to collect rubber. As in times past, they cleared their garden sites before leaving and returned to the village in time to burn them over and plant. The necessity to provide all their own subsistence limited the rubber producing season to three months, mid-June to mid-September, out of a possible seven. This parallels closely the earlier phases of Northeastern Algonkian fur production, when the Indians' need to obtain their own meat supply by aboriginal cooperation techniques limited fur production and conflicted with their increased desire for Western manufactures.

During the nineteenth century (and to the present day) the Mundurucú, like the Algonkians and in fact most aborigines, had been acquiring a seemingly insatiable appetite for the utilitarian wares and trinkets of civilization. Firearms increased their efficiency in warfare and hunting, especially the individual hunting carried on during the rubber season when one or two families lived in isolation adjacent to their rubber trees. In communal hunts, the game could be surrounded and the range and velocity of the weapons were not so crucial to success. Other items, too, became necessities to the Mundurucú. Contrary to popular belief that nudity is beneficial to tropical peoples, there are various reasons why clothing is desirable in the Amazon. Insect stings greatly annoy the Indians, and at night the temperature drops to from 55° to 65° F. Clothing, however, is expensive, and only in recent years has it been used consistently in some Mundurucú villages. The movement toward covering the body entailed the development within two generations of a sense of shame comparable to that of Europeans. The Mundurucú, especially the women, have also acquired a desire for finery for the sake of display. They have also developed a taste for many strictly non-utilitarian goods, such as the Brazilian raw cane rum and the beads and ornaments purveyed by the trader.

A full and adequate description of the growth of Mundurucú dependence upon trade would require a separate treatise, for reliance upon manufactured goods entailed further dependence upon many adjuncts of these goods. For example, firearms required powder and lead, while garments of factory-woven cloth had to be made and repaired with scissors, thread, and needles. The substitution of metal pots for native ones of clay and of manufactured hammocks for the native product has reached the point where many young women now do not know how to make these articles. The Mundurucú barely remember that their forebears used stone axes and bamboo knives, and they would be helpless without the copper toasting pan used to make manioc flour.

Despite the flourishing trade in gewgaws, the allure of most trade goods lay more in their sheer utility than in their exotic qualities. The increased efficiency of the Mundurucú economy made possible by steel tools must have been enormous.

The parallels in these basic processes of acculturation between the Mundurucú and the Montagnais are probably to be found also among most aborigines. In the case of the Mundurucú, the displacement of aboriginal crafts by commercial goods better suited to meet local needs, both old and new, inexorably led to increased dependency of the people upon those who furnished these goods and therefore to a greater involvement in economic patterns external to their own culture.

The Mundurucú families, like those of the Algonkians, became dependents of the trading posts. More than a century ago, Bates related that Brazilian traders made seasonal expeditions to trade with the Mundurucú. After rubber became important in the Amazon, permanent trading posts were established on the upper Tapajós River. These posts, whether owned by individuals or companies, exercised such control over tracts of rubber-producing forest that they compelled the rubber collector to trade exclusively with them. They accomplished this by their power of dispossession and by holding the collector in debt. The traders among the Mundurucú were never able to obtain title of ownership to the rubber regions within Mundurucú country proper, but they made the Indians dependent upon them in a very real sense through their credit arrangements. In time, all of the Mundurucú villages came under the control of various traders, who were so influential by virtue of being necessary to the Indians that they were able to appoint the "chief," in violation of Indian tradition, and thereby intensified their control over the Indians.

The progressive weakening of the hereditary chief, whose authority was based upon aboriginal activities, was furthered by the decline in warfare. The post-white warfare, although frequently mercenary in character and auxiliary to Portuguese occupation and expansion, continued the native pattern of authority. The Indians were paid in trade goods. When, at the end of the nineteenth century, the central Amazon region had been pacified, the military help of the Mundurucú was no longer needed. Meanwhile, rubber collecting had become the principal means by which the Indians acquired foreign trade articles. Since the Indians were important to rubber production in labor-starved Amazonia, they were pushed to greater efforts by the traders. Increased devotion of the Mundurucú to rubber production correspondingly interfered with their warfare; for in earlier times the rubber season was the time for war. When in 1914 a Franciscan mission was established in their midst, the earlier political and economic basis of Mundurucú warfare was so undermined that the admonitions of the priests that they live in peace were quite effective.

At the end of the second stage of Mundurucú acculturation, only bonds of kinship and economic collectivity in producing food for the group held Mundurucú society together. Much of the old structure was gone. The chieftaincy had been undermined, warfare had ended, and reliance upon the outside economy was taking effect. During the nineteenth century, increasing numbers of Mundurucú who had difficulties with their co-residents were able to leave their villages permanently. Many others left in order to participate more fully in the rubber economy.

Full dependency upon rubber collection is not compatible with village life. Since the aboriginal Mundurucú villages were located several days foot travel from the rubber areas fringing the rivers, a family participating both in collective village life and the rubber economy had to migrate seasonally between its village and its house in the rubber area. Families living in this manner could spend only three to four months in rubber production. The only way the Indians can devote their full efforts to rubber tapping is to leave the villages of the interior savannah and live permanently near the rubber trees along the river banks. A large portion of the Mundurucú, whose increased need of and desire for trade goods could no longer be satisfied by the yield of only three months' work in the rubber avenues, have made this choice.

These families represent the third stage of Mundurucú acculturation. Their resettlement in the rubber regions, however, has occurred in two ways. The first is a direct and complete adaptation to rubber collection, which can be studied in many contemporary inland villages. People desiring to increase their income from barter improve their rubber avenue house to make it more comfortable during the rains, plant gardens, and remain there. Although they maintain relationships with the inland villages, the loci of their social lives lie increasingly within the orbit of the communities of scattered families dependent upon the trading posts. The final step in their incorporation into the local Brazilian economy and the culmination of this acculturative process will come when they abandon horticulture to devote full time to work in the rubber avenues, and, like their Brazilian neighbors and the Western Montagnais, depend upon trade for the bulk of their food supply.

The second mode of readaptation to the rubber economy, while ending in the same type of settlement pattern and social organization as the first, involves passage through an intermediate stage. The previously mentioned mission on the Cururú River had indifferent success in attracting the Mundurucú until the 1920s, when a policy of trading with the Indians was adopted. The missionaries were honest and generous in their commercial relations, and rubber-tapping became more profitable to the Indians. Their intensified collecting activities resulted in a general movement to the banks of the Cururú River, and by the 1930s many interior villages had been abandoned.

The migrants settled so heavily on the river banks that they were able to nucleate in new villages. These villages, however, lacked the men's organization, division of labor, and collective patterns which structured the old type villages. Although the population shift from the old to new villages was heavy, it involved individual families rather than whole villages. The new villages grew as additional nuclear families arrived from the savannah communities. During this period of growth, since the new villages consisted of families, many of which had not previously been connected with one another, each family had to carry on the subsistence activities which were formerly the function of the extended family and village. Gardens were cleared and planted by husband and wife with whatever aid their children were capable of giving. Fish, taken by family members from the nearby rivers, rapidly replaced game formerly taken in collective hunts as the major source of protein. Meanwhile, increased rubber production enabled the Indians to buy the hooks, lines, and canoes with which fishing was made more effective. As the new villages grew larger, the atomistic division of labor was perpetuated, and the nuclear family became the basic unit of production.

Political authority on the Cururú River was almost nonexistent. The migrants began to trade as individuals, first with the missionaries and later with the newly established Indian Post. This economic trend stripped the "chiefs" of one of their last remaining functions, and their role was reduced to that of intermediary between the villagers and the priests and Indian agent.

The amorphously structured villages which arose on the banks of the Cururú River represent a transition to the family level and are not the culmination of adaptation to the ecology of rubber collection. Most of the residents of the Cururú River still have to reside away from their villages during the rubber season, but the easy communication made possible by canoe transportation allows the majority to return to rubber production after planting their gardens.

The new individualism and fragmented division of labor, combined with facets of the old culture which had become dysfunctional in the new situation, contributed to the disorganization of Cururú River society. The political authority of appointed "chiefs" was now a means of extending the influence of the whites. The continuing migration of young men from the remaining primitive villages of the savannahs caused an oversupply of men on the Cururú River, and conflicts over women became rife. Owing to the endless squabbles in villages which had lost their aboriginal basis of integration, dissidents moved off to live at their rubber avenues or formed new and smaller villages. This fission process is still going on. Concomitantly, the Mission and the Indian Post are becoming more important as focal points in a new mode of integration of the Mundurucú. Over one-third of the Cururú River population make their rainy season homes at these agencies, which serve as centers of trade and of social and religious gatherings. It is from the Post and Mission, also, that the lines of authority now radiate.

COMPARATIVE SUMMARY

The accompanying table presents the major phases of acculturation in summary form, as abstracted from the historical continua. The basic acculturative factors in both cases exerted parallel influences, although the two societies were substantively different until the final culmination was reached. There were four causal factors common to each. First, both became involved in a mercantile, barter economy in which the collector of wild products was tied by bonds of debt and credit to particular merchants. Such involvement also occurred widely among native peoples who produced crops or livestock. This arrangement must be distinguished from cash transactions, in which, owing to the impersonality of money as a medium of exchange, the primary producer has greater freedom of choice as to with whom he will deal. In a pure credit-barter economy, all transactions are based on a personal relationship between the principals; the merchant must be able to rely upon the continued patronage of the primary producer whereby the latter liquidates past debts while assuming new ones. It seems to be a basic procedure that the pre-literate Indian is kept in debt by the trader. While the latter can manipulate accounts at will, and no doubt is frequently guilty of malfeasance, he usually allows the Indian to buy beyond his means. The debtor-producer is selling his future production, and the creditor will not extend payment unless assured of delivery. Where such an economy is found, it is common for merchants to refuse to deal with primary producers who are in debt to another merchant. This is a "gentleman's agreement" in the Amazon, although it is frequently violated by wandering traders. Second, the growing ties of dependency upon the traders are at the expense of collective bonds within the respective societies. Reliance upon individuals and institutions outside the native social system are intensified by a steady increase in demand and need for manufactured goods. This, as we have seen, goes beyond the mere initial allure of Western tools and ornaments. Luxuries soon became necessities—a process that can be found in our own culture. Third, while crude latex and animal furs are very unlike articles, they imply a common cultural-ecological adaptation. Both are natural products having a reliable occurrence in worthwhile quantity within an area which can be most efficiently exploited by one man. Both require conservation, for careless exploitation can seriously reduce the number of furbearing animals, or render rubber trees worthless. The producer has an incentive to maintain the productivity of his resources. Finally, both rubber trees and fur animals are sufficiently dispersed to require that persons exploiting them live or work at some distance from one another.

These factors of change were essentially the same among both Mundurucú and Montagnais, and they were introduced through contact with the outside world. Their initial effects upon the aboriginal cultures were somewhat dissimilar, owing to aboriginal differences between the two groups. Whereas the Mundurucú chief served at first as intermediary with the trader, this seems not to have been true of the Montagnais chief. Montagnais family heads, however, traded on behalf of their sons. For a short time, this pattern was followed by many Mundurucú during the period immediately after the Mundurucú chief had ceased to act as intermediary with the trader. After the breakdown of extended kinship bonds in both groups, individuals traded completely on their own.

The native kinship organization persisted longer among the Mundurucú than among the Montagnais, and this has been a factor in perpetuating village life today among the less acculturated Indians east of the Tapajós River. Aboriginal Mundurucú kinship structure was more extensive and socially integrative than that of the Montagnais. Moreover, the aboriginal production of subsistence crops survives even among Mundurucú families living in isolation in their rubber avenues. The Mundurucú still produce all their own subsistence, although there are some changes in emphasis, technique, and organization.

The Brazilian rubber tapper—the white man who has gone into the forest or the Indian of mixed blood who is completely acculturated and enmeshed in the mercantile economy—usually buys all his food from the trader and devotes the season when he could be growing his own food to tapping rubber or to working off his debt to the trader by performing personal services. At present, we know of only one case of a Mundurucú who bought most of his food, but we can confidently predict that, as the population becomes more acculturated toward dependency in all ways upon the larger society, an ever-increasing number will buy food. When

Tabular Comparison

Mundurucú	*Montagnais*
1. Pre-rubber	**1. Pre-fur**
Village consists of men's house, matrilocal extended family households; population divided into patrilineal clans and moieties.	Nomadic composite band hunts large migratory game animals.
Village males form collective hunting and garden-clearing group.	Frequent band breakup during winter scarcity.
Household females form the horticultural unit.	Amalgamation of several winter groups for summer hunting and fishing.
Intensive warfare for headhunting and as mercenaries allied to whites; partial dispersal of villagers in dry season for fishing and war.	Chieftainship weak and shifting—leader of winter group; no summer band chief.
Chief the war leader and representative of villages in trade of manioc flour.	Residence bilocal, frequent shifts of winter group membership.
2. Marginal involvement	**2. Marginal involvement**
Chief continues as mediator with trader, but is now often trader-appointed—trader gains influence.	Trade by family heads—leaders do not trade for followers.
Dry season population dispersal for rubber production rather than fishing and war—war continues, but lessened in importance.	Trapping secondary to subsistence hunting—subsistence still gotten traditionally, basic social patterns persist.
Basic pre-rubber economy and settlement pattern unchanged.	No trapping territory.
Continuing displacement of aboriginal crafts.	Linkage to trading posts.
3. Transitional	**3. Transitional**
Further displacement of native crafts, increased need of trade goods, increased dependence on trader.	Further displacement of native crafts, increased need of trade goods, increased dependence on trader.
Chieftainship undermined due to new type chiefs who now represent the trader.	Increased fur production interferes with subsistence hunting.
Agricultural cycle and village life inhibit larger rubber production.	Individual trade conflicts with group solidarity.
Trend toward individual trade.	
4. Convergence and culmination	**4. Convergence and culmination**
A. Intermediate	Fur trapping now predominant; winter provisions purchased.
Move to new villages in rubber regions.	Winter groups not necessary with end of collective hunt—family or individual hunting gives greater efficiency, allows conservation.
Chief now intermediary with Indian agent and missionaries.	Shift of economic interdependencies from group to trader.
Individual trade, individualized subsistence economy—end of men's house and traditional village—village held together only by weakening kin ties and sociability.	Emergence of a chief who serves as intermediary with Indian agents and missionaries.
Centripetal factors (e.g., sorcery, sexual rivalry) cause fission of these villages and results in B, below.	Nuclear family basic unit at all times of year.
B. Dispersal (follows upon 3 or 4A)	Trapper maintains and transmits right to a delimited hunting territory exploited only by his family.
Leadership no longer integrative.	
Individual trade undercuts kin obligations.	
Conflict with agricultural cycle resolved by moving to rubber avenue—family now in isolation except for trade bonds.	

they are no longer able to feed themselves by their own efforts, they will have effectively become *caboclos,* or neo-Brazilian backwoodsmen.

The acculturative factors operated in two somewhat different ways among both the Mundurucú and Montagnais. First, they created a succession of modifications in the native societies, which gradually converged toward typological identity in the final family level. Second, during this evolution of the total groups they produced deviant families which broke away from their fellow tribesmen to devote themselves entirely to tapping or trapping. It was not until the processes had nearly reached their culmination that the surviving but greatly modified native society began to disintegrate.

Among the Mundurucú the bonds of leadership and kinship had undergone a steady and slow attrition during one hundred years. The end of warfare had robbed Mundurucú culture of a great deal of its vitality, and the chief was reduced to a mere figurehead, manipulated by the trader and the religious and governmental agencies. Work in the rubber avenues and dependence upon the trader had served to sever and weaken ties within the society. At the final point of transition to isolated residence, and total divorce from traditional communal life, the Mundurucú were not much more closely integrated than the Montagnais.

The culmination of the long acculturative processes shows a high degree of structural parallelism. Both Mundurucú and Montagnais populations are divided into loosely integrated and dispersed communities centering about particular trading posts with which the individual families have ties. The Indians still recreate, associate, and intermarry with one another, but the nuclear family is now the stable socioeconomic unit. It is the highest level of integration found among the native population itself, but it is linked to the nation through the intermediary of a regional economy. The integration of the family with the national level is highly specialized and limited. These families do not yet share a substantial part of the common denominator of the national culture or even of the regional sub-cultures of their non-Indian neighbors.

There is a final phase, which, though occurring at different dates in the different localities, is characterized by assimilation of the Indians as a local sub-culture of the national sociocultural system and virtual loss of identity as Indians. At this point, the acculturational processes and results diverge, since the Indians participate to a much greater extent in the national culture. So long as the families maintain their marginal relation with the national society, they are quite unlike the basic populations of the nations in which they lived and much more like one another. When, however, they learn the national language, intermarry extensively with non-Indians, and acquire many of the non-Indian values and behavior patterns, they have to be classed with the special regional sub-cultures that have developed in portions of these nations.

It can be predicted that the drastic shift in mode and level of integration will do much to hasten the loss of cultural distinctiveness. Fortes has cogently expressed the relationship between social structure and formal culture content in such a situation:

> I would suggest that a culture is a unity insofar as it is tied to a bounded social structure. In this sense I would agree that the social structure is the foundation of the whole social life of any continuing *society.* . . . The social structure of a group does not exist without the customary norms and activities which work through it. We might safely conclude that where structure persists there must be some persistence of corresponding custom, and where custom survives there must be some structural basis for this.

FURTHER COMPARISONS

We can delimit and refine the Mundurucú-Algonkian parallel by the cross-cultural examination of structural changes caused by acculturation in other areas. We will not seek further parallels, however, but will discuss cultures in which divergence appears manifest. One instance of such apparent divergence is the Northwest Coast, where the fur trade at first strengthened or intensified rather than weakened the aboriginal social structure. The florescence of the potlatch and class system on the Northwest Coast as a result of new wealth in trade goods is a thesis which has been ably expounded by a number of students. It would be very misleading, however, to consider *any* trade in furs as the crucial factor. What really matters is *individual trapping of fur-bearing animals.* The sea otter was the principal fur bartered by most Northwest Coast tribes, and collection involved neither individual effort nor delimited territories. The amount of land trapping was probably fairly limited and in any event did not offset the cultural effects of the great salmon wealth which created surpluses rarely if ever paralleled by hunting, gathering, and fishing people.

The trapping activities of the Skagit of Puget Sound more nearly paralleled those of the Northeastern Algonkians, according to Collins' description:

> The [trading] posts played an important part in altering the economy of the Indians. First, they encouraged a shift in their hunting habits. The skins in which the traders were most interested were beaver and land otter. These animals had small value in the aboriginal economy, since they were less desirable for food than deer or elk, for example. At the traders' behest, however, hunters pursued these animals eagerly. Another economic shift took place when the hunters, instead of killing game for meat, began to exchange skins for food.

The result of this trade was, however, quite different from its effects in Eastern Canada.

The effects of these changes upon Skagit social organization were pronounced. Distinctions in social rank began to be more marked—a shift made possible since, though social mobility had always been within the grasp of any person of good descent who could acquire the distinction of wealth, new sources of wealth were now available.

The new wealth acquired by the Skagit was funnelled into the class structure and ultimately the potlatch. The difference, then, between the processes of change which occurred among Northwest Coast and Northeastern Canadian groups is that the former integrated the new wealth into a *pre-existent* class structure created and perpetuated by a fishing economy. Among the latter, since there were no cultural means or goals promoting the concentration of surplus wealth in the hands of a select few, the benefits rebounded to all persons. The same was true of Mundurucú society which also was unstratified. The differences between the Skagit on one hand as opposed to the Mundurucú and Montagnais on the other are attributable to the stratification of society among the former, which in turn is partially explainable by the greater aboriginal resources of the Skagit. In effect, this constitutes a difference of level of socio-cultural integration.

The impact of trapping upon a pre-existing social structure can be even better appraised among the Carrier of the interior of British Columbia, where the wealth in salmon was far less than on the coast. The fur trade among the

Blackwater River Carrier involved intimate interaction with Northwest Coast groups, especially the Bella Coola. Goldman summarizes the effects of this contact upon the simple, bilateral Carrier hunting bands:

> Undoubtedly the Bella Coola, like all Northwest Coast tribes, became relatively wealthy as a result of this trade. And in Bella Coola where wealth was the decisive factor in building rank, the fur trade must have been particularly welcome. And the lowly interior Carrier who hunted for furs in order to trade with the Bella Coola, who traded them to the whites, became an important part of the scheme of elevating one's rank. Although a Bella Coola did not gain valuable prerogatives from a Carrier son-in-law, if he could get a monopoly upon his furs he could make enough wealth to purchase new prerogatives. And as the Bella Coola benefited by this trade, so did the Alkatcho Carrier. The latter took up products obtained on the coast and traded them to the Carrier villages eastward on the Blackwater River drainage. As they obtained guns and steel traps, economic productivity spurted so that they were able to build up the necessary property surpluses for potlatching. Potlatching obligations in turn stimulated economic activity, and the degree to which they were able to potlatch made possible the full integration of crests as honorific prerogatives.

Given our previous hypotheses, developments more or less parallel to those in Eastern Canada might be expected. But these Carrier did not trade with European traders; they dealt instead with stratified Northwest Coast tribes in the context of an economic system, the rationale of which was the validation of rank by potlatch. As the following example of the Stuart Lake Carrier suggests, direct trade with the whites and the end of potlatching result ultimately in the family trapping territory system.

The effect of the fur trade among the Carrier of Stuart Lake to the north of the Blackwater River ran a similar course but culminated in family trapping territories, according to Steward's research. In pre-white times, the wealth of salmon fisheries, although far less than those of the coastal tribes, had provided some surplus, while contacts with the Tsimshian of the Skeena River had introduced a pattern for channeling this surplus to nobles who controlled the fishing rights of large territories in the name of matrilineal moieties. This wealth circulated through small-scale potlatches. The fur trade, carried on directly with the whites more than through coastal contacts, created a new source of wealth and intensified the native pattern. Although furs were trapped by individual moiety members, a noble had rights to a certain percentage of the furs taken in his moiety's territory.

In the course of about 50 years, however, several processes combined to bring about individual trapping territories as among the Indians of eastern Canada. Most importantly, the new wealth in trade goods brought hardware that was of value to individuals. Pressures mounted to force the nobles to divide the trapping territories among their own children rather than to pass them on intact to their sister's sons, who had traditionally inherited their titles and rights. This process was aided by the activities of the Catholic missionary-ethnologist Father Morice, who effectively undermined the native religious sanctions of the class of nobles, and by the government, which banned potlatching. The older pattern survives only in isolated localities, where it is carried on clandestinely. At Fort St. James on Stuart Lake, where there is located a Hudsons' Bay Trading Post and some few hundred whites and Indians, the processes have reached a culmination almost identical to that of the Montagnais.

Present-day Carrier society at Stuart Lake consists of individual families that have exclusive rights to certain trap-lines that are registered with and protected by the Provincial Government. The family is the kinship and economic unit [Steward].

It seems likely that the Blackwater River Carrier have not yet reached the final stage of acculturation. The same may be true of the Skagit. The critical consideration is whether wealth in salmon among these tribes was so great that it offset the importance of trapping. This was not the case at Stuart Lake. On the lower Skeena River, salmon are so important that canneries have been built, and the Tsimshian and Tlingit have given up fur trapping to become commercial fishermen and cannery laborers.

Certain Plains Indians in North America also engaged in the fur trade but developed in distinctive ways. This is another illustration of the need to examine specific features in the taking of furs. There is a significant ecological difference between the collection of fur on the Great Plains and in the coniferous forests of Canada that lies essentially in the difference between hunting and trapping. It is incomplete and misleading therefore to make comparisons simply on the basis of "fur trading." In the Great Plains, buffalo hides were the chief item traded, whereas in eastern Canada, small, non-gre-

garious and non-migratory animals were trapped. The trade on the Plains resulted in an emphasis upon the buffalo hunt beyond the needs of subsistence and served to strengthen the collective and cooperative techniques traditionally used in the pursuit of migratory herds. Moreover, band cohesion in the Plains was enhanced by acquisition of the horse and gun and by intensification of warfare, the latter carried on in part to obtain horses.

It is possible that a non-stratified society which acquires surplus wealth may develop a class structure, but this involves special conditions not ordinarily found among collectors of wild products. Some of the North American Plains Indians showed an incipient development of a class society in the late eighteenth and early nineteenth centuries, but the tribes were decimated by epidemics and overwhelmed by the advancing frontier when intensified wealth and significant prestige differences had begun to emerge. A parallel between the Plains and the Mundurucú can be found in the increased authority of chiefs owing to their functions as intermediaries between the traders and the Indians. Jablow notes such a florescence of political controls among the Cheyenne, and Lewis specifically states of Blackfoot trade:

In periods of monopoly [of the Indian trade by one company] the fur trade had a positive effect, that is, it increased the prestige and authority of the chiefs. In periods of competition it had a disruptive effect, that is, it weakened the power of the chiefs.

The Plains band chief traded a commodity which was obtained by collective effort. The Mundurucú chief served as middleman in the pre-rubber period when trade in manioc flour, which was also communally produced, was of primary importance. But he eventually lost his position when individually produced rubber became predominant. The Tenetehara Indians of northeastern Brazil have been in contact with civilization longer than the Mundurucú, but, according to Wagley and Galvao, the village chiefs and extended family heads still have a central role in the trading of collectively produced manioc flour and palm oils. It seems apparent that, lacking some other basis for political authority, it is difficult for leaders to maintain control over trade in individually produced goods.

Our formulations, in effect, state that when certain acculturative factors, defined functionally rather than formally, are present, the core of a culture will change in expectable and predictable ways. These formulations assume the constancy of certain other preconditions, which, though well worth investigation of themselves, can be regarded as given factors for methodological purposes.

This can best be exemplified in our present cases by reference to the basic, though incompletely explained, acculturative factor common not only to the Mundurucú and Naskapi but to most primitive peoples throughout the world. This factor can be stated simply as follows: *When goods manufactured by the industrialized nations with modern techniques become available through trade to aboriginal populations, the native people increasingly give up their home crafts in order to devote their efforts to producing specialized cash crops or other trade items in order to obtain more of the industrially made articles.* The consequences of this simple though world-wide factor are enormous, even though they vary in local manifestation. The phenomenon is of such a high order of regularity that special explanations must be sought for the few departures from it.

The main hypothesis arising from the present study is that: *When the people of an unstratified native society barter wild products found in extensive distribution and obtained through individual effort, the structure of the native culture will be destroyed, and the final culmination will be a culture type characterized by individual families having delimited rights to marketable resources and linked to the larger nation through trading centers.* Tappers, trappers, and no doubt other collectors come under this general statement.

NOTES

1. The acculturational phenomena described in this article were apparently found among many, although not all, Northeastern Algonkians, including native groups of New England as well as Canada. Speck, Steward, and others have considered this probem for many years. They were also found among certain Mackenzie Basin Athabaskans, as Jenness has shown. A very comparable case of acculturational process was studied by Steward among the British Columbia Carrier. These cases will be cited in the concluding comparative section. The Montagnais are taken as our principal example because Eleanor Leacock studied them in detail from this point of view.

PART VII   Ideology, Language, and Values

40

SOCIOLOGICAL ASPECTS
OF THE RELATION BETWEEN LANGUAGE AND PHILOSOPHY

LEWIS S. FEUER

LANGUAGE is the primary fact which concerns contemporary philosophy. Men have been speaking and writing for a long time, but it is only recently that the task of philosophy has been said to be the analysis of language. Ethical perplexities, social anxieties, the nature of scientific knowledge, religious speculations, are held not to be directly the problems of the philosopher. They enter his study by way of a domain of languages and sub-languages. This preoccupation with language is itself an unsual phenomenon in our intellectual history. It challenges the sociologist of philosophic ideas for an explanation, and it leads one to wonder upon what evidence philosophers have accepted the doctrine of linguistic primacy.

Bertrand Russell has for many years been the leading proponent of the importance of the analysis of language. More than a half-century ago, he wrote: "That all sound philosophy should begin with an analysis of propositions, is a truth too evident, perhaps to demand a proof." None the less, Russell sought to defend this "truth" with a sociological argument concerning the causes of philosophic beliefs. A large part of Western philosophy, Russell affirmed, was determined by the notion that every proposition must consist of a subject and a predicate. "Any philosophy," he said, "which uses either substance or the Absolute will be found, on inspection, to depend on this belief. Kant's belief in an unknowable thing-in-itself was largely due to the same theory." In his later writings, Russell often recurred to the sociological argument for the linguistic determination of philosophic ideas. "We have to guard," he wrote, "against assuming that grammar is the key to metaphysics," an assumption which he believed had been made by traditional philosophy. He re-

From *Philosophy of Science*, 20(2): 85–100. Copyright © 1953 by the Williams and Wilkins Company, Baltimore, Md. 21202, U.S.A. Reprinted by permission of the publisher and the author. Lewis S. Feuer is Professor of Philosophy, University of Toronto.

ferred with approval to the views of the philologist Sayce. "Sayce maintained that all European philosophy since Aristotle has been dominated by the fact that philosophers spoke Indo-European languages, and therefore supposed the world, like the sentences they were used to, necessarily divisible into subjects and predicates." The linguistic interpretation of philosophic history was central in Russell's thinking, but it was never supported with the requisite historical data. It took on the character of a postulate whose proof was commended to others. He thus declared that "a great book might be written showing the influence of syntax on philosophy; in such a work, the author could trace in detail the influence of the subject-predicate structure of sentences upon European thought, more particularly in the matter of 'substance.' "

In this essay, I shall try to show why this great book could not be written.

Our problem is a sociological one. The linguistic school adheres to the sociological doctrine that the structures of languages have been the primary determinant of philosophies. I shall try to show that the available evidence is against this sociological theory. When writers like Russell speak of the influence of syntax on philosophy, they are presumably speaking of a verifiable sociological causal relation. And in what follows, I shall approach the problem as one in the sociology of philosophic ideas. There is overwhelming evidence that the structure of languages has had no primary, determining effect on men's philosophies.

The philologist Sayce, upon whose authority Russell relies, declared: "Had Aristotle been a Mexican, his system of logic would have assumed a wholly different form." We cannot perform this experiment, but we can show how the same metaphysics has arisen among peoples with radically different languages, and how the most diverse types of philosophies have arisen among men who used the same language. And, to begin with, we can show how syntactical variations have not been accompanied by corresponding differences in metaphysics.

SYNTACTIC VARIATION NOT CORRELATED WITH CHANGES IN PHILOSOPHIC IDEAS

The linguistic interpretation of the history of philosophy affirms that the forms of language, the mode of syntax, tend to be projected by thinkers as the substance of reality. Linguistic determinants, of which the thinker is often unconscious, are thus held to shape his metaphysical outlook. Part of the contribution of philosophical linguistics is then believed to be its bringing in to clear consciousness the hitherto unconscious influence of syntactical forms. What philological facts are at variance with the linguistic interpretation of philosophy? There are many languages, in the first place, in which gender is a syntactical category, for instance, Latin, French, German, Spanish. In English, we don't assign gender to "the table," but the French say "la table." We cannot, however, affirm that this difference in syntax reflects itself in a corresponding distinction between English and French philosophy. Perhaps the distinction in gender early reflected motivations toward metaphysics which Freud has illumined. It may be that primitive philosophers once projected the masculine and feminine principles throughout nature. Perhaps the progenitors of the feminine *l'étendue* and the masculine *le temps* conceived of space as a female receptacle, and time as a cosmic male organ. A philosophical psychoanalyst might perceive in Alexander's theory, that time is the "mind" of space, a weakened version of the more forthright primitive metaphysics. He might even regard the emergent qualities as the offspring of the sexual union of space and time. The origins of the classifications of gender, however, remain obscure. If one finds that the "earth" and the names of trees are conceived as feminine after the fruit-bearing analogy, there are still such strange facts as that words for "table, thought, fruit" are masculine in one language and feminine in another. As Jespersen says, "It is certainly impossible to find any single governing principle in this chaos." Whatever the origin of gender, its grammatical structure has within historic times been no determinant of metaphysics. If grammar itself was once founded on an unconscious metaphysic, this linkage is now so vestigial as to have no appreciable bearing on the structure of philosophic ideas.

In many languages, to take another group of facts, there is a tendency to get rid of the subjunctive mood. "In Danish and in Russian there are only a few isolated survivals; in English the subjunctive has since Old English times been on retreat, though from the middle of the nineteenth century there has been a literary revival of some of its uses." The trend is toward stating the content of traditional contrary-to-fact conditional sentences in the indicative mood.

To what is this decline of the subjunctive mood to be attributed? It is difficult to say, for grammarians are not clear as to what characterizes the use of the subjunctive in Aryan languages. It seems to denote a certain hesitation, or doubt, or anxiety concerning the reality of the proposed situation. Perhaps it was once culturally more important to indicate the doubts, anxieties, uncertainties of the speaker. With the decline of social anxieties, the cultural need for a differentiated subjunctive mood may have lessened. But whatever the causes of syntactical change, one cannot say that the fortunes of the subjunctive mood have been reflected in corresponding philosophic doctrines. The character of Danish and Russian philosophic speculations is not correlated with the low estate of the subjunctive. The anguish and anxiety of Kierkegaard could express itself in an idiom which was discarding the subjunctive mood.

Ring Lardner's baseball player, like his fellow Americans, was unaware of the existence of the subjunctive mood. His syntax conformed to that law of laziness which, according to Sayce, is the basic cause of change in language. Perhaps the promptings of laziness are involved in the decline of the subjunctive. There is no evidence, however, that the American public has been influenced by an unconscious metaphysical revolt against contrary-to-fact conditional significances.

French metaphysicians and French positivists use the same idiom with the same structure; the grammar they use has not predetermined them to a common mould. Descartes, Comte, and Bergson used the same language with the same grammatical structure. Their modes of thought are diverse, but each could state his philosophy with lucidity in the same syntax.

Again, we might ask what has been the philosophical bearing of the phenomenon of double or cumulative negation. Languages as varied as those of Russian, Spanish, Magyar, and Bantu exhibit this syntactical form. Two negatives in these languages do not cancel each other; on the purely linguistic level, it is not true in their syntaxes that not-not p = p. Do these languages then promote some special alternative logic or metaphysics? Not at all. As Jespersen says, the function of double negation is not as a logical, but as a psychological device. A layer of negative coloring is spread throughout a whole sentence instead of being localized in one part. Where repeated negatives are not used for emphasis, they may serve to convey attitudes of hesitancy. "This is not unknown to me" conveys a reticence not present in "I know this." Double negation can thus express either a strengthened negative or a weakened positive.

In the common American language, as H. L. Mencken says, "the double negative is so freely used that the simple negative appears to be almost abandoned." The title of a once-popular song, "I ain't never done nothing to nobody no time," abundantly illustrates the vulgar syntactical form. There is no evidence, however, that the American proletariat has developed a metaphysic of dialectic negation to higher powers.

The syntax of cumulative negation has never in any historic language been the cause for the formulation of some non-Aristotelian logic. In all languages, moreover, when it is made clear that negative expressions are to refer to the same word, such expressions do cancel each other. The manifest, syntactical rules do not reach down into an unconscious metaphysic of "negation" other than the two-valued logic of truth and falsehood. Grammar does not legislate its corresponding metaphysics.

Especially do we see this to be the case with respect to the syntactical differences among languages in the expression of time-relations. The different tense-systems do not involve corresponding differences in the metaphysics of time. The usage of the "dramatic present" illustrates well how a syntactical form is without metaphysical consequence. It has been observed that the language of uneducated people narrates past events by using the "dramatic present." "One need only listen to the way in which people of humblest ranks relate incidents that they have witnessed themselves to see how natural, nay inevitable, this form is" [Jesperson]. The style of Damon Runyon is indeed contrived around such a use of the "dramatic present." There is no evidence, however, that either the humblest persons or the sophisticated denizens of Broadway have been led by their elementary

syntax to deny the distinction between past and present, or to insist that the present alone is real.

Many languages, furthermore, have no future tense, and make use of such devices instead as the use of the present tense to convey futurity. There is no evidence that the people who use these languages have therefore confounded the present with the future in a metaphysical sense.

Similarly, there are some American Indian languages in which the terms for day-before-yesterday and day-after-tomorrow are the same. This usage has not led to a metaphysics in which the immediate past and the immediate future are identified. The time-experience of certain Indian tribes differs in some respects from our own. Their days are not punctuated with clocks and calendars. They have no exact chronologies, and they place events in approximate order by reference to memorable events and periods in their own life-histories. They have no weekly recurrence of a Sabbath. Withal, there are basic aspects to the human experience of time which are universal—the distinctions between past, present and future, the irreversibility of time; and no linguistic usage or cultural outlook can negate these common properties of human experience.

The evidence of primitive languages is especially crucial in the consideration of the bearing of syntax on philosophy. The syntax and vocabulary of primitive languages are an outgrowth of dealings with concrete objects. One would then expect that there would be a syntactical resistance on the part of primitive peoples to Western philosophies and religious ideas, a resistance which, in view of the tremendous linguistic differences, might well ensure the non-comprehension of those ideas. Such, however, is not the case. Franz Boas' conclusions on this matter are directly to the point:

In primitive culture people speak only about actual experiences. They do not discuss what is virtue, good, evil, beauty; the demands of their daily life, like those of our uneducated classes, do not extend beyond the virtues shown on definite occasions by definite people, good or evil deeds of their fellow tribesmen, and the beauty of a man, a woman, or of an object. They do not talk about abstract ideas. The question is rather whether their language makes possible the expression of abstract ideas. It is instructive to see that missionaries, who in their eagerness to convert natives have been compelled to learn their languages, have had to do violence to the idioms in order to convey to the natives their more or less abstract ideas, and that they have always found it possible to do so and be understood. Devices to develop generalized ideas are probably always present and they are used as soon as the cultural needs compel the natives to form them.

"It is true," Boas writes, "that in many languages it would be difficult to express the generalized statements of philosophic science, because the categories imposed by the structure of the grammar are too specific." However, he adds, "It is not true that primitive languages are unable to form generalized concepts."

Languages are flexible instruments. When the cultural need for the expression of abstract ideas is felt, the appropriate devices are used to achieve this expression. But it is the cultural need which is decisive. The character of the language-instrument does not itself shape the idea to be expressed. A given language, for instance, may seem to be well suited by its syntactical forms to lead its users to a belief in metaphysical universals. But in the absence of certain cultural demands, such a belief will not be found. Empiricists, for instance, often hold that the expression of adjectival situations through the use of nouns gives rise to the belief that there are abstract entities, universals, denoted by these nouns. When one says "this flag has whiteness" instead of "this flag is white," one is supposed to be on the path to Platonic realism. For "whiteness" as a noun is thought to mislead one into the belief that it symbolizes an abstract entity. Primitive languages, however, often have this grammatical usage without giving evidence of a tendency toward Platonic metaphysics. Franz Boas describes this mode of primitive syntax:

It is not unimportant to recognize that in primitive languages, here and there, our adjectival ideals are expressed by nouns. A poor person may be conceived as a person who has poverty; a sick person as a person who has sickness; and it is not necessary that these qualities should be conceived as concrete objects. Sickness is often conceived, but poverty or size is not. We also find cases in which the structure of the sentence demands the frequent use of abstract nouns, as when the Kwakiutl Indian of Vancouver Island says to a girl, "Take care of your womanhood"; when the Eskimo speaks of the smallness or largeness of an object; or when the Dakota Indian speaks of strength and goodness.

The grammar of abstract nouns does not seem to have predisposed the Kwakiutl, Eskimo, or Dakota Indians toward a Platonic metaphysic. The causal sources of Platonism are still obscure, but it is noteworthy that the distinguished historical scholar, F. M. Cornford, finds its basis in socio-cultural rather than in linguistic phenomena: "you could build the whole structure of Platonism round that central scheme for the reform of society. What we call the theory of Forms or Ideas, and the whole conception of the universe that goes with it, could be represented, not unfaithfully, as deducible from the moral thesis." The motivation toward a "participationist" metaphysics seems to have derived from the early influences of the totemestic social order. Totemism, as Jane Harrison said, was also an epistemology. Value attitudes, emotional projections, social perspectives—these are the founts which nurture the diverse modes of metaphysical ideas. The language one uses is shaped and mis-shaped to express the metaphysical ideas which its users are trying to project. Some languages may be more malleable and expressive in certain respects than others. But every language lends itself to the appropriate tinkering required to convey the new meanings. At most, a language may be a minor agency of syntactical resistance or syntactical propensity toward certain philosophic views. It has none of the proportions of importance, however, with which it is endowed by linguistic philosophers.

THE DIFFUSION OF A COMMON PHILOSOPHY THROUGH DIFFERENT SYNTAXES

The Aristotelian metaphysics has not been the exclusive property of the Indo-European languages. It is often overlooked that it was propounded and highly developed by Arabic and Hebrew thinkers even before it was espoused by the medieval Christian philosophers. The syntax of the Semitic language differs markedly from the European tongues, but Semitic syntactical rules proved no insuperable obstacle to the formulation of the Aristotelian ideas. Words were invented to express the novel metaphysical ideas. The Talmudists had been singularly averse to speculative notions, but the medieval Jewish philosophers contrived the necessary forms to convey the foreign concepts. The Jewish philosophers derived their knowledge of Aristotle through the intermediary of Averroes. Averroes himself did not know Greek; his commentaries were based on Arabic translations from either the original Greek or from Syriac translations. When, during the twelfth century, the fanatical sect of Almohades in Spain forbade the study of philosophy, Averroes' own works in their original Arabic were almost completely lost. His writings, however, had meanwhile been translated into Hebrew, and it was in this form that they first spread through Europe. Aristotle was imported into Western Europe with Semitic bills of lading.

There were some misrepresentations of Aristotle's ideas which arose as they were refracted from one linguistic medium to another, Syriac, Arabic, Hebrew, Latin. The outstanding fact, however, is that problems of syntax and terminology were surmounted with relative ease to achieve an expression of Aristotelian metaphysics in the Semitic languages. Slight differences in metaphor had no bearing on the effective statement of common metaphysical ideas. The medieval Jewish philosopher would translate the "self-existent" essence of substance with the phrase "sheyiyeh omed biphnai atsmoh," which affirms literally, "that which will be standing by itself." "Self-existent" was conveyed by a phrase "standing by itself." The metaphor of "standing" did not, however, obstruct the formation of the idea of self-existent substance. Words took on new significances; to ask "whether the universals are only in the mind," the medieval Jewish philosophy would say, "im haklallim haym b'saychel l'vad," and the use of the word "haklallim," though derived from a familiar root, was not to be found in Biblical or Talmudical sources. Some translations would have behavioristic overtones,— "rational" was expressed by "m'daber," which literally is the participle "speaking," "quantity" was translated by "hakamah," "the how much." When Crescas discusses the existence of God, his terminology has an empirical flavor. "God exists" is translated "haeloh nimtzah," that is, "God is found." There is no simple verb "to exist" in classical Hebrew; in that language, things are found or not found, and the verb "matzoh," to find, is one of homely human action. The absence of the abstract verb "to exist" was no barrier to the discussions of the proofs for God's existence. The diffusion of metaphysical culture thus takes place across boundaries of syntax.

The notions of "being," indeed, were explicated in Hebrew despite the fact that ordinary noun-clauses in that language are without a copula of any kind. The syntactical relation between subject and predicate in such sentences is expressed, as in mathematical logic, by mere juxtaposition. The use of the verb "hayoh" in a sense near to that of a copula becomes frequent only in the later Books of the Bible. The Hebraic sensitivity to problems of existence does not, however, seem to have been affected by their syntactical omission of "being" as a copulative form.

THE SOCIAL SOURCES OF LINGUISTIC METAPHORS

When we leave the Mediterranean basin, and move our study to the Far East, we are in lands which were relatively unaffected by any diffusion of philosophic ideas. The Chinese language and writing are profoundly different from the European. We would expect, if the linguistic theory were true, that the Chinese culture would therefore be incapable of evolving philosophic ideas similar to those of Western civilization. Bertrand Russell, after his travels and teaching in China, wrote a book on that country in which he speculated briefly on the probable influence of the Chinese language on its philosophy. He inclined to agree with the view of a Chinese thinker that the alphabetical civilizations are fickle and lack solidity. He quoted the latter's words:

Certainly this phenomenon can be partially explained by the extra-fluidity of the alphabetical language which cannot be depended upon as a suitable organ to conceive any solid ideas. . . . [As for the Chinese language] it is invulnerable to storm and stress. It has already protected the Chinese civilization for more than forty centuries. It is solid, square, and beautiful, exactly as the spirit it represents.

If the Chinese language possesses such sociological powers of durability, we would expect that it would have nourished such a doctrine as the substance-attribute philosophy. Free from the atomicities and unstable transciences of the alphabetical languages, it would be predisposed to see unchanging solidities in things, whereas Western philosophy would, by contrast, be characterized by an underlying aversion to enduring substances. Actually, no such correlations hold.

There have been Chinese philosophers who developed doctrines akin to those of classical Western philosophy. Kung-sun Lung, early in the third century B.C., elaborated a doctrine, for instance, which was very much like the Platonic theory of universals. His word "chih," which meant "pointers," conveyed a notion similar to "universals." Kung said: "Things in every instance involve universals, but universals do not point to the material world. If there were no universals, things could not be described as 'things' . . . The fact that the material world has no universals springs from each single thing having a name. A name is itself not a universal." And there have been Chinese philosophers such as Mo Ti, who formulated an empirical outlook:

The words of our Master Mo: the universally true way of learning by investigation whether a thing exists or not, is, without question, by means of the actual knowledge (on the evidence) of everybody's ears and eyes. If it has been heard and seen, then it is undoubtedly to be taken as existing. If no one has heard of it or seen it, then it is undoubtedly to be taken as non-existing.

Chinese philosophy, on the whole, has not, however, been preoccupied with the problems which have been the especial concern of Western philosophers. Theory of knowledge, for instance, has not developed in China; anxieties concerning the existence of the external world, the haunting presence of things in-themselves and unknowables, are not characteristic of Chinese thought. Evidently this indifference to epistemology does not derive from the structure of its language. The Chinese language has no inflections, no declensions or conjugations, in our sense of the terms. Nevertheless, as Max Müller once said, "there is no shade of thought which cannot be rendered in Chinese."

The distinctive characteristics of Chinese philosophy are an expression, according to Fung-Yu-Lan, its recent leading historian, of the social, economic, and technological traits of Chinese civilization. Fung agrees that epistemologic questions are not "problems" to the Chinese thinker. "Whether the table that I see before me is real or illusory, and whether it is only an idea in my mind or is occupying objective space, was never seriously considered by Chinese philosophy." Not that the Chinese had somehow learned the positivist critique of non-experimental questions. Rather, the farmer's outlook had uniquely conditioned the outlook of the Chinese philosopher. "What farmers have to deal with, such as the farm and crops, are all things which they immediately apprehend. And in their primitivity and innocence, they value

what they thus immediately apprehend. It is no wonder then, that their philosophers likewise take the immediate apprehension of things as the starting point of their philosophy." The agricultural setting of Chinese thought similarly impressed itself upon John Dewey during his sojourn in the Far East:

China is agrarian, agricultural; everyone knows that fact. But while we know it, we forget how long and how stable is their agriculture. The title of a book by an American agriculturalist, *Farmers of Four Thousand Years,* is infinitely significant when we reflect upon it.

We may venture the hypothesis, furthermore, that the intensity of Chinese family life, the "we-feeling," kept the sense of reality and involvedness with things strong. The Chinese individual was not afflicted with loneliness or emotional isolation; it is striking that epistemologic subjectivism begins to torment philosophers with the onset of the age of economic individualism.

Where linguistic influences are operative in the modes of formulation within Chinese philosophy, they are the lines of transmission for more underlying socio-economic determinants of modes of thought. Expressions of the Chinese language reflect the agricultural life of a great land-domain. Fung states their close relationship:

China is a continental country. To the ancient Chinese their land was the world. There are two expressions in the Chinese language which can both be translated as the world. One is "all beneath the sky" and the other is "all within the four seas". To the people of a maritime country such as the Greeks, it would be inconceivable that expressions such as these could be synonymous. But that is what happens in the Chinese language, and it is not without reason.

The metaphors, however, which are embedded in the linguistic expressions are without any significant impact on the varieties of Chinese philosophy. The metaphors in time lose even any recessive efficacy; people become unaware of them. They are then curiosities for the social philologist, but they are not the source of an unconscious metaphysic which permeates the minds of their users.

Occasionally a metaphor will help give a philosophy a vogue which it might not otherwise have enjoyed. The syntax of the English language was common to both William James and Josiah Royce, to the pluralistic empiricist and the monistic idealist. Syntax did not impose its inevitable impress upon their philosophies. Both of them were aware that their doctrines were in different ways at variance with ordinary syntactical forms, the plurality of self-existent qualities as much so as the Reality which was the presumable immanent subject of all propositions. But James made use of a metaphor of the American language which brought friends to his philosophy among the citizenry at large. He spoke of the pragmatic method as a way of realizing the "cash value" of words. Sensitive to the American idiom, he had also described his God as one who does a retail, not a wholesale business. And James' call for confidence in God, for a faith akin to that which wins a man "promotions, boons, appointments" smacks of a salesman turned theologian, who writes his theology with the help of phrases from a manual on "How To Win Friends and Influence People." These were linguistic metaphors, but James found to his consternation that his philosophy was henceforth linked to them. In vain, he protested against the description of pragmatism "as a characteristically American movement, a sort of bobtailed scheme of thought, excellently fitted for the man on the street, who naturally hates theory and wants cash returns immediately."

What is remarkable, furthermore, is that James' financial metaphors were so infectious that they infiltrated the language of his avowed opponents. Josiah Royce thus found himself criticizing James in James' own vocabulary of business enterprise. Pragmatism, Royce argued, would be unable to meet the calls for cash payments; it would have to confess bankruptcy. An Absolute Pragmatism, a central cosmic reserve bank, with hard metaphysical bullion, would be required, he argued, to guarantee the otherwise inflationary, wild-cat finance of the plural, independent banks. The American business culture thus embraced its philosophers in its idiom. Pragmatist and absolute idealist both found themselves speaking its language. But such influences do not pertain to the syntactical forms of the English language. The pecuniary metaphors were rather part of the content of the American idiom, more immediately responsive to cultural changes than syntactical forms. And as such, these expressions are the direct vehicles for socio-economic influences on philosophy. By contrast, the grammatical forms remain in the background, invariant, unchanging while the diverse philosophies arise to compete

with each other under diverse cultural circumstances.

INADEQUACY OF THE DOCTRINE OF LINGUISTIC RELATIVITY

The linguistic interpretation of the history of thought has given rise to a special epistemological doctrine which may be called "linguistic relativity." According to this doctrine, each language defines for its users a unique cultural universe, one which includes within itself a unique physical universe as well. There is, according to this view, no world of common physical uniformities and facts which is the same for all cultures. As B. L. Whorf, a leading proponent of this theory, says: "We are thus introduced to a new principle of relativity, which holds that all observers are not led by the same physical evidence to the same picture of the universe, unless their linguistic backgrounds are similar. . . ." Every language is thus held to impose a kind of linguistic *a priori* on the forms for the analysis and description of nature. The grammar of each language, Whorf states, "is not merely a reproducing instrument for voicing ideas but rather is itself the shaper of ideas, the program and guide for the individual's mental activity, for his analysis of impressions, for his synthesis of his mental stock in trade. . . . We dissect nature along lines laid down for us by our native languages."

On what kind of evidence does the so-called principle of linguistic relativity rest? Various facts are adduced such as the difference in Eskimo linguistic usage from ours. The Eskimo would regard our use of "snow" as too large and inclusive. We use the same word to denote falling snow, snow on the ground, snow packed hard like ice, slushy snow, flying snow—in short, all the varieties of snow. But an Eskimo has different words for falling snow and slushy snow, "he would say that falling snow, slushy snow, and so on are sensuously and operationally different, different things to contend with; he uses different words for them and other kinds of snow."

Do such facts, however, establish a principle of linguistic relativity? Far from it. Rather, they illustrate the principle that where the specific differences among similar events are more important in the life of the people than the membership in the general class, the people's language may not include the abstract, general term for the class in question. Specific functions are then more emphasized than the abstract class membership. To the Eskimo, in his struggle with his material environment, the differences in the varieties of snow are what are important. "Snow" in the abstract would be co-terminous with his known physical universe, an unchanging background to his struggle for existence. What does concern him in vital ways are the variations of his world—is the ice, for example, such as can be carved for a house? His purposes differ from ours, and perceived differences, which are unimportant for us, are those to which he must most attend. The Eskimo's language does not, however, impose a specific metaphysics. He works with his day-by-day objects in an empirical spirit, he acknowledges the uniformities and causal processes of nature. As for his religious beliefs in spirits and the powers of the charms of his shamans, they bear no relationship to the structure of his language.

Categories that are unessential to a given culture, says Boas, will on the whole not be found in its language. Categories, on the other hand, that are culturally important will be found in detail. A society in which the distinction between paternal and maternal lines is socially important will have a suitable distinctive terminology. Our society lacks such a vocabulary. The obligatory categories similarly vary from one people to another. We say: "the man killed the bull," but in one Indian language, epistemological niceties are insisted upon. One has to specify the source of information, its location, and whether the data are seen, heard, or inferred. One would say: "this man kill as seen by me that bull." But, as Boas further points out, "the relational functions of grammar have certain principles in common all over the world." Every language will set forth determinate relations between a subject and predicate, verb and adverb, noun and attribute. Whatever the differences in environment, a common world of spatio-temporal objects confronts all men, and there are common properties to the matter-of-fact dealings of all peoples with nature.

Different languages emphasize different relations of men to nature, but the segments which are emphasized do not define incommensurable universes. Each culture can be informed in its own language concerning the limitations of its experience; if it wishes to, if it needs to, it can add to the resources of its language. The Hebraists in Israel have thus taken an ancient language, and expanded its vocabulary so that

textbooks of electro-dynamics can be written in the idiom of the prophets. The "principle of linguistic relativity" argues that there are incommensurable cultural universes. An incommensurable cultural universe would be an unknown one. The fact of linguistic communication, the fact of translation, belies the doctrine of relativity.

The "will to be untranslatable" grows during an era of cultural regression and ethrocentrism. An old Italian proverb has it, *Traduttori, traditori* ("Translators are traitors"). And the Talmud likewise said that the oral law was not written down, because God feared that otherwise it would be translated into Greek, and he wished to keep it the special mystery of his people. The later rabbis mourned the Septuagint translation of the Bible with a day of fasting. Linguistic relativity is the doctrine of untranslatability in modern guise.

We might indeed regard the "principle of linguistic relativity" as a pseudo-sociological hypothesis. A doctrine which is stated in the language of sociology but which no sociological observation could possibly confirm is a pseudo-sociological hypothesis. For instance, since we use English, we are held at once to be precluded from understanding, let us say, the Chinese civilization and world-standpoint. When we show that a Chinese can understand us, and we the Chinese, it is argued that such an Asian has been contaminated by Western European culture. And since the very fact of communication is "evidence" of such contamination, it follows that we couldn't possibly introduce a negative instance to this hypothesis. In short, it is not an empirical, scientific theory. How it itself could be discovered, how the relativist has escaped his own linguistic a priori to know, for example, the details of the Hopi a priori is incomprehensible. For he does manage to state the Hopi perspective in English, and this, if his doctrine were true, he should be unable to do.

The "principle of linguistic relativity" is an instance of a phenomenon among thinkers which we might call "illegitimate diffusion." When the theory of physical relativity acquired its world renown, there was a tendency for theorists in other departments to run riot with the words of "relativity." The psychological and social sciences, for instance, began to discover "frames of reference" everywhere. Economic classes, social observers, different philosophies—all of these were variously denoted as "frames of reference." The immense prestige of the physical theory of relativity was the covert, emotive argument for the adoption of these "relativities." As a matter of fact, none of these usages have any significant analogy to the physical theory.

In physical science, a body which is described as a "frame of reference" conforms to certain conditions. Thus it is stipulated that laws of nature will be invariant for all frames of reference. Although time measurements and distance measurements vary with respect to different observers, there is a space-time interval between events which is invariant for all frames of reference, moving uniformly relative to one another. But linguistic relativity, with its incommensurable universes, has forgotten the invariant world which is common to all observers. And whereas the physical theory was an attempt to explain certain unusual experimental findings, the linguistic theory arose from no counterpart of a Michelson-Morley experiment in communication. It is rather a projective superimposition upon the facts, and indeed, essentially contrary to their sense.

Despite his theory, the linguistic relativist always has had a marked ability for transcending his own linguistic a priori. "Our language," says Whorf, "gives us a bipolar division of nature. But nature herself is not thus polarized." We are thus informed that: "Nature herself, apart from any definition or determination by an a priori linguistic scheme, is not polarized." We evidently have no difficulty in stating propositions which escape the net of the linguistic a priori, and the relativist himself joins in this easy transcendence. A language is not a "frame of reference" in any sense which can give rise to a doctrine of linguistic relativity.

COMMON HUMAN EXPERIENCE AND UNIVERSAL CATEGORIES

A common, universal, scientific mode of thinking manages to express itself in all languages. It is the linguistic aspect of the common struggle of men everywhere for survival in the midst of their environment. There is the imprint on all languages of those categories and distinctions which facilitate the matter-of-fact causal reasoning without which men could not cope with their problems of biologic existence. As Malinowski said:

The categories derived from the primitive use will also be identical for all human languages, in spite of the many superficial diversities. For man's essential nature is identical and the primitive uses of language are the same. . . . The fundamental grammatical categories, universal to all human languages, can be understood only with reference to the pragmatic Weltanschauung of primitive man. . . .

Language can undertake vagaries only after it has fulfilled the minimum tasks of assistance in living. Jespersen has vividly described the common, human logic which is found in different linguistic guises:

When we examine languages, we do indeed find many things which imply the existence of a fundamental common nature in human beings all the world over. Some features of language are due to a common humanity: they show themselves just because the individuals who speak the languages are human beings. . . . This is certain that we see everywhere in the history of languages a uniform striving to be quit of the same superfluous distinctions and to reduce the grammatical apparatus to the simplest possible, to a system in which the great innersyntactical, logical, or rational categories are denoted sharply and unmistakeably. Such distinctions as those between one and more, he and she, between animate and inanimate, between past, present, and future, between the three persons—distinctions which in the infancy of language were chaotically coupled with one another and with obscure ideas of a quite different kind—come by this means to stand out sharper and sharper, while a logic common to all mankind breaks radiantly through the barriers of linguistic expressions.

The syntax of any given language may be regarded as composed of two kinds of forms and distinctions, those which correspond to natural realities and those which are projected by the languages upon realities. We might call the former "realistic syntactical distinctions" and the latter "projective syntactical distinctions." The distinction of gender, for instance, as applied to inanimate objects is an example of the latter. Now Russell believes that logical analysis of "the properties of language may help us to understand the structure of the world." He holds that study of syntax enables us to "arrive at considerable knowledge concerning the structure of the world," and as an example of such knowledge, he mentions our acknowledgment of relations as part of the non-linguistic constitution of the world. Where Russell errs is in his belief that it is the study of syntax which has led to such knowledge. The occurrence of syntactical forms is no guarantee that there are corresponding forms in nature. The distinction of gender, as we have said, is one such non-corresponding form. Our acknowledgment of relations is one founded on our actual experience of relations, and if a language were to lack relational forms, we would say so much the worse for that language. We must turn to extra-linguistic facts in order to decide which syntactical forms correspond to natural realities, and which don't. The natural world is the extra-linguistic criterion with which we judge the extent to which linguistic forms accurately conform to the structure of things. Language is not an autonomous metaphysical organon, and Russell's view that language by itself is a guide to the world's structure is an example of that faith in the "omnipotence of thought," to use Freud's expression, which is the hallmark of the unrealistic, unscientific, magical mode of thought.

Linguistic philosophers have expressed the view that incorrect grammar leads to erroneous metaphysical belief. Correct grammar, it is added, is neutral as to rival metaphysical beliefs [Max Black]. What, however, do we mean by an "incorrect grammar"? It is a classification of linguistic forms which is founded not upon the forms in function but upon an antecedent metaphysics. The Latin grammarians, influenced by Aristotle's metaphysics and not by Latin as it was used, held that every sentence must consist of a subject and a predicate. Academic prejudice applied the dominant metaphysics to the facts of speech, and grammar, which, indeed, is an empirical science of speech habits, was transformed into an a priori set of metaphysical rules. The prestige of Roman civilization promoted a species of linguistic imperialism. As Jespersen states: "Latin has been considered for centuries the supreme language, and extolled for its logic. It was easy then for people to make the mistake of thinking that everything in Latin grammar was pure logic, and that in the other languages only what agreed with Latin could be logically defended." One grammarian in 1861 wrote that to say "It is me" rather than "It is I" was "nothing else than the grossest sin against the first and simplest and most incontrovertible laws of thought and grammar." Latin provincialism overlooked the fact that nothing in logic makes it mandatory for the predicative to stand in the same case as the subject; the Russian and Finnish languages, for instance, sometimes employ different cases.

The formulations of the Latin grammarians were an intrusion, a superimposition of metaphysical dogma upon the empirical forms of speech. Their procedure was analogous to the intrusion of Aristotelian metaphysic, or Hegel's metaphysic, upon the forms and laws of physical science. We can say that incorrect grammar leads to erroneous metaphysics only in the same sense as we can say that incorrect physics leads to erroneous metaphysics. Moreover, there is an important distinction between linguistic forms in use and the grammarian's version of these linguistic forms. As an empirical matter, we have seen that empirical linguistic forms do not have a primary role in determining people's philosophies. And we have seen that the grammarian's description of a language errs when it projects some favorite metaphysics upon the empirical forms of speech. But the source of the grammarian's metaphysics is not his language; it is an extrapolative use of metaphysics which had extra-linguistic origins.

The great linguistic revolutions in the history of philosophy have come when men turned from the scholarly, honorific language to the language of common people. The archaic classical language was the depository of an accumulated vested interest in meaningless terms. The vernacular language, by contrast, was closer to the homespun verifiable realities. Meaningless terms stand out more conspicuously when they are introduced into the vernacular because the latter is closely connected with the everyday necessities of biologic existence. The literary classical language, on the other hand, has led a life immured in monasteries, dissociated from the practical concerns of men. No wonder that this dissociation of language from the controls of action finally produces a situation, as Veblen says, where "classical learning acts to derange the learner's workmanlike aptitudes." So that Descartes wrote in his momentous linguistic manifesto: "If I write in French which is the language of my country, rather than in Latin which is that of my teachers, this is because I hope that those who avail themselves only of their natural reason in its purity may be the better judges of my opinions than those who believe only in the writings of the ancients" (Discourse on Method, Part IV). The change from Latin to the vernacular, as Morris Cohen once said, revealed the emptiness of received systems.

The significance of these historic linguistic decisions has not been by way of a new choice of syntactical determinants. It is also true that the vernacular idiom could in time become encrusted with its own growth of meaningless verbiage. At the crucial juncture of historic change, however, the vernacular was the medium of empirically minded people, those whose minds had not been stamped with the schoolmen's metaphysics. The use of the vernacular was an appeal to fresh social and scientific determinants for philosophy, to open-mindedness rather than tradition. The significance of the vernacular was sociological, not syntactical; its significance was that it opened the windows of science to the fresh sight and evidence of all men, that it cleared the air of clerical vested interest.

The contemporary notion that the special task of philosophy is the analysis of syntax is, we suggest, an ideological formula, a projective definition. Such a definition promotes the separation of philosophy from the actualities of life-decisions; it defines a philosophical realm which has a scholastic autonomy, and proposes indeed that philosophers are lexicographers, the formulators of the next edition of dictionaries. If philosophies are linked to social institutions, if every philosophy is the perspective of a socio-cultural universe, it follows that the critique of philosophies will tend to lead the philosopher toward a criticism of their socio-cultural sources. The analysis of philosophies then becomes their socio-analysis. By contrast, the linguistic interpretation of philosophic thought provides a haven for those who would avoid commitment to matters of fact or social standpoint. Philosophic thought then becomes an unconscious filibuster in which the underlying aim is not to decide problems. Men's thinking, their agency as problem-solving animals, is thus inverted from its biologic role; it becomes a professional device for indefinitely postponed decision. The linguistic interpretation of philosophy is an ideological, projective formula in the sense that it would repress those cultural and psychological conflicts which are the generative source of philosophic history.

It used to be said that man is a speaking animal. Probably it would be more truthful to speak of him as a stammering, stuttering animal. Clarity of speech will come to him when the deep conflicts within him are resolved, when his anxieties are reduced. That is why philosophy cannot rest with the critique of language.

41

LANGUAGE, THOUGHT, AND CULTURE

PAUL HENLE

ORDINARILY, language is taken for granted. Its fluent and easy use leads to the assumption that it is a transparent medium for the transmission of thought. Because it offers no apparent obstacle to our customary flow of ideas, one assumes that it is a vehicle equally fitted to convey any beliefs. Scientifically, it is assumed to be of interest to linguists and perhaps to psychologists interested in child development or aphasia, but that is all. Such a conception

of language has been challenged by a number of linguists and anthropologists. Edward Sapir, more than twenty years ago, maintained that:

> The relation between language and experience is often misunderstood. Language is not merely a more or less systematic inventory of the various items of experience which seem relevant to the individual, as is so often naively assumed, but is also a self-contained, creative symbolic organization, which not only refers to experience largely-acquired without its help but actually defines experience for us by reason of its formal completeness and because of our unconscious projection of its implicit expectations into the field of experience.

Sapir added that the force of this claim could be realized only when the relatively similar

Indo-European languages were compared with widely differing languages such as those indigenous to Africa and America.

Benjamin Lee Whorf in a series of papers has developed Sapir's claim, maintaining that a language constitutes a sort of logic, a general frame of reference, and so molds the thought of its habitual users. He claimed also that, where a culture and a language have developed together, there are significant relationships between the general aspects of the grammar and the characteristics of the culture taken as a whole. To substantiate these theses, Whorf made a comparison of American Indian languages, notably Hopi, with European languages. Among the latter, he found the differences so insignificant in comparison to the differences from Hopi that he grouped them all together under the general title of SAE (Standard Average European).

If Whorf and his followers are right, the study of language takes on a new importance in the social sciences. Its place in psychology is greatly expanded, and it becomes of primary significance in all studies of culture. It may even provide the focal point about which the social sciences can best be integrated. For this reason we shall devote [this paper] to an examination of the thesis, beginning with a consideration of terms and then proceeding to discussions first of the relation of language to thought and then of the connection between language and culture.

Since the connections which can be established between language, thought, and culture depend in part, of course, on the definitions of the terms involved, it is to this problem that we first turn. Such an analysis is particularly necessary before trying to establish relationships between thought and language. Ordinarily, language is the chief evidence for the existence and character of thought and, if Whorf's claim is to be anything more than a truism, the relevant aspects of the two must be clearly distinguished and kept separate.

We may begin by looking for aspects of language which are clearly separable from thought and which may be compared to it. Vocabulary, meaning by this simply the list of words to be found in the language, would clearly be one such item. Comparing this with the vocabulary of another language one might obtain some idea of the peculiarities of the language in question, or, at least, of the difference in the two vocabularies. These differences might be compared with differences in ideas and opinions commonly expressed in the two languages. Another even more striking characteristic of languages is the mode of inflection, and diverse languages may be compared to see if differences here are connected with differences in what is expressed in the language. Again, the manner of sentence formation is a linguistic element, isolable from the content of a language and comparable with it. In some cases, also, terms in different languages, designating the same phenomena, belong to different word classes, so that, for example, what is represented by a noun in one language may be represented by a verb in another. This again is a concrete difference capable of being compared with the content of the two languages.

In the category which we have generically referred to as thought, perception must be included, as well as what may be called the conceptual organization of experience. Thus, Whorf reports that in Shawnee the cleaning of a gun with a ramrod is described by something close to directing "a hollow moving dry spot by means of a tool." This certainly shows a difference in organization—the emphasis in English being on the things, the physical objects, and the emphasis in Shawnee being elsewhere. According to some theories, differences in organization of this sort, if carried far enough, result in differences in philosophies. In any case they would show a difference in thought to be related to differences of language.

This enumeration of elements of language and thought would hardly be controversial. On bringing culture into the problem, however, one is faced with an anthropological controversy as to just what culture includes. We shall not attempt to settle the dispute, but shall merely outline the view which is most useful for comparison with language, without making any claims for this view in any other connection. A good statement of it makes culture "all those historically created designs for living, explicit and implicit, rational, irrational and nonrational, which exist at any given time as potential guides for the behavior of men." From this standpoint, culture constitutes the set of modes of procedure or the guides to living which are dominant in a group. These are thought of not as isolated but as functionally interrelated, clustering together to form certain *themes,* a theme being a higher-level generalization. Generalizations of the lower level are simply those directly based on instances of conduct, constituting patterns of behavior. Generalizations of these patterns constitute themes, each theme containing notions exemplified in a number of patterns of behavior. Themes need not be consistent, and as Opler has noticed such themes as "old age is desired and respected" and "all persons must continually validate their positions by participation in activities defined as peculiar to that position" may both be operative in the same culture. Indeed the limitation of one theme by the operation of another conflicting one may be necessary to the survival of the society.

The problem, then, which Whorf poses may be restated a little more explicitly: What is the relationship between the mechanisms of language such as vocabulary, inflection, and sentence formation on the one hand and either perception and organization of experience or the broad patterns of behavior on the other? This question is reasonably specific, except for the sort of relation involved. Obviously, the most desirable and least controversial goal would be simply to set up correlations to show that certain linguistic elements vary, say, with certain aspects of culture. Given the correlations, it would not be necessary to assign causal priority, but there still could be inferences from one side to the other. In dealing with the relationship between vocabulary and the interests of a society there is enough direct evidence to indicate such a correlation, but hardly so with any of the other relationships. In these cases, collateral evidence must enter and, in part, must take the form of showing reason to believe that a correlation would be found if more evidence were available. This prediction of the correlation is made by claiming causal connections between various factors. Even in the case of the relationship between vocabulary and culture, this sort of evidence helps substantiate the evidence of direct correlation. We see every reason to believe, as part of our common-sense psychology, that a people should have words for objects with which they are concerned and that they should lack words for objects with which they have fewer dealings. We are therefore more ready to accept as adequate the evidence which exists for the connection between the two.

To claim a causal relation between language and culture is not, of course, to say which influences the other. Either may be the causal agent, both may be joint effects of a common cause, or there may be mutual causal action. Indeed this latter is to be expected with continuing factors such as language and culture. The connections which we shall investigate in the next section will be largely causal.

With this brief discussion of the factors involved, we may turn to the evidence for relationships. It will be convenient to begin with the evidence for a connection between language and thought and to open the discussion with a consideration of the relationship between vocabulary and perception. Languages differ notoriously in vocabulary, and this difference is generally correlated with a difference in environment. Thus, Whorf notices that Eskimo languages have a variety of words for different kinds of snow where we have only one. Aztec is even poorer than we in this respect, using the same word stem for cold, ice, and snow. Sapir gives detailed evidence over a broader field in claiming that the vocabulary of a language clearly reflects the physical and social environment of a people. Indeed, the complete vocabulary of a language would be "a complex inventory of all the ideas, interests, and occupations that take up the attention of the community. . . ." He notices that among the Nootka of the northwest coast, marine animals are defined and symbolized with precise detail. Some desert people reserve the detailed lexicon for berries and other edible food plants. Similarly, the Paiute, a desert people, speak a language which permits the most detailed description of topographical features, a necessity in a country where complex directions may be required for the location of water holes. Sapir points out that what holds for the physical environment, holds even more clearly for the social. Status systems in various cultures, however complex, and differentiations due to occupations are all mirrored in languages.

So far, the argument merely shows that vocabulary reflects the environment of a people. Since the culture is largely dependent on this environment, especially where technology is relatively undeveloped, we have an argument suggesting at least that vocabulary and general ways of acting are effects of a common cause, so one may be an index to the other.

All this still says nothing concerning perception and would have little to do with it, if perception were merely a matter of recording what is presented. This is not the case, however, and there is abundant evidence to show that perception is influenced by mental set. Such effects of mental set have been summarized by Bruner and Goodman in a now classical paper. They say:

. . . subjects can be conditioned to see and hear things in much the same way as they can be conditioned to perform such overt acts as knee jerking, eye blinking, or salivating. Pair a sound and a faint image frequently enough, fail to present the image, and the subject sees it anyway when the sound is presented. Any student of suggestion, whether or not he has pursued Bird's exhaustive bibliography of the literature on the subject, knows that. Not perception? Why not? The subject sees what he reports as vividly as he sees the phi-phenomenon.

In addition, they point out, reward and punishment, experience, and social factors may all be of influence. Their own research goes on to show that children overestimate the size of coins, that the amount of overestimation is, in general, dependent upon the value of the coin, that the error is greater with coins than with cardboard discs of the same size, and that it is greater with poor than with rich children. Clearly, as they say, it will not do to consider a perceiver as a "passive recording instrument of rather complex design."

The question then becomes one of whether knowing an item of vocabulary—at least one which has application to sense experience— constitutes a set directed toward perceiving in terms of this word. The existence of such a set would mean noticing those aspects of the environment which pertained to the application of the term and tending to neglect others. Direct evidence on the point is not available, but it seems reasonable to conjecture that there is such a set. There is strong motivation to learn the language of a society on the part of children and newcomers, for only through knowing the language can wants be satisfied and communication be established. Ability to use the words of a language is thus prized, and this desire is reinforced by the discovery that the vocabulary is useful in dealing with the environment. Given the motivation to learn the language it is reasonable to infer a set favoring the application of it and so an influence on perception.

It would seem then to be consistent with what we know of mental set on other grounds to assume that the world appear different to a person using one vocabulary than it would to a person using another. The use of language would call attention to different aspects of the environment in the one case than it would in the other. Numerous illustrations of this sort may be given. The Navaho, for example, possess

color terms corresponding roughly to our "white," "red," and "yellow" but none which are equivalent to our "black," "gray," "brown," "blue," and "green." They have two terms corresponding to "black," one denoting the black of darkness, the other the black of such objects as coal. Our "gray" and "brown," however, correspond to a single term in their language and likewise our "blue" and "green." As far as vocabulary is concerned, they divide the spectrum into segments different from ours. It would seem probable that on many occasions of casual perception they would not bother to notice whether an object were brown or gray, and that they would merely avoid discussions as to whether a shade of color in a trying light was blue or green, but they would not even make the distinction.

This example must not be taken as showing that the Navahos are incapable of making color distinctions which are familiar to us. They do not suffer from a peculiar form of color-blindness any more than we do since we lack words for the two sorts of black which they distinguish. The point is rather that their vocabulary tends to let them leave other distinctions unnoticed which we habitually make.

If we are right in claiming an influence of vocabulary on perception, it might be expected that vocabulary would influence other aspects of thought as well. The divisions we make in our experience depend on how we perceive and so would be subject to the same linguistic influence as perception. Once again, one would expect the influence to run in both directions. If, in thinking about the world, one has occasion to use certain ideas, one would expect them to be added to the vocabulary, either directly or through metaphor; this is probably the primary influence. Once the term is in the vocabulary, however, it would constitute an influence both on perception and conception.

Inflections also were listed among the linguistic items which might have an influence on thought. Since grammatical forms are less subject to change than vocabulary, such an influence, if it exists, would be far more pervasive than that of vocabulary. We shall contend that there is an influence and that it is similar to that of vocabulary, influencing perception by calling attention to certain aspects of experience rather than to others.

The way in which inflections most often operate may be illustrated by means of a hypothetical example. Suppose we have a verb-stem, say A, and suppose that, at some early stage of the language, A is used by itself. At a later stage, let us suppose that it seemed desirable to add tense indicators to the verb, representing, say, past, present, and future. These might be suffixed and might be schematized by Ax, Ay, and Az. Since every situation in which A was formerly used was one in which a suffix was applicable, a simplification would naturally suggest itself. The stem form was no longer needed by itself, since one of the suffixed forms would always be appropriate, yet it was easier to pronounce than any of them. It would naturally, therefore, be used in place of one of the suffixed forms with the meaning of that form. Thus, Ax might be abbreviated to A. Although this would be a convenience in conversation it would have the effect of depriving the language of any word having the old meaning of A. This might be no loss, but it would require an increase in thought in order to use the language. No longer could one simply notice that the conditions for the application of the stem word were present and proceed to use it. One would be required to notice in addition which of the suffixes applied. In order to speak of one aspect of experience, it would be necessary to notice—and speak of—another as well. This might be called a *forced observation* induced by inflection. Tense, discussed above, represents only one sort of forced observation, and it is apparent that the use of an English verb requires observations regarding number and person as well.

The use of the term "forced observation" must not be construed to imply that a speaker of a language is conscious of being compelled to notice certain aspects of his environment. Most often he makes these observations naturally, almost unconsciously, and certainly with no feeling of constraint. Nor, of course, is the force actual or physical. A person can use the English vocabulary, disregarding distinctions of tense and person, and, under favorable circumstances, make himself understood. Under usual and less favorable circumstances, however, he will not be understood and, in any case, he risks ridicule. This is the only external compulsion. Habitual use of the language provides an internal compulsion.

The observations which are forced differ in different languages. Thus Kluckhohn and Leighton comparing English with Navaho say:

English stops with what from the Navaho point of view is a very vague statement—"I drop it." The Navaho must specify four particulars which the English leaves either unsettled or to inference from context :
1. The form must make clear whether "it" is definite or just "something."
2. The verb stem used will vary depending upon whether the object is round, or long, or fluid, or animate, etc., etc.
3. Whether the act is in progress, or just about to start, or just about to stop, or habitually carried on, or repeatedly carried on, must be rigorously specified . . .
4. The extent to which the agent controls the fall must be indicated . . .

Dorothy Lee has noticed that, in a similar fashion, Wintu requires the indication in suffixes of the evidence on which a statement is based thus forcing an observation. She says:

He (the Wintu) cannot say simply *the salmon is good.* That part of *is good* which implies the tense (now) and the person (it) further has to contain one of the following implications: (the salmon is good) I see, I taste (or know through some sense other than sight), I infer, I judge, I am told.

Just as is the case with vocabulary, one may claim that the forced observations imposed by inflections constitute a mental set. Because it must be mentioned in speaking, the time of an action is more likely to receive the attention of a user of English than of a user of Wintu. Again, it is easy to make a statement in English without considering the evidence for it. A Wintu might be expected to be more perceptive in this respect. The influence here is similar to that exerted by vocabulary except that it is concentrated on relatively fewer items—those which form the basis of inflection—and so is stronger with regard to these.

Finally, under the heading of language comes the factor of sentence structure. While again one would expect that the primary influence runs from thought and social needs to sentence structure, there may be a reciprocal influence as well.

To take the case of English and the SAE languages generally, there seem to be two dominant forms of sentence: first, what may be called the subject-predicate type of statement, of which "The book is red" may be taken as a paradigm; and second, what may be called the actor-action type, of which "John runs" or "John loves Mary" are typical. In the first type there is no action, merely a quality attributed to a subject, in the second the subject is thought of as taking an action. In either case, however, the subject typically is an enduring object—something recognizable through time. Even when the subject is not an object in this sense, the tendency is to speak of it as if it were. Thus, an automobile mechanic will talk of fixing the timing on a car in much the same terms that he speaks of fixing the tire, even though the timing is simply a relation of events while the tire is an object. One may claim that speaking of fixing the timing in this way is metaphorical, and this may be, but the point is that the metaphor proceeds via the conception of a stable physical object.

This tendency is pervasive in our language. In general, events are spoken of as if they were stable objects, and, in speech at least, much of the fluidity of passing experience seems to be lost. This tendency, as Whorf has noticed, extends even to time itself. We speak of it and even think of it as a substance of indefinite extent. We may isolate a segment of it in the same sense that we may cut a link of sausage, and we may save five minutes in something like the sense that we save a scrap of meat.

Such ways of looking at the world are of importance, not merely in the organization of the details of experience, but also for philosophy, in particular for logic and metaphysics. Classic logic took the subject-predicate form of statement as basic and insisted that any logical manipulations must be confined to this form. Sentences of the form "John loves Mary" had to be twisted until loving Mary was considered a predicate of John. Various arguments were classified and tested in terms of the relations between subject and predicate. While this conception of logic is almost completely rejected at present, there is no doubt that it was a major influence on thought up to the present century.

In metaphysics the notion of subject and predicate appears in a somewhat different form. One of the classic philosophic problems has been that of explaining the integration and organization of our sense-perception. It makes no difference whether one considers sensations given in isolation or presented in Gestalten, the problem still remains of relating the observations of one time with those of another. The classic answer to the problem, already fully developed in Aristotle, is that the universe is composed of *substances* and that everything perceived is an attribute of some substance. Substances or substance—whether there was only one substance in the universe, or many, depended on the

philosopher—were thought of as continuing through time and, in some cases, even as lasting forever, and so connecting the perceptions of one time with those of another. Thus the broadest description of the universe according to most of the Western philosophic tradition would be to say that the world consists of substances and their attributes. The parallel between the metaphysical substance, which had, or was modified by, qualities, and the logical subject, which had, or was modified by, predicates, was apparent—so much so that substance was often defined as that which is always subject and never predicate. By the same parallel, attributes corresponded to predicates.

Much of the philosophy of this century has been a polemic against these conceptions. The older logic has been displaced by one which allows a predicate to connect several subjects and in which the whole notion of subject has nothing like its classical importance. In metaphysics, such otherwise divergent writers as Whitehead, Russell, and Bergson have agreed in rejecting the classical formulations of substance. Both the close parallel between substance and subject and the connection between classical logic and grammar have been deprecated. Thus Russell has insisted: " 'Substance,' in a word, is a metaphysical mistake, due to the transference to the world-structure of the structure of sentences composed of a subject and a predicate." Having noticed this connection between SAE language and philosophy, we may turn to the contrast of both of them to the thought and language of the Hopi which Whorf has pointed out in considerable detail. There are five principal points of divergence, and it will be seen that they represent differences either in grammar or in the conception of time. These major linguistic differences occur in the following points: (1) plurality and numeration, (2) nouns of physical quantity, (3) phases of cycles, (4) temporal forms of verbs, and (5) duration, intensity, and tendency. Each of these calls for some discussion.

1. SAE uses plurals and cardinal numbers, not merely for actual aggregates given all at once, but also for aggregates which Whorf calls "imaginary" such as ten days, which cannot be given in one perception. Hopi does not use plurals in this latter case and where we would speak of ten days as an aggregate, the Hopi would say "until the eleventh day" or "after the tenth day."

There is a temptation to dismiss this difference between SAE and Hopi modes of speaking merely as a difference in idiom, having no significance for the underlying thought. If the preference for "ten days" rather than "after the tenth day" were considered alone, this would undoubtedly be the proper explanation. A difference in thought-pattern of the sort that Whorf is trying to show cannot rest on any single instance of linguistic usage, however striking it may be. Only the multiplication of instances makes it less probable that one is faced with a casual difference in manner of speaking and more probable that one is dealing with a difference in the mode of thought. Thus the total weight of evidence which Whorf presents is of importance rather than any single item.

2. Whorf distinguishes two sorts of SAE nouns, individual nouns, denoting bodies with definite outlines (e.g., a tree, a stick, a man) and mass nouns, denoting "homogeneous continua without implied boundaries" (e.g., water, wood, meat, etc.). Where it is desirable to indicate boundaries for a mass noun, we do so by such phrases as "pane of glass," "piece of soap," "cup of coffee," "bag of flour," etc. The prevalence in such phrases of a combination of a term for a container with one for contents paves the way, Whorf thinks, for the philosophic notion of the world as a combination of form and matter. Such a theory he claims is instantly acceptable to common sense: "It is so through linguistic habit. Our language patterns often require us to name a physical thing by a binomial that splits the reference into a formless item plus a form."

Hopi nouns, in contrast, always have an individual sense, even though the boundaries of some objects are vague or indefinite. There is no contrast between individual and mass nouns, hence no reference to container or body-type, and no analogy to provide the dichotomy of form and matter.

3. In SAE terms like "summer," "morning," and "hour" which indicate phases of cycles are treated in much the same way as other nouns. They may serve as grammatical subjects and objects and may be pluralized and used with number-terms in the same way as nouns for physical objects. Even "time" is treated as a mass-noun. Hopi is quite different in this respect. Terms denoting phases of cycles are linguistically distinct from nouns and constitute a separate form-class called temporals. Whorf says: "There is no objectification as a region,

an extent, a quantity, of the subjective duration-feeling. Nothing is suggested about time except the perpetual "getting later" of it. And so there is no basis here for a formless item answering to our 'time.' "

4. Our system of tenses divides time into three distinct sections, past, present, and future and thereby aids in the objectification of time which is conceived by analogy to space. There are some difficulties with the scheme, notable in the variety of uses to which the present tense is put, and these, Whorf claims, are responsible for confusions of thought.

Hopi verbs have no tenses but only validity-forms, aspects and modal forms linking clauses. There are three validity forms: one indicating simply that the speaker is reporting a past or present event, another indicating the speaker's expectation, and a third showing that he is making a statement generally recognized to be true. Aspect forms report differing degrees of duration in respect to the event, and the modal forms, employed only when an utterance includes two verbs or clauses, show relations, including temporal relations, between the two clauses. This grammatical structure, according to Whorf, avoids the objectification of time.

5. SAE languages express duration, intensity, and tendency through spatial metaphors. Thus:

We express duration by long, short, great, much, quick, slow, etc.; intensity by large, great, much, heavy, light, high, low, sharp, faint, etc.; tendency by more, increase, grow, turn, get, approach, go, come, rise, fall, stop, smooth, even, rapid, slow, and so on through an almost inexhaustible list of metaphors that we hardly recognize as such since they are virtually the only linguistic media available. The non-metaphorical terms in this field, like early, late, soon, lasting, intense, very, tending, are a mere handful, quite inadequate to the needs.

Hopi on the contrary has no such metaphors, but expresses duration, intensity, and tendency literally, without any trace of the spatial figures found in SAE. There is even a special class of terms, the "tensors," constituting a separate part of speech, to express these factors, and it is a very large class of terms. Other linguistic devices are used as well.

Whorf sums up the influence of these linguistic differences on thought by saying that speakers of SAE tend to see the world in terms of things, the things themselves built up of a formless stuff given a determinate form. Nonspatial entities are conceived by spatial metaphor. The Hopi, on the other hand, seem

. . . to have analyzed reality largely in terms of *events* (or better "eventing"), referred to in two ways, objective and subjective. Objectively, and only if perceptible physical experience, events are expressed mainly as outlines, colors, movements, and other perceptive reports. Subjectively, for both the physical and non-physical, events are considered the expression of invisible intensity-factors, on which depend their stability and persistence, or their fugitiveness and proclivities. It implies that existents do not "become later and later" all in the same way; but some do so by growing, like plants, some by diffusing and vanishing, some by a procession of metamorphoses, some by enduring in one shape till affected by violent forces. In the nature of each existent able to manifest as a definite whole is the power of its own mode of duration; its growth, decline, stability, cyclicity, or creativeness.

A similar connection between grammatical forms and prevalent modes of thought has been noticed in Wintu by Dorothy Lee. Each Wintu verb has two related forms to be used under different circumstances. The first category of stems, she finds, indicates among other things, that the subject participates as a free agent in the activity described by the verb. In contrast to this:

. . . to this stem of Category II is attached a suffix whose underlying meaning seems to be that of natural necessity and which corresponds to the modal suffixes of Category I. This suffix is used to express, all in one, futurity, causality, potentiality, probability, necessity; to refer to an inevitable future which might, can and must be, in the face of which the individual is helpless. Category II has reference to a state of being in which the individual is not a free agent.

This difference in verb categories is significant as mirroring the prevalent conception of the universe. In part, the Wintu feels he can control his environment; for the rest, it is completely beyond him. This underlying metaphysics is summed up as follows:

The Wintu has a small sphere wherein he can choose and do, can feel and think and make decisions. Cutting through this and circumscribing it is the world of natural necessity wherein all things that are potential and probable are also inevitable, wherein existence is unknowable and ineffable.

Here again, then, is a parallel between thought about the world in its broadest aspects and major grammatical categories. The aspect of grammar emphasized is different from the aspects prominent in Whorf's investigation, but the major conclusion is the same.

Before leaving this topic of the relation between language and thought, it may be well to notice what we have and have not sought to establish. We have looked for connections and causal relationships between language on the one hand and thought on the other. We have claimed an influence of vocabulary and inflection, acting primarily on perception, and an influence of methods of combination, affecting thought primarily at a more abstract level. In neither case have we claimed, nor would we want to claim, that language is the sole influence or even the primary influence. In neither case have we claimed that the causal relationship does not also run in the other direction as well. Because of the enduring character of language and the fact that a population changes in time, it well may be that language considered in the large is molded by environmental conditions, social organization, and prevalent modes of thought. This would not prevent language being an influence on thought in the development of the individual, and this is all we have claimed. Next, we have made no claim that a study of a language by itself would suffice to show the general character of thought of its users. Some general knowledge of the culture of the speakers would be required, and, indeed, it is doubtful that one could get the necessary intimacy with the language without this broader knowledge of the culture.

Neither, finally, have we argued that there is any compulsive influence of language upon thought, that language makes impossible all but certain modes of perception and organization of expression. Since perception and the organization of experience are ordinarily manifested only through language, the point being made here may be made in another way. In natural languages, the elements we have been considering—vocabulary, inflection and modes of sentence structure—do not make it impossible to express certain things, they merely make it more difficult to express them. In artificial languages of the sort with which a logician deals, the vocabulary is fixed. The rules for combination of symbols are explicit and the types of manipulation permissible are specified. In such model languages, one can often show that a given expression cannot be stated in the language. The situation is different in natural languages, however. Vocabulary may grow by the addition of new words or metaphorical extension of old ones, syntactical rules may sometimes be sacrificed without loss of intelligibility, and it would be difficult to show that any given expression cannot go into the language. At least it need be no part of the present argument that there are such impossibilities of expression. All we have contended is that certain linguistic features make certain modes of perception more prevalent or more probable, not that they completely rule out others. Similarly, in showing metaphysical implications of language, we have not meant to say that conflicting views would be inexpressible in the language. After all, Whorf, while arguing that the prevailing Hopi metaphysics is radically different from that inherent in the SAE languages, has given his account of the Hopi philosophy in an SAE language. Bergson, whose thought in retrospect appears to have greater affinities to typical Hopi modes of thought than to SAE, was highly successful in expressing himself in an SAE language.

It should be noted parenthetically, that in showing a connection between linguistic forms and metaphysics, we have not, of course, intended any implication concerning the truth of the rival systems. If Aristotle comes closer to the inherent SAE metaphysics than Bergson, it does not follow that he is more—or less— likely to be correct. The fact, which we have just seen, that a metaphysics may run counter to that typical of the language in which it is written shows, moreover, that metaphysical thought cannot be entirely linguistically conditioned.

The contention of this section, then, is that language is one of the factors influencing perception and the general organization of experience. This influence need not be primary or unique or compelling, but neither is it negligible.

In the discussion of the relations of language to culture there is at least the advantage of greater objectivity over the preceding section. There, in discussing the relation of language to thought, it was exceedingly difficult to determine the thought side of the comparison. In discussion of the influence of various linguistic elements on perception, the evidence was indirect and consisted in contending that, from what we know of mental set, we would expect these factors to constitute sets influencing perception. The only likely alternative to this procedure would be some sort of projective technique used to test whether speakers of different languages perceived ambiguous figures in radically different ways. Even here, the perception would be marked by its linguistic formulation, and it would probably be necessary to

ask the subject to reproduce what was seen after an interval of time rather than to state what was seen. Even if users of different languages showed markedly different results, there would still be the problem of showing that the difference depends on language rather than on a set induced by other environmental factors. The extreme difficulty of administering such tests, as well as their inconclusive nature, leaves the kind of evidence we have cited as good as any which is likely to become available in the near future.

In discussing the relationship between language and the broader aspects of thought, the situation was somewhat, though not a great deal, better. There was at least direct evidence, a connection between grammatical forms and general characteristics of Western thought and philosophy. Here the grammatical forms could be described with relative assurance, but the evidence as to the dominant trends of Western philosophy, while a very widely held view, is merely an interpretation of an historical record. Similarly, when Whorf contrasted SAE and Hopi characteristic modes of thought, these represented interpretations, and interpretations based on a feeling for a social atmosphere rather than on anything so definite as a written record. While it represents the work of a sensitive observer based on long acquaintance with the people studied, and so constitutes valuable evidence, still, it is the sort of evidence characteristic of the beginning of a science rather than of an advanced stage.

In tracing the connection of language and culture, it is easier to give the evidence in a precise form. As in any scientific work there is, of course, an element of interpretation in generalizing from specific acts to patterns and from patterns to broader themes, but at least there are interpretations of individual acts which are public and verifiable. Though this line of investigation presents great difficulties and lacks the precision which it may later acquire, still it has a more hopeful outlook. Since, moreover, thought is concerned with, and so influenced by, general aspects of culture, this latter investigation of the relation of language to culture may be the key to the problem of the preceding section.

As before, we may consider vocabulary, inflections, and the building of compounds as the elements of language to be compared with patterns of culture. We have noticed before that there is a close relationship between vocabulary and environment, and, since the general patterns of behavior which we have taken as definitive of culture are equally a function of environment, one would expect a correlation with vocabulary. Certainly, one needs words for the objects involved in habitual action and, conversely, words which have no use in discourse are not likely to remain long in any active sort of vocabulary. Because of the very function of language, it may be taken for granted that language and culture are related in this way, and this conclusion would not generally be regarded as controversial.

With regard to the role played by inflections and modes of word-combination, there is, however, more room for dispute. In a discussion of the Hopi language which embraces both these points, Whorf has argued that differences between SAE and Hopi grammar correspond, not merely to differences in modes of thought, but to differences in the cultures as well. These differences center about differences in the conception of time.

In Hopi, we have noticed, days are not totaled by use of cardinal numbers, but are referred to by their order. It is as if, Whorf says, different days were thought of as successive reappearances of the same entity rather than as completely separate and distinct slices of time. Since time is viewed as having this sort of continuity, special importance attached to preparations for what is done at one time might be expected to leave its impress on reappearances of the same time. Preparation constitutes a relatively important part of Hopi life and involves such factors as prayer, practicing, rehearsing, as well as various magic rites and even mere good wishes to a project, to say nothing of the types of preparation considered relevant in SAE. Whorf says:

Hopi "preparing" activities again show a result of their linguistic thought background in an emphasis on persistence and constant insistent repetition. A sense of the cumulative value of innumerable small momenta is dulled by an objectified, spatialized view of time like ours, enhanced by a way of thinking close to the subjective awareness of duration, of the ceaseless "latering" of events.

And this difference in views of time, as we have seen, he holds to be a direct consequence of the structures of the languages.

In complete contrast to the Hopi treatment of time is the quantified, spatialized view in-

volved in the SAE languages. Whorf finds correlated with this the prevalence of:

1. Records, diaries, book-keeping, accounting, mathematics stimulated by accounting;
2. Interest in exact sequence, dating, calendars, chronology, clocks, time wages, time graphs, time as used in physics;
3. Annals, histories, the historical attitude, interest in the past, archaeology, attitudes of introjection towards past periods, e.g., classicism, romanticism.

Whorf also attributes interest in speed and in saving time to this quantitative treatment of time. Some of the differences between Hopi and SAE cultures, therefore, seem explicable in terms of the differing treatments of time and this, as was argued in the preceding section, depends on differences in the grammatical structures of the languages.

Hoijer, in working with the Navaho, has reached a similar conclusion as to the relation of grammatical categories to culture. He dealt, first of all, with Navaho verb forms and found in them a parallel to general traits of the society. Navaho verbs may be divided into two types, the neuter and the active. The neuter verbs represent states or conditions and show an absence of movement or action. Some represent qualities, such as being blue, or thin, or tall. Active verbs, on the other hand, represent events, actions, and movements. While at first sight the two kinds appear quite different, Hoijer finds in analyzing the types of neuter verbs that each represents a withdrawal of motion of a certain sort. He summarizes his results as follows:

. . . it would appear that Navaho verb categories center very largely about the reporting of events, or better, "eventings." These eventings are divided into neuters, eventings solidified, as it were, into states of being by virtue of the withdrawal of motion, and actives, eventings in motion. . . .
But this is not all. A careful analysis of the meanings of Navaho verb bases, neuter and active, reveals that eventings themselves are conceived, not abstractly for the most part, but very concretely in terms of the movements of corporeal bodies, or of entities metaphorically linked with corporeal bodies. Movement itself is reported in painstaking detail, even to the extent of classifying as semantically different the movements of one, two, or several bodies, and sometimes distinguishing as well between movements of bodies differentiated by their shape and distribution in space.

Extending the discussion to other aspects of the language, Hoijer finds a similar emphasis on motion and notices a strong cultural parallel. He says:

> To summarize: in three broad speech patterns, illustrated by the conjugation of active verbs, the reporting of actions and events, and the framing of substantive concepts, Navaho emphasized movement and specifies the nature, direction, and status of such movement in considerable detail. Even the neuter category is relatable to the dominant conception of a universe in motion, for, just as some one is reported to have described architecture as frozen music, so the Navaho define position as a resultant of the withdrawal of motion.
>
> Parallels to this semantic theme may be found in almost every aspect of Navaho culture taken as a whole. Even today the Navaho are fundamentally a wandering, nomadic folk, following their flocks from one pasturage to another. Myths and legends reflect this emphasis most markedly, for both Gods and culture heroes move restlessly from one holy place to the next, seeking by their motion to perfect and repair the dynamic flux which is the universe.

Hoijer also finds an additional parallel between the Navaho language and culture, which this time involves a somewhat different aspect of the grammar, the sentence structure. He finds that the actor-action pattern of sentence so common in SAE is foreign to Navaho. A person is associated with an action, rather than being the author or cause of it. Motion and position are treated as being inherent in an object, rather than as being induced by some agent. Hoijer notices how consonant this is with the general Navaho attitude toward nature as reported by Kluckhohn and Leighton. They say that the Navaho does not seek to control nature or believe in doing so; rather, he attempts to influence it, often through songs and ritual. This lack of agency toward nature, as shown in practice, is mirrored in the grammatical construction which does not speak in terms of acting upon an object.

While this evidence adduced by Whorf and Hoijer is certainly striking, there is a question as to just how much it shows. Whorf himself was quite modest in his claims, maintaining that "there are connections but not correlations or diagnostic correspondences between cultural norms and linguistic patterns." Hoijer, however, wishes to go farther and claims that Whorf has understated his case, that more can be made of the correspondence. The attempt to establish correlations would certainly present a program for future investigations, though it is unlikely that more can be claimed for it at present as a general method. Hoijer, as we have just observed, found a striking parallel between the movement expressed in Navaho verb-forms and the general mobility of Navaho life, but it is doubtful that one would be even tempted to generalize and expect such correlations with mobility among all peoples. Certainly, many more studies like Hoijer's are required, extending over a wide range of languages, before much warrant could be given such a generalization. It is worth noticing also that Whorf's study of Hopi does not give verb-forms anything like the prominence that Hoijer gives them. The point would seem to be that every culture may, perhaps, be correlated with some aspect of the language accompanying it, but there is not yet enough evidence to suggest what this aspect may be without actual examination of the case. For the present it is necessary to study both the language and the culture to trace parallels, and so there can be no diagnostic employment of the correlations discovered. Only after many more studies of this sort would it be possible even to suggest which features of a grammar might in general be expected to correlate with a culture. This is not, of course, to condemn the investigations which have been made, but merely to point out that they stand at the beginning of a vast inquiry. More data are required before it is even possible to formulate specific hypotheses; but this is often the case at the start of a new science.

42

LINGUISTIC RELATIVITY:
THE VIEWS OF BENJAMIN LEE WHORF

MAX BLACK

THE welcome appearance of a collection of Whorf's scattered writings,[1] together with an illuminating memoir and introduction and a fuller bibliography than has hitherto been available, makes it possible to see the work of that remarkable man in something like its astonishing entirety. Few books of equal importance are as interesting: it would take a dull reader to be indifferent to Whorf's views.

Competent experts have praised Whorf's technical contributions to the study of American Indian languages. But these are overshadowed by his remarkable and still controversial pronouncements about the relations between language, culture, and mental process, to which this discussion will be devoted.

The aim of rendering what Whorf called "linguistic relativity" sufficiently precise to be tested and criticized encounters formidable obstacles in his writings: variant formulations of the main points are often inconsistent, there is much exaggeration, and a vaporous mysticism blurs perspectives already sufficiently elusive.

The dominating thought is happily expressed in the quotation from Sapir that Whorf himself used as an epigraph for his best essay:

Human beings do not live in the objective world alone, nor alone in the world of social activity as ordinarily understood, but are very much at the mercy of the particular language which has become the medium of expression for their society. It is quite an illusion to imagine that one adjusts to reality essentially without the use of language and that language is merely an incidental means of solving problems of communication and reflection. The fact of the matter is that the "real world" is to a large extent unconsciously built up on the language habits of the group.

This has been called the "Sapir-Whorf hypothesis."

I believe Whorf is committed to the following ten propositions, each of which needs elucidation:

(1) Languages embody "integrated fashions of speaking" or *"background linguistic systems,"* consisting of prescribed modes of expressing thought and experience.

(2) A native speaker has a distinctive *"conceptual system"* for "organizing experience"; and (3) a distinctive *"world-view"* concerning the universe and his relations to it.

(4) The background linguistic system partially determines the associated conceptual system; and (5) partially determines the associated world-view.

(6) Reality consists of a "kaleidoscopic flux of impressions."

(7) The "facts" said to be perceived are a function of the language in which they are expressed; and (8) the "nature of the universe" is a function of the language in which it is stated.

(9) Grammar does not reflect reality, but varies arbitrarily with language.

(10) Logic does not reflect reality, but varies arbitrarily with language.

(1) *Languages incorporate "background linguistic systems."* For uses of the quoted expression, see pages 212, 247, and elsewhere; "integrated fashion of speaking" (p. 158) and "pattern system" (p. 252) are approximate synonyms.

A recurring difficulty is that of distinguishing the "background" from the language itself and so preventing Whorf's main contentions from degenerating into tautology. That a given language imposes an inherited vocabulary and grammar upon its users is too obvious to require mention; but of course Whorf means more than this. The "background" has to be a *subsystem* composed of "patterns" that are *meaningful* to the native speaker no less than to the investigating linguist.

To take an illustration: Whorf claims to discover a category of gender in English (pp. 68,

From *Philosophical Review*, 68 (1959): 228–238. Reprinted by permission of the publisher and the author. Max Black is Professor of Philosophy, Cornell University.

90 ff.) which, unlike gender in Romance languages, is genuinely functional. Here and throughout Whorf recognizes some linguistic categories, but not all, as genuinely having meaning. For him "any scientific grammar is necessarily a deep analysis into relations" (p. 68) and "linguistics is essentially the quest of MEANING" (p. 73, capitals in original).

In isolating *significant* categories, Whorf proceeds as follows: Formal criteria of somewhat heterodox kinds define the linguistic category; the linguistic analyst (Whorf) then searches for the "idea" that "unifies" the category (p. 81); which is then expressed in the linguist's metalanguage. Ideally, some verifiable predictions about admissible constructions in the language should result. A paradigm of the method is Whorf's isolation of three classes of Hopi verbs (pp. 107–109). Though he begins by using non-semantical criteria, he characteristically presses on until he has satisfied himself about three underlying "concepts." There result what Whorf calls "covert categories" or "cryptotypes" (pp. 88, 89, 92), grammatical classes not marked by invariable morphemic tags, but recognizable by the distinctive interactions of their members with the contexts in which they can occur.

This outcome may remind philosophers of "semantical types" or even of Wittgenstein's "depth grammar." Nor need the most toughminded of professional linguists feel any qualms about the identification of cryptotypes, since the relevant criteria are *formal*.

The chief difficulty lies in the claim that the cryptotypes *have meaning* for the unsophisticated native speaker. Whorf speaks of "a sort of habitual consciousness" (p. 69); of "a submerged, subtle, and elusive meaning" (p. 70); of a "formless idea" (p. 71), a "rising toward fuller consciousness . . . of linkage bonds" (p. 69), and so on. But it is hard to believe that the ordinary speaker is aware of a grammatical classification that takes all the virtuosity of a Whorf to discover. I doubt that the average English speaker realizes that the particle *"un-"* can only be prefixed to transitive verbs of a "covering, enclosing, and surface attaching meaning" (p. 71) that constitute a prototype. Whorf himself must have the concept since he succeeds in expressing it; but the man in the English street simply uses *"un-"* in happy ignorance. Here I think Whorf commits the *linguist's fallacy* of imputing his own sophisticated attitudes to the speakers he is studying.

The heuristic value of the notion of a cryptotype is manifested in its capacity to induce verifiable predictions (cf. the discussion of the imaginary verb *to flimmick* at p. 71); the rest is mythical psychology.

(2) *A native speaker his a distinctive "conceptual system" for "organizing experience."* The underlying picture is of an undivided continuum arbitrarily dissected by language. Whorf speaks of the "segmentation of nature" (p. 240) and the "artificial chopping up of the continuous spread and flow of existence" (p. 253); he says "we dissect nature" (pp. 213, 214) and "cut" it up (p. 213) when we "organize it into concepts" (p. 213), and all this "largely because, through our mother tongue, we are parties to an agreement to do so, not because nature itself is segmented in that way exactly for all to see" (p. 240).

Let us try this out on color words. We have only a poor handful of uncompounded color words for referring to the millions of observably different components of the color solid; and other languages select the color labels in ways strikingly different—Navaho splits our *black* into two colors and lumps *blue* and *green* together. (But the Navaho are just as good at discriminating colors as we are!)

Here is as favorable a case for Whorf's thesis as can be imagined; yet to apply his ways of talking about the undisputed facts would be to engender confusion. The vocabulary of the operating theatre ("cutting," "chopping," "dissecting," "segmenting") is out of place; to speak is not to butcher, *pace* Bergson and other critics of analysis. To dissect a frog is to destroy it, but talk about the rainbow leaves it unchanged. The case would be different if it could be shown that color vocabularies influence the perception of colors, but where is the evidence for that? If we treat Whorf's talk about "segmentation" as excusable rhetoric, there remains only the complaint that classification is arbitrary.

Is the discreteness of our vocabulary to count as a sporadic or a universal defect? When Whorf talks of everybody seeing the constellation Ursa Major in the same way (p. 164) he seems to admit that language is sometimes adequate to reality; but he inclines to treat the case as exceptional, and the Milky Way serves his metaphysics better than the Big Dipper. He subscribes, consciously or not, to the ancient metaphysical lament that to describe is *necessarily* to falsify. The flat unsatisfying answer is that Whorf, like many others, has succumbed to the muddled notion that the function of speech is to *reinstate* reality. Well, the best recipe for apple pie can't be eaten—but it would be odd to regard that as an inadequacy.

How can language generate a "conceptual system"? If we were to accept the view that reference to somebody's-having-a-concept-of-something is a compendious way of talking about certain related capacities to distinguish objects, to respond to them differentially, and especially to talk about them, we might agree to regard "thinking as the [a?] function which is largely linguistic" (p. 66). But having-a-concept cannot be straightforwardly identified with ability to use the corresponding word.

We must admit that human beings have far more concepts (distinctive cognitive capacities) than words for expressing them—as the example of colors amply shows. Even if symbolization is essential to thought, a place must be left for *ad hoc* symbols, nonverbal tokens, and other ways of thinking without using dictionary words.

Consequently, inferences from vocabulary to cognitive capacities are always precarious. If the presence of a word actively in use suggests the existence of a corresponding concept, absence of a word shows almost nothing. A striking example is provided by Whorf's observation that the Hopi have no name for the kiva (p. 205). Now it is hardly to be supposed that they have no concept of a "structure so highly typical of pueblo culture and so intimately connected with their religion" (*ibid*.).

Were we able, as we are not, to infer from a given vocabulary to corresponding cognitive capacities, a further inferential leap would be needed to show that different languages incorporate different conceptual systems. The admitted possibility of translation from any language into any other renders the supposed relativity of such systems highly dubious.

Whorf is most interested in what might be called *structural concepts,* typically expressed by grammatical features. He makes much of the fact that the statement "It is a dripping spring" (an odd example, by the way) is expressed in Apache by a very different construction, inadequately rendered by "As water, or springs, whiteness moves downwards" (p. 241). Whorf adds: "How utterly unlike our way of thinking!" But what is the evidence that the

Apache *thinks* differently? The difficulty is that the hypostatized structural concepts are so bound to the defining grammatical constructions that it becomes hard to conceive of any extra-linguistic verification. Having the concept of a predicate (for all except the linguist or the philosopher) is about the same as using a language that insists upon the use of predicates, and Whorf's contention reduces to saying that one cannot speak grammatically without using a particular grammar. It is a far cry to the assumption that to speak grammatically is to mold "reality" into a structure isomorphic with the grammar. Here, again, Whorf commits the "linguist's fallacy."

(3) *A native speaker has a distinctive "world-view" concerning the universe and his relations to it.* Or, as we might say, every man is his own metaphysician. Every language crystallizes "the basic postulates of an unformulated philosophy" (p. 61) and "conceals a META-PHYSICS" (p. 58, capitals in the original).

I understand this to mean that every language incorporates a distinctive set of general categories applicable to the universe and a set of ontological propositions involving those categories. In English, according to Whorf, the relevant categories include "time," "space," "substance," and "matter" (p. 138). We are said to "see existence through a binomial formula that expresses any existent as a spatial form plus a spatial formless continuum related to the form as contents [sic] is related to the outlines of its container. Nonspatial existents are imaginatively spatialized and charged with similar implications of form and continuum" (p. 147). Whorf may be saying that the dominant categories in English are either substance-plus-property or form-plus-matter—the first literally applicable to a physical body of a definite outline, the second to a tangible container with fluid contents. These categories, he suggests, are then applied by "extension" and "metaphor" to cases where they cannot literally fit, so that all our descriptions tend to be "objectified" and "spatialized." (This is no vaguer than Whorf's own account, though occasionally he speaks as if "Newtonian space, time, and matter" (pp. 152, 153) were what he meant by the "form-plus-substance dichotomy" (p. 152).)

Consider now the Hopi "metaphysics": Here, we are told, there is no explicit or implicit reference to time, nor are there "our familiar contrasts of time and space" (p. 58); instead, we have "two grand cosmic forms, which as a first approximation in terminology we may call MANIFESTED and MANIFESTING (or UNMANIFEST) or, again, OBJECTIVE and SUBJECTIVE" (p. 59). The "subjective" realm includes all that is yet to happen, but conceived of as "mental," as something "burgeoning" and "fermenting" in a conative, spiritual activity that embraces natural and animal phenomena as well as human activity (p. 62); the "objective" realm consists of present and past manifestations of this universal spiritual striving (p. 59). The Hopi think of reality mainly in terms of *events* (p. 147): objectively these are constituted by such directly perceptible features as outlines, colors, movements (p. 147), subjectively as "the expression of invisible intensity factors, on which depend their stability and persistence, or their fugitiveness and proclivities" (p. 147). How much of all this would the average Hopi recognize? Perhaps it might leave him as dumbfounded as a Greek peasant reading Aristotle.

So much for the supposed contrast between the metaphysics implicit in the Hopi language and the metaphysics of "standard average Europeans." Now for some comments.

The idea that a given language commits its users to a distinctive philosophy has been memorably expressed by Lichtenberg: "Our false philosophy is incorporated in our whole language; we cannot reason without, so to speak, reasoning wrongly. We overlook the fact that speaking, no matter of what, is itself a philosophy." One cannot help feeling that an idea that has appealed to thinkers as diverse as von Humboldt, Cassirer, and Wittgenstein must have something to be said for it.

An extreme form of the view rejected by Whorf might hold language to be no more than an external representation of an independent content, so that the relation between the two would be like that of a garment to the body it clothes. But this is plainly indefensible: speech is often an integral part of a wider activity, as the much-discussed case of "performatory language" sufficiently demonstrates. So far we must certainly agree with Whorf and Sapir. But the denial that language is a separable garment for an independently existing reality merely announces a program and offers no arguable thesis. Whorf goes much further in making specific contentions about the "implicit meta-

physics" underlying English and other European languages.

Consider a single inference from grammar to underlying metaphysics. Starting from the alleged fact that "our normal sentence" contains a subject before the verb (p. 242), Whorf goes on to say, "we therefore read action into every sentence, even into 'I hold it'" (p. 243). And again "We think of it [i.e., *holding*] and even see it as an action because language formulates it in the same way as it formulates more numerous expressions, like 'I strike it,' which deal with movements and changes" (p. 243).

But what is it to "read" action into a sentence? Can it be anything more than *using* the transitive verb? One formal mark of an "action" in the narrow sense is the possibility of adding distinctive modifiers: a man may strike (to use Whorf's example) slowly, jerkily, energetically, and so on. Now if somebody were to attach these adverbs to the verb "to hold" that would be sufficient indication that he was "reading action" into the verb. I suppose a child might say he was holding his hat slowly, and the poet is allowed a similar license; but otherwise the conceptual confusion is too gross to occur.

Still more dubious are Whorf's broader delineations of the unformulated metaphysics. He says that we "objectify" our "awareness of time and cyclicity" and explains: "I call it [our conception of time] OBJECTIFIED, or imaginary, because it is patterned on the OUTER world. It is this that reflects our linguistic usage" (pp. 139–140). And again, "concepts of time lose contact with the subjective experience of 'becoming later' and are objectified as counted QUANTITIES, especially as lengths, made up of units as a length can be visibly marked off into inches. A 'length of time' is envisioned as a row of similar units, like a row of bottles" (p. 140).

But what is it to "objectify"? Is it more than the fact that we use words like "long" and "short" in connection with time intervals? Objectification is supposed to be shown by our interest in exact records, in calculation, and in history (p. 153). But if so, "objectification" seems to shift its meaning. I doubt if we can even imagine what it would be like to "treat time as if it were space": I doubt whether this phrase has any definite meaning for Whorf or his readers.

Whorf concedes that there is no observable difference in the behavior of speakers of languages having markedly different grammars: "The Hopi language is capable of accounting for and describing correctly, in a pragmatic or operational sense, all observable phenomena of the universe" (p. 58). I suppose therefore that the Hopi can estimate time intervals and supply dates, so that even if Whorf is right in his remarkable statement that their language "contains no reference to 'time,' either explicit or implicit" (p. 58), they may be expected to have pretty much the same concept of time that we have. Of course, much depends on what one means by "implicit": if the Hopi manage to get along without any reference to time, one would like to know their secret.

The fact is that the metaphysics that Whorf envisages is not the "unformulated and naive world-view" of the layman, but the sophisticated construction of a metaphysician. Shorn of its fanciful appendages, the philosophy that Whorf professes to discern in "standard average European" looks uncommonly like a bowdlerized version of some scholia from Newton's *Principia*. To the contention that this is *the* metaphysics embodied in the Western languages (only awaiting formulation by the analyst) the sufficient answer is that Descartes—another "standard average European"—was led to a metaphysical system radically different. Languages that Hume and Hegel could use with equal fluency can hardly embody a unique philosophy.

(4) *The background linguistic system partially determines the associated conceptual system; and* (5) *partially determines the associated world-view.* I have chosen to say "partially determines" in both cases, though it is hard to decide what Whorf's final opinion was about the relation. A much cited passage denies "that there is anything so definite as 'a correlation' between culture and language" (p. 139) and Whorf says emphatically that "there are connections but not correlations or diagnostic correspondences between cultural norms and linguistic patterns" (p. 159). But in these passages Whorf is discussing inferences from linguistic features to specific cultural features such as hunting practices (p. 139) or "the existence of Crier Chiefs" (p. 159). In saying, "The idea of 'correlation' between language and culture, in the generally accepted sense of correlation, is certainly a mistaken one" (p. 139, n. 1), he is referring to culture as a constellation of observ-

able practices and institutions. But in talking about the connection with "habitual thought" he consistently implies a tighter bond: language "imposes" contrasts on us (p. 55), our dominant categories are "creatures" of language (p. 162), our thoughts are "controlled" (p. 252) by "inexorable systems" (p. 257)—and similarly in many other places.

I have already argued that Whorf identified the "conceptual system" and the "world view" with the language in which they were expressed, while also confusedly thinking of them as distinct. No wonder then that he is led to think of the connection as "inexorable": if "thought" is defined as an aspect of "language" the connection between the two becomes one of logical necessity.

(6) *Reality consists of a kaleidoscopic flux of impressions.* This "flux" (p. 213) is uncommonly like James's "stream of thought." Whorf is under the spell of a conception of "raw experience" (p. 102) that is "more basic than language" (p. 149), where all is motion and impermanence and even the contrast between past and present has yet to arise: "If we inspect consciousness we find no past, present, future, but a unity embracing consciousness. EVERYTHING is in consciousness, and everything in consciousness Is, and is together" (pp. 143–144). And the "real time" of consciousness is a *becoming*: "Where real time comes in is that all this in consciousness [the global unity of experience] is 'getting later,' changing certain relations in an irreversible manner" (p. 144).

Well, it is futile to argue against this picture: insistence upon the continuity and flow of experience is unexceptionable but empty, since nothing imaginable is being denied; but it is a bold leap to the contention that customary reference to time-intervals and temporal relations involves falsification. When Whorf claims that "if 'ten days' be regarded as a group it must be as an 'imaginary,' mentally constructed group" (p. 139), he must be taking the logic of counting to require the simultaneous existence of the things counted. Perhaps the best to be said for Whorf's metaphysics is that in all its amateurish crudity it is no worse than some philosophical systems that have had a considerable vogue.

Yet Whorf manages after all to express his philosophy. In describing the "deeper process of consciousness" upon which language is "a superficial embroidery" (p. 239) he refutes his own claim that "no individual is free to describe nature with absolute impartiality" (p. 239). Here is the familiar paradox that all general theories of the relativity of truth must brand themselves as biased and erroneous. The standard defense of claiming a privileged position for the theory's own promulgator takes the quaint form in Whorf of a hope that the linguist "familiar with very many widely different linguistic systems" (p. 214) may be free from the metaphysical biases of any. But if Whorf's linguistic studies led him to a Bergsonism that he might have read in the French, it is conceivable that a Greek-reading Hopi might have been led to the delighted discovery of Aristotelian substance as the prime reality.

Whorf's own metaphysics supplies him with a supposed "canon of reference for all observers, irrespective of their languages or scientific jargon" (p. 163), that allows him to appraise languages in terms of their relative ontological adequacy. So he is led, surprisingly, to praise a language that "cannot say 'a wave' " as being "closer to reality in this respect" (p. 262), or to suggest that the Hopi language is a better vehicle for physics than the European languages. But if he were to abstain from metaphysics altogether, on the ground of the incurable relativity of all conceptual systems, his own included, his position would hardly suffer. For the desired relativity might still be argued on the basis of intralinguistic comparisons, just as we establish the relativity of geometries without reference to a supposed absolute and nongeometrical knowledge of space. Such intralinguistic comparisons will in any case be needed, since the detour into dubious ontology cannot excuse the theorist from the detailed demonstration of variation of grammatical structure. Abandoning the metaphysical substructure would have the additional advantage of permitting argument between thinkers who will need a good deal of persuasion before they become Bergsonians.

This examination threatens to become tedious and need not be prolonged, since enough has been said to reveal the basic difficulties of Whorf's position. I have been particularly interested throughout in the extent to which Whorf's outlook was controlled by philosophical conceptions. It would have been presumptuous to rush in where so many linguists fear to tread, were not so much philosophy entwined with the linguistics. I do not wish the negative conclusions reached to leave an impression that Whorf's writings are of little value. Often enough in the history of thought the unsoundest views have proved the most suggestive. Whorf's mistakes are more interesting than the carefully hedged commonplaces of more cautious writers.

NOTES

1. *Language, Thought, and Reality: Selected Writings of Benjamin Lee Whorf.* Edited and with an introduction by John B. Carroll. Foreword by Stuart Chase. (New York, John Wiley and Sons, Inc., 1956, pp. x, 278.) A valuable feature is the inclusion of a number of Whorf's hitherto unpublished manuscripts. Subsequent editions ought to include an index. [NOTE: All page references in this paper refer to this edition of Whorf's book. Eds.]

43

BELIEF AND KNOWLEDGE

GODFREY LIENHARDT

We have imprisoned our own conceptions, by the lines which we have drawn in order to exclude the conceptions of others.—S. T. COLERIDGE, *Biographia Literaria*

CONFLICT between religion and natural science, concerning the origin and status of Man, disturbed many scholars of the last century not only intellectually but also in their personal lives. Charles Darwin, who had originally intended to become a clergyman of the Established Church, recalled that even when an undergraduate he did not 'in the least doubt the strict and literal truth of every word in the Bible.' Sir James Frazer had been brought up in a devout and affectionate Presbyterian family, where he had 'learned the Shorter Catechism by heart and accepted its teaching without question as the standard of orthodoxy.' Like so many others of the time, both of them came to reject the doctrines in which they had been reared, which were too narrow, or too narrowly understood, to accommodate their mature experience.

Even the religion of educated Europeans of their own class was thus associated for them as for others like them with an immaturity of sentiment and reason, a timid or obstinate traditionalism, which they had personally outgrown. Still more compounded of error and misunderstanding, arising from false analogical reasoning, and ignorance of natural causes, laws and processes therefore appeared the religion of uneducated, unscientific peoples who were assumed to have remained closer to an original psychological infancy of mankind.

Tylor's theory of the basis of religion, and Frazer's of the nature of magic, illustrate the approach of many Victorian writers to these topics. . . . Tylor's minimal definition of religion as 'a belief in spiritual beings'—this simplest form of religion, 'animism' as he called it—

From *Social Anthropology*, Chap. 6. Copyright © 1964 by Oxford University Press, London. Reprinted by permission of the publisher and the author. Godfrey Lienhardt is Lecturer in Social Anthropology and African Sociology, Oxford University.

arose, he thought, when primitive peoples had reflected upon their experience of immaterial forms in dreams, or considered the difference between a living man and his corpse. Primitive Man, considering these mysteries and anxious for an explanation, would infer the existence of a human soul, immaterial and separable from the body. From this he would develop the idea of other souls and spirits 'from the tiniest elf that sports in the long grass up to the heavenly Creator and Ruler of the world, the Great Spirit.'

According to one of Frazer's most influential theories, magical practices were to be explained by a 'law of sympathy' governing primitive thought. From this 'law' followed such common beliefs as that gold might be used to cure jaundice, or that a person might be injured by the magical treatment of his nail- or hair-clippings. Things which had a striking quality in common, like the yellowness of gold and jaundice, or which had once been in intimate contact, were believed to affect one another. This is, of course, a true account of common beliefs, and Frazer's categories of 'imitative' and 'contagious' magic still have some value; but he was too ready to regard this descriptive formulation as a conclusion to his investigation.

For Tylor and more particularly Frazer, primitive religion and magic were erroneous means towards a knowledge and control of human circumstances, and particularly of the physical world, which in their day men of science had really begun to achieve by rational methods. In France, the more philosophical Lévy-Bruhl posited a primitive mentality quite different in orientation from that of modern philosophers and scientists, a synthesizing, affective, poetic mentality which neither made, nor aimed at making, the distinctions of European logic. In primitive thought, men and natural beings and objects might 'participate' mystically in one another's existence, as when among people who hold totemic beliefs a man and his totemic animal are supposed in some sense to share a common life.

Early inquiry into such matters, particularly in Britain, much oversimplified the problems of translation and interpretation of exotic ideas and customs. Original texts from native informants were very few. The scholars who claimed to understand 'primitive mentality' knew nothing of the languages in which it was expressed, and had no intimate experience of the actual social and physical conditions of the peoples whose beliefs they confidently interpreted. Consequently much of their interpretation was the result of simple introspection, of supposing themselves in foreign circumstances and imagining how they themselves would then think and act.

Yet the Victorian anthropologists had at least begun seriously to collect and sift evidence about the beliefs of remote cultures which were often absurdly misunderstood by other educated men. They were prepared to compare, as well as contrast, 'savages' with themselves, and they tried to understand some principles of symbolic thought and action on a wide comparative basis. If for them the primitive gods, and possibly all gods, were products of a more or less uninstructed human reason and imagination, they were still examples of 'gods' to be studied, and not 'idols,' 'devils' or mere mumbo-jumbo, as they were sometimes made to appear by those who viewed them entirely from the standpoint of their own absolute revealed religious orthodoxies. When a traveller as influential as Sir Samuel Baker could tell the Ethnological Society of London (in 1866) that the Dinka and Shilluk of the Upper Nile had no religion 'nor is the darkness of their minds enlightened by even a ray of superstition,' it was as well to have a Tylor to rebuke his opinionated ignorance.

Further, perhaps partly because some of them had themselves exchanged one framework of convictions for another in moving outside religious faiths they had once professed, anthropologists had begun to explore how far truths and beliefs, which seemed self-evidently and absolutely valid to those nurtured in them, were actually contingent upon particular social and historical circumstances.

Here the French sociologists of the *Année Sociologique*—Durkheim, Mauss, Hubert and others—were more systematic, and conscious of their aims, than their British or American counterparts, who gave less thought to the difference between sociological and psychological generalizations. For Frazer and others, the explanation of religious and magical beliefs and customs lay ultimately in the working of the individual human mind; and they readily assumed that their own minds were sufficiently representative of 'the human mind,' if at its most subtle and efficient. The French, more sociologically, insisted that the very possibilities of thought and experience were given in a social tradition, which its bearers inherited rather than chose.

There were thus distinctively *collective* ideas and modes of behaviour which moulded the individual mind and conscience differently in different societies. As Durkheim wrote:

. . . there is in every society a certain group of phenomena which may be differentiated from those studied by the other natural sciences. When I fulfil my obligations as brother, husband or citizen, when I execute my contracts, I perform duties which are defined, externally to myself and my acts, in law and custom. Even if they conform to my own sentiments, and I feel their reality subjectively, such reality is still objective, for I did not create them; I merely inherited them through my education . . .

Similarly the church member finds the beliefs and practices of his religious life ready-made at birth; their existence prior to his own implies their existence outside himself. . . .

From such theoretical starting points, these French writers proposed a sociology of ideas and beliefs in which such seemingly fundamental and intuitive notions as those of time, of space, and of classification were examined in relation to social conditions.

Anthropological insistence upon the necessity of interpreting belief and custom as relative to social circumstance has sometimes laid the subject open to charges of a total relativism. Logically, such a relativism would bring the validity of anthropological findings themselves into question, for if all expressions of 'truth' were *merely* relative to social conditons, then there would be nothing to choose between, say, an anthropologist's interpretation of witchcraft and that of a witch.

But a sociology of ideas and convictions does not necessarily imply that the sociologist himself makes no critical judgment as to their greater or lesser validity. He maintains only that no informed judgment can properly be made unless the notions under consideration are first seen as part of the whole social situation which defines their meaning. Thus, to refer to an earlier example, the giving of bridewealth in marriage might appear superficially to resemble purchase of women, but on closer inspection is seen to be a different kind of transaction. Whether that transaction is commendable, is a question of a different order.

In this concern for the detailed social context, social anthropology in this century seems to have developed in a way parallel to some historical and literary studies (one thinks at random of Collingwood, Namier, Beljame, L. C. Knights), though professional scholars in these other subjects not unnaturally tend to judge it still by the earlier writings which first made an impact on the cultivated reader. In the first chapter of his work *The Greeks and their Gods* (1950) W. K. C. Guthrie, for example, has given a judicious criticism of the eclecticism of earlier anthropological writers in the field of classical studies—Frazer, Jane Harrison, Gilbert Murray—which differs little in principle from that which any living social anthropologist might produce. They tended too easily to interpret details of classical custom in the light of isolated ethnological facts culled from here and there from quite different peoples and circumstances—Australian aborigines, African kingdoms and so forth. But today, any anthropologist trying to understand the religion of his chosen area would accept the principle laid down by Guthrie for his study of the Greeks, that:

. . . our primary task is to see the religion of Greece in the historical setting of Greek modes of thought and expression, the life of the city state or Boeotian farm, religion as it was affected by the Persian invasion or the Peloponnesian war, above all religion in a small sea-girt country in an East Mediterranean climate.

Modern anthropological works are similarly grounded in the specificity of very local circumstances. Moreover, the anthropologist has usually had the opportunity of directly experiencing these himself, and needs not recreate a foreign way of life by the application of an imaginative scholarship to literature.

But the task does not end with an understanding of specific circumstances only. Though social anthropologists no longer select details of beliefs from all over the world, to fit them together in comprehensive theories of the universal characteristics of totemism, ancestor-worship, witchcraft or the like, they still try to reach conclusions which have some relevance for the interpretation of material other than their own. A movement of thought between general themes and specific detail, with the inten-

tion of reaching a better understanding of both, is encouraged, in teaching, from the beginning. What this actually involves may be suggested by considering anthropological treatment of notions that seem most conspicuously and self-evidently false to people who have not been brought up to assume their truth—beliefs in witchcraft.

It seems to be generally taken for granted in modern Western society that the complex of beliefs and acts indicated by the word 'witchcraft' arise from superstitious delusion. Yet in the European past, men whose intellectual brilliance is in other respects unquestioned accepted witchcraft as a fact, and belief in it therefore cannot be regarded as utterly incompatible with an educated, critical and even scientific intelligence. In the *Religio Medici,* Sir Thomas Browne held that those who denied the reality of witchcraft were themselves witches, thus (and in a way characteristic of witchcraft-thought) interpreting arguments against his own belief so as to confirm it. Francis Bacon, who also believed in witchcraft (though perhaps partly because it was more prudent to appear to do so in the time of the intensely witch-conscious King James I), observed that '. . . the act of envy hath something in it of witchcraft, so there is no other cure of envy than the cure of witchcraft, that is, remove the lot as they call it and lay it on another. . . .' Here, the real existence of witchcraft is predicated where most of us, probably, would be inclined to accept first the existence of envy, and regard witchcraft as a set of fears and superstitions stemming from that vice.

European witchcraft notions were commonly fitted into a Christian theological system, so that witches were regarded as in league with the Devil or other evil spirits in the Christian struggle between good and evil, and persecuted for that reason. Margaret Murray and those whom her zealous writings convince, similarly see European witchcraft largely as an opposition by organized adherents of a pagan religion surviving from pre-Christian times, to later Christian orthodoxy.

An anthropological interpretation of witchcraft must however take into account ethnological evidence from other societies where the special historical and theological circumstances which gave European witchcraft its particular form do not exist, and here the information from Africa and some of the Indians of North America is particularly rich.

First we have to try to divest the term 'witchcraft' of the confusion of associations which it has in popular thought. It is commonly associated with 'magic,' for example; yet there are many who, like Prospero, might properly be called magicians, but who are certainly not witches. Again, the European belief that witches are in communication with evil spirits is not found everywhere, and cannot therefore be said to be an essential feature of all witchcraft.

Witchcraft, basically, entails attributing many of the evils of life to evil in some other persons, who usually by arcane means attack the health and prosperity of their victims. For the sake of clarity, anthropologists have tended to use the term 'witchcraft' to denote primarily a supposed *psychic* act, producing harm which may not even be held to be entirely deliberately planned. In witchcraft so considered, the witch may not know himself what he has done until, having been accused, he is declared guilty by divination, the consultation of oracles, or some other means of 'smelling out' witches.

Then, given his own initial conviction—which he shares with his accusers—that such baneful influences do emanate from one person to another, and in the often highly suggestible condition induced by the methods of inquiry which have identified him as a witch, he may well admit his guilt. Hence the numerous confessions obtained, whether legalistically as under the courts and tortures of Europe, or by the clairvoyant means of investigation often used in Africa. Confessions then seem to provide further proof of the existence of witches.

This entirely psychic act, 'witchcraft,' may be distinguished from 'sorcery,' in which there is a conscious and overt intention to injure expressed in the recitation of some malevolent formula or the symbolic use of material means of causing harm. In the complex of relationships of hatred and suspicion to which both these words refer, the element of 'witchcraft' as defined above is not empirically observable. It is wholly in the mind and its imaginings, and no proof of this witchcraft that would satisfy a modern court of law could be adduced, though sometimes the presence of a physical substance said to represent it is established by postmortem. The workings of sorcery on the other hand might be seen and heard if the sorcerer were caught reciting his formula or using his medicines. They can exist therefore outside the mind, even though their real effects are, from a modern point of view, also in the imagination.

Hence, though a modern court of law might not believe that a sorcerer was capable of producing the harm he intended by the means he actually employed, his intention to do so could be demonstrable without his own confession. Courts in Africa today have in such cases adopted something of the attitude of Thomas Hobbes referred to by Parrinder in his short study, *Witchcraft:* 'I think not that their witchcraft [here one might say 'sorcery'] is any real power but yet that they are justly punished for the false belief they have that they can do such mischief, joined with their purpose to do it if they can.'

In practice among people who take such matters seriously, this analytic distinction between sorcery and witchcraft is not always clearly drawn and may not be drawn at all. 'Witches' and 'sorcerers' may represent anything from persons who are materially innocent of any offense except that of having incurred suspicion, fear and enmity, to members of covens of power-seeking occultists, capable in extreme cases (as far as carefully sifted legal evidence can show) of acts of ritual cannibalism.

This very confusion and overlapping of notions, this interplay of imagination and knowledge, confirm beliefs in witchcraft and sorcery. Those who have done no more than glance at a baby which has then fallen sick, or have merely excited distaste for some feature of their physical appearance, or envy for their success, may come to be suspected of vile secret acts of malice. Yet there is some reason for distinguishing analytically between 'witchcraft' and 'sorcery' on the lines indicated. Some peoples do in their own thought make a comparable distinction, and it is one which (as in witchcraft cases tried in modern courts of law) may have practical consequences. And as a matter of general principle, a social anthropologist is required as far as possible to discard the associative thought which *promotes* belief in order to *study* belief, reducing compound experiences and notions as far as possible to constituent elements. No social phenomenon can be adequately studied merely in the language and categories of thought in which the people among whom it is found represent it to themselves.

The effects attributed to witchcraft or sorcery —sickness, misfortune, death—are as real to believers in witchcraft as to sceptics. The 'effects' in themselves raise no anthropological problem.

But the causes to which such effects are at-tributed, and the form of argument by which they are identified as the results of witchcraft, do create a problem of interpretation for those who deny the validity of witchcraft belief.

Professor Michael Polanyi, in *Personal Knowledge* (1957), tried to clarify this prob-lem, basing his argument partly on the rich ma-terial from the Azande of the Sudan, and from that detailed and brilliantly analysed ethno-graphic information has suggested general con-clusions about the nature of our belief and knowledge, quite outside the world of Zande witchcraft.

The Azandes' beliefs in witchcraft, like those of other peoples, start from the observed facts of misfortune and differential luck; the desire to explain these; and the assumption that the reasons for them are in other people. 'Witch-craft' for Azande is thus a term used to some extent like 'providence' or 'chance' in England; but behind it is a more searching explanatory in-tention. 'Witchcraft' accounts primarily for the particular manifestations rather than general characteristics, of human unhappiness.

A Zande who has cultivated his garden to the best of his ability, let us say, following a'l locally prescribed procedures, has a bad yield because of some pest. He recognizes that it is the pest that has ruined his crop, but he is not content to let the matter rest there. He wants to know why it is *his* particular crop that has failed, when others promise a fine harvest. Brought up to explain misfortune and death, by 'witchcraft,' and to believe that witches and other secret enemies may be identified by the consultation of oracles, he turns to the oracles to discover who may be responsible for his bad luck.

Of the several kinds of Zande oracle, the most authoritative is *benge,* a poison adminis-tered to chickens whose reactions to it vary, and are interpreted as positive or negative an-swers to questions asked of the poison oracle. A Zande text gives some indication of how this works:

Benge is the wood from which they [Azande] derive oracles. If a man's relative dies he consults *benge* about his death in order to find out the witch who killed him. . . .
    A Zande catches some chickens today and takes them to *benge.* He mixes *benge* with a little water and he seizes a chicken and pours *benge* into his beak, and addresses *benge* thus: 'Benge, benge, you are in the throat of the chicken. I will die this year, *benge* hear it, twist the fowl round and round and

lay down its corpse. It is untrue, I will eat my eleusine this year and the year after, let the fowl survive.' If he will not die the fowl survives. If he will die the fowl dies in accordance with the speech of *benge*.

Such beliefs can be shown to have several important functions and effects in Zande society. For instance witchcraft beliefs represent a kind of popular psychology and moral philosophy, since the people whom a Zande expects to be-witch him, and whose names are likely to be put before the oracle, are those whom he thinks have reason to dislike him. These also are likely to be those whom he himself dislikes. To suspect witchcraft, then, is to assess motive and inten-tion. Also (since the wing of a fowl that has died from *benge* in an oracular consultation may be sent to the witch identified by it, to blow upon to 'cool' his witchcraft) the result is to deal openly and frankly with the minor irri-tations of human relationships before they ac-cumulate into determined hatred. Writing of a very different people, the Navaho Indians of North America, the late Clyde Kluckhohn con-cluded that

In a society where the relative strength of anticipa-tion of punishment for overt aggression is high, witchcraft allows imaginary aggression. Witchcraft channels the displacement of aggression, facilitating emotional adjustment with a minimum disturbance of social relationships.

Therefore also:

Witchcraft belief allows the verbalization of anxiety in a framework that is understandable and that implies the possibility of doing something.
    Witches (who are living indivduals) are poten-tially controllable by the society; the caprices of environment are not.

But when all allowance has been made for such positive functions of witchcraft beliefs, it should not be forgotten that the practice may sometimes involve sorcery too—the actual performance of acts of aggression, 'ritual' cannibalism and the inversion of accepted values which among the Navaho, according to Kluckhohn, are inhibited by being performed in the imagination.

Zande acceptance of witchcraft and oracles has another function more specific to Zande society. When legal cases lie for injury—for witchcraft, adultery, or other wrongs which it is easy to suspect but difficult to prove—and the evidences from different primary consulta-tions of the oracle are contradictory, then the

oracles of princes are regarded as final. Thus
the regressions of doubt and conflict of opinions
in matters which, by their very nature, cannot
become clear by demonstrable proofs, have an
end in the attribution of infallibility to the
oracles of rulers. The princes' oracles then have
legal and political functions, in bolstering the
system of rule and providing a means of settling
issues which must otherwise, to the detriment
of effective law, remain in dispute.

Evans-Pritchard emphasized that the Azande
were not able or not prepared to put their whole
system of beliefs in witchcraft, oracles and
magic to any test which would call the validity
of the whole into question. They would not, for
example, test the poison on the fowl as though
it were simply a natural poison, without putting
any question to it at all, for this would be a
foolish waste of poison. When an oracle contradicted itself, answering 'yes' and 'no' to exactly the same question, they would not doubt
the value of oracles in general. They would
merely argue that in this particular case there
had been some fault in the procedure or the
poison.

Polanyi has considered the implications of
this Zande system of belief for our understanding of the stability of belief and the 'fiduciary
basis of knowledge' as he calls it, more generally. The Azande accept on traditional faith
the assumption upon which their whole system
of thought rests, and which, since it involves
circular argument, defeats particular doubts:

So long as each doubt is defeated in its turn, its
effect is to strengthen the fundamental convictions
against which it was raised. 'Let the reader consider
(writes Evans-Pritchard) any argument that would
utterly demolish all Zande claims for the power of
the oracles. If it were translated into Zande modes
of thought it would serve to support their entire
structure of belief.' Thus the circularity of a conceptual system tends to reinforce itself by contact
with every fresh topic.

The stability of belief, then, is shown by 'the
way it denies to any rival conception the ground
in which it might take root':

. . . a new conception, e.g. that of natural causation,
which would take the place of Zande superstition,
could be established only by a whole series of relevant instances, and such evidence cannot accumulate
in the minds of people if each of them is disregarded in its turn for lack of the concept that
would lend significance to it.

Such is a philosopher's and scientist's account

of what anthropologists have called 'collective
representations,' categories of thought which
are absolutely assumed among members of a
given society. In Polanyi's words, 'by holding
the same set of presuppositions they mutually confirm each other's interpretation of
experience.'

Anthropologists have commonly followed
Frazer, Malinowski and others, in distinguishing 'magic' from 'religion' by reference to the
attitude of the practitioner and the techniques
employed. Magic in this view achieves its ends
through formulae and acts which are held to
be intrinsically effective in a quasi-deterministic
way; it is thus, according to Frazer, an erroneous form of science. Religion on the other
hand involves a sense of dependence upon
higher powers, whose help is supplicated and
anger propitiated, but who are not subject to
man's absolute control.

At the time when native categories of priest,
sorcerer, doctor and witch were badly confused
by Europeans, sometimes with resulting injustice as when priests were punished as sorcerers
or 'witch-doctors' for example, there was something to be said for this effort to clarify our
own terms. Also in many cultures the people
themselves do commonly distinguish between
mystical operations undertaken for private individual ends, often at the expense of other members of the society, and those which are openly
performed for the benefit of all. Durkheim and
his followers based their religious sociology on
a universally acknowledged division of activities
and objects into 'sacred' and 'profane' and demonstrated up to a point that 'the sacred' was
closely connected with the social, while the profane or secular embraced matters of private
individual interest. Durkheim and his colleagues
thus rejected those many minimal definitions of
religion which made belief in gods or spirits
a necessary distinguishing feature. They turned
instead to a study of the relations between these
two domains, the sacred, set apart from common life and hedged round by taboos and special
prohibitions and observances, and the profane.
And these were not to be regarded as simply
opposed to one another (as good to evil, for
example) but as radically different in kind.
They were as two different worlds, and to pass
from the profane to the sacred man must, in
effect, be born anew, as is represented in so
many rites of initiation, purification and con-
secration all over the world.

But attempts at working definitions and classification are only a beginning, and can sometimes direct attention from the central problems. Whether we call the particular notions and actions we study magical or religious or magico-religious (a compound word which itself indicates that such terms raise difficulties) our interest is in the nature of belief and knowledge, and of symbolic action and expression, in specific social contexts. Zande witchcraft notions, as we have seen, involve a systematic interpretation of human experience which, for Azande, is given a particular kind of order and coherence in their witchcraft philosophy. Behind that philosophy also, if not frequently invoked, is a conception of a Divinity, a First Cause, in which the order of the whole world is grounded.

Among many other peoples, beliefs in witchcraft are less in evidence and play a smaller explanatory role. It is then what we should call 'religious' beliefs (or among many today, political ideologies or the theories of natural science) that provide an ultimate framework for men's understanding of themselves and the world. The creeds of the Presbyterian and Anglican churches had once done so for Frazer, Darwin and their likes, before creeds seemed to exclude truth rather than symbolize it.

In discussing magical and religious beliefs and rites we are considering particular humans' apprehensions of underlying order in their world, ways of discovering and announcing that order, and means of adapting themselves to it. With this in mind, it is instructive to consider first, rather than traditional religions, certain relatively modern cults whose genesis is well-documented; for in ancient religions the accretions of centuries sometimes make it difficult to isolate boldly the fundamental principles of religious belief and action. We shall consider then two relatively new religions: the Ghost Dance religions which spread among many North American Indian tribes at the end of the last century; and the hundreds, and probably thousands, of separatist sects and native churches which, evolving their own forms of religious beliefs and rites, have broken away from Christian missionary churches in Africa.

The Ghost Dance religion is a general term referring to a number of separate religious revivals spreading among many different American Indian groups at various times in the course of the nineteenth century. They had in common the belief that by performing certain ritual dances and other ceremonies, and adhering to ethical and other prescriptions revealed in dreams to leaders who taught them to their followers, they would in Lucy Mair's phrase 'bring an ideal world into being.' The dances and other rituals would unite men with their ancestors—hence the general name 'Ghost Dance'—in a world and way of life which fulfilled many traditional Indian aspirations, though war and all quarrelsomeness, particularly among Indians, were forbidden.

Of the varieties of Ghost Dance (known in the vernacular by various names) I confine myself to one well-described complex studied by Alexander Lesser and described in *The Pawnee Ghost Dance Hand Game* (1933). The incorporation of an old Indian guessing and gambling game into the new rituals is of special interest in this religion.

By the end of the nineteenth century the Pawnee, whose ancestral territories lay between the Mississippi and the Rocky Mountains, where they had originally lived by horticulture and hunting, had become displaced and demoralized wards of the United States government. Their culture and traditional forms of enjoyment—hunting, dancing, gambling and feasting—had suffered seriously through the civilizing efforts of missionaries and government officials. In 1892, says Lesser, 'after the best efforts of the Pawnee to adjust themselves to living alongside the white man, the tribe had come to a cultural impasse, with nothing to look forward to and nothing to live by.'

In the 1890's, various forms of the Ghost Dance, and the visions and rules connected with it, were spreading from a centre among the Californian Paiute to neighbouring Indians and then much more widely afield. In 1891 Frank White, a Pawnee Indian away from home, took part in the Ghost Dance among the Comanche and Wichita Indians of Oklahoma.

Under the influence of the dance and the drug peyote, White fell into a trance, and in a vision saw a village in which a figure described as 'the Messiah,' and his people, were dancing and singing. He joined the dance, and learnt songs in his own Pawnee language. Later in the year he returned north to organize the dance and introduce connected rituals and doctrines among his own people. People were to prepare for the coming of the kingdom by dancing and other activities and abstentions, especially by abstaining from ploughing.

To turn away from certain practical activities and renounce certain material goods and advantages are features of millenarian movements in other parts of the world; but here also it is consistent with what seems to have been a deeply felt Indian revulsion against the white man's unrestrained exploitation of the earth. As one prophet expressed it:

You ask me to plow the ground. Shall I take a knife and tear my mother's bosom? Then when I die she will not take me to her bosom to rest. You ask me to dig for stone. Shall I dig under her skin for her bones? Then when I die I cannot enter her body to be born again. . . .

It was of course basically the Americans' appetite for developing the continent which had resulted in the dispossession and degradation of the Indians. Frank White's religion was to create a different scale of values, and one in part recovered from an Indian past.

At first White taught the few songs he knew, some of them in Wichita and Arapaho, and organized the singers and the dancers in a simple form of liturgy. As more and more people joined his original group, the arrangements became more complex and formalized. White and his acolytes used a special sacred tipi where the dancers had their faces painted, and from where they came out to lead the dance. In dancing, the congregation fell into trances and made contact with another world:

From time to time those who fell would get up and tell what they had seen. Each had a message from the other world, and had learned songs. These visions became sanctions not only for special developments of the Ghost Dance and of the hand game, but also for important revivals of old aspects of Pawnee life, before this had ceased to function.

Those who acted and believed in this way (now as it were members of a church) were to be saved, and live on in an Indian Paradise when, as was predicted and imminently expected, a high wind would destroy the whites and the half-castes.

The ritual and ceremonial surrounding the Ghost Dance involved most importantly a preliminary pipe-smoking ceremony, with special actors and elaborately formalized gestures, in which a blessing was given to the dancers. For the performance of all these ceremonies, the area of ground around White's tipi was divided up for the 'rituale' as a choreographer divides a stage, or as a church is divided, to give sacred meanings to special orientations. The cardinal points of the compass in particular

had religious meanings attached to them. Connected with such religious meanings, there were also symbolic representations drawn partly from Indian and partly from Christian sources. Thus, one who was referred to as 'the Child of the Father in Heaven' is said to have appeared in a vision to teach the ritual and the doctrine of the smoke offering, parts of which were connected in meaning with a complex traditional star mythology. To this mythology Christ's crucifixion was assimilated since a cross was the Pawnee sign for 'star.'

With this eclectic integration of myths, beliefs, and rites, went an elaborate and coherent symbolism. Eagle or crow feathers were worn by some of the participants because the Pawnee thought of the eagle and the crow as high- and far-flying birds with penetrating vision and knowledge of distant matters. Their feathers were held to assist in producing the visionary states of the Ghost Dance. More particularly the crow was thought of as a bird which could find what it searched for, and would help people to find what they had lost—basically their old integrity. It is interesting to note that as Frank White's Ghost Dance religion developed, the eagle and crow, whose feathers had originally been used according to individual preference or knowledge, began to be seen in symbolic opposition, according to their different qualities, and were associated with opposing sides in the ritual Hand Game which formed an important adjunct to the Ghost Dance. Here is a simple example of the growth of a 'liturgy' and 'rituale,' through the formalization of features which had first been accidental or haphazard, however imaginatively appropriate.

The traditional hand games of the North American Indians were originally guessing and gambling games, in which opposing teams, in pairs of individuals, guessed in which hand their opponents concealed a counter, though in forms of play of extreme elaboration and complication. Tallies were kept by the leaders, bets were placed on the results, and that team won which guessed most accurately. The games were basically competitions to show who had the greater 'luck,' which the Indians thought of as a positive quality—even quantity—or virtue, prestigious in itself and necessary for the successful conduct of life.

In the Hand Game played as an adjunct to the Ghost Dance religion, the gambling element was removed. Richer ceremonial and insignia were introduced, some of them drawn from old

Pawnee symbolism of colours and natural objects. Tally sticks, for example, were made of the traditionally sacred cedar and dogwood, and were divided up into groups associated with different directions, basically the northern and southern horizons, which in turn were associated with different colours, the dark for the northern horizon, the bright for the southern horizon. There were altars with ordered arrangements of the sacred pipes and other *materia sacra*. The opponents or players took up their positions in formal relation to the altars. All this and much more elaboration of symbolic action developed around the fundamental interest of the Indians in solemnly discovering which had the greater 'luck'—or, to put it into terms which perhaps convey more of the real meaning in our own culture, which was more blessed.

This local Indian religion exhibits some common basic features of religion everywhere, even where the deep element of social protest and overwhelming nostalgia for the past—specific features of the Ghost Dance—are not significantly present: that is, myth, here represented by visions, coming from beyond present practical experience, which validates formal rituals and ceremonials; the doctrine of obligations and abstentions, here fairly simple, which this ritual and mythological complex carries with it; the quest for insight, and truth represented in many religions as 'illumination,' and the creation in ritual and myth of a particular and coherent pattern of meanings, in terms of which the worshippers understand the order of the world and their relation to it. These go with differentiation of roles of the actors in the sacred play (here in the Ghost Dance Hand Game, the word 'play' is even literally appropriate) and the evaluation of spaces and objects in the material world according to the position they are assigned in this whole structure of thought and imagination and action. (Very widespread, in this evaluation, are sets of symbolic oppositions: good/evil, sky/earth, male/female, etc. The opposition of right and left, often equated respectively with the fortunate and the unfortunate, the male and the female, and the strong and the weak, has particularly interested social anthropologists since Robert Hertz's *La Prééminence de la Main Droite* (translated by Rodney and Claudia Needham in *Death and the Right Hand,* 1960).

Two more, and shorter examples, further illustrate this characteristic activity of the religious imagination in symbolic and poetic

thought. Those whom Sundkler in his *Bantu Prophets in South Africa* (1948) has called 'the Zionists' are independent native churches in South Africa, deriving ultimately from an American pentecostal church. They have developed different forms of syncretist religion with emphasis on healing, speaking with tongues, and purification by rites and the observation of taboos. Of one such church, Sundkler writes:

. . . Zionists regard their Zion Church as the court of heaven. The positions in the church house at T— of prophet X's Salem Church show clearly how the church is a replica of the heavenly temple: at the altar is sitting prophet X himself, 'the Judge' (*u Mahluli*) in episcopal vestments. . . . If he is absent . . . he has gone to the vestry where he is speaking to God through his 'Heavenly Telephone'. Near the altar are also the twelve prophets and the twelve apostles, the former in purple, the latter in white. In front of these are seated the Brides and Bridegrooms of the Lamb, some eighty to a hundred young men and girls, all in white. In the four corners of the nave of the church four men in white vestments stand silently: they are the four cardinal points, North, South, East, and West. The 'Hospital' is—logically—in the middle of the church: here are gathered the sick and those who are specially set aside to pray for them. . . .

and he adds: "Their collective experience has provided a consistent "dream-geography" of heaven.'

Here then, again, a religion provides a distinctive patterning of experience, a map of the psyche and the world which, for believers, is held to represent the situation of man in true proportion and scale. This aspect of religions is well and succinctly illustrated in a detail from the religion of another American Indian prophet of the type earlier described, the prophet Smohalla.

In this great work *The Ghost Dance Religion and the Sioux Outbreak of 1890* . . . James Mooney gives a description of the religion and doctrine of Smohalla, in which he reproduces a sketch of the heraldic flag which flew from his flagstaff. [See p. 447.] The field was yellow, representing the yellow grass of summer in that part of the world. The green border represented the boundaries of the world, green suggesting the moist greenery of mountains, and the band outside and above this was blue with a white star. The patch in the centre was red. Smohalla described his flag in the following terms:

This is my flag, and it represents the world. God

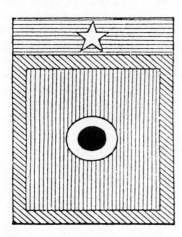

told me to look after my people—all are my people. There are four ways in the world—north and south and east and west. I have been in all those ways. This is the centre. I live here. The red spot is my heart—everybody can see it. The yellow grass grows everywhere around this place. The green mountains are far away all round the world. There is only water beyond—salt water. The blue [referring to the blue cloth strip] is the sky, and the star is the north star. That star never changes; it is always in the same place. I keep my heart on that star. I never change.

In Melanesia, cults have arisen which have as part of their object to gain for their adherents European manufactured goods, knowns as 'cargo,' which hitherto seem to have arrived only for Europeans. For this reason they are known as 'cargo cults' or 'cargo movements.' . . . K. O. L. Burridge, in *Mambu* (1960), describes how

participants . . . engage in a number of strange and exotic rites and ceremonies the purpose of which is, apparently, to gain possession of European manufactured goods . . . Large decorated houses, or 'aeroplanes' or 'ships' made of wood, bark and palm thatch bound together with vines, may be built to receive the goods, and participants may whirl, shake, chant, dance, foam at the mouth or couple promiscuously in agitated attempts to obtain the cargo they want.

But something other than greed for material possessions is involved. Burridge says:

The most significant theme in cargo movements seems to be moral regeneration: the creation of a new man, the creation of new unities, the creation of a new society. . . . And both new man and new society are to be a true amalgam or synthesis, not a mixture of European and Kanaka forms and ideals.

These are religions largely created or initiated

by charismatic leaders, as Max Weber called them, and bear the marks of consistency of a single dominating personality. But even then their coherence is not that of a logically thought out, rational scheme of ideas produced by one mind only. After the initial appeal of the leader's definition and interpretation of a particular social experience, others make their contributions to ritual and doctrine. The 'vision' of one man then becomes accepted by his followers as a source of their distinctive collective experience, of which their own visions are part. D. F. Pocock observes in *Social Anthropology* (1961):

These societies . . . were being subjected to a gathering flood of external experience which finally increased beyond the 'stretch' of the indigenous categories that might render it meaningful . . . The social forms of communication appear inadequate. The society is as near to atomization as it could be. The last resort is a new stress upon the individual as that society conceives it, an emphasis upon history, upon individual possession by spirits, upon the individually inspired leader.

Messianic and millennarian cults arise in special historical circumstances, involving usually a strong sense of social deprivation in their adherents; but, eccentric in some details as these religions may be, we can see in them basic characteristics of other religions in which the historical factors affecting the growth of ritual and doctrine are more difficult to ascertain. In such religions, it is traditional teaching, more or less formalized according to the society, which establishes in the minds of believers a particular interpretation of cosmic order—a cosmogony, cosmology and sometimes a cosmography—and a confidence in prescribed means of understanding and adapting to that order

Religious conceptions and symbolism then unify the understanding of human experience, by emphasizing certain aspects of it (which differ from religion to religion) and placing them in a significant order and relationship one with another. Thus it is that the crises of human life—birth, initiation, marriage, death—are surrounded by rites and ceremonies in great variety, as Van Gennep observed in his great study of them, *Les Rites de Passage*. By initiation ceremonies, for example, the young are made into adults, and their relations with the whole community then change. It is not unusual in these ceremonies for the initiate to undergo a symbolic death, so he may be born again as an adult. In ceremonies at death again, the relations between the dead and the living are defined and ordered. Secondary burial, when after a period the corpse is disinterred and re-buried, among some peoples establishes the deceased as now finally one of the dead, where-as before he had not fully as we say 'passed over.' A Nuer man for whom the mortuary ceremonies had been performed during a long absence from home, when his death had been presumed, but who returned alive, was still re-garded, so we are told, as a living ghost in the village.

Integration, whether of the self, the com-munity, or the universe, is a characteristic, explicit religious concern. In an ancient Egyp-tian hymn to Ptah-tanu, quoted by Max Muller in his *Introduction to the Science of Religion* (1873), the god is made a figure of this in-tegration: '. . . thou hast put together the earth, thou hast united thy limbs, thou hast reckoned thy members, what thou hast found apart, thou hast put in its place . . .' and in a passage from a contemporary life of the Emperor Akbar quoted by the same author, the King is repre-sented as having a divinely conferred insight into order and unity behind the diversity of appearance:

. . . for a king possesses, independent of men, the ray of Divine wisdom, which banishes from his heart everything that is conflicting. A king will therefore sometimes observe the element of har-mony in a multitude of things, or sometimes, reversely, a multitude of things in that which is apparently one.

In this picture of the enlightened ruler, ideal-ized as it is, there is yet an element of sociolog-ical truth. The actual social role of leaders like the Grand Sanusi of Cyrenaica or 'divine kings' (like the King of the Shilluk) does in part de-rive from their religious status. By placing them theoretically above local oppositions among their people this status sometimes enables them to symbolize a deeper unity, putting them, more than others, in a position to reconcile those who are in conflict.

Numberless and immensely varied cos-mogonic and cosmological myths also represent, with rich imagery, the establishment and nature of the cosmic orders of different peoples, and which provide the full context of their religious practices. A common theme in these myths is the creation of a physically and morally ordered universe, out of chaos and darkness. The Maori of New Zealand, according to Elsdon Best,

speak of an original state of 'night' before Sky and Earth appeared. This 'night', in Maori, sig-nifies not only simple nighttime, but also the underworld of the dead, and the period of human existence before birth and after death. It implies the darkness of the unknown, from which a sequence of forces and conditions de-veloped generating, eventually, the intelligible Maori universe into being. Maori interest in genealogy leads them to explain the develop-ments of this earliest period by genealogical tables recited, in varying versions by a trained priestly class, and in which personified forces appear as ancestors of a kind. One such table has

. . . such names as Te Kune, Te Pupuke, Te Hihiri, Te Mahara, Te Hinengaro, and Te Manako, ere coming to the primal parents Sky and Earth. These expressions may be rendered as 'the conceiving', 'the flowing forth' (or swelling), 'the persevering' (or thinking), 'the thought' (or power of thinking), and 'the longing' or desiring.

Next in this Maori Genesis come Sky and Earth, then close together. From their mating many gods of the Maori pantheon were born:

. . . When these children were born, the Earth Mother was shrouded in darkness, the only sign of light was the feeble glimmer of a glow-worm . . . Sky and Earth were in close contact, for the Sky parent was closely embracing the Earth Mother . . .

The god Tane, one of the children of this mat-ing and the progenitor of mankind, then pro-posed to his brothers that the parents should be separated, 'that the Sky should be forced upward that they might enjoy freedom of move-ment and the air of space'. His brother Whiro (the god personifying evil, darkness and death) objected, and when Tane succeeded in separat-ing Sky and Earth, remained within the Earth. Tane brought light and life to men, and sym-bolizes light, life and fertility.

In this much abbreviated version of the com-plex Maori mythologies dealing with the crea-tion, are features very similar to some in creation myths told by peoples with whom the Maori could have had no historical contact. An original chaos, dark and undifferentiated, gives way to a particular ordered world with a space for human beings to live in and the light by which they can see and know. Among many peoples, it is some human act which creates an initial separation of Sky and Earth. This so often figured also as a separation of

God and Man, and is therefore logically the origin of religious practice, in representing the differentiation and separation of the divine and the human. Very widespread are myths which explain the division of Sky and Earth, and God and Man, by the act of a woman. According to the Dinka of the Sudan the first woman, trying to pound more grain than God had allowed for human requirements, struck God and the Sky with a long-handled pestle. Offended, God withdrew from the earth, and men have since had to propitiate him, especially in sickness and death, both originally unknown.

The idea that the creation of the world was a giving of reality to mere appearance or potential, the emergence of the actual, palpable world from a dream or thought, is found in myth. It appears very clearly in the following, from the Uitota Indians of South America— one example of the poetic metaphysic with which the social anthropologist (and the depth psychologist, from whom in this field we may have much to learn) is often presented:

In the beginning there was nothing but mere appearance. Nothing really existed. It was a phantasm, an illusion, that our father touched; something mysterious it was that he grasped. Nothing existed. Through the agency of a dream our father, He-who-is-appearance-only Nainema, pressed the phantasm to his breast and then was sunk in thought. Not even a tree existed that might have supported this phantasm, and only through his breath did Nainema hold this illusion attached to the thread of a dream. He tried to discover what was at the bottom of it, but he found nothing. 'I have attached that which was non-existent', he said. There was nothing. Then our father tried again and investigated the bottom of this something and his fingers sought the empty phantasm.
He tied the emptiness to the dream thread, and pressed the magical glue substance on it. Thus by means of his dream did he hold it like the fluff of raw cotton.
He seized the bottom of the phantasm and stamped upon it repeatedly, allowing himself finally to rest upon the earth of which he had dreamt.
The earth phantasm was now his. Then he spat out saliva repeatedly so that forests might arise. He lay upon the earth and set the covering of heavens above it. He drew from the earth the blue and white heavens and placed them above.

Here, and also in Maori belief appears a theme to which early writers on 'primitive religion' often did little justice: the very high value set on the power of thought, on knowledge, intelligence and insight. In *La Pensée Sauvage* (1962) Professor Lévi-Strauss has con- vincingly illustrated the practical, even systematic, knowledge which many peoples once thought to lack intellectual curiosity actually seek, and obtain, by exploring their environment.

Knowledge and intelligence are all the more conditions of survival and success where the material advantages of our own kind of civilization are lacking. It is knowledge and intelligence, often represented also in trickery, cunning and deceit, which characterize what are called the 'culture heroes' who are held to have contributed much to the spiritual and cultural heritage of the societies to which they belong.

But when Jacob deceives his father and tricks Esau, or when some other heroic trickster (sometimes a man or demiurge, sometimes figured in folklore as an animal—the hare, the spider, the coyote are well-known examples) outwits his enemies and even his friends, we should be wrong to conclude that the peoples who admire these acts do not also in their ordinary lives set some store by truthfulness and uprightness. These heroic deceptions are remembered as showing the power and value of cleverness and knowledge, often associated with luck or blessing also. Ethical judgments are here irrelevant or are suspended. Hence 'holy' men, even in religions which contain a strong ethical teaching, are not always personally exemplars of the conventional morality of their societies.

People now brought up in the traditions of the universal religions are accustomed indeed to a more direct integration of ethical and religious prescription. St Augustine pointed to this in arguing the superiority of Christianity to paganism: the pagan gods, for him when converted from them, were inferior in that they gave no moral teaching and were themselves represented as committing shameful acts. But in many pagan societies, as often in practice in our own, it is the parents and the elders who primarily inculcate morality. The gods, or some of the gods, are simply its ultimate sanction. In themselves, they are beyond human moralizing.

It will have been apparent that religions and magical 'beliefs', as we call them, are often for those who hold them rather a kind of knowledge and theory of the nature of the universe and of man. From this point of view, there is some point of comparison between such beliefs and the theories of natural science. Robin Horton has even suggested that a modern physicist might become aware of 'a logical resemblance between the gods of primitive peoples and the ultimate particles and other theoretical entities of his own science.'

The differences of course are very marked, and most particularly in the quest for certain kinds of universal truths which characterizes the procedure of natural science. Magical and religious beliefs or theories may indeed be attested *in* experience, either of the individual or the community of believers; but they are not systematically and coldly tested *against* experience over as wide a range of instances as possible. Hence the many occasions when magical or religious expectations are not satisfied in practice are not set against the few when they are. There is a well-known passage in Livingstone's *Missionary Travels* in which a conversation (perhaps not entirely *ipsissima verba*) between Livingstone and an African Rain-Doctor or Rain-Maker underlines this difference. Livingstone accuses the Rain-Doctor of waiting for the clouds, then using his medicines and taking the credit for having brought the rain. The Rain-Doctor replies:

. . . we are both doctors and not deceivers. You give a patient medicine. Sometimes God is pleased to heal him by means of your medicine. Sometimes not—he dies. When he is cured, you take the credit for what God does. I do the same. Sometimes God grants us rain, sometimes not. When he does, we take the credit of the charm. When a patient dies you don't give up trust in your medicine. Neither do I when no rain falls . . .

The medical doctor answers:

I give medicine to living creatures within my reach, and can see the effect though no cure follows. . . . God alone can command the clouds. Only try and wait patiently. God will give us rain without your medicines.

To which the Rain-Doctor says:

Well, I always thought white people were wise until this morning. Whoever thought of making a trial of starvation? Is death pleasant then?

Ironically the Rain-Doctor's beliefs had some-more in common with those of modern scientific rain-makers than had those of Livingstone. The Rain-Doctor thought to make rain by the use of medicines and techniques, and it is by 'medicines' and techniques that clouds are seeded today, whatever also may be thought to be the efficacy of prayer.

As religious and magical beliefs involve definitions of physical, intellectual and moral order,

part of religious practice consists in the attempt to discover the relations between that order and particular events and situations of human life. Religious and magical practices are thus often concerned with the searching out of truths which, it is thought, men must know for their own good, and which go beyond common knowledge or purely rational deduction. Zande witch-doctors and oracles, the visions of the Ghost Dance and ecstasies of the Bantu prophets' congregations, the supposedly superior wisdom and insight of divine kings—all these are examples of this urgent interest in truths which are thought to lie beyond practical or purely rational investigation.

Among the Polynesians the spiritual power or *mana* (a word which, like *taboo* from the same part of the world, has become an anthropological term) of a priest was demonstrated in the truth of his predictions, and from all over the world there are examples of the value set upon a superior grasp of 'truth', whether of past, present or future—in the visionary medicine men or *shamans* of the Eskimo, in African priests and diviners, in the mystics and saints and prophets of the universal religions, and even in the petty clairvoyants of our own rationalistic civilization. These are more discredited in theory, perhaps, than in practice, as the business of horoscopes, prediction and so on shows. A Maori diviner, seeking the cause of sickness, expresses this constituent of religious and magical practice in his spell or prayer:

A seeking a searching
To seek whither?
To search the land, to seek the origin,
To seek out the base, to search the unknown
To seek out the *atua* [spirit]
May it be effectual

Another aspect of it is implied in the solemn custom of calling the gods to reveal, or witness or guarantee truth in trials by ordeal, swearing of oaths and the consultation of oracles.

Sacrifice is the central act of many religions: and on this subject Dr Sundkler quotes a revealing statement by one of the foremost founders of independent African churches, a Zulu named Isaiah Shembe. 'Isaiah Shembe,' he says, 'though reticent in speaking to Europeans on the subject of sacrifices, nevertheless insisted on the need of them: "They hold people together by blood. The Gate of Heaven is opened through sacrifices." '

There are overtones of Christian teaching

here, especially in the reference to Heaven. But the suggestion that sacrifice in some sense 'holds people together' does not derive exclusively from Christianity, still less from the peculiarities of belief of this African sect. Looking at sacrifice in the simple, factual, even naturalistic way in which an anthropologist must begin his study, it is possible to see considerable sociological truth in Shembe's view, quite apart from any theological or mystical meaning it may also have.

Many different kinds of sacrifice have been distinguished—sacrifice as a gift to the gods; as a sign of communion with them and a way of gaining strength from them; sacrifice as atonement, as self-abnegation, as immolation or destruction for the divinity, and so forth. But sacrifice in general involves the notion of an offering; and among the commonest types of sacrificial offerings are those made by so many peoples of the world for the dead ancestors of their own families.

Such offerings are found not only among so-called primitive peoples but also in the literate civilizations of Eastern and Western antiquity. They vary much in kind, from expressions of filial regard—small gifts of food or drink or other symbolic acts of commemoration—to blood sacrifice itself. The motives behind the services rendered to ancestors, ghosts, or family gods, are similarly varied.

Yet there is a common element in what is often rather misleadingly called 'ancestor worship.' Whatever the nature of the offering, or the reason behind it, it does perpetuate the memory of the dead; and it does acknowledge that the living and the dead belong to a single community, wider than that of the living alone. And this is not simply a pious belief. There obviously is continuity, biological and cultural, between the living and the dead. We are partly formed by the past, even the distant past. Sacrificial offerings for ancestors symbolically recognize this. Further, those who remember their dead together, and share the same dead, also of necessity emphasize their living relationships among themselves: commemoration of the ancestor is affirmation of the range of relationships he created among the living, a holding together of all those who count him important in their past.

So in the many societies, both historical and of the present, where family, kin, and lineage are of more importance than in our kind of state common sacrifice is a sign of common interests, and an act which asserts and promotes them. It represents a common life, and not only on an ideal or metaphorical plane, but in the day-to-day practical affairs of human co-operation. Sometimes this may be observed in detail in the very way in which the flesh of a sacrificial animal is shared. Among some Nilotic peoples of the Sudan, oxen are the preferred victims: the ox is brought out and tethered to a peg in the centre of the people: they pray and invoke the gods over it; the priest, in some cases, leads the prayers which are repeated by the congregation. Sicknesses and misfortunes are put 'upon the back' of the victim. In its death it will carry them away—another Christian theme which is not exclusively Christian. Finally, the beast is killed and its flesh is divided according to strict rule among different groups within the family and the community. The officiating priest has his allotted portions, as do the mother's and the father's kin of those making the sacrifice, the old people of the community and so on. The whole beast therefore actually figures in its body the social relationships of those present at its death. The integrity of the local society is incarnate, as it were, in the victim.

A similar theme of holding people together, and the recognition of a common life in religious acts—though not strictly in sacrifice—may be found in some forms of totemism. Among many peoples, the relationship existing between whole groups of people—notably those claiming common descent and belonging to the same clan is symbolized by a totem. Totems are of many kinds, but are often one or another species of animal, sometimes regarded as an ancestor of the clan. A common totem therefore stands for a community of interests of one sort or another as McLennan recognized. Among the Australian aborigines, let us say, a clan which has as its totem the kangaroo will pay special attention to kangaroos, and perform ceremonies from time to time to increase their numbers.

Members of that clan are thus related in the kangaroo, and identified as a group with common interests by reference to the animal. On ceremonial occasions, pieces of the flesh of the totemic animal may be solemnly eaten, often by old men or guardians of the group. Earlier writers—Robertson Smith and Durkheim among them—saw in this eating of the flesh of a totem, which was also in some sense sacred, one of the elemental features of all sacrifice: communion with the god and between the worshippers in the eating of its flesh. This interpretation would not fit what we now know of the varied forms of totemism; certainly there are peoples who do not interpret the eating of the flesh of the victim after sacrifice as a religious communion. Yet again the sharing of a sacrificial beast, or of the flesh of a totemic animal, is in fact a sign and reaffirmation of relationship and community of interest.

What are these common interests? In those societies where the state does not offer its protection an individual depends first on his kinsmen. To be without kin, by chance or war or other misfortune, is to be in danger, to be helpless. So an isolated individual must find a group which will accept him—first perhaps as a friend, or servant; then in some sense as a kinsman. And either he, or his descendants, are finally guaranteed full protection when they are admitted, according to their place, to a full share in the sacrificial rites. Members of a well-defined political community sacrifice together; and those who sacrifice together have their share of protection by that community. So a sacrifice may often involve expressions of hostility to enemies —even displays against death itself. People sacrifice not only positively for themselves, but negatively against those forces that would destroy them.

The service of family ancestors and family gods, or even of clan ancestors and clan gods, is the duty of groups of kinsmen: others are ultimately excluded from such family cults. Along with these cults in many societies there are others, which embrace wider communities, not only of kin but also of neighbours and fellow tribesmen or townsmen. Those who live in the same territory, who share a land and co-operate in its protection and prosperity, then have gods to which sacrifice and other services may be rendered on behalf of the whole population of a town or region.

There is little or no evidence for supposing that the worship of the gods of such larger communities is everywhere a later historical development than cults of ancestors and family gods. Both kinds of cult often exist side by side, as do their adherents; together they reflect the total complex order of the communities which are drawn together in them. Also many—perhaps all—'polytheistic' peoples seem to exhibit at times a monotheistic train of thought. The various gods and spirits presiding over the fortunes and interests of different sections of the society and different aspects of the physical world may on occasion be seen as manifesta-

tions, not, it is true, of one supreme personal God, but at least of a single divine principle informing all the gods. For the ancient Greeks too, it would appear, Zeus, though a distinct divine figure, could also stand for the gods, divinity in the abstract.

Gods of various kinds seem to merge in this single notion of 'the divine' when peoples have in mind the human community as a whole in relation to higher powers. Sacrifice even to commemorate particular family ancestors or the guardian spirits of a clan or a place, is often accompanied by service to a divinity of all men. In Dinka sacrifices I have seen, two separate victims may be offered, one to the totemic spirits of the clan providing the sacrifice, and one to a god in the sky who watches over all the human creation. It is as though the act of sacrifice itself, turning men's attention to a kind of being different from and superior to their own, also suggests, besides local ties and loyalties, a widening circle of common human concerns.

But the bonds that might hold together a potentially universal society can scarcely be suggested, felt, and known, except in the experience which unites much smaller groups of people —the family, the clan, the village or town or guild. So it is that these particular experiences of communal living are symbolized in local deities; and sacrifice, the central feature of service of the gods, focuses attention upon the common values of the worshippers in focusing attention on the gods. From an anthropological view it is finally irrelevant whether or not these gods exist outside living human consciousness of them. Nor do we need to inquire into the deeper personal, spiritual and psychological grounds of sacrifice. The sociological meaning of sacrifice has begun to be suggested when we have accepted it as a way of serving the gods, and seen what those gods mean in relation to social life and human relations, how they correspond to the sharing of interests within different communities and sections of communities. From this point of view sacrifice to a common god is a sign and a strengthening of the common life. From other points of view it has other meanings.

If the sociological point of view, as far as it goes, has some truth in it, we see why it is that so widely throughout the world the situation of sacrifice is thought to demand peace and agreement between those who sacrifice together. In the ordinary course of social life, even members of a single and affectionate family may be at odds with each other; but in a religious ceremony it is often explicitly required that these differences should at least appear to be overcome. So, to give one of many examples, it is said that the duties of a high priest among the Gã peoples of Ghana are:

. . . not only to officiate at public worship, and give the god its daily or weekly libations, but to interpret to the people the wishes of the god . . . The peace of the town is one of his first concerns . . . He does not like his children to quarrel . . . (M. J. Field, *Religion and Medicine of the Gã People,* 1937).

And if public worship, of which sacrifice in one form or another is often the typical act, springs from a community of interest, so it demands, and probably to some extent creates, a group at peace within itself.

Sacrifice therefore often plays an important part in ceremonies for confirming a peace. In an account of a peace-making ceremony among the Shilluk, this is represented in an unusual image. After the victim had been speared and fallen, we are told:

The two factions moved close together. The

animal was then cut open, and some of the contents of the stomach were taken by the old men, and thrown on the young men. The thought was that the animal eats a bit here and a bit there, but in the stomach it all becomes one mass. Even so the individuals of the two factions were to become one.

Here it seems that collective sacrifice expresses and confirms the intentions of those who offer it to regard themselves as members of a single peaceful community. The concerns of any one become the concerns of all; as is seen very clearly in the general primitive belief in the efficacy of public sacrifice for curing those individuals who are sick and helping those who are barren. Why it should be that beliefs in the sacrificial death of a victim as a means to life and harmony for the people are so widely held raises other and different questions. There may be other means of producing the same effects; but that sacrifice does, as Shembe said, 'hold people together' would seem to be a belief founded on practical experience among many people of the world. It has been upon this ground of experience that so many different theological inquiries and reflections have been based.

44

SOCIAL BELIEFS AND INDIVIDUAL THINKING IN TRIBAL SOCIETY

MAX GLUCKMAN

MANCHESTER University does not require its professors to give inaugural lectures, and though I have to introduce a new subject to the University, I have not the opportunity within its walls to state officially and publicly how social anthropology approaches its problems. When your Society honoured me with a request for a lecture, I felt it was an occasion which should serve as an inaugural lecture. I was therefore

From *Memoirs of the Manchester Literary Society,* 1949–50, 91(5): 73–98. Copyright © 1949 by Max Gluckman. Reprinted by permission of the author. Max Gluckman is Professor of Social Anthropology, Manchester University.

pleased when your Committee selected, from the list of lectures I offered it, a subject which would allow me to present, partly through my own field research, some reflections on a classic study by my colleague, Professor E. E. Evans-Pritchard of Oxford—his study of *Witchcraft, Oracles and Magic among the Azande of the Anglo-Egyptian Sudan.* Tonight I concentrate on one aspect of that study—the form which scepticism takes in primitive society.

One day while travelling in Barotseland, in North-Western Rhodesia, I shot a crocodile. A crocodile yields valuable ingredients for the Barotse magician and sorcerer, and my paddlers began to claim various parts of the carcase. One, Mubita, claimed the claws. I asked Mubita why he wanted these, and he replied that he would put a claw on the prow of his dugout canoe: then if his dugout were stolen a crocodile would pursue the thief and take him. Nor would it be a simple crocodile that would seize the man as he travelled by dugout or fished in the waters of the Barotse Plain. This crocodile would take the thief when he was far from water; it would travel miles overland to seize him in some unlikely place. I asked Mubita, "do people really fear these claws?" and Mubita replied, "honest men will fear them." I want to examine some of the implications of this reply.

From infancy, every individual is moulded by the culture of the society into which he is born. All human beings see, but we now know, for example, that how they see shapes and colours is to some extent determined by this process of moulding. More than this, their ability to describe their perceptions depends on the categories contained in their respective languages. *A fortiori*, an individual's emotional reactions and his complex ideas for dealing with his fellows and with nature are derived from his culture. For example, the development of romantic love in our own civilisation can be traced, and it produces behaviour very different from that involved in sexual mating as such. We are indoctrinated now to believe that everyone has somewhere, somehow, to find an ideal mate: this is shrieked at us by advertisements of soaps and scents, by songs and films, and stated more quietly by folk and fairy-tales and novels. Though African men and women fall in love with each other they do so with different sentiments. In 1883 a Cape Government Commission presented a report on African laws and customs. Some old Fingo had complained to the Commission of the increasing number of illegitimate births and runaway marriages: "It is all this thing called love. We do not understand it. This thing called love has been introduced." An anthropologist writing about marriage among the Bemba of North-Eastern Rhodesia records: "I once amazed a group of elderly Bemba by telling them an English folktale about the difficulties experienced by a Prince in winning the hand of his bride—glassy mountains, chasms, dragons, giants and the like. An old chief present was genuinely astonished. 'Why not take another girl?' he said." Of course, individuals are not perfectly moulded.

Even in these societies this thing called love may creep in. When it does, the stricken individual is believed to have been bewitched. So that if a Barotse man is too attached to his wife, is extravagantly jealous for her, or spends too much time with her, his fellows shake their heads and fear she has seduced him from his senses with strong medicines.

For though all known primitive societies have marriage and the family, the individual family is less important, compared with other kinship groups, than in our society. A man's strongest attachments are those to his blood-kin reckoned to many degrees, and all marriages tend to be marriages of state with other groups of blood-kin. Therefore Lozi say: "Do not confide in your wife, confide in your sister. Tomorrow she may be someone else's wife; your sister is always your sister." One observer has even said, in summary, a man sleeps with his wife, loves his sister, and seeks companionship with other men. Moreover in these polygamous societies the ideal for a man is to be married to many wives, and a wife must share the love of her husband with other wives. The isolation of individual families in separate houses, and with this isolation the high importance of the bonds between man and wife, which are characteristic of our society, are reflected in sentiments about love between men and women which are incompatible with the structure of African societies. The emotions of loving a man or woman, and the ideas about relations between lovers and sweethearts, husbands and wives, are therefore ways of feeling and thinking which are contained in the specific social relations of a particular society.

Perceptions, emotions, evaluations of right and wrong, ideas of the causes of events—in short, whole systems of thought and feeling—thus exist transcendentally, independently of the individuals in whom they appear. They are what the French sociologists call *collective representations*, which pass from generation to generation, learnt in behaviour, contained in proverb and precept, in technology and convention and ritual, and, with the development of writing, in books. A man's psyche is social, not organic. Therefore a Londoner's baby brought up in an African tribe would be an African and an African baby reared in London by Londoners would be a Londoner. That this moulding by culture can occur later in life is evidenced by the report in 1686 of some shipwrecked Dutch seamen in South East-Africa on a Portuguese wrecked there forty years before: "This Portuguese had been circumcised and had a wife, children, cattle and land; he spoke only the African language, having forgotten everything, his God included."

Scholars who compare the modes of thought of primitive peoples with their own, are accustomed to compare the primitive's social beliefs about what we call witchcraft, magic, ancestral spirits, etc., with those parts of his reasoning which a modern scientist employs in his laboratory or a philosopher in his study—and, if I may say so, usually exclusively in those confined precincts. Inevitably the primitive does not emerge from this comparison as a Western philosopher or scientist. "There's ne-er a villain in all Denmark but he's an arrant knave"—a man who believes in witchcraft believes in witchcraft. But beliefs in witchcraft and ancestor spirits form only a part of the total ideas which a primitive society provides for its members. All primitive societies have highly developed technologies in which is implicit a considerable amount of what we may call scientific knowledge. Relatively to our technological and scientific knowledge, theirs is small, but it is vast relatively to its absence among other animals. It is true, too, that few primitive societies have the scientific attitude which deliberately queries, tests and develops existing knowledge. Nevertheless, I ask you not to forget that the societies which I discuss tonight have a considerable technical knowledge. Malinowski described the awareness of dynamics which is implicit in the Trobriand Islanders' construction of outrigger canoes. I myself have recorded for the Lozi of Barotseland a wide technical knowledge which is accurate and scientific. They live in a large plain on the Upper Zambezi which is flooded each year, and they have to take into account types of soils, vegetation, the time of the flood's coming and its depth in different places, rainfall and temperature in different months, fertility of soils and the use of manure and phosphates and rotation, in order to decide where and how to make their gardens and when to plant these and to what crops. Some gardens they build up above the waters, other places they drain. Government experts describe this Lozi agriculture as remarkable, and say that they can suggest no improvements in it without long experimentation. The Lozi have twenty-two recorded methods of catching fish with nets, dams, traps and weapons, and to use these they have to smelt and work iron, make string and rope from roots and bark, construct dugouts and paddles, and know the movements of fish with the rise and fall of the flood. Their legal system is well-developed and includes many basic concepts of our own, such as tort and crime, public and private law, equity and the doctrine of the reasonable man. In their political constitution I have found the doctrine of the separation of powers, the principle of the representation of the different estates of the nation, etc., so well worked out, that when I described this constitution to our Professor of Government he retorted disbelievingly, "They must have read Dicey's *Law of the Constitution.*" These ideas occupy the main spheres of action in primitive society, and I ask you to bear this in mind during the following analysis. Though I speak about beliefs in witchcraft, they are used, as you will see, together with scientific beliefs.

As crudely described in Haggard's account of Gagool in *King Solomon's Mines,* in Seabrook's books about Voodoo, or in the *Wide World Magazine,* from which most of us get our ideas of witchcraft and magic, these beliefs in witchcraft appear to be amusing, stupid and grotesque. We now know, from Evans-Pritchard's analysis, that they are marked by acute perception and logic.

It is generally believed that in a primitive society the course of events is: a man believes he has been bewitched, therefore he falls ill and may die. This, if it ever occurs, is rare. In practice, an African suffers some misfortune, such as illness or crop failure, and he blames it on a witch, against whom he proceeds to take action. This is the rationale imposed on the African because he is born into a society which believes that misfortunes are caused by witches. But the witch is not the whole cause of the misfortune. To every misfortune there is a "how?" and a "why?" That is, we may ask, "how did this man die?" and answer, "because he was run over by a motor car and his skull was fractured." Empirical observation and medical science give the answer. There is also the problem, "why that motor-car ran over that man at that place at that time?" To this there are various answers, all of them more or less theological. The African distinguishes the why and the how of misfortunes as clearly as we do. What he explains with the statement, "I am ill because I am bewitched," is why he is ill now when for some months he has been well and when all his neighbours about him are still well. In epidemics, other beliefs are invoked.

Similarly, a man blames a witch if his crops, planted in good soil, fail where his neighbours' crops flourish or if his cattle drop their calves while his neighbours' cattle do not. If a man goes hunting and is killed by an elephant, the African sees clearly that he was killed because the elephant trampled on him, and Africans know that elephants are mighty and fearful beasts. But the death of the hunter involves a series of problems: why was this hunter killed and not another hunter, why by that elephant and not by that elephant, why on this hunt and not another hunt? The answer is, because a witch had bewitched him. That is, a witch brought that elephant and that man at that place and moment together so that the man was killed. Or men sit in the shade of a granary raised on logs, and the granary, its supports eaten away by termites, falls on them and crushes them. This is witchcraft. The African, who is an acute observer, knows that termites eat wood, and when a granary's supports are thus eaten it collapses. But why did this granary fall at the particular moment when these particular men were sitting under it? Witchcraft.

Witchcraft is thus a theory of causation but it is a theory which explains causal links which modern scientists do not attempt, cannot attempt, to explain. Other people ascribe the particularity of phenomena to ancestor spirits, providence, kismet, the will or retribution of God; the sceptical scientist can only say it is chance, the coincidence of two chains of events in space-time. That science cannot answer the central problem of witchcraft belief is well illustrated by Professor Monica Wilson. She reports that a well-educated Pondo teacher in South Africa said that his child died of typhus because he was bewitched. Professor Wilson remonstrated that typhus was caused by an infected louse. The teacher replied: "I know that it was a louse from a person ill with typhus which gave my child typhus and that he died of typhus, but why did the louse go to my child, and not to the other children with whom he was playing?"

The belief in witchcraft thus provides explanations for the particularity of misfortunes. It does not for the African provide the whole interpretation of the misfortune. The belief in witchcraft does not exclude empirical observation and scientific understanding; on the contrary, witchcraft belief embraces and uses empirical observation and scientific understanding. The witch has to cause misfortune through disease, termites eating wood, elephants, crop-blight, and all these exist in their own right and have their own effects on men's lives. So much is this so among the Azande, that even the death of a warrior in battle has to be avenged on a witch, who has used the enemy as his tool. Here the witch has caused this enemy and not another, in this battle and not another battle, to kill this man and not another man. The natural causes of misfortunes frequently cannot be reacted to, especially with African techniques; the belief in witchcraft selects a witch as the socially significant cause against whom action can be taken.

Not every kind of accident or ill may be ascribed to witchcraft. His ability to blame witches for misfortunes does not mean that the African fails to recognise lack of skill and moral lapses. For an unskilled potter to say that his pots broke in firing because he was bewitched, would not convince his fellows if he had left pebbles in the clay, but the skilled potter who had followed all the rules of his craft would be supported in saying this. If a younger hunter were foolish enough to approach the elephant herd from up-wind and they charged upon him, he would be blamed for his stupidity; if an old hunter did this, he would be blamed for asking for trouble, though clearly a witch must have made him depart from his usual care. Or while the man's own kin would say that he was killed because he was bewitched, other people might blame it on his lack of skill. For the same beliefs are not categorically imposed on all, but different peoples use different beliefs according to their status in the situation.

Similarly, it would not be a sound defence for a criminal to plead that he did wrong because he was bewitched to do so, for it is not believed that witchcraft makes a man lie, steal, commit adultery, or betray his chief. Evans-Pritchard stresses that

since Azande recognise plurality of causes, and it is the social situation that indicates the relevant one, we can understand why the doctrine of witchcraft is not used to explain every failure and misfortune. It sometimes happens that the social situation demands a commonsense, and not a mystical, judgment of cause. . . . Only on one occasion have I heard a Zande plead that he was bewitched when he had committed an offence and this was when he lied to me, and even on this occasion everybody present laughed at him and told him that witchcraft does not make people tell lies.

If a man murders another tribesman with knife or spear he is put to death. It is not necessary in such a case to seek a witch, for an objective towards which vengeance may be directed is already present. If, on the other hand, it is a member of another tribe who has speared a man, his relatives, or his prince, will take steps to discover the witch responsible for the event.

It would be treason to say that a man put to death on the orders of his king for an offence against authority was killed by witchcraft. . . . For here the social situation excludes the notion of witchcraft as on other occasions it pays no attention to natural agents and emphasises witchcraft.

In these instances

it is the natural cause and not the mystical cause that is selected as the socially significant one. In these situations witchcraft is irrelevant and, if not totally excluded, is not indicated as the principal factor in causation. As in our own society a scientific theory of causation, if not excluded, is deemed irrelevant in questions of moral and legal responsibility, so in Zande society the doctrine of witchcraft, if not excluded, is deemed irrelevant in the same situations. We accept scientific explanations of the causes of disease, and even of the causes of insanity, but we deny them in crime and sin because here they militate against law and morals which are axiomatic. The Zande accepts a mystical explanation of misfortune, sickness and death, but he does not allow this explanation if it conflicts with social exigencies expressed in laws and morals.

What is this witch who is believed to cause misfortunes?—or, rather, who can be blamed for certain misfortunes after they occur? And how does he work his evil? Anthropologists, following Evans-Pritchard, distinguished two kinds of mystical evildoers. There are sorcerers who are believed to use black magic to harm people—that is, they are believed to attack others by using certain ingredients, uttering spells and performing rites. We would classify the witches in *Macbeth* as sorcerers. Witches, on the other hand, are people who have certain physiological or anatomical characteristics, usually inherited, which enable them to do harm in a mystical fashion. In our culture, the person who has the evil eye or tongue is a witch. Among the Azande, witchcraft is a condition of the intestine which, as revealed by autopsy, is probably a passing state of digestion. The sorcerer is supposed to kill his enemy by such means as putting medicine in a quill and stabbing his footprints. The ill-power of a witch leaves his body, in some mysterious form, and acts on the soul of his enemy's organs. It is probable that Africans rarely perform sorcery:

they would soon see that it is not effective. It is certain that the power of witchcraft does not exist. But here again we must remember that as the belief in witchcraft operates in social life, the chain of behaviour starts at the other end. A man suffers misfortune and explains its occurrence by blaming it on a witch; he does not suspect he is being bewitched and therefore suffers a misfortune. So that when he suffers the misfortune, he sets about finding the witch responsible for it. For Africans do not worry, except in a general way, about who are witches until they are attacked.

The witch at work is discovered by various kinds of oracles and means of divination. No recorded technique of divination will directly name the witch. The most important Zande technique is to give a substance, prepared under very special conditions, to chickens while asking a question. According as the question is framed, the chicken will vomit the substance or be killed by it to answer "yes" or "no." This substance, which is used throughout Africa, is probably a strychnine for that is a poison which is unpredictable, by dose, in its effects. Therefore its operation cannot be controlled. The oracle is used for several purposes: to decide whether, if you take a certain course of action, such as marrying your daughter to some man now, witchcraft will affect its success; to select from a number of otherwise equally suitable sites for your new homestead that one where witchcraft will not prevent you from prospering; to decide whether, if you go hunting tomorrow, you will kill game, and the presence or absence of witchcraft determines whether you will or not; and so on. If you are seeking the witch who has afflicted you with misfortune, you put to the oracle a number of names of your personal enemies, those who have cause to hate you or whom you have cause to hate. To these names the oracle-poison, acting in the chickens, answers "yes" or "no" by killing or sparing the chickens. Ultimately it must answer "yes" to someone's name, and your witch is indicated. In most tribes the system of beliefs does not allow you to use the oracle to find an unknown thief of your property, or lover of your wife. The thief is magically punished by methods such as putting crocodile claws on your dugout, or using medicines which will cause lightning to strike him. As we have seen, Mubita thought honest men would fear these crocodile claws— seeing them on the dugout, the honest man might not take the dugout. The determined thief takes the dugout and risks the mystical retribution. (Honest British fear burglar alarms, thieves do not.) Obviously, if you know the thief you sue him in court, and you sue in court the detected lover of your wife. If you suspect your wife is committing adultery, and you cannot catch her lover, you give her a magical substance which will not harm you or her but which will afflict an adulterer with a most unpleasant disease. This is justifiable for the Zulu among whom divorce is rare; it is sorcery among the Lozi where divorce is very frequent, since it will afflict a woman's new husband. In short, the oracle is used mainly to detect a witch who has been at work or the threat of witchcraft to some projected enterprise.

Other techniques of divination work similarly. The Azande rub two grooved boards together, while asking questions, and the boards stick for "yes" but continue sliding for "no." Or they put two different species of twigs into a termites' nest, and "yes" or "no" depends on which twig is more eaten by the termites. The Zulu consult diviners in the fashion of our nursery game, "hot" or "cold." They go in a party to the diviner who begins to recite a list of possible—and limited—contingencies which may be troubling them: something is lost, cattle are dying, someone is ill. The clients all this time clap and chorus, "We agree, we agree," and as he gets on the trail they clap more quickly and chorus more loudly. When he has fixed on, say, illness, he begins to specify, it is a man, it is a woman, it is a child, and so on, gradually narrowing his answers. Ultimately, on the basis of his knowledge of the people and local gossip, he may name as sorcerer the one they suspect; if he does not know them, he indicates, with their help, the sorcerer by social definition—it is a man or woman, old or young, related in such-and-such a way to the afflicted person. Witchdoctors, too, work themselves up by dances and magical substances to choose the guilty person from among names which may have been given them by the sufferer.

Quite clearly, in this way a personal enemy of the sufferer is always detected as the witch. Therefore early writers on African life described the system as fraudulent and witch-doctors as cheats. One of Evans-Pritchard's major contributions is to show that the "fraud-ulence" is the most reasonable and sensible part of the whole system. For it holds that witchcraft does not harm people haphazardly, but the witch attacks people he hates, has

quarrelled with, of whom he is envious. So that when a man falls ill (and people should not be ill), or his crops fail (which they should not do on good soil), or he suffers other misfortune, he says that someone who envied him his many children, the favour of his chief, or his good employment with Europeans and his resulting fine clothes, therefore hated him and has used medicines or evil power to do him ill. The theory of witchcraft is thus, as well as being a theory of causation, a theory of morals, for witches and sorcerers are bad people, hating, grudging, envious, spiteful. Clearly the sorcerer, the man who goes out of his way to use black magic, is immoral. The system of belief also stresses the immortality of witchcraft even though it is a constitutional, often inherited, power. For on the one hand there are wicked people who wish others ill, but because they have not witchcraft cannot do harm mystically unless they use sorcery; and there are good people who have witchcraft in them but because they are moral do not use this power so that it remains, as the Africans put it, "cool" inside them. On the other hand there is the immoral man who has the power to bewitch and uses that power. Since people are only interested in whether their fellows are witches when they suffer misfortunes, they seek among their personal enemies for those who may have this power. They think of someone with whom they have quarrelled and suspect him of the evil deed. Thus witchcraft as a theory of causes of misfortunes reflects the personal relations between the sufferer and his fellows, and acts as a theory of moral judgments on what is good and bad.

Evans-Pritchard, while he was among the Azande, wrote this passage to summarise their ideas and feelings on this point:

All those near a prince or European become objects of envy, malice, and all uncharitableness. The princes bear each other no love. They fear medicines and the encroachment of their brothers on their domains. Courtiers vie with one another to obtain the favour of their prince and are intensely jealous of each other. The young fear and envy the old. The old fear and envy the young. Every man has his enemies, those against whom he has long-standing grudges. He is certain that someone is injuring him. Within the household there is often bitter, though maybe concealed, jealousy between wives, between brothers, between sisters. In the family itself the wife often hates and tricks her husband, and the husband is unceasingly jealous of his wife and bullies her. Children hate and sometimes fear their fathers. A man's crop is successful, his nets are full of game, his termites swarm, and he is convinced that he has become the butt of his neighbours' jealousy and will be bewitched. His crops fail, his nets are empty, his termites do not swarm, and by these signs he knows that he has been bewitched by his jealous neighbour. How the misfortunes of others please a Zande. Nothing is more pleasing, more assuring to him, more flattering to his self-esteem, than the downfall of another. The loss of his prince's favour strikes a man down and his friends are rich in consolations but poor in sympathy. Almost morbidly sensitive they view every remark, every slight allusion by others in conversation, as a veiled attack on themselves, a concealed dart of malice. And if witchcraft is behind ill-will, slander, tale-telling, well, then a Zande may well fear his neighbours and may well be indignant at their hostility to him, for misfortune will surely dog him.

When Europeans as outside observers say that fraud and cheating underlie accusations of witchcraft, this has no meaning, but Africans themselves are aware of what these processes of selection imply. Clearly it is reasonable that the man who bewitches you should be your personal enemy. The sufferer who wishes to abolish the witchcraft harming him, above all people does not wish to make a deliberately false accusation, for what good is it to him if he detects the wrong person as witch? But he does accuse personal enemies. This the African appreciates quite clearly. His view of any particular accusation will vary according to his status in the situation. The sufferer and his close kin may be convinced it is justified, the accused consider it false, and outsiders, if they are not indifferent, support one or the other. In Zululand I lived with an important and wealthy governor of a district, who was also adviser to the Zulu king. Cheek by jowl with his homestead, was the homestead of his cousin, linked to him through his father's father. In Zulu, they are brothers. The cousin's wife died after a long and painful illness, and, after brooding on it a while, the widower burst out with an accusation that the governor, who had always hated him, had killed her by sorcery. The whole district was upset by the quarrel. I discussed the case with an old diviner, who himself hunted witches. Yet fully aware of psychical projection, he concluded: "Obviously the accusation is absurd. Why should the governor hate his younger brother? The governor has political power and the main family herd. His brother thinks the governor hates him, because he hates the governor." So that the African knows that often a man accuses not someone who hates him, or who is envious of

him, but someone whom he envies or hates. He may even stress this when he is himself accused, or if for any reason he sides with the accused though he is not directly involved, but he forgets it when he makes an accusation.

When a man accuses another of witchcraft, his course of action will depend on many circumstances. His reaction may be socially determined, as, for example, by whether witchcraft is a crime punished by the state, or a tort for which compensation is paid to the sufferer. Where the misfortune is something which cannot be remedied, such as the breaking of pots in firing, the sufferer may accept it as witchcraft, just as we would say, "Bad luck." But when witchcraft is making him ill and may cause him to die, when it is blighting his crop, or when by divination he finds that it is threatening him in the future, he does not sit down under it helplessly. He has to scotch its evil working. This he does by changing his course of action, or by using protective magic which will stop the witchcraft and possibly kill the witch, or by calling in a diviner to find out who is the witch so that he can be put out of action, or the witch be persuaded to withdraw his witchcraft. Among the Azande, the accuser may send the wing of the chicken which died to the witch's name, by the hand of an intermediary, to the alleged witch. The accused, probably unconscious of any evil intent, is constrained by social norms to behave in a gentlemanly fashion; that is, he takes water in his mouth, blows it over the wing, and declares that if it is his witchcraft that has done harm, he was unaware of it, and he spurts water to cool his witchcraft and show his moral innocence. He may not believe the accusation to be a valid one, but he does not formulate his doubt by querying the validity of oracles. He will say to himself that the accuser did not really make a test but sent the wing of a chicken he had just killed; or that if he did make a test the oracle-poison was not sound, or a taboo of its use was broken; or he may conclude that the real witch by his evil power had distorted the working of the oracle. He doubts not the system, but the validity of the particular accusation against him, and he has to cast his doubts in the dogma of the system, by using other beliefs within it. Thereby he confirms his own acceptance of the system as a whole.

Obviously the system could not work if the oracles of private individuals legally pinned guilt. The accuser would make his charge from the verdict of his oracles or the diviner he had consulted, the accused reject the charge with his oracles or by consulting another diviner. The final verdict is given by superior authority, the oracles or witchdoctors of the chief, and these cannot be queried. In his heart, a convicted man may believe that the witch has controlled the working of the chief's oracles, or that his enemy has bribed the man who consulted them for the chief, but it is treason openly to question these oracles—an offence against the chief.

Normally, a man only goes to the chief to get a verdict against the alleged witch after a kinsman has died, when vengeance is enjoined. Here the witchcraft beliefs are related to the existence of the kin-group as a vengeance-group. Nowadays, this open action is prohibited by European authority. In some tribes therefore people make vengeance-magic against the witch. But they do not identify the witch and try to kill him by magic: were they to do so, they would soon observe that it does not work. Vengeance-magic is made against the unknown witch, as against the unknown thief or adulterer, and as people die in the neighbourhood, the oracles are asked, "Was this one the witch?" Ultimately they answer "yes," and vengeance is achieved. The other man's kin meantime start making magic to avenge his death.

This very brief summary of how beliefs in witchcraft, oracles and magic work, emphasises that we cannot deduce the mode of thinking of individuals within a primitive society directly from the social beliefs and attitudes of that society. Very many scholars writing on social problems like to begin their analyses with a statement of what primitive man thought or did, they use the comparison to highlight their analyses of our own ideas. As anthropologists see it, what they do is to give a stereotyped presentation of what they would think were they, savants and scientists of our civilisation, presented with the social beliefs of primitive society. But I hope this analysis has brought out that the thinking processes of man in primitive society are more complex, and that neither his character nor the nature of his mind nor his views of the universe can be simply derived from selected beliefs of his culture, particularly the myths and mystical beliefs. It would be as absurd to deduce the character and thought of modern man from the theory of relativity combined with the Credo. Man in primitive society is as complex a character as man in modern society, made up of as many contradictory prej-

udices and principles. I stressed at the outset that his being is moulded by his culture, and that his culture provides him with beliefs and attitudes with which to handle his relations both with other individuals and with nature. I have given but a part of the core of witchcraft beliefs, and primitive societies have many other systems of beliefs. I must stress too that though I have spoken for convenience sake as if these beliefs belong to all primitive societies, there are many which have no developed doctrine of witchcraft: some have elaborate ancestor-cults, others totem-cults, and so on. But I hope I have shown that the beliefs are not hard and fast rules which can be applied mechanically. They are often, when presented schematically, contradictory. But individuals make use of different beliefs within the system from situation to situation, for in actual life these beliefs become significant in action, not as ideas in the people's minds. In using them, Africans reason quite logically and sensibly, and show psychological insight as penetrating as our own. The system is not irrational and the behaviour it entails is not incomprehensible to us. If they were, Evans-Pritchard would not have been able to interpret them to us. While he was among the Azande, he lived as if he believed in witchcraft, and he says he found it as sensible a way as any of ordering his affairs.

The essence of the system is that it must work reasonably; and the African insists on this. One morning it was reported to me that an old Lozi friend was very ill. I went to see him and he told me he had been awakened by a singing in his ears and found he was almost deaf, with pus pouring from them. He sent for a diviner-magician. This man said he had been attacked by a sorcerer who had sent the resurrected body of a dead man to put medicines about the homestead. The magician proceeded to remedy the ill by various magical rites. One of the patient's wives collapsed in a faint, and he drove out the magician for being a fraud who was killing his wife. He sent his other two wives to consult another diviner. I asked what he had paid the fraud and was told a chicken. When I went on to ask him whether he had claimed it back, he laughed and said "no; I saw that he was a cheat, but it is because he is a poor man who is trying to get a little food and money." His wives then brought the verdict from the second diviner. This was as follows: the patient had previously been very ill with a serious disease and had been cured by an old woman, who had then taught him to cure the disease. The previous night she had gone past his village and did not stop to greet him and exchange gifts: the disease had reawakened, become angry, and struck him down. He immediately exclaimed: *"Kwautwahala!"*—"That is understandable," or, as we would say, "That is reasonable." He continued to sicken and eventually died, nor could all my pleading, supported by a prince, son to the king he had loyally served, induce him to agree to go to hospital. He and his family were convinced that European doctors might be able to wash out his ears—they asked me to do it—but could not cure the mystical cause of his illness. Yet clearly this man was no fool, prevented by absurd beliefs from making empirical observations or understanding human motivation: he saw quite clearly that one diviner was a fraud and suspected his pecuniary motives. This did not prevent him from consulting another diviner.

The system of beliefs is reasonable enough, even to us, but even anthropologists consider its premises invalid. We do not believe that misfortunes are caused by witchcraft or sorcery. In fact it is impossible to disprove that they are so caused, though it is equally impossible to prove it. You will remember that Flecker's *Hassan* said that the man who thinks he is wise believes nothing till the proof, the man who is wise believes everything till the disproof. His truly wise man would undoubtedly believe in witchcraft. For in a sense, psychologically at least, it is true. We cannot disprove that witches are to blame for individuals' misfortunes, since the belief answers problems that are not answered by our scientific theories. These are shared crudely by Africans, in the sense that they know that fire burns, that seeds in fertile soils when rain falls produce crops, and that a man dies if he is crushed by an elephant or the fall of a granary. Even today intellectually it is difficult to disprove, as we have seen where the Pondo teacher thought his child got typhus because a witch sent an infected louse to it. We can expand the "how" of misfortunes without disposing of the "why."

The system is psychologically satisfying in that within it, reasonably enough, enemies are accused, and the actual charges made, for the suffering individuals, validate the system. Those accused may doubt the charges, but, as we have seen, only by expressing their doubts through invoking other beliefs within the system. For the beliefs are lived, not thought out, and no individual views the whole of it at once so that he can discover its contradictions and inconsistencies. People use those parts that suit them in particular stiuations. Moreover, the system is so cast that it accords with reality, or reality can always be recast to accord with it. Magic does not attempt the impossible: rain-magicians try to make rain in the rainy season, not in the dry months. Vengeance-magic and magic against thieves and adulterers are used against unspecified individuals.

Wherever the system might conflict with reality, at crucial points where it could be checked, its beliefs are vague and deal with transcendant non-observable facts: the witch works at night with the soul of his witchcraft on the soul of his enemy's organs; the soul of the poison-oracle finds out the witchcraft. The theory is a complete whole, in which every part buttresses every other part. Illness proves that a witch is at work, he is discovered by divination, he is persuaded to withdraw his witchcraft—the patient recovers, as most patients do recover. Or the witch is attacked with magic. It is virtually impossible for the African to find a flaw in the system which will disprove the system as a whole. We have seen that scepticism exists and is not socially repressed until it comes to the verdict of the chief's oracles. Evans-Pritchard writes that the "absence of formal and coercive doctrines permits Azande to state that many, even most, witch-doctors are frauds. No opposition being offered to such statements they leave the main belief in the prophetic and therapeutic powers of witch-doctors unimpaired. Indeed, scepticism is included in the pattern of belief in witch-doctors. Faith and scepticism are alike traditional. Scepticism explains failures of witch-doctors, and being directed towards particular witch-doctors even tends to support faith in others." Even the witch-doctor who works by sleight of hand to carry out certain enterprises of his craft believes that there are doctors who have the magic to make this unnecessary; and could the trickster but get that magic, he feels he would not have to resort to trickery. "In this web of belief every strand depends upon every other strand, and a Zande cannot get out of its meshes because this is the only world he knows. The web is not an external structure in which he is enclosed. It is the texture of his thought and he cannot think that his thought is wrong. Nevertheless, his beliefs are not absolutely set but are variable and fluctuating to allow for different situations and to permit empirical observation and even doubts." A man cannot think without his thoughts, and his thoughts are the moulding of his brain by the beliefs of his society. Even today, it is difficult for an educated African to formulate his doubts outside the system. I once heard a Lozi clerk defend the belief that a sorcerer can kill an enemy by stabbing his footprints with a quill full of medicines. His companion retorted: "What, even if he is wearing shoes?"

This sort of system of beliefs is characterised by what Evans-Pritchard has called secondary elaboration of belief. Failures can be interpreted within the system by invoking other beliefs. Every year before the Trade Winds bring the rains, Zulu call in special magicians to treat their villages against lightning. Most villages are not struck, but if a man's village *is* struck, he will say the magician was bad, his medicines were poor, a taboo was broken, a witch wielded the lightning, or Heaven itself was too powerfully determined to strike that village. We reason no more logically. If your house, which you have protected with lightning conductors, is nevertheless struck, you may say that the workman was bad, the wires poor, the charge was too strong. You do not rush to the Royal Society to deny the validity of scientific theory.

Few individuals are wholly conditioned, and some are very sceptical. Today, in Africa, one meets these more frequently. The greatest sceptic of witchcraft I knew was an illiterate old man of over 70 who had grown up at court. He denied everything. In Central Africa there is a widespread belief that to be successful you need magic and to get the magic you must kill one of your kinsfolk. This old man told me that his nephew in this way sold the life of a younger brother to a magician for magic of success in working for Europeans. He did not pay the magician, who came to the old man and demanded his fee. The old man drove him out and rebuked his nephew: "See, you have lost your brother and you are not successful." To my query, he replied that naturally he had not reported this: the culprit would have been hanged, and, as they had lost one young man, why lose another? Again, his brothers-in-law sold the life of their sister, his wife, for hunting magic, and when they did not pay the fee the magician came to tell him of the crime. He drove the magician out, saying it was none of his business; he had lost a wife but could easily get another, his brothers-in-law had use-

lessly lost a sister who could not be replaced. The people around considered he should have reported the murderers: is the true sceptic always a bad citizen? This old man's younger brother once sold his life, but it was to a magician who did not have this bad magic. He came to the old man and demanded an ox to wash his name. The youngster, confronted, showed his guilt, and his elder brother delivered over the ox. His only comment was: "I told my brother, 'see, you are a fool, you have lost us an ox.'"

Generally, however, the sceptic does not question the whole system, but only individual parts of it. Scepticism is doubt about particular individuals, particular medicines, particular accusations and not of the whole. This is necessarily so, because few individuals are in a position to generalise; they have not enough information about the workings of the whole system. Kings have, and they live outside it: some of them have been utter sceptics. Within certain limits, otherwise, it is necessary that scepticism should exist, to explain failures, unexpected observations, and so on. For the sceptic queries within a system of beliefs, not as a detached outsider. Heresy has always been as restricted by social ideas as orthodoxy.

I have dealt on the whole with the intellectual structure of this system of ideas. However, the system arises from the type of social relations which characterise African society, and these are conditioned by the basic economic framework. Though, as we have seen, African tribes possess science and developed techniques of production, African economies are stationary. Their tools are simple, and a man can produce little beyond what he can himself consume. The goods he does produce are simple and primary: food to eat, grass and mud houses to live in, skins or barkcloth or a little woven cotton to wear. Any one man's ability to consume these primary foods is limited. A chief cannot himself use the milk, meat and skins he gets from his comparatively vast herds of cattle; he cannot build himself a palace luxuriously furnished or bedeck himself and his wives with jewellery. Trade exists, but though it may involve the exchange of different goods these are still primary goods—vegetable products for fish or meat, pots for mats, honey for milk, and so on. Therefore these societies had—and still largely have—necessarily an egalitarian standard of living. . . . Nevertheless, these men do not produce merely sufficient goods to maintain their families. Tremendous energy is devoted to the accumulation of goods for re-distribution. In the Trobriand Islands, men feed not their own wives, but their sisters, so that after each harvest there is a general portage of much of the fruits of the year from each man's garden to his brother-in-law's village.

Logically, given only this type of goods, a man can only do one of two things with his surplus: he can destroy it or give it away. The solution of destruction is found in all societies in the form of feasts: it is most highly developed in the *potlatch* of the American Indians of British Columbia. Here men strive to accumulate goods to destroy at feasts given to rivals: they burn blankets and seal-oil and cast valuable coppers into the sea. To regain face, the rival must set to work in order to give a greater feast to his former host. We have similar types of behaviour, which Veblen termed conspicuous consumption and which O. Henry satirised in his millionaires. But in primitive economies there is no choice between investment and feasting.

To give these *potlatch* feasts, an Indian of status has to have the support of his kinsmen and subordinates; alone, he can never accumulate enough to become a significant competitor in feastgiving. In the meagre continent of Africa, men do not indulge in this direct destruction but they use their wealth to support their kinsmen and other dependents. Even the chief can only use the products of his herds and gardens to support people, and he can only redistribute to his subjects the many loads of tribute they yield to him. There are wealthy men, who from that wealth get political power, but they cannot use their wealth to achieve a higher standard of living. Nor can they exploit the labour of their subjects or slaves. When the Zulu king Shaka built a new capital he sent out thousands of men to get the materials: each returned, after a march of twenty miles to unnecessarily distant forests, bearing a single sapling. Slaves tended to be treated as kinsmen: without clock, calendar, or profit, they could not be worked to raise greatly their masters' standard of living, nor was there any enterprise in which the masters could invest the surplus products of their labour.

One marked feature of the beliefs in witchcraft clearly arises from the stationary limitations of these economies. This is that any man who is unusually productive or has too many windfalls of luck suspects he is in danger of being bewitched, and is suspected by others of

using witchcraft to steal their fertility and luck. This cast to the system is consistent with the economic structure. The beliefs have persisted and for a time proliferated in the new relations established by Western conquest, but they are not compatible with our civilisation's emphasis on individual productivity. Changes in economic relations will shatter the system. At present, the beliefs act with the colour bar to fetter African productivity. I knew a man who had abandoned living in his extra-fine house and moved to a hovel because envy had induced witches to attack him unceasingly.

Furthermore, the productive groups involved in this economy are generally small, almost self-subsistent, groups of kin, even where they are organised within kingdoms of some hundreds of thousands of people. Social relationships are undifferentiated. Men hold land by virtue of status, arising from birth into a widely extended kinship system; they live and co-operate in almost every activity with these kin. Relations are personal, face to face, and are not integrated within a large impersonal institutional framework. Each social relationship embraces many interests. It is a system without economic cleavages to produce class differentiation, and over long periods of time, despite quarrels and increase in numbers, the pattern has persisted, duplicating itself again and again in new areas and new generations.

The beliefs in witchcraft are related also to the organisation of society in these small, self-subsistent, repetitive groups. As most relations are intensely personal, all events tend to be explained by what occurs inside these personal relations. Success is bought palpably at others' cost. In our society an action in court exists only where we can show direct injury received; in primitive society every misfortune tends to be cast as a tort and a witch can be prosecuted for causing it. Thus like ideas of how men and women love one another, beliefs in witchcraft are rooted in social relations, and ultimately are a way of thinking about social relationships. For they imply that you blame your misfortunes or depend for your prosperity, which is due to the absence of witchcraft and the blessing of ancestral-spirits, on your relations with your kinsmen and neighbours. If these are bad, you are in danger. In any particular society, charges of witchcraft fly along certain lines of social tension, between fellow-wives of one man, against daughters-in-law or sisters-in-law, against jealous brother or nephew. Women above all possess this evil power. Therefore the beliefs, being particular to certain relationships, are not examined as a system. Here again these beliefs are not compatible with our wide-scale impersonal society.

Before passing to the wider lessons implied by this analysis, I indicate summarily that what we have said of ideas about witchcraft is true too of political ideas. In these stationary economies organised in small self-subsistent groups, it is virtually impossible for the people to conceive of other systems. If he lives in a kingdom, a man cannot be a republican. Kings fear rivals, not revolutionaries. Where a king rules inefficiently or tyrannously, men do not query the institution of kingship, but rise in rebellion to defend the kingship against the bad king. Invariably they rise behind another member of the royal family, who in attacking his kinsman-king strengthens and does not weaken the kingship, or his family's title to it, since the fight is for the values of the kingship. Every civil war reunites the nation about the kingship.

Thus kingship is an absolute value. A man can query whether a particular king is ruling adequately, or is the true heir; he does not—one may almost say cannot—query the kingship itself. Even should an individual become sceptical of the worth of kingship itself, he cannot alter the structure of his society by producing a repulican party. For his only redress against a bad king, or some act of tyranny, is to make someone else king. Since there is no scope for exploitation, in our sense of the word, to create classes, there occur only individual acts of injustice, the resentment against which is canalised into rebellions which defend the system. Thus, in political behaviour, scepticism exists, but it becomes focused on the worth of individuals, not on the offices they hold. Above all, the politico-economic structure functions so that the outcome of doubt and querying is to strengthen the existing pattern and the social beliefs in it.

Certain general conclusions emerge. Anthropologists, in elucidating these kinds of problems, have among other things demonstrated the basic similarity of all humankind, under various different guises in different cultures. They have helped to demolish the myth of constitutional differences between the races of mankind. But . . . I want to conclude by touching briefly on certain problems raised by this study about our own modes of thought.

Had I the time, I could indicate in detail how we reason similarly within our systems of ideas. I give one or two examples. Let us take the common beliefs that Jews are grasping or Negroes immoral. The very phrases, so often heard, "he is a decent Jew" or "he is a decent Negro," by implication strengthen the beliefs that Jews or Negroes as classes of people are not decent—just as querying one witchdoctor strengthens faith in witchdoctorhood.

Again, I remember finding on a friend's bookshelves before the war a collection of anti-Hitler cartoons from all over the world. I turned to the title page and saw the imprint "Leipzig: collected by Ernest Hanfstaengel," who was personal aide-de-camp to Hitler. Those cartoons which portrayed Hitler as a fool, a beast, a mountebank, etc., were re-published by the Nazis in Germany to prove to Germans that Germany was encircled, and that other lands were ruled by Communistic Capitalistic Jews who allowed these vilifications of the Führer. The moral of propaganda is clear: direct assault on a closed system of ideas is immensely difficult, since the system absorbs the attacks and converts them to strengthen itself. That lice carry typhus is easily absorbed into the belief in witchcraft.

For it is not necessary that a system of beliefs about social relations should be consistent, since social life is lived through a series of varied situations which evoke different, even contradictory, beliefs. I would go further and suggest that all systems of ideas about social relations have been in the past, and tend still to be, cast in this form: inchoate, inconsistent, malleable, flexible, fluctuating, variable—capable of absorbing the evidence that seems to contradict the system within the system so as to strengthen it, yet nevertheless logical and reasonable. Read any newspaper of any political faith and you will find within it men thinking about witchcraft. Ultimately faith in certain ideals and confidence in certain moral rules which arise from social relations, dominate over empirical observations and scientific scepticism about social behaviour.

African beliefs about witchcraft or kingship or love between men and women persisted since the pattern of their social structure was a repetitive pattern. Now that they are swallowed by our society new types of social relationships, rather than new ideas, are attacking the systems as wholes. The new patterns of beliefs are similarly constructed. Africans are suspicious of and hostile to Government. A District Officer in my seminar at Oxford suggested that the op- position of Muslim Emirs in Northern Nigeria to female education could be overcome by tak- ing them to see girls' schools in the Middle East. I suggested that if visiting these persuaded Emirs to agree to schools for girls in their own countries, they would begin to attack the Gov- ernment for not giving them more or good enough schools, even for not having compelled them to have these schools before. Another officer told us this had in fact happened in his district. This does not apply to Africans alone. I have analysed the "social thinking" of Euro- peans in Africa—it is basically similar.

We have very many different systems of be- lief, for ours is a rapidly changing, hetero- geneous society. Around us we see constantly how difficult it is for the protagonists of old morals or beliefs, or new morals and beliefs, to meet in argument. For beliefs and morals, viewed instituionally or as they appear in the psyches of individuals, are full of preconcep- tions and prejudices, and are invoked in specific situations, not viewed schematically. New situations are interpreted by each party in terms of its own premises. If two politicians or moralists can hardly meet, it is even more difficult for people to integrate diverse systems of ideas. At a summer school of the Rationalist Press Association I heard rationalists assail sci-

entists as morally responsible for the destruction of the last war, yet more people died under crude weapons and by the withholding of food and the medicines that modern science has found than were killed by highly complex weapons. Clearly every system of ideas to inter- pret social relationships, established or emerg- ing, is as closed as the system of beliefs in witchcraft.

Thus comparative studies of primitive peo- ples help to make us aware how far the way in which we think about social relations is in- fluenced by our social beliefs and how we formulate our own participation in the structure of society. Nevertheless, I would say that we have advanced in understanding of the social and psychical, as well as of the natural, world. Social relations are beginning to assume a shape which gives us the opportunity to examine them scientifically as well as ethically. If we can be made aware of the distorting structure of our systems of ideas, we are greatly helped not only to more objective observation of social behaviour, but also to mutual under- standing. However, this examination may make us politically impotent. We must remember that the structure of a social situation presents a moral choice between limited ends and values with all the disadvantages that choice may entail.

45

ON NORMS AND VALUES

JUDITH BLAKE and KINGSLEY DAVIS

THE meaning of "norm" in everyday usage is ambiguous. It often refers to a statistical reg- ularity, as when we say that one's temperature is "normal" or that a man who has been sick has resumed his "normal" activities. On the

From Robert Faris (Ed.), *Handbook of Modern Sociology.* Copyright © 1964 by Rand McNally and Company. Reprinted by permission of the pub- lisher and the authors. Judith Blake is Associate Professor of Demography and Kingsley Davis is Professor of Sociology, both at the University of California, Berkeley.

other hand, it may indicate an accepted stand- ard or model, as in the phrase "set the norm" or "conform to ethical norms." In sociology the same ambiguity is found, although ostensibly, at least, when a formal definition is given, the second meaning is stipulated. Thus the term is presumably employed, as is done in the present chapter, to designate any standard or rule that states what human beings should or should not think, say, or do under given circumstances.

In this strict sociological usage, the most important element is the *should,* for it clearly implies two important propositions: first, that actual behavior *may* differ from the norm; second, that it *will* differ from the norm unless some effort or force is exerted to bring about conformity. The sociological use of the term generally assumes, without always saying so, that norms are shared to some extent. A purely private, or individual, view of what people should do or think is a norm, but unless it is shared by others, it has no social significance.

Anything in society which pertains to norms, including statements concerning their nature, rationalizations justifying them, and reactions to their violation, may be designated by the adjective "normative." Employed in this way, the word is seen to refer to an entire aspect of human society. It also refers to an element in individual behavior, as when we say that someone's actions are influenced by "normative" factors.

Construed in this way, the normative aspect of human society and human behavior is broad in coverage but conceptually distinct. It embraces, for example, the notion of "values," which are the goals or principles in terms of which specific norms are claimed to be desirable. For example, the rule that political officials should be elected is justified, or "explained," by saying that popular election is necessary if "democracy" is to be realized. The rule itself is the norm, but the value, democracy, is part of the normative reasoning. Disembodied values —i.e., values without any norms through which they can be collectively achieved—are, like purely private norms, sociologically irrelevant.

The "normative" further embraces the inner and outer compulsions (generally called "sanctions") which tend to enforce conformity. A banker who embezzles funds must contend, even when he is successful, with the efforts of others to catch him and with his own ideas of the potential dangers if he is caught. His behavior is therefore "normatively oriented," not so much because of the sheer rule prohibiting embezzlement as because of the sanctions against violation of the rule.

WHY THE NORMATIVE PLAYS A CRUCIAL ROLE IN SOCIOLOGY

The reason that sociology has given a great deal of attention to norms is clear. Human society, as distinct from insect and animal societies, is in part organized and made possible by rules of behavior. By contrast, the intricate interactions of an ant colony or a beehive, like those of a prairie dog village, are governed mainly by instinctive reactions to natural and social stimuli. Such interactions may involve learning to some degree, but this learning, if it occurs, is mainly a matter of habituation to (hence remembrance of) particular environmental stimuli, to which a stereotyped response becomes affixed. In human groups, on the other hand, instinctive responses are channeled or even repressed by the enforcement of behavioral rules that are transmitted by symbolic communication. These rules differ in character from one group to another, and thus help to account for differences in behavior among human societies. For insects and animals, however, behavior tends to be nearly identical from one group to another within the same species, varying only with external conditions. Obviously, then, if the structure of human societies is to be understood, if human behavior is to be adequately explained, the normative aspect must be dealt with. A biologist, habituated to viewing behavior as a function of a physical organism reacting to physical stimuli presented by the environment and other organisms, is apt to bring the same outlook to his analysis of human conduct. If he does so in the concrete sense of offering a complete explanation of some social phenomenon, he is "biologizing" human society. This fallacy is no less bizarre than the opposite—namely, an explanation of some aspect of insect or animal society in terms of presumed norms governing behavior.

Not only does the role of norms account for the difference between human sociology and biology, but it helps account for the division of labor between sociology and economics. In general, economics assumes a normative framework in terms of which the process of production and exchange takes place. Sociology, on the other hand, in trying to understand the way the entire society works (not merely its economic system) has to deal with the norms themselves. For instance, a popular economics textbook points out that in the United States the distribution of income is influenced by the fact that women and Negroes are kept out of certain good jobs and are sometimes paid less for the same job (Samuelson, 1961). If this fact were due to differences in capacity between the races or the sexes, it would come under the economic system of explanation, because the "human resources" available to enter into production would be different. But, finding that "there are numerous jobs which either sex or race can do equally well," the author attributes the discrimination to "prejudice." As an economist he is not obliged to explain why this prejudice occurs (the word is not even in the index), although, as he says, it affects something he is concerned with, the distribution of income. He takes the prejudice for granted, whereas the sociologist must explain its existence by accounting for the norms governing differential hiring and pay. One way in which he does this is by examining nonoccupational roles. The norms governing women's participation in the labor force certainly have something to do with their particular role within the family.

If it be granted that social norms affect behavior, then the totality of norms, or at least the totality of major norms, within a society can be expected to have some consistency, or order. Otherwise, the social system would not approximate a "system," and the society would tend to fall to pieces and be absorbed by another one which was orderly. It follows that an important aspect of the study of social organization is the study of the "normative order."

VALUES AND NORMS

So far we have tried to distinguish the normative factor in behavior and to assess the reasons for its importance to sociology. Let us now admit that this "factor" is quite diverse in character and try to distinguish some of its elements or parts.

Probably the greatest single distinction within the normative realm is that between something variously called values, sentiments, themes, or ethical principles, on the one hand, and the specific rules of conduct, thought, and speech on the other. The line between the two is always fuzzy (Is the doctrine of freedom of the press, for example, a norm or a value?), but the attempt to separate them has been made again and again in sociological and philosophical thought. Apparently the reasons for this effort have varied, but two seem to stand out. Investigators have felt it necessary to probe beyond external behavior to the motives that impel behavior. In addition, since subjective phenomena seem bewildering in the number and variety of their expressions, observers have felt that it must be possible to reduce them to a few recurrent, underlying principles, or perhaps "real motives." In any case, the task of finding these subjective forces or entities has been complicated by the fact that human beings not only act but give reasons for their actions. An observer must therefore decide whether to accept the reason given or to judge that, through ignorance or deception, it is not the real one. Not only do persons give private reasons, but there are official versions of what are the proper reasons for given kinds of conduct.

An early attempt to separate the essential values from the kaleidoscope of external manifestations was made by Vilfredo Pareto. In his general treatise on sociology (1935) he not only distinguished basic subjective factors but sought to use them in the analysis of social structure and social change. Underlying the countless rules and rites, verbal arguments and rationalizations (or "derivations"), he thought he could distill a few recurrent motives, or themes, which he called "residues," and which he thought responded to corresponding sentiments. The social system was, for him, a "social equilibrium" consisting of these sentiments acting as forces, and "social dynamics" was, in large part, a matter of the "circulation of the elite" in which differential strength of the various sentiments among the social classes was the main explanatory principle.

Pareto was a student of advanced societies and therefore had to deal with the limitless sophistries of thought which came from the mouths and pens of priests, philosophers, statesmen, scholars, journalists, scientists, and other literate specialists and pleaders. He had to deal with conflicts and differences of opinion. For this reason he had particularly to wrestle with the problem of how to cope with the verbal arguments and explanations in getting to the actual motives hidden behind them. For William Graham Sumner, on the other hand, the problem was somewhat different. This great student of the norms drew his materials mostly from reports about primitive tribes. He therefore was required to pay little or no attention to written expressions of human thought as objects of study and did not need to consider seriously the supernatural and magical explanations that primitive people gave for their norms. In contrast to Pareto, therefore, he barely recognized anything like general principles or abstract values, and when he did, he saw them as consequences rather than determinants of the norms themselves, which he called folkways and mores.

All are forced to conform, and the folkways dominate social life. They seem true and right, and arise into mores as the norm of welfare. Thence are produced faiths, ideas, doctrines, religions, and philosophies, according to the stage of civilization and the fashion of reflection and generalization.

Both Pareto and Sumner refused to take the explanations people give for their norms or their conduct at face value. But Pareto sought to find behind the explanations a few basic motives or sentiments, while Sumner emphasized the norms themselves, simply regarding the verbal expressions of people as part of the normative system.

It seems that in general the literature dealing with norms has followed both men in certain respects, regardless of whether or not it was actually influenced directly by them. There has been a tendency to draw materials and inspiration, as Sumner did, from studies of preliterate villagers. Hence conflict, deviation, and the complexity of verbal statement and argument have been minimized. This line of treatment has of course been prominent among the social anthropologists, but it has been present too in the work of Talcott Parsons and some of his students. Due to the emphasis on *different* societies in anthropological thought, the search for values tended to take a new turn. It became a search for the particular underlying values, cultural themes, or ethos of each particular society. This development raised in turn the question of whether the values of one society had any relation to the values of another. In other words, is cultural relativity absolute, or is there a single set of values, of which those of different societies are simply variant expressions? Pareto had made it clear that he regarded the sentiments as having "social utility"; Sumner thought that the folkways and mores were adaptive, keeping the society in touch with reality and contributing to its survival. Presumably, in anthropological and sociological thought since Emile Durkheim and Bronislaw Malinowski, the values must have a *function* in society; but the question is obscure because, for many social scientists at least, what is taken as a value may be disfunctional, and what is functional may not be valued.

The search for a particular set of values which then explain or enlighten us concerning the social system is Paretian in character, all the more so if the values are considered to be a single set which may simply vary in strength from one group to another. This approach has apparently been followed by Parsons. Although his "value-orientations" are seemingly applicable to entire societies and appear relatively free from the complications of deviancy, group conflict, and deception (being to this extent Sumnerian), he does have, like Pareto, a single set which are then used as explanatory devices. It is perhaps an exaggeration to say so, but it does seem as if the ease of explanation provided by the value-attitudes is facilitated by the fact that, as "pattern-variables," their classification is given in pairs. If, in a given society or group, a phenomenon is not explicable in terms of "universalism," "achievement orientation," and "specificity," it surely will be explicable in terms of "particularism," "ascription," and "diffuseness."

An interesting addition to the literature on values arises from the attempt to investigate them empirically in complex rather than primitive societies. When this is done by going to people and asking them about their attitudes and preferences, the old problem of what to do with verbal expressions, which may conceal as well as divulge, is raised again. For the most part it appears that these studies tend to construe values simply as expressions of opinion, feeling, or preference, accepting verbal statements of subjects more or less at face value. In doing so, the task of finding a few "underlying motives" which can be used for all mankind is given up, although the search may still be for a few values held to characterize the particular group or society. The reduction of "values" to verbally stated attitudes is illustrated by one study of "courtship values" which asked students what trait or quality they preferred in "dates." The results showed, for example, that male students stress "desirable physical appearance" in their "dates." [1]

Empirical, quantitative research may prove the best antidote to the idea that there is a set of subjective entities or forces which, once posited, can be used to explain human behavior. This idea seems to be a trap, because the values, sentiments, or motives are always inferred, and hence have no better status for causal analysis than the observable phenomena from which they are inferred. Furthermore, since the implication is that there are only a few such entities—or even one, if the single "ethos" of a whole society is being depicted—

the inferred items are so remote from the observed behavior that it is doubtful whether any two analysts working independently would reach the same results. Our skepticism is increased by what we take to be the lack of sociological usefulness in previous classifications of the motives of man. The most notable of these was the list of four wishes of W. I. Thomas (1927).

There is, of course, a distinction to be made between the standards involved in judgments, on the one hand, and the application of those standards in specific judgments, on the other. Thus, in regard to social behavior, it is one thing to say that parents prefer sons to daughters, and quite another to say that parents feel they should treat their daughters in a certain way under given circumstances. Presumably, a preference for sons is a value, but it says nothing concrete concerning parental conduct and it has no sanctions. A norm, on the other hand, says that a given line of conduct must, or should, be followed. Thus a preference for sons in the United States does not mean that female infanticide is permitted or that boys are given more clothes. What, then, is the utility of the distinction between values and norms?

Whatever the utility may be, it surely is not that of designating cause and effect. Presumably a norm "exemplifies" a value, but this does not mean that the norm is *caused* by the value it exemplifies, or that the value is the motive and the norm simply the expression of this motive with respect to behavior. Such a mode of explanation is extremely tempting, not only because it is the way people think anyway—that is, the individual always has a reason for doing whatever he does—but also because it gives an unfailing mode of explaining norms and behavior. The flaw, however, lies in the question of logic and evidence. Can we accept as true people's verbal description of their values? These may be nothing more than a rationalization of the norms—as when, for instance, someone justifies the exclusion of married women from jobs on the ground that a woman's place is in the home. Can we adopt some indirect technique of getting verbal statements of values, thus deceiving the subject into revealing what he would not reveal if he knew our purpose? Such a technique still makes the assumption that the values are consciously held and are rationally connected with norms and conduct—an old-fashioned view controverted by voluminous evidence. Can we then take people's statements and *reinterpret* them to get at

"underlying" values? Yes, provided we wish to make the questionable assumption that verbal statements inevitably reflect real values, and provided we admit that the process of symbolic reinterpretation in itself has no empirical controls and consequently may differ radically from one observer to another.

In practice, we tend to find the best evidence of values in the norms themselves. If people manifest a dislike of cheating in examinations, of dishonest advertising in business, and of unnecessary roughness in sports, we infer something like a value of "fair competition." Such a process of reasoning may help us to insert the motivational linkages and thus integrate a body of diverse information. At bottom, however, it is a classification. Its usefulness does not extend to causal explanation, because the inferred value comes only from the specific norms themselves and hence cannot be used as an explanation of those norms. In other words, unless we have evidence independent of the norms themselves, we cannot logically derive norms from values. Independent evidence, if obtainable, may show that the so-called values are nonexistent, that they are consequences of the norms, or that they derive from a third factor which is also responsible for the norms.

It is the norms, not the values, that have the pressure of reality upon them. It is the norms that are enforced by sanctions, that are subject to the necessity of action and the agony of decision. It is therefore the norms that represent the cutting edge of social control. In this regard Sumner seems to have been more correct than some of his successors, for he emphasized the importance of the folkways and mores in understanding society rather than the vague, slippery ideologies, rationalizations, and generalizations people use in justifying their observance or nonobservance of norms.

A more satisfactory use of "values" in sociological analysis is to abandon them as causal agents and to recognize them frankly as sheer constructs by which we attempt to fill in the subjective linkages in the analysis of social causation. For example, the movement of peasants to cities during the process of industrialization is not "explained" by saying that they prefer the bright lights of the city to the drab monotony of the village. Only when the evolving economic and social situation in both the village and the city are taken into account can we begin to explain this recurrent major social phenomenon. It helps us understand the process, however, if we can get some inkling of how the peasant's feelings and thoughts take shape in view of these conditions; and so we try to put together a model of his mental reactions and test it out against various kinds of empirical evidence, including his verbal statements.

THE FALLACY OF NORMATIVE DETERMINISM

We raise the question of causation with respect to values and norms because we believe that conceptual distinctions unrelated to empirical investigation are empty exercises. For the same reason, we wish to push on to the wider question of normative causation in general, apart from the distinction between values and norms. In doing so, we come to one of the most confused and at the same time basic issues in sociology and social anthropology. No one can doubt that norms exercise *some* influence on behavior, but the question of *how much* influence they exercise is highly debatable. At times, sociologists and social anthropologists have seemed to adopt an extreme view by treating the normative system as the sole object of analysis or as the sole determinant of social phenomena. This has usually been done by implicit assumption and careless overstatement rather than by deliberate doctrine, and it has been camouflaged at times by a seemingly broader position of cultural determinism. At any rate, it is a position that affords a good point of departure in analyzing the interrelation between norms and other factors in behavior.

At its most naive level, normative determinism takes the fact that norms *are meant* to control behavior as the basis for assuming that they *do* control it. The only task of social science is then to discover the particular norms in any given society. By this reasoning, nearly all social scientists in Latin America are trained in the law rather than in statistics and social research. The law, being the crystallization of the normative order, is assumed to be what one needs to know. At a more sophisticated level, the assumption is made that the independent variable consists in "cultural configurations," "basic value-orientations," or "the institutional system," which determines everything else in a society. This has a doctrinal side—e.g., in statements about the nature of man—as well as a methodological side. An anthropologist states

with approval that national character studies assume that

each member of a society is systematically representative of the cultural pattern of that society, so that the treatment accorded infant or immigrant, pupils or employees or rulers, is indicative of the culturally regular character-forming methods of that society (Mead).

C. Kluckhohn expresses a common dictum when he says that the constants in human life from one society to another "arise out of the biological nature of the species" and its fixed environment, whereas the variations arise from culture. Each culture, he says, has a "grammar." "The function of linguistic grammar is to control the freedom of words so that there is no needless congestion of the communication traffic. The grammar of culture, in general, likewise makes for orderliness."

According to this view, the avenue to understanding actual societies is to understand their cultures. The term culture has a bewildering and altogether too convenient variety of definitions. Sometimes it is used so broadly as to cover all material products of man, all social behavior, all ideas and goals. Used in this way, it includes society itself, and therefore the cultural determinism of social phenomena becomes a tautology. Frequently, however, the term culture is used primarily in the sense of a normative system. In this case we get what may be called a "blueprint theory" of society, namely, that there is a set of "culture-patterns" which are, so to speak, laid down in advance and followed by the members of the society. The determinism implicit in this view is indicated by such phrases as "handed down," "shaped by his culture," "ultimate values," "culture-bound," "way of life," and others.

The way of life that is *handed down* as the social heritage of every people does more than *supply* a set of skills for making a living and a *set of blueprints* for human relations. Each different way of life *makes its own assumptions* about the ends and purposes of human existence . . . (Italics supplied) (C. Kluckhohn).

Similarly, Parsons and his followers have placed heavy emphasis on value-orientations as the key to sociological analysis. In the hands of some, this emphasis gets translated into dogma; for example, "Values determine the choices men make, and the ends they live by" (Stein and Cloward, 1958).

Under the assumption of the supremacy of the norms and "dominant" value-orientations, the chief research method of the social disciplines becomes that of questioning informants. The investigator asks a member of the society what people are *supposed* to do, and hence the normative pattern will emerge. The informant necessarily knows the "culture," because he lives it and is determined by it.

Any member of a group, provided that his position within that group is specified, is a perfect sample of the group-wide pattern on which he is acting as an informant (Mead).

Furthermore, with this reliance on norms and values as determinants of social phenomena, peculiar importance is naturally given to "socialization," normally interpreted to mean the acquisition, or "internalization," of the norms. According to Parsons:

There is reason to believe that, among the learned elements of personality in certain respects the stablest and most enduring are the major value-orientation patterns and there is much evidence that these are "laid down" in childhood and are not on a large scale subject to drastic alteration during adult life. There is good reason to treat these patterns of value-orientation, as analyzed in terms of pattern variable combinations, as the core of what is sometimes called "basic personality structure."

Most of the sociologists and anthropologists who stress culture, culture patterns, norms, value-attitudes, and such concepts would deny that they are determinists. They would say they are abstracting—treating behavior *as if* it were determined by the normative system. In practice, however, the emphasis on values and norms leads, as critics have been quick to point out, to deficiencies in the scientific understanding of real societies. The gravest deficiency arises, ironically, in the failure to deal adequately with norms themselves. As long as the cultural configurations, basic value-attitudes, prevailing mores, or what not are taken as the starting point and principal determinant, they have the status of unanalyzed assumptions. The very questions that would enable us to understand the norms tend not to be asked, and certain facts about society become difficult, if not impossible, to comprehend. For instance, an assumption of normative primacy renders it difficult to explain deviancy and crime, although the real world plainly exhibits a great deal of normative violation. If one is to understand deviancy, one must ask why societies frequently

reward violation more heavily than conformity to the norms; why legitimate authority is one of the most widespread bases of illegitimate power; why ego and alter so frequently disagree on norms applicable to their relationship; why any action, no matter how atrocious, can be justified in terms of the verbal formulas in which norms and values are couched. Furthermore, the origin and appearance of new norms and their constant change—again facts of social existence—become incomprehensible under an assumption of normative sovereignty.

Worse yet, the deceptive ease of explanation in terms of norms or value-attitudes encourages an inattentiveness to methodological problems. By virtue of their subjective, emotional, and ethical character, norms, and especially values, are among the world's most difficult objects to identify with certainty. They are bones of contention and matters of disagreement. The assumption that for each society there is one norm or one value regarding a given aspect of behavior is in most instances untrue. Insofar as an investigator uses norms or values as explanatory principles for concrete behavior, he therefore tends to be explaining the known by the unknown, the specific by the unspecific. His identification of the normative principles may be so vague as to be universally useful, i.e., anything and everything becomes explicable. Thus, if Americans spend a great deal of money on "alcoholic beverages, theater and movie tickets, tobacco, cosmetics, and jewelry," the explanation is simple: They have a good-time ideology. If, on the other hand, they devote themselves to hard work, it is because they have "an Evil-but-perfectible definition of *human nature,*" in contrast to the fiesta-loving Mexicans. If "superficial intimacy is easy in America," it is "because of the cult of the average man." If, on the other hand, there is a lack of social intimacy between Negro and white, it is because of a "racism" value. The cynical critic might advise that, for convenience in causal interpretation, the values of a "culture" should always be described in pairs of opposites.

Explicit definitions, when given, demonstrate the nebulous character of "value." Here, for example, is the definition of "value-orientation" in a 437-page book on value-orientations:

Value orientations are complex but definitely patterned (rank-ordered) principles, resulting from the transactional interplay of three analytically dis-

tinguishable elements of the evaluative process—
the cognitive, the affective, and the directive elements—which give order and direction to the
ever-flowing stream of human acts and thoughts as
these relate to the solution of "common human"
problems (F. Kluckhohn and Strodtbeck, 1961).

We learn in the paragraphs explaining this
definition that "value-orientations" differ from
"basic values"! Also we are told that, instead
of "amalgamating" the cognitive and affective
elements, as do Hallowell, Whorf, and C. Kluckhohn, this definition "separates" them.

Presumably if one's interpretation is in terms
of norms rather than values, one is on firmer
ground. Yet the difficulty of proving the existence of the norm is great. As a consequence,
there is a tendency to take regularities in behavior as the evidence of the norm. When this
is done, to explain the behavior in terms of the

norm is a redundancy. Seen in this light, statements such as the following are also redundant:
"Knowledge of a culture makes it possible to
predict a good many of the actions of any
person who shares that culture." (C. Kluckhohn, 1949). Why not simply say, "Knowledge
of behavior in a society makes it possible to
predict behavior in that society"? Of course,
if norms are taken to be regularities of behavior, they have no analytical significance at all;
they are then merely another name for behavior
itself, and cannot contribute to an understanding
of behavior.

NOTES

1. The Index of the first 25 volumes of the
American Sociological Review contains 45 articles
under the heading of "values."

Structuralism and Formal Analysis

46

STUDIES IN ETHNOSCIENCE

WILLIAM C. STURTEVANT

THIS paper is a survey and explication of a new approach in ethnography—of what one might well call "the New Ethnography" were it not for that label's pejorative implications for practitioners of other kinds of ethnography. The method has no generally accepted name, although one is clearly required. "Ethnoscience" perhaps has the widest acceptance, in conversation if not in print, and has the advantage of freshness. However, some of this word's undesirable implications should be disavowed: "The term 'ethnoscience' is unfortunate for two reasons—first, because it suggests that other kinds of ethnography are *not* science, and second because it suggests that folk classifications and folk taxonomies *are* science" (Spaulding 1963). Although the name may have been chosen partly because of the first of these implications, it would be impolitic if not impolite to insist on it; in any case, the method should stand or fall on its own merits. To dispose adequately of the second implication would require a discourse on the definition and philosophy of science. It is perhaps sufficient to remark that the most appropriate meaning to assign to the element "science" here (but not necessarily elsewhere) is, essentially, "classification." This restricted implication has been well expressed by G. G. Simpson in a somewhat similar context:

The necessity for aggregating things (or what is operationally equivalent, the sensations received from them) into classes is a completely general characteristic of living things. . . . Such generalization, such classification in that sense, is an absolute, minimal requirement of adaptation, which in turn is an absolute and minimal requirement of being or staying alive. . . . We certainly order our perceptions of the external world more fully, more constantly, and more consciously than do any other organisms. . . . Such ordering is most conspicuous

From *American Anthropologist*, 66(2): 99–131, special issue on "Transcultural Studies in Cognition," June, 1964. Copyright © 1964 by the American Anthropological Association. Reprinted by permission of the publisher and the author. William C. Sturtevant is Curator of Ethnology, Bureau of American Ethnology, Smithsonian Institution.

in the two most exclusively human and in some sense highest of all our activities: the arts and sciences. . . . The whole aim of theoretical science is to carry to the highest possible and conscious degree the perceptual reduction of chaos . . . . the most basic postulate of science is that nature itself is orderly. . . . All theoretical science is ordering (Simpson 1961: 3–5).

"Ethnoscience" is appropriate as a label because it may be taken to imply one interpretation of such terms as "ethnobotany," "ethnogeography," etc.—although it is important to emphasize that the approach is a general ethnographic one, by no means limited to such branches of ethnography as are often called by the names of recognized academic "arts and sciences" coupled with the prefix "ethno-." This prefix is to be understood here, in a special sense: it refers to the system of knowledge and cognition typical of a given culture. Ethnoscience differs from Simpson's "theoretical science" ı that it refers to the "reduction of chaos" achieved by a particular culture, rather than to the "highest possible and conscious degree" to which such chaos may be reduced. To put it another way, a culture itself amounts to the sum of a given society's folk classifications, all of that society's ethnoscience, its particular ways of classifying its material and social universe. Thus, to take an extreme example, the "ethnopornography" of the Queensland aborigines is what *they* consider pornography—if indeed they have such a category—rather than what was considered pornography by the Victorian ethnologist who titled the last chapter of his monograph on Queensland aboriginal culture "ethno-pornography," warned that "the following chapter is not suitable for perusal by the general reader," and described under this heading such topics as marriage, pregnancy and childbirth, menstruation, "foul language," and especially genital mutilations and their social and ceremonial significance (Roth 1897:169–84). Similarly, "ethnohistory" is here the conception of the past shared by the bearers of a particular culture, rather than (the more usual sense) the history (in our terms) of "ethnic groups;" "ethnobotany" is a specific cultural conception of the plant world, rather than (again the more usual sense) a description of plant uses arranged under the binomials of our own taxonomic botany.

It is not a new proposal that an important aspect of culture is made up of the principles by which a people classify their universe. A rather clear statement to this effect was made by Boas (1911:24–26); the notion was hinted at by Durkheim and Mauss (1903:5–6); Malinowski clearly stated that "the final goal, of which an Ethnographer should never lose sight. . . . is, briefly, to grasp the native's point of view, his relation to life, to realise *his* vision of *his* world" (1922:25). Even E. B. Tylor can be understood in the same sense, when he warned that the ethnologist "must avoid that error which the proverb calls measuring other people's corn by one's own bushel" (1881:410). However, the explicit definition of culture as a whole in these terms, and the proposition that ethnography should be conceived of as the discovery of the "conceptual models" with which a society operates, was first stated quite recently in an elegant, brief paper by Goodenough:

A society's culture consists of whatever it is one has to know or believe in order to operate in a manner acceptable to its members, and to do so in any role that they accept for any one of themselves. . . . It is the forms of things that people have in mind, their models for perceiving, relating, and otherwise interpreting them. . . . Ethnographic description, then, requires methods of processing observed phenomena such that we can inductively construct a theory of how our informants have organized the same phenomena. It is the theory, not the phenomena alone, which ethnographic description aims to present (Goodenough 1957: 167–68).

It has long been evident that a major weakness in anthropology is the underdeveloped condition of ethnographic method. Typologies and generalizations abound, but their descriptive foundations are insecure. Anthropology is in the natural history stage of development rather than the "stage of deductively formulated theory" (Northrop 1947), it is history rather than science (Kroeber 1952:52–78), it has not discovered a fundamental unit comparable to the physicists' atom (a common complaint, variously worded; e.g., Kluckhohn 1953:517, Spuhler 1963). One may try to make the best of this situation by insisting that one prefers to remain a historian or a humanist, or one

may look for improvement in ethnography. Taking the latter choice, the best strategy is not, I think, to seek to modify existing generalizations on the basis of intensive field work of the traditional sort in one or two societies (Leach 1961a, 1961b), nor to elaborate *a priori* typologies and apply them to more and more old descriptions by means of fancy retrieval procedures, hoping that the errors and incommensurabilities in the descriptive sources will balance out in the statistical manipulations used to yield generalizations. It is on this latter score that Needham (1962) attacks Murdock's methods (e.g., 1953, 1957), justifiably although intemperately. An interesting methodological contrast of this sort is provided by the exchange between Goodenough (1956b) and Fischer (1958) on Trukese residence rules: Goodenough pointed out the descrepancies resulting from his and Fischer's attempts to apply the usual *a priori* typology of residence in their independent censuses of Truk as a basis for urging that ethnographers should drop this method and substitute the search for the rules significant to the bearers of a particular culture in their own choices of residence. Fischer responded by tinkering with the *a prior* typology to take account of the Trukese peculiarities Goodenough had noted—yet there is no guarantee that the next culture examined will fit his new typology any better than Truk fitted the old one.

What is needed is the improvement of ethnographic method, to make cultural descriptions replicable and accurate, so that we know what we are comparing. Ethnoscience shows promise as the New Ethnography required to advance the whole of cultural anthropology.

The ethnoscientific approach is now about ten years old and has a rapidly growing body of practitioners in general agreement on methods and aims, in close communication with each other, and sharing an enthusiasm for the rehabilitation and revivification of ethnography. There are several excellent programmatic general statements about ethnoscience (Conklin 1962a; Frake 1962; Wallace 1962), which include (usually simplified) examples. However, most previous discussions and exemplifications have been couched in such terms that many anthropologists assume that what is being described is not ethnography but some kind of linguistics or "kinship algebra" or both, so that there may now be room for a more informal, less technical characterization.

The sections which follow attempt to present briefly and in rather general terms the main features of ethnoscience as a method, and to indicate some of the areas in which further work is needed. Usually, examples are either not given, or not described in sufficient detail for adequate comprehension of their relevance. The sources cited should be examined for more complete exemplification.

PRINCIPLES

1. ETICS AND EMICS

If a folk classification is ever to be fully understood, an ethnoscientific analysis must ultimately reduce to a description in terms approximating culture-free characteristics. Colors may be among the significant features in a folk taxonomy of plants; but color itself is classified by principles which differ from culture to culture, hence is a domain which must be analyzed ethnoscientifically before the botanical folk taxonomy is translatable into our terms (Conklin 1955). Enough is known about color, and the classificatory features involved are ordinarily sufficiently concrete, so that the color classification of a given culture may be relatable to culture-free physical and physiological features. Obviously there are very few aspects of culture where reductionism of this type is even remotely foreseeable. In domains where such reduction is not yet possible, the local perceptual structure may nevertheless be largely discoverable, even though incompletely translatable (see now Frake 1964:134). In fact, in some domains the very difficulties in observation which prevent the outside observer from analyzing the significant features in culture-free terms also force the bearers of the culture to utilize explicit verbalized defining attributes in learning and communicating about their own folk classification—hence make easier the discovery of attributes on this level—in contrast to classifications where the objects and their attributes are so concrete and frequent that the classifications may be well learned by exemplification rather than description (Frake 1961:124–25). Nevertheless, full understanding of a culture or an aspect of a culture and particularly its full description in a foreign language require the ultimate reduction of the significant attributes of the local classifications into culture-free terms.

Lamb's discussion of the relationship between his semantic and sememic strata, and the parallel relationship between the phonetic and phonemic strata (Lamb 1964:75–77), is highly relevant here.

Culture-free features of the real world may be called "etics" (Pike 1954). The label may also be applied to features which are not truly culture-free, but which at least have been derived from the examination of more than one culture, or to the sum of all the significant attributes in the folk classifications of all cultures. Most of ethnography has operated with characterisitcs of this sort; ethnology has devoted much attention to the accumulation and systematization of features which *might* be significant in any folk classification, but it has given little attention to comparison of folk classifications or their principles as such. These results are by no means wasted from the point of view of ethnoscience: the ethnographer's knowledge of etics assists him in discovering the locally-significant features by guiding his initial observations and formulation of hypotheses.

Pike contrasts an etic approach with one which he calls emic, which amounts to an ethnoscientific one: an attempt "to discover and describe the behavioral system [of a given culture] in its own terms, identifying not only the structural units but also the structural classes to which they belong" (French 1963:398). An emic description should ultimately indicate which etic characters are locally significant. The more we know of the etics of culture, the easier is the task of ethnoscientific analysis. Thus the great attention to kinship in the past, as well as the great amount of knowledge concerning cultural variability in kinship terminologies (the basic paper on the etics of kinship being a half century old [Kroeber 1909]) is one reason why emic analyses of kinship are easier than those of art, or law, or religion. Better knowledge, at least among anthropologists, of the physiology and physics of color than of taste or smell more readily permits an ethnoscientific analysis of color, even though it is clear (Conklin 1955) that a folk domain including color need not be congruent with what the physicists understand by color. It seems probable that the vast accumulation of anthropological (both ethnological and archeological) knowledge of the etics of material culture will allow the ethnoscientific approach to be quite readily applied in this presently-neglected field. Furthermore, in

material culture the objects classified are concrete and easily examined and usually readily
observable in many examples during the time
available for normal field work—in contrast to
diseases, deities, etc. In classifications of concrete but natural, noncultural phenomena such
as plants and animals, the range of variation
which is classified is both extreme and beyond
the direct control of the classifiers, who must
select only certain features to which classificatory significance is given (Lévi-Strauss
1962b:73–74). But with cultural artifacts the
corpus is smaller and the significant features
are largely produced by the classifiers and hence
should be more distinctive and more readily
recognizable; also the ethnographer can here
subject at least some of the features to controlled variation in order to test informants'
reactions to their significance (cf. Berlin and
Romney 1964 for an illustration of some of
these advantages).

The nature of learning and of communication
implies that a culture consists of shared classifications of phenomena, that not every etic difference is emic. But it should be emphasized that
an emic analysis refers to one society, to a set
of interacting individuals. Cross-cultural comparison, if we take culture in Goodenough's
sense, is another level of analysis which involves
the comparison of different emic systems. There
is no reason why one should expect to find
emic regularities shared by cultures differing
in space or time. Thus Dundes' "emic units in
the structural study of folktales" (1962) are
not emic units in the sense here intended, insofar as the "system" of which they are analytical
units is comparative (an etically defined "motif,"
"tale," or "tale type," whose actual manifestations in different cultures are treated as
"variants"). On the other hand, Lévi-Strauss'
brief characterization of some of the defining
attributes of the "gustèmes" of the English,
French, and Chinese cuisines (1958:99–100) is
a comparison of the emics of different cultures,
although the emic analysis of each of the three
cuisines is not presented in sufficient detail to
be convincing. Even so, "slippage back and
forth between individual systems and any and all
systems, as context for structural relevance, re-
curs in his [Lévi-Strauss'] work" also; "the first
step in a resolution of the problem . . . is to
refer structural contrast exclusively to within
the domains of individual systems, where its
cognitive basis can be empirically warranted"
(Hymes 1964:45, 16).

2. DOMAINS

One of the most important principles of
ethnoscience, and one of those most often overlooked, is the necessity for determining in a
nonarbitrary manner the boundaries of the
major category or classification system being
analyzed, i.e., for discovering how a domain is
bounded in the culture being described rather
than applying some external, cross-cultural definitions of the field. If this is not done, the description of the internal structuring of the
domain is likely to be incomplete if not entirely
erroneous, and the utility of the analysis for
predicting the classificatory placement of new
instances will suffer. (See now Hymes 1964:16–
18.)

Any two cultures differ in the way they
classify experience. Everyone with any familiarity with more than one realizes that this
is true for the lower, more specific classificatory
categories, and trivial examples are easily found.
But we cannot assume that the higher, more
general levels of the folk classifications of different cultures will coincide either; there is no
reason to suppose that the total range of a set
of categories will match that of the "corresponding" set in another culture even though the
ranges of the lower categories in the two sets
are different.

Thus every anthropologist recognizes that
"uncle" is not a universal category, but most
seem to suppose that "relative" or "kinship" is
—i.e., that a set of categories defined by consanguinity and affinity is everywhere a "natural"
set, that features such as ritual relationships
must somehow be always outside the core system; the term "fictive kinship" is significant of
the analytical bias. In contrast, Conklin (1964)
specifically does not assume that "kinship" is a
domain everywhere bounded in the same
manner.

It is also customary to assume that everywhere there are just two systems of kinship
terms: those used in "reference" and those
used in "address." Thus an *a priori* decision
is made as to the significant defining features
and the number of coexistent systems. Such an
analysis of the American kinship system blurs
many distinctions: "mother's brother" and
"father's brother" are required instead of
"uncle" in some referential contexts; different
forms of address are often used to differentiate
co-resident "grandmothers" or "mothers" (Mo

vs WiMo/HuMo); such terms as "father, dad, daddy, pop, old man" are not synonymous.

The classic distinction between terms of address and terms of reference is not of much help in dealing with the American system. It tends to obscure certain important processes, partly, at least, because it presumes that there is a single term used in all referential contexts. . . . In the contemporary American system the wide variety of alternate forms allows them to differentiate a variety of different contexts (Schneider and Homans 1955: 1195–96).

It seems probable that these "alternate forms" would turn out to be quite systematically structured, that several domains could be specified, were the contexts to be analyzed ethnoscientifically. One would expect a higher degree of agreement between informants in the usage of these terms if the contexts were discovered by the observation of natural situations or the asking of natural questions than is the case when informants are asked (e.g. Lewis 1963) to sort the "alternates" into contexts which are supplied ahead of time by the investigator, even though he himself is an American.

Frake (1960:58–59) has made the same point with regard to the Eastern Subanun. Conklin (1951) described several Tagalog "coexisting sets of relationship terms," with their defining contexts. Swartz (1960) shows the relevance of situational environments to the choice between two Trukese terms. According to Chao's analysis (1956), there are three major sets of Mandarin Chinese kinship terms, which are not entirely synonymous even in their kinterm referents; furthermore, the contexts in which Chinese "terms of address" (pronouns, kinship terms, proper names, and titles) are used can be analyzed in terms of the intersection of seven main categories of hearers and ten main categories of person spoken of or addressed (Chao 1956). Presumably this kind of situation is quite general. Yet Norbeck can still conclude a discussion of the "errors" in Morgan's schedule of Japanese kinship terms by urging "the importance of making clear distinctions between terms of address and terms of reference" (1963:214) when it is clear from his preceding discussion (and from Befu and Norbeck 1958) that there are many more than two systems here, and that some of Morgan's "errors" in fact represent accurate reporting of one of these systems.

The arbitrary delimitation of major domain boundaries persists in kinship studies even though the analytical procedures here are the most developed ones in ethnography. It is an even more obvious fault in other areas. Many of the difficulties, for example, in discussions of "primitive art" are seen in a new light when one ceases to assume that "art" is a universal category. The assumption that "cultures . . . have in common . . . a uniform system of classification. . . . a single basic plan" (Murdock 1945:125) is stifling to ethnoscientific analysis.

There may be domains—perhaps kinship is one of them—which are more nearly universal than others, where cross-cultural comparison would show greater sharing of significant features for higher level taxa than for lower level ones. But this is a significant hypothesis to be tested by the comparison of domains from different cultures, each analyzed without prejudice, rather than being a postulate determining the delimitation of domains to be analyzed. Prior assumption of the universality of domains, as in much work on kinship and other domains (e.g. color), prejudges the case and masks some of the variability the explication of which is a classical task of anthropology.

But procedures for the definition of domains are not yet well worked out—this remains one of the more difficult problem areas of ethnoscience (Conklin 1962a:124, 1964; Öhman 1953; Voegelin and Voegelin 1957). However, the problems do not differ in kind from those involving the identification of categories on lower levels, or the discovery of significant contexts or environments.

3. TERMINOLOGICAL SYSTEMS

Research in ethnoscience so far has concentrated on classifications as reflected by native terminology, on "discerning how people construe their world of experience from the way they talk about it" (Frake 1962:74).

The analysis of a culture's terminological systems will not, of course, exhaustively reveal the cognitive world of its members, but it will certainly tap a central portion of it. Culturally significant cognitive features must be communicable between persons in one of the standard symbolic system of the culture. A major share of these features will undoubtedly be codable in a society's most flexible and productive communication device, its language (Frake 1962: 75; cf. Conklin 1962a, Goodenough 1957, Lounsbury 1963).

The main evidence for the existence of a category is the fact that it is named. As a result, the analyst faces the problem of locating *segregates* (segregate: "any terminologically-distinguished . . . grouping of objects," Conklin 1962a:120–21; Frake 1962:76). Much work on the "Sapir-Whorf hypothesis" has assumed that any morpheme, word, or grammatical construction labels a category of meaning, that the semantic structure of a language is built up only of these units. But it is clear that contrasting categories within a terminological system, and within a single level of a system, are frequently named with units whose positions in the strictly linguistic system vary markedly—morpheme, word, phrase, etc. (Conklin 1962a; Frake 1961, 1962; Lounsbury 1956:190–92). These labels of classificatory categories, whatever their grammatical status, have been called "lexemes." Alternatively, a lexeme is a "meaningful form whose signification cannot be inferred from a knowledge of anything else in the language" (Conklin 1962a:121; see also Weinreich 1963:145–46; Lamb's use of the term [1964] is nearly equivalent). Thus for example "stool" is a lexeme in English, and kwêi chéi ('stool') is a lexeme in Burmese labelling an approximately equivalent segregate, even though kwêi ('dog') and chéi ('leg(s)') are also nouns occurring independently as labels for other segregates. The analyst must differentiate between lexemes and other linguistic forms of similar grammatical status which do not serve as segregate labels. The solution of this problem depends partly on knowledge of the language, both comprehension of it and technical knowledge of its structure. Comprehension is required because translation prior to semantic analysis causes insuperable difficulties because of the incommensurability of the semantics of any two languages (Conklin 1962a:125–27 gives a nice example). Furthermore, in practice much of the best data comes from observing linguistic behavior outside the formal eliciting situation with an informant. One task of ethnoscience, in fact, can be viewed as the solution of the old problem of translation.

Knowledge of the linguistic structure is necessary because the category names belong to two systems, one linguistic and one nonlinguistic; or, in Lamb's terms (1964), because lexemes are related by representation to both the morphemic and sememic strata. "While identity between the two planes is incomplete, it is a useful starting-point from which to describe the lack of isomorphism actually found" (Weinreich 1963:117). Lamb (1964:62–66) catalogs

the different possible discrepancies between units on different strata.

The many discussions within linguistics of the relevance of meaning to the analysis of phonology and grammar apply here also; even if form and meaning are in principle independent, or at least not insomorphic, and if (as some have maintained) an appeal to meaning is methodologically unsound in linguistic analysis, nevertheless the practice of linguistic field work has established that in order to get the job done within a reasonable time, on the basis of a corpus of practical size, it is essential to appeal to meaning in some manner—by the same or different test, the pair test, or some less explicit test where the linguist is analyzing his own native language (see Voorhoeve 961:41–42 on the semantic element in such tests). The converse applies to ethnoscientific analysis: although the two systems are not entirely congruent, the overlap is sufficient so that an "appeal to linguistic form" is a very useful field technique in working out a terminological system. In fact, the development of ethnoscience will certainly eventually assist strict linguistics in handling the "problem of meaning."

Efforts to discover nonterminological systems in such areas as behavior units (Barker 1963; Barker and Barker 1961; Barker and Wright 1955), folktales (Lévi-Strauss 1955; Leach 1961c), and values (Kluckhohn 1956, 1958) have not employed rigorous, replicable procedures for identifying units without the application of criteria foreign to the cultures analyzed; in this regard they differ little from many previous ethnographies. These studies attempt to discover classifications without first establishing the communication systems by which they are transmitted.

Nonlinguistic communication systems are also structured. Birdwhistell's work with kinesics (1952) and Hall's with proxemics (the structuring of space in interpersonal relations) (1963a, 1963b) are concerned with establishing the units of the codes, and to some extent with discovering categories of meanings, but both jump to rather anecdotal cross-cultural comparisons before working out the structure of any one system. The nonisomorphism of sememic and lower strata can be expected to hold here also. Other communication systems are also relevant, including paralanguage (voice qualities and nonlinguistic vocalizations; see Trager 1958). Material culture resembles language in some important respects: some artifacts—for example, clothing—serve as arbitrary symbols for meanings (i.e., noniconic signs [Goodenough 1957]) and occur in a limited number of discrete units whose combinability is restricted. Possibly complex phenomena of esthetics would yield to a similar approach. Studies in these areas are potentially of much importance for ethnography, and it seems wise not to restrict the meaning of ethnoscience to the study of *terminological* systems.

4. PARADIGMS AND COMPONENTIAL ANALYSIS

A key concept in ethnoscience is that of the contrast set. This is a class of mutually exclusive segregates which occur in the same culturally relevant environment (setting, context, substitution frame, surroundings, situation, etc.). These segregates "share exclusively at least one defining feature"—i.e., that which characterizes the environment in which they occur (Conklin 1962a:124; cf. Frake 1962:78–79). The domain of the set is the total range of meanings of its segregates.

The notion of contrast is relative to the environment within which it occurs. Thus the mutual exclusion in English between 'ant' and 'ship' (Conklin 1962a:127) or between 'hamburger' and 'rainbow' (Frake 1962:79) is not contrast in this sense, because the environment which they share is not culturally revelant. As Frake (1962:79) puts it, "In writing rules for classifying hamburgers I must say something about hot dogs, whereas I can ignore rainbows. Two categories contrast only when the difference between them is significant for defining their use. The segregates 'hamburger' and 'rainbow,' even though they have no members in common, do not function as distinctive alternates in any uncontrived classifying context." Although 'ant,' 'ship,' 'hamburger,' and 'rainbow' are all 'things,' the sub-sets of 'things' to which they belong are so far removed from each other that these four segregates themselves are never distinctive alternates. Any culturally significant partitioning of 'things' would involve contrasts between segregates on a much higher level. Lower level environments are of primary importance—in this case, for example, the environment in which such segregates as 'hamburger,' 'hotdog,' and 'cheeseburger' contrast, and the environments in which such adjacent segregates as 'sandwich,' 'pie,' and 'something to eat' occur (Frake 1962:78–82).

One may conceive of a contrast set containing only one segregate; if, as seems likely, there are no complete synonyms, then every segregate does occur in an environment which no other segregate shares. But "contrast" implies that the set contain at least two segregates, and the term is normally understood in this way. Since these minimal two contrast in the same environment, each must have some unique feature of meaning.

A paradigm is a set of segregates which can be partitioned by features of meaning, i.e., a set some members of which share features not shared by other segregates in the same set (Chafe 1962; Conklin 1962a:132; Goodenough 1956a:197, 202; Lounsbury 1960:127–28, 1962). A set of only two segregates can be considered a paradigm, but normally the term is applied to sets of three or more segregates, so that at least some of the sub-sets consist of two or more segregates sharing some feature of meaning.

It is important to note that while all contrast sets are paradigmatic, not all paradigmatic sets are *complete* contrast sets. A paradigmatic set may not be equivalent to its containing contrast set: it is possible to analyze paradigmatically a collection of items which do not *exclusively* share any feature, which do not exhaust the membership of a class occurring in a single environment (Conklin 1964). Thus Burling (1963a) has made a paradigmatic analysis of a set of "core kinship terms" which however do not form a complete contrast set—there is no culturally relevant environment which differentiates these terms from the other Garo kinship terms. A parallel example from phonology (where a paradigm involves phonetic rather than semantic features) is Chafe's (1962:338–39) paradigm of English consonant phonemes, which excludes some phonemes (*l, r,* perhaps also *y, w, h*) which are included in the relevant contrast set.

This difference between a paradigm and a contrast set is not always recognized in ethnoscientific work. Yet if the analysis is required to reflect the cognitive system of the bearers of the culture, before attempting a paradigmatic analysis one should show that one is dealing with a complete contrast set, that there is a culturally relevant environment in which all and only the segregates in the set occur. This is the problem of definition of domains seen from a somewhat different angle.

A componential analysis is an analysis of a paradigm in terms of the defining features, the "dimensions of contrast" or "criterial attributes" of the segregates in the set. The aim is to discover the "rule for distinguishing newly encountered specimens of [a] category from contrasting alternatives" (Frake 1962:83). The procedure is to search for the minimum features of meaning which differentiate segregates in the set. Each feature has two or more contrasting values, termed "components." Each segregate is then defined in terms of the presence or irrelevance of each component; i.e., a bundle of components defines the segregate. It is normally assumed that the number of componential dimensions will be smaller than the number of segregates they define. The paradigm may then be viewed as a multidimensional structure, in which the categories are placed according to the componential dimensions. (Useful references on componential analysis include Conklin 1962a, 1964; Frake 1962; Wallace 1962; Lounsbury 1956, 1962; Goodenough 1956a; Sebeok 1946; Chafe 1962. Lamb's [1964] sememes are similar to, if not identical with, the semantic components of these authors.)

There are two points of view regarding such componential analyses (Burling 1964). According to one of them, the componential analysis should reflect the classificatory principles utilized by the bearers of the culture, the components should be "cognitively salient;" such an approach has been labeled an aim for "psychological reality" (Wallace and Atkins 1960:64). However, this is a difficult requirement: such features are often not consciously formulated, and furthermore different bearers of the same culture may utilize different features and yet share the same categories and communicate perfectly (Wallace 1962). The other position is what Wallace and Atkins (1960:64) refer to as an aim for "structural reality," and what Lounsbury (1964) calls a "formal account." This position drops at this point the requirement that an ethnoscientific analysis should reflect the cognitive world of the bearers of the culture being analyzed. Having discovered the culturally significant sets and their included units, say these workers, we now try to determine the most economical componential analysis which will define (or "generate") their paradigmatic relationship—we are concerned only with predictability, economy, and inclusiveness, not any longer with cognitive saliency. Others take an intermediate position, and allow the use of hints from the culture in deciding between variant componential solutions which are equally or nearly equally economical—for there will often

(if not always) be such variants, and furthermore the criterion of economy (simplicity, parsimony) is not an easy one to define and apply (see Wells 1963:42 on this last point). Romney and D'Andrade (1964) discuss this problem, and illustrate some testing procedures for determining the cognitive saliency of alternate componential analyses of the same set of terms. Cancian (1963) has illustrated another method, which may be used to evaluate a componential analysis of a multi-position classification. If it is possible to determine the position in this classification of some items whose exact position is not known to all informants familiar with the classification, the correctness of the components used in setting up the classification can be tested by means of the magnitude of informants' errors in placing items unknown to them. If errors are extreme, the classification is shown to be erroneously understood by the ethnographer. "When an informant makes an error that results from lack of precise information, he is most likely to approximate the truth in terms that are meaningful to him" (Cancian 1963:1073).

Weinreich (1963:148–49) points out that componential analysis is more appropriate in some domains than in others. In a given culture, some domains will be more highly patterned; in these, "distinguishing components recur in numerous sets of signs, [whereas] the bulk of the vocabulary is of course more loosely structured and is full of components unique to single pairs, or small numbers of pairs," of segregates. While componential analysis is still possible in these latter "non-terminologized fields," Weinreich suggests that the cognitive saliency of components will be greater in the more structured domains and the validity of the componential analysis can be more readily checked by informants' reactions in these domains.

It is important to note that not every componential analysis is ethnoscientific. Semantic and ethnoscientific studies have adapted the method from its use in another area, phonology (e.g. Harris 1944). When semantic componential analysis is applied to paradigms which are not complete contrast sets, the results are not strictly ethnoscientific. Furthermore, the method essentially amounts to focusing on the differentiating features of a classification rather than on its categories or pigeonholes. Hence any classification is amenable to analysis resembling a componential one, and the technique is very useful for extending and elaborating purely etic typologies having nothing to do with ethnoscience. Thus, for example, Pike (1943) was able to improve greatly on existing compendia of articulatory phonetics by attending to the distinctive features of previous phonetic typologies, and extending and recombining them to to produce new phonetic types and a more logical classification. Similarly, Balfet (1952) produced the best available typology of basketry techniques by abstracting the components of previous classifications and re-arranging them to produce logical grids with many new classificatory slots, some of them as yet unknown in actual specimens even though fully possible. Malkiel (1962) describes a typology of dictionaries which explicitly borrows from the method of componential analysis.

5. TAXONOMIES

Different segregates within a folk classification may be related to each other in various ways: as part to whole, as sequential or developmental stage to stage, as different grades of intensity, etc. (Conklin 1962a:129, 1962b; Frake 1964). The kind of relationship between segregates which has so far received the most attention is that of inclusion; segregates related in this way form a taxonomy—a folk taxonomy in the case of folk classifications. In a taxonomy, there is a series of hierarchical levels, with each segregate at one level included in (only) one segregate at the next higher level. It is sometimes possible to analyze componentially a contrast set which forms one level of a folk taxonomy, but it is impossible to analyze in this way the whole taxonomy, even though the boundaries of the whole must define a domain: a single contrast set is limited to one taxonomic level (Conklin 1962a:128, 1964; Frake 1962).

A single folk classification may contain sets of segregates interrelated in different ways. From one point of view, any folk classification is a taxonomy since the domain or environment of the whole classification may be taken to define the most inclusive taxonomic level. But if the segregates within such a classification are not further related by inclusion, the taxonomy has only two levels and is relatively uninteresting as such; what is then more interesting is the kind of nontaxonomic relationship between the lower level segregates. A folk taxonomy of more than two levels, interesting as such, may also contain within it segregates which are interrelated in some nontaxonomic way (e.g., as

developmental stages) which together form a domain which itself is placed within a taxonomic series.

Some attention has been devoted to folk taxonomies, particularly in ethnobotany, and the prospects are good for comparisons of folk taxonomic principles intra- and interculturally, but much of the methodology still requires attention. Further discussion will be found in Conklin's recent (1962a) excellent general treatment of folk taxonomies.

6. DISCOVERY PROCEDURES

Since the ethnoscientific method aims at discovering culturally relevant discriminations and categorizations, it is essential that the discovery procedures themselves be relevant to the culture under investigation. While arbitrary stimuli— i.e., stimuli foreign to the culture—may yield nonrandom responses, the patterning involved derives from the cognitive system of the bearers of the culture, and the principles of this system are not likely to be made clear by answers to the wrong questions. Regularities will appear if one measures continental European manufactured goods with an American or British yardstick, but measuring with a meter stick will much more readily reveal the principles of the system relevant in European culture.

If an ethnography is to reflect the cognitive system of the bearers of a culture, the validity of the description depends on the discovery procedures. Hypotheses must be checked in the field situation, and revised if they turn out not to fit the field data. Thus it is impossible to make a strictly ethnoscientific analysis of data previously collected, by oneself or by someone else, according to different procedures. Any componential or similar analysis made of such old data must be treated as an inadequately checked hypothesis. Structural re-statements of even the best old field data may prove impossible. Lévi-Strauss illustrates some difficulties which

result from our ignorance of the observations (real or imaginary), facts, or principles which inspire the [folk] classifications. The Tlingit Indians say that the wood worm is "clever and neat," and that the land-otter "hates the smell of human excretion." The Hopi believe that owls exert a favorable influence on peach trees. If these attributes were taken into account in placing these animals in a [folk] classification of beings and objects, one could search indefinitely for the key, were not these minute but precious indications furnished by chance (Lévi-Strauss 1962b: 81; my translation).

Criterial attributes must be investigated in the field.

The general principle here is widely recognized, but only very recently has attention been devoted to making explicit the discovery procedures involved. Discussion and exemplification so far have concentrated on the use of questions in the native language and *chosen from the customary repertory* of the culture being studied. Frake's explication of interlinked topics and responses of queries in Subanun is an excellent example. His general suggestions on distinguishing questions which are appropriate to particular topics from those which are inappropriate (1964:143–44) should be particularly noted. Sarles (1963) describes a related procedure, in this case applied to Tzotzil, for identifying questions and their responses in conversational texts, determining acceptable permutations of the questions, and manipulating these to discover classes of appropriate responses. Metzger and Williams, in a series of papers as yet only partly published, have emphasized the discovery, selection, and use of question "frames" appropriate for eliciting specific folk classifications, particularly among the Tzeltal and Ladinos of Chiapas (Metzger 1963; Metzger and Williams 1962a, 1962b, 1962c, 1963a, 1963b). These papers are important particularly in that the frames utilized are explicitly stated, as a means of ensuring replicability and demonstrating the reliability of the analyses. Conklin (1964) has suggested some improvements in the genealogical method applicable to field studies of kinship systems, including the use of question frames, the recording of conversations in native settings, and the use of "ethnomodels" or native metaphors and diagrams of classifications (including diagrams volunteered by informants to aid in explaining to the ethnographer and influenced by observation of the ethnographer's charting attempts).

The emphasis on the classes of responses elicited by appropriate questions is beginning to show the expectable extreme complexity of the cognitive map of any culture, with multitudinous interlocking and overlapping contrast sets. Even so, these papers concentrate on the discovery of categories and their significant environments; as yet insufficient attention has been devoted to the development of reliable techniques for elucidating the further underlying complexities in cognitively salient semantic components.

I have already mentioned the relevance of ethnoscientific methods to material culture, where the possibility of pointing to and manipulating concrete objects may partially replace the use of question frames and the reliance on terminological systems in eliciting significant categories and contrasts. Another area where similar comparison of concrete cultural manifestations may be possible is music. Recent published discussions by ethnomusicologists of their problems in developing appropriate notation systems imply, at least to a nonspecialist, that the etics in this field have developed to the point where the application of ethnoscientific methods would resolve many difficulties and lead to a true *ethno*musicology (see Bright 1963:28–31).

EXAMPLES

Despite considerable discussion of ethnoscience in recent years, there have been relatively few applications of the methods in the only context in which they matter: intensive field work. This section provides an annotated bibliography of most but not all of the published or nearly published ethnographic reports which qualify as ethnoscience, insofar as I am aware of them. I comment also on some publications which will not so qualify, but which are of interest in this connection because of similarities or contrasts in method or theory.

1. PRONOMINAL AND CASE PARADIGMS

Analysis in terms of semantic components was first applied to paradigms of affixes, particularly to sets where the components are at least sometimes overt, i.e., components "with separate phonemic identities" (Lounsbury 1956: 161–62; in Lamb's [1964] terms, where there is simple representation between the sememic, lexemic, and morphemic strata). In these instances, the contrast set is defined morphologically, in terms of its linguistic environment. The first development of the methods is due to Roman Jakobson, who applied them in an analysis of the semantic components of the Russian case system (Jakobson 1936). This was followed by Trubetzkoy's (1937) componential analysis of the Slovak case system (with some comparison of Slavic case systems on the same basis), and by Sebeok's (1946) analysis of the Finnish and Hungarian case systems and comparison of the structural principles of the two.

Lotz (1949) followed with an analysis of the Hungarian pronominal suffixes, which included a diagram exhibiting the suffixes in a structure whose dimensions consist of semantic oppositions. Wonderly, pointing out (in effect) that Sebeok's components are much less overt than Lotz's, analyzed the pronominal suffixes of two dialects of Quechua in terms of semantic components which are covert in that each morpheme is associated with two components, but where the distributional classes of the morphemes are associated with the components on a one-to-one basis (Wonderly 1952). In the use of distribution to validate the semantic components, Wonderly's treatment resembles Harris' (1948) analysis of the Hebrew pronominal paradigm—but Harris identified the components solely in terms of the shared linguistic environments of the morphemes, and did not attempt to identify shared features of meaning (Lounsbury 1956:162). D. Thomas (1955) gives a componential analysis of Ilocano pronouns which utilizes both semantic and distributional criteria. A similar analysis for another Philippine language, Maranao, is briefly outlined by McKaughan (1959); but according to his analysis the forms are not affixes, yet he gives no evidence that the paradigm is a complete contrast set. A very similar componential structure is indicated for the pronominals of a third Philippine language, Hanunóo, where the morphemes are also not affixes; but Conklin (1962:134–36) is careful to demonstrate that the paradigm is a complete contrast set. He includes a dimensional diagram of the type introduced by Lotz (1949), as does Berlin (1963) in his componential analysis of Tzeltal pronominals (a more complex system than the Philippine ones), and Austerlitz (1959) in his componential analysis of Gilyak pronouns. In a footnote, Austerlitz (1959:104) notes the possibility of reducing the three pairs of oppositions of his analysis to two, by introducing a rule of order of application of the oppositions. The semantic components involved make clear the implications of an alternative application of forms glossed 'thou' and 'ye' in addressing a single person, and an alternative between 'he, she' and 'thou' in addressing one's spouse.

In a fascinating paper, Brown and Gilman (1960) have analyzed in detail a somewhat similar alternative in European languages (English, French, Italian, Spanish and German; Slobin [1963] finds the analysis to be applicable to Yiddish also). They describe the rules for selecting, now and in the past, between the two singular pronouns normally glossed 'familiar' and 'polite.' There turn out to be a whole series of correlates of choice between the two, which Brown and Gilman reduce to two basic semantic binary oppositions, power or status (superior-inferior) and solidarity or intimacy (solidary-nonsolidary), discussing their association with features of social structure, political ideology, and affective style. The relationship between these dimensions is complex enough so that it would be difficult to diagram, and further complexities are introduced by ongoing changes which the authors demonstrate both by historical data and by data on individual variation in present usage. In another paper, Brown and Ford (1961) show the relevance of the same dimensions to choices between a variety of forms of address in modern American English which are not grammatically obligatory, unlike the pronouns previously analyzed (the dimensions governing the selection of pronouns are here said to hold for 20 languages of Europe and India, and for Japanese). Brown's emphasis on social correlates and his detailed examination of the semantic dimensions in various behavioral contexts might well be combined with a more explicitly componential analysis and more careful delimitation of domain boundaries. Probably some of Brown's methods are adaptable to the problem of determining the cognitive saliency of semantic components in this and similar domains. Brown alludes to some interconnections between usages of kinship terms and other terms of address. An approach similar to his might elucidate some of the semantic dimensions of choice between alternative or "variant" kinship terms, and it would be particularly interesting to apply similar techniques to the study of the complex and often interrelated kinship, status, and personal address terminological systems of Southeast and Eastern Asia (see Koentjaraningrat 1960:107–14, for an example).

2. KINSHIP TERMINOLOGIES

Componential analysis was first applied to kinship terminologies in simultaneous and independent inventions by Ward H. Goodenough and Floyd G. Lounsbury in 1947–1949. In each case the breakthrough was the result of training by Murdock in the etics of kinship, plus thorough knowledge of descriptive linguistics (where componential analysis was then used in phonology), plus an acquaintance with the philosopher Charles W. Morris' work on the theory of signs. Both shared also some exposure to mathematics and learning theory (Lounsbury, in conversation, November, 1960). Goodenough published first, giving a methodological statement together with a componential analysis of the Trukese kinship terminology he had collected in the field (1951:103–10). In a pair of important papers appropriately published in a 1956 issue of *Language* dedicated to A. L. Kroeber, both authors set out careful theoretical and methodological treatments, Goodenough's illustrated by a revision of his Trukese analysis and Lounsbury's by a structural analysis of the Pawnee terminology collected by an Indian Agent in 1863 for Lewis Henry Morgan (Goodenough 1956a, Lounsbury 1956). Wallace and Atkins (1960) have analyzed and compared the methods of these two papers in some detail. An important difference not noted by Wallace and Atkins—although it is related to the problem of metaphors which they do discuss—is that Goodenough makes plain (more so in his earlier monograph [1951:103–107] than in his methodological paper [1956a]) that the paradigm he is analyzing is also a complete contrast set. He is able to do this because he was concerned while in the field with identifying the boundaries of the domain glossed 'kinship.' Lounsbury (1956), however, is not able to do this, since he is analyzing a set of terms collected long ago with unknown sampling procedures. He goes further, and explicitly excludes some of the terms listed by Morgan, making his selection on the basis of *a priori* criteria (1956:163).

Since these ground-breaking papers, a number of other kinship terminologies have been analyzed componentially, with variations in techniques of analysis in methods of presentation, and in the extent of discussion of methodological problems. Conklin's unpublished Ph.D. thesis (1954:80) included a brief componential analysis of Hanunóo consanguineal terms of reference, influenced by Goodenough's monograph (1951) and by knowledge of Lounsbury's Pawnee analysis prior to its publication. Romney and Epling (1958) gave a componential analysis of Kariera kinship terminology, pointing out

some of the behavioral correlates of the semantic features. Pospisil (1960) gave componential definitions for the Kapauku terminology, and followed this with a classification of the terms in an outline which has some of the characteristics of a key (cf. Conklin 1962b, 1964). Frake's treatment of Subanun kinship (1960: 58–63) emphasizes the nonarbitrary delimitaion of domains, the determination of complete contrast sets, the environmental features determining selection between alternative sets of terms, and the investigation of behavioral correlates of the kinship categories, as well as presenting a well-diagrammed componential analysis. Wallace and Atkins (1960) illustrate their theoretical discussion with a componential analysis of some American-English consanguineal terms of reference, admitting that for purposes of simplified illustration they use an arbitrarily delimited paradigmatic set.

Conant (1961) presented an interesting "componential comparison" of "Jarawa kin systems of reference and address," emphasizing eliciting procedures for maintaining the Jarawa distinctions between the two systems, pointing out that the system of address here involves "non-kin terms" ("which have meanings and usages not restricted to kinship") in the same contrast set with kin terms, and discussing problems of establishing the psychological reality of the componential analysis (including evaluation of disagreements between informants). One of his conclusions from the comparison is that the Jarawa address system has more behavioral correlates than the reference system. In contrast, Grimes and Grimes (1962) restrict their componential analysis of Huichol terminology to those terms of reference "that are amenable to simple structural statement" (1962:104). Yet within this arbitrary boundary, they are concerned with criteria of cultural relevance—for example, in setting up an unusual dimension of "distance from ego" because it accords well with some other characteristics of the social structure.

Epling (1961) published a detailed analysis of Njamal terminology, in which he assumed that his componential description is the psychologically real one. Burling (1962) challenged this assumption by presenting an alternative componential analysis of the same set of terms. He greatly simplified the componential formulae required, mainly be defining components specifically relevant to this system rather than following Epling (1961:155) in using only dimensions as defined by Kroeber (1909) plus one from Lounsbury (1956). Burling also discussed some of the problems in applying the criterion of economy in choosing between different componential analyses, and emphasized that this criterion, difficult as it is, is not the same as the criterion which demands cognitive saliency for a componential analysis. In a later paper using his own Garo data and influenced by recent developments in linguistics, Burling (1963a) modified the usual procedures of componential analysis by selecting a set of "core terms" which are readily analyzable componentially, then using these terms "as building blocks to provide definitions for the remaining kinship terms used by the Garo," these latter being labelled "derived terms" (1963a:80). He disavowed any implication of psychological reality for this scheme. A third paper combines the two points, in an analysis of Burmese kinship terminology (Burling 1963b). Here he presents two full analyses of a set of referential terms, one of them componential in the usual sense, and the other using a method similar to the one he had previously applied to the Garo system. While Burling gives some evidence that certain features of the second analysis better reflect the Burmese cognitive system, he again disavows an interest in using this kind of criterion to choose between alternative analyses.

Lounsbury's recent work (1962, 1964) has concentrated on increasing the parsimony of componential analyses. The two papers cited deal with the Seneca consanguineal terminology (1962) and with some general techniques for simplifying analyses by the application of "generative rules" resembling those used by Burling but more elegantly stated and of more general application. As before, Lounsbury is concerned with improving the logic of the analytical method. He does point out possible sociological correlates, but he views "formal accounts" such as his, which operate with criteria of parsimony and sufficiency, as logically prior to "functional accounts" (Lounsbury 1964). The criterion of sufficiency requires that the analysis correctly account for all the empirial data in hand; but since the data he uses derive from fieldwork not oriented towards his problems (e.g., his Seneca data are largely from Lewis Henry Morgan) he cannot be certain that his paradigms represent complete contrast sets—thus the "root meaning" or common semantic feature defining the domain of a paradigm is that feature shared by all the forms of the set, but the additional phrase "and no others" which would define a complete contrast set is missing (Lounsbury 1962)—and the adequacy of his analytical models is tested by their ability to account for data which is at least secondary as compared to the primary field data against which ethnographic theories should be tested if they are to be adequate cultural descriptions. There can be little doubt, however, that Lounsbury's improvements in analytical method will be very valuable to ethnographers interested in gauging the cognitive saliency of structural analyses: procedures for developing additional alternative models should help in discovering the one (or more than one) which is the most "real" for a given culture, and it is not difficult to conceive of cognitive saliency for generative rules such as Lounsbury's. Furthermore, his models are already enabling him to devise ethnological typologies much more powerful than previous ones for cross-cultural comparisons of kinship terminologies and their correlates.

Romney and D'Andrade (1964) have again demonstrated the possibility of alternative componential analyses of the same paradigm—in this case, the restricted set of American-English terms previously analyzed by Wallace and Atkins (1960). The results of their testing of informants to determine the cognitive saliency of the variant analyses imply that it might be useful to use some such tests as an aid in the construction of models, rather than using tests to compare formal models previously devised.

Conklin (1964) emphasizes the desirability of combining "in actual field situations, recording activities, analytic operations, and evaluative procedures." The evaluative procedures on which he concentrates involve "the discovery of locally recognized contrasts, within recurrent ethnogenealogical settings." This paper is important for its many suggestions for methodological improvement, particularly in the development of more rigorous field techniques. It is illustrated by a detailed presentation of the Hanunóo kinship system as analyzed by these methods.

An advance in a new direction has been made by Friedrich (1963), who uses componential analyses to reconstruct the evolution of the Russian kinship system from the Proto-Indo-European period to the present, giving particularly detailed analyses of the Old Russian and Modern Russian terminologies. He demonstrates the advantages of such an approach over previous methods for reconstructing the history of kinship terminologies.

3. COLOR TERMINOLOGIES

Useful contrasts with the problems of ethno-scientific analysis of kinship are provided by recent work on color terminologies. Some such domain is probably universal, but it is very clear here that domain boundaries vary from culture to culture. Conklin's analysis of Hanunóo color terminology (1955) provides a good starting point. Several features of this overly brief account are too often overlooked: (1) The culturally relevant domain, for which Hanunóo lacks a covering lexeme, is *not* equivalent to that labelled "color" in English, since it involves semantic dimensions additional to those of hue, saturation, and brightness which delimit the domain in English; (2) This being the case, the basic structure of the terminology system would not have been discovered had the ethnographer restricted his investigation to the use of artificial stimuli such as color chips; (3) Discovery of the taxonomic nature of the system required observation of Hanunóo behavior in contrastive situations normal to them; (4) The "two levels" of contrast described for this system are relevant to it, not proposed as a cultural universal, and even the Hanunóo second, more specific, level (not here analyzed) is said to include several sublevels. The first two points particularly have not been attended to in other studies—including those which cite this paper as a model. Eliciting procedures such as those recommended by Ray (1952, 1953) and those used by Lenneberg and Roberts (1956), Landar, Ervin, and Horowitz (1960), and Goodman (1963) will not reveal such criterial attributes as moisture, surface texture, etc., as may exist (cf. Newman's remarks quoted by Lenneberg and Roberts 1956:23), nor will they make evident the nature of different co-existing systems which may occur (e.g., special color terminologies for horses in Navaho [Landar, Ervin, and Horowitz 1960:371 n. 12] and Papago [O'Neale and Dolores 1943], or for cattle in Nuer [Evans-Pritchard 1940:41–45]). Nevertheless, work to date provides nice illustrations of the cultural relativity of semantic distinctions. Taking only the spectral dimension of hue, the most central feature for cross-cultural equating of 'color' domains, one could now add Hanunóo (Conklin 1955), Navaho (Landar,-Ervin, and Horowitz 1960), Malayalam (Goodman 1963), and perhaps Zuni (Lenneberg and Roberts 1956) to the chart Gleason (1955:4 and 1961:4) gives comparing the very different placement and number of basic categorizations made by English, Shona, and Bassa.

Probably color terminologies are everywhere taxonomies of at least three levels. The relation of inclusion which defines a taxonomy is well illustrated by the specific studies of Hanunóo, Navaho, and Malayalam. All have a domain 'color' (sometimes lacking a lexeme) at the most inclusive level, with a small number of basic or primary terms at "Level I," and with a great number of more specific terms, all included under one or another of the basic terms, at "Level II" (probably usually with further levels below this). However, the Zuni research did not investigate this point but evidently assumed that the artificial testing situation itself would elicit terms on the same taxonomic level; deductions as to probable primary terms in Zuni can be made from the data provided as to which terms were most frequently used, but neglect of levels of contrast certainly accounts for some of the variability between subjects in the Zuni experiments.

Conklin (1955) gives a componential analysis of the four Level I Hanunóo terms; the other authors are prevented from making such analyses by their concentration of contrasts along the dimension of hue. The Navaho study gives more detail than the others on more specific Level II color terminology and mentions several dimensions on this level, but does not analyze them componentially One step which should now be taken is to investigate levels below the primary level in a folk taxonomy of color; it is evident that this will be a considerably more difficult task than the analysis of Level I terms.

The research of Lenneberg and others (Lenneberg 1961; Landar, Ervin, and Horowitz, 1960; and references in both) on "color codability" has shown interesting variation between speakers of the same and of different languages in the extent of agreement on the application of terms to specific colors, on the width of overlap of terms measured against scaled stimuli, and on the relationship between the folk terminology and abilities to recognize and discriminate between colors. The domain would seem to be particularly useful for such tests of the effects of folk classification—culture—on behavior, because different areas of the same taxonomy vary in the extent to which individuals agree on categorization, and vary in the discreteness and degree of criteriality of semantic features, and because at least some of the distinguishing features are relatively easy to codify and display in testing materials.

4. OTHER DOMAINS

It is instructive to compare what has been accomplished and what can be envisaged in the analysis of color terminologies with the possibilities in the domain of smell and taste. In these areas English has a relatively small and weakly terminologized vocabulary, and, particularly in comparison to color, the etics involved are very poorly known. Thus Aschmann (1946) lists a number of Totonac stems in a domain which may reasonably be glossed 'smell,' in the form of a taxonomy with eight primary categories each labelled with a basic root, with a quite vague characterization of the meaning of each of these eight roots. Each class is in turn subdivided by terms for more specific 'smells,' but the lack of relevant etics forces Aschmann to define each more specific term merely by listing objects characterized by that 'smell.' Each term on this lower level consists of the root labelling the higher class, plus an affix; these affixes recur with the different roots in the set, but the lack of etics prohibits the recognition of any features of meaning which may be associated with the affixes. It would be possible to determine, with informants, whether Aschmann's analysis represents a true folk taxonomy and whether this has more than three levels, but the lack of appropriate etics would make it exceedingly difficult if not impossible to identify critical attributes.

A domain in which smells and tastes in turn might be expected to serve frequently as criterial attributes is that of cuisine. Lévi-Strauss' brief suggestion for the analysis of "gustèmes" (1958:99–100) influenced L.-V. Thomas (1960) in description of the Diola cuisine. But this first attempt of any length must be said to have failed. Thomas listed and described the principal Diola recipes, but grouped them according to an arbitrary imposed scheme. He then took up the binary oppositions suggested by Lévi-Strauss, plus a few of his own, and applied them as *a priori* descriptive devices to the whole cuisine—without any effort to account exhaustively for the corpus he had just presented, and without any attempt to discover any Diola classifications of foods or recipes other than that implicitly recognized by his (incomplete) mention of Diola names for the recipes described. The oppositions were not even related to the distinctions between individual recipes. As Thomas remarks, it is surprising that more attention has not been devoted to cuisines by ethnographers. The domain should yield readily to an ethnoscientific approach.

Ethnobiology is frequently cited in illustration of ethnoscientific methods, particularly the study of folk taxonomies. A great deal of work in this field is partially relevant, in that it has frequently been realized (although also too often ignored) that the species and genus categorizations of other cultures normally do not coincide with those of Western science. A good example is Bulmer's (1957) discussion of bird naming practices among the Kyaka of the New Guinea highlands. He recognizes differences between the Kyaka and scientific classifications, but tends to assume, for example, that apparent synonymy represents ignorance or confusion without testing for levels of contrast or the effects of setting (he does note that names for hawks are more accurately—i.e., more consistently—applied to specimens seen in flight than to the rare specimens seen dead). Malkin's papers on the ethnozoology of the Seri, Sumu, and Cora (1956a, 1956b, 1958) are unusual in the attention devoted to the higher level taxa in the folk taxonomies, and to native knowledge of such subjects as the sex differentiation, development, and food habits of local animals. But Malkin's approach is to evaluate ethnozoological knowledge in terms of scientific zoology—to see whether the distinctions and characteristics known to scientific zoologists are locally recognized—rather than to investigate the nature and principles of the local systems of zoological knowledge. An early work which exhibits some of the same merits and faults, and is still worth attention for its detailed description of a system of ethnozoological knowledge, is that by Henderson and Harrington (1914).

Studies of any sort in ethnozoology are rare. There are, however, hundreds of publications relating to ethnobotany, which are emic or ethnoscientific in varying degrees (again, an unusually sophisticated early example must be credited to Harrington: Robbins, Harrington, and Freire-Marreco 1916). Despite the importance of the domain, the previous interest in the topic, the usual explicit taxonomic structure of the terminology, and the relative ease with which names may be tied to specimens and 'translated' into scientific terminology, there is only one full-scale ethnoscientific investigation of ethnobotany: that in Conklin's dissertation on Hanunóo (1954). Some of this material as well as ethnoscientific analyses of many related domains appears in his monograph on Hanunóo agriculture (1957). But the analysis of the Hanunóo classification of plants together with the corpus of terms on which it is based, and a great deal of material on the significance of plants in other areas of Hanunóo culture, remain unpublished. Some illustrations taken from this research are presented in a methodological context in Conklin's recent paper on folk taxonomies (1962a).

Frake's ethnoscientific treatment of Subanun disease diagnosis (1961) is important as a demonstration of the utility of the new methods in a quite different domain, but even more so for its emphasis on ethnographic analytic techniques. The system is a multilevel taxonomy. Among the points taken up by Frake are problems involved in the extensive occurrence of the same term at different levels of contrast, the relation between hierarchic levels and sets consisting of stage names, and methods for the discovery of the significant attributes of categories via verbal descriptions (possible because other methods for learning distinctive features here are difficult for both Subanun and ethnographer). To explain why some areas of the Subanun folk taxonomy of diseases are more elaborated than others, Frake advances the general hypothesis that "the greater the number of distinct social contexts in which information about a particular phenomenon must be communicated, the greater the number of different levels of contrast into which that phenomenon is categorized" (1961:121).

In another ethnoscientific study of medicine, Metzger and Williams (1963a) have investigated several aspects of the roles of Tzeltal curers. Again, emphasis is placed on discovery procedures—in this case particularly question frames. One interesting feature of the Tzeltal situation is that while there are clear criteria for placing curers into two classes, one more highly valued than the other, these are not in general groups with fixed and widely recognized membership; yet the choice of a curer is clearly very important to the patient, and Metzger and Williams succeed in indicating how such choices are made.

The research of Barker and his coworkers in the "psychological ecology" of the "behavior systems" of American and English children (Barker and Wright 1955; Barker and Barker 1961; Barker 1963) converges in several respects with ethnoscience (awareness of the convergence is apparently one-sided: Barker et al. do not cite ethnographers or linguists, nor relevant work in systematic biology). These authors emphasize their concern with the inherent segments of the normally occurring "stream of behavior," as opposed to the artificial "tesserae" into which behavior is segmented in more usual psychological investigations. They are interested in the discovery and analysis of natural "behavior units" and in the classification and interrelationships of such units, the identification and segmentation of their significant behavioral and nonbehavioral environments or "settings," and the relations between these environments and the behavior units. Their requirements for a "natural unit" are less stringent than those of ethnoscience: it is sufficient for them that the investigator does not himself influence the behavior he is observing, and that his segmentation is not entirely arbitrary. It is not required that the units be cognitively salient to the subjects. Thus, speaking of behavior settings, Barker and Barker (1961:467) write:

Because the list of settings which we have identified reads, for the most part, like a common-sense directory of a town's businesses, organization meetings, school classes, and so forth, it is sometimes overlooked that their identification involves highly technical operations and precise ratings of interdependence. . . . the precise quantitative criterion which we have used to establish the limits of behavior settings. . . . was selected so that the settings would fall within the usual range of laymen's discrimination. Nevertheless, the criteria for their identification are not lay criteria.

Reliability is measured by agreement between observers trained in the special analytical method, and while subjects are observed in detail, their own terminology for units of behavior or environment is not thoroughly investigated and their own perception of units is otherwise deemphasized. It is assumed that there is a "normal behavior perspective," i.e., a normal size for perceived units, which varies between subjects, rather than that the size of perceived units is determined by the environment (with variations in judgments on artificial questionnaires being more the result of varying interpretations of the directions given than of differences between individuals' behavior perspectives). The behavior units are not viewed as a separate system, a folk classification, which is actualized in the stream of behavior. Quite plainly, familiarity with the notions of contrast sets, and of levels of contrast, would be advantageous.

The "behavioral segments" investigated by Richard N. Adams in rural Guatemala (1962) superficially resemble Barker's "behavior units." But Adams' approach is explicitly ethnoscientific, he concentrates on local terminology as an indicator of "reported acts," and says his segments must be distinguished from the preceding and following phases of the continuum by formal attribute differences recognized by the actors. He is concerned also that the classification of these acts reflects the participants' cognition. Adams' early results indicate considerable success in identifying natural segments and their sequential arrangements; he recognizes the existence of unsolved problems in componential analysis (including that of the cognitive saliency of components).

O. E. Klapp (1962) has published an intriguing study of American "social types"—more than 800 "informal" roles which have explicit colloquial names. The domain makes good sense intuitively to an American. Klapp fully recognizes that his social types represent a terminological folk classification specific to American culture, and he approaches a nonrigorous analysis of the semantic components involved. But he provides no explicit description of the boundaries of the domain, his higher level taxa are artificial rather than folk taxa, and he is little concerned with the structural relations between social types. While this folk classification is certainly more "weakly terminologized" than such domains as kinship or "institutionalized offices" (both excluded by Klapp), it seems probable that a more ethnoscientific approach, with attention to complementary distribution and levels of contrast, would show it to be more highly structured and more hierarchical than does Klapp's description.

I stop at this point, in the hope that sufficient examples have been given to illustrate the new approach; however, I do not mean to imply that there are not a number of other studies which are clearly ethnoscientific, and many more which are partially so.

CONCLUSIONS

It is claimed that ethnoscience is a general ethnographic method. It may be useful to indicate a few of the classical interests of ethnology to which the relevance of the new methods is already quite obvious. The measurement and significance of individual variation among bearers of a culture is touched on in ethnoscientific contexts by Frake (1964), Romney and D'Andrade (1964), and Metzger (1963), among others. Lévi-Strauss (1962a, 1962b) has devoted much attention recently to symbolism seen as the equating and movement between folk classifications in different domains. It seems likely that there are great differences between cultures in the pervasiveness of symbolic or metaphoric equation between folk classifications; the Dogon (Hopkins 1963; Griaule and Dieterlen 1954; Palau Marti 1957:53ff.) and the Ancient Chinese (Bodde 1939) seem to exhibit such symbolism to a higher degree than is indicated by the usual ethnographic literature for most other cultures. Perhaps this is best viewed as one aspect of the interlinking of domains noted by Frake (1964:141); the manner in which these networks may be revealed by Frake's interlinking queries promises to clarify some of the meanings of the concept of function in cultural analysis. Barnett's view of the process of innovation makes particularly obvious the relevance of ethnoscience to the study of culture change. He sees innovation as essentially a process of cognitive reorganization, where innovators substitute an element from one folk classification into another, and this often by a sort of idiosyncratic metaphorical equating of different domains (Barnett 1961; see Wallace 1961:ch. 4 for a critical expansion of this idea.) Adams (1962), in a somewhat similar approach to culture change, is examining changes in the formal definitions and the frequency of occurrence of behavioral segments.

Ethnoscience raises the standards of reliability, validity, and exhaustiveness in ethnography. One result is that the ideal goal of a complete ethnography is farther removed from practical attainment. The full ethnoscientific description of a single culture would require many thousands of pages published after many years of intensive field work based on ethnographic methods more complete and more advanced than are now available. Hence emphases in ethnography will continue to be guided by ethnological, comparative, interests. Some domains will receive more attention than others.

In the present state of interest in cross-cultural comparisons, continued ethnoscientific emphasis on domains such as kinship is assured.

Existing generalizations require testing, and new theories require development, by the comparison of ethnographic statements which reveal the relevant structural principles. It is the classificatory principles discovered in ethnography which should be compared, not the occurrence of categories defined by arbitrary criteria whose relevance in the cultures described is unknown (cf. Goodenough 1956b:36–37).

But fuller development of ethnographic method and theory, and also intracultural comparisons to determine the "nature of culture" or the nature of cognition, the generality and interrelations of classificatory and other cognitive principles and processes within any one culture, both require that the New Ethnography be applied to a variety of domains, not just to areas of much current interest in ethnological theory.

Cross-cultural comparison of the logic of classification requires a great deal more knowledge of the varying logics of different domains in the same culture, as well as better ethnographies of different cultures.

It is probable that the number, kind, and "quality" of these logical axes [of relations between classificatory categories] are not the same in different cultures, and that the latter could be classed as richer or poorer according to the formal properties of the reference systems they appeal to in erecting their classificatory structures. However even cultures less endowed in this respect operate with logics of several dimensions, of which the inventorying, analysis, and interpretation require a richness of ethnographic and general data which is too often lacking (Lévi-Strauss 1962b: 85–86; my translation).

Ethnoscientific work so far has concentrated on the sorts of cognitive structure involved in selection classes: the interrelations of categories considered as sets of possible alternatives under varying environmental conditions. Little attention has yet been paid to the methods required for the investigation of the sort of structures involved in the rules of combination, the temporal or spatial ordering of co-occurring categories from different selection classes. To understand "how natives think" we need to know about both kinds of structure.

REFERENCES

ADAMS, RICHARD N.
> 1962   The formal analysis of behavioral segments: A progress report. MS. read at the 61st Annual Meeting of the American Anthropological Association, Chicago, November 16, 1962.

ASCHMANN, HERMAN
> 1946   Totonac categories of smell. Tlalocan 2(2):187–189. Azcapotzalco, D. F., México.

AUSTERLITZ, ROBERT
> 1959   Semantic components of pronoun systems: Gilyak. Word 15(1): 102–109.

BALFET, HELENE
> 1959   La Vannerie: Essai de classification. L'Anthropologie 56(3–4): 259–280.

BARKER, ROGER G., ed.
> 1963   The stream of behavior: Explorations of its structure & content. New York, Appleton-Century-Crofts.

BARKER, ROGER G. and LOUISE SHEDD BARKER
> 1961   Behavior units for the comparative study of cultures. In Studying Personality Cross-culturally, B. Kaplan, ed. New York, Row, Peterson, pp. 457–476.

BARKER, ROGER G. and HERBERT F. WRIGHT
> [n.d.; 1955] Midwest and its children: The psychological ecology of an American town. Evanston, Row, Peterson.

BARNETT, H. G.
> 1961   The innovative process. Kroeber Anthropological Society Papers 25:25–42. Berkeley.

BEFU, HARUMI and EDWARD NORBECK
1958 Japanese usages of terms of relationship. Southwestern Journal of Anthropology 14(1):66–86.

BERLIN, BRENT
1963 A possible paradigmatic structure for Tzeltal pronominals. Anthropological Linguistics 5(2):1–5.

BERLIN, BRENT and A. KIMBALL ROMNEY
1964 Descriptive semantics of Tzeltal numeral classifiers. [*In* Transcultural studies in cognition, American Anthropologist (June 1964), pp. 79–98.]

BIRDWHISTELL, RAY L.
[n.d.; preface dated 1952] Introduction to kinesics: An annotation system for analysis of body motion and gesture. Louisville, University of Louisville.

BOAS, FRANZ
1911 Introduction. *In* Handbook of North American Indian Languages, part 1, Boas, ed. Bureau of American Ethnology Bulletin 40.

BODDE, DIRK
1939 Types of Chinese categorical thinking. Journal of the American Oriental Society 59(2):200–219.

BRIGHT, WILLIAM
1963 Language and music: Areas for cooperation. Ethnomusicology 7(1):26–32.

BROWN, ROGER and MARGUERITE FORD
1961 Address in American English. Journal of Abnormal and Social Psychology 62(2):375–385.

BROWN, ROGER and ALBERT GILMAN
1960 The pronouns of power and solidarity. *In* Style in Language, T. A. Sebeok, ed. Cambridge, Massachusetts, Technology Press of M.I.T.; New York, John Wiley, pp. 253–276.

BULMER, RALPH
1957 A primitive ornithology. Australian Museum Magazine 12(7): 224–229.

BURLING, ROBBINS
1962 A structural restatement of Njamal kinship terminology. Man 62: 122–124 (art. 201).
1963a Garo kinship terms and the analysis of meaning. Ethnology 2(1): 70–85.
1963b Burmese kinship terminology. Manuscript.
1964 Cognition and componential analysis: God's truth or hocus pocus. American Anthropologist 66(1):20–28.

CANCIAN, FRANK
1963 Informant error and native prestige ranking in Zinacantan. American Anthropologist 65(5):1068–1075.

CHAFE, WALLACE L.
1962 Phonetics, semantics, and language. Language 38(4):335–344.

CHAO, YUEN REN
1956 Chinese terms of address. Language 32(1):217–241.

CONANT, FRANCIS P.
1961 Jarawa kin systems of reference and address; a componential comparison. Anthropological Linguistics 3(2):19–33.

CONKLIN, HAROLD C.
1951 Co-existing sets of relationship terms among the Tanay Tagalog. Unpublished MS., read at the 50th Annual Meeting of the American Anthropological Association, Chicago.

1954   The relation of Hanunóo culture to the plant world. Unpublished Ph.D. dissertation in anthropology, Yale University.

1955   Hanunóo color categories. Southwestern Journal of Anthropology 11(4):339–344.

1957   Hanunóo agriculture: A report on an integral system of shifting cultivation in the Philippines. FAO Forestry Development Paper No. 12. Rome, Food and Agriculture Organization of the United Nations.

1962a   Lexicographical treatment of folk taxonomies. *In* Problems in Lexicography, F. W. Householder and S. Saporta, eds., Indiana University Research Center in Anthropology, Folklore, and Linguistics Publication 21 [and] International Journal of American Linguistics 28 (2) part 4, pp. 119–141.

1962b   Comment [on Frake 1962]. *In* Anthropology and Human Behavior, T. Gladwin and W. C. Sturtevant, eds., Washington, Anthropological Society of Washington, pp. 86–91.

1964   Ethnogenealogical method. *In* Explorations in Cultural Anthropology: Essays Presented to George Peter Murdock, W. H. Goodenough, ed. New York, McGraw-Hill. (In press.)

DUNDES, ALAN

1962   From etic to emic units in the structural study of folk-tales. Journal of American Folklore 75(296):95–105.

DURKHEIM, EMILE and M. MAUSS

1903   De quelques formes primitives de classification; contribution à l'étude des représentations collectives. L'Année Sociologique 6: 1–72.

EPLING, P. J.

1961   A note on Njamal kin-term usage. Man 61:152–159 (art. 184).

EVANS-PRITCHARD, E. E.

1940   The Nuer: A description of the modes of livelihood and political institutions of a Nilotic people. Oxford, Clarendon Press.

FISCHER, J. L.

1958   The classification of residence in censuses. American Anthropologist 60(3):508–517.

FRAKE, CHARLES O.

1960   The Eastern Subanun of Mindanao. *In* Social Structure in Southeast Asia, G. P. Murdock, ed. Viking Fund Publications in Anthropology 29, pp. 51–64.

1961   The diagnosis of disease among the Subanun of Mindanao. American Anthropologist 63(1):113–132.

1962   The ethnographic study of cognitive systems. *In* Anthropology and Human Behavior, T. Gladwin and W. C. Sturtevant, eds. Washington, Anthropological Society of Washington, pp. 72–85, 91–93.

1964   Notes on queries in ethnography. [*In* Transcultural studies in cognition, American Anthropologist (June 1964), pp. 132–145.]

FRENCH, DAVID

1963   The relationship of anthropology to studies in perception and cognition. *In* Psychology: A Study of a Science, vol. 6, S. Koch, ed. New York, McGraw-Hill, pp. 388–428.

FRIEDRICH, PAUL

1963   An evolutionary sketch of Russian kinship. Proceedings of the 1962 Annual Spring Meeting of the American Ethnological Society, pp. 1–26.

GLEASON, H. A., JR.

1955, 1961 An introduction to descriptive linguistics. 1st ed., New York,

Henry Holt & Co., 1955; Rev. ed., New York, Holt, Rinehart & Winston, 1961.

GOODENOUGH, WARD H.

1951   Property, kin, and community on Truk. Yale University Publications in Anthropology 46.

1956a   Componential analysis and the study of meaning. Language 32(2): 195–216.

1956b   Residence rules. Southwestern Journal of Anthropology 12(1): 22–37.

1957   Cultural anthropology and linguistics. *In* Report of the 7th Annual Round Table Meeting on Linguistics and Language Study, Paul L. Garvin, ed. Monograph Series on Languages and Linguistics No. 9, Institute of Languages and Linguistics, Georgetown University, Washington, pp. 167–173. [Also published in Bulletin of the Philadelphia Anthropological Society 9(3):3–7, 1956, Philadelphia.]

GOODMAN, JOHN STUART

1963   Malayalam color categories. Anthropological Linguistics 5(5): 1–12.

GRIAULE, MARCEL and GERMAINE DIETERLEN

1954   The Dogon. *In* African Worlds: Studies in the Cosmological Ideas and Social Values of African Peoples, Daryll Forde, ed. London, Oxford University Press for the International African Institute, pp. 83–110.

GRIMES, JOSEPH E. and BARBARA F.

1962   Semantic distinctions in Huichol (Uto-Aztecan) kinship. American Anthropologist 64:104–114.

HALL, EDWARD T.

1963a   Field methodology in proxemics. Unpublished lecture before the Anthropological Society of Washington, March 19, 1963.

1963b   Proxemics: The study of man's spatial relations. *In* Man's Image in Medicine and Anthropology, Iago Galdston, ed. Monograph IV, Institute of Social and Historical Medicine, The New York Academy of Medicine, New York, International Universities Press, Inc., pp. 422–445.

HARRIS, ZELLIG S.

1944   Simultaneous components in phonology. Language 20(4):181–205.

1948   Componential analysis of a Hebrew paradigm. Language 24(1): 87–91. (Reprinted on pp. 272–274 of Readings in Linguistics, 2nd ed., M. Joos, ed. New York, American Council of Learned Societies, 1958.)

HENDERSON, JUNIUS and JOHN PEABODY HARRINGTON

1914   Ethnozoology of the Tewa Indians. Bureau of American Ethnology Bulletin 56.

HOPKINS, NICHOLAS S.

1963   Dogon classificatory systems. Anthropology Tomorrow 9(1):48–54. Chicago.

HYMES, DELL H.

1964   Directions in (ethno-) linguistic theory. [*In* Transcultural studies in cognition, American Anthropologist (June 1964), pp. 6–56.]

JAKOBSON, ROMAN

1936   Beitrag zur allgemeinen Kasuslehre; Gesamtbedeutungen der russischen Kasus. Travaux du Cercle Linguistique de Prague 6

(Études dédiées au Quatrième Congrès de Linguistes): 240–288. Prague.

KLAPP, ORRIN E.

1962 Heroes, villains, and fools: The changing American character. Englewood Cliffs, New Jersey, Prentice-Hall, Inc.

KLUCKHOHN, CLYDE K. M.

1953 Universal categories of culture. *In* Anthropology Today: An Encyclopedic Inventory, A. L. Kroeber, ed. Chicago, University of Chicago Press, pp. 507–523.

1956 Toward a comparison of value-emphases in different cultures. *In* The State of the Social Sciences, L. D. White, ed. Chicago, University of Chicago Press, pp. 116–132.

1958 The scientific study of values. *In* University of Toronto Installation Lectures: Three Lectures (by N. Frye, C. K. M. Kluckhohn, and V. B. Wigglesworth), Toronto, University of Toronto Press, pp. 26–54.

KOENTJARANINGRAT, R. M.

1960 The Javanese of south central Java. *In* Social Structure in Southeast Asia, G. P. Murdock, ed. Viking Fund Publications in Anthropology 29, pp. 88–115.

KROEBER, A. L.

1909 Classificatory systems of relationship. Journal of the Royal Anthropological Institute 39:77–84. [Reprinted on pp. 175–181 of Kroeber 1952.]

1952 The nature of culture. Chicago, University of Chicago Press.

LAMB, SYDNEY M.

1964 The sememic approach to structural semantics. [*In* Transcultural studies in cognition, American Anthropologist (June 1964), pp. 57–78.]

LANDAR, HERBERT J., SUSAN M. ERVIN, and ARNOLD E. HOROWITZ

1960 Navaho color categories. Language 36(3):368–382.

LEACH, E. R.

1961a Pul Eliya, a village in Ceylon. Cambridge, University Press.

1961b Rethinking anthropology. London School of Economics Monographs on Social Anthropology 22.

1961c Lévi-Strauss in the Garden of Eden: An examination of some recent developments in the analysis of myth. Transactions of the New York Academy of Sciences, ser. 2, 23 (4):386–396.

LENNEBERG, ERIC H.

1961 Color naming, color recognition, color discrimination: A reappraisal. Perceptual and Motor Skills 12(3):375–382. Missoula, Montana.

LENNEBERG, ERIC H. and JOHN M. ROBERTS

1956 The language of experience; a study in methodology. Indiana University Publications in Anthropology and Linguistics 13 [and] International Journal of American Linguistics Memoir 13.

LÉVI-STRAUSS, CLAUDE

1955 The structural study of myth. Journal of American Folklore 68(270):428–444.

1958 Anthropologie structurale. Paris, Plon.

1962a Le Totémisme aujourd'hui. Paris, Presses Universitaires de France.

1962b La Pensée sauvage. Paris, Plon.

LEWIS, LIONEL S.

1963 Kinship terminology for the American parent. American Anthropologist 65(3):649–652.

LOTZ, JOHN
1949 The semantic analysis of the nominal bases in Hungarian. Travaux du Cercle Linguistique de Copenhague 5:185–197. Copenhagen.

LOUNSBURY, FLOYD G.
1956 A semantic analysis of the Pawnee kinship usage. Language 32 (1):158–194.
1960 Similarity and contiguity relations in language and in culture. *In* Report on the 10th Annual Round Table Meeting on Linguistics and Language Studies, Richard S. Harrell, ed. Georgetown University Monograph Series on Languages and Linguistics, No. 12. Washington, pp. 123–128.
1962 The structural analysis of kinship semantics. *In* Preprints of Papers for the Ninth International Congress of Linguists, Cambridge, Massachusetts, M.I.T., pp. 583–588. [Full final version is in press in the Proceedings of the Congress, The Hague, Mouton & Co.]
1963 Linguistics and psychology. *In* Psychology: A Study of a Science, vol. 6, S. Koch, ed. New York, McGraw-Hill, pp. 552–582.
1964 A formal account of the Crow and Omaha-type kinship terminologies. *In* Explorations in Cultural Anthropology: Essays Presented to George Peter Murdock, W. H. Goodenough, ed. New York, McGraw-Hill. (In press.)

MALINOWSKI, BRONISLAW
1922 Argonauts of the Western Pacific. London, George Routledge & Sons, Ltd.

MALKIEL, YAKOV
1962 A typological classification of dictionaries on the basis of distinctive features. *In* Problems in Lexicography, Fred W. Householder and Sol Saporta, eds., Indiana University Research Center in Anthropology, Folklore, and Linguistics Publication 21 [and] International Journal of American Linguistics 28(2), part 4, pp. 3–24.

MALKIN, BORYS
1956a Seri ethnozoology: A preliminary report. Davidson Journal of Anthropology 2(1): 73–83. Seattle.
1956b Sumu ethnozoology: Herpetological knowledge. *Ibid.* 2(2):165–180.
1958 Cora ethnozoology, herpetological knowledge; a bioecological and cross cultural approach. Anthropological Quarterly 31(3):73–90. Washington.

McKAUGHAN, HOWARD P.
1959 Semantic components of pronoun system: Maranao. Word 15(1): 101–102.

METZGER, DUANE
1963 Some ethnographic procedures. MS. read at annual meeting of Southwestern Anthropological Association, Riverside, California, April 11–13.

METZGER, DUANE and GERALD WILLIAMS
1962a The patterns of primary personal reference in a Tzeltal community. Unpublished paper, Anthropology Research Projects, Preliminary Report, Stanford.
1962b Procedures and results in the study of native cognitive systems: Tzeltal firewood. Unpublished paper, Anthropology Research Projects, Preliminary Report, Stanford.

1962c Tenejapa medicine II: Sources of illness. Unpublished paper, Anthropology Research Projects, Preliminary Report, Stanford.

1963a Tenejapa medicine I: The curer. Southwestern Journal of Anthropology 19(2):216–34.

1963b A formal ethnographic analysis of Tenejapa Ladino weddings. American Anthropologist 65(5), pp. 1076–1101.

MURDOCK, GEORGE PETER

1945 The common denominator of cultures. *In* The Science of Man in the World Crisis, Ralph Linton, ed. New York, Columbia University Press, pp. 123–142.

1953 The processing of anthropological materials. *In* Anthropology Today, A. L. Kroeber, ed. Chicago, University of Chicago Press, pp. 476–487.

1957 World ethnographic sample. American Anthropologist 59:664–87.

NEEDHAM, RODNEY

1962 Notes on comparative method and prescriptive alliance. Bijdragen tot de Taal-Land-en Volkenkunde 118(1) (Anthropologica 3): 160–82. 's-Gravenhage.

NORBECK, EDWARD

1963 Lewis Henry Morgan and Japanese terms of relationship: Profit through error. Southwestern Journal of Anthropology 19(2):208–15.

NORTHROP, F. S. C.

1947 The logic of the sciences and the humanities. New York, Macmillan.

OHMAN, SUZANNE

1953 Theories of the "linguistic field." Word 9(2):123–34.

OLMSTED, DAVID L.

1950 Ethnolinguistics so far. Studies in Linguistics, Occasional Papers 2. Norman, Oklahoma.

O'NEALE, LILA M. and JUAN DOLORES

1943 Notes on Papago color designations. American Anthropologist 45(3):387–97.

PALAU MARTI, MONTSERRAT

1957 Les Dogon. [Ethnographic Survey of Africa, Western Africa, French Series, No. 4.] Paris, Presses Universitaires de France [for the] Institut International Africain.

PIKE, KENNETH L.

1943 Phonetics: A critical analysis of phonetic theory and a technic for the practical description of sounds. University of Michigan Publications, Language and Literature vol. 21.

1954 Emic and etic standpoints for the description of behavior. *In* his Language in Relation to a Unified Theory of the Structure of Human Behavior, Part I, Preliminary Edition. Glendale, Summer Institute of Linguistics, pp. 8–28.

POSPISIL, LEOPOLD

1960 The Kapauku Papuans and their kinship organization. Oceania 30(3):188–205.

RAY, VERNE F.

1952 Techniques and problems in the study of human color perception. Southwestern Journal of Anthropology 8(3):251–259.

1953 Human color perception and behavioral response. Transactions of the New York Academy of Sciences, ser. 2, 16(2):98–104.

ROBBINS, WILFRED WILLIAM, JOHN PEABODY HARRINGTON, and BARBARA FREIRE-MARRECO
    1916   Ethnobotany of the Tewa Indians. Bureau of American Ethnology
            Bulletin 55.

ROMNEY, A. KIMBALL and ROY GOODWIN D'ANDRADE
    1964   Cognitive aspects of English kin terms. [*In* Transcultural studies
            in cognition, American Anthropologist (June 1964), pp. 146–170.]

ROMNEY, A. KIMBALL and PHILIP J. EPLING
    1958   A simplified model of Kariera kinship. American Anthropologist
            60(1):59–74.

ROTH, WALTER E.
    1897   Ethnological studies among the north-west-central Queensland
            aborigines. Brisbane, Edmund Gregory; and London, Queens-
            land Agent-General's Office.

SARLES, HARVEY B.
    1963   The question-response system in language. Manuscript.

SCHNEIDER, DAVID M. and GEORGE C. HOMANS
    1955   Kinship terminology and the American kinship system. American
            Anthropologist 57(6):1194–1208.

SEBEOK, THOMAS A.
    1946   Finnish and Hungarian case systems: Their form and function.
            Acta Instituti Hungarici Universitatis Holmiensis, Series B, Lin-
            guistica 3. Stockholm.

SIMPSON, GEORGE GAYLORD
    1961   Principles of animal taxonomy. New York, Columbia University
            Press.

SLOBIN, DAN I.
    1963   Some aspects of the use of pronouns of address in Yiddish. Word
            19(2):193–202.

SPAULDING, ALBERT C.
    1963   The course of anthropological research as viewed from the Na-
            tional Science Foundation. Unpublished paper, read before the
            annual meeting of the Central States Anthropological Society,
            Detroit, Michigan, May 17.

SPUHLER, J. N.
    1963   *Review of* Mankind Evolving by Th. Dobzhansky. American An-
            thropologist 65(3):683–84.

SWARTZ, MARC J.
    1960   Situational determinants of kinship terminology. Southwestern
            Journal of Anthropology 16(4):393–97.

THOMAS, D.
    1955   Three analyses of the Ilocano pronoun system. Word 11(2):204–
            208.

THOMAS, L.-V.
    1960   Essai d'analyse structurale appliquée à la cuisine diola. Bulletin de
            l'Institut Français d'Afrique Noire, sér. B, 22(1–2):328–345.

TRAGER, GEORGE L.
    1958   Paralanguage: A first approximation. Studies in Linguistics 13
            (1–2):1–12. Buffalo.

TRUBETZKOY, N. S.
    1937   Gedanken über die slovakische Deklination. Sborník Matice Slo-
            venskej 15:39–47. [Not seen.]

TYLOR, EDWARD B.
    1881   Anthropology, an introduction to the study of man and civiliza-
            tion. New York, D. Appleton & Co.
VOEGELIN, CHARLES F. and FLORENCE M. VOEGELIN
    1957   Hopi domains; a lexical approach to the problem of selection.
            Indiana University Publications in Anthropology and Linguistics
            14 [and] International Journal of American Linguistics Memoir
            14.
VOORHOEVE, JAN
    1961   Linguistic experiments in syntactic analysis. *In* Creole Language
            Studies No. II, Proceedings of the Conference on Creole Language
            Studies . . . , R. B. Le Page, ed. London, Macmillan & Co., Ltd.,
            pp. 37–60.
WALLACE, ANTHONY F. C.
    1961   Culture and personality. Studies in Anthropology [1], New York,
            Random House.
    1962   Culture and cognition. Science 135(3501):351–57.
WALLACE, ANTHONY F. C. and JOHN ATKINS
    1960   The meaning of kinship terms. American Anthropologist 62(1):
            58–80.
WEINREICH, URIEL
    1963   On the semantic structure of language. *In* Universals of Language,
            Joseph H. Greenberg, ed. Cambridge, Massachusetts, The M.I.T.
            Press, pp. 114–171.
WELLS, RULON
    1963   Some neglected opportunities in descriptive linguistics. Anthro-
            pological Linguistics 5(1):38–49.
WONDERLY, WILLIAM L.
    1952   Semantic components in Kechua person morphemes. Language
            28(3):366–376.

47

THE PSYCHIC UNITY OF
HUMAN GROUPS

ANTHONY F. C. WALLACE

ONE of the most hoary assumptions of the uniformitarian viewpoint is the belief that a society will fall apart and its members scatter if they are not threaded like beads on a string of common motives. Numerous sources may be quoted which attest to the "common thread" belief. Thus Aberle, Cohen, Davis, Levy, and

Sutton, in an essay on the functional prerequisites of a human society, include as prerequisites a "shared, articulated set of goals." Fromm asserts that a nuclear character structure must be shared by "most members of the same culture" in order for the culture to continue; socialization must make people "want to act as they have to act." Durkheim's thesis that society depends for integration upon the "common sentiments" of its members is a similar view. Honigmann expresses the position in the plaintive assertion, "In any community, there must be some congruence between what different people do, believe, and feel, otherwise social order would be impossible." Margaret Mead has carried the argument to the point where cultural heterogeneity (as, for example, in contemporary United States) is conceived as almost *ipso facto* pathogenic:

. . . in a heterogeneous culture, individual life experiences differ so markedly from one another that almost every individual may find the existing cultural forms of expression inadequate to express his peculiar bent, and so be driven into more and more special forms of psychosomatic expression.

Social philosophers, less humane than the scientists quoted above, but equally disturbed by the problems of their societies, at times have found the "common motive" theme a congenial one, and have used the threat of social disintegration and individual degeneration to justify measures for the standardization of sentiments.

It is, however, impossible to demonstrate empirically that any social system is operated by individuals all driven by the same motives; indeed, the data of personality-and-culture studies, as well as clinical observation, show conclusively that a sharing of motives is not necessary to a sharing of institutions. But how about a sharing of cognitions? Is cognitive sharing a functional prerequisite of society? Here we enter the domain of the ethnographer who may not wish to tread the spongy ground of motive-analysis, but finds it both necessary and painless to make inferences from overt behavior about cognitive matters, such as the criteria for discrimination of kinsmen by terminological category, the substantive beliefs about the order of the cosmos, and the rules of procedure by which a shaman arrives at his differential diagnosis over a sick child. The minimum task of the ethnographer, of course, is simply to describe overt human behavior. "Description," in this minimum sense, is the formulation of a set of statements which will predict, for the ethnographer, what a class of subjects will do and say under various circumstances. Accordingly, any complete ethnographic statement will include a specification of both a configuration of circumstances and of a behavior sequence which a class of subjects produces (presumptively as a result of learning) whenever that configuration presents itself. Usually, the "circumstances" which elicit a certain behavior sequence on the part of one class of subjects will include the acts and utterances of another class of sub-

jects. Therefore, most ethnographic descriptions primarily concern repetitive patterns of reciprocal interaction in which the behaviors of each class of subjects are the circumstance for the behaviors of the other class of subjects.

It has been sometimes assumed that such systems of reciprocal interaction, in which different classes of subjects play specialized roles, as well as general norms describing constant act-and-circumstance relations for a single class of subjects, require not merely a set of cognitive maps, but a uniformity of cognitive maps among the participants for their continued successful operation. Thus, for example, in their previously quoted essay on the functional prerequisites of a human society, Aberle, Cohen, Davis, Levy, and Sutton postulate the necessity of "shared cognitive orientations," as well as "shared, articulated set of goals." Yet what few formal attempts have been made, by techniques such as componential analysis, to define the cognitive maps necessary to culturally correct behaviors have demonstrated unambiguously that it is often possible for the ethnographer to construct several different maps, each one of which will predict adequately the overt behavior of subjects. Let us therefore now ask the question directly: Is it necessary that all participants in a stable socio-cultural system have the same "map" of the system in order that they may select the correct overt behaviors under the various relevant circumstances?

MINIMAL SOCIO-CULTURAL SYSTEMS

A system may be defined as a set of variable entities (persons, objects, customs, atoms, or whatever) so related that, first, some variation in any one is followed by a predictable (i.e., non-random) variation in at least one other; second, that there is at least one sequence of variations which involves all of the entities.

Let us define the properties of the least complex system which an ethnographer might describe. Such a system must satisfy the following minimum requirements: first, that two parties, A, and B, the initiator and respondent, respectively, interact; second, that each completion of one sequence of interactions be followed, sooner or later, by a repetition of the same sequence. Using the convention that the acts of A are represented by the symbols a_i, and those of B by the symbols b_j, and that temporal relationship is represented by the symbol $\rightarrow$, to be read "is followed by," we assert that the simplest such system has the following structure:

$$a_1 \longleftrightarrow b_1$$

Since it is legitimate to regard the sense of the symbol $\rightarrow$, "is followed by," as a reasonable interpretation of the logical relationship of material implication (whenever x, then y), we may refer to the structure $a_1 \longleftrightarrow b_1$ as a *primary equivalence structure* (ES_1). In such a structure, whenever A does a_1, then (sooner or later) B does b_1; and whenever B does b_1, then (sooner or later) A does a_1.

Interaction structures of ES_1 type seem patently too simple to serve as useful models of the components of socio-cultural systems. The *secondary equivalent structure* (ES_2), however, looks more interesting:

Here, we may interpret acts a_1 and b_1 as instrumental acts and acts a_2 and b_2 as consummatory acts. The distinguishing features of ES_2 is that the consummatory act of each party is released by (but is not necessarily exclusively conditional upon) the instrumental act of the other. The equivalence between a_1 and b_1 describes the repetitive nature of the interaction. A whimsical but culturally valid example of a secondary equivalence structure is provided by a little ritual commonly found among the present inhabitants of the eastern coast of the United States (its wider distribution, in time and space, is unknown to me). When a child loses one of his baby teeth, he places the tooth under his pillow at night when he goes to bed; the parent, after the child has fallen asleep, then comes and replaces the tooth with a coin ($a_1 \rightarrow b_1$). The child, on awakening, takes the coin and buys candy with it ($b_1 \rightarrow a_1$). (Possibly, he thereby loosens another tooth, if it is caramel candy!) The parent, meanwhile, after replacing the tooth with a coin, delightedly reports the transaction to his spouse ($a_1 \rightarrow b_1 \rightarrow b_2$). And with the next tooth he sheds, the child, who has observed that tooth-placing is followed by candy and who likes candy, repeats a_1 and thus continues the process ($b_1 \rightarrow a_1$). This simple custom is

(for reasons which I shall mention later) not unlike the silent trade, so widely reported among primitive peoples. It may be diagrammed as follows:

More complex structures, involving two parties, can obviously be constructed out of the same relationships. Thus, a tertiary equivalence structure (ES_3) has the form:

$$
\begin{array}{ccc}
a_1 & \longleftrightarrow & b_1 \\
a_2 & \longleftrightarrow & b_2 \\
a_3 & & b_3
\end{array}
$$

Structures of quaternary and still higher degree evidently can be made by a simple process of extension. Structures involving more than two persons also can be designed, although they are more difficult to represent on a plane surface. In general, we can consider that the two-party secondary equivalence structure, which we have suggested as the smallest practical model of a stable socio-cultural system, is only one of a class of equivalence structures ^mES_n, where $m > 1$ denotes the number of parties to the system, and $n > 1$ denotes the number of levels of equivalences $a_i \longleftrightarrow b_j$ incorporated. It would be interesting to investigate in detail the logical properties of these systems and to speculate that, in principle, *any* socio-system, involving m parties in repetitive interaction, can be described by some equivalence structure of the class ^mES_n. However, these exercises would carry us beyond the purposes of this paper.

We now conclude that the simplest possible social-interaction system that an ethnographer might describe has the form of a two-person secondary equivalence structure. This structure is, however, a model of what the ethnographer perceives; it is the ethnographer's cognitive map. We wish now to discover with what combination of maps, α_i and β_j, held by the two parties A and B, the ethnographer's model is compatible.

MINIMAL COGNITIVE MAPS OF PARTICIPANTS IN SOCIO-CULTURAL SYSTEMS

At this point, we must make explicit two conventions which have been employed in the foregoing analysis. These are: first, that the ethnographer's map is valid ("true"); second, that the systems are "perfect," in the sense that there are no exceptions to the regularity of the relationships indicated by the symbols →. We know, of course, that in "real life" ethnographers make errors and that human behavior is not perfectly predictable. Although it would not invalidate the reasoning to introduce these qualifications (since a probabilistic logic would do just as well as the strict two-valued logic we are using), it would make the demonstrations more tedious. These conventions are now also applied to the cognitive maps maintained by the participants: we assume that each participant's map is valid ("true"); and we assume that the relationships are two-valued ("yes" or "no" rather than a probabilistic "maybe").

We have suggested already that a_1 and b_1 be regarded as "instrumental" acts and a_2 and b_2 as "consummatory." It is important to recognize that this classification is only a relative one; that is to say, a_1 is instrumental with respect to a_2, and b_1 with respect to b_2. In teleological terms, A does a_1 "in order to be able" to do a_2, and B does b_1 "in order to be able" to do b_2. But we do not actually need to invoke any panel of needs, drives, tensions, instincts, or whatever, the satisfaction of which makes an act ultimately consummatory, since we assume that the maps validly describe real events. It is therefore true by definition that neither A nor B will continue to participate in the system unless, first, each perceives that, *within the limits of the system,* his ability to perform his own consummatory act depends upon his partner performing his instrumental act; second, that when he performs his own instrumental act, its function is to elicit his partner's instrumental act; third, that he repeatedly performs his own instrumental act.

The simplest (but not the only) possible cognitive maps for A and B respectively, which satisfy the foregoing requirements, are the following:

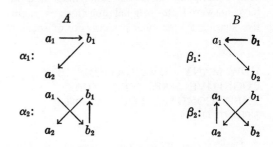

These maps are to be interpreted as follows:

α_1: A knows that whenever he does a_1, B will respond with b_1, and A will then perform a_2.

α_2: A knows that whenever he does a_1, B will respond with b_2 and then b_1, and A will then perform a_2.

β_1: B knows that whenever he does b_1, A will respond with a_1, and B will then perform b_2.

β_2: B knows that whenever he does b_1, A will respond with a_2 and then a_1, and B will then perform b_2.

Each possible combination of these cognitive maps will yield a structure which is identical with, or logically implies, $^2ES_2$. Thus:

$$\alpha_1 \wedge \beta_1 =$$

$$\alpha_1 \wedge \beta_2 =$$

$$\alpha_2 \wedge \beta_1 =$$

$$\alpha_2 \wedge \beta_2 =$$

We have now demonstrated that at least four cognitive maps, in addition to the ethnographer's, are compatible with the continued existence of a simple system of social interaction. The four maps of the participant parties can exist in four possible combinations, each of which sums to $^2ES_2$ or to a form which implies $^2ES_2$. Evidently, it is not *necessary* that both participants share the same map; and we have answered our original question: is cognitive sharing a functional prerequisite of society?

HOW MANY COMBINATIONS OF COGNITIVE MAPS WILL YIELD THE SECONDARY EQUIVALENCE STRUCTURE?

Even a casual inspection comparison of the ethnographer's model with the four participants' models will suggest that a number of unique cognitive maps are possible which are different from, but contain, either or both of the A structures, and/or either or both of the B structures. The basic model of $^2ES_2$ itself, for instance, contains both α_1 and β_1; $^2ES_2$ added to itself will yield $^2ES_2$; $^2ES_2$ added to α_1 will yield $^2ES_2$; $^2ES_2$ added to β_1 will yield $^2ES_2$, and so on. Let us therefore inquire, out of curiosity, just how many unique combinations of α-maps and β-maps there are where the sum equals, contains, or implies $^2ES_2$, with the proviso that each component α-map include either, or both, α_1 and α_2, and each component β-map include either, or both, β_1 and β_2. The number is well over a million. The number of unique α-maps is over a thousand and the number of unique β-maps is also over a thousand. Thus, it is apparent that even when one considers extremely simple systems, a very large number of different cognitive maps of such systems are, for all practical purposes, interchangeable as system components.

What are the implications of these considerations? Evidently cognitive sharing is not *necessary* for stable social interaction. The two parties to systems of form $^2ES_2$ do not need to know what the "motives" of their partners in the interchange are. Indeed, they need not even correctly know *who* their partners are. In the tooth exchange ritual alluded to earlier, the child at first believes that a good fairy, whom he never sees, takes the tooth, for motives unexplained, and leaves the coin. This relationship is not unlike the silent trade. Later, the child may know that the parents are responsible but does not "let on," from a benevolent wish not to spoil his parents' fantasies about *his* fantasies. One or the other or both of the parties may be able to perform his consummatory act *only* after the partner performs his instrumental act; or other circumstances may also permit it. But, the advocate of togetherness may argue,

whether or not it is necessary that *all* members of society share *all* cognitive maps, they must share at least *one*. Such an argument, however, is not convincing. No criteria known to the writer would specify what one map it is functionally necessary that all members of a given society should share. Recourse cannot be had to the empirical argument that all members of all societies are *known* to share at least one map, for the data to support such an argument do not exist. And merely demonstrating that some defined group of human individuals, or even all the members of some one society, share a particular map, is irrelevant to the discussion. (Such a society would have to be a peculiarly simple and at the same time clairvoyant one, anyway.) Two or more parties may indeed share a common cognitive map, but such a circumstance is, in a sense, wasteful, since at least two, and therefore all, of these maps must be larger than the minimally necessary ones. And only when each actor is cognizant of the other's "motive" (consummatory act), can the actors' cognitive maps be identical and still contribute to system maintenance.

It may appear to be a bleak prospect to consider that human beings characteristically engage in a kind of silent trade with all their fellow men, rarely or never actually achieving cognitive communality. Indeed, one may suspect that the social sciences have nourished the idea of cognitive sharing for so long, just because the world would may seem rather a lonely place if the wistful dream of mutual identification is abandoned. Still another anxiety may now arise: for an implication of our researches is that individuals can produce a socio-cultural system which is beyond their own comprehension. If, for instance, α_k is as complex a map as A can maintain, and β_l is as complex as B can maintain, their sum (*unless* they are identical) will be a structure *containing* $^2ES_2$, but in its totality *more* complex than one or both of them can grasp. If one of these parties be an anthropologist, who is attempting to construct a general ES which he will call "culture," then, alas, he may be a participant-observer in a socio-cultural system which is more complex than he can describe ethnographically! Even if he cannot describe the system fully, he must be able to construct a cognitive map which is more complex than that of any of his subject's.

But perhaps the most significant point to be made is a relatively practical one, growing out of concerns with the application of anthropological knowledge to psychiatric research. A principal problem for the research anthropologist, in a mental hospital setting, is to explain how a person comes to be extruded from his socio-cultural system. Is it because he is a "deviant," one whose cognitive maps are not shared by other members of the community? Or is it because he has been unable to maintain stable cognitive maps sufficiently complex for them to sum to an equivalence structure with those of his fellows? From the viewpoint of the organization of diversity, it would appear that the most generally adequate explanation is the latter: particularly in a large and complex society, equivalence structures normally will be the articulation of uniquely private cognitive worlds, anyway. The measure of individual survival will not be conformity, but complementarity.

IS COGNITIVE NON-SHARING A FUNCTIONAL PREREQUISITE OF SOCIETY?

Finally, we ask whether the fact that cognitive sharing is not a *necessary* condition of society does not mask an even more general point. Not only *can* societies contain subsystems, the cognitive maps of which are not uniform among participants; they *do,* in fact, invariably contain such systems. Ritual, for instance, is often differently conceptualized by viewers and performers; public entertainment similarly is variously perceived by professional and audience: the doctor (or shaman) and patient relationship demands a mutual misunderstanding. Even in class and political relationships, complementary roles (as, for instance, between the holders of "Great" and "Little" Traditions) are notoriously difficult to exchange. Administrative personnel and leaders generally must understand the system on a "higher" level of synthesis than their subordinates, a level which demands a different, because more abstract, cognitive map. Indeed, we now suggest that human societies may characteristically *require* the non-sharing of certain cognitive maps among participants in a variety of institutional arrangements. Many a social sub-system simply will not "work" if all participants share common knowledge of the system. It would seem therefore that cognitive *non*-uniformity may be a functional desideratum of society (although, by

the criteria we have used above, it is certainly not a formal prerequisite any more than is uniformity). For cognitive non-uniformity subserves two important functions: (1) it permits a more complex system to arise than most, or any, of its participants can comprehend; (2) it liberates the participants in a system from the heavy burden of knowing each other's motivations.

If socio-cultural organization is not necessarily dependent upon a community of motives or cognitions, then by what psychological mechanism is it achieved and maintained? This mechanism is evidently the perception of partial equivalence structures. By this is implied the recognition—as the result of learning—that the behavior of other people under various circumstances is predictable, irrespective of knowledge of their motivation, and thus is capable of being predictably related to one's own actions. Evidently, groups, as well as individuals, can integrate their behaviors into reliable systems by means of equivalence structures, without extensive motivational or cognitive sharing. The equivalence structure model should be congenial to that tradition in social anthropology which interests itself in the relations between organized groups. Thus, reciprocal interactions between the representatives of geographically separate groups as alien as American Indian tribes and colonial or state governments have proceeded for centuries, with only minimal sharing of motives or understanding, on a basis of carefully patterned equivalences. Similar observation might be made of the relations between castes, social classes, professional groups, kin groups, factions, parties, and so forth. In no case is it *necessary* that a basic personality or a basic cognitive framework be shared, but it is necessary that behaviors be mutually predictable and equivalent.

Thus, we may say that as any set of persons establish a system of equivalent behavioral expectancies, an organized relationship comes into existence. Such a system of equivalent mutual expectancies may be termed an *implicit contract,* in the general sense of the word "contract." In this sense, and not in the sense of any formal document, society is, as Rousseau intuited, built upon a set of continually changing social contracts which are possible only because human beings have cognitive equipment adequate to their maintenance and renewal. Culture can be conceived as a set of standardized models of such contractual relationships, in which the equivalent roles are specified and available for implementation to any two parties whose motives make their adoption promising. The relationship is based not on a sharing, but on a complementarity of cognitions and motives. Marital relationship, entry into an age grade, the giving of a feast—in all such contracts, the motives may be diverse, but the cognitive expectations are standardized. Thus, the relationship between the driver of a bus and the riders is a contractual one, involving specific and detailed mutual expectancies. The motives of drivers and riders may be as diverse as one wishes; the contract establishes the system. From this standpoint, then, it is *culture* which is shared (in the special sense of institutional contract) rather than personality, and culture may be conceived as an invention which makes possible the maximal organization of motivational diversity. This it is able to accomplish because of the human (not uniquely human, but pre-eminently so) cognitive capacity for the perception of systems of behavioral equivalence.

FALLACIES, FADS, AND SPECIALIZATIONS

The progress of research in culture-and-personality is, at times, hampered by the common use of fallacious metaphors and by faddish enthusiasms for particular jargons and techniques. But it is important to distinguish between fad and fallacy, on the one hand, and legitimate specialization, on the other.

Conspicuous examples of the fallacious metaphor are the frequently mishandled words "internalization," "impact," and "mold." Thus, it is sometimes said that personality *is* (ontologically) culture "internalized" in the individual; that culture change has an "impact" on the individual; that culture "molds" the individual. Such expressions, and theoretical formulations based on them, are meaningless in any literal sense. As Radcliffe-Brown once remarked, "To say of culture patterns that they act upon an individual . . . is as absurd as to hold a quadratic equation capable of committing a murder." As we observed in connection with systems analysis, culture and personality are constructs of different "logical type," in Russell's sense; that is to say, the concept of a culture is a set of propositions about some of the same propositions which are included within

the concept of one or more of the personalities within the society. Thus, to use transitive metaphors like "internalize," "impact," "mold," and so on, to describe the relation between culture and personality, is precisely comparable to claiming that a circle has an "impact on," or "molds," the points which constitute it, or that the points are "internalizations" (or "expressions," or "phrasings," or "transforms") of the equation describing the circle.

The obverse of the "internalization" fallacy is the "statistical fallacy," which offers an enumeration of the properties of individual persons as if it were a description of a social or cultural system, without any demonstration that a non-random relationship obtains among the dimensions considered. Such statistical "structures" are mere archival material unless a systematic relationship among the dimensions can be demonstrated.

Fads in culture-and-personality, as in other fields of endeavor, are sometimes difficult to distinguish from new specializations. Thus, to some, the projective techniques have been a fad, now happily passing; to others, they appear as legitimate, highly specialized tools which will be continuously refined and employed by a few individuals concerned with particular kinds of problems for a very long time. The fad for projective techniques saw them being used for a time uncritically, as novelties, by dozens of field workers, often in inappropriate situations. Now that the fad stage has worn off and sober reflection has begun, the projective techniques will be used by fewer but better-trained persons for the special tasks to which they are suited, or to which they may be adapted; and we may expect continuous improvement of the tools themselves and of their interpretation as this specialization continues.

A similar observation may be made with respect to a number of conceptual schemes and research procedures "borrowed" from other disciplines. Psychoanalysis, for instance, is a highly specialized branch of psychiatry, particularly successful in dealing with the character disorders and symptomatic neuroses of upper- and middle-class people who can afford and will accept protracted verbal treatment. Much of psychoanalytic theory has been, in one form or another, used by culture-and-personality workers. For a time, it was something of a fad to sprinkle psychoanalytic jargon over the pages of ethnographic reports, like the water of baptism, in order to make them read like personality descriptions. This faddish misuse of psychoanalytic theory, by both psychiatrists and anthropologists, is waning; what remains is a specialized body of concepts and research techniques that will continue to be used wherever profitable by properly trained men. Comparable remarks may be made about the utility of communication theory, reinforcement learning theory, the life history, and other special techniques and bodies of knowledge. Their incorporation into anthropological thought is regularly accompanied by inflated claims that they are universal theoretical or methodological solvents, and students flock to try them out. Enthusiasm wanes when they are recognized as being useful only in solving particular kinds of problems, and they assume the humbler but more enduring role of specializations.

48

THE ETHNOGRAPHIC STUDY OF COGNITIVE SYSTEMS

CHARLES O. FRAKE

WORDS FOR THINGS

A RELATIVELY simple task commonly performed by ethnographers is that of getting names for things. The ethnographer typically performs this task by pointing to or holding up the apparent constituent objects of an event he is describing, eliciting the native names for the objects, and then matching each native name with the investigator's own word for the object. The logic of the operation is: if the informant calls object X a *mbubu* and I call the object X a *rock,* then *mbubu* means *rock.* In this way are compiled the ordinary ethnobotanical monographs with their lists of matched native and scientific names for plant specimens. This operation probably also accounts for a good share of the native names parenthetically inserted in so many monograph texts: "Among the grasses (*sigbet*) whose grains (*bunga nen*) are used for beads (*bitekel*) none is more highly prized than Job's tears (*glias*)." Unless the reader is a comparative linguist of the languages concerned, he may well ask what interest these parenthetical insertions contain other than demonstrating that

the ethnographer has discharged a minimal obligation toward collecting linguistic data. This procedure for obtaining words for things, as well as the "so-what" response it so often evokes, assumes the objective indentifiability of discrete "things" apart form a particular culture. It construes the name-getting task as one of simply matching verbal labels for "things" in two languages. Accordingly, the "problem-oriented" anthropologist, with a broad, cross-cultural perspective, may disclaim any interest in these labels; all that concerns him is the presence or absence of a particular "thing" in a given culture.

If, however, instead of "getting words for things," we redefine the task as one of finding the "things" that go with the words, the eliciting of terminologies acquires a more general interest. In actuality not even the most concrete, objectively apparent physical object can be identified apart from some culturally defined system of concepts. An ethnographer should strive to define objects according to the conceptual system of the people he is studying. Let me suggest, then, that one look upon the task of getting names for things not as an exercise in linguistic recording, but as a way of finding out what are in fact the "things" in the environment of the people being studied. This paper consists of some suggestions toward the formulation of an operationally explicit methodology for discerning how people construe their world of experience from the way they talk about it. Specifically these suggestions concern the analysis of terminological systems in a way which reveals the conceptual principles that generate them.

In a few fields, notably in kinship studies, anthropologists have already successfully pushed an interest in terminological systems beyond a matching of translation labels. Since Morgan's day no competent student of kinship has looked upon his task as one of simply finding a tribe's words for "uncle," "nephew," or "cousin." The recognition that the denotative range of kinship categories must be determined empirically in each case, that the categories form a system, and that the semantic contrasts underlying the system are amenable to formal analysis, has imparted to kinship studies a methodological rigor and theoretical productivity rare among ethnographic endeavors. Yet all peoples are vitally concerned with kinds of phenomena other than genealogical relations; consequently there is no reason why the study of a people's concepts of these other phenomena should not offer a theoretical interest comparable to that of kinship studies.

Even with reference to quite obvious kinds of material objects, it has long been noted that many people do not see "things" quite the way we do. However, anthropologists in spite of their now well-established psychological interests have notably ignored the cognition of their subjects. Consequently other investigators still rely on stock anecdotes of "primitive thinking" handed down by explorers, philologists, and psychologists since the nineteenth century. Commonly these anecdotes have been cited as examples of early stages in the evolution of human thought—which depending on the anecdotes selected, may be either from blindly concrete to profoundly abstract or from hopelessly vague to scientifically precise. A typical citation, purporting to illustrate the primitive's deficient abstractive ability, concerns a Brazilian Indian tribe which allegedly has no word for "parrot" but only words for "kinds of parrots." The people of such a tribe undoubtedly classify the birds of their environment in some fashion; certainly they do not bestow a unique personal name on each individual bird specimen they encounter. Classification means that individual bird specimens must be matched against the defining attributes of conceptual categories and thereby judged to be equivalent for certain purposes to some other specimens but different from still others. Since no two birds are alike in every discernible feature, any grouping into sets implies a selection of only a limited number of features as significant for contrasting kinds of birds. A person learns which features are significant from his fellows as part of his cultural equipment. He does not receive this information from the birds. Consequently there is no necessary reason that a Brazilian Indian should heed those particular attributes which, for the English-speaker, make equivalent all the diverse individual organisms he labels "parrots." Some of this Indian's categories may seem quite specific, and others quite general, when compared to our grouping of the same specimens. But learning that it takes the Indian many words to name the objects we happen to group together in one set is trivial information compared to knowing how the Indian himself groups these objects and which attributes he selects as dimensions to generate a taxonomy of avifauna. With the latter knowledge we learn what these people regard as significant about birds. If we can arrive at comparable knowledge about their concepts of land animals, plants, soils, weather, social relations, personalities, and supernaturals, we have at least a sketch map of the world in the image of the tribe.

The analysis of a culture's terminological systems will not, of course, exhaustively reveal the cognitive world of its members, but it will certainly tap a central portion of it. Culturally significant cognitive features must be communicable between persons in one of the standard symbolic systems of the culture. A major share of these features will undoubtedly be codable in a society's most flexible and productive communication device, its language. Evidence also seems to indicate that those cognitive features requiring most frequent communication will tend to have standard and relatively short linguistic labels. Accordingly, a commonly distinguished category of trees is more likely to be called something like "elm" by almost all speakers rather than labelled with an ad hoc, non-standardized construction like, "You know, those tall trees with asymmetrical, serrated-edged leaves." To the extent that cognitive coding tends to be linguistic and tends to be efficient, the study of the referential use of standard, readily elicitable linguistic responses —or *terms*—should provide a fruitful beginning point for mapping a cognitive system. And with verbal behavior we know how to begin.

The beginning of an ethnographic task is the recording of what is seen and heard, the segmenting of the behavior stream in such a way that culturally significant noises and movements are coded while the irrelevant is discarded. Descriptive linguistics provides a methodology for segmenting the stream of speech into units relevant to the structure of the speaker's language. I assume that any verbal response which conforms to the phonology and grammar of a language is necessarily a culturally significant unit of behavior. Methodologies for the structural description of a non-verbal behavior are not correspondingly adequate in spite of important contributions in this direction by such persons as Pike and Barker and Wright. By pushing forward the analysis of units we know to be culturally relevant, we can, I think, more satisfactorily arrive at procedures for isolating the significant constituents of analogous and interrelated structures. The basic methodological concept advocated here—the determination of the set of contrasting responses appropriate to a given, culturally valid, eliciting context—should ultimately be applicable to the "semantic" analysis of any culturally meaningful behavior.

SEGREGATES

A terminologically distinguished array of objects is a *segregate*. Segregates are categories, but not all categories known or knowable to an individual are segregates by this definition. Operationally, this definition of a segregate leaves a problem: how do we recognize a "term" when we hear one? How do we segment the stream of speech into category-designating units?

The segmentation of speech into the grammatically functioning units revealed by linguistic analysis is a necessary, but not sufficient, condition for terminological analysis. Clearly no speech segment smaller than the minimal grammatical unit, the morpheme, need be considered. However, the task requires more than simply a search for the meanings of morphemes or other grammatical units. The items and arrangements of a structural description of the language code need not be isomorphic with the categories and propositions of the message. Linguistic forms, whether morphemes or larger constructions, are not each tied to unique chunks of semantic reference like baggage tags;

rather it is the use of speech, the selection of one statement over another in a particular socio-linguistic context, that points to the category boundaries on a culture's cognitive map.

Suppose we have been studying the verbal behavior accompanying the selection and ordering of items at an American lunch counter. The following text might be typical of those overheard and recorded:

"What ya going to have, Mac? Something to eat?"

"Yeah. What kind of sandwiches ya got besides hamburgers and hot dogs?"

"How about a ham 'n cheese sandwich?"

"Nah . . . I guess I'll take a hamburger again."

*   *   *

"Hey, that's no hamburger; that's a cheeseburger!"

*   *   *

The problem is to isolate and relate these speech forms according to their use in naming objects. Some, but apparently not all, orderable items at a lunch counter are distinguished by the term *something to eat*. A possibility within the range of 'something to eat' seems to be a set of objects labelled *sandwiches*. The forms *hamburger, hot dog, ham 'n cheese sandwich,* and *cheeseburger* clearly designate alternative choices in lunch-counter contexts. A customer determined to have a 'sandwich' must select one of these alternatives when he orders, and upon receipt of the order, he must satisfy himself that the object thrust before him—which he has never seen before—meets the criteria for membership in the segregate he designated. The counterman must decide on actions that will produce an object acceptable to the customer as a member of the designated segregate. The terminological status of these forms can be confirmed by analysis of further speech situations, by eliciting utterances with question frames suggested to the investigator by the data, and by observing non-verbal features of the situation, especially correlations between terms used in ordering and objects received.

In isolating these terms no appeal has been made to analysis of their linguistic structure or their signification. *Sandwich* is a single morpheme. Some linguists, at any rate, would analyze *hot dog* and even *hamburger* as each containing two morphemes, but, since the meaning of the constructions cannot be predicted from a knowledge of the meaning of their morphological constituents, they are single "lexemes" or "idioms." *Ham'n cheese sandwich* would not, I think, qualify as a single lexeme; nevertheless it is a standard segregate label whose function in naming objects cannot be distinguished from that of forms like *hot dog*. Suppose further utterances from lunch-counter speech show that the lexically complex term *something to eat* distinguishes the same array of objects as do the single morphemes *food* and *chow*. In such a case, a choice among these three terms would perhaps say something about the social status of the lunch counter and its patrons, but it says nothing distinctive about the objects designated. As segregate labels, these three frequently-heard terms would be equivalent.

Although not operationally relevant at this point, the lexemic status of terms bears on later analysis of the productivity of a terminological system. In contrast, say, to our kinship terminology, American lunch-counter terminology is highly productive. The existence of productive, polylexemic models such as *ham 'n cheese sandwich* permits the generation and labelling of new segregates to accommodate the latest lunch-counter creations. However, the non-intuitive determination of the lexemic status of a term requires a thorough analysis of the distinctive features of meaning of the term and its constituents. Such an analysis of the criteria for placing objects into categories can come only after the term, together with those contrasting terms relevant to its use, has been isolated as a segregate label.

CONTRAST SETS

In a situation in which a person is making a public decision about the category membership of an object by giving the object a verbal label, he is selecting a term out of a set of alternatives, each with classificatory import. When he asserts "This is an *X*," he is also stating that it is *not* specific other things, these other things being not everything else conceivable, but only the alternatives among which a decision was made. In lunch-counter ordering, 'hamburger,' 'hot dog,' 'cheeseburger,' and 'ham and cheese sandwich' are such alternatives. Any object placed in one of these segregates cannot at the same time belong to another. Those culturally appropriate responses which are distinctive alternatives in the same kinds of situations —or, in linguistic parlance, which occur in the

same "environment"—can be said to *contrast*. A series of terminologically contrasted segregates forms a *contrast set*.

Note that the cognitive relation of contrast is not equivalent to the relation of class exclusion in formal logic and set theory. The three categories 'hamburger,' 'hot dog,' and 'rainbow' are mutually exclusive in membership. But in writing rules for classifying hamburgers I must say something about hot dogs, whereas I can ignore rainbows. Two categories contrast only when the difference between them is significant for defining their use. The segregates 'hamburger' and 'rainbow,' even though they have no members in common, do not function as distinctive alternatives in any uncontrived classifying context familiar to me.

TAXONOMIES

The notion of contrast cannot account for all the significant relations among these lunch-counter segregates. Although no object can be both a hamburger and a hot dog, an object can very well be both a hot dog and a sandwich or a hamburger and a sandwich. By recording complementary names applied to the same objects (and eliminating referential synonyms such as *something to eat* and *food*), the following series might result:

Object A is named: *something to eat, sandwich, hamburger*

Object B is named: *something to eat, sandwich, ham sandwich*

Object C is named: *something to eat, pie, apple pie*

Object D is named: *something to eat, cherry pie*

Object E is named: *something to eat, ice-cream bar, Eskimo pie.*

Some segregates include a wider range of objects than others and are sub-partitioned by a contrast set. The segregate 'pie' *includes* the contrast set 'apple pie,' 'cherry pie,' etc. For me, the segregate 'apple pie' is, in turn, sub-partitioned by 'French apple pie' and 'plain (or 'ordinary') apple pie' Figure 1 diagrams the sub-partitioning of the segregate 'something to eat' as revealed by naming responses to objects A—E.

Again it is the use of terms, not their linguistic structure, that provides evidence of in-

something to eat				
sandwich		pie		ice-cream bar
ham-burger	ham sandwich	apple pie	cherry pie	Eskimo pie
OBJECTS: A	B	C	D	E

FIGURE 1. Sub-partitioning of the segregate 'something to eat' as revealed by naming responses to objects A-E.

clusion. We cannot consider 'Eskimo pie' to be included in the category 'pie,' for we cannot discover a natural situation in which an object labeled *Eskimo pie* can be labeled simply *pie*. Thus the utterance, "That's not a sandwich; that's a pie," cannot refer to an Eskimo pie. Similar examples are common in English. The utterance, "Look at that oak," may refer to a 'white oak' but never to a 'poison oak.' A 'blackbird' is a kind of 'bird,' but a 'redcap' is not a kind of 'cap.' For many English speakers, the unqualified use of *American* invariably designates a resident or citizen of the United States; consequently, for such speakers, an 'American' is a kind of 'North American' rather than the converse. One cannot depend on a particular grammatical construction, such as one of the English phrasal compounds, to differentiate consistently a single cognitive relation, such as that of inclusion. Because English is not unique in this respect, the practice of arguing from morphological and syntactic analysis directly to cognitive relations must be considered methodologically unsound.

Segregates in different contrast sets, then, may be related by inclusion. A system of contrasts sets so related is a *taxonomy;* this definition does not require a taxonomy to have a unique beginner, i.e., a segregate which includes all other segregates in the system. It requires only that the segregates at the most inclusive level form a demonstrable contrast set.

Taxonomies make possible a regulation of the amount of information communicated about an object in a given situation (compare: "Give me something to eat" with "Give me a French apple pie a la mode"), and they provide a

hierarchal ordering of categories, allowing an efficient program for the identification, filing, and retrieving of significant information. The use of taxonomic systems is not confined to librarians and biologists; it is a fundamental principle of human thinking. The elaboration of taxonomies along vertical dimensions of generalization and horizontal dimensions of discrimination probably depends on factors such as the variety of cultural settings within which one talks about the objects being classified, the importance of the objects to the way of life of the classifiers, and general properties of human thinking with regard to the number of items that the mind can cope with at a given time. Determining the precise correlates of variations in taxonomic structure, both intra-culturally and cross-culturally, is, of course, one of the objectives of this methodology.

In order to describe the use of taxonomic systems and to work out their behavioral correlates, evidence of complementary naming must be supplemented by observations on the socio-linguistic contexts that call for contrasts at particular levels. One could, for example, present a choice between objects whose segregates appear to contrast at different levels and ask an informant to complete the frame: "Pick up that ———." Suppose we have an apple pie on the counter next to a ham standwich. The frame would probably be completed as "Pick up that pie." If, however, we substitute a cherry pie for the ham sandwich, we would expect to hear "Pick up that apple pie." Variations on this device of having informants contrast particular objects can be worked out depending on the kind of phenomena being classified. Some objects, such as pies and plants, are easier to bring together for visual comparison than others, such as diseases and deities.

Another device for eliciting taxonomic structures is simply to ask directly about relations of inclusion: "Is *X* a kind of *Y?*" Since in many speech situations even a native fails to elicit a term at the level of specification he requires, most, if not all, languages probably provide explicit methods for moving up and down a taxonomic hierarchy:

"Give me some of that pie." "What kind of pie d'ya want, Mac?"

"What's this 'submarine' thing on the menu?" "That's a kind of sandwich."

Once a taxonomic partitioning has been worked out it can be tested systematically for terminological contrast with frames such as "Is that an X?" with an expectation of a negative reply. For example, we could point to an apple pie and ask a counterman:

1. "Is that something to drink?"
2. "Is that a sandwich?"
3. "Is that a cherry pie?"

We would expect the respective replies to reflect the taxonomy of lunch-counter foods:

1. "No, it's something to eat."
2. "No, it's a pie."
3. "No, it's an apple pie."

(Admittedly it is easier to do this kind of questioning in a culture where one can assume the role of a naive learner.)

In employing these various operations for exploring taxonomic structures, the investigator must be prepared for cases when the same linguistic form designates segregates at different levels of contrast within the same system ('man' vs. 'animal,' 'man' vs. 'woman,' 'man' vs. 'boy'); when a single unpartitioned segregate contrasts with two or more segregates which are themselves at different levels of contrast ("That's not a coin; it's a token." "That's not a dime; it's a token"); and when incongruities occur in the results of the several operations (terminological contrasts may cut across sub-hierarchies revealed by complementary naming; explicit statements of inclusion may be less consistent than complementary naming).

ATTRIBUTES

Our task up to this point has been to reveal the structure of the system from which a selec-

tion is made when categorizing an object. When you hand a Navajo a plant specimen, or an American a sandwich, what is the available range of culturally defined arrays into which this object can be categorized? Methodological notions of contrast and inclusion have enabled us to discern some structure in this domain of cognitive choices, but we still have not faced the problem of how a person decides which out of a set of alternative categorizations is the correct one in a given instance. How does one in fact distinguish a hamburger from a cheeseburger, a chair from a stool, a tree from a shrub, an uncle from a cousin, a jerk from a slob?

A mere list of known members of a category —however an investigator identifies these objects cross-culturally—does not answer this question. Categorization, in essence, is a device for treating new experience as though it were equivalent to something already familiar. The hamburger I get tomorrow may be a quite different object in terms of size, kind of bun, and lack of tomatoes from the hamburger I had today. But it will still be a hamburger—unless it has a slice of cheese in it! To define 'hamburger' one must know, not just what objects it includes, but with what it contrasts. In this way we learn that a slice of cheese makes a difference, whereas a slice of tomato does not. In the context of different cultures the task is to state what one must know in order to categorize objects correctly. A definition of a Navajo plant category is not given by a list of botanical species it contains but by a rule for distinguishing newly encountered specimens of that category from contrasting alternatives.

Ideally the criterial attributes which generate a contrast set fall along a limited number of dimensions of contrast, each with two or more contrasting values or "components." Each segregate can be defined as a distinctive bundle of components. For example, the plant taxonomy of the Eastern Subanun, a Philippine people, has as its beginner a contrast set of three segregates which together include almost all of the more than 1,400 segregates at the most specific level of contrast within the taxonomy. This three member contrast set can be generated by binary contrasts along two dimensions pertaining to habit of stem growth (see Table I). Applications of componential analysis to pronominal systems and kinship terminologies have made this method of definition familiar. The problem remains of demonstrating the cognitive saliency of componential solutions—to what ex-

TABLE I. Defining attributes of the contrast set of stem habit in the Subanun plant taxonomy.

Contrast Set	Dimensions of Contrast	
	Woodiness	*Rigidity*
gayu 'woody plants'	W	R
sigbet 'herbaceous plants'	W̄	R
belagen 'vines'	W̄	R̄

tent are they models of how a person decides which term to use?—and of relating terminological attributes to actual perceptual discriminations. As a case of the latter problem, suppose we learn that informants distinguish two contrasting plant segregates by calling the fruit of one 'red' and that of the other 'green.' We set up 'color' as a dimension of contrast with values of 'red' and 'green.' But the terminology of 'color' is itself a system of segregates whose contrastive structure must be analysed before color terms can serve as useful defining attributes of other segregates. Ultimately one is faced with defining color categories by referring to the actual perceptual dimensions along which informants make differential categorizations. These dimensions must be determined empirically and not prescribed by the investigator using stimulus materials from his own culture. By careful observation one might discover that visual evaluation of an object's succulence, or other unexpected dimensions, as well as the traditional dimensions of hue, brightness, and saturation, are criterial to the use of "color" terms in a particular culture.

Whether aimed directly at perceptual qualities of phenomena or at informants' descriptions of pertinent attributes, any method for determining the distinctive and probabilistic attributes of a segregate must depend, first, on knowing the contrast set within which the segregate is participating, and, second, on careful observations of verbal and non-verbal features of the cultural situations to which this contrast set provides an appropriate response.

This formulation has important implications for the role of eliciting in ethnography. The distinctive "situations," or "eliciting frames," or "stimuli," which evoke and define a set of contrasting responses are cultural data to be discovered, not prescribed, by the ethnographer. This stricture does not limit the use of preconceived eliciting devices to prod an informant into action or speech without any intent of defining the response by what evoked it in this instance. But the formulation—prior to observa-

tion—of response-defining eliciting devices is ruled out by the logic of this methodology which insists that any eliciting conditions not themselves part of the cultural-ecological system being investigated cannot be used to define categories purporting to be those of the people under study. It is those elements of *our informants'* experience, which *they* heed in selecting appropriate actions and utterances, that this methodology seeks to discover.

OBJECTIVES

The methodological suggestions proposed in this paper, as they stand, are clearly awkward and incomplete. They must be made more rigorous and expanded to include analyses of longer utterance sequences, to consider nonverbal behavior systematically, and to explore the other types of cognitive relations, such as sequential stage relations and part-whole relations, that may pertain between contrast sets. Focusing on the linguistic code, clearer operational procedures are needed for delimiting semantically exocentric units ("lexemes" or "idioms"), for discerning synonomy, homonymy, and polysemy, and for distinguishing between utterance grammaticalness (correctly constructed code) and utterance congruence (meaningfully constructed message). In their present form, however, these suggestions have come out of efforts to describe behavior in the field, and their further development can come only from continuing efforts to apply and test them in ethnographic field situations.

The intended objective of these efforts is eventually to provide the ethnographer with public, non-intuitive procedures for ordering his presentation of observed and elicited events according to the principles of classification of the people he is studying. To order ethnographic observations solely according to an investigator's preconceived categories obscures the real content of culture: how people organize their experience conceptually so that it can be transmitted as knowledge from person to person and from generation to generation. As Goodenough advocates in a classic paper, culture "does not consist of things, people, behavior, or emotions," but the forms or organization of these things in the minds of people. The principles by which people in a culture construe their world reveal how they segregate the pertinent from the insignificant, how they code and retrieve information, how they anticipate events, how they define alternative courses of action and make decisions among them. Consequently a strategy of ethnographic description that gives a central place to the cognitive processes of the actors involved will contribute reliable cultural data to problems of the relations between language, cognition, and behavior; it will point up critical dimensions for meaningful cross-cultural comparison; and, finally, it will give us productive descriptions of cultural behavior, descriptions which, like the linguists' grammar, succinctly state what one must know in order to generate culturally acceptable acts and utterances appropriate to a given socio-ecological context,

49

COGNITION AND COMPONENTIAL ANALYSIS: GOD'S TRUTH OR HOCUS-POCUS?

ROBBINS BURLING

I

MANY anthropologists have been attracted by procedures of formal semantics, such as componential analysis, and some have noted the possibility of alternative solutions. To my knowledge, however, none have given consideration to the total number of alternative solutions that are logically possible, and to the implications of that number for the problem of indeterminacy, and to the implications of indeterminacy for semantic analysis. Componential analysis is applied to a set of terms which form a culturally relevant domain and proceeds by recognizing semantic distinctions (components) which apportion the terms of the set into contrasting sub-sets, such that every item is distinguished from every other item by at least one component. Subsets can be arrived at in many alternative ways, however, and in the following discussion I will first consider the wide number of possible choices (II). Then I will consider the relation of the number of possibilities to the "cognitive" status of solu-

From *American Anthropologist*, 66: 20–28; with comments by Dell H. Hymes and Charles O. Frake and a rejoinder by Robbins Burling, *American Anthropologist*, 66: 116–122. Reprinted by permission of the publisher and the authors. Robbins Burling is Associate Professor of Anthropology, University of Michigan. Dell H. Hymes is Professor of Anthropology, University of Pennsylvania, and Charles O. Frake is Associate Professor of Anthropology, Stanford University.

tions, and conclude by stating what limited but real value I consider componential analyses to have (III).

II

My first objective will be to clarify the ways in which the items in a set may be distinguished from each other and divided among individual cells. The theoretical possibilities are most easily understood by considering very small sets of items. If we have a set of only one item, there is no problem of partitioning at all. Two items can presumably be distinguished in only one way, allowing only one possible division of a set of two terms. If there are three items in the set (call the items *a, b, c*) the possibilities become slightly more complex. For a first partition, one has three obvious choices: use a component which separates *a* from *b* and *c;* one which separates *b* from *a* and *c;* or one which separates *c* from *a* and *b*. As a matter of fact, any two of these components acting together will partition the set of three items completely, so that, to start with, there are three possible componential analyses of a set of three items (Figure 1). However, one further possibility must also be allowed for. After a first partition (which, let us say, separates *a* from *b* and *c*) it is possible to make a second partition which distinguishes *b* from *c*, but which is irrelevant for *a*. Such components have been regularly

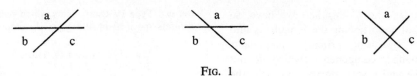

FIG. 1

used in analyses which have actually been carried out. For instance, in giving a semantic analysis of the third person singular pronouns in English, one might first suggest an animate/inanimate distinction to separate *it* on the one hand from *he* and *she* on the other. A second component, separating male from female can distinguish *he* from *she*, but sex is simply irrelevant for *it*. If we recognize this type of secondary partitioning, which makes use of a component that is significant for some but not all of the items in the set, three additional methods of discretely partitioning a set of three items become possible—for instance, a component distinguishing *a* from *b* and *c*, together with a second component separating *b* from *c* but irrelevant for *a*. This makes six possible analyses in all (Figure 2).

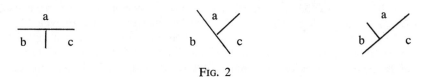

FIG. 2

When we consider a set of four items, the possibilities increase considerably. In the hope of keeping the discussion as clear as possible, I will arbitrarily label the items *a, b, c,* and *d,* and I will call any partition which is significant over the entire set a "primary component." A component which is significant for less than the total number of items of the set I will call a "secondary component." A secondary component can only act after the particular sub-set to which it applies has been set off and distinguished either by one of the primary components or by a more inclusive secondary component. The initial partition of any set must always be made by a primary component. To label particular components I will use abbreviations of the following type: *ab/cd* means a component that divides the set of four items into two sub-sets, *ab* on the one hand and *cd* on the other. Secondary components can be labeled by such formulae as *bc/d,* which would indicate a component which acts after *a* has been separated from the others and which is not itself applicable to *a* but which distinguishes *b* and *c* from *d*.

In a set of four items, seven different primary components can be recognized. These fall into two distinctive types, which I will call *Type I* and *Type II,* respectively.

Type I   a/bcd   b/acd   c/adb   d/abc
Type II   ab/cd   ac/bd   ad/bc

These primary components can be combined in various ways to produce "discrete" but "non-redundant" solutions to the set. By a "discrete" solution I mean an analysis which apportions each item into a separate cell and which distinguishes between every pair of items by at least one component. By a "non-redundant" solution I mean an analysis in which no component can be eliminated without breaking down the distinction between at least one pair of items. Both discreteness and non-redundancy have implicitly been considered desirable in componential analysis. The discrete but non-redundant solutions, using the primary components only, are as follows:

A. Any three Type I components: 4 possible solutions.
B. Any two Type II components: 3 possible solutions.
C. Any one of the Type II components may be combined with any of four pairs of Type I components. The Type I components must be chosen to partition the sets already set up by the Type II components. For instance, ab/cd can be combined with any one of the following pairs of Type I components, but with no others:

a/bcd and c/abd
a/bcd and d/abc
b/acd and d/abd
b/acd and d/abc

Combining each of the three Type II components with the four appropriate Type I components gives: 12 possible solutions: $3 \times 2 \times 2$.

Taking A, B, and C together, we have, so far, 19 ways of apportioning the four items into discrete cells by using primary components only. If secondary components (which do not cut across the entire set) are used as well, the possibilities increase. We can recognize two types of secondary components, those which make a distinction among three items and those which distinguish only two. These can be added to the earlier types and called Types III and IV. There are, respectively, 12 and 6 Type III and Type IV components, as follows:

Type III		a/bc	b/ac	c/ab	
		a/bd	b/ad	d/ab	
		a/cd	c/ad	d/ac	
		b/cd	c/bd	d/bc	
Type IV	a/b	a/c	a/d	b/c	b/d	c/d

Several new possibilities now arise by which components of the several Types can be combined to obtain discrete but non-redundant solutions.

D. Any two Type I components acting together may be combined with any one of four Type III components: a/bcd and b/acd, for instance, may be combined with any of the four Type III components which distinguish c from d.

E.g. a/bcd, b/acd, c/ad
24 solutions: $(3+2+1) \times 4$

E. Any two Type I components acting together may be combined with one particular Type IV component:

E.g. a/bcd, b/acd/ c/d
6 solutions: $(3+2+1) \times 1$

F. Any Type I component when acting with any Type II component may be combined with any one of four Type III components: a/bed with ab/cd fails to distinguish only c and d. Any of the four Type III components which do distinguish cd from d will complete the job.

E.g. a/bcd, ab/cd, c/bd
48 solutions: $4 \times 3 \times 4$

G. Any Type I component acting together with any Type II component can then be combined with one particular Type IV component. I.e. once a choice of the Type I and Type II components has been made, one and only one of the Type IV components will complete the partitioning:

E.g. a/bcd, ab/cd, c/d
12 solutions: $4 \times 3 \times 1$

H. Any Type II component may be combined with the two Type IV components which redivide the sub-sets specified by the Type II component.

E.g. ab/cd with a/b with c/d
3 solutions: $3 \times 1 \times 1$

I. Any Type I component together with any one of three Type III components (one of the three which do not include the item designated by the letter to the left of the slash in the Type I component which was chosen) can then be combined with one particular Type IV component to complete the partitioning.

E.g. a/bcd with b/cd with c/d
12 solutions: $4 \times 3 \times 1$

In D through I, by combining primary and secondary components, we have added 105 possible analyses to the 19 which use primary components only for a total of 124 ways in which a set of four terms can be discretely but non-redundantly apportioned into cells by the application of components. Clearly with five or more items the possibilities would rapidly become astronomical.

One hundred and twenty-four possible analyses for four items may seem surprising, but they do not exhaust the complications. Others deserve at least brief mention: 1) *Homonomy.* Analysts of kinship terminology have occasionally found it expedient to provide two different formulae for a single term and suggest that it has (by such an analysis) two different meanings. 2) *Empty semantic spaces.* Authors of some semantic analyses have pointed out that when a number of components cross-cut each other in several ways, it may be found that there is no lexeme at all for some particular combination of components. 3) *Non-binary components.* There is no necessary reason why an analysis must be confined to binary distinctions, although some workers seem to have felt them to be esthetically more pleasing and my discussion has been limited to them. 4) *Parallel components.* There seems no reason to suppose that in real systems only a single distinction can separate the same sub-sets, though in the abstract formulation given here only one distinction is possible. 5) *Redundancy.* Finally, there seems no real reason to limit the available analyses to the non-redundant ones, except that by admitting redundant analyses, we open the way to vastly increased possibilities: ab/cd/ac/bd, and a/bcd form a discrete analysis of four items. It is redundant since the third component can be eliminated without destroying the discreteness of the solution. Redundant components have not traditionally been allowed in semantic analyses, though it is difficult to justify this limitation as a matter of principle. Homonomy, empty spaces, non-binary distinctions, parallel components, and redundant solutions all add considerable complexity to the possibilities for analysis of a set of terms. In principle, the number of possible analyses becomes infinite.

III

Readers may doubt whether this abstract and formalistic argument has any great relevance to the practical analysis of real systems. Later, I will try to suggest that it does, but since its relevance is entirely dependent upon one's objectives in conducting a semantic analysis, we must be clear about our objectives before considering its relevance.

Anthropologists who have advocated the use of componential analysis and similar formal methods as a way of studying the meaning of sets of terms seem to have had two contrasting objectives. Their first and more modest goal has been to specify the conditions under which each term would be used. The problem has been posed in the following way: What do we have to know in order to say that some object is to be called by a given term? That is, analysts have searched for a set of rules which would unambiguously state the criteria by which it could be decided whether or not a particular term could be applied to some object, and the test for the validity of the analysis has been the accuracy with which it predicts such naming. If it can be used to predict what term will be used for a particular object, then this is taken to justify the analysis.

The more ambitious objective of the method is to use it to lead us to an understanding of the criteria by which speakers of the language themselves decide what term to use for a particular item. This view was suggested in Goodenough's original paper when he said, "[the semantic analyst] aims to find the conceptual units out of which the meanings of linguistic utterances are built . . ." and more forcefully by Wallace: "The problem is to define the taxonomic system itself—that is, to explicate the rules by which users of the terms group various social and genealogical characteristics into concepts." Frake described one of his papers as containing ". . . some suggestions toward the formulation of an operationally-explicit methodology for discovering how people construe their world of experience from the way they talk about it."

These two objectives differ in an important way. Specifically, any of hundreds or thousands of logically alternative solutions might predict which term can be used, but the success of that prediction does not demonstrate that the speaker of the language uses the same scheme, or indicate whether or not all speakers use the same one.

It is a long and difficult leap from an analysis which is adequate in the sense of discriminating which term should be used to denote an object to that particular analysis which represents the way in which people construe their world. I will try to suggest briefly that the difficulty is not a purely hypothetical one by considering the attempts that have been made to analyze such sets as botanical and disease terminology. Conklin (1962) and Frake (1961, 1962) have suggested that such terms can be arranged into a hierarchical taxonomy. In colloquial English, for instance, (not necessarily in the special English of taxonomic botany) we have a class of objects which we call plants, and within the class of plants we have a class of trees. Within the class of trees is a class of "needled trees" (which, in my part of the country where little account is taken of broad-leafed evergreens, seems nearly synonymous with "evergreen"). "Needled trees" include "pines" and "pines" in turn include "jack pines." At each taxonomic level are other coordinate terms: "Flowers" and "bushes" may be coordinate with "trees"; "palms" and "leafy trees" with "needled trees"; "spruce" and "hemlocks" with "pines"; and "white" and "Norway pines" with "jack pines" (Figure 3). Taxonomies existed for plants in all languages long before Linnaeus codified the idea and laid the basis for systematic biology.

A taxonomy of the sort suggested by this example constitutes a special form of componential analysis. After a primary component has been used to divide the entire set of terms, the next distinction is a secondary component which divides one of the sub-sets but which typically does not cross the first component into the other sub-set. Each component operates only within a single undifferentiated set which has been set off by earlier components but which is not yet divided itself. Intersecting com-

PLANTS

ETC.	BUSHES	FLOWERS	TREES			
	ETC.		LEAFY TREES	PALM TREES	NEEDLED TREES	
	ETC.		ETC.	ETC.	SPRUCE	HEMLOCK	PINE

FIG. 3

ponents may be used for botanical terminology as well as for kinship, but they have less commonly been recognized.

It is my feeling that the analyses of terms into hierarchical taxonomies that have lately been discussed have rather glossed over the problems of indeterminacy. In fact, in my example I also glossed over some difficult problems of this sort. I am not at all certain, for instance, that "flower" and "bush" are really coordinate to "tree." Perhaps on the basis of size English speakers distinguish "trees" from "bushes," and "bushes" from "plants" (homonymous, but not synonymous with "plants" used as a general cover term for the entire set), and then on the basis of use, divide "plants" into "flowers," "vegetables," and "weeds." What about "cedars"? Are they "needled trees"? Not really, of course, but they are not "leafy trees" either. Should "balsam," "hemlock," and "spruce" be classed together as "short needled trees" (Christmas trees) as opposed to "pines"? Or should they all have equivalent taxonomic status? What is the essential "cognitive" difference between hemlock and spruce? Is it gross size, type of needle, form of bark, or what? I do not know how to answer these questions, but they are the types of questions which must be answered before any single semantic analysis can claim to represent the cognitive organization of the people, or even claim to be much more than an exercise of the analyst's imagination. The questions which I raise about English botanical terms represent precisely the sort of indeterminacy that arose in the abstract example which began this paper.

Analyses of terms in exotic languages may obscure the range of possible alternatives. For instance, Frake discusses some disease terms in Subanun, a language of Mindanao, and he makes appealing suggestions for their analysis;

yet I cannot help wondering if he does not convey an unjustified certainty in the particular analysis he offers. Frake gives a diagram of the same form as my diagram of English plant terms (Figure 3), in which certain skin diseases are assigned to various taxonomic categories and sub-categories. Not knowing the language, the reader can hardly question the data, and yet he may still wonder if this diagram is any less subject to question than my diagram of plant terms. This is particularly the case since Frake does not give a complete analysis of all disease terms, but limits himself to examples which illustrate the problems he is considering, and he implies that once having solved the problems one may easily provide the full analysis. In fact, in my judgment, the field of structural semantics has had a surfeit of programmatic articles, glowing with promise of a new ethnography, and a dearth of substantive descriptions of whole systems or definable subsystems.

Students who claim that componential analysis or comparable methods of semantic analysis can provide a means for "discovering how people construe their world" must explain how to eliminate the great majority of logical possibilities and narrow the choice to the one or few that are "psychologically real." I will not be convinced that there are not dozens or hundreds of possible analyses of Subanun disease terms until Frake presents us with the entire system fully analyzed and faces squarely the problem of how he chooses his particular analysis. In the meantime, I will doubt whether any single analysis tells us much about people's cognitive structure, even if it enables us to use terms as a native does.

The hope that we could somehow use our knowledge of language to gain understanding of the workings of the human mind has had a long history. Whorf's ideas have fallen into disrepute largely because the relationships which he claimed to see between patterns of language and patterns of thought could be checked only from the side of language. The language patterns were there to be sure, but how, except through intuition, could one tell whether the patterns corresponded to anything else? Structural semantics has the advantage over Whorf's more naive ideas in that it attempts to relate two observable types of data with one another—language use and events in the non-linguistic world. I cannot see that it has any advantage over Whorf's procedures in gaining an understanding of cognition.

This conclusion may sound harsh, but it does not imply that "structural semantics" is useless. There is a real problem of formulating rules which will predict the use of terms, or to put it another way, of specifying the relationship between terms, on the one hand, and events and situations in our extra-linguistic experience, on the other. In still other words, it is legitimate to try to specify precisely what terms "mean." The exercise of carrying out a formal analysis, moreover, is certainly useful in checking the completeness and adequacy of one's data, in exactly the same way that writing up a grammatical statement may make one aware of previously unimagined possibilities, whether or not these are attributed to the speaker. If nothing else, a precise statement of the objects to which terms are applied is certainly a help to someone wishing to learn the language or use behavior which will be effective. I am convinced that componential analysis and other formal semantic methods can help us in this task. As we learn more about all aspects of language use and its relation to non-linguistic events and as we bring studies of various semantic domains into harmony with each other and take wider and wider account of all aspects of behavior, we may be able to narrow down the alternatives. I expect, however, that a large degree of indeterminacy will always remain. I can be proven wrong by analyses which admit to no alternatives, but until such analyses are given, I will regard it as gratuitous to attribute our analyses to the speakers.

Linguists, in referring to attitudes toward grammatical analyses, have sometimes made a distinction between the "God's truth" view and the "hocus-pocus" view (Householder). When a linguist makes his investigation and writes his grammar, is he discovering something about the language which is "out there" waiting to be described and recorded or is he simply formulating a set of rules which somehow work? Similarly, when an anthropologist undertakes a semantic analysis, is he discovering some "psychological reality" which speakers are presumed to have or is he simply working out a set of rules which somehow take account of the observed phenomena? The attitude taken in this paper is far over on the "hocus-pocus" side. It is always tempting to attribute something more important to one's work than a tinkering with a rough set of operational devices. It certainly sounds more exciting to say we are "discovering the cognitive system of the people" than to admit that we are just fiddling with a set of rules which allow us to use terms the way others do. Nevertheless, I think the latter is a realistic goal, while the former is not. I believe we should be content with the less exciting objective of showing how terms in language are applied to objects in the world, and stop pursuing the illusory goal of cognitive structures.

DISCUSSION OF BURLING'S PAPER
Dell H. Hymes

This paper makes an original and important contribution to the development of componential analysis, when it shows that there exist a large and expanding number of logical possibilities for the internal structure of members of a set, and when it draws some implications from that fact for cognitive validity. The paper, it seems to me, however, is an accurate criticism only of some, not all, existing practice. I do not share the author's pervading skepticism, and should like to stress ways in which the difficulty he raises can be and is being met.

The main thing is to observe that the total number of logical possibilities is fully pertinent only if all solutions have an equal chance of being arrived at. Not all solutions do have an equal chance of being arrived at, however, if the practice of the work by Conklin and Frake, cited in the paper, is followed. One must consider here the point made in Conklin (1955), as to finding out what questions members of the culture themselves ask in categorizing experience, a point which he has elaborated, contrasting semantic structure with arbitrary arrangement, in comments to Frake (1962), regarding analysis of American coins. In general, componential analysis, as practiced and advocated by Goodenough, Conklin, Frake, is question-dependent, dependent upon the questions asked by participants in the culture.

One major consequence of such practice is that investigation allows members of the culture to reveal the existence of various types of relations among members of a set, e.g., hierarchical relations of class inclusion. The point is that the revealing of a type of relation eliminates some logically possible alternative solutions. Taking hierarchy as an example, if a and b are found to be kinds of c, then $c/a+b$ holds; both $a/b+c$ and $b/a+c$ are eliminated.

Another major consequence is the attention given to techniques for eliciting and ascertaining cognitively pertinent features, by use of native drawings, culturally relevant objects, etc. Again, the point is that the discovery of semantic content for componential dimensions may serve to eliminate some logically possible alternative solutions. If a contrasts with b as to one feature, and both with c as to another, then again $c/a+b$ is indicated (although the kind of relation, hierarchical or other, remains open thus far), not $a/b+c$ or $b/a+c$.

Another way of coming at the status of the difficulty raised by Burling is to distinguish between (a) making the right *sorting*, which can be formal and cognitively empty, since it involves only putting the discriminated items into relation with each other, and (b) making the right *assignment* of semantic features to the dimensions of the sorting. Logical possibilities, as discussed here, apply only to the former. There are, indeed, great problems of indeterminacy and dubious validity, since, even if the one and only right sorting is achieved, its semantic basis may be unknown or unknowable. To use an example for which I am indebted to a conversation some years ago with Fred W. Householder, Jr., I may be able to predict that you will sort berry A and berry B, but not know whether by size, color, shape, imagined taste, or what; and to predict that you will group berry A and berry B together as against berry C, and group all as subtypes of berry type D, yet still be no wiser as to why. In fact, however, sorting and assignment are interdependent in the empirical field investigations of Frake and Conklin, and contextual and other evidence can be obtained which permit facts of sorting and the semantic content of the relationship, to give evidence for each other, in the course of developing a theory for the set as a whole. Given a set—and it is vital to note that the

existence and conditions of relevance of a set must also be empirically determined—the possible sortings, and the possibly pertinent semantic features, are both finite in number; and one sorting usually will eliminate some features as possible, while particular features usually will eliminate some sortings.

The distinction between sorting and assignment is in effect a distinction between a model, taken as accounting for the way in which the set is organized, and an explanation, which is involved in prediction of naming, thus making the organization intelligible or motivated. Within the range of logically possible alternatives, all are equivalent as models in the sense that each satisfies the criterion of sorting out the terms of the set. Even if one sorting and one model can be decided upon, no explanation or interpretation of how the sorting is done is given. Burling notes this, but does not seem to realize that explanation is involved in the prediction of naming, which he discusses and advocates as a goal, and which he seems to think can be accomplished by any logically possible model.

If an analyst claims only to have found a set of components which make a distinction everywhere native speakers do, the spectre of many logically possible cognitive alternatives is real; but prediction of naming has not been accomplished. To predict naming is to treat the analysis as generative, as accounting for the acceptability and non-acceptability of acts of naming, including, by implication, acts of naming novel objects. To predict the naming of novel objects introduces the possibility, indeed necessity of discriminating among alternative solutions in terms of the semantic features validly pertinent to designating an item as X, Y or not in the set. In favorable cases, one can vary the possibilities and get responses which eliminate a good deal of indeterminacy, pinpointing pertinent features, e.g., by triad tests as Romney has done with American kinship. (Note that the problem is in principle the same as that being investigated in acoustic phonetics with regard to alternative orderings of a phonemic system, and the criteria actually employed by native hearers to distinguish the members.)

There are, of course, additional considerations which give credence to the validity of an analysis, such as informant explicitness and consistency. Frake's problem in Subanun was the opposite of the predicament described by

Burling. There was no difficulty in getting agreement as to the criteria discriminating different terms; rather, the difficulty was in getting agreement on the term to be used in a given instance of predicting naming. All knew the criteria for being an instance of *X,* but might disagree as to whether or not a given instance met the criteria. Also, it is impressive when an analysis brings order out of confusion, supported by contextual evidence, as in the case of Haugen's analysis of Icelandic terms of orientation on the basis of Einarsson's data, and Frake's resolution of the seeming confusion of usage of a term, once the fact of implicit answers at different levels of the native hierarchic taxonomy was found.

It remains that not all indeterminacy may be removed, and, as Goodenough has noted, the fact may itself be significant. Some areas of experience are more elaborately and more consistently terminologized than others, and this in itself tells us something interesting about the cognitive system of a group. Sometimes overt variation in accounts given by informants can be explicated, providing the basis for experimental test. Thus, Miss Joan Davlin has found a remarkable variety of reasons and reasoning for the distinction between "books" and "magazines," but the major criteria can all be referred to an underlying distinction in the temporal dimension as to periodicity of publication. The latter contrast seems to be the source of the major features recognized and used by informants, though itself not offered by any.

In sum, Burling's skepticism and analysis is a valuable corrective to simplistic and bandwagon approaches to componential analysis, which, when valid, is hard work indeed. One must balance skepticism with the positive things that can be done, however, unless one intends the skepticism to apply not only to a new technique (new techniques seem often to spur such skepticism), but to most of anthropology, whenever it refers to values, orientations, attitudes, beliefs, or any other notion which imputes the presence of something inside people.

So far as the best current work is concerned, the strategy is to discover questions which reveal native sortings and the features which discriminate semantically for native speakers, and to integrate the two. The analyst who follows such a strategy is never in the situation of having to consider all logically possible sortings. His field procedure secures elimination of many of them by members of the culture, and he does all he can to devise questions, techniques, predictions which will discriminate among the alternatives that may remain.

The full force of Burling's critique applies only to that part of current practice which consists, so to speak, of sitting at a desk with a set of terms uncertainly constituting a native set, and playing with analysis into dimensions uncertainly corresponding to native features. There are people whose conception of componential analysis answers to the description, but they are not the ones cited in the present paper.

FURTHER DISCUSSION OF BURLING
Charles O. Frake

Given two competing ethnographic statements (the operational derivation of each from an ethnographic record being equally clear), the best statement is the one which most adequately accounts for the widest range of behavior. If two statements differ in their implications for behavior, then a choice between them can only be made in one way: by testing them against the behavior of the people being described. I can see no other criterion of "reality" or "truth" —be it psychological, structural, or God's— available to the investigator or, for that matter, to persons in a society learning to be "native actors." A person learning to speak and behave in a culturally appropriate manner is "just fiddling with a set of rules which allow him to use terms [and otherwise behave] the way others do." If this is hocus-pocus, then there is no God's truth—either for the investigator or his subjects. The important thing is to write ethnographic statements whose implications for behavior are explicit and which can therefore be tested against competing statements.

I agree with Burling that the field has had more than its share of programmatic statements. Substantive descriptions are badly needed, and the intent of the programmatic statements was presumably to stimulate the production of such descriptions, not to generate more programmatic statements.

BURLING'S REJOINDER

The criticisms which Frake and Hymes level against my paper boil down to the suggestion that there are more ways to rid ourselves of the problems of indeterminacy than I admit, and that I have been unfair to various authors who have grappled with these problems and who have suggested ways out. I will start by admitting partial guilt. In my enthusiasm for the logical possibilities I did underplay the efforts of Frake, Conklin, and others to work out operationally explicit procedures by which they hope to arrive at determinate solutions. Hymes is quite right in pointing out that such procedures have been a central topic of several of their papers. I find Hymes' distinction between a "sorting" and an "assignment" particularly helpful in clarifying the discussion, and he is of course entirely correct when he points out that my discussion of the logical possibilities refers only to the former. The primary purpose of my paper, in fact, was to show just what an enormous gap there is between such a sorting and some particular assignment which claims to say something about the culture, or about the cognition of the people. I did try to suggest, even if too briefly, that there are possibilities of escape when I said, "As we learn more about all aspects of language use and its relation to non-linguistic events and as we bring studies of various semantic domains into harmony with each other and take wider and wider account of all aspects of behavior, we may be able to narrow down the alternatives," but apparently I did not elaborate on this enough. Nevertheless, having said this much, I would also assert that the real question is not whether these problems have been raised and struggled with, but whether the proposed techniques are adequate to the task of solving them. Hymes and Frake seem to believe that they are. I still have to be persuaded. I perceive two questions upon which we disagree: an empirical question, "Can enough of the alternatives be eliminated to make the technique live up to its promise?"; and an epistemological one, "Can even a gross reduction in alternatives ever tell us anything about cognition?" I will first comment briefly on the epistemological question.

Though it sounds banal, let me assert my belief that the best analysis is the one that most successfully predicts (corresponds to, describes, explains) behavior, and by behavior I include not only the use of terms (which was the subject of my paper), but also non-verbal behavior, and even the way people talk about their own terminology. Frake seems to agree when he says that there is no other criterion of "reality" except to test it against behavior, and this must mean that cognition is inferable only

from behavior, but I find it difficult to square this with some of his other statements. When he says, for instance, that his strategy will contribute data to problems of "the relations between language, cognition, and behavior," I am puzzled, for if cognition is entirely reducible to behavior, then I do not see how we can possibly investigate the relation *between* behavior and cognition. (Was this not the Whorfian fallacy?) When Hymes accuses me of skepticism about "most of anthropology, whenever it refers to values, orientations, attitudes, beliefs, or any other notion which imputes the presence of something inside people," he is correct. I am entirely skeptical about getting "inside people" via their behavior; but if I thought this constituted "most of anthropology," I wouldn't be here. Quite possibly, I simply misunderstand terms like "conceptualization" and "cognition"; and if these terms are nothing but shorthand ways of talking about behavior, I have no objection to them; but then I do object to trying to investigate the relation between behavior and cognition. Conceivably, however, our misunderstanding rests upon more subtle differences in our epistemological assumptions.

The question of whether the proposed techniques are sufficient to eliminate most alternatives, regardless of our assumptions about cognition, is, happily, more subject to empirical testing; and it is foolish for us to argue about it abstractly. My only justification for writing yet another programmatic article was that I have tried to analyse various sets of terms, and I have not found the proposed methods adequate. I have faced horrendous problems of alternative possibilities, and I felt that part of the difficulty stemmed from the logical problems raised in my paper. My colleagues may well be more clever and successful in these analyses than I. But when Goodenough suggests an intricate distinction between "lineal," "ablineal," and "co-lineal" to help in the ordering of English kin terms, I am not persuaded that he is approaching anyone's cognitive system, though he is certainly proposing a scheme that works. When Frake confidently tells us that for a Subanun "A case of *nuka* may eventually develop into one of 23 more serious diseases" (not "about 23" or "over 20" but just "23") I suspect the imposition of a spurious precision. I have no idea how many ways a "sore" can develop in English, and I doubt whether the number can be counted in a meaningful way. This is an example of what I felt to be "unjustified certainty in the particular analysis offered" when I quite unfairly seemed to be implying that Frake was unaware of the problems I raise. I am pleased when Conklin tells us that the decisive cognitive division among the American units of monetary exchange is between "coins" and "bills" or when Haugen shows that Icelandic *norðr, austr, suðr,* and *vestr* do not always mean the cardinal directions north, east, south, and west, but may also mean "in the direction leading ultimately to the north (east, south, west) quarter of the island," but we hardly need the elaborate terminology and complex methodological apparatus which has grown up around componential analysis to tell us these things.

Proponents of formal semantics have promised far more than a distinction between coins and bills or between books and magazines. They have held out the hope for analyses in other domains which would approach in elegance those which have already been done on kinship terms. I yield to no one in my admiration for

Goodenough's analysis of Trukese kinship terminology, but Goodenough showed that his methods were possible by giving us an analysis of a whole system, and not by simply suggesting methods and illustrating them on scattered and artificially simple examples. In discussing my fear of the residue of indeterminacy, I said, "I can be proved wrong by analyses which admit to no alternatives." But is it too much to ask for demonstrations of the technique on whole systems other than kinship or pronouns? One need not go off to exotic parts of the world to do this. English would really be a better test case, since readers could more easily judge the results. How about a full analysis of American folk terminology for trees? I have the nagging fear that the reason full analyses have not been given is because the methods advocated are not equal to the goals. I would really like to be proved wrong, for I think componential analysis is lots of fun, but I will only be persuaded by substantive descriptions, not by methodological arguments.

50

SOME COMMENTS ON FORMAL ANALYSIS
OF GRAMMATICAL AND SEMANTIC SYSTEMS

MURIEL HAMMER

INTRODUCTION

THE relationship between the "native's" structuring of reality and the alien analyst's structuring of reality comes up from time to time as a serious methodological question in social science. It arises in a number of forms. It has recently been prominent in discussions of componential analysis and generative grammar but has also been of some interest in more general social theory (for example, Does a clan need to be a named group? Is there class structure in a society without class consciousness—and,

From *American Anthropologist,* 68: 362–373. Reprinted by permission of the publisher and the author. Muriel Hammer is Senior Scientist (Biometrics), New York State Department of Mental Hygiene and Columbia University.

of course, the much larger problems of the relationship between stated norms and observed practices).

The attribution of more fundamental "truth" to the native's structuring than to the analyst's structuring often goes unquestioned. The more fundamental truth, then, quite naturally, becomes the criterion of validity for the analyst's work. Consideration of all the ontological and epistemological assumptions underlying this approach would be a very large undertaking; but it may be worthwhile to consider the implications of a few of these assumptions, with particular reference to two somewhat related areas of work in which they seem currently to be especially relevant. To focus the discussion, major attention will be given to specific works by Wallace [1] on semantic or componential analysis, and Chomsky [2] on transformational or generative grammar.

The main issue hinges on the distinction between open and closed systems, and the relationship between empirical and formal analysis. Related to this are questions about the appropriateness of formal and empirical criteria of adequacy for structural analysis, about the nature of change and how it relates to structural analysis, and about the connection between logical derivatives and different orders of empirical consequences.

An example, particularly of the last point, may be useful. It can easily be demonstrated that there cannot be a system with all three of the following characteristics:

(a) Sub-groups are hierarchically ordered; if A is higher than B, and B is higher than C, then A is higher than C.

(b) A man marries a woman of a higher-status sub-group.

(c) There is no set of people who cannot marry.

Clearly, if (a) is true, then either (b) or (c) cannot be true, since the highest status group of men and the lowest status group of women could not marry in accord with (b). But these characteristics are, in fact, described for Kachin marriage (Leach 1954). What happens, simply, is that the rules of the system are not empirically pushed to perfect consistency of application; at the bottom status levels (a) is weakened in that hierarchical distinctions are allowed to blur, while at the top, geographical distance "covers" for hierarchy and men marry non-local women. Thus, the empirical consequence that is derivable from the logical contradiction is that the system *cannot* operate consistently on the basis of the formulated rules and must involve departures from them at the logical "weak points," top and bottom.

Rather than discuss abstractly the questions raised above, this paper will consider them first in the context of Chomsky's criteria for grammar and then in terms of Wallace's discussion of "cognitive process" as revealed by componential analysis.

FINITE GRAMMARS AND "NATIVE SPEAKERS' INTUITION"

For Chomsky, a grammar is a theory of a language. He deals with a language as a set of sentences and states that in a natural language ". . . there are infinitely many sentences." The grammar of a language L is ". . . a device that generates all of the grammatical sequences of L and none of the ungrammatical ones." He goes on to say that "One requirement that a grammar must certainly meet is that it be finite"; and later, "Clearly, every grammar will have to meet certain *external conditions of adequacy* [italics his]; e.g., the sentences generated will have to be acceptable to the native speaker." Again, after stating that the proper goal of linguistic science should be that of ". . . developing an evaluation procedure for grammars . . . ," he says ". . . it is necessary to state precisely (if possible, with operational, behavioral tests) the external criteria of adequacy for grammars." He then mentions two other kinds of criteria which are concerned with internal standards (primarily simplicity) and cross-language generality.

There is no logical difficulty in a finite set of rules governing the production of a non-finite set or sequence of units. Euclidean geometry may be infinite; its rules are a finite, relatively simple set. Arithmetic and geometric series are infinite, and are generated by application of a (presumably) finite set of rules. But is a grammar really finite? Certainly no *complete* grammar of a natural language has ever really been accomplished or, to my knowledge, seriously attempted. While this may be a function of the unwieldy length that would be required or the relative lack of elegance, it is perhaps not even theoretically true that a grammar of a natural language is finite.

Let us first consider the listing procedures utilized in many "rules," in conjunction with the non-finiteness of vocabulary (whether for an individual or a language community). If it is possible to increase the number of units in the relevant "pool" (i.e., to make new words), then a comprehensive list of units governed by the rule in question is not only practically impossible, but theoretically impossible. Grammatical finiteness would then be preserved only if there is a finite set of rules governing all potential increases to the relevant pool (like the number system's "+1"), on the basis of which absolute prediction were possible of the lists in which each possible new unit would be included and the lists from which it would be excluded. If the linguistic "behavior" of any unit added to a language (or idiolect) were subject to "purely" linguistic conditions, such absolute prediction might be theoretically possible (though presumably not feasible). If, however, it is subject to influence from factors which are *accidental* from the point of view of the language, then absolute prediction depends, even theoretically, not only on the finiteness of the linguistic rules but on the finiteness of rules of the *total* complex of extra-linguistic systems whose influence has now entered consideration.

If it is agreed that no natural system—physical, biological, or cultural—is a closed system, then the demand for a finite set of rules governing the operation of the system—particularly if formulated *in absolute terms*—must be rejected as inapplicable.

The difference is important. In the search for a finite, generative grammar formulated in absolute terms, Chomsky holds the native speaker as ultimate criterion of grammaticalness. Disagreement among native speakers then must signify different languages; error of judgment is defined out of existence, and, along with it, change. Novelty is retained, but not change. New utterances can, as promised, be generated infinitely, but there is no way to modify the rules themselves. Yet it is clearly the case that the rules governing a language do change, and it may be suggested that they change not randomly but also according to rule. It is perfectly allowable to treat a language as if it were a static and closed system, to construct a system which is modeled on the basis of selected characteristics of a natural language, but precisely and exhaustively bounded to make it an eternal entity, subject to logical criteria of analysis. But it is not then permissible to use real speakers to provide the criteria for correctness and adequacy of analysis. It is, in fact, not possible to do so. Whatever may be the "locus" of the sentences that have not yet occurred but would be grammatical if they did, it may be assumed to be in the same vague terrain which also includes the locus of the rules that are in process of changing; and both loci must in some sense be attributed to these native speakers.

That the intuitive linguistic knowledge of the native speaker is not a simple criterion can readily be demonstrated. Hill (1958) has shown disagreement as to the grammaticalness of a set of sentences used as illustrations by Chomsky; years earlier, Leonard (1938) showed marked disagreements within a sample of educated, native English-speaking judges including linguists, English teachers, writers, and others,

on a number of expressions including very common ones such as "It's me." If it is objected, as Chomsky seems to do, that linguistic variations, even within a language community, are theoretically beside the point, since they merely indicate that the grammars appropriate to a number of idiolects are not identical, two new problems arise: first, one must somehow account for communication, since people do in fact speak to each other, and the grammaticalness of an utterance is relevant to such communication; and second, I think it can be shown that even our criterion individual has more than one grammar. He will accept sentences in speech that he will reject if they are written; he will accept in conversation sentences he will reject in a formal speech; he will produce sentences that he himself finds unacceptable if he listens to them; he will make judgments about grammaticalness inconsistently. (As a matter of fact, much of the time he doesn't speak in "sentences.") As a methodological problem this variability need not be an insurmountable difficulty, but in terms of linguistic theory it cannot be ignored. Which set of norms is "the grammar" even for an individual? Must not the grammatical rules be conditional on *extralinguistic* context?

If a grammar is sought which is *not* pragmatically conditional, one possible approach is the setting up of two connected grammars, one of maximal range and one of minimal range. The maximal range grammar would presumably be the simpler and more general set of rules governing the body of productions—let us restrict ourselves here to sentences—which might under some (but unspecified) conditions be considered acceptable in the language. The minimal range grammar would add those restrictions necessary for the production of only those sentences which are always formally acceptable. (It is of course not logically necessary that the set of rules be simpler for the maximal range grammar; it may well be the reverse. In any case, the relationship between these two grammars, as well as among the several grammars relevant to differing pragmatic definitions, needs exploration.) This approach, however, while not quite pragmatically conditional, is still not sufficiently freed of the speakers of the language to produce a finite grammar. Limitation to the minimal range grammar at a given time does not itself create the required speaker-free conditions for a finite grammar, but does perhaps provide an explicit basis for the construction of an artificially bound system completely comprehended in a finite set of rules. The criterion for any rule would not be the responses of the native speaker but the rule's contribution to coherence or elegance (etc.) of the set of rules for the constructed system; and, ultimately, its contribution to the construction of a system which permits manipulations yielding statements of relationship that cannot be worked out by dealing directly with the empirical material (e.g.—"holes" in the phonemic system).

The adequacy of the constructed system as a grammar for a particular language cannot really be evaluated. On the reasonable assumption that no grammar can ever perfectly predict the speakers' behavior (either in the production of sentences or in judgments about them), evaluative criteria would require greater specification than the seemingly simple requirement that all and only the "grammatical" sentences of the language be generated by the system. Putting aside the problem that this "simple" requirement begs the question of grammaticalness, the problems of selection of test-sentences, test-speakers, and weighting of results must be dealt with. Do we prefer a grammar which produces no errors, but has not the capacity to produce many of the sentences speakers consider perfectly correct, or one which allows the production of all correct sentences but also many that are not, or one with some intermediary degree of error and omission? We obviously cannot say, without some higher-order criterion. It is perfectly possible that very different grammars will be found most adequate for the criteria we would want to use in the differing contexts of teaching English to foreign students, decoding electronically recorded messages, writing poetry, assisting in psychiatric diagnosis, and in mechanical translation, for example. Within the last-mentioned, the grammars most adequate to translation from Hebrew to English, French to English, and English to French may again differ. The point here is not that a grammar must be "useful," but only that if its "adequacy" is to be evaluated, it must be evaluated with respect to something more exact, less varied, than a speaker's intuitive knowledge.

To put the matter in different terms, if there is no clear single external criterion of adequacy —and I believe there is not—then the choice among possible grammars must remain a function of the interests of the investigators (and those they communicate with). It would seem that there may be partial exceptions to this: (1)

in the case of choice between two grammars which formally handle a selected body of material equally well, but only one of which also handles an additional body of material, the more inclusive grammar seems clearly preferable, and (2) in the case of choice between two grammars which formally handle the same selected body of material, one more simply than the other, the simpler grammar seems clearly preferable. More generally, then, choice between grammars which differ only (or primarily) along a single dimension can be made. This is primarily a formal criterion, even though it involves the handling of a body of empirical material. At this point, however, a distinction should be made among formal models. We are not dealing with purely formal models like mathematics. The elements of the models of interest here derive from empirical concerns: thus the choice of units, their definition, the operations and relations utilized, are all initially influenced by the empirical interest that elicits the model. Nevertheless, the criteria of evaluation for the model must be formal; external criteria will necessarily be arbitrary.

To summarize briefly before turning to componential analysis, it has been argued here that finite formal grammars must be evaluated fundamentally in formal terms, that the rules involved in linguistic behavior are not a finite set because natural languages are not closed systems, and that the speakers of the language are not an appropriate source of evaluative criteria for a formal, finite grammar.

COMPONENTIAL ANALYSIS AND "PSYCHOLOGICAL REALITY"

Similar considerations apply to componential analysis of kinship. Let us first look at several statements from the introductory section of Wallace's article on "Culture and Cognition."

One of the products of modern studies in ethnographic method has been an increasing awareness that the research operations of the ethnographer produce primarily not naturalistic or statistical descriptions of regularities in overt behavior but descriptions of the rules which the actors are presumably employing, or attempting to employ, in the execution and mutual organization of this behavior. A second product of these methodological studies is the recognition that a set of such related rules forms a *calculus which describes cognitive process.* . . . What he [the ethnographer] does, . . . is to infer the system of rules which *these people are attempt-*

ing to apply. The assurance that he is on the way to an adequate understanding of these rules will be given him *by the logical completeness of the system he infers and by his ability, when using it, to produce behavior which an expert will reward* by saying, in effect, "That's right; that's good; now you've got it." Sometimes, of course, a sociologist or a psychologist will say to him, "But it is the behavior that is real, not the abstract system which no one actually applies perfectly and completely and which is merely the asymptote of the real curve of behaviors." To this the investigator simply replies that culture—conceived in this sense as a collection of formal calculi—is just as real as algebra, Euclidean geometry, and set theory, which are also "merely" the asymptotes of the "real" behavior of fallible students, professional mathematicians, and machines (Italics mine).

Wallace, like Chomsky, thus sets forth for the evaluation of the analyst's system of rules both formal criteria—"the logical completeness of the system he infers"—and external or empirical criteria—"his ability . . . to produce behavior which an expert will reward . . ." (the expert, of course, being native to the cultural group studied). (There is, incidentally, confusion here of the kind of knowledge involved in familiarity and skill with the kind of knowledge involved in analysis. An entomologist is, after all, not expected to carry honey around in his belly.) Wallace further makes explicit the relationship between the cultural "native" and the desired product of analysis: the latter is "the system of rules which these people are attempting to apply" and it "describes cognitive process."

One further quotation is necessary:

The commitment to describe the psychological reality of culture requires that not just any model which predicts some overt class of action be accepted, but only that model which is used as a system of reckoning by the actor. Not infrequently it can be demonstrated that two systems of reckoning will yield the same result in overt behavior. For example, there are several different ways to compute the square root of a number; the task in culture and cognition would be, not simply to find *a* way, but to find *the* way being actively employed by a person or a group. The technical problem of determining which of two equally predictive models corresponds best to the model actually being used by the subject requires the introduction of problems of choice which were not a part of the originally predicted behavior and which precede it in the chain of reckoning.

At this point, Wallace and Chomsky do not correspond—Chomsky does not (at least on the surface) demand that the speaker *use* the gram-marian's rules, but only that both ultimately arrive at the same sentence-judgments. Wallace goes further, and asks that the rules themselves correspond to "psychological reality."

The arguments against using concepts like "psychological reality," in this way are too well known to need repetition (i.e., one cannot get at it directly, or know when one "has" it, etc.). In view of this fact, however, and of the fact that it nevertheless continues to be used, it may be worth dealing with the values of such a concept, and considering possible ways of retaining those values without entering the domain of invisible, undefinable criteria. Reference to psychological reality (or cognitive process) is presumably not meant by Wallace to exclude overt behavior; it is meant to transcend it, in the sense that no one set of behaviors can be specified which is regularly the critical set, so that some overriding criterion must be introduced. Since we are unable to define the overriding criterion, we name it in a way which does not lend itself to being identified prematurely with concrete behavior. The obvious alternative solution is to define the overriding criterion. This solution is not suggested facetiously, although such a criterion would be exceedingly difficult to define.

Wallace illustrates the method of componential analysis using American-English consanguineal reference terminology. He shows that the 15 important kin types (or terms) may be formally defined along the three dimensions of sex, generation, and lineality. To decide whether this is an "adequate" analysis let us consider several empirical observations that might be made of American-English kin terminology:

(1) Reference terms like "uncle" and "aunt" are used by natives to refer to individuals with no consanguineal relationship to Ego. These individuals include the spouses of parents' siblings (even when they are childless), sometimes parents' siblings of one's own spouse, and for some, but not all Egos, long-term close friends of Ego's parents. Ego readily responds to specific questions about his uncles and aunts by distinguishing parents' friends from the others as "not really related."

(2) Some Egos at some times distinguish named categories according to generation and lineality within the "cousin" category. The terms used include "first cousins" and "second cousins," and sometimes "cousins once removed." Questioning of natives about the defi-

nitions of these terms, and the kin to whom they refer, elicits highly varied responses.

(3) When there are large age discrepancies within the same kin category, Ego tends to qualify his use of the reference term for some of them by assertions like, "He's really my uncle but he's my age," or by including the "deviant" relative in the "wrong" kin category such as "cousin."

(4) Some Egos qualify their use of the reference term for specific individuals in terms of their history of interactions—for example, "He's more my brother really than my cousin because my mother brought him up."

(5) Natives give vague and inconsistent responses to questions involving extension of kinship to distant cousins and such persons as first cousins' spouses or mother's brother's wife's sister and her husband. A plausible hypothesis is that extension of kinship terms to such individuals is a function of the family's network of interactions, rather than any combination of the three dimensions cited.

Many other observations could be added to reinforce the conclusion that sex, generation, and lineality are not adequate as dimensions of the American-English kinship terminological reference system. Romney and d'Andrade suggest a fourth dimension, reciprocity, as an improvement in terms of native speakers' (in this case, high school students) responses to subsets of kin terms.

However, such a conclusion about inadequacy is initially in the wrong domain if the dimensions formally work for the phenomena selected as within the boundaries of the system analyzed. The question of *adequacy to the selected system* must be asked in formal terms (e.g., is there a simpler or more elegant or more general solution?). The question of *adequacy to empirically observable usage* can only be asked with reference to some specified kind of utility (e.g., what is the system's relevance to some sets of kin-behavior other than terms, or to variation in term-usage with variation in situation, etc.).

The classic "application" of componential analysis of kinship to ethnographic data (Kroeber 1909) may be paraphrased as follows: (1) assuming the same set of biologically related individuals for all humans; (2) assuming the culturally specific sets of terms of reference and persons to whom they refer as given in ethnographic descriptions; (3) defining a limited set of dimensions on the basis of which these biologically related individuals may be categorized by these terms of reference; and (4) assuming (implicitly) the basic formal criterion of economy of analysis, Kroeber finds that the kinship systems he deals with differ in terms of the particular dimensions used, the number of dimensions used, and the internal consistency—or relative redundancy—of use of those dimensions. The number and internal consistency of dimension-use, according to Kroeber, reflect a bi-polar distribution which corresponds to the older dichotomy between "descriptive" and "classificatory" systems, or to "political" and "kin-based" societies. It should be noted that while the particular purpose of Kroeber's analysis does provide an external criterion of adequacy of the underlying formal analyses— i.e., a way of distinguishing two general types— the external criterion in this case has nothing to do with the behavior (or cognition) of the native informants. They, of course, were the source of the data on kinship terms and their referents, but they were not in any other way relevant to the analysis. If the data were correct and the analyses were formally proper, the native informant's confession or denial that he uses those dimensions would have no bearing on Kroeber's results. Morgan's own use of kinship data may be seen as componential analysis which was then organized within a theory involving premises about covariation of named categories and social distinctions and about differential rates of change in cultural characteristics. One source of difficulty in evaluating some of Morgan's work is the lack of separation between the formal and the empirical aspects of the theory.

One further kind of comment on componential analysis should be considered here. Burling (1964) has provided the simple arithmetic for the complex issue involving the very large number of componential analyses possible for even a small number of items. Hymes (1964) has argued that independently elicited information on the informants' principles of "sorting" can eliminate from consideration many logical possibilities. It should be said, first, that componential analysis does not deal with a number of separate items, but with an informant-produced sorting of those items into named sets (such as mo bro+fa bro+mo si hu+fa si hu). The analyst extracts possible principles for such a sorting. On the whole, the number of possible alternatives is *reduced* rather than *increased* when the number of items is larger, since the analyst is *not* free to sort them. But let us look again at the nature of "cognitive reality." If my informant sorts a series of items in such a way that all the yellow objects (triangular and circular) are in one group, and all the blue objects (triangular and square) are in another, and he tells me he is sorting on the basis of shape, he may, of course, be joking, lying, or stupid, or he may be rationalizing (poorly) a set of behaviors whose abstract logical principles he never learned, does not consciously use, and does not really know. The example above may be too simple to be believable, but anyone who has ever tried to give road map directions to a place he gets to with ease, or explain the construction of plural nouns to a child, or the basis of his recognizing as Elizabethan a particular piece of music he has not heard before will realize that people can often "sort" reliably without having information on their sorting principles. Far worse, they may readily give information on principles they are simply not using. Verplanck (1962) summarizes relevant experimental work on this question, indicating that subjects' statements of the rules they were using and the sortings they actually made, could be experimentally controlled *essentially independently of each other.* If I want to know how he will talk about his rules for sorting, I need to study that; but if I want to know how he will sort, I had better not study his stated rules.

In the same article already cited, Wallace states with perfect clarity a position which seems to me to contradict the demand for psychological reality. He points out:

> Now, just as the ethnographer may invent a taxonomic model which will predict satisfactorily how a speaker will refer to his kinsmen but which does not describe how the speaker reckons kinfolk, so it is possible that two members of the same society may produce similar or complementary behaviors without sharing the same cognitive model.

His resolution of the apparent paradox is to ask for a "metacalculus" which deals with the "diverse calculi of particular individuals or subgroups cooperating to maintain stable systems of relationships. . . ." But such a calculus cannot be presumed to have any "psychological reality" for anyone except, perhaps, the ethnographer.

CONCLUSION

It also seems quite clear that cultural systems, in Wallace's sense of sets of rules, have actual indeterminacy, which is not merely a function of incomplete or inadequate analysis. There are, at any time, potential value conflicts (i.e., conflicts between operative principles) which simply have not yet arisen. When they arise, the conditions under which they arise will affect their resolution, and new principles will have been created. Furthermore, the systems of rules will be affected by the partly chance question of *which* conflicts arise, and in what sequence. A set of rules analyzed systematically has the power of producing a number of logical derivatives which are not obvious in less formal descriptions of the same basic data. These cannot form the basis of simple predictions of future behavior, but they can make explicit the nature of the potential conflicts (still in formal terms) and thus the alternatives available *within the framework of analysis, assuming sets of posited conditions apply when the conflict arises.* In those cases where there is good empirical information on the changing conditions which affect the phenomena that are the source of the data assumed in the formal analyses, and where the logical derivatives of those analyses involve few alternatives, predictions may be quite good. Failing these requirements, they will not be. But the formal analyses provide the *only* possible basis of dealing systematically with this kind of indeterminancy. To insist that they can not be evaluated in terms of the native's cognitive structure is not, I think, to minimize their importance. On the contrary, their freedom from native intuition is a source of their power.

It may be suggested then that componential analyses, like grammars of a language, are finite and formal, and, thereby, unlike the behaviors utilized in their derivation. They may be evaluated in formal terms. Selection of external criteria of adequacy is necessarily and quite properly arbitrary. The arbitrariness (from the formal point of view) of the external criteria need not, however, be capricious. Formal analyses derive their advantage in large measure from the wide scope of their applicability and from the clarity with which internal characteristics such as consistency are revealed. The most effective use to be made of them, therefore, involves the subjecting of a diversity of conditions to the same essential analysis—as sugugested in Chomsky's generality criterion—and the derivation of hypotheses about change of structure from the conflicts within a system or between systems when analyzed jointly.

The questions to which formal and empirical analyses are most appropriately addressed are fundamentally different. "Explanation" requires both to be joined; and the process of joining them raises the most complex and scientifically least well treated methodological questions.

It may be necessary to state here that I am exaggerating the degree of separation possible between formal and empirical study. Any empirical analysis must of necessity utilize formal structures, categories, modes of connection; and formal analyses cannot be entirely empty, even if they only use points, lines, numbers, and equal signs.

But they are distinct, and the blurring of the distinction is not a good thing for the study of human society. It leads to ethnographies with no behavioral data, and to theories with no generality.

Questions about what people say and do, where they live, how many of them there are, what parts of their environment they use and how they use it, all require empirical answers. These are not simple questions to answer, and the structuring the questions require in order to allow for investigation makes some formalization essential. They are, however, quite different questions from those dealing with dimensions of social categorization, or with principles of maintenance and change of systems, or with structural definition of a code, or with the formal changes implied by the addition of a fifth member to a four-member unit.

Social explanation demands that we know both; improper merging of the two procedures neither. It is generally recognized that data pushed and mutilated at the altar of a theory is improper as an empirical report; it seems less well recognized that *formal* systems must be judged primarily by formal criteria. The crossing of the criteria is proper only as a secondary procedure, and only partially. That is, for a given purpose these data or this formal system may or may not be to the point, may be more or less satisfactory. Their validity must be evaluated in other terms.

NOTES

1. Anthony F. C. Wallace, "Culture and Cognition," *Science* (1962), 135: 351–357.
2. Noam Chomsky, *Syntactic Structures*, The Hague, 1957.

51

STRUCTURAL ANALYSIS IN LINGUISTICS AND IN ANTHROPOLOGY

CLAUDE LÉVI-STRAUSS

LINGUISTICS occupies a special place among the social sciences, to whose ranks it unquestionably belongs. It is not merely a social science like the others, but, rather, the one in which by far the greatest progress has been made. It is probably the only one which can truly claim to be a science and which has achieved both the formulation of an empirical method and an understanding of the nature of the data submitted to its analysis. This privileged position

From *Structural Anthropology*. Copyright © 1963 by Basic Books, Inc., Publishers, New York. Reprinted by permission of the publisher and the author. Claude Lévi-Strauss is Professor of Social Anthropology, Collège de France, Paris.

carries with it several obligations. The linguist will often find scientists from related but different disciplines drawing inspiration from his example and trying to follow his lead. *Noblesse oblige.* A linguistic journal like *Word* cannot confine itself to the illustration of strictly linguistic theories and points of view. It must also welcome psychologists, sociologists, and anthropologists eager to learn from modern linguistics the road which leads to the empirical knowledge of social phenomena. As Marcel Mauss wrote already forty years ago: "Sociology would certainly have progressed much further if it had everywhere followed the lead of the linguists. . . ." The close methodological analogy which exists between the two disciplines imposes a special obligation of collaboration upon them.

Ever since the work of Schrader it has been unnecessary to demonstrate the assistance which linguistics can render to the anthropologist in the study of kinship. It was a linguist and a philologist (Schrader and Rose) who showed the improbability of the hypothesis of matrilineal survivals in the family in antiquity, to which so many anthropologists still clung at that time. The linguist provides the anthropologist with etymologies which permit him to establish between certain kinship terms relationships that were not immediately apparent. The anthropologist, on the other hand, can bring to the attention of the linguist customs, prescriptions, and prohibitions that help him to understand the persistence of certain features of language or the instability of terms or groups of terms. At a meeting of the Linguistic Circle of New York, Julien Bonfante once illustrated this point of view by reviewing the etymology of the word for uncle in several Romance languages. The Greek θεῖος corresponds in Italian, Spanish, and Portuguese to *zio* and *tio;* and he added that in certain regions of Italy the uncle is called *barba.* The "beard," the "divine" uncle —what a wealth of suggestions for the anthropologist! The investigations of the late A. M. Hocart into the religious character of the avuncular relationship and the "theft of the sacrifice" by the maternal kinsmen immediately come to mind. Whatever interpretation is given to the data collected by Hocart (and his own interpretation is not entirely satisfactory), there is no doubt that the linguist contributes to the solution of the problem by revealing the tenacious survival in contemporary vocabulary of relationships which have long since disap-

peared. At the same time, the anthropologist explains to the linguist the bases of etymology and confirms its validity. Paul K. Benedict, in examining, as a linguist, the kinship systems of Southeast Asia, was able to make an important contribution to the anthropology of the family in that area.

But linguists and anthropologists follow their own paths independently. They halt, no doubt, from time to time to communicate to one another certain of their findings; these findings, however, derive from different operations, and no effort is made to enable one group to benefit from the technical and methodological advances of the other. This attitude might have been justified in the era when linguistic research leaned most heavily on historical analysis. In relation to the anthropological research conducted during the same period, the difference was one of degree rather than of kind. The linguists employed a more rigorous method, and their findings were established on more solid grounds; the sociologists could follow their example in "renouncing consideration of the spatial distribution of contemporary types as a basis for their classifications." But, after all, anthropology and sociology were looking to linguistics only for insights; nothing foretold a revelation.

The advent of structural linguistics completely changed this situation. Not only did it renew linguistic perspectives; a transformation of this magnitude is not limited to a single discipline. Structural linguistics will certainly play the same renovating role with respect to the social sciences that nuclear physics, for example, has played for the physical sciences. In what does this revolution consist, as we try to assess its broader implications? N. Troubetzkoy, the illustrious founder of structural linguistics, himself furnished for the answer to this question. In one programmatic statement, he reduced the structural method˙ to four basic operations. First, structural linguistics shifts from the study of *conscious* linguistic phenomena to study of their *unconscious* infrastructure; second, it does not treat *terms* as independent entities, taking instead as its basis of analysis the *relations* between terms; third, it introduces the concept of *system*—"Modern phonemics does not merely proclaim that phonemes are always part of a system; it *shows* concrete phonemic systems and elucidates their structure"—; finally, structural linguistics aims at discovering *general laws,* either by induction "or . . . by logical deduction, which would give them an absolute character."

Thus, for the first time, a social science is able to formulate necessary relationships. This is the meaning of Troubetzkoy's last point, while the preceding rules show how linguistics must proceed in order to attain this end. It is not for us to show that Troubetzkoy's claims are justified. The vast majority of modern linguists seem sufficiently agreed on this point. But when an event of this importance takes place in one of the sciences of man, it is not only permissible for, but required of, representatives of related disciplines immediately to examine its consequences and its possible application to phenomena of another order.

New perspectives then open up. We are no longer dealing with an occasional collaboration where the linguist and the anthropologist, each working by himself, occasionally communicate those findings which each thinks may interest the other. In the study of kinship problems (and, no doubt, the study of other problems as well), the anthropologist finds himself in a situation which formally resembles that of the structural linguist. Like phonemes, kinship terms are elements of meaning; like phonemes, they acquire meaning only if they are integrated into systems. "Kinship systems," like "phonemic systems," are built by the mind on the level of unconscious thought. Finally, the recurrence of kinship patterns, marriage rules, similar prescribed attitudes between certain types of relatives, and so forth, in scattered regions of the globe and in fundamentally different societies, leads us to believe that, in the case of kinship as well as linguistics, the observable phenomena result from the action of laws which are general but implicit. The problem can therefore be formulated as follows: Although they belong to *another order of reality,* kinship phenomena are *of the same type* as linguistic phenomena. Can the anthropologist, using a method analogous *in form* (if not in content) to the method used in structural linguistics, achieve the same kind of progress in his own science as that which has taken place in linguistics?

We shall be even more strongly inclined to follow this path after an additional observation has been made. The study of kinship problems is today broached in the same terms and seems to be in the throes of the same difficulties as was linguistics on the eve of the structuralist revolution. There is a striking analogy between certain attempts by Rivers and the old lin-

guistics, which sought its explanatory principles first of all in history. In both cases, it is solely (or almost solely) diachronic analysis which must account for synchronic phenomena. Troubetzkoy, comparing structural linguistics and the old linguistics, defines structural linguistics as a "systematic structuralism and universalism," which he contrasts with the individualism and "atomism" of former schools. And when he considers diachronic analysis, his perspective is a profoundly modified one: "The evolution of a phonemic system at any given moment is directed by the *tendency toward a goal.* . . . This evolution thus has a direction, an internal logic, which historical phonemics is called upon to elucidate." The "individualistic" and "atomistic" interpretation, founded exclusively on historical contingency, which is criticized by Troubetzkoy and Jakobson, is actually the same as that which is generally applied to kinship problems. Each detail of terminology and each special marriage rule is associated with a specific custom as either its consequence or its survival. We thus meet with a chaos of discontinuity. No one asks how kinship systems, regarded as synchronic wholes, could be the arbitrary product of a convergence of several heterogeneous institutions (most of which are hypothetical), yet nevertheless function with some sort of regularity and effectiveness.

However, a preliminary difficulty impedes the transposition of the phonemic method to the anthropological study of primitive peoples. The superficial analogy between phonemic systems and kinship systems is so strong that it immediately sets us on the wrong track. It is incorrect to equate kinship terms and linguistic phonemes from the viewpoint of their formal treatment. We know that to obtain a structural law the linguist analyzes phonemes into "distinctive features," which he can then group into one or several "pairs of oppositions." Following an analogous method, the anthropologist might be tempted to break down analytically the kinship terms of any given system into their components. In our own kinship system, for instance, the term *father* has positive connotations with respect to sex, relative age, and generation; but it has a zero value on the dimension of collaterality, and it cannot express an affinal relationship. Thus, for each system, one might ask what relationships are expressed and, for each term of the system, what connotation—positive or negative—it carries regarding each of the following relationships: generation, collaterality, sex, relative age, affinity, etc. It is at this "micro-sociological" level that one might hope to discover the most general structural laws, just as the linguist discovers his at the infra-phonemic level or the physicist at the infra-molecular or atomic level. One might interpret the interesting attempt of Davis and Warner in these terms.[1]

But a threefold objection immediately arises. A truly scientific analysis must be real, simplifying, and explanatory. Thus the distinctive features which are the product of phonemic analysis have an objective existence from three points of view: psychological, physiological, and even physical; they are fewer in number than the phonemes which result from their combination; and, finally, they allow us to understand and reconstruct the system. Nothing of the kind would emerge from the preceding hypothesis. The treatment of kinship terms which we have just sketched is analytical in appearance only; for, actually, the result is more abstract than the principle; instead of moving toward the concrete, one moves away from it, and the definitive system—if system there is—is only conceptual. Secondly, Davis and Warner's experiment proves that the system achieved through this procedure is infinitely more complex and more difficult to interpret than the empirical data. Finally, the hypothesis has no explanatory value; that is, it does not lead to an understanding of the nature of the system and still less to a reconstruction of its origins.

What is the reason for this failure? A too literal adherence to linguistic method actually betrays its very essence. Kinship terms not only have a sociological existence; they are also elements of speech. In our haste to apply the methods of linguistic analysis, we must not forget that, as a part of vocabulary, kinship terms must be treated with linguistic methods in direct and not analogous fashion. Linguistics teaches us precisely that structural analysis cannot be applied to words directly, but only to words previously broken down into phonemes. *There are no necessary relationships at the vocabulary level.* This applies to all vocabulary elements, including kinship terms. Since this applies to linguistics, it ought to apply *ipso facto* to the sociology of language. An attempt like the one whose possibility we are now discussing would thus consist in extending the method of structural linguistics while ignoring its basic requirements. Kroeber prophetically foresaw this difficulty in an article written many years ago.[2] And

if, at that time, he concluded that a structural analysis of kinship terminology was impossible, we must remember that linguistics itself was then restricted to phonetic, psychological, and historical analysis. While it is true that the social sciences must share the limitations of linguistics, they can also benefit from its progress.

Nor should we overlook the profound differences between the phonemic chart of a language and the chart of kinship terms of a society. In the first instance there can be no question as to function; we all know that language serves as a means of communication. On the other hand, what the linguist did not know and what structural linguistics alone has allowed him to discover is the way in which language achieves this end. The function was obvious; the system remained unknown. In this respect, the anthropologist finds himself in the opposite situation. We know, since the work of Lewis H. Morgan, that kinship terms constitute systems; on the other hand, we still do not know their function. The misinterpretation of this initial situation reduces most structural analyses of kinship systems to pure tautologies. They demonstrate the obvious and neglect the unknown.

This does not mean that we must abandon hope of introducing order and discovering meaning in kinship nomenclature. But we should at least recognize the special problems raised by the sociology of vocabulary and the ambiguous character of the relations between its methods and those of linguistics. For this reason it would be preferable to limit the discussion to a case where the analogy can be clearly established. Fortunately, we have just such a case available.

What is generally called a "kinship system" comprises two quite different orders of reality. First, there are terms through which various kinds of family relationships are expressed. But kinship is not expressed solely through nomenclature. The individuals or classes of individuals who employ these terms feel (or do not feel, as the case may be) bound by prescribed behavior in their relations with one another, such as respect or familiarity, rights or obligations, and affection or hostility. Thus, along with what we propose to call the *system of terminology* (which, strictly speaking, constitutes the vocabulary system), there is another system, both psychological and social in nature, which we shall call the *system of attitudes.* Although it is true (as we have shown above) that the study of systems of terminology places us in a situation analogous, but opposite, to the situation in which we are dealing with phonemic systems, this difficulty is "inversed," as it were, when we examine systems of attitudes. We can guess at the role played by systems of attitudes, that is, to insure group cohesion and equilibrium, but we do not understand the nature of the interconnections between the various attitudes, nor do we perceive their necessity. In other words, as in the case of language, we know their function, but the system is unknown.

Thus we find a profound difference between the *system of terminology* and the *system of attitudes,* and we have to disagree with A. R. Radcliffe-Brown if he really believed, as has been said of him, that attitudes are nothing but the expression or transposition of terms on the affective level. The last few years have provided numerous examples of groups whose chart of kinship terms does not accurately reflect family attitudes, and vice versa. It would be incorrect to assume that the kinship system constitutes the principal means of regulating interpersonal relationships in all societies. Even in societies where the kinship system does function as such, it does not fulfill that role everywhere to the same extent. Furthermore, it is always necessary to distinguish between two types of attitudes: first, the diffuse, uncrystallized, and non-institutionalized attitudes, which we may consider as the reflection or transposition of the terminology on the psychological level; and second, along with, or in addition to, the preceding ones, those attitudes which are stylized, prescribed, and sanctioned by taboos or privileges and expressed through a fixed ritual. These attitudes, far from automatically reflecting the nomenclature, often appear as secondary elaborations, which serve to resolve the contradictions and overcome the deficiencies inherent in the terminological system. This synthetic character is strikingly apparent among the Wik Munkan of Australia. In this group, joking privileges sanction a contradiction between the kinship relations which link two unmarried men and the theoretical relationship which must be assumed to exist between them in order to account for their later marriages to two women who do not stand themselves in the corresponding relationship. There is a contradiction between two possible systems of nomenclature, and the emphasis placed on attitudes represents an attempt to integrate or transcend this contradiction. We can easily agree with

Radcliffe-Brown and assert the existence of "real relations of interpendence between the terminology and the rest of the system." Some of his critics made the mistake of inferring, from the absence of a rigorous parallelism between attitudes and nomenclature, that the two systems were mutually independent. But this relationship of interdependence does not imply a one-to-one correlation. The system of attitudes constitutes, rather, a dynamic integration of the system of terminology.

Granted the hypothesis (to which we wholeheartedly subscribe) of a functional relationship between the two systems, we are nevertheless entitled, for methodological reasons, to treat independently the problems pertaining to each system. This is what we propose to do here for a problem which is rightly considered the point of departure for any theory of attitudes—that of the maternal uncle. We shall attempt to show how a formal transposition of the method of structural linguistics allows us to shed new light upon this problem. Because the relationship between nephew and maternal uncle appears to have been the focus of significant elaboration in a great many primitive societies, anthropologists have devoted special attention to it. It is not enough to note the frequency of this theme; we must also account for it.

Let us briefly review the principal stages in the development of this problem. During the entire nineteenth century and until the writings of Sydney Hartland, the importance of the mother's brother was interpreted as a survival of matrilineal descent. This interpretation was based purely on speculation, and, indeed, it was highly improbable in the light of European examples. Furthermore, Rivers' attempt to explain the importance of the mother's brother in southern India as a residue of cross-cousin marriage led to particularly deplorable results. Rivers himself was forced to recognize that this interpretation could not account for all aspects of the problem. He resigned himself to the hypothesis that *several* heterogeneous customs which have since disappeared (cross-cousin marriage being only one of them) were needed to explain the existence of a *single* institution. Thus, atomism and mechanism triumphed. It was Lowie's crucial article on the matrilineal complex [3] which opened what we should like to call the "modern phase" of the problem of the avunculate. Lowie showed that the correlation drawn or postulated between the prominent position of the maternal uncle and matrilineal descent cannot withstand rigorous analysis. In fact, the avunculate is found associated with patrilineal, as well as matrilineal, descent. The role of the maternal uncle cannot be explained as either a consequence or a survival of matrilineal kinship; it is only a specific application "of a very general tendency to associate definite social relations with definite forms of kinship regardless of maternal or paternal side." In accordance with this principle, introduced for the first time by Lowie in 1919, there exists a general tendency to *qualify attitudes*, which constitutes the only empirical foundation for a theory of kinship systems. But, at the same time, Lowie left certain questions unanswered. What exactly do we call an avunculate? Do we not merge different customs and attitudes under this single term? And, if it is true that there is a tendency to qualify all attitudes, why are only certain attitudes associated with the avuncular relationship, rather than just any possible attitudes, depending upon the group considered?

A few further remarks here may underline the striking analogy between the development of this problem and certain stages in the evolution of linguistic theory. The variety of possible attitudes in the area of interpersonal relationships is almost unlimited; the same holds true for the variety of sounds which can be articulated by the vocal apparatus—and which are actually produced during the first months of human life. Each language, however, retains only a very small number among all the possible sounds, and in this respect linguistics raises two questions: Why are certain sounds selected? What relationships exist between one or several of the sounds chosen and all the others? Our sketch of the historical development of the avuncular problem is at precisely the same stage. Like language, the social group has a great wealth of psycho-physiological material at its disposal. Like language too, it retains only certain elements, at least some of which remain the same throughout the most varied cultures and are combined into structures which are always diversified. Thus we may wonder about the reason for this choice and the laws of combination.

For insight into the specific problem of the avunculate we should turn to Radcliffe-Brown. His well-known article on the maternal uncle in South Africa [4] was the first attempt to grasp and analyze the modalities of what we might call the "general principle of attitude qualification." We shall briefly review the fundamental ideas of that now-classic study.

According to Radcliffe-Brown, the term *avunculate* covers two antithetical systems of attitudes. In one case, the maternal uncle represents family authority; he is feared and obeyed, and possesses certain rights over his nephew. In the other case, the nephew holds privileges of familiarity in relation to his uncle and can treat him more or less as his victim. Second, there is a correlation between the boy's attitude toward his maternal uncle and his attitude toward his father. We find the two systems of attitudes in both cases, but they are inversely correlated. In groups where familiarity characterizes the relationship between father and son, the relationship between maternal uncle and nephew is one of respect; and where the father stands as the austere representative of family authority, it is the uncle who is treated with familiarity. Thus the two sets of attitudes constitute (as the structural linguist would say) two pairs of oppositions. Radcliffe-Brown concluded his article by proposing the following interpretation: In the final analysis, it is descent that determines the choice of oppositions. In patrilineal societies, where the father and the father's descent group represent traditional authority, the maternal uncle is considered a "male mother." He is generally treated in the same fashion, and sometimes even called by the same name, as the mother. In matrilineal societies, the opposite occurs. Here, authority is vested in the maternal uncle, while relationships of tenderness and familiarity revolve about the father and his descent group.

It would indeed be difficult to exaggerate the importance of Radcliffe-Brown's contribution, which was the first attempt at synthesis on an empirical basis following Lowie's authorative and merciless criticism of evolutionist metaphysics. To say that this effort did not entirely succeed does not in any way diminish the homage due this great British anthropologist; but we should certainly recognize that Radcliffe-Brown's article leaves unanswered some fundamental questions. First, the avunculate does not occur in all matrilineal or all patrilineal systems, and we find it present in some systems which are neither matrilineal nor patrilineal. Further, the avuncular relationship is not limited to two terms, but presupposes four, namely, brother,

sister, brother-in-law, and nephew. An interpretation such as Radcliffe-Brown's arbitrarily
isolates particular elements of a global structure
which must be treated as a whole. A few
simple examples will illustrate this twofold
difficulty.

The social organization of the Trobriand Islanders of Melanesia is characterized by matrilineal descent, free and familiar relations between father and son, and a marked antagonism
between maternal uncle and nephew. On the
other hand, the patrilineal Cherkess of the Caucasus place the hostility between father and son,
while the maternal uncle assists his nephew and
gives him a horse when he marries. Up to this
point we are still within the limits of Radcliffe-
Brown's scheme. But let us consider the other
family relationships involved. Malinowski
showed that in the Trobriands husband and
wife live in an atmosphere of tender intimacy
and that their relationship is characterized by
reciprocity. The relations between brother and
sister, on the other hand, are dominated by an
extremely rigid taboo. Let us now compare the
situation in the Caucasus. There, it is the
brother-sister relationship which is tender—to
such an extent that among the Pschav an only
daughter "adopts" a "brother" who will play
the customary brother's role as her chaste bed
companion. But the relationship between spouses
is entirely different. A Cherkess will not appear
in public with his wife and visits her only in
secret. According to Malinowski, there is no
greater insult in the Trobriands than to tell a
man that he resembles his sister. In the Caucasus
there is an analogous prohibition: It is forbidden
to ask a man about his wife's health.

When we consider societies of the Cherkess
and Trobriand types it is not enough to study
the correlation of attitudes between *father/son*
and *uncle/sister's son*. This correlation is only
one aspect of a global system containing four
types of relationships which are organically
linked, namely: *brother/sister, husband/wife,
father/son,* and *mother's brother/sister's son*.
The two groups in our example illustrate a
law which can be formulated as follows: In both
groups, the relation between maternal uncle
and nephew is to the relation between brother
and sister as the relation between father and
son is to that between husband and wife. Thus
if we know one pair of relations, it is always
possible to infer the other.

Let us now examine some other cases. On
Tonga, in Polynesia, descent is patrilineal, as

among the Cherkess. Relations between husband
and wife appear to be public and harmonious.
Domestic quarrels are rare, and although the
wife is often of superior rank, the husband
". . . is nevertheless of higher authority in all
domestic matters, and no woman entertains the
least idea of rebelling against that authority."
At the same time there is great freedom between nephew and maternal uncle. The nephew
is *fahu,* or above the law, in relation to his
uncle, toward whom extreme familiarity is permitted. This freedom strongly contrasts with
the father-son relationship. The father is *tapu;*
the son cannot touch his father's head or hair;
he cannot touch him while he eats, sleep in his
bed or on his pillow, share his food or drink,
or play with his possessions. However, the
strongest *tapu* of all is the one between brother
and sister, who must never be together under
the same roof.

Although they are also patrilineal and patrilocal, the natives of Lake Kutubu in New
Guinea offer an example of the opposite type
of structure. F. E. Williams writes: "I have
never seen such a close and apparently affectionate association between father and son. . . ."
Relations between husband and wife are characterized by the very low status ascribed to
women and "the marked separation of masculine and feminine interests. . . ." The women,
according to Williams, "are expected to work
hard for their masters . . . they occasionally protest, and protest may be met with a beating."
The wife can always call upon her brother for
protection against her husband, and it is with
him that she seeks refuge. As for the relationship between nephew and maternal uncle, it is
". . . best summed up in the word 'resepct' . . .
tinged with apprehensiveness," for the maternal
uncle has the power to curse his nephew and
inflicts serious illness upon him (just as among
the Kipsigis of Africa).

Although patrilineal, the society described
by Williams is structurally of the same type
as that of the Siuai of Bougainville, who have
matrilineal descent. Between brother and sister
there is ". . . friendly interaction and mutual
generosity. . . ." As regards the father-son
relationship, Oliver writes, ". . . I could discover little evidence that the word 'father'
evokes images of hostility or stern authority or
awed respect." But the relationship between the
nephew and his mother's brother "appears to
range between stern discipline and genial mutual
dependence. . . ." However, ". . . most of the

informants agreed that all boys stand in some awe of their mother's brothers, and are more likely to obey them than their own fathers. . . ." Between husband and wife harmonious understanding is rare: ". . . there are few young wives who remain altogether faithful . . . most young husbands are continually suspicious and often give vent to jealous anger . . . marriages involve a number of adjustments, some of them apparently difficult. . . ."

The same picture, but sharper still, characterizes the Dobuans, who are matrilineal and neighbors of the equally matrilineal Trobrianders, while their structure is very different. Dobuan marriages are unstable, adultery is widespread, and husband and wife constantly fear death induced by their spouse's witchcraft. Actually, Fortune's remark, "It is a most serious insult to refer to a woman's witchcraft so that her husband will hear of it" appears to be a variant of the Trobriand and Caucasian taboos cited above.

In Dobu, the mother's brother is held to be the harshest of all the relatives. "The mother's brother may beat children long after their parents have ceased to do so," and they are forbidden to utter his name. There is a tender relationship with the "navel," the mother's sister's husband, who is the father's double, rather than with the father himself. Nevertheless, the father is considered "less harsh" than the mother's brother and will always seek, contrary to the laws of inheritance, to favor his son at the expense of his uterine nephew. And, finally, "the strongest of all social bonds" is the one between brother and sister.

What can we conclude from these examples? The correlation between types of descent and forms of avunculate does not exhaust the problem. Different forms of avunculate can coexist with the same type of descent, whether patrilineal or matrilineal. But we constantly find the same fundamental relationship between the four pairs of oppositions required to construct the system. This will emerge more clearly from the diagrams which illustrate our examples. The sign + indicates free and familiar relations, and the sign — stands for relations characterized by hostility, antagonism, or reserve (Figure 1). This is an oversimplification, but we can tentatively make use of it. We shall describe some of the indispensable refinements farther on.

The synchronic law of correlation thus suggested may be validated diachronically. If we summarize, after Howard, the evolution of

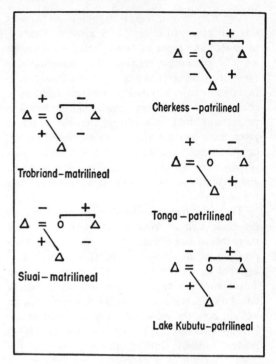

FIGURE 1

family relationships during the Middle Ages, we find approximately this pattern: The brother's authority over his sister wanes, and that of the prospective husband increases. Simultaneously, the bond between father and son is weakened and that between maternal uncle and nephew is reinforced.

This evolution seems to be confirmed by the documents gathered by Léon Gautier, for in the "conservative" texts (Raoul de Cambrai, Geste des Loherains, etc.), the positive relationship is established chiefly between father and son and is only gradually displaced toward the maternal uncle and nephew.

Thus we see that in order to understand the avunculate we must treat it as one relationship within a system, while the system itself must be considered as a whole in order to grasp its structure. This structure rests upon four terms (brother, sister, father, and son), which are linked by two pairs of correlative oppositions in such a way that in each of the two generations there is always a positive relationship and a negative one. Now, what is the nature of this structure, and what is its function? The answer is as follows: This structure is the most elementary form of kinship that can exist. It is, properly speaking, *the unit of kinship*.

One may give a logical argument to support this statement. In order for a kinship structure to exist, three types of family relations must always be present: a relation of consanguinity, a relation of affinity, and a relation of descent—in other words, a relation between siblings, a relation between spouses, and a relation between parent and child. It is evident that the structure given here satisfies this threefold requirement, in accordance with the scientific principle of parsimony. But these considerations are abstract, and we can present a more direct proof for our thesis.

The primitive and irreducible character of the basic unit of kinship, as we have defined it, is actually a direct result of the universal presence of an incest tabooo. This is really saying that in human society a man must obtain a woman from another man who gives him a daughter or a sister. Thus we do not need to explain how the maternal uncle emerged in the kinship structure: He does not emerge—he is present initially. Indeed, the presence of the maternal uncle is a necessary precondition for the structure to exist. The error of traditional anthropology, like that of traditional linguistics, was to consider the terms, and not the relations between the terms.

Before proceeding further, let us briefly answer some objections which might be raised. First, if the relationship between "brothers-in-law" is the necessary axis around which the kinship structure is built, why need we bring in the child of the marriage when considering the elementary structure? Of course the child here may be either born or yet unborn. But, granting this, we must understand that the child is indispensable in validating the dynamic and teleological character of the initial step, which establishes kinship on the basis of and through marriage. Kinship is not a static phenomenon; it exists only in self-perpetuation. Here we are not thinking of the desire to perpetuate the race, but rather of the fact that in most kinship systems the initial disequilibrium produced in one generation between the group that gives the woman and the group that receives her can be stabilized only by counter-prestations in following generations. Thus, even the most elementary kinship structure exists both synchronically and diachronically.

Second, could we not conceive of a symmetrical structure, equally simple, where the sexes would be reversed? Such a structure would involve a sister, her brother, brother's wife, and brother's daughter. This is certainly a theoretical possibility. But it is immediately eliminated on empirical grounds. In human society, it is the men who exchange the women, and not vice versa. It remains for further research to determine whether certain cultures have not tended to create a kind of fictitious image of this symmetrical structure. Such cases would surely be uncommon.

We come now to a more serious objection. Possibly we have only inverted the problem. Traditional anthropologists painstakingly endeavored to explain the origin of the avunculate, and we have brushed aside that research by treating the mother's brother not as an extrinsic element, but as an immediate *given* of the simplest family structure. How is it then that we do not find the avunculate at all times and in all places? For although the avunculate has a wide distribution, it is by no means universal. It would be futile to explain the instances where it is present and then fail to explain its absence in other instances.

Let us point out, first that the kinship system does not have the same importance in all cultures. For some cultures it provides the active principle regulating all or most of the social relationships. In other groups, as in our own society, this function is either absent altogether or greatly reduced. In still others, as in the societies of the Plains Indians, it is only partially fulfilled. The kinship system is a language; but it is not a universal language, and a society may prefer other modes of expression and action. From the viewpoint of the anthropologist this means that in dealing with a specific culture we must always ask a preliminary question: Is the system systematic? Such a question, which seems absurd at first, is absurd only in relation to language; for language is the semantic system par excellence; it cannot but signify, and exists only through signification. On the contrary, this question must be rigorously examined as we move from the study of language to the consideration of other systems which also claim to have semantic functions, but whose fulfillment remains partial, fragmentary, or subjective, like, for example, social organization, art, and so forth.

Furthermore, we have interpreted the avunculate as a characteristic trait of elementary structure. This elementary structure, which is the product of defined relations involving four terms, is, in our view, the true *atom of kinship.* Nothing can be conceived or given beyond the fundamental requirements of its structure, and, in addition, it is the sole building block of more complex systems. For there are more complex systems; or, more accurately speaking, all kinship systems are constructed on the basis of this elementary structure, expanded or developed through the integration of new elements. Thus we must entertain two hypotheses: first, one in which the kinship system under consideration operates through the simple juxtaposition of elementary structures, and where the avuncular relationship therefore remains constantly apparent; second, a hypothesis in which the building blocks of the system are already of a more complex order. In the latter case, the avuncular relationship, while present, may be submerged within a differentiated context. For instance, we can conceive of a system whose point of departure lies in the elementary structure but which adds, at the right of the maternal uncle, his wife, and, at the left of the father, first the father's sister and then her husband. We could easily demonstrate that a development of this order leads to a parallel splitting in the following generation. The child must then be distinguished according to sex—a boy or a girl, linked by a relation which is symmetrical and inverse to the terms occupying the other peripheral positions in the structure (for example, the dominant position of the father's sister in Polynesia, the South African *nhlampsa,* and inheritance by the mother's brother's wife). In this type of structure the avuncular relationship continues to prevail, but it is no longer the predominant one. In structures of still greater complexity, the avunculate may be obliterated or may merge with other relationships. But precisely because it is part of the elementary structure, the avuncular relationship re-emerges unmistakably and tends to become reinforced each time the system under consideration reaches a crisis—either because it is undergoing rapid transformation (as on the Northwest Coast), or because it is a focus of contact and conflict between radically different cultures (as in Fiji and southern India), or, finally, because it is in the throes of a moral crisis (as was Europe in the Middle Ages).

We must also add that the positive and negative symbols which we have employed in the above diagrams represent an over-simplification, useful only as a part of the demonstration. Ac-

tually, the system of basic attitudes comprises at least four terms: an attitude of affection, tenderness, and spontaneity; an attitude which results from the reciprocal exchange of prestations and counter-prestations; and, in addition to these bilateral relationships, two unilateral relationships, one which corresponds to the attitude of the creditor, the other to that of the debtor. In other words there are: mutuality (=), reciprocity (±), rights (+), and obligations (—). These four fundamental attitudes are represented in their reciprocal relationships in Figure 2.

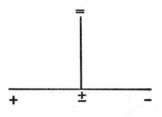

FIGURE 2

In many systems the relationship between two individuals is often expressed not by a single attitude, but by several attitudes which together form, as it were, a "bundle" of attitudes (as in the Trobriands, where we find both mutuality *and* reciprocity between husband and wife). This is an additional reason behind the difficulty in uncovering the basic structure.

We have tried to show the extent to which the preceding analysis is indebted to outstanding contemporary exponents of the sociology of primitive peoples. We must stress, however, that in its most fundamental principle this analysis departs from their teaching. Let us cite as an example Radcliffe-Brown:

The unit of structure from which a kinship is built up is the group which I call an "elementary family," consisting of a man and his wife and their child or children. . . . The existence of the elementary family creates three special kinds of social relationship, that between parent and child, that between children of the same parents (siblings), and that between husband and wife as parents of the same child or children. . . . The three relationships that exist within the elementary family constitute what I call the first order. Relationships of the second order are those which depend on the connection of two elementary families through a common member, and are such as father's father, mother's brother, wife's sister, and so on. In the third order are such as father's brother's son and mother's brother's wife. Thus we can trace, if we have genealogical information, relationships of the fourth, fifth or n^{th} order.

The idea expressed in the above passage, that the biological family constitutes the point of departure from which all societies elaborate their kinship systems, has not been voiced solely by Radcliffe-Brown. There is scarcely an idea which would today elicit greater consensus. Nor is there one more dangerous, in our opinion. Of course, the biological family is ubiquitous in human society. But what confers upon kinship its socio-cultural character is not what it retains from nature, but, rather, the essential way in which it diverges from nature. A kinship system does not consist in the objective ties of descent or consanguinity between individuals. It exists only in human consciousness; it is an arbitrary system of representations, not the spontaneous development of a real situation. This certainly does not mean that the real situation is automatically contradicted, or that it is to be simply ignored. Radcliffe-Brown has shown, in studies that are now classic, that even systems which are apparently extremely rigid and artificial, such as the Australian systems of marriage-classes, take biological parenthood carefully into account. But while this observation is irrefutable, still the fact (in our view decisive) remains that, in human society, kinship is allowed to establish and perpetuate itself only through specific forms of marriage. In other words, the relationships which Radcliffe-Brown calls "relationships of the first order" are a function of, and depend upon, those which he considers secondary and derived. The essence of human kinship is to require the establishment of relations among what Radcliffe-Brown calls "elementary families." Thus, it is not the families (isolated terms) which are truly "elementary," but,

rather, the relations between those terms. No other interpretation can account for the universatility of the incest taboo; and the avuncular relationship, in its most general form, is nothing but a corollary, now covert, now explicit, of this taboo.

Because they are symbolic systems, kinship systems offer the anthropologist a rich field, where his efforts can almost (and we emphasize the "almost") converge with those of the most highly developed of the social sciences, namely, linguistics. But to achieve this convergence, from which it is hoped a better understanding of man will result, we must never lose sight of the fact that, in both anthropological and linguistic research, we are dealing strictly with symbolism. And although it may be legitimate or even inevitable to fall back upon a naturalistic interpretation in order to understand the emergence of symbolic thinking, once the latter is given, the nature of the explanation must change as radically as the newly appeared phenomenon differs from those which have preceded and prepared it. Hence, any concession to naturalism might jeopardize the immense progress already made in linguistics, which is also beginning to characterize the study of family structure, and might drive the sociology of the family toward a sterile empiricism, devoid of inspiration.

NOTES

1. "Structural Analysis of Kinship," *American Anthropologist,* 1935.
2. "Classificatory Systems of Relationship," *Journal of the Royal Anthropological Institute,* 1909.
3. "The Matrilineal Complex," *U. of California Publications in American Archaeology and Ethnology,* XVI, No. 2 (1919).
4. "The Mother's Brother in South Africa," *South African Journal of Science,* 1924.

52

CLAUDE LÉVI-STRAUSS—
ANTHROPOLOGIST AND PHILOSOPHER

EDMUND LEACH

As with Darwin and Freud and many other famous men Claude Lévi-Strauss, Professor of Social Anthropology at the Collège de France, needs to be judged on two quite different levels. First we may ask: 'What has he contributed to the particular scientific discipline in which he is a professional expert?' and secondly: 'What is the basis of his public celebrity?' The treatment which is now being accorded to Lévi-Strauss' work in French intellectual journals suggests that he should be looked upon as an original thinker of the first rank. He is beginning to be spoken of as a philosopher, the founder of 'structuralism,' on a par with Sartre, the founder of existentialism.[1] How should we judge him in this role?

A fellow anthropologist like myself is not perhaps the best kind of person to answer this sort of question. I can make judgments about Lévi-Strauss' skill as an analyst of ethnographic materials, but when it comes to his still embryonic but potentially much more grandiose reputation as a philosopher I am not only out of my depth but somewhat unsympathetic to his position.

In this 20th century, 'idealist' attitudes are not at all respectable and Lévi-Strauss himself emphatically rejects any suggestion that his arguments must imply an idealist foundation. But this is awkward. The elements in Lévi-Strauss' thought which I find most interesting all seem to me to be idealist in tone; yet these are precisely the points at which Lévi-Strauss feels that I misunderstand his intentions. Readers of this essay should bear this discrepancy in mind.

At the outset of his academic career Lévi-Strauss was associated with Marcel Mauss, the principal pupil and collaborator of Emile Durkheim. This means that there is substantial common ground between the social anthropology of Lévi-Strauss and the social anthropology of

From *New Left Review,* 34 (Nov.–Dec., 1965): 12–27. Reprinted by permission of the publisher and the author. Edmund Leach is Reader in Social Anthropology, Cambridge University.

his British colleagues, for the latter likewise trace their intellectual descent in a direct line back to Durkheim. But the common ground is treated in very different ways. Whereas the British show an obsessional interest in particulars and an exaggerated suspicion of generalization, Lévi-Strauss is at his best when talking in completely general terms and at his weakest when demonstrating the fit of his general theory with the tiresome details of particular cases. This difference is partly a matter of national temperament, the French love of logical order, the British love of practical experiment, but it is also the outcome of history. In all countries the 20th-century Founding Fathers of anthropology favoured grandiose generalization. They thought of anthropology as the study of Man, the whole species of *homo sapiens,* and their objective was to discover facts which were universally true of all men everywhere, or at least of all men at 'a particular stage of development.' They showed great ingenuity in the construction of logically plausible schemes of universal human evolution and they then used ethnographic evidence simply as 'illustration,' arguing (without justification) that the primitive peoples of the modern world were really very ancient peoples whose development had somehow been arrested. Lucretius had managed just as well in the 1st century BC without dragging in the ethnography at all.

But with the turn of the century, British social anthropologists executed a complete *volte face.* Under the influence of W. H. R. Rivers, an experimental psychologist, they began to concentrate their efforts on the detailed ethnographic description of particular societies. The history and social organization of a single tribe is not perhaps a subject of such general and enthralling interest as the History of Mankind but, for a scientist, a few verifiable facts about the former are worth any number of mere guesses about the latter. Generally speaking, things have stayed that way. For over half a century the distinguishing quality of British social anthropology has been the superlatively high standards of its ethnographic description and analysis. But along with this bias towards empiricism goes a limitation of objectives. Pushed to define his subject a British social anthropologist is likely to say that his concern is with 'the principles of organization in small scale societies.' For him *social structure* is something which 'exists' at much the same level of objectivity as the articulation of the human skeleton or the functional-physiological interdependence of the different organs of the human anatomy. In contrast, Lévi-Strauss still retains the grander more macrocosmic viewpoint of the 19th century; he is concerned with nothing less than the structure of the human mind, meaning by 'structure' not an articulation which can be directly observed but rather a logical ordering, a set of mathematical equations which can be demonstrated as functionally equivalent (as in a model) to the phenomenon under discussion.

THE TOTAL TRANSACTION

Some of the critical formative influences on Lévi-Strauss' thinking are quite easy to detect. An early item is Mauss' 'Essai sur le don.' In this celebrated essay Mauss used two detailed ethnographic descriptions of primitive systems of ritual exchange (Malinowski's account of the Trobriand *kula* and Boas' account of the Kwakiutl *potlatch*) as the foundation for a broad generalization about the nature of social action. Sociologists (and social anthropologists) are concerned with 'man in society,' with systems of relationships rather than with individuals in isolation. Mauss' insight was to recognize that the concept of 'relationship' is itself an abstraction from something quite concrete. We say of two individuals that they are 'in relationship' when we see that they are in communication, that is when they pass 'messages' to one another, and these messages are conveyed through material media, sound waves in the air, ink scribbles on a piece of paper, the symbolic value embodied in a gift of flowers. The 'gift,' that is to say the material thing which passes from one individual to the other, is an 'expression' of the relationship, but the quality of the relationship is something both more abstract and more mysterious. The recipient of a gift, whether of words or of things, feels coerced by it, he is not only compelled

to receive he is also compelled to reciprocate. Mauss' original treatment of this theme borders on the mystical and Lévi-Strauss' own much more subtle elaborations of the idea always hover on the edge of metaphysics. This perhaps is unavoidable.

Mauss' essay contains another very fundamental idea, that of the *prestation totale*. A person to person interaction is never an isolated event but only part of a total set of transactions widely dispersed through space and through time. A particular gift has significance because of its comparability and contrast with other transactions, not only those between the same actors, but also those which are taking place round about between other members of the same communication system.

As developed by Lévi-Strauss this theme links up directly with his view that in any cultural system the conventional modes of person to person interaction constitute a language which can be decoded like any other language. But a language is not just an inventory of words, it is a complex structure of syntax and grammar which is all of a piece. Indeed individual words have little or no meaning in themselves; the meaning arises from the context in which they appear and the grammatical conventions of the language as a whole. One does not need to be a professional linguist to see that this is true of *words;* Lévi-Strauss' originality is that he applies the same kind of argument to all kinds of conventional action and also to the thematic symbols which appear in myth and ritual. This doctrine, that actions, events, ideas can never be assessed in isolation but only as part of a total system, is not peculiar to Lévi-Strauss, it was present much earlier in the writings of the theoretical sociologists (e.g. Comte, Marx, Durkheim, Weber) and of the functionalist social anthropologists (e.g. Malinowski and Radcliffe-Brown) and even in Freud's view of the human personality, but it contrasts sharply with the philogenetic view of history in which each event is unique in itself, a derivative of its chronological antecedents, and also with various brands of historical anthropology in which each 'custom' is treated as an isolate with a particular discoverable 'origin.' Earlier varieties of functionalism have assumed that the 'purpose' or 'need' served by the interconnectedness of cultural phenomena is of an economic or political or physiological kind . . . the parts of the social system function together so as to

(a) preserve the system in its struggle against the natural environment (Marx)
(b) preserve the system as such 'in good health' (Durkheim, Radcliffe-Brown)
(c) satisfy the biological needs of the individual members of society (Malinowski).

Lévi-Strauss' functionalism is not only of larger scale, in that his 'totalty' is, generally speaking, the whole of humanity rather than the whole of one particular society, but his emphasis on 'communication' gives the whole argument a novel twist and suggests a possible utility for other concepts taken over direct from general communication theory, e.g. binary oppositions, Markoff chains, redundancy. But while Lévi-Strauss' anthropology has a new look, he has not really made any fundamental new discoveries; rather he has presented familiar materials in a different way, so that modern techonological discoveries in other fields, such as those which are ordinarily associated with computer languages and systems theory, suddenly acquire a possible relevance for the understanding of human behaviour in general.

THE PROTOTYPE OF 'PRIMITIVE MAN'

Between 1935 and 1939 Lévi-Strauss held a post as Professor of Sociology at the University of São Paulo, Brazil. In successive long vacations he conducted anthropological fieldwork among a variety of primitive tribal peoples of the interior, notably a tiny group of Amazonian nomads, the Nambikwara.

In a strictly academic sense the resulting formal monograph seems of rather indifferent quality when compared with the sort of thing that English writers (influenced by Malinowski) had already produced at a much earlier date, but the direct experiences of primitive life left a deep and lasting impression. The curious autobiographical travel book *Tristes Tropiques,* which first established Lévi-Strauss' reputation as an intellectual (as distinct from being an anthropologist) is principally an account of his personal reaction to the situation of the Amazonian Indians as he saw them. In retrospect these people have become for Lévi-Strauss the prototype of 'primitive man,' and when, as in his latest volume, *Le Cru et le Cuit,* he discusses the myths of the Bororo and the Mundurucu he writes as if he were displaying for our attention the characteristics of untutored savages everywhere. It is this kind of generality

which gives Lévi-Strauss' work its wide appeal. Anthropologists become interesting when they talk about Man—all men, including you and me. Yet it is precisely this same generality which makes Lévi-Strauss' professional (British) colleagues suspicious. They have carefully cultivated an expertise by which one culture is sharply distinguished from another; they are alarmed by those strands in the Lévi-Strauss brand of structuralism which seem to reduce all men to a single pattern.

'Seem to' is the operative expression here. Lévi-Strauss constantly wobbles precariously between the study of Man and the study of particular peoples. When he is talking about Man, it is the 'human mind' which becomes the creative agent responsible for the miracle of culture and this 'human mind' is an aspect of the human brain, something shared by all members of the species *homo sapiens.* But when he is talking about particular peoples, a slightly different kind of entity has to be reified. One of the most interesting chapters in *Tristes Tropiques* is entitled 'A Native Society and its Style.' I can warmly recommend it to anyone trying to get to grips with the 'variations-on-a-theme' aspects of the structuralist thesis. But this chapter starts off as follows:

The ensemble of a people's customs has always its particular style; they form into systems. I am convinced that the number of these systems is not unlimited and that human societies, like individual human beings (at play, in their dreams, or in moments of delirium) never create *absolutely*: all they can do is to choose certain combinations from a repertory of ideas which it should be possible to reconstitute. For this one must make an inventory of all the customs which have been observed by oneself or others, the customs pictured in mythology, and the customs evoked by both children and grown-ups in their games. The dreams of individuals, whether healthy or sick, and psycho-pathological behaviour should also be taken into account.

Note how, in this quotation 'human societies' are credited with a limited creative capacity directly analogous to that of 'individual human beings.' This is very difficult. Lévi-Strauss claims that he does not share Durkheim's very idealist concept of a 'Group Mind' or 'Collective Conscience' yes it is hard to see how a passage such as the above can be given any sense without the introduction of some such metaphysical formulation.

A third landmark experience in Lévi-Strauss' development was his association in New York,

during the latter part of the war, with the linguist Roman Jakobson. The latter was responsible for introducing into America the concepts
and procedures of the Prague school of structural linguistics, and the emphasis on 'binary
opposition' and 'distinctive features' which permeates Jakobson's linguistics has been assimilated *en bloc* into Lévi-Strauss' system of
structural anthropology. A paper written at that
time and published in the second issue of *Word,*
a journal originally launched by Jakobson and
his friends, has become a key reference for
anyone interested in Lévi-Strauss' ideas.[2]

Sixteen years later the same two authors col-
laborated on a lemon-squeezer analysis of the
structure of a poem by Baudelaire. Those who
find the peculiarities of marriage preferences
and South American mythology too far off the
beaten track may learn something of structuralism by studying this exercise in literary criticism, which most people find preposterous,
exasperating and fascinating all at once.

MARX AND FREUD

Freud has a place in the Lévi-Straussian
scheme but it is not easy to assess. He is extensively referred to only in one book, yet a
number of Lévi-Strauss' more difficult arguments seem to parallel comparable obscurities
in the Freudian system. Freud's final model of
the human psyche postulated an opposition between an animal Id and a human Ego, mediated
by the Super-Ego, an internalized parent, an
'unconscious conscience.' The Super-Ego is a
precipitate of the cultural environment but it
only needs a slight deviation from Freudian
orthodoxy to turn Super-Ego into a metaphysical Jungian 'collective unconscious.' As indicated already, Lévi-Strauss' system entails a
rather similar triad: Nature, Culture and a mediator which is mostly a structural aspect of the
human brain, but sometimes a much more generalized *Geist*-like entity the *esprit humain*—
the Human Mind—which seems hardly distinguishable from a personified human society.

Finally Marx. Lévi-Strauss persistently maintains that he is a Marxist and on occasion he
will use specific Marxist terms such as *praxis.*
Likewise he refers to the 'undeniable primacy
of the infrastructures' which I interpret as
meaning that the style of a culture is limited
by the state of its technology in relation to the
physical environment and by the degree to

which that environment has already been modified by human action. But Lévi-Strauss' position
seems far removed from that of historical determinism in any simple sense. On the contrary
he is constantly emphasizing the enormous variability of culture and laying stress on the mutual interdependence of the variations rather
than on their chronological development or on
the superiority of one system as against another. Cultural differences, in Lévi-Strauss'
analysis, are analogous to the differences between the individual pieces in Bach's 30 Gold-
berg variations: they are played in sequence
one after another and there is a sense in which
the last is an evolutionary development from
the first, but the later variations are neither
superior nor inferior to the earlier ones and the
elimination of any one would reduce the merit
of all. It is very difficult for anyone who is not
highly expert in the appropriate form of discourse to say whether such a position can
properly be said to be Marxist or even to
understand where Marx comes into it at all.
Marx, it is said, 'stood Hegel on his head' and
if Lévi-Strauss has turned Marx inside out we
are perhaps more or less back at the beginning.
A strain of Hegelian dialectic is very prominent in all of Lévi-Strauss' writing. Every thesis
serves to generate its own antithesis and the
opposition between thesis and antithesis will
then be resolved by a mediating synthesis which
in turn generates a new antithesis. For Hegel
this was a process in the development of ideas,
for Marx it is a process in the development of
political-economic systems, for Lévi-Strauss it is
simply 'dialectic,' a basic characteristic of the
human mind which expresses itself in verbal
classifications, in the structure of myth, in
varieties of marriage regulation.

Any reader of Lévi-Strauss must find it very
difficult to decide just how he views the role of
the historical situation as an active factor in
the historical process. In some of his earlier
writings there is a definite undertow of evolutionism—'generalized' exchange is more highly
evolved than 'restricted' exchange, class structures may evolve out of 'generalized' exchange.
I don't think that he has ever actually repudi-
ated this position; he has simply talked about
something else. His chosen field is the analysis
of 'elementary' structures; 'complex' structures
are left to others. On the other hand he can
hardly be said to be an enthusiast for the idea
of Progress.

The conclusion of *Tristes Tropiques* stresses

the transitoriness of all human endeavour. 'The world began without the human race and will end without it. The institutions, manners and customs which I shall have spent my life in cataloguing and trying to understand are an ephemeral efflorescence of the creative process in relation to which they are meaningless, unless it be that they allow humanity to play its destined role' . . . And a few lines later we learn that civilization is a 'prodigiously complicated mechanism' whose 'true function' is simply to increase the entropy of the Universe. Whatever meaning one may attach to such rhetoric, this is not the voice of Marxist optimism. Yet this position does involve a kind of historical determinism: 'As he moves forward within his environment, Man takes with him all the positions that he has occupied in the past, and all those he will occupy in the future. As in a Greek drama, destiny will work itself out in the end no matter how the individual characters exercise their free choices meanwhile. The last move of the game is check-mate whatever you do. Despite the implicit pessimism, the passage which I have just cited really contains the nub of the structuralist argument. Social phenomena are to be thought of as particular expressions of persistent generalized mathematical functions. What happens in the future is not predetermined in its details but it is predestined in its overall shape since it is simply a transformation of what is already existent and of what has already happened in the past. The more we go forward, the more we stay in the same place; the last act of Hamlet is already foreshadowed in the opening scene even though the beholder is still quite unaware of that which is to come. 19th century brands of evolutionism assumed that, by ratiocination and planning, Man could not only know where he was heading for but could ensure that he got there in the shortest possible time. Lévi-Strauss' brand of destiny is of a much more ambiguous kind but it is far from being an unprecedented novelty. Sophocles and the authors of the Old Testament and the legendary Lord Buddha would all have understood his thesis very well.

THE MODEL

Lévi-Strauss' first really major work was *Les Structures Elémentaires de la Parenté* (1949). It is a work of technical anthropology mainly devoted to making a wide ranging set of comparisons between the formal marriage rules of Australian Aborigines and those of various tribal peoples of South East Asia. Marriage, for Lévi-Strauss, is not simply a matter of establishing a legal basis for the domestic family, it is an *alliance* resulting from a contractual exchange between two groups—the group of the husband and the group of the bride. The exchange can take different forms . . . it may involve direct reciprocity, an exchange of sisters between two men, or delayed reciprocity: 'We give you a woman now; you give back to us one of her daughters', or generalized reciprocity within a larger system: 'We give you a woman in exchange for cattle; we will use the cattle to obtain a woman from elsewhere.'

Although British social anthropologists admire the way that Lévi-Strauss displays these systems, which are distributed seemingly at random over vast areas of the map, as dialectical variations of a single theme, many would question whether formal marriage rules can have the importance which Lévi-Strauss supposes and some would challenge quite radically his whole approach to kinship behaviour and kinship terminology. They also question the evolutionist undercurrent. As mentioned already Lévi-Strauss has argued that different systems of marital organization can have different absolute merit in that one may be more resistant than another to the ravages of history, or one may serve to hold together larger agglomerations of people than another. On this basis generalized marriage exchange is to be regarded as a later more sophisticated development than the direct reciprocal type. But generalized exchange also has its weaknesses which must lead towards the development of a class hierarchy in which inferiors render women as tribute to their superiors, and this is the beginning of caste hypergamy. Such condensation of what is really a rather subtle argument is outrageously unfair but it will indicate why the empirically minded British anthropologists have not responded very favourably to this extreme exercise in grand scale theory.

In the decade before Lévi-Strauss published his book his British colleagues, working mainly from African data, had developed a substantial body of theory about the importance of principles of descent and inheritance as factors in maintaining the continuity of society.[3] In the African systems where descent functions as a principle of group solidarity (e.g. 'the children of Israel,' 'the House of David'), marriage is usually looked upon as a personal matter serving to distinguish the individual from his fellow group members. Lévi-Strauss certainly added something important when he showed that marriage alliance, like descent, *can* function so as to preserve the structural continuity of a social system and he also took a genuine step forward when he showed that the South East Asian kinship systems which he talks about can be thought of as 'variations on a theme' in relation to the better known systems of the Australian Aborigines, but in the British view, his generalizations were far too sweeping. Since the 'elementary structures' which he discusses are decidedly unusual they seem to provide a rather flimsy base for a general theory. The British, who pride themselves on their detailed studies of particular systems, have also been horrified by the scale and superficiality of Lévi-Strauss' comparisons. In order to cover so much ground in such small space Lévi-Strauss was ruthlessly selective in his selection of what he took to be significant evidence and there are places when he seems to have misread his sources altogether.

But though *Structures* is best regarded as a splendid failure it does contain one fundamental idea of great importance; this is the notion, distilled from Mauss and Freud and Jakobson, that social behaviour (the transactions which take place between individuals), is always conducted by reference to a conceptual scheme, a model in the actor's mind of how things are or how they ought to be. And the essential characteristic of this model is that it is logically ordered. Lévi-Strauss recognizes that the actual behaviour of actual individuals may be full of irregularity and improvisation. But these practices are nevertheless an expression of the actors' orderly ideal scheme just as the ideal scheme is itself a programme for action produced by the *praxis* of the whole society. As his ideas have developed Lévi-Strauss has come to see himself more and more as being concerned with the logical structures which are to be found not *in* the empirical facts themselves but *at the back of* the empirical facts.

The analogy is with language. The grammar and syntax and sound discriminations of a language are what make it possible for a sentence to convey a meaning, but the linguist who seeks to investigate such structures has to go to the patterning of the sounds not to the meaning of the message. And so also in psycho-analytical dream interpretation. The basic assumption is that the actual dream, which here corresponds

to a 'practice,' is an ephemeral trivial matter, but it is at the same time a precipitate of something much more important and more enduring, a logical puzzle in the dreamer's conceptual system.

If we accept this approach, it is understandable that Lévi-Strauss should have moved directly from a study of over-formalized ideal systems of marriage regulation, which he presumed to provide the logic at the back of actual kinship behaviour, to a study of the structure of myth. Lévi-Strauss' first essay in this field was published in English in 1955 [4] and in the intervening years he has published a great deal on the subject both in English and in French. So far as ordinary anthropology is concerned his procedures represent a radical departure from previous orthodoxies though tnere are links with George Dumezil's comparative studies of Indo-European religions and also with techniques employed for many years by students of European folk-tales.

THE INNER STRUCTURE OF MYTHS

For the past 50 years the orthodox British anthropological view has been quite unambiguous. Myth can only be understood in its cultural context; within that context it provides the 'charter for social action,' that is to say it stands behind social practice in much the same way as Lévi-Strauss' 'structurally ordered conceptual scheme' stands behind actual social behaviour. But where, for Lévi-Strauss and the Marxists, words like *structure, praxis,* and *ideology* are very broad notions corresponding to the thoughts and actions of whole classes of humanity at a particular stage of development, the British anthropologists' ordinary use of *myth* is narrowly specific; a myth is a particular tale about the past which serves to justify a particular type of action in the present within the context of a particular cultural milieu. Against this background the two fundamental peculiarities of Lévi-Strauss' myth analysis are, firstly his 19th century willingness to talk about myths in themselves without close reference to social context, and secondly his view that significance can only emerge from a study of contrast. This second principle implies that while he is never prepared to expound a single myth considered in isolation he will readily tackle the seemingly much more difficult task of analysing and interpreting a whole set of marginally related tales. He presumes that such tales, considered as a total set, develop out of repeated transformations of the elements of a single persisting structural theme, and it is this persisting structure which must be the analyst's chief concern.

The significance of a set of myths does not lie in the meaning of the stories in any straightforward sense but in the relations between the stories. There is an analogy with music. What we first hear is a tune, a melody; but the experience of music is not just a collection of tunes. What the musically sensitive person responds to is the structure of the music as a totality, the complexities of counterpoint and of harmony and the relations between a theme and its variations. Likewise in drama, what distinguishes a powerful, emotionally significant, play from a triviality is not a quality of the story but a quality of the inner structure to which we can respond even when we cannot consciously recognize what it is. Lévi-Strauss' thesis is that the inner structures of myth systems are everywhere much the same and he is concerned to show us what these structures are. The analogy with linguistics is very close. There are linguists who are solely concerned with the analysis of the grammar, syntax, phonology, etc., of particular languages, and there are other linguists who set out to discover general principles which apply to all forms of human speech. The two kinds of study are mutually interdependent but, up to a point, they are separate fields of investigation. As Lévi-Strauss sees it, the type of localized functionalist analysis favoured by British anthropologists corresponds to the particular description of a particular language; his own contribution to social anthropology corresponds to general linguistic theory. But just as general linguistics is in no way concerned with the particular meaning of particular sentences but only with the mechanics of how sentences can convey information, so also the logic of Lévi-Strauss' position leads him to lose inteerst in the meaning of particular myths. Instead he concentrates all his attention on how myths come to mean anything at all.

Even so there are certain fundamental contradictions in the human situation with which all human beings must come to terms. In so far as myth provides a way of dealing with these universal puzzles, there is a limited sense in which even the meaning of all mythical systems is the same. For example it is universally true

that man is both an animal (a creature of Nature) and different from an animal (in that he is a creature of Culture); it is universally true that although all sensible men are fully aware that every individual is destined to die, yet many sensible men manage to persuade themselves that, on a metaphysical plane, some form of immortality is possible; it is universally true that through a process of enculturation men come to believe, at a sub-liminal level, that 'mothers' and 'sisters' and 'wives' are women of quite different kinds towards whom quite distinct types of sexual behaviour are appropriate. One common function of myth is to provide a deeply felt justification for such culturally basic yet non-rational attitudes as these.

AN ORDERLY WORLD

Anyone who wishes to see how this doctrine works out in practice must examine for himself some of Lévi-Strauss' own writings. The principle is expounded in 'The Structural Study of Myth'; the most satisfying practical exercises are 'La Geste d' Asdival' and *Le Cru et le Cuit*.

Parallel with investigations into the structure of myth Lévi-Strauss has pursued investigations into the structure of human thought as such. *La Pensée Sauvage*, with its separate preface, *Le Totémism Aujourdhui*, does not postulate, in 19th century evolutionist manner, a mythopoeic phase of civilization which we have left behind, it assumes rather that the style of thinking which is typical of very primitive societies is present also in much of our own thinking process; we too are totemites only at one remove.

The essentials of Lévi-Strauss' argument here seem to me to be the following:

(a) The world of Nature, the unmodified environment into which man is born, exists in its own right and is governed by order; the processes of biology are not just random accidents. In this respect the human brain is a part of Nature.

(b) Nevertheless this order in Nature is to a large extent inaccessible to us as conscious beings. The human brain is not in the least like a camera. Our capacity to achieve technological mastery over our surroundings does not derive from any capacity to see things as they actually are, but rather from the fact that the brain is capable of reproducing transformations of structures which occur 'out there' in Nature and then responding to them. In other words Lévi-Strauss seems to postulate that the structure and workings of the human brain are analogous to those of a very complicated kind of computer; it is the nature of this computer that it sorts out any information which is fed into it through the sense organs in accordance with the 'programme' to which it is adjusted. The result of this sorting process is to present to the individual consciousness an impression of an orderly world, but this orderliness of the perceived world is not necessarily closely fitted to the orderliness of Nature, it is an orderliness that has been imposed on the sensory information by the structures built into the computer programme. The 'programme' (this is my term, not Lévi-Strauss') is partly an endowment of heredity . . . that is to say it arises from the intrinsic characteristics of the brain of *homo sapiens* and partly it is a feed-back from the cultural environment in which the individual has been raised. Particularly important here are the categories of the individual's ordinary spoken language which have the effect of presenting the speaker's sense perceptions to himself as an organized system. Lévi-Strauss likens this organizing capacity of the human brain to the activities of a *bricoleur* or handiman who creates fantastic and only partly useful objects out of old junk, the residues of history and anything that comes to hand. All that one can affirm about the final product is that, to the beholder, the world will appear to be an organized place, but there is an almost unlimited range of possibilities about just how the organization will be achieved. Hence the extraordinary variety of human culture despite the unity of human nature. The basic bricks out of which cultural order is constructed are verbal categories and *La Pensée Sauvage* is really an inquiry into just how far the content of such categories is arbitrary and how far it is predetermined by the nature of the real objects which are being categorized.

Lévi-Strauss claims to be a Marxist materialist and he firmly rejects any suggestion that he believes in 'idealism'—the view that things only exist in so far as they are known. Yet his position seems in some respects akin to that of an idealist in that he appears to argue that what we know is only very marginally related to what actually exists. Moreover since our actions are governed by what we know (or rather by

what we think) it would seem logical to conclude that it doesn't really matter very much what kind of reality lies at the back of the verbal categories. It is worth reflecting that the famous medieval controversy between the realists (idealists) and the nominalists (empiricists) arose over an argument about the meaning of a passage on Porphyry's *Introduction to the Categories of Aristotle* which raised the question of (a) whether species exist of themselves or only in the mind; (b) whether if subsistent they are corporeal or incorporeal; and (c) whether they are separated from sensible things or placed in them. This seems a very good description of the theme of Lévi-Strauss' *La Pensée Sauvage*. The fact that his topic is a very old one does not mean that he has nothing new to say, but it does perhaps suggest that the novelty of his style of presentation should not lead us into excessive enthusiasm.

TOTEMISM

From the anthropological (as distinct from the philosophical) point of view the most interesting aspect of this part of Lévi-Strauss' work is that he has brought back into fashion an out-of-date topic, the study of totemism. In its new guise 'totemism,' as such, really disappears; it becomes just one specialized variety of a universal human activity, the classification of social phenomena by means of categories derived from the non-social human environment.

The process by which words can be made to convey information is vastly more complex than is ordinarily understood by those who lack linguistic sophistication. The meaning of a word is not just the gloss which is attached to it in a dictionary, it is also something that derives from the social situation in which the word is uttered, its position in relation to other words in the sentence, and the punning associations which the word denotes sub-liminally both for the speaker and listener. We ourselves use language in a variety of different ways but, in particular, we have a literary language as well as a spoken language. 'Written speech' is addressed to strangers who are out of sight; it must therefore be unambiguous; whatever information is to be conveyed must be there in the pattern of the words. But 'spoken speech' is addressed to acquaintances in direct face-to-face relations, and, in this case, the exchange of words is only a part of the total communicative transaction which is also conducted by other forms of action such as 'gesture,' 'gift giving,' 'role playing,' etc. One distinguishing feature of *La Pensée Sauvage* is that the individuals who are in communication are always in face-to-face relationships so that speech and action are not nearly so sharply distinguished as is commonly the case among 'educated' (i.e. literate) people. But, in literate civilizations, words are not *just* a means of *transmitting* information, they are *also* a means of *storing* information. By inversion, this raises a problem which Lévi-Strauss has thought about in a new and very interesting way. Every culture, primitive as well as sophisticated, is faced with problems of information storage and information retrieval. Primitive savages, such as Australian Aborigines or Kalahari Bushmen, are very far from being ignorant fools. On the contrary, they have such an intimate knowledge of the resources of the local environment that they are able to live with considerable comfort in terrain which more 'civilized' people consider uninhabitable. How is this done? In the absence of books, how is the essential 'scientific' information stored away and transmitted from generation to generation?

Lévi-Strauss' answer to this problem runs something like this: When sophisticated people store information in books or computer tapes or gramophone records they do so by means of structured codes. Specially designed objects in the external world (books, etc.) are subjected to an ordering process which serves as a store of information; other men using the same codes can then read back the information by analysing the patterns which have been imposed on the material objects.

But in primitive society, as in any other, *all* objects in the external world are ordered by the mere process of subjecting them to verbal categories, and the way things in the world are classified is *itself* a form of information storage. The words of an ordinary vernacular language do not reflect natural kinds but sets of things which are of value and relevance for the speaker of the language, and the way such words are associated and patterned in relation to one another serves to store information in the same way as the information on this printed page is stored in the patterning of the conventional printed signs.

In addition to its dual function of imposing order on, and storing up information about, the external world, verbal classification has the further important function of imposing order upon the speaker's own human society. In an objective sense, a human society is just an undifferentiated crowd of human individuals, but this is not how it seems to the actor who is a member of the system. For this human actor, society as a whole is divided into named groups, within which individuals have different named statuses, and it is these groups and statuses which determine how individuals shall react towards one another. The novelty of Lévi-Strauss' approach to totemism (which is a development from a position adopted a generation earlier by Radcliffe-Brown) lies in his recognition that a major characteristic of totemic systems is that the actors use the same verbal classifications to impose order upon the human society as they use to impose order on the natural environment.

In all normal colloquial languages all species of living things, recognized as existing in the natural environment, are treated as elements in a single total system. The members of a particular species are not then distinguished by a simple list of positive characteristics but rather by a list of binary discriminations.

Thus for us 'the dog is the companion of man' and the word 'dog' connotes a whole set of discriminations such as:

dog is like man in that it is organic not inorganic, warm blooded not cold blooded, inedible not edible, mammal not bird, tame not wild, lives in the house not outside, is a personality with a name not just a member of a species.

dog is unlike man in that it is four-footed not two-footed, furry not hairless, incapable of speech, has a personal name which is similar to but usually different from that of a man, and so on.

What I am saying here is that, in arriving at any particular discrimination, such as: 'What is the difference between a dog and a man?' we really use a kind of matrix classification which simultaneously distinguishes one set of criteria which are common to both dog and man and another set of criteria which differentiate dog and man. In the computer-like language of the mind the word 'dog' instantaneously embodies this whole matrix of binary discriminations as well as many more.

The peculiarity of totemic societies is that the discriminations which are applied to animal species are of a kind that are applicable also to human groups so that the difference between one human group and another is felt to be of the same kind as the difference between one animal species and another. This is not a *stupid* way of thinking, it is simply an *economical* way of thinking; it is analogous to running several different programmes through the same computer at the same time, all using the same computer language. If the programmes have been set up correctly there will be no confusion.

LÉVI-STRAUSS' IMPORTANCE

Lévi-Strauss has not resolved all the anthropological problems posed by totemism. In particular it has been argued that by concentrating his attention on objective distinctions such as those in his formula:—*fresh: putrid: : raw: cooked=Natural process*: *Cultural process* he has pushed on one side those subjective distinctions which are at the base of religious attitudes (e.g. clean/dirty, good/bad, sacred/profane) and that in consequence, in Lévi-Strauss' analysis, the mystical aspects of totemism (which have traditionally been considered its very essence) are not so much explained as simply ignored. All the same, by shifting attention away from the oddity of religious attitudes being addressed to animal species to the much more general problem of the relation between social classifications and natural kinds, he has made a very old hat suddenly look fresh and interesting.

This is where Lévi-Strauss' importance lies. He puts familiar facts together in unfamiliar ways and thereby provokes thought about fundementals. *La Pensée Sauvage* contains an astonishing chapter in which the author sets out to demonstrate that the structure of the Indian caste system is a logical transformation from the structure of the totemic order of the Australian Aborigines. Intellectual fireworks of this kind do not in themselves enlarge our understanding of either the caste order or of Australian totemism, but they do challenge us to think more deeply about what is specifically human about human society. In Lévi-Strauss' view it is much more important to understand the difference between Culture and Nature than

to bother with scholastic arguments about how Oriental Despotism is related to Feudalism in the sequence of historical determinism.

Finally I should like to offer a brief warning to those who, like myself, find it a lot easier to read English than to read French. Lévi-Strauss chooses and arranges his words with scrupulous care so that in the original the result often has a poetic quality in that a sentence may contain a variety of harmonic ambiguities over and above what appears to be said on the surface. This faces his translators with a difficult if not impossible task. Paradoxically some of the really difficult passages seem quite straight forward in English simply because the built-in opacity cannot be reproduced in translation. Philosophers who attempt in this way to talk about the unsayable are almost bound to be misunderstood. But even misunderstanding can be a mental stimulus. I think we can pin down fairly precisely just where the misunderstanding is most likely to arise.

To go back to the beginning. In supposing that the individual human brain operates somewhat after the fashion of a computer in selecting and sorting and comparing patterned structures Lévi-Strauss is very much in contemporary fashion, but the philosophical difficulty is how to move from the level of the individual to the level of the group. Social anthropologists are primarily interested in behaviours which are characteristic *not* of individuals acting in isolation and *not* of the whole human species but of individuals in the context of their cultural situation; and human cultures vary to a quite astonishing degree. Lévi-Strauss seems to be trying to use the model of the computer-like human brain to provide a representation of the workings of whole societies within a system of such societies. At a conscious level he apparently rejects the abstract metaphysical notion of 'group mind,' which an equivalance between individual and society might invite, yet he seems to come back to the same point from two directions, firstly by reifying society and treating it as an active creative entity *like* an individual, and secondly by asserting that the pure individual, the 'I,' has no separate existence at all.

This seems to me a strictly anti-nominalist position in the classical sense and one which is surely very hard to square with materialism or empiricism or any other down to earth concern with observable facts. It is this aspect of the matter which makes British social anthropologists cagey if not actively hostile.

NOTES

1. For a list of recent commentaries on the work of Lévi-Strauss see *L'Arc* (Aix-en-Provence) Issue No. 26, 1965, pp. 85–87. This issue of *L'Arc* is itself wholly concerned with Lévi-Strauss and includes at pp. 77–84 a comprehensive bibliography of his writings.

2. 'L'analyse structurale en linguistique et en anthropologie.' *Word*. Vol. I, No. 2, pp. 1–12. Reprinted in *Anthropologie Structurale* (Paris) 1958

(English version in *Structural Anthropology* (New York) 1963, Chapter 2).

3. For a survey of this work see M. Fortes 'The Structure of Unilineal Descent Groups,' *American Anthropologist*. Vol. 55 (1953), pp. 17–39.

4. 'The Structural Study of Myth,' *Journal of American Folklore* Vol. 68 (1955), No. 270, pp. 428–44. Revised version in *L'Anthropologie Structurale* (Paris) 1958.

53

THE CEREBRAL SAVAGE:
ON THE WORK OF CLAUDE LÉVI-STRAUSS

CLIFFORD GEERTZ

Today I sometimes wonder if I was not attracted to anthropology, however unwittingly, by a structural affinity between the civilisations which are its subject matter and my own thought processes. My intelligence is neolithic.—TRISTES TROPIQUES

WHAT, after all, is one to make of savages? Even now, after three centuries of debate on the matter—whether they are noble, bestial, or even as you and I; whether they reason as we do, are sunk in a demented mysticism, or possessors of higher forms of truth we have in our avarice lost; whether their customs, from cannibalism to matriliny, are mere alternatives, no better and no worse, to our own, or crude precursors of our own now out-moded, or simply passing strange, impenetrable exotica amusing to collect; whether they are bound and we are free, or we are bound and they are free—after all this we still don't know. For the anthropologist, whose profession it is to study other cultures, the puzzle is always with him. His personal relationship to his object of study is, perhaps more than any other scientist, inevitably problematic. Know what he thinks a sav-

age is and you have the key to his work. You know what he thinks he himself is and, knowing what he thinks he himself is, you know in general what sort of thing he is going to say about whatever tribe he happens to be studying. All ethnography is part philosophy, and a good deal of the rest is confession.

In the case of Claude Lévi-Strauss, Professor of Social Anthropology in the *Collège de France* and the centre right now of a degree of general attention which men who spend their lives studying far-off peoples do not usually get, sorting out the spiritual elements from the descriptive is particularly difficult. On the other hand, no anthropologist has been more insistent on the fact that the practice of his profession has consisted of a personal quest, driven by a personal vision and directed toward a personal salvation.

I owe myself to mankind just as much as to knowledge. History, politics, the social and economic universe, the physical world, even the sky, all surround me in concentric circles and I can only escape from those circles in thought if I concede to each of them some part of my being. Like the pebble which marks the surface of the wave with circles as it passes through it, I must throw myself into the water if I am to plumb the depths.

On the other hand, no anthropologist has made

greater claims for ethnology as a positive science:

... The ultimate goal of the human sciences is not to constitute man but to dissolve him. The critical importance of ethnology is that it represents the first step in a process which includes others. Ethnographic analysis tries to arrive at invariants beyond the empirical diversity of societies. . . . This initial enterprise opens the way for others . . . which are incumbent on the natural sciences: the reintegration of culture into nature and generally of life into the whole of its physico-chemical conditions. . . . One can understand, therefore, why I find in ethnology the principle of all research.

In Lévi-Strauss' work the two faces of anthropology—as a way of going at the world and as a method for uncovering lawful relations among empirical facts—are turned in toward one another so as to force a direct confrontation between them rather than (as is more common among ethnologists) out away from one another so as to avoid such a confrontation and the inward stresses which go with it. This accounts both for the power of his work and for its general appeal. It rings with boldness and a kind of reckless candour. But it also accounts for the more intra-professional suspicion that what is presented as High Science may really be an ingenious and somewhat roundabout attempt to defend a metaphysical position, advance an ideological argument, and serve a moral cause.

There is, perhaps, nothing so terribly wrong about this, but, as with Marx, it is well to keep it in mind, lest an attitude toward life be taken for a simple description of it. Every man has a right to create his own savage for his own purposes. Perhaps every man does. But to demonstrate that such a constructed savage corresponds to Australian Aborigines, African Tribesmen, or Brazilian Indians is another matter altogether.

The spiritual dimensions of Lévi-Strauss' encounter with his object of study, what trafficking with savages has meant to him personally, are particularly easy to discover, for he has recorded them with figured eloquence in a work which, though it is very far from being a great anthropology book, or even an especially good one, is surely one of the finest books ever written by an anthropologist: *Tristes Tropiques*. Its design is in the form of the standard legend of the Heroic Quest—the precipitate departure from ancestral shores grown familiar, stultify-

ing, and in some uncertain way menacing (a philosophy post at a provincial *lycée* in Le Brun's France); the journey into another, darker world, a magical realm full of surprises, tests and revelations (the Brazilian jungles of the Cuduveo, Bororo, Nambikwara, and Tupi-Kawahib); and the return, resigned and exhausted, to ordinary existence ("farewell to savages, then, farewell to journeying") with a deepened knowledge of reality and the obligation to communicate what one has learned to those who, less adventurous, have stayed behind. The book is a combination autobiography, traveller's tale, philsosophical treatise, ethnographic report, colonial history, and prophetic myth.

For what, after all, have I learnt from the masters I have listened to, the philosophers I have read, the societies I have investigated and that very Science in which the West takes a pride? Simply a fragmentary lesson or two which, if laid end to end would reconstitute the meditations of [Buddha] at the foot of his tree.

The sea journey was uneventful, a prelude. Reflecting upon it twenty years later he compares his position to that of the classical navigators. They were sailing toward an unknown world, one hardly touched by mankind, a Garden of Eden "spared the agitations of 'history' for some ten or twenty millennia." He was sailing toward a spoiled world, one which these navigators (and the colonists who followed them) had destroyed in their greed, their cultural arrogance, and their rage for progress. Nothing was left of the terrestrial Garden but remnants. Its very nature had been transformed and had become "historical where it once was eternal, and social where it once was metaphysical." Once the traveller found civilisations radically different from his own awaiting him at the end of his journey. Now he finds impoverished imitations of his own, set off here and there by the relics of a discarded past. It is not surprising that he finds Rio disappointing. The proportions are all wrong. Sugar Loaf Mountain is too small, the bay is placed the wrong way round, the tropical moon seems overblown with only shanties and bungalows to set it off. He arrived as a delayed Columbus to make a flattening discovery: "the tropics are not so much exotic as out of date."

Ashore, the descent into the depths begins. The plot thickens, grows phantasmagorial and arrives at a denouement wholly unforeseen. There are no Indians in the outskirts of São Paulo as he had been promised in Paris by, of all people, the head of the *École Normale.* Where in 1918 two-thirds of the state was marked on the map as "unexplored territory, inhabited only by Indians," not a single native Indian was left in 1935 when, in search of "a human society reduced to its basic expression," he took up his post as Professor of Sociology in the new university there. The nearest were several hundred miles away on a reservation; but they were not very satisfying. Neither true Indians nor true savages, "they were a perfect example of that social predicament which is becoming ever more widespread in the second half of the 20th century: they were 'former savages,' that is to say [ones] on whom civilisation had been abruptly forced; and, as soon as they were no longer 'a danger to society,' civilisation took no further interest in them. . . ." None the less, the encounter was instructive, as all initiations are, for it disabused him of "the ingenuous and poetical notion of what is in store for us that is common to all novices in anthropology" and so prepared him to confront with more objectivity the less "contaminated" Indians with whom he was to have to do later.

There were four groups of these, each a little further into the jungle, a little more untouched, a little more promising of final illumination. (*1*) The Caduveo in the middle Paraguay intrigued him for their body tattoos in whose elaborate designs he thought he could see a formal representation of their aboriginal social organisation, by then largely decayed. (*2*) The Bororo, deeper into the forest, were rather more intact. Their numbers had been radically reduced by disease and exploitation, but they still lived in the old village pattern and struggled to maintain both their clan system and their religion. (*3*) Deeper yet, the childlike Nambikwara were so simple that he could find in their political organisation—a matter of small, constantly reforming nomadic bands led by temporary chiefs—support for Rousseau's theory of the social contract. (*4*) And finally, near the Bolivian border, in "Crusoe country," gnosis appeared at last at hand in the form of the Tupi-Kawahib, who were not only uncontaminated, but, the savant's dream, *unstudied:*

Nothing is more exciting for an anthropologist than the prospect of being the first white man to penetrate a native community. . . . In my journey I was to re-live the experience of the travellers of old; at the same time I should be faced with that moment, so crucial to modern thought, at which a community, which had thought itself complete, perfected, and self-sufficient, is made to realize that it is nothing of the kind. . . . The counter-revelation in short: the fact that it is not alone in the world, that it is but part of a vast human ensemble, and that to know itself it must first look at the unrecognisable image of itself in that mirror of which one long-forgotten splinter was about to give out, for myself alone, its first and last reflection.

With such great expectations it came then as a distinct disappointment that rather than providing a purified vision of primitivity these ultimate savages proved intellectually inaccessible, beyond his grasp. He, quite literally, could not communicate with them.

I had wanted to pursue "the Primitive" to its furthest point. Surely my wish has been gratified by these delightful people whom no white man had seen before me, and none would ever see again? My journey had been enthralling and, at the end of it, I had come upon "my" savages. But alas—they were all too savage. . . . There they were, all ready to teach me their customs and beliefs and I knew nothing of their language. They were as close to me as an image seen in a looking-glass. I could touch, but not understand them. I had at one and the same time my reward and my punishment, for did not my mistake, and that of my profession, lie in the belief that men are not always men? That some are more deserving of our interest and our attention because there is something astonishing to us in their manners. . . . No sooner are such people known, or guessed at, than their strangeness drops away, and one might as well have stayed in one's own village. Or if, as in the present case, their strangeness remained intact, then it was no good to me, for I could not even begin to analyse it. Between these two extremes, what are the equivocal cases which afford us [anthropologists] the excuses by which we live? Who is, in the end, the one most defrauded by the disquiet we arouse in the reader? Our remarks must be pushed a certain distance if we are to make them intelligible, and yet they must be cut off half-way, since the people whom they astonish are very like those for whom the customs in question are a matter of course. Is it the reader who is deceived by his belief in us? Or ourselves, who have not the right to be satisfied before we have completely dissolved that residuum which gave our vanity its pretext?

At the end of the Quest there waited thus not a revelation but a riddle. The anthropologist seems condemned either to journey among men whom he can understand precisely because his own culture has already contaminated them, covered them with "the filth, *our* filth, that we have thrown in the face of humanity," or among those who, not so contaminated, are for

that reason largely unintelligible to him. Either
he is a wanderer among true savages (of whom
there are precious few left in any case) whose
very otherness isolates his life from theirs or he
is a nostalgic tourist "hastening in search of a
vanished reality . . . an archaeologist of space,
trying in vain to repiece together the idea of the
exotic with the help of a particle here and a
fragment of debris there." Confronted with
looking-glass men he can touch but not grasp,
and with half-ruined men "pulverised by the
development of Western civilisation," Lévi-
Strauss compares himself to the Indian in the
legend who had been to the world's end and
there asked questions of peoples and things and
was disappointed in what he heard. "I am the
victim of a double infirmity: what I see is an
affliction to me; what I do not see a reproach."

Must the anthropologist therefore despair?
Are we never to know savages at all? No, because there is another avenue of approach to
their world than personal involvement in it—
namely, the construction out of the particles
and fragments of debris it is still possible to
collect (or which have already been collected)
of a theoretical model of society which, though
it corresponds to none which can be observed
in reality, will none the less help us towards an
understanding of the basic foundations of human existence. And this is possible because
despite the surface strangeness of primitive men
and their societies they are, at a deeper level, a
psychological level, not alien at all. The mind
of man is, at bottom, everywhere the same: so
that what could not be accomplished by a drawing near, by an attempt to enter bodily into
the world of particular savage tribes, can be
accomplished instead by a standing back, by
the development of a general, closed, abstract,
formalistic science of thought, a universal grammar of the intellect. It is not by storming the
citadels of savage life directly, seeking to penetrate their mental life phenomenologically (a
sheer impossibility) that a valid anthropology
can be written. It is by intellectually reconsti-
tuting the shape of that life out of its filth-
covered "archaeological" remains, reconstructing
the conceptual systems that, from deep beneath
its surface, animated it and gave it form.

What a journey to the heart of darkness
could not produce, an immersion in structural
linguistics, communication theory, cybernetics
and mathematical logic can. Out of the disappointed romanticism of *Tristes Tropiques* arose

the exultant scientism of Lévi-Strauss' other
major work, *La Pensée Sauvage* (1962).

La Pensée Sauvage actually departs from an
idea first set forth in *Tristes Tropiques* with respect to the Caduveo and their sociological
tattoos: namely, that the totality of a people's
customs always forms an ordered whole, a
system. The number of these systems is limited.
Human societies, like individual human beings,
never create out of whole cloth but merely
choose certain combinations from a repertory
of ideas anteriorly available to them. Stock
themes are endlessly arranged and rearranged
into different patterns: variant expressions of
an underlying ideational structure which it
should be possible, given enough ingenuity, to
reconstitute. The job of the ethnologist is to
describe the surface patterns as best he can, to
reconstitute the deeper structures out of which
they are built, and to classify those structures,
once reconstituted, into an analytical scheme—
rather like Mendelyeev's periodic table of the
elements. After that "all that would remain for
us to do would be to recognise those [structures]
which [particular] societies had in fact adopted."
Anthropology is only apparently the study of
customs, beliefs, or institutions. Fundamentally
it is the study of thought.

In *La Pensée Sauvage* this governing notion
—that the universe of conceptual tools available
to the savage is closed and he must make do
with it to build whatever cultural forms he
builds—reappears in the guise of what Lévi-
Strauss calls "the science of the concrete."
Savages build models of reality—of the natural
world, of the self, of society. But they do so
not as modern scientists do by integrating abstract propositions into a framework of formal
theory, sacrificing the vividness of perceived
particulars for the explanatory power of generalised conceptual systems, but by ordering
perceived particulars into immediately intelligible wholes. The science of the concrete
arranges directly sensed realities—the unmistakable differences between kangaroos and
ostriches, the seasonal advance and retreat of
flood waters, the progress of the sun or the
phases of the moon. These become structural
models representing the underlying order of
reality as it were analogically. "Savage thought
extends its grasp by means of *imagines mundi*.
It fashions mental constructions which render
the world intelligible to the degree that they
contrive to resemble it."

This uncanonical science ("which we prefer to call 'primary' rather than 'primitive'") puts a philosophy of finitude into practice. The elements of the conceptual world are given, prefabricated as it were, and thinking consists in fiddling with the elements. Savage logic works like a kaleidoscope whose chips can fall into a variety of patterns while remaining unchanged in quantity, form, or colour. The number of patterns producible in this way may be large if the chips are numerous and varied enough, but it is not infinite. The patterns consist in the disposition of the chips *vis-à-vis* one another (*i.e.,* they are a function of the relationships among the chips rather than their individual properties considered separately). And their range of possible transformations is strictly determined by the construction of the kaleidoscope, the inner law which governs its operation. And so it is too with savage thought. Both anecdotal and geometric, it builds coherent structures out of "the odds and ends left over from psychological or historical process."

These odds and ends, the chips of the kaleidoscope, are images drawn from myth, ritual, magic, and empirical lore. (How, precisely, they have come into being in the first place is one of the points on which Lévi-Strauss is not too explicit, referring to them vaguely as the "residue of events . . . fossil remains of the history of an individual or a society.") Such images are inevitably embodied in larger structures—in myths, ceremonies, folk taxonomies, etc.—for, as in a kaleidoscope, one always sees the chips distributed in *some* pattern, however ill-formed or irregular. But, as in a kaleidoscope, they are detachable from these structures and arrangeable into different ones of a similar sort. Quoting Franz Boas that "it would seem that mythological worlds have been built up, only to be shattered again, and that new worlds were built from the fragments," Lévi-Strauss generalises this permutational view of thinking to savage thought in general. It is all a matter of shuffling discrete (and concrete) images—totem animals, sacred colours, wind directions, sun deities or whatever—so as to produce symbolic structures capable of formulating and communicating objective (which is not to say accurate) analyses of the social and physical worlds.

Consider totemism. Long regarded as an autonomous, unitary institution, a kind of primitive nature worship to be explained in terms of mechanical theories of one sort or another—evolutionist, functionalist, psycho-analytic, utilitarian—it is for Lévi-Strauss only a special case of this overall tendency to build conceptual schemes out of particular images.

In totemism, a logical parallel is (quite subconsciously) postulated between two series, one natural and one cultural. The order of differences between the terms on one side of the parallel is isomorphic with the order of differences between the terms on the other side. In the simplest case, the apparent physical differences between animal species—bear, eagle, turtle, etc.—are put into correspondence with the sociological differences between social groups—clans *A, B, C,* and so on. It is not the specific characteristics of bear, eagle, and turtle as such which are critical—fox, rabbit, and crow would have served as well—but the sensible contrast between any pair of them. It is upon this that the savage seizes to represent intellectually to himself and to others the structure of his clan system. When he says that the members of his clan are descended from bear but those of his neighbour's from eagle he is not giving forth with a bit of illiterate biology. He is saying, in a concrete metaphorical way, that the relationship between his clan and his neighbours is analogous to the perceived relationship between species.

Considered term by term, totemic beliefs are simply arbitrary. "History" has cast them up and "history" may ultimately destroy them, alter their role, or replace them with others. But seen as an ordered set they become coherent, for they are able then to represent symbolically another sort of set similarly ordered: allied, exogamous, patrilineal clans. And the point is general. The relationship between a symbolic structure and its referent, the basis of its *meaning,* is fundamentally "logical," a coincidence of form—not affective, not historical, not functional. Savage thought is frozen reason and anthropology is, like music and mathematics, "one of the few true vocations."

Or like linguistics. For in language too the constituent units—phonemes, morphemes, words—are, from a semantic point of view, arbitrary. Why the French call a certain kind of animal *"chien"* and the English call it *"dog,"* or why English forms its plurals by adding *"-s"* and Malay forms its by doubling roots are not the sorts of questions linguists—structural linguists, at any rate—any longer consider it profitable to ask except in historical terms. It is only when ordered, by the rules of grammar and syntax, into utterances—strings of speech embodying propositions—that significance emerges and communication is possible. And in language too this guiding order, this *ur*-system of forms in terms of which discrete units are shuffled in such a way as to turn sound into speech, is subconscious. It is a deep structure which a linguist reconstitutes from its surface manifestations. One can become conscious of one's grammatical categories by reading linguistic treatises just as one can become conscious of one's cultural categories by reading ethnological ones. But, as acts, both speaking and behaving are spontaneous performances fed from underground springs. Finally, and most important, linguistic study (and, along with it, information theory and class logic) also defines its basic units, its constituent elements, not in terms of their common properties but their differences; *i.e.*, by contrasting them in pairs. Binary opposition— that dialectical chasm between plus and minus which computer technology has rendered the *lingua franca* of modern science—forms the basis of savage thought as it does of language. And indeed it is this which makes them essentially variant forms of the same thing: communications systems.

With this door open all things are possible. Not just the logic of totemic classifications but of any classificatory scheme at all—plant taxonomies, personal names, sacred geographies, cosmologies, hair styles among the Omaha Indians, or design motifs on Australian bullroarers—can *en principe,* be exposed. For they always trace down to an underlying opposition of paired terms—high and low, right and left, peace and war, etc.—expressed in concrete images, palpable concepts, "beyond which it is, for intrinsic reasons, both useless and impossible to go." Further, once certain of these schemas, or structures are determined, they can then be related to one another—*i.e.*, reduced to a more general, and "deeper" structure embracing them both. They are shown to be mutually derivable from each other by logical operations—inversion, transposition, substitution: all sorts of systematic permutations— just as one transforms an English sentence into the dots and dashes of Morse code or turns a mathematical expression into its complement by changing all the signs. One can even move between different levels of social reality—the exchange of women in marriage, the exchange

of gifts in trade, the exchange of symbols in ritual—by demonstrating that the logical structures of these various institutions are, when considered as communication schemes, isomorphic.

Some of these essays in "socio-logic" are, like the analysis of totemism, persuasive and enlightening as far as they go. (In as much as any metaphysical content or affective aura these beliefs may have is vigorously excluded from attention, this is not really so very far.) Others, like the attempt to show that totemism and caste are capable ("by means of a very simple transformation") of being reduced to variant expressions of the same general underlying structure are at least intriguing if not precisely convincing. And others, like the attempts to show that the different ways in which horses, dogs, birds and cattle are named form a coherent three-dimensional system of complementary images cross-cut by relations of inverted symmetry, are triumphs of self-parody. They are exercises in "depth interpretation" farfetched enough to make even a psycho-analyst blush. It is all terribly ingenious. If a model of society which is "eternal and universal" can be built up out of the débris of dead and dying societies—a model which reflects not time, nor place, nor circumstance but (this from *Totemism*) "a direct expression of the structure of the mind (and behind the mind, probably of the brain)"—then this may well be the way to build it.

For what Lévi-Strauss has made for himself is an infernal culture machine. It annuls history, reduces sentiment to a shadow of the intellect, and replaces the particular minds of particular savages in particular jungles with the Savage Mind immanent in us all. It has made it possible for him to circumvent the impasse to which his Brazilian expedition led—physical closeness and intellectual distance—by what perhaps he always really wanted—intellectual closeness and physical distance. "I stood out against the new tendencies in metaphysical thinking which were then [*i.e.*, in 1934] beginning to take shape," he wrote in *Tristes Tropiques,* explaining his dissatisfaction with academic philosophy and his turn towards anthropology.

Phenomenology I found unacceptable, in so far as it postulated a continuity between experience and reality. That one enveloped and explained the other I was quite willing to agree, but I had learnt . . . that there is no continuity in the passage between the two and that to reach reality we must first repudiate experience, even though we may later reintegrate it into an objective synthesis in which sentimentality plays no part.

As for the trend of thought which was to find fulfilment in existentialism, it seemed to me to be the exact opposite of true thought, by reason of its indulgent attitude toward the illusions of subjectivity. To promote private preoccupations to the rank of philosophical problems is dangerous . . . excusable as an element in teaching procedure, but perilous in the extreme if it leads the philosopher to turn his back on his mission. That mission (he holds it only until science is strong enough to take over from philosophy) is to understand Being in relation to itself, and not in relation to oneself.

The High Science of *La Pensée Sauvage* and the Heroic Quest of *Tristes Tropiques* are, at base, but "very simple transformations" of one another. They are variant expressions of the same deep underlying structure: the universal rationalism of the French Enlightenment. For all the apostrophes to structural linguistics, information theory, class logic, cybernetics, game theory, and other advanced doctrines, it is not de Saussure, or Shannon, or Boole, or Weiner, or von Neumann who is Lévi-Strauss' real *guru* (nor, despite the ritual invocation of them for dramatic effect, Marx or Buddha)—but Rousseau!

Rousseau is our master and our brother. . . . For there is only one way in which we can escape the contradiction inherent in the notion of the position of the anthropologist, and that is by reformulating, on our own account, the intellectual procedures which allowed Rousseau to move forward from the ruins left by the *Discours sur l'Origine de l'Inégalité* to the ample design of the *Social Contract,* of which Emile reveals the secret. He it is who showed us how, after we have destroyed every existing order, we can still discover the principles which allow us to erect a new order in their stead.

Like Rousseau, Lévi-Strauss' search is not after all for men, whom he doesn't much care for, but for Man, with whom he is enthralled. It is, as much in *La Pensée Sauvage* as in *Tristes Tropiques,* the jewel in the lotus he is after. The "unshakable basis of human society" is not really social at all but psychological—a rational, universal, eternal, and thus (in the great tradition of French moralism) virtuous mind.

Rousseau ("of all the *philosophes* the nearest to being an anthropologist") demonstrates the method by which the paradox of the anthropological traveller—who comes either too late to find savagery or too early to appreciate it —can at last be solved. We must, as he did, develop the ability to penetrate the savage mind by employing (to provide Lévi-Strauss with what he perhaps least needs, another *expression*) what might be called epistemological empathy. The bridge between our world and that of our subjects (extinct, opaque, or merely tattered) lies not in personal confrontation—which, so far as it occurs, corrupts both them and us. It lies in a kind of experimental mind-reading. And Rousseau, "trying on [himself] modes of thought taken from elsewhere or merely imagined" (in order to demonstrate "that every human mind is a locus of virtual experience where what goes on in the minds of men, however remote they may be, can be investigated"), was the first to undertake it. One understands the thought of savages neither by mere introspection nor by mere observation, but by attempting to think as they think and with their materials. What one needs, aside from obsessively detailed ethnography, is a neolithic intelligence.

The philosophical conclusions which for Lévi-Strauss follow from this postulate—that savages can only be understood by re-enacting their thought processes with the débris of their cultures—add up, in turn, to a technically reconditioned version of Rousseauian moralism.

Savage ("wild," "undomesticated") modes of thought are primary in human mentality. They are what we all have in common. The civilised ("tamed," "domesticated") thought patterns of modern science and scholarship are specialised productions of our own society. They are secondary, derived and, though not unuseful, artificial. Although these primary modes of thought (and thus the foundations of human social life) are "undomesticated" like the "wild pansy"—that spectacularly untranslatable pun which gives *La Pensée Sauvage* its title—they are essentially intellectual, rational, logical, not emotional, instinctive, or mystical. The best— but in no sense perfect—time for man was the neolithic (*i.e.,* post-agricultural, pre-urban) age: what Rousseau (who, contrary to the usual stereotype of him, was not a primitivist) called *société naissante.* For it was then that this mentality flourished, producing, out of its "science of the concrete," those arts of civilisation—agriculture, animal husbandry, pottery, weaving, food conservation and preparation, etc.—which still provide the foundations of our existence.

It would have been better for man had he kept to this "middle ground between the indolence of the primitive state and the questing activity to which we are prompted by our *amour propre*"—instead of abandoning it, by some unhappy chance, for the restless ambitiousness, the pride and egoism, of mechanical civilisation. But he *has* left it. The task of social reform consists in turning us again towards that middle state, not by drawing us back into the neolithic but by presenting us with compelling reminders of its human achievements, its sociological grace, so as to draw us forward into a rational future where its ideals—the balancing of self-regard with general sympathy—will be even more fully realised. And it is a scientifically enriched anthropology ("legitimising the principles of savage thought and restoring them to their rightful place") which is the appropriate agency of such reform. Progress towards humanness—that gradual unfolding of the higher intellectual faculties Rousseau called *perfectibilité*—was destroyed by cultural parochialism, armed with a half-grown science. Cultural universalism, armed with a mature science, will once more set it in motion.

If [the human] race has so far concentrated on one task, and one alone—that of building a society in which Man can live—then the sources of strength on which our remote ancestors drew are present also in ourselves. All the stakes are still on the board, and we can take them up at any time we please. Whatever was done, and done badly, can be begun all over again: "The golden age [wrote Rousseau] which blind superstition situated behind or ahead of us is *in us.*" Human brotherhood acquires a palpable significance when we find our image of it confirmed in the poorest of tribes, and when that tribe offers us an experience which, when joined with many hundreds of others, has a lesson to teach us.

But perhaps more interesting than this modernised profession of a classical faith in (to use Hooker's phrase) "the perpetual and general voice of men" is what the fate of such an attempt to set King Reason back upon his throne in the guise of the Cerebral Savage will be in today's world. However much it is set round with symbolic logic, matrix algebra, or structural linguistics, can we—after all that has happened since 1762—still believe in the sovereignty of the intellect?

After a century-and-a-half of investigations into the depths of human consciousness which have uncovered vested interests, infantile emotions, or a chaos of animal appetites, we now have one which finds there the pure light of natural wisdom that shines in all alike. It will doubtless be greeted, in some quarters, with a degree of welcome, not to say relief. Yet that such an investigation should have been launched from an anthropological base seems distinctly surprising. For anthropologists are forever being tempted—as Lévi-Strauss himself once was—out of libraries and lecture halls, where it is hard to remember that the mind of man is no dry light, into "the field," where it is impossible to forget it. Even if there are not many "true savages" out there any more there are enough vividly peculiar human individuals around to make any doctrine of man which sees him as the bearer of changeless truths of reason—an "original logic" proceeding from "the structure of the mind"—seem merely quaint, an academic curiosity.

That Lévi-Strauss should have been able to transmute the romantic passion of *Tristes Tropiques* into the hyper-modern intellectualism of *La Pensée Sauvage* is surely a startling achievement. But there remain the questions one cannot help but ask. Is this transmutation science or alchemy? Is the "very simple transformation" which produced a general theory out of a personal disappointment real or a sleight-of-hand? Is it a genuine demolition of the walls which seem to separate mind from mind by showing that the walls are surface structures only, or is it an elaborately disguised evasion necessitated by a failure to breach them when they were directly encountered? Is Lévi-Strauss writing, as he seems to be claiming in the confident pages of *La Pensée Sauvage*, a prolegomena to all future anthropology? Or is he, like some uprooted neolithic intelligence cast away on a reservation, shuffling the débris of old traditions in a vain attempt to revivify a primitive faith whose moral beauty is still apparent but from which both relevance and credibility have long since departed?

SELECTED BIBLIOGRAPHY

Since this is a *selected bibliography* we should like to emphasize that items included here were chosen for their general theoretical interest and because they might serve as leads to some of the additional and important literature.

PART I: OVERVIEW

BANTON, MICHAEL (General Ed.).

    1965 *The relevance of models for social anthropology.* Association of Social Anthropologists of the Commonwealth (ASA) Monographs 1. London: Tavistock.

    1966a *Political systems and the distribution of power.* ASA Monographs 2. London: Tavistock.

    1966b *Anthropological approaches to the study of religion.* ASA Monographs 3. London: Tavistock.

    1966c *The social anthropology of complex societies.* ASA Monographs 4. London: Tavistock.

BENEDICT, RUTH.

    1948 Anthropology and the humanities. *American Anthropologist,* 55: 5–16.

BIDNEY, DAVID.

    1953 *Theoretical anthropology.* New York: Columbia University Press.

BLACK, MAX (Ed.).

    1961 *The social theories of Talcott Parsons.* Englewood Cliffs, N.J.: Prentice-Hall.

BOAS, FRANZ.

    1940 *Race, language and culture.* New York: Macmillan.

COPELAND, JOHN W.

    1963 Culture and man: Leslie A. White's thesis re-examined. *Southwestern Journal of Anthropology,* 19: 109–120.

DOLE, GERTRUDE E., and ROBERT L. CARNIERO (Eds.).

    1960 *Essays in the science of culture in honor of Leslie A. White.* New York: Thomas Y. Crowell.

DUBOIS, CORA (Ed.).

    1960 *Lowie's selected papers in anthropology.* Berkeley: University of California Press.

EVANS-PRITCHARD, E. E.

    1951 *Social anthropology.* London: Cohen and West.

FARIS, ROBERT E. L. (Ed.).

    1964 *Handbook of modern sociology.* Chicago: Rand McNally.

FIRTH, RAYMOND.

    1951 Contemporary British social anthropology. *American Anthropologist,* 53: 474–489.

FIRTH, RAYMOND (Ed.).

    1957 *Man and culture: an evaluation of the work of Bronislaw Malinowski.* London: Routledge and Kegan Paul.

FORDE, DARYLL.

    1947 The anthropological approach in social science. Presidential Address, Section H, British Association for the Advancement of Science. London.

GOLDSTEIN, LEON J.

    1955 Bidney's humanistic anthropology. *Review of metaphysics,* 8: 493–509.

1957 On defining culture. *American Anthropologist*, 59: 1075–1081.

GROSS, LLEWELLYN (Ed.).

1967 *Sociological theory: inquiries and paradigms.* New York: Harper and Row.

HARRIS, MARVIN.

1964 *The nature of cultural things:* New York: Random House.

HOMANS, GEORGE.

1950 *The human group.* New York: Harcourt, Brace.

KLUCKHOHN, CLYDE.

1939 The place of theory in anthropological studies. *Philosophy of Science*, 6: 328–344.

KROEBER, ALFRED L.

1952 *The nature of culture.* Chicago: University of Chicago Press.

1955 History of anthropological thought. In William L. Thomas, Jr. (Ed.), *Yearbook of anthropology.* Chicago: University of Chicago Press.

KROEBER, ALFRED L., and CLYDE KLUCKHOHN

1952 *Culture: A critical review of concepts and definitions.* Papers of the Peabody Museum of American Archaeology and Ethnology, Harvard University, Vol. XLVII, No. 1. Cambridge, Mass.

LEACH, EDMUND R.

1961 *Rethinking anthropology.* London School of Economics Monographs on Social Anthropology No. 22. London: Athlone Press.

LÉVI-STRAUSS, CLAUDE.

1966a Anthropology: its achievements and future. *Current Anthropology*, 7: 124–127.

1966b The scope of anthropology. *Current Anthropology*, 7: 112–123.

LOWIE, ROBERT H.

1937 *The history of ethnological theory.* New York: Farrar and Rinehart.

MADDEN, EDWARD H. (Ed.).

1960 *The structure of scientific thought: an introduction to philosophy of science.* Boston: Houghton Mifflin.

MALINOWSKI, BRONISLAW.

1931 Culture. In *Encyclopedia of the Social Sciences*, Vol. 4: 421–646.

1944 *A scientific theory of culture and other essays.* Chapel Hill: University of North Carolina Press.

MARTINDALE, DON.

1960 *The nature and types of sociological theory.* New York: Houghton Mifflin.

MARX, KARL.

1959 *Karl Marx: selected writings in sociology and social philosophy.* (Ed. by T. B. Bottomore and M. Rubel.) London: Watts.

MURDOCK, GEORGE P.

1951 British social anthropology. *American Anthropologist*, 53: 465–473.

NADEL, S. F.

1951 *The foundations of social anthropology.* Glencoe, Ill.: Free Press.

NATANSON, MAURICE (Ed.).

1963 *Philosophy of the social sciences: a reader.* New York: Random House.

PARSONS, TALCOTT.

1951 *The social system.* Glencoe, Ill.: Free Press.

PARSONS, TALCOTT, EDWARD SHILS, KASPAR NAEGELE, and JESSE PITTS (Eds.).

1961 *Theories of society.* (2 vols.) Glencoe, Ill.: Free Press.

POCOCK, D. F.
    1961   *Social anthropology.* London: Sheed and Ward.

POPPER, KARL.
    1963   *The open society and its enemies.* (2 vols.) Princeton: Princeton University Press.

RADCLIFFE-BROWN, A. A.
    1957   *A natural science of society.* Glencoe, Ill.: Free Press.

REDFIELD, ROBERT.
    1953   *The primitive world and its transformation.* Ithaca, N.Y.: Cornell University Press.

REDFIELD, MARGARET PARK (Ed.).
    1962   *Human nature and the study of society: the papers of Robert Redfield,* Vol. I. Chicago: University of Chicago Press.

STERN, B. J.
    1929   Concerning the distinction between the social and the cultural. *Social forces,* 8: 264–271.

STOCKING, GEORGE W., JR.
    1965   "Cultural Darwinism" and "philosophical idealism." In E. B. Tylor, A special plea for historicism in the history of anthropology. *Southwestern Journal of Anthropology,* 21: 130–147.

VENABLE, VERNON.
    1946   *Human nature: the Marxian view.* New York: Alfred A. Knopf.

WEBER, MAX.
    1946   *From Max Weber: essays in sociology.* (Trans. and ed. by H. H. Gerth and C. Wright Mills.) New York: Oxford University Press.

WHITE, LESLIE A.
    1949   *The science of culture.* New York: Farrar, Straus.
    1959   The concept of culture. *American Anthropologist,* 61: 227–251.

WOLF, ERIC R.
    1964   *Anthropology.* Englewood Cliffs, N.J.: Prentice-Hall.

PART II: EXPLANATION IN SOCIAL SCIENCE

BARNETT, HOMER G.
    1953   *Innovation: the basis of cultural change.* New York: McGraw-Hill.
    1965   Laws of socio-cultural change. *International Journal of Comparative Sociology,* 6: 207–230.

BARTLEY, W. W.
    1962   Achilles, the tortoise, and explanation in science and history. *British Journal for the Philosophy of Science,* 13: 15–33.

BERGMANN, GUSTAV
    1962   Purpose, function, scientific explanation. *Acta Sociologica,* 5: 225–238.

BRAITHWAITE, R. B.
    1953   *Scientific explanation.* Cambridge, England: Cambridge University Press.

BRODBECK, MAY.
    1959   Models, meaning and theories. In L. Gross (Ed.), *Symposium on sociological theory.* New York: Harper and Row.
    1962   Explanations, predictions, and "imperfect" knowledge. In H. Feigl and G. Maxwewll (Eds.), *Minnesota studies in the phi-*

losophy of science, Vol. 3. Minneapolis: University of Minnesota Press.

BROWN, ROBERT.
1963 *Explanation in social science.* Chicago: Aldine Publishing Company.

BUETTNER-JANUSCH, JOHN.
1957 Boas and Mason: particularism versus generalization. *American Anthropologist*, 59: 318–324.

CAMPBELL, N. R.
1921 *What is science?* London: Methuen.

DiRENZO, GORDON J. (Ed.).
1966 *Concepts, theory and explanation in the behavioral sciences.* New York: Random House.

DRAY, WILLIAM.
1957 *Laws and explanation in history.* New York: Oxford University Press.

DURKHEIM, EMILE.
1951 *Suicide.* (Ed. by G. Simpson.) Glencoe, Ill.: Free Press.

GARDINER, PATRICK.
1952 *The nature of historical explanation.* London: Oxford University Press.

GELLNER, ERNEST.
1958 Time and theory in social anthropology. *Mind.* 67: 182–202.

GIBSON, QUENTIN.
1960 *The logic of social inquiry.* New York: Humanities Press.

GOLDSTEIN, LEON J.
1957 The logic of explanation in Malinowskian anthropology. *Philosophy of Science*, 24: 156–166.
1959 Ontological social science. *American Anthropologist*, 61: 290–298.

GOODENOUGH, WARD H.
1963 *Cooperation in change: an anthropological approach to community development.* New York: Russell Sage Foundation.

HEMPEL, CARL G.
1965 *Aspects of scientific explanation and other essays in the philosophy of science.* New York: Free Press.

HOMANS, G. C., and D. M. SCHNEIDER.
1955 *Marriage, authority and final causes.* Glencoe, Ill.: Free Press.

KAHL, RUSSELL (Ed.).
1963 *Studies in explanation: a reader in the philosophy of science.* Englewood Cliffs, N.J.: Prentice-Hall.

KEMENY, JOHN G.
1959 *A philosopher looks at science.* Princeton: D. Van Nostrand.

KUHN, THOMAS S.
1962 *The structure of scientific revolutions.* Chicago: University of Chicago Press.

MANDELBAUM, MAURICE.
1957 Societal laws. *British Journal for the Philosophy of Science*, 8: 211–224.
1961 Historical explanation: the problem of "covering laws." *History and Theory*, 1: 229–242.

NAGEL, ERNEST.
1961 *The structure of science.* New York: Harcourt, Brace and World.

NAGEL, ERNEST, and CARL HEMPEL.
1952 Symposium: problems of concept and theory formation in the

social sciences. In *Science, language, and human rights*. Philadelphia: University of Pennsylvania for the American Philosophical Association.

PITT, J.
1959   Generalizations in historical explanation. *Journal of Philosophy*, 56: 578–586.

POPPER, KARL.
1957   The aim of science. *Ratio*, 1: 24–35.
1959   *The logic of scientific discovery*. London: Hutchinson.
1963   *Conjectures and refutations*. London: Routledge and Kegan Paul.

RAPOPORT, ANATOL.
1959   Uses and limitations of mathematical models in social science. In L. Gross (Ed.), *Symposium on sociological theory*. New York: Harper and Row.

REX, JOHN.
1961   *Key problems of sociological theory*. London: Routledge and Kegan Paul.

RUDNER, RICHARD.
1966   *Philosophy of social science*. Englewood Cliffs, N.J.: Prentice-Hall.

TOULMIN, STEPHEN.
1953   *The philosophy of science*. London: Hutchinson University Library, Hutchinson House.
1963   *Foresight and understanding*. New York: Harper and Row (Harper Torchbook).

WEBER, MAX.
1947   *The theory of social and economic organization*. (Trans. by A. M. Henderson and T. Parsons. Ed. by T. Parsons.) New York: Oxford University Press.

WAX, MURRAY.
1956   The limitations of Boas' anthropology. *American Anthropologist*, 58: 63–74.

PART III: METHODOLOGY

ABEL, THEODORE.
1948   The operation called Verstehen. *American Journal of Sociology*, 54: 211–218.

ADAMS, RICHARD N.
1962   The community in Latin America: a changing myth. *Centennial Review*, 6: 409–434.

ARENSBERG, CONRAD M., and SOLON T. KIMBALL.
1965   *Culture and community*. New York: Harcourt, Brace and World.

BIERSTEDT, ROBERT.
1959   Nominal and real definitions in sociological theory. In L. Gross (Ed.), *Symposium on sociological theory*. New York: Harper and Row.

BRODBECK, MAY.
1954   On the philosophy of the social sciences. *Philosophy of Science*, 21: 140–156.
1958   Methodological individualisms: definition and reduction. *Philosophy of Science*, 25: 1–22.

CARNEIRO, ROBERT L.
    1962   Scale analysis as an instrument for the study of cultural evolution. *Southwestern Journal of Anthropology*, 18: 149–169.

DURKHEIM, EMILE.
    1938   *The rules of sociological method.* (Ed. by George E. G. Catlin.) Chicago: University of Chicago Press.

EDEL, ABRAHAM.
    1959   The concept of levels in social theory. In L. Gross (Ed.), *Symposium on sociological theory*. New York: Harper and Row.

EGGAN, FRED.
    1955   Social anthropology: methods and results. In F. Eggan, (Ed.), *Social anthropology of North American Indian tribes*. 2d ed. Chicago: University of Chicago Press.

EISENSTADT, S. M.
    1961   Anthropological studies of complex societies. *Current Anthropology*, 2: 201–210. (See also "Comments" by J. A. Barnes and A. L. Epstein *et al.*, 2: 210–222.)

EVANS-PRITCHARD, E. E.
    1965   The comparative method in social anthropology. In E. E. Evans-Pritchard, *The position of women and other essays*. London: Faber and Faber.

FISCHER, JOHN L.
    1958   The classification of residence in censuses. *American Anthropologist*, 60: 508–517.

FRANK, PHILIP G. (Ed.).
    1961   *The validation of scientific theories.* New York: Collier.

GLUCKMAN, MAX (Ed.).
    1964   *Closed systems and open minds: the limits of naivety in social anthropology.* Chicago: Aldine Publishing Company.

GOODENOUGH, W. H.
    1963   Some applications of Guttman scale analysis to ethnography and culture theory. *Southwestern Journal of Anthropology*, 19: 235–250.

GOULDNER, ALVIN W., and RICHARD A. PETERSON.
    1962   *Notes on technology and the moral order.* New York: Bobbs-Merrill.

HOBHOUSE, L. T., C. C. WHEELER, and M. GINSBURG.
    1930   *The material culture and social institutions of the simpler peoples.* London: Chapman and Hall.

JARVIE, I. C.
    1961   Nadel on the aims and methods of social anthropology. *British Journal for the Philosophy of Science*, 12: 1–24.
    1964   *The revolution in anthropology.* London: Routledge and Kegan Paul.

JESSOR, RICHARD.
    1958   The problem of reductionism in psychology. *Psychological Review*, 65: 170–178.

KAPLAN, ABRAHAM.
    1964   *The conduct of inquiry: methodology for behavioral science.* San Francisco: Chandler.

KAUFMANN, F.
    1944   *Methodology in the social sciences.* New York: Oxford University Press.

KÖBBEN, A. J. F.
>
> 1952 New ways of presenting an old idea: the statistical method in social anthropology. *Journal of the Royal Anthropological Institute*, 82: 129–146.
>
> 1967 Why exceptions? the logic of cross-cultural analysis. *Current Anthropology*, 8: 3–19. (See also "Comments" by M. Altschuler *et al.*, 8: 19–34.)

LESSER, ALEXANDER.

> 1961 Social fields and the evolution of society. *Southwestern Journal of Anthropology*, 17: 40–48.

LEVY, MARION J., JR.

> 1950 Some basic methodological difficulties in the social sciences. *Philosophy of Science*, 17: 287–301.

LEWIS, OSCAR.

> 1955 Comparisons in cultural anthropology. In William L. Thomas, Jr. (Ed.), *Yearbook of anthropology*. Chicago: University of Chicago Press.

McEWEN, WILLIAM J.

> 1963 Forms and problems of validation in social anthropology. *Current Anthropology*, 4: 155–169. (See also "Comments" by Harold E. Driver *et al.*, 4: 169–183.)

MAQUET, JACQUES.

> 1964 Objectivity in anthropology. *Current Anthropology*, 5: 47–55.

MANDELBAUM, MAURICE.

> 1955 Societal facts. *British Journal of Sociology*, 6: 305–317.

MARTINDALE, DON.

> 1959 Sociological theory and the ideal type. In L. Gross (Ed.), *Symposium on sociological theory*. New York: Harper and Row.

MOORE, FRANK W. (Ed.).

> 1961 *Readings in cross-cultural methodology*. New Haven, Conn.: Human Relations Area Files Press.

MURDOCK, GEORGE P.

> 1949 *Social structure*. New York: Macmillan.

NAGEL, ERNEST, P. SUPPES, and A. TARSKI (Eds.).

> 1962 *Logic, methodology, and philosophy of science: proceedings of the 1960 international congress*. Stanford, Calif.: Stanford University Press.

NADEL, S. F.

> 1952 Witchcraft in four African societies: an essay in comparison. *American Anthropologist*, 54: 18–29.

NAROLL, R.

> 1956 A preliminary index of social development. *American Anthropologist*, 58: 687–715.

RAULET, HARRY M.

> 1959 A note on Fischer's residence typology. *American Anthropologist*, 61: 108–112. (See also reply by Fischer, 61: 679–681.)

SCHAPERA, I.

> 1953 Some comments on comparative method in social anthropology. *American Anthropologist*, 55: 353–366.

SCHNEIDER, DAVID M., and KATHLEEN GOUGH (Eds.).

> 1961 *Matrilineal kinship*. Berkeley and Los Angeles: University of California Press.

STEWARD, JULIAN, *et al.*

> 1956 *The people of Puerto Rico*. Urbana: University of Illinois Press.

SRINIVAS, M. N. (Ed.).
   1958   *Method in social anthropology: selected essays by A. R. Rad-cliffe-Brown.* Chicago: University of Chicago Press.
TYLOR, E. B.
   1899   On a method of investigating the development of institutions; applied to the laws of marriage and descent. *Journal of the Royal Anthropological Institute,* 18: 245–273.
WEBER, MAX.
   1949   *On the methodology of the social sciences.* (Trans. and ed. by E. A. Shils and H. A. Finch.) New York: Free Press.

PART IV: FUNCTIONALISM, EVOLUTION, AND HISTORY

A. STRUCTURE AND FUNCTION

ABERLE, D. F., A. K. COHEN, A. K. DAVIS, M. J. LEVY, JR., and F. X. SUTTON.
   1950   The functional prerequisites of a society. *Ethics,* 60: 100–111.
BARBER, BERNARD.
   1956   Structural-functional analysis: some problems and misunderstandings. *American Sociological Review,* 21: 129–135.
BREDEMEIER, HARRY C.
   1955   The methodology of functionalism. *American Sociological Review,* 20: 173–180.
CARLSSON, GOSTA.
   1962   Reflections on functionalism. *Acta Sociologica,* 5: 201–224.
COSER, LEWIS.
   1956   *The functions of social conflict.* Glencoe, Ill.: Free Press.
COULT, ALLAN D.
   1962   An analysis of Needham's critique of the Homans and Schneider theory. *Southwestern Journal of Anthropology,* 18: 317–335.
DAVIS, KINGSLEY.
   1959   The myth of functional analysis as a special method in sociology and anthropology. *American Sociological Review,* 24: 752–772.
DURKHEIM, EMILE.
   1947   *The division of labor in society.* Glencoe, Ill.: Free Press.
FIRTH, RAYMOND.
   1955   Function. In William L. Thomas, Jr. (Ed.), *Yearbook of anthropology.* Chicago: University of Chicago Press.
   1964   *Essays on social organization and values.* London School of Economics Monographs on Social Anthropology No. 28.
FRIED, MORTON H.
   1957   The classification of corporate unilineal descent groups. *Journal of the Royal Anthropological Institute,* 87: 1–29.
FORTES, MEYER.
   1953   The structure of unilineal descent groups. *American Anthropologist,* 55: 17–41.
GLUCKMAN, MAX.
   1959   *Custom and conflict in Africa.* Glencoe, Ill.: Free Press.
   1963   *Order and rebellion in tribal Africa; collected essays.* London: Cohen and West.
GOLDSCHMIDT, WALTER.
   1966   *Comparative functionalism.* Berkeley and Los Angeles: University of California Press.

GOULDNER, ALVIN.
  1959 Reciprocity and autonomy in functional theory. In L. Gross
        (Ed.), *Symposium on sociological theory.* New York: Harper
        and Row.
HEMPEL, CARL G.
  1959 The logic of functional analysis. In L. Gross (Ed.), *Symposium
        on sociological theory.* New York: Harper and Row.
HIELD, WAYNE.
  1954 The study of change in social science. *British Journal of Sociol-
        ogy,* 5: 1–11.
HOMANS, GEORGE C.
  1941 Anxiety and ritual: the theories of Malinowski and Radcliffe-
        Brown. *American Anthropologist,* 43: 164–172.
LEACH, EDMOND R.
  1954 *Political systems of highland Burma: a study of Kachin social
        structure.* Cambridge, Mass.: Harvard University Press.
LESSER, ALEXANDER.
  1935 Fuctionalism in social anthropology. *American Anthropologist,*
        37: 386–393.
LEVY, M. J., JR.
  1952 *The structure of society.* Princeton, N.J.: Princeton University
        Press.
LOCKWOOD, DAVID.
  1956 Some remarks on the "social system." *British Journal of Soci-
        ology,* 7: 134–146.
MERTON, ROBERT K.
  1957 *Social theory and social structure.* (Rev. ed.) Glencoe, Ill.: Free
        Press.
NADEL, S. F.
  1957 *The theory of social structure.* Glencoe, Ill.: Free Press.
NAGEL, ERNEST.
  1956 A formalization of functionalism: with special reference to its
        application in the social sciences. In Ernest Nagel, *Logic without
        metaphysics.* Glencoe, Ill.: Free Press.
NEEDHAM, RODNEY.
  1962 *Structure and sentiment.* Chicago: University of Chicago Press.
RADCLIFFE-BROWN, A. R.
  1952 *Structure and function in primitive society.* Glencoe, Ill.: Free
        Press.
SPIRO, MELFORD, E.
  1952 Ghosts, Ifaluk and teleological functionalism. *American Anthro-
        pologist,* 54: 497–503.
  1953 A typology of functional analysis. *Explorations,* 1: 74–95.
  1961 Sorcery, evil spirits, and functional analysis: a rejoinder. *Amer-
        ican Anthropologist,* 63: 820–824.
VAN DEN BERGHE, PIERRE L.
  1963 Dialectic and functionalism: toward a theoretical synthesis.
        American Sociological Review, 28: 695–705.
VOGT, EVON Z.
  1960 On the concepts of structure and process in cultural anthropology.
        American Anthropologist, 62: 18–33.
WORSLEY, PETER M.
  1956 The kinship system of the Tallensi: a revaluation. *Journal of the
        Royal Anthropological Institute,* 86: 37–75.

B. EVOLUTION

BARRINGER, H. R., G. I. BANKSTEN, and R. W. MACK (Eds.).
   1965   *Social change in developing areas; a reinterpretation of evolutionary theory.* Cambridge, Mass.: Schenkman.
BOCK, KENNETH E.
   1952   Evolution and historical process. *American Anthropologist,* 54: 486–496.
   1963   Evolution, function and change. *American Sociological Review,* 28: 229–237.
CHILDE, V. GORDON.
   1951a *Social evolution.* London and New York: H. Schuman.
   1951b *Man makes himself.* New York: New American Library.
GERARD, R. W., CLYDE KLUCKHOHN, and ANATOL RAPOPORT.
   1956   Biological and cultural evolution. *Behavioral Science,* 1: 6–34.
GOLDMAN, IRVING.
   1955   Status rivalry and cultural evolution in Polynesia. *American Anthropologist,* 57: 680–697.
   1959   Evolution and anthropology. *Victorian Studies,* 3: 55–75.
GOLDSCHMIDT, WALTER.
   1959   *Man's way.* New York: Henry Holt.
GOLDSTEIN, LEON J.
   1967   Theory in anthropology: development or causal? In Llewellyn Gross (Ed.), *Sociological theory: inquiries and paradigms.* New York: Harper and Row.
HUXLEY, JULIAN.
   1956   Evolution, cultural and biological. In William L. Thomas (Ed.), *Current anthropology.* Chicago: University of Chicago Press.
KELLER, ALBERT G.
   1931   *Societal evolution.* New York: Macmillan.
LEEDS, ANTHONY.
   1964   Brazilian careers and social structure; an evolutionary model and case history. *American Anthropologist,* 66: 1321–1347.
MAINE, HENRY.
   1861   *Ancient law.* London: John Murray.
MEAD, MARGARET.
   1964   *Continuities in cultural evolution.* New Haven and London: Yale University Press.
MEGGERS, BETTY (Ed.).
   1959   *Evolution and anthropology.* Washington, D.C.: Anthropological Society of Washington.
MOORE, WILBERT E.
   1963   *Social change.* Englewood Cliffs, N.J.: Prentice-Hall.
MORGAN, LEWIS H.
   1910   *Ancient society.* Chicago: Charles H. Kerr. (First published in 1877).
MUNRO, THOMAS.
   N.d.   *Evolution in the arts, and other theories of culture history.* Cleveland: Cleveland Museum of Art.
OPLER, MORRIS E.
   1962   Two converging lines of influence in cultural evolutionary theory. *American Anthropologist,* 64: 524–527.
SAHLINS, MASHALL D., and ELMAN R. SERVICE (Eds.).
   1960   *Evolution and culture.* Ann Arbor: University of Michigan Press.

SERVICE, ELMAN R.
    1960   Kinship terminology and evolution. *American Anthropologist*, 62: 747–763.
    1962   *Primitive social organization: an evolutionary perspective.* New York: Random House.

STEWARD, JULIAN H.
    1955   *Theory of culture change: the methodology of multilinear evolution.* Urbana: University of Illinois Press.

TAX, SOL (Ed.).
    1960   *The evolution of man: man, culture and society.* Vol. II in S. Tax (Ed.), *Evolution after Darwin.* Chicago: University of Chicago Press.

TYLOR, E. B.
    1871   *Primitive culture.* (2 vols.) London: John Murray.

WHITE, LESLIE A.
    1959   *The evolution of culture.* New York: McGraw-Hill.

C. HISTORY

BELLAH, ROBERT N.
    1959   Durkheim and history. *American Sociological Review*, 24: 447–461.

BOCK, KENNETH E.
    1956   *The acceptance of histories: toward a persepctive for social science.* Berkeley: University of California Press.

CARR, EDWARD HALLET.
    1962   *What is history?* New York: Alfred A. Knopf.

CHILDE, V. GORDON.
    1954   *What happened in history.* (Rev. ed.) Harmondsworth, England: Penguin Books.

COCHRAN, THOMAS C., *et al.*
    1954   *The social sciences in historical study.* New York: Social Science Research Council Bulletin No. 64.

COLLINGWOOD, R. G.
    1946   *The idea of history.* Oxford: Clarendon Press.

EVANS-PRITCHARD, E. E.
    1962   Anthropology and history. In E. E. Evans-Pritchard, *Essays in social anthropology.* London: Faber and Faber.

GARDINER, PATRICK (Ed.).
    1959   *Theories of history: readings from classical and contemporary sources.* Glencoe, Ill.: Free Press.

GEERTZ, CLIFFORD.
    1965   *The social history of an Indonesian town.* Cambridge, Mass.: M.I.T. Press.

GOTTSCHALK, LOUIS (Ed.).
    1963   *Generalization in the writing of history.* Chicago: University of Chicago Press.

HOOK, S. (Ed.).
    1963   *Philosophy and history.* New York: New York University Press.

HUGHES, H. STUART.
    1964   *History as art and science.* New York: Harper and Row.

KROEBER, ALFRED L.
    1935   History and science in anthropology. *American Anthropologist*, 38: 539–569.

1944   *Configurations of culture growth.* Berkeley: University of California Press.

1963   *An anthropologist looks at history.* (Ed. by Theodora Kroeber.) Berkeley and Los Angeles: University of California Press.

MANDELBAUM, MAURICE.

1938   *The problem of historical knowledge.* New York: Liveright.

MEYERHOFF, H. (Ed.).

1959   *The philosophy of history in our time.* New York: Doubleday (Doubleday Anchor Books).

NADEL, GEORGE H. (Ed.).

1965   *Studies in the philosophy of history: selected essays from "History and theory."* New York: Harper and Row (Harper Torchbooks).

NAGEL, ERNEST.

1960   Determinism in history. *Philosophy and phenomenological research,* 20: 291–317.

POPPER, KARL R.

1964   *The poverty of historicism.* New York: Harper and Row.

TEGGART, FREDERICK J.

1941   *Theory and processes of history.* Berkeley: University of California Press.

WARE, C. F. (Ed.).

1940   *The cultural approach to history.* New York: Columbia University Press.

WATKINS, J. W. N.

1957   Historical explanation in the social sciences. *British Journal for the Philosophy of Science,* 8: 104–117.

PART V: CULTURE AND PERSONALITY

ABERLE, D. F.

1951   The psychosocial analysis of a Hopi life-history. *Comparative Psychology Monographs,* 21: 1–133.

BARNOUW, VICTOR.

1963   *Culture and personality.* Homewood, Ill.: Dorsey Press.

BARRY, H., I. CHILD, and M. K. BACON.

1959   Relation of child training to subsistence economy. *American Anthropologist,* 61: 51–63.

BENEDICT, RUTH.

1946   *The chrysanthemum and the sword: patterns of Japanese culture.* Boston: Houghton Mifflin.

COHEN, YEHUDI A. (Ed.).

1961   *Social structure and personality: a casebook.* New York: Holt, Rinehart and Winston.

DuBois, CORA.

1944   *The people of Alor.* Minneapolis: University of Minnesota Press.

ERIKSON, ERIK.

1950   *Childhood and society.* New York: W. W. Norton.

FREUD, SIGMUND.

1937   *Civilization and its discontents.* (Trans. by Joan Riviere.) London: Hogarth.

FROMM, ERICH.

1941   *Escape from freedom.* New York: Farrar and Rinehart.

GERTH, H., and C. WRIGHT MILLS.
 1953 *Character and social structure*. New York: Harcourt, Brace.
GOFFMAN, ERVING.
 1961 *Encounters: two studies in the sociology of interaction*. Indianapolis: Bobbs-Merrill.
HALLOWELL, A. IRVING.
 1955 *Culture and experience*. Philadelphia: University of Pennsylvania Press.
HARING, DOUGLAS (Ed.).
 1948 *Personal character and cultural milieu*. Syracuse: Syracuse University Press.
HONIGMANN, JOHN J.
 1954 *Culture and personality*. New York: Harper.
HOOK, S. (Ed.).
 1959 *Psychoanalysis, scientific method, and philosophy*. New York: New York University Press.
HSU, FRANCIS L. K. (Ed.).
 1961 *Psychological anthropology: approaches to culture and personality*. Homewood, Ill.: Dorsey Press.
INKELES, ALEX, and D. LEVINSON.
 1954 National character: the study of modal personality and sociocultural systems. In G. Lindzey (Ed.), *Handbook of social psychology*, Vol. 2. Cambridge, Mass.: Addison-Wesley.
KAPLAN, BERT.
 1954 *A study of Rorschach responses in four cultures*. Papers of the Peabody Museum of American Archeology and Ethnology, Harvard University, 42, No. 2.
KAPLAN, BERT (Ed.).
 1961 *Studying personality cross-culturally*. Evanston, Ill.: Row, Peterson.
KARDINER, ABRAM.
 1939 *The individual and his society*. New York: Columbia University Press.
 1945 *The psychological frontiers of society*. New York: Columbia University Press.
KLUCKHOHN, C., H. A. MURRAY, and D. SCHNEIDER (Eds.).
 1952 *Personality in nature, society, and culture*. (2d ed.) New York: Alfred A. Knopf.
LINDESMITH, ALFRED R., and ANSELM L. STRAUSS.
 1950 A critique of culture-personality writings. *American Sociological Review*, 15: 587–600.
LINTON, RALPH.
 1945 *The cultural background of personality*. New York: Appleton-Century-Crofts.
MARX, MELVIN H. (Ed.).
 1963 *Theories in contemporary psychology*. New York: Macmillan.
MEAD, MARGARET.
 1951 The study of national character. In D. Lerner and H. Laswell (Eds.), *The policy sciences*. Stanford, Calif.: Stanford University Press.
MINER, H., and G. DEVOS.
 1960 *Oasis and casbah*. Ann Arbor: University of Michigan Press.
ORLANSKY, HAROLD.
 1949 Infant care and personality. *Psychological Bulletin*, 46: 1–48.

RACHMAN, STANLEY (Ed.).

    1963   *Critical essays on psychoanalysis.* New York: Macmillan.

SARGENT, S. S., and MARIAN W. SMITH (Eds.).

    1949   *Culture and personality.* Proceedings of an Inter-Disciplinary Conference under the Auspices of the Viking Fund. New York: Viking Fund.

SPIRO, MELFORD E.

    1950   Human nature in its psychological dimension. *American Anthropologist,* 56: 19–30.

WALLACE, ANTHONY F. C.

    1951   Culture and personality: the natural history of a false dichotomy. *Psychiatry,* 14: 19–46.

    1952   *The modal personality of the Tuscarora Indians as revealed by the Rorschach test.* Bureau of American Ethnology Bulletin 150.

    1956   Mazeway resynthesis: a biocultural theory of religious inspiration. *Transactions of the New York Academy of Sciences,* 18, Series 11: 626–638.

    1962a The new culture-and-personality. In Thomas Gladwin and William Sturtevant (Eds.), *Anthropology and human behavior.* Washington D.C.: Washington Anthropological Society.

    1962b *Culture and personality.* New York: Random House.

WHITING, BEATRICE (Ed.).

    1963   *Six cultures: studies of child rearing.* New York: John Wiley.

WHITING, J. W. M., and I. CHILD.

    1953   *Child training and personality.* New Haven, Conn.: Yale University Press.

PART VI: ECOLOGY

ADAMS, RICHARD N., *et al.*

    1959   *Plantation systems of the new world.* Social Science Monographs 7. Washington, D.C.: Pan American Union.

ALTSCHULER, MILTON.

    1959   On the environmental limitations of Mayan cultural development. *Southwestern Journal of Anthropology,* 14: 189–198.

CONKLIN, HAROLD C.

    1957   *Hanunóo agriculture: a report on an integral system of shifting cultivation in the Philippines.* FAO Forestry Development Paper No. 12. Rome: Food and Agriculture Organization of the United Nations.

COTTRELL, FRED.

    1955   *Energy and society.* New York: McGraw-Hill.

FERDON, EDWIN J., JR.

    1959   Agricultural potential and the development of cultures. *Southwestern Journal of Anthropology,* 15: 1–19.

FORDE, C. DARYLL.

    1934   *Habitat, economy and society.* New York: Harcourt, Brace.

FRAKE, CHARLES O.

    1962   Cultural ecology and ethnography. *American Anthropologist,* 64: 53–59.

FREEMAN, J. D.

    1955   *Iban agriculture, a report on the shifting cultivation of hill rice by the Iban of Sarawak.* Colonial Research Studies Vol. 18. London: Her Majesty's Stationery Office.

FRIED, MORTON H.
  1952 Land tenure, geography and ecology in the contact of cultures. *American Journal of Economics and Sociology*, 11: 391–412.

GEERTZ, CLIFFORD.
  1963 *Agricultural involution; the process of ecological change in Indonesia.* Berkeley: University of California Press.

HARRIS, MARVIN.
  1959 The economy has no surplus? *American Anthropologist* 61: 185–199.
  1966 The cultural ecology of India's sacred cattle. *Current Anthropology*, 7: 51–59 (See also "Comments" by Nirmal K. Rose et al., 7: 60–66.)

HELM, JUNE.
  1962 The ecological approach in anthropology. *American Journal of Sociology*, 67: 630–639.

KROEBER, ALFRED L.
  1939 *Cultural and natural areas of native North America.* Berkeley: University of California Press.

LATTIMORE, OWEN.
  1940 *Inner Asian frontiers of China.* New York: American Geographical Society Research Series No. 21.
  1962 *Studies in frontier history; Collected Papers, 1928–58.* Paris: Mouton.

LEEDS, ANTHONY, and ANDREW P. VAYDA (Eds.).
  1965 *Man, culture and animals.* Washington, D.C.: American Association for the Advancement of Science. Publication No. 78.

LEIGHLY, JOHN (Ed.).
  1963 *Land and life: a selection from the writings of Carl Ortwin Sauer.* Berkeley and Los Angeles: University of California Press.

MEGGERS, BETTY J.
  1954 Environmental limitations on the development of culture. *American Anthropologist*, 56: 801–824.

MISHKIN, B.
  1940 *Rank and warfare among the Plain Indians.* Monographs of the American Ethnological Society 3. New York.

PALERM, A., ERIC R. WOLF, WALDO R. WEDEL,
BETTY J. MEGGERS, JACQUES M. MAY, and LAWRENCE KRODER.
  1960 *Studies in human ecology.* Social Science Monographs III. Washington, D.C.: Anthropological Society of Washington and Pan American Union.

SAHLINS, MARSHALL D.
  1955 Esoteric efflorescence in Easter Island. *American Anthropologist*, 57: 1045–1052.
  1959 *Social stratification in Polynesia.* Seattle: University of Washington Press.
  1961 The segmentary lineage: an organization of predatory expansion. *American Anthropologist*, 63: 322–345.

SECOY, FRANK RAYMOND.
  1953 *Changing military patterns on the Great Plains.* Monographs of the American Ethnological Society 21. New York.

SLATER, MIRIAM K.
  1959 Ecological factors in the origin of incest. *American Anthropologist*, 61: 1042–1059.

SPROUT, HAROLD, and MARGARET SPROUT.
>   1965   *The ecological perspective on human affairs.* Princeton, N.J.: Princeton University Press.

STEWARD, JULIAN H. (Ed.).
>   1955   *Irrigation civilization: a comparative study.* Social Science Monographs 1. Washington, D.C.: Pan American Union.

SWEET, LOUISE E.
>   1965   Camel riding of North Arabian Bedouin: a mechanism of ecological adaptation. *American Anthropologist,* 67: 1132–1150.

THOMAS, WILLIAM L., JR. (Ed.).
>   1956   *Man's role in changing the face of the earth.* Chicago: University of Chicago Press.

WAGNER, PHILIP L.
>   1960   *The human use of the earth.* Glencoe, Ill.: Free Press.

WAGNER, PHILIP L., and MARVIN W. MIKESELL (Eds.).
>   1962   *Readings in cultural geography.* Chicago: University of Chicago Press.

WEBB, WALTER PRESCOTT.
>   1931   *The great plains.* New York: Grosset and Dunlap.

WILBERT, JOHANNES (Ed.).
>   1961   *The evolution of horticultural systems in native South America: causes and consequences.* Anthropologica Supplement Publication No. 2. Caracas, Venezuela.

PART VII: IDEOLOGY, LANGUAGE, AND VALUES

ALBERT, ETHEL M.
>   1956   The classification of values. *American Anthropologist,* 58: 221–248.

AYER, A. J.
>   N.d.   *Language, truth, and logic.* New York: Dover Books. (First published in 1935.)

BELLAH, ROBERT.
>   1957   *Tokugawa religion; the values of pre-industrial Japan.* Glencoe, Ill.: Free Press.

BENEDICT, RUTH.
>   1934   *Patterns of culture.* New York and Boston: Houghton Mifflin.

BERGMAN, GUSTAV.
>   1951   Ideology. *Ethics,* 61: 205–218.

BROWN, R. W., and E. H. LENNEBERG.
>   1954   A study in language and cognition. *Journal of Abnormal and Social Psychology,* 49: 454–462.

CHAFE, WALLACE (Ed.).
>   1963   *Aspects of language and culture.* Proceedings of the American Ethnological Society. Seattle: University of Washington Press.

CHOMSKY, N.
>   1959   Review of *Verbal behavior* by B. F. Skinner (New York: Appleton-Century-Crofts, 1957). *Language,* 35: 26–58.

DuBois, CORA.
>   1955   The dominant value profile of American culture. *American Anthropologist,* 57: 1232–1239.

DURKHEIM, EMILE, and M. MAUSS.
>   1963   *Primitive classification.* (Trans. and ed. by Rodney Needham.) London: Cohen and West.

FORDE, DARYLL (Ed.).

    1954   *African worlds: studies in the cosmological ideas and social values of African peoples.* London: Oxford University Press.

GELLNER, ERNEST.

    1959   *Words and things; a critical account of linguistic philosophy and a study in ideology.* London: Victor Gollancz.

GREEN, ROBERT W. (Ed.).

    1959   *Protestantism and capitalism: the Weber thesis and its critics.* Boston: D. C. Heath.

GUMPERZ, J., and DELL HYMES (Eds.).

    1964   *The ethnography of communication. American Anthropologist,* 66 (6), Part 2.

HALLOWELL, A. IRVING.

    1960   Ojibwa ontology, behavior, and world view. In Stanley Diamond (Ed.), *Culture in history: essays in honor of Paul Radin.* New York: Columbia University Press.

HOIJER, H.

    1954   *Language in culture.* American Anthropological Association Memoir No. 79. Menasha, Wis.: George Banta Co. for the Association.

HORTON, ROBIN.

    1962   The Kalabari world view: an outline and interpretation. *Africa,* 32: 197–219.

HYMES, DELL (Ed).

    1964   *Language in culture and society: a reader in linguistics and anthropology.* New York: Harper and Row.

KLUCKHOHN, CLYDE.

    1952   Values and value orientations in the theory of action: an exploration in definition and classification. In Talcott Parsons and Edward A. Shils (Eds.), *Toward a general theory of action.* Cambridge, Mass.: Harvard University Press.

    1953   Universal categories of culture. In A. L. Kroeber (Ed.), *Anthropology today.* Chicago: University of Chicago Press.

    1956   Toward a comparison of value-emphases in different cultures. In Leonard White (Ed.), *The state of the social sciences.* Chicago: University of Chicago Press.

    1959   The scientific study of values. In *Three lectures* (1958). Toronto: University of Toronto Press.

LEE, DOROTHY D.

    1940   A primitive system of values. *Philosophy of Science,* 7: 355–379.

    1944   Linguistic reflection of Wintu thought. *International Journal of American Linguistics,* 10: 181–187.

    1949   Being and value in a primitive culture. *Journal of Philosophy,* 46: 401–415.

LENNEBERG, ERIC H.

    1960   Language, evolution, and purposive behavior. In Stanley Diamond (Ed.), *Culture in history, essays in honor of Paul Radin.* New York: Columbia University Press.

LINSKY, LEONARD (Ed.).

    1952   *Semantics and the philosophy of language.* Urbana: University of Illinois Press.

MANDELBAUM, DAVID G. (Ed.).

    1951   *Selected writings of Edward Sapir in language, culture and personality.* Berkeley: University of California Press.

MAQUET, J. J.
    1951   *The sociology of knowledge.* (Trans. by John Locke.) Boston: Beacon Press.

MOORE, WILBERT E., and MELVIN M. TUMIN.
    1949   Some social functions of ignorance. *American Sociological Review,* 14: 787–795.

MORRIS, E. W.
    1955   *Signs, language and behavior.* New York: George Braziller.

OPLER, MORRIS.
    1945   Themes as dynamic forces in culture. *American Journal of Sociology,* 51: 198–206.

REDFIELD, ROBERT.
    1952   Primitive world view. *Proceedings of the American Philosophical Society,* 96: 30–36.

VOGT, EVON Z.
    1951   *Navaho veterans: a study of changing values.* Cambridge, Mass.: Papers of the Peabody Museum of American Archeology and Ethnology, Harvard University, 41, No. 1.

VOGT, EVON, Z., and THOMAS F. O'DEA.
    1953   A comparative study of the role of values in social action in two southwestern communities. *American Sociological Review,* 18: 645–654.

VOGT, EVON Z., and J. M. ROBERTS.
    1956   A study of values. *Scientific American,* 195 (1): 25–31.

WALLACE, ANTHONY F. C.
    1956   Revitalization movements. *American Anthropologist,* 58: 264–281.

WEBER, MAX.
    1958   *The protestant ethic and the spirit of capitalism.* (Trans. by Talcott Parsons.) New York: Charles Scribner's Sons.

WHORF, BENJAMIN.
    1956   *Language, thought and reality.* New York: John Wiley.

PART VIII: STRUCTURALISM AND FORMAL ANALYSIS

BOLINGER, DWIGHT.
    1965   The atomization of meaning. *Language,* 41: 555–573.

COLBY, B. N.
    1966   Ethnographic semantics: a preliminary survey. *Current Anthropology,* 7: 3–17. (See also "Comments" by Olga Akhmanova *et al.,* 7: 18–32.)

CONKLIN, HAROLD C.
    1955   Hanunóo color categories. *Southwestern Journal of Anthropology,* 11: 339–344.

FODOR, J. A., and J. J. KATZ (Eds.).
    1964   *The structure of language: readings in the philosophy of language.* Englewood Cliffs, N.J.: Prentice-Hall.

FRAKE, C. O.
    1961   The diagnosis of disease among the Subanun of Mindanao. *American Anthropologist,* 63: 11–32.

GOODENOUGH, WARD H.
    1956   Componential analysis and the study of meaning. *Language,* 32: 195–216.

1964 *Explorations in cultural anthropology: essays in honor of George Peter Murdock.* New York: McGraw-Hill. (Contains a number of essays on ethnographic semantics and formal analysis.)

HAMMEL, E. (Ed.).
1965 *Formal semantic analysis. American Anthropologist,* 67 (5), Part 2.

KATZ, J. J., and J. A. FODOR.
1963 The structure of a semantic theory. *Language,* 39: 170–210.

KROEBER, ALFRED L.
1909 Classificatory systems of relationship. *Journal of the Royal Anthropological Institute,* 39: 77–84.

LEACH, E. R.
1961 Lévi-Strauss in the garden of Eden: an examination of some recent developments in the analysis of myth. *Transactions of the New York Academy of Sciences,* Ser. II, 23 (4): 386–396.

LÉVI-STRAUSS, CLAUDE.
1949 *Les structures elementaires de la parente.* Paris: Presses Universitaires de France.
1963a *Totemism.* (Trans. from the French by Rodney Needham.) Boston: Beacon Press.
1963b *Structural anthropology.* New York: Basic Books.
1964 *Tristes tropiques.* (Trans. from the French by John Russell.) New York: Atheneum.
1966 *The Savage mind.* Chicago: University of Chicago Press.

LIVINGSTONE, FRANK B.
1959 A formal analysis of prescriptive marriage systems among the Australian aborigines. *Southwestern Journal of Anthropology,* 15: 361–372.

LOUNSBURY, FLOYD G.
1956 A semantic analysis of Pawnee kinship usage. *Language,* 32: 158–194.
1964 The structural analysis of kinship semantics. In Horace G. Lunt (Ed.), *Proceedings of the ninth international congress of linguists.* The Hague: Mouton.

METZGER, D., and G. E. WILLIAMS.
1963 A formal ethnographic analysis of Tenejapaladino weddings. *American Anthropologist,* 65: 1076–1101.

MURPHY, ROBERT F.
1963 On Zen Marxism: filiation and alliance. *Man,* 21: 17–19.

NUTINI, HUGO G.
1965 Some considerations on the nature of social structure and model building: a critique of Claude Lévi-Strauss and Edmund Leach. *American Anthropologist,* 67: 707–731.

ROMNEY, K., and R. D'ANDRADE (Eds.).
1964 Transcultural studies in cognition. *American Anthropologist,* 66 (3), Part 2.

SAHLINS, MARSHALL D.
1966 On the Delphic writings of Claude Lévi-Strauss. *Scientific American,* 214 (6): 131–136.

SCHEFFLER, HAROLD W.
1966 Structuralism. *Yale French Studies,* 36–37: 66–88.

SCHOLTE, BOB.
1966 Epistemic paradigms: some problems in cross-cultural research on social anthropological history and theory. *American Anthropologist,* 68: 1192–1201.

SEBAG, LUCIEN.
    1964 *Marxisme et structuralisme*. Paris: Payot.
SHUBIK, MARTIN (Ed.).
    1964 *Game theory and related approaches to social behavior*. New
            York: John Wiley.
WALLACE, ANTHONY, F. C.
    1962 Culture and cognition. *Science,* 135: 351–357.
WALLACE, ANTHONY, F. C., and JOHN ATKINS.
    1960 The meaning of kinship terms.. *American Anthropologist,* 62: 58–
            80.
ZIFF, P.
    1960 *Semantic analysis*. Ithaca, N.Y.: Cornell University Press.